Hornbook Series and Basic Legal Texts
Nutshell Series

and

Black Letter Series

of

WEST PUBLISHING COMPANY
P.O. Box 64526
St. Paul, Minnesota 55164–0526

Accounting

FARIS' ACCOUNTING AND LAW IN A NUT-SHELL, 377 pages, 1984. Softcover. (Text)

Administrative Law

AMAN AND MAYTON'S HORNBOOK ON ADMINISTRATIVE LAW, Approximately 750 pages, 1993. (Text)

GELLHORN AND LEVIN'S ADMINISTRATIVE LAW AND PROCESS IN A NUTSHELL, Third Edition, 479 pages, 1990. Softcover. (Text)

Admiralty

MARAIST'S ADMIRALTY IN A NUTSHELL, Second Edition, 379 pages, 1988. Softcover. (Text)

SCHOENBAUM'S HORNBOOK ON ADMIRALTY AND MARITIME LAW, Student Edition, 692 pages, 1987 with 1992 pocket part. (Text)

Agency—Partnership

REUSCHLEIN AND GREGORY'S HORNBOOK ON THE LAW OF AGENCY AND PARTNERSHIP, Second Edition, 683 pages, 1990. (Text)

STEFFEN'S AGENCY-PARTNERSHIP IN A NUTSHELL, 364 pages, 1977. Softcover. (Text)

NOLAN–HALEY'S ALTERNATIVE DISPUTE RESOLUTION IN A NUTSHELL, 298 pages, 1992. Softcover. (Text)

RISKIN'S DISPUTE RESOLUTION FOR LAWYERS VIDEO TAPES, 1992. (Available for purchase by schools and libraries.)

American Indian Law

CANBY'S AMERICAN INDIAN LAW IN A NUTSHELL, Second Edition, 336 pages, 1988. Softcover. (Text)

Antitrust—see also Regulated Industries, Trade Regulation

GELLHORN'S ANTITRUST LAW AND ECONOMICS IN A NUTSHELL, Third Edition, 472 pages, 1986. Softcover. (Text)

HOVENKAMP'S BLACK LETTER ON ANTITRUST, Second Edition approximately 325 pages, April 1993 Pub. Softcover. (Review)

HOVENKAMP'S HORNBOOK ON ECONOMICS AND FEDERAL ANTITRUST LAW, Student Edition, 414 pages, 1985. (Text)

SULLIVAN'S HORNBOOK OF THE LAW OF ANTITRUST, 886 pages, 1977. (Text)

Appellate Advocacy—see Trial and Appellate Advocacy

Art Law

DUBOFF'S ART LAW IN A NUTSHELL, Second Edition, approximately 325 pages, 1993. Softcover. (Text)

Banking Law

LOVETT'S BANKING AND FINANCIAL INSTI-

Banking Law—Cont'd

TUTIONS LAW IN A NUTSHELL, Third Edition, 470 pages, 1992. Softcover. (Text)

Civil Procedure—see also Federal Jurisdiction and Procedure

CLERMONT'S BLACK LETTER ON CIVIL PROCEDURE, Third Edition, approximately 350 pages, May, 1993 Pub. Softcover. (Review)

FRIEDENTHAL, KANE AND MILLER'S HORNBOOK ON CIVIL PROCEDURE, Second Edition, approximately 1000 pages, May 1993 Pub. (Text)

KANE'S CIVIL PROCEDURE IN A NUTSHELL, Third Edition, 303 pages, 1991. Softcover. (Text)

KOFFLER AND REPPY'S HORNBOOK ON COMMON LAW PLEADING, 663 pages, 1969. (Text)

SIEGEL'S HORNBOOK ON NEW YORK PRACTICE, Second Edition, Student Edition, 1068 pages, 1991. Softcover. (Text) 1992 Supplemental Pamphlet.

SLOMANSON AND WINGATE'S CALIFORNIA CIVIL PROCEDURE IN A NUTSHELL, 230 pages, 1992. Softcover. (Text)

Commercial Law

BAILEY AND HAGEDORN'S SECURED TRANSACTIONS IN A NUTSHELL, Third Edition, 390 pages, 1988. Softcover. (Text)

HENSON'S HORNBOOK ON SECURED TRANSACTIONS UNDER THE U.C.C., Second Edition, 504 pages, 1979, with 1979 pocket part. (Text)

MEYER AND SPEIDEL'S BLACK LETTER ON SALES AND LEASES OF GOODS, Approximately 300 pages, 1993. Softcover. (Review)

NICKLES' BLACK LETTER ON COMMERCIAL PAPER, 450 pages, 1988. Softcover. (Review)

STOCKTON AND MILLER'S SALES AND LEASES OF GOODS IN A NUTSHELL, Third Edition, 441 pages, 1992. Softcover. (Text)

STONE'S UNIFORM COMMERCIAL CODE IN A NUTSHELL, Third Edition, 580 pages, 1989. Softcover. (Text)

WEBER AND SPEIDEL'S COMMERCIAL PAPER IN A NUTSHELL, Third Edition, 404 pages, 1982. Softcover. (Text)

WHITE AND SUMMERS' HORNBOOK ON THE UNIFORM COMMERCIAL CODE, Third Edition, Student Edition, 1386 pages, 1988. (Text)

Community Property

MENNELL AND BOYKOFF'S COMMUNITY PROPERTY IN A NUTSHELL, Second Edition, 432 pages, 1988. Softcover. (Text)

Comparative Law

FOLSOM, MINAN AND OTTO'S LAW AND POLITICS IN THE PEOPLE'S REPUBLIC OF CHINA IN A NUTSHELL,   451 pages, 1992. Softcover. (Text)

GLENDON, GORDON AND OSAKWE'S COMPARATIVE LEGAL TRADITIONS IN A NUTSHELL. 402 pages, 1982. Softcover. (Text)

Conflict of Laws

HAY'S BLACK LETTER ON CONFLICT OF LAWS, 330 pages, 1989. Softcover. (Review)

SCOLES AND HAY'S HORNBOOK ON CONFLICT OF LAWS, Student Edition, 1160 pages, 1992. (Text)

SIEGEL'S CONFLICTS IN A NUTSHELL, 470 pages, 1982. Softcover. (Text)

Constitutional Law—Civil Rights

BARRON AND DIENES' BLACK LETTER ON CONSTITUTIONAL LAW, Third Edition, 440 pages, 1991. Softcover. (Review)

BARRON AND DIENES' CONSTITUTIONAL LAW IN A NUTSHELL, Second Edition, 483 pages, 1991. Softcover. (Text)

ENGDAHL'S CONSTITUTIONAL FEDERALISM IN A NUTSHELL, Second Edition, 411 pages, 1987. Softcover. (Text)

MARKS AND COOPER'S STATE CONSTITUTIONAL LAW IN A NUTSHELL, 329 pages, 1988. Softcover. (Text)

Constitutional Law—Civil Rights—Cont'd

NOWAK AND ROTUNDA'S HORNBOOK ON CONSTITUTIONAL LAW, Fourth Edition, 1357 pages, 1991. (Text)

VIEIRA'S CONSTITUTIONAL CIVIL RIGHTS IN A NUTSHELL, Second Edition, 322 pages, 1990. Softcover. (Text)

WILLIAMS' CONSTITUTIONAL ANALYSIS IN A NUTSHELL, 388 pages, 1979. Softcover. (Text)

Consumer Law—see also Commercial Law

EPSTEIN AND NICKLES' CONSUMER LAW IN A NUTSHELL, Second Edition, 418 pages, 1981. Softcover. (Text)

Contracts

CALAMARI AND PERILLO'S BLACK LETTER ON CONTRACTS, Second Edition, 462 pages, 1990. Softcover. (Review)

CALAMARI AND PERILLO'S HORNBOOK ON CONTRACTS, Third Edition, 1049 pages, 1987. (Text)

CORBIN'S TEXT ON CONTRACTS, One Volume Student Edition, 1224 pages, 1952. (Text)

FRIEDMAN'S CONTRACT REMEDIES IN A NUTSHELL, 323 pages, 1981. Softcover. (Text)

KEYES' GOVERNMENT CONTRACTS IN A NUTSHELL, Second Edition, 557 pages, 1990. Softcover. (Text)

SCHABER AND ROHWER'S CONTRACTS IN A NUTSHELL, Third Edition, 457 pages, 1990. Softcover. (Text)

Copyright—see Patent and Copyright Law

Corporations

HAMILTON'S BLACK LETTER ON CORPORATIONS, Third Edition, 732 pages, 1992. Softcover. (Review)

HAMILTON'S THE LAW OF CORPORATIONS IN A NUTSHELL, Third Edition, 518 pages, 1991. Softcover. (Text)

HENN AND ALEXANDER'S HORNBOOK ON LAWS OF CORPORATIONS, Third Edition,

Student Edition, 1371 pages, 1983, with 1986 pocket part. (Text)

Corrections

KRANTZ' THE LAW OF CORRECTIONS AND PRISONERS' RIGHTS IN A NUTSHELL, Third Edition, 407 pages, 1988. Softcover. (Text)

Creditors' Rights

EPSTEIN'S DEBTOR-CREDITOR LAW IN A NUTSHELL, Fourth Edition, 401 pages, 1991. Softcover. (Text)

EPSTEIN, NICKLES AND WHITE'S HORNBOOK ON BANKRUPTCY, Approximately 1000 pages, January, 1992 Pub. (Text)

NICKLES AND EPSTEIN'S BLACK LETTER ON CREDITORS' RIGHTS AND BANKRUPTCY, 576 pages, 1989. (Review)

Criminal Law and Criminal Procedure—see also Corrections, Juvenile Justice

ISRAEL AND LaFAVE'S CRIMINAL PROCEDURE—CONSTITUTIONAL LIMITATIONS IN A NUTSHELL, Fourth Edition, 461 pages, 1988. Softcover. (Text)

LaFAVE AND ISRAEL'S HORNBOOK ON CRIMINAL PROCEDURE, Second Edition, 1309 pages, 1992 with 1992 pocket part. (Text)

LaFAVE AND SCOTT'S HORNBOOK ON CRIMINAL LAW, Second Edition, 918 pages, 1986. (Text)

LOEWY'S CRIMINAL LAW IN A NUTSHELL, Second Edition, 321 pages, 1987. Softcover. (Text)

LOW'S BLACK LETTER ON CRIMINAL LAW, Revised First Edition, 443 pages, 1990. Softcover. (Review)

SUBIN, MIRSKY AND WEINSTEIN'S THE CRIMINAL PROCESS: PROSECUTION AND DEFENSE FUNCTIONS, Approximately 450 pages, February, 1993 Pub. Softcover. Teacher's Manual available. (Text)

Domestic Relations

CLARK'S HORNBOOK ON DOMESTIC RELA-

Immigration Law—Cont'd

PROCEDURE IN A NUTSHELL, Third Edition, 497 pages, 1992. Softcover. (Text)

Indian Law—see American Indian Law

Insurance Law

DOBBYN'S INSURANCE LAW IN A NUTSHELL, Second Edition, 316 pages, 1989. Softcover. (Text)

KEETON AND WIDISS' INSURANCE LAW, Student Edition, 1359 pages, 1988. (Text)

International Law—see also Sea, Law of

BUERGENTHAL'S INTERNATIONAL HUMAN RIGHTS IN A NUTSHELL, 283 pages, 1988. Softcover. (Text)

BUERGENTHAL AND MAIER'S PUBLIC INTERNATIONAL LAW IN A NUTSHELL, Second Edition, 275 pages, 1990. Softcover. (Text)

FOLSOM'S EUROPEAN COMMUNITY LAW IN A NUTSHELL, 423 pages, 1992. Softcover. (Text)

FOLSOM, GORDON AND SPANOGLE'S INTERNATIONAL BUSINESS TRANSACTIONS IN A NUTSHELL, Fourth Edition, 548 pages, 1992. Softcover. (Text)

Interviewing and Counseling

SHAFFER AND ELKINS' LEGAL INTERVIEWING AND COUNSELING IN A NUTSHELL, Second Edition, 487 pages, 1987. Softcover. (Text)

Introduction to Law—see Legal Method and Legal System

Introduction to Law Study

HEGLAND'S INTRODUCTION TO THE STUDY AND PRACTICE OF LAW IN A NUTSHELL, 418 pages, 1983. Softcover. (Text)

KINYON'S INTRODUCTION TO LAW STUDY AND LAW EXAMINATIONS IN A NUTSHELL, 389 pages, 1971. Softcover. (Text)

Judicial Process—see Legal Method and Legal System

SINHA'S JURISPRUDENCE (LEGAL PHILOSO-

PHY) IN A NUTSHELL. Approximately 350 pages, 1993. Softcover. (Text)

Juvenile Justice

FOX'S JUVENILE COURTS IN A NUTSHELL, Third Edition, 291 pages, 1984. Softcover. (Text)

Labor and Employment Law—see also Employment Discrimination, Workers' Compensation

LESLIE'S LABOR LAW IN A NUTSHELL, Third Edition, 388 pages, 1992. Softcover. (Text)

NOLAN'S LABOR ARBITRATION LAW AND PRACTICE IN A NUTSHELL, 358 pages, 1979. Softcover. (Text)

Land Finance—Property Security—see Real Estate Transactions

Land Use

HAGMAN AND JUERGENSMEYER'S HORNBOOK ON URBAN PLANNING AND LAND DEVELOPMENT CONTROL LAW, Second Edition, Student Edition, 680 pages, 1986. (Text)

WRIGHT AND WRIGHT'S LAND USE IN A NUTSHELL, Second Edition, 356 pages, 1985. Softcover. (Text)

Legal Method and Legal System—see also Legal Research, Legal Writing

KEMPIN'S HISTORICAL INTRODUCTION TO ANGLO-AMERICAN LAW IN A NUTSHELL, Third Edition, 323 pages, 1990. Softcover. (Text)

REYNOLDS' JUDICIAL PROCESS IN A NUTSHELL, Second Edition, 308 pages, 1991. Softcover. (Text)

Legal Research

COHEN AND OLSON'S LEGAL RESEARCH IN A NUTSHELL, Fifth Edition, 370 pages, 1992. Softcover. (Text)

COHEN, BERRING AND OLSON'S HOW TO FIND THE LAW, Ninth Edition, 716 pages, 1989. (Text)

Legal Writing and Drafting

MELLINKOFF'S DICTIONARY OF AMERICAN

Legal Writing and Drafting—Cont'd

LEGAL USAGE, 703 pages, 1992. Softcover. (Text)

SQUIRES AND ROMBAUER'S LEGAL WRITING IN A NUTSHELL, 294 pages, 1982. Softcover. (Text)

Legislation—see also Legal Writing and Drafting

DAVIES' LEGISLATIVE LAW AND PROCESS IN A NUTSHELL, Second Edition, 346 pages, 1986. Softcover. (Text)

Local Government

MCCARTHY'S LOCAL GOVERNMENT LAW IN A NUTSHELL, Third Edition, 435 pages, 1990. Softcover. (Text)

REYNOLDS' HORNBOOK ON LOCAL GOVERNMENT LAW, 860 pages, 1982 with 1990 pocket part. (Text)

Mass Communication Law

ZUCKMAN, GAYNES, CARTER AND DEE'S MASS COMMUNICATIONS LAW IN A NUTSHELL, Third Edition, 538 pages, 1988. Softcover. (Text)

Medicine, Law and

HALL AND ELLMAN'S HEALTH CARE LAW AND ETHICS IN A NUTSHELL, 401 pages, 1990. Softcover (Text)

JARVIS, CLOSEN, HERMANN AND LEONARD'S AIDS LAW IN A NUTSHELL, 349 pages, 1991. Softcover. (Text)

KING'S THE LAW OF MEDICAL MALPRACTICE IN A NUTSHELL, Second Edition, 342 pages, 1986. Softcover. (Text)

Military Law

SHANOR AND TERRELL'S MILITARY LAW IN A NUTSHELL, 378 pages, 1980. Softcover. (Text)

Mining Law—see Energy and Natural Resources Law

Mortgages—see Real Estate Transactions

Natural Resources Law—see Energy and Natural Resources Law, Environmental Law

TEPLY'S LEGAL NEGOTIATION IN A NUTSHELL, 282 pages, 1992. Softcover. (Text)

Office Practice—see also Computers and Law, Interviewing and Counseling, Negotiation

HEGLAND'S TRIAL AND PRACTICE SKILLS IN A NUTSHELL, 346 pages, 1978. Softcover (Text)

Oil and Gas—see also Energy and Natural Resources Law

HEMINGWAY'S HORNBOOK ON THE LAW OF OIL AND GAS, Third Edition, Student Edition, 711 pages, 1992. (Text)

LOWE'S OIL AND GAS LAW IN A NUTSHELL, Second Edition, 465 pages, 1988. Softcover. (Text)

Partnership—see Agency—Partnership

Patent and Copyright Law

MILLER AND DAVIS' INTELLECTUAL PROPERTY—PATENTS, TRADEMARKS AND COPYRIGHT IN A NUTSHELL, Second Edition, 437 pages, 1990. Softcover. (Text)

Products Liability

PHILLIPS' PRODUCTS LIABILITY IN A NUTSHELL, Third Edition, 307 pages, 1988. Softcover. (Text)

Professional Responsibility

ARONSON AND WECKSTEIN'S PROFESSIONAL RESPONSIBILITY IN A NUTSHELL, Second Edition, 514 pages, 1991. Softcover. (Text)

LESNICK'S BEING A LAWYER: INDIVIDUAL CHOICE AND RESPONSIBILITY IN THE PRACTICE OF LAW, 422 pages, 1992. Softcover. Teacher's Manual available. (Coursebook)

ROTUNDA'S BLACK LETTER ON PROFESSIONAL RESPONSIBILITY, Third Edition, 492 pages, 1992. Softcover. (Review)

WOLFRAM'S HORNBOOK ON MODERN LEGAL ETHICS, Student Edition, 1120

Professional Responsibility—Cont'd
pages, 1986. (Text)

WYDICK AND PERSCHBACHER'S CALIFOR-
NIA LEGAL ETHICS, 439 pages, 1992.
Softcover. (Coursebook)

Property—see also Real Estate Transactions, Land Use, Trusts and Estates

BERNHARDT'S BLACK LETTER ON PROPER-
TY, Second Edition, 388 pages, 1991.
Softcover. (Review)

BERNHARDT'S REAL PROPERTY IN A NUT-
SHELL, Second Edition, 448 pages,
1981. Softcover. (Text)

BOYER, HOVENKAMP AND KURTZ' THE
LAW OF PROPERTY, AN INTRODUCTORY
SURVEY, Fourth Edition, 696 pages,
1991. (Text)

BURKE'S PERSONAL PROPERTY IN A NUT-
SHELL, Second Edition, approximately
400 pages, May, 1993 Pub. Softcover.
(Text)

CUNNINGHAM, STOEBUCK AND WHIT-
MAN'S HORNBOOK ON THE LAW OF PROP-
ERTY, Second Edition, approximately
900 pages, May, 1993 Pub. (Text)

HILL'S LANDLORD AND TENANT LAW IN A
NUTSHELL, Second Edition, 311 pages,
1986. Softcover. (Text)

Real Estate Transactions

BRUCE'S REAL ESTATE FINANCE IN A
NUTSHELL, Third Edition, 287 pages,
1991. Softcover. (Text)

NELSON AND WHITMAN'S BLACK LETTER
ON LAND TRANSACTIONS AND FINANCE,
Second Edition, 466 pages, 1988. Soft-
cover. (Review)

NELSON AND WHITMAN'S HORNBOOK ON
REAL ESTATE FINANCE LAW, Second
Edition, 941 pages, 1985 with 1989
pocket part. (Text)

Regulated Industries—see also Mass
Communication Law, Banking Law
GELLHORN AND PIERCE'S REGULATED IN-
DUSTRIES IN A NUTSHELL, Second Edi-
tion, 389 pages, 1987. Softcover.

(Text)

Remedies

DOBBS' HORNBOOK ON REMEDIES, Second
Edition, approximately 1000 pages,
April, 1993 Pub. (Text)

DOBBYN'S INJUNCTIONS IN A NUTSHELL,
264 pages, 1974. Softcover. (Text)

FRIEDMAN'S CONTRACT REMEDIES IN A
NUTSHELL, 323 pages, 1981. Softcover.
(Text)

O'CONNELL'S REMEDIES IN A NUTSHELL,
Second Edition, 320 pages, 1985. Softcover. (Text)

Sea, Law of

SOHN AND GUSTAFSON'S THE LAW OF
THE SEA IN A NUTSHELL, 264 pages,
1984. Softcover. (Text)

Securities Regulation

HAZEN'S HORNBOOK ON THE LAW OF SE-
CURITIES REGULATION, Second Edition,
Student Edition, 1082 pages, 1990.
(Text)

RATNER'S SECURITIES REGULATION IN A
NUTSHELL, Fourth Edition, 320 pages,
1992. Softcover. (Text)

Sports Law

CHAMPION'S SPORTS LAW IN A NUT-
SHELL,. Approximately 300 pages,
January, 1993 Pub. Softcover. (Text)

SCHUBERT, SMITH AND TRENTADUE'S
SPORTS LAW, 395 pages, 1986. (Text)

Tax Practice and Procedure

MORGAN'S TAX PROCEDURE AND TAX
FRAUD IN A NUTSHELL, 400 pages, 1990.
Softcover. (Text)

Taxation—Corporate

SCHWARZ AND LATHROPE'S BLACK LET-
TER ON CORPORATE AND PARTNERSHIP
TAXATION, 537 pages, 1991. Softcover.
(Review)

WEIDENBRUCH AND BURKE'S FEDERAL IN-
COME TAXATION OF CORPORATIONS AND
STOCKHOLDERS IN A NUTSHELL, Third
Edition, 309 pages, 1989. Softcover.
(Text)

Taxation—Estate & Gift—see also Estate Planning, Trusts and Estates

McNulty's Federal Estate and Gift Taxation in a Nutshell, Fourth Edition, 496 pages, 1989. Softcover. (Text)

Peat and Willbanks' Federal Estate and Gift Taxation: An Analysis and Critique, 265 pages, 1991. Softcover. (Text)

Taxation—Individual

Dodge's The Logic of Tax, 343 pages, 1989. Softcover. (Text)

Hudson and Lind's Black Letter on Federal Income Taxation, Fourth Edition, 410 pages, 1992. Softcover. (Review)

McNulty's Federal Income Taxation of Individuals in a Nutshell, Fourth Edition, 503 pages, 1988. Softcover. (Text)

Posin's Federal Income Taxation, Second Edition, approximately 650 pages, May, 1993 Pub. Softcover. (Text)

Rose and Chommie's Hornbook on Federal Income Taxation, Third Edition, 923 pages, 1988, with 1991 pocket part. (Text)

Taxation—International

Doernberg's International Taxation in a Nutshell, 325 pages, 1989. Softcover. (Text)

Bishop and Brooks' Federal Partnership Taxation: A Guide to the Leading Cases, Statutes, and Regulations, 545 pages, 1990. Softcover. (Text)

Burke's Federal Income Taxation of Partnerships in a Nutshell, 356 pages, 1992. Softcover. (Text)

Schwarz and Lathrope's Black Letter on Corporate and Partnership Taxation, 537 pages, 1991. Softcover. (Review)

Taxation—State & Local

Gelfand and Salsich's State and Local Taxation and Finance in a Nutshell, 309 pages, 1986. Softcover. (Text)

Torts—see also Products Liability

Kionka's Black Letter on Torts, 339 pages, 1988. Softcover. (Review)

Kionka's Torts in a Nutshell, Second Edition, 449 pages, 1992. Softcover. (Text)

Prosser and Keeton's Hornbook on Torts, Fifth Edition, Student Edition, 1286 pages, 1984 with 1988 pocket part. (Text)

Trade Regulation—see also Antitrust, Regulated Industries

McManis' Unfair Trade Practices in a Nutshell, Third Edition, approximately 450 pages, 1993. Softcover. (Text)

Schechter's Black Letter on Unfair Trade Practices, 272 pages, 1986. Softcover. (Review)

Trial and Appellate Advocacy—see also Civil Procedure

Bergman's Trial Advocacy in a Nutshell, Second Edition, 354 pages, 1989. Softcover. (Text)

Clary's Primer on the Analysis and Presentation of Legal Argument, 106 pages, 1992. Softcover. (Text)

Dessem's Pretrial Litigation in a Nutshell, 382 pages, 1992. Softcover. (Text)

Goldberg's The First Trial (Where Do I Sit? What Do I Say?) in a Nutshell, 396 pages, 1982. Softcover. (Text)

Hegland's Trial and Practice Skills in a Nutshell, 346 pages, 1978. Softcover. (Text)

Hornstein's Appellate Advocacy in a Nutshell, 325 pages, 1984. Softcover. (Text)

Jeans' Handbook on Trial Advocacy, Student Edition, 473 pages, 1975. Softcover. (Text)

Trusts and Estates

ATKINSON'S HORNBOOK ON WILLS, Second Edition, 975 pages, 1953. (Text)

AVERILL'S UNIFORM PROBATE CODE IN A NUTSHELL, Second Edition, 454 pages, 1987. Softcover. (Text)

BOGERT'S HORNBOOK ON TRUSTS, Sixth Edition, Student Edition, 794 pages, 1987. (Text)

MCGOVERN, KURTZ AND REIN'S HORNBOOK ON WILLS, TRUSTS AND ESTATES–INCLUDING TAXATION AND FUTURE INTERESTS, 996 pages, 1988. (Text)

MENNELL'S WILLS AND TRUSTS IN A NUTSHELL, 392 pages, 1979. Softcover. (Text)

SIMES' HORNBOOK ON FUTURE INTERESTS, Second Edition, 355 pages, 1966. (Text)

TURANO AND RADIGAN'S HORNBOOK ON NEW YORK ESTATE ADMINISTRATION, 676 pages, 1986 with 1991 pocket part. (Text)

WAGGONER'S FUTURE INTERESTS IN A NUTSHELL, 361 pages, 1981. Softcover. (Text)

Water Law—see also Environmental Law

GETCHES' WATER LAW IN A NUTSHELL, Second Edition, 459 pages, 1990. Softcover. (Text)

Wills—see Trusts and Estates

Workers' Compensation

HOOD, HARDY AND LEWIS' WORKERS' COMPENSATION AND EMPLOYEE PROTECTION LAWS IN A NUTSHELL, Second Edition, 361 pages, 1990. Softcover. (Text)

*

McCORMICK ON EVIDENCE

Fourth Edition

By

John William Strong

General Editor

Rosenstiel Professor of Law, University of Arizona

Contributing Authors

Kenneth S. Broun

Henry Brandis Professor of Law, University of North Carolina

George E. Dix

A.W. Walker Centennial Professor of Law, The University of Texas

Michael H. Graham

Professor of Law, University of Miami

D. H. Kaye

Regents Professor of Law, Arizona State University

Robert P. Mosteller

Professor of Law, Duke University

E. F. Roberts

Edwin H. Woodruff Professor of Law, The Cornell Law School

This book is an abridgement of "McCormick on Evidence, Fourth Edition, Volumes 1 & 2, Practitioner Treatise Series".

HORNBOOK SERIES®

WEST PUBLISHING CO.

ST. PAUL, MINN., 1992

This is an abridgement of "McCormick on Evidence, Fourth Edition, Volumes 1 & 2, Practitioner Treatise Series", West Publishing Co., 1992.

Hornbook Series, Westlaw, the West Publishing Co. Logo and the key symbol appearing on the front cover are registered trademarks of West Publishing Co. Registered in U.S. Patent and Trademark Office.

Library of Congress Cataloging-in-Publication Data

McCormick, Charles Tilford, 1889–1963.
    McCormick on evidence / by John William Strong, general editor ; contributing authors, Kenneth S. Broun . . . [et al.].
        p.   cm. — (Hornbook series)
    Includes index.
    ISBN 0–314–90350–X
    1. Evidence (Law)—United States. I. Strong, John William, 1935–
. II. Broun, Kenneth S. III. Title. IV. Series.
    KF8935.M29   1992b   92–22645
                                                     CIP

ISBN 0–314–90350–X

    McCormick, Evidence 4th Ed. HB
    1st Reprint—1993

PRINTED ON 10% POST CONSUMER RECYCLED PAPER

Preface to the Student Edition

The appearance of the present volume is a sufficient departure from the traditional format of McCormick on Evidence to require a word of explanation.

The first edition of the treatise, and the only one personally authored by Professor McCormick, was clearly intended principally as a resource for students of Evidence. It provided a trenchant, concise, and readily accessible statement of the basic principles of the subject, largely unencumbered by exhaustive citations of authority. For those users in need of fuller historical treatment, or of compilation of multiple authorities, plentiful citations to the treasure trove of Wigmore's 3rd edition were provided.

In the ensuing forty years, subsequent editions of the book have increasingly departed from the original pattern by the addition of ever more citations of authority. Several factors have contributed to the process. The striking growth of the law, particularly following the appearance of the Federal Rules, contributed to this accretion. So too, undoubtedly, did changing academic fashion with its emphasis on the proliferation of citations. But the main cause of the metamorphosis of the book into the form exhibited by the recently published 4th edition has been its substantial and continued popularity with the bench and bar. These groups, of course, require not only statements of basic principles, but also the identification of entry points for comprehensive research into the multiplicity of narrower questions not treatable in a basic work.

The described process which has inevitably led to the two-volume format of McCormick on Evidence, 4th edition, but it has understandably had its critics among law teachers and students. The essence of this criticism, has been that when used as a conventional study aid, or as the text supporting a problem method approach to the study of Evidence, a wealth of citations is not only unneeded but is the occasion of unwanted bulk and expense. It is in response to comments in this vein that the present one-volume student edition, largely free of citations of authority, is offered. Only those footnotes have been retained which are thought to be indispensable to the student users. Specifically, these include citations to case decisions so notable as to be discussed by name in the text, and cross references to related discussions elsewhere in the treatise.

The text itself remains virtually identical with that of the parent volume. No excisions of either chapters or sections have been made, and in only a few instances has wording been revised in the interest of additional clarity. It is hoped that substantial identity of text will ease the task of those who may find it necessary to move from the student edition to the practitioner's work in search of supporting authority. To this end, the section numbers in the two editions are in all instances identical.

One final and much regretted novelty in the present edition is the absence of Edward W. Cleary as General Editor and contributing author. The late Professor Cleary served us not only as general editor of the second and third editions of McCormick, but also as reporter for the Supreme Court's Advisory Committee on the Federal Rules of Evidence. Professor Cleary's contributions to the development of the Law of Evidence were significant, and he was valued as a scholar and as a friend by all of the present authors of this treatise. It is appropriate that the 4th edition be dedicated to his memory.

JOHN WILLIAM STRONG

June, 1992
Tucson, Arizona

WESTLAW® Overview

McCormick on Evidence offers a detailed and comprehensive treatment of the basic rules and principles of evidence law. To supplement the information supplied in this treatise, researchers can access WESTLAW. WESTLAW is a computer-assisted legal research service of West Publishing Company.

The law of evidence on WESTLAW includes case law, statutes, court rules and orders, administrative materials and commentary databases. To help research the law of evidence, a WESTLAW appendix is included in this edition. This appendix provides information on databases, search techniques and sample research problems so that you can coordinate WESTLAW research with this book.

THE PUBLISHER

*

Summary of Contents

TITLE 7. RELEVANCY AND ITS COUNTERWEIGHTS

TITLE 8. DEMONSTRATIVE EVIDENCE

TITLE 9. WRITINGS

TITLE 10. THE HEARSAY RULE AND ITS EXCEPTIONS

TITLE 11. JUDICIAL NOTICE

TITLE 12. BURDEN OF PROOF AND PRESUMPTIONS

TITLE 13. ADMINISTRATIVE EVIDENCE

Table of Contents

TITLE 3. ADMISSION AND EXCLUSION

TITLE 4. COMPETENCY

TITLE 5. PRIVILEGE: COMMON LAW AND STATUTORY

TITLE 8. DEMONSTRATIVE EVIDENCE

TITLE 9. WRITINGS

TITLE 10. THE HEARSAY RULE AND ITS EXCEPTIONS

TITLE 11. JUDICIAL NOTICE

TITLE 12. BURDEN OF PROOF AND PRESUMPTIONS

TITLE 13. ADMINISTRATIVE EVIDENCE

McCORMICK
ON EVIDENCE

*

Title 1

INTRODUCTION

Chapter 1

PREPARING AND PRESENTING
THE EVIDENCE

Table of Sections

§ 1. Planning and Preparation of Proof as Important as the Rules of Evidence

The law of evidence is the system of rules and standards by which the admission of proof at the trial of a lawsuit is regulated. But it should be emphasized that this trial stage, when proof is offered and the rules of evidence come into play, is a late stage in a long process. Thus, every case which will be encountered, dealing with a dispute over a rule of evidence or its application, presents a situation in which the lawyers concerned have been required to shoulder many other tasks in the planning and production of testimony, and in anticipation of problems of presentation of proof at the trial under the law of evidence, long before any question of evidence law is presented to the court. As a reminder, some of these earlier stages in the problem of proof will be mentioned in this chapter.

§ 2. Preparation for Trial on the Facts, Without Resort to the Aid of the Court

The client must be interviewed to ascertain the facts, and these interviews should include a tactful but searching cross-examination to overcome the client's natural tendency to confine the story to the facts favorable to himself. The witnesses who have firsthand knowledge of the transaction in controversy must likewise be interviewed, and where possible, their written statements taken.[1] Apart from the ordinary eyewitnesses, it is increasingly necessary to arrange for the employment of technical experts, such as physicians in personal injury cases, chemists and physicists in patent litigation, engineers and architects in contro-

§ 2

1. See § 3 infra concerning the right to interview witnesses.

2

versies over construction contracts, psychiatrists in criminal cases, and handwriting experts in disputes over the genuineness of documents. To prepare himself to testify, and to give to counsel the information he will need to frame his questions at the trial, the expert must usually be furnished with a detailed request for an investigation and report upon specific questions. Also, it will often be necessary to assemble available documentary evidence, such as contracts, letters, receipts, loose-leaf records, deeds, certified copies of conveyances, judgments, and decrees. Other physical evidence, such as the revolver of the attacker and the perforated coat of the victim in a murder case, or a sample of the goods in an action for breach of warranty, should be discovered and preserved for use at the trial. The lawyer, moreover, must be fertile in planning for the production of all those aids to the senses which quicken the jury's interest in and understanding of the testimony, such as photographs, motion picture films, X-ray photographs, plats, diagrams, and models. If pertinent, scientific evidence must be prepared. Where practicable, the task of proof should be lightened by securing written stipulations from opposing counsel of the existence of facts not in controversy, such as the execution of documents, or the ownership of a vehicle, or of premises, involved in the suit. If it is anticipated that the terms of a document in the possession of the adversary will need to be proved by use of a copy, written notice to produce the original at the trial must be given to opposing counsel.

Manifestly, all of this preparation must be planned, and the plan will develop as new information is disclosed, but as the trial approaches, a definite program must be formulated. Each fact involved in the claim or defence should be listed, with the witnesses and documents by which it will be proved. This may well be supplemented by a list of the witnesses in the order in which they will be called, including the subjects upon which they will be examined, and a separate list of exhibits, including witnesses who are to authenticate each exhibit. Finally, and most important, at the last minute before the witnesses are to go on the stand, the counsel who calls them must talk to each in order to ascertain what he is prepared to swear, to cause him to refresh his memory, if necessary, by reading his signed statement, and to warn him of the probable line of the adversary's cross-examination.

§ 3. Invoking the Aid of the Court in Preparing for Trial: Right to Interview Witnesses: Discovery and Depositions: Requests for Admission: Pretrial Conferences

From time to time the question arises whether counsel should have an unfettered opportunity to interview a witness. Resort to the court may be required to settle the matter. The question usually arises when opposing counsel has instructed a witness not to "talk", or to "talk" only upon conditions, or much less commonly when a court places limitations upon interviews. Generally, it is said that a criminal defendant has the right to an opportunity to interview witnesses privately. Apparently the prosecution in a criminal case has a similar right. There is an emerging similar right for both parties in civil cases. Nevertheless, there are a few situations in which a court may refuse to interfere when witnesses are advised by counsel to limit interviews or refuse interviews. The witness sought to be interviewed is free to refuse an interview. Despite the existence of discovery devices, the right to an opportunity to interview is important in trial preparation.

The official discovery procedures in the various jurisdictions are treated at length in treatises and one-volume works concerning the subjects of civil and criminal procedure. Consequently, only a very short and summary review of these procedures is included here.

In addition to preparation for trial without the use of any official pretrial procedures, adequate preparation requires the use of official procedures that are made available once a lawsuit has been commenced. Since the pleadings in civil cases may be fairly general and need not outline the opponent's factual case in any detail in many jurisdictions, the rules for civil cases in many states provide for fairly thorough discovery processes by which each party may discover the facts and possible evidence in the case, and at least ascertain in part what detailed fact issues may arise for trial, as well as the opponent's positions concerning factual matters.

One of the most important discovery procedures in civil cases is undoubtedly the procedure by which each party may orally examine the other under oath and may likewise examine any persons who may possibly have any knowledge of the subject matter of the lawsuit. Over half the states have substantially copied the federal rules for this procedure. Although an order for a commission authorizing an officer to preside at such an oral examination is still required in some states, the procedure for taking oral depositions more often specifies only a notice to the person to be examined and a subpoena requiring him to appear at a certain time and place for the examination before a notary public, plus a notice of the examination to the opposing party, if he is not the person to be examined. In many jurisdictions, following the lead of the federal discovery process for civil cases, the examination upon oral deposition may seek information "reasonably calculated to lead to the discovery of admissible evidence" even if the information will not be admissible at the trial. In these jurisdictions, effective employment of the taking of oral depositions will enable a party to discover the evidence both for and against his positions concerning the facts.

In civil cases, written interrogatories may also be directed to the opponent in many states, and he will be required to answer them. Usually these interrogatories are used hand in hand with the procedure of taking oral depositions. Further, a party is often permitted to secure an order requiring the adversary to permit him to examine all papers and things—even real property—relating to the subject matter of the suit. At least in personal injury suits, and sometimes in other suits in which the physical or mental condition of a party is in issue, an order for exami-

nation of the condition of the party may be secured in over half the states. Further, although not strictly speaking a discovery device, a party may in many states send requests for admissions to his opponent who must either admit or deny the detailed requests.

Finally, the pretrial hearing or conference is authorized for civil cases in many jurisdictions, although it has not necessarily been frequently used in all of them. When the case is approaching the time for trial, usually two or three weeks before the date set, the judge summons counsel for both sides, and sometimes the parties, and seeks to settle all preliminary questions of pleading, to ascertain the scope of the dispute, and to secure agreements as to the facts not really at issue. The original federal rule mentions, as among the objects of the hearing:

"(1) The simplification of the issues;

* * *

"(3) The possibility of obtaining admissions of fact and of documents which will avoid unnecessary proof;

"(4) The limitation of the number of expert witnesses;

"(5) The advisability of a preliminary reference of issues to a master for findings to be used as evidence when the trial is to be by jury" * * *.

Pretrial conference can serve as a vehicle for reaching agreement upon various factual issues, although it will not necessarily have that result.

A final step that should be mentioned before concluding this summary of ways in which the aid of the court is invoked in civil cases in the preparation for trial on the facts, is the procurement of the issuance and service of writs of subpoena for the witnesses who are to be used at the trial. In the case of a document or other physical evidence held by another, the party who desires its production at the trial may secure a subpoena duces tecum addressed to the possessor commanding him to attend the trial as a witness and to bring with him the document or other object.

It should be mentioned that the use of some of the above-described discovery devices may result in testimony and other evidence which may be introduced into evidence at the trial. The testimony upon the taking of oral or written depositions may be introduced under varying circumstances. Under rules similar to the federal rules, the deposition testimony of an opposing party may be introduced virtually without any conditions. The most common conditions for the introduction of deposition testimony of persons other than witnesses are the requirements expressed in the federal rules of civil procedure. Depositions are also admissible under the terms of the federal rules of evidence.[1]

The proper use of all these pretrial devices for trial preparation is, of course, in and of itself an important art.

Discovery procedures available to a criminal defendant should also be mentioned. Only in somewhat recent times have rules or statutes been enacted to provide for any true discovery procedures for criminal defendants, and these procedures are limited. The Crime Control Act of 1970 provides for taking depositions primarily for the preservation of the evidence of the witness (for future use as evidence) and not for the purpose of discovery of facts. For the first time depositions were authorized on motion of the government.[2] A broad discovery provision concerning discovery and examination by defendant of reports, tests, grand jury testimony, books, papers, documents, tangible objects, and places is provided for by Rule 16 of the federal criminal rules. A more limited provision is made in the federal rules for discovery of matters of this kind by the government.

In the various states, all manner of miscellaneous and limited provisions which might have some limited use for discovery of facts exist, but no detailed review will be attempted here.

§ 4. The Order of Presenting Evidence at the Trial

Under the usual order of proceeding at the trial, including a trial under the Federal Rules of Evidence, the plaintiff, who has the burden of establishing his claim, will first introduce the evidence to prove the facts necessary to enable him to recover, e.g., the making of the contract sued on, its breach, and the amount of damages. At this stage the plaintiff will bring forward successively all the witnesses on whom he will rely to establish these facts, together with the documents pertinent for this purpose, which will be offered when they have been authenticated by the testimony of the witnesses. During this stage each witness of the plaintiff will first be questioned by the plaintiff's counsel, upon direct examination, then cross-examined by opposing counsel, and these examinations may be followed by re-direct and re-cross examinations. When all of the plaintiff's witnesses to his main case have been subjected, each in turn, to this process of questioning and cross-questioning, the plaintiff signifies the completion of his case in chief by announcing that he rests.

Then the defendant presents the witnesses (and also the documents and other tangible evidence) in support of his case. At this stage the defendant will produce evidence not only in denial of the plaintiff's claim, such as evidence that a contract sued on was never actually agreed on, or in a negligence case that some bodily injury was not permanent as claimed by the plaintiff, but also in support of any affirmative defenses which the defendant has pleaded, such as the defense of fraud in the procurement of a contract sued on, or the making of a release of a personal injury claim. Here again each witness's story on direct examination is subject to be tested by cross-examination and supplemented on re-direct, etc., before he leaves the stand. When the defendant has thus completed the presentation of his proof of affirmative defenses, if any, and his evidence in denial of the plaintiff's claims, the defendant announces that he rests.

The plaintiff is now entitled to another turn at bat. He may now present his case in

1. See § 254 infra.

2. 18 U.S.C.A. § 3503. See Wright, Federal Practice and Procedure: Criminal § 241.

rebuttal. The plaintiff is not entitled to present at this stage witnesses who merely support the allegations of the complaint, but is confined to testimony which is directed to refuting the evidence of the defendant, unless the court in its discretion permits him to depart from the regular order of proof. The plaintiff's witnesses in rebuttal may be new ones, but he may often recall witnesses who testified for him on the case in chief, to answer some point first raised by the defendant's witnesses. In this, as in the other stages, the witness may not only be examined on direct, but cross-examined and re-examined. When the plaintiff's case in rebuttal is finished, he closes his case. If new points are brought out in the plaintiff's rebuttal evidence, the defendant may meet them by evidence in rejoinder, otherwise he closes his case at once. When both parties have announced that they have closed, the hearing on the facts comes to an end and the trial proceeds with the argument of counsel and the court's instructions to the jury.

To sum up: The stages of the hearing of the facts are

(1) the plaintiff's main case, or evidence in chief,

(2) the defendant's case or evidence in defense,

(3) the plaintiff's evidence in rebuttal, and

(4) the defendant's evidence in rejoinder.

In each of these stages, all of the witnesses to the facts appropriate at the particular period will be called by the party, and the examination of each witness may pass through these steps:

(1) the direct examination, conducted by the party who calls the witness,

(2) the cross-examination by the adversary,

(3) re-direct, and

(4) re-cross.

Under Federal Rule of Evidence 611(a), the above-described order of a trial is ordinarily followed, but the court "shall exercise reasonable control over the mode and order of interrogating witnesses and presenting evidence so as to (1) make the interrogation and presentation effective for the ascertainment of the truth, (2) avoid needless consumption of time, and (3) protect witnesses from harassment or undue embarrassment." The judge usually will not have sufficient reason to change the stages of the hearing as described above. The primary focus of the rule is the control of the steps for examination of witnesses as described above and the nature of examination of witnesses.

Title 2

EXAMINATION OF WITNESSES

Chapter 2

THE FORM OF QUESTIONS ON DIRECT: THE JUDGE'S WITNESSES: REFRESHING MEMORY

Table of Sections

§ 5. The Form of Questions: (a) Questions Calling for a Free Narrative Versus Specific Questions

The art of direct examination of your own witness, and of telling a composite story from the mouths of your own witnesses, is far more important, though perhaps less difficult, than the art of cross-examination. One of the problems of tactics is whether the information which a particular witness will give can best be elicited by a succession of questions about specific facts and happenings or will be brought out more effectively by a general question. In the latter case, the attention of the witness will be directed to the incident in litigation by asking him whether he was on the scene at the time and then requesting him to tell what he saw and heard on that occasion. This latter method, narrative testimony, may often be more effective. The narrative does not seem to come from the counsel,

as it might when specific interrogation is employed. If the witness has a good memory, a good personality, and some effectiveness in speaking, his spontaneous statement of his own story may well be more interesting and impressive. Scientific tests give some indication that spontaneous narrative is more accurate (because less influenced by suggestion) while the fully interrogated testimony is, naturally, more complete in its representation of the facts. Specific interrogation may be desirable to ensure the presentation of facts in proper order; to give the witness confidence in the courtroom; to supplement the testimony properly by visual aids, demonstrative evidence, and writings; to prevent dull testimony; and to accomplish a variety of other purposes.

If a witness is to be examined by the narrative method, counsel must plan to be ready to interrupt with specific questions, if necessary, or to supplement the narrative by specific questions which bring out omitted facts.

Under the prevailing view, there is no general rule of law requiring or preferring either form of questioning. Courts have emphasized the danger that when asked to tell his story the witness will include hearsay or other incompetent testimony, but a proper caution by court or counsel, on the adversary's request, will usually prevent this. True, if the improper statement comes out in the story, there is only the remedy of striking out that part of the evidence. There is also a danger that counsel may waive an objection if he does not interrupt promptly and move to strike. But the need for eliciting what the witness knows in the most vivid and accurate way is an interest to be balanced against the need of the adversary for a fair opportunity to object. The guiding principle is that the trial judge has a discretion, not reviewable except for abuse, to control the form of examination, to the end that the facts may be clearly and expeditiously presented; hence he may permit either of the methods discussed. It is believed, however, that whenever circumstances make narrative testimony feasible, its use is likely to be in the interest of the examining party and of the accurate disclosure of the truth, and that the use of this method will seldom be curbed by enlightened judges, except, perhaps, in criminal trials when it may entail the risk that testimony will be given concerning a matter which is not constitutionally admissible.

These principles are consistent with Federal and Revised Uniform Rule (1974) 611(a), which provide:

The court shall exercise reasonable control over the mode and order of interrogating witnesses and presenting evidence so as to (1) make the interrogation and presentation effective for the ascertainment of the truth, (2) avoid needless consumption of time, and (3) protect witnesses from harassment or undue embarrassment.

§ 6. The Form of Questions: (b) Leading Questions

In the preceding section, the method of soliciting the free and unguided narrative of the witness on direct examination is compared with the method of drawing out testimony by specific questions. A danger of the latter method is that the witness may acquiesce in a false suggestion. The suggestion itself may plant the belief in its truth. Some studies have confirmed the convictions of judges that this danger is greater than one who has had no experience with trials would suppose. And, regardless of his beliefs, a friendly or pliant witness may follow suggestions on direct examination. On the other hand, it can be urged that there is little reason for barring suggestive questions. In many instances, at least, the objection is trivial.

Nevertheless, subject to all of the conditions and limitations that are discussed in the remainder of this section, objections to leading questions have been preserved by the common law and by Rule 611(c) of the Federal and Revised Uniform Rules of Evidence.

A leading question then is one that suggests to the witness the answer desired by the examiner. A question may be leading because of its form, but often the mere form of a question does not indicate whether it is leading. The question which contains a phrase like "did he not?" is obviously and invariably leading, but almost any other type of question may be leading or not, dependent upon the content and context. It is sometimes supposed that a question which can be answered yes or no is by that fact marked as leading, and the beginner may seek refuge in the form of a neutral alternative ("State whether or not * * *") to escape the charge of leading. But quite often the former kind of question will not be leading and equally often the latter kind will be. The whole issue is whether an ordinary man would get the impression that the questioner desired one answer rather than another. The form of a question, or previous questioning, may indicate the desire, but the most important circumstance for consideration is the extent of the particularity of the question itself. If the question describes an incident in detail and asks if the incident happened, the natural inference is that the questioner expects an affirmative answer. Or if one alternative branch of a question is concrete and detailed and the other vague ("Was the sound like the scream of a woman in fear or was it otherwise?") the impression is that the first alternative is suggested. On the other hand, if a question is sufficiently neutral ("At what time did this occur?") or sufficiently balanced ("Was the water hot or cold?"), it is not leading.

As we have seen, the normal practice is for the careful lawyer to interview in advance all witnesses whom he expects to call for direct examination to prove his own case. This practice is entirely proper, but it does create a probability that the lawyer and the witness will have reached an *entente* which will make the witness especially susceptible to suggestions from the lawyer. On the other hand, when counsel cross-examines a witness called by the adversary, he may have had no opportunity to talk to the witness previously, and in any event there is less likelihood of an understanding between them about the facts. Hence the practice: upon objection, the judge will ordinarily forbid leading questions on direct examination and will ordinarily permit them on cross-examination. But the entire matter of the allowability of leading questions is discretionary, and the judge's action will not be reviewed unless it is charged that it amounted to, or contributed to, the denial of a fair trial.

When the normal assumption about the relation between the witness and the examining counsel or his client appears unfounded, the usual practice is reversed. If, on direct, the witness appears hostile to the examiner, or reluctant, or unwilling, the danger of suggestion disappears, and the judge will permit leading questions, and conversely, if on cross-examination the witness appears to be biased in favor of the cross-examining party, counsel may be prohibited from leading.

In various other situations, leading questions are permitted. They may be used to bring out preliminary matters, such as the name and occupation of the witness; or to elicit matters not substantially in dispute. They may be employed to suggest a subject or topic, as distinguished from an answer. Additional relaxations are grounded in necessity. Thus, the judge, when need appears, will ordinarily permit leading questions to children, or to witnesses so ignorant, timid, weak-minded, or deficient in the English language, that they cannot otherwise be brought to understand what information is sought. It is recognized, especially as to children, that in these cases, the danger of false suggestion is at its highest, but it is better to face that danger than to abandon altogether the effort to bring out what the witness knows. Similarly, when a witness has been fully directed to the subject by non-leading questions without securing from him a complete account of what he is believed to know, his memory is said to be "exhausted" and the judge may permit the examiner to ask questions which by their particularity may revive his memory but which of necessity may thereby suggest the answer desired.

In some jurisdictions, there is a long-standing practice that permits leading questions to a witness who, for impeachment purposes, is to testify to a statement of a previous witness that is inconsistent with the testimony of that witness. Necessity again is said to be the basis of the practice. It might otherwise be impossible to call attention to the subject of the testimony. It has been argued, however, that the practice should not be followed.

§ 7. The Form of Questions: (c) Misleading and Argumentative Questions

The examiner may not ask a question that merely invokes the witness's assent to the questioner's inferences from or interpretations of the facts proved or assumed. This kind of question is subject to objection as "argumentative" but the trial court has a wide range of discretion in enforcing the rule, particularly on cross-examination where such questions are more frequent. A still more common vice is for the examiner to couch the question so that it assumes as true matters to which the witness has not testified, and which are in dispute between the parties. The danger here is two-fold. First, if the examiner is putting the question to a friendly witness, the recitation of the assumed fact may suggest the desired answer; and second, whether the witness is friendly or hostile, the answer is likely to be misleading. Oftentimes, the question will be so separate from the assumption that if the witness answers the question without mentioning the assumption, it is impossible to ascertain whether the assumption was ignored or affirmed.

Occasionally questions are considered objectionable because they are too broad or too indefinite. Often this objection is in reality an objection of lack of relevancy.

The principles mentioned in this section are not expressed specifically in the Federal or Revised Uniform Rules (1974), but they may be enforced by the trial court in its discretion under Rules 403 and 611(a). As to Rule 403 see § 185 infra. For wording of Rule 611(a) see text supra at § 5.

§ 8. The Judge May Examine and Call Witnesses

Under the Anglo–American adversary trial system, the parties and their counsel have the primary responsibility for finding, selecting, and presenting the evidence. However, our system of party-investigation and party-presentation has some limitations. It is a means to the end of disclosing truth and administering justice; and for reaching this end the judge may exercise various powers.

Prominent among these powers is the power to call and question witnesses.

Under the case law and Federal Rule of Evidence 614(b) the judge has discretion to examine any witness to clarify testimony or to bring out needed facts which have not been elicited by the parties. Also, it is sometimes said that the judge may have a duty to question witnesses, but the exercise of such a duty does not appear to have been enforced by any appellate court decisions.

In those states—the great majority—in which the judge does not have power to comment on the weight of the evidence, the judge's questioning in jury cases must be cautiously guarded so as not to constitute an implied comment. Thus, if the judge uses leading questions, suggesting the desired answer, the questions may strongly imply that the desired answer is the truth, and thus may offend the rule against comment. Subject to the limitation that a leading question may constitute prohibited comment, it has been held that the policy against leading questions by counsel, namely, that of avoiding false testimony elicited by partisan suggestion,[1] has no application in general to judges, whose office is to be impartial. This reasoning seems somewhat questionable. Also, questions which are aimed at discrediting or impeaching the witness, though allowable for counsel, when asked by the judge may often— not always—intimate the judge's belief that the witness has been lying, and thus be an implied comment on the weight of the testimony.

In the federal courts and in the few states where the common law power to comment is retained, and in judge-tried cases in all jurisdictions, these restrictions on leading questions and impeaching questions are relaxed. Nevertheless, even then, the judge, though he has a wide power to examine witnesses, must avoid extreme exercises of the power to question, just as he must avoid extreme exercises of the power to comment. He must not assume the role of an advocate or of a prosecutor. If his questions are too partisan or even if they are too extensive, he faces the risk that the appellate court will find that he has crossed the line between judging and advocacy. However, the mere number of questions put by the judge should not be a crucial factor. The nature of the questions is the most important matter.

Not only may the judge examine witnesses called by the parties, but in his discretion he may also, for the purpose of bringing out needed facts, call witnesses whom the parties might not have chosen to call. The power to call witnesses has perhaps most often been exercised when the prosecution expects that a

---

1. See § 6 supra.

necessary witness will be hostile and desires to escape the necessity of calling him and being cumbered by the traditional rule against impeaching one's own witness. Under the Federal Rules of Evidence, although a party may impeach the party's own witness, Fed.R.Evid. 607, the prosecutor may not wish to call a witness and thereby be identified with the witness. The prosecutor may then invoke the judge's discretion to call the witness, Fed.R.Evid. 614(a), in which event either party may cross-examine and impeach him. Another use of the power, implemented by statute in some jurisdictions, is to mediate the battle of partisan expert witnesses employed by the parties, through the judge's resumption of his ancient power to call an expert of his own choosing, or one agreed upon by the parties, to give impartial testimony to aid him or the jury in resolving a scientific issue. But the judge's power of calling witnesses in aid of justice is general and is not necessarily limited to meeting these particular needs.

§ 9. Refreshing Recollection

It is abundantly clear from everyday observation that the latent memory of an experience may be revived by an image seen, or a statement read or heard. This is a part of the group of phenomena which the classical psychologists have called the law of association. The recall of any part of a past experience tends to bring with it the other parts that were in the same field of awareness, and a new experience tends to stimulate the recall of other like experiences. The effect of a reminder, encountered in reading a newspaper or in the conversation of a friend, which gives us the sensation of recognizing as familiar some happening which we had forgotten, and prompts our memory to bring back associated experiences, is a frequently encountered process.

As we have seen,[1] the interviewing of witnesses by counsel who will examine them in court is a necessary step in preparing for trial. It is at this stage that the memory of the witness can best be refreshed about the facts of the case, by giving her the opportunity to read her own written statements previously made, or the letters, maps, or other documents in the case. It is only when this review of the data is insufficient to enable the witness to recall the facts while testifying that refreshing her memory on the stand is advisable. If it is matter which a jury would suppose she should remember unaided, the use of a crutch lessens their confidence in the testimony.

At trials, the practice has long been established that in interrogating a witness counsel may hand her a memorandum to inspect for the purpose of "refreshing her recollection," with the result that when she speaks from a memory thus revived, her testimony is what she says, not the writing. This is the process of *refreshing recollection at the trial* in the strict and accurate sense.

But when this simple but helpful expedient had become established, it was natural for counsel to seek to carry it a step further. If the witness, being shown the writing, states that her memory is not revived thereby and that she cannot testify from a refreshed recollection, she may indicate on looking at the writing, that she recognizes it as a memorandum made by her when the facts were fresh in her mind, and *therefore,* though she has no present memory of the transaction described, she is willing to testify that the facts were correctly recited in the memorandum. Thus the writing itself becomes the evidence. We now recognize this latter situation as quite a different process from the process of *refreshing recollection.* In the process of refreshing recollection, the witness testifies orally on her present refreshed memory; when her memory is not jogged, she merely relies upon her written recital of things remembered in the past as a basis for introducing the writing.

The procedure of tendering a memorandum to the witness is followed in both cases but the underlying justification in the newer situation is quite different. It rests on the relia-

§ 9

1. See § 2 supra.

bility of a writing which the witness swears is a *record of her past recollection,* and the writing is introduced into evidence. Appropriate safeguarding rules have been developed for this latter kind of memoranda, requiring that they must have been written by the witness or examined and found correct by her, and that they must have been prepared so promptly after the events recorded that the events must have been fresh in the mind of the witness when the record was made or examined and verified by her. In this volume these latter memoranda are considered separately, as a possible exception to the hearsay rule.[2]

Apparently, the earlier English cases of genuine refreshment of recollection imposed no restriction upon *the use of memoranda at the trial to refresh.* The memoranda were not required to have been written by the witness or under her direction, or to have been made near in time to the event. In the later-developed practice of introducing records of *past recollection,* restrictions of this kind were imposed with good reason. Since, however, the old name of "refreshing recollection" was given to both practices, it was natural that the restrictions developed for one kind of memoranda should be applied to the other.

Which is the wiser practice, the rule of the older cases, championed by Wigmore and by most present-day courts, to the effect that any memorandum, without restriction of authorship, time, or correctness, may be used when the purpose is to revive memory; or the rule requiring that the memorandum to refresh must meet the same tests as the record of past recollection? Even if the latter requirement is an historical or analytical blunder, it will be none the worse for that if it is a safeguard needed in the search for truth.

It is true that any kind of stimulus, "a song, or a face, or a newspaper item," may produce the "flash" of recognition, the feeling that "it all comes back to me now." But the genuineness of the feeling is no guaranty of the correctness of the image recalled. The danger that the mind will "remember" something that never happened is at least as great here as in the case of leading questions. "Imagination and suggestion are twin artists ever ready to retouch the fading daguerrotype of memory."

Thus, decisions which import into the realm of refreshing memory at the trial the requirements developed for memoranda of past recollection recorded, namely, the requirements that the witness must have made the writing or have recognized it as correct, and that the making or recognition must have occurred at the time of the event or while it was fresh in memory, have a plausible basis in expediency.

Nevertheless, most courts today when faced with the clear distinction between the two uses of the memoranda, will adhere to the "classical" view that any memorandum or other object may be used as a stimulus to present memory, without restriction by rule as to authorship, guaranty of correctness, or time of making. On balance, it would seem that this liberality of practice is the wiser solution because there are other sufficient safeguards to protect against abuse. See Fed. R. Evid. 612. The first safeguard is the power of control by the trial judge. It is a preliminary question for her decision whether the memorandum actually does refresh, and from the nature of the memorandum and the witness's testimony she may find that it does not. Moreover, in the exercise of her discretion to control the manner of the examination, as in the case of leading questions, she may decline to permit the use of the aid to memory where she regards the danger of undue suggestion as outweighing the probable value.

The second safeguard is the rule which entitles the adverse party, when the witness seeks to resort to the memorandum, to inspect the memorandum so that she may object to its use if ground appears, and to have the memorandum available for her reference in cross-examining the witness. With the memorandum before her, the cross-examiner has a

---

2. See Ch. 28 infra. But if the memorandum was prepared by the witness it may be admissible as a non-hearsay statement. See § 251 infra.

good opportunity to test the credibility of the witness's claim that her memory has been revived, and to search out any discrepancies between the writing and the testimony. This right to demand inspection has in the past usually been limited to writings used by the witness on the stand, but the reasons seem in general equally applicable to writings used by the witness to refresh her memory before she testifies. The subject of inspection and use of writings to which the witness has referred prior to testifying at the trial is discussed at the end of the instant section.

Not only may the adversary inspect the memoranda used to refresh memory during the examination of a witness, but she may submit them to the jury for their examination. On the other hand, the party offering the witness may not do so unless the memoranda constitute independent evidence and are not barred by the hearsay rule. The cardinal rule is that unless they may be introduced under the hearsay rule or one of its exceptions, they are not evidence, but only aids in the giving of evidence. Consequently, a copy may be used without accounting for the original.

The line between using the writing as an aid to memory and basing one's testimony upon it as a correct record of past memory is sometimes shadowy. Must it be shown that the witness has no present recollection of the matters embodied in the memorandum before she can use it as an aid to memory? It is sometimes said, even as a matter of case law under the Federal Rules of Evidence, that this must appear, but it is believed that the requirement is unsound. The witness may believe that she remembers completely but on looking at the memorandum she would be caused to recall additional facts. As the Chinese proverb has it, "The palest ink is clearer than the best memory." On the other hand, there is here the ever-present danger that a suggestive witness may think that she remembers a fact because she reads it. It seems eminently a matter for discretion, rather than rule. Similarly, it would seem that a witness may recognize from present memory the correctness of successive facts set out in a memo-

randum, but that she may be unable, despite this recognition, to detail those facts from memory without continuing to consult the writing. Accordingly, the statement that a witness once refreshed must speak independently of the writing seems too inflexible, and it is believed that the matter is discretionary and that the trial judge may properly permit the witness to consult the memorandum as she speaks, especially where it is so lengthy and detailed that even a fresh memory would be unable to recite all the items unaided.

As mentioned previously in the instant section, various cases have refused to enforce a demand for production at trial of matter reviewed by a witness to refresh memory prior to testifying. However, there have been some decisions to the contrary. The most important factor in this trend has been the adoption of Federal Rule of Evidence 612 with the provision that if a witness uses a writing to refresh her memory for the purpose of testifying, before testifying, an adverse party is entitled to have the writing produced at the hearing, to inspect it, to cross-examine the witness thereon, and to introduce into evidence those portions which relate to the testimony of the witness, although only if the court in its discretion determines such production is necessary in the interests of justice.

A writing consulted to refresh memory may be a privileged one, e.g. a letter written by the client-witness to her attorney giving details of the case. In this event, the possibility of conflict arises between the disclosure requirement and the rule that confidential communications between attorney and client are privileged against disclosure. Should the act of consulting the writing be given the effect of a waiver of the privilege? Spelling out a waiver when the writing is consulted by the witness while testifying appears to present no problem; for a witness in effect to say that she can consult the writing while testifying in open court but refuse to allow the opposing party or her counsel to see what the writing is, would so undermine credibility that the claim seems simply not to be made. In fact, usual practice is for examining counsel to establish the bona fides of what is going on by having the witness explain the nature of the document being consulted, and tendering it to opposing counsel. The problem area is when the writing is consulted in advance of trial as an aspect of preparation and in addition is privileged. Ordinarily the privilege involved will be either attorney-client[3] or the qualified privilege for "work product",[4] and the problem of waiver is discussed further in connection with those privileges.[5]

A further matter which must be considered in connection with Federal Rule of Evidence 612 is the relationship between that rule and Rule 26.2 of the Federal Rules of Criminal Procedure, which is the replacement for the so-called Jencks Act, 18 U.S.C.A. § 3500. It is discussed in a later section.[6]

The use of hypnosis as a technique for refreshing the recollection of witnesses is treated in the chapter on scientific and experimental evidence.[7]

3. See generally Ch. 10 infra.
4. See § 96 infra.
5. See § 93 infra.

6. See § 97 infra.
7. See § 206 infra.

Chapter 3

THE REQUIREMENT OF FIRSTHAND KNOWLEDGE: THE OPINION RULE: EXPERT TESTIMONY

Table of Sections

§ 10. The Requirement of Knowledge From Observation

The common law system of proof is exacting in its insistence upon the most reliable sources of information. This policy is apparent in the Opinion rule, the Hearsay rule and the Documentary Originals rule. One of the earliest and most pervasive manifestations of this attitude is the rule requiring that a witness who testifies to a fact which can be perceived by the senses must have had an opportunity to observe, and must have actually observed the fact. See Fed.R.Evid. 602. The same requirement, in general, is imposed upon declarations coming in under exceptions to the hearsay rule, that is, the declarant must so far as appears have had an opportunity to observe the fact declared.

This requirement may easily be confused with the hearsay rule which bars the repetition of out-of-court statements described as hearsay under that rule.[1] Technically, if the testimony of the witness on its face and in form purports to be testimony of observed facts, but the testimony is actually repetition of statements of others, the objection is that the witness lacks firsthand knowledge. If the form of the testimony indicates the witness is repeating out-of-court statements, the hearsay objection possibility is raised. Often courts have disregarded this distinction.

§ 10

1. See § 247 infra.

The burden of laying a foundation by showing that the witness had an adequate opportunity to observe is upon the party offering the testimony. By failing to object the adversary waives the preliminary proof, but not the substance of the requirement, so that if it later appears that the witness lacked opportunity, or did not actually observe the fact, his testimony will be stricken. If under the circumstances proved, reasonable men could differ as to whether the witness did or did not have adequate opportunity to observe, then the testimony of the witness should come in, and the jury will appraise his opportunity to know in evaluating the testimony.

In laying this foundation of knowledge, it is allowable for the examiner to elicit from the witness the particular circumstances which led him to notice or observe or remember the fact.

While the law is exacting in demanding firsthand observation, it is not so impractical as to insist upon preciseness of attention by the witness in observing, or certainty of recollection in recounting the facts. Accordingly, when a witness uses such expressions as "I think," "My impression is," or "In my opinion," this will be no ground of objection if it appears that he merely speaks from an inattentive observation, or an unsure memory, though it will if the expressions are found to mean that he speaks from conjecture or from hearsay.

One who has no knowledge of a fact except what another has told him cannot, of course, satisfy the present requirement of knowledge from observation. When the witness, however, bases his testimony partly upon firsthand knowledge and partly upon the accounts of others, the problem is one which calls for a practical compromise. Thus when he speaks of his own age, or of his kinship with a relative, the courts will allow the testimony. And when the witness testifies to facts that he knows partly at first hand and partly from reports, the judge, it seems, should admit or exclude according to the reasonable reliability of the evidence.

THE OPINION RULE

§ 11. The Evolution of the Rule Against Opinions: Opinions of Laymen

The opinion rule, though it developed from practices and expressions of the English courts, was enforced more generally, and far more inflexibly, here than in the mother country. In the first place a rule against "opinions" may have had a different meaning for the English judge. We are told that in English usage of the 1700's and earlier, "opinion" had the primary meaning of "notion" or "persuasion of the mind without proof or certain knowledge." It carried an implication of lack of grounds, which is absent from our present-day meaning of the term "opinion" in this country. We use the word as denoting a belief, inference, or conclusion without suggesting that it is well- or ill-founded.

The requirement that witnesses must have personal knowledge, already discussed in the preceding section, was a very old rule, having its roots in medieval law, which demanded that they speak only "what they see and hear." The classic dictum of Coke in 1622, that "It is no satisfaction for a witness to say that he 'thinketh' or 'persuadeth himself'" [1] and Mansfield's statement in 1766, "It is mere opinion, which is not evidence" [2] are to be understood as condemning testimony when not based upon personal knowledge. Statements founded only on hearsay or conjecture would fall under this ban. But as Wigmore interprets the historical evidence, there was not until the 1800's any recognition of an opinion rule which would exclude inferences by witnesses possessing personal knowledge. [3]

By the middle of the 1800's the disparagement of "mere opinion" in the sense of a notion or conjecture not rooted in observation had emerged into a much more questionable

§ 11

1. Adams v. Canon, Dyer 53b, quoted 7 Wigmore, Evidence § 1917, p. 2 (Chadbourn rev.1979).

2. Carter v. Boehm, 3 Burr. 1905, 1918 (1766) quoted 7 Wigmore, Evidence § 1917, p. 7 (Chadbourn rev.1978).

3. 7 Wigmore, Evidence § 1917 (Chadbourn rev.1979).

canon of exclusion. This was the doctrine that witnesses generally must give the "facts" and not their "inferences, conclusions, or opinions."

This classic formula, based as it is on the assumption that "fact" and "opinion" stand in contrast and hence are readily distinguishable, proved to be the clumsiest of all the tools furnished the judge for regulating the examination of witnesses. It is clumsy because its basic assumption is an illusion. The words of the witness cannot "give" or recreate the "facts," that is, the objective situations or happenings about which the witness is testifying. Drawings, maps, photographs, even motion pictures, are only a remote and inaccurate portrayal of those "facts", and how much more distant approximations of reality are the word pictures of oral or written testimony. There is no conceivable statement however specific, detailed and "factual," that is not in some measure the product of inference and reflection as well as observation and memory. The difference between the statement, "He was driving on the left-hand side of the road" which would be classed as "fact" under the rule, and "He was driving carelessly" which would be called "opinion" is merely a difference between a more concrete and specific form of descriptive statement and a less specific and concrete form. The difference between so-called "fact," then, and "opinion," is not a difference between opposites or contrasting absolutes, but a mere difference in degree with no recognizable line to mark the boundary.

If trial judges are given the task of distinguishing on the spur of the moment between "fact" and "opinion", no two judges, acting independently, can be expected to reach the same results on the same questions. Of course, it is true that many recurring questions have been used and hence have been customarily classified as calling for "fact" or "opinion", but in a changing world there will constantly be presented a myriad of new statements to which the judge must apply the distinction. Thus, good sense demands that the trial judge be accorded a wide range of discretion at least in classifying evidence as

"fact" or "opinion," and probably in admitting evidence even where found to constitute opinion. Various courts have expressed this viewpoint. It is incorporated in Federal Rule of Evidence and Revised Uniform Rule of Evidence (1974) 701.

The recognition of the impossibility of administering the opinion standard as a mandatory rule, however, came but slowly. The alleviation of the strictness of the standard was at first limited to cases of strict necessity. This rule as stated in the cited case, which in form of statement excludes opinion except in the circumstances listed, remains as the "orthodox" view in fewer and fewer state courts, but in states which have not adopted the Federal Rules of Evidence (or a similar set of rules) the actual practice in the trial of cases is becoming, if indeed it has not always been, far more liberal than the older formulas, and might more accurately be reflected in a formula expressed by some courts that sanction the admission of opinions on grounds of "expediency" or "convenience" rather than "necessity." The so-called "short-hand rendition" rule seems to incorporate this more liberal notion. "Convenience" is a principle incorporated in Federal Rule of Evidence 701.

It is believed that the standard actually applied by many of the trial judges of today includes the principle espoused by Wigmore, namely that opinions of laymen should be rejected only when they are superfluous in the sense that they will be of no value to the jury. The value of opinions to the jury is the principal test of Federal Rule of Evidence and Revised Uniform Rule of Evidence (1974) 701. It seems fair to observe that the prevailing practice in respect to the admission of the opinions of non-expert witnesses may well be described, not as a rule excluding opinions, but as a rule of preference. The more concrete description is preferred to the more abstract. Moreover, it seems that the principal impact of the rule is upon the form of examination. The questions, while they cannot suggest the particular details desired, else they will be leading, should nevertheless call for the most specific account that the witness can give. For example, he must not be asked,

"Did they agree?" but "What did they say?" When recognized as a matter of the form of the examination rather than the substance of the testimony—again, a difference of degree— the opinion rule, like other regulations of form, such as the control over leading questions and questions calling for a free narrative and over the order of proof is seen to fall naturally in the realm of discretion. Furthermore, it seems that this habit and tradition of Anglo–American lawyers to examine about specific details is a valuable heritage. The problem is to preserve this scientific habit of approach but yet to curb the time-wasting quibbling over trivial objections on the ground of "opinion" which may still be heard in those courts which attempt a literal application of the older formulas.

One solution is simply to eliminate the matter of lay opinion from the category of things governed by rules. Supporters would find a sufficient substitute in the natural desire of a lawyer to present a detailed case as being the most convincing technique and in the ability of the adversary on cross-examination to expose the non-existence or inconsistency of details not developed on direct. Of course, Federal Rule of Evidence and Revised Uniform Rule of Evidence 701 does not embody the above solution, but it does present a viable alternative solution. Under Rule 701 and Rule 602, the witness must have personal knowledge of matter that forms the basis of testimony of opinion; the testimony must be based rationally upon the perception of the witness; and of course, the opinion must be helpful to the jury (the principal test). Contrary to some decisions under case law, provided personal knowledge is adequately established the witness need not relate the observed matters that are the basis of opinion, although the judge should have discretion to require preliminary testimony of the facts observed. Finally, Rule 403 permits exclusion of inferences that are prejudicial, confusing, misleading or time-wasting.

§ 12. The Relativity of the Opinion Rule: Opinions on the Ultimate Issue

As pointed out in the next preceding section, the terms "fact" and "opinion" denote merely a difference of degree of concreteness of description or a difference in nearness or remoteness of inference. The opinion rule operates to prefer the more concrete description to the less concrete, the direct form of statement to the inferential. But there is still another variable in the equation. The purpose of the testimony has had an effect on the degree of concreteness required. In the outer circle of collateral facts, near the rim of relevancy, evidence in general terms will be received with relative freedom, but as we come closer to the hub of the issue, the courts have been more careful to call for details instead of inferences.

The trial judge may well be more liberal in the use of his discretion to admit opinions and inferences as to collateral matters and less liberal in order to see that the concrete details are brought out as to more crucial matters. Is it expedient to go further and to tie his hands by a rule forbidding opinion-evidence as to these "ultimate" matters?

Undoubtedly there is a kind of statement by the witness which amounts to no more than an expression of his general belief as to how the case should be decided or as to the amount of unliquidated damages which should be given. It is believed all courts would exclude such extreme expressions. There is no necessity for this kind of evidence; to receive it would tend to suggest that the judge and jury may shift responsibility for decision to the witnesses; and in any event it is wholly without value to the trier of fact in reaching a decision.

But until about 35 years ago, a very substantial number of courts had gone far beyond this commonsense reluctance to listen to the witness's views as to how the judge and jury should exercise their functions and had announced the general doctrine that witnesses would not be permitted to give their opinions or conclusions upon an ultimate fact in issue.

The reason was sometimes given that such testimony "usurps the function" or "invades the province" of the jury. Obviously these expressions were not intended to be taken literally, but merely to suggest the danger that the jury might forego independent analysis of the facts and bow too readily to the opinion of an expert or otherwise influential witness.

Although the rule had been followed in many states prior to 1942, a trend began to abandon or reject it with the result that now in a majority of state courts an expert may state his opinion upon an ultimate fact, provided that all other requirements for admission of expert opinion are met. The trend culminated in the adoption of Federal Rule of Evidence 704(a):

> Except as provided in subdivision (b), testimony in the form of an opinion or inference otherwise admissible is not objectionable because it embraces an ultimate issue to be decided by the trier of fact.

Some courts had already adopted the rule that opinions of laymen on ultimate facts were not precluded. Other general rules of admissibility for such opinions may, however, preclude them in particular instances, e.g., opinions as to how the case should be decided and the like. Under the most liberal rules those opinions would be excludable on the ground that their value is outweighed by "the danger of unfair prejudice, confusion of issues, or misleading the jury, or by considerations of undue delay, waste of time, or needless presentation of cumulative evidence."

This change in viewpoint concerning "ultimate fact" opinion resulted from the fact that the rule excluding opinion on ultimate facts is unduly restrictive, with many possible close questions of application. The rule can often unfairly obstruct the presentation of a party's case, to say nothing of the illogic of the notion that opinions on ultimate facts usurp the function of the jury. In jurisdictions in which the prohibitive rule is retained, there must be difficult and confusing questions whether an opinion concerns an ultimate fact.

Regardless of the rule concerning admissibility of opinion upon ultimate facts, courts do not permit opinion on a question of law, unless the issue concerns a question of foreign law.[1] Nor do the Federal Rules of Evidence permit opinion on law except questions of foreign law.

A court which does not ban opinion on the ultimate issue as such may nevertheless condemn a question phrased in terms of a legal criterion not adequately defined by the questioner so as to be correctly understood by laymen, the question being interpreted by the court as calling for a legal opinion. But it is often convenient or desirable to use questions that are not intended to call forth any legal conclusion but that are phrased in terms of some legal standard familiar to lawyers. There is thus a problem of interpretation of the questions.

The problem has arisen often in relation to testimony on the issue of capacity to make a will. Thus, a court taking the view that there may be opinion upon an ultimate issue would approve a question, "Did X have mental capacity sufficient to understand the nature and effect of his will?" but would frown on the question, "Did X have sufficient mental capacity to make a will?" because the latter question may be incorrectly understood by the witness and the jury if they do not know the law's definition of "capacity to make a will." But a court which prohibits generally opinions on the ultimate issue might condemn both forms of questions, or even one where the questioner breaks down "testamentary capacity" into its factual elements as legally defined. Similar problems may arise in respect to such issues as undue influence, total and permanent disability, negligence, and the like.

On the whole, it is thought that the danger that these questions phrased in terms of "legal conclusions" will be understood as calling for a conclusion or opinion of law is very slight, since they will seldom be asked except when the popular meaning is approximately the same as the legal meaning. In a jurisdiction where there is no general rule against opinions on the ultimate issue, it seems that a request by the adversary that the questioner define his terms should be the only recourse.

§ 12

1. See § 335 infra.

Federal Rule of Evidence 704(b) provides that when the mental state or condition of a defendant in a criminal case is in issue (such as premeditation in homicide, lack of predisposition in entrapment, or when the true affirmative defense of insanity has been raised), an expert witness may not testify that the defendant did or did not have the mental state or condition constituting an element of the crime charged or of a defense thereto. Rule 704(b) seeks to eliminate the confusing spectacle of competing medical experts testifying to directly contradictory conclusions as to the ultimate legal issue to be found by the trier of fact. Presumably the medical expert is able to answer the questions, "Was the accused suffering from a mental disease or defect?"; "Explain the characteristics of the mental disease and defect."; and "Was his act the product of that disease or defect?" However, the expert may not answer the question "Was the accused able to appreciate the nature and quality of his acts", or "Was the accused able to appreciate the wrongfulness of his acts?" Whether Rule 704(b) is having its intended effect of substantially moderating the battle of experts when mental state or condition is an issue remains to be determined.

§ 13. Expert Witnesses: Subjects of Expert Testimony: Qualifications: Cross–Examination

An observer is qualified to testify because he has firsthand knowledge of the situation or transaction at issue. The expert has something different to contribute. This is the power to draw inferences from the facts which a jury would not be competent to draw.

To warrant the use of expert testimony two general elements are required. First, some courts state that the subject of inference must be so distinctively related to some science, profession, business or occupation as to be beyond the ken of laymen. Some cases say that the judge has discretion in administering this rule. Other cases will admit expert opinion concerning matters about which the jurors may have general knowledge if the ex-

pert opinion would still aid their understanding of the fact issue. This latter standard is included within the terms of Federal Rule of Evidence and Revised Uniform Rule of Evidence 702. In fact, Rule 702 should permit expert opinion even if the matter is within the competence of the jurors if specialized knowledge will be helpful, as it may be in particular situations.

Second, the witness must have sufficient skill, knowledge, or experience in or related to the pertinent field or calling as to make it appear that his opinion or inference will probably aid the trier in the search for truth. The knowledge may be derived from reading alone in some fields, from practice alone in some fields, or as is more commonly the case, from both. While the court may rule that a certain subject of inquiry requires that a member of a given profession, as a doctor, an engineer, or a chemist be called; usually a specialist in a particular branch within a profession will not be required. However, the practice in respect to experts' qualifications has not for the most part crystallized in specific rules, but is recognized as a matter for the trial judge's discretion reviewable only for abuse. Reversals for abuse are rare.

There is also the question of whether opinion evidence is admissible if the court believes that the state of the pertinent art or scientific knowledge does not permit a reasonable opinion to be asserted even by an expert. Also, expert opinion need not be admitted if the court believes that an opinion based upon particular facts cannot be grounded upon those facts.

On cross-examination in the process of probing the witness' qualifications, experience, bases, and assumptions opposing counsel may require the expert to disclose the facts, data, and opinions underlying the expert's opinion not previously disclosed. See Fed. R.Evid. 705. With respect to facts, data, or opinions forming the basis of the expert's opinion, disclosed on direct examination or during cross-examination, the cross-examiner may explore whether, and if so how, the nonexistence of any fact, data, or opinion or the existence of a contrary version of the fact, data, or opinion supported by the evidence, would affect the expert's opinion. Similarly the expert may be cross-examined with respect to material reviewed by the expert but upon which the expert does not rely. Counsel is also permitted to test the knowledge, experience, and fairness of the expert by inquiring as to what changes of conditions would affect his opinion, and in conducting such an inquiry, subject to the requirements of Fed. R.Evid. 403, the cross-examiner is not limited to facts finding support in the record. It is, however, improper to inquire of the expert whether his opinion differs from another expert's opinion, not expressed in a learned treatise, if the other expert's opinion has not itself been admitted in evidence. An expert witness may, of course, be impeached with a learned treatise, admissible as substantive evidence under Fed.R.Evid. 803(18). A hypothetical question may be employed upon cross-examination in the court's discretion.

Cross-examination of an expert directed at establishing bias through financial interest is proper. In this context the cross-examiner may seek to establish (1) financial interest in the case at hand by reason of remuneration for services, including services performed which enabled him to testify, (2) continued employment by a party, or (3) the fact of prior testimony for the same party or the same attorney. When it comes to questions directed toward establishing (1) the amount of previous compensation from the same party, (2) the relationship between the expert's income from testifying on behalf of a party or a category of party and total income of the expert, or (3) the mere fact of prior testimony most frequently on behalf of other persons or entities similarly situated, the common law authority indicates lack of agreement. Such inquiries be permitted.

While the precise scope of cross-examination of expert witnesses rests within the discretion of the trial court, this discretion should not be applied in a narrow or restricted manner, especially with respect to experts who deal in opinions as to matters truly not in the common knowledge and experience of laymen.

§ 14. Grounds for Expert Opinion: Hypothetical Questions

The traditional view has been that an expert may state an opinion based on his first-hand knowledge of the facts, or based upon facts in the record at the time he states his opinion, or based partly on firsthand knowledge and partly on the facts of record. If the opinion is to be based on the facts of record, such facts must be in the expert's possession by virtue of the expert having been present at the taking of the testimony of those facts, or they may be furnished to the expert prior to testimony of any opinion by including them in a hypothetical question that asks the expert to assume their truth and state a requested opinion based upon them. However, these methods of eliciting expert opinion have been subject to much criticism; and in response, they are permitted but have been liberalized in the growing number of jurisdictions that have adopted the Federal and Revised Uniform Rule of Evidence 705, as well as in some other jurisdictions. Two major general changes have been made. First, on direct examination an expert may state an opinion without prior disclosure of the underlying data or facts, leaving the process of disclosure of such data to the opponent on cross-examination, if the opponent desires disclosure. Second, specified types of facts and data which are not in the record and which are inadmissible are proper grounds for the expert's opinion. At the same time, in these more liberal jurisdictions the traditional methods and procedures for eliciting expert opinion may still be employed. The traditional views mentioned above are considered in this section, referring to their use when pertinent in the liberal jurisdictions, and the more recent liberal rules, mentioned above in general, are discussed in Sections 15 and 16.

If an expert witness has firsthand knowledge of material facts, he may describe what he has observed and give his inferences therefrom under both traditional views and Federal Rules of Evidence 703 and 705. When the expert has no firsthand knowledge of the situation at issue, and has made no firsthand investigation of the facts, then traditionally the required method of securing the benefit of the expert's skill is by asking the expert to assume certain facts and then on these assumed facts to state opinions or inferences. These questions are known as hypothetical questions, and the rules regulating their form and content have perhaps been developed more on the basis of theoretical logic than on the basis of practicalities. At the discretion of the judge hypothetical questions are permissible under the Federal Rules of Evidence and other liberal rules.

In most jurisdictions with the more traditional views mentioned above it has been permissible to have an expert witness in court during the taking of testimony, and then when the expert is called as a witness to simplify a hypothetical question by merely asking the witness to assume the truth of the previous testimony heard by the witness, or some specified part of it, and to state an opinion upon that assumption. Again this practice is permissible in the discretion of the court under the Federal Rules of Evidence and other liberal rules. The practice has some advantages and some limitations. Two obvious requirements are that the assumed facts must be clear to the jury and must not be conflicting. Otherwise the jury will not be given any aid. A question which asks the witness to assume the truth of one previous witness's testimony will usually meet these requirements, but as the range of assumption is widened to cover the testimony of several witnesses, or all the testimony for one side, the risk of infraction of these requirements is increased; and when a hypothetical question covers all the testimony in the case, the question manifestly will be approved only when the testimony on the issue relating to the question is not conflicting and is brief and simple enough for the jury to recall its outlines without having them recited.

The type of hypothetical questions just discussed, namely those based on other testimony in the case, satisfy the basic traditional requirement imposed on all hypothetical questions—that the facts assumed must be supported by evidence in the case. This rule should not be a requirement for hypothetical questions in jurisdictions which follow the Federal Rules of Evidence. Assuming a jurisdiction in which the requirement exists, the requirement is based on the notion that if the answering opinion is founded on premises of fact which the jury, for want of evidence, cannot find to be true, then they are equally disabled from using the answering opinion as the basis for a finding. Direct testimony supporting the fact assumed is not required. It is sufficient if the fact is fairly inferable from the circumstances proved. Moreover, the supporting evidence need not have been already adduced if the interrogating counsel gives assurance that it will be. Further, it is no objection that the supporting evidence is controverted. The proponent is entitled to put his side of the case to the witness for his opinion. However, it is thought there is a possible danger that, by omitting some of the facts, the proponent may present an unfair and inadequate picture to the expert and that the jury may give undue weight to the answer without considering its faulty basis. What safeguards have been supplied? Some decisions have required that all facts material to the question should be embraced in the hypothesis, but this viewpoint seems undesirable because it is likely to multiply disputes as to the sufficiency of the hypothesis, and may tend to cause counsel, out of abundance of caution, to propound questions so lengthy as to be wearisome and almost meaningless to the jury. The more expedient and more widely prevailing view is that there is no rule requiring that all material facts be included. The safeguards are that the adversary may on cross-examination supply omitted facts and ask the expert if his opinion would be modified by them, and further that the trial judge if he deems the original question unfair may in his discretion require that the hypothesis be reframed to supply an adequate basis for a helpful answer.

As indicated in Section 16, infra, however, none of these traditional rules governing the requirements for hypothetical questions has furnished sufficient safeguards against evils arising from the use of these questions.

§ 15. Expert's Opinion Based on Reports of Others and Inadmissible or Unadmitted Data and Facts

A question calling for a direct opinion based upon firsthand knowledge of an expert is so direct, simple, and thus effective that a party may for similar reasons desire to obtain an opinion based upon reports of others. There formerly was a majority view, however, that a question is improper if it calls for the witness' opinion on the basis of reports that are not in evidence or are inadmissible in evidence under the hearsay rule (without reciting their contents as hypotheses, to be supported by other evidence as to their truth). The essential reason in support of this view seemed to be that the jury was asked to accept as evidence the witness' inference, based upon someone's hearsay or upon other inadmissible facts which were presumably not supported by any evidence at the trial and which therefore the jury had no basis for finding to be true. Want of knowledge could also be asserted. This view was also taken when the witness was asked to give a similar direct (not hypothetical) opinion, not merely on the basis of reports, facts and data of this kind, but on these matters supplemented by the witness' own observation of the person or matter in question. However, in this latter situation there has been a strong case law trend toward a contrary view. (There is also a suggested view that opinions based upon hearsay should be less objectionable if they are opinions upon subject matters that have an indirect relation to the fact issues in the case, rather than opinions directly concerning the facts in issue.) The above trend was another trend in the area of evidence law which culminated in a broader view in Federal Rule of Evidence 703, which has been adopted in various state jurisdictions. Of course, under Rule 703 (and Rule 705) an expert may give a direct opinion upon facts and data, including reports, which are inadmissible or not introduced into evidence, provided the reports or other data are "of a type reasonably relied upon by experts in the particular field in forming opinions or inferences upon the subject." This view is justified on the ground that an expert in a science is competent to judge the reliability of statements made to him by other investigators or technicians. He is just as competent indeed to do this as a judge and jury are to pass upon the credibility of an ordinary witness on the stand. If the statements, then, are attested by the expert as the basis for a judgment upon which he would act in the practice of his profession, it seems that they should ordinarily be a sufficient basis even standing alone for his direct expression of professional opinion on the stand, and this argument is reinforced when the opinion is founded not only upon reports but also in part upon the expert's firsthand observation. The data of observation will usually enable the expert to evaluate the reliability of the statement.

The principal problem presented by Rule 703 is the interpretation of the language quoted above. The key language consists of the words, "reasonably relied upon" as further modified in the rule. The liberal approach is that the judge may rely on the expert's view in judging whether the standard of the rule is met at least in matters in which the judge is not equipped to "second guess" the expert. There is also a restrictive approach to the effect that if the data would have been or was excluded from the record as hearsay and can not meet a test of circumstantial trustworthiness for an exception to the hearsay rule, the standard of Rule 703 is not met.

An example may best illustrate the concept of trustworthiness identical or equivalent to that of statements admissible pursuant to a hearsay exception required under the restrictive approach. Assume the following facts: Plaintiff's warehouse burned to the ground. The insurance company asserts arson in defending an action on the insurance policy. The defendant insurance company lists as potential witnesses for trial an expert from the local fire department arson squad and an arson investigator employed by a company to conduct such investigations. The fire department arson expert arrived on the scene about twenty minutes after the first firefighter arrived. The expert is prepared to testify that the fire was deliberately set.

The fire department arson expert in support of this opinion relies upon oral statements made by a firefighter on the scene describing observations during the first few minutes fighting the fire. The arson expert may reasonably rely on oral statements of another firefighter relating matters of personal knowledge; experts customarily rely on such statements, and because the statements are made pursuant to a business duty to report, they are sufficiently trustworthy to make such reliance reasonable. In addition, the fire department arson expert relies upon the results of laboratory tests on material the firefighters removed from the wreckage. Because these laboratory tests were conducted in the course of a regularly conducted business activity, the arson expert may reasonably rely on these results.

The arson expert also relies on two additional statements. The first statement, made by a firefighter on the scene, relates that ten minutes after the firefighter arrived a bystander calmly reported seeing a man run out of a building shortly before it caught fire. The second statement, made by another firefighter, relates that the firefighter saw Harold Jones standing at the corner watching the fire and that Harold Jones is rumored among the firefighters to be a professional arsonist. Although arson experts customarily may rely on these types of statements, neither statement is sufficiently trustworthy to make such reliance reasonable. Applying the better restrictive approach to analyzing trustworthiness, the expert may not "reasonably" rely on the statement by a bystander who is under no business duty to report, possessing no indicia of trustworthiness beyond that of hearsay statements at large. A statement by a member of the expert's organization reporting a rumor, a statement not based upon personal knowledge of the underlying facts, similarly is a hearsay statement insufficiently trustworthy to be "reasonably" relied upon

even if experts in the field customarily rely on such statements.

Neither approach is flawless. The difficulty with the liberal approach is that a party can employ an expert witness to place untrustworthy facts, data, or opinions before the jury. Under the restrictive approach, a court may exclude material on which an expert may actually rely in the expert's practice. On balance the restrictive approach is preferable.

The judge and the attorneys may treat the matter in a hearing under Rule 104. A problem under Rule 703 in criminal cases is whether the defendant should or must have the opportunity of cross-examination of the persons who originated the data upon which an expert relies under the language of Rule 703. Rule 703 should probably be followed unless a government expert is in effect being used solely to bring before the jury otherwise inadmissible matter (particularly, inadmissible hearsay). A similar solution should be employed where the criminal defendant's mental health expert relies on the defendant's out of court statements to support an opinion where insanity is a defense.

Of course, almost all expert opinion embodies hearsay indirectly, a matter which the courts recognize and accept.

§ 16. Should the Hypothetical Question Be Retained?

The hypothetical question is an ingenious and logical device for enabling the jury to apply the expert's scientific knowledge to the facts of the case. Nevertheless, it has been largely a failure in practice and an obstruction to the administration of justice. If we require that it recite all the relevant facts, it becomes intolerably wordy. If we allow, as most courts do, the interrogating counsel to select such of the material facts as he sees fit, we tempt him to shape a one-sided hypothesis. Those expert witnesses who have given their views seem to agree that this partisan slanting of the hypothesis is the fatal weakness of the practice. The legal writers who have studied the problem seem equally agreed in condemnation.

What is the remedy? It seems hardly practicable to require the trial judge to undertake such a preliminary study of the case as would be necessary to enable him to make the selection of the significant facts to be included. It would be feasible for the questions to be framed by both counsel in conference with the judge, either at a pretrial hearing or during the trial, with the jury excluded. But this is wasteful of time and effort. The only remaining expedient is the one generally advocated, namely, that of dispensing with the requirement that the question be accompanied by a recital of a hypothesis, unless the proponent elects to use the hypothetical form, or unless the trial judge in his discretion requires it. This is the procedure authorized by Federal and Revised Uniform Rule of Evidence (1974) 705 and a few other statutes and rules. It is for the cross-examiner to bring out the basis for the expert's opinion if that is desired. Manifestly, this does not lessen the partisanship of the question or the answer, but it does simplify the examination and removes the occasion for imperiling the judgment by mistakes in the form of hypothetical questions. Rule 705 does, however, give the judge discretion to require prior disclosure of basis facts, and it may be assumed that he will do so when there has not been adequate opportunity to discover them in advance, especially in criminal cases.

§ 17. Proposals for Improvement of the Practice Relating to Expert Testimony

In common law countries we have the contentious, or adversary, system of trial, where the opposing parties, and not the judge as in other systems, have the responsibility and initiative in finding and presenting proof. Advantageous as this system is in many respects, its present application in the procurement and presentation of expert testimony is widely considered a sore spot in judicial administration. There are two chief points of weakness in the use of experts. The first is the choice of experts by the party, who will naturally be interested in finding, not the best scientist, but the "best witness." As an English judge has said:

> " * * * the mode in which expert evidence is obtained is such as not to give the fair result of scientific opinion to the Court. A man may go, and does sometimes, to half-a-dozen experts * * * He takes their honest opinions, he finds three in his favor and three against him; he says to the three in his favor, 'will you be kind enough to give evidence?' and he pays the three against him their fees and leaves them alone; the other side does the same * * * I am sorry to say the result is that the Court does not get that assistance from the experts which, if they were unbiased and fairly chosen, it would have a right to expect." [1]

The second weakness is that the adversary method of eliciting scientific testimony, by direct and cross-examination in open court, frequently upon hypothetical questions based on a partisan choice of data, is ill-suited to the dispassionate presentation of technical data, and results too often in overemphasizing conflicts in scientific opinions which a jury is incapable of resolving.

A potential remedy for the first weakness worthy of serious consideration lies in the use of trial judges common law power to call experts. Cases are recorded as early as the 14th century—before witnesses were heard by juries—of the summoning of experts by the judges to aid them in determining scientific issues. The existence of the judge's power to call witnesses generally and expert witnesses particularly seems well recognized in this country. It has been declared by rules and statutes in a substantial number of states empowering the trial judge to summon expert witnesses of his own choosing. Some of these provisions apply to scientific issues in any

Spiller, 6 Ch.D. 412 (1877).

§ 17

1. Jessel, M.R., in Thorn v. Worthington Skating Rink Co., L.R. 6 Ch.D. 415, 416 (1876), note to Plimpton v.

case, civil or criminal, some are limited to criminal cases and some refer to issues of sanity in criminal cases. The principle is implemented in the carefully drafted Model Expert Testimony Act approved in 1937 by the Commissioners on Uniform State Laws,[2] and embodied in abbreviated form in the former and present Uniform Rules of Evidence and Federal Rule of Evidence 706. The further mechanism of establishing panels of impartial experts designated by groups in the appropriate fields, from which panel court appointed experts would be selected, should also be considered. An American Bar Association committee has approved in principle this procedure for impartial medical expert witnesses.

It would not only be helpful to reduce the partisan element in the selection of experts, it is also important that the contentious character of the presentation of the results of the expert's investigation be modified. Otherwise, the "battle of experts" might merely evolve into a battle of examiner and cross-examiner in the interrogation of the official expert at the trial. In some kinds of controversies a well-devised plan of scientific investigation and report may operate to reduce greatly the need for contested trials in court. In the Uniform Act, it is provided that the court may require a conference of the experts, whether chosen by the court or the parties, so that they may as far as possible resolve together, in the light of the knowledge and observations of all of them, their differences of view and their difficulties in interpreting the data. As a result, there will be possibilities of a complete agreement which may practically settle the issue for the parties. If not, it will at least make clear the area of agreement and may narrow the controversy within manageable limits. Two or more experts, it is provided, may join in a single report. At the trial, moreover, the individual report of the expert witness, or a joint report, may be read to the court and jury as a part of his testimony, and he may be cross-examined thereon. (In any event, each expert may be required to

file a report which is subject to inspection.) The Act dispenses with the requirement of the use of the hypothetical question.

In evaluating the potential utility of court appointed experts as a remedy to the partisan nature of expert witness testimony, it is important to keep in mind that the expanded use of court appointed experts is not without its critics. It has been argued in opposition to the court appointment of an expert witness that there is no such thing as a truly impartial expert and, even assuming such an expert does exist, why should it be assumed that the court has the ability to discern him. In addition, the procedure associated with the employment of the expert at trial could foster excessive emphasis by the trier of fact on this witness' opinion at the expense of the adversary system.

There are other features of the common law procedure which greatly hamper the effectiveness of expert testimony. Among these are, first, the unsuitability of the jury, a body of laymen usually required to be unanimous, as a tribunal for appraising scientific evidence; second, the rules of privilege, especially the physician-patient privilege and the privilege against self-incrimination;[3] and third, the occasional employment by the courts of standards of liability, which do not accord with the scientific standards which the experts are accustomed to use as criteria, as in the case of the "understanding of right and wrong" test of responsibility of insane persons.

Finally, it should be borne in mind that the need for better employment by the courts of the resources of technicians and scientists goes beyond the use of expert witnesses. A judge has said:

"The methods of courts might well be supplemented by the use of well tested examples of administrative tribunals, of expert investigators acting for the court—engineers, scientists, physicians, economic and social investigators, as needed—in addition to, not in substitute for, similar experts acting for the parties * * *.

---

2. The Act is set out in 1937 Handbook, Nat'l Conf. Com'rs on Unif.State Laws 339–348.

3. See §§ 99 and 134 infra.

"Why should not judge and jury in cases involving multitudinous scientific exhibits, or scientific questions, have the benefit of the assistance of those competent to organize such data and analyze such questions? Why should not courts have adequate fact finding facilities for all kinds of cases? Boards of directors do. Administrative tribunals do. The parties, and in a large sense the public, have an interest in the decision of cases on whole truth, not on partial understanding. The machinery and expert staffs developed by the interstate commerce commission, state public service commissions, and workmen's compensation boards have values for fact finding which may profitably be studied in reference to judicial reorganization * * * *"[4]

The judicial tradition has known an abundance of procedures which are well adapted to the utilizing of the services and knowledge of experts. Perhaps pretrial conferences could be designed more specifically to deal with matters involving expert opinion. Most important is the power, often regulated by statute or rule, but in any event presumably one of the latent, "inherent" judicial powers, of referring a question to a master, referee, auditor or similar officer, standing or special. The reference may contemplate merely an investigation and report, or a hearing followed by a report or a preliminary decision. It has been urged that these traditional procedures be more widely used and more effectively prescribed by statute. It is suggested likewise that the courts make wider use of the technical resources of the sister branch of the government, the administrative commissions. It may be predicted that all of these opportunities of the courts for using expert knowledge less clumsily may eventually be employed more widely in the future. They would not merely be useful as aids to a more intelligent final trial of an issue in this context of employment of expert knowledge, but it is likely they would more and more often render trial unnecessary.

§ 18. Application of the Opinion Rule to Out-of-Court Statements

Does the opinion rule apply to statements made out of court, and offered in court under some exception to the hearsay rule? If we accept the traditional view that the opinion rule is a categorical rule of exclusion, rejecting a certain definable type of evidence, it is natural to assume that if this kind of evidence is excluded when elicited from a witness on the stand, it should also be rejected when offered in the form of the repetition in court of what some narrator has said out of court. Consequently, many decisions have simply discussed the admissibility of opinions contained in hearsay declarations as if they had been given by a witness on the stand, and have rejected or admitted them accordingly, although common sense doubtless has an unspoken influence toward a more liberal treatment of the out-of-court opinions. If on the other hand we adopt the view to which the courts seem now to be tending namely, that the opinion rule is not an absolute rule of exclusion, but rather a relative rule for the examination of witnesses, preferring when it is feasible the more concrete form of examination to the more general and inferential,[1] then it becomes obvious that the opinion rule has no sensible application to statements made out of court. Sustaining an objection to counsel's question to a witness as calling for an "opinion" is usually not a serious matter since counsel can in most cases easily reframe the question to call for the more concrete statement. But to reject the statement of the out-of-court narrator of what he observed, as in a dying declaration, on the ground that the statement is too general in form to meet the courtroom rules of interrogation mistakes the function of the opinion rule and may shut out altogether a valuable item of proof. Many of the cases, and Wigmore, have taken this view as to admissions,[2] and it is believed that it is

4. Justice Harold M. Stephens, What Courts can Learn from Commissions, 21 A.B.A.J. 141, 142 (1933). Also, see generally, Ch. 37 infra.

§ 18

1. See §§ 11, 12 supra.

2. See § 256 infra. Compare the similar problem presented in respect to evidence of inconsistent state-

in the process of prevailing as to the other classes of declarations coming in under exceptions to the hearsay rule.[3]

Of course, the speciously similar question of the want of personal knowledge of the declarant should be distinguished. If it appears that the out-of-court declarant had not observed at first hand the fact declared, this goes not to form but to substance and is often fatal to admissibility if the statement is offered to prove the fact.[4]

---

ments to impeach, § 35 infra. See treatment of the various exclusions and exceptions to the hearsay rule in Chapters 25–33 infra.

3. As to dying declarations see § 313 infra.

4. See §§ 313 and 280 infra. But the situation is to the contrary with respect to admissions, see § 255 infra and the entry of items in business records, see § 290 infra.

Chapter 4

CROSS–EXAMINATION AND SUBSEQUENT EXAMINATIONS

Table of Sections

§ 19. The Right of Cross–Examination: Effect of Deprivation of Opportunity to Cross–Examine

For two centuries, common law judges and lawyers have regarded the opportunity of cross-examination as an essential safeguard of the accuracy and completeness of testimony, and they have insisted that the opportunity is a right and not a mere privilege. This right is available, of course, at the taking of depositions, as well as on the examination of witnesses at the trial. And the premise that the opportunity of cross-examination is an essential safeguard has been the principal justification for the exclusion generally of hearsay statements,[1] and for the admission as an exception to the hearsay rule of reported testimony taken at a former hearing when the present adversary was afforded the opportunity to cross-examine.[2] State constitutional

§ 19

1. See § 245 infra.

2. See § 302 infra.

provisions guaranteeing to the accused the right of confrontation have been interpreted as codifying this right of cross-examination, and the right of confrontation required by the Sixth Amendment of the federal constitution in general guarantees the accused's right to the opportunity of cross-examination in criminal proceedings.

What are the present consequences of a denial or failure of the right? There are several common situations. First, a party testifying on his own behalf may unjustifiably refuse to answer questions necessary to a complete cross-examination. Here it is generally agreed that the adversary is entitled to have the direct testimony stricken out, a result that seems warranted.

Second, a non-party witness may similarly refuse to be cross-examined, or to answer proper questions of the cross-examiner. Here the case is a little less clear, but the expressions of some judges and writers seem to sanction the same remedy of excluding the direct. This minimizes the temptation for the party to procure the witness's refusal, a collusion which is often hard to prove and protects the right of cross-examination strictly. There is also some authority for the view that the matter should be left to the judge's discretion. Finally, there is support for the notion that if the privilege against self-incrimination is invoked upon cross-examination to questions which go to the credibility of the witness and are otherwise collateral or immaterial, the testimony on direct examination should not be stricken, or at the least the judge should have an area of discretion in making his ruling on that matter.

Third, the witness may become, or purport to become, sick or otherwise physically or mentally incapacitated, before cross-examination is begun or completed. Many of such cases arouse suspicion of simulation, particularly when the witness is a party, and consequently the party's direct examination will often be excluded. In the case of the non-party witness, the same result is usually reached, but, at least in civil cases, it is arguable that this result should be qualified so that the judge is directed to exclude unless he is clearly convinced that the incapacity is genuine, in which event he should let the direct testimony stand. He should then be authorized to explain to the jury the weakness of such uncross-examined evidence. Temporary incapacity may change this result, as indicated below.

The fourth situation is that of the death of the witness before the cross-examination. Here again it is usually said that the party thus deprived of cross-examination is entitled to have the direct testimony stricken, unless, presumably, the death occurred during a postponement of the cross-examination consented to or procured by him. In case of death there seems no adequate reason for excluding the direct testimony, except that exclusion may well be required if the witness is a state's witness in a criminal case. It has been suggested that exclusion of the direct should be discretionary but no matter how valuable cross-examination may be, common sense tells us that the half-loaf of direct testimony is better than no bread at all. To let the direct testimony stand was the accepted practice in equity. It is submitted that except for the testimony of the state's witnesses in criminal cases the judge should let the direct testimony stand but should be required on request to instruct the jury in weighing its value to consider the lack of opportunity to cross-examine.

The above results may be modified in certain situations. It has been held that where the incapacity is temporary the cross-examiner may not insist upon immediate exclusion of the direct testimony, but must be content with the offer of a later opportunity to cross-examine even when this makes it necessary for him to submit to a mistrial.

It has been assumed in the preceding paragraphs that, though some cross-questions may have been answered, a failure to secure a complete cross-examination would be treated as if cross-examination had been wholly denied. It seems, however, that a cross-examination, though cut off before it is finished, may yet under the circumstances be found to have been so substantially complete as to satisfy the requirement of opportunity to cross-examine. It also appears that cross-examination may be regarded in the particular situation as having been sufficient as to part of the direct testimony to allow that part to stand though the rest must be stricken.

Finally, the infringement of the right of cross-examination may come, not from the refusal or inability of the witness, but from the action of the judge. The judge, as we shall see, has wide discretionary control over the *extent* of cross-examination upon particular topics, but the denial of cross-examinations altogether, or its arbitrary curtailment upon a proper subject of cross-examination will be ground for reversal.

§ 20. Form of Interrogation

In contrast with direct examination, cross-examination may usually be conducted by leading questions. See Fed.R.Evid. 611(c). The cross-examiner's purpose in the main is to weaken the effect of the direct testimony, and furthermore, the witness is usually assumed to be a more or less uncooperative one. Consequently the danger of undue acquiescence in the examiner's suggestions is not ordinarily present. However, when it appears that the witness is biased in favor of the cross-examiner, and likely to be unduly yielding to the suggestions of leading questions the judge in many jurisdictions may restrain the asking of them, and in those jurisdictions where the scope of cross-examination is limited, if the examiner goes beyond the proper field of cross-examination he may be required to refrain from leading the witness. There are, on the other hand, a number of somewhat illogical decisions which permit leading questions on cross-examination even though the witness appears biased in favor of the cross-examiner.

§ 21. Scope of Cross–Examination: Restriction to Matters Opened Up on Direct: The Various Rules

The practice varies widely in the different jurisdictions on the question whether the cross-examiner is confined in his questions to the subjects testified about in the direct examination, and if so to what extent.

The traditional rule of wide-open cross-examination. In England and some of the states, the simplest and freest practice prevails. In these jurisdictions, the cross-examiner is not limited to the topics which the direct examiner has chosen to open, but is free to cross-examine about any subject relevant to any of the issues in the entire case, including facts relating solely to the cross-examiner's own case or affirmative defense.

The "restrictive" rule, in various forms, limiting cross-examination to the scope of the direct. The majority of the states have agreed in the view that the cross-examination must be limited to the matters testified to on the direct examination. This general rule was adopted by Federal Rule of Evidence 611(b). This doctrine can be employed narrowly to restrict the cross-questions to those relating only to the same acts or facts, and, perhaps, those occurring or appearing at the same time and place. The doctrine has often been formulated in a way to suggest this meaning. Thus, the cross-examination has been said to be limited to "the same points" brought out on direct, to the "matters testified to," to the "subjects mentioned," and the like. Slightly more expansive is the extension to "facts and circumstances connected with" the matters stated on direct, but this still suggests the requirement of identity of transaction, and proximity in time and space. Seemingly a much wider extension is accomplished by another variation of the formula. This is the statement that the cross-examination is limited to the matters opened in direct and to facts tending to explain, contradict, or discredit the testimony given in chief, and even more widely, facts tending to rebut any "inference or deduction" from the matters testified on direct. There is little consistency in the expression and the use of formulas, even in the same jurisdiction. All express criteria are too vague to be employed with precision. Assuming that cross-examination is somehow to be limited to the subject matter of the direct examination, the subject matter of questions on direct examination can always be defined in particular instances with greater or lesser generality regardless of the general formulas.

In defining the subject matter of the direct examination Federal Rule of Evidence 611(b) should be interpreted to include the broader views expressed above, a viewpoint that is not inconsistent with the provision that the court may permit inquiry into additional matters as if on direct.

All these limiting formulas have a common escape valve, namely, the notion that where part of a transaction, contract, conversation, or event has been revealed on direct, the remainder may be brought out on cross-examination. The fact that this is substantially a mere statement of the converse of the limiting rule itself does not detract from its usefulness as an added tool for argument. This particular rule of completeness is unaffected by Federal Rule of Evidence 106, which does not apply to cross-examination after testimony upon direct. Another escape valve for appeal purposes is the notion that the trial judge has a certain amount of discretion in ruling upon the scope of cross-examination.

The half-open door: cross-examination extends to any matters except cross-examiner's affirmative case. A third view as to the scope of cross-examination would take a middle course between the two extremes. Under this view, now mostly obsolete, the cross-examiner could question the witness about any matters relevant to any issue in the action, except facts relating only to the cross-examiner's own affirmative case, such as defendant's affirmative defenses or cross-claims, or in case of a plaintiff, his new matter in reply. This rather liberalized standard in some instances served as a half-way house, for a time, for courts which later turned to the "wide-open" practice. It has the merit, as compared with the restrictive practice, of lessening dispute by widening the ambit of examination. Its present drawback is that it would often be difficult to determine, particularly under the liberal pleading rules of today, whether the matter inquired about does relate solely to

the examiner's "distinct grounds of defense or avoidance."

§ 22. Cross–Examination to Impeach Not Limited to the Scope of the Direct

One of the main functions of cross-examination is to afford an opportunity to elicit answers which will impeach the veracity, capacity to observe, impartiality, and consistency of the witness; and yet the direct can seldom be expected to touch explicitly on the points to which impeachment is directed. Accordingly, the rule prevails, even in jurisdictions adopting the most restrictive practice, that cross-examination to impeach is not, in general, limited to matters brought out in the direct examination. This view is adopted in Federal Rule of Evidence 611(b).

§ 23. Practical Consequences of the Restrictive Rules: Effect on Order of Proof: Side–Effects

It is sometimes asserted that the only "essential" difference between the "wide-open" and the restrictive rules as to scope of cross-examination is in the time or stage at which the witness may be called upon to testify to the facts inquired about. Thus the difference between the rules would be primarily in their effect upon the order of proof. Under the "wide-open" rule the witness may be questioned on the new matter on cross-examination, whereas under the restrictive rules the cross-examiner can merely postpone the questions until his own next stage of putting on proof, and then call the witness and prove the same facts. This difference is, of course, a substantial difference, but in many instances a mere postponement of the questions will not necessarily be the result of a ruling excluding a cross-question as not in the scope of the direct. Unless the question is vital and he is fairly confident of a favorable answer, the cross-examiner will at the least take considerable risk if he calls the adversary's witness at a later stage as his own, and will often be motivated to abandon the inquiry. Getting concessions from the opponent's witness while his story is fresh is worth trying for. To call the perhaps unfriendly witness later when his first testimony is stale is usually a much less effective expedient. Also promotion of orderly presentation of proof, supposedly promoted by restrictive rules, may not be an effective reason in particular cases in which a party has injected an issue by one witness but not by a second witness who may not be cross-examined on the issue although he may have knowledge relevant to that issue.

A ruling excluding questions as not within the scope of the direct is not the only consequence of the restrictive rule. There are many collateral effects. Thus the courts adopting the restrictive practice often say that if the cross-examiner, perhaps without objection, cross-examines on new matter he makes the witness his own. This notion is stated in Federal Rule of Evidence 611(b). This being so, he is normally forbidden to ask leading questions about the new matter, and under the traditional rule against impeaching one's own witness [1] may be precluded from impeaching the witness as to those facts. But because one may impeach one's own witness under Federal Rule of Evidence 607, one would not be precluded from impeaching the witness concerning the new matter brought out pursuant to Rule 611(b). Furthermore, the application of the restrictive rule so as to exclude unfavorable testimony from the plaintiff's witness which could otherwise be elicited on cross-examination, may save the plaintiff from a directed verdict at the close of his case in chief. This is usually a tactical advantage, affording the plaintiff a wider possibility for strengthening his case from his opponent's witnesses, even though the unfavorable testimony of the cross-examined witness may be later elicited by the defendant in the course of his own case in defense, and standing undisputed may thus ultimately result in a directed verdict, anyway. Finally, in one situation, the restrictive rule may become a rule of final exclusion, not a rule of postponement. This is

the situation where the witness has a privilege not to be called as a witness by the cross-examiner. Thus, the privilege of the accused, and of the spouse of the accused, not to be called by the state in a criminal case may prevent the prosecutor from eliciting the new facts at a later stage, if he cannot draw them out on cross-examination.[2]

§ 24. The Scope of the Judge's Discretion Under the Wide–Open and Restrictive Rules

When Gibson, C.J.[1] and Story, J.[2] introduced the innovation upon the orthodox "wide-open" cross-examination, by suggesting that questioning about new matter was not proper at the stage of cross-examination, they thought of their admonitions as relating solely to the order of proof. Traditionally the order of proof and the conduct and extent of cross-examination have been said to be specially subject to discretionary control by the trial judge.

Accordingly, the earlier cases and many of the more recent cases in jurisdictions adopting the restrictive rule in any of its forms, emphasize the power of the trial judge in his discretion to allow deviations. It has been said, indeed, that both the courts following the wide-open and those adopting the restrictive practice "recognize the discretionary power of the trial court to allow variations from the customary order and decline ordinarily to consider as an error any variation sanctioned by the trial court." If this statement were fully true, the hazards of injustice at the trial, or of reversals on appeal, in the administration of either rule would not be substantial. But the statement probably paints too bright a picture.

In the states adopting "the scope of the direct" test, trial courts and lawyers tend to find it easier to administer the test as a rule

---

§ 23

1. This rule, however, has now been much liberalized in many jurisdictions. See § 38 infra.

2. See §§ 25, 26 infra.

§ 24

1. In Ellmaker v. Buckley, 16 Sarg. & Rawles 72 (Pa.1827).

2. In Philadelphia & Trenton Railroad Co. v. Stimpson, 39 U.S. (14 Pet.) 448 (1840).

than as a flexible standard of discretion. Also, appellate courts have reversed many cases for error in the application of the test, although there is a trend to give a greater scope of power to the trial judge.

In jurisdictions following the traditional wide-open view, there seems to have been little tendency to apply the general notion that the order of proof is discretionary. The tradition has not been shaped in terms of order of proof, but in the language of a right to cross-examine upon the whole case. The situation which puts the most strain upon the wide-open rule is the one where a party, usually the plaintiff, finds himself compelled at the outset to call from the adversary's camp either the party himself or some ally or employee to prove up a formal fact not substantially in dispute. Shall the adversary be allowed to disrupt the proponent's case at this stage by cross-examining the willing witness about matters of defense unrelated to the direct examination? This is an appealing situation for the exercise of a discretion to vary from the wide-open practice and to require the cross-examiner to call the witness for these new matters when he puts on his own case. So far, however, as the decisions examined reveal, the power is not emphasized in the "wide-open" jurisdictions.

§ 25. Application of Wide–Open and Restrictive Rules to the Cross–Examination of Parties: (a) Civil Parties

In the cross-examination of party witnesses two situations are to be distinguished, namely, the hostile cross-examination by the adversary of a party who calls himself as a witness in his own behalf, and the friendly cross-examination by the counsel of a party who has been called as an adverse witness by his opponent. In the first situation, in jurisdictions following the restrictive rules it is sometimes held that while the range of discretion to permit the relaxation of the restrictive practice is wider, the general limitation to the "scope of the direct," based on the maintenance of the normal order of proof is still applicable. However, relaxation of the re-

strictive practice *only* for parties as mentioned above does not appear to be authorized by Federal Rule of Evidence 611(b). A few cases, however, without much discussion of reasons have said that upon the hostile cross-examination of a party, the limitation to the scope of the direct will not be applied. Of course, in the "wide-open" states the usual freedom from the restriction is accorded without question.

When a party calls the adverse party as a hostile witness, it is usually provided by statute or rule that he may question him "as upon cross-examination," i.e., he may ask leading questions, and that he is not "bound" by the answers of the adverse witness, which means chiefly that he may impeach the testimony by showing inconsistent statements. When this examination, savoring so nearly of a cross-examination, is concluded, there is a view that gives no right to the party to be further examined immediately by his own counsel, but gives the judge a discretion to permit it or to require that his examination be deferred until the witness-party's own "case" is put on. Most jurisdictions, however, permit the immediate further examination of the witness by his own counsel. Presumably upon request the trial judge would forbid leading questions, see Fed.R.Evid. 611(c), and there is no tendency here in the restrictive states to relax for this "cross-examination" of a friendly witness, the usual restrictions limiting the questions to the scope of the direct.

§ 26. Application of Wide–Open and Restrictive Rules to the Cross–Examination of Parties: (b) The Accused in a Criminal Case

As a means of implementing the prescribed order of producing evidence by the parties, the restrictive rules limiting cross-examination to the scope of the direct or to the proponent's case are arguably burdensome, but they are understandable. The cross-examiner who has been halted has at least a theoretical remedy. He may call the witness for questioning when he puts on his own next stage of evidence. However, when the restrictive practice is applied to the accused in a criminal case, as it is in jurisdictions that follow that practice generally, the accused may carefully limit his direct examination to some single aspect of the case such as age, sanity, or alibi and then invoke the court's ruling that the cross-examination be limited to the matter thus opened. This restrictive practice has been criticized. Of course, there is no problem of the accused escaping searching inquiry on the whole case if the scope of cross-examination is "wide-open."

Regardless of whether the result under the restrictive rule may be desirable, it may be that the scope of cross-examination of the accused in a criminal case is not controlled solely by evidence case law, and statutes or rules governing the matter.[1] Federal Rule 611(b) is not intended to govern the extent to which an accused in a criminal case who testifies thereby waives the privilege against self-incrimination.[2] The outer limits of cross-examination may well be controlled, at least in the future, by constitutional doctrine concerning the extent to which the accused waives his privilege of self-incrimination by taking the stand and testifying. Some judicial language suggests that under the Fifth Amendment of the United States Constitution the waiver should extend only to questioning concerning matters mentioned upon direct examination. If this position ultimately prevails, state practice would be governed by the constitutional limits of waiver, making "wide-open" cross-examination of criminal defendants, and perhaps even extremely liberal restrictive rules, unconstitutional.

§ 27. Merits of the Systems of Wide–Open and Restricted Cross–Examination

The principal virtue claimed for the restrictive rules is that they tend to require the parties to present their *facts* in due order, first the facts on which the plaintiff has the burden, then those which the defendant must prove, and so on, following the prescribed

stages.[1] Avoided is the danger, mentioned in section 24 supra, that one party's plan of presenting *his* facts will be interrupted by the interjection on cross-examination of new and damaging matters which constitute his adversary's case. This interjection, if permitted, lessens the impact and persuasiveness of the proponent's facts. The nice case which he planned to lay out fact by fact has been muddled and complicated during its very presentation by new and doubt-raising facts drawn out in cross-examination of the proponent's own witnesses. The regular order of presenting the two parties' "cases" by separate stages is thus modified. The "case," formerly a single melody, becomes convertible to counterpoint.

It must be remembered, however, that like all rules of order, the common law order of proof by "cases" or stages, is to some extent arbitrary. Two witnesses cannot be allowed to speak at once, so some rules must be worked out as to who shall call the witnesses and in what order. A further rule, however, that a witness who knows many facts about the case shall be allowed to tell only certain ones at his first appearance, and as to others must be called later, seems even more artificial. The freer system under the wide-open practice by which on the direct examination the regular order of proof of the "cases" of the respective parties is maintained, but under which the adversary is free to draw out all the damaging facts on cross-examination, has a natural order of its own. The procedure by which each witness successively may be caused to tell all he knows about the case, is a system which would be followed spontaneously in any informal investigation untrammeled by rules. It serves the convenience of witnesses and may appear to the jury as a natural way of developing the facts. Moreover, to the objection that diversion into new paths upon cross-examination lessens the unity and persuasiveness of the direct examiner's presentation of his case, we may raise the doubt

§ 26

1. See generally § 132 infra.
2. See § 134 infra.

§ 27

1. See § 4 supra.

whether the direct examiner is in justice entitled to the psychological advantage of presenting his facts in this falsely simple and one-sided way. Is he in justice entitled to this clear impact on the jury's mind, to this favorable first impression which, though to be answered later, may be hard to dislodge?

Another factor is the consideration of economy of time and energy. Obviously, the wide-open rule presents little or no opportunity for dispute in its application. The restrictive practice in all its forms, on the other hand, can be productive in the courtroom of bickering over the choice of the numerous variations of the "scope of the direct" criterion, and of their application to particular cross-questions. These controversies are often reventilated on appeal, and there may be the possibility of reversal for error. Observance of these vague and ambiguous restrictions is a matter of constant and hampering concern to the cross-examiner. If these efforts, delays and misprisions were the necessary incidents to the guarding of substantive rights or the fundamentals of fair trial, they might be worth the cost. As the price of the choice of an obviously debatable regulation of the order of evidence, the sacrifice seems misguided. The American Bar Association's Committee for the Improvement of the Law of Evidence for the year 1937–38 said this:

> "The rule limiting cross-examination to the precise subject of the direct examination is probably the most frequent rule (except the Opinion rule) leading in trial practice today to refined and technical quibbles which obstruct the progress of the trial, confuse the jury, and give rise to appeal on technical grounds only. Some of the instances in which Supreme Courts have ordered new trials for the mere transgression of this rule about the order of evidence have been astounding.

> "We recommend that the rule allowing questions upon any part of the issue known to the witness * * * be adopted * * *."[2]

2. See 6 Wigmore, Evidence § 1888, p. 711 (Chadbourn rev. 1976) where the relevant part of the Committee's report is set out in full.

There are thus strong reasons for the "wide-open" rule.

§ 28. Cross-Examination About Witness's Inconsistent Past Writings: Must Examiner Show the Writing to the Witness Before Questioning About Its Contents?

A fatal weakness of liars is letter writing. Betraying letters are often inspired by mere boastfulness, sometimes by greed or other reasons. Properly used they have destroyed many a fraudulent witness. An eminent trial lawyer makes these suggestions to the attacking cross-examiner:

> "* * * There is an art in introducing the letter contradicting the witness' testimony. The novice will rush in. He will obtain the false statement and then quickly hurl the letter in the face of the witness. The witness, faced with it, very likely will seek to retrace his steps, and sometimes do it skillfully, and the effect is lost.

> "The mature trial counsel will utilize the letter for all it is worth. Having obtained the denial which he wishes, he will, perhaps, pretend that he is disappointed. He will ask that same question a few moments later, and again and again get a denial. And he will then phrase—and this requires preparation—he will then phrase a whole series of questions not directed at that particular point, but in which is incorporated the very fact which he is ready to contradict—each time getting closer and closer to the language in the written document which he possesses, until he has induced the witness to assert not once, but many times, the very fact from which ordinarily he might withdraw by saying it was a slip of the tongue. Each time he draws closer to the precise language which will contradict the witness, without making the witness aware of it, until finally, when the letter is sprung, the effect as compared with the other method is that, let us say, of atomic energy against a firecracker."[1]

§ 28

1. Nizer, The Art of Jury Trial, 32 Corn.L.Q. 59, 68 (1946). An instructive, similar suggestion as to the technique of "exposure by document" is found in Love, Docu-

However, in some courts there may be an obstacle in the way of this effective method. This is the rule in *Queen Caroline's Case,* pronounced by English judges in an advisory opinion in 1820.[2] The significant part of the opinion for present purposes is the pronouncement that the cross-examiner cannot ask the witness about any statements made by the witness in writing, or ask whether the witness has ever written a letter of a given purport, without *first* producing the writing or letter and exhibiting it to the witness, and permitting the witness to read the writing or such part of it as the cross-examiner seeks to ask him about. Thus, in vain is the potential trap laid before the eyes of the bird. While reading the letter the witness will be warned by what he sees not to deny it and can quickly weave a new web of explanation.

The rule that the writing must first be shown to the witness before he can be questioned about it was thought by the judges to be an application of the established practice requiring the production of the original document *when its contents are sought to be proved.*[3] This notion was a misconception in at least two respects. First, the cross-examiner is not seeking to prove *at this stage* the contents of the writing by the answers of the witness. On the contrary, his zealous hope is that the witness will deny the existence of the letter. Second, the original documents rule is a rule requiring the production of the document as proof of its contents to the judge and jury, not to the witness. So obstructive did the powerful Victorian cross-examining barristers find the rule in the *Queen's Case* that they secured its abrogation by Parliament in 1854.[4]

When urged upon them, this practice requiring exhibition to the witness was usually accepted without question by American courts and occasionally by legislators. It is believed, however, that actual invocation of the rule in trials is relatively infrequent in most states in which the rule has not been changed, and

that the generality of judges and practitioners in these jurisdictions are unaware of this possible hidden rock in the path of the cross-examiner.

So far, the rule has been discussed as it works in the situation where the cross-examiner is seeking to uncover in a dramatic and devastating fashion the perjury of a calculating witness. In this situation, the rule seems to blunt one of counsel's sharpest weapons of exposure. But the weapon may be misdirected. Innocent and well-meaning witnesses write letters and forget their contents and later testify mistakenly to facts inconsistent with the assertions in the letters. Their forgetfulness may need to be revealed, and their present testimony thus discredited to that extent. Arguably, however, they should not be invited by subtle questioning to widen the gap between their present statements and their past writings, and then be devastated by a dramatic exposure. Under this viewpoint, the judge should be vested with the discretion whether to permit the questioning about the writing without requiring its exhibition to the witness.

In recognition of the disadvantages of the rule of *Queen Caroline's Case,* Federal Rule of Evidence 613(a) abolishes the rule by permitting the cross-examination without prior showing of the writing to the witness, and substitutes the requirement that the writing be shown or disclosed to opposing counsel on request as an assurance of good faith on the part of the cross-examiner.

§ 29. The Standard of Relevancy as Applied on Cross–Examination: Trial Judge's Discretion

There are three main functions of cross-examination: (1) to shed light on the credibility of the direct testimony, (2) to bring out additional facts related to those elicited on direct, and (3) in states following the "wide-

---

mentary Evidence, 38 Ill.Bar J. 426, 429–30 (1950). See also 4 Belli, Modern Trials § 63.30 (2d ed. 1982).

  2. 2 B. & B. 284, 129 Eng.Rep. 976, 11 Eng.Rul.C. 183 (1820).

  3. This rule, also called the best evidence rule, is developed in Ch. 23 infra.

  4. St. 17 & 18 Vict. c. 125, § 24.

open" rule, to bring out additional facts which tend to elucidate any issue in the case. As to cross-examination designed to serve the second or third of these functions, there seems to be no reason why the usual standard of relevancy as applied to testimony offered on direct examination should not equally be applied to facts sought to be elicited on cross-examination.

As to the first function, that of evaluating the credibility of the evidence given on direct, the purpose is contrastingly different. Here the test of relevancy is not whether the answer sought will elucidate any of the main issues, but whether it will to a useful extent aid the court or jury in appraising the credibility of the witness and assessing the probative value of the direct testimony. There are many recognized lines of questioning for this purpose, none of which is commonly relevant to the main issues. In general the principles stated in this section are pertinent under Federal Rule of Evidence and Revised Uniform Rule of Evidence 611(b), which authorize cross-examination concerning "matters affecting the credibility of the witness." A familiar type is the question or series of questions, often used as preliminary questions on cross-examination, inquiring as to residence and occupation, designed to place the witness in his setting. A further common question is, "Have you talked to anyone about this case?" Another is the testing or exploratory type of question. In asking this kind of question, the cross-examiner (who it will be remembered may not have the advantage of having previously interviewed the witness) will ask disarming questions often remote from the main inquiry, which are designed to test by experiment the ability of the witness to remember detailed facts of the nature of those which he recited on direct, or his ability accurately to perceive such facts, or his willingness and capacity to tell the truth generally, without distortion or exaggeration. This is part of the tradition and of the art of cross-examination and many of the famous instances of dramatically devastating cross-examinations are of this type. The courts recognize that a rule limiting questions to those relevant to the main issues would cripple the usefulness of this kind of examination. A final instance of evaluative cross-examination is the direct attack by impeaching questions seeking to show such matters as bias, inconsistent statements, or conviction of crime.

As to all the lines of inquiry mentioned in the next preceding paragraph, designed to shed light on the credibility of the witness and his direct testimony, the criteria of relevancy are vague, and the purpose of the cross-examiner is often experimental. Accordingly too tight a rein upon the cross-examiner may unduly curb the usefulness of the examination. On the other hand, dangers of undue prejudice to the party or the witness and of waste of time from extended exploration are apparent. Consequently, the trial judge has a recognized discretionary power to control the extent of examination. This exercise of discretion will only be reviewed for abuse resulting in substantial harm to the complaining party. An examination of a large number of these cases leaves the impression that in practice abuse is more often found when complaint is made that the judge has unduly curbed the examination than when undue extension of the discretion to permit the questioning is charged.

§ 30. The Cross–Examiner's Art

A cursory and general examination of the art of cross-examination, gleaned from the prolific writing on the subject, may serve to aid the beginning advocate by bringing him some of the wisdom lawyers have learned from hard experience and may also serve to aid in considering the discussion in the next succeeding section, which attempts to appraise the significance of cross-examination.

Preparation is the key. Certainly, some lawyers seem to have a native talent for conducting effective cross-examination. A great Victorian advocate, Montagu Williams, seemed to share this view when he said, "I am by trade a reader of faces and minds." Today, however, the stress is upon thorough preparation, not upon sudden sallies of inspiration. Improvisation is often necessary but its results are small compared to those from planned questions based on facts dug out before trial. The steps in preparation are explained in many of the works concerning the art of cross-examination. Not all steps can be taken as to all adverse witnesses. Nor can every case bear the expense of thorough preparation. Nevertheless, preparation before trial is the only soil from which, in the day-to-day run of cases, successful cross-examination can grow. At the trial, some lawyers recommend that notes in preparation for later questions should be made by an associate or by the client, rather than by the examiner. Oral suggestions to the examiner in court should be avoided.

No cross-examination without a purpose. As we have seen, these purposes may be, first, to elicit new facts, qualifying the direct, or in some states bearing on any issue in the case; second, to test the story of the witness by exploring its details and implications, in the hope of disclosing inconsistencies or impossibilities; and third, to prove out of the mouth of the witness, impeaching facts known to the cross-examiner such as prior contradictory statements, bias and conviction of crime. In considering any of these objectives, but particularly the latter two, the cross-examiner must be conscious that the odds are slanted against him. An unfavorable answer is more damaging when elicited on cross-examination. It is hard for a cross-examiner to win his case on cross-examination; it is easy for him to lose it. Accordingly, if the witness has done no harm on direct examination, a cross-examination for the second or third purpose is usually ill-advised. There remains the witness whose direct testimony has been damaging, or even threatens to be destructive of the cross-examiner's case if the jury believes it. Cross-examination will usually be needed, and whether the object shall be a skirting reconnaissance distant from the crucial issues, or a frontal attack on the story or the credit of the witness, will depend on the availability of impeaching material disclosed by preparation and on a judgment of the risks and advantages of the holding defence or the counterattack.

A question directed to a crucial or critical fact on which the outcome of the case depends should seldom be asked an adverse witness unless the cross-examiner is reasonably confident the answer will be favorable. Similarly, broad questions which open the door for an eager witness to reinforce his direct testimony with corroborating circumstances, e.g., "How do you explain?" or "How did it happen?" are usually ill-advised. If a discrepant fact has been drawn out on cross-examination, it is often better to wait and stress the inconsistency in argument than to press the witness with it. It is the responsibility of the proponent's counsel to elicit an explanation, if any, on redirect.

In conducting a testing or exploratory examination, for obvious reasons it is inadvisable to follow the order of the witness's direct testimony. "If the witness is falsifying, jump quickly with rapid-fire questions from one point of the narrative to the other, without time or opportunity for a connected narrative: backward, forward, forward, backward from the middle to the beginning, etc."

Cross-examine for the jury, not for your client. It is often a temptation to the cross-examiner to display his wit and skill before his client, or to feed the vengeful feelings of the latter toward opposing witnesses by tripping and humiliating them upon cross-examination. Frequently these small victories upon collateral inquiries are easy to secure. The odds between the experienced advocate and the witness, nervous in new surroundings, are not even. The cross-examiner needs constantly to remind himself that the jury is keenly aware of this inequality of position, and that each juror is prone to imagine himself in the shoes of the witness. Better results with the witness, and a better impression upon the jury will usually flow from tact and consideration than from bulldozing and ridicule. The cloak falls more easily in the sunshine than in the hurricane. In the rare case when the cross-examiner is convinced that a crucial witness is dishonest and that he can demonstrate it, the attack must be pressed home to the jugular. But the cross-examiner should always be mindful of his duty to use his skills and weapons justly and fairly, and also of the need so to conduct himself that the jury, with its latent sympathy for witnesses, will be impressed with his fairness.

Make one or two big points; end on a high note. When the cross-examiner has led up to and secured an important admission, he should not dull the edge of the effect by too many explanatory details, nor risk a recantation by calling for a repetition. He should pass on to another important point if he has one, and end the examination when his last big point is made. "When you have struck oil stop boring."

While the above generalities are worthwhile general guideposts, the cross-examiner must adapt his techniques to the specific situation he faces. Of course, different experts might well use different techniques in cross-examining the same witness at a particular trial.

§ 31. Cross–Examination Revalued

Early Victorian writers on advocacy exaggerated the strategic significance of cross-examination as affecting the outcome of trials. One of them wrote, "There is never a cause contested, the result of which is not mainly dependent upon the skill with which the advocate conducts his cross-examination." [1] This stands in contrast with the view of Scarlett, a great "leader" of a later day, who said, "I learned by much experience that the most useful duty of an advocate is the examination of witnesses, and that much more mischief than benefit generally results from cross-examination. I therefore rarely allowed that duty to be performed by my colleagues. I cross-examined in general very little, and more with a view to enforce the facts I meant to rely upon than to affect the witness's credit,—for the most part a vain attempt." [2] Reed, who was one of our most sensible American writers on trial tactics, expresses the

modern informed opinion when he says, "Sometimes a great speech bears down the adversary, and sometimes a searching cross-examination turns a witness inside out and shows him up to be a perjured villain. But ordinarily cases are not won by either speaking or cross-examining." [3] At the same time, most lawyers who write concerning the art of cross-examination still believe that failure to use this tool can lose a case. To the advocate of today, it is often a means of gleaning additional facts but it is also still employed as a means of attack upon the credit of the direct testimony of the witness whenever possible. Cross-examination of experts seems important in many instances. In fact, Federal Rule of Evidence 705 makes the opportunity to cross-examine particularly important if, as the rule permits, only an opinion in effect is elicited. Thus while cross-examination does not loom large as a determinant of victory in many cases, it still may be an important ingredient in other cases.

In the appraisal of policies upon which the modernizing of the existing system of evidence rules must be based, it seems that a similar evaluation of cross-examination as an engine for discovering truth is called for. The present assumption is that the statement of a declarant or witness, if opportunity for cross-examination is not afforded, is so fatally lacking in reliability that it is not even worth hearing in a court of justice, and that the opportunity for cross-examination is indispensable. Now obviously cross-examination is a useful device to secure greater accuracy and completeness for the witness's testimony as a whole, and in the hands of a skillful advocate will often—not always—expose fraud or honest error in the witness. But it has its own hazards of producing errors. It is, in truth, quite doubtful whether it is not the honest but weak or timid witness, rather than the rogue, who most often goes down under the fire of a cross-examination. Certainly every witness in judicial proceedings should

§ 31

1. Quoted from Cox, The Advocate 434, in Reed, Conduct of Lawsuits 277 (2d ed. 1912).

2. Memoir of Lord Abinger 75, quoted in Reed, supra note 1 at 278.

3. Reed, supra note 1 at 276.

in fairness be made available for cross-examination by the opponent wherever possible. But the premise that where cross-examination is not possible, as in the case of out-of-court statements, or as in the case of a witness who dies before cross-examination, the statement or testimony should generally be excluded for that reason alone, seems ill-founded. Cross-examination, it is submitted, should be considered as useful but not indispensable as an agency of discovering truth, and absence of opportunity to cross-examine should only be one factor to be weighed in determining whether the statement or testimony should be received. Such an approach to hearsay problems might lead us to conclude that when opportunity to cross-examine a witness is permanently cut off without fault of either party, the direct testimony should nevertheless be received as suggested in a previous section. It might lead us to further conclude that hearsay statements should be admitted if the statement was made by the declarant on personal knowledge and reported by the witness at first hand, and if the declarant is now dead or unavailable for cross-examination or, on the other hand, if the declarant is alive and still available for cross-examination. Perhaps written statements should be admitted wherever production for cross-examination can fairly be dispensed with.

It should be noted, however, that although these modern viewpoints are supportable, there remains a special problem concerning the criminal defendant's right of cross-examination under the Fifth, Sixth, and Fourteenth Amendments of the federal constitution and the scope of the right as it affects interrupted cross-examination and the scope of the hearsay rule.[4]

§ 32. Redirect and Subsequent Examinations

One who calls a witness is normally required to elicit on his first examination, the direct, all that he wishes to prove by him. This norm of proving everything so far as

feasible at the first opportunity is manifestly in the interest of fairness and expedition. Whether the cross-examiner is limited to answering the direct is, as we have seen, a matter as to which our jurisdictions are divided, with a much greater number favoring the restrictive rule.[1] As to the redirect, however, and all subsequent examinations, there is no such division and the practice is uniform that the party's examination is normally limited to answering any new matter drawn out in the next previous examination of the adversary. It is true that the judge under his general discretionary power to vary the normal order of proof may permit the party to bring out on redirect examination some matter which is relevant to his case or defense and which through oversight he has failed to elicit on direct. Under Federal Rule of Evidence 611(a) the judge has broad discretion over the scope of redirect. But the reply to new matter drawn out on cross-examination is the normal function of the redirect, and examination for this purpose is often a matter of right, though its extent is subject to control in the judge's discretion.

A skillful re-examiner may often draw the sting of a lethal cross-examination. The reply on redirect may take the form of explanation, avoidance, or qualification of the new substantive facts or matters of impeachment elicited by the cross-examiner. The direct approach, such as "What did you mean by" or "What was your reason for" a statement made by the witness on cross-examination, may often be proper, but a mere reiteration of assertions previously made on the direct or cross-examination is not usually sanctioned, although the judge has an area of discretion in this matter.

The rule of completeness, which permits proof of the remainder of a transaction, conversation, or writing when a part thereof has been proven by the adversary, so far as the remainder relates to the same subject-matter, is often invoked by the re-examiner. This principle is not abrogated by Federal Rule of

---

4. See § 19 supra, and § 252 infra.

1. See § 21 supra.

Evidence 106.[2] Moreover, the principle of curative admissibility,[3] under which evidence that is irrelevant or otherwise incompetent may sometimes be allowed to be answered by the adversary, is likewise frequently resorted to by the examiner on redirect.

Recross-examination, following the rule of first opportunity mentioned above, is normally confined to questions directed to the explanation or avoidance of new matter brought out on redirect.

2. See § 56 infra.

3. See § 57 infra.

Chapter 5

IMPEACHMENT AND SUPPORT

Table of Sections

§ 33. Introductory: The Stages of Impeachment and the Modes of Attack

There are five main modes of attack upon the credibility of a witness. The first, and probably the most effective and most frequently employed, is an attack by proof that the witness on a previous occasion has made statements inconsistent with his present testimony. The second is an attack by a showing that the witness is partial on account of emotional influences such as kinship for one party or hostility to another, or motives of pecuniary interest, whether legitimate or corrupt. The third is an attack upon the character of the witness. The fourth is an attack by showing a defect of capacity in the witness to observe, remember or recount the matters testified about. The fifth is proof by other witnesses that material facts are otherwise than as testified to by the witness under attack.[1] Finally, it might be observed that lack of religious belief is not available as a basis of attack on credibility. Some of these attacks

§ 33

1. See § 49 infra.

are not specifically or completely treated by the Federal or Revised Uniform Rules of Evidence, but they are generally authorized by those rules.

The process of impeachment may be employed in two different stages. First, the facts discrediting the witness or his testimony may be elicited from the witness himself upon cross-examination. A good faith basis for the inquiry is required. Certain modes of attack are limited to this stage; it is said, "You must take his answer." Second, in some situations, the facts discrediting the witness are proved by extrinsic evidence, that is, the assailant waits until the time for putting on his own case in rebuttal, and then proves by a second witness or by documentary evidence, the facts discrediting the testimony of the witness attacked.[2]

There is a cardinal rule of impeachment. Never launch an attack which implies that the witness has lied deliberately, unless you are convinced that the attack is justifiable, and is essential to your case. An assault which fails often produces in the jury's mind an indignant sympathy for the intended victim.

It is believed that, in general, there is less practical emphasis upon impeachment of witnesses than formerly, and that the elaborate system of rules regulating the practice and scope of impeachment which has been developed in the past is now applied with less strictness and is simplified by confiding the control less to rules and more to judicial discretion.

§ 34. Prior Inconsistent Statements: Degree of Inconsistency Required

When a witness testifies to facts material in a case, the opponent may have available proof that the witness has previously made state-

ments that are inconsistent with his present testimony. Under a modern view of the hearsay rule, some or all such previous statements would be admissible as substantive evidence of the facts stated. This viewpoint is discussed in the chapter concerning hearsay.[1] However, under the more traditional views of hearsay these previous statements will often be inadmissible as evidence of what they state because they constitute hearsay and are not within any exceptions to the hearsay rule.[2] Even though inadmissible hearsay as evidence of the facts stated, they are nevertheless admissible for the limited purpose of impeaching the witness.[3] See Fed.R.Evid. 613(b). Subject to the extension that prior inconsistent statements are admissible as substantive evidence because they are defined as not hearsay if they were made under oath subject to the penalty of perjury at a trial, hearing or other proceeding, or in a deposition, see Fed.R.Evid. 801(d)(1)(A), the Federal and Revised Uniform Rules of Evidence preserve this traditional view.

It is important to note that the treatment of inconsistent statements in this chapter is confined to the situation in which the statements are introduced for impeachment purposes but may not be used as substantive evidence (over proper objection of the opponent).[4] For this purpose, the making of the previous statements may be drawn out in cross-examination of the witness himself, or if on cross-examination the witness has denied making the statement, or has failed to remember it,[5] the making of the statement may be proved by another witness; but under the Federal and Revised Uniform Rule of Evidence 613(b) the making of the statement may also be brought out by the second witness without prior inquiry of the witness who made it.[6] This form of impeachment is sometimes called "self-contradiction". It is to be distinguished from the

---

2. See §§ 45 and 49 infra.

§ 34

1. See § 251 infra.

2. See generally Chapter 24 infra.

3. The use of unconstitutionally obtained evidence for purposes of impeachment is discussed in § 182 infra.

4. The use of prior inconsistent statements as substantive evidence is discussed in § 251 infra.

5. See § 37 infra.

6. See § 37 infra. This discussion assumes the matter is noncollateral, §§ 36 and 49 infra.

mere production of other evidence as to material facts conflicting with the evidence of the assailed witness. The mere production of other evidence that conflicts with the evidence of a witness is discussed in a later section.[7]

The theory of attack by prior inconsistent statements is not based on the assumption that the present testimony is false and the former statement true but rather upon the notion that talking one way on the stand and another way previously is blowing hot and cold, and raises a doubt as to the truthfulness of both statements. More particularly the prior statement, assuming it is inadmissible as substantive evidence under the hearsay rule, may be used in this context only as an aid in judging the credibility of the testimony with which the previous statement is inconsistent. To create the above-mentioned doubt by introduction of the previous statement of the witness, what degree of inconsistency between the testimony of the witness and his previous statement is required? The language of some of the cases seems overstrict in suggesting that a contradiction must be found, and under the more widely accepted view any material variance between the testimony and the previous statement will suffice. Accordingly, if the former statement fails to mention a material circumstance presently testified to, which it would have been natural to mention in the prior statement, the prior statement is sufficiently inconsistent. Again, an earlier statement by the witness that he had no knowledge of facts now testified to, should be provable. Seemingly the test should be, could the jury reasonably find that a witness who believed the truth of the facts testified to would have been unlikely to make a prior statement of this tenor? The Federal and Revised Uniform Rule of Evidence 613 do not expressly indicate a test for inconsistency. The liberal rules for inconsistency expressed herein should govern. Thus, if the previous statement is ambiguous and according to one meaning would be inconsistent with the testimony, it should be admitted for the jury's consideration. In applying the criterion of material inconsistency reasonable judges will be likely to differ, and a fair range of discretion should be accorded to the trial judge. Moreover, it is to be hoped that instead of restricting the use of prior statements by a mechanical use of the test of inconsistency, the courts will lean toward receiving such statements in case of doubt, to aid in evaluating the testimony. The statements, indeed, having been made when memory was more recent and when less time for the play of influence has elapsed, are often inherently more trustworthy than the testimony itself.[8] A logical extension of this reasoning justifies the admission of prior testimony about an independent and unrelated event so similar to testimony now given as to arouse suspicion of fabrication.

§ 35. Prior Inconsistent Statements: Opinion in Form

If a witness, such as an expert, testifies in terms of opinion, of course all courts will permit impeachment by showing a previous expression by the witness of an inconsistent opinion. More troublesome is the question which arises when the witness testifies to specific facts and then is sought to be impeached by prior inconsistent expressions of opinion. For example, in a collision case the plaintiff's witness testifies to particular facts inculpating the driver of a bus involved in the accident. The opponent proposes to show that the witness said just after seeing the collision, "The bus was not to blame."

Should the opinion rule be applied to exclude such an impeaching statement? The early American tradition of a strict rule against opinions has been much relaxed in recent trial administration.[1] What was once supposed to be a difference in kind between fact and opinion is now regarded as a difference in degree only.[2] Wigmore considers that the rule goes no further than to exclude opin-

7. See § 45 infra.

8. See Ch. 24 infra.

§ 35

1. See §§ 11, 12, 17 supra.

2. See §§ 11, 12 supra.

ion as superfluous when more concrete statements could be resorted to.[3] Thus, the principal practical value of the opinion rule is as a regulation of trial practice requiring the examining counsel to bring out his facts by more specific questions if practicable, before resorting to more general ones. For this reason, it is a mistake of policy to apply it to any out-of-court statements whatsoever, since no such controls are possible.[4] Moreover, when the out-of-court statement is not offered at all as evidence of the fact asserted, but only to show the asserter's inconsistency, the whole purpose of the opinion rule, to improve the objectivity and hence reliability of testimonial assertions, is quite inapplicable. Hence, though many earlier decisions, influenced perhaps by a statement in Greenleaf[5] and a casual English holding at *nisi prius*,[6] and some later opinions, exclude impeaching statements in opinion form, the trend of holdings and the majority view is in accord with the commonsense notion that if a substantial inconsistency appears the form of the impeaching statement is immaterial. This view is indirectly authorized by Federal and Revised Uniform Evidence Rule 701 because of the broad scope of that opinion rule.

§ 36. Prior Inconsistent Statements: Extrinsic Evidence: Previous Statements as Substantive Evidence of the Facts Stated

On cross-examination we have seen that strict rules of relevancy are relaxed, and generally the trial judge in his discretion may permit the cross-examiner to inquire about any previous statements inconsistent with assertions, relevant or irrelevant, which the witness has testified to on direct or cross. At this stage, there is no strict requirement that the previous impeaching statements must not deal with "collateral" matters. But as appears in the next paragraph, if the inquiry on cross-examination is as to inconsistent statements about "collateral" matters, the cross-

examiner must "take the answer"—he cannot bring on other witnesses to prove the making of the alleged statement. Or if, as under the Federal and Revised Uniform Rules of Evidence, extrinsic evidence of inconsistent statements may be introduced before such cross-examination, the intrinsic evidence must not concern collateral matters.

Extrinsic evidence, that is, the production of attacking witnesses, for impeachment by inconsistent statements, is sharply narrowed for obvious reasons of economy of time and attention. The tag, "You cannot contradict as to collateral matters," applies, and here the meaning is that to impeach by extrinsic proof of prior inconsistent statements, the statements must have as their subject facts relevant to the issues in the cause. This analysis of collateral matter should be followed generally under the Federal and Revised Uniform Rules of Evidence (in the introduction of inconsistent statements to impeach by extrinsic evidence).

A distinct but somewhat cognate notion is the view that if a party interrogates a witness about a fact which would be favorable to the examiner if true, and receives a reply which is merely negative in its effect on examiner's case, the examiner may not by extrinsic evidence prove that the first witness had earlier stated that the fact was true as desired by the inquirer. An affirmative answer would have been material and subject to be impeached by an inconsistent statement, but a negative answer is not damaging to the examiner, but merely disappointing, and may not be thus impeached. In this situation the policy involved is not the saving of time and confusion, as before, but the protection of the other party against the hearsay use by the jury of the previous statement. With respect to the Federal and Revised Uniform Rules of Evidence view see § 38.

As previously indicated,[1] inconsistent statements of a witness are primarily treated in this chapter upon the assumption that they

---

3. 7 Wigmore, Evidence § 1918 (Chadbourn rev. 1978).

4. See § 18 supra.

5. Greenleaf, Evidence § 449 (3d ed. 1846).

6. Elton v. Larkins, 5 Car. & P. 385, 172 Eng.Rep. 1020 (1832).

§ 36

1. See § 34 supra.

may be inadmissible as substantive evidence on the issues in the case under the traditional hearsay rule as administered in numerous states, and under the limited conditions in the Federal and Revised Uniform Rules of Evidence (1974) 801(d)(1). Of course, taking into account the limited federal exemption in jurisdictions in which it is effective, and under the hearsay rule exceptions effective in the various jurisdictions, particular inconsistent prior statements of a witness may be admissible as substantive relevant evidence as well as for impeachment purposes. However, under another view, all prior inconsistent statements of a person who is available as a witness at the trial or testifies may be considered substantive evidence, not barred by the hearsay rule, and thus not restricted to the purpose of impeachment. This latter viewpoint is discussed in § 251.

§ 37. Prior Inconsistent Statements: Requirement of Preliminary Questions on Cross–Examination as "Foundation" for Proof by Extrinsic Evidence

In 1820 in the answers of the judges in *Queen Caroline's Case,* it was announced: "If it be intended to bring the credit of a witness into question by proof of anything he may have said or declared touching the cause, the witness is first asked, upon cross-examination, whether or not he has said or declared that which is intended to be proved." [1] Thus was crystallized a practice which was previously occasional and discretionary. Only later and gradually was it almost universally accepted in this country. It came to be applied to both written and oral inconsistent statements.[2] The purposes of this traditional requirement are (1) to avoid unfair surprise to the adversary, (2) to save time, as an admission by the witness may make extrinsic proof unnecessary, and (3) to give the witness in fairness a chance to explain the discrepancy.

To satisfy the requirement the cross-examiner will ask the witness whether the witness made the alleged statement, giving its substance, and naming the time, the place, and the person to whom made. The purpose of this particularity is, of course, to refresh the memory of the witness as to the supposed statement by reminding the witness of the accompanying circumstances. If the witness denies the making of the statement, or fails to admit it, for example by saying "I don't know" or "I don't remember", then the requirement of "laying the foundation" is satisfied and the cross-examiner, at the next stage of giving evidence, may prove the making of the alleged statement. If, however, the witness unequivocally admits the making of the supposed statement, may the cross-examiner still choose to prove it again by another witness? Wigmore, with some support, suggests that the cross-examiner may, but the prevailing view is to the contrary and in the usual situation this seems the more expedient practice.

Under Federal and Revised Uniform Rule 613 the only requirements for introducing prior inconsistent written or oral statements of a witness are (1) that in questioning the witness concerning written statements or the substance of the statements, they shall be shown or disclosed to the opposing counsel upon request, and (2) after introduction of the inconsistent statements by cross-examination of the witness or without prior warnings of any kind by extrinsic evidence, the witness shall be afforded the opportunity at a later appropriate stage of the proceedings to deny or explain them and opposing counsel shall have the opportunity to question the witness at an appropriate later time about them. The opportunity of the witness to explain or deny later and the opportunity of the opposing counsel to question later can itself be ignored in the discretion of the judge "in the interests of justice."

The Federal and Revised Uniform Rules of Evidence thus on their face adopt a liberal view, abolishing the notion that the witness must on cross-examination be shown an inconsistent statement or be advised of its con-

---

§ 37

1. 2 Brod. & Bing. 284, 313, 129 Eng.Rep. 976 (1820).

2. See § 28 supra.

tents before being questioned about its substance in any way, and abandoning the requirement that the above-mentioned traditional foundation questions must be put to the witness on cross-examination before extrinsic evidence of the statement is introduced, i.e., before other witnesses testify to it or before an inconsistent writing is introduced.

As the Advisory Committee's Note to Federal Rule 613 indicates, "[t]he traditional insistence that the attention of the witness be directed to the statement on cross-examination is relaxed in favor of simply providing the witness an opportunity to explain and the opposite party an opportunity to examine on the statement, with no specification of any particular time or sequence." The Advisory Committee's Note suggests that Rule 613 facilitates the questioning of collusive witnesses by permitting several such witnesses to be examined before disclosure of a joint prior inconsistent statement. That rather infrequent benefit hardly explains Rule 613 dispensing with the requirement that a foundation be laid on cross-examination. The rationale for Rule 613 in fact derives from a combination of two factors: (1) that Rule 801(d)(1) as proposed by the Advisory Committee and the Supreme Court gave substantive effect to all prior inconsistent statements, and (2) perceived lawyer incompetence.

To understand why the Advisory Committee proposed Rule 613 one must keep in mind that if prior inconsistent statements are admissible only for purposes of impeachment, the foundation requirement fosters the use of such statements to affect credibility while discouraging the trier of fact from giving them substantive consideration. In practice, the foundation requirement served to place a prior statement in juxtaposition to the testimony at trial of the witness sought to be impeached. In addition, by enabling the witness to admit a prior statement as his own, the foundation requirement reduced the likelihood that extrinsic evidence of the prior inconsistent statement would be introduced, evidence that is much harder for the jury not to accept substantively. Under the scheme of the proposed evidence rules, however, all prior incon-

sistent statements were to be admissible as substantive evidence pursuant to Rule 801(d)(1). With the substantive admissibility of all such prior statements this objective fostered by the foundation requirement was no longer relevant and a practical consideration became paramount. Trial lawyers for some unknown reason often forget to lay or in some cases never learned how to lay a proper foundation for extrinsic evidence. The Advisory Committee politely referred to such forgetfulness or incompetence as the "dangers of oversight." With substantive admissibility, these "oversight[s]" could be legitimized by permitting introduction of prior inconsistent statements at any time so long as the witness was eventually given an opportunity to deny or explain.

As enacted by Congress, however, Rule 801(d)(1) does not permit the substantive admission of all prior inconsistent statements. Thus the traditional foundation requirements' utility in encouraging the jury to consider a prior inconsistent statement solely as an indication of credibility and not as substantive evidence remains relevant. Since all prior inconsistent statements are not substantively admissible, counsel should not have the unfettered right to introduce extrinsic evidence of such a statement before the witness has an opportunity to admit, deny, or explain the declaration. Initial introduction of extrinsic evidence permits a prior statement to be placed before the trier of fact on multiple occasions and under circumstances encouraging the statement's acceptance as substantive evidence. Accordingly, federal courts and state courts operating under an identical scheme should and do require under Rule 403 and Rule 611 that the traditional foundation be laid on cross-examination prior to the introduction of extrinsic evidence with respect to prior inconsistent statements admissible solely to impeach unless the interests of justice otherwise require.

If the witness attacked is not on the stand but the testimony introduced was given in a deposition or at some other trial, most prior decisions otherwise applying the traditional requirements exclude the inconsistent statement unless the foundation question was asked at the prior hearing. In this situation, at the discretion of the judge, the Federal and Revised Uniform Rule 613 should not require the opportunity of any denial or explanation by the witness or questioning by the opposing counsel. When otherwise applicable, all of the above traditional requirements should be abandoned in the case of depositions based upon written interrogatories (which must be prepared in advance) or in the case of inconsistent statements made after the prior testimony was taken.

If a party takes the stand as a witness, and the adversary desires to use a prior inconsistent statement of the witness, the statement is receivable in two aspects, first as the admission of the opposing party, and second, as an inconsistent statement to impeach the witness. In the first aspect, it is relevant evidence upon the fact issues; in the second aspect, it is not. In jurisdictions requiring traditional foundation questions for impeachment, the requirement is almost universally held inapplicable. There is less danger of surprising a party than a witness, and the party will have ample opportunity for denial or explanation after the inconsistent statement is proved. In these jurisdictions the courts on occasion may inadvertently assume that the requirement applies to the party-witness. Sometimes courts have imposed the requirement if the proponent offers the statement only for impeachment, and one court held the judge has discretion to impose the requirement of a foundation question as prerequisite to proof of a party-witness admission. These niggling qualifications seem hardly worth their salt and in jurisdictions which otherwise require the foundation question the sensible practice is the simple one of dispensing with the "foundation" entirely in respect to parties' admissions.

Federal and Revised Uniform Rule 613 have nothing to do with the introduction and admission into evidence of admissions of parties, even if the admissions have some effect on the credibility of the party as a witness. Nor do the rules have any impact upon the introduction of a hearsay statement pursuant to a hearsay exception contained in Federal and Revised Uniform Rules 803 even when the out of court declarant testifies. However, Federal and Revised Uniform Rule 613 is applicable when a prior inconsistent statement is admitted as substantive evidence solely by virtue of Federal and Revised Uniform Rule 801(d)(1)(A).

Again in jurisdictions in which a foundation question is required and it is overlooked, the judge should have discretion to consider such factors as the lack of knowledge of the inconsistent statement on the part of the impeacher when the witness was cross-examined, the importance or unimportance of the testimony under attack, and the practicability of recalling the witness for denial or explanation, and in the light of these circumstances to permit the impeachment without the foundation or to permit departure from the traditional time sequence if it seems fairer to do so.

§ 38. Prior Inconsistent Statements: Rule Against Impeaching One's Own Witness

The common law rule forbidding a party to impeach her own witness, which has been modified to an extent indicated later in this section or abandoned, is of obscure origin but probably is a late manifestation of the evolution of the common law trial procedure from an inquisitorial to a contentious or adversary system. The prohibition was general, applying to all forms of impeachment. It applied not only to attack by inconsistent statements but to attack on character, or by a showing of bias, interest or corruption. It did not, however, forbid the party to introduce other evidence to dispute the facts testified to by her witness.

Among the reasons, or rationalizations, found for the rule are, first, that the party by calling the witness to testify vouches for the trustworthiness of the witness, and second, that the power to impeach is the power to coerce the witness to testify as desired, under the implied threat of blasting the character of the witness if the witness does not. The answer to the first reason is that, except in a few instances such as character witnesses or expert witnesses, the party has little or no choice of witnesses. The party calls only those who happen to have observed the particular facts in controversy. The answers to the second reason are (a) that it applies only to two kinds of impeachment, the attack on character and the showing of corruption, and (b) that to forbid the attack by the calling party leaves the party at the mercy of the witness and the adversary. If the truth lies on the side of the calling party, but the witness's character is bad, the witness may be attacked by the adversary if the witness tells the truth; but if the witness tells a lie, the adversary will not attack, and the calling party, under the rule, cannot. Certainly it seems that if the witness has been bribed to change the story, the calling party should be allowed to disclose this fact to the court.

The most important, because most effective, kind of impeachment, is by inconsistent statements and most of the cases that have applied the rule are of this type. It is difficult to see any justification for prohibiting this sort of showing as to the reliability of a witness who has testified contrary to a previous position. Perhaps there is a fear that the previous statement will be considered by the jury as substantive evidence of the facts asserted if, as in various jurisdictions, the statement for that purpose will be hearsay.[1] Except in those jurisdictions which have altogether abandoned it, the common law rule against impeaching one's own witness persists for the most part with respect to attacks showing bias and attacks upon character. On the other hand, it has been relaxed in a number of jurisdictions by statute or decision insofar as it prohibits impeachment by inconsistent statements. A provision in the draft of the Field Code of Civil Procedure in 1849 found fruit in the English Common Law Procedure Act of 1854, as follows (St. 17 & 18 Vict. c. 125, § 22): "[1] A party producing a witness shall not be allowed to impeach his credit by general evidence of bad character; [2] but he may, in case the witness shall in the opinion

of the judge prove adverse, [3] contradict him by other evidence, [4] or by leave of the judge prove that he has made at other times a statement inconsistent with his present testimony." This statute was copied in a few states. Other states, following the example of Massachusetts in 1869, have adopted the English statute except for omitting the troublesome condition that the witness must have proved "adverse." Some courts have reached a similar result by decision.

These statutes and similar decisions open the door to the most important type of impeachment of one's own witness, namely, prior inconsistent statements. But whether the extension is derived from statute or decision, two troublesome qualifications have been imposed on the reform by some courts. The first is that the party seeking to impeach must show that she is surprised at the testimony of the witness. The second is that she cannot impeach unless the witness' testimony is positively harmful or adverse to her cause, reaching further than a mere failure ("I do not remember," "I do not know") to give expected favorable testimony. These limitations are explainable only as attempts to safeguard the hearsay policy by preventing the party from proving the witness' prior statements in situations where it appears that its only value to the proponent will be as substantive evidence of the facts asserted. The rule against substantive use of the statements, and the soundness of its policy, as well as growing authority to the contrary, is the theme of a subsequent section.[2]

The rule that prohibits or limits the impeachment of one's own witness is being abandoned in more and more jurisdictions. Abandonment is accomplished by Federal and Revised Uniform Rule of Evidence (1974) 607. The standard methods of impeachment are permitted under these rules. There is some dispute whether and under what circumstances impeachment of one's own witness will be impermissible because of prejudice to the opposing party, particularly in criminal

---

1. See § 251 infra.

2. See § 251 infra.

cases. It has been widely held that the prosecution in a criminal case may not employ a prior inconsistent statement to impeach a witness it has called as a "mere subterfuge" or for the "*primary* purpose" of placing before the jury substantive evidence which is not otherwise admissible. Application of the "mere subterfuge" or "*primary* purpose" caveat focuses upon the content of the witness' testimony as a whole. Thus if the witness' testimony is important in establishing any fact of consequence significant in the context of the litigation, the witness may be impeached as to any other matter testified to by means of a prior inconsistent statement. While the power to attack the character of one's own witness may often be of little value to the attacker, and is often of little moment to the administration of justice, subject to the foregoing limitation, a rule against the showing of prior inconsistent statements of one's own witness to aid in evaluating the testimony of the witness is a serious obstruction to the ascertainment of truth, even in criminal cases. From the standpoint of a defendant in a criminal case, there is also a possibility of urging that forbidding a defendant from attacking a witness called by the defendant is unconstitutional in particular instances.[3]

§ 39. Partiality

Case law recognizes the slanting effect upon human testimony of the emotions or feelings of the witness toward the parties or the self-interest of the witness in the outcome of the case or in matters somehow related to the case. Partiality, or any acts, relationships or motives reasonably likely to produce it, may be proved to impeach credibility. While the Federal Rules of Evidence does not in terms refer to attacking the witness by showing bias, interest, corruption, or coercion, it clearly contemplates the use of the above-mentioned grounds of impeachment. A good faith basis for the inquiry is required.[1] In fact, in criminal cases the defendant has a conditional constitutional right to so attack the credibility of government witnesses. The power of the trial judge to impose limits on the above grounds for attacking a witness is mentioned later in this section.

The kinds and sources of partiality are too infinitely varied to be reviewed exhaustively, but a few of the common instances may be mentioned. *Favor* or friendly feeling toward a party may be evidenced by family or business relationship, by employment by a party or the party's insurer, or by sexual relations, or by shared membership in an organization, or by particular conduct or expressions by the witness evincing such feeling. It is commonly held in collision cases that when a witness appears for defendant the fact that he has made a claim against the defendant and has been paid a sum in settlement tends to show bias in favor of defendant.[2] Similarly, *hostility* toward a party may be shown by the fact that the witness has had a fight or quarrel with him, or has a lawsuit pending against him, or has contributed to the defense or employed special counsel to aid in prosecuting the party. In criminal cases, the feeling of the witness toward the victim sheds light on his feeling toward the charge. *Self-interest* of the witness is manifest when he is himself a party, or a surety on the debt sued on. It may be shown likewise as reflecting on his interest that he is being paid by a party to give evidence, even though payment beyond regular witness fees may as in the case of an expert be entirely proper. *Self-interest* may be shown also in a criminal case when the witness testifies for the state and it is shown that an indictment is pending against him, that the witness has not been charged with a crime, has been promised leniency, has been granted immunity, is awaiting sentence, is being held in protective custody, or that he is an accomplice or co-indictee in the crime on trial. Self-interest in an extreme form may be manifested in *corrupt* activity by the witness such as seeking to bribe another witness,

---

3. Chambers v. Mississippi, 410 U.S. 284 (1973).

§ 39

1. See § 49 infra.

2. See § 266 infra.

or by taking or offering to take a bribe to testify falsely, or by the making of other similar charges on other occasions without foundation. The trial court has a great deal of discretion in deciding whether particular evidence indicates partiality. A large majority of appellate decisions examined approved the ruling of the trial judge on this score.

Preliminary question. A majority of the courts impose the requirement of a foundation question as in the case of impeachment by prior inconsistent statements. Before the witness can be impeached by calling other witnesses to prove acts or declarations showing partiality, the witness under attack must first have been asked about these facts on cross-examination. There is pre-rules federal case authority to this effect. Fairness to the witness is most often given as the reason for the requirement, but the saving of time by making unnecessary the extrinsic evidence seems even more important. Some courts, adhering to the analogy of inconsistent statements, make a difference between declarations and conduct evidencing partiality, requiring the preliminary question as to the former and not as to the latter. But as suggested in a leading English case, words and conduct are usually intermingled in proof of partiality, and "nice and subtle distinctions" should be avoided in shaping this rule of trial practice. Better require a "foundation" as to both or neither. It seems that jurisdictions recognizing the requirement should recognize also a discretion in the judge to dispense with it when mere matters of indisputable relationship, such as kinship, are concerned, or where the foundation was overlooked and it is not feasible to recall the witness, or where other exceptional circumstances make it unfair to insist on the prerequisite.

A minority of holdings do not require any warning question on cross-examination of the principal witness as a preliminary to the introduction of extrinsic evidence of partiality. The Federal and Revised Uniform Rules (1974) are silent on the subject. The discretion granted the judge in Rule 611(a) is adequate authority to follow the same pattern for partiality as that actually employed for prior

inconsistent statements. Thus following the preferred method for impeachment by a prior inconsistent statement, the witness under attack should first be asked about acts or statements showing partiality on cross-examination.

Cross-examination and extrinsic evidence; main circumstances. We have seen that in many states the impeacher must inquire as to the facts of partiality on cross-examination as the first step in impeachment. It seems arguable that if the witness fully admits the facts claimed to show partiality, the impeacher should not be allowed to repeat the same attack by calling other witnesses to the admitted facts. And it is held that when the main circumstances from which the partiality proceeds have been proven, the trial judge has a discretion to determine how far the details, whether on cross-examination or by other witnesses, may be allowed to be brought out. After all, impeachment is not a central matter, and the trial judge, though he may not deny a reasonable opportunity at either stage to prove the partiality of the witness, has a discretion to control the extent to which the proof may go. He has the responsibility for seeing that the sideshow does not take over the circus. This result is indicated by decisions on the facts in several cases under the Federal Rules of Evidence. It follows from the power of the trial judge to "exercise reasonable control" under the terms of Rule 611(a). On the other hand, if the witness on cross-examination denies or does not fully admit the facts claimed to show bias, the attacker has the right to prove those facts by extrinsic evidence. In courtroom parlance, facts showing bias are not "collateral," and the cross-examiner is not required to "take the answer" of the witness, but may call other witnesses to prove them. There are similar holdings under the Federal Rules of Evidence.

§ 40. Character: In General

The character of a witness for truthfulness or mendacity is relevant circumstantial evidence on the question of the truth of particular testimony of the witness. The discussion of the rules which have developed as to character-impeachment will reveal certain general questions of balancing policies. Among them are these: How far in any particular situation does the danger of unfair prejudice against the witness and the party calling her from this type of impeachment outweigh the probable value of the light shed on credibility? Again, should the field of character-impeachment be limited so far as practicable to attack on the particular character trait of truthfulness or should it extend to "general" character for its undoubted though more remote bearing upon truthfulness, on the notion that the greater includes the lesser? [1]

It seems probable, moreover, that the tendency is to use this form of attack more and more sparingly. It was part of the melodrama of the pioneer trial to find "the villain of the piece." It fits less comfortably into the more businesslike atmosphere of the present courtroom. Moreover, as a method of advocacy, the danger to the attacker is great if the attack fails of its mark, or if it is pressed too far. Finally, it is hoped lawyers are conscious of their duty not to ask a question that the lawyer has no reasonable basis to believe is relevant designed to degrade a witness or other person.

§ 41. Character: Misconduct, for Which There Has Been No Criminal Conviction

The English common law tradition of "cross-examination to credit" permits counsel to inquire into the associations and personal history of the witness, including any particular misconduct which would tend to discredit his character, though it has not been the basis for conviction of crime. (This is the kind of misconduct referred to in this section unless otherwise indicated.) Under the common law tradition the courts trusted the disciplined

discretion of the bar to avoid abuses. In this country, there is a confusing variety of decisions, occasionally even in the same jurisdiction. At present, however, it can be said generally that the majority of courts limit cross-examination concerning acts of misconduct as an attack upon character to acts which have a significant relation to the credibility of the witness. This is the view adopted by Federal Rule of Evidence 608(b). Particular instances of conduct satisfying this standard will normally involve dishonesty or false statement, i.e., active misrepresentation, as employed in Federal Rule of Evidence 609(a)(2).[1] Some courts permit an attack upon character by fairly wide-open cross-examination upon acts of misconduct which show bad moral character and can have only an attenuated relation to credibility. Finally, a number of courts prohibit altogether cross-examination as to acts of misconduct for impeachment purposes. This latter view is arguably the fairest and most expedient practice because of the dangers otherwise of prejudice (particularly if the witness is a party), of distraction and confusion, of abuse by the asking of unfounded questions, and of the difficulties, as demonstrated in the cases on appeal, of ascertaining whether particular acts relate to character for truthfulness.

The above-mentioned notions should be distinguished from the showing of conduct which indicates partiality, the showing of conduct as an admission, and the showing of conduct for impeachment by contradiction.[2]

In this country, the danger of victimizing witnesses and of undue prejudice to the parties has led most of our courts which permit the showing of acts of misconduct under the rules mentioned above, to recognize that cross-examination concerning acts of misconduct is subject to a discretionary control by the trial judge. Some of the factors that may, it seems sway discretion, are (1) whether the

---

§ 40

1. See the general discussion of relevancy and its counterweights in Ch. 16 infra, and of the relevancy of character evidence in various other situations in Ch. 17 infra.

§ 41

1. See § 42 infra.

2. See § 39 supra re partiality, §§ 261–267 infra re admissions by conduct, and § 45 infra re impeachment by contradiction. Inconsistent conduct is yet another subject. See § 37 supra.

testimony of the witness under attack is crucial or unimportant, (2) the relevancy of the act of misconduct to truthfulness, depending upon the rule followed in the jurisdiction in that respect, (3) the nearness or remoteness of the misconduct to the time of trial, (4) whether the matter inquired into is such as to lead to time-consuming and distracting explanations on cross-examination or re-examination, (5) whether there is undue humiliation of the witness and undue prejudice. A good faith basis for the inquiry is required.[3]

In the formative period of evidence law, there came to be recognized, as a sort of vague corollary of the privilege against self-incrimination, a privilege of a witness not to answer questions calling for answers which would degrade or disgrace him, provided such questions were not material to the issues in the case. The privilege, though sporadically recognized from time to time during the 1800s, has in the present century been generally abandoned, except as it is encysted in the Codes of a few states. The practical protection to the witness is not so effective as that given by courts which prohibit such cross-examination altogether, since the prohibitory rule will be invoked by counsel or by the court of its own motion, whereas the privilege must be claimed by the witness, and such a claim is almost as degrading as an affirmative answer. Taking a somewhat intermediate position Federal and Revised Uniform Rule of Evidence (1974) 611(a) gives the court discretion to prevent harassment or embarrassment of witnesses when they are cross-examined pursuant to Rule 608(b) concerning acts of misconduct.

In jurisdictions which permit character-impeachment by proof of misconduct for which no conviction has been had, an important curb is the accepted rule that proof is limited to what can be brought out on cross-examination. Thus, if the witness stands his ground and denies the alleged misconduct, the examiner must "take his answer," not that he may not further cross-examine to extract an ad-

mission, but in the sense that he may not call other witnesses to prove the discrediting acts.[4] This rule is adopted by Federal Rule of Evidence 608(b).

A further important curb is the privilege against self-incrimination. While a witness who without objecting makes a partial disclosure of incriminating matter cannot then invoke the privilege when asked to make the disclosure complete,[5] it seems clear that the mere act of testifying cannot be regarded as a waiver of the privilege with respect to inquiry on cross-examination into criminal activities for the purpose of attacking his credibility. While an accused, unlike an ordinary witness, has an option whether to testify at all, exacting such a waiver as the price of taking the stand leaves little of the right to testify in one's own behalf. Therefore Federal Rule of Evidence and Revised Uniform Rule of Evidence 608(b) provide that the giving of testimony by any witness, including an accused, does not waive the privilege as to matters relating only to credibility.

§ 42. Character: Conviction of Crime

At common law the conviction of a person of treason or any felony, or of a misdemeanor involving dishonesty or false statement (crimen falsi), or the obstruction of justice, rendered the convicted person altogether incompetent as a witness. These were said to be "infamous" crimes. By statutes or rules which are virtually universal in the common law world, this primitive absolutism has been abandoned and the disqualification for conviction of crime has been abrogated, and by specific provision or by decision has been reduced to a mere ground of impeachment of credibility. Just as the common law definition of disqualifying crimes was not very precise, so also the abrogating statutes and rules are correspondingly indefinite, and the resulting definitions of crimes for which a conviction shall be ground of impeachment vary widely among the states that have not adopted Federal Rule of Evidence 609.

---

3. See § 49 infra.
4. See also § 49 infra.

5. For more detailed discussion, see § 140 infra.

A rule that would limit impeachment to conviction of crimes that involve dishonesty or false statement would be fairly definite for administrative purposes but not an arbitrary criterion for fairness purposes.

The Federal Rule governing impeachment by proof of conviction of crime is the product of compromise. Crimes of "dishonesty or false statement," regardless of the punishment therefor, may be used against any witness, including an accused. Other crimes punishable by less than imprisonment in excess of one year are never usable. Against an accused who takes the stand or criminal defense witnesses, crimes punishable by death or imprisonment in excess of one year may be used, if the court determines that the probative value of the conviction outweighs its prejudicial effect on the defendant; in civil cases or against all witnesses other than the accused in criminal cases such crimes are usable unless the court determines that the probative value of the conviction is substantially outweighed by its prejudicial effect. Factors appropriate for consideration in the balancing process are (1) the nature of the crime, (2) recency of the prior conviction, (3) similarity between the crime for which there was prior conviction and the crime charged, (4) the importance of defendant's testimony, and (5) the centrality of the credibility issue. Crimes involving "dishonesty or false statement," regardless of the punishment or against whom used, do not require balancing of probative value against prejudice.

The nature of specific offenses properly included within the phrase "dishonesty and false statement" has been subject to debate. The Report of the Conference Committee stated:

By the phrase "dishonesty and false statement" the Conference means crimes such as perjury or subornation of perjury, false statement, criminal fraud, embezzlement, or false pretense, or any other offense in the nature of crimen falsi, the commission of which involves some element of deceit, untruthfulness, or falsification bearing on the accused's propensity to testify truthfully.

Arguably under the view of the Report of the Conference Committee limiting the phrase "dishonesty or false statement" to crimes involving crimen falsi little meaning attaches to the term "dishonesty," with the possible exception of embezzlement. The controversy appeared in reported decisions trying to give meaning to the term "dishonesty or false statement" with respect to convictions involving petty larceny, robbery, shoplifting and narcotics. It quickly became settled, however, that crimes involving solely the use of force such as assault and battery, and crimes such as drunkenness and prostitution do not involve "dishonesty or false statement," while the crime of fraud does.

The pattern that has emerged from the cases evidences a willingness to follow the Report of the Conference Committee and define "dishonesty or false statement" as a crime "which involves some element of deceit, untruthfulness, or falsification bearing on the accused's propensity to testify truthfully." Several additional crimes have now been held on their face to meet this definition. On the other hand, federal courts and most state courts are unwilling to conclude that offenses such as petty larceny, shoplifting, robbery, possession of a weapon, and narcotic violations are per se crimes of "dishonesty or false statement." A physical attempt to remain undetected does not alone make the crime one involving dishonesty or false statement. However, if the party wishing to employ a conviction not considered per se a crime of "dishonesty or false statement" is able to show by going behind the judgment that the particular conviction rested upon facts establishing deceit, untruthfulness or falsification, i.e., involved some element of active misrepresentation, the prior conviction may be employed to impeach credibility.

The use of any conviction is subject to time limits.

Convictions in any state or in federal court are usable to impeach. Though a judgment against a lawyer of suspension or disbarment for criminal misconduct is not technically a conviction, it has been held to be provable to impeach. In statutes relating to proceedings in juvenile courts it is frequently provided that an adjudication of delinquency shall not be used in evidence against the child in any other court and shall not be deemed a "conviction." These statutes are usually construed as precluding the finding from being used as a conviction to impeach credibility. In various jurisdictions, as under the Federal Rule of Evidence 609(d), this matter is dealt with in detail by general evidence rules or statutes. Sometimes juvenile adjudications are admissible under such provisions.

By case law a pardon does not prevent the use of the conviction to impeach. The Federal Rule of Evidence 609(c) adopts the same rule under stated conditions. By the predominant view, including Federal Rule of Evidence 609(e), the pendency of an appeal does not preclude the use of the conviction for this purpose. Most courts hold that lapse of time may prevent use of a conviction too remote in time if the judge in his discretion finds that under the circumstances it lacks probative value. The Federal Rule of Evidence 609(b) is more specific. It provides that evidence of a conviction is not admissible if a period of more than ten years has elapsed since the date of the conviction or of the release of the witness from the confinement imposed for that conviction, whichever is the later date, unless the court determines, in the interests of justice, that the probative value of the conviction supported by specific facts and circumstances substantially outweighs its prejudicial effect. Case authority is divided respecting the use of a judgment based upon a plea of *nolo contendere*. Federal Rule of Evidence 609 should permit its use.

The general rule in other situations is that proof of an official record must if feasible be made by the use of a certified or examined copy, in preference to oral testimony of its contents. The rule was applied in England to proof of records of conviction, so as to preclude the cross-examiner from asking about convictions. This practice still lingers in a few states, but the inconvenience of the requirement, and the obvious reliability of the answer of a witness acknowledging his own conviction, have led most jurisdictions, by statute, rule, or decision, to permit the proof to be made either by production of the record or a copy, or by the oral statement of the convicted witness himself. Here the cross-examiner need not "lay a foundation" for proof by copy or record, nor is he bound to "take the answer" if the witness denies the conviction, but may prove it by the record. It is common practice for the party who calls a witness with a provable criminal record to bring out the prior conviction on direct examination. This process was never treated as impeachment of a party's own witness but rather as anticipatory disclosure designed to reduce the prejudicial effect of the evidence if revealed for the first time on cross-examination.[1] Anticipatory disclosure is particularly common when the criminal defendant testifies on his own behalf.

How far may the cross-examiner go in his inquiries about convictions? He may ask about the name of the crime committed, i.e. murder or embezzlement. It will certainly add to the pungency of the impeachment where the crime was an aggravated one if he may ask about the circumstances, for example, whether the murder victim was a baby, the niece of the witness. And it has been suggested by a few courts that since proof by record is allowable, and the record might show some of these circumstances, the cross-examination should at least be permitted to touch all the facts that the record would. On the whole, however, the more reasonable practice, minimizing prejudice and distraction from the issues, is the generally prevailing one that beyond the name of the crime, the time and place of conviction, and sometimes the punishment; further details such as the name of the victim and the aggravating circumstances may not be inquired into.

It may be thought that if the impeacher is precluded from showing details and circum-

§ 42
1. As to impeaching one's own witness, see § 38 supra.

stances of aggravation, the witness should similarly be cut off from explaining or extenuating the conviction or denying his guilt. Certainly it is impractical and forbidden to retry the case on which the conviction was based. And many cases forbid any explanation, extenuation or denial of guilt even by the witness himself on redirect. This rule is a logical consequence of the premise of conclusiveness of the judgment. It does not, however, satisfy our feeling that some reasonable outlet for the instinct of self-defense by one attacked should be conceded, if it can be done without too much damage to the business at hand. Accordingly a substantial number of courts, while not opening the door to a retrial of the conviction, do permit the witness himself to make a brief and general statement in explanation, mitigation, or denial of guilt, or recognize a discretion in the trial judge to permit it. Wigmore aptly terms it a "harmless charity to allow the witness to make such protestations on his own behalf as he may feel able to make with a due regard to the penalties of perjury."

The sharpest and most prejudicial impact of the practice of impeachment by conviction (as is true also of cross-examination as to misconduct, see § 42, above) is upon one particular type of witness, namely, the accused in a criminal case who elects to take the stand. If the accused is forced to admit that he has a "record" of past convictions, particularly if the convictions are for crimes similar to the one on trial, there is an obvious danger that the jury, despite instructions, will give more heed to the past convictions as evidence that the accused is the kind of man who would commit the crime on charge, or even that he ought to be put away without too much concern with present guilt, than they will to the legitimate bearing of the past convictions on credibility. The accused, who has a "record" but who thinks he has a defense to the present charge, is thus placed in a grievous dilemma. If he stays off the stand, his silence alone will prompt the jury to believe him guilty. If he elects to testify, his "record" becomes provable to impeach him, and this again is likely to doom his defense. Where

does the balance of justice lie? Most prosecutors would argue with much force that it would be misleading to permit the accused to appear as a witness of blameless life, and this argument has prevailed widely. An intermediate view, between permitting convictions generally to be introduced and excluding all convictions of the accused to impeach him as a witness, is a proposal that the convictions be restricted to those supposedly bearing directly upon character for truthfulness. Another intermediate view, but with the disadvantage of uncertainty, was a rule which would permit the introduction of prior convictions of the defendant-witness in the discretion of the judge, who was to balance in each instance the possible prejudice against the probative value of the conviction as to credibility. As already noted earlier in this section the Federal Rule of Evidence is a compromise that in effect combines the above two notions in a specific manner. In Pennsylvania, the accused who takes the stand is shielded, under certain circumstances, from cross-examination as to misconduct or conviction of crime when offered to impeach but not from proof of conviction by the record of conviction. Finally, the former Uniform Rule provided that if the accused does not offer evidence supporting his own credibility the prosecution shall not be allowed, on cross-examination or otherwise, to prove for impeachment purposes his conviction of crime. The variety of solution, both actual and proposed, indicate the stubborn and troublesome nature of the problem.

In view of the difficulties encountered in the balancing approach, the suggestion has been made that the "mere fact" method be substituted for convictions punishable by death or imprisonment in excess of one year. The method is described as follows:

[T]he proper procedural approach is simply to ask the witness the straight-forward question as to whether he had ever been convicted of a crime. The inquiry must end at this point unless the witness denies that he has been convicted. In the event of such denial the adverse party may then in the presentation of his side of the case produce and file in evidence the record of any such conviction. If the witness admits prior conviction of a crime, the inquiry by his adversary may not be pursued to the point of naming the crime for which he was convicted. If the witness so desires he may of his own volition state the nature of the crime and offer any relevant testimony that would eliminate any adverse implications; for example, the fact that he had in the meantime been fully pardoned or that the crime was a minor one and occurred many years before.[2]

The suggestion has also been made that impeachment of the accused by showing of prior convictions is an unconstitutional procedure, but at present, this result is not established.

§ 43. Character: Impeachment by Proof of Opinion or Bad Reputation

In most jurisdictions the impeacher may attack the character of a witness by using the following question formula with another witness:

"Do you know the general reputation at the present time of William Witness in the community in which he lives, for truth and veracity?"

"Yes."

"What is that reputation?"

"It is bad."

This routine is the distillation of traditions which became established in a majority of American courts. It was the result of choices between alternative solutions, some wise, some seemingly misguided.

Misguided it seems is the first choice of the doctrine that this attack on character for truth must be in the abstract, debilitated form of proof of reputation. By what is apparently a misreading of legal history, the American courts have in the past generally prohibited proof of character by having a witness describe his belief or opinion of the character of the second witness under attack when the belief or opinion is based upon experience with the witness under attack and upon observation of his conduct. The limitation to

reputation has been defended on the ground that to let in opinion from observation would provoke distracting side-issues over disputes about specific conduct of the witness attacked, since the impeaching witness may be cross-examined about the grounds of his opinion. Furthermore, a difficult assessment of the impeaching witness might be necessary. These dangers undoubtedly exist, and the controversies would need to be held to reasonable limits by the judge. However, the question is whether the choice of reputation instead of experience and observation has not eliminated most of the objectivity from the attempt to appraise character, and has not encouraged the parties to select those who will give voice, under the guise of an estimate of reputation, to prejudice and ill-will. The hand is the hand of Esau, but the voice is the voice of Jacob. And, in addition, reputation in modern, impersonal urban centers is often evanescent, fragile, or actually non-existent.

Based upon reasons such as those stated above, the Federal Rule of Evidence 608(a) and the Revised Uniform Rule of Evidence 608(a) permit attack upon character by opinion, while at the same time retaining the traditional attack upon character by reputation. Various aspects of this rule are considered throughout the remainder of this section.

The courts also have faced here a further choice—a recurrent one in various phases of character-impeachment—namely, shall the inquiry be as to "general character," or as to other specific types of bad traits such as sexual immorality, or shall it be directed solely and specifically to the trait of veracity? Surely it is clear that in this elusive realm of reputation as to character it is best to reach for the highest degree of relevancy that is attainable. Fortunately the great majority of our courts have taken this view and have limited the inquiry to "reputation for truth and veracity." Opinion, as well as reputation, pursuant to Federal and Revised Uniform Rule of Evidence 608(a) is likewise limited. Only a few jurisdictions open the door, in

---

2. McArthur v. Cook, 99 So.2d 565, 567 (Fla.1957).

addition, to reputation for "general character" or "general moral character," and fewer still permit proof of reputation for specific traits other than veracity.

The crucial time when the character of the witness under attack has its influence on his truth-telling is the time when he testifies. But obviously reputation takes time to form and is the resultant of earlier conduct and demeanor, so that it does not precisely reflect character at a later date. The practical solution is to do what most courts actually do, that is, (1) to permit the reputation-witness to testify about the impeachee's "present" reputation as of the time of the trial, if he knows it, and (2) to permit testimony as to reputation (which is usually a settled, continuing condition) as of any time before trial which the judge in his discretion finds is not too remote to be significant. This practice should be permitted by Federal Rule of Evidence 608(a). The opinion of the witness permitted by the federal rule should have a similar time relation to the trial.

As to place of reputation, the traditional inquiry is as to general reputation for veracity "in the community where he lives." The object of this limitation of place is obviously to restrict evidence of repute, to reputation among the people who know him best. The limitation was appropriate for the situation in England (and less so in America) before the Industrial Revolution, when most people lived either in small towns or in rural villages. But as an exclusive limitation it would not be appropriate in this country today, where a person may be little known in the suburb or city neighborhood where he lives, but well known in another locality where he spends his workdays or in several localities where he does business from time to time. Thus, today it is generally agreed that proof may be made not only of the reputation of the witness where he lives, but also of his repute, as long as it is "general" and established, in any substantial community of people among whom he is well known, such as the group with whom he works, does business or goes to school. These standards should apply under Federal Rule of Evidence 608(a). The trial

judge has a reasonable need of discretion to determine whether the reputation sought to be proved among the group in question meets these standards.

Other problems arise when the attack on character is by opinion as authorized by Federal Rule of Evidence 608(a). Although it appears that an opinion of a lay person should be based on some firsthand knowledge pursuant to Rule 602 so that the opinion can be based on rational perception and be of aid to the jury as required by Rule 701, acts of misconduct cannot be brought out from the witness on direct examination because Rule 608(b) prohibits evidence of such acts by extrinsic evidence. An adequate preliminary showing to meet the requirements of Rule 701 would be made by evidence of sufficient acquaintance with the witness to be attacked. Impeachment by experts is considered in the next section.

§ 44. Defects of Capacity: Sensory or Mental

Any deficiency of the senses, such as deafness, or color blindness or defect of other senses which would substantially lessen the ability to perceive the facts which the witness purports to have observed, should of course be provable to attack the credibility of the witness, either upon cross-examination or by producing other witnesses to prove the defect. Probably the limits and weaknesses of human powers of perception should be studied more widely by judges and lawyers in the interest of a more accurate and objective administration of justice.

As to the mental qualities of intelligence and memory, a distinction must be made between attacks on competency and attacks on credibility, the subject of this section. Sanity in any general sense is not the test of competency, and a so-called insane person is generally permitted to testify if he is able to report correctly the matters to which he testifies and if he understands the duty to speak the truth. Even more clearly, Federal Rule of Evidence 601, for use at least in federal question cases in federal courts, disassociates the subject of sanity or insanity from the subject of competency of witnesses to testify, although one could be sufficiently incompetent so that one's testimony would be barred if one did not have the capacity to recall or observe, understand the duty to tell the truth, or have the capacity to have personal knowledge. Manifestly, however, the fact of mental "abnormality" either at the time of observing the facts or at the time of testifying will be provable, on cross or by extrinsic evidence, as bearing on credibility, often, as under the federal rules, in the discretion of the court. The use of expert opinion as extrinsic evidence in this situation is discussed in the last part of this section.

What of defects of mind within the range of normality, such as a slower than average mind or a poorer than usual memory? These qualities reveal themselves in a testing cross-examination by a skilled questioner. May they be proved by other witnesses? The decisions are divided. It seems eminently a case for discretion. The trial judge would determine whether the crucial character of the testimony attacked and the evaluative light shed by the impeaching evidence overbalance the time and distraction involved in opening this side-dispute. The development of standardized tests for intelligence and their widening use in business, government and the armed forces, suggest that they may eventually come to serve as useful aids in the evaluation of testimony.

Abnormality, we have seen, is a horse of a different color. It is a standard ground of impeachment. One form of abnormality exists when one is under the influence of drugs or drink. If the witness was under the influence at the time of the happenings which he reports in his testimony or is so at the time he testifies, this condition is provable, on cross or by extrinsic evidence, to impeach. Habitual addiction stands differently. It is generally held that the mere fact of chronic alcoholism is not provable on credibility. On the other hand, as to drug addiction to which more social odium has been attached, many decisions allow it to be shown to impeach, even without evidence that it did in the particular

case affect truth-telling, although more courts, absent a particular showing of effect on the witness's veracity, would exclude it. Most federal cases agree. In respect to both addictions the excluding courts seem to have the better of the arguments. It can scarcely be contended that there is enough scientific agreement to warrant judicial notice that addiction in and of itself usually affects credibility. Certainly it is pregnant with prejudice. On the other hand, there is an increasing recognition among non-legal authorities that addiction may in various instances be linked with personality and other defects which do bear upon credibility.

In recent decades with the growth in importance of psychiatry, the testimony of psychiatrists upon issues of sanity in cases of wills and crimes has become familiar to the legal profession. Naturally, the use of expert psychiatric testimony as to mental disorders and defects suggests itself as a potential aid in determining the credibility of crucial witnesses in any kind of litigation. In one type of case, namely sex offenses, Wigmore and other commentators have urged the indispensable value of this kind of testimony, and in the past it has been approved by the courts. But Wigmore's positions that females who testify they have been sexually molested or attacked may often report such matters falsely, and that a judge should *always* be sure that the female victim—witness's social history and mental makeup are the subject of examination and testimony by a qualified physician, have been the subject of penetrating critical analysis of the basis for these views. Most courts now hold that the matter of psychiatric testimony generally is one in the discretion of the trial judge, and many of these courts hold that the discretion to order an examination and permit such testimony should be exercised only for compelling reasons or in compelling circumstances. Such circumstances are not at all clear; definite limiting conditions should at the least be developed; and in fact there is limited state authority that there should be no power at all to order a psychiatric examination and admit resulting testimony in trials for rape.

Various courts have tended to take the position that there may be impeachment of principal witnesses in other cases by expert psychiatric opinion. On the other hand, insofar as published opinions indicate, the federal courts have been disinclined to exercise their discretion to permit attacks by experts on mental capacity affecting credibility. If there is ground for believing that a principal witness is subject to some mental abnormality that may affect his credibility, a need for employment of the resources of psychiatry may exist. Many courts today would accept the principle that psychiatric evidence should be received, at least in the judge's discretion, when its value outweighs the cost in time, distraction, and expense and other disadvantages. The value seems to depend first upon the importance of the appraised witness's testimony, and second upon the opportunity of the expert to form a reliable opinion. This first factor, the importance of the testimony, is a relevant factor at least from the standpoint of policy considerations relating to the feasibility and desirability of subjecting witnesses (even party-witnesses) to an ordeal of psychiatric attack which may or may not be justified. The above-mentioned second factor, opportunity to form a reliable opinion, raises difficulties. An opinion based solely upon a hypothetical question seems almost valueless here. Only slightly more reliable is an opinion derived from the subject's demeanor and his testimony in the courtroom. Most psychiatrists would say that a satisfactory opinion can only be formed after the witness has been subjected to a clinical examination. A discretionary power has been recognized in a few instances, granting the judge the power to order an examination of a prosecuting witness, but the conditions for exercising that discretion are unclear. It seems the power to exercise discretion should exist in any type of case, to be exercised not only upon the bases of whether undue expenditure of time or expense and undue distraction will result, but

also upon the bases of whether the witness is a key witness and whether there are substantial indications that the witness is suffering from mental abnormality at the time of trial or was so suffering at the time of the happening about which he testifies. Only if there is no power to order an examination should expert opinion on the bases of courtroom observation and reading of the record be considered. Even then, permitting opinion based upon such material seems very questionable.

Expert opinion on character for truthfulness or untruthfulness authorized by Federal and Revised Uniform Rule 608(a) should probably be distinguished from the subject discussed above, opinion of mental capacity to tell the truth. Thus Rule 608(a) should not be considered direct authority for the type of opinion testimony discussed in this section.

§ 45. Impeachment by "Contradiction" [1]

"Contradiction" may be explained as follows. Statements are elicited from Witness One, who has testified to a material story of an accident, crime, or other matters, to the effect that at the time he witnessed these matters the day was windy and cold and he, the witness, was wearing his green sweater. Let us suppose these latter statements about the day and the sweater to be "disproved." This may happen in several ways. Witness One on direct or cross-examination may acknowledge that he was in error. Or judicial notice may be taken that at the time and place it could not have been cold and windy, e.g., in Tucson in July. But commonly disproof or "contradiction" is attempted by calling Witness Two to testify to the contrary, i.e., that the day was warm and Witness One was in his shirt-sleeves. It is in this latter sense that the term "contradiction" is used in this section.

---

§ 45

1. The extent to which evidence obtained in violation of a constitutional right may be used to impeach is treated in § 182 infra. The use of treatises to impeach experts is dealt with in § 321 infra.

What impeaching value does the contradiction have in the above situation? It merely tends to show—for Witness One may be right and Witness Two may be mistaken—that Witness One has erred or falsified as to certain particular facts, and therefore is capable of error or lying, and this should be considered negatively in weighing his other statements. But all human beings have this capacity and all testimony should be discounted to some extent for this weakness. It is true that the trial judge in his discretion may permit the cross-examiner to conduct a general test of the power of Witness One to observe, remember and recount facts unrelated to the case, to "test" or "explore" these capacities.[2] To permit a dispute, however, about such extraneous or "collateral" facts as the weather and the clothing of Witness One, that are material only for "testing" the witness, by allowing the attacker to call other witnesses to disprove them, is not practical. Dangers of surprise, of confusion of the jury's attention, and of time-wasting are apparent.

Therefore, many courts maintain the safeguarding rule that a witness may not be impeached by producing extrinsic evidence of "collateral" facts to "contradict" the first witness's assertions about those facts. A matter is "collateral" if the matter itself is not relevant in the litigation to establish a fact of consequence,[3] i.e., not relevant for a purpose other than mere contradiction of the in-court testimony of the witness. If the collateral fact sought to be contradicted is elicited on cross-examination, this safeguarding rule is often expressed by saying that the answer is conclusive or that the cross-examiner must "take the answer." By the better view, if the "collateral" fact happens to have been drawn out on direct, the rule against contradiction should still be applied. The danger of surprise is lessened, but waste of time and confusion of issues stand as objections.

§ 46. Beliefs Concerning Religion

As indicated in a subsequent section,[1] the common law required as a qualification for taking the oath as a witness, the belief in a God who would punish untruth. This rule grew up in a climate of custom and assumptions which today seem primitive and archaic. It has quite generally been abandoned in most common law jurisdictions. General provisions like that in the Illinois constitution to the effect that "no person shall be denied any civil or political rights, privilege or capacity on account of his religious opinions" have been construed in many states to abrogate the rule of incompetency to take the oath. Nor is belief in God required by the Federal Rules of Evidence 601 or 603.

The general tendency, as indicated in Sections 43 and 65, has been to convert the old grounds of incompetency to testify, such as interest and infamy, into grounds of impeaching credibility, and this principle of conversion has sometimes been expressly enacted in constitutional provisions and in statutes. Should the principle be applied so as to permit the credibility of a witness to be attacked by showing that she is an atheist or an agnostic and does not believe in Divine punishment for perjury? The greater number of courts that answered the question at all said no, either by interpreting general provisions such as that quoted above from the Illinois constitution, or by mandate of specific constitutional, statutory, or rule language. Thus many states recognize a privilege of the witness not to be examined about her own religious faith or beliefs, except so far as the judge in her discretion finds that the relevance of the in-

2. See § 29 supra.

3. See generally § 49 infra.

§ 46

1. See § 63 infra.

quiry upon some substantive issue in the case outweighs the interest of privacy and the danger of prejudice. A few, either reasoning from the conversion of grounds of incompetency into grounds for impeachment or following specific provisions, may allow this ground of impeachment. It is to be observed, however, that the common law analogy would not extend to permit inquiry into particular creeds, faiths or affiliations except as they shed light on the witness's belief in a God who will punish untruth.

There is a strong reason why the legislatures and courts should, in addition to recognizing the privilege of a witness not to answer to her own religious beliefs, forbid the party to impeach by bringing other witnesses to attack the faith of the first one. This reason of course is that there is no basis for believing that the lack of faith in God's avenging wrath is today an indication of greater than average untruthfulness. Without that basis, the evidence of atheism is simply irrelevant upon the question of credibility.

Federal Rule of Evidence 610 provides:

> Evidence of the beliefs or opinions of a witness on matters of religion is not admissible for the purpose of showing that by reason of their nature the witness' credibility is impaired or enhanced.

§ 47. Supporting the Witness

Impeachment is not a dispassionate study of the capacities and character of the witness, but is regarded in our tradition as an *attack* upon his credibility. Under our adversary system of trials the opponent must be given an opportunity to meet this attack by evidence sustaining or rehabilitating the witness. One general principle, operative under both case law and the Federal Rules of Evidence, is that in the absence of an attack upon credibility no sustaining evidence is allowed. A second truism is that when there has been evidence of impeaching facts the proponent may bring contradictory evidence asserting the untruth of the alleged impeaching facts. Such a denial is always relevant and generally allowable.

A discussion of rehabilitation and support of witnesses is more readily organized around the techniques employed than in terms of principle, just as was seen to be the case with respect to impeachment. The two most common specific methods that are attempted are (1) introduction of supportive evidence of good character of the witness attacked, and (2) introduction of consistent statements of the witness who has been attacked. The most common rehabilitation problem is whether these two types of rehabilitation evidence may be introduced in connection with the various methods of impeachment that have been attempted, as outlined in the previous sections of this chapter. The general test for solution is whether evidence of the good character of the witness or of his consistent statements is logically relevant to explain the impeaching fact. The rehabilitating facts must meet a particular method of impeachment with relative directness. The wall, attacked at one point, may not be fortified at another and distinct point. Credibility is a side issue and the circle of relevancy in this context may well be drawn narrowly. How narrowly is a question of degree as to which reasonable courts differ.

When may the party supporting the witness, who has been attacked by one of the impeachment methods discussed in this chapter, offer evidence of good character of the witness for truth? See Fed.R.Evid. 608(a). Certainly attacks by evidence of bad reputation, bad opinion of character for truthfulness, conviction of crime, or eliciting from the witness on cross-examination acknowledgment of misconduct which has not resulted in conviction, will all open the door to character support. The evidence of good character for truth is logically relevant to meet these kinds of impeachment. Moreover, a slashing cross-examination may carry strong accusations of misconduct and bad character, which the witness's denial will not remove from the jury's mind. If the judge considers that fairness requires it, he may permit evidence of good character, a mild palliative for the rankle of insinuation by such cross-examination.

Corrupt conduct of a witness of a sort to show bias should also seemingly be regarded as including an attack on veracity-character and thus warranting character support, but impeachment for bias or interest by facts not involving corruption, such as proof of family relationship, may not be met by proof of good character for truth.

Attempts to support the witness by showing his good character for truth have resulted in contradictory conclusions when the witness has been impeached by evidence of an inconsistent statement, or has been met by the adversary's evidence denying the facts to which the witness has so testified. If the witness has been impeached by the introduction of an inconsistent statement, the greater number of courts permit a showing of his good character for truth, but if the adversary has merely introduced evidence denying the facts to which the witness testified, the greater number of cases will not permit a showing of the witness's good character for truth. Convenient as automatic answers to these seemingly minor trial questions may be, surely it is unrealistic to handle them in a mechanical fashion. A more sensible view is the notion that the judge should consider in each case whether a particular impeachment for inconsistency or a conflict in testimony, or either of them, amounts in net effect to an attack on character for truth and should exercise his discretion accordingly to admit or exclude the character-support. It has been suggested this view is embodied in the Federal Rules of Evidence.

Turning to the attempts to rehabilitate or support a witness by introduction of a prior statement consistent with his present testimony after the credibility of the witness has been attacked in some way, a similar question arises. What kind of attack upon the witness opens the door to evidence of prior statements by the witness consistent with his present story on the stand? When the attack takes the form of impeachment of character, by showing misconduct, convictions or bad reputation, it is generally agreed that there is no color for sustaining by consistent statements. The defense does not meet the assault. Fur-

ther, if the attacker has charged bias, interest, corrupt influence, contrivance to falsify, or want of capacity to observe or remember, the applicable principle is that the prior consistent statement has no relevancy to refute the charge unless the consistent statement was made *before* the source of the bias, interest, influence or incapacity originated. The above results should ordinarily be reached under Federal Rule of Evidence 801(d)(1)(B).

There is much division of opinion on the question whether impeachment by inconsistent statements opens the door to support by proving consistent statements. A few courts hold generally that the support is permissible. This rule has the merit of easy application in the court room. Some courts, since the inconsistency remains despite all consistent statements, hold generally that it does not. But certain modifications or even a complete departure from these general rules should be recognized. If the attacked witness denies the making of the inconsistent statement then some courts consider that the evidence of consistent statements near the time of the alleged inconsistent one, is relevant to fortify his denial. Again, if in the particular situation, the attack by inconsistent statement is accompanied by, or interpretable as, a charge of a plan or contrivance to give false testimony, then proof of a prior consistent statement *before* the plan or contrivance was formed, tends strongly to disprove that the testimony was the result of contrivance. Here all courts agree. It is for the judge to decide whether the impeachment amounts to a charge of contrivance, and ordinarily this is the most obvious implication. If it does not, then it may often amount to an imputation of inaccurate memory. If so the consistent statement made when the event was recent and memory fresh should be received in support. Recognition of these modifications would leave it still open to these courts to exclude various statements procured after the inconsistent statement, and thus to discourage pressure on witnesses to furnish successive counter-statements.

The above modifications could be the governing rules in the interpretation of the Federal Rules of Evidence. Under a broader viewpoint the judge has at least practical discretion under Rules 401 and 403 to determine whether any particular circumstances justify admission of consistent statements to rehabilitate the witness. This interpretation is a basically different approach. Yet it would permit judges to discourage pressure for successive counter statements of witnesses.

The fact of a complaint of rape and in some instances the details of the complaint have been held admissible. Both the fact of complaint and, where allowed, the details of the complaint may be admissible on the theory of rehabilitating or bolstering the complaining witness, but since this evidence may also come in as substantive evidence under some theories, the matter is dealt with later.[1] Likewise, prior consistent statements of identification may be admissible substantively or to rehabilitate, but because prior identifications may be admissible as substantive evidence and also involve constitutional requirements, the subject is also discussed elsewhere.[2]

§ 48. Attacking the Supporting Character Witness

Under Federal and Revised Uniform Rule of Evidence (1974) 608(b)(2) and generally at common law a witness who has testified as to his favorable opinion or the good reputation of another witness ("principle witness") for truth and veracity[1] can be cross-examined with respect to prior acts of the principal witness, if probative of untruthfulness. Specific instances of conduct sufficiently probative of untruthfulness not having resulted in a conviction[2] will normally involve dishonesty or false statement.[3] Extrinsic evidence with respect to specific instances of conduct of the principal witness not resulting in a conviction

is not admissible; the cross-examiner must take the witness' answer.[4]

A character witness testifying to the reputation of the principal witness as to truthfulness, may testify on direct examination and be cross-examined concerning with whom, where, and when the witness actually discussed the reputation of the principal witness. Opinion testimony must be based upon personal knowledge of the principal witness by the character witness; the extent of the relationship with the principal witness is a proper subject of inquiry on cross-examination.

When a character witness testifies as to the reputation of the principal witness for truthfulness, the proper question on cross-examination with respect to specific instances of conduct of the principal witness at common law is "Have you heard?". Where the testimony of the character witness is in the form of an opinion, the proper form of the question at common law is either "Do you know?" or "Are you aware?". The foregoing distinction, while correct in theory, is of such slight practical importance that it could easily be eliminated if elimination has not already been accomplished.[5] The character witness may be asked not only about the specific acts of the principal witness probative of untruthfulness, but also may be cross-examined concerning familiarity with convictions as well as arrests, rumors, reports, indictments, etc., concerning the principal witness. Such matters have a natural bearing upon the reputation of the principal witness and character witness' opinion of the principal witness. Lack of familiarity with such matters is relevant to an assessment of the basis for the character witness' testimony. Familiarity with such matters explores the character witness' standard of "truthfulness" or "untruthfulness." Whatever the form of the question, the cross-examin-

---

§ 47

1. See § 272.
2. See § 251 infra.

§ 48

1. For a discussion of when good character testimony is admissible to support the character of a witness for truth and veracity, see § 47 supra.

2. See § 42 supra with respect to the admissibility of prior convictions to impeach.

3. See § 41 supra.

4. See § 49 infra.

5. See § 191 infra.

er must, of course, have a good faith basis supporting the inquiry.

Inquiry on cross-examination of the character witness as to acts of the principal witness probative of untruthfulness not resulting in a conviction will be precluded if the court determines that the probative value of such cross-examination is substantially outweighed by the danger of unfair prejudice. The rather tenuous nature of character testimony as to truth and veracity in the first place, coupled with the inherent risk of unfair prejudice associated with such cross-examination when the principal witness is also a party, militate in favor of the court exercising its discretion in favor of prohibiting inquiry into specific acts. In fact, a blanket prohibition upon cross-examination as to specific acts of the principal witness is well recommended.

§ 49. Contradiction: Collateral and Non–Collateral Matters; Good Faith Basis

On cross-examination, every permissible type of impeachment that may be employed during cross-examination has as one of its purposes the testing of the credibility of the witness. The use of extrinsic evidence to contradict is more restricted due to considerations of confusion of the issues, misleading the jury, undue consumption of time, and unfair prejudice raised by the introduction of so-called collateral matters. If a matter is considered collateral, the testimony of the witness on direct or cross-examination stands— the cross-examiner must take the witness' answer; extrinsic evidence, i.e., evidence offered other than through the witness himself, in contradiction is not permitted. If the matter is not collateral, extrinsic evidence may be introduced disputing the witness' testimony on direct examination or denial of truth of the facts asserted in a question propounded on cross-examination.

A matter is non-collateral if the matter is itself relevant in the litigation to establish a fact of consequence, i.e., relevant for a purpose other than mere contradiction of the in-court testimony of the witness. Matters bearing directly upon the credibility of the witness in a manner other than merely through contradiction or self-contradiction, such as (1) bias, interest, corruption, or coercion, (2) alcohol or drug use, (3) deficient mental capacity and (4) want of physical capacity or absence of actual employment of physical capacity to acquire personal knowledge are also non-collateral and may be contradicted by other evidence. Impeachment of a witness' character for truthfulness by means of a prior conviction is also non-collateral.[1] However, impeachment of a witness' character for truthfulness by means of specific instances of conduct not resulting in a conviction is collateral. Similarly, employment of a specific instance of conduct on cross-examination to impeach reputation or opinion testimony as to a pertinent character trait of the principal is treated as a collateral matter.[2] Finally, a third category of non-collateral creating a test of necessity exists. A witness may be contradicted as to a part of his testimony where as a matter of human experience he would not be mistaken if the thrust of his testimony was true. To illustrate, if the witness had testified that he was going east on Main proceeding from A to B following behind the defendant's car and that the sun didn't affect his vision, the fact one has to go west on Main to get from A to B places in question the entirety of the witness' testimony. Treatment of specific instances of conduct offered to impeach as collateral is based upon an assessment of the lack of probative value of extrinsic proof contradicting the denial given by the witness upon the credibility of the witness in comparison to the dangers of unfair prejudice, confusion of the issues, misleading the jury, and waste of time. These three categories were developed at common law to permit introduction of extrinsic evidence relating to the credibility of a witness as now mandated in the federal court by Rule 403—where the probative value of the evidence is not substantially outweighed by trial concerns including the danger of unfair

---

1. See § 42 supra.

2. See § 48 supra and § 191 infra.

prejudice. However extrinsic evidence meeting the foregoing test of non-collateral may nevertheless be excluded if in the particular instance at hand the dangers specified in Rule 403 predominate. Thus extrinsic evidence being non-collateral is a necessary but not sufficient condition for admissibility.

Consider the following illustration. Bob is called to testify that the color of the traffic light facing Apple Street was red at the time of an automobile accident he witnessed at the corner of Apple and Main. On direct examination, Bob testifies that he was proceeding east on Apple Street heading toward the Piagano's Pizza Restaurant which was located on the corner of Apple and Peach. On cross-examination counsel asks, "Isn't it true that Piagano's Pizza Restaurant is located on Apple three blocks east of Peach at Maple?" Although this question is permissible as potentially affecting the jury's assessment of Bob's power of recollection and concern for detail, if Bob continues to maintain that the restaurant is on Peach Street, extrinsic evidence may not be offered during the cross-examiner's case in chief as to the location of the restaurant. The matter is collateral, because the location of the restaurant is not relevant in the litigation other than to contradict the testimony of the witness. Even if Bob denied on cross-examination making a prior statement in which he allegedly said that the restaurant was on Apple and Maple, extrinsic evidence establishing the prior statement would be inadmissible because the matter remains collateral. On the other hand, the color of the traffic light is non-collateral, i.e., the color of the traffic light is itself otherwise relevant in the case. Thus contradictory evidence that the light facing Apple Street was green is admissible. Similarly, if Bob denies on cross-examination having previously stated that the traffic light was green, extrinsic evidence establishing Bob's prior inconsistent statement is admissible.

Assuming Bob is then asked on cross-examination if he was wearing his glasses while driving, a yes answer may be contradicted by extrinsic evidence that his only pair of glasses was being repaired at the time of the accident. Evidence disputing the acquisition of personal knowledge by the witness of facts relevant in the case is non-collateral. Similarly, if Bob denied on cross-examination that his wife was related to the plaintiff, extrinsic evidence of such a fact would be admissible. Evidence of partiality of the witness is non-collateral. Extrinsic evidence offered to establish bias, interest, corruption, or coercion of the witness may be admitted following denial by the witness of a fact giving rise to such an inference when put to the witness on cross-examination. Finally, restructuring the initial illustration, if Piagano's Pizza Restaurant is in fact located on Birch Street, and its location on Birch in relation to Bob's location prior to leaving for the restaurant would naturally place Bob on Main, and not Apple, as he approached the intersection, extrinsic evidence of the location of the restaurant would be admissible on the ground that error as to the location of the restaurant brings into question the trustworthiness of Bob's entire testimony. Bob may have seen the light facing Main, and not the light facing Apple. To illustrate, assume there is no left turn allowed from Apple onto Main. To go left you have to turn right before the intersection and then left onto Main thus winding up on Main and not Apple when approaching the intersection. This type of left turn structure is found in New Jersey.

Extrinsic evidence concerning a collateral matter may be admitted under the doctrine of "door opening." Admissibility of evidence under the notion of "door opening" tends to arise where the government seeks to introduce evidence on rebuttal to contradict specific factual assertions raised during the direct examination of the criminal defendant.[3]

The application of the standard theory of collateral contradiction discussed in this section has been criticized for use under the Federal Rules of Evidence on the ground that the result is a mechanically applied doctrine without consideration of properly pertinent

---

3. See § 57 infra.

matters. It has been urged that the discretionary approach of Rule 403 should be substituted. However, various federal opinions do mention "collateral" evidence. As previously mentioned, Federal Rules of Evidence 401–403, which govern impeachment by contradiction, are entirely consistent with the "collateral" doctrine as discussed in this section; Rule 403 is explicit in the discretion granted the trial judge to admit or exclude contradictions found relevant under Rule 401. Of course, the label, "collateral" should not be used mechanically.

A good faith basis on the part of examining counsel as to the truth of the matter contained in questions propounded to a witness on cross-examination is required. Innuendoes and insinuations of inadmissible or nonexistent matters are improper. Thus counsel on cross-examination may not ask Bob, "Isn't it true that Piagano's is located on Birch?" without having a reasonable basis in fact for believing that Piagano's is in fact on Birch and not Apple. Nor may counsel on cross-examination inquire of Bob whether his wife was related to the plaintiff absent a good faith basis. Note that the requirement of a good faith basis applies only when the cross-examiner is effectively asserting in the form of a question the truth of a factual statement included within the question. If the cross-examiner is merely inquiring whether something is or is not true, a good faith basis is not required. Thus the question, "Your glasses were being repaired at the time of the accident, weren't they?" requires a good faith basis, while the question, "Were you wearing your glasses at the time of the accident?" does not. The principle of a good faith basis applies in the laying of a foundation for impeachment by prior inconsistent statement. Moreover the examining party must have the intent and ability to introduce extrinsic evidence establishing the making of the statement as to a non-collateral matter in the event the making of the statement is not admitted by the witness.[4]

4. See § 37 supra.

§ 50. Exclusion and Separation of Witnesses

If a witness hears the testimony of others before he or she takes the stand, the witness will find it much easier to deliberately tailor his or her own story to that of other witnesses. Witnesses may also be influenced subconsciously. In either event, the cross-examiner will find it more difficult to expose fabrication, collusion, inconsistencies or inaccuracies with respect to witnesses who have heard others testify. Separation prevents improper influence during the trial by prohibiting witness to witness communication both inside and outside of the courtroom.

At common law the court in its discretion may exclude witnesses in the interests of the ascertainment of truth. Rather than adopting a discretionary approach, Federal and Revised Uniform Rule of Evidence (1974) 615 treat the exclusion of witnesses as a matter of right: "At the request of a party, the court shall order witnesses excluded." The court is also empowered to order exclusion on its own motion. A request to exclude witnesses is often referred to as "invoking the rule on witnesses." No time period is specified in which to make the request. Several standards have been applied in determining whether a failure of the court to order exclusion of a witness requires a reversal of the judgment.

Not all witnesses may be excluded and separated. Neither case law nor Rule 615 authorizes exclusion of (1) a party who is a natural person, (2) an officer or employee of a party which is not a natural person designated as its representative by its attorney which includes an investigative agent of the government, or (3) a person whose presence is shown by the party to be essential to the presentation of the cause. An example of a witness whose presence may be essential is an expert witness. It is certainly essential to give counsel the benefit of an expert's assistance while an expert for the other party is testifying.

Similarly, assistance may be necessary in connection with other technical matters as to which counsel lacks sufficient familiarity to try the case effectively on his own. A strong argument can be made for also permitting the presence of an expert witness who intends to give an opinion at trial based in part on evidence presented at trial. Exclusion and separation does not extend to rebuttal witnesses or witnesses called to impeach credibility.

While Rule 615 does not explicitly provide for the separation of witnesses, courts have inherent authority to take further measures designed to prevent communication between witnesses, such as ordering them to remain physically apart, ordering them not to discuss the case with one another, and ordering them not to read a transcript of the trial testimony of another witness.

If a witness violates an order of exclusion or sequestration, the appropriate remedy is committed to the sound discretion of the court. The court may refuse to permit a witness to testify, declare a mistrial, or instruct the jury to weigh the credibility of the witness in light of the witness' presence in court or discussions with another witness. The court may also hold the witness in contempt. The thrust of judicial opinion is against the simple remedy of disqualifying the witness. Unfortunately once it is decided to permit the witness to testify, the alternatives of comment or contempt are not without their drawbacks. The best remedy is to avoid the problem as much as possible by the court impressing upon both the witness and counsel in the first place the importance of obeying the court's ruling excluding and separating the witness.

Title 3

ADMISSION AND EXCLUSION

Chapter 6

THE PROCEDURE OF ADMITTING AND EXCLUDING EVIDENCE

Table of Sections

§ 51. Presentation of Evidence: Offer of Proof

At the outset, it should be noted that our adversary system imposes on the parties the burden of presenting evidence at the trial pursuant to rules and practices that make it clear when proof has been presented so that it is officially introduced and thereupon can be considered by the trier of fact in the resolution of fact issues. The rules of practice concerning presentation of evidence, offers of proof, and the taking of objections are thus slanted to secure this result.

The presentation of things such as writings, photographs, knives, guns, and all kinds of tangible things often proves troublesome to neophytes. There are variations in local pro-

cedures, but the process may be shortly and generally described here. The party wishing to introduce any sort of evidence of this type should first have the thing marked by the clerk for identification as an exhibit for the party. Having had the thing marked by the clerk for identification as an exhibit, the proponent should "lay the foundation" for its introduction as an exhibit by having it appropriately identified or authenticated by the testimony of a witness who is qualified to identify or authenticate it.

Next, the proposed exhibit should be submitted to the opposing attorney for his inspection, at least upon his request, and then the proponent should present it to the judge, stating, e.g., "Plaintiff offers this (document or object, describing it), marked, 'Plaintiff's Exhibit No. 2' for identification, as Plaintiff's Exhibit No. 2." At this point, the opponent may make his objection to its receipt in evidence, and the judge will make his ruling upon the objection. Assuming the judge rules that the thing will be accepted in evidence, if it is a writing, it may be read to the jury by the counsel offering it or by the witness, or if it is a thing it may be shown, or passed, to the jury, in the discretion of the judge or in accordance with local custom or rules, for inspection by the jury.

Of course, the usual way of presenting oral testimony is to call the witness to the stand and ask him questions. Normally, (but not always) the opponent is required to object to testimony by objections to the questions of the examiner before the witness answers the questions.[1] Ordinarily, the admissibility of testimony is thus decided by the judge's sustaining or overruling objections to questions. If the court sustains an objection to a question, the witness is prevented from answering the question and from testifying to that extent.

In such case, for two reasons, the proponent of the question should ordinarily make "an offer of proof", Fed.R.Evid. 103(a)(2). The usual practice is for the proponent to state to the judge what the witness would say if he were permitted to answer the question and what he expects to prove by the answer to the question. While a secondary reason for an offer of proof is that it permits the judge to consider further the claim for admissibility, the primary reason is to include the proposed answer and expected proof in the official record of the trial, so that in case of appeal upon the judge's ruling, the appellate court may understand the scope and effect of the question and proposed answer in considering whether the judge's ruling sustaining an objection was proper. The trial court must usually require this offer of proof to be made out of the hearing of the jury. Federal Rule of Evidence 103(c) requires this be done to the extent practicable. It is also important to

note that upon cross-examination the requirement can be relaxed.

For the purpose of appeal, a question, in the context of the record, may itself so specifically indicate the purport of the expected answer that the appeal court will consider the propriety of the ruling upon the question without an offer of proof. But when, as is more usual, an offer of proof is required before the appellate court will consider a ruling sustaining an objection to a question, the statement constituting the offer of proof must be reasonably specific and must state the purpose of the proof offered unless the purpose is apparent. Where the offered testimony suggests a question as to its materiality or competency, the offer of proof must indicate the facts on which relevancy or admissibility of the testimony depends. These matters apply to Federal Rule of Evidence 103.

If counsel specifies a purpose for which the proposed evidence is inadmissible and the judge excludes, counsel cannot complain of the ruling on appeal though it could have been rightly admitted for another purpose.

If part of the evidence offered, as in the case of a deposition, a letter, or a conversation, is admissible and a part is not, it is incumbent on the offeror, not the judge, to select the admissible part. If counsel offers both good and bad together and the judge rejects the entire offer, the offeror may not complain on appeal.

The method of offer of proof described above assumes there is a witness upon the stand who is being questioned. Suppose, however, that there are several witnesses who are available, but not in court, to prove a line of facts, and the judge's rulings on the law have indicated that he will probably exclude this line of testimony, or the judge rules in advance that the line of testimony is inadmissible. Must the party produce each of these witnesses, question them, and on exclusion, state the purport of each expected answer? A few decisions have said that this procedure must be followed before an effective ruling can be secured. Obviously it would often be a

§ 51

1. See § 52 infra.

wasteful performance which witnesses, counsel, and judge would desire to avoid. The better view is that it is not invariably essential, but that a sufficient offer of proof may be made without producing the witnesses, if it is sufficiently specific and if there is nothing in the record to indicate a want of good faith or inability to produce the proof.

§ 52. Objections

If the administration of the exclusionary rules of evidence is to be fair and workable the judge must be informed promptly of contentions that evidence should be rejected, and the reasons therefor. The initiative is placed on the party, not on the judge. The general approach, accordingly, is that a failure to object to an offer of evidence at the time the offer is made, assigning the grounds, is a waiver upon appeal of any ground of complaint against its admission. Federal Rule of Evidence 103(a)(1) is in Accord. It is important to note, however, that this usual approach is modified by the doctrine of plain error, which is discussed at the end of this section.

Time of Making: Motions to Strike. Consistently with the above approach, counsel is not allowed to gamble upon the possibility of a favorable answer, but must object to the admission of evidence as soon as the ground for objection becomes apparent. Usually, in the taking of testimony of a witness an objection is apparent as soon as the question is asked, since the question is likely to indicate that it calls for inadmissible evidence. Then counsel must, if opportunity affords, state her objection before the witness answers. But sometimes an objection before an answer to a question is not feasible. A forward witness may answer before counsel has a chance to object. A question which is not objectionable may be followed by an objectionable unresponsive answer. Or, after the evidence is received, a ground of objection to the evidence may be disclosed for the first time in the later course of the trial. In all these cases, an "after-objection" may be stated as soon as the ground appears. The proper technique for such an objection is to phrase a motion to strike out the objectionable evidence, and to request an instruction to the jury to disregard the evidence. Counsel should use the term "motion to strike," as just indicated, but it seems that any phraseology which directs the judge's attention to the grounds as soon as they appear, and asserts the objection, should be sufficient.

In the taking and subsequent use at the trial of depositions on oral or written questions, the time when objections must be made to the questions and answers is a matter variously regulated by rules and statutes in the different jurisdictions. Usually objections going to the "manner and form" of the questions or answers, such as objections to leading questions or disclaimers of unresponsive answers—sometimes opinions and secondary evidence are put in this class—, must be made at the time of taking the deposition and disposed of upon motion before the trial. Objections going to the "substance," such as relevancy and hearsay, may usually be urged for the first time when the deposition is offered in evidence at the trial.

If evidence was introduced at the first trial of a case, and an available objection was not made at the first trial, may the same evidence when tendered at a second trial of the same case be effectively objected to at the second trial for the first time? See § 259 infra.

Motions in Limine. A motion for an advance ruling on the admissibility of evidence is a relatively modern device for obtaining rulings on evidence before the evidence is sought to be introduced. The purpose of such motions may be to insulate the jury from exposure to harmful inadmissible evidence or to afford a basis for strategic decisions. Advance rulings upon objections may be sought prior to trial or at the trial in advance of the presentation of the evidence. The usual rule is that the judge has a wide discretion to make or refuse to make advance rulings, although it has been held that such advance rulings may not be had. Unless the decision of a motion first requires a factual background of the evidence as it develops at the trial, and as long as the matter is left primarily within the discretion of the trial judge, the use of a motion in limine to make advance objections for the purposes mentioned above should be encouraged. In view of some case disagreement, it has been recommended that objections that have been overruled at a hearing on a motion in limine should be repeated at the trial and where an objection has been sustained an offer of proof should be made at trial to make sure that appeal rights are preserved. If motions in limine are to be permitted as a means of advance objection, there are also instances when it would be desirable to permit such motions by the future proponent of evidence.

The instant type of motion should be distinguished from motions for suppression of evidence which may be required,[1] as well as from hearings on preliminary fact questions at the trial.[2]

General and Specific Objections. The precept constantly urged is that objections must be accompanied by a reasonably definite statement of the grounds, that is to say, that objections must reasonably indicate the appropriate rules of evidence as reasons for the objections made. These objections are labeled specific objections in contrast to so-called general objections which assign no such grounds for the objection. One purpose of the requirement is that the judge may understand the question raised and that the adversary may have an opportunity to remedy the defect, if possible. This precept does not *per se* ban the use of general objections (objections which state no grounds) at the trial, but rather it is one that is enforced to a certain extent on appeal. Thus the second purpose of the requirement is to make a proper record for the reviewing court in the event of an appeal. If the judge *overrules* a general objection, the objecting party may not ordinarily complain of the ruling on appeal by urging a valid ground not mentioned when the objection was made. However, there are three exceptional situations in which this rule on appeal may not be followed—in which the appeal court

will consider whether a valid ground of objection resulted in an erroneous overruling although it was, of course, not stated by the general objection made to the trial judge. The first is that, if the ground for exclusion should have been obvious to judge and opposing counsel without stating it, the want of specification of the ground is immaterial for purposes of complaining on appeal of the judge's action in overruling the general objection. This exception is clear good sense. Second, it has also been said that if the evidence is not admissible for any purpose, the general objection may be sufficient to secure on appeal a review of the judge's action in overruling the objection. This exception is arguably not effective and may not make sense for if the ground is not apparent, it seems there is still need for specification for appeal purposes. Third, it has been suggested that if the omitted ground was one that could not have been obviated, the general objection may serve to secure consideration on appeal of an unstated specific ground for objection. It is believed that this exception overlooks the consideration that though the objection to the particular evidence could not have been obviated, yet if the ground of objection had been stated the judge and adverse counsel might have appreciated its force, and the offer might have been excluded or withdrawn, and the adversary might have introduced other evidence to fill the gap. Thus this third exception is not authorized under Federal Rule Evid. 103(a)(1).

As a result of the above-mentioned rules, a trial judge's action in overruling a general objection will usually be supported on appeal. And if the trial judge *sustains* a general objection, the upper court is again charitable toward the trial judge's ruling. "When evidence is *excluded* upon a mere general objection, the ruling will be upheld, if any ground in fact existed for the exclusion. It will be assumed, in the absence of any request by the opposing party or the court to make the objection definite, that it was understood, and that

1. See § 183 infra.

the ruling was placed upon the right ground." [3]

Examples of general objections are "I object;" or objections on the ground that the evidence is "inadmissible," "illegal," "incompetent," or is not proper testimony for the jury; or an objection "on all the grounds ever known or heard of". One of the most overworked forms is an objection on the ground that the evidence is "incompetent, irrelevant and immaterial." Its rhythm and alliteration have seduced some lawyers to employ it as a routine and meaningless ritual, a "vain repetition." Thus, courts frequently treat this form as equivalent merely to the general objection, "I object." The word "incompetent" as applied to evidence means no more than inadmissible, and thus cannot be said to state a ground of objection. However, the terms, "irrelevant and immaterial," do state, though general in terms, a distinct and substantial ground for exclusion. A requirement that the objector state specifically wherein the evidence, as applied to the particular issues, is irrelevant or immaterial, as some courts seem to demand, seems in many situations unduly burdensome as involving the difficulties usually associated with proving a negative. It would be far more practical to consider the irrelevancy objection in this general form as the equivalent of a specific objection with the qualification that if the judge has any doubt of relevancy, she may call upon the proponent to explain the purpose of the proof.

While an objection of irrelevancy in general form has on occasion been held sufficient to raise a claim of prejudice in the sense of arousing personal animus against the party, it would seem in principle that such an objection should not carry with it the matters listed in Rule 403, under the Federal Rules. These matters can readily be raised specifically and do not entail the burden of establishing a negative mentioned above.

Objections should be specific not only with respect to the statement of grounds, but also with respect to a particular part of an offer, in view of another rule as to saving error for

appeal. If evidence sought to be introduced consists of several statements or items tendered as a unit, e.g., a deposition, a letter, a conversation, a transcript of testimony or the like, and if the objection is to the whole of the evidence when parts are subject to the objection made and parts are not, the judge will not be put in error for overruling the objection. It is not the judge's duty to sever the bad parts if some are good. Obviously such a rule should not be administered rigidly by the appellate courts but with due concession, if need be, to the realities of the particular trial situation.

Even more clearly, if evidence offered is properly admissible on a particular issue, but not upon some other issue, or is admissible against one party but not against another, an objector who asks that this evidence be excluded altogether, though she assigns grounds, cannot complain on appeal if her objection is overruled. She should have asked that the admission of the evidence be limited to the particular purpose or party.

On appeal, the *overruling* of an untenable specific objection will not be overturned because there was a tenable ground for exclusion which was not urged in the trial court.

If an untenable specific objection is *sustained*, there is authority that the appellate court will uphold the ruling if there is any other ground for doing so, even though not urged below. There is no point in ordering a retrial if the evidence would then be excluded on the proper ground. However, some qualifications must be made. If the correct objection, had it been made, could have been obviated, or admissible evidence could have been substituted, then a retrial seems appropriate. If a ruling upon the proper objection at the second trial would involve the judge's discretion, a new trial would be appropriate unless the judge on remand determines that her discretion would be exercised in favor of exclusion. A similar result should follow where findings of fact are required as a preliminary to determining admissibility.

3. Tooley v. Bacon, 70 N.Y. 34, 37 (1877).

Repetition of Objections. A offers testimony by one witness which his adversary, B, thinks is inadmissible. B objects, and the objection is *sustained.* In such event, if A offers similar testimony by the same or another witness, B must of course repeat her objection if she is to complain of the later evidence. Suppose, however, the first objection is *overruled.* Must B then repeat her objection when other like evidence similarly objectionable is offered? A few decisions intimate that she must, a practice which places B in the invidious semblance of a contentious obstructor, and conduces to waste of time and fraying of patience. Most courts, however, hold that B is entitled to assume that the judge will continue to make the same ruling and she need not repeat the objection. It seems that the consequence of this view should be, that the first objection remains good and is not waived, and that in addition, the reach of this objection extends to all similar evidence subject to the same objection. It seems that in any jurisdiction where the practice in this respect is at all doubtful, it is a wise precaution for objecting counsel to ask the judge to have the record show that it is understood that the objection goes to all other like evidence, and when later evidence is offered, to have it noted that the earlier objection applies.

The Exception. Closely associated with the objection but distinct from it in the classic common law practice was the exception. The Federal rules and the practice in many states have dispensed with exceptions, and have provided that for all purposes formerly served thereby, "it is sufficient that a party, at the time the ruling or order of the court is made or sought, makes known to the court the action which the party desires the court to take or his objection * * * and the party's grounds therefor."[4] Nevertheless, for reasons such as an attempt to impress a jury, some attorneys persist in making statements that they except to a ruling in jury cases in jurisdictions in which exceptions are unnecessary.

The Tactics of Objecting. Jurors want to know the facts and they may well look upon objections as attempts to hide the facts, and upon successful objections as the actual suppression of facts. If this description of the jury's attitude is sound, certain consequences as to desirable tactics seem to follow.

No objections should be made unless there is reason to believe that the making of the objection will do more good than harm. If an objection has little chance of being sustained, at the trial or on appeal, it should usually not be made. It has also been pointed out that objections to leading questions, or to opinion evidence, frequently result in strengthening the examiner's case by requiring her to elicit the testimony in more concrete and convincing form. In general, objections should be few and should be directed only to evidence which if admitted will be substantially harmful, and then only if the objector believes she can obtain a favorable ruling at the trial or upon appeal.

Finally, since objections are usually made in the jury's presence, the manner of the objector and the terms of the objection are important. An objection should be stated so that it does not appear to rest merely upon some technical rule. Thus, an objection to a copy under the original writing-best evidence rule should not be stated solely in terms of "secondary evidence" but should also be grounded upon the safer reliability of the original writing. The objection of "hearsay," for example, should be expanded by an explanation of the need, in justice and fairness, for producing the original informant so that the jury may see him, and his sources of knowledge may be explored.

Withdrawal of Evidence. The Federal and revised Uniform Rules of Evidence (1974) do not in terms deal with the subject of withdrawal of evidence. A reasonable interpretation of Rule 611(a), however, would include permitting withdrawal as an aspect of the court's discretionary control over the presentation of evidence. Such discretion could be exercised in accordance with the following

---

4. Fed.R.Civ.P. 46; Fed.R.Crim.P. 51.

acceptable case law principles. If a party has introduced evidence which is not objected to and which turns out to be favorable to the adversary, it has sometimes been intimated that the offering party may withdraw the evidence as of right. The accepted rule seems to be, however, that such a withdrawal is not of right. Rather, the adversary is entitled to have the benefit of the testimony as it bears in her favor, unless the special situation makes it fair for the judge in her discretion to permit the withdrawal. On the other hand, if the evidence is admitted over the adversary's objection, and the proponent later decides to yield to the objection, and asks to withdraw the evidence, the court may revoke its ruling and permit the withdrawal.

Plain Error Rule. Many of the criteria for the so-called "harmless error" rule and the "plain error" rule are similar, but the two concepts so labeled should be distinguished. Federal and Revised Uniform Rule of Evidence (1974) 103 defines "harmless error" generally by its opening statement, "Error may not be predicated upon a ruling which admits or excludes evidence unless a substantial right of a party is affected * * *." Plain error is defined in Rule 103(d) as follows, "Nothing in this rule precludes taking notice of plain errors affecting substantial rights although they were not brought to the attention of the court." Thus harmless error denotes error in rulings which is not cause for reversal; plain error denotes error sufficiently serious to justify considering it on appeal despite a failure to observe the usual procedural requirements for saving error for review. This subsection is confined to plain error. It has been observed that for error not to be harmless the courts speak as though the error must be prejudicial to the appellant, but for plain error the error must have very prejudicial effects, yet little difference can be found in the ways these concepts are applied in actual cases.

For many reasons, including the hesitation of appellate courts to interfere with lower court trial responsibilities,[5] lack of details on appeal that relate to the question of whether there was very prejudicial error, and the possible questionable effect of claimed plain error on trials and their results, there appears to be a tendency to avoid a holding that plain error occurred even in criminal cases. A holding of plain error is more likely to be the cause for reversal in errors involving the constitutional rights of criminal defendants. Reversals on the basis of plain error are much less common in civil cases than in criminal cases, perhaps in part because liberty and life are not involved as a motive to apply the doctrine and thus interfere with the usual adversary trial system.

The application of the doctrine depends upon a case to case analysis.

§ 53. Preliminary Questions of Fact Arising on Objections

The great body of the law of evidence consists of rules that operate to exclude relevant evidence. Examples are the hearsay rule, the rule preferring original writings, and the various rules of privilege for confidential communications. These exclusionary rules are all "technical" in the sense that they have been developed by a special professional group, namely judges and lawyers, and in the further sense that for long-term ends they sometimes obstruct the ascertainment of truth in the particular case. Many if not most of these technical exclusionary rules, and the exceptions thereto, are in terms conditioned upon the existence of certain facts. Thus a copy of a writing will not be received unless the original is lost, destroyed, or otherwise unavailable.[1] Suppose a copy is offered and there is conflicting evidence as to whether the original is destroyed or intact. The judge of course ascertains and announces the rule of evidence law setting up the criterion of admission or exclusion, but who is to decide whether the original is lost, destroyed or unavailable—the preliminary question of fact upon

---

5. See § 55 infra.

1. See § 230 infra.

§ 53

which hinges the *application* of the rule of evidence law?

Issues of fact are usually left to the jury, but there are strong reasons here for not doing so. If the special question of fact were submitted to the jury when objection was made, cumbersome and awkward problems about unanimity would be raised. If the judge admitted the evidence (the copy as above) to the jury and directed them to disregard it unless they found that the disputed fact existed, the aim of the exclusionary rule would likely be frustrated, for two reasons. First, the jury would often not be able to erase the evidence from their minds, if they found that the conditioning fact did not exist. They could not if they would. Second, the average jury would not be interested in performing this intellectual gymnastic of "disregarding" the evidence. They are intent mainly on reaching their verdict in a case in accord with what they believe to be true, rather than in enforcing the long-term policies of evidence law.

Accordingly, under the traditional view and the generally accepted principle the trial judge decides with finality those preliminary questions of fact upon which depends the admissibility of an item of evidence that is objected to under an exclusionary rule of evidence such as the hearsay rule.[2] This principle is incorporated in Federal and Revised Uniform Rule of Evidence (1974) 104(a). The same practice extends to the determination of preliminary facts conditioning the application of the rules as to competency and privileges of witnesses. On all these preliminary questions the judge, on request, will hold a hearing in which each side may produce evidence.

The foregoing discussion involves situations where the admissibility of evidence is attacked, and it is sought to be excluded under a "technical" exclusionary rule. Those situations are to be distinguished from another type of situation, namely those in which the relevancy, i.e. probative value, of a fact offered in evidence depends on the existence of another, and preliminary, fact. As the Advis-

ory Committee's Note to Federal Rule of Evidence 104(b) observes:

> Thus when a spoken statement is relied upon to prove notice to X, it is without probative value unless X heard it. Or if a letter purporting to be from Y is relied upon to establish an admission by him, it has no probative value unless Y wrote or authorized it. Relevance in this sense has been labelled "conditional relevancy." Morgan, Basic Problems of Evidence 45–56 (1962).

These factual questions of conditional relevancy are to be distinguished from questions whether particular evidence is relevant as a matter of law, such as whether evidence that accused purchased on the day before a murder a weapon of the type used in the killing is relevant. Questions of the latter nature are, of course, for the judge, as are matters of law generally.

The factual questions of conditional relevancy are well within the competency of juries and involve the kind of questions with which we are accustomed to see juries deal. Did A say such-and-such? Did B hear him? Did C sign the letter offered in evidence? And so on. Jury trials would be curtailed greatly if judges gave the final decisions on these questions. The judge is not, however, eliminated from the picture but divides his responsibility with the jury in the following manner. The judge requires the proponent to bring forward evidence from which the jury could find the existence of the preliminary fact. The opposing party may then bring in disputing evidence. If on all the evidence the judge determines that the jury could not find the existence of the preliminary fact, he excludes the evidence. Otherwise, the question is for the jury.

The procedure described above was and is followed at common law and is embodied in Federal and Revised Uniform Rule of Evidence (1974) 104(b), which reads:

> When the relevancy of evidence depends on the fulfillment of a condition of fact, the court shall admit it upon, or subject to, the intro-

---

2. See § 162 infra, for rules concerning the admission of confessions of a criminal defendant.

duction of evidence sufficient to support a finding of the fulfillment of the condition.

Some situations have not readily lent themselves to treatment as a member of either of the two groupings discussed above and accordingly require further discussion.

First, confessions are subject to their own special rules, which are treated elsewhere.[3]

Second, in cases involving offers of dying declarations some courts have given the jury a share in deciding the preliminary question whether declarant had the settled, hopeless expectation of death required for that exception to the hearsay rule.[4] This pattern is not followed by Federal and Revised Uniform Rule of Evidence (1974) 104.

Third, in a troublesome group of cases the preliminary fact question coincides with one of the ultimate disputed fact-issues that the jury will normally decide. Several examples may be given. (1) In a bigamy prosecution where the first marriage is disputed, the second wife is offered as a state's witness, and defendant objects under a statute disqualifying the wife to testify against her husband. (2) Plaintiff sues on a lost writing, and defendant contends that it was not lost because it never existed. (3) In a prosecution for conspiracy, the state offers an alleged declaration by a co-conspirator made during the course of and in furtherance of the conspiracy. Defendants deny that the conspiracy ever existed. The results that have been reached lack much in the way of consistency.

In Example (1) the preliminary question involves the competency of the witness, a question for the judge at common law or under Rule 104(a) if it were not for the overlap with the jury issue whether she was the wife. To allow the judge to decide her competency seems not to embarrass the jury trial in any way; his decision need not be communicated to the jury; and additional useful evidence may be made available. Accordingly the cases have tended to leave the decision to the judge. In Example (2) the preliminary

question whether a writing was lost is for the judge at common law or under Rule 104(a), but evidently it cannot have been lost if it never existed. Aside from the question of loss, the execution of the document would be a jury question, with the preliminary question of authentication for admissibility purposes one for the jury at common law or under Rule 104(b). The basic issue in the case quite clearly is whether the original writing ever existed; the question whether it has been lost is subsidiary. Sound judgment appears to call for decision of the basic question by the jury, rather than having it subsumed into the judge's question. This is the result, both by decision and under Rule 1008, for if the judge decided that the writing never existed and excludes the secondary evidence, the case is ended without ever going to the jury on the central issue. In Example (3), at common law the cases were divided as to whether the judge should make the preliminary determination whether a conspiracy existed and defendant and declarant were members of it, or the judge should admit the evidence upon a prima facie showing, instructing the jury to disregard it if they found these matters not proved. Supporting the first position is the view that, by rather casual analysis, the judge is dealing with the applicability of a supposed hearsay exception for declarations by a co-conspirator, with the preliminary question to be decided by the judge. This reasoning leads to application of Rule 104(a) under the Federal and Revised Uniform Rules. Under one analysis of the definition of hearsay, however, virtually all declarations by co-conspirators will be found to qualify as "verbal acts,"[5] and hence not hearsay in the first place. This reasoning would lead to the jury's making the preliminary determination, after screening by the judge, as a question of conditional relevancy, whether at common law or under Rule 104(b). Whatever the merits of these positions, the fact is that the United States Su-

---

3. Infra § 162.

4. The nature of the requirement is discussed in § 310 infra.

5. Infra § 259.

preme Court in Bourjaily v. United States,[6] declared that under the Federal Rules of Evidence determining the admissibility of a statement of a coconspirator is solely a matter for the court, Rule 104(a), and that the court in making its determination must apply the more probably true than not true (preponderance) standard of proof. This result is probably the result of two considerations: the difficulty, and to some extent unreality, of submitting the preliminary question to the jury, and the understandable wish to extend judicial control over the use of conspiracy charges by prosecutors.

§ 54. Availability as Proof of Evidence Admitted Without Objection

As indicated in section 52, a failure to make a sufficient objection to evidence which is incompetent waives any ground of complaint as to the admission of the evidence. But it has another effect, equally important. If the evidence is received without objection, it becomes part of the evidence in the case, and is usable as proof to the extent of the rational persuasive power it may have. The fact that it was inadmissible does not prevent its use as proof so far as it has probative value. The incompetent evidence, unobjected to, may be relied on in argument, and alone or in part may support a verdict or finding. This principle is almost universally accepted. The Federal and Revised Uniform Rules of Evidence are silent on this subject but raise no doubt as to the continued applicability of the rules in this section. The principle applies to any ground of incompetency under the exclusionary rules. It is most often invoked in respect to hearsay, but it has been applied to evidence vulnerable as secondary evidence of writings, opinions, evidence elicited from incompetent witnesses or subject to a privilege, or subject to objection because of the want of authentication of a writing, of the lack-of-knowledge qualification of a witness, or of the expertness qualification. Relevancy and probative worth, however, stand on a different footing.

6. 483 U.S. 171 (1987).

If the evidence has no probative force, or insufficient probative value to sustain the proposition for which it is offered, the want of objection adds nothing to its worth and it will not support a finding. It is still irrelevant or insufficient. However, the failure to object to evidence related to the controversy but not covered by the pleadings, may amount to the informal framing of new issues. When this is held to have been the result, the failure to object on the ground that the evidence is not relevant to any issue raised by the pleadings is waived, and the evidence will support the proponent's side of the new informal issue.

§ 55. Waiver of Objection

A failure to assert an objection promptly and specifically is a waiver.[1] What other conduct is a waiver?

Demand for inspection of a writing. One party, D, gives notice to his opponent, O, to produce a document, and O does produce it at the trial. Thereupon in open court D asks to inspect it, and is allowed to do so. The document if offered by O would be inadmissible, except for the notice, production, and inspection. Do these facts preclude D from objecting when the document is offered by O? England, Massachusetts, and a few other states have said yes, D is precluded from objecting. This result was based at first upon the notion that it would be unconscionable to permit the demanding party to examine the private papers of the producing party without being subjected to some corresponding risk on his own part. A later case, however, has justified the result on the ground that the party who is called on in open court before a jury to produce a writing for inspection may be suspected of evasion or concealment unless he is given the privilege of introducing the writing. Cases from other states recognize that the older policy against compelled disclosure to his adversary of relevant writings in possession of a party is now outmoded and that the prevailing policy is just the opposite, namely,

1. See § 52 supra.

that of exerting pressure for full disclosure except for privileged matter. Accordingly, these states reject the rule, and permit him to assert any pertinent objection if the producing party offers the writing. This rule is consistent with Federal and Revised Uniform Rule of Evidence (1974) 103(a)(1). It should be emphasized that the older policy is inconsistent with the pretrial discovery policy of the federal and similar civil discovery rules, which have been adopted widely in the states. The matter today is in fact largely not totally historical.

Failure to object to earlier like evidence. A party has introduced evidence of particular facts without objection. Later he offers additional evidence, perhaps by other witnesses or writings, of the same facts or a part thereof. May the adversary now object, or has he waived his right by his earlier quiescence? It is often summarily stated in the opinions that he is precluded from objecting. But in opinions where the question is carefully discussed it is usually concluded that the mere failure to object to other like evidence is not a waiver of objection to the new inadmissible evidence. This concept should be applied under the Federal and Revised Uniform Rules of Evidence. Of course, an overruling of this new objection will frequently not be prejudicial, but that is a different question. The practice of the best advocates of withholding objection unless it is clear that the evidence would be damaging is in the interest of dispatch of business and would be encouraged by the nonwaiver rule. On the other hand, when the evidence of the fact, admitted without objection, is extensive, and the evidence though inadmissible has some probative value, the trial judge should be conceded a discretion to find that the objector's conduct has amounted to a waiver. Again, this condition upon the previously stated rule should be followed under the Federal and Revised Uniform Rules of Evidence.

The Offering of Like Evidence by the Objector. If it happens that a party who has objected to evidence of a certain fact himself produces evidence from his own witness of the

same fact, he has waived his objection. This result should be reached under the Federal and Revised Uniform Rules of Evidence. However, when his objection is made and overruled he is required and entitled to treat this ruling as the "law of the trial" and to explain or rebut, if he can, the evidence which has come in over his protest. Consequently, it will not be a waiver if he cross-examines the adversary's witness about the matter, even though the cross-examination entails a repetition of the fact, or if he meets the testimony with other evidence which under the theory of the objection would be inadmissible. The Federal and Revised Uniform Rules of Evidence should not change the above results. The closely related question of whether he may so meet the testimony by extrinsic evidence at all is considered in Section 57. Generally, he may do so.

Exclusion by Judge in Absence of Objection. A party's failure to object usually waives the objection and precludes the party from complaining if the evidence is let in.[2] But the failure by the party does not of itself preclude the trial judge from excluding the evidence on his own motion if the witness is disqualified for want of capacity or the evidence is incompetent, and he considers that the interests of justice require the exclusion of the testimony. The Federal and Revised Uniform Rules of Evidence in Rule 611(a) and elsewhere grant the judge sufficiently broad powers to follow the principles outlined in this paragraph. There is much evidence, however, such as reliable affidavits or copies of writings, which though inadmissible under the technical exclusionary rules, may be valuable in the particular situation and which the trial judge in the absence of objection would not be justified in excluding. It is only when the evidence is irrelevant, unreliable, misleading, or prejudicial, as well as inadmissible, that the judge should exercise his discretionary power to intervene. Privileged evidence, such as confidential communications between husband and wife, should be treated differently. The privileges protect the outside interests of the holders, not the interest of the parties in securing

2. See § 52 supra.

justice in the present litigation. Accordingly, in case privileged matter is called for, and the holder is present, the judge may if necessary explain the privilege to the holder, but will not assert it of his own motion; but if the holder is absent the judge, in some jurisdictions, has a discretionary power to assert it in his behalf.

§ 56. The Effect of the Introduction of Part of a Writing or Conversation

Two important considerations come into play when a party offers in evidence a portion only of a writing, or of an oral statement or conversation. The first is the danger of admitting the portion only, thereby wresting a part of such a body of expressions out of its context. "The fool hath said in his heart, there is no God," [1] where the last phrase only is quoted, is an example of the possibilities of distortion. This danger, moreover, is not completely averted by a later, separate, supplying of the relevant omitted parts. The distorted impression may sometimes linger, and work its influence at the subconscious level. Second is the opposing danger of requiring that the whole be offered, thereby wasting time and attention by cumbering the trial and the record, in the name of completeness, with passages and statements which have no bearing on the present controversy.

In the light of these alternatives, is a party who seeks to give in evidence part of a writing or statement required to offer it in entirety, or at least all of it that is relevant to the facts sought to be proved? The prevailing practice seems to permit the proponent to prove only such part as he desires. However, to guard against the danger of an ineradicable false first impression, the adversary should and, within the court's discretion, will be permitted to require the proponent to prove so much as pertains to the fact sought to be proved, that is, all that explains or is useful in interpreting the part proved. Federal and Revised Uniform Rule of Evidence (1974) 106 specifies

this rule for writings or recorded statements. It is sometimes stated that the additional writing or recorded statement may be admitted only if otherwise admissible. However, since admissibility includes principles governing the operation of the concept of waiver of objection through "door opening", otherwise inadmissible evidence often does in fact become admissible. Ultimately, whether otherwise inadmissible evidence offered to explain, modify, qualify, or otherwise shed light on the part already received is admitted should depend upon whether its probative value in such regard is substantially outweighed by dangers of unfair prejudice, confusion of the issues, misleading the jury, or waste of time.

As to the adversary's other alternative the cases are much clearer and more consistent. She may wait until her own next stage of presenting proof, and then merely by reason of the fact that the first party has introduced a part, she has the right to introduce the remainder of the writing, recording, statement, correspondence, former testimony, or conversation so far as it relates to the same subject matter and hence tends to explain and shed light on the meaning of the part already received. This right is subject to the qualification set forth above where the remainder is inadmissible.

§ 57. Fighting Fire With Fire: Inadmissible Evidence as Opening the Door

One party offers evidence which is inadmissible. Because the adversary fails to object, or because he has no opportunity to do so, or because the judge erroneously overrules an objection, the inadmissible evidence comes in. Is the adversary entitled to answer this evidence, by testimony in denial or explanation of the facts so proved? It has been stated that in some jurisdictions the adversary is not entitled to so meet the evidence, in others he may do so, and finally in some he may do so if he would be prejudiced by rejection of efforts to

§ 56

1. The oft-repeated classic illustration, see 7 Wigmore, Evidence § 2094 (Chadbourn rev. 1978).

meet the evidence; but that in reaching these results many of the decisions seem merely to affirm the action of the trial court. However, most of the courts seem to say generally that "one who induces a trial court to let down the bars to a field of inquiry that is not competent or relevant to the issues cannot complain if his adversary is also allowed to avail himself of the opening." Federal cases have on occasion applied this general notion in various situations.

Judicial pronouncements do not settle the question as to how the trial judge should deal with the problem. Because of the many variable factors affecting the solution in a particular case, the diverse situations do not lend themselves easily to generalizations. The following conclusions, having some support in the decisions, are submitted as reasonable:

(1) If the inadmissible evidence sought to be answered is irrelevant and not prejudice-arousing, the judge, to save time and to avoid distraction of attention from the issues, should refuse to hear answering evidence; but if he does hear it, under the prevailing view, the party opening the door has no standing to complain.

(2) If the evidence, though inadmissible, is relevant to the issues and hence presumably damaging to the adversary's case, or though irrelevant is prejudice-arousing to a material degree, and if the adversary has seasonably objected or moved to strike, then the adversary should be entitled to give answering evidence as of right. By objecting he has done his best to save the court from mistake, but his remedy by assigning error to the ruling is not an adequate one. He needs a fair opportunity to win his case at the trial by refuting the damaging evidence. This situation should be distinguished from the question, considered in section 55, whether the prior objection is waived if the answering evidence is permitted.

(3) If again the first inadmissible evidence is relevant, or though irrelevant is prejudice-arousing, but the adversary has failed to object or to move to strike out, where such an objection might apparently have avoided the harm, then the allowance of answering evidence should rest in the judge's discretion. He should weigh the probable influence of the first evidence, the time and distraction incident to answering it, and the possibility and effectiveness of an instruction to the jury to disregard it. However, here various courts have indicated that introduction of the answering evidence is a matter of right.

(4) In any event, if the inadmissible evidence, or even the inquiry eliciting it, is so prejudice-arousing that an objection or motion to strike cannot have erased the harm, then it seems that the adversary should be entitled to answer it as of right.

It will be noted that the question discussed in this section as to rebutting inadmissible evidence, is a different one from whether a party's introduction of evidence inadmissible under some exclusionary rule (such as hearsay or secondary evidence of writings) gives license to the adversary to introduce other evidence which is inadmissible under the same exclusionary rule but which bears on some different issue or is not relevant to the original inadmissible evidence. The doctrine of "opening the door" has not been extended to that extent.

§ 58. Admissibility of Evidence Dependent on Proof of Other Facts: "Connecting Up"

Very often the relevancy or admissibility of evidence of a particular fact hinges upon the proof of other facts. Thus, proof that a swaying automobile passed a given spot at a certain time, or that a conversation was had by the witness at a given time and place with an unidentified stranger, will become relevant and significant only when the automobile is identified as the defendant's, or the stranger is shown to be the deceased for whose death the plaintiff is suing. So evidence of acts and declarations may not become material or admissible until shown to be those of an agent of the other party, and a copy of a writing may not become competent evidence until the original is proven to be lost or destroyed. Some of these missing facts may be thought of, in terms of the logic of pleading or argument, as preliminary to the fact offered, some as co-ordinate with it. It matters not. In either event, often only one fact can be proven at a time or by a given witness, and the order of convenience in calling witnesses or of clear presentation may not in a particular case be the order of logical statement.

Who decides the order of facts? In the first instance, the offering counsel does so by making the offer. The court in its general discretionary supervision of the order of proof, may, to avoid a danger of prejudice or confusion, require that the missing fact be proved first. But it seldom does, and the everyday method of handling the situation when the adversary objects to the relevancy or the competency of the offered fact is to permit it to come in conditionally, upon the assurance, express or implied, of the offering counsel that she will "connect up" the tendered evidence by proving, in the later progress of his case, the missing facts. Federal and Revised Uniform Rules of Evidence 104(b) and 611(a) give the court this same authority.

In a long trial, however, where the witnesses are many and the facts complex, it is easy for the offering counsel to forget the need for making the required "connecting" proof, and for the judge and the adversary to fail to observe this gap in the evidence. Who invokes the condition subsequent, upon such a breach? The burden is placed upon the objecting party to renew the objection and invoke the condition. By the majority view this is to be done by a motion to strike out the evidence conditionally received, when the failure of condition becomes apparent. It seems that it does become apparent when the offering party completes the particular stage of the case in which the evidence was offered, and that when she "rests" without making the missing proof, the adversary should then move to strike, failing which, she cannot later claim as of right to invoke the condition. Some weight should be given, however, to the duty assumed by the offering party in promising to furnish the connecting proof, and recognition of this can best be given by according the trial judge a discretion to allow the adver-

sary to invoke the condition, if the continuing availability of the missing proof makes it fair to do so, at any time before the case is submitted to the jury or before final judgment in a judge-tried case. Though some courts have considered the difference in form material, it seems that a motion to strike, a motion to withdraw the fact from the jury, or a request that the jury be instructed to disregard the evidence should each be regarded as a sufficient invocation of the condition. The discussion in this paragraph is compatible with Federal and Revised Uniform Rules of Evidence 104(b) and 611(a).

To be distinguished from the practice described above of conditional admission pending further proof, is the practice of admitting evidence provisionally where objection is made, subject to a later ruling on the objection in the light of further consideration when the case has been more amply developed. Here again the objecting counsel, to preserve the objection, must renew the objection before the case is concluded. The practice occasionally seems appropriate enough in a judge-tried case but where the trial is with a jury there is danger that letting the evidence in, even provisionally, may make an impression that a later ruling of exclusion may not erase—a danger that here seems unnecessary to incur. Accordingly this practice, though doubtless in the realm of discretion, has been criticised. It should be avoided.

§ 59. Evidence Admissible for One Purpose, Inadmissible for Another: "Limited Admissibility"

An item of evidence may be logically relevant in several aspects, as leading to distinct inferences or as bearing upon different issues. For one of these purposes it may be admissible but for another inadmissible. In this frequently arising situation, subject to the limitations outlined below, the normal practice in case law and under the Federal and Revised Uniform Rule of Evidence (1974) 105 is to admit the evidence. The interest of the adversary is to be protected, not by an objection to its admission, but by a request at the time of the offer for an instruction that the jury is to consider the evidence only for the allowable purpose. Such an instruction may not always be effective, but admission of the evidence with the limiting instruction is normally the best available reconciliation of the respective interests. It seems, however, that in situations, where the danger of the jury's misuse of the evidence for the inadmissible purpose is great, and its value for the legitimate purpose is slight or the point for which it is admissible can readily be proved by other evidence, the judge's power to exclude the evidence altogether is clear in case law and under the Federal and Revised Uniform Rule of Evidence 403.

Similarly, subject to the restrictions stated in the above and following paragraphs, evidence may frequently be admissible as against one party, but not as against another, in which event the practice is to admit the evidence, with an instruction, if requested, that the jury are to consider it only as to the party against whom it is admissible.

However, limiting instructions are not sufficient to insure against misuse by the jury of the confessions or admissions of a codefendant who does not take the stand when the confessions or admissions implicate the defendant. A violation of the Sixth Amendment right to confront witnesses results.[1] This rule is applicable in state courts. However if the case against the defendant was so overwhelming, apart from a confession or an admission of a codefendant, that its admission into evidence was harmless beyond a reasonable doubt, the Supreme Court will not require reversal. It can not be concluded generally that if one purpose of two or more uses of evidence against a criminal defendant violates constitutional rights of the defendant, the evidence is completely inadmissible.

§ 60. Admission and Exclusion of Evidence in Trials Without a Jury

The rules of evidence at common law and pursuant to the Federal and Revised Uniform Rules of Evidence (1974) apply on their face in trials without a jury. Nevertheless as Thayer states, our law of evidence is to a great extent a "product of the jury system * * * where ordinary untrained citizens are acting as judges of fact." In addition, judges possess professional experience in valuing evidence greatly lessening the need for exclusionary rules. The feeling of the inexpediency of these restrictions as applied to judges has caused courts to say that the same strictness will not be observed in applying the rules of evidence in judge only trials as in trials before a jury, and it is difficult to avoid reaching the same result under the Federal and Revised Uniform Rule of Evidence (1974).

The most important influence in encouraging trial judges to take this attitude toward evidence rules in nonjury cases is a rule obtaining in most appellate courts. These courts have said that in reviewing a case tried without a jury the admission of inadmissible evidence over objection will not ordinarily be a ground of reversal if there was admissible evidence received sufficient to support the findings. The judge will be presumed to have disregarded the inadmissible and relied on the admissible evidence. If the judge errs, however, in the opposite direction, by excluding evidence which ought to have been received, the judge's ruling will of course be subject to reversal if it is substantially harmful to the losing party. On the other hand, some appellate courts decisions decline to apply the presumption when the evidence was objected to and the objection overruled. Moreover the presumption may everywhere be rebutted by a showing to the contrary. Possible methods of making the requisite showing include statements from the bench, and specific reliance upon improperly admitted evidence contained in specific findings of fact either prepared separately or as part of an opinion or memorandum of decision.

In practice, considerations of waste of time, predictability and consistency fostering lawyer preparation and the orderly conduct of

§ 59

1. See § 279 infra.

the trial lead most trial judges to apply the rules of evidence in a nonjury trial to exclude evidence that "is *clearly* inadmissible, privileged, or too time consuming in order to guard against reversal." Where the admissibility of evidence is, however, debatable, the contrasting attitudes of the appellate courts toward errors in receiving and those excluding evidence seem to support the wisdom of the practice adopted by many experienced trial judges in nonjury cases of provisionally admitting all debatably admissible evidence if objected to with the announcement that all questions of admissibility will be reserved until the evidence is all in. In considering the objections if renewed by motion to strike at the end of the case, the judge will lean toward admission rather than exclusion and at the end will seek to find clearly admissible testimony on which to base his findings of fact. This practice will lessen the time spent in arguing objections and will ensure that appellate courts will have in the record the evidence that was rejected as well as that which was received. This will often help to make an end of the case.

*

Title 4

COMPETENCY

Chapter 7

THE COMPETENCY OF WITNESSES

Table of Sections

§ 61. In General

The common law rules of incompetency have been undergoing a process of piecemeal revision by statutes for over a century, so that today most of the former grounds for excluding a witness altogether have been converted into mere grounds of impeaching his credibility.

Since the disqualification of witnesses for incompetency is thus dwindling in importance, and since the statutory modifications and the modifications in states which have adopted the Federal Rules of Evidence or the Revised Uniform Rules of Evidence, vary from state to state, a development here of the law in the different jurisdictions is not justified. The common law grounds of incompetency and the general lines of statutory and rule change are summarized in the following sections.

§ 62. Mental Incapacity and Immaturity: Oath or Affirmation

There is no rule which excludes an insane person as such, or a child of any specified age, from testifying, but in each case the traditional test is whether the witness has intelligence enough to make it worthwhile to hear him at all and whether he feels a duty to tell the truth. Is his capacity to perceive, record, recollect, and narrate, such that he can probably bring added knowledge of the facts? The major reason for disqualification of the persons mentioned in this section to take the stand is the judges' distrust of a jury's ability to assay the words of a small child or of a deranged person. Conceding the jury's deficiencies, the remedy of excluding such a witness, who may be the only person available who knows the facts, seems inept and primitive. Though the tribunal is unskilled, and the testimony difficult to weigh, it is still better to let the evidence come in for what it is worth, with cautionary instructions.

Revised Uniform Rule of Evidence 601 and the first sentence of Federal Rule of Evidence 601 reflect the above and additional reasoning by providing every person is competent to be a witness unless "otherwise provided" in the rules. The only general competency requirements "otherwise provided" by the Federal and Revised Uniform Rules of Evidence (1974) are contained in Rule 603 which requires that every witness declare that he will testify truthfully by oath or affirmation and Rule 602 which requires that the witness possess personal knowledge. Together these rules require that (1) the witness have the capacity to accurately perceive, record and recollect impressions of fact (physical and mental capacity), (2) the witness in fact did perceive, record and can recollect impressions having any tendency to establish a fact of consequence in the litigation (personal knowledge), (3) the witness declare that he will tell the truth, understand the duty to tell the truth (oath or affirmation), as well as understand the difference between the truth and a lie or fantasy, and (4) the witness possess the capacity to comprehend questions and express himself understandably, where necessary with aid of an interpreter, Rule 604 (narration). Before a witness will be permitted to testify, evidence must be introduced sufficient to support a finding of personal knowledge, i.e., that the witness had the capacity to and actually did observe, receive, record, and can now recollect and narrate impressions obtained through any of his senses having any tendency to establish a fact of consequence, and the witness must declare by oath or affirmation that he will testify truthfully. No other personal qualifications of a witness are required. No mental qualification is specified. The Advisory Committee's Note reasons that standards of mental capacity have proved elusive, few

witnesses were actually disqualified, and moreover that a witness wholly without mental capacity is difficult to imagine. However, while mental incapacity is not a specified ground of incompetency, testimony of a witness whose mental capacity has been seriously questioned may still be excluded on the grounds that no reasonable juror could possibly believe that the witness in fact possesses personal knowledge, or understands the difference between the truth and a lie or fantasy and the duty to tell the truth.

Competency of a witness to testify thus requires a minimum ability to observe, record, recollect and recount as well as an understanding of the duty to tell the truth. Where the capacity of a witness has been brought into question, the ultimate question is whether a reasonable juror must believe that the witness is so bereft of his powers of perception, recordation, recollection, and narration as to be so untrustworthy as a witness as to make his testimony lack relevancy. Such a test of competency has been characterized as requiring minimum credibility. The trend is to resolve doubts as to minimum credibility of the witness in favor of permitting the jury to hear the testimony and judge the credibility of the witness for itself. Thus mental capacity generally functions as an effect on the weight to be given to testimony rather than precluding admissibility. Nevertheless testimony of a witness passing the text of minimum credibility may be excluded on the basis of perceived trial dangers such as misleading or confusing the jury and unfair prejudice.

§ 63. Religious Belief

Belief in a divine being who, in this life or hereafter, will punish false swearing was a prerequisite at common law to the capacity to take the oath. Members of many major religions could meet the test, but members of other religions, as well as atheists and agnostics, could not. This ground of incapacity has fortunately been abandoned in most state jurisdictions, either by explicit state constitutional or statutory provisions, or by expansive interpretation of state provisions forbidding deprivation of rights for religious beliefs, or by changing the common law "in the light of reason and experience," or because such a requirement would be inconsistent with our law and with the spirit of our institutions, or by adoption of the Federal Rules of Evidence or the Revised Uniform Rules of Evidence 601 and 603. In any event, this rule of incapacity appears to be prohibited in any state or federal court by the first and fourteenth amendments of the federal constitution. A witness can object to an oath directly or inferentially stating his belief in God, but it has been held that routinely swearing witnesses to tell the truth using the phrase, "so help me God," does not vitiate a trial, when the witnesses have not objected. Probably the loser has no standing to object on appeal in such a case, but it is conceivable that in some circumstances he could make a strained argument that he has an interest and is affected. Inquiry into the religious opinions of the witness for impeachment purposes is discussed in another section.[1]

§ 64. Conviction of Crime

The common law disqualified altogether the witness who had been convicted of treason, felony, or a crime involving fraud or deceit. In England and in most of the states during the last hundred years this disqualification has been swept away by legislation. In 1917, the Supreme Court of the United States determined that "the dead hand of the common law rule" of disqualification should no longer be applied in criminal cases in the federal courts. The disqualification is not recognized in Federal Rule of Evidence and Revised Uniform Rule of Evidence (1974) 601. In a few states, however, it has been retained for conviction of perjury and subornation thereof. These statutes are now of questionable validity under a holding of the Supreme Court of the United States that declared unconstitutional Texas statutes which barred the persons charged or convicted as co-participants in the same crime from testifying for each other.

§ 65. Parties and Persons Interested: The Dead Man Statutes

By far the most drastic of the common law rules of incompetency was the rule that excluded the testimony of the parties to the lawsuit and of all persons having a direct pecuniary or proprietary interest in the outcome. In effect, this rule imposed a disability upon the party to testify in his own behalf and conferred upon him a privilege not to be used as a witness against himself by the adversary. The disability had the specious justification of preventing self-interested perjury; the privilege had not even a specious excuse. It is almost unbelievable that the rule could have continued in force in England until the middle of the 19th century, and in this country for a few decades longer. In England, the reform was sweeping, and no shred of disqualification in civil cases remains.

In this country, however, a compromise was forced upon the reformers. The objection was raised that in controversies over transactions, such as contracts, or other events where one party had died and the other survived, hardship and fraud would result if the surviving parties or interested persons were permitted to testify to the transaction or the event. The survivor could testify though the adverse party's lips would be sealed in death. This is a seductive argument. It was accepted in nearly all the early statutes, at a time when the real dispute was whether the general disqualification should be abolished or retained, and the concession for survivors' cases undoubtedly seemed a minor one. But the concession where it still exists has now become so ingrained a part of judicial and professional habits of thinking that it is hard to dislodge by argument.

Accordingly, statutes in many states provide that the common law disqualification of parties and interested persons is abolished, except that they remain disqualified to testify concerning a transaction or communication with a person since deceased in a suit prose-

1. See § 46 supra.

cuted or defended by the executor or administrator of the decedent. However, it is often provided by the statute or by case law that the surviving party or interested person may testify if called by the adversary, i.e., by the executor or administrator, thus abrogating the privilege feature of the common law rule. The practical consequence of these statutes is that if a survivor has rendered services, furnished goods or lent money to a man whom he trusted, without an outside witness or admissible written evidence, he is helpless if the other dies and the representative of his estate declines to pay. The survivor's mouth may even be closed in an action arising from a fatal automobile collision, or in a suit upon a note or an account which the survivor paid in cash without taking a receipt.

Most commentators agree that the expedient of refusing to listen to the survivor is, in the words of Bentham, a "blind and brainless" technique. In seeking to avoid injustice to one side, the statute-makers ignored the equal possibility of creating injustice to the other. The temptation to the survivor to fabricate a claim or defense is obvious enough, so obvious indeed that any jury will realize that his story must be cautiously heard. A searching cross-examination will usually, in case of fraud, reveal discrepancies inherent in the "tangled web" of deception. In any event, the survivor's disqualification is more likely to balk the honest than the dishonest survivor. One who would not balk at perjury will hardly hestitate at suborning a third person, who would not be disqualified, to swear to the false story.

The lawmakers and courts are being brought to see the blindness of the traditional survivors' evidence acts, and liberalizing changes are being adopted. A few states have provided that the survivor may testify, but his testimony will not support a judgment unless corroborated by other evidence. Others authorize the trial judge to permit the survivor to testify when it appears that his testimony is necessary to prevent injustice. Both of these solutions have reasonably apparent drawbacks which are avoided by a third type of statute that sweeps away the disqualification entirely and permits the survivor to testify without restriction, but seeks to minimize the danger of injustice to the decedent's estate by admitting any writings of the deceased or evidence of oral statements made by him, bearing on the controversy, both of which would ordinarily be excluded as hearsay.

Federal Rule of Evidence (except in diversity cases) and Revised Uniform Rule of Evidence (1974) 601 abandon the instant disqualification altogether. Not all states which have copied the Federal Rules have done so.

Interest, then, as a disqualification in civil cases has been discarded, except for the fragmentary relic retained in the survivors' evidence statutes. The disqualification of parties defendant in criminal cases which at common law prevented the accused from being called as a witness by either side has been abrogated in England and in this country to the extent it disabled the defendant to testify in his own behalf, but it survives to the extent that the prosecution cannot call him. In this form, it is a rule of privilege, and constitutes one aspect of the privilege against self-incrimination, treated in a later section.[1]

While the disqualification of parties and persons interested in the result of the lawsuit has thus been almost entirely swept away, the fact of interest of the witness, whether as a party or otherwise, is by no means disregarded. It may be proved to impeach credibility,[2] and in most jurisdictions the court will instruct that a party's testimony may be weighed in the light of his interest.

§ 66. Husbands and Wives of Parties

Closely allied to the disqualification of parties, and even more arbitrary and misguided, was the early common law disqualification of the husband or wife of the party. This disqualification prevented the party's husband or wife from testifying either for or against

1. See §§ 116, 131, infra.

2. See § 39 supra.

the party in any case, civil or criminal. Doubtless we should classify the disability of the husband or wife as a witness to testify *for* the party-spouse as a disqualification, based upon the supposed infirmity of interest, and the rule enabling the party-spouse to prevent the husband or wife from testifying *against* the party as a privilege.

Of course, the common law rule has been modified. In the majority of jurisdictions statutes have made the husband or wife fully competent to testify for or against the party-spouse in civil cases. In criminal cases, the disqualification of the husband or wife to testify for the accused spouse has been removed, but it is sometimes provided that the prosecution may not call the spouse, without the consent of the accused spouse, thus preserving for criminal cases the privilege of the accused to keep the spouse off the stand altogether. In some jurisdictions either spouse may claim the privilege. In federal criminal cases only the spouse who is to be called by the prosecution as a witness may claim the privilege. Federal Rule of Evidence 501 presents an unusual situation in the federal rule system. In other jurisdictions spouses may be called to the stand to testify just as any other witnesses.

Even at common law the instant privilege was withheld from the husband in criminal prosecutions against him for wrongs directly against the person of the wife. The statutes which retain the instant privilege usually broaden this exception to include prosecution of any "crime committed by one against the other" and various other miscellaneous exceptions. There is some disagreement concerning the time in which the instant privilege exists, but most courts regard the initial time at which it comes into being as the date of the creation of the marriage and the terminal date as the date of termination of marriage, as by divorce.

Several procedural questions may arise. The holder of the privilege must be ascertained. There is disagreement whether it is error for the prosecution to call the spouse to the stand in a criminal case thereby forcing the accused spouse or the witness' spouse to object in the presence of the jury. Most courts protect the privilege by denying the right to comment upon its exercise.

The privilege is sometimes applied to extrajudicial statements of the spouse.

The privilege has sometimes been defended on the ground that it protects family harmony. But family harmony is nearly always past saving when the spouse is willing to aid the prosecution. The privilege is an archaic survival of a mystical religious dogma and of a way of thinking about the marital relation that is today outmoded.

Both the instant privilege, and the ancient disqualification, must be clearly distinguished from another privilege—the privilege against disclosure of confidential communications between husband and wife. It is discussed in another place.[1]

§ 67. Incompetency of Husband and Wife to Give Testimony on Non-access

In 1777, in an ejectment case where the issue of the legitimacy of the claimant was raised, Lord Mansfield delivered a pronouncement which apparently was new-minted doctrine, "that the declarations of a father or mother cannot be admitted to bastardize the issue born after marriage * * * it is a rule founded in decency, morality and policy, that they shall not be permitted to say after marriage that they have had no connection and therefore that the offspring is spurious * * *."[1] This invention of the great jurist though justly criticised by Wigmore as inconsistent, obstructive and pharisaical,[2] was followed by later English decisions until abrogat-

---

§ 66

1. See Ch. 9 infra.

§ 67

1. Goodright v. Moss, 2 Cowp. 291, 98 Eng.Rep. 1257 (1777).

2. 7 Wigmore, Evidence § 2064 (Chadbourn rev. 1978).

ed by statute, and has been accepted by some courts in this country. A few courts have wisely rejected it by construing the general statutes abolishing the incompetency of parties and of spouses as abolishing this eccentric incompetency also, but other courts have not yielded to this argument. The points of controversy in the application of the rule are (a) whether it is limited strictly to evidence of non-access, or whether it extends to other types of evidence showing that some one other than the husband is the father, (b) whether the rule is limited to proceedings wherein legitimacy is in issue or extends to suits for divorce where the question is adultery rather than the legitimacy of the child, and (c) whether it is confined to prohibiting the testimony of husband and wife on the stand, or extends to excluding evidence of the previous admissions or declarations of the spouse. In view of the impolicy of the rule it is believed that in all these instances the more restrictive application is to be preferred.

§ 68. Judges, Jurors and Lawyers

A judicial officer called to the stand in a case in which she is not sitting as a judge is not disqualified by his office from testifying. But when a judge is called as a witness in a trial before her, her role as witness is manifestly inconsistent with his customary role of impartiality in the adversary system of trial. Nevertheless, under the older view she was in general regarded as a competent witness, though she might have a discretion to decline to testify. This view is preserved in some state statutes but is subject to criticism. A second view is that the judge is disqualified from testifying to material, disputed facts, but may testify to matters merely formal and undisputed. This distinction is not easy to draw, and formal matters nearly always can be proved by other witnesses. Accordingly the third view, for which support is growing, that a judge is incompetent to testify in a case which she is trying, seems the most expedient one. It is embodied in Federal and Revised

Uniform Rule of Evidence 605. This rule provides for an "automatic" objection.

A somewhat similar danger to the impartial position of the tribunal is present when a juror sitting in a case is called as a witness. Thus Federal and Revised Uniform Rule of Evidence (1974) 606(a) provides that the juror is incompetent as a witness. By adoption of this rule in state jurisdictions, substantial inroads have been made on the traditional common law and the statutes to the contrary.

There is a separate traditional doctrine that a juror is incompetent to testify in impeachment of the juror's verdict. While once criticized, this doctrine is now firmly entrenched in the decisions. Barring juror impeachment of the verdict promotes the finality of verdicts and encourages frank and free jury deliberation, while discouraging harassment of jurors by losing parties. A few courts would abandon the rule of disqualification, and would permit jurors to broadly testify to misconduct and irregularities which are ground for new trial. For protection of finality they would trust to a doctrine which excludes, as immaterial, evidence as to the expressions and arguments of the jurors in their deliberations and evidence as to their own motives, beliefs, mistakes and mental operations generally, in arriving at their verdict. Federal and Revised Uniform Rule of Evidence (1974) 606(b) adopt the conservative traditional doctrine based upon prior federal case law. First these rules do not equate with, or govern, grounds for a new trial, but merely govern the competency of jurors to testify concerning the jury process. Second, in addition to jurors' thought processes, discussions, motives, beliefs, and mistakes, they exclude irregular juror conduct in the jury room. Third, they do not exclude juror testimony of extraneous prejudicial influences. Fourth, they do not preclude testimony of others about their knowledge of jury misconduct.

To be distinguished from these rules of incompetency and exclusion, is the doctrine which has the support of Wigmore[1] and of some judicial expressions, to the effect that

§ 68

1. 8 Evidence § 2346 (McNaughton rev. 1961).

each juror has a privilege against the disclosure in court of her communications to the other jurors during their retirement.

At common law and under Federal and Revised Uniform Rule of Evidence 601 a lawyer for a party is not as such incompetent to testify. Nevertheless, the court has wide discretion to refuse to permit a lawyer to testify in favor of his client. Discretion will often be exercised to prevent such testimony where other sources of evidence as to the fact of consequence are available or where the necessity for testimony by the lawyer could have been avoided. Even where no other witness is available and the lawyer is willing to withdraw, discretion will sometimes be exercised in favor of preventing the lawyer from testifying.

The ABA Model Rules of Professional Conduct, Rule 3.7, Lawyer as Witness, enacted in 1983, provides as follows:

(a) A lawyer shall not act as advocate at a trial in which the lawyer is likely to be a necessary witness except where:

(1) the testimony relates to an uncontested issue

(2) the testimony relates to the nature and value of legal services rendered in the case; or

(3) disqualification of the lawyer would work substantial hardship on the client.

(b) A lawyer may act as advocate in a trial in which another lawyer in the lawyer's firm is likely to be called as a witness unless precluded from doing so by [conflict of interest] Rule 1.7 or Rule 1.9.

§ 69. Firsthand Knowledge and Expertness

Two other rules, already considered, may be related to the subject of competency of witnesses. These rules are the requirement that a witness testifying to objective facts must have had means of knowing them from observation,[1] and the rule that one who would testify to his inference or opinion in matters

requiring special training or experience to understand, must be qualified as an expert in the field.[2] It should be noted that unlike most of the other rules of competency, which go to the capacity of the witness to speak at all, these last are directed to his capacity to speak to a particular matter.

§ 70. The Procedure of Disqualification

Under the earlier common law practice, the witness was not sworn until she was placed upon the stand to begin her testimony. Before the oath was administered the adversary had an opportunity to object to her competency and the judge or counsel would then examine the witness touching upon her qualifications, before she was sworn as a witness. This was known as a voir dire examination. Traditionally when the witness is first called to the stand to testify, the opponent has been required to challenge her competency, if grounds of challenge are then known to her.

Except possibly for diversity cases, the situation described above is quite different from that prescribed by Federal Rule of Evidence 601 in the federal courts, because of the limited scope of the subject of competency of witnesses. The situation is also different under the Revised Uniform Rule of Evidence 601. In effect the procedure for challenging judges and jurors as witnesses is prescribed by Rules 605 and 606.[1] In federal criminal cases the privilege of the spouse witnesses to object to being called by the prosecution may probably be exercised before the spouse witness takes the stand. Since the objections of incapacity and immaturity do not bear upon competency but rather upon credibility, these matters need not be raised before the witness begins to testify. Even in diversity cases in federal court, the federal court should not be bound by the exact procedures of objection followed in any particular state.

§ 69

1. See § 10 supra.
2. See § 13 supra.

§ 70

1. See § 68 supra.

Finally, under both case law and the Federal and Revised Uniform Rules of Evidence, the offering party must first show knowledge or expertness of the witness, usually by questioning the witness to show the witness is qualified.[2]

If a question of fact is disputed or doubtful on the evidence, the trial judge sitting with a jury does not submit this question of fact to the jury, except questions whether the witness has firsthand knowledge.[3] As with all similar issues of fact arising in the determination of the admissibility of evidence [4] the judge decides the preliminary issue and sustains or rejects accordingly the challenge to the witness or the objection to evidence.

In federal court the procedure for determining the competency of a child witness is governed by statute.[5]

2. See §§ 10, 13 supra.
3. See § 69.

§ 71. Probable Future of the Rules of Competency

The rules which disqualify witnesses who have knowledge of relevant facts and mental capacity to convey that knowledge are serious obstructions to the ascertainment of truth. For a century the course of legal evolution has been in the direction of sweeping away these obstructions. To that end Federal Rules of Evidence 601 through 606 (deleting the second sentence of Rule 601), or the similar rules of the Revised Uniform Rules of Evidence should be adopted in more state jurisdictions. Congress should exercise the power to adopt these rules without qualification for diversity cases.

4. See § 53 supra.
5. 18 U.S.C.A. § 3509(c).

*

Title 5

PRIVILEGE: COMMON LAW AND STATUTORY

Chapter 8

THE SCOPE AND EFFECT OF THE
EVIDENTIARY PRIVILEGES

Table of Sections

§ 72. The Purposes of Rules of Privilege: (a) Other Rules of Evidence Distinguished

The overwhelming majority of all rules of evidence have as their ultimate justification some tendency to promote the objectives set forward by the conventional witness' oath, the presentation of "the truth, the whole truth, and nothing but the truth." Thus such prominent exclusionary rules as the hearsay rule, the opinion rule, the rule excluding bad character as evidence of crime, and the original documents (or "Best Evidence") rule, have as their common purpose the elucidation of the truth, a purpose which these rules seek to effect by operating to exclude evidence which is unreliable or which is calculated to prejudice or mislead.

By contrast the rules of privilege, of which the most familiar are the rule protecting against self-incrimination and those shielding the confidentiality of communications between husband and wife, attorney and client, and physician and patient, are not designed or intended to facilitate the fact-finding process or to safeguard its integrity. Their effect instead is clearly inhibitive; rather than facilitating the illumination of truth, they shut out the light.

Rules which serve to render accurate ascertainment of the truth more difficult, or in some instances impossible, may seem anomalous in a rational system of fact-finding. Nevertheless, rules of privilege are not without a rationale. Their warrant is the protection of interests and relationships which, rightly or wrongly, are regarded as of sufficient social importance to justify some sacrifice of availability of evidence relevant to the administration of justice.

The interests allegedly served by privileges, as might be expected, are varied. The great constitutional protections which have evolved around self-incrimination, confessions, and unlawfully obtained evidence are considered elsewhere. They are commonly classed as privileges.

Of the rules treated here, a substantial number operate to protect communications made within the context of various professional relationships, e.g., attorney and client, physician and patient, clergyman and penitent. The rationale traditionally advanced for these privileges is that public policy requires the encouragement of the communications without which these relationships cannot be effective. This rationale, today sometimes referred to as the utilitarian justification for privilege, found perhaps its strongest supporter in Dean Wigmore who seems to have viewed it as the chief, if not the exclusive, basis for privilege. Wigmore's views have been widely accepted by the courts, and have largely conditioned the development of thinking about privilege.

More recently another, and analytically distinct, rationale for privilege has been advanced. According to this theory certain privacy interests in the society are deserving of protection by privilege irrespective of whether the existence of such privileges actually operates substantially to affect conduct within the protected relationships. Thus, while it has been suggested that communications between

husband and wife and physician and patient do not have their genesis in the inducement of the privileges accorded them, some form of these privileges is nevertheless seen as justified on the alternative basis that they serve to protect the essential privacy of certain significant human relationships. Given its comparatively recent origin, this latter rationale probably has not operated as a conscious basis for either the judicial or legislative creation of existing privileges. Today's judicial tendency to pour new wine into old bottles, however, may serve to make the nonutilitarian theory a factor in the subsequent development of thinking about privilege.

It is open to doubt whether all of the interests and relationships which have sometimes been urged as sufficiently important to justify the creation of privileges really merit this sort of protection bought at such a price. Moreover, even if the importance of given interests and relationships be conceded, there remain questions as to whether evidentiary privileges are appropriate, much less sufficient, mechanisms for accomplishing the desired objectives. In any event, it is clear that in drawing their justifications from considerations unrelated to the integrity of the adjudication process, rules of privilege are of a different order than the great bulk of evidentiary rules.

§ 72.1   The Purposes of Rules of Privilege: (b) Certain Rules Distinguished

As developed in a subsequent section,[1] true rules of privilege may be enforced to prevent the introduction of evidence even though the privilege is that of a person who is not a party to the proceeding in which the privilege is involved. This characteristic serves to distinguish certain other rules which, like privileges, are intended to encourage or discourage certain kinds of conduct. Among these latter rules may be included those excluding offers of compromise[2] and subsequent remedial

§ 72.1

1.   § 73 infra.

2.   See § 266 infra.

measures following an injury.[3]

Functionally, the policies toward which these latter rules are directed may be fully realized by implementing the rules only in litigation to which the person sought to be actuated by the rule is a party. For example, the rule excluding evidence of offers of compromise is designed to encourage compromise; admitting the evidence in a case to which the offeror is not a party will in no wise operate to discourage compromises. Accordingly, such rules may be asserted only by a party. This consideration, in addition to the fact that these rules are also justified in part by considerations relating to relevancy, makes classification as rules of privilege analytically imprecise.

Again, true rules of privilege operate generally to prevent revelation of confidential matter within the context of a judicial proceeding. Thus, rules of privilege do not speak directly to the question of unauthorized revelations of confidential matter outside the judicial setting, and redress for such breaches of confidence must be sought in the law of torts or professional responsibility.

§ 73. Procedural Recognition of Rules of Privilege

In one important procedural respect, rules of privilege are similar to other evidentiary rules. The fact that most exclusionary rules are intended to protect the integrity of the fact-finding process while rules of privilege look toward the preservation of confidences might lead the casual reflector to conclude that the former will operate inexorably to exclude untrustworthy evidence while the latter will only be enforced at the option of the holder of the privilege. Such, we know, is not the case. Neither set of rules is self-executing: rules of exclusion, no less than rules of privilege, must be asserted to be effective, and if not asserted promptly will ordinarily be waived. Instead, the distinction in purpose between the two types of rules is reflected by a difference in the persons who may claim

their benefit and, perhaps today, in what forum.

§ 73.1 Procedural Recognition of Rules of Privilege: (a) Who May Assert?

This difference in foundation between the two groups of rules manifests itself in another line of cleavage. The rule of exclusion or preference, being designed to make the trial more efficient as a vehicle of fact disclosure, may be invoked as of right only by the person whose interest in having the verdict follow the facts is at stake in the trial. Thus, when evidence condemned by one of these rules is offered, only the adverse party may object, unless the judge elects to interpose. But by contrast, if the evidence is privileged, the right to object does not attach to the opposing party as such, but to the person vested with the outside interest or relationship fostered by the particular privilege. True, other persons present at the trial, including the adverse party, may call to the court's attention the existence of the privilege, or the judge may choose to intervene of his own accord to protect it, but this is regarded as having been done on behalf of the owner of the privilege.

The right to complain on appeal is a more crucial test. If the court erroneously recognizes an asserted privilege and excludes proffered testimony on this ground, of course the tendering party has been injured in his capacity as litigant and may complain on appeal. But if a claim of privilege is wrongly denied, and the privileged testimony erroneously let in, the distinction which we have suggested between privilege and a rule of exclusion would seem to be material. If the adverse party to the suit is likewise the owner of the privilege, then, while it may be argued that the party's interest *as a litigant* has not been infringed, most courts decline to draw so sharp a line, and permit him to complain of the error.

Where, however, the owner of the privilege is not a party to the suit, it is somewhat difficult to see why this invasion of a third

3. See § 267 infra.

person's interest should be ground of complaint for the objecting party, whose only grievance can be that the overriding of the outsider's rights has resulted in a fuller fact-disclosure than the party desires. It has not been thought necessary to afford this extreme sanction in order to prevent a break-down in the protection of privilege. In at least two classes of privileges, the privileges against self-incrimination [1] and against the use of evidence secured by unlawful search or seizure,[2] this distinction has been clearly perceived and the party is quite consistently denied any ground for reversal, despite the constitutional bases of the two privileges. The results in cases of erroneous denials of other privileges are more checkered; a considerable number of the older cases seem to allow the party to take advantage of the error on appeal.

The California Code of Evidence, one of the few modern codifications to address the question, is clear-cut. It provides: "A party may predicate error on a ruling disallowing a claim of privilege only if he is the holder of the privilege, except that a party may predicate error on a ruling disallowing a claim of privilege by his spouse * * *." [3]

§ 73.2   Procedural Recognition of Rules of Privilege: (b) Where May Privilege Be Asserted?—Rules of Privilege in Conflict of Laws

Under traditional choice of law doctrine all rules of evidence, including those of privilege, were viewed as procedural and thus appropriately supplied by the law of the forum. This approach naturally tended to suppress any consideration of the differences in purpose clearly existing between rules of exclusion and preference on the one hand, and rules of privilege on the other.

Modern conflict of laws analysis, by contrast, inclines toward resolution of choice of law questions through evaluation of the policy interests of the respective jurisdictions which have some connection with the transaction in litigation. Under this approach, the forum will almost invariably possess a strong interest in a correct determination of the facts in dispute before its courts, and therefore a strong interest in the application of its rules of exclusion and preference. By contrast, the forum may have virtually no interest in applying its rules of privilege in a case where the relationship or interest sought to be promoted or protected by the privilege had its contacts exclusively with another jurisdiction.

Thus, for example, if a given professional relationship is carried out exclusively in State X which itself does not extend a privilege to protect that relationship, there would seem to be no compelling reason for the forum, State Y, to apply its own rules of privilege, thus denying its court the benefit of helpful evidence. No interest either of the forum or of State X argues for recognition of the forum's privilege in such a case.

In short, though case law to date is somewhat sparse, the basic difference in purpose between rules of privilege and other rules of evidence should prove of increasing significance in the resolution of choice of law problems.

§ 74.   Limitations on the Effectiveness of Privileges: (a) Risk of Eavesdropping and Interception of Letters

Since privileges operate to deny litigants access to every person's evidence, the courts have generally construed them no more broadly than necessary to accomplish their basic purposes. One manifestation of this tendency is to be seen in the general rule that a privilege operates only to preclude testimony by parties to the confidential relationship. Accordingly, a number of older decisions held that an eavesdropper may testify to confidential communications, and that a letter, otherwise confidential and privileged, is not protected if it is purloined or otherwise intercepted by a third person. This principle, how-

§ 73.1

1. See § 120 infra.

2. See § 175 infra.

3. West's Ann.Cal.Evid.Code § 918.

ever, has only infrequently been carried to the extent of allowing a privilege to be breached if the interception is made possible by the connivance of a party to the confidential relationship.

Though the same general rule is still sometimes applied, most modern decisions do no more than hold that a privilege will not protect communications made under circumstances in which interception was reasonably to be anticipated. Certainly, a qualification of the traditional rule in terms of the reasonable expectations of the privileged communicator may provide a desirable common law readjustment to cope with the alarming potential of the modern eavesdropper. While in earlier times the confidentiality of privileged communications could generally be preserved by a modest attention to security, homespun measures will hardly suffice against the modern panoply of electronic paraphernalia.

The vastly enhanced technology of eavesdropping has drawn a variety of legislative reactions more directly responsive to the problem. These have included state statutes prohibiting wiretapping and electronic surveillance and denying admissibility to evidence obtained in violation. Such provisions are of course in addition to that protection which may rest on constitutional grounds. Moreover, statutes and rules defining the privileges have begun to include provisions entitling the holder to prevent anyone from disclosing a privileged communication.

§ 74.1 Limitations on the Effectiveness of Privileges: (b) Adverse Arguments and Inferences From Claims of Privilege

The underlying conflict comes most clearly in view in the decisions relating to the allowability of an adverse inference from the assertion of privilege. Plainly, the inference may not ordinarily be made against a party when a witness for that party claims a privilege personal to the witness, for this is not a

matter under the party's control.[1] But where the party himself suppresses evidence by invoking a privilege given to him by the law, should an adverse inference be sanctioned? The question may arise in various forms, for example, whether an inquiry of the witness, or of the party, calling for information obviously privileged, may be pressed for the pointed purpose of forcing the party to make an explicit claim of the privilege in the jury's hearing, or again, whether the inference may be drawn in argument, and finally, whether the judge in the instructions may mention the inference as a permissible one.

Under familiar principles an unfavorable inference may be drawn against a party not only for destroying evidence, but for the mere failure to produce witnesses or documents within his control.[2] No showing of wrong or fraud seems to be required as a foundation for the inference that the evidence if produced would have been unfavorable. Why should not this same conclusion be drawn from the party's active interposing of a privilege to keep out the evidence? A leading case for the affirmative is Phillips v. Chase,[3] where the court said:

> "It is a rule of law that the objection of a party to evidence as incompetent and immaterial, and insistence upon his right to have his case tried according to the rules of law, cannot be made a subject of comment in argument. * * * On the other hand, if evidence is material and competent except for a personal privilege of one of the parties to have it excluded under the law, his claim of the privilege may be referred to in argument and considered by the jury, as indicating his opinion that the evidence, if received, would be prejudicial to him."

An oft-quoted statement by Lord Chelmsford gives the contrary view:

> "The exclusion of such evidence is for the general interest of the community, and therefore to say that when a party refuses to permit professional confidence to be broken,

§ 74.1

1. See § 73 supra, and more particularly as to self-incrimination § 120 infra.

2. See § 264 infra.

3. 201 Mass. 444, 480, 87 N.E. 755, 758 (1909), writ of error dismissed 216 U.S. 616.

everything must be taken most strongly against him, what is it but to deny him the protection which, for public purposes, the law affords him, and utterly to take away a privilege which can thus only be asserted to his prejudice?" [4]

The first of these arguments is based upon an unfounded distinction between incompetent and privileged evidence, namely, a supposition that the privilege can be waived and the incompetency cannot. As we have seen, both may be waived with equal facility. As to the second, it may be an overstatement to say that permitting the inference "utterly takes away" the privilege. A privilege has its most substantial practical benefit when it enables a party to exclude from the record a witness, document, or line of proof which is essential to the adversary's case, lacking which he cannot get to the jury at all on a vital issue. The inference does not supply the lack of proof.[5] In other situations, the benefit accruing from a successful claim of privilege will depend upon circumstances. It is evident, however, that in a case which does survive a motion for a directed verdict or its equivalent, allowing comment upon the exercise of a privilege or requiring it to be claimed in the presence of the jury tends greatly to diminish its value. In Griffin v. California [6] the Supreme Court held that allowing comment upon the failure of an accused to take the stand violated his privilege against self-incrimination "by making its assertion costly." Whether one is prepared to extend this protection to all privileges probably depends upon his attitude towards privileges in general and towards the particular privilege involved. The cases, rather naturally, are in dispute. It is submitted that the best solution is to recognize only privileges which are soundly based in policy and to accord those privileges the fullest protection. Thus comment, whether by judge or by counsel, or its equivalent of re-

quiring the claim to be made in the presence of the jury, and the drawing of inferences from the claim, all would be foreclosed.

§ 74.2   Limitations on the Effectiveness of Privileges: (c) Constitutional Limitations on Privilege

A hitherto unrecognized source of limitations on privilege in criminal cases has in recent years emerged as a result of decisions of the Supreme Court dealing with the Compulsory Process and Confrontation Clauses of the Constitution of the United States.

The three cases which have figured in this development are Washington v. Texas,[1] Davis v. Alaska,[2] and United States v. Nixon.[3] In Washington v. Texas, the Court held the provisions of the compulsory process clause binding upon states as a component of due process, and struck down a Texas statute which rendered persons charged or convicted as co-participants in the same crime incompetent to testify for one another. The Court's decision stressed the "absurdity" of the statute and specifically held only that the constitutional provision is violated by "arbitrary rules that prevent whole categories of defense witnesses from testifying * * * *"[4] The Court expressly disclaimed any implied disapproval of testimonial privileges which it noted are based upon quite different considerations.

In Davis v. Alaska, the Court held that the confrontation clause was violated by application of a state statute privileging juvenile records where the result was to deny the defendant the opportunity to elicit on cross-examination the probationary status of a critical witness against him. Recognizing the strength of the state policy in favor of preserving the confidentiality of juveniles' records, the Court nevertheless held that this policy must yield to the superior interest of

---

4. Wentworth v. Lloyd, 10 H.L.Cas. 589, 591 (1864).

5. See § 264 infra.

6. 380 U.S. 609 (1965).

§ 74.2

1. 388 U.S. 14 (1967), on remand 417 S.W.2d 278 (Tex.Cr.App.).

2. 415 U.S. 308 (1974).

3. 418 U.S. 683 (1974).

4. Washington v. Texas, 388 U.S. 14, 22 (1967), on remand 417 S.W.2d 278 (Tex.Cr.App.).

the defendant in effective confrontation. Significantly, the Court's decision did not compel disclosure of the juvenile record, but only remanded the case for further proceedings not inconsistent with the Court's opinion.

Finally, in United States v. Nixon, the Court held that a claim of absolute privilege of confidentiality for general presidential communications in the performance of the office would not prevail "over the fundamental demands of due process of law in the fair administration of criminal justice. The generalized assertion of privilege must yield to the demonstrated, specific need for evidence in a pending criminal trial." [5]

Taken together, and despite the somewhat distinctive fact situations involved, these cases fairly raise the question as to the viability of a claim of privilege when a criminal defendant asserts: (1) a need to introduce the privileged matter as exculpatory, or (2) a need to use the privileged matter to impeach testimony introduced by the state. The question is of course not altogether a novel one. Privileges running in favor of the government, such as the informer's privilege, have long been qualified to accommodate the defendant's rights of confrontation. [6] Similarly, the state has frequently been precluded from relying upon the testimony of a witness whose claim of privilege on self-incrimination grounds prevents effective cross-examination. [7]

A number of state decisions, purporting to give effect to the constitutional holdings of Davis and Nixon, have resolved conflicts between the rights of a defendant on the one hand and claims of private privilege on the other by overriding the latter and forcing (or attempting to force) the testimony of the privilege holder.

Despite such decisions, the extent to which protection of the interests of a criminal defendant constitutionally requires invasion of private privilege was never clear, and has been placed even further in doubt in the decision of the Supreme Court in Pennsylvania v. Ritchie.[8] In Ritchie, the defendant, charged with rape and other related crimes, sought pretrial access to files of a state child protective agency. The defendant's chief interest in the files, which were protected by a qualified privilege under state statute, was to discover material of possible use in the cross-examination of his daughter, the complaining witness. The state supreme court, relying on Davis, held that the defendant had the right to inspect the files in question by virtue of the Confrontation and Compulsory Process clauses. The Supreme Court reversed this portion of the state judgment, a majority of the court concurring that the defendant was entitled only to have the file inspected in camera by the trial court. Only four justices, however, joined in the plurality opinion which based this result on due process grounds and stated that the Pennsylvania court's reliance on Davis was "misplaced" and that the confrontation clause creates only a "trial" right.

Not surprisingly, the Ritchie decision has been accorded a variety of interpretations. The seemingly preferable resolution of the Ritchie problem, and one adopted by several courts, is to require that the defendant make a showing that there is reasonable ground to believe that failure to produce material which has been found privileged will be likely to impair defendant's right of confrontation. Once such a showing is made, the state must then obtain the privilege holder's waiver for purposes of an in camera inspection and, if the matter is found relevant, for trial presentation; otherwise the privilege-holder's testimony will be inadmissible. However, many decisions have failed to find that the defendant's constitutional rights require even so limited an intrusion on private privilege.

Even more dubious today is any right of the criminal defendant to obtain and present matter protected by private privilege which is relevant to the issues of the case but has no direct bearing upon the credibility of a witness for the prosecution.

---

5. 418 U.S. 683, 713 (1974).

6. Roviaro v. United States, 353 U.S. 53 (1957).

7. See § 19 supra.

8. 480 U.S. 39 (1987).

§ 75. The Sources of Privilege

The earliest recognized privileges were judicially created, the origin of both the husband-wife and attorney-client privileges being traceable to the received common law.[1] The development of judge-made privileges, however, virtually halted over a century ago. Though it is impossible definitely to ascribe a reason for this cessation, a contributing factor was undoubtedly a judicial tendency to view privileges from the standpoint of their hindrance to litigation. Certainly the vantage point of the legal profession in general, and of the judiciary in particular, is such as to force into prominence the more deleterious aspects of privilege as impediments to the fact-finding process. By contrast, many of the beneficial consequences claimed for privilege can be expected to be observable only outside the courtroom, and even then are often difficult of empirical demonstration.

Perhaps as a consequence, during the 19th century the source of newly created privileges shifted decisively from the courts to the legislatures. New York enacted the first physician-patient privilege in 1828, and the vast majority of new privileges created since that time have been of legislative origin. The trend extended to codification even of the preexisting common law privileges, and today the husband-wife and attorney-client privileges are statutorily controlled in most states.

It may be argued that legitimate claims to confidentiality are more equitably received by a branch of government not preeminently concerned with the factual results obtained in litigation, and that the legislatures provide an appropriate forum for the balancing of the competing social values necessary to sound decisions concerning privilege. At the same time, while there is no doubt that some of the statutorily created privileges are soundly based, legislatures have on occasion been unduly influenced by powerful groups seeking the prestige and convenience of a professionally based privilege. One result of the process has been that the various states differ substantially in the numbers and varieties of privilege which they recognize.

Until very recently, the heavy consensus of opinion among commentators has favored narrowing the field of privilege, and attempts have been made, largely without success, to incorporate this view into the several 20th century efforts to codify the law of evidence. The draftsmen of both the Model Code of Evidence and the 1953 Uniform Rules of Evidence favored limitations on the number and scope of privileges. The final versions of both of these codifications, however, contained the generally recognized common law and statutory privileges substantially unimpaired.

The Federal Rules of Evidence as proposed by the Advisory Committee and approved by the Supreme Court contained provisions recognizing and defining nine non-constitutional privileges: required reports, attorney-client, psychotherapist-patient, husband-wife, clergyman-communicant, political vote, trade secrets, secrets of state and other official information, and identity of informer. In addition, proposed Rule 501 specifically limited the privileges to be recognized in the federal courts to those provided for by the Rules or enacted by the Congress.[2] When the Rules were submitted to the Congress the privilege provisions excited particular controversy, with the result that all of the specific rules of privilege were excised from the finally enacted version of the Rules.[3]

The failure of Congress to enact specific rules of privilege left the Federal Rules of Evidence with a large gap when viewed as a

---

§ 75

1. See §§ 78 and 87 infra.

2. Deleted Federal Rule 501, 56 F.R.D. 230, reads:

Except as otherwise required by the Constitution of the United States or provided by Act of Congress, and except as provided in these rules or in other rules adopted by the Supreme Court, no person has a privilege to:

(1) Refuse to be a witness; or

(2) Refuse to disclose any matter; or

(3) Refuse to produce any object or writing; or

(4) Prevent another from being a witness or disclosing any matter or producing any object or writing.

3. For the text of Fed.R.Evid. 501 as adopted by the Congress, see note 2 supra.

potential model code for possible adoption by the states. Therefore, in promulgating the Revised Uniform Rules of Evidence (1974), based almost entirely on the Federal Rules, the National Conference of Commissioners on Uniform State Laws included specific rules of privilege. These are substantially the version of the Federal Rules submitted to Congress, but contain some notable changes. Some states adopting rules or codes based upon the Federal Rules have adopted the proposed Federal Rules concerning privilege, others have adopted the Uniform Rules on this subject, and some have retained their antecedent rules of privilege.

§ 76.　The Current Pattern of Privilege

The failure of Congress to enact specific rules of privilege for the federal courts effectively precluded any immediate prospect of substantial national uniformity in this area. It is arguable that, in light of the strength and contrariety of views which the subject generates, hope for such a consensus was never realistic. In any event, the present form of Federal Rule of Evidence 501 perpetuates a fluid situation in the federal law of privilege and affords the states little inducement to adopt identical or similar schemes of privilege. The variegated pattern of privilege in both federal and state courts, described below, thus seems likely to remain the case for the foreseeable future.

§ 76.1　The Current Pattern of Privilege: (a) Privilege in Federal Courts

The Proposed Federal Rules of Evidence recognized only privileges emanating from federal sources and their enactment would have created a unitary scheme of privilege applicable to all cases regardless of jurisdictional ground. The congressionally enacted rules, however, establish a bifurcated system of privilege rules. Federal Rule of Evidence 501 provides:

> Except as otherwise required by the Constitution of the United States or provided by Act of Congress or in rules prescribed by the Supreme Court pursuant to statutory authority,

the privilege of a witness, person, government, State, or political subdivision thereof shall be governed by the principles of the common law as they may be interpreted by the courts of the United States in the light of reason and experience. However, in civil actions and proceedings, with respect to an element of a claim or defense as to which State law supplies the rule of decision, the privilege of a witness, person, government, State, or political subdivision thereof shall be determined in accordance with State law.

Under Rule 501, then, common law, "as interpreted * * * in the light of reason and experience," will determine the privileges applicable in federal question and criminal cases, while privileges in diversity actions will derive from state law. In the former types of cases, it seems likely that the rules promulgated by the Supreme Court will prove influential as indicators of "reason and experience." But it is also apparent that the intent of Rule 501 is not to limit the number and type of privileges recognized to those included in the proposed rules. A significant question exists whether this freedom should be used to recognize and apply state privileges in cases where Rule 501 does not require such to be done.

The situation with respect to cases in which state law provides the rule of decision, primarily diversity cases, is somewhat clearer. Presumably a federal court today would not, as was sometimes done prior to the enactment of Rule 501, enforce a privilege in a diversity case which is not recognized by applicable state law. A major question remains, however, as to the process by which the existence or absence of an "applicable" state privilege will be determined in conflict of law situations.

It has been argued that, given the status of Rule 501 as an Act of Congress, the federal courts, in determining the applicable state law of privilege are not constrained to accept state conflict of laws principles. Though this position has been supported by a number of commentators, a majority of the cases decided since enactment of the Federal Rules have continued to follow the doctrine of Klaxon Co. v. Stentor Electric Manufacturing Co.[1] and thus to look to state choice of law rules in determining what state's privilege should be applied.

§ 76.2 The Current Pattern of Privilege: (b) State Patterns of Privilege

State patterns in the recognition of privileges vary greatly. As developed in succeeding chapters, all states possess some form of husband-wife,[1] and attorney-client privilege.[2] All afford some protection to certain government information.[3] Most, though not all, allow at least a limited privilege to communications between physician and patient.[4] In addition several other privileges are worthy of specific mention.

Though probably not recognized at common law, a privilege protecting confidential communications between clergymen and penitents has now been adopted in all 50 states. Wigmore's seemingly grudging acceptance of the privilege perhaps reflects the difficulty of justifying its existence on exclusively utilitarian grounds, since at least where penitential communications are required or encouraged by religious tenets, they are likely to continue to be made irrespective of the presence or absence of evidentiary privilege. A firmer ground appears available in the inherent offensiveness of the secular power attempting to coerce an act violative of religious conscience. Implementing a decent regard for religious convictions while at the same time avoiding making individual conscience the ultimate measure of testimonial obligation has proved to be attended by some difficulties. Early statutory forms of the privilege undertook to privilege only penitential communications "in the course of discipline enjoined by the church" to which the communicant belongs. This limitation, however, has been urged to be unduly, perhaps unconstitutional-

ly, preferential to the Roman Catholic and a few other churches. The statutes have, accordingly, generally been broadened. Revised Uniform Rule of Evidence (1974) 505 is typical in extending the privilege generally to "confidential communication[s] by a person to a clergyman in his professional character as spiritual advisor." It remains an open question whether even such an ecumenical privilege can withstand an appropriate challenge based upon the establishment clause of the First Amendment.

The privilege is generally held to be that of the communicant and accordingly waivable by him, though some states expressly confer an independent privilege on the clergyman.

One of the most persistently advocated privileges for many years, but particularly during the past decade, has been one shielding journalists from being testimonially required to divulge the identities of news sources. The rationale asserted for this privilege is analogous to that underlying the long-standing governmental informers privilege and is exclusively utilitarian in character. Thus, it is contended that the news sources essential to supply the public's need for information will be "dried up" if their identities are subject to compelled disclosure. Numerous attempts to have the privilege enacted by federal statute have failed, and it is not one of those privileges incorporated into the Revised Uniform Rules of Evidence (1974). Moreover, the argument that a journalist's privilege is constitutionally to be implied from the First Amendment guarantee of a free press was rejected by the Supreme Court in Branzburg v. Hayes. However, taking note that this rejection did not command an absolute majority of the Court, a substantial number of lower federal courts have undertaken to recognize a qualified journalist's privilege which may be penetrated by appropriate showings on the part of the party desiring the privileged information. Though occasionally referred to as a

§ 76.1

1. 313 U.S. 487 (1941).

§ 76.2

1. See Ch. 9 infra.

2. See Ch. 10 infra.

3. See Ch. 12 infra.

4. See Ch. 11 infra.

common law creation, the privilege has generally been said to derive from the First Amendment. Some form of privilege for journalists has been created by statute, or in a few cases by judicial decision, in a substantial number of states. A few state courts have also found the privilege to be implied by state constitutional provision. Unlike other professional privileges, it is generally conceived as belonging to the journalist, to be claimed or waived irrespective of the wishes of the news source.

Communications to accountants are privileged in perhaps a third of the states. This privilege is most closely analogous to that for attorney-client, though the social objective to be furthered is arguably a distinguishable and lesser one.

In recent years much attention has been bestowed upon the plight of the rape victim, and some sort of sexual assault victim-counselor privilege has been created by statute or court decision in a substantial number of states. Such a privilege can claim a substantial basis in public policy, but inevitably comes into conflict with the constitutional rights of the criminal defendant.

Even broader acceptance has been achieved by the principle that protection by evidentiary privilege is necessary for the deliberations of medical review committees.

There is occasional recognition of privilege for communications to confidential clerks, stenographers and other "employees" generally, school teachers, school counselors, participants in group psychotherapy, nurses, marriage counselors, private detectives, and social workers. A privilege for parent-minor child communications has been recommended and has received some scanty judicial approval, as has a privilege for scientific researcher-subject.

An attempt to obtain recognition of a federal privilege protecting against disclosure of confidential peer review materials of academic institutions was rejected by the Supreme Court in University of Pennsylvania v. E.E.O.C.[5]

§ 77. The Future of Privilege

Despite the rejection by the Congress of the Proposed Federal Rules of Evidence relating to privilege and the resultant failure to effect substantive changes in this area, several concurrent developments may portend certain new directions in the development of the law of privilege.

The vehemence of the attacks leveled at certain of the proposed Federal Rules on privilege suggests that the basic concept of evidentiary privilege, despite its deleterious consequences for the administration of justice, will not be abandoned in the foreseeable future. Many of these attacks, predictably, came from groups specifically interested in the preservation or creation of particular privileges. Much more significantly, the cause of privilege was also espoused by an unprecedentedly large segment of the academic community. The latter response was in large part precipitated by a generalized concern over the increasing intrusiveness of modern society into human privacy, a concern reflected in several Supreme Court decisions conferring constitutional status upon certain aspects of privacy.

While the ultimate strategic significance of evidentiary privilege as a bastion for defending privacy values may be doubted, the focus on privacy as an operative basis for the recognition of some privileges is believed to be a healthy and overdue development. At the optimum, it may offer a theoretical basis for a more satisfactory accommodation than has heretofore been achieved between the legitimate demands for freedom against unwarranted intrusion on the one hand and the basic requirements of the judicial system on the other.

The traditionally felt need, stemming largely from Wigmore's dictum, to justify all privileges in terms of their utilitarian value leads not only to the assertion of highly questionable sociological premises, but also, affords little prospect for meaningful reconciliation of values in this area. Traditional evidentiary

5. 493 U.S. 182 (1990).

privilege necessarily paints with a broad brush since the achievement of utilitarian objectives requires privileges which are essentially absolute in character. But if it is recognized that not all privileges are based on identical considerations or will have identical effects if allowed in litigation, it will be seen that not all privileges need make such large demands. If the object aimed at is not the inducement of conduct in certain relationships but the protection of individual privacy from unnecessary or trivial intrusions, the implementation of the privilege is amenable to the finer touch of the specific solution. Thus, a decision in the particular case that sufficiently grave considerations demand disclosure will, to be sure, impact adversely on the privilege holder, but no more extended societal interest will be impaired.

Another factor may also contribute to a greater use of qualified or conditional privileges which are subject to suspension on ad hoc determination of particular need for evidence in a given case. It is already clear that the law of privilege must to some extent ac-commodate to the developing rights of criminal defendants under the Confrontation and Compulsory Process Clauses.[1] At the same time it is desirable, whenever possible, to avoid a choice between the automatic and total override of privilege whenever a criminal defendant asserts a need for privileged matter, and the dismissal of the charges if the privilege is to be sustained. At least in those instances where accomplishment of the privilege objective does not necessitate absolute protection, an in camera weighing of the potential significance of the matter sought as against the considerations of privacy underlying the privilege may represent a desirable compromise.

Though necessarily entailing a certain amount of procedural inconvenience and a considerable amount of judicial discretion, this solution has recommended itself to a number of commentators and courts. It is perhaps reasonable to predict that an increased involvement of judges in the general area of privacy and confidentiality may be in the making.

§ 77

1. See § 74.2, supra.

Chapter 9

THE PRIVILEGE FOR MARITAL COMMUNICATIONS

Table of Sections

§ 78. History and Background and Kindred Rules

We are dealing here with a late offshoot of an ancient tree. The older branches are discussed in another chapter.[1] Those earlier rules, to be sharply distinguished from the present doctrine, are first, the rule that the spouse of a party or person interested is disqualified from testifying for the other spouse, and second, the privilege of a party against having the party's husband or wife called as an adverse witness. These two earlier rules forbid the calling of the spouse as a witness at all, for or against the party, regardless of the actual testimony to be elicited, whereas the privilege presently discussed is limited to a certain class of testimony, namely communications between the spouses or more broadly in some states, information gained on account of the marital relation.

The movement for procedural reform in England in the first half of the 1800s found expression in the evidence field in agitation for the break up of the system of disqualification of parties and spouses. One of the auxiliary reasons which had been given to justify the disqualification of spouses was that of preserving marital confidences. As to the disqualification of spouses the reform was largely accomplished by the Evidence Amendment Act, 1853. On the eve of this legislation, Greenleaf writing in this country in

§ 78

1. See § 66 supra.

1842, clearly announced the existence of a distinct privilege for marital communications, and this pronouncement was echoed in England by Best in 1849, though seemingly there was little or no support for such a view in the English decisions. Moreover, the Second Report of 1853 of the Commissioners on Common Law Procedure, after rejecting the arguments for the outmoded rules of disqualification, calls attention to the special danger of "alarm and unhappiness occasioned to society by * * * compelling the public disclosure of confidential communications between husband and wife * * *" and declares that "[a]ll communications between them should be held to be privileged."

However, though the policy supporting a privilege for marital communications had thus been distinctly pointed out, there had been little occasion for its judicial recognization, since the wider disqualifications of the spouses of parties left small possibility for the question of the existence of such a privilege to arise.

Nevertheless, the English Act of 1853, mentioned above, after it abolished the disqualification of husbands and wives of the parties, enacted that "no husband shall be compellable to disclose any communication made to him by his wife during the marriage, and no wife shall be compellable to disclose any communication made to her by her husband during the marriage." [2] Moreover, nearly all the states in this country, while making spouses competent to testify, have included provisions disabling them from testifying to communications between them.

In the light of this history the Court of Appeal in England has denied that there was any common law privilege for marital communications. In this country, however, the courts have frequently said that the statutes protecting marital communications from disclosure are declaratory of the common law. Moreover, some courts have even held the "common law" rule to be in effect without benefit of statute, at least until legislatively abrogated.

In addition to the vitality which it has displayed in the courts, the rule discussed here has been viewed by some legal commentators as the most defensible of the various forms of marital privilege. However, Federal Rule of Evid. 505 as approved by the Supreme Court but deleted by the Congress, recognized no privilege for confidential communications between spouses, limiting the privilege to that of an accused in a criminal proceeding to prevent his spouse from testifying against him. The marital privilege under the Revised Uniform Rules, limited under the 1974 version of those rules to a privilege of the accused to prevent disclosure of confidential communications, was subsequently broadened by amendment of Uniform Rule of Evidence 504. The revised rule recognizes a privilege for adverse spousal testimony as well as one for confidential communications in criminal cases, and extends the latter privilege to civil cases as well. Under Federal Rule of Evidence 501, as adopted by Congress, the federal courts have continued to recognize a marital communications privilege as effective by common law.

§ 79. What Is Privileged: Communications Only, or Acts and Facts?

Greenleaf, arguing in 1842 for a privilege distinct from marital incompetency, and furnishing the inspiration for the later statutes by which the privilege was formally enacted, spoke only of "communications" and "conversations." Those later statutes themselves (except one or two) sanctioned the privilege for "communications" and for nothing beyond. Accordingly it would seem that the privilege should be limited to *expressions* intended by one spouse to convey a meaning or message to the other. These expressions may be by words, oral, written or in sign-language, or by expressive acts, as where the husband opens a trunk before his wife and points out objects therein to her. Moreover, the protection of the privilege will shield against indirect disclosure of the communication, as where a

2. St. 16 & 17 Vict. c. 83, § 3.

husband is asked for his wife's whereabouts which he learned only from her secret communication. It seems, nevertheless, that logic and policy should cause the courts to halt with communications as the furthest boundary of the privilege, and a substantial number have held steadfast at this line.

An equal or greater number of courts, however, have construed their statutes which say "communications" to extend the privilege to acts, facts, conditions, and transactions not amounting to communications at all. One group seems to announce the principle that acts done privately in the wife's presence amount to "communications." Another would go even further and say that any information secured by the wife as a result of the marital relation and which would not have been known in the absence of such relation is protected. Some at least of this latter group would hold that information secured by one spouse through observation during the marriage as to the health, or intoxication, habitual or at a particular time, or the mental condition of the other spouse, would be protected by the privilege.

All extensions beyond communications seem unjustified by the theory of this privilege. The attitude of the courts in these cases seems to reflect a confusion with the quite distinguishable purpose of preserving family harmony by disqualifying one spouse from giving any testimony whatsoever against the other.[1] Whatever the merits of the latter principle, its attempted implementation under the guise of a communications privilege can only lead to anomalous results, for the bulk of the cases involve factual situations in which the marriage has already been destroyed. It is believed a different attitude would be wiser, namely that of accepting the view that privileges in general, and this privilege for marital confidences in particular, are inept and clumsy devices for promoting the policies they profess to serve, but are extremely effective as stumbling blocks to obstruct the attainment of justice. Accordingly, at the very least, the movement should be toward restriction of these devices rather than their expansion through theoretically dubious applications.

A specific instance of development in the proper direction has recently been evident in statutes and cases which exclude from the protection of the privilege communications in furtherance of crime or fraud. This exception, long recognized to restrict the cognate privilege for attorney-client communications, seems amply justified in the present context as well.

§ 80. The Communication Must Be Confidential

Most statutes expressly limit the privilege to "confidential communications." However, even where the words used are "any communication" or simply "communications," the notion that the privilege is born of the "common law" and the fact that the pre-statutory descriptions of the privilege had clearly based it upon the policy of protecting confidences,[1] have actuated most courts to read into such statutes the requirement of confidentiality. Communications in private between husband and wife are assumed to be confidential, though of course this assumption will be strengthened if confidentiality is expressly affirmed, or if the subject is such that the communicating spouse would probably desire that the matter be kept secret, either because its disclosure would be embarrassing or for some other reason. However, a variety of factors, including the nature of the message or the circumstances under which it was delivered, may serve to rebut a claim that confidentiality was intended. In particular, if a third person (other than a child of the family) is present to the knowledge of the communicating spouse, this stretches the web of confidence beyond the marital pair, and the communication is unprivileged. If children of the family are present this likewise deprives the conversation of protection unless the children

§ 79

1. See § 66, supra.

§ 80

1. See § 78 supra.

are too young to understand what is said. The fact that the communication relates to business transactions may show that it was not intended as confidential. Examples are statements about business agreements between the spouses, or about business matters transacted by one spouse as agent for the other, or about property or conveyances. Usually such statements relate to facts which are intended later to become publicly known. To cloak them with privilege when the transactions come into litigation would be productive of special inconvenience and injustice.

§ 81. The Time of Making the Communication: Marital Status

The privilege is created to encourage marital confidences and is limited to them. Consequently, communications between the husband and wife before they were married, or after their divorce are not privileged. And attempts to assert the privilege by participants in "modern" living arrangements argued to be the functional equivalents of marriage have to date uniformly been rejected by the courts. The requirement of a valid marriage may be satisfied by a valid common law marriage, if it can be proved, but a bigamous marriage will not suffice. This latter holding should, by analogy to other privileges, be relaxed where the party seeking the benefit of the privilege was ignorant of the status of the other purported spouse. It is suggested that there is no meaningful distinction to be drawn between this latter situation and that in which a communication made during a purported marriage, later annulled for fraud by the victim of the fraud, has been held privileged.

What of a husband and wife living apart? It has been said that the privilege "should not apply when the parties are living in separation and especially, as in this case, so living under articles of separation, and the one making the communication is actively hostile to the other." Against the view, however, may be urged the consideration that communication in this context is far more likely to be related to preservation of the marriage than

are the vast bulk of admittedly privileged communications. This fact, coupled with the pragmatic difficulty involved in determining when hostility between the spouses has become implacable, argues for the more easily administered approach of terminating the privilege only upon a decree of divorce. In any event, this latter view is generally adopted.

§ 82. Hazards of Disclosure to Third Persons Against the Will of the Communicating Spouse

The weight of decision seems to support the view that the privilege does not protect against the testimony of third persons who have overheard (either accidentally or by eavesdropping) an oral communication between husband and wife, or who have secured possession or learned the contents of a letter from one spouse to another by interception, or through loss or misdelivery by the custodian. There is one important qualification which many if not most of the cases announce, namely that the privilege will not be lost if the eavesdropping, or the delivery or disclosure of the letter be due to the betrayal or connivance of the spouse to whom the message is directed. Just as that spouse would not be permitted, against the will of the communicating spouse, to betray the confidence by testifying in court to the message, so he or she may not effectively destroy the privilege by out-of-court betrayal.

The first-mentioned doctrine, that the eavesdropper or the interceptor of the letter may testify to the confidential message, is sometimes supported on the ground that the particular statute is phrased in terms of incompetency of the spouses to testify to the communication, and should not be extended to disqualify third persons. Perhaps it may better be sustained on the more general view that since the privilege has as its only effect the suppression of relevant evidence, its scope should be confined as narrowly as is consistent with reasonable protection of marital communications.

In this latter view, it seems, since the communicating spouse can ordinarily take effective precautions against overhearing, he should bear the risk of a failure to use such precautions. Moreover, if he sends a messenger with a letter, he should ordinarily assume the risk that the chosen emissary may lose or misdeliver the message. The rationale that the spouses may ordinarily take effective measures to communicate confidentially tends to break down where one or both are incarcerated. However, communications in the jailhouse are frequently held not privileged, often on the theory that no confidentiality was or could have been expected.

As has been observed elsewhere, the development of sophisticated eavesdropping techniques has led to curbs upon their use and upon the admissibility of evidence obtained thereby.[1] It has also led to including in rules governing privileged communications provisions against disclosure by third persons.

If the spouse to whom the letter is addressed dies and it is found among the effects of the deceased, may the personal representative be required or permitted to produce it in court? Here is no connivance or betrayal by the deceased spouse, and on the other hand this is not a disclosure against which the sender could effectively guard. If the privilege is to be held, as most courts do,[2] to survive the death of one of the spouses, it seems that only a court which strictly limits the effect of the statute to restraining the spouses themselves from testifying, could justify a denial of the privilege in this situation.

§ 83. Who Is the Holder of the Privilege? Enforcement and Waiver

Greenleaf in 1842, in foreshadowing the protection of marital communications, wrote of the projected rule as a "privilege" based on "public policy." Many legislatures, however, when they came to write the privilege into law phrased the rule simply as a survival in this special case of the ancient incompetency of the spouses, which the same statutes undertook to abolish or restrict. So it is often provided that the spouses are "incompetent" to testify to marital communications. Consequently, the courts frequently overlook this "common law" background[1] of privilege, and permit any party to the action to claim the benefit of the rule by objection. Doubtless counsel often fail to point out that privilege, not incompetency, is the proper classification, and that the distinctive feature of privilege is that it can only be claimed by the holder or beneficiary of the privilege, not by a party as such.[2] The latter principle is clearly correct.

Who is the holder? Wigmore's argument, that the policy of encouraging freedom of communication points to the communicating spouse as the holder, seems convincing. Under this view, in the case of a unilateral oral message or statement, of a husband to his wife, only the husband could assert the privilege, where the sole purpose is to show the expressions and attitude of the husband. If the object, however, were to show the wife's adoption of the husband's statement by her silence, then the husband's statement and her conduct both become her communication and she can claim the privilege. Similarly, if a conversation or an exchange of correspondence between them is offered to show the collective expressions of them both, either it seems could claim privilege as to the entire exchange.

A failure by the holder to assert the privilege by objection, or a voluntary revelation by the holder of the communication, or of a material part, is a waiver. The judge, however, may in some jurisdictions in his discretion protect the privilege if the holder is not present to assert it, and objection by a party not the holder may serve the purpose of invoking this discretion, though the party may not complain if the judge fails to protect this privilege belonging to the absent spouse.

§ 82

1. See § 74 supra, and §§ 169, 176 infra.

2. See § 85 infra.

§ 83

1. See § 78, supra.

2. See § 73, supra.

§ 84. Controversies in Which the Privilege Is Inapplicable

The common law privilege against adverse testimony of a spouse was subject to an exception in cases of prosecution of the husband for offenses against the wife, at least those of violence. When nineteenth century statutes in this country limited and regulated this privilege and the incompetency of spouses as witnesses and defined the new statutory privilege for confidential communications the common law exception above mentioned was usually incorporated and extended, and frequently other exceptions were added. Under these statutes it is not always clear how far the exceptions are intended to apply only to the provisions limiting the competency of the spouses as witnesses, or whether they apply also to the privilege for confidential communications. Frequently, however, in the absence of a contrary decision, it is at least arguable that the exception does have this latter application, and in some instances this intent is clearly expressed. Any other result would, in principle, indeed be difficult to justify.

The types of controversies in which the marital communication privilege is made inapplicable vary, of course, from state to state. They may be derived from express provision, from statutory implication, or from decisions based upon common law doctrine. They may be grouped as follows:

1. Prosecutions for crimes committed by one spouse against the other or against the children of either. Besides statutes in general terms, particular crimes, most frequently family desertion and pandering, are often specified, and as to these latter the withdrawal of the privilege for communications is usually explicit.

2. Actions by one of the spouses against an outsider for an intentional injury to the marital relation. Thus far this exception has been applied, sometimes under statutes, sometimes as a continuation of common law tradition, chiefly in actions for alienation of affection or for criminal conversation. It is usually applied to admit declarations expressive of the state of affection of the alienated spouse.

3. Actions by one spouse against the other. Some of the statutes are in this broader form. Some apply only to particular kinds of actions between them, of which divorce suits are most often specified. This exception for controversies between the spouses, which should extend to controversies between the representatives of the spouses, seems worthy of universal acceptance. In the analogous case of clients who jointly consult an attorney, the clients are held to have no privilege for such consultation in controversies between themselves.[1] So here it seems that husband and wife, while they would desire that their confidences be shielded from the outside world, would ordinarily anticipate that if a controversy between themselves should arise in which their mutual conversations would shed light on the merits, the interests of both would be served by full disclosure.

4. A criminal prosecution against one of the spouses in which a declaration of the other spouse made confidentially to the accused would tend to justify or reduce the grade of the offense.

§ 85. If the Communication Was Made During the Marriage, Does Death or Divorce End the Privilege?

The incompetency of husband or wife to testify for the other, and the privilege of each spouse against adverse testimony are terminated when the marriage ends by death or divorce.[1] The privilege for confidential communications of the spouses, however, was based, in the mind of its chief sponsor, Greenleaf, upon the policy of encouraging confidences, who thought that encouragement required not merely temporary but permanent secrecy. The courts in this country have accepted this need for permanent protection—though it may be an unrealistic assumption—and about one-half of our statutes codifying the privilege

§ 84

1. See § 91 infra.

§ 85

1. See § 66, supra.

explicitly provide that it continues after death or divorce. In fact, this characteristic accounts for a large proportion of the attempted invocations of the communications privilege, since if the marriage has not been terminated one of the other, more embrasive marital privileges will frequently apply. But it is probably in these cases where the marital tie has been severed that the supposed policy of the privilege has the most remote and tenuous relevance, and the possibilities of injustice in its application are most apparent. Wigmore points out that in this area, "there must arise occasional instances of hardship where ample flexibility should be allowed in the relaxation of the rule."

In the famous English case of Shenton v. Tyler, the court was faced with one of those instances of hardship. The plaintiff sued a widow and alleged that her deceased husband had made an oral secret trust, known to the widow, for the benefit of plaintiff, and sought to interrogate the widow. The widow relied on sec. 3 of the Evidence Amendment Act, 1853, as follows: " * * * no wife shall be compellable to disclose any communication made to her during the marriage." The court rejected the Greenleaf theory of a common law privilege for communications surviving the end of the marriage, and was "unable to find any warrant for extending the words of the section by construction so as to include widowers and widows and divorced persons." However debatable may be the court's position that there was no common law privilege for marital communications,[2] it seems clear that the actual holding that the privilege for communications ends when the marriage ends is preferable in policy to the contrary result reached under American statutes and decisions.

§ 86. Policy and Future of the Privilege

The argument traditionally advanced in support of the marital communications privilege is that the privilege is needed to encourage marital confidences, which confidences in turn promote harmony between husband and wife. This argument, now reiterated for almost a century and a half, obviously rests upon certain assumptions concerning the knowledge and psychology of married persons. Thus it must be assumed that spouses will know of the privilege and take its protection into account in determining to make marital confidences, or at least, which is not the same thing, that they would come to know of the absence of the privilege if it were withdrawn and be, as a result, less confiding than at present.

In the absence of any empirical validation, these propositions have appeared highly suspect to many, though not all, commentators. Thus the most convincing answer to the argument of policy appears to be that the contingency of courtroom disclosure would almost never (even if the privilege did not exist) be in the minds of the parties in considering how far they should go in their secret conversations. What encourages them to fullest frankness is not the assurance of courtroom privilege, but the trust they place in the loyalty and discretion of each other. If the secrets are not told outside the courtroom there will be little danger of their being elicited in court. In the lives of most people appearance in court as a party or a witness is an exceedingly rare and unusual event, and the anticipation of it is not one of those factors which materially influence in daily life the degree of fullness of marital disclosures. Accordingly, we must conclude that, while the danger of injustice from suppression of relevant proof is clear and certain, the probable benefits of the rule of privilege in encouraging marital confidences and wedded harmony is at best doubtful and marginal.

Probably the policy of encouraging confidences is not the prime influence in creating and maintaining the privilege. It is really a much more natural and less devious matter. It is a matter of emotion and sentiment. All of us have a feeling of indelicacy and want of decorum in prying into the secrets of husband and wife.

---

2. See § 78, supra.

As pointed out in an earlier section,[1] this "privacy" rationale, particularly in the case of marital privilege, has been widely advanced in recent years. It may be hoped that increasing recognition of the true operative basis for affording privilege to the marital partners will in turn draw with it acceptance of the logical implications of that rationale, and that the privilege can accordingly be reshaped into a less anomalous form.

A desirable first step is to recognize that delicacy and decorum, while worthy and deserving of protection, will not stand in the balance where there is a need for otherwise unobtainable evidence critical to the ascertainment of significant legal rights. This disproportion, together with the consideration that maintenance of privacy as a general objective is not critically impaired by its sacrifice in cases of particular need, argues for treating this privilege as a qualified one. This view, in turn, would remove much of the felt need to hedge the privilege narrowly about with not completely logical exceptions and qualifications, perhaps largely out of the fear that a more liberal ambit of the privilege will inexorably lead to loss of critical evidence in future cases.

Again, a particularly anomalous characteristic of the present privilege, if protection of marital privacy be accepted as its justification, is its extension to testimony sought after the termination of the marriage by death or divorce. This extension, which accounts for the majority of seriously deleterious consequences of the privilege, arguably serves, at most, the quite inferior privacy interest in the confidences of past marriages. The practical consequences of eliminating this feature would differ little from those occasioned by placing the privilege, as is sometimes done today, in the hands of the testifying spouse or former spouse. However, the expedient suggested here is thought more compatible with the evolving theory of the privilege.

Finally, though the time is yet far removed, it may someday be recognized that a communications privilege, however appropriate to professional relationships, is highly unsuited to the marital context, being at some points too broad and at others too narrow appropriately to protect the essential private aspects of marriage.

§ 86

1. See § 72, supra.

Chapter 10

THE CLIENT'S PRIVILEGE: COMMUNICATIONS BETWEEN CLIENT AND LAWYER

Table of Sections

§ 87. Background and Policy of the Privilege: (a) Theoretical Considerations

The notion that the loyalty owed by the lawyer to his client disables him from being a witness in his client's case is deep-rooted in Roman law. This Roman tradition may or may not have been influential in shaping the early English doctrine of which we find the first traces in Elizabeth's time, that the oath and honor of the barrister and the attorney protect them from being required to disclose, upon examination in court, the secrets of the client. But by the eighteenth century in England the emphasis upon the code of honor had lessened and the need of the ascertainment of truth for the ends of justice loomed larger than the pledge of secrecy. So a new justification for the lawyer's exemption from disclosing his client's secrets was found. This theory, which continues as the principal rationale of the privilege today, rests upon three propositions. First the law is complex and in order for members of the society to comply

120

with it in the management of their affairs and the settlement of their disputes they require the assistance of expert lawyers. Second, lawyers are unable to discharge this function without the fullest possible knowledge of the facts of the client's situation. And last, the client cannot be expected to place the lawyer in full possession of the facts without the assurance that the lawyer cannot be compelled, over the client's objection, to reveal the confidences in court. The consequent loss to justice of the power to bring all pertinent facts before the court is, according to the theory, outweighed by the benefits to justice (not to the individual client) of a franker disclosure in the lawyer's office.

This clearly utilitarian justification, premised on the power of the privilege to elicit certain behavior on the part of clients, has a compelling common-sense appeal. The tendency of the client in giving his story to his counsel to omit all that he suspects will make against him is a matter of every day professional observation. It makes it necessary for the prudent lawyer to cross-examine his client searchingly about possible unfavorable facts. In criminal cases the difficulty of obtaining full disclosure from the accused is well known, and would certainly become an absolute impossibility if the defendant knew that the lawyer could be compelled to repeat what he had been told.

These justifications, however, have never been convincing to all. Jeremy Bentham, perhaps the most famous of the privilege's critics to date, argued that the privilege is not needed by the innocent party with a righteous cause or defense, and that the guilty should not be given its aid in concerting a false one. Betham's apocalyptic division of the client world into righteous and guilty seems somewhat naive in a time when even the best-intended may doubt their compliance with an ever more overwhelming body of law. Nevertheless, none can deny the privilege's unfortunate tendency to suppress the truth, and it has commonly been urged that it is only the greater benefit of increased candor which justifies the continuation of the privilege. Wigmore, the great champion and architect of the privilege, subscribed to this view, though he acknowledged that "Its benefits are all indirect and speculative; its obstruction is plain and concrete." [1]

The trend of recent years toward attempted empirical verification of the intuitive judgments of the past has lent a special cogency to Wigmore's assessment. For the degree of efficacy of the privilege in achieving its avowed aims, speculated to be quite low by critics, is ironically likely to prove undemonstrable by reason of the privilege itself. Despite these difficulties, it is of course possible to proceed from the Cartesian postulate that the privilege effects some unknown and unknowable marginal alteration in client behavior. But such minimal claims, even when combined with efforts to structure the privilege so as to confine its operation to contexts in which it will most probably have an effect, seem to fall short of an adequate justification.

As a possible ancillary justification, it is today suggested with increasing frequency that considerations of privacy should play a role in supporting and ultimately defining the privilege. To date, this rationale has achieved only very little recognition in the courts as a supporting, much less a sufficient, justification for the attorney-client privilege. It is probable that the ultimate fate of this theory will depend upon the success of its advocates in suggesting what implications for the parameters for the privilege are implied by such a rationale.

At the present time it seems most realistic to portray the attorney-client privilege as supported in part by its traditional utilitarian justification, and in part by the integral role it is perceived to play in the adversary system itself. Our system of litigation casts the lawyer in the role of fighter for the party whom he represents. A strong tradition of loyalty attaches to the relationship of attorney and

---

§ 87

1. 8 Wigmore, Evidence § 2291, p. 554 (McNaughton rev. 1961).

client, and this tradition would be outraged by routine examination of the lawyer as to the client's confidential disclosures regarding professional business. To the extent that the evidentiary privilege, then, is integrally related to an entire code of professional conduct, it is futile to envision drastic curtailment of the privilege without substantial modification of the underlying ethical system to which the privilege is merely ancillary.

The foregoing state of affairs is clearly less than optimum from the standpoint that predictability in the application of the privilege, logically indispensable for any utilitarian effect, is largely lacking in many areas. Advocates of the supposedly inviolate privilege of yesteryear perceive even greater uncertainties interjected by the increasing uses of in camera inspection to determine the legitimacy of claims of privilege, and even in some jurisdictions the use of a balancing test to determine whether the privilege will be honored. While a balancing approach to the privilege is not totally consistent with the privilege's current rationales, it is suggested that increased use of these expedients will ultimately result in a fairer, surer, and more rational administration of the privilege than could be achieved through the traditional methodology of controlling its scope through the liberal extension of exceptions and application of waiver doctrine.

A clear statement of the scope of the privilege as now generally accepted is embodied in the Revised Uniform Evid.Rules (1986).[2]

2. Revised Uniform Rule of Evidence (1986 amendment) 502:

(a) **Definitions.** As used in this rule:

(1) A "client" is a person, public officer, or corporation, association, or other organization or entity, either public or private, who is rendered professional legal services by a lawyer, or who consults a lawyer with a view to obtaining professional legal services from him.

(2) A representative of the client is one having authority to obtain professional legal services, or to act on advice rendered pursuant thereto, on behalf of the client.

(3) A "lawyer" is a person authorized, or reasonably believed by the client to be authorized, to engage in the practice of law in any state or nation.

(4) A "representative of the lawyer" is one employed by the lawyer to assist the lawyer in the rendition of professional legal services.

(5) A communication is "confidential" if not intended to be disclosed to third persons other than those to whom disclosure is made in furtherance of the rendition of professional legal services to the client or those reasonably necessary for the transmission of the communication.

(b) **General Rule of Privilege.** A client has a privilege to refuse to disclose and to prevent any other person from disclosing confidential communications made for the purpose of facilitating the rendition of professional legal services to the client (1) between himself or his representative and his lawyer or his lawyer's representative, (2) between his lawyer and the lawyer's representative, (3) by him or his representative or his lawyer or a representative of the lawyer to a lawyer or a representative of a lawyer representing another party in a pending action and concerning a matter of common interest therein, (4) between representatives of the client or between the client and a representative of the client, or (5) among lawyers and their representatives representing the same client.

(c) **Who May Claim the Privilege.** The privilege may be claimed by the client, his guardian or conservator, the personal representative of a deceased client, or the successor, trustee, or similar representative of a corporation, association, or other organization, whether or not in existence. The person who was the lawyer or the lawyer's representative at the time of the communication is presumed to have authority to claim the privilege but only on behalf of the client.

(d) **Exceptions.** There is no privilege under this rule:

(1) *Furtherance of Crime or Fraud.* If the services of the lawyer were sought or obtained to enable or aid anyone to commit or plan to commit what the client knew or reasonably should have known to be a crime or fraud;

(2) *Claimants Through Same Deceased Client.* As to a communication relevant to an issue between parties who claim through the same deceased client, regardless of whether the claims are by testate or intestate succession or by inter vivos transaction;

(3) *Breach of Duty by a Lawyer or Client.* As to a communication relevant to an issue of breach of duty by the lawyer to his client or by the client to his lawyer;

(4) *Document Attested by a Lawyer.* As to a communication relevant to an issue concerning an attested document to which the lawyer is an attesting witness;

(5) *Joint Clients.* As to a communication relevant to a matter of common interest between or among two or more clients if the communication was made by any of them to a lawyer retained or consulted in common, when offered in an action between or among any of the clients; or

(6) *Public Officer or Agency.* As to a communication between a public officer or agency and its lawyers unless the communication concerns a pending investigation, claim, or action and the court deter-

§ 87.1   Background and Policy of the Privilege: (b) Modern Applications

The application of the privilege for the benefit of a corporate client, as distinguished from a natural person, was never questioned until a federal district court in 1962 held that a corporation is not entitled to claim the privilege.[1] The decision attracted wide attention and much comment, most of which was adverse, until reversed on appeal.[2] There seems to be little reason to believe that the issue will arise soon again.

The scope of the privilege in the corporate context, however, has presented an exceptionally troublesome question which is even yet not fully resolved. The difficulty is basically one of extrapolating the essential operating conditions of the privilege from the paradigm case of the traditional individual client who both supplies information to, and receives counsel from, the attorney. Are both of these aspects of the relationship to be protected in the corporate setting, in which the corporate agents in a position to furnish the pertinent facts are not necessarily those empowered to take action responsive to legal advice based upon those facts? Early decisions focused upon the first half of this dichotomy, and extended the privilege expansively to communications from any "officer or employee" of the client corporation. This emphasis was dramatically reversed by the case of City of Philadelphia v. Westinghouse Electric Corp.,[3] which propounded a "control group" test under which the privilege was restricted to communications made by those corporate functionaries "in a position to control or even to take a substantial part in a decision about any action which the corporation may take upon the advice of the attorney."

The "control group" theory was widely, though not universally, followed by the courts until the 1981 decision of the Supreme Court in Upjohn Co. v. United States.[4] While the Court specifically declined in Upjohn to attempt the formulation of a definitive rule, it did specifically reject the control group principle as one which "cannot * * * govern the development of the law in this area." The principal deficiency which the Court noted as inherent in the control group test is its failure to recognize the function of the privilege as protecting the flow of information to the advising attorney. The opinion does suggest limitations however, in that such information will be privileged only if: (1) it is communicated for the express purpose of securing legal advice for the corporation; (2) it relates to the specific corporate duties of the communicating employee; and (3) it is treated as confidential within the corporation itself.

The Upjohn decision evoked a large amount of commentary, much of which has been critical. In addition to the decision's failure to articulate the scope of the privilege of corporations more clearly, another frequent criticism has been Upjohn's reliance upon a utilitarian rationale without at the same time limiting the privilege to instances where it is likely to be effective for its stated purpose. Thus a lower level corporate employee sufficiently sophisticated to factor an evidentiary privilege into his decision to communicate with a corporate attorney is unlikely to be reassured by a privilege which is waivable in the exclusive discretion of the corporation. At a minimum, the privilege should apply only to corporate employees who either have, or are expressly conferred, the power to assert the privilege.

Though the Upjohn decision is not rested upon constitutional grounds, and is thus not

---

mines that disclosure will seriously impair the ability of the public officer or agency to process the claim or conduct a pending investigation, litigation, or proceeding in the public interest.

§ 87.1

1. Radiant Burners, Inc. v. American Gas Association, 207 F.Supp. 771 (N.D.Ill.1962).

2. Radiant Burners, Inc. v. American Gas Association, 320 F.2d 314, 98 A.L.R.2d 228, and note, (7th Cir.1963).

The case is remarkable for the number of amici curiae briefs urging reversal including briefs from the Chicago Bar Ass'n, the Illinois State Bar Ass'n, and the American Bar Ass'n.

3. 210 F.Supp. 483 (E.D.Pa.1962), mandamus and prohibition denied sub nom. General Electric Co. v. Kirkpatrick, 312 F.2d 742 (3d Cir.1962), cert. denied 372 U.S. 943.

4. 449 U.S. 383 (1981).

binding upon the states, it has had considerable influence outside the federal system. At the same time, some states continue to subscribe to the control group test, thus adding the identity of the forum in which the privilege will ultimately be asserted to other sources of uncertainty as to its scope.

An *Upjohn* extension of the corporate attorney-client privilege almost necessitates extension of the privilege in other organizational structures. While under the control group test the scope of the corporate privilege might be roughly likened to that available to a proprietorship, extension to lower level employees without a corresponding extension to employees of various other entities is probably politically as well as theoretically indefensible. Where the entity in question is governmental, however, significantly different considerations appear, which have led a number of states substantially to limit the privilege for such entities.

As noted above, there are situations which draw into question the application of the conventional rule that a corporation's privilege may be asserted or waived by the management of the corporation. One such situation is the derivative stockholder's action, in which both parties claim to be acting in the corporate interest. In the leading case of Garner v. Wolfinbarger,[5] the court addressed the problem thus raised by recognizing a qualified privilege on the part of the corporate management, but one which may be pierced by a showing of good cause by the shareholders. Subsequent decisions, however, have found the "mutuality of interest" between management and shareholders relied upon in *Garner* to be lacking in a variety of similar situations.

§ 88. The Professional Relationship

The privilege for communications of a client with his lawyer hinges upon the client's belief that he is consulting a lawyer in that capacity and his manifested intention to seek professional legal advice. It is sufficient if he reasonably believes that the person consulted is a lawyer, though in fact he is not. Communications in the course of preliminary discussion with a view to employing the lawyer are privileged though the employment is in the upshot not accepted. The burden of proof rests on the person asserting the privilege to show that the consultation was a professional one. Payment or agreement to pay a fee, however, is not essential. But where one consults an attorney not as a lawyer but as a friend or as a business adviser or banker, or negotiator, or as an accountant, or where the communication is to the attorney acting as a "mere scrivener" or as an attesting witness to a will or deed, or as an executor or as agent, the consultation is not professional nor the statement privileged. There is some conflict in the decisions as to whether the privilege is available for communications to an administrative practitioner who is not a lawyer. However, the privilege will generally be applicable even where the services performed by a lawyer are not necessarily available only from members of the legal profession.

Ordinarily an attorney can lawfully hold himself out as qualified to practice only in the state in which he is licensed, and consultation elsewhere on a continuing basis would traditionally not be privileged, but exceptionally by custom he might lawfully be consulted elsewhere in respect to isolated transactions, and Revised Uniform Evidence Rule (1986 amendment) 502(a)(3) requires only that he be authorized or reasonably be believed to be authorized "in any state or nation."

Traditionally, the relationship sought to be fostered by the privilege has been that between the lawyer and a private client, but more recently the privilege has been held to extend to communications to an attorney representing the state. However, disclosures to the public prosecuting attorney by an informer are not within the attorney-client privilege, but an analogous policy of protecting the giving of such information has led to the recognition of a privilege against the disclosure of the identity of the informer, unless the trial judge finds that such disclosure is necessary in the interests of justice. Communications to an attorney appointed by the court to serve the

---

5. 430 F.2d 1093 (5th Cir.1970), cert. denied 401 U.S. 974.

interest of a party are of course within the privilege. A communication by a lawyer to a member of the Board of Governors of the state bar association, revealing a fraudulent conspiracy in which he had been engaged and expressing his desire to resign from the practice of law was held not privileged.

Wigmore argued for a privilege analogous to the lawyer-client privilege for "confessions or similar confidences" made privately by persons implicated in a wrong or crime to the judge of a court. As to judges generally there seems little justification for such a privilege if the policy-motive is the furtherance of the administration of justice by encouraging a full disclosure. Unlike the lawyer the judge needs no private disclosures in advance of trial to enable him to perform his functions. In fact such revelations would ordinarily embarrass rather than aid him in carrying out his duties as a trial judge. The famous case of Lindsey v. People,[1] however, raised the question whether the judge of a juvenile court does not stand in a special position with regard to confidential disclosures by children who come before him. The majority of the court held that when a boy under promise of secrecy confessed to the judge that he had fired the shot that killed his father the judge was compellable, on the trial of the boy's mother for murder, to divulge the confession. The court pointed out that a parent who had received such a confidence would be compellable to disclose. In the case of this particular court the need for encouraging confidences is clear, but in most cases the most effective encouragement will come from the confidence-inspiring personality of the judge, even without the aid of assurances of secrecy. The court's conclusion that the need for secrecy for this type of disclosure does not outweigh the sacrifice to the administration of justice from the suppression of the evidence seems justifiable.

§ 89. Subject–Matter of the Privilege: (a) Communications

The modern justification of the privilege, namely, that of encouraging full disclosure by

the client for the furtherance of the administration of justice,[1] might suggest that the privilege is only a one-way one, operating to protect communications of the client or his agents to the lawyer or his clerk but not vice versa. However, it is generally held that the privilege will protect at least those attorney to client communications which would have a tendency to reveal the confidences of the client. In fact, only rarely will the attorney's words be relevant for any purpose other than to show the client's communications circumstantially, or to establish an admission by the client by his failure to object. Accordingly, the simpler and preferable rule, adopted by a number of statutes and the Revised Uniform Evidence Rules (1974) and by the better reasoned cases, extends the protection of the privilege also to communications by the lawyer to the client.

An even more embracive view, adopted by statute in a few states, would protect against disclosure by the attorney of any knowledge he has gained while acting as such, even information obtained from sources other than the client. Such an extension finds no justification in the modern utilitarian theory of the privilege. In any event, the more widely prevailing rule does not bar divulgence by the attorney of information communicated to him or his agents by third persons. Nor does information so obtained become privileged by being in turn related by the attorney to the client in the form of advice.

The commonly imposed limitation of protection to communications passing between client and attorney, while logically derived from the policy rationale of the privilege, does raise certain problems of construction where the information acquired by the attorney does not come in the conventional form of oral or written assertions by the client. Initially it is fairly easy to conclude, as most authority holds, that observations by the lawyer which might be made by anyone, and which involve no communicative intent by the client, are

1. See § 87 supra.

not protected. Conversely, testimony relating intentionally communicative acts of the client, as where he rolls up his sleeve to reveal a hidden scar or opens the drawer of his desk to display a revolver, would as clearly be precluded as would the recounting of statements conveying the same information. Much more problematic are cases in which the client delivers tangible evidence such as stolen property to the attorney, or confides facts enabling the attorney to come into the possession of such evidence. Here the decisions are somewhat conflicting, reflecting the virtual impossibility of separating the act of confidence which may legitimately be within the privilege from the preexisting evidentiary fact which may not. To resolve the dilemma, one carefully reasoned argument is that the privilege should not operate to bar the attorney's disclosure of the circumstances of acquisition, since to preclude the attorney's testimony would offer the client a uniquely safe opportunity to divest himself of incriminating evidence without leaving an evidentiary trial.

Difficulties also arise in applying the communications-only theory when one assisting the lawyer, e.g., an examining physician, learns and communicates to the lawyer matters not known to the client. The privilege seems to apply with respect to the communication itself. If the physician is considered as aligned with the client, his knowledge would be that of the client and not privileged; but if aligned with the lawyer, the privilege seems to apply, as held in the leading case.

The application of the privilege to writings presents practical problems requiring discriminating analysis. A professional communication in writing, as a letter from client to lawyer for example, will of course be privileged. These written privileged communications are steadily to be distinguished from preexisting documents or writings, such as deeds, wills, and warehouse receipts, not in themselves constituting communications between client and lawyer. As to these preexisting documents two notions come into play. First, the client may make communications

about the document by words or by acts, such as sending the document to the lawyer for perusal or handing it to him and calling attention to its terms. These communications, and the knowledge of the terms and appearance of the documents which the lawyer gains thereby are privileged from disclosure by testimony in court. Second, on a different footing entirely stands the question, shall a lawyer who has been entrusted with the possession of a document by his client be subject to an order of court requiring him to produce the document at the trial or in pretrial discovery proceedings whether for inspection or for use in evidence? The policy of encouraging full disclosure does of course apply to encouraging the client to apprise his lawyer of the terms of all relevant documents, and the disclosure itself and the lawyer's knowledge gained thereby as we have seen are privileged. It is true also that placing the documents in the lawyer's hands is the most convenient means of disclosure. But the next step, that of adding to the privilege for communications a privilege against production of the preexisting documents themselves, when they would be subject to production if still in the possession of the client, would be an intolerable obstruction to justice. To prevent the court's gaining access to a relevant document a party would only have to send it to his lawyer. So here this principle is controlling: if a document would be subject to an order for production if it were in the hands of the client it will be equally subject to such an order if it is in the hands of his attorney. An opposite conclusion would serve the policy of encouraging the client to make full disclosure to his lawyer right enough, but reasonable encouragement is given by the privilege for communications *about* documents, and the price of an additional privilege would be intolerably high. There are other doctrines which may impel a court to recognize a privilege against production of a preexisting document,[2] but not the doctrine of privilege for lawyer-client communications.

2. See § 96 infra.

§ 90. Subject–Matter of the Privilege: (b) Fact of Employment and Identity of the Client

When a client consults an attorney for a legitimate purpose, he will seldom, but may occasionally, desire to keep secret the very fact of consultation or employment of the lawyer. Nevertheless, consultation and employment are something more than a mere private or personal engagement. They are the calling into play of the services of an officer licensed by the state to act in certain ways in furtherance of the administration of justice, and vested with powers of giving advice on the law, of drafting documents, and of filing pleadings and motions and appearing in court for his client, which are limited to this class of officers.

Does the privilege for confidential communications extend to the fact of consulting or employing such an officer, when intended to be confidential? The traditional and still generally applicable rule denies the privilege for the fact of consultation or employment, including the component facts of the identity of the client, such identifying facts about him as his address and occupation, the identity of the lawyer, and the payment and amount of fees. Similarly, factual communications by the lawyer to the client concerning logistical matters such as trial dates are not privileged.

Several reasons have been advanced as a basis for denying protection to the client's identity, most notably that "the mere fact of the engagement of counsel is out of the rule [of privilege] because the privilege and duty of silence do not arise until the fact is ascertained." Additionally, it is said that a party to legal proceedings is entitled to know the identity of the adversary who is putting in motion or staying the machinery of the court. Such propositions, however, shed little light on the real issue, i.e., whether client anonymity is in some cases essential to obtaining the proper objectives of the privilege.

The inadequacy of a purely simplistic rule excluding client identity from the coverage of

the privilege was revealed by the facts of the leading case of Baird v. Koerner,[1] in which the court upheld a claim of privilege by an attorney who had mailed a check for back taxes to the IRS on behalf of an anonymous client. Any other result on the facts of *Baird* would seem inconceivable, and the decision has served a wholesome purpose by introducing an element of flexibility into the general rule. However, a number of decisions following *Baird* arguably vastly extended the exceptions to the rule. Thus it was variously stated that exception is made "when the disclosure of the client's identity by his attorney would have supplied the last link in a existing chain of incriminating evidence * * *," or "where * * * a strong probability exists that disclosure of such information would implicate the client in the very criminal activity for which legal advice was sought." Such decisions may have blazed a false trail in making the exceptions to the rule turn too largely upon the question of the severity of potential harm to the client rather than upon considerations germane to the privilege.

Today, happily, there is a marked trend toward refocusing upon the essential purpose of the privilege by extending its protection to client identity and fee arrangements only if the net effect of the disclosure would be to reveal the nature of a client communication. It is to be hoped that this approach will increasingly serve to deny protection where agencies performed by attorneys are no necessary part of the attorney's unique role nor appropriate for immunization from public disclosure and scrutiny. One who reviews the cases in this area will be struck by the prevailing flavor of chicanery and sharp practice pervading most of the attempts to suppress proof of professional employment, and general application of a rule of disclosure seems the approach most consonant with the preservation of the repute of the lawyer's high calling. At the same time, much should depend upon the client's objective in seeking preservation of anonymity, and cases will arise in which

§ 90

1. 279 F.2d 623 (9th Cir.1960).

protection of the client's identity is both proper and in the public interest.

§ 91. The Confidential Character of the Communications: Presence of Third Persons and Agents: Joint Consultations and Employments: Controversies Between Client and Attorney

It is of the essence of the privilege that it is limited to those communications which the client either expressly made confidential or which he could reasonably assume under the circumstances would be understood by the attorney as so intended. This common law requirement seems to be read into those statutes which codify the privilege without mentioning the confidentiality requirement. A mere showing that the communication was from client to attorney does not suffice, but the circumstances indicating the intention of secrecy must appear. Wherever the matters communicated to the attorney are intended by the client to be made public or revealed to third persons, obviously the element of confidentiality is wanting. Similarly, if the same statements have been made by the client to third persons on other occasions this is persuasive that like communications to the lawyer were not intended as confidential.

Questions as to the effect of the presence of persons other than the client and the lawyer often arise. At the extremes answers would be clear. Presumably the presence of a casual disinterested third person within hearing to the client's knowledge would demonstrate that the communication was not intended to be confidential. On the other hand if the help of an interpreter is necessary to enable the client to consult the lawyer his presence would not deprive the communication of its confidential and privileged character. Moreover, in cases where the client has one of his agents attend the conference, or the lawyer calls in his clerk or confidential secretary, the presence of these intermediaries will be assumed not to militate against the confidential nature of the consultation, and presumably this would not be made to depend upon whether the presence of the agent, clerk or secretary was in the particular instance reasonably necessary to the matter in hand. It is the way business is generally done and that is enough. As to relatives and friends of the client, the results of the cases are not consistent, but it seems that here not only might it be asked whether the client reasonably understood the conference to be confidential but also whether the presence of the relative or friend was reasonably necessary for the protection of the client's interests in the particular circumstances.

When two or more persons, each having an interest in some problem, or situation, jointly consult an attorney, their confidential communications with the attorney, though known to each other, will of course be privileged in a controversy of either or both of the clients with the outside world, that is, with parties claiming adversely to both or either of those within the original charmed circle. But it will often happen that the two original clients will fall out between themselves and become engaged in a controversy in which the communications at their joint consultation with the lawyer may be vitally material. In such a controversy it is clear that the privilege is inapplicable. In the first place the policy of encouraging disclosure by holding out the promise of protection seems inapposite, since as between themselves neither would know whether he would be more helped or handicapped, if in any dispute between them, both could invoke the shield of secrecy. And secondly, it is said that they had obviously no intention of keeping these secrets from each other, and hence as between themselves it was not intended to be confidential. In any event, it is a qualification of frequent application and of even wider potentiality, not always recognized. Thus, in the situation mentioned in the previous paragraph where a client calls into the conference with the attorney one of the client's agents, and matters are discussed which bear on the agent's rights against the client, it would seem that in a subsequent controversy between client and agent, the limitation on the privilege accepted in the joint consultation cases should furnish a controlling analogy.

One step beyond the joint consultation where communications by two clients are made directly in each other's hearing is the situation where two parties separately interested in some contract or undertaking, as in the case of borrower and lender or insurer and insured, engage the same attorney to represent their respective interests, and each communicates separately with the attorney about some phase of the common transaction. Here again it seems that the communicating client, knowing that the attorney represents the other party also, would not ordinarily intend that the facts communicated should be kept secret from him. Whether the doctrine of limited confidentiality should be applied to communications by an insured to an agent of the insurer bound by contract to provide the defense for both has provoked differing judicial reactions. Where the statement is made directly to the attorney hired by the insurer, there is no question that the privilege applies in an action brought by a third person, nor does it seem disputed that there is no privilege where the controversy is between the insured, or someone claiming under him, and the company itself over the company's liability under the policy.

The weight of authority seems to support the view that when client and attorney become embroiled in a controversy between themselves, as in an action by the attorney for compensation or by the client for damages for the attorney's negligence, the seal is removed from the attorney's lips. Though sometimes rested upon other grounds it seems that here again the notion that as between the participants in the conference the intention was to disclose and not to withhold the matters communicated offers a plausible reason. As to what is a controversy between lawyer and client the decisions do not limit their holdings to litigations between them, but have said that whenever the client, even in litigation between third persons, makes an imputation against the good faith of his attorney in respect to his professional services, the

curtain of privilege drops so far as necessary to enable the lawyer to defend his conduct. Perhaps the whole doctrine, that in controversies between attorney and client the privilege is relaxed, may best be based upon the ground of practical necessity that if effective legal service is to be encouraged the privilege must not stand in the way of the lawyer's just enforcement of his rights to be paid a fee and to protect his reputation. The only question about such a principle is whether in all cases the privilege ought not to be subject to the same qualification, that it should yield when the evidence sought is necessary to the attainment of justice.

§ 92. The Client as the Holder of the Privilege: Who May Assert, and Who Complain on Appeal of Its Denial?

A rule regulating the *competency* of evidence or of witnesses—a so-called "exclusionary" rule—is normally founded on the policy of safeguarding the fact-finding process against error, and it is assertable by the party against whom the evidence is offered. The earmarks of a *privilege,* as we have seen, are first, that it is not designed to protect the fact-finding process but is intended to protect some "outside" interest, other than the ascertainment of truth at the trial, and second, that it cannot be asserted by the adverse party as such, but only by the person whose interest the particular rule of privilege is intended to safeguard.[1] While once it was conceived that the privilege was set up to protect the lawyer's honor, we know that today it is agreed that the basic policy of the rule is that of encouraging clients to lay the facts fully before their counsel. They will be encouraged by a privilege which they themselves have the power to invoke. To extend any benefit or advantage to someone as attorney, or as party to a suit, or to people generally, will be to suppress relevant evidence without promoting the purpose of the privilege.

Of course, a party may be the holder of a privilege.

§ 92
1. See the discussion in § 72, supra of the distinction between competency and privilege.

Accordingly it is now generally agreed that the privilege is the client's and his alone, and Revised Uniform Rule (1974) 502(b) vests the privilege in the client. It is thought that this would be recognized even in those states which, before modern notions of privilege and policy were adequately worked out, codified the rule in terms of inadmissibility of evidence of communications, or of incompetency of the attorney to testify thereto. These statutes are generally held not to be intended to modify the common law doctrines.

It is not surprising that the courts, often faced with statutes drafted in terms of obsolete theories, and reaching these points rarely and usually incidentally, have not worked out a consistent pattern of consequences of this accepted view that the rule is one of privilege and that the privilege is the client's. It is believed that the applications suggested below are well grounded in reason and are supported by some authority, whether of text or decision.

First, it is clear that the client may assert the privilege even though he is not a party to the cause wherein the privileged testimony is sought to be elicited. Second, if he is present at the hearing whether as party, witness, or bystander he must assert the privilege personally or by attorney, or it will be waived. Third, in some jurisdictions, if he is not present at the taking of testimony, nor a party to the proceedings, the privilege may be called to the court's attention by anyone present, such as the attorney for the absent client, or a party in the case, or the court of its own motion may protect the privilege. Fourth: While if an asserted privilege is erroneously sustained, the aggrieved party may of course complain on appeal of the exclusion of the testimony, the erroneous denial of the privilege can only be complained of by the client whose privilege has been infringed. This opens the door to appellate review by the client if he is also a party and suffers adverse judgment. If he is not a party, the losing party in the cause, by the better view is

without recourse. Relevant, competent testimony has come in, and the privilege was not created for his benefit. But the witness, whether he is the client or his attorney, may refuse to answer and suffer an adjudication of contempt and may, in some jurisdictions at least, secure review on habeas corpus if the privilege was erroneously denied. This remedy, however, is calculated to interrupt and often disrupt progress of the cause on trial. Does a lawyer on the witness stand who is asked to make disclosures which he thinks may constitute an infringement of his client's privilege, owe a duty to refuse to answer and if necessary to test the judge's ruling on habeas corpus or appeal from a judgment of contempt? It seems clear that, unless in a case of flagrant disregard of the law by the judge, the lawyer's duty is merely to present his view that the testimony is privileged, and if the judge rules otherwise, to submit to his decision.

§ 93. Waiver

Since as we have seen, it is the client who is the holder of the privilege, the power to waive it is his, and he alone, or his attorney or agent acting with his authority, or his representative may exercise this power. In the case of the corporation, the power to claim or waive the privilege generally rests with corporate management, i.e., ultimately with the board of directors.

Waiver may be found, as Wigmore points out, not merely from words or conduct expressing an intention to relinquish a known right, but also from conduct such as partial disclosure which would make it unfair for the client to invoke the privilege thereafter.[1] Finding waiver in situations in which forfeiture of the privilege was not subjectively intended by the holder is consistent with the view, expressed by some cases and authorities, that the essential function of the privilege is to protect a confidence which, once revealed

§ 93
1. 8 Wigmore, Evidence § 2327 (McNaughton rev. 1961).

by any means, leaves the privilege with no legitimate function to perform. Logic notwithstanding, it would appear poor policy to allow the privilege to be overthrown by theft or fraud, and in fact most authority requires that to effect a waiver a disclosure must at least be voluntary.

Given the scope of modern discovery and the realities of contemporary litigation, a question of great practical importance today is whether a voluntary but inadvertent disclosure should result in waiver. In earlier times, the burden of avoiding such a disclosure of privileged, and the consequent waiver of the privilege, was relatively slight compared to that encountered today where enormous quantities of documents may be sought by an opponent through discovery. Under current conditions, some privileged material is likely to pass through even the most tightly woven screen. Since the consequences of such an oversight are potentially staggering, the question is raised as to whether traditional waiver doctrine ought to be modified. Not surprisingly, the decisions in the area have been somewhat divergent. However, while some courts apparently still adhere to a rather strict approach to waiver, others have considered factors such as the excusability of the error, whether prompt attempt to remedy the error was made, and whether preservation of the privilege will occasion unfairness to the opponent. The costs of attempting to avoid waiver under a strict rule would argue strongly for modification along these lines, and it is believed that the decisions are tending in this direction.

Turning then to the specific contexts in which waiver may be argued to occur, it will be recalled that as noted in an earlier section the commencement of a malpractice action against the attorney by the client will constitute a waiver of the privilege by the latter.[2] There are, in addition, a variety of other types of actions in which the advice of an attorney will sometimes be relied upon in support of a claim or defense. It has accordingly become established that if a party interjects the "ad-

vice of counsel" as an essential element of a claim or defense, then that party waives the privilege as to all advice received concerning the same subject matter. While there can be no doubt of the desirability of a rule preventing a party from relying upon the advice of counsel as the basis of a claim or defense while at the same time frustrating a full exploration of the character of that advice, the problem of defining when such an issue has been interjected is an extremely difficult one. The cases are generally agreed that filing or defending a lawsuit does not waive the privilege. By contrast, specific reliance upon the advice either in pleading or testimony will generally be seen as waiving the privilege. Some decisions have gone much further, and have extended the doctrine broadly to cases in which a mental state asserted by the client is sought to be shown inconsistent with the advice of counsel. Such extensions seem dubious lacking full acceptance of the Benthamite principle that the privilege ought to be overthrown to facilitate the search for truth.

Of course, if the holder of the privilege fails to claim his privilege by objecting to disclosure by himself or another witness when he has an opportunity to do so, he waives his privilege as to the communications so disclosed.

By the prevailing view, which seems correct, the mere voluntary taking the stand by the client as a witness in a suit to which he is party and testifying to facts which were the subject of consultation with his counsel is no waiver of the privilege for secrecy of the communications to his lawyer. It is the communication which is privileged, not the facts. If on direct examination, however, he testifies to the privileged communications, in part, this is a waiver as to the remainder of the privileged consultation or consultations about the same subject.

What if the client is asked on cross-examination about the communications with his lawyer, and he responds without asserting his claim of privilege? Is this a waiver? Unless

2. Section 91, supra.

there are some circumstances which show that the client was surprised or misled, it seems that the usual rule that the client's failure to claim the privilege when to his knowledge testimony infringing it is offered, would apply here, and that the decisions treating such testimony on cross-examination as being involuntary and not constituting a waiver are hardly supportable.

How far does the client waive by calling the attorney as a witness? If the client elicits testimony from the lawyer-witness as to privileged communications this obviously would waive as to all consultations relating to the same subject, just as the client's own testimony would. It would seem also that by calling the lawyer as a witness he opens the door for the adversary to impeach him by showing his interest. And it seems reasonable to contend as Wigmore does that if the client uses the lawyer to prove matter which he would only have learned in the course of his employment this again should be considered a waiver as to related privileged communications. But merely to call the lawyer to testify to facts known by him apart from his employment should not be deemed a waiver of the privilege. That would attach too harsh a condition on the exercise of the privilege. Unless the lawyer-witness is acting as counsel in the case on trial, there is no violation of the Code of Professional Responsibility, and if he is, it recognizes that his testifying may be essential to the ends of justice. Moreover, these are matters usually governed not by the client but by the lawyer, to whom the ethical mandate is addressed.

In an earlier section [3] discussing a witness' use of a writing to refresh his recollection for purposes of testifying, it was pointed out that, under both common law and Federal Evidence Rule 612, if a witness consulted a writing to refresh his recollection while testifying, opposing counsel is entitled to inspect it, to cross-examine the witness upon it, and to introduce in evidence portions that relate to the testimony of the witness. It was further pointed out that if the document were privileged, e.g. an attorney-client communication, such act of consultation would effect a waiver of the privilege.[4] And finally, the problem area was said to be when the privileged writing was consulted by the witness prior to testifying. At common law authority generally was against requiring disclosure of writings consulted prior to testifying, and under that view the problem of waiver of privilege does not arise. However, an increasing number of cases have allowed disclosure, and Federal Evidence Rule 612 gives the trial judge discretion to order disclosure. Should this discretionary power of the judge extend also to deciding whether a waiver of privilege has occurred? Or should it be said that on the one hand waiver never occurs, or on the other that it always occurs? The Report of the House Committee on the Judiciary took a strict no-waiver position,[5] but no language to that effect was incorporated in Rule 612. Nor was there included any specific provision that privilege should always be waived. The discretionary provision was inserted almost as a matter of necessity to limit disclosure of the potentially vast volume and variety of documents that might be consulted before testifying to those truly bearing on the testimony of the witness, and similar considerations are pertinent to the waiver question. While the cases are mixed, the preferred view seems to be that the judge's discretion extends not only to the threshold question whether connection with the testimony is sufficient to warrant disclosure but also to the question whether its importance is sufficient to override the privilege, given all the circumstances.

When at an earlier trial or stage of the case the privilege has been waived and testimony as to the privileged communications elicited without objection, the prevailing view is that this is a waiver also for any subsequent hearing of the same case.

3. See § 9 supra.

4. See § 9 supra.

5. "The Committee intends that nothing in the Rule be construed as barring the assertion of a privilege with respect to writings used by a witness to refresh his memory." House Comm. on Judiciary, Fed.Rules of Evidence, H.R.Rep. No. 650, 93d Cong., 1st Sess., p. 13 (1973).

This result has traditionally be justified on the ground that once the confidence protected by the privilege is breached the privilege has no valid continuing office to perform. It should be noted, however, that the same result may here be supported by the distinguishable consideration that to allow a subsequent claim of the privilege would unfairly disadvantage the opponent who has reasonably assumed that the evidence would be available. The same reasons seem to apply where the waiver was publicly made upon the trial of one case, and the privilege later sought to be asserted on the hearing of another case.

Should the same rule of once published, permanently waived, apply to out-of-court disclosures made by the client or with his consent? Authority is scanty, but it seems that if the client makes or authorizes public disclosure, this should clearly be a waiver. Even where the privileged matter is privately revealed, or authorized to be revealed, to a third person, waiver has generally resulted and this conclusion may be supported by analogy to the cases which deny privilege when a third person is present at the consultation.[6] At the same time, it has been pointed out that considerations of fairness to the opponent rarely enter in where the disclosure is neither public nor made in the context of the litigation.

§ 94. The Effect of the Death of the Client

The accepted theory is that the protection afforded by the privilege will in general survive the death of the client. But under various qualifying theories the operation of the privilege has in effect been nullified in the class of cases where it would most often be asserted after death, namely, cases involving the validity or interpretation of a will, or other dispute between parties claiming by succession from the testator at his death. This result has been reached by different routes. Sometimes the testator will be found to have waived the privilege in his lifetime, as by directing the attorney to act as an attest-

ing witness. Wigmore argues, as to the will contests, that communications of the client with his lawyer as to the making of a will are intended to be confidential in his lifetime but that this is a "temporary confidentiality" not intended to require secrecy after his death and this view finds approval in some decisions. Other courts say simply that where all the parties claim under the client the privilege does not apply. The distinction is taken that when the contest is between a "stranger" and the heirs or personal representatives of the deceased client, the heirs or representatives can claim privilege, and they can waive it. Even if the privilege were assumed to be applicable in will contests, it could perhaps be argued that since those claiming under the will and those claiming by intestate succession both equally claim under the client, each should have the power to waive.

This doctrine that the privilege is ineffective, on whatever ground, when both litigants claim under the deceased client has been applied to suits by the heirs or representatives to set aside a conveyance by the deceased for mental incapacity and to suits for the enforcement of a contract made by the deceased to make a will in favor of plaintiff. The cases encountered where the party is held to be a "stranger" and hence not entitled to invoke this doctrine are cases where the party asserts against the estate a claim of a promise by the deceased to pay, or make provision in his will for payment, for services rendered. It may well be questioned whether the deceased would have been more likely to desire that his attorney's lips be sealed after his death in the determination of such claims than in the case of a controversy over the validity of the will. The attorney's offered testimony would seem to be of more than average reliability. If such testimony supporting the claim is true, presumably the deceased would have wanted to promote, rather than obstruct, the success of the claim. It would be only a short step forward for the courts to apply here the notion that the privilege is "personal" to client, and to hold that in all cases death terminates

6. See § 91 supra.

the privilege. This could not to any substantial degree lessen the encouragement for free disclosure which is the purpose of the privilege.

§ 95. Consultation in Furtherance of Crime or Fraud

Since the policy of the privilege is that of promoting the administration of justice, it would be a perversion of the privilege to extend it to the client who seeks advice to aid him in carrying out an illegal or fraudulent scheme. Advice given for those purposes would not be a professional service but participation in a conspiracy. Accordingly, it is settled under modern authority that the privilege does not extend to communications between attorney and client where the client's purpose is the furtherance of a future intended crime or fraud. Advice secured in aid of a legitimate defense by the client against a charge of past crimes or past misconduct, even though he is guilty, stands on a different footing and such consultations are privileged. If the privilege is to be denied on the ground of unlawful purpose, the client's guilty intention is controlling, though the attorney may have acted innocently and in good faith. As to when the client must be shown to have had the guilty purpose, the traditional and apparent majority rule is that the purpose must exist at the time the legal advice is sought.

Must the judge, before denying the claim of privilege on this ground find as a fact, after a preliminary hearing if contested, that the consultation was in furtherance of crime or fraud? This would be the normal procedure in passing on a preliminary fact on which the admissibility of evidence depends, but here this procedure would facilitate too far the use of the privilege as a cloak for crime. As a solution, some courts have cast the balance in favor of disclosure by requiring only that the one who seeks to avoid the privilege bring forward evidence from which the existence of an unlawful purpose could reasonably be found. Even this limitation seems needless when, as is commonly the case, the examining counsel has sufficient information to focus the inquiry by specific questions, thus avoiding any broad exploration of what transpired between attorney and client.

Questions arise fairly frequently under this limitation upon the privilege in the situation where a client has first consulted one attorney about a claim, and then employs other counsel and brings suit. At the trial the defense seeks to have the first attorney testify to disclosures by the client which reveal that the claim was fabricated or fraudulent. This of course may be done, but if the statements to the first attorney would merely reveal variances from the client's later statements or testimony, not sufficient to evidence fraud or perjury, the privilege would stand.

It has been questioned whether the traditional statement of the area of the limitation, that is in cases of communications in aid of crime or fraud, is not itself too limited. Wigmore argues that the privilege should not be accorded to communications in furtherance of any deliberate scheme to deprive another of his rights by tortious or unlawful conduct. Stricter requirements such as that the intended crime be *malum in se* or that it involve "moral turpitude," suggested in some of the older decisions, seem out of place here where the only sanction proposed is that of opening the door to evidence concededly relevant upon the issue on trial. There further seems no apparent reason why the exception should not be applied equally to the work product privilege.

§ 96. Protective Rules Relating to Materials Collected for Use of Counsel in Preparation for Trial: Reports of Employees, Witness–Statements, Experts' Reports, and the Like

A heavy emphasis on the responsibility of counsel for the management of the client's litigation is a characteristic feature of the adversary or contentious system of procedure of the Anglo–American tradition. The privilege against disclosure in court of confidential communications between lawyer and client as we have seen, is largely supported in modern times by the policy of encouraging free disclosure by the client in the attorney's office to enable the lawyer to discharge that responsibility.[1] The need for this encouragement is understood by lawyers because the problem of the guarded half-truths of the reticent client is familiar to them in their day-to-day work.

Closely allied to this felt need of promoting a policy of free disclosure by the client to enable the lawyer to do the work of managing his affairs most effectively in the interests of justice, is a feeling by lawyers of a need for privacy in their work and for freedom from interference in the task of preparing the client's case for trial. Certainly if the adversary were free at any time to inspect all of the correspondence, memoranda, reports, exhibits, trial briefs, drafts of proposed pleadings, and plans for presentation of proofs, which constitute the lawyer's file in the case, the attorney's present freedom to collect for study all the data, favorable and unfavorable, and to record his tentative impressions before maturing his conclusions, would be cramped and hindered.

The natural jealousy of the lawyer for the privacy of his file, and the court's desire to protect the effectiveness of the lawyer's work as the manager of litigation, have found expression, not only as we have seen in the evidential privilege for confidential lawyer-client communications, but in rules and practices about the various forms of pretrial discovery. Thus, under the old chancery practice of discovery, the adversary was not required to disclose, apart from his own testimony, the evidence which he would use, or the names of the witnesses he would call in support of his own case. The same restriction has often been embodied in, or read into, the statutory discovery systems.

Counterbalancing this need for privacy in preparation, of course, is the very need from which the discovery devices spring, namely, the need to make available to each party the widest possible sources of proof as early as may be so as to avoid surprise and facilitate preparation. The trend has been in the direction of wider recognition of this latter need, and the taboo against the "fishing expedition" has yielded increasingly to the proposition that the ends of justice require a wider availability of discovery than in the past. Accordingly there has developed an impressive arsenal of instruments of discovery, including interrogatories to the adverse party, demands for admissions, oral and written depositions of parties and witnesses, production of documents or things, entry upon land, and physical and mental examinations. In recent years some disenchantment with discovery has surfaced with claims that it was used as an instrument of harassment, was unduly time-consuming, and was excessively costly. Some amendments to the Federal Rules of Civil Procedure are presently under way dealing largely with increased involvement of trial judges and are not likely to have a substantial direct impact upon the matters here under discussion. We turn then to examine the extent to which the increase in the scope of discovery has served to diminish privacy of preparation.

Attorney–Client privilege. In the first place, of course, it is recognized that if the traditional privilege for attorney-client communications applies to a particular writing which may be found in a lawyer's file, the privilege exempts it from pretrial discovery proceedings, such as orders for production or questioning about its contents in the taking of depositions. On the other hand, if the writing has been in the possession of the client or his agents and was there subject to discovery, it seems axiomatic that the client cannot secure any exemption for the document by sending it to an attorney to be placed in his files.

How do these distinctions apply to a report made by an agent to the client of the results of investigation by himself or another agent of facts pertinent to some matter which later becomes the subject of litigation, such as a business dispute or a personal injury. It has usually been held that an agent's report to his principal though made in confidence is not privileged as such, and looked on as a mere preexisting document it would not become

§ 96

1. See § 87 supra.

privileged when sent by the client-principal to his lawyer for his information when suit is brought or threatened. The problem frequently arises in connection with proceedings for discovery of accident reports by employees, with lists of eyewitnesses, and in connection with signed statements of witnesses attached to such reports or secured separately by investigators employed in the client's claim department or by an insurance company with whom the client carries insurance against liability. Revised Uniform Evidence Rule (1986) 502(b) extends the privilege to confidential communications for the purpose of facilitating the rendition of legal services to the client to communications "(4) between representatives of the client or between the client and representatives of the client * * *." The import of this provision remains largely unexplored.

Whether a communication by the client's agent, on behalf of the client, to the latter's attorney would be privileged, has been discussed elsewhere. Under the Supreme Court decision in Upjohn Co. v. United States [2] the attorney-client privilege will protect intra-corporate communications made for the purpose of securing legal advice if, additionally, the communication relates to the communicating employee's assigned duties and is treated as confidential by the corporation. The communications in question were made by the employees directly to General Counsel and other lawyers representing the corporation in the investigation. An analogous rule would seem appropriate for application to agency situations not involving corporations.

By contrast, routine reports of agents made in the regular course of business, before suit is brought or threatened, have usually, though not always, been treated as pre-existing documents which not being privileged in the client's hands do not become so when delivered into the possession of his attorney. It is clear, however, that these classifications are not quite mutually exclusive and that some cases will fall in a doubtful borderland. And the law is in the making on the question

whether a report of accident or other casualty, by a policy-holder or his agents to a company insuring the policy-holder against liability, is to be treated as privileged when the insurance company passes it on to the attorney who will represent both the company and the insured. Reasonably the insurance company may be treated as an intermediary to secure legal representation for the insured, by whom the confidential communications can be transmitted as through a trusted agent. A report to a liability insurer can have no purpose other than use in potential litigation.

Work product. The discussion thus far has centered upon the extent to which the attorney-client privilege, just as any other privilege, can be invoked as a bar to discovery. Another, and much more frequently encountered limitation upon discovery of materials contained in the files of counsel, is furnished by the so-called "work product" doctrine, exempting trial preparations, in varying degrees, from discovery.

On June 14, 1946, the Advisory Committee on Federal Rules of Civil Procedure recommended the following amendment to Federal Rule 30(b):

> The court shall not order the production or inspection of any writing obtained or prepared by the adverse party, his attorney, surety, indemnitor, or agent in anticipation of litigation or in preparation for trial unless satisfied that denial of production or inspection will unfairly prejudice the party seeking the production or inspection in preparing his claim or defense or will cause him undue hardship or injustice. The court shall not order the production or inspection of any part of the writing that reflects an attorney's mental impressions, conclusions, opinions, or legal theories, or, except as provided in Rule 35, the conclusions of an expert.

The Supreme Court took no action on the proposed amendment but on January 3, 1947, handed down the decision in Hickman v. Taylor,[3] which is summarized below.

---

2. 449 U.S. 383 (1981).

3. 329 U.S. 495 (1947).

A tugboat, while helping tow a B. & O. Railroad carfloat, sank in the Delaware river, drowning five of the crew. Three days later, the two partner-owners of the tug and their underwriters hired Fortenbaugh's law firm to defend them against potential litigation arising from the drownings and to sue the railroad for damage to the tug. After a public Steamboat Inspectors' hearing, at which the four survivors testified, Fortenbaugh obtained signed statements from them. He also interviewed other persons, in some instances making memoranda. One action for death under the Jones Act was filed, the other death claims being settled. Plaintiff's Interrogatory 38 asked whether statements of witnesses were obtained; if written, copies were to be furnished; if oral, the exact provisions were to be set forth in detail. Upon refusal to comply, the two owners and Fortenbaugh were adjudged in contempt. The Third Circuit Court of Appeals reversed, and the Supreme Court granted certiorari.

During oral argument, the following exchange occurred:

Mr. Justice Jackson: What would be the practical effect in the daily functioning of our judicial system if we order counsel to produce as requested in Interrogatory 38?

Mr. Fortenbaugh: In my judgment, interviews will go unrecorded, unpleasant sources will not be pursued, and counsel will be tempted to keep files under his bed at home.

The Supreme Court affirmed the judgment of the Court of Appeals. The problem, said the Court, was to balance the interest in privacy of a lawyer's work against the interest supporting reasonable and necessary inquiries. Proper preparation of a client's case demands that information be assembled and sifted, legal theories be prepared, and strategy be planned "without undue and needless interference." [4] If the product of this work (interviews, statements, memoranda, etc.) were available merely on demand, the effect on the legal profession would be demoralizing. Discovery may be had where relevant and non-privileged facts, necessary for preparation of the opposing party's case, remain hidden, or the witness unavailable. The burden is on the party seeking to invade the privacy of the lawyer to show justification; this is "implicit in the rules as now [in 1947] constituted." [5] Rule 34 requires a showing of good cause for an order to produce documents, and Rule 30(b) gives the judge authority to limit examination upon the taking of a deposition when it appears that the examination is being conducted in bad faith or so as to annoy, embarrass, or oppress. Here no attempt was made to show need for the written statements. And as for the oral statements, to require Fortenbaugh to reproduce them would have a highly adverse effect upon the legal profession, making the lawyer more an ordinary witness than an officer of the court. Under the circumstances of this case, no showing could be made that would justify requiring disclosure of the mental impressions of counsel as to what the witnesses told him.

Considerable disagreement in the lower courts as to the meaning of Hickman v. Taylor followed that decision, no doubt resulting at least in part from the labored path followed by the Court to the conclusion that the matter of a qualified work product privilege was in fact covered by its own rules as then written. Finally after more than 20 years, the Court in 1970 adopted an amended Rule 26(b), with subdivision (3) directed in specific terms to the scope of the qualified work product protection. Nonetheless, Hickman v. Taylor remains a "brooding omnipresence," much cited and quoted by the courts, and in fact still governs an important area of the qualified work product protection. [6]

These salient provisions of Rule 26(b)(3) should be noted:

(1) In terms its work product immunity extends only to "documents and tangible things," yet discovery of documents constituted only one-half the subject of Hickman v. Taylor. The other half, i.e. mental impres-

---

4.   329 U.S. at 511.

5.   329 U.S. at 512.

6.   See Upjohn Co. v. United States, 449 U.S. 383, 397–402 (1981).

sions and the like, receives only pendant mention in the second sentence of Rule 26(b)(3), discussed in paragraph (5) below.

(2) The document or thing must have been "prepared in anticipation of litigation or for trial." If this scope seems unduly limited, it must be remembered that litigation is the frame of reference for work product. When the lawyer is engaged in rendering other services, e.g. the drafting of a contract, information which he needs will most likely be communicated by the client, falling within the attorney-client privilege. Information from outside sources is peculiarly a characteristic of the litigation situation.

(3) Hickman v. Taylor on its facts dealt only with work produced by an attorney, leaving open a troublesome question as to the status of the product of claim adjusters, investigators, and the like. The rule, however, is specific, speaking of documents prepared "by or for another party or by or for that other party's representative (including his attorney, consultant, surety, indemnitor, insurer, or agent)."

(4) The requirement of need is spelled out "only upon a showing that the party seeking discovery has substantial need of the materials in the preparation of his case and that he is unable without undue hardship to obtain the substantial equivalent of the materials by other means."

(5) The judge in ordering discovery of covered materials is directed to "protect against disclosure of the mental impressions, conclusions, opinions, or legal theories of an attorney or other representative of a party concerning the litigation." Literally read, the rule appears to protect mental impressions and the like of the lawyer only against disclosure that would be incidental to disclosure of documents and tangible things, in this regard being absolute in terms. If, however, counsel had not reduced a witness' statement to writing and counsel's deposition were taken in an effort to discover what the witness had said, Rule 26(b)(3) literally would not apply. Under these circumstances, however, it seems inconceivable that courts would not fall back upon Hickman v. Taylor and require an ex-

traordinarily strong showing of need, as has indeed been the case.

(6) A person, whether a party or a witness, is entitled to a copy of his own statement merely by requesting it; no showing of need is required.

The rule, it should be observed, does not immunize facts, or the identities of persons having knowledge of facts, or the existence of documents as contrasted with the documents themselves. Nor does the rule spell out the breadth of application or the duration of the qualified privilege that it recognizes. Does it apply at trial? Can it be invoked in other proceedings? Case law is meagre.

A further provision of revised Rule 26(b)(4) permits, in proper circumstances, discovery of facts and opinions of experts whom the party expects to call as witnesses at trial or who have been retained but are not expected to testify.

§ 97. Discovery in Criminal Cases: Statements by Witnesses

The development of discovery in criminal cases has, for a variety of reasons, lagged far behind that available in the civil area. The pros and cons of the continuing debate on the subject are outside the scope of the present treatment, though it is pertinent to observe that the trend seems clearly in the direction of more liberal discovery in the criminal area. This expansion of criminal discovery, like its earlier civil analogue, has raised the question whether "work product" should be afforded protection, and even the more advanced rules and proposals on the subject do undertake to provide such protection.

A distinguishable question which has drawn considerable attention is whether disclosure should be granted of material at, as opposed to before, trial. At a fairly early date, both federal and state decisions had espoused the view that when the statements of prosecution witnesses contradicting their trial testimony are shown to be in the hands of the government the defendant is entitled to demand their production at the trial. But despite this background, the famous *Jencks* [1] case was widely viewed as a startling incursion into new territory. The Supreme Court held in that case that the trial court had erroneously denied defense requests to inspect reports of two undercover agents who were government witnesses. It was not required, said the Court, that defendant show that the reports were inconsistent with the witnesses' testimony; if they related to the same subject, defendant was entitled to make the decision whether they were useful to the defense. The dissent condemned the holding as affording the criminal "a Roman holiday for rummaging through confidential information [in government files] as well as vital national secrets." This view was echoed in widespread protests by the press, by the Department of Justice, and in the halls of Congress where the so-called Jencks Act of 1959 was hastily enacted. Despite this background, the Act was for the most part a codification of the decision which had been so vehemently attacked. The Act has now been superseded by Rule 26.2 of the Federal Rules of Criminal Procedure. However, the terms of the Act must be considered in examining the effect of Rule 26.2, as will appear from the subsequent discussion.

Subsection (a) of the Act as amended provided that no statement by a government witness or prospective witness should be the subject of subpoena, discovery, or inspection until the witness has testified on direct examination in the trial. Subsection (b) provided that after a witness called by the government has testified on direct the court should, on motion of defendant, order the government to produce any statement (as later defined) relating to the subject matter of his testimony. Under subsection (c) the court will in case of question examine the statement and excise portions not related to the testimony. If, under subsection (d), the government elects not to comply with the order to produce, the testimony is to be stricken or, if justice re-

quires, a mistrial is to be declared. In subsection (e), "statement" as used in subsections (b), (c), and (d) is defined; the definition is very precise and narrow, designed to include only statements that beyond any reasonable question represent with a very high precision the words used by the witness. It will be observed that subsection (a) was designed to bar disclosure of any statement of a witness, regardless of how precise or imprecise a rendition it might be, unless and until the witness had testified for the government. After that testimony had been given, then disclosure was allowed and required but only as to highly precise statements, as defined in (e). If a writing were not a statement at all, in the broad sense of (a), the Act did not affect it. Writings which were statements in the broad sense of (a), but not within the strict definition of (e), or within (e) but whose maker did not testify, remained locked away, except as they might be obtainable under Brady v. Maryland, or under Evidence Rule 612 discussed below.

For the most part Rule 26.2 transposed the Act into the Federal Rules of Criminal Procedure. Some changes must, however, be noted. Rule 26.2 does not contain the prohibition of subsection (a) of the Act against compelling disclosure of a statement, in the broad sense, unless and until the witness has testified on direct. Thus Rule 26.2 deals only with compelling production of statements within the strict definition of subsection (e) of the Act, which is retained as subdivision (F) of the Rule. But as a companion to Rule 26.2, there was at the same time added to Rule 17 of the Criminal Rules, which deals with subpoenas, a new subdivision (h):

> Statements made by witnesses or prospective witnesses may not be subpoenaed from the government or the defendant under this rule, but shall be subject to production only in accordance with the provisions of Rule 26.2.

While superficially this may appear to constitute no more than a relocation of subsection

---

§ 97

1. Jencks v. United States, 353 U.S. 657 (1957) (prosecution of labor union official for filing false non-Commu-

nist affidavit with NLRB).

(a) of the Act, in fact the separation undermines the force of any argument that Rule 26.2 controls all statements of witnesses and prospective witnesses, in the broad sense, and leaves it effective only with regard to statements as narrowly defined in subdivision (F) of Rule 26.2. This is important in connection with the relationship between Rule 26.2 and Evidence Rule 612, discussed below.

A further highly significant change effected by Rule 26.2 was the expansion of coverage to include statements by defense witnesses and prospective witnesses as well as those for the government. This change was stimulated by the Supreme Court's decision in United States v. Nobles.[2] As under the Act, the penalty for refusal is striking of the testimony, with the further provision that if the refusing party is the government a mistrial may be declared if justice requires. A defendant cannot, of course, be allowed to abort a trial by refusing to deliver a statement.

And in 1983, a related amendment to Rule 12(i) had the effect of extending the provisions of Rule 26.2 to pretrial hearings of motions to suppress evidence. In an earlier section attention was directed to the need to examine the relationship between Criminal Rule 26.2 and Evidence Rule 612. That section pointed out that when a witness while testifying refers to a writing to refresh his memory, an opposing party is entitled to inspect it, to cross-examine upon it, and to introduce in evidence portions related to the testimony of the witness; if the reference for refreshing was prior to testifying, access to and use of the writing is subject to the court's discretion. If the writing consulted for refreshment is the statement of a witness or prospective witness,

the potential for conflict between Criminal Rule 26.2 and Evidence Rule 612 is seen. If the writing is a statement within the strict definition of Rule 26.2(F), the conflict is in reality no more than an overlap, as under either rule disclosure is required once the witness has testified on direct. But when the statement is a statement in the broad sense, as under subsection (a) of the Act, but not within the strict definition of subsection (e) of the Act, the construction in *Palermo*[3] as previously observed, was that no disclosure was available. The confusion is compounded by the fact that Rule 612 opens with the phrase, "Except as otherwise provided in criminal proceedings by section 3500 of title 18, United States Code * * * " and has not been amended. What is the effect of the exception? Does subsection (a) of the Act continue with its former effect? Did *Palermo* survive, pro tanto, the subsequent enactment of Rule 612? A satisfactory resolution probably lies only in the legislative sphere. Meanwhile a look at fundamentals may suggest a satisfactory construction. Both the Act (and Rule 26.2) and Rule 612 are directed to testing the credibility of witnesses. One pursues that end by giving access to statements which, if inconsistent, undoubtedly qualify for impeachment by that route. The other pursues the same end by giving access to materials generally, whether statements or not, which may have influenced the memory and narrative of the witness. Both can operate side by side without real conflict. The tangle is one of language, not of goals. This result is fairly reachable within the present language in view of the disappearance of subsection (a) of the Act, as noted above.

---

2.   422 U.S. 225 (1975).

3.   Palermo v. United States, 360 U.S. 343 (1959).

Chapter 11

THE PRIVILEGE FOR CONFIDENTIAL INFORMATION SECURED IN THE COURSE OF THE PHYSICIAN–PATIENT RELATIONSHIP

Table of Sections

§ 98. The Statement of the Rule and Its Purpose

The common law knew no privilege for confidential information imparted to a physician. When a physician raised the question before Lord Mansfield whether he was required to disclose professional confidences, the great Chief Justice drew the line clear. "If a surgeon was voluntarily to reveal these secrets, to be sure, he would be guilty of a breach of honor and of great indiscretion; but to give that information in a court of justice, which by the law of the land he is bound to do, will never be imputed to him as any indiscretion whatever." [1]

§ 98
1. The Duchess of Kingston's Trial, 20 How.St.Trials 573 (1776).

The pioneer departure from the common law rule was the New York statute of 1828 which in its original form was as follows: "No person authorized to practice physic or surgery shall be allowed to disclose any information which he may have acquired in attending any patient, in a professional character, and which information was necessary to enable him to prescribe for such patient as a physician, or to do any act for him as a surgeon."

Another early act which has been widely copied is the provision of the California Code of Civil Procedure of 1872, § 1881, par. 4, "A licensed physician or surgeon cannot, without the consent of his patient, be examined in a civil action as to any information acquired in attending the patient which was necessary to enable him to prescribe or act for the patient."

The rationale traditionally asserted to justify suppression in litigation of material facts learned by a physician is the encouragement thereby given to the patient freely to disclose all matter which may aid in the diagnosis and treatment of disease and injury. To obtain this end, so the argument runs, it is necessary to secure the patient from disclosure in court of potentially embarrassing private details concerning health and bodily condition. The validity of this utilitarian justification of the privilege has been questioned by many on the ground that the average patient, in consulting a physician, will have his thoughts centered upon his illness or injury and the prospects for betterment or cure, and will spare little thought for the remote possibility of some eventual disclosure of his condition in court. Accordingly, if an assurance of confidentiality has little importance in the play of forces upon the patient, it might well be concluded that the privilege is largely ineffective in attaining its avowed objective. Despite these arguments, however, the number of states adhering to the common law and refusing any general physician-patient privilege has slowly but steadily dwindled.

Over the same period, there has been a strong trend toward the recognition of two related but distinguishable privileges protecting, respectively, communications between psychiatrist and patient and psychologist and patient. Though the former profession, being medically trained, has always come within the ambit of the older physician-patient privilege where that privilege is recognized, it has been cogently argued that accepted practice in the treatment of mental illness involves considerations not encountered in other medical contexts. The following statement is frequently quoted in this regard.

> Among physicians, the psychiatrist has a special need to maintain confidentiality. His capacity to help his patients is completely dependent upon their willingness and ability to talk freely. This makes it difficult if not impossible for him to function without being able to assure his patients of confidentiality and, indeed, privileged communication * * *. A threat to secrecy blocks successful treatment.

The uniqueness of the psychiatrist-patient relationship led to the inclusion in the proposed Federal Rules of Evidence of a psychotherapist-patient privilege even though no general physician-patient privilege was suggested. The Revised Uniform Rules (1974) retained this privilege, but make the rule optionally one extending to confidential communication to a physician as well as to a psychotherapist. In the same vein, several of the states which continue to reject a general physician-patient privilege have enacted privileges applicable to the more limited psychotherapeutic context. And, recognizing that the treatment of mental illness is carried out by clinical psychologists as well as by psychiatrists, several states have enacted psychologist-patient privileges.

Even in the absence of statute, some privilege-like protection of certain aspects of the physician-patient relationship appears to be emerging as a function of federal constitutional guarantees of the right of privacy. In Whalen v. Roe,[2] the constitutionality of a New York statute creating a state data bank of the names and addresses of persons obtaining certain drugs by medical prescription was chal-

___

2. 429 U.S. 589 (1977).

lenged, *inter alia,* on the ground that patients would be deterred from obtaining appropriate medication by the apprehension that disclosure of their names would stigmatize them as drug addicts. Though garbed in constitutional vestments as an impairment of the right to make personal decisions, this argument bears a striking resemblance to the traditional rationale of privilege. While upholding the statute in *Whalen,* the Supreme Court did so on the basis of reasoning which strongly suggests the existence of some constitutional right on the part of patients to preserve confidentiality with respect to medical treatment.

Subsequent decisions of lower federal and state courts evidence considerable disagreement concerning the nature and scope, and even the existence, of the constitutionally based right intimated to exist in *Whalen.* A majority of the cases considering the point have involved information conveyed during psychotherapeutic treatment, a context in which the traditional utilitarian justification has been urged to possess particular validity. Nevertheless, even cases of the latter sort have generally been resolved on the particular facts against the claimant of privilege, and it would appear clear that any constitutional right to privacy in medical information is a highly qualified one.

§ 99. Relation of Physician and Patient

The first requisite for the privilege is that the patient must have consulted the physician for treatment or for diagnosis looking toward treatment. If consulted for treatment it is immaterial by whom the doctor is employed. Usually, however, when the doctor is employed by one other than the patient, treatment will not be the purpose and the privilege will not attach. Thus, when a driver at the request of a public officer is subjected to a blood test for intoxication, or when a doctor is appointed by the court or the prosecutor to make a physical or mental examination, or is employed for this purpose by the opposing party, or is selected by a life insurance company to make an examination of an applicant

for a policy or even when the doctor is employed by plaintiff's own lawyers in a personal injury case to examine plaintiff solely to aid in preparation for trial, the information secured is not within the present privilege. But when the patient's doctor calls in a consultant physician to aid in diagnosis or treatment, the disclosures are privileged.

If the patient's purpose in the consultation is an unlawful one, as to obtain narcotics in violation of law, or as, by some authority, a fugitive from justice to have his appearance disguised by plastic surgery, the law withholds the shield of privilege.

It has been held that where a doctor has attended a mother in her confinement and the newborn child, the child is a patient and can claim privilege against the doctor's disclosure of facts as to the apparent maturity of the child at birth.

After the death of the patient the relation is ended and the object of the privilege can no longer be furthered. Accordingly, it seems the better view that facts discovered in an autopsy examination are not privileged.

§ 100. Subject Matter of the Privilege: Information Acquired in Attending the Patient and Necessary for Prescribing

Statutes conferring a physician-patient privilege vary extensively, though probably a majority follow the pioneer New York and California statutes in extending the privilege to "any information acquired in attending the patient." [1] Understandably, these provisions have been held to protect not only information explicitly conveyed to the physician by the patient, but also data acquired by examination and testing. Other statutes appear facially to be more restrictive and to limit the privilege to communications by the patient. This appearance, however, may frequently be misleading, for statutes of this sort have been construed to provide a privilege fully as broad as that available elsewhere. The confusion is further compounded by a line of authority

§ 100

1. See § 98 supra.

which holds that facts observable by anyone without professional knowledge or training are not within the privilege.

While the information secured by the physician may be privileged, the fact that he has been consulted by the patient and has treated him, and the number and dates of his visits, are not within the shelter of the privilege.

The extent to which the privilege attaches to the information embodied in hospital records is discussed in the chapter on Business Records.[2]

§ 101. The Confidential Character of the Disclosure: Presence of Third Persons and Members of Family: Information Revealed to Nurses and Attendants: Public Records

We have seen that the statutes existing in many states codifying the privileges for marital communications and those between attorney and client usually omitted the requirement that to be privileged such communications must have been made in confidence. Nevertheless, the courts have read this limitation into these statutes, assuming that the legislatures must have intended this common law requirement to continue.[1] The statutes giving the patient's privilege for information gained in professional consultations again omit the adjective "confidential."[2] Should it nonetheless be read in, not as a continuation of a common law requirement, but as an interpretative gloss, spelled out from policy and analogy? Certainly the policy arguments are strong. First is the policy of holding all privileges within reasonable bounds since they cut off access to sources of truth. Second, the argument that the purpose of encouraging those who would otherwise be reluctant, to disclose necessary facts to their doctors, will be adequately served by extending a privilege for only such disclosures as the patient wishes to keep secret.

This principle of confidentiality is supported by those decisions which hold that if a casual third person is present with the acquiescence of the patient at the consultation, the disclosures made in his presence are not privileged, and thus the stranger, the patient and the doctor may be required to divulge them in court. Whether this principle is to be applied when the stranger is a police officer who has escorted the patient to the hospital or doctor's office should, it would seem, turn on whether meaningful acquiescence on the patient's part is to be found on the facts.

If, however, the third person is present as a needed and customary participant in the consultation, the circle of confidence may be reasonably extended to include him and the privilege will be maintained. Thus the presence of one sustaining a close family relationship to the patient should not curtail the privilege. And the nurse present as the doctor's assistant during the consultation or examination, or the technician who makes tests or X-ray photographs under the doctor's direction, will be looked on as the doctor's agent in whose keeping the information will remain privileged. But the application of strict agency principles in this context would seem inconsistent with the realities of modern medical practice, and the preferable view is that of the courts which have based their decisions upon whether the communication was functionally related to diagnosis and treatment.

Many courts on the other hand do not analyze the problems in terms of whether the communications or disclosures were confidential and professional, but rather in terms of what persons are intended to be silenced as witnesses. This seems to be sticking in the bark of the statute, rather than looking at its purpose. Thus these courts, if casual third persons were present at the consultation, will still close the mouth of the doctor but allow the visitor to speak. And if nurses or other attendants or technicians gain information necessary to treatment they will be allowed by these courts to speak (unless the privilege

2. See § 293 infra.

§ 101

1. See §§ 80, 91 supra.

2. See § 98 supra.

statute specifically names them) but the physician may not.

When the attending physician is required by law to make a certificate of death to the public authority, giving his opinion as to the cause, the certificate should be provable as a public record, despite the privilege. The duty to make a public report overrides the general duty of secrecy, and in view of the availability of the record to the public, the protection of the information from general knowledge, as contemplated by the privilege, cannot be attained. Accordingly, under the prevailing view, the privilege does not attach.

Today, state and local laws increasingly impose upon physicians requirements to report various types of patient information related to the public health and safety, e.g., the treatment of gunshot wounds, venereal disease, mental illness, and the occurrence of fetal death. Generally, state schemes for the collection and preservation of such data and its use by appropriate authorities have been upheld as against challenges based either upon a constitutional right of privacy or the professional privilege. In some instances, e.g., the reporting of gunshot wounds, the privilege has been held to be qualified to the extent of the reporting requirement, with the result that the physician may testify to any fact included within the report. Conversely, where the physician's report is not required the physician would remain precluded from testifying to the facts in the report, though there is some authority that the privilege, being testimonial, does not bar use of the report to generate other admissible evidence. Many of the reporting systems, however, obviously do not envision general disclosure of the data collected, and maintenance of some degree of confidentiality may in fact be indispensable to constitutionality.

§ 102. Rule of Privilege, Not Incompetency: Privilege Belongs to the Patient, Not to an Objecting Party as Such: Effect of the Patient's Death

As has been pointed out in the discussion of privileges generally,[1] the rule which excludes

disclosures to physicians is not a rule of incompetency of evidence serving the end of protecting the adverse party against unreliable or prejudicial testimony. It is a rule of privilege protecting the extrinsic interest of the patient and designed to promote health, not truth. It encourages free disclosure in the sickroom by preventing disclosure in the courtroom. The patient is the person to be encouraged and he is the holder of the privilege.

Consequently, he alone during his lifetime has the right to claim or to waive the privilege. If he is in a position to claim it and does not, it is waived and no one else may assert it. If the patient is not present, is unaware of the situation, or for some other reason is unable to claim the privilege, it is generally held that the privilege may be asserted on his behalf by a guardian, personal representative, or the health care provider, the latter being frequently held to have an enforceable duty to invoke the privilege in the absence of waiver by the patient. This necessary rule has unfortunately demonstrated considerable potential for allowing health care providers to advance personal interests under the guise of vindicating the privilege. It is to be hoped that it will not ultimately prove beyond judicial ingenuity in cases of this sort to allow the patient the ultimate decision as to whether the privilege will be invoked.

The adverse party as such has no interest to protect if he is not the patient, and thus cannot object as of right, and should have no right to complain on appeal if the patient's privilege is erroneously denied.

The whole supposition of the patient-privilege legislation, that the patient's fear of revelation in court of the information he gives the doctor will be such as to discourage free disclosure, is highly speculative. To think that he is likely to be influenced by fear that such revelations may occur after his death seems particularly fanciful. A rule that the privilege terminated with the patient's death

§ 102

1. See § 72 supra.

would have reached a common-sense result which would have substantially lessened the obstructive effect of the privilege. The courts, however have not taken this tack but hold that the privilege continues after death. Nevertheless, in contests of the survivors in interest with third parties, e.g., actions to recover property claimed to belong to the deceased, actions for the death of the deceased, or actions upon life insurance policies, the personal representative, heir or next of kin, or the beneficiary in the policy may waive the privilege, and, by the same token, the adverse party may not effectively assert the privilege. In contests over the validity of a will, where both sides—the executor on the one hand and the heirs or next of kin on the other—claim under and not adversely to the decedent, the assumption should prevail that the decedent would desire that the validity of his will should be determined in the fullest light of the facts. Accordingly in this situation either the executor or the contestants may effectively waive the privilege without the concurrence of the other.

§ 103. What Constitutes a Waiver of the Privilege?

The physician-patient statutes, though commonly phrased in terms of incompetency, are nevertheless held to create merely a privilege for the benefit of the patient, which he may waive.

Generally it is agreed that a contractual stipulation waiving the privilege, such as is frequently included in applications for life or health insurance, or in the policies themselves, is valid and effectual.

Another context in which the privilege is waived anticipatorily is that in which a testator procures an attending doctor to subscribe his will as an attesting witness. This action constitutes a waiver as to all facts affecting the validity of the will.

The physician-patient privilege, like most other privileges, may also be waived in advance of trial by a disclosure of the privileged information either made or acquiesced in by the privilege holder. Obviously, the law has

no reason to conceal in court what has been freely divulged on the public street, and the only question in such cases becomes the voluntariness of the revelation and the scope of the waiver.

Waiver in connection with litigation is an area in which substantial changes have occurred in recent years. A shrinking from the embarrassment which comes from exposure of bodily disease or abnormality is human and natural. It is arguable that legal protection from exposure is justified to encourage frankness in consulting physicians. But it is not human, natural, or understandable to claim protection from exposure by asserting a privilege for communications to doctors at the very same time when the patient is parading before the public the mental or physical condition as to which he consulted the doctor by bringing an action for damages arising from that same condition. This, in the oft-repeated phrase, is to make the privilege not a shield only, but a sword.

The conclusion mandated by these considerations clearly is that a patient voluntarily placing his or her physical or mental condition in issue in a judicial proceeding waives the privilege with respect to information relative to that condition. Failure to find a waiver from assertion of a claim or defense predicated upon a physical or mental condition has the awkward consequence of effectively frustrating discovery on a central issue of the case unless one of a variety of temporizing expedients is pressed into service to accommodate the outmoded rule.

Happily today the once prevalent rule that no waiver results from raising a claim or defense has been widely reversed by statute. Thus, at present, the crucial questions concern the types of issues which sufficiently implicate a party's physical or mental condition, and what actions by a party serve to raise these issues within the meaning of the modern statutes. A claim for damages for personal injuries is of course the paradigm example, and will clearly waive the privilege in all jurisdictions where such waiver by filing is possible at all. Claims for damages for mental suffering have been treated similarly, but here some discernment is called for lest the privilege be seen to evaporate upon the filing of any claim whatsoever. With respect to defenses, a distinction is clearly to be seen between the allegation of a physical or mental condition, which will effect the waiver, and the mere denial of such a condition asserted by the adversary, which will not.

A much litigated point since the conversion to more liberal rules of waiver has been whether a waiver effected by filing a claim or defense will permit the waiving party's adversary in litigation to contact physicians on an ex parte basis. Those decisions approving such contacts stress the economies of informal discovery and the anomaly of treating any witness as "belonging" to a party, considerations which suffice to make permissibility of ex parte contact the better rule. The contrary position, however, has been taken by a slightly greater number of courts, and possesses a substantial rationale in the consideration that the waiver following upon the filing of a claim or defense extends only to information relevant to the condition relied upon. It may well be that this limitation is quite likely to be substantially disregarded in an ex parte situation.

In the criminal area, waiver under the modern statutes has been seen to flow from assertion of the defenses of insanity and diminished responsibility.

Because of the principles discussed above, there will today be fewer occasions in which a cause will come on for trial with the patient's privilege still intact. Since the possibility still exists, however, it should be briefly considered how the privilege may be waived in trial.

How far does the patient's testifying waive the privilege? Doubtless, if the patient on direct examination testifies to, or adduces other evidence of, the communications exchanged or the information furnished to the doctor consulted this would waive in respect to such consultations. When, however, the patient in his direct testimony does not reveal any privileged matter respecting the consultation, but testifies only to his physical or mental condi-

tion, existing at the time of such consultation, then one view is that, "where the patient tenders to the jury the issue as to his physical condition, it must in fairness and justice be held that he has himself waived the obligation of secrecy." This view has the great merit of curtailing the scope of an obstructive privilege, but there are a number of courts which hold that the patient's testimony as to his condition without disclosure of privileged matter is not a waiver. If the patient reveals privileged matter on cross-examination, without claiming the privilege, this is usually held not to be a waiver of the privilege enabling the adversary to make further inquiry of the doctors, on the ground that such revelations were not "voluntary." The counter-argument, that the failure to assert the privilege should be a complete waiver, seems persuasive.

If the patient examines a physician as to matters disclosed in a consultation, or course of treatment, of course this is a waiver and opens the door to the opponent to examine him about any other matters then disclosed. And if several doctors participated jointly in the same consultation or course of treatment the calling of one to disclose part of the shared information waives objection to the adversary's calling any other of the joint consultants to testify about the consultation, treatment or the results thereof. Liberal courts go further and hold that calling by the patient of one doctor and eliciting privileged matter from him opens the door to the opponent's calling other doctors consulted by the patient at other times to bring out any facts relevant to the issue on which the privileged proof was adduced. It is not consonant with justice and fairness to permit the patient to reveal his secrets to several doctors and then when his condition comes in issue to limit the witnesses to the consultants favorable to his claims. But a substantial number of courts balk at this step.

Though the privilege continues after death of the patient, it may then be waived by the personal representative of the decedent. And where the personal representative is involved in litigation over the decedents estate with other persons claiming through the decedent, or where heirs-at-law are in opposition to one another, any one of the parties may waive the privilege.

§ 104. Kinds of Proceedings Exempted From the Application of the Privilege

The wide variation among state statutes creating and defining the physician-patient privilege renders it difficult to generalize usefully concerning the types of proceedings exempted from the operation of the privilege. Even where the Uniform Rule has been adopted, one or more qualifications have commonly been engrafted upon it. And though the now widely-adopted patient-litigant exception has undoubtedly reduced somewhat the differential application of the privilege, there remain many instances in which the holder of the privilege will not come within that exception. In short, it is indispensable to consult local statutes on the present point.

Probably the most common pattern to be observed in the statutes is that of a broadly defined privilege, applicable to both civil and criminal proceedings, to which a variety of specific exceptions are then attached. But there are states which deny the privilege in criminal cases generally, or in felony cases, or in cases of homicide.

With respect to other exceptions, the privilege has long been viewed as unworkable in worker compensation cases, and in medical malpractice cases and will generally be unavailable in these contexts. In more recent years, proceedings involving child abuse have claimed the attention of the legislatures, and these proceedings are now the most commonly singled out as involving policy considerations more weighty than those underlying the privilege. Other types of proceedings found withdrawn from the operation of the privilege are commitment proceedings, prosecutions for some types of drug offenses, and will contests.

The privilege is also sometimes withdrawn in child custody proceedings.

§ 105. The Policy and Future of the Privilege

Some statements of Buller, J., in 1792 in a case involving the application of the attorney-client privilege seem to have furnished the inspiration for the pioneer New York statute of 1828 on the doctor-patient privilege. He said: "The privilege is confined to the cases of counsel, solicitor, and attorney. * * * It is indeed hard in many cases to compel a friend to disclose a confidential conversation; and I should be glad if by law such evidence could be excluded. It is a subject of just indignation where persons are anxious to reveal what has been communicated to them in a confidential manner. * * * There are cases to which it is much to be lamented that the law of privilege is not extended; those in which medical persons are obliged to disclose the information which they acquire by attending in their professional characters."[1]

These comments reveal attitudes which have been influential ever since in the spread of statutes enacting the doctor-patient privilege. One attitude is the shrinking from forcing anyone to tell in court what he has learned in confidence. It is well understood today, however, that no such sweeping curtain for disclosure of confidences in the courtroom could be justified. Another is the complete failure to consider the other side of the shield, namely, the loss which comes from depriving the courts of any reliable source of facts necessary for the right decision of cases.

Perhaps the main burden of Justice Buller's remarks, however, is the suggestion that since the client's disclosures to the lawyer are privileged, the patient's disclosures to the doctor should have the same protection. This analogy has probably been more potent than any other argument, particularly with the lawyers

§ 105

1. Wilson v. Rastall, 4 Term, Rep. 753, 759, 100 Eng. Rep. 1287 (K.B.1792).

in the legislatures. They would be reluctant to deny to the medical profession a recognition which the courts have themselves provided for the legal profession. Manifestly, however, the soundness of the privilege may not be judged as a matter of rivalry of professions, but by the criterion of the public interest.

Some of the analytical weaknesses of the utilitarian rationale of the privilege, except in the psychotherapeutic context, have been noted earlier.[2] To these must be added the perplexities and confusions arising from judicial and legislative attempts to render tolerable a rule which essentially runs against the grain of justice, truth, and fair dealing. The uncertainties of application of a privilege so extensively and variously qualified and restricted should suffice conclusively to rebut any continuing effort to justify it on utilitarian grounds, for no one familiar with the vagaries of its operation will be disposed to repose confidence in its protection. Those not so knowledgeable will often find it a snare and a delusion.

A more tenable argument, however, has been increasingly advanced in recent years. This view holds that the privilege should not be viewed as operating to inspire the making of medical confidences but rather as protecting such confidences once made. In support of this position it is contended that the legitimate interest in the privacy of the physician-patient relationship should not be subject to casual breach by every litigant in single-minded pursuit of the last scrap of evidence which may marginally contribute to victory in litigation. While it is true that the privilege will occasionally be seen operating to prevent such unwarranted intrusions, it is debatable whether the value of such protection is sufficiently great to justify both the suppression of critical evidence in other cases and the costs of administering a highly complex rule.

Complete abolition of the privilege, however, appears a utopian hope given current political realities. Perhaps the happiest realizeable alternative is that long followed by the state of North Carolina, which qualifies its statutory privilege with the provision that "the court, either at trial or prior thereto * * * may compel such disclosure when, in his opinion, the same is necessary to a proper administration of justice." Such a statute, perceptively and sensitively applied, would not only allow protection of privacy against trivial intrusion but would draw from the privilege the threat of injustice which it has long carried.

---

2. See § 98 supra.

Chapter 12

PRIVILEGES FOR GOVERNMENTAL SECRETS

Table of Sections

§ 106. Other Principles Distinguished

In discussing the evidential privileges and rules of exclusion in respect to the production and admission of writings and information in the possession of government officers, it is well to mark off at the outset some other principles which may hinder the litigant seeking facts from the government, but which are beyond our present inquiry. Among them are these: (a) questions of substantive privilege of government officers from liability for their acts and words, (b) questions as to the general exemption of the chief executive and other high officers from judicial process to enforce their appearance or attendance or to compel them to give evidence, and (c) questions as to the irremovability of official records.

§ 107. The Common Law Privileges for Military or Diplomatic Secrets and Other Facts the Disclosure of Which Would Be Contrary to the Public Interest

Since the turn of the century the activities of government have multiplied in number and widened in scope, and the need of litigants for the disclosure and proof of documents and other information in the possession of government officials has correspondingly increased. When this need is asserted and opposed, the resultant question requires a delicate and judicious balancing of the public interest in the secrecy of "classified" official information against the public interest in the protection of the claim of the individual to due process of law in the redress of grievances.

It is generally conceded that a privilege and a rule of exclusion should apply in the case of writings and information constituting military or diplomatic secrets of state. Clearly, there is no more substantial justification for secrecy than that the material protected is vital to the security of the nation. Congress has formalized this privilege in the criminal context by the enactment of the Classified Information Procedures Act (CIPA),[1] the provisions of which recognize a power in the executive branch to determine that public disclosure of classified information shall not be made in a criminal trial. Where such a determination prevents the defendant from disclosing classified information in his defense, the court is empowered to dismiss the indictment or information or afford the defendant appropriate lesser relief.

Wigmore seems to regard it as doubtful whether the denial of disclosure should go further than this, but state statutes in this country sometimes state the privilege in broader terms, and the English decisions seem to have accepted the wide generalization that official documents and facts will be privileged whenever their disclosure would be injurious to the public interest. Whether this wider principle is justified in point of policy is open to serious question.

§ 108. Qualified Privileges for Government Information: The Constitutional Presidential Privilege: Common Law Privileges for Agency Deliberations and Law Enforcement Files

The case of United States v. Nixon[1] brought into sharp focus both the limits of the long-standing executive privilege protecting diplomatic and military secrets and the distinguishable question as to whether some broad-er privilege protects confidential communications between the President and his or her immediate advisors. The decision of the Supreme Court in that case, while apparently recognizing a constitutionally based privilege of this nature, nevertheless held that the privilege is a qualified one and subject to invasion upon a showing of demonstrable need for evidence relevant to a criminal proceeding. The presidential privilege has occasioned considerable discussion by constitutional scholars, but will, for all of its importance to our system of government, rarely be encountered.

Of much greater everyday significance is the enormous quantity of information produced, collected, and compiled by the governmental agencies which have proliferated since the end of World War II. Only an infinitesimal amount of this governmental information will fall within the previously discussed privilege protecting military and diplomatic secrets. What then of the vast remainder?

Until fairly recently, this great store of information, though not within the ambit of any well-defined evidentiary privilege, was as a practical matter extremely difficult or impossible to obtain. Prior to its amendment in 1958, the so-called Federal Housekeeping Act[2] was assumed by administrators to authorize the issuance of regulations requiring governmental personnel in the actual possession of governmental documents and records to decline to produce them even when served with a subpoena issued by a court. The validity of these regulations was consistently upheld by the Supreme Court, and though the cases never went to the extent of holding that the Act created a statutory privilege the practical effect was that private litigants were unable to obtain needed information.

The overall accessibility of governmental information has more recently been dramatically increased by new legislation. In 1958, the Federal Housekeeping Act was amended by the Congress to include a provision removing any possible implication that the Act was

§ 107

1.   18 U.S.C.A.App. § 1 et seq.

§ 108

1.   418 U.S. 683 (1974).
2.   5 U.S.C.A. § 822, R.S. § 161 (1875).

intended to create a statutory privilege,[3] and the intent of this amendment has been observed in subsequent court decisions. Access to governmental information has been even more substantially increased with the enactment by the Congress,[4] and by many state legislatures, of Freedom of Information legislation. While these statutes are directed toward availability of information for the public in general and the news media in particular their importance in clearing the way for discovery in litigation will be readily apparent. To proceed under the federal Freedom of Information Act no standing or particularized need for the desired information need be shown, and any person is eligible to proceed under the provisions of the statute. For present purposes, however, the important question is the extent to which the FOIA affects the question of evidentiary privilege for governmental information.

At the time of the enactment of the original federal FOIA in 1966, there was clearly some protection extended by the courts to sensitive government information which did not rise in importance to the level of military or diplomatic secrets. Thus there was in existence a qualified common law privilege protecting some aspects of government agency policy deliberations, and another, less clearly defined, shielding agency investigative files. In enacting the FOIA, Congress recognized the desirability of maintaining some degree of confidentiality in these areas and thus included them within the exemption provisions of the act.

The FOIA itself, of course, does not address the question of evidentiary admissibility, and thus cannot be said to be a statutory enactment of the privileges in question. At the same time, it is obvious that the two are critically interrelated, and that the exemption provisions mark the outermost limits of the privileges. For it would be anomalous in the extreme to deny evidentiary admission on grounds of confidentiality to material available on request to even the casually interested. A moment's reflection, however, will suggest that the converse does not hold, and that the evidentiary privileges might meaningfully and reasonably be viewed as protecting *less* than the total sum of information denied the general public under the FOIA exceptions. Such a differentiation is justifiable on the ground that the litigant's interest in access to evidence will sometimes be stronger than the ordinary citizen's interest in merely obtaining information. It has accordingly been held that not all information exempt from disclosure under the exceptions to FOIA will necessarily be protected by privilege if sought by discovery processes for purposes of litigation. The foregoing synopsis will suggest that the multitudinous decisions construing the exception provisions of FOIA will be of varying precedential value concerning the scope of the privileges discussed below.

(a) The Agency Policy Deliberations Privilege.

This privilege protects communications made between governmental personnel, or between governmental personnel and outside consultants, which consist of advisory opinions and recommendations preliminary to the formulation of agency policy. Like other communications privileges, that protecting governmental agency deliberations seeks to encourage a free flow of communication in the interest of some larger end, in this instance the objective of establishing agency policy only after consideration of the full array of contrasting views on the subject. Here, as elsewhere, it is assumed that total candor will be enhanced, and the quality of governmental decision-making correspondingly improved, by an assurance of at least qualified confidentiality.

Other contributory policies supporting the recognition of this privilege have been said to be that it avoids premature and potentially

---

3. P.L. 85–619, 72 Stat. 547 (1958). The Act in its present form reads: "The head of an Executive department or military department may prescribe regulations for the government of his department, the conduct of its employees, the distribution and performance of its business, and the custody, use, and preservation of its records, papers, and property. This section does not authorize withholding information from the public or limiting the availability of records to the public." 5 U.S.C.A. § 301.

4. 5 U.S.C.A. § 552.

misleading public disclosure of possible agency action, and assures that governmental decision-makers will be judged solely upon the quality of their decisions without regard to the quality of other options considered and discarded.

To come within the rationale of the privilege, the matter sought to be kept confidential must have been communicated prior to the finalization of the policy at which it was directed, and must have constituted opinion or evaluation as opposed to the mere reporting of objective facts. It is not, however, material whether the communication reflected the view which ultimately became embodied in agency policy, or even whether the communication was considered or totally ignored by the decision-maker. The privilege is that of the government, and would appear to be claimable indefinitely since it is terminated neither by the adoption of the policy concerned nor by the death of the author of the privileged matter. As further discussed below, the privilege is a conditional one only, and is therefore subject to invasion upon a sufficient showing of necessity.

The question of privilege for government agency deliberations has arisen only infrequently in the context of state government. Many of the states enacting state FOIA statutes have included exemption provisions protecting policy development materials from mandatory disclosure under the statutes. Where the question of a true evidentiary privilege has arisen, i.e., where the material is sought for introduction into evidence rather than simply as information, a majority of the states passing on the question have upheld the existence of a qualified privilege on the federal model. The root of the privilege on the state level has almost invariably been said to be the doctrine of separation of powers.

(b) The Privilege for Information and Files Relating to Law Enforcement.

Prior to the enactment of the federal FOIA and its state counterparts, a privilege protecting the investigative results of government agencies appears to have been sporadically recognized but ill-defined, frequently being treated as but an aspect of a more comprehensive but amorphous privilege for "government information." Clearly, however, disclosure of the files of law enforcement agencies may seriously hamper enforcement efforts by discouraging or compromising confidential informants, disclosing the existence, targets, or methods of investigation, or facilitating defense of a criminal prosecution or civil enforcement proceeding by revealing the nature of the case in preparation. Congress recognized the legitimacy of these concerns in the enactment of a highly specific exemption to the FOIA, which in the most recent iteration of the statute expands its protection to "records or information compiled for law enforcement purposes." Today the exemption and the privilege, at least in federal law, seem inextricably intertwined, leaving no practical reason for distinguishing between them.

To come within the ambit of the privilege, the investigation must be one directed at the enforcement of the law, criminal or civil, and must be conducted by an agency charged by law with law enforcement functions. Though it has been said that the privilege, unlike that for agency policy deliberations, expires with the governmental undertaking to which the privileged matter relates, this seems an overly broad generalization. It is clear, however, that the protection here afforded is conditional, and in the unusual sense that it will not attach at all failing an initial government demonstration that production "could reasonably be expected to" bring about one or more of the harms specified by the statute.

With regard to state law in this area, some states expressly confer privilege upon law enforcement records by statute, while others possess "classical" official information statutes which would cover at least some of such records under the rubric of communications made by or to a public officer in official confidence when the public interest would suffer from disclosure. However, it would appear that where a state FOIA is in effect, state courts will accord that statute primacy in determining the maximum sweep of this privilege.

§ 109. Effect of the Presence of the Government as a Litigant

To the extent that the Freedom of Information Act is available as a means for obtaining government records and information for use in evidence, as discussed in the preceding section, no distinction is made between situations where the litigation is between parties other than the government and those where the government is a party. However, when procedures other than under the Act are resorted to, the difference may be substantial.

When the government is not a party and successfully resists disclosure sought by a party, the result is simply that the evidence is unavailable, as though a witness had died, and the case will proceed accordingly, with no consequences save those resulting from the loss of the evidence. This approach to dealing with the impact of governmental privilege upon litigation between third parties causes no insuperable difficulties where the privilege is a conditional one, or where the privileged matter does not bear crucially on the central issues of the case. Its appropriateness has been questioned, however, where the successful invocation of the absolute privilege in favor of diplomatic or military secrets makes impossible any approximation of a full presentation of the issues. Whether or not dismissal of the cause is warranted where the sovereign has rendered its courts incapable of fairly trying the issues, dismissal has been granted at the behest of the government where continued litigation by adversary means threatens partial or indirect exposure of the protected secret.

The presence of the government in court as a litigant, whether as the moving party in a civil or criminal proceeding, or by virtue of consenting to be sued as a defendant, raises the possibility that an exercise of privilege may be sanctioned by ordinary judicial enforcement measures. Accordingly, in a criminal prosecution the court may give the government the choice of making disclosure of matters of significance to the defense or suffering dismissal of the proceeding; any executive immunity is waived and the government cannot as litigant invoke an evidentiary privilege, e.g., for military secrets, while at the same time seeking to proceed affirmatively with respect to the subject matter.

As the plaintiff in a civil action, the government is of course subject to the ordinary rules of discovery, and may face dismissal of its action if through the invocation of privilege it deprives the defendant of evidence useful to the defense. There would, however, seem to be no reason why the government, as distinguished from other litigants, should inexorably face dismissal for failure to make discovery under any and all circumstances. Thus it has been suggested that only where the governmental claim of privilege shields evidence of such importance as to deny the defendant due process should dismissal automatically result.

Where the government is defendant, as under the Tort Claims Act, an adverse finding cannot be rendered against it as the price of asserting an evidentiary privilege. This is not one of the terms upon which Congress has consented that the United States be subjected to liability. Thus where the plaintiff's action cannot be made out without disclosure of the privileged matter the plaintiff will remain remediless, though in light of the extreme nature of this result some courts will go to some lengths to avoid it.

§ 110. The Scope of the Judge's Function in Determining the Validity of the Claim of Privilege

When the head of department has made a claim of privilege for documents or information under his control as being military or diplomatic secrets is this claim conclusive upon the judge? United States v. Reynolds,[1] which remains the Supreme Court's most recent and comprehensive ruling on the privilege, has been extensively mined for the answer to this question. The generally accepted conclusions are that while the judiciary is not to defer totally to the "caprice" of the executive, the judicial role is a limited one and focused largely upon the process of claiming the privilege rather than upon the merits of

§ 110

1. 345 U.S. 1 (1953).

its invocation. Thus, the privilege must be claimed by the head of the executive department having charge of the material, and the statement of this official must indicate personal consideration of the claim, the identity (so far as possible) of the privileged material, and the reasons supporting the claim. In some instances, no more will be necessary in order to enable the court to rule in favor of the claim, but it is not unusual for the government to further support its claim with an in camera affidavit and perhaps other matter. Whatever material is considered by the court, the standard applied is whether there exists a reasonable danger that disclosure will damage national security. If the answer to this question is in the affirmative, the privilege is absolute, and cannot thereafter be affected by any amount of need on the part of a litigant.

Once we leave the restricted area of military and diplomatic secrets, however, a greater role for the judiciary in the determination of governmental claims of privilege becomes not only desirable but necessary. The head of an executive department can appraise the public interest of secrecy as well (or perhaps in some cases better) than the judge, but his official habit and leaning tend to sway him toward a minimizing of the interest of the individual. Under the normal administrative routine the question will come to him with recommendations from cautious subordinates against disclosure and in the press of business the chief is likely to approve the recommendation about such a seemingly minor matter without much independent consideration. The determination of questions of fact and the applications of legal standards thereto in passing upon the admissibility of evidence and the validity of claims of evidential privilege are traditionally the responsibility of the judge. As a public functionary he has respect for the executive's scruples against disclosure and at the same time his duties require him constantly to appraise private interests and to reconcile them with conflicting public policies; he may thus seem better qualified than the executive to weigh both interests understandingly and to strike a wise balance.

McCormick, Evidence 4th Ed. HB—5

The foregoing considerations largely explain the fact that privileges running in favor of government, other than that for military and diplomatic secrets, are uniformly held to be qualified ones only. Thus, where these privileges are claimed, it is for the judge to determine whether the interest in governmental secrecy is outweighed in the particular case by the litigant's interest in obtaining the evidence sought. A satisfactory striking of this balance will, on the one hand, require consideration of the interests giving rise to the privilege and an assessment of the extent to which disclosure will realistically impair those interests. On the other hand, factors which will affect the litigant's need will include the significance of the evidence sought for the case, the availability of the desired information from other sources, and in some instances the nature of the right being asserted in the litigation. Here, as with other qualified privileges, the possibility of in camera inspection by the court offers a practical expedient for testing the claim of privilege without, by that testing process, destroying irretrievably the secrecy which the privilege is designed to preserve.

§ 111. The Privilege Against the Disclosure of the Identity of an Informer

Informers are shy and timorous folk, whether they are undercover agents of the police or merely citizens stepping forward with information about violations of law, and if their names were subject to be readily revealed, this enormously important aid to law enforcement would be almost cut off. On this ground of policy, a privilege is recognized in respect to disclosure of the identity of an informer, who has given information about supposed crimes to a prosecuting or investigating officer or to someone for the purpose of its being relayed to such an officer. The privilege runs to the government or state, and may be invoked by its officers who as witnesses or otherwise are called on for the information, and runs also, according to some authority, to one charged with being an informer, and when neither the government nor the informer is represented at the trial, in some jurisdictions the judge as in other cases of privilege [1] may invoke it for the absent holder. It is disputed whether the privilege is confined to disclosure of identity or extends also to the contents of the communication. Seldom will the contents of the statement be competent if the name is undisclosed, but it is believed that the policy of the privilege does not apply to shielding the purport of the communication from disclosure. Of course, if revealing the contents will in the circumstances probably reveal the identity of the informer, the privilege should attach.

The privilege has two important qualifications, one obvious and the other not so obvious but just. The first is that when the identity has already become known to "those who would have cause to resent the communication," the privilege ceases. The second is that when the privilege is asserted by the state in a criminal prosecution, and the evidence of the identity of the informer becomes important to the establishment of the defence, the court will require the disclosure, and if it is still withheld, that the prosecution be dismissed. While the inherent fairness of this second exception is apparent, it poses difficulties of implementation if the privilege is not to be rendered meaningless by automatic defense allegations of the informer's potential value as a witness. To avoid this result the expedient widely used, and sometimes seemingly required, is an in camera hearing on the nature of the informer's probable testimony. The trial court may then assess the balance between the value of that testimony to the defense and the significance of the considerations underlying the privilege in the particular case.

In recent years, factors closely analogous to those giving rise to the informer's privilege have led to extensive recognition of a similar privilege protecting the confidentiality of police surveillance locations.

§ 112. Statutory Privileges for Certain Reports of Individuals to Government Agencies: Accident Reports, Tax Returns, etc.

A policy faintly similar to that which has prompted the common law privilege for the identity of informers may be thought to have some application to all reports required by law to be made by individuals to government agencies, giving information needed in the administration of their public functions. If the statements may be used against the reporters, they may in some degree be discouraged from making full and true reports. On the other hand, these reports often deal with facts highly material in litigation, and an early report to government may be reliable and pressingly needed for ascertainment of the facts. The latter interest has prevailed with the courts, and in the absence of a statutory provision creating the privilege there is no privilege for these reports. In the legislative halls, however, when bills requiring such reports are proposed, the supposed need for encouraging frank and full reports frequently looms large to the proponents of the measures, and statutory privileges for reports of highway and industrial accidents and returns of property and income for taxation are common. The soundness of a policy extending greater protection to these reports than is required by constitutional guarantees is dubious, and in some instances seems to imply a greater need for accuracy in governmental statistic gathering than in judicial fact-finding. But where the policy is effectively adopted by statute, its unwisdom is submitted not to justify judicial incursions upon the protection ostensibly afforded.

§ 113. The Secrecy of Grand Jury Proceedings—(a) Votes and Expressions of Grand Jurors; (b) Testimony of Witnesses

The taking of evidence by grand jurors and their deliberations have traditionally been shrouded in secrecy. The ancient oath administered to the grand jurors bound them to

1. See § 73 supra.

keep secret "the King's counsel, your fellows' and your own."

Several objectives are commonly suggested as being promoted by the policy of secrecy: to guard the independence of action and freedom of deliberation of the accusatory body, to protect the reputations of those investigated but not indicted, to prevent the forewarning and flight of those accused before publication of the indictment, and to encourage free disclosure by witnesses. The procedure for attaining them assumes two forms, somewhat loosely described as "privilege." The first is a privilege against disclosure of the grand jurors' communications to each other during their deliberations and of their individual votes. The propriety of such a measure as an assurance of free and independent deliberation can scarcely be doubted, though it may be of slight practical importance in view of the infrequency with which these communications and votes will be relevant to any material inquiry. The second of these privileges involves disclosure of the testimony given by witnesses before the grand jury, and as an area of substantial controversy deserves thoughtful scrutiny.

While the grand jury in its origins may in considerable measure have been an instrument of and subservient to the crown, its position as an important bulwark of the rights of English citizens was established by the end of the 17th century. This latter aspect is evident in the provision of the Fifth Amendment of the Constitution of the United States requiring presentment or indictment as a precondition of prosecution for a capital or infamous crime. During this period the grand jury's independence of incursion by both prosecution and defense appears to have been well recognized, and prosecutors were admitted to its councils only by suffrance. However, the decline in the feeling of need for the grand jury as a protector of individual liberties which caused its abolition in England seems in this country to have led to a return of the grand jury, in its accusatorial capacity, to the role of subordinate arm of the prosecution, operating to a degree as rubber stamp but on occasion as a powerful instrumentality of discovery. Thus we find statutes and rules providing for the presence of prosecuting attorneys and stenographers except when the grand jury is deliberating or voting.

The veil of secrecy surrounding grand jury proceedings does not preclude all subsequent disclosure and use of the testimony and other material presented there. In the federal system prosecutors have long had the use of grand jury material in criminal prosecutions stemming from the grand jury's investigations. Such use is perfectly consistent both with the practical operation of the grand jury and with the central purpose of that body which justifies its broad investigatory powers.

Government use of grand jury material for purposes other than criminal prosecution, however, e.g., in a regulatory proceeding dealing with the same facts, is an abuse of the grand jury system, and the federal statutory provisions regulating such use have occasioned a great deal of litigation.

Two 1983 decisions of the Supreme Court have clarified the statutory provisions and imposed significant limitations on access to grand jury materials by government agencies. In the first of these decisions, United States v. Sells Engineering, Inc.,[1] the Court held that government attorneys other than those working on the criminal matters before the grand jury are not automatically entitled to access to grand jury materials without a court order, and further that to obtain such an order not only must the requirements of the statute be met, but also a "particularized need" for the material must be shown. And, in United States v. Baggot,[2] the Court held that the Internal Revenue Service was not entitled to court ordered access to grand jury materials in connection with a civil tax investigation because such an investigation is not "prelimi-

---

§ 113

1. 463 U.S. 418 (1983). The same requirement was imposed with respect to state officials who request federal grand jury material in Illinois v. Abbott & Associates, Inc., 460 U.S. 557 (1983).

2. 463 U.S. 476 (1983).

nary to or in connection with a judicial proceeding" as required by the rule.

In the federal system, then, government agencies would appear to have little advantage over civil litigants seeking access to grand jury material. The latter continue to face the necessity of demonstrating, as earlier required more generally in United States v. Procter & Gamble Co.,[3] a "particularized need" for the material. This requirement, though frequently condemned by commentators, has consistently been reasserted by the Supreme Court. In short, it seems clear that federal grand jury secrecy will continue to enjoy substantial protection for the foreseeable future.

Among others having a potential need for access to transcripts of testimony before a grand jury, perhaps the strongest case may be made for the criminal defendant. The right of an accused to a copy of his own recorded grand jury testimony is today recognized by statute or rule in a number of states and in the federal courts. Considerations of basic fairness (and the inapplicability of the justifications for grand jury secrecy in this context) argue strongly for this access. The question of defense access to the testimony of other grand jury witnesses earlier drew what has been characterized as a "curiously ambiva-

lent" response from the Supreme Court. This question has now largely been resolved in the defendant's favor by an amendment to the Jencks Act[4] which confers a right to such material with respect to government witnesses once they have testified on direct. No infringement of the objectives of secrecy mentioned at the beginning of this section can result from this measure of disclosure, and it would seem to constitute the least acceptable minimum for state as well as federal courts.

Despite the stringent language of the federal rule imposing secrecy on grand jury proceedings, witnesses are pointedly omitted from the enumeration of persons bound by its provisions, and the rule seems to place no obstacle in the way of the practice of "debriefing" witnesses after they have given testimony. That a federal judge has authority to administer an oath of secrecy to grand jury witnesses has long been questioned. More recently, a state statute prohibiting a grand jury witness from ever disclosing the testimony before the grand jury was held by the Supreme Court to violate the First Amendment as applied to a witness wishing to disclose information independently acquired by him to which he had testified before the grand jury.[5]

---

3. 356 U.S. 677 (1958).
4. 18 U.S.C.A. § 3500; Fed.R.Crim.P. 26.2.

5. Butterworth v. Smith, 494 U.S. 624 (1990).

Title 6

PRIVILEGE: CONSTITUTIONAL

Chapter 13

THE PRIVILEGE AGAINST
SELF–INCRIMINATION

Table of Sections

§ 114. The History of the Privilege: (a) Origin of the Common Law Privilege

Because of relatively widespread doubt as to the wisdom of the privilege against self-incrimination, the origin and development of the rule have been of special interest to legal scholars. Unfortunately important aspects of the matter are still clouded with doubt. What is known suggests that the privilege had its roots in opposition to the use of the *ex officio* oath by the English ecclesiastical courts and that its development was intimately intertwined with the political and religious disputes of early England. The most significant ambiguity is whether the privilege as finally applied in the common law courts after 1700 represented a logical extension of principle underlying earlier opposition to the procedures of ecclesiastical courts, or rather, whether it represented condemnation by association of a procedure not inherently inconsistent with prevailing values.

Prior to the early 1200s, trials in the ecclesiastical courts had been by ordeal or compurgation oath, the formal swearing by the party and his oath helpers. Under the influence of Pope Innocent III, however, there was introduced into the ecclesiastical courts the "jusjurandum de veritate dicenda" or inquisitorial oath. Unlike the procedure used in the administration of the compurgation oath, the inquisitorial oath involved active interrogation of the accused by the judge in addition to the accused's uncomfortable consciousness of his oath to reveal the entire truth of the matter under inquiry. There was some formal limitation upon the power of the ecclesiastical courts to use this new device. An accused could not be put to his oath in the absence of some presentation, which could take the form of formal accusation by one who thereby became a party to the resulting proceeding, denunciation to the court by one unwilling to become a party, or the accused's

"popular reputation" as guilty of the subject of the inquiry.[1] The extent to which these restrictions were observed in practice is open to doubt. Mary Hume Maguire asserts that "in England *ex officio* procedure as practiced recognized little necessity of presentment by 'common report' or 'violent suspicion.' The judge *ex officio,* i.e., by virtue of his office as judge, summoned the party into court, and instituted action." In practice then, an individual could be called before the court and made to respond to a broad inquiry into his affairs without regard to the nature or strength of the accusations against him.

The precise nature of the early opposition to the practices of the ecclesiastical courts is in dispute. Wigmore argues that the first three centuries of opposition were based solely upon a desire to limit the potentially expansive jurisdiction of the ecclesiastical courts. Maguire, on the other hand, asserts that in addition to the jealousy of jurisdiction there was "steady and growing opposition to the administration of the oath itself as 'repugnant to the ancient customs of our Realm' and contrary to the spirit of the common law."

In any case, opposition to the oath became much greater when the procedure was adopted by two new courts and used for essentially political purposes. In 1487 the Court of the Star Chamber was authorized to pursue its broad political mandate by means of the oath. The Star Chamber was not even subjected to the requirement of presentation that theoretically provided protection from broad "fishing inquisitions" by the ecclesiastical courts. About one hundred years later the same procedure was authorized for the Court of the High Commission in Causes Ecclesiastical, established to maintain conformity to the recently established church. The freewheel-

§ 114

1. M. Maguire, Attack of the Common Lawyers on the Oath Ex Officio, in Essays in History and Political Theo-

ry in Honor of Charles H. McIlwain (1936), p. 203.

ing methods of these politically-minded courts—including the use of torture—undoubtedly stimulated a great deal of additional opposition to the oath procedures.

Required self-incrimination and the use of the oath were not confined to the ecclesiastical courts and the courts of High Commission and Star Chamber. In criminal trials the accused was expected to take an active part in the proceedings, often to his own detriment. He was examined before trial by justices of the peace, and the results of this examination were preserved for use by the judge at trial. Only in limited classes of cases was the examination under oath. This was not out of tenderness for the accused, but rather because it was believed that administering an oath would unwisely permit the accused to place before the jury an influential denial of guilt made under oath. When formally accused, the defendant was required to plead and submit to trial; failure to do so sometimes resulted in extreme forms of torture. Once trial had begun, the accused was subject to vigorous interrogation. He again was not placed under oath, but this again was because permitting him to take the oath would make available too easy a means of avoiding liability. Responding to Wigmore's suggestion that there was no opposition to inquisitorial procedures in the common law courts, Maguire cites a series of petitions sent to the Crown in the mid 1300s from Commons, urging the king to prohibit in the King's Council the use of the oath procedure found objectionable in the ecclesiastical courts. It is not clear, however, whether the basis for this complaint was the use of the oath procedure itself or the abuse of it by putting individuals to their oaths in the absence of a presentation.

Whatever its nature, opposition to the procedures of the High Commission and the Star Chamber was greatly stimulated by the efforts of John ("Freeborn John") Lilburn, a vocal opponent of the Stuarts (although he later collided with the Parliament's government). Arrested upon a charge before the

Star Chamber involving the printing or importing of heretical and seditious books, Lilburn denied these charges under the Attorney–General's interrogation. When asked about other matters, however, he refused to respond. For his failure to take a legal oath, he was whipped and pilloried. Undaunted, Lilburn applied to Parliament. In 1641 Commons voted that the sentence was illegal and voted reparation; in 1645, the House of Lords concurred that the sentence was illegal and must be vacated. Broader legislative relief preceded Lilburn's, when in 1641 the Long Parliament passed a bill to abolish the Courts of High Commission and Star Chamber and to prohibit the administration of an *ex officio* oath requiring an answer to "things penal." It is possible, however, that this did not prevent the ecclesiastical courts from using the oath procedure upon proper presentment or in penal matters lying within the ecclesiastical jurisdiction.

After 1641, the common law courts began to apply to their own procedure some of the restrictions that had been urged for their ecclesiastical counterparts. The reform, however, affected only the trial procedure; the practice of pre-trial examination (and use of the results at trial) remained unmodified until 1848. But there is general agreement that by 1700 extraction of an answer in any procedure in matters of criminality or forfeiture was improper.

It is difficult to draw many helpful conclusions from the historical origin of the privilege. Wigmore accepts Bentham's suggestion that the privilege as ultimately applied in the common law courts was essentially a matter of overkill.[2] After early opposition to the scope of the jurisdiction of the ecclesiastical courts, Bentham asserts, attention was turned to their abuse of the oath whereby an individual was put to his oath without proper presentment. This procedure, pursuant to which an individual was required to respond accurately and fully to broad questions con-

---

2. Id., at 292, citing J. Bentham, Rationale of Judicial Evidence, in 7 The Works of Jeremy Bentham 456, 462 (Bowring ed. 1843).

cerning his activities, was sometimes accompanied by torture and became the vehicle for effectuating the policies of foreign popes, bigoted prelates suppressing religious diversity, and dictatorial kings. Because of strong emotional feeling against the abuse of the procedure, the common law courts unnecessarily and illogically (according to Bentham) accepted the proposition that not only was it improper to compel an individual to respond to interrogation when no charge had been made against him, but also that it was inherently improper to compel him to respond at all. Wigmore and Bentham find no basis for the latter proposition in the history of opposition to the oath procedure. But perhaps this is too narrow a reading of the historical material. Even if the initial objection was only to the impropriety of putting individuals to their oath without presentation, this policy suggests at least limited objection to the use of information extracted from the mouth of the accused as the basis for a criminal prosecution. This early suspicion of compulsory self-incrimination—even if it extended only to situations where compulsion was exerted before an accusation had been made by some other method—is in no way inconsistent with later condemnation of the practice in broader circumstances. In fact both seem to be based upon a feeling that compelling an individual to provide the basis for his own penal liability should be limited because the position in which it places the individual—making a choice between violating a solemn oath and incurring penal liability—weighs against important policies of individual freedom and dignity. At first, there may have been agreement that the need to secure sufficient evidence for conviction from one whom there was significant reason to believe was guilty outweighed the invasion of personal dignity. But the decision of the common law courts in the later 1600s that even this did not outweigh the policy can certainly be viewed as consistent with and a logical extension of the opposition to the procedures of the ecclesiasti-cal courts and the courts of Star Chamber and High Commission.

§ 115. The History of the Privilege: (b) Development of the Privilege in America

There is significant disagreement regarding the early development of the privilege in America. Wigmore asserts that the privilege "remained an unknown doctrine" in the colony of Massachusetts for a generation after 1641.[1] Pittman, however, concludes that significant opposition to testimonial compulsion developed in the New England colonies after 1640 as well as in England and for largely the same reasons.[2] According to him, the Puritans sought removal of the right to compel self-incriminating testimony because they saw it as a means by which New England magistrates, who claimed divine authority, enforced compliance with an established church.

There is some evidence of the privilege in early colonial America. Pittman concludes that the privilege in regard to an accused was fairly well established in the New England colonies before 1650 and in Virginia soon after. In any case, it was inserted in the constitutions or bills of rights of seven American states before 1789, and has since spread to all state constitutions except those of Iowa and New Jersey. In both of the latter states, however, it was accepted as a matter of non-constitutional law.

Disagreement also exists concerning the source of the provision in the Fifth Amendment to the federal constitution. The first two editions of Wigmore's treatise argued that "the real explanation of the Colonial convention's insistence upon it would seem to be found in the agitation then going on in France against the inquisitorial feature of the Ordinance of 1670." Pittman, however, argues that the stream of influence was in fact running towards France from the American colonies at this time and that the colonies' own experience with high-handed prerogative

---

§ 115

1. 8 Wigmore, Evidence § 2250 (McNaughton rev. 1961), p. 293.

2. Pittman, The Colonial and Constitutional History of the Privilege Against Self-Incrimination in America, 21 Va.L.Rev. 763, 775 (1935).

courts provided the incentive for the drive to insert the privilege into the Bill of Rights. Wigmore's treatise now agrees.[3] In addition, Pittman suggests, American statesmen recognized there existed conflicts of interest and authority in the new nation much the same as underlay the conflict between the Church and the Crown in England. The Fifth Amendment privilege, he concludes, not only was an answer to numerous instances of colonial misrule but was a shield against "the evils that lurk[ed] in the shadows of a new and untried sovereignty."

Whatever the source of the Fifth Amendment privilege, Malloy v. Hogan,[4] decided in 1964, held it applicable to the states by virtue of the Fourteenth Amendment. Mr. Justice Brennan, speaking for the Court, relied heavily upon the line of Supreme Court decisions holding use of coerced confessions in state criminal prosecutions a denial of due process of law. Despite the Court's initial position that the coerced confession rule did not rest upon the Fifth Amendment privilege, the line of cases, as the Court read them in *Malloy*, soon abandoned that position and came to accept fully the underlying federal standard governing admissibility which in turn was based upon the Fifth Amendment privilege:

The shift reflects recognition that the American system of criminal prosecution is accusatorial, not inquisitorial, and that the Fifth Amendment privilege is its essential mainstay. * * * Governments, state and federal, are thus constitutionally compelled to establish guilt by evidence independently and freely secured, and may not by coercion prove a charge against an accused out of his own mouth. Since the Fourteenth Amendment prohibits the states from inducing a person to confess through 'sympathy falsely aroused' * * * or other like inducement far short of 'compulsion by torture' * * * it follows *a fortiori* that it also forbids the States to resort to imprisonment, as here, to compel him to answer questions that might incriminate him. The Fourteenth Amendment secures against

state invasion the same privilege that the Fifth Amendment guarantees against federal infringement—the right of a person to remain silent unless he chooses to speak in the unfettered exercise of his own will, and to suffer no penalty * * * for such silence.[5]

Not only is the Fifth Amendment privilege binding upon the states under *Malloy,* but the Court also made clear that its application in state courts must be consistent with federal constitutional standards. Rejecting the contention that the availability of the federal privilege to a witness in a state proceeding should be determined according to a less stringent standard than is applicable in a federal proceeding, the Court responded, "It would be incongruous to have different standards determine the validity of a claim of privilege based on the same feared prosecution, depending on whether the claim was asserted in a state or federal court. Therefore, the same standards must determine whether an accused's silence in either a federal or state proceeding is justified."[6]

§ 116. The History of the Privilege: (c) Development of the Two Branches of the Privilege—The Privilege of an Accused in a Criminal Proceeding and the Privilege of a Witness

Historically, the privilege developed from objections to the procedure whereby the ecclesiastical courts were able to compel one against whom no charge had been made to respond in incriminating fashion to broad questions posed to him. Nevertheless, when the common law courts began to apply the privilege in their own proceedings, it soon became clear that the privilege could be invoked not only by a defendant in a criminal prosecution but also by a witness whose conviction could not procedurally be a consequence of the proceeding. There is no historical indication that this was recognized as an important step in the growth of the privilege. Whatever the rationale of the English courts

---

3. 8 Wigmore, Evidence § 2250 (McNaughton rev. 1961), p. 294.

4. 378 U.S. 1 (1964).

5. Malloy v. Hogan, 378 U.S. 1, 7–8 (1964).

6. Malloy v. Hogan, 378 U.S. 1, 9–14 (1964).

for refusing to restrict the privilege to one himself on trial for a criminal offense, it was not discussed in the written decisions.

The early state constitutional provisions as well as the Fifth Amendment language permit a construction that prohibits only compulsion to cause an individual to give oral testimony in a criminal proceeding in which he is a defendant. Several authorities have argued that this was their original meaning. This position is strengthened by the fact that early American cases upholding a witness's refusal to answer relied not on existing state constitutional provisions but rather on the existence of the common law privilege which clearly encompassed a witness in a criminal or civil proceeding.

In any case, the Fifth Amendment privilege was not formally broadened beyond the apparent initial intent of the state provisions until a century after its adoption. In Counselman v. Hitchcock,[1] decided in 1892, the Supreme Court rejected the government's contention that the constitutional privilege extended a narrower privilege than the common law and that under the Fifth Amendment a witness could invoke the protection only when called upon to testify in a criminal case in which he was the accused. The precise holding was relatively narrow—that one called before a grand jury could invoke the privilege because the grand jury proceeding was a "criminal case" within the meaning of the amendment—but the language portended a broader expansion of the privilege. Thirty years later, in holding the privilege available to a bankrupt sought to be examined concerning his estate, the Court could say with confidence:

"The Government insists, broadly, that the constitutional privilege against self-incrimination does not apply in any civil proceeding. The contrary must be accepted as settled. The privilege is not ordinarily dependent upon the nature of the proceeding in which the testimony is sought or is to be used. It applies

alike to civil and criminal proceedings, wherever the answer might tend to subject to criminal responsibility him who gives it. The privilege protects a mere witness as fully as it does one who is also a party defendant."[2]

It is now generally accepted that the state constitutional provisions as well as that of the Fifth Amendment may be invoked by one whose testimony is sought in a proceeding other than a criminal prosecution in which he is the defendant. In view of the application of the federal privilege to the states,[3] however, it is now the scope of the federal privilege which is of primary importance. It is also clear that the right of one not a defendant in a criminal case to decline to provide information tending to show that he has committed a criminal offense is merely one aspect of the broad privilege against self-incrimination. But there are significantly different problems raised when the privilege is invoked by one not a defendant in a criminal prosecution. There is, therefore, analytical value in considering separately the two aspects or "branches" of the privilege: the privilege of the accused in a criminal proceeding, and the privilege of one not an accused (usually referred to as the privilege of a witness).

§ 117. The History of the Privilege: (d) Current Status of the Privilege

Much recent self-incrimination discussion has focused upon the Supreme Court's construction of the Fifth Amendment's privilege. In some senses, this is unfortunate. Similar privileges are recognized in all states as a matter of either or both state constitutional provision or case law,[1] and versions of the privilege are sometimes embodied in statutory provisions or court rule. Commentators and courts have increasingly recognized state courts' right and perhaps duty to construe state constitutional and statutory provisions "independently" of the Supreme Court's construction of even identically-phrased federal

§ 116

1. 142 U.S. 547 (1892).
2. McCarthy v. Arndstein, 266 U.S. 34, 40 (1924).
3. See § 117 infra.

§ 117

1. See § 115, supra.

constitutional provisions. This jurisprudence of "new federalism" emphasizes that there is no single privilege against compelled self-incrimination. Specifically, discussion of legal protection against compelled self-incrimination must recognize the possibility that state law provides citizens with greater protection than does the Fifth Amendment privilege.

How state courts should construe their own constitutional and statutory provisions raises broad general questions of judicial construction. State courts, when construing state provisions, are not bound to analyses used by the Supreme Court in construing the Fifth Amendment, although the federal tribunal's analyses are useful as points of reference for how state law would best be developed. Most significantly, state courts are not bound to accept the Supreme Court's conclusions as to which policies are entitled to judicial consideration or to the comparative weight to be given those policies that are relevant.

State privileges sometimes differ in phraseology from the Fifth Amendment. Seldom, however, do these differences in terminology strongly suggest how current questions of construction should be resolved. The Fifth Amendment provides that no person is to be "compelled in any criminal case to be a witness against himself." State constitutional provisions, in contrast, sometimes specify that no person may be "compelled to give evidence against himself." While this suggests the possibility that the protection afforded by the state provisions is broader, it is difficult to regard the difference in language as necessarily controlling.

Courts often accept that the "intent" or original understandings of the framers or adopters of state provisions, if it can be ascertained, should determine the current content of those provisions. But seldom is there reliable evidence of any understandings relevant to those issues confronting modern courts. Perhaps, then, the major issue raised by state constitutional self-incrimination provisions is whether state courts should regard the Supreme Court's construction of the Fifth Amendment as presumptively appropriate for their state provisions well. Under such an interpretive approach, a state provision will be construed as the Supreme Court has construed the Fifth Amendment privilege, unless the proponent of a broader (or narrower) interpretation comes forward with convincing evidence of original understanding or policy considerations appropriate for judicial consideration.

Despite widespread acknowledgement by state courts that they have the power to construe state privileges independent of the Supreme Court's construction of the Fifth Amendment, state tribunals have in fact tended to follow the federal Court's case law. In the sections that follow, some state courts' deviations from the Supreme Court's Fifth Amendment constructions will be noted and discussed. These decisions, however, are exceptions to the general tendency of state courts to incorporate into state law the content which the Supreme Court had developed in the Fifth Amendment context.

§ 118. Policy Foundations of the Modern Privilege

Inquiry into the policies that do or might support the privilege often seems a frustrating and perhaps fruitless task. Despite the privilege's rich history, vigorous arguments have been made that the dangers of the Court of Star Chamber no longer exist and that the privilege has outlived its rationale. Even proponents of the privilege acknowledge that its popularity and acceptance was not based upon a careful scrutiny of its rationale and that its incorporation into our legal tradition occurred without thorough examination. Modern discussion has tended to undertake largely de novo development of justifications.

Whether a conceptually adequate justification exists may have little significance to the basic questions under modern law. Supreme Court discussions of the Fifth Amendment privilege often contain references to the justifications for and purposes served by it, but the Court has acknowledged that "the privilege has never been given the full scope which the values it helps to protect suggest." [1] Moreover, "[t]he policies behind the privilege are varied, and not all are implicated in any given application of the privilege." [2] Stuntz notes that judicial and academic writings tend to be dominated by standard explanations for the privilege that fail to explain adequately even the basic aspects of Fifth Amendment privilege law, "leading to a widespread sense that many of [the Fifth Amendment privilege's] rules and limitations are simply inexplicable." [3]

Opponents of the privilege make several principle points beyond simply arguing the lack of a satisfactory and principled basis for the privilege. First, the privilege deprives the state of access to a valuable source of reliable information, the subject of the investigation himself, and therefore purchases whatever values it attains at too great a cost to the inquiry for truth. The subject may be an especially valuable source of information when the alleged crime is one of the sophisticated "white collar" offenses, and in such situations the privilege may deny the prosecution access to the *only* available information. Moreover, the privilege may as a practical matter be impossible to implement effectively. Although the law may extend the theoretical right to remain silent at no or minimal cost, in fact it is inevitable that inferences will be drawn from silence and that the inferences will be acted upon. Since these inferences are drawn from inherently ambiguous silence, they are less reliable than inferences from other sources, including compelled self-incriminatory testimony. The result is that one who chooses to invoke the privilege is not protected, but rather is subjected to potential prejudice in a manner ill designed to promote even his own best interest.

Rationales for the privilege can usefully be divided into systemic ones—based on the role of the privilege in maintaining a valuable criminal justice system—and individual ones—resting on the value of the privilege in implementing the interests or values of those suspected or accused of crime. These rationales may overlap, as is demonstrated by the argument that the privilege serves as a valuable means of preventing the conviction of innocent criminal defendants. One who is under the strain of actual or potential accusation, although innocent, may be unduly prejudiced by his own testimony for reasons unrelated to its accuracy. For example, he may have physical traits or mannerisms that would cause an adverse reaction from the trier of fact. He might, under the strain of interrogation, become confused and thereby give an erroneous impression of guilt. Or, his act of testifying may permit the prosecution to introduce his prior criminal convictions, ostensibly for impeachment purposes, and the trier of fact may uncritically infer his guilt from these. The privilege affords such an individual the opportunity to avoid these dangers possibly flowing from discussing an incriminating situation and thereby creating an unreliable but prejudicial impression of guilt.

Whether these considerations support the privilege is at best problematic. Few defendants may give misleading impressions of guilt, and juries may be more skilled at evaluating evidence than is sometimes believed. Even when there is a significant risk that testifying will create an erroneous impression of guilt, practical considerations are likely to lead many defendants to testify nevertheless. To the extent that these risks are real ones, other reforms in criminal procedure might better protect against them; the admissibility of prior convictions to impeach, for example, might be limited.

The privilege may also protect the innocent in less direct ways. It constitutes one part— but an important part—of our accusatorial system which requires that no criminal punishment be imposed unless guilt is established by a large quantum of especially reliable evidence. By denying the prosecution access to what is regarded as an inherently suspect type of proof—the self-incriminating admis-

§ 118

1. Schmerber v. California, 384 U.S. 757, 762 (1966).
2. McGautha v. California, 402 U.S. 183, 214 (1971).

3. Stuntz, Self–Incrimination and Excuse, 88 Colum.L.Rev. 1227, 1228 (1988).

sions of the accused—the privilege forces the prosecution to establish its case on the basis of more reliable evidence, thus creating an additional assurance that every person convicted is in fact guilty as charged. Others, however, argue that the privilege is an ineffective means of encouraging the making of the guilt-innocence decision on reliable evidence. In many situations, for example, it denies defendants the right to call witnesses whose testimony might well be reliable and exculpatory.

Other systemic arguments run that the privilege serves to deny governments powers that might otherwise be abused, particularly in especially sensitive areas. It may also serve to maintain public confidence in the legal system by preventing the degeneration of trials into spectacles that many would find offensive. Of course, the privilege may in fact do neither. Public confidence in the legal system, to the contrary, may even be reduced when courts are compelled to eschew what appears to be the most reliable sources of information. To the extent that the privilege does accomplish these purposes, it may do so inefficiently, as by failing to identify and restrain those governmental powers most offensive and likely to be abused or those aspects of criminal procedure most offensive to the population in general.

Recent defenses of the privilege have tended to rely less upon systemic rationales than upon individual ones. These arguments, which again somewhat overlap, suggest that the privilege prevents the treatment of suspects and defendants in ways that would be offensive to notions of "privacy" or "individual autonomy." As the privilege applies to out-of-court law enforcement interrogation, for example, it may serve to prohibit interrogation techniques that, given the public's increased sensitivities, may now be as offensive as physical torture was at the time of the privilege's development.

As applied in either the in-court or out-of-court situations, the privilege may prevent

the treatment of suspects and accuseds in ways that are unacceptably "cruel." Intolerable cruelty may arise simply from compelling the accused to participate in the process itself. Or, the privilege may prevent the treatment of such persons in ways unacceptable because such treatment is inconsistent with developed notions of human dignity. Even a guilty person, for example, may be regarded as retaining aspects of dignity that are violated when that person is compelled to actively participate in the process of bringing punitive sanctions down upon him.

Gerstein [4] has developed a somewhat similar argument based on privacy concerns: Most persons apprehended for a crime which they have committed regard themselves as a part of the same moral community as those who are the victims of criminal offenses. They regard the commission of an offense as a moral as well as a legal matter. For such persons, a confession involves not simply submission to legal liability but the acknowledgement of moral wrongdoing and often the revelation of remorse. A person's judgments of his own moral blameworthiness is special and perhaps unique and thus peculiarly private. This sort of "information"—self-acknowledgment of moral blameworthiness—is so "private" that the individual ought to have full control over it. Even if the courts are empowered to convict an accused of a crime, they should not be empowered to force him to publicly make the judgment by which he condemns himself in his own conscience. He ought to be able to decide whether to share this only with his God or those to whom he feels bound by trust and affection.

A related argument runs that compelling even a guilty person to choose among incriminating himself, committing perjury, or suffering penalties such as contempt citation requires such a difficult or offensive choice that the privilege is justified by the need to prevent that choice. Exactly why the choice presented by this "cruel trilemma" [5] is so of-

---

4. Gerstein, Privacy and Self–Incrimination, 80 Ethics 87 (1970).

5. See Murphy v. Waterfront Commission, 378 U.S. 52, 55 (1964) (Fifth Amendment privilege reflects, among other things, "our unwillingness to subject those suspect-

fensive is not entirely clear. Perhaps it is because a person's natural instincts and personal interests so strongly suggest that he should lie in an effort to avoid criminal liability that it is somehow unfair to punish him for following those instincts. If no reasonable person could be expected to do other than what the witness did, fairness seems offended by punishing him. Perhaps the choice is offensive simply because the state is forcing the person to act. In many cases, Judge Frank argued, "the state would be forcing him to commit a crime and then punishing him for it." Yet the law often puts witnesses and others to choices that seem no less difficult or "unfair," and to single out persons—most of them in the position because of their own criminal acts—for solicitude may be inappropriate.

Stuntz argues that other efforts to explain the privilege unsatisfactorily assume that the activity protected is in some sense "justified." He suggests that a more satisfactory explanation rests on quite different excuse grounds. Were the privilege not recognized, our legal system would be compelled to make available an excuse defense to those defendants who, when called as a prosecution witness, perjured themselves rather than admit guilt. But such a defense would invoke quite heavy systemic costs. By removing the deterrents to perjury, for example, the defense would lead to a flood of perjurious testimony impairing juries' ability to accurately resolve cases. Recognizing the privilege avoids the need to pay those costs.

The Fifth Amendment and other versions of the privilege can only be regarded as supported by varying combinations of the considerations discussed above. Particular requirements imposed by them often must rest upon combinations of some but less than all of the considerations. The core situation covered by all versions of the privilege, direct trial examination of the sworn defendant under threat of contempt citations as to whether he committed the crime charged, implicates all of

these considerations to a singularly significant degree. Whether or not other situations come within the privilege, however, must depend upon what considerations are implicated, the comparative weight given those considerations, and the degree to which they are implicated. The variety of purposes and rationales that can be called into play and the absence of historical or other guidelines for applying those purposes and rationales, however, means that courts have extraordinary flexibility in constructing policy analyses with which to address particular issues presented by the privilege in its various forms.

§ 119. Procedural Manner of Effectuating the Privilege

Because of the variety of situations to which the privilege may apply, it might be asserted in any of a wide variety of ways. How the privilege may or must be invoked depends in part upon whether the holder is asserting the privilege of an accused in a criminal prosecution or rather that of a witness. A witness in an in-court proceeding, therefore, will ordinarily invoke the privilege as a response to particular questions asked on direct or cross-examination.[1] An accused, on the other hand, ordinarily need not affirmatively "invoke" his privilege, as he is entitled even not to be called as a witness.

As the privilege applies to out-of-court situations, invoking it becomes more complicated. A suspect compelled to make out-of-court admissions may raise his privilege as the basis for objecting to the later reception of those admissions into evidence against him. Criminal or other penalties may be attached to a requirement which a person believes, as applied to his situation, compels protected self-incrimination. In such situations, the holder of the privilege may first assert it as a defense to a criminal prosecution for failure to comply with the requirement.

How and when the holder of the privilege *must* assert it in order to realize its full pro-

ed of crime to the cruel trilemma of self-accusation, perjury or contempt").

1. See § 137 infra.

tection is discussed in the sections that follow. This is closely interwined with the substance of the privilege, as in some situations it is clear that a person's failure to assert the privilege means that his self-incriminating disclosures are not "compelled" within the meaning of the privilege.[2]

Is a person entitled to a judicial determination as to the merits of his claim to the privilege before he must decide whether or not to make self-incriminating disclosures and thus risk a penalty for improperly refusing to testify or provide information? In most situations, such as in-court testimony, a witness who asserts the privilege is afforded a ruling on his claim by the trial judge. If the trial judge determines that his claim is not a valid one, the witness is given—as a matter of practice if not of absolute right—an opportunity to testify before contempt penalties are assessed. In Garner v. United States,[3] Garner asserted that he was entitled as a matter of Fifth Amendment mandate to a procedure that would give him a ruling on his claim to the privilege before he had to make a choice that could subject him to criminal liability. This, the majority concluded, was in essence a contention that the Fifth Amendment guarantees a preliminary-ruling procedure for testing the validity of specific assertions of the privilege. Such a procedure might best serve the interests of both the Government and the holder of the privilege, the majority acknowledged, but the Fifth Amendment does not require it:

> What is at issue here is principally a matter of timing and procedure. As long as a valid and timely claim of privilege is available as a defense to a taxpayer prosecuted for failure to make a return, the taxpayer had not been denied a free choice to remain silent merely because of the absence of a preliminary judicial ruling on his claim.[4]

This was said after the majority earlier concluded that good faith but erroneous reliance upon the privilege would be a defense to criminal prosecution, but the language used does not incorporate that conclusion. Whether the holder of the privilege may be penalized by prosecution or citation for contempt for good faith but mistaken reliance on the privilege, then, remains unclear.

§ 120. Personal Nature of the Privilege

Courts frequently describe the privilege against compelled self-incrimination as being personal in nature. These often offhand comments are sometimes, however, somewhat misleading.

The privilege is clearly personal in the sense that only the person who is at risk of incrimination can invoke it. A witness, therefore, cannot refuse to provide information on the ground that it would incriminate someone else and thus intrude upon their interests. If a lawyer is called as a witness before a grand jury, for example, he cannot rely on the privilege as a basis for refusing to respond to questions on the ground that the answers would incriminate his client. A criminal defendant cannot invoke the privilege of witnesses, codefendants, or even coconspirators or accomplices. Nor, generally speaking, can a criminal defendant successfully complain that the self-incrimination rights of such persons were violated in the litigation process.

There has been some suggestion that the personal nature of the privilege means that it can only be invoked by the personal act or statement of the holder and thus that a lawyer cannot invoke it on behalf of the holder. This is unnecessary and undesirable. When a lawyer, acting under authorization of the client and on behalf of the client, invokes the client's privilege, there is nothing to be gained by requiring the client to invoke the privilege himself. On the other hand, it is reasonable (and perhaps necessary)[1] to require that the decision as to whether or not to invoke the privilege be made by the client and not the

---

2. See §§ 125, 136, 137, 139 infra.
3. 424 U.S. 648 (1976).
4. Id. at 665.

§ 120

1. See §§ 134, 140, infra.

lawyer. If the lawyer's authorization is in reasonable doubt, the trial judges should have authority to require that the client's authorization be established.

§ 121. General Scope of the Privilege: (a) Protection Against Criminal Liability

The privilege protects its holders only against the risk of *legal criminal liability*. Despite vigorous objection, it has been uniformly held to provide no protection against the disgrace and practical excommunication from society which might result from disclosure of matter which, under the circumstances, could not give rise to criminal liability.

If the risk of criminal liability is removed there is no privilege. It is clear, then, that the privilege does not apply when prosecution and conviction is precluded by passage of the period of limitations, pardon, prior acquittal, or a grant of immunity,[1] although whether on particular facts the risk of liability is in fact removed may present a difficult question. When prior conviction removes the risk of criminal liability, then the privilege is similarly rendered inapplicable. Whether that risk is actually removed by prior conviction, however, presents some special problems.

If direct appeal from a conviction is pending or remains available, a convicted defendant might, despite his conviction, harbor hope that his conviction will be reversed on appeal and that any disclosures he makes would be used to incriminate him upon any retrial that follows. Because of this possibility, the courts have generally held that a convicted defendant retains the protection of the privilege until appeal is exhausted or until the time for appeal expires. As the Maryland court recognized,[2] despite the low statistical likelihood of reversal on appeal, the risk of a retrial is not so remote as to constitute a negligible risk under the prevailing standard. Whether the possibility that a conviction might be invalidated in collateral attack should affect the availability of the privilege is another matter. Because collateral attack is generally available at any time, finding that the risk of retrial after a successful attack of this sort preserves protection would dramatically expand the protection of the privilege. The best solution is to treat the possibility of successful collateral attack and retrial as raising the question of whether the facts present a "real and appreciable" danger of incrimination.[3] In the absence of some specific showing that collateral attack is likely to be successful, a conviction should be regarded as removing the risk of incrimination and consequently the protection of the privilege.

A convicted defendant might also invoke the protection of the privilege on the ground that disclosures might cause him to receive a more severe penalty for the crime of which he has been convicted than would otherwise be imposed. This raises the question of what disadvantages in a criminal proceeding other than formal conviction are within the protection of the privilege. Is, in other words, increased severity of sentence a type of "incrimination" within the meaning of the privilege?

In Estelle v. Smith[4] the Supreme Court held that the Fifth Amendment protected an accused person from compelled disclosures that increased the risk of being sentenced to death although not the risk of conviction for capital murder. In explanation, however, it offered only that it could find no basis for distinguishing between the guilt and penalty issues. There is no principled basis on which *Smith* could be distinguished from other situations in which compelled disclosure would increase the risk of sentence severity but short of death. The lower courts have generally assumed that the privilege protects an accused or even a convicted defendant against compelled disclosures that might increase the severity of the punishment.

---

§ 121

1. See § 143 infra.

2. See Ellison v. State, 310 Md. 244, 528 A.2d 1271 (1987).

3. See § 122 infra.

4. 451 U.S. 454 (1981).

On the other hand, in *Smith* the Court assumed that a finding of competency to stand trial would not be "incrimination" within the meaning of the Fifth Amendment. Hence, that provision does not prohibit compulsion upon an accused to provide information that could at most increase the risk of his being found competent. In Minnesota v. Murphy [5] the Court turned to later aspects of the criminal process and indicated in dictum that revocation of probation would not be "incrimination" within the meaning of the Fifth Amendment and that therefore a probationer has no right to invoke the privilege on the basis that his answers would increase the risk of his probation being revoked. The *Smith* discussion can be explained on the ground that a finding of competency leads to no imposition of liability of any sort, but merely removes a procedural barrier to proceeding with the criminal prosecution. The *Murphy* dictum is more difficult to reconcile with *Smith's* holding that the privilege protects against an increase in severity of the penalty imposable upon conviction, because in some senses probation revocation reflects a significant change in the severity of the penalty visited upon one guilty of an offense. Lower courts have, however, followed *Murphy*.

It is clear that the privilege does protect against the risk of conviction for what are technically criminal offenses and equally clear that it does not protect against the imposition of liability for damages on the basis of traditionally civil causes of action. Whether it protects against types of liability that are between these two poles is less clear. In 1886, the Supreme Court held that "proceedings instituted for the purpose of declaring the forfeiture of a man's property by reason of offenses committed by him, though they may be civil in form, are in their nature criminal." [6] Thus the Fifth Amendment privilege protects against forfeiture, at least where such action is based on conduct that could also serve as the basis for a criminal prosecu-

tion. In Application of Gault,[7] the Court held that the federal constitutional privilege protected against compelled disclosures that could lead to a finding that a child was delinquent. This determination apparently rested largely upon the fact that such a finding could result in a loss of liberty which the Court concluded was indistinguishable from the imprisonment that might follow criminal conviction. But in Baxter v. Palmigiano,[8] the Court almost offhandedly held that disciplinary penalties imposed upon convicted prison inmates were not "incrimination" and did not themselves invoke the protection of the Fifth Amendment privilege. Two years later, the Court held that a civil penalty imposed under the Federal Water Pollution Control Act for discharge of harmful substances into navigable waters was not "incrimination" within the Fifth Amendment meaning.[9]

This line of decisions came to a head in Allen v. Illinois,[10] in which the Court considered whether the Fifth Amendment protected against being found a sexually dangerous person under the nominally civil Illinois Sexually Dangerous Persons Act. Under the Act, a person may be found a sexually dangerous person only upon proof that he has engaged in criminal sexual misconduct. If such a finding is made, he can be committed for an indeterminate period to a maximum-security institution run by correctional authorities. Generally, the Court held, the legislature's designation of liability as civil in nature will be sufficient to take it out of Fifth Amendment coverage. A "civil" label must be disregarded and the Fifth Amendment applied, however, upon " 'the clearest proof' that 'the statutory scheme [is] so punitive either in purpose or effect as to negate [the State's] intention' that the proceeding be civil * * *." The Illinois courts had determined that the proceedings were essentially civil in nature. Allen failed to make the required showing that the scheme was punitive in purpose or effect. Contrary to indications in *Gault*, the

---

5. 465 U.S. 420 (1984).

6. Boyd v. United States, 116 U.S. 616, 634 (1886).

7. 387 U.S. 1 (1967).

8. 425 U.S. 308 (1976).

9. United States v. Ward, 448 U.S. 242 (1980).

10. 478 U.S. 364 (1986).

fact that liability may result in involuntary incarceration is insufficient to require application of the privilege.

Under *Allen,* a litigant seeking to establish that the Fifth Amendment protects against a nominally civil form of liability has a difficult task and is unlikely to succeed. In that case, the Court assumed that the Fifth Amendment privilege does not protect against compulsory hospitalization for mental illness. Lower courts have held that the privilege does not protect members of the bar against disciplinary proceedings or judges against judicial discipline. Nor is an administrative proceeding to suspend a commercial pilot's license criminal or "quasi-criminal" so as to invoke the fifth amendment privilege. Protection similarly does not extend to liability for civil contempt of court although it probably does extend to criminal contempt.

§ 122. General Scope of the Privilege: (b) Requirement of a "Real and Appreciable" Risk of Incrimination

Early in the development of the federal constitutional privilege it was established that the danger of incrimination must be "real and appreciable." A danger only "imaginary and unsubstantial" would not support invocation of the privilege.[1] This formulation of the required risk developed from the English decision in Queen v. Boyles.[2] A witness asserted the danger of parliamentary impeachment as a basis for invoking the privilege. Rejecting this, the court held:

[T]he danger to be apprehended must be real and appreciable, with reference to the ordinary operation of the law in the ordinary course of things—not a danger of an imaginary and unsubstantial character, having reference to some extraordinary and barely possible contingency, so improbable that no reasonable man would suffer it to influence his conduct.[3]

This formulation of the required risk is still widely accepted. In several early decisions, the United States Supreme Court invoked it as a basis for holding the privilege inapplicable.[4] But as now applied, at least in most contexts, this required risk is generally present. This is best illustrated by the cases in which a question inquires into sexual activity that is technically violative of criminal prohibitions that are seldom and perhaps never enforced. Courts have sustained claims of the privilege in these situations often without inquiry into whether the likelihood of criminal prosecution is so remote as to render the risk of incrimination imaginary and unsubstantial. Some courts have expressly embraced what seems to be the functional rule: it is sufficient that information sufficiently implicates a person in activity that is formally criminalized, and the courts will not inquire further into such matters as the probability of actual prosecution. This makes good sense, given the difficulties of formulating an adequate criterion for the required probability and the greater problems that would arise in applying any such standard to all but the easiest cases.

Application of the general requirement of a real and appreciable risk to some more specific problems in the administration of the privilege does present difficulties. These are considered elsewhere in this chapter in connection with the compulsory production of documents and tangible items[5] and the task of determining whether a witness's response to a question is sufficiently related to criminal liability to support invocation of the privilege.[6]

§ 123. General Scope of the Privilege: (c) Incrimination Under the Laws of Another Jurisdiction

A witness may assert the privilege on the basis of concern regarding criminal liability

§ 122

1. Brown v. Walker, 161 U.S. 591, 608 (1896).
2. 1 B. & S. 311, 121 Eng.Rep. 730 (K.B.1861).
3. Id. at 330, 121 Eng.Rep. at 738.
4. Brown v. Walker, 161 U.S. 591 (1896) (possibility of conviction under laws of another sovereign a danger of an imaginary and unsubstantial character); Rogers v. United States, 340 U.S. 367, 374–75 (1951) (after witness had admitted holding office of treasurer of Communist Party, disclosure of acquaintance with her successor presents no more than a mere imaginary possibility of increasing the danger of prosecution).

5. See § 128, infra.
6. See § 139, infra.

in the courts of a jurisdiction other than the one in which the witness's testimony is being sought. These situations can be divided as follows: (a) a witness in either state or federal court claims danger of incrimination under the laws of a foreign country; (b) a witness in a state court claims danger of incrimination under the laws of another state; (c) a witness in a state court claims danger of incrimination under federal law; and (d) a witness in a federal court claims a danger of incrimination under state law.

Traditionally, most courts took the position that the privilege protected only against incrimination under the laws of the sovereign which was attempting to compel the incriminating information. In part, the basis for such holdings was the view that the risk of prosecution by another sovereign was so low as not to invoke protection under the privilege. It has also been argued, however, that this result follows from the rationale for the privilege. To the extent that the privilege is based upon concern regarding brutality and other such excesses that a sovereign might commit when attempting to compel a person's assistance in achieving his own conviction, that risk is seldom presented when the only potential criminal liability lies under the laws of another jurisdiction. In such cases, the compelling sovereign is unlikely to have sufficient interest in incriminating the person to perform acts which invoke the rationale for the privilege.

With regard to the Fifth Amendment privilege, this traditional position was rejected by the Supreme Court in Murphy v. Waterfront Commission.[1] Murphy and several others had been subpoenaed to testify before the Waterfront Commission of New York Harbor regarding a work stoppage at certain New Jersey piers. They were granted immunity from prosecution under New York and New Jersey law but invoked their Fifth Amendment privilege on the ground that their responses would tend to incriminate them under federal law. The Supreme Court agreed that the Fifth Amendment privilege protects state witnesses from liability under federal as well as state law. Noting the high degree of cooperation among jurisdictions, it reasoned without extended discussion that most and perhaps all of the policies and purposes of the Fifth Amendment privilege are defeated when a witness possessing protection against incrimination under both state and federal law can be "whipsawed" into incriminating himself under both bodies of law by simply being called as a witness in the courts of first one and then the other jurisdiction. The defense of the traditional view noted earlier was dismissed as based upon too narrow a view of those policies supporting the Fifth Amendment privilege.

The court recognized, however, that to expand Murphy's Fifth Amendment protection in state courts to include protection against incrimination under federal law without providing the states with a means of obtaining his testimony would ignore the interests that both levels of Government have in investigating and prosecuting crime. Consequently, it held that when a state compels testimony incriminating under federal law, as for example under a grant of immunity, the Federal Government is prohibited from making any incriminating use of that compelled testimony and its fruits. Since Murphy and his companions were thus adequately protected against the use of their compelled testimony in securing their federal convictions, they could be compelled to testify.

Murphy expressly resolved only situation (c) above. But it removed any conceptual basis for the traditional view that the privilege was inapplicable in situations (b) and (d). In both situations, witnesses have protection. But the jurisdiction seeking their testimony may nevertheless compel it if the witness can be assured that the compelled testimony and evidence derived from it cannot be used to incriminate him under the laws of the other jurisdiction. This assurance is provided by the federal constitutional prohibitions against the use of coerced "confessions" in either federal or state protections.

§ 123

1. 378 U.S. 52 (1964).

There is, then, general agreement that a federal witness is protected against incrimination under state law and that a state witness is protected against incrimination under the law of other states. Similarly, it is clear that in either situation the witness can be granted immunity by the forum jurisdiction and compelled to answer and that neither the testimony nor evidence derived from it will be usable in the other jurisdiction. Whether a witness who invokes the privilege on the ground that the testimony may incriminate her only under the laws of another jurisdiction can be compelled to testify without a grant of local immunity is not clear. Perhaps, in the absence of an assertion of the privilege by the witness and a grant of immunity overriding it, the testimony is not sufficiently "compelled" to assure its exclusion in the other jurisdiction.

Situation (a) above remains unresolved. The Supreme Court has noted but not addressed it.[2] Chief Justice Burger expressed the view that there is a "fair prospect" that a majority of the Court would hold that the Fifth Amendment protects against the risk of incrimination under the laws of a foreign nation. The *Murphy* dictum, he reasoned, if "carried to its logical conclusion, would support such an outcome."[3]

The functional underpinning of *Murphy,* however, may well not apply here. *Murphy's* holding undoubtedly rested in part upon the Court's conclusion that the costs of extending coverage could be kept manageable by permitting the forum jurisdiction to compel testimony by assuring that the state under whose laws the witness was incriminated could not use that compelled testimony. No similar conclusion could be reached if the Fifth Amendment were held to protect against the incrimination under the law of foreign countries. United States courts, of course, could not assure that the courts of those countries would not use testimony or derivative evidence obtained in American courts under threat of contempt. Consequently, the result of such an expansion of Fifth Amendment coverage might well mean that the testimony would be rendered totally unavailable in the United States, since no effective immunity or its equivalent could be provided the witness. This might well be too high a cost to pay for taking the *Murphy* dictum to its logical conclusion.

Lower federal courts have shown a strong tendency to avoid the question by readily concluding that witnesses have not shown a sufficient risk of incrimination under the law of foreign countries. In the case of efforts to resist testifying before a grand jury, courts have insisted upon a showing that sealing the grand jury testimony would not eliminate the risk or reduce it to insignificance. To the extent that they have addressed the basic question, lower federal courts have tended towards the view that Fifth Amendment protection does not extend to incrimination under the laws of foreign countries. The leading case is probably United States v. (Under Seal) (Araneta).[4] In concluding that the Fifth Amendment did not protect the witnesses against incrimination under the laws of the Philippines, the court was clearly influenced by its concern that a holding to the contrary would mean that the United States would sometimes be totally barred from obtaining evidence within its reach because a foreign sovereignty could use that evidence in a manner not permitted in the United States. Such a position, it reasoned, would compromise the national sovereignty and thus would be unacceptable.

§ 124. General Scope of the Privilege: (d) Activity Compelled Must Be "Testimonial"

The Fifth Amendment privilege and those of almost all states protect only against com-

---

2. See Zicarelli v. New Jersey State Commission of Investigation, 406 U.S. 472, 478–481 (1972).

3. Araneta v. United States, 478 U.S. 1301, 1304 (1986) (granting stay pending filing of petition for certiorari).

4. 794 F.2d 920, 925–28 (4th Cir.1986), cert. denied 479 U.S. 924.

pulsion to engage in *testimonial* self-incriminating activity. Both the rationale and the meaning of this limitation, however, are subject to some dispute despite extensive treatment of the matter in two major recent cases, Doe v. United States [1] and Pennsylvania v. Muniz.[2]

As early as 1910, the United States Supreme Court held that the Fifth Amendment privilege was not violated when an accused was compelled to put on a blouse for purposes of determining whether it fitted him.[3] "[T]he prohibition * * *," declared the Court, "is a prohibition of the use of physical or moral compulsion to exact communications * * *." [4] This approach was reaffirmed in Schmerber v. California.[5] Explaining that the privilege "protects an accused only from being compelled to testify against himself, or otherwise provide the state with evidence of a testimonial or communicative nature," the Court held that blood extracted from a non-consenting suspect, "although an incriminating product of compulsion, was neither [his] testimony nor evidence relating to some communicative act or writing by [him. Thus] it was not inadmissible on privilege grounds."

Precisely why the Fifth Amendment privilege is limited to compulsion to engage in "testimonial" activity was not directly addressed until *Doe* and the Court's discussion in that case is not particularly satisfactory. In *Doe,* the Court first noted that so limiting the privilege is consistent with the history of the Fifth Amendment privilege and its predecessors, which were historically intended to prevent the use of legal compulsion to extract sworn communications from accuseds of facts which would incriminate them. The variety of policies served by the privilege are served when the privilege is applied to spare an accused from having to reveal his knowledge, thoughts and beliefs with the Government, and thus limiting the privilege to such situations is consistent with those policies.

The Court acknowledged that those policies would be served to some extent by applying the privilege more broadly. Precisely why that does not permit or require a broader formulation of the privilege's protection was not carefully developed. "[T]he scope of the privilege," the *Doe* majority reiterated from *Schmerber,* "does not coincide with the complex of values it helps to protect." But this observation is of little help in explaining why the testimonial requirement is imposed to determine the extent to which the scope will coincide with those values. *Doe* simply assumed that the Court's prior case law established that the protected interests in "privacy, fairness, and restraint of governmental power" are not impermissibly offended by compelling the accused to cooperate in the prosecution's use of his body to develop "highly incriminating testimony." The Court apparently conceded that the privilege is based in part upon the need to limit the Government's ability to compel the accused to "assist in his prosecution" in a broader sense, and that this purpose would be served by expanding the privilege to nontestimonial situations. But it stressed that other federal Constitutional provisions also serve that same purpose, apparently so effectively that the Fifth Amendment need not be developed so as to provide additional limits.

Despite *Doe* and the Court's 1990 decision in *Muniz,* whether particular activity is "testimonial" and thus cannot be compelled under the Fifth Amendment remains a "difficult question." In *Doe,* the Court approved the formulation urged by the Government: an act is "testimonial" within the meaning of the Fifth Amendment privilege if it "explicitly or implicitly, relate[s] a factual assertion or disclose[s] information." Citing from Wigmore's treatise, it offered further that this means that compelled action is "testimonial" only if the action is sought as an indication of the subject's intentional expression of his knowl-

§ 124

1. 487 U.S. 201 (1988).
2. 496 U.S. 582 (1990).
3. Holt v. United States, 218 U.S. 245 (1910).

4. Id. at 252–253.
5. 384 U.S. 757 (1966).

edge or belief concerning factual matters.[6] This approach was reaffirmed in *Muniz.*

Apparently this means that the privilege is implicated when, but only when, the Government imposes compulsion to cause the subject to act in a manner that the subject intends as a disclosure of his perception of, or belief as to, factual matters. Consequently, it is not sufficient that the government seeks by compulsion to learn the subject's thoughts. The privilege prohibits only compulsion to require the subject to intentionally reveal his thoughts. Conduct consisting of flight from the scene of a crime, for example, reveals the person's thoughts—his consciousness of his own guilt. But the conduct—the flight—is not an intentional communication by the subject of the contents of those thoughts and thus it is not testimonial.

Physical as well as verbal activity may be testimonial under this definition. The "vast majority" of verbal statements will be testimonial, because "[t]here are very few instances in which a verbal statement, either oral or written, will not convey information or assert facts."[7]

Whether activity—especially nonverbal conduct—is "testimonial" and thus within the privilege so defined has proven to sometimes be a troublesome question, but some situations create no reasonable question. Compelling a suspect to simply cooperate so that officials may observe the suspect's physical characteristics clearly involves no "testimonial" activity on the suspect's part. Consequently, compelling a person to appear in a lineup for observation of his physical characteristics is permissible. Requiring a suspect to submit to the extraction of a blood sample was held in *Schmerber* not to be compulsion of testimonial conduct, and nothing has cast doubt upon the Court's 1910 holding[8] that compelling a suspect to don an item of cloth-

ing to reveal whether it fits is similarly only coercing nontestimonial activity.

In the context of compelled production of documents,[9] the Court has made clear that a person's act of producing an item in response to a subpoena may involve tacit acknowledgements that the item exists, that the respondent has access to it, and that the item produced is believed by the respondent to be the one demanded. In some situations at least, the act of producing the item therefore has a testimonial component and thus invokes the Fifth Amendment privilege. This "act of production" rule, of course, need not be limited to the subpoenaed document context and has been held to apply to evidence that a criminal suspect, in response to an officer's demand, produced a controlled substance from his car. By his act of producing the substance, the suspect tacitly acknowledged the incriminating fact that he was aware of its presence in his vehicle.

In South Dakota v. Neville,[10] the majority found "considerable force" in the argument that a suspect's refusal to participate in a breath test for blood alcohol was like flight and thus noncommunicative conduct rather than a testimonial communication. It did not, however, resolve the matter. The Court has also held, apparently without qualification, that the privilege does not prohibit compelling suspects to provide voice[11] or handwriting samples[12] despite the possibility that in some situations suspects' responses might contain tacit acknowledgements that are difficult to distinguish from the testimonial aspects of responding to a subpoena for items. Whether a lie detector or polygraph examination would involve testimonial activity remains unclear.

In *Muniz,* the Court addressed the application of the Fifth Amendment to a stationhouse sobriety test which involved several categories of "compelled" activity. The offi-

6. *Doe,* supra note 1, at 211, citing 8 J. Wigmore, Evidence § 2265 p. 386 (McNaughton rev. 1961).

7. *Doe,* supra note 1, at 213, cited in *Muniz,* supra note 2, at 2648.

8. Holt v. United States, 218 U.S. 245, 252–53 (1910).

9. See generally § 128 infra.

10. 459 U.S. 553 (1983).

11. United States v. Dionisio, 410 U.S. 1, 7 (1973).

12. Gilbert v. California, 388 U.S. 263, 266 (1967).

cer conducting the test first asked Muniz his name, address, height, weight, eye color, date of birth, and current age. Next, in an apparent effort to test Muniz' ability to calculate, he asked, "Do you know what the date was of your sixth birthday?" Finally, the officer instructed him, as he performed several physical dexterity tests, to count. Controversy focused upon the second "sixth birthday" question, to which Muniz had responded, "No, I don't."

Justice Brennan, speaking for a bare majority of five justices, explained that this question did not require exploration of the "outer boundries of what is 'testimonial,'" because the "core meaning" of that concept made clear that Muniz' response to the question was testimonial. That the police were seeking to ascertain the physical nature of Muniz' brain processes was not controlling, he continued, if that inquiry was pursued by means that called for testimonial responses from the suspect. The question posed to Muniz called for such a response, because it demanded that he communicate his perception or belief concerning his mental processes and their result. Functionally, he was communicating that he believed or knew that he was unaware of the date of his sixth birthday and, therefore, that he could not calculate it.

This result was required, Justice Brennan developed further, by applying a functional analysis using the rationale for the privilege. At its core, the privilege is designed to protect those suspected of crime from modern-day analogues of the historic trilemma of self-accusation, perjury or contempt. "Whatever else it may include * * *," he explained, "the definition of 'testimonial' evidence articulated in *Doe* must encompass all responses to questions that, if asked of a sworn suspect during a criminal trial, could place the suspect in the 'cruel trilemma.'" Muniz was confronted with such a trilemma. The custodial environment "precluded" silence. He was, then, left with the choice of truthfully admitting he did not know the date of his sixth birthday, and thus incriminating himself, and misrepresenting that he did know it and offering an incorrect date in support.

The majority assumed that the first questions—as to Muniz' name, address, height, weight, eye color, date of birth, and current age—did call for testimonial responses, but found that they were not obtained in violation of the applicable *Miranda* requirements. It found no need to reach the question of whether self-incriminatory responses to a demand to count aloud during the physical dexterity tests would be "testimonial." On the other hand, the Court made clear that the Fifth Amendment did not bar the officers from compelling Muniz to speak in order to determine whether he would slur his words. Slurred speech and other evidence of lack of muscular coordination do not involve testimonial components and thus their compelled demonstration does not invoke the Fifth Amendment privilege.

Four members of the Court, in an opinion by Chief Justice Rehnquist, took issue with the majority's conclusion that Muniz' answer to the sixth birthday question was testimonial. They did not offer an alternative comprehensive definition of "testimonial" activity, but simply argued that the question called only for a demonstration by Muniz as to his ability "to do a simple mathematical exercise." This, they concluded, was no different from compelling Muniz to demonstrate his physical ability to perform tasks involving normal unimpaired coordination. "If the police may require Muniz to use his body in order to demonstrate the level of his physical coordination," the Chief Justice argued, "there is no reason why they should not be able to require him to speak or write in order to determine his mental coordination."

The lower courts have found almost no compelled activities testimonial in nature. Authorities have been permitted to compel submission to blood, hair and saliva sampling and cooperation in a neutron activation test designed to determine whether the suspect recently fired a gun. Prior to *Muniz*, the lower courts had tended to find most sobriety tests beyond the protection of the privilege, and had found the privilege inapplicable even to procedures involving the recitation of the alphabet, activity of the sort on which *Muniz* reserved judgment.

Despite the Supreme Court's construction of the Fifth Amendment privilege as limited to compulsion to engage in "testimonial" activity, states remain free to define the protection afforded by their constitutional, statutory, or case law privileges more broadly. Few have done so, however, and the clear trend is towards defining protection under state provisions as no broader than that afforded by the Fifth Amendment.

The New Jersey Supreme Court, in the context of private papers, has defined the state's case law privilege as protecting the privacy interest in the contents of certain private papers. This is considered in more detail below.[13] Traditionally, there was considerable support in case law for the proposition that some state privileges prohibited any compelled activity—whether testimonial or not—that gave rise to incriminating evidence or information implicating the person so compelled. After the Utah Supreme Court's rejection of this position in 1985, however, apparently only Georgia still adheres to this approach.

Under the approach of the Georgia court, the privilege prohibits only compulsion to engage in *affirmative actions* that are self-incriminating. It does, therefore, prohibit compelling a suspect to produce a handwriting exemplar. But it does not bar compelled but passive submission to a surgical procedure required for removal of a bullet from the suspect's body, the taking of blood and urine samples for chemical analysis, or the removal of a suspect's shoes. Such a construction of the privilege is somewhat suggested by the terms of some formulations of it, as for example those providing that no person "shall be compelled to give evidence against himself." Such nuances in terminology have not, however, been regarded as of much significance.

Whether the rationales of the privilege can support such a broad construction is problematic. To the extent that the privilege is designed to minimize cruelty, perhaps that purpose might be best effectuated by prohibiting compulsion to engage in any volitional affirmative act, since such situations provide an incentive to engage in potentially abusive persuasion until the subject complies. As the Utah court noted in the leading recent rejection of this position, however, other constitutional provisions are available to condemn excessive coercion.[14] Moreover, the incentive for extreme—and thus cruel—persuasive measures is greatest in situations where communicative cooperation is sought, because there the subject retains the power to control the contents of the sought response. Any use of a suspect himself to develop evidence with which to bring about his own downfall might be regarded as offending privacy concerns underlying the privilege; the more "affirmative" the compelled participation by the suspect, the greater the privacy intrusion might be. It is doubtful, however, whether today privacy considerations are of sufficient significance in supporting the privilege to serve as a foundation for defining its scope. Difficulties in determining what forms of cooperation are sufficiently "affirmative" to come within a prohibition against compelled affirmative cooperation argue against defining the scope of a privilege in those terms. Yet—as *Doe* and *Muniz* illustrated—defining the privilege as limited to "testimonial" activity may present no less serious difficulties. Nevertheless, state courts are unlikely to construe their privileges as prohibiting compelled nontestimonial incriminating conduct even insofar as it involves affirmative actions by the accused.

§ 125. General Scope of the Privilege: (e) Compulsion

There is agreement that the privilege applies only when self-incriminatory and testimonial activity is "compelled." What compulsion means varies with the context of the testimonial activity, although the recent his-

---

13. See § 127 infra.

14. American Fork City v. Cosgrove, 701 P.2d 1069, 1074 (Utah 1985), citing Utah Const. Art. I, § 7 (guarantee of due process).

tory of the privilege has involved significant expansion of the concept of compulsion.

Traditionally, the privilege was limited to situations in which "legal" compulsion—compulsion imposed under authority of law—was exerted upon the witness. Consequently, the privilege was regarded as inapplicable to police questioning, since law enforcement officers have no authority to compel answers to their inquiries. In Miranda v. Arizona,[1] however, the Supreme Court rejected this approach as a matter of Fifth Amendment law and held the privilege implicated in out-of-court custodial interrogation by police. Reasoning that coverage of such activity was necessary to avoid rendering the privilege at trial a mere empty formality, the Court rejected the requirement that the compulsion be legal. The Fifth Amendment privilege applies to and protects citizens in situations in which their freedom to abstain from self-incrimination "is curtailed in any significant way."

On the other hand, the requirement of compulsion is the conceptual basis for many of the procedural requirements that must be met for successful reliance upon the privilege and consequently serves to limit its effect. Most important, as a general rule, compulsion is present only if a witness has asserted a right to refuse to disclose self-incriminating information and this refusal has been overridden. "The answers of such a witness to questions put to him are not compelled within the meaning of the Fifth Amendment," the Court held, "unless the witness is required to answer over his valid claim of the privilege."[2]

In Minnesota v. Murphy,[3] the Court explained that this rule is inapplicable in three "well-defined" situations where the circumstances so suggest that the person's ability to make a free choice is impaired as to render inappropriate a requirement that the person expressly articulate a desire not to incriminate himself. One is where a citizen is subjected to custodial law enforcement interroga-

tion. There, *Miranda* recognizes that the Fifth Amendment applies and imposes certain requirements even if the person does not first affirmatively assert a desire to avoid self-incrimination.

Another situation is where a person is confronted with such significant potential penalties for invoking the privilege that his failure to do so cannot reasonably be regarded as a free choice. Finally, the requirement of an assertion of the desire to remain silent has not been required in cases in which federal tax requirements imposed on gamblers require potentially incriminating filings with the government. Given especially that claiming the privilege would itself be self-incriminating in this situation, no such affirmative action is required.

The need for compulsion also explains the recent holdings that the Fifth Amendment privilege does not protect the contents of self-incriminatory documents from compelled production.[4] Since the person's arguably "testimonial" act of putting incriminatory information in the papers occurred before and without any effect from the compulsion of a later subpoena for those papers, the testimonial and self-incriminating act of so disclosing that information was not compelled within the meaning of the privilege.

In South Dakota v. Neville,[5] the Supreme Court made clear that the compulsion must be "impermissible." At issue in *Neville* was the admissibility of a driver's refusal to submit to a blood alcohol test, offered by the prosecution as evidence of the driver's intoxication. To the extent that the refusal was testimonial,[6] any compulsion exerted upon him to take the test did not render his refusal compelled within the meaning of the Fifth Amendment privilege. The criminal process often requires suspects and defendants to make choices, the Court explained, and the Fifth Amendment does not necessarily preclude this:

§ 125

1. 384 U.S. 436 (1966).

2. Minnesota v. Murphy, 465 U.S. 420, 427 (1984).

3. 465 U.S. 420 (1984).

4. See generally §§ 127–128, infra.

5. 459 U.S. 553 (1983).

6. See § 124, supra.

[T]he values behind the Fifth Amendment are not hindered when the state offers a suspect the choice of submitting to the blood-alcohol test or having his refusal used against him. * * * [T]he state could legitimately compel the suspect, against his will, to accede to the test. Given, then, that the offer of taking a blood-alcohol test is clearly legitimate, the action becomes no *less* legitimate when the State offers a second option of refusing to take the test, with the attendant penalties for making that choice.[7]

The refusal, therefore, is not an act coerced by the officer and trial use of evidence of that refusal is not barred by the privilege.

§ 126. General Scope of the Privilege: (f) Burdens on Exercise of the Privilege

Prohibited compulsion upon a witness to provide self-incriminating testimony may be indirect as well as the traditional threat of contempt if he refuses to testify. Consequently, the privilege provides protection against some officially imposed disadvantages being attached to a witness's invocation of the privilege. In Malloy v. Hogan,[1] the Supreme Court described the Fifth Amendment privilege as including not only the right to remain silent in the face of incriminatory questions but also a right "to suffer no penalty * * * for such silence." "Penalty" has been defined as any sanction which makes assertion of the Fifth Amendment privilege "costly."

In the event that such a penalty has been imposed, the witness is entitled to appropriate relief. If the witness provides self-incriminatory testimony in response to the threat of that penalty, the admissions are to be regarded as impermissibly compelled and hence inadmissible against the witness. If the witness nevertheless refuses to provide the demanded answers and the penalty is imposed, the witness is entitled to relief from that penalty.

In a series of decisions implementing this rule, the United States Supreme Court has held that a teacher may not be discharged solely because he invoked his privilege before a congressional committee,[2] that an attorney cannot be disbarred because in reliance upon the privilege he refused to produce documents during a judicial investigation into his alleged professional misconduct,[3] that a police officer may not be dismissed for refusing to sign a general waiver of immunity during an investigation of the "fixing" of traffic tickets,[4] that architects called before grand juries investigating public contracts cannot on the basis of their refusal to waive their privilege be barred from state public contracting for five years,[5] and that an officer of a political party cannot be barred from party or public office for five years because he refused to testify or waive immunity when called before a grand jury to testify concerning the conduct of his office.[6] Of course, Griffin v. California[7] forbids drawing any inference against an accused from the accused's failure to testify in the criminal prosecution.[8]

In contrast to this line of cases, however, stands Baxter v. Palmigiano.[9] A prison inmate who was the subject of disciplinary proceedings, the Court held, could invoke his privilege on the ground that the conduct he would have to admit might subject him to criminal prosecution. But, it continued, the privilege was not violated if disciplinary authorities were permitted to consider his invocation of the privilege as tending to show that he committed the disciplinary infraction. *Baxter* cited and apparently approved the "prevailing rule," long applied by the lower courts, that the Fifth Amendment does not forbid the drawing of adverse inferences against the parties to civil actions when they

---

7. *Neville*, supra note 5, at 565 (emphasis in original).

§ 126

1. 378 U.S. 1 (1964).

2. Slochower v. Board of Higher Education, 350 U.S. 551, 558 (1956).

3. Spevack v. Klein, 385 U.S. 511, 514 (1967).

4. Gardner v. Broderick, 392 U.S. 273, 278–79 (1968).

5. Lefkowitz v. Turley, 414 U.S. 70, 83 (1973).

6. Lefkowitz v. Cunningham, 431 U.S. 801, 807 (1977).

7. 380 U.S. 609 (1965).

8. See § 132, infra.

9. 425 U.S. 308 (1976).

invoke the privilege during that litigation. It emphasized, however, that the "penalty" involved—the finding that the disciplinary infraction was established—could not be based entirely upon the inference from the inmate's invocation of the privilege.

Precisely why the adverse inference permitted in *Baxter* survived Fifth Amendment attack while other penalties have not is not clear. *Griffin*, of course, is closest to *Baxter*, since both involved a penalty in the form of an actual or potential adverse inference. In *Baxter*, the Court suggested that among the relevant considerations were the more severe impact upon the holder of the privilege in *Griffin* situations, the punitive aspect of criminal prosecutions encouraging more use—or perhaps misuse—of an opportunity to draw an adverse interest, and the existence of more important governmental interests in *Baxter* situations that would be frustrated by prohibiting an adverse inference. It is also possible, given the majority's reliance upon the requirement in *Baxter* that other evidence existed to justify the "penalty," that the Court gave some weight to what it perceived as the reduction of the impact of the adverse inference assured by this requirement. This is supported by Lefkowitz v. Cunningham,[10] in which the Court characterized *Baxter* as both (a) "giv[ing] no more probative value [to the inference from invoking the privilege] than the facts of the case warranted" and (b) permitting the inference to be used only as "one of a number of factors to be considered by the trier of fact in assessing [the] penalty." In contrast, the penalty held impermissible in *Cunningham* was imposed solely and automatically upon the basis of Cunningham's invocation of the privilege.

The Court returned to the problem in Minnesota v. Murphy,[11] in which Murphy claimed that the state threatened to revoke his probation if he did not waive his Fifth Amendment self-incrimination rights and answer questions concerning his involvement in another offense. His answers, he argued, were therefore compelled and inadmissible.

After reviewing "the so-called 'penalty' cases," the Court concluded that those "made clear that the State could not constitutionally carry out a threat to revoke probation for the legitimate exercise of the Fifth Amendment privilege." Reaffirming *Cunningham's* discussion of *Baxter*, it suggested that Murphy's reliance upon the Fifth Amendment was one of a number of factors to be considered in determining whether Murphy had violated his probation.

Lower courts have understandably had some difficulty determining the extent to which the Supreme Court's penalty cases limit the disadvantages that can be attached to exercises of the privilege. A Minnesota court, for example, considered a custody order that appeared to require a parent, as a prerequisite to regaining custody of the children, to cooperate fully in an evaluation by acknowledging his prior criminal abuse of the children. In a confusing discussion finding this permissible, the majority characterized the threatened termination of rights to the children as not a prohibited "sanction for exercise of a constitutional right," but rather "the necessary result of [the parent's] failure to rectify parental deficiencies" and a permissible exercise by the state of "its right and obligation to protect these children."

Most lower courts read *Baxter* as permitting an adverse inference to be drawn from a party's invocation of the privilege, subject to the qualification that the inference cannot itself necessarily determine whether relief is granted to the other party. A Maryland court, for example, read *Baxter* as requiring that a jury told of a civil defendant's invocation of the privilege in response to requests for admissions must be instructed that it could, but need not, infer from the defendant's invocation of the privilege that the answers would be adverse to the defendant.

Penalty issues most commonly arise when a party to civil litigation permissibly invokes the privilege during discovery. It is agreed that where this occurs, courts have right pow-

---

10. 431 U.S. 801 (1977), discussed at note 6 supra.

11. 465 U.S. 420 (1984).

er to respond appropriately even if this results in a disadvantage being placed upon the party who invoked the privilege. The purpose of such action, and the objective of the court in fashioning an appropriate response for a particular case, should not be to sanction the party who invoked the privilege but rather to provide a remedy for the party disadvantaged by his opponent's reliance upon the privilege. The rationale for responsive action applies with particular vigor when the plaintiff invokes the privilege, since fundamental notions of fairness are violated if a party comes into court seeking relief from another and then relies upon his privilege to conceal information that might defeat his claim.

Trial courts have considerable discretion in fashioning relief when a party invokes the privilege in response to discovery demands. They should take particular care in exercising that discretion, however, to prevent a plaintiff from obtaining relief on facts rendered incomplete by the plaintiff's reliance upon the privilege. A civil defendant's involuntary involvement in a lawsuit suggests that in fashioning a remedy for his invocation of the privilege, more weight be given to his self-incrimination interests. Dismissal or the striking of pleadings is clearly permissible, at least in some cases, even where the defendant has invoked the privilege. But the constitutionally-based need to minimize penalization of the exercise of a fundamental right requires that alternatives—such as delaying the civil litigation pending resolution of criminal matters—be considered first.

§ 127. The Privilege as Related to Documents and Tangible Items: (a) Limits on Use of "Private" Papers

Boyd v. United States [1] has long provided the basis for speculation and sometimes assumption that the Fifth Amendment provides special and extremely broad protection for certain "private papers." Under this approach, the private content of these documents is within the scope of the privilege's protection, with the result that the government is barred not only from using those documents against their author in court but also from compelling him to produce them or perhaps even seizing them during the course of an otherwise reasonable search. The conceptual basis for this position was never entirely clear, but seemed to rest upon the combined effect of the Fifth Amendment's privilege and the Fourth Amendment's protection against unreasonable searches and seizures. It was regarded as related to, and perhaps a part of, the Fourth Amendment's "mere evidence" rule, a prohibition against the seizure and use of items that were neither contraband nor instruments or fruits of crime but of value to the prosecution because they were evidence that a crime was committed or that a particular person committed it.

In 1967, the Supreme Court abandoned the "mere evidence" rule as a Fourth Amendment prohibition [2] but—apparently referring to private papers and perhaps objects—pointedly left undecided "whether there are items of evidentiary value whose very nature precludes them from being the object of a reasonable search or seizure." Nine years later, in Fisher v. United States, [3] the Court rejected much of Boyd's analysis and specifically disapproved Boyd's suggestion that the Fifth Amendment protects privacy interests in private items under circumstances that do not involve compelled testimonial self-incrimination. Fisher held that the Fifth Amendment did not bar compelled production of financial records from a citizen or his attorney, but the Court noted that it was not resolving whether the Fifth Amendment would shield a citizen from compulsion to produce "private papers." It left no doubt, however, that to the extent compelled production of such papers was constitutionally limited on the basis of the privacy of the contents of those records, that limitation would come from the Fourth Amendment rather than the Fifth Amendment's self-incrimination provision. Later that year, the

§ 127

1. 116 U.S. 616 (1886).

2. Warden v. Hayden, 387 U.S. 294 (1967).

3. 425 U.S. 391 (1976).

Court held in Andresen v. Maryland [4] that if business papers had been obtained in a search reasonable under Fourth Amendment standards, the Fifth Amendment prohibited neither their seizure nor their use.

United States v. Doe [5] reaffirmed that whether the Fifth Amendment prohibits the compelled production of documents turns upon whether the act of production is an incriminating testimonial communication, a matter addressed in the next section.[6] But *Doe* involved only business records. Justice O'Connor concurred, commenting that implicit in the Court's analysis was that "the Fifth Amendment provides absolutely no protection for the contents of private papers of any kind." Justice Marshall, joined by Justice Brennan, on the other hand, expressed the view that the Court's opinion had not reconsidered the matter of private papers in general and that it remained open.

Most lower courts read *Fisher, Andresen* and *Doe* as removing any remaining vitality of the old *Boyd* rule. There is, however, some lingering discomfort with the absence of either a holding or explicit and unqualified language to that effect joined by a majority of the Court. Consequently, a number of courts prefer to regard the matter as not yet definitely settled but to conclude that any Fifth Amendment protection as might remain is limited to a small category of rather intensely personal papers and perhaps documents, such as diaries.

The Fourth Circuit, in contrast, has held that *Boyd* remains viable and thus that the Fifth Amendment prohibits the compelled production of private papers held in a personal capacity.[7] In explanation, it offered:

[T]he forced disclosure of private incriminating information jeopardizes the individual's right to keep at least that aspect of himself which is reflected in his private papers free from the intrusive hands of the government. Implicit in the cherished right to "pursue hap-

piness" is the concomitant right to express one's own thoughts free from the government's exaction of those thoughts upon penalty of one's liberty.[8]

Despite the Supreme Court's failure formally to declare its death, *Boyd's* protection for the contents of even intimately personal documents has lost all life. In *Fisher,* the majority rejected *Boyd's* rationale. Personal privacy is among the purposes served by the Fifth Amendment privilege. But as the Court has repeatedly emphasized, the coverage of the Fifth Amendment does not reflect the full ramifications of all of its rationales. *Fisher* made clear that the role of privacy in supporting the Fifth Amendment is not important enough to justify giving privacy interests much if any role in defining Fifth Amendment coverage. The Fifth Amendment privilege will not "serve as a general protector of privacy," even in the limited context of private papers.

The resulting limited effect of the privilege is illustrated by State v. Barrett,[9] in which the prosecution introduced a journal written by the defendant and obtained from his attorneys by means of a subpoena. In addition to its incriminating entries, the journal contained entries relating Barrett's feelings regarding his pending divorce and the dispute concerning custody of a child. Obtaining the journal, the court held, did not implicate the Fifth Amendment, since the subpoena was directed against Barrett's attorneys and demanded no testimonial actions by Barrett. The Fifth Amendment provided no protection relating to the private contents of the journal, so the prosecution's use of it in evidence similarly did not implicate that provision.

Denying Fifth Amendment protection to private papers is particularly appropriate for reasons that were not yet clear at the time of *Boyd.* As the Court emphasized in *Fisher,* the Fourth Amendment has become the primary

---

4. 427 U.S. 463 (1976).

5. 465 U.S. 605 (1984).

6. See § 128 infra.

7. United States v. (Under Seal), 745 F.2d 834 (4th Cir.1984), vacated as moot 471 U.S. 1001, on remand 763 F.2d 662 (4th Cir.).

8. 745 F.2d at 840.

9. 401 N.W.2d 184 (Iowa 1987).

federal constitutional source of protection for privacy interests, at least as those are endangered by official action taken as part of criminal investigations. This, however, was not clear until Katz v. United States [10] in which the Court announced that whether official activity was covered by the Fourth Amendment depended largely upon whether it intruded upon a reasonable expectation of privacy held by the subject of the investigation. *Boyd,* of course, was decided far earlier when this Fourth Amendment emphasis upon privacy had not yet developed.

Moreover, excluding personal papers from Fifth Amendment protection makes practical sense. If personal papers are covered by the Fifth Amendment, that provision makes them totally unavailable to the government. The Fourth Amendment, on the other hand, has the flexibility to accommodate the possibility that the government might be permitted to search for, seize, and use personal documents only if the government meets unusually stringent requirements designed to assure that citizens are subjected to such an extreme intrusion upon their privacy only if exceptionally significant public interests are served.

State courts remain free, of course, to construe their state provisions more broadly. The New Jersey Supreme Court has construed the state's common law privilege as retaining a *Boyd*-like protection for the content of certain private papers. This position rests upon the state court's conclusion that the nature and therefore the scope of the state privilege differs significantly from that of the Fifth Amendment as construed in *Fisher* and *Doe.*

Even the New Jersey court, however, construes this protection as limited. Business records of a sole proprietorship, for example, are not sufficiently private in content to be immune from subpoena, although protection would apparently be extended to a person's personal checking account records, cancelled checks and perhaps banking statements and

tax returns. Other state courts have shown no inclination to give state privileges a construction that differs so fundamentally from that given the Fifth Amendment by the Supreme Court.

§ 128. The Privilege as Related to Documents and Tangible Items: (b) Compulsory Production

The subpoena power has traditionally included the ability to compel the person to whom the subpoena is directed to produce papers, documents, and other physical items. A subpoena which so directs the production of items is generally called a subpoena *duces tecum.* Self-incrimination considerations impose some limitations upon this use of the subpoena power, but the nature and scope of those limitations has been a problem of long-standing concern.

Boyd v. United States,[1] decided in 1886, was widely understood as holding that the Fifth Amendment prohibited compelled production and use as evidence of "purely evidentiary" items, the seizure of which was prohibited by the Fourth Amendment. This, of course, included many documents which could be characterized as of purely and exclusively evidentiary significance. By 1976, however, Fisher v. United States [2] confirmed what was by that time quite clear from other case law developments: the Fifth Amendment prohibits only compulsion to make incriminating testimonial communications, so it does not address compulsion upon a person to produce documents containing previously-made disclosures, if the compelled act of production itself does not constitute a self-incriminating and testimonial communication. Any doubt as to this was removed by United States v. Doe.[3]

Under *Fisher* and *Doe,* application of the Fifth Amendment to compelled production of documents or items is a matter of applying the requirements that the compelled activity

---

10. 389 U.S. 347 (1967).

§ 128

1. 116 U.S. 616 (1886).

2. 425 U.S. 391 (1976).

3. 465 U.S. 605 (1984).

be "testimonial" [4] and that the compelled disclosure create a "real and appreciable risk" of self-incrimination.[5] This does not turn upon the contents of any documents that are involved; whether those documents embody previously-made testimonial communications is of no significance, because any such communications were completed before the compulsion was applied and thus cannot be the products of that compulsion. Instead, the question is whether the "act of production" itself—which *is* compelled by the subpoena—involves a self-incriminating testimonial communication. If the item happens to be a document, this does not turn upon the contents of that document. Consequently, whether the item involved is a document or not is largely and perhaps entirely irrelevant to whether the Fifth Amendment is invoked by its compelled production.

By producing an item in response to a subpoena a person may make one or more of several explicit or implicit representations: (a) they believe that items described by the subpoena exist; (b) they believe that such items are within their possession or control; and (c) they believe that the items produced are within the description of the subpoena. Any such representations are unquestionably testimonial communications, although they may be made by conduct rather than by explicit words. *Fisher* and *Doe* establish that whether the Fifth Amendment applies to a demand for production of items focuses upon these potential representations flowing from the act of production. This, in turn, will usually depend upon whether any such communications as might be involved in a particular case involve a real and appreciable risk of incrimination.

Fisher makes clear that the analysis requires careful consideration, on the facts of the particular case, of what additional information those communications will provide the government. In *Fisher*, the subpoenas called for production of various documents of a sort generally created by accountants preparing tax returns for their clients. Apparently the

government was already aware—from the returns—that the subjects had employed accountants to prepare the returns. With regard to the first two possible representations distinguished above, the Court concluded that the existence and location of the papers involved was "a foregone conclusion" and any confirming communication provided by compliance with the subpoenas did not add sufficiently to the Government's information to invoke the privilege.

In regard to the third type of representation distinguished above, the *Fisher* Court noted the theoretical possibility that a taxpayer's production of items could be used to authenticate those items if and when they were later offered as evidence against him in a criminal trial. The risk of such use of a person's act of production, it noted, has been the prevailing recent justification for regarding the Fifth Amendment as barring enforcement of a documentary subpoena. On the facts of *Fisher*, however, the Court concluded that this theoretical possibility did not "represent a substantial threat of self-incrimination." The taxpayers whose Fifth Amendment rights were at issue had not personally prepared the documents sought. Consequently, they could not vouch for the "accuracy" of them; therefore, any acknowledgment implicit in the taxpayers' production of the documents would not be admissible to authenticate those documents, since the taxpayers lacked first-hand knowledge as to what those documents in fact were. Because the testimonial communication tacitly made by production could not in fact be used for this purpose, making it would not be "incriminating" as is necessary to invoke the protection of the Fifth Amendment privilege.

Doe, however, involved different documents—the respondent's telephone records, bank account records, business records, and cancelled checks of his businesses. Both the District Court and the Court of Appeals had concluded that on the facts of the case, neither the existence of documents of this sort

---

4. See generally § 124 supra.

5. See generally § 122 supra.

nor the respondent's possession or control of any such documents as did exist was a foregone conclusion as had been the case in *Fisher*. The Supreme Court was unwilling to overturn this finding. The respondent's testimonial representation, by his act of producing documents, that such documents both existed and were within his control would create a "substantial and real" risk of incrimination, the Court therefore concluded, and consequently the lower courts had not erred in sustaining the respondent's claim of the privilege in response to the subpoenas.

Doe confirms the Court's observation in *Fisher* that whether the tacit admissions made by responding to a subpoena for items are sufficiently testimonial and incriminating to invoke the privilege "do not lend themselves to categorical answers" and will often "depend on the facts and circumstances of particular cases * * *." [6] The Court's deference to the lower tribunals' conclusion in *Doe* also makes clear that trial courts have substantial discretion in making the necessary determinations.

In *Doe,* the Government conceded and the Court agreed that the federal immunity statute permitted the Government to overcome the Fifth Amendment problem by giving the respondent immunity from the results of the acknowledgements he makes by his act of production of the documents sought. This has been done in subsequent cases. Since *Fisher* and *Doe* make clear that one subpoenaed to produce documents has no Fifth Amendment protection for the contents of those documents, such a grant of immunity removes the risk of incrimination and renders the subpoenas enforceable.

The analysis required in these cases is illustrated by Marano v. Holland.[7] Prior to trial, the defendant Marano was compelled to produce a ten page autobiography and a diary written by his mother. Under *Fisher* and *Doe,* the court concluded, the Fifth Amendment would be implicated only if Marano's act of production had significant and testimonial incriminating effects. As the documents were never admitted into evidence, Marano's tacit acknowledgements as to their existence, custody and authenticity had no incriminating significance. The Fourth Amendment, however, was implicated. Whether and under what circumstances private papers can be demanded of a suspect has never been definitively resolved by the Supreme Court, and the *Marano* court did not attempt a definitive answer. An "absolute minimum," it held, would be probable cause to believe the papers constitute relevant evidence. Since that had not been shown as a basis for the order demanding production, the demand that Marano produce the papers violated the Fourth Amendment.

§ 129. The Privilege as Related to Corporations, Associations, and Their Agents: (a) The Privilege of the Organization

Although at common law only a natural person could be convicted of a crime, it is now clear that corporations and sometimes even unincorporated entities can be criminally liable by virtue of acts performed by agents of the organizations. A subpoena *duces tecum* may be directed to a corporation itself rather than to the officers or agents of the organization, although it is obvious that compliance will have to be accomplished through the actions of the organization's agents. And, of course, information that tends to incriminate an organization may be sought from agents of that organization. When agents of an organization are directed to testify or to produce documents or items, may they decline to do so on the basis that such action will incriminate the organization?

The Fifth Amendment issue was addressed in Hale v. Henkel,[1] involving a corporation. Hale, officer of that corporation, was required both to testify and to produce corporate documents over his objection that to do so would

---

6. Fisher v. United States, supra note 2, 425 U.S. at 410.

7. 179 W.Va. 156, 366 S.E.2d 117 (1988).

§ 129

1. 201 U.S. 43 (1906).

tend to incriminate the corporation. This was permissible, the Court held, relying in part upon the personal nature of the Fifth Amendment privilege; any privilege the corporation might have would be personal to it, and Hale could not invoke it on the corporation's behalf.

More substantively, the Court also held that the corporation had no privilege under the Fifth Amendment. It reasoned that a corporation, unlike a natural person, is "a creature of the State" holding privileges subject to the laws of the State and the terms of its charter. Legislatures reserve a right to investigate such organizations to assure that they have not exceeded their powers and to conduct such investigations by demanding even self-incriminating information from the organizations. This is reasonable, since otherwise many investigations into possible abuses by corporations of their immense power would necessarily fail, because such abuses could only be ascertained by information obtained from the organizations themselves.

In United States v. White,[2] the Court held that an unincorporated labor union had no privilege that could be invoked on its behalf. It suggested, in the course of its discussion, that many of the rationales for the privilege support its limitation to "natural individuals." Organizations, for example, do not possess the "dignity" which is offended by compelled self-incrimination. Similarly, an organization cannot be subjected to torture or "equally reprehensible methods that are necessary to compelling self-incrimination or that are invited by the right to do so.

It is now clear that the Fifth Amendment privilege is possessed only by natural persons. This position rests on the dual grounds that, first, many of the rationales of the privilege would not be served by extending it to organizations and, second, that so extending it would impede particularly difficult investigations of suspected organizational wrongdoing and thus involve exceptional social costs. State courts remain free, of course, to construe state privileges as affording protection to such entities, but there is little reason—or rush—to do so. Whatever policies support the privilege's continued vitality, they apply with insufficient force to such organizations to outweigh the numerous contrary considerations.

§ 130. The Privilege as Related to Corporations, Associations, and Their Agents: (b) Agents' Ability to Invoke Their Personal Privilege

As developed in the previous section, a witness who is an agent of an organization may not decline to testify or produce items or documents on the basis that to do so would incriminate the organization. But may the agent resist demands to testify or produce items on the basis of his own personal privilege, that is, on the ground that compliance would incriminate him personally? The "collective entity" rule, first developed in Wilson v. United States,[1] greatly restricts the ability of organizational agents to do so on the basis of their Fifth Amendment privilege.

In *Wilson*, a subpoena was issued to the corporation of which Wilson was president, demanding production of corporate records in the possession of Wilson. He resisted the subpoena on the ground that the records would personally incriminate him. Rejecting his argument, the Court emphasized that to permit a corporate agent to invoke his personal privilege would, to a significant extent, frustrate the purposes of denying a privilege to the corporation itself. The government's interest in access to corporate records would be difficult or impossible to effectuate if those in custody of them could resist production on the basis of their personal privilege. Moreover, the impact upon the corporate agents is somewhat mitigated by the fact that such agents, when they assume their positions of responsibility and custody of corporate records, to some extent assume the risk that their personal privilege will be lost.

---

2. 322 U.S. 694 (1944).

§ 130

1. 221 U.S. 361, 377–85 (1911).

In later cases, *Wilson's* approach was expanded to representatives of many nonincorporated organizations. The Court has also held that the agent's disability outlives the organization. Thus a person who was an agent of a now-defunct corporation but still retains the corporation's records must produce them regardless of the personally self-incriminating impact.[2]

Wilson's collective entity rule can be stated as follows: an organizational agent who holds organizational documents and items in a representative capacity has no right to resist a demand for production of those documents or items on the basis of his personal Fifth Amendment privilege.

There is some uncertainty as to the extent to which the collective entity rule applies when an organizational agent is requested to do more than physically produce organizational documents or items. In *Wilson*, the Court commented that, despite its holding that the agent must produce the documents, the agent "may decline to utter upon the witness stand a single self-incriminating word."[3] But this may not be the case.

In Curcio v. United States,[4] an agent of a labor union was subpoenaed to produce certain union records. He appeared and testified that the records had been prepared but were no longer in his possession. When asked about the whereabouts or possession of the records, he invoked his privilege. Upholding his right to do so, the Supreme Court rejected the Government's argument that an organizational agent's duty is to either produce the records or explain or account under oath for their nonproduction regardless of the personally incriminating consequences of doing so. It suggested, however, that an organizational agent might have no right to resist responding to questions merely "auxiliary to the production" of documents he is duty-bound to produce. This, in turn, might require the agent to identify the documents or authenticate them for admission into evidence. Such

limited oral testimony, the Court suggested, might merely require explicit oral acknowledgement of what is implicitly represented by the act of production, and thus not increase the risk of incrimination beyond what is required of the witness under *Wilson* and its progeny. But the matter was not resolved, because the questions asked in *Curcio* went beyond what would be permitted under this reasoning. Lower courts, however, have held that witnesses may be required to give such authenticating oral testimony as well as to produce the items.

In Braswell v. United States[5] the Supreme Court considered whether the collective entity rule survived the Court's restructuring of its approach to the effect of the Fifth Amendment's privilege upon compulsory production of documents.

The rationale for the *Fisher–Doe* emphasis upon the act of production, Braswell argued, suggests that an organizational agent should be entitled to invoke his personal privilege. The agent's act of production is clearly compelled by the subpoena. If it is both testimonial and self-incriminating to the agent, the agent should—in the absence of a grant of immunity—be entitled to invoke the privilege. *Wilson* and cases relying on it did not focus upon the self-incriminating and testimonial significance of the act of production, Braswell urged, and therefore simply did not deal with the implication of that for the organizational agent.

The *Braswell* majority, however, disagreed and held that the collective entity rule had survived *Fisher* and *Doe* largely unscathed. Chief Justice Rehnquist acknowledged for the Court that *Fisher* and *Doe* did embark upon a new course of Fifth Amendment analysis. But the increased emphasis upon the act of production under those cases did not render the collective entity rule obsolete. The agent's "assumption of his representative capacity" still leads to certain obligations, including that of producing organizational doc-

---

2. Wheeler v. United States, 226 U.S. 478, 489–90 (1913); Grant v. United States, 227 U.S. 74, 79–80 (1913).

3. *Wilson,* supra note 1, at 385.

4. 354 U.S. 118 (1957).

5. 487 U.S. 99 (1988).

uments regardless of the self-incriminating repercussions. It is also still the case that permitting a claim of privilege by the agent would be "tantamount to a claim of privilege by the corporation," and thus would circumvent the privilege's inapplicability to such organizations. Accepting Braswell's argument, moreover, "would have a detrimental impact on the Government's efforts to prosecute 'white collar crime,' one of the most serious problems confronting law enforcement authorities." In an apparent attempt to reconcile conceptually the result with the emphasis in *Fisher* and *Doe* upon protecting any testimonially self-incriminating act involved in production, the Court offered that when a corporation custodian produces corporation documents, "the custodian's act of production is not deemed a personal act, but rather an act of the corporation."

Having thus reaffirmed the basic collective entity rule, the Court proceeded to limit its effects. Among the implications flowing from the personally incriminating effects of the agent's actions, the Chief Justice indicated, is a prohibition against the prosecution's use of his act of production against him individually. Suppose, for example, the Government subpoenas the records of Corporation A from X, president of that corporation. X produces the record. Later, X is prosecuted and the prosecution wishes to show that X possessed the records and was aware of their contents. To prove this, the prosecution may show: (a) X was president of Corporation A; (b) documents of this sort are generally in possession of and familiar to the president of an organization like Corporation A; and (c) these documents were produced by an agent of Corporation A in response to a subpoena for documents of this sort. But the prosecution may *not* show that X himself personally produced the documents on behalf of Corporation A.

Braswell, in effect, provides a superceding "rationale" for the collective entity rule carefully tailored to what is now regarded as the limited intrusion upon interests protected by the privilege. Only the agent's incriminatory act of production invokes privilege concerns. By providing that an organizational agent is automatically entitled to functional immunity from the use against him of the testimonial aspects of his act of production, *Braswell* removes the incriminating aspect of that compelled act of production. After *Braswell*, it is even arguable that the collective entity rule is no longer an exception to the privilege. The organizational agent has no right to resist compelled production because the agent is automatically protected from the prosecution's use against him of that aspect of his compliance that invokes privilege protection.

As in other areas, state courts remain free to construe state privileges as affording broader protection in this context to organizational agents. The Massachusetts Supreme Court, in Commonwealth v. Doe,[6] rejected the *Braswell* analogy and construed its state constitutional provision as permitting a corporate representative to invoke his personal privilege in response to a subpoena for corporate documents. *Braswell*, it reasoned, rested largely upon a fiction that the state tribunal would not adopt:

> The act of production is demanded *of the witness* and the possibility of self-incrimination is inherent in that act. The witness's status as a representative does not alter the fact that in so far as he is a natural person he is entitled to the protection of [the state constitutional privilege]. It would be factually unsound to hold that requiring *the witness* to furnish corporate records, the act of which would incriminate him, is not *his act*. * * * His status as custodian of the corporation's records does not require that he lose his individual privilege under [the state privilege].[7]

Apparently responding to the Supreme Court's suggestion that some notion of the agent's assumption of responsibility supports *Wilson's* holding, the Massachusetts court held that under the state provision the agent loses the personal privilege only if the record established that the agent's actions in the

---

6. 405 Mass. 676, 544 N.E.2d 860 (1989).

7. 405 Mass. at 680–81, 544 N.E.2d at 862 (emphasis in original).

particular case constituted a "knowing and intelligent" waiver. Since the record did not support a finding that Doe was aware that by accepting his corporate position and custody of the records he was surrendering some of his constitutional protection, no such waiver theory was available. Finally, and apparently in response to *Braswell's* concern regarding white collar crime investigations, the court commented that the terms of the privilege simply do not permit a balancing of state interests against defendants' interests as a means of determining whether the privilege applies.

Under *Wilson's* collective entity rule, a witness is deprived of the right to rely on his personal privilege to resist a demand for documents or items only if there is a collective entity sufficient to invoke the rule, the documents or items sought are those of the entity, and the witness has them in his capacity as an agent of the entity. With regard to the first requirement, the case law suggests that a corporation will generally if not always be a sufficient collective entity.

Unincorporated associations present greater difficulties. Bellis v. United States [8] suggests that the unit must be recognizable as an entity apart from its individual members, probably on the basis of its performance of organized and institutional activity. Further:

> The group must be relatively well organized and structured, and not merely a loose, informal association of individuals. It must maintain a distinct set of organizational records, and recognize rights in its members of control and access to them.[9]

A labor union, of course, is a sufficient unit to invoke the rule. And *Bellis* itself makes clear that a partnership will often be sufficient.

The partnership in *Bellis* was a law firm that had been in existence for nearly fifteen years and had three partners and six employees. It maintained a bank account and held itself out as an entity with an independent institutional identity. Size is relevant but not necessarily determinative, the Court com-

mented. "[A]n insubstantial difference in the form of [a] business enterprise," it continued, should not control. Despite their noncorporate nature, partnerships such as law and stock brokerage firms are often large, impersonal, and perpetual in duration. The personal interest of any particular partner in the financial records of the organization is "highly attenuated." A different case might be presented, the Court noted, if the partnership had been a "small family" one or if "there were some other pre-existing relationship of confidentiality among the partners."

The records must also be organizational records held by the witness in his capacity as an agent of the entity. The Court of Appeals for the District of Columbia Circuit has suggested that the agency rationale for the collective entity rule indicates that agency law provides an appropriate source for standards. Disclaiming any intention of providing a definitive test, the court posed the controlling question as whether, with regard to the development and possession of the particular records at issue, the witness acted within the scope of his agency relationship with the entity. In the case before it, the witness—an officer of the corporation—had opened a bank account in the name of the corporation. His only argument that he possessed the records of that account in a personal rather than representative capacity was that he had used the account for funds stolen from the corporation. This, the court held, was insufficient under *Wilson* itself to remove the records of the account from the scope of the agency relationship.

§ 131. The Privilege of an Accused in a Criminal Proceeding: (a) Definition of an Accused in a Criminal Proceeding

The privilege confers significantly different rights upon one who is the accused in a criminal proceeding as compared to one who is simply a witness in a criminal or other proceeding. An accused, unlike a witness, has not simply the right to withhold self-incrimi-

---

8. 417 U.S. 85 (1974).

9. Id. at 92–93.

nating responses to inquiries but also the right to be free of the inquiries themselves. It is, therefore, important to know when a person who is the subject of an official investigation becomes an accused in a criminal proceeding and entitled to the protection that accompanies this status.

The traditional view has been that an individual does not become an accused until the criminal process has been formally brought to bear upon him. Thus at such preliminary and investigatory proceedings as a grand jury investigation, a coroner's inquest, and perhaps a preliminary hearing, the suspect or subject of the proceedings has no right to refuse all cooperation in the matter.

The Supreme Court has shown no inclination to abandon this position as a matter of Fifth Amendment law. While it has not addressed the issue directly, for example, the Court has suggested that the target of a grand jury investigation has no Fifth Amendment right to refuse to appear and take the witness stand when subpoenaed.[1]

The propriety of this approach depends in large part upon what functions of the privilege of an accused is emphasized. An accused is afforded extraordinary protection by the privilege partly to avoid emphasizing to the trier of fact that he is invoking the privilege. This minimizes the risk that an adverse inference will be drawn from his doing so. Of course, this rationale supports the traditional position, since until formal proceedings have been commenced and the accused is brought before the trier of fact, this risk is not presented.

On the other hand, the extraordinary protection afforded an accused probably also rests in part on a perception that the risks to the interests implicated increases as a case progresses towards a trial. The prosecution's increased focus exclusively upon the accused when formal charges have been made to some extent increases the risk of the sort of overzealous activity that endangers interests protected by the privilege. To the extent that this rationale supports distinguishing the accused from other witnesses, the traditional position appears too inflexible. The privilege, under this approach, would best require examination of procedures such as grand jury appearances to determine whether they pose sufficient risks of this sort to justify or require that suspects involved in them be treated as "accuseds" and given a right to refuse to have queries put to them.

State courts may, of course, regard these or other considerations as indicating that state privileges should confer the status of an accused in a criminal proceeding upon one who is the subject of such preliminary proceedings. The New York Court of Appeals, for example, has read that state's constitution as giving one who is the target of an investigation a right not to be examined before the investigating grand jury. Again, however, a more flexible approach may best reconcile the conflicting considerations; thus a target witness might be guaranteed special protections but, if those are provided, required to submit to questioning.

§ 132. The Privilege of an Accused in a Criminal Proceeding: (b) Inferences From and Comment Upon the Accused's Reliance Upon the Privilege

A criminal defendant clearly has a right not to be penalized at trial for invoking his rights under the privilege. Such penalization can occur in a number of ways, ranging from a judge explicitly basing a finding of guilt upon the defendant's reliance upon the privilege to a prosecutor subtly encouraging a jury to give significance to a defendant's protection actions. The right to be free from penalties is, however, somewhat qualified. These qualifications are best developed by separate discussion of two situations. The first consists of those in which a defendant on trial complains

§ 131

1. Cf. United States v. Washington, 431 U.S. 181, 183–84 n. 2 (1977) (target of grand jury investigation has no right to be warned of target status); United States v. Mandujano, 425 U.S. 564 (1976) (grand jury target called as witness had no right to counsel inside grand jury chambers).

that he is being penalized for invoking the privilege in that trial. The second consists of situations in which the defendant complains of penalization for having invoked the privilege in prior proceedings or out-of-court before the present trial began.

Fifth Amendment Protection for Failure to Testify in Present Trial. It is clear that the fact that a defendant declined to testify at his criminal trial cannot be considered as tending to prove his guilt in that trial. Implementing this, however, has proven a troublesome problem in administering the privilege.

In Griffin v. California,[1] the Supreme Court held that the Fifth Amendment privilege was violated by a prosecutor's argument which urged the jury to draw an inference of guilt from a defendant's failure to testify when his testimony could reasonably have been expected to deny or explain matters proved by the prosecution and a jury instruction that authorized the jury to draw that suggested inference. So encouraging the jury to infer guilt from the defendant's reliance upon the privilege, the Court concluded, constituted an impermissible penalty for exercising the privilege, despite the risk that even without argument or instruction the jury might do it anyway. "What the jury may infer given no help from the court is one thing," noted the Court. "What they may infer when the court solemnizes the silence of the accused into evidence against him is quite another."[2]

Despite the implications of *Griffin,* defendants are seldom able to attack a conviction on the direct basis that their failures to testify in their own defense were taken into account in finding them guilty. Courts will generally not permit efforts to establish that jurors actually relied upon such impermissible considerations, and even apparently unambiguous admissions by trial judges sitting without juries have failed to persuade appellate courts to overturn convictions.

Griffin obviously bars the trial judge from telling the jury that it may infer guilt from the defendant's failure to testify. Nevertheless, the Supreme Court has apparently upheld instructions authorizing the jury to draw an inference from certain unexplained evidence, despite the risk that this might result in penalization of the defendant's failure to testify.[3] But lower courts sometimes find *Griffin* error in trial judges' comments or instructions that call juries' attention to the defendant's failure to testify or implicitly invite the jury to consider it.

Griffin makes clear that a prosecutor's argument can give rise to Fifth Amendment error and prosecutors' "direct" references to defendants' failure to testify are universally recognized as violations of *Griffin.* So-called "indirect" comments, however, have given rise to significant difficulty.

Most—although not all—lower courts have adopted an approach under which *Griffin* and the Fifth Amendment are violated if the prosecutor "manifestly intended" to comment on the defendant's silence or if the character of the comment was such that a jury would "naturally and necessarily" construe it as a comment on the defendant's failure to testify. Given the nature of this standard, it is appropriate and probably inevitable that appellate tribunals defer significantly to trial judges' characterizations of particular comments, since trial judges are in a uniquely advantageous position to assess how juries might respond to such comments. A wide variety of prosecution arguments or comments present difficult issues under this sort of approach.

Probably the single most difficult and frequently encountered problem in applying this standard arises when the prosecution argues to the jury that its evidence is uncontradicted or unrefuted. The Supreme Court has twice decided cases involving such situations, but

§ 132

1. 380 U.S. 609 (1965).

2. Id. at 614.

3. In Barnes v. United States, 412 U.S. 837 (1973), the Court upheld an instruction permitting the jury to infer knowledge that property was stolen from evidence of possession of recently-stolen property, if the possession was not satisfactorily explained. Without elaboration, it simply commented that this could not fairly be understood as a comment on the defendant's failure to testify. 412 U.S. at 846 n. 12.

neither decision provides much guidance for lower courts.[4] Generally, prosecutors are, of course, free to emphasize to juries the defense's failure to rebut prosecution evidence. But if on the facts of the particular case the only or perhaps even most likely source of such rebuttal is the defendant's personal testimony, such argument may become an impermissible comment upon the defendant's failure to waive his privilege and offer that testimony.

Fifth Amendment Protection From Penalties for Previous Invocations of the Privilege. How much defendants are protected from disadvantages based on having invoked the privilege prior to the present trial is less clear and certainly more limited. This is particularly so when at the present trial the defendant testifies in his own defense and the prosecution seeks to use his prior invocation of the privilege in cross-examination and impeachment.

In Raffel v. United States,[5] the Supreme Court held that a defendant who testified at trial had no federal constitutional protection against cross-examination concerning his failure to testify at a prior trial on the same charge. This seemed to rest largely on a waiver notion, as the Court stressed that a defendant who takes the witness stand subjects himself to such cross-examination as is generally permitted. But other language in the opinion suggested that the basis of decision was rather that such a defendant has no right that warrants protection. Any Fifth Amendment right to be free from penalties for invoking the privilege, the Court suggested, extends only to penalties imposed in the same trial or proceeding in which the defendant involved the privilege.

In Doyle v. Ohio,[6] however, the Court held that a testifying defendant could not, under the Due Process Clause, be cross-examined concerning his pretrial silence after being taken into custody and given *Miranda* warnings. Jenkins v. Anderson,[7] held that this protec-

tion did not extend to cross-examination based on silence prior to either arrest or *Miranda* warnings. Then, in Fletcher v. Weir,[8] no constitutional bar was found to cross-examination on the basis of silence after arrest but prior to administration of *Miranda* warnings. Whether *Raffel* survived *Griffin* and *Doyle* depends in large part upon *Doyle's* rationale.

Doyle itself appeared to rest in part upon the Court's perception that a defendant's silence could be either reliance upon his Fifth Amendment right to remain silent or incriminating consciousness of guilt; its significance was "insoluably ambiguous." This suggested the underlying constitutional deficiency in *Doyle* was the risk of jury speculation as to the most appropriate inference. So read, *Doyle* would have little significance for *Raffel's* holding. But other parts of the *Doyle* opinion suggested that this ambiguity was significant only because it created a risk that the jury would give weight to what was in fact an invocation by the defendant of his Fifth Amendment right to silence. Under this construction, the basic constitutional defect was, as in the *Griffin* situation, the drawing of an inference of guilt from invocation of the privilege. *Doyle*, then, could have been read as expanding *Griffin* to bar drawing an adverse inference from an accused's pretrial reliance upon the privilege. So read, *Doyle* would obviously cast doubt upon *Raffel's* continued vitality insofar as *Raffel* rested upon an assumption that an accused has no right at trial to be free from penalties for relying on the privilege prior to that trial.

In *Jenkins* and *Fletcher,* the Court disclaimed any reliance upon either constitutionally-prohibited jury speculation or *Griffin*-like penalization of a pretrial exercise of the privilege. *Doyle*, the Court made clear, rested exclusively upon the "fundamental unfairness" inherent in informing a suspect that he has a right to remain silent and then using that silence against him. In neither *Jenkins*

---

4. Lockett v. Ohio, 438 U.S. 586, 595 (1978); United States v. Hastings, 461 U.S. 499, 505 (1983).

5. 271 U.S. 494 (1926).

6. 426 U.S. 610 (1976).

7. 447 U.S. 231 (1980).

8. 455 U.S. 603 (1982) (per curiam).

nor *Fletcher* had the defendants received the *Miranda* admonition that they had the right to remain silent. Consequently, the prosecution's later use of their silence did not present the unfairness inherent in *Doyle*.

Even *Doyle* does not apply if, after the warnings, the arrested defendant does not rely upon his right to remain silent but rather makes an affirmative statement to officers. If he testifies at trial, there is no constitutional bar to cross-examination of him concerning inconsistencies between his pretrial statement and his trial testimony.[9] Moreover, if a testifying defendant affirmatively claims to have given police an exculpatory statement consistent with his testimony, his silence after the warnings can be used to rebut this. On the other hand, an invocation of *Miranda* rights protected under *Doyle* was not rendered admissible by the defendant's assertion at trial of an insanity defense, even though the defendant's ability and inclination to assert his rights arguably was highly probative on the insanity question.[10]

As a matter of Fifth Amendment law, then, *Raffel* remains effective. A defendant who testifies has no federal constitutional protection against cross-examination concerning invocations of the privilege at previous proceedings or out-of-court before trial. Only if a defendant was officially told before trial that he had an apparently unqualified right to remain silent will his subsequent out-of-court silence be constitutionally unavailable to the prosecution.[11]

Raffel and its Supreme Court progeny involved impeachment of a testifying defendant with his prior reliance upon the privilege. Can a defendant's pretrial silence or failure to testify at a prior trial be used as substantive evidence of guilt?

Griffin's rationale can easily and appropriately be extended and *nontestifying* defendants consequently can be regarded as entitled to be free from inferences from and comments upon prior reliance upon the Fifth Amendment, even if that reliance occurred in a previous trial or out-of-court. There is no reason to limit *Griffin* to penalties imposed in the same judicial proceeding in which the defendant exercised his rights under the privilege. *Raffel* can be read as based upon the waiver made by a defendant's act of taking the witness stand. This waiver best construed extends only so far as its rationale and therefore permits the prosecution only to use his prior reliance upon the privilege to challenge his credibility. No such waiver has been made when the defendant does not testify. When he does testify, there is no reason to construe the waiver as permitting the prosecution to use his prior reliance on the privilege as substantive evidence of his guilt.

Lower courts have in fact tended to bar the prosecution from substantive use of defendants' previous invocations of the privilege. The First Circuit, for example, read the Supreme Court's case law as establishing that "where a defendant does not testify at trial it is impermissible to refer to any fifth amendment rights that defendant has exercised."[12]

This position raises the difficult question of what constitutes a protected invocation by the defendant of his Fifth Amendment rights. Is simple silence or a barebones refusal to speak sufficient, or must such silence be shown to have been based upon reliance on a known legal right to remain silent?

Under general Fifth Amendment rules, of course, a person must affirmatively assert his rights under the provision. If this approach applies, a defendant must probably show more to obtain protection than that he was silent in a pretrial context. Under Miranda

---

9. Anderson v. Charles, 447 U.S. 404, 408 (1980) (per curiam).

10. Wainwright v. Greenfield, 474 U.S. 284 (1986).

11. This does not, of course, address the very different question of whether, as a matter of nonconstitutional evidence law, prior silence in reliance upon the privilege should and will be admissible for even limited impeach-

ment purposes. Grunewald v. United States, 353 U.S. 391 (1957), Stewart v. United States, 366 U.S. 1 (1961), and United States v. Hale, 422 U.S. 171 (1975) were all decided on such nonconstitutional grounds. *Jenkins,* supra note 7, at 237 n. 4. See generally § 160 infra.

12. Coppola v. Powell, 878 F.2d 1562, 1567 (1st Cir. 1989).

v. Arizona,[13] however, suspects undergoing custodial interrogation are exempted from this need to affirmatively assert their Fifth Amendment rights. Perhaps a similar approach should be taken in at least some pretrial silence situations. The informal, accusatory and inherently coercive nature of the out-of-court situations often involved, arguably make explicit invocation of the privilege unrealistic. On the other hand, the requirement of official compulsion suggests that the defendant must, at the time of his silence, have been officially detained or at least aware of the presence of law enforcement officers. In such situations, a defendant should be protected by *Griffin* from the trial use of his pretrial silence to prove his guilt.

State Law Protection. Some lower courts have expressed considerable dissatisfaction with the holdings in *Fletcher* and *Jenkins,* construing *Doyle* as barring trial use of defendants' pretrial silence only if the defendants had been previously admonished that they had a right to remain silent. Even under the *Fletcher–Jenkins* rationale, they have reasoned, use of silence in pre-*Miranda* warning situations is as unfair as use of silence after *Miranda* warnings. Governmental entities have developed and so widely publicized the *Miranda* rights that many and perhaps almost all suspects—whether individually warned or not—have been officially encouraged to believe that they have an unqualified right to remain silent. Using silence by unwarned suspects to impeach them, then, is arguably as fundamentally unfair as the similar use of silence by admonished defendants.

Some state courts have recognized state law prohibitions against impeachment or substantive use of silence before administration of *Miranda* warnings or even before arrest or custody. These decisions sometimes rest on state constitutional grounds, although a number of state courts have declined to go beyond *Doyle–Fletcher–Jenkins* as a matter of state constitutional law. State tribunals have been more willing to invoke nonconstitutional evidence doctrine as a basis for barring use at trial of defendants' pretrial silence prior to the administration of the *Miranda* warning concerning a right to silence.

§ 133. The Privilege of an Accused in a Criminal Proceeding: (c) Instructing the Jury Regarding the Privilege

Whether instructions directing jurors to give no weight to a defendant's failure to testify can in fact be effective, of course, is open to dispute. In Carter v. Kentucky,[1] the Supreme Court nevertheless held that the Fifth Amendment requires trial judges upon request to instruct juries that no inferences are to be drawn from defendants' failure to testify. "No judge can prevent jurors from speculating about why a defendant stands mute in the face of a criminal accusation," the Court reasoned, "but a judge can, and must if requested to do so, use the unique power of the jury instruction to reduce that speculation to a minimum."[2]

It is widely recognized, however, that reasonable persons differ with regard to when, if ever, such an instruction is likely to do more good than harm. The instruction, of course, reminds jurors of the defendant's failure to testify and emphasizes it albeit by stressing the law's demand that the failure be given no significance. Some lawyers, in at least some situations, believe that the giving of such an instruction increases rather than decreases the likelihood that the jury will actually consider the defendant's failure to testify. In light of this, may or should such an instruction be given if the defendant does not request it or if the defendant actively opposes it?

In Lakeside v. Oregon,[3] the Supreme Court found no Fifth Amendment defect in a trial judge's giving of such an instruction over the defendant's objection. *Griffin* was concerned only with adverse comment, the Court reasoned. It then rejected as "speculative" Lake-

---

13.   384 U.S. 436 (1966); see generally § 148, infra.

§ 133

1.   450 U.S. 288 (1981).

2.   450 U.S. at 303.

3.   435 U.S. 333 (1978).

side's argument that the jury might, in the absence of instructions, take no notice of his failure to testify but if given cautionary instructions might totally disregard those directives and draw an inference from his failure to testify. Sound nonconstitutional policy may direct that a trial judge respect a defendant's desire that cautionary instructions not be given, the Court commented, and states remain free to prohibit cautionary instructions over defendants' objection as a matter of state law.

It is difficult to find any significant interests furthered by the giving of such an instruction over the defendant's objection. Moreover, in light of the uncertainty as to whether and when such an instruction is more favorable to an accused than the absence of any instruction, there is little reason to permit the instruction if the defendant affirmatively objects. As the Maryland court observed:

> Since the instruction is a right of the defendant, for his benefit, but because the beneficial effect of the instruction may be uncertain in some circumstances, it follows that the decision whether the instruction is given should lie with the defendant.[4]

An increasing number of jurisdictions so provide, sometimes by statute, and sometimes by constitutional or nonconstitutional case law.

A special problem is presented by multiple defendant trials, where one of several nontestifying defendants seeks such an instruction but the others oppose it. There seems widespread agreement, however, that in this situation the *Carter* right of the defendant who wishes the instruction must prevail, and the instruction must be given. It would, however, be sound to avoid any specific reference in these instructions to the passivity or rights of those defendants who object to the instruction.

If an instruction is given, care should be taken to phrase it so as to minimize any

possible suggestion that the defendant's failure to testify might be because he is guilty and taking the stand would require him to acknowledge that fact. Thus the instructions should explain the defendant's right as one not to testify rather than one not to incriminate himself, as the latter phraseology suggests that the likely reason for not testifying is to avoid having to admit guilt. The Massachusetts court has even suggested that trial judges avoid reference to defendants' "refusal" or "neglect" to testify.

§ 134. The Privilege of an Accused in a Criminal Proceeding: (d) "Waiver" of the Privilege by Voluntary Testimony

A criminal accused's extensive rights under the privilege are diminished by his act of testifying in his own behalf during the trial. Unlike the situation of a witness, who loses the privilege only by testifying to incriminating facts,[1] the accused suffers this reduction in his rights merely by testifying, regardless of the incriminatory content of his testimony. In Brown v. United States[2] the Supreme Court explained:

> "[The accused] has the choice, after weighing the advantage of the privilege against self-incrimination against the advantage of putting forward his version of the facts and his reliability as a witness, not to testify at all. He cannot reasonably claim that the Fifth Amendment gives him not only this choice but, if he elects to testify, an immunity from cross-examination on the matters he has himself put in dispute. It would make of the Fifth Amendment not only a humane safeguard against judicially coerced self-disclosure but a positive invitation to mutilate the truth a party offers to tell."[3]

Whether the accused's loss of certain advantages under the privilege rests on a waiver rationale is not entirely clear. If so, of course, the accused should suffer this decreased protection only upon proof that his

---

4. Hardaway v. State, 317 Md. 160, 167, 562 N.E.2d 1234, 1237 (1989).

§ 134

1. See § 140 infra.

2. 356 U.S. 148 (1958).

3. 356 U.S. at 155–56.

decision to testify reflected an informed as well as voluntary decision. Despite the extensive use of "waiver" language in the discussions, however, the courts show little inclination to require any such proof regarding the accused's initial decision. *Brown's* discussion suggests that the defendant's loss of Fifth Amendment protection rests less upon waiver principles than upon a forfeiture-like rationale, under which even self-incriminatory cross-examination is regarded as a reasonable burden to place upon the accused's decision to testify regardless of whether he anticipated this at the time he testified.

Whether the loss of protection rests upon a waiver or forfeiture rationale is not resolved by case law concerning trial judges' duties to admonish defendants concerning their right to testify or not. Most courts hold that a trial judge has no duty to admonish a represented defendant who seeks to testify that he has a right not to do so, although the trial judge may have discretion—or perhaps even a duty—to intervene if it appears that the defendant does not understand the situation. Some courts hold that an unrepresented defendant must be so admonished. When an admonishment is appropriate, the courts have indicated that it need not be extensive and even suggested that it must not be. This, however, seems to reflect less an assumption that the defendant's decision need not be an intelligent one than a concern that an elaborate admonishment may impose improper pressure upon a defendant.

The major problem in applying this rule has been defining the extent to which an accused loses the protection of the privilege by testifying. Traditionally, many courts have taken the position that a defendant who testifies becomes subject to cross-examination under the jurisdiction's applicable rules and loses the right to invoke the privilege in response to any question proper under those rules. Under this approach, a testifying defendant may be questioned concerning all matters related to the case and his credibility, regardless of whether he addressed those mat-

ters on direct examination. He may not invoke his privilege on the ground that answers to such questions would incriminate him further regarding the offenses for which he is being tried. Nor can he invoke it on the ground that his answers would incriminate him for other offenses, except when the questions tending to do so are asked only for impeachment purposes.[4]

A defendant's loss of protection by virtue of testifying in his own defense should not be tied to the jurisdiction's rules concerning permissible cross-examination. Some jurisdictions restrict cross-examination to matters testified to on direct examination, while others permit cross-examination on all phases of the case.[5] There is no reason why the scope of an important constitutional right should vary depending upon the jurisdiction's choice of a cross-examination rule. The scope of cross-examination is essentially a matter of control over the order of production of evidence. The primary policy served by limiting cross-examination is the orderly conduct of the trial; ordinary witnesses usually have no legitimate interest that is affected by the scope of permitted cross-examination. Defining the protection of the privilege, on the other hand, involves the "fairness" of requiring defendants to forfeit the protection of the privilege in order to place their own versions of the facts before triers of fact. This affects defendants' interests which are, generally speaking, protected by the privilege. The scope of protection retained by a testifying defendant should not be tied to the scope of cross-examination of the ordinary witness.

Several alternatives exist to the traditional approach that ties the scope of remaining protection to the scope of permissible cross-examination of a regular witness. One would regard the accused as having lost the privilege as to all aspects of the offense to which he has testified. This has the advantages of simplicity and ease of application. It may not, however, adequately relate the reduction of protection to the rationale for reducing

---

4. See § 41 supra as to claiming the privilege on cross-examination directed to impeachment.

5. See § 21 supra.

protection, that is, the defendant's decision to testify. An accused's basic right under the privilege is not simply one to avoiding taking the stand but rather one to be free from compelled testimonial self-incrimination regarding the offense for which he is on trial as well as others. To automatically regard a defendant who testifies in his own defense as having lost all protection under the privilege regarding the offense for which he is being tried is to deprive him of important protection under the privilege without regard to whether this degree of deprivation is justified by the defendant's triggering action.

Another approach, taken by an increasing number of courts, prohibits a testifying defendant from invoking the privilege only when cross-examination is reasonably related to the subject matter of his direct examination. Courts taking this approach, however, tend to construe this criterion broadly and to find no right to refuse to respond to questions with relatively attenuated relation to the matters inquired into on direct examination. This formulation of the testifying defendant's remaining protection seldom leads to results different from those that would be reached under the traditional approach.

The rationale for requiring a testifying defendant to submit to cross-examination is primarily if not exclusively to provide reasonable assurance that his testimony, like that of other witnesses, is subjected to procedures believed to provide assurance of accuracy. A defendant should neither be invited nor permitted, in the Supreme Court's *Brown* language, "to mutilate the truth [he] offers to tell." The extent to which a defendant forfeits the privilege by testifying should be related to this rationale for decreased protection because of his testifying. Emphasis should be placed on the ability of the prosecution to subject the accused's testimony on direct examination to scrutiny regarding its truth. Thus a defendant who testifies should have no right to invoke the privilege regarding questions on cross-examination that the trial court, in the exercise of discretion, determines

are necessary to provide the prosecution with a reasonable opportunity to test the defendant's assertions on direct.

Such an approach to defining the scope of a testifying defendant's loss of protection is consistent with the position, reflected in the Federal Rules,[6] that a testifying witness does not automatically lose the right to invoke the privilege regarding matters relating only to credibility. This approach was recently adopted by the New York Court of Appeals, which characterized the underlying problem as finding an accommodation between the defendant's interest in testifying in his own defense and the prosecution's interest in being able to mount "a balanced evidentiary response." Implicit in the court's analysis is the assumption that the prosecution is entitled to elicit responses from a testifying defendant that are further incriminating only if doing so is necessary to test the accuracy of what the defendant has asserted on direct examination.

If a defendant has testified in his own defense and impermissibly refused to respond to cross-examination in mistaken reliance upon his privilege, what action should or may the trial court take? As in the case where an ordinary witness invokes the privilege on cross-examination,[7] the trial court has substantial discretion as to how to respond. But in view of a defendant's particularly important interest in having his version of the events go to the trier of fact, a trial judge should be especially reluctant to strike the defendant's testimony on direct examination and should do so only after considering and rejecting alternative measures such as striking only part of the testimony on direct examination or directing that the jury consider in assessing the defendant's credibility his improper reliance upon his privilege.

A defendant suffers the reduction in protection described above only upon "testifying." Does a defendant testify and thus subject himself to cross-examination if he demonstrates some physical characteristic to the jury or

---

6. See § 41 supra.

7. See § 140 infra.

otherwise participates in the trial other than by traditional sworn oral testimony from the witness stand? In several cases, for example, defendants sought opportunities to demonstrate their voices for juries but without subjecting themselves to cross-examination. The courts have assumed that if, but only if, the defendants' proposed actions would be "nontestimonial" [8] the trial courts could permit the defendant to make the demonstration without submitting to cross-examination. Since in the pretrial context a defendant's compelled demonstration of his physical characteristics seems clearly to be nontestimonial, his voluntary demonstration of them during trial is necessarily also nontestimonial and does not require that he submit to cross-examination.

The loss of protection has traditionally been regarded as effective throughout the proceeding in which the accused testifies. During that proceeding the privilege does not reattach if the accused physically leaves the witness stand, and he can be recalled and required to testify again if this is otherwise procedurally proper. On the other hand, testifying in one "proceeding" does not preclude the accused from invoking the privilege in a separate and independent proceeding. A defendant who testified in one trial is not, for example, barred from relying on the privilege in a second trial on the same charge. And a defendant who testifies at the guilt stage of a trial retains his right to rely on the privilege if he is convicted and the sentencing hearing is held before the jury.

§ 135. Special Problems: (a) Limits on Compelled Defense Disclosure to the Prosecution Imposed by the Privilege

The increasing liberality with which discovery is granted to defendants in criminal litigation has brought demands that discovery be made a "two-way" street, with the result that legislation, court rules, and judicial decisions have increasingly created certain defense duties to make disclosure to the prosecution. These duties may involve only notice of intent to rely upon certain "defenses"—such as alibi or insanity—at trial. Or, they may require greater detail regarding the defense trial case, such as the place the defense will attempt at trial to show that the defendant was at the time of the offense. Disclosure may require only that the defense provide factual information that defense trial evidence will later reveal, such as the names, addresses and "statements" of persons that the defense will call as witnesses. Or, it may require revelation of information that is affirmatively incriminating and which the defense would not, of course, attempt to prove at trial.

Requirements of such defense disclosure raise a number of complex issues concerning appropriate criminal justice policy and infringement of defendants' rights. This section considers only the possibility that some required disclosure of this sort violates defendants' privilege against compelled self-incrimination.

In two major decisions the Supreme Court greatly limited defendants' Fifth Amendment protection from such disclosure requirements. In Williams v. Florida,[1] the Court found no Fifth Amendment violation in a requirement that the defendant provide pretrial notice of intent to claim alibi and disclose to the prosecution where the defense evidence would tend to show the defendant was, as well as the names and addresses of witnesses the defense intended to call to support the claim of alibi. Reasoning that the requirement did nothing more than accelerate disclosure which the defense would otherwise make at trial, the Court reasoned that "[n]othing in the Fifth Amendment privilege entitles a defendant as a matter of constitutional right to await the end of the State's case before announcing the nature of his defense * * * " [2] This rationale, if applied to defense disclosure generally,

---

8. See generally § 124 supra.

§ 135

1. 399 U.S. 78 (1970).

2. Id. at 85.

would permit compelled pretrial disclosure of any information which the defense would otherwise disclose during trial. It would not, however, deny Fifth Amendment protection to potentially damaging information which the defense would not itself use at trial. *Williams* seemed to assume that defendants could not be compelled to make such disclosure.

But this was cast into doubt by United States v. Nobles.[3] The defense wished to call a defense investigator to testify to statements made by prosecution witnesses inconsistent with their trial testimony, but the trial court ruled that if this was done the defense would have to permit the prosecution to inspect those portions of the investigator's written report relevant to the statements at issue. The Supreme Court found no Fifth Amendment bar to compelling Nobles to make such disclosure, reasoning that the Fifth Amendment protects a defendant only against being personally compelled to make testimonial disclosures. Because the investigator's report contained only testimonial disclosures made by persons other than the defendant, it concluded, disclosure under compulsion would involve no compelled testimonial activity by the defendant.

Where the defense strategy "waives" objection to inquiry into an area, lower courts have permitted broad compelled disclosure. Thus a defendant was held to have no right to resist a demand that counsel produce a report from an expert who had examined the defendant but would not testify at trial, where the defendant's plea of insanity had opened up the area of criminal responsibility.

Lower courts differ, however, on whether the Fifth Amendment permits compelled disclosure regarding information the defense will not itself later offer, when the defense has not so waived inquiry into the area. The Washington Supreme Court held that the Fifth Amendment permitted the trial court to compel defense counsel to disclose transcripts, notes and summaries of interviews between defense investigators and state witnesses. *Nobles,* the court reasoned, permits such compelled disclosure as long as the defense is not required to provide the state with access to information from the defendant himself. A New Jersey court, on the other hand, read Fifth Amendment protection as much broader and concluded that a defendant need not reveal the names of persons he did not intend to call as witnesses but who possessed information affirmatively incriminating the defendant.

If *Nobles'* rationale is applied logically, the role of the Fifth Amendment privilege in limiting defense disclosure is quite limited. It provides no protection against compelled disclosure, during or before trial, concerning information possessed by defense counsel but obtained from sources other than the defendant's communications to counsel. Despite *Nobles'* suggestion, the Court's rationale even suggests that defense counsel can be compelled to disclose information developed from information provided by the defendant. Since the compulsion to disclose would be applied only after the defendant provided the information, the defendant's testimonial disclosure cannot be regarded as "compelled" within the meaning of self-incrimination law.[4]

State law versions of self-incrimination, of course, might impose more stringent limits upon prosecutorial disclosure. The leading authority for such a position is the California Supreme Court's decision in In re Misener.[5] Article I, § 15 of the West's Ann.Cal. Const., the court reasoned, prohibits any compelled disclosure by the defendant that might conceivably lighten the prosecution's burden of proving the defendant's guilt. Consequently, the privilege against compelled self-incrimination invalidates statutory authority for the trial court to order, after a defense witness has testified, the defense to give the prosecution statements by the witness relating to the witness's testimony on direct.

---

3. 422 U.S. 225 (1975).

4. See generally § 125, supra, discussing the requirement of "compulsion."

5. 38 Cal.3d 543, 213 Cal.Rptr. 569, 698 P.2d 637 (1985).

The *Misener* court was unpersuaded by the argument that defendants who call such witnesses waive state constitutional protection concerning information relevant to cross-examination. Defendants may by calling such witnesses give up any right they have to preserve those witnesses from full and vigorous cross-examination, it reasoned, but they do not also waive their right to refuse to provide the prosecution with the means to conduct such cross-examination.

The *Misener* court also found several grounds for rejecting *Nobles'* reliance upon the personal nature of the privilege. Defense counsel often locate witnesses by using defendants' statements, the court first reasoned, so disclosure of witnesses' statements would frequently involve indirect disclosure of defendants' statements in violation of *Nobles*. Most significantly, however, the court also simply rejected *Nobles* as addressing only the federal constitutional requirement. By implication, then, *Misener* holds that the California state constitutional privilege is not completely "personal to the defendant" and, at least in some situations, bars required production of information that does not constitute a compelled testimonial communication by the accused.

The *Nobles* approach rejected in *Misener* properly gives self-incrimination principles a relatively minor role in placing constitutional limits upon the extent to which defendants can be compelled to give the prosecution disclosure. Whether the prosecution should be permitted access to information in the defense's possession depends primarily upon whether such access in inconsistent with an appropriate balance of advantage between the defense and prosecution. Defining appropriate constitutional limits upon how this balance may be struck is a task best performed primarily by provisions other than those guaranteeing the right to be free from compelled self-incrimination.

Under Wardius v. Oregon,[6] for example, the general Fifth and Fourteenth Amendment demand of due process requires that compelled disclosure be reasonably reciprocal. In *Wardius,* the Court held invalid a notice of alibi requirement that unlike the Florida provision at issue in *Williams* imposed upon the prosecution no duty to disclose witnesses to be offered in rebuttal of the alibi. Such an analysis addresses the major underlying concerns more directly and hence more effectively than self-incrimination scrutiny.

Compelled disclosure may also impede defense counsel's ability to marshall the facts and evidence necessary to prepare a defense, and thus affect counsel's ability to function effectively. This concern is at most tangentially related to self-incrimination policies, and is best addressed as raising potential violations of the right to adequate representation by counsel or perhaps as violating the attorney-client privilege.

Any provision for disclosure by the defense must also respect the holding of Brooks v. Tennessee[7] that the Fifth Amendment privilege confers a right upon a defendant to testify in his own defense as well as to remain silent. A defendant must be permitted to exercise this choice "in the unfettered exercise of his own will," and consequently a defendant cannot be limited to testifying before any other defense witnesses. This would seem to bar any requirement that a defendant make a preliminary commitment either to testify or to avoid doing so. Whether it would be violated by something less, as by a requirement that a defendant give nonbinding notice that he may testify, is unclear.

Misener rests upon the California Supreme Court's unusually expansive perception of the state constitutional privilege, and its holding has been rejected on this ground by other courts. In California, *Misener* was apparently "overruled" by 1990 amendments to the state constitution.

This is appropriate. *Misener's* holding relies upon considerations substantially beyond those reasonably regarded as embodied in prohibitions against compelled self-incrimination. *Williams* and *Nobles* reflect a more reason-

---

6. 412 U.S. 470 (1973).

7. 406 U.S. 605 (1972).

ably limited perception of the privilege and its role in limiting the prosecution's access to the fruits of defense investigative efforts.

§ 136. Special Problems: (b) Psychiatric Examinations of the Criminal Defendant

Psychiatric examinations of a criminal defendant may be ordered by the trial court for any of numerous purposes, including evaluating the defendant's competence to stand trial, gathering evidence concerning anticipated defenses such as insanity, or gathering information bearing upon the most appropriate sentence to be imposed if conviction results. A psychiatrist who has examined a defendant for one purpose may be later called upon to testify on a different issue. This variety of purposes complicates the task of determining the relevance of the privilege against compelled self-incrimination to such examinations.

The initial question is whether the privilege applies at all. If the examiner merely observes characteristics of the defendant's behavior, there is no testimonial activity on the defendant's part to be protected. In Estelle v. Smith,[1] the Supreme Court left open the possibility that the Fifth Amendment might be inapplicable to an examination at which this was actually the case. In *Smith*, however, the Court concluded that the psychiatrist had in fact relied upon the defendant's communicated remarks, such as his recitation of the details of the crime charged. Given that, the Court concluded, the state's later use of the psychiatrist's testimony implicated the Fifth Amendment. Other courts have been similarly reluctant to conclude that defendants' verbal responses during such examinations are nontestimonial.

An examination may be said to involve no compulsion if the defendant is not required to respond to particular questions. This, however, ignores the practical pressure upon a defendant even in the absence of formal compulsion. *Smith* makes clear that, for Fifth Amendment purposes, the same considerations as implicate the privilege in station-house police questioning also require its application when a defendant in custody is compelled to submit to an examination even if she is not specifically required to answer questions put to her.

Whether the responses called for are incriminating is somewhat more difficult. In *Smith*, the Supreme Court commented that if the results of an examination are confined to determining the accused's competency to stand trial, no Fifth Amendment issue would be presented. This is apparently because a finding of competency simply removes a potential bar to trial of the accused and thus does not constitute "incrimination" within the meaning of the Fifth Amendment privilege. But *Smith* makes equally clear that if the results of the examination are used against the defendant on the question of guilt or innocence or in support of a severe penalty[2] upon conviction, the defendant's responses are incriminating and the Fifth Amendment applies.

If the Fifth Amendment applies, what does it require? In *Smith*, the Court held that the similarity between the compelled examination and custodial law enforcement questioning called for a *Miranda*-like warning to the defendant that his statements made during the examination could be used against him and that he had the right to remain silent. Moreover, the admonishments must sometimes go further. In *Smith*, the results of the interview were used by the state at Smith's capital sentencing procedure in support of its case for imposition of the death penalty; the Court made clear that the admonishments would have to inform the accused of this particular potential use of his admissions during the interview. Although the Court did not specifically indicate that the accused has a right not to have the interview begun, this is implied in the Court's explicit requirement that after the warning the defendant "volun-

---

§ 136

1. 451 U.S. 454 (1981).

McCormick, Evidence 4th Ed. HB—6

2. See § 121, supra.

tarily consent" to the examination. Whether a defendant has a right to the presence of counsel was not before the Court and therefore was not resolved, but the Court indicated a distaste for extending this aspect of *Miranda* to psychiatric examinations.

Smith was a death penalty case, and the Court clearly left open the possibility that its holding would not necessarily apply to other situations. No principled distinction between capital and other cases is possible, however.

The major issue after *Smith* is the extent to which these requirements are relaxed when the defendant has asserted—or will assert—a defense implicating her mental condition. There is widespread agreement that when a defendant asserts a defensive matter that involves reliance upon a claim of psychological abnormality, otherwise applicable Fifth Amendment protections are at least somewhat diluted. At a minimum, the defendant can be compelled to submit to an examination by a psychiatrist without the need for the *Smith* cautions. The leading judicial discussion, by then Judge Scalia,[3] rejected a waiver analysis as an obvious fiction. Instead, Judge Scalia explained, a defendant's assertion of such a defense puts into issue difficult issues, and the defendant's mental status is the primary source of potentially reliable evidence on those issues. Assuming substantial flexibility in Fifth Amendment doctrine, he then reasoned that in these situations Fifth Amendment protections must fall because of overwhelmingly important and "fair" countervailing considerations: the "unreasonable and debilitating effect" that full application of the Fifth Amendment would have "upon society's conduct of a fair inquiry into the defendant's culpability." This discussion has been cited with approval by the Supreme Court[4] and has been widely relied upon by other lower tribunals.

The cases leave unclear how and to what extent efforts can be made to compel a defendant to participate in such an examination. A Colorado court, for example, recently declined to address whether a defendant has a right to "terminate" an interview. Thus the psychiatrist properly continued an interview despite the defendant's "initial reluctance" to discuss certain topics. In finding no Fifth Amendment violation, the court stressed that no evidence had been presented that the defendant's ultimate disclosures "were coerced or involuntary in any way, or * * * the result of surreptitious mental invasion." An examiner, it concluded, can continue questions beyond and despite a defendant's "expressed reluctance" to discuss a particular topic. Whether a defendant could be specifically ordered to fully respond to an examiner's queries and penalized upon refusal, or even whether an examination can continue over a defendant's explicit and sustained desire to end the examination, therefore, remain open.

If a defendant is examined under the mere permissive standards applicable when she has asserted a mental abnormality defense, can her admissions to the examiner be used not simply to rebut the defensive matter raised by the defendant but rather as substantive evidence that the defendant committed the offense? Statutes frequently bar this. Courts have often assumed that this is required by self-incrimination law as well.

The rationale for dilution of the protection generally afforded by the privilege suggests that the prosecution be limited in its use of the resulting evidence to the matter that justified the dilution. If a defendant loses at least some of the protection of the privilege because of her insertion into the case of a mental abnormality issue, the prosecution should be permitted to use the fruits of the privilege's relaxation only on that issue. This was recognized by the New Hampshire Supreme Court, which held that upon defense request, a trial jury must be instructed to consider the prosecution's expert testimony, based on a compelled examination, only on those issues to which the defendant's mental abnormality issue related.

---

3. United States v. Byers, 740 F.2d 1104, 1111–1115 (D.C.Cir.1984) (plurality opinion).

4. Buchanan v. Kentucky, 483 U.S. 402, 423 (1987).

A defendant most often becomes subject to a compelled examination under this rule when she asserts a traditional defense of insanity. But the courts have quite liberally expanded the exception to include other situations in which a defensive assertion necessarily involves a claim of mental abnormality. The Fifth Circuit has suggested that *Smith's* holding applies whenever the defendant introduces "mental status evidence that may fairly be characterized as expert testimony." Where this is the case, but only where it is, the prosecution's only effective means of countering the defendant's assertion is by expert testimony, and despite her privilege the defendant may be compelled to participate in an examination permitting the prosecution to develop such testimony.

Consistent with such an approach, relaxed self-incrimination standards have been held applicable when the defendant claims so-called "diminished capacity." Fifth Amendment requirements were similarly held inapplicable when a defendant, at sentencing, introduced testimony by drug treatment and rehabilitation counselors that he was capable of rehabilitation. Moreover, the prosecution has been held entitled to have the defendant examined by an expert of its choosing where the defendant was likely at her murder trial to offer psychological testimony supporting her claim that because she suffered from battered woman's syndrome she was entitled to acquittal on self-defense grounds.

These holdings are appropriate. As the New Hampshire Supreme Court noted, the rationale for relaxing self-incrimination standards in such situations is to permit the prosecution a reasonable opportunity to test defendants' claims based on mental abnormality. This rationale applies regardless of whether defendants' efforts involve assertions of what are technically "defenses" that admit the elements of the crime charged.

§ 137. The Privilege of a Witness: (a) Invoking the Privilege

Non-defendant witnesses are privileged only to decline to respond to inquiries, not to be free from those inquiries designed to elicit responses self-incriminatory in nature. The nature of the privilege for non-defendant witnesses means that the requirements for invoking it are somewhat different than those applicable when the holder of the privilege is an accused in a criminal proceeding. Most importantly, a witness must submit to questioning and invoke the privilege in response to each specific question. A witness has no right to refuse either to appear or to be sworn as a witness. If a witness is asked a series of questions, the witness must ordinarily assert the privilege in response to each one. A "blanket" objection to a line of questioning on self-incrimination grounds generally will not constitute an effective assertion of the privilege. In limited situations, however, such a "blanket objection"—as, for example, a "running objection" to an entire "line of questioning"—may be effective, at least if specifically accepted by the trial judge.

Outside of the courtroom context, the same general rule governs. While the privilege applies when a person is required to provide information or when a party to litigation is required to respond to pretrial discovery requests, the person or party cannot simply fail or refuse to respond but must explicitly and specifically invoke the privilege. Thus in *Garner v. United States,*[1] the defendant's filing of federal income tax returns containing self-incriminating information rendered those returns admissible in a later criminal prosecution. His failure to invoke the privilege at the time of the filing of the returns deprived him of any ability to rely on the privilege regarding information in those returns. Similarly, a witness being deposed has been held to a duty to raise the privilege during the deposition process. He cannot answer fully but later effectively assert the privilege when some particular litigative use is made of the answers. In exceptional situations in which the assertion of the privilege might itself be self-incriminating, however, a witness may be able to simply remain silent and later avoid

1. 424 U.S. 648 (1976).

penalization for refusal to answer on the basis of the privilege.

Courts justify the requirement that witnesses so raise their privilege on the basis of the limited protection afforded witnesses by the privilege in this context and the need to accommodate considerations other than the witnesses' interest in avoiding compelled self-incrimination. Parties to litigation have obvious interests in being able to produce relevant testimony, and society as a whole has an important interest in the accurate and efficient resolution of litigation. The trial judge and not the witness himself must determine whether a witness's claim of the privilege is justified. Requiring specific assertion of the privilege when the testimony or information is sought permits efficient resolution of witnesses' claims in a manner that accommodates these other interests. A claim of the privilege by a witness alerts the court and the parties to the need to immediately inquire into the basis for that claim when the facts are fresh and can most accurately be developed. It also guides that inquiry by identifying the nature of the possible incriminatory risks that must be investigated.

Ordinarily, it is desirable that the jury not know that a witness has invoked the privilege, since neither party to litigation is entitled to draw any inference from a witness's invocation. Therefore, if a party anticipates that his witness will invoke the privilege, he should alert the trial court of this. The witness's invocation and the court's inquiry into the justification for the witness's reliance on the privilege should take place out of the presence of the jury. But where it is not clear in advance whether a witness will invoke the privilege, a trial judge has discretion whether to interrupt the presentation of the case to conduct an anticipatory inquiry or, instead, to proceed despite the risk that the jury will therefore observe the witness's reliance on the privilege.

Special problems of potentially constitutional dimensions are presented when the prosecution in a criminal case is permitted to make substantial inquiries before the jury of a witness who responds by relying on the privilege. In Namet v. United States,[2] the Supreme Court suggested that prosecution misconduct sufficient to render a conviction invalid might occur if the prosecution, knowing that a witness will invoke the privilege, calls that witness before the jury and then makes a "conscious and flagrant attempt to build its case out of inferences arising from use of the [self-incrimination] privilege." Alternatively, such action creates significant risk that the jury will rely upon an inference of the defendant's guilt from the witness's invocation of the privilege or from the questions themselves. This might constitute an impermissible use of "testimony" not subject to cross-examination by the defendant. In Douglas v. Alabama,[3] the Court gave constitutional status to the second possibility, holding that a defendant's Sixth Amendment right to effective cross-examination was violated when the prosecution was permitted to extensively question a witness regarding a pretrial statement implicating the defendant and the witness refused on self-incrimination grounds to respond to all questions.

Lower courts apply a multi-factor analysis to determine whether error is committed when a prosecution witness is questioned before the jury and invokes his privilege. Among the relevant considerations are the prosecutor's certainty that the witness will invoke the privilege, the number and nature of the questions as to which the privilege is invoked, whether other evidence has been introduced on those matters as to which the jury might draw an inference from the witness's invocation of the privilege, and the giving—and likely effectiveness—of an instruction to the jury to draw no inference from the witness's action.

A witness may lose Fifth Amendment protection by a failure to raise it in the necessary manner even if that failure is not the result of a decision that meets the traditional requirements for a waiver of a constitutional

2. 373 U.S. 179 (1963).

3. 380 U.S. 415 (1965).

right. This, the Court explained in Minnesota v. Murphy,[4] is because a witness is not *compelled* to incriminate himself unless he has asserted a right to refuse to provide the information and that assertion has been rejected.[5] The case law dealing with the required manner of asserting the privilege, then, does not address the waiver of a right but rather whether there is any right at issue.

Whether compulsion is necessarily lacking unless a witness has asserted his right to refuse to answer is, as a practical matter, quite problematic. The Court's reasoning may be that witnesses simply cannot, as a purely factual matter, regard themselves as compelled to respond unless they unsuccessfully assert their privilege. This is probably incorrect. Ignorance or confusion might well leave a witness so convinced that he is required to respond to questions into incriminating topics that the witness perceives nothing to be gained from asserting a right to remain silent. Alternatively, the Court's rationale may be that no reasonable person could regard these demands as being for self-incriminating answers. This, however, adds a disturbingly objective aspect to the protection afforded by the privilege. As applied to a witness, the privilege thus appears to protect only against compulsion that would objectively be recognized as containing no qualification rendering it inapplicable to self-incriminating answers.

From a practical perspective, of course, the Court's approach makes imminent sense. If a witness was able to invoke the privilege long after his testimony, elaborate and difficult inquiry into his earlier mental processes would be necessary. Witnesses might ultimately be able to deprive the prosecution of evidence developed from disclosures made knowingly and voluntarily but later recognized as unwise. Requiring a witness to assert the privilege when the matter arises greatly minimizes these difficulties. Whether or not the privilege actually applies can then be investigated immediately and determined most reliably and efficiently. If the trial court determines that the witness has a right to withhold the demanded answers, the prosecution can make a considered choice whether to challenge further the witness's right to rely on the privilege, to grant immunity and thus obtain the answers at the cost so incurred or, to simply abandon the question and thus avoid the trouble and risks involved in attempting to overcome the witness's reliance on the privilege.

The Supreme Court's approach must be justified on the ground that these advantages are so important as to outweigh the costs. Primary among those costs is the likelihood that witnesses will at least occasionally be denied the protection of the Fifth Amendment privilege although they revealed incriminating information under the perception that they were legally obligated to do so.

§ 138. The Privilege of a Witness: (b) The Right to Be Warned and to Counsel

Generally speaking, if a trial judge becomes aware that the questioning of a witness raises the risk that the witness by responding will incriminate himself, the trial judge has substantial discretion as to whether and how to respond. The judge may, for example, stop the questioning briefly to warn the witness that she may decline to give self-incriminating answers and perhaps assure that the witness has a clear opportunity to assert a desire to withhold answers. When this is done, it is clearly best done out of the presence of the trial jury. The judge may also take more drastic steps as, for example, by temporarily stopping the trial so that the witness may consult with an attorney and even by appointing an attorney to consult with the witness.

Ordinarily, however, this process protects only the interests of the witness. Noncompliance with any requirements as might apply does not prejudice the legitimate interests of the parties, so they may not complain of the

---

4. 465 U.S. 420, 426–440 (1984).

5. See generally § 125, supra.

trial judge's failure to take adequate steps to protect the interests of the witnesses.

The matter becomes more delicate in a criminal trial when the judge becomes concerned that a defense witness's self-incrimination rights may be placed in unfair jeopardy. The witness's self-incrimination interests, of course, are no less in such situations. But the defense has a particularly important interest that is also affected—the defendant's Sixth Amendment right to present all potentially exculpatory evidence. As the Supreme Court recognized in Webb v. Texas,[1] trial judges' efforts to protect defense witnesses' interests may impermissibly intrude upon defendants' right to produce evidence.

Perhaps the most that can be generally said with confidence in such situations is that trial judges have a special duty to seek an accommodation between witnesses' self-incrimination interests and defendants' interests in full production of relevant evidence. The judge is not barred from alerting the witness to her self-incrimination right, but the judge's authority to caution the witness "should be exercised sparingly and with great caution." In deciding whether and how to proceed, the judge should consider—among other factors— the actual risk of the witness being prosecuted, and must take special care to assure that any decision not to testify is that of the witness herself. The West Virginia Supreme Court has suggested that trial judges are well advised to include admonishments that might encourage witnesses to testify, such as statements that a witness who testifies may invoke the privilege during her testimony. Of course, the prosecution's interest in being able to challenge the credibility of defense testimony must also be given adequate consideration. The witness must therefore be alerted to the duty after testifying on direct examination to submit to appropriate cross-examination.[2]

Different and perhaps more difficult questions are posed by questioning of witnesses in grand jury proceedings, particularly where a witness is a "target" of the grand jury's concern. Such witnesses seem clearly to not yet be "accuseds," entitled to defendants' right not to be called as witnesses. Although they are entitled to refuse on self-incrimination grounds to respond to particular questions, the Supreme Court has been quite reluctant to impose further and more specific Fifth Amendment requirements in this area for two reasons. First, the Court perceives the grand jury as unlikely to place improper pressure upon those being questioned, because of the civilian composition of the bodies and judicial supervision of them. Second, the Court regards the flexibility of grand jury procedure as important to the bodies' ability to perform their tasks. Expansion of witnesses' rights might reduce this flexibility and impede grand jury effectiveness.

Specifically, the Court has refused to extend to even target witnesses under grand jury questioning the *Miranda* rights afforded suspects undergoing law enforcement custodial interrogation. In United States v. Mandujano,[3] the prosecutor had informed the grand jury witness that, despite his indigency, he was entitled to representation but that the lawyer would have to remain outside the grand jury room although he would be available for consultation. The Court characterized this as "plainly a correct recital of the law," and noted that under "settled principles" a grand jury witness is not entitled to have his lawyer present inside the grand jury room. Because of the reduced risk to the suspect's self-incrimination rights and the increased danger that lawyers' involvement would be disruptive, suspects questioned by grand juries have no Fifth Amendment right to the presence of an attorney. It is likely that they have the right to consult with an attorney before responding to particular questions, although they can be required to leave the grand jury room to do so.

Since there is no right to the presence of counsel, obviously a grand jury target witness

§ 138

1. 409 U.S. 95 (1972).

2. See § 140, infra.

3. 425 U.S. 564 (1976).

has no Fifth Amendment right to full *Miranda* warnings. But does the witness have a right to a lesser or modified warning? The Supreme Court has specifically declined to decide whether a grand jury witness has a Fifth Amendment right to be warned that she has the right to decline to answer questions on self-incrimination grounds.[4] It has made clear, however, that a simple and comprehensive statement by a prosecutor as to witnesses' right to refuse answers would meet any such right as might exist.[5] In United States v. Washington,[6] the Court failed to reach whether a witness who is the target of a grand jury investigation is entitled, upon being subpoenaed to testify, to a "target warning" informing him that he is a target of the inquiry. But the Court's discussion made clear it was not favorably disposed to finding any such requirement. Both target and non-target witnesses, the Court commented, have the same right against compelled self-incrimination during a compelled grand jury appearance. Since target witness status does not affect the scope of constitutional protection, it continued, a warning of such status would add nothing of value in protecting Fifth Amendment rights in this area.

The *Washington* majority's reasoning is wanting. While both target and nontarget witnesses have the same Fifth Amendment rights, those rights are as a practical matter placed at substantially greater risk when a witness is a target. Whether grand jury target witnesses should be entitled to greater rights—with regard to warnings or representation—should turn on whether those practical risks to the privilege are great enough to warrant such increased protective efforts.

Despite—or perhaps because of—the Supreme Court's reluctance to find rigorous Fifth Amendment rights in this context, a number of states have gone beyond the Court's position. The Indiana Supreme Court, for example, has held—apparently re-

lying on the state constitutional self-incrimination provision—that all grand jury witnesses must be told the general nature of the investigation and that they may refuse to answer incriminating questions. Target witnesses must also be told of their right to counsel. The New Jersey Supreme Court has construed its common law self-incrimination privilege to require that target witnesses be told that they are targets and of their right not to incriminate themselves. Statutes or court rules sometimes go further, as by creating a right to an appointed attorney with whom the witness may consult. Under some statutes, at least target witnesses are entitled to have counsel appear with them inside the grand jury chambers. Concerns that so involving counsel in the grand jury process may disrupt grand jury proceedings or reduce its flexibility by creating an adversary atmosphere are sometimes met by making clear that counsel may simply advise the witness and, by implication, may not object to questions or procedures or even to address the grand jurors on behalf of the target witness.

§ 139. The Privilege of a Witness: (c) Determination Whether a Specific Response Would Be Incriminatory

Determining whether a specific demanded response is sufficiently incriminatory to be within the protection of the privilege presents a more difficult task than the more general undertaking of defining the required risk[1] of "incrimination."[2] In some cases, of course, the matter is clear because the question on its face calls for an incriminating response. The difficulties arise from facially innocent questions, as, for example, "Do you know John Bergoti?" When a witness invokes the privilege in response to such a question, three questions are raised: (a) who decides whether the response is incriminatory; (b) what criterion should be used to determine the propriety of the witness's invocation of the privilege;

---

4. United States v. Washington, 431 U.S. 181, 190 (1977).

5. United States v. Washington, 431 U.S. 181 (1977).

6. 431 U.S. 181 (1977).

1. See § 122 supra.

2. See § 121 supra.

and (c) who bears the burdens of producing information or facts on which the decision can be made and of proof on the ultimate question?

As to (a), it is settled that the witness himself is not the final arbiter of whether his invocation is proper. Rather, the court itself must determine whether the refusal to answer is in fact justifiable under the privilege. Any other position would subordinate the effective operation of the judicial system to the desires of witnesses. Whether formally giving the court this power and responsibility in fact enables the court to decide whether particular questions are actually incriminatory, however, turns in large part upon the criterion to be applied and the availability of facts for application of that standard.

As to question (b), the traditional statement of the criterion has been that "the Court must see, from the circumstances of the case, and the nature of the evidence which the witness is called to give, that there is reasonable ground to apprehend danger to the witness from his being compelled to answer."[3]

With regard to question (c), the witness invoking the privilege was traditionally required to produce sufficient information from which the court could find a sufficient risk of incrimination and perhaps even to convince the court that such a risk existed. A requirement that the witness produce information, however, clearly creates some risk that a witness may be required to incriminate himself as a means of establishing that he has a right not to do so. The classic defense of the traditional position was put by Judge Learned Hand:

> Obviously a witness may not be compelled to do more than show that the answer is likely to be dangerous to him, else he would be forced to disclose those very facts which the privilege protects. Logically, indeed, he is boxed in a paradox, for he must prove the criminatory character of what it is his privilege to protect because it is criminatory. The only practica-

ble solution is to be content with the door's being set a little ajar, and while at times this no doubt partially destroys the privilege * * * nothing better is available.[4]

The dilemma of a witness is best illustrated by those cases in which a witness believes that an accurate response would be inconsistent with earlier testimony and thus increase the risk of prosecution for perjury. To demand any explanation, of course, would require the witness to alert authorities to the possibility of perjury and perhaps stimulate an investigation that would lead to prosecution and conviction.

The traditional answers to questions (b) and (c) have been cast into doubt by Hoffman v. United States,[5] which is the point of reference for modern application of the Fifth Amendment privilege and most other formulations of the right. Petitioner Hoffman, subpoenaed before a federal grand jury, declined to answer any questions regarding recent contacts with one Weisberg, a witness who had not responded to a subpoena issued by the grand jury. The Court of Appeals held that Hoffman had not made a sufficient showing of the relationship between his possible responses and criminal liability to support his reliance upon the privilege; the Supreme Court reversed.

"To sustain the privilege," the Court explained, "it need only be evident from the implications of the question, in the setting in which it was asked, that a responsive answer to the question or an explanation of why it cannot be answered might be dangerous because injurious disclosure could result."[6] In addressing this, the trial judge should have considered the purpose of the grand jury investigation, Hoffman's admitted long acquaintance with Weisberg, general knowledge that the chief occupation of some individuals is criminal activity, and that one person with a criminal record (which Hoffman had) called before a grand jury might be hiding another person also called. After itself examining

---

3. Mason v. United States, 244 U.S. 362, 365 (1917).

4. United States v. Weisman, 111 F.2d 260, 262 (2d Cir.1940) (Hand, J.).

5. 341 U.S. 479 (1951).

6. Id. at 486–487.

these factors, the Court concluded that "in this setting it was not 'perfectly clear, from a careful consideration of all the circumstances in the case, that the witness is mistaken, and that the answer[s] *cannot possibly* have such tendency' to incriminate." [7]

Despite its prominence, *Hoffman's* implications are not clear. The Court's first statement is consistent with traditional doctrine—unless the court can conclude that further inquiry would create a danger of injurious disclosure it cannot sustain a claim of privilege, and if this conclusion cannot be drawn from circumstances already available for scrutiny, the witness has the obligation to bring the necessary circumstances to the attention of the court. But the Court's second statement indicates that a trial judge may not refuse to sustain the privilege unless he can conclude that the witness's invocation is improper. This, of course, would reallocate at least the burden of producing information and indicates that in the absence of a sufficient factual basis for the conclusion, the claim of privilege must be allowed.

Lower courts disagree on how *Hoffman* is to be read. Some construe it as requiring that a witness's claim to the privilege be sustained unless it is perfectly clear from all the circumstances that the answer to the question cannot possibly have any tendency to incriminate the witness. This suggests that the party seeking the witness's testimony over the witness's claim of the privilege has both the burden of producing information or evidence on which the witness's claim can be evaluated and—once that information or evidence is produced—of persuading the trial judge that the required risk of incrimination is absent. Other courts read *Hoffman* as sometimes at least imposing upon a witness invoking the privilege some obligation to support that claim.

Perhaps *Hoffman* directs what the Missouri Supreme Court has described as a "rational basis" approach. This would not impose upon a witness the burden of convincing the judge that the answer might incriminate him, but it

would—where the risk is not otherwise obvious—require the witness or his attorney to describe, in general terms, a rational basis on which the answer could conceivably incriminate him. This burden could be met without producing evidence or testimony, as for example by argument of counsel presenting logical possibilities.

Hoffman is probably best read as leaving the burden of persuasion upon the party seeking to override a witness's claim to the privilege. But where the question, considered in light of the evidence in the case and other information properly taken into account, is one which the trial judge could reasonably regard as presenting no more than an imaginary and unsubstantial risk of incrimination, the claimant has the burden of putting into the record—by evidence, logical argument, or persuasion—a basis for regarding that conclusion as insufficiently supported.

The combination of the relaxed requirements for determining the required risk of incrimination [8] and the minimal showing required on the facts of particular cases means that witnesses' claims to the privilege are seldom rejected. In an exceptional Idaho case, however, a civil party refused to respond to discovery questions inquiring as to his age, educational attainment, professional or vocational training or experience, specialized skills, and employment history. To support his claim to the privilege, he offered only that if he had been employed in some sort of fraud, his responses to the questions might be a "link in the chain" needed for prosecution. Under *Hoffman,* the Idaho court held, this was not a sufficient showing of the required risk to support the refusal to respond.

Whatever the abstract requirements, it is clear that trial judges have considerable flexibility in applying them. Whether to hold a factual hearing is discretionary, although it would probably be impermissible to reject a witness's claim to the privilege without granting the witness's request for a factual hearing at which he would have an opportunity to

---

7. Id. at 488.

8. See § 122 supra.

establish the basis for his claim. As *Hoffman* itself made clear, the judge is not limited to the formal record in the case but may consider news media reports, general information, and perhaps even specific factual information which he has from other sources. In an effort to minimize the risk that a witness will have to make incriminatory disclosures to establish that he is not required to do so, some courts have entertained *ex parte* submissions. Whether these are fair to the party seeking the testimony is problematic, and in some cases are unlikely to be effective in eliminating the witness's dilemma.

As in other situations, state courts are of course free to construe state formulations of the privilege as more protective of the underlying rights than the Fifth Amendment as applied in *Hoffman*. The Missouri Supreme Court has concluded that even if the Fifth Amendment imposes no more than a requirement that a witness describe a "rational basis" for concluding that an answer will incriminate, the result is an unacceptable risk that the privilege will be lost in the process of establishing its applicability. Consequently, it has held that under the Missouri state constitutional privilege:

> "[O]nce a witness claims the privilege afforded him under [the state] provision, a rebuttable presumption arises that the witness' answer might tend to incriminate him, a presumption that can be rebutted by a demonstration by the party seeking the answer that such answer 'cannot possibly' have such tendency to incriminate."

This has been recognized as more protective than the federal privilege. Other courts, perhaps for that reason, have not embraced it.

§ 140. The Privilege of a Witness: (d) "Waiver" by Disclosure of Incriminating Facts

The accused in a criminal proceeding forfeits the privilege to a significant extent by the mere act of testifying. Since a witness has no privilege to decline to testify, this same approach cannot be used to determine when a witness has lost the right to invoke the privilege. Consequently, whether and to what extent a witness is deprived of the right to invoke the privilege focuses instead upon the disclosure that the witness has already made.

The leading case is Rogers v. United States[1] in which Rogers had testified before a grand jury to having held the office of Treasurer of the Communist Party and to having had possession of its membership lists and books until January of 1948, at which time she turned them over to another. When asked the identity of the person to whom she gave them, she declined to answer. Affirming a sentence for contempt, the Supreme Court found that in view of her prior testimony, she was not justified in declining on Fifth Amendment self-incrimination grounds to reveal the name of the person to whom the documents had been given. Under the well-accepted rule, explained the Court, a witness who has voluntarily revealed self-incriminating facts without invoking the privilege cannot invoke that privilege to avoid further disclosure of the details of the incriminating information.

There are several aspects of uncertainty regarding *Rogers'* rationale and, correspondingly, its application. First, must the witness's testimony, in order to deprive the witness of the right to invoke the privilege, constitute a knowing and intelligent waiver as is often required for the loss of an important constitutional right? If so, no loss of the privilege would occur unless the witness understood, while testifying, the extent to which the testimony would mean that the privilege could not be later invoked. While the *Rogers* opinion is not entirely clear on this point, the Court seems not to have based the witness's loss of the privilege on waiver principles. Consequently, it is not necessary that the initial testimony meet the traditional "knowing and intelligent" test before the witness may be compelled to testify further.

§ 140

1. 340 U.S. 367 (1951).

Second, does *Rogers* rest in significant part upon the need to avoid distortion of evidence? If so, whether a particular case presents the risk of such distortion would be significant in determining whether the witness had lost the right to invoke the privilege. In *Rogers,* the Court commented that to permit a claim of the privilege "would open the way to distortion of facts by permitting a witness to select any stopping place in the testimony." Perhaps *Rogers'* holding rests in part on the basis that whatever remaining interest the witness has in being able to invoke the privilege is outweighed by the general risk that witnesses' arbitrary decisions to invoke the privilege and thus preclude further inquiry into matters about which they have testified will lead to triers of fact having to resolve cases on the basis of distorted and misleadingly incomplete evidence. This risk may have been perceived as sufficiently great that case-by-case inquiry into whether it is presented by particular situations is unnecessary. In Klein v. Harris,[2] however, the Second Circuit found this consideration so important as to require, before a witness is found to have lost the ability to invoke the privilege, a determination that on the facts of the case "the witness' prior statements have created a significant likelihood that the finder of fact will be left with and prone to rely on a distorted view of the truth." Generally, however, most lower courts appear to regard the need to avoid distortion as a consideration supporting a witness's loss of the privilege but not as part of the criterion for determining whether in particular situations a witness may invoke the privilege.

Third, is *Rogers* simply an application of the general requirement that a demanded answer be incriminating?[3] With regard to each question as to which Rogers had invoked her privilege, the Court considered her prior testimony and inquired whether, in light of that testimony, "the answer to that particular question would subject the witness to a 'real danger' of further crimination." Rogers had no right to invoke the privilege with regard to the question at issue, the Court concluded, because the answer, considered in light of her prior testimony, would not increase her danger of prosecution and conviction. Reading *Rogers* as simply an application of the requirement that an answer be incriminating eliminates any need for recourse to waiver or distortion considerations and suggests a criterion for applying it.

Most lower courts assume that this is the conceptual basis for the *Rogers* rule and incorporate this into the analysis for determining whether a witness has lost the right to rely on the privilege. Under this approach, a court inquires whether, in view of the witness's prior disclosures, the answer to the question at issue would increase the risk of incrimination. As the Ninth Circuit has noted, a witness must be accorded considerable lattitude in deciding when to stop responding to questions: "A contrary rule would involve the witness in a dilemma that would vitiate the privilege: invoking the privilege too soon could be contempt of court, while invoking it too late would inadvertently 'waive' the privilege."[4] Consistent with this approach, lower courts find relatively few situations in which they are willing to reject witnesses' assertions that further answers would increase the risk of incrimination. This is, of course, also consistent with the increasingly-accepted position that a witness who testifies does not lose the right to refuse to respond to questions as to separate crimes unrelated to her direct testimony and relevant only to her credibility.[5]

Several special problems are sometimes presented when witnesses in criminal prosecutions invoke their privilege. If the witness has already given testimony damaging to the defendant and invokes the privilege in response to the defendant's cross-examination, the situation implicates defendants' Sixth Amendment right to effective confrontation of witnesses presented against them.[6] In such

---

2. 667 F.2d 274 (2d Cir.1981).

3. See § 123 supra.

4. Matter of Seper, 705 F.2d 1499, 1501 (9th Cir.1983).

5. See § 41, supra.

6. Other aspects of claims of the privilege by witnesses are discussed in § 120 supra.

situations, the court must appraise the impact of the witness's action upon the defendant's ability to test the credibility of the testimony already given. The assessment must include "the nature of the excluded inquiry, whether the field of inquiry was adequately covered by the other questions that were allowed, and the overall quality of the cross-examination viewed in relation to the issues actually litigated at trial." If the witness's invocation of the privilege does preclude effective cross-examination, the witness's testimony on direct examination must be struck. On the other hand, if the witness's action does not have this effect, no such action need be taken. Where the witness invokes the privilege only regarding questions on matters collateral to the direct examination, as for example with regard to matters bearing only on the witness's general credibility, it is less likely that the defendant's ability to cross examine will be sufficiently affected as to require the striking of the testimony on direct. The trial judge can properly consider measures short of striking the witness's direct testimony, such as having the witness invoke the privilege before the jury or instructing the jury to consider the testimony in light of the defendant's reduced ability to cross-examine.

A somewhat different situation is presented if a defense witness invokes the privilege in response to the prosecution's efforts to cross-examine. The prosecution, of course, is entitled to a fair opportunity to test the credibility of the defense testimony, and in an appropriate case the trial court can properly strike a defense witness's testimony on direct examination. But such action endangers the defendant's Sixth Amendment right to present testimony and trial judges should consequently be reluctant to impose this drastic remedy. Again, less severe alternatives—such as striking only those portions of the testimony on direct which cannot be adequately tested on cross-examination—should be considered. If, however, the witness's actions frustrate the entire cross-examination process, striking that testimony is permissible and proper.

A witness's loss of the privilege by testifying to incriminating facts, like a defendant's loss of the privilege by simply testifying, is of limited duration. Generally, it applies throughout but not beyond the "proceeding" in which the witness has given the incriminating testimony. Witnesses' privilege, however, has given rise to more dispute as to what constitutes the "proceeding" in which the witness has no right to invoke the privilege in response to certain questions.

There is agreement that disclosure of incriminating facts in one criminal trial does not bar a witness from refusing to testify as to those same matters in another criminal trial. The same is true of a witness who has testified in a prior civil trial; the witness's testimony in the first trial may be admissible in the second trial,[7] but the witness is entitled to invoke the privilege in the second trial even if she did not in the first.

More dispute exists concerning the effect of disclosure at an early stage of what is a single unit of litigation. Much of the case law has concerned the ability of a witness who makes self-incriminating disclosures during grand jury testimony to later invoke the privilege when called as a witness at the trial. Ellis v. United States,[8] held that grand jury disclosure precluded the witness from invoking the privilege at trial. Most courts, however, hold to the contrary. Consistent with this approach, testimony at a pretrial hearing has been held not to deprive a witness of the right to invoke the privilege at trial. The New York Court of Appeals has even held that a prosecution witness later recalled by the defense as a defense witness was entitled to invoke her privilege in her second trip to the witness stand, reasoning that her testimony during her second appearance could subject her to criminal liability for perjury.

Ellis unwisely extends a witness's loss of his privilege beyond the "proceeding" in which he testifies. In theory, a witness should not ordinarily be subject to additional legal detriment by being required to repeat

---

7. See §§ 301–308 infra.

8. 416 F.2d 791 (D.C.Cir.1969).

testimony previously given. But in the excitement and confusion that may be generated by the second appearance, the witness might make admissions beyond those previously made. Reaffirming earlier self-incriminating admissions may encourage prosecution as a practical matter. Testimony during the second appearance might, as the New York court noted, increase the risk of liability for perjury based on the first appearance. The traditional rule that a witness's loss of the privilege by testifying lasts only during that "proceeding" in which the witness testified is consistent with the spirit of the privilege.

§ 141. Agreement to Waive the Privilege

It is clear from the previous discussion that an accused person forfeits his privilege to a significant extent by testifying in his own behalf and that one not an accused by testifying to incriminating matters loses the right under certain circumstances to decline to elaborate on those or related matters. But may one agree in advance to forego the protection of the privilege and later be held to that promise? Few discussions of the matter are satisfactorily conclusive, but the Supreme Court has recently drastically reduced the potential effectiveness of any such contractual commitment.

Wigmore [1] takes the position that a contract, either expressed or implied, to waive the privilege is, if otherwise enforcible, binding upon the party who agrees to waive the privilege. While the contract will not be specifically enforced (i.e., the party will not be held in contempt for refusal to testify) unless there is also a fiduciary duty or some other important public policy involved, it will be given effect in determining rights between the parties to the agreement. Little authority is cited, although Wigmore's position is more lenient than that of the original Uniform Rules (1953), which stated that one who

would otherwise have a privilege "has no such privilege" if he has contracted with anyone not to claim it.[2]

The effectiveness of any agreement of this nature respecting a constitutional privilege was minimized by Stevens v. Marks.[3] Stevens, a New York police officer, had, under threat of discharge from his employment, signed a waiver which the Court interpreted as purporting to have the effect of depriving him of his privilege as well as any immunity to which he might be entitled under New York Law. Reversing Stevens' contempt conviction for refusing to testify, the Court assumed that the waiver was initially valid but held that no justification appeared for denying the petitioner the right to withdraw it. Therefore, his effort to withdraw it and rely on his privilege was effective. Whether "administrative inconvenience" occasioned by withdrawal might in some situations mean that withdrawal would be ineffective was left open, since no such inconvenience was shown in the case.

In light of Stevens, it is unlikely that an agreement to waive the privilege can be fully enforced—that is, that the person can be held in contempt for refusing to answer self-incriminating questions—except perhaps where it can be shown that the prosecution relied to its detriment on that agreement and thus permitting the defendant to invoke the privilege would significantly prejudice the prosecution. In several recent Illinois cases, witnesses have been held in contempt for invoking their privilege as a basis for refusing to testify in other proceedings, despite a plea bargaining agreement to waive the privilege and testify. Under Stevens, such a result is inappropriate unless the prosecution can demonstrate significant prejudice as a result of reliance upon those plea bargains.

If a person who agrees to waive the privilege is penalized in some way other than by being held in contempt for refusal later to

1. 8 Wigmore, Evidence § 2275(a) (McNaughton rev. 1961).

2. Original Uniform Rule 37 (1953). No corresponding provision appears in the Revised Uniform Evid.Rules (1974).

3. 383 U.S. 234 (1966).

testify, the situation would be most appropriately analyzed as raising the issue whether an impermissible burden has been imposed on the exercise of the privilege.[4] If the exercise of the privilege constitutes a breach of an agreement between private parties, the matter should be regarded as essentially private. Any burden imposed on the party who exercised his privilege in violation of the agreement would not be a state-imposed disadvantage. It would, therefore, be beyond the scope of the protection of the privilege.

§ 142. The "Required Records" Exception

Many governmental regulatory schemes require for their success the development and maintenance of records by those regulated and reasonable access by the government to those records. Since these regulatory schemes are often enforced at least in part by criminal penalties, the privilege against compelled self-incrimination potentially interferes with their implementation. In response to this, the Supreme Court has developed what has become known as the "required records" exception to some of the demands of the Fifth Amendment privilege.

This exception finds application in two major situations. First, a witness has no right under the privilege to invoke the Fifth Amendment in response to a demand that records or related documents be produced if those records come within the required records rule. Second, a person may be criminally punished for failing to comply with requirements of a regulatory scheme within the required records doctrine, even if such compliance involves actual or potential testimonial self-incrimination.

Compelled Production. The required records doctrine first developed in response to efforts to avoid compelled production of records required by regulatory schemes. It was recognized by the Supreme Court in Shapiro v. United States. Shapiro, a wholesale

fresh produce dealer, was subject to the wartime Emergency Price Control Act of 1942.[1] Regulations promulgated under the Act required that anyone subject to the Act "preserve for examination by the Office of Price Administration all his records, including invoices, sales tickets, cash receipts, or other written evidences of sale or delivery * * *" and that he keep records of the kind he customarily had kept. In response to a subpoena *duces tecum*, Shapiro produced the materials required by the Act. When he was subsequently prosecuted for violation of the Act, he asserted as a plea in bar that the compulsory production of the materials had given him immunity, or, if no such immunity had been conferred, that the statute under which he was being prosecuted was therefore unconstitutional. Rejecting his argument, the Court held that production of the material at issue could constitutionally be required of Shapiro without granting him immunity. It assumed that some limits exist on the Government's ability to require the keeping and production of records, but these limits were clearly not overstepped where "there is a sufficient relation between the activity sought to be regulated and the public concern" that the Government can constitutionally prohibit or regulate the basic activity and require the keeping of particular records.

As later developed the *Shapiro* doctrine requires that all of three requirements be met. First, the purposes of the government's activity must be "essentially regulatory." Second, the records required and demanded must be of the sort that the regulated persons or businesses would customarily keep. Third, the records must have assumed some "public aspects." Yet in application these requirements are quite easily met.

The first requirement focuses upon the nature of the government's purpose in imposing the regulatory scheme. Simply because the government relies in part upon criminal sanctions does not mean that the scheme is not essentially regulatory. Generally, the judi-

---

4. See § 126 supra.

1. 335 U.S. 1 (1948).

cial inquiry is simply whether the regulatory scheme is a generally-permissible one. If so, a demand for records kept pursuant to it meets the first *Shapiro* requirement.

The second requirement is generally regarded as turning upon the type of records usually kept in connection with the regulated activity. In United States v. Lehman,[2] for example, the court stressed that the language of the subpoena limited the demand "to exactly those records [one] would normally keep" in the cattle dealing business at issue in the case.

The third requirement may be the most troublesome to apply, because of uncertainty as to what public aspects must exist and what is required to establish them. Unquestionably, the records need not be "public" in the sense that the general public has access to them or a right of access. Rather, the question is generally posed as whether the records are closely enough related to a sufficiently important "public" interest. In an unusual refusal to apply the required records rule, for example, the Seventh Circuit held that even if the Internal Revenue Code required taxpayers to keep records supporting claims made in tax returns, the limited nature of the taxpayer-Internal Revenue Service relationship was insufficient to give the records the "public aspects" that the *Shapiro* rule requires.

As applied to compulsory production, the required records exception has been the subject of vigorous criticism. *Shapiro*, critics have urged, offers no satisfactory conceptual basis for the exception. It can only be explained on the basis of a balancing of interests; in some situations, the public need for citizen cooperation to make regulatory schemes effective outweighs the interest of those regulated in being free from compelled self-incrimination. This approach, of course, is inconsistent with what some regard as the absolute terms of the privilege. Insofar as it permits circumvention of the privilege by sim-

ply requiring that records be kept, it invites abuse. If the three requirements developed for its application were narrowly defined and rigorously applied, this might greatly reduce the risk of abuse. But the ease with which those requirements are met suggests that the risk of abuse remains.

Perhaps the original justification for the exception is tied to what was at the time of *Shapiro* the widely-accepted notion that the privilege provided protection against the self-incriminating *contents* of documents.[3] *Shapiro's* flexible balancing approach may have been an acceptable manner of limiting what was perceived as essentially the privacy protection afforded by this aspect of the privilege. Under Fisher v. United States[4] and United States v. Doe,[5] however, it is now clear that in the compelled production context the privilege provides only limited protection from the testimonially-incriminating aspects of the "act of production."[6] In view of the narrow limitations which the privilege imposed upon compelled production of documents, and the relative ease with which that limited protection can be negated by a grant of use immunity,[7] as questionable an exception as the required records rule may have become unjustified.

Nevertheless, the courts have refused to read *Fisher* and *Doe* as superseding the required records rule or so removing its justification as to demand that it be abandoned. State courts remain free, of course, to construe their state privileges as embodying no similar exception, but they have not done so.

The flexibility and continued vitality of the doctrine as part of the Fifth Amendment was illustrated in 1990 by Baltimore City Department of Social Services v. Bouknight.[8] After Bouknight's abused child was found within the jurisdiction of the juvenile court, she accepted custody of him subject to conditions and further orders of the court. Fearing that the child had been abused or even killed, the

---

2. 887 F.2d 1328 (7th Cir.1989).

3. See generally § 127 supra.

4. 425 U.S. 391 (1976).

5. 465 U.S. 605 (1984).

6. See generally § 128 supra.

7. See generally § 143 infra.

8. 493 U.S. 549 (1990).

court later directed Bouknight to produce him. She resisted in reliance upon the Fifth Amendment, arguing that by producing the child she would be acknowledging control over him and that this might aid the State in prosecuting her. Finding that she could be compelled to produce the child, the Court relied heavily upon *Shapiro* and explained that decision as resting on the principle that "[w]hen a person assumes control over items that are the legitimate object of the government's non-criminal regulatory powers, the ability to invoke the privilege is reduced." This same principle applied in *Bouknight*. By finding the child within the jurisdiction of the juvenile court, the state subjected him to a noncriminal regulatory scheme. When Bouknight accepted custody, she assumed certain obligations attending that custody, including that of producing the child for "inspection." The "required records" exception, or at least the principle on which it is based, is obviously not limited to records and may render the privilege unavailable as a bar to compelled production of other items where custody of them is pursuant to a noncriminal regulatory scheme.

On the other hand, in *Bouknight* the Court suggested that the prosecution might be barred from using against Bouknight in later criminal prosecution the testimonial aspects of Bouknight's act of producing the child.[9] If this is the case, the required records doctrine as applied to compulsory production of existing records has little remaining significance. Such automatic immunity from the very limited protected aspects of compelled production removes the risk of incrimination and thus for any need for an exception to the privilege.

Compliance With Regulatory Scheme Requirements. Regulatory schemes often require registration, payment, reporting, or similar activities that those regulated might reasonably regard as increasing the risk of their criminal prosecution and conviction, often for violations of the enforcement provisions of the regulatory scheme but sometimes for other crimes as well. The privilege against compelled self-incrimination may be violated by these requirements and consequently may prohibit punishment of one who fails to comply with the requirements. But a somewhat different aspect of the required records doctrine than the one discussed above sometimes permits such punishment.

After several quite confusing decisions involving attacks upon such schemes that did not consider the relationship between the schemes and *Shapiro's* required records doctrine, the Court in 1968 turned to that question in a trilogy of cases—Marchetti v. United States,[10] Grosso v. United States,[11] and Haynes v. United States.[12] The Court assumed that under regulatory schemes sufficiently like that in *Shapiro*, those regulated would have no Fifth Amendment protection from the requirements and could therefore be penalized for noncompliance. But it held that neither of the two federal statutory schemes at issue—the occupational tax provisions of the federal wagering tax statutes and the firearm registration requirements of the National Firearms Act—met the requirements of the exception for required records as it had been developed in *Shapiro*. The Court's application of *Shapiro* to the federal wagering tax requirements illustrates the deficiencies.

First, the Government's purpose was not essentially regulatory. While its principal interest was the collection of revenue and not the punishment of gamblers, the required information was demanded from a select group of persons inherently suspected of criminal activity. Second, what was required was not simply the creation and production of records of a sort customarily kept. Those subject to the Act were required to provide information about wagering activities unrelated to any records which might have been kept. Third, the records or information did not have sufficient "public aspects." All that supported such a characterization of the information

---

9. 493 U.S. at 561, citing Braswell v. United States, 487 U.S. 99 (1988), discussed in § 143 infra.

10. 390 U.S. 39 (1968).

11. 390 U.S. 62 (1968).

12. 390 U.S. 85 (1968).

demanded was "[t]he Government's anxiety to obtain information known to a private person." This could not alone give the information the public aspect required under *Shapiro,* because that would virtually nullify the privilege in this context.

An amended version of the National Firearms Act was upheld by the Supreme Court in United States v. Freed.[13] Primary emphasis was placed on an inserted immunity provision, which provided that information or evidence obtained from an application submitted in compliance with the statute's requirements could not be used, "directly or indirectly," against the person who provided it in a criminal proceeding for a violation of law occurring prior to or concurrently with the filing of the application. Lower courts have upheld other statutory schemes requiring that self-incriminating information be provided to officials if those providing the information are protected against its use. If those compelled to provide the information are protected from its incriminating use, the scheme is valid despite its focus upon persons suspected of criminal activity and despite its purpose of enforcing the criminal prohibitions.

Several reporting schemes lacking prohibitions against the use of self-incriminating information have been struck down by lower courts on the basis of reasoning that emphasized the absence of protection similar to that in the federal statute upheld in *Freed.* Such schemes raise the real current vitality of the required records doctrine, especially if under *Bouknight* those who simply produce records are automatically protected from prosecutorial use against them of their act of production. Under these schemes, persons are required to create and maintain records in a manner that involves compelled testimonially activity far different in nature from the limited testimonial aspects of producing records.

If the required records doctrine is still viable, these lower court decisions oversimplify the self-incrimination issue and may well be wrongly-decided. In some regulatory situations those regulated can probably be required to create, maintain and produce even self-incriminatory records without running afoul of the Fifth Amendment, even in the absence of any protection from the use of these records or information in them as evidence of criminal guilt. When this is permissible is so difficult to discern, however, and the costs of use immunity is so low, that legislative drafters have often preferred to avoid the problem by prohibiting the self-incriminatory use of information provided by the required reporting or disclosure.

§ 143. Removing the Danger of Incrimination: Immunity and Immunity Statutes

Since the privilege protects only against formal legal liability,[1] which is a matter of legal mandate, the privilege does not apply if the risk of criminal liability is removed. Among the ways in which this risk can be removed is by the granting of immunity.

Generally, neither trial courts nor prosecutors are regarded as having inherent power to grant immunity to witnesses, so the ability of either to provide immunity depends upon specific legislative authorization. As the Missouri Supreme Court explained, the immunity power "is subject to such abuse" that whether and when immunity should be granted is best left for legislative decision. Immunity is properly available only after legislative deliberation and development of "carefully drawn legislation" that minimizes the risk of abuse and misapplication. Some courts, however, have found inherent power in prosecutors to grant immunity.

Where courts are faced with situations in which witnesses have relied upon unauthorized "grants" of immunity, they will often grant relief in reliance upon a doctrine of "equitable immunity." This is a remedial doctrine, however, and does not legitimize or authorize an original effort to grant immunity. When it applies, it may provide only limited relief. The Colorado Supreme Court,

---

13. 401 U.S. 601 (1971).

1. See § 121 supra.

for example, has held that a witness improperly promised during interrogation that she could not be prosecuted was adequately protected by exclusion of her self-incriminating statements and was not entitled to have a prosecution dismissed.

The major issue raised by immunity has the been the scope of protection that is necessary or desirable in order to render the privilege inapplicable. In 1892, the Supreme Court held in Counselman v. Hitchcock [2] that an immunity statute which conferred limited "use immunity"—that is, protection from the subsequent use of the witness's immunized testimony against the witness in a criminal prosecution—was inadequate under the Fifth Amendment where it did not also protect the witness from the use of evidence obtained by using immunized testimony—that is, derivative evidence—as well as the testimony itself. Dictum in the Court's opinion was widely regarded as committing the Court to the position that "transactional immunity"—that is, immunity from prosecution for those transactions about which the witness testified under immunity—was necessary to render the Fifth Amendment privilege unavailable to a witness.

The major concern regarding "use immunity," even if expanded to protect the witness from use of both his testimony itself and derivative evidence, is that it may be ineffective in practice because of the difficulty of determining whether evidence offered by the prosecution was in fact derived from the immunized testimony. In Kastigar v. United States,[3] the Fifth Amendment issue was squarely addressed. Under the Fifth Amendment privilege, the Court held, a grant of transactional immunity is not necessary in order to compel a witness to testify over an assertion of his privilege. The sole concern of the privilege, reasoned the majority, is the prevention of compulsion to give testimony that leads to the infliction of penalties affixed to criminal acts. "Immunity from the use of compelled testimony, as well as evidence derived directly and indirectly therefrom, af-

fords this protection." Turning to the longstanding concerns regarding the implementation of such grants of use immunity, the Court held that once a defendant establishes that he has previously testified under a grant of immunity concerning matters related to his prosecution, the prosecution—upon defense objection—must affirmatively prove that the evidence it offers against the defendant is derived from a legitimate source wholly independent of the previously compelled testimony.

Justice Marshall dissented in *Kastigar,* urging that, given practical realities, a grant of use and derivative use immunity cannot eliminate all possibility that compelled testimony will operate to convict the immunized witness. Information relating to the source of the prosecution's evidence, and thus to any possible taint by immunized testimony, is "uniquely within the knowledge of the prosecuting authorities." Usually, a mere assertion by the prosecution that it obtained offered evidence independent of immunized testimony will be sufficient to meet its burden under the majority's holding. Only if the prosecution is willing to give the defense access to information suggesting otherwise will the defense have any chance of prevailing. Moreover, given the size and nature of "the investigative bureaucracy," those prosecuting a case may simply not be aware of reliance by others in that organization upon immunized testimony. A prosecutor's good faith belief that his evidence is independent may simply be unfounded.

Kastigar's approach has been rejected in several decisions holding that state constitutional privileges can be rendered inapplicable only by a grant of transactional immunity. Some decisions rely to some extent upon traditional indicators of "framers' intention." But generally the state court decisions requiring transactional immunity as a matter of state constitutional law rest upon the state courts' concern that in practice there is insufficient assurance that a prosecution permitted

---

2.   142 U.S. 547 (1892).

3.   406 U.S. 441 (1972).

under *Kastigar* will in fact be based upon actually independent evidence.

Whether or not transactional immunity is required by the Fifth Amendment or state constitutional privileges, it may be desirable as a matter of sound policy. Justice Marshall's concerns regarding the effectiveness of use immunity, although perhaps not strong enough to render use immunity inadequate as a matter of constitutional law, may be sufficient to dictate a legislative policy that the privilege be rendered unenforceable only upon a grant of immunity from prosecution for any offense arising out of the transaction about which a witness is compelled to testify. If a jurisdiction provides by statute for only such transactional immunity, of course, a witness is entitled to such protection as a matter of statutory law regardless of whether the witness has a constitutional right to such protection.

Generally, then, the availability of immunity to witnesses is closely tied to statutory authority for such immunity and statutorily-provided procedures for conferring and enforcing it. Unfortunately, such statutes vary widely. Prior to 1970, federal statutory law contained over fifty immunity provisions, each applicable to limited situations. In 1970, Congress repealed these and substituted a general immunity statute authorizing the granting of use and derivative use immunity. Some states have similarly enacted generally-applicable immunity provisions. In others, however, immunity is governed by numerous, varied, and specific provisions often similar to pre–1970 federal law. The major models available for state reform in this area are the federal statute and Rule 732 of the Uniform Rules of Criminal Procedure (1974) which—unlike the federal provision—provides for transactional immunity.

The major issue presented by statutory immunity procedure is what if any actions by the prosecution or judge are necessary to confer immunity upon a witness. Early immunity provisions sometimes conferred transactional immunity upon any witnesses who tes-

tified regarding a particular matter. This was subject to clear abuse; prosecutors could "accidentally" grant immunity to guilty parties, and a guilty person could even secure protection from prosecution by creating an opportunity to volunteer testimony concerning the matter. The immunity provision of the original Interstate Commerce Act, as amended in 1893 after *Counselman,* served as the model for many of the numerous specific federal statutory provisions superseded in 1970 by the general federal immunity statute. In 1906, this provision was construed as providing immunity even upon a witness who, without being subpoenaed, volunteered information. Congress immediately responded by amending the provision to make it applicable only to witnesses who testified under subpoena.

Later, Congress added to some federal immunity provisions but not others a requirement that the witness first invoke his privilege. In United States v. Monia,[4] the Supreme Court held that where an immunity statute contained no such provision, a subpoenaed witness received immunity even if he never asserted a right to refuse to testify in reliance on the privilege. The result was that prosecutors sometimes unintentionally conferred immunity upon guilty persons by subpoenaing them as witnesses at a time when the prosecutors had little or no indication that the persons subpoenaed had been guilty of criminal involvement in the matters about which their testimony was sought.

In order to avoid these problems, an immunity statute is best drafted so as to require several specific steps before immunity is granted. First, the witness must invoke his right under the privilege not to answer. Second, prosecuting authorities must make application to the court for immunity. Third, the court must determine whether immunity should in fact be granted, although it is clear that ordinarily the court should defer to the prosecution's judgment that the need for the testimony at issue justifies the loss of the ability to prosecute the witness or—if only use

4. 317 U.S. 424 (1943).

immunity is involved—the ability to use the witness' testimony and its fruits. If the court approves the prosecution's application, the court should make certain that the witness understands both that he is required by law to answer questions and that he is protected by the grant of immunity. Many modern statutes, including the federal provision, provide for such a procedure, although some state statutes still create the risk that a witness will be accidentally granted immunity by being subpoenaed or even permitted to voluntarily testify.

Increased reliance upon "use and derivative use" immunity has resulted in considerable concern regarding the scope of the "taint" of the immunized testimony. More specifically, the issue is what under *Kastigar* the prosecution must, upon challenge, prove is "independent" of the defendant's testimony given pursuant to a grant of use immunity. It is clear that the prosecution must, at a minimum, demonstrate that the evidence it offers would have been known and available to it had the defendant not testified. Probably this applies even to cross-examination, so that *Kastigar* is violated if a prosecutor's consideration of a defendant's immunized testimony causes the prosecutor to elicit significant testimony on cross-examination of defense witnesses.

But must the prosecution also show that it has made no "nonevidentiary" use of the immunized testimony? In the leading case for a broad reading of *Kastigar,* United States v. McDaniel,[5] the Eighth Circuit held that the prosecution has a heavy burden of this sort, at least when the evidence shows that the prosecutor who tried the case against the defendant was aware of the defendant's immunized testimony. *Kastigar,* the court concluded, requires that the prosecution not use the immunized testimony for such nonevidentiary uses as "assistance in focusing the investigation, deciding to initiate prosecution, refusing to plea-bargain, interpreting evidence, planning cross-examination, and otherwise generally planning trial strategy." Moreover, the

prosecution must prove that no such use was made of the immunized testimony.

Other courts, however, have read *Kastigar* as limited to evidentiary use of immunized testimony. In United States v. Byrd,[6] for example, the Eleventh Circuit held that *Kastigar* did not prohibit a prosecutor from considering immunized testimony in deciding to reindict a defendant. Since in many situations the prosecution would be unable to make such a showing, the court reasoned, prosecution would be barred and the result would be that the witness-defendant would receive what amounted to transactional immunity. This, however, would be inconsistent with *Kastigar,* which specifically held that use immunity was constitutionally sufficient.

If a witness who has given immunized testimony is later prosecuted and testifies in his own defense, his immunized testimony may not be used to impeach him.[7] Even if the immunized testimony tends reliably to suggest that the witness-defendant is committing perjury and thus should not be believed, the Supreme Court has made clear this use of the testimony is not permissible. Immunized testimony is "the essence of coerced testimony" and thus inadmissible in light of the Fifth and Fourteenth Amendments' bar upon the use of compelled self-incrimination.

Immunity, whether transactional or use immunity, does not protect the witness from prosecution for perjury committed in the giving of the immunized testimony and the testimony relied upon as being false may, of course, be used in the prosecution. It is less clear whether immunized testimony may be used to prove that the witness committed perjury during other testimony, either before or after the immunized testimony, and there is lower court authority for the proposition that a grant of immunity must protect the witness against the use of immunized testimony in a prosecution for perjury committed at a previous time.

5. 482 F.2d 305 (8th Cir.1973).

6. 765 F.2d 1524 (11th Cir.1985).

7. New Jersey v. Portash, 440 U.S. 450, 459–460 (1979).

Multijurisdictional aspects of immunity create special difficulties, given that testimony may well have incriminating implications in more than one jurisdiction. If state A grants a witness transactional immunity and the witness gives testimony with incriminating implications in state B as well as state A, what flexibility does state B have to prosecute? If state A's grant of transactional immunity had to be given full effect in state B, this would raise serious federalism concerns regarding the right or ability of one state to frustrate the criminal process of another state. But the few cases addressing the matter seem agreed that Fifth Amendment concerns are satisfied if state B, in effect, grants the witness use immunity. While this may impose a significant burden upon state B's prosecutors, this is necessary to protect state A's ability to compel testimony and to enforce its own laws; it does not frustrate state B's right similarly to enforce its own criminal prohibitions.

A special problem is presented when a defendant requests or demands immunity for defense witnesses. Demands of this sort are often accompanied by claims that grants of immunity are necessary to implement the defendants' Sixth Amendment right to compel testimony for defensive purposes. Defendants' claims generally encounter the initial problem of authority to grant them relief. Statutory provisions for immunity often require that the prosecution seek the immunity, and some courts have rejected defendants' claims on the ground that the courts have no authority to grant immunity on the motion of the defense. The leading case supporting these defendants' position, Government of Virgin Islands v. Smith,[8] reasoned in part that this problem could be overcome by simply dismissing a prosecution where the Government's failure to seek immunity was unacceptable to the trial court, although it also concluded that federal district courts have inherent power to grant immunity to defense witnesses in limited situations, as where a witness has exculpatory information. To the extent that trial courts have authority to grant immunity to defense witnesses over the prosecution's resistance, or to the extent that they can threaten dismissal to encourage the prosecution to seek such immunity, it is clear that the power is to be exercised sparingly.

8. 615 F.2d 964 (3d Cir.1980).

Chapter 14

CONFESSIONS

Table of Sections

§ 144. "Confessions" and Admissibility

Among the most frequently-raised evidentiary issues in criminal litigation are those relating to the admissibility of self-incriminating statements or admissions by the defendant. These issues are the subject of the present Chapter.

Definition of "Confession." Traditional analysis sometimes required inquiry into whether a self-incriminating statement by a defendant was a "confession" within a rather specialized meaning of that term. This is seldom necessary today, although some legal requirements do apply only or differently to confessions as contrasted with other self-incriminating statements.

When such distinctions must be made, a confession is generally described as a statement admitting or acknowledging all facts necessary for conviction of the crime at issue.

An "admission," in contrast, consists of an acknowledgment of one or more facts tending to prove guilt but not of all the facts necessary to do so.

Both confessions and admissions are sometimes distinguished from so-called "exculpatory statements." The latter are defined as assertions by the accused intended at the time made to exculpate him but which, by the time of trial, tend to show his guilt. A frequent use of exculpatory statements by the prosecution in criminal litigation is to offer them in conjunction with other evidence tending to show their falsity. The jury is then asked to infer from the fact that the defendant offered a false exculpatory statement that he was conscious of his own guilt and, ultimately, that he was in fact guilty. Exculpatory statements may also, of course, be used to prove guilt in circumstantial ways other than this "consciousness of guilt" route.

Most of the major limitations upon the admissibility of confessions also apply to admissions and exculpatory statements. This chapter, therefore, will assume unless a particular discussion requires otherwise that no distinction is appropriately drawn among self-incriminating acknowledgements. "Confession," "admission," and "statement" will generally be used interchangeably.

Manner of Proving Confessions. A confession may, of course, consist of an oral admission by the defendant and the state may prove such an oral statement; the absence of a written embodiment does not preclude admission of the oral confession into evidence. When there is a written document purporting to embody the defendant's out-of-court admission, the matter becomes somewhat more complicated. A written confession, like any other proffered documentary evidence, requires authentication.[1] But there is no requirement that the defendant have signed the document. It is sufficient that the defendant has otherwise adopted the substance of the

written document, as where there is proof that it was read to him and that he orally acknowledged that it accurately reflected his earlier oral admissions. Even when there is no evidence of such adoption by the defendant, a written or typed document is admissible if there is other testimony that it accurately reflects what the defendant orally said at the relevant time.

Theory of Admissibility. Confessions and admissions are out-of-court statements quite frequently offered to prove the truth of matters asserted therein and thus are potentially subject to exclusion pursuant to the prohibition against hearsay. Nevertheless, there is general agreement that the prosecution is entitled to introduce confessions. The conceptual basis for this position is, however, somewhat unclear. If the justification for the admissibility of confessions turns upon whether confessions are within the rationale of one or more of the traditional exceptions to the prohibition against hearsay, certain difficulties arise.

Wigmore[2] and Morgan[3] group together in one exception to the hearsay rule statements made by criminal defendants and those made by parties to civil litigation. This exception is based, in their view, upon the assumption that the major justification for excluding hearsay is the unavailability of the declarant for cross-examination. Since both criminal defendants and parties to civil litigation are available for examination during trial, the argument goes, the rationale for the hearsay prohibition does not apply.

There are several weaknesses in this explanation. First, historically out-of-court statements of criminal defendants were admissible before a party to a civil suit became a competent witness.[4] Thus under this explanation the exception would have preceded its justification. Second, a criminal defendant is not available for examination during trial in the same sense as a party to civil litigation. The

---

§ 144

1. For discussion of authentication requirements, see §§ 218–228 infra.

2. 3 Wigmore, Evidence § 816 (Chadbourn rev. 1970).

3. Morgan, Admissions as an Exception to the Hearsay Rule, 30 Yale L.J. 355 (1921).

4. See generally § 65, supra.

privilege against compulsory self-incrimination embodied in the Fifth Amendment and state constitutions gives a criminal defendant the right to decline to submit to either direct or cross-examination at trial; a party to civil litigation has no such right. The criminal defendant may, of course, waive this protection and testify as to matters relating to the making of a confession or its contents. But justifying a confession exception to the hearsay rule on defendant's ability to waive their self-incrimination privilege may be inconsistent with the solicitude with which the privilege is now treated.[5]

The hearsay exception for declarations against interest has also been offered as a basis admitting out-of-court statements of an accused. This, too, is subject to question. That a declaration was, at the time it was made, against the penal interests of the declarant was not traditionally considered sufficient to bring it within this exception.[6] Moreover, the confession rule includes statements—especially admissions and exculpatory statements—which were not against even the penal interests of the declarant at the time they were made and thus would not come within this version of the exception.

These conceptual difficulties in bringing the confession rule within the rationale of a traditional exception to the hearsay rule are simply bypassed by the Federal Rules of Evidence and substantial other modern thought which do not classify admissions of a party-opponent, including confessions, as hearsay at all.[7] Thus the admissibility of self-incriminating statements need not be evaluated in terms of compliance with any other traditional exception to the prohibition against hearsay but is left free to be considered *de novo*.[8]

A confession, especially one that survives the multiple attacks that can be made upon its admissibility under modern law, is sufficiently reliable evidence of the defendant's guilt to deserve consideration by the jury. While a defendant can contradict a confession via personal trial testimony only by waiving his self-incrimination rights, nevertheless this opportunity is available. On balance, the generally high probative value of this kind of evidence and the availability of means to address any doubts concerning reliability that might arise in particular cases support admission into evidence. It may be useful, however, to approach the entire area of confession law with sensitivity to the likelihood that there may be some tension between the general rule permitting the prosecution to introduce such evidence, on the one hand, and the general prohibition against hearsay, on the other.

Exclusionary Confession Law Rules. Given the general principle that defendants' confessions are admissible to prove guilt, confession law becomes primarily a collection of rules that prevent the use of particular categories of confessions. To some extent, some confession law rules are examples of the sort of exclusionary sanctions discussed in Chapter 15. Under these, exclusion of confessions is mandated by a perceived need to implement policies other than the accurate ascertainment of the "truth." For example, the requirements that confessions be excluded if they are shown to be sufficiently related to an unlawful arrest [9] and—perhaps—to a delay in presenting the defendant before a judicial officer following arrest [10] are designed to maximize compliance with the rules governing arrest and prompt presentation.

The traditional voluntariness requirement,[11] on the other hand, is more closely related to the objective of accurate ascertainment of guilt or innocence at trial. The modern requirement [12] still to some extent serves that function. Although the federal constitutional requirement must be applied without reference to the accuracy of particular confes-

---

5. See § 132, supra.

6. See § 318 infra. The current trend is to consider a penal interest sufficient to satisfy the exception. Id.

7. See § 254 infra.

8. See generally the discussion in § 254 infra.

9. See § 157 infra.

10. See § 156 infra.

11. See § 146 infra.

12. See § 147 infra.

sions, the requirement itself—on a more general level—is based in part on the assumption that involuntary confessions are more likely than voluntary ones to be inaccurate.

Other modern requirements, such as the well-known *Miranda* rules,[13] are less directly related to accuracy concerns, although to some extent they are designed to assure voluntariness and hence reliability. But these requirements, even more than the modern voluntariness demands, are also intended to prevent certain types of law enforcement conduct that is regarded as offensive for reasons totally unrelated to the accuracy of resulting confessions.

§ 145. Corroboration and Independent Proof of the *Corpus Delicti*

Despite the absence of any clear demand in English law, early American decisions embraced a requirement that in order for a conviction based upon a confession to be sustained, the confession must have been corroborated by other evidence introduced at trial. After the Massachusetts Supreme Court adopted such a requirement in 1984, apparently all American states as well as the federal courts have embraced such a requirement. In many jurisdictions, it has been incorporated into statute or court rule.

Rationale for Requirement. The requirement has traditionally been based upon concern that convictions might result from false confessions. Whether other considerations also support it is less clear. It has been argued that the corroboration requirement serves to combat coercive or otherwise improper police practices in securing confessions. At best the requirement achieves this objective indirectly, and the function is perhaps more effectively accomplished by other legal requirements relating to confessions. It is possible, although unlikely, that the requirement might be supported on the basis

that it tends to encourage other and more desirable police investigatory practices than interrogation of suspects.

Despite widespread agreement that the requirement is based upon a need to assure accuracy, there has been little consensus on what potential sources of inaccuracy are of major concern. The Washington court has indicated that the rule is designed to combat, first, risks of inaccuracy arising from misinterpretation or misreporting by witnesses who testify to what defendants admitted and, second, risks of inaccuracy with regard to what defendants said. These latter sources of inaccuracy, the court continued, include not only force or coercion but also the possibilities that a confession was "based upon a mistaken perception of the facts or law, or falsely given by a mentally disturbed individual."[1]

Some courts regard the objectives of the requirement as more modest. A Maryland court, for example, commented that the requirement serves the more limited purpose of preventing a mentally unstable person from confessing to and being convicted of a crime that never occurred.

The corroboration requirement rests upon the dual assumptions that such risks of inaccuracy are serious ones and that juries are unable or disinclined to recognize and accommodate these risks. Since juries are likely to accept confessions uncritically, the demand for corroboration provides a minimal requirement assuring that an untrustworthy confession alone will not lead to conviction.

There are several quite different formulations of the requirement, two of which are variations of what is often called the requirement of independent proof of the *corpus delicti*. The third, applied by the federal courts and some state tribunals, is a more flexible approach.

Independent Proof of the Corpus Delicti. The traditional formulation of the requirement, still applied by most jurisdictions, de-

---

13. See §§ 148–152 infra.

§ 145

1. City of Bremerton v. Corbett, 106 Wash.2d 569, 576, 723 P.2d 1135, 1139 (1986).

mands that there be some evidence other than the confession that tends to establish the *corpus delicti*. Generally, the evidence need not do so beyond a reasonable doubt, and if sufficient independent evidence exists, that independent evidence *and* the confession may both be considered in determining whether guilt has been proved beyond a reasonable doubt.

There is some dispute regarding the definition of *corpus delicti*, which literally means the "body of the crime." To establish guilt in a criminal case, the prosecution must ordinarily show that (a) the injury or harm constituting the crime occurred; (b) this injury or harm was done in a criminal manner; and (c) the defendant was the person who inflicted the injury or harm. Wigmore maintains that *corpus delicti* means only the first of these, that is, "the fact of the specific loss or injury sustained," and does not require proof that this was occasioned by anyone's criminal agency.[2] Some courts have agreed. This approach was adopted by the Massachusetts court, which reasoned that the objective of the corroboration requirement was a quite limited one—guarding against convictions for "imaginary crimes"—and that the restrictive definition of *corpus delicti* best tailored the requirement to serve this limited purpose.

Most courts, however, define *corpus delicti* as involving both (a) and (b). This means that the corroborating evidence must tend to show the harm or injury and that it was occasioned by criminal activity. It need not, however, in any manner tend to show that the defendant was the guilty party. Thus in a homicide case, the *corpus delicti* consists of proof that the victim died and that the death was caused by a criminal act, but it need not tend to connect the defendant on trial with that act.

The traditional approach has been to require that the elements of the offense be carefully distinguished and that the corroborating evidence tend to show each of those elements. A growing number of courts, however, are abandoning the strict requirement

that the corroborating evidence tend to prove all elements of the *corpus delicti*. Thus the corroborating evidence need only tend to show the "major" or "essential" harm involved in the offense charged and not all of the elements technically distinguished. This tendency is most pronounced in homicide cases, where defendants are often tried for offenses that involve requirements beyond simply the causing of death in a criminal manner. There is even some authority for the proposition that the corroborating evidence need only tend to show the commission of an offense, and that this will be sufficient to support conviction for a technically different offense to which the defendant confessed.

Felony murder cases have posed the problem with special difficulty. Under the traditional application of the *corpus delicti* formulation, the elements of felony murder include the predicate felony as well as the fact of death and the causing of it in a criminal way; thus, corroborating evidence would have to tend to prove that predicate felony. Most courts, however, have balked at this and have held that the corroborating evidence need not tend to prove the predicate felony.

However formulated, the requirement of independent proof of the *corpus delicti* is easily met in practice. The New York court has observed that the "requirements of the rule are not rigorous." At least where the incriminating statement is a full confession, only "slight" corroborating evidence is often required, and this can be circumstantial as well as direct.

Evidence Establishing Trustworthiness of Confession. In Opper v. United States,[3] the Supreme Court held as a matter of federal evidence law that a conviction in federal court could not rest upon an uncorroborated confession. Without extensive explanation, it continued, the "better rule" would not require that the corroborating evidence establish the *corpus delicti* but rather that it be "substantial independent evidence which would tend to establish the truthfulness of the state-

---

2. 7 Wigmore, Evidence § 2072, pp. 524–525 (Chadbourn rev. 1978).

3. 348 U.S. 84 (1954).

ment."[4] A growing number of state courts have adopted this position. In Smith v. United States,[5] the Court added that the *Opper* analysis requires corroboration for those elements of the offense "established by admissions alone." Even given *Smith's* holding, this approach is clearly more flexible than the requirement that the corroborating evidence tend to establish the *corpus delicti*.

The major advantage of the trustworthiness approach is that it provides some protection against conviction on the basis of inaccurate confessions while avoiding serious problems involved in the *corpus delicti* formulation. Application of the *corpus delicti* formulation may have been a relatively simple task that accomplished the purpose of the corroboration requirement when crimes were few and were defined in simple and concise terms. But modern statutory criminal law has increased the number and complexity of crimes. Simply identifying the elements of the *corpus delicti* thus provides fertile ground for dispute. Requiring that the corroborating evidence tend to establish each element once the *corpus delicti* is defined may pose an unrealistic burden upon the prosecution without significantly furthering the requirement's objective of providing appropriate, although minimal, assurance against conviction on the basis of inaccurate confessions. This is especially the case with regard to crimes that may not have a tangible *corpus delicti,* such as attempt offenses, conspiracy, tax evasion and similar offenses. As applied to modern crimes, the trustworthiness approach may be easier than the *corpus delicti* rule to apply, as effective in accomplishing the underlying purpose, and less likely to lead to occasionally unreasonable results.

"Confessions" and "Admissions." There is general agreement that the corroboration requirement applies not only to "confessions"—defined as complete and conscious admissions of guilt to a crime—but also to "admissions"—acknowledgments of facts relevant to guilt—and even to exculpatory statements, because all involve the risks which the requirement is designed to reduce. The requirement is not limited to statements made to law enforcement officers and consequently applies to statements made to private persons. A lower court holding that the requirement applied only to statements made during custodial interrogation was rejected by the Washington Supreme Court, which reasoned that the underlying risk is present in other situations as well. But a judicial confession or admission, made in court, does not require corroboration.

Admissibility Requirement and Role of Judge and Jury. The sufficiency of corroboration is generally presented and addressed as a matter of the sufficiency of the prosecution's evidence to convict. Judicial discussions are, however, often couched in terms that suggest the requirement also goes to admissibility. Under such an approach, production of corroborating evidence is required to render the out-of-court confession admissible. Appellate courts applying this formulation of the requirement virtually never find reversible error from its violation, because trial judges are universally agreed to have discretionary control over the order of the evidence. Thus, admission of a confession without sufficient corroborating evidence does not require reversal if, at the close of the evidence, there is sufficient corroborating evidence.

This does not resolve how trial judges *should* proceed. Several appellate courts have directed trial judges to require the prosecution to produce sufficient independent evidence before accepting proffers of out-of-court incriminating statements. If a trial judge admits a confession and then later concludes that the prosecution has not fulfilled its promise to introduce sufficient corroborating evidence, his only courses of action are to strike the confession and instruct the jury to disregard it or to declare a mistrial. Neither, of course, is satisfactory, given the difficulty any jury would have in disregarding evidence of a confession. Thus a trial judge who accepts a confession subject to later corroboration will

---

4. 348 U.S. at 93.

5. 348 U.S. 147 (1954).

be under considerable pressure to find subsequently-offered corroboration sufficient. If the requirement goes to admissibility, then, trial judges most appropriately exercise their discretion by demanding the corroborating evidence before entertaining an offer of the confession at issue.

Whether the requirement is one of admissibility, sufficiency of the evidence, or both, it obviously is to be applied in at least the first instance by the trial judge. If the judge finds the confession admissible, or the corroborating evidence sufficient for the case to go to the jury, or both, does the corroboration requirement now become a jury question? Obviously, the jury must evaluate the sufficiency of the evidence as a whole. The real question is whether the jury should be instructed, in determining the sufficiency of the evidence to convict, to go through any particular analysis because of the corroboration requirement.

Wigmore assumes that the trial judge applies the rule first, and if the case goes to the jury, the "same question" is then posed for the jury, which must address "without reference to the judge's ruling, whether the corroboration exists to satisfy them." [6] Some courts certainly regard the jury as playing a role in applying the requirement. At least a few appear to conceptualize the jury's evaluation as the major one, with the judge's ruling merely a preliminary screening decision.

Other courts have taken far different approaches. The Virginia Supreme Court, for example, has held that a defendant is not entitled to have the jury instructed that it should consider whether a confession has been adequately corroborated. Application of the *corpus delicti* rule is for the trial judge, and the jury has no power to "overrule" the judge's decision on that. While the jury passes on the sufficiency of the evidence, which necessarily includes proof of the *corpus delicti*, this task is adequately accomplished under general instructions.

Future of Corroboration Requirement. Wigmore maintains that no corroboration rule is needed and that existing requirements are, in the hands of unscrupulous defense counsel, "a positive obstruction to the course of justice." [7] Commentators have generally agreed. Given the development of other confession law doctrines, especially Fifth Amendment protections as promulgated in *Miranda* and the voluntariness requirement, concerns regarding law enforcement interrogation practices do not provide significant support for the corroboration requirement. Whether courts can properly retain the doctrine for the purpose of encouraging investigatory techniques other than interrogation is at best questionable, but the corroboration requirement as applied cannot be regarded as effectively providing significant pressure for pursuing such other procedures.

Similarly, the requirement as administered is quite unlikely to provide much protection against inaccuracies resulting from mistakes in reporting, suspects' misunderstandings of the law or facts, or pressures too subtle to invoke *Miranda* or voluntariness protection. Perhaps, as the Massachusetts court concluded, the requirement can be justified only as a safeguard against the very unusual case in which a false confession has been made "by a person suffering a mental or emotional disturbance or some other aberration." It is unlikely that any protection it provides in such situations, or in any others, could not also be provided by careful scrutiny of the evidence by a conscientious judge. The requirement may, however, serve to trigger such scrutiny in appropriate cases by trial judges otherwise too rushed by the press of business to recognize such evidentiary deficiencies.

If a requirement of corroboration is to be retained, there is little justification for formulating it as demanding independent evidence of each element of the *corpus delicti* technically distinguished. Nor is there sufficient need to submit the matter to the jury, as long as the jury is adequately sensitized to the need to find all elements of the crimes charged beyond a reasonable doubt. The Supreme

---

6. 7 Wigmore, Evidence § 2073, p. 531 (Chadbourn rev. 1978).

7. 7 Wigmore, Evidence § 2070 p. 510 (Chadbourn rev. 1978).

Court's *Opper* approach is adequate to serve such need as exists. Thus trial judges should have a duty to assure, if the prosecution's case rests upon the defendant's out-of-court admission, that the prosecution has produced reasonable evidence other than that admission to establish the trustworthiness of the admission or confession.

§ 146. Voluntariness (a) The Common Law Rule

The common law rule requiring voluntariness of an out-of-court confession as a condition for admission into evidence is of relatively recent origin. Early English case law developed a requirement that a "confession" proceeding from fear, menace or duress be rejected by the judge, but "confession" here meant essentially a plea of guilty that eliminated the requirement of evidence. Until the mid–1700s, English law imposed no requirements on the admissibility of what are now regarded as confessions, i.e., defendants' out-of-court admissions offered as evidence of guilt.

Between the Restoration of 1660 and 1775, the English courts came to apply the limits developed for pleas to out-of-court confessions, although the formal reports contained few traces of this development or its rationale. In 1775, Lord Mansfield provided in an offhand comment what Wigmore characterizes as the first full and clear judicial expression of the voluntariness requirement as applied to what modern law regards as confessions: "The instance has frequently happened, of persons having made confessions under threats or promises: the consequence as frequently has been, that such examinations and confessions have not been made use of against them on their trial."[1] Early discussions made clear that the rationale for this approach was the perceived lack of reliability of statements motivated not by guilt but by a desire to avoid discomfort or to secure some favor.

As originally developed in the English courts, the requirement was applied so as to exclude only those confessions given under circumstances raising reasonable doubt as to their accuracy. But during the early 1800s, judicial attitudes towards confessions changed and offers of confessions were greeted with increasing skepticism. Wigmore complains that the doctrine was applied to exclude confessions "upon the slightest pretext." Even Greenleaf, who was generally cautious concerning confessions,[2] acknowledged that the rule "has been sometimes extended quite too far, and has been applied to cases, where there could be no reason to suppose that the inducement had any influence upon the mind of the prisoner."

In its first confession case, Hopt v. Utah,[3] the Supreme Court of the United States adopted as a matter of federal evidence law what it characterized as the well-developed common law requirement of voluntariness. That requirement, the Court explained, commands that a confession be held inadmissible

> when the confession appears to have been made either in consequence of inducements of a temporal nature, held out by one in authority, touching the charge preferred, or because of a threat or promise by or in the presence of such a person, which, operating upon the fears or hopes of the accused, in reference to the charge, deprives him of that freedom of will or self-control essential to make his confession voluntary within the meaning of the law.[4]

§ 147. Voluntariness (b) Modern Standards

Voluntariness is imposed as a constitutional prerequisite to the admissibility of confessions by the Fifth and Fourteenth Amendments to the United States constitution and also by state constitutional analogues to those provi-

---

§ 146

1. Rudd's Case, 1 Leach Cr.C. 115, 118, 168 Eng.Rep. 160, 161 (1775).

2. S. Greenleaf, A Treatise on the Law of Evidence § 214 (3rd ed. 1846).

3. 110 U.S. 574 (1884).

4. 110 U.S. at 585.

sions. On a nonconstitutional level, statutes sometimes impose a requirement of voluntariness, and in other situations case law is likely to do much the same thing. The relationships among these potentially different requirements of voluntariness and between these voluntariness requirements and other constitutional requirements—such as those self-incrimination requirements developed in *Miranda* and state law analogues [1] and the more general right to counsel [2]—present some of the most difficult questions of constitutional confession law.[3]

Despite the variety of different sources that might impose requirements of voluntariness, most discussion and litigation has concerned the requirement imposed by the Fourteenth Amendment's guarantee of due process. The content of this requirement is consequently the point of reference of discussions of voluntariness whatever the source of the specific requirement being discussed.

Development of Federal Constitutional Requirement. Only thirteen years after it embraced the voluntariness requirement as a matter of evidence law in Hopt v. Utah,[4] the Supreme Court—in Bram v. United States [5]—commented that whenever an issue arises in federal criminal trials as to the voluntariness of a confession, "the issue is controlled by that portion of the Fifth Amendment to the Constitution of the United States, commanding that no person 'shall be compelled in any criminal case to be a witness against himself.'" This, the Court continued, embodied the common law rule of voluntariness.

Because the Fifth Amendment was not held binding on the states until 1964,[6] the *Bram* analysis did not impose the voluntariness requirement upon the states as a matter of federal constitutional law. The Court's 1936 holding in Brown v. Mississippi,[7] however,

made clear that a state court conviction resting upon a confession extorted by brutality and violence violated the accused's general right to due process guaranteed by the Fourteenth Amendment. Subsequent cases established that any use in a state criminal proceeding of a coerced confession violated the federal standard. After the Fifth Amendment was applied to the states, the Court characterized the due process standard developed in *Brown* and its progeny as "the same general standard which [is] applied in federal prosecutions—a standard grounded in the policies of the privilege against self-incrimination." [8]

Content of the Federal Constitutional Requirement. In Blackburn v. Alabama,[9] the Supreme Court explained that "a complex of values underlies the stricture against use by the state of confessions which, by way of convenient shorthand, this Court terms involuntary." These values were significantly clarified—and perhaps restricted—by the Court's important 1986 decision in Colorado v. Connelly.[10]

The traditional criterion for determining the admissibility of a confession challenged under the voluntariness requirement was articulated by Justice Frankfurter in 1961:

The ultimate test * * * [is] voluntariness. Is the confession the product of an essentially free and unconstrained choice by its maker? If it is, if he has willed to confess, it may be used against him. If it is not, if his will has been overborne and his capacity for self-determination critically impaired, the use of his confession offends due process.[11]

Physical coercion or the threat of it, of course, necessarily shows that the defendant's will was overborne and his confession involuntary. But the Court was increasingly presented with claims of "psychological" rather than

§ 147

1. See §§ 148–152 infra.

2. See § 153 infra.

3. These are explored in the context of two particularly difficult issues in §§ 154 (promises) and 155 (deception), infra.

4. 110 U.S. 574 (1884).

5. 168 U.S. 532 (1897).

6. See § 115 supra.

7. 297 U.S. 278 (1936).

8. Davis v. North Carolina, 384 U.S. 737, 740 (1966).

9. 361 U.S. 199 (1960).

10. 479 U.S. 157 (1986).

11. Culombe v. Connecticut, 367 U.S. 568, 602 (1961).

physical coercion. Application of the voluntariness standard became more difficult as cases increasingly relied upon these claims of more subtle influences than were presented by the earlier decisions.

Since 1961 the constitutional question of voluntariness has been carefully distinguished from the question of the accuracy or reliability of particular confessions. In Rogers v. Richmond,[12] the Court held that due process did not permit a trial court to resolve the admissibility of a confession challenged on voluntariness grounds by using "a legal standard which took into account the circumstances of probable truth or falsity." Evidence that a challenged confession (or some subpart of it) is accurate, then, is totally irrelevant to the voluntariness inquiry.

The common law background of the due process requirement suggests that among its objectives has been the protection of defendants from confessions that are unreliable. Prior to *Connelly,* there was little to suggest that the requirement of voluntariness had lost its concern with accuracy in the process of constitutionalization. Rogers v. Richmond was not inconsistent with this approach. A prohibition upon case-by-case consideration of accuracy is not inconsistent with the proposition that involuntary confessions are excluded in part because as a general matter they tend to be so subtly unreliable that juries and judges are likely to give them more weight than can objectively be justified.

In *Connelly,* however, the Court apparently cut the voluntariness analysis loose from any mooring on accuracy concerns. Acknowledging that the statement before it might be "quite unreliable," the Court continued that "this is a matter to be governed by the evidentiary laws of the forum * * * and not by the Due Process Clause of the Fourteenth Amendment." The "aim" of the federal provision, it announced, "is not to exclude presumptively false evidence, but to prevent fundamental unfairness in the use of evidence, whether true or false."

Justice Frankfurter's classic voluntariness discussion suggests that among the concerns of due process was that a defendant at trial be free of any prior self-incriminating admission that did not reflect a "an essentially free and unconstrained choice" by the defendant. In *Connelly,* the Court held that the Fourteenth Amendment's due process requirement of voluntariness imposed no such absolute requirement. Official and coercive activity "is a necessary predicate to the finding that a confession is not 'voluntary' within the meaning of the Due Process Clause of the Fourteenth Amendment." In the absence of this predicate, a defendant's mental condition, no matter how much it may in actual fact have prevented his decision to confess from being a meaningful exercise of choice, cannot render his confession "involuntary."

Pre–*Connelly* case law reflected an increasing emphasis in the Court's voluntariness cases upon the need to discourage offensive law enforcement conduct used to elicit confessions. But arguably there was little indication that such conduct was an absolute prerequisite. *Connelly,* however, makes clear that this is now the case. A confession extracted from a defendant by actual physical force applied by a private person acting only in his private capacity, for example, is not involuntary within the meaning of the due process rule because it is not the result of official misconduct.

Connelly did not render the suspect's decision making process irrelevant to voluntariness. Once official coercion is established, the inquiry turns to whether as a result the defendant's will was overborne. In resolving this, the defendant's mental condition and its effect upon his susceptibility to coercion of the sort established is relevant. Case law indicates, the Court noted, that the more subtle the forms of psychological persuasion used in a case, the more significant the suspect's mental condition becomes in resolving voluntariness.

Connelly provided little guidance for determining what constitutes the official coercion

---

12. 365 U.S. 534 (1961).

necessary to require the Fourteenth Amendment analysis to proceed to the mind of the suspect. *Connelly's* facts illustrate the difficulty. Connelly was mentally ill and experienced a "voice" telling him either to confess to a murder or kill himself. He approached a uniformed Denver police officer and, explaining that his conscience was bothering him, volunteered an incriminating statement concerning the offense. In response to questions asked by the bewildered officer, Connelly denied that he had been drinking but stated that he had, in the past, been a patient in several mental hospitals. The Court, after developing the due process standard, summarily concluded that the taking and later the trial use of Connelly's statement to the officer did not violate the Fourteenth Amendment.

The *Connelly* Court distinguished Blackburn v. Alabama,[13] in which police learned during the interrogation that Blackburn had a history of mental problems. The Court continued:

> The police exploited this weakness with coercive tactics: "the eight-to-nine-hour sustained interrogation in a tiny room which was upon occasion literally filled with police officers; the absence of Blackburn's friends, relatives, or legal counsel; [and] the composition of the confession by the Deputy Sheriff rather than by Blackburn."[14]

Apparently, then, these factors—at least under the circumstances presented—were enough to demonstrate coercive police conduct triggering voluntariness analysis. In determining whether the impact of this coercion upon Blackburn had overborne his will, Blackburn's mental impairment could be considered.

It is less clear what role Blackburn's mental impairment could play in determining that the police activity was coercive. *Connelly* leaves no doubt that the Court perceived as critical the fact that the officers knew of Blackburn's impairment and "exploited" it. Does this mean that officers' subjective desire to "use" a suspect's known impairment to

persuade him to confess is what is important? Is it sufficient in itself to establish coercive activity? *Connelly* leaves these questions unanswered.

Pre–*Connelly* Supreme Court case law reflected consideration of numerous factors in evaluating a voluntariness challenge. The Court gave significant weight to the time of the day or night of the interrogation, the length of interrogation, the quality of the conditions in which the defendant was held before confessing, and similar matters. These have been evaluated in light of various characteristics of the accused that presumably affect the impact of these factors upon the accused. Thus the Court has found suggestion of involuntariness in the accused's youth, physical illness, injury, or infirmity, low educational level, and little or no prior experience with law enforcement practices and techniques. Whether or not officers warned the suspect of his right to silence and explained that right, where there is no specific obligation to do so, is relevant to voluntariness; in any case, the extent of the suspect's actual appreciation of his rights is clearly significant.

Lower courts have been somewhat slow to accept fully the need to find official coercion before inquiring as to defendants' actual subjective circumstances and reactions. In part, this may reflect reluctance to give up their traditional prerogative to evaluate confession decisions on the "totality of the circumstances." But it may also reflect such courts' view that the concept of official coercion is so vaguely defined that it can generally be found on most facts by courts predisposed to find it. Consequently, despite its analytical importance, the requirement of official coercion does not impose a significant practical barrier to proceeding with voluntariness analysis and thus there is some reluctance to attribute considerable actual significance to it.

Subrequirement of "Intelligence." Criteria for effective waivers of self-incrimination and

---

13. 361 U.S. 199 (1960).

14. *Connelly,* supra note 10, 479 U.S. at 165, quoting from Blackburn v. Alabama, 361 U.S. 199, 207–208 (1960).

general constitutional rights to counsel [15] have stressed the need to inquire separately into "voluntariness" and "intelligence" of suspects' waiver decisions. Does the general requirement of "voluntariness" include a subrequirement of "intelligence" that demands that the suspect be found to have been actually aware of some information? Logic suggests that a suspect cannot make an acceptable decision to confess—one that would render his confession admissible under general voluntariness law—unless at a minimum he was aware that he had a legal right to remain silent or at least not to make a self-incriminatory admission.

Nothing in the Supreme Court's due process voluntariness law, however, suggests any need for this awareness, or at least any need for specific findings on the matter as a condition of finding a confession voluntary. To the contrary, in a general review of voluntariness law, the Court commented that in none of its decisions had the Court required that the prosecution prove "as part of its initial burden" on voluntariness that the defendant was aware of his right to refuse to answer police queries.[16] This suggests that although the defendant's awareness of his right is relevant, there is no absolute requirement that he be shown to have been cognizant of his legal right to decline a self-incriminating admission. Thus a trial court finding of due process voluntariness does not rigidly demand a specific factual finding by the court of such awareness.

Comparison With Self–Incrimination Waiver Standards. A confession given during custodial interrogation is subject to specific self-incrimination requirements, particularly those developed from the Fifth Amendment in *Miranda* and its progeny.[17] Among those requirements are the need for the prosecution to prove effective waivers of the right to counsel and to remain silent.[18] In such situations, do the self-incrimination requirements supersede those of the more general voluntariness requirement? Specific aspects of this question are developed in several other sections of this chapter.[19]

On a general level, some courts have indicated that where both the general voluntariness and the more specific self-incrimination requirements apply, the former requires a more general and flexible inquiry than the latter. Under this approach, the voluntariness of a *Miranda* waiver requires an essentially factual inquiry concerning the suspect's state of mind. But if the self-incrimination waivers were effective, the voluntariness of the confession is an additional and different question. Analysis of the voluntariness issue involves more subtle integration into the analysis of the underlying policy considerations and the balancing of competing considerations. Ultimately, resolution of the voluntariness claim requires a relatively subjective conclusion as to whether the means used to obtain the confession are compatible with the underlying policy considerations.

Connelly's apparent determination that *Miranda* waivers require little if anything more than due process voluntariness [20] means that discussions of such considerations as intoxication and psychological abnormality on the "voluntariness" of *Miranda* waivers [21] and their "intelligence" [22] are applicable to the more general due process issue as well.

Dissatisfaction With Due Process Voluntariness. The Supreme Court's willingness in *Miranda* [23] to impose upon the states the quite rigid self-incrimination requirements developed in the case reflected significant dissatisfaction with the due process voluntariness standard. Several aspects of the voluntariness requirement probably gave rise to this

---

15. See §§ 151 and 152 infra (voluntariness and intelligence of self-incrimination waivers) and § 153 infra (general right to counsel requirements).

16. Schneckloth v. Bustamonte, 412 U.S. 218, 226–227 (1973).

17. See § 148 infra.

18. See §§ 151–152 infra.

19. See § 154 (promises) and § 155 (deception) infra. See generally §§ 151–152 infra.

20. See § 151 infra.

21. See § 151 infra.

22. See § 152 infra.

23. See § 148 infra.

dissatisfaction. First, the voluntariness rule gave little precise guidance to law enforcement officers as to what the law required. Inherent in the "totality of the circumstances" approach is an analysis in which few specific facts of each case are specifically identified as sufficient in themselves to require routine avoidance. As a result, officers motivated to look to the case law to determine what they could do found little guidance.

Second, the *Miranda* opinion itself suggests that the Court concluded that the voluntariness test was inherently inadequate to deal with the more subtly coercive methods of interrogation that the Court saw as replacing overt brutality as the major threat to constitutionally-protected interests affected by the interrogation process. If federal constitutional law was to deal with the risks to protected interests posed by these techniques, the Court concluded, it could not continue to rely almost exclusively upon due process voluntariness.

Third, the Court became sensitive to the tendency of voluntariness inquiries to devolve into a swearing match between the defendant, giving one version of the interrogation, and the officers, presenting another. Too often such conflicts were uncritically resolved in favor of the officers. Defendants' inability to recreate in court what transpired in the interrogation room deprived them of much or all of the value of the voluntariness doctrine.

Finally, the Court was frustrated with the continuing administrative burden posed by the voluntariness rule. Serious efforts to apply it, especially to claims of subtle psychological coercion, required significant trial court time. Appellate review, if properly undertaken, similarly was time consuming. The Supreme Court itself had reviewed numerous cases in an effort to provide guidance to the lower courts regarding the manner in which they should deal with these claims. Yet despite this effort on all levels, the voluntariness rule provided few returns. Problems raised by subtle interrogation techniques had not been addressed, practical guidelines for interrogating officers had not been developed,

and recurring instances of what the Court regarded as clearly impermissible interrogation practices demonstrated that the costs being paid for the voluntariness rule were not deterring prohibited interrogation practices.

State Law and Statutory Voluntariness Requirements. Statutory and state constitutional requirements of voluntariness need not, of course, be construed as having the same contents as the due process requirement. State courts have not often addressed this possibility, perhaps because due process voluntariness is so flexible a standard that cases are often more easily resolved by manipulating that standard than by justifying acceptance of a different criterion.

As lower courts confront the implications of *Connelly's* limitations on due process voluntariness, however, they are likely to be more receptive to arguments that statutory or state constitutional voluntariness requirements are not subject to an absolute requirement of official coercion. Such arguments may find support in pre-*Connelly* state cases imposing absolute requirements that confessing defendants have made meaningful decisions to confess.

§ 148. Self–Incrimination Standards (a) *Miranda* Requirements

In 1966, the Supreme Court's dissatisfaction with due process voluntariness culminated in Miranda v. Arizona,[1] which has become the focus of subsequent confession law development and analysis.

On the doctrinal level, *Miranda*'s significance lies, first, in its holding that custodial law enforcement interrogation implicated the Fifth Amendment's privilege against compelled self-incrimination. Previously, the privilege had widely been regarded as limited to those situations in which the questioner had a legal right to compel answers. Since law enforcement officers had no legal authority to penalize refusals to answer their questions, the traditional view had been that questioning by such officers did not implicate the

§ 148

1.   384 U.S. 436 (1966).

privilege. Rejecting this approach, the Court reasoned in *Miranda* that "[a]s a practical matter, the compulsion to speak in the isolated setting of the police station may well be greater than in courts or other official investigations [where the legal power to compel answers may be exercised]."[2]

The focus of the Court's concern in *Miranda* was what the Court perceived as the "inherently compelling pressures" of custodial interrogation which, without proper safeguards, inevitably work "to undermine the individual's will to resist and to compel him to speak where he would not otherwise do so freely." In support, it canvassed manuals and texts used by law enforcement, noting recommendations that interrogating officers isolate suspects, proceed as if guilt is clear and inquire only as to the reasons for committing the crime, offer moral or legal excuses for the criminal activity, alternate displays of sympathy and hostility (the "Mutt and Jeff" technique), and use trickery. Modern in-custody interrogation, it stressed, is "psychologically rather than physically oriented" and inherently involves "compulsion." In the absence of protective devices, "no statement obtained from the defendant [in this context] can truly be the product of free choice."

Miranda "Prophylactic" Requirements. To implement the privilege in the custodial interrogation context, the Court developed what have come to be characterized as *per se* or "prophylactic" rules—requirements that are designed to assure that specific decisions are legally acceptable but which, for protective purposes, apply even to situations where on the facts the suspects' decisions may not have fallen below standards imposed by the law. Specifically, a confession obtained in violation of these requirements must, as a matter of Fifth Amendment law, be excluded from evidence even if application of voluntariness standards to the particular facts of the case would not lead to a conclusion that the confession was involuntary.

Although this has been somewhat overshadowed by later developments, it is clear that

the *Miranda* Court regarded the major source of protection for those undergoing custodial interrogation as the right to counsel. The suspect's Fifth Amendment interests, reasoned the majority, can only be protected by affording the suspect an attendant right to counsel. This means not simply the right to consult with counsel before questioning, "but also to have counsel present during any interrogation * * *." Counsel must be available regardless of the financial ability of the suspect. Consequently, an attorney must be provided at public expense for those indigent defendants who wish the assistance of counsel.

The most well-known *Miranda* requirement is that of warnings. While "no talismanic incantation" of the language used in the opinion is necessary,[3] officers must give the suspect essentially the following admonitions:

1. You have the right to remain silent;

2. Anything you say can [and will] be used against you in court;

3. You have the right to consult with a lawyer and to have the lawyer with you during interrogation; and

4. If you cannot afford an attorney, one will be appointed for you prior to any questioning if you so desire.

The first three elements are "absolute prerequisite[s]" to acceptable custodial interrogation. Failure to give even one of them cannot be "cured" by evidence that the suspect was already aware of the substance of the omitted warning[s]. Omission of the fourth element, on the other hand, is not fatal if the suspect was known to already have an attorney or to have ample funds to secure one. If, however, there is any doubt as to the applicability of the fourth element, this will be resolved against the prosecution. The warnings must be given prior to any interrogation.

Waivers of Miranda Rights. Neither the right to remain silent nor its attendant right to counsel during interrogation is mandatory. Both are subject to waiver. In all cases

2. 384 U.S. at 461.

3. California v. Prysock, 453 U.S. 355, 359 (1981).

where the prosecution offers at trial a self-incriminating statement made during custodial interrogation, it must show a voluntary and intelligent waiver of the privilege against self-incrimination itself. If the statement was made during interrogation at which no lawyer was present on the suspect's behalf, the prosecution must also show an effective waiver of the right to counsel.

Unfortunately, the Court's discussions sometimes fail to acknowledge that these waivers often occur at quite different times and present quite different issues. The waiver of the privilege, as a practical matter, does not occur until the suspect actually makes an incriminating admission. The waiver of the right to counsel, on the other hand, must occur before interrogation begins. In the numerous cases in which an accused waives counsel but makes no incriminating admissions until after extended questioning, the two waivers are quite distinct. Depending upon what occurred during the interrogation, the waiver of the privilege itself may be subject to defects that could not have tainted the earlier waiver of counsel.

Post-*Miranda* developments establish that the Court failed to anticipate the frequency with which suspects would waive the assistance of counsel. *Miranda* itself suggests that the Court assumed that suspects would usually invoke the right to counsel and that counsel would in fact be present. Counsel's presence, in turn, would either assure that no self-incriminating statement was made by the defendant or, if one was made, that it was given under circumstances that rendered it so obviously an effective waiver of the privilege that seldom would the use of the statement at trial present difficult issues concerning the waiver's effectiveness.

In fact, of course, the overwhelming majority of statements obtained during custodial interrogation offered at trials are obtained during questioning conducted without coun-

sel. In many and probably most of those cases in which a viable admissibility issue is presented, that issue concerns the adequacy of the evidence on waiver. *Miranda* waiver law, then, has taken on a prominence that the *Miranda* Court itself almost certainly did not foresee.

Miranda waivers need not be "express," the Court reaffirmed in North Carolina v. Butler.[4] Obviously, evidence that the suspect specifically articulated that she was aware of the right and was choosing not to exercise it constitutes strong—but not necessary—evidence of waiver. At the other extreme, *Miranda* itself makes clear that waiver will not be presumed from a suspect's silence after the warnings or from the fact that the suspect eventually provided a confession. In intermediate situations, the question is whether the evidence before the court regarding what the defendant did and said permits a finding that the prosecution has proved by a preponderance of the evidence that the defendant was aware of the right and both voluntarily and intelligently chose not to exercise it.

Later sections consider in detail the requirements that waivers be both voluntary[5] and intelligent.[6]

Additional Prophylactic Rules. Despite the rigor with which the *Miranda* Court fashioned *per se* Fifth Amendment requirements out of the very general language of the constitutional provision, post-*Miranda* decisions have shown no inclination to continue this approach by developing more such requirements.[7] This was made obvious in Moran v. Burbine,[8] in which the evidence indicated that police had misled Burbine's counsel into believing that Burbine would not be interrogated. Burbine's counsel consequently made no further efforts to contact Burbine, who nevertheless was interrogated, waived his rights, and gave an incriminating statement.

Burbine urged the Court to adopt what would have been in essence a *per se* rule

---

4. 441 U.S. 369 (1979).

5. See § 151 infra.

6. See § 152 infra.

7. The one exception is the strict prohibition against approaching a suspect who invokes the right to counsel. See § 150 infra.

8. 475 U.S. 412 (1986).

requiring police to inform a suspect of an attorney's efforts to reach him. The Court acknowledged that such a rule "might add marginally to *Miranda's* goal of dispelling the compulsion inherent in custodial interrogation." "[O]verriding practical considerations," however, argued against such a rule. The complexity that would accompany any such rule would decrease *Miranda's* clarity and ease of application. Further, such a requirement would cause some suspects to decline to make voluntary but self-incriminating statements and thus "work a substantial and * * * inappropriate shift in the subtle balance struck in [*Miranda*]."

Generally, then, whether a confession is rendered inadmissible by circumstances involving no violation of the basic rules developed in the *Miranda* opinion itself turns upon whether those circumstances demonstrate that the defendant's waivers were ineffective.

Congressional "Overruling" of Miranda. Congress has purported, for purposes of federal criminal prosecutions, to "overrule" *Miranda's* basic exclusionary holding. In 1968, as part of the Omnibus Crime Control and Safe Streets Act of 1968, Congress passed what is now Section 3501 of Title 18 of the United States Code. Section 3501(a) provides that in a criminal prosecution brought by the United States or by the District of Columbia, a confession "shall be admissible in evidence if it is voluntarily given." Under section 3501(b), the trial judge determining voluntariness is directed to consider, among other things, whether or not the defendant had been advised that he was not required to make a statement, that any statement made could be used against him, and that he had the right to the assistance of counsel. Also to be considered is whether the defendant was in fact without the assistance of counsel during interrogation and the giving of the confession. But "[t]he presence or absence of any of [these] factors * * * need not be conclusive on the issue of voluntariness of the confession."

This legislation does not attempt to negate the *Miranda* holdings that a suspect undergoing custodial interrogation is entitled to the assistance of counsel or that she is entitled to

the four-part warning. It does, however, purport to change *Miranda's per se* exclusionary remedy and to make violations of the suspect's rights merely factors relevant to the voluntariness inquiry which, in turn, determines the admissibility of the confession. The statute remains untested in litigation, apparently because federal prosecutors are unwilling to risk convictions by relying on the statute in order to press the federal courts to consider whether the statute exceeded Congressional power.

State Constitutional Miranda-like Requirements. State courts are, of course, free to read state constitutional self-incrimination provisions as imposing the same requirements which *Miranda* found in the Fifth Amendment privilege. Such action would seem to be a prerequisite to state law holdings that state law imposes more stringent versions of specific *Miranda* requirements than are demanded by Supreme Court case law. A few state courts have explicitly embraced the *Miranda* requirements as independently required by state constitutions.

Even those state court decisions addressing the interrogation protections imposed by state constitutional self-incrimination provisions, however, have failed to comprehensively consider the propriety of reading constitutional self-incrimination provisions as imposing requirements as specific as those mandated by *Miranda* and as requiring the exclusion of confessions that are not in fact "involuntary." Whatever its ultimate propriety, *Miranda* certainly reflected an aggressive and debatable exercise of judicial power to develop general language in a constitution. State courts seem reluctant to confront whether they have authority to act similarly and—if so—whether they should do so. Consequently, state courts inclined to impose requirements more stringent than those imposed by the Supreme Court's case law have tended to eschew development of state law versions of *Miranda* based on state constitutional self-incrimination privileges. Rather, they have tended to rely upon state constitutional explicit grants of the right to counsel.[9]

§ 149. Self–Incrimination Requirements (b) Applicability of *Miranda*

Miranda applies[1] only if two threshold requirements are established: the defendant must have been in "custody" at the time of the statement and the statement must have been the result of "interrogation." Post–*Miranda* construction of these requirements has significantly limited the impact of *Miranda*. If either or both of these requirements are not met, due process voluntariness generally provides the only federal constitutional restriction on the use of a confession,[2] and the prosecution's task of establishing admissibility is greatly eased.

Miranda did not purport to address all problems raised by the use of out-of-court incriminating admissions but rather only the especially high risks to the privilege created by "custodial interrogation." In developing the contents of those terms, the Court has attempted to define them so that *Miranda* applies where, but only where, the interests protected by the privilege are subjected to the extraordinary risks that stimulated development of the *Miranda* rights. Even where both requirements are met, there are several firmly established exceptions to the *Miranda* requirements and another that is quite likely to be adopted by the Court.

Custody. In Orozco v. Texas,[3] the Court refused to define custody as meaning only "stationhouse custody." Thus it applied *Miranda* to questioning of a suspect in his own bedroom, where officers had entered and surrounded the bed in which he was lying. *Miranda* applied because the suspect had been "deprived of his freedom in [a] significant way." The fact that the suspect was in custody for an offense other than that about which

the officers questioned him was held not to render *Miranda* inapplicable in Mathis v. United States.[4] On the other hand, *Miranda* does not apply if custody does not actually exist, the Court held in Oregon v. Mathiason,[5] even if the interrogation takes place in a "coercive environment."

Does "custody" require some actual restraint of the suspect by an officer, or is it sufficient that the suspect reasonably perceive that the officer would not permit this? The suspect might anticipate that the officer would either prevent the suspect from leaving or—if the confrontation occurs on the suspect's "territory"—would insist upon remaining despite the suspect's demand that the officer leave. In Berkemer v. McCarty,[6] in a closely-related context, the Court stressed that whether a suspect is in custody for *Miranda* purposes turns upon how a reasonable person would understand her status. This emphasis meshes well with *Miranda's* rationale. The underlying risks that justify *Miranda* extraordinary requirements can have an impact upon a suspect only when the suspect is aware of the coercive nature of his situation. The suspect's perception, then, is the appropriate focus of the criterion for determining whether *Miranda* applies.

"Custody" in this literal sense is not—at least always—alone sufficient to trigger *Miranda*. In Berkemer v. McCarty,[7] the Court refused to hold *Miranda* applicable to all situations in which the suspect had been literally deprived of his freedom and held it inapplicable to questioning during "an ordinary traffic stop." Such stops do not, for several reasons, create sufficient risk to the privilege to justify application of *Miranda's* extraordinary requirements. First, such detentions are brief, and motorists recognize this. There is little

---

9. See generally § 153 infra.

§ 149

1. There is widespread agreement among the lower courts that *Miranda* does not apply to questioning by a private person acting in his private capacity.

2. In some noncustodial situations, the Sixth Amendment right to counsel applies; see generally § 153 infra.

3. 394 U.S. 324 (1969).

4. 391 U.S. 1, 4–5 (1968).

5. 429 U.S. 492, 495 (1977) (per curiam).

6. 468 U.S. 420 (1984).

7. 468 U.S. 420 (1984).

risk that motorists will fear detention until the officer is provided with the answers he seeks. Second, traffic stops usually involve only one or two officers confronting the motorist in a public place. The atmosphere will generally lack the "police dominat[ion]" giving rise to the inherent coercion with which *Miranda* is concerned.

But, the Court continued, *Miranda* applies to questioning following an arrest even for a minor traffic offense. It relied primarily upon the difficulties of articulating, developing and applying any exception for minor offenses, but it also stressed the absence of convincing evidence that the risks of coercion following arrest for minor offenses is sufficiently low to render the rationale for *Miranda* inapplicable. *Miranda,* then, applies if an officer makes a "formal arrest," even for a minor offense. "Formal arrest" was not defined, but the Court apparently intended to require an explicit announcement by the officer to the motorist that the motorist was being arrested.

Noting the risks that officers might circumvent a rule limiting *Miranda* to formal arrest situations, the Court further announced that *Miranda* would apply even in the absence of a formal arrest if a motorist "is subjected to treatment that renders him 'in custody' for practical purposes." Again, this was not defined. The Court made clear, however, that practical custody did not turn upon the officer's subjective intentions. "[T]he only relevant inquiry," it observed, "is how a reasonable man in the suspect's position would have understood his situation."

Does *Miranda* apply to questioning during a nonarrest field detention for investigatory purposes, so-called "*Terry* stops," [8] permitted under Fourth Amendment law upon "reasonable suspicion" that the person is engaged in criminal activity? A person so stopped and questioned, of course, "is not obligated to respond." [9]

The Supreme Court has not ruled directly on whether that right is protected by *Mi-*

randa's prophylactic requirements, but in *McCarty* the Court assumed that *Miranda* did not apply to *Terry* stops. "The comparatively nonthreatening character of detentions of this sort" the Court offered, "explains the absence of any suggestion in our opinions that *Terry* stops are subject to the dictates of *Miranda.*" Lower courts have shared this assumption that *Miranda* is inapplicable.

McCarty's assumption that *Miranda* does not apply to investigatory stops is questionable, and a reasonable case can be made for applying to investigatory detentions at least a version of *Miranda.* Such detentions are more likely than traffic stops to be conducted in isolated and therefore "police dominated" circumstances. Citizens who know what to expect as a result of a traffic stop may have less familiarity with investigatory detentions and consequently may be less certain that such detentions will in fact be brief and that there is little risk of adverse consequences from their refusal to respond to questions. Thus the risks to the privilege in such situations may be more akin to those posed to it during post-arrest questioning than to the reduced risks arising from traffic stop inquiries.

Literal application of *Miranda,* on the other hand, would quite clearly be unrealistic. Counsel, retained or appointed, could not be provided in the field situation. Delaying questioning until the subject is moved to the stationhouse so that counsel could be provided would delay questioning and make it so cumbersome that the value of investigatory detentions would be eliminated. Moreover, requiring a subject to submit to movement to the stationhouse as a condition of invoking his Fifth Amendment rights might well offend Fourth Amendment values. The Fifth Amendment cannot reasonably be read as extending the right to counsel to *Terry* stop questioning or, of course, as requiring that the subjects be told they have such a right. The right to remain silent applies, however, and is arguably at particular risk. Self-incrimination considerations might, then, re-

---

8. See Terry v. Ohio, 392 U.S. 1 (1968).

9. Berkemer v. McCarty, 468 U.S. 420, 439 (1984).

quire at least a pre-questioning admonition as to that right.

Interrogation. Although *Miranda* itself made clear that its requirements applied only when a suspect was being interrogated, the meaning of this prerequisite was not addressed until 1980 and Rhode Island v. Innis.[10] In *Innis,* the Court refused to limit *Miranda* to situations involving "express interrogation:"

> [T]he term "interrogation" under *Miranda* refers not only to express questioning, but also to any words or actions on the part of the police (other than those normally attendant to arrest and custody) that the police should know are reasonably likely to elicit an incriminating response from the suspect.[11]

Whether law enforcement conduct is the "functional equivalent" of express questioning and triggers *Miranda* focuses primarily upon the perspective of the suspect. Evidence that the words or conduct at issue were intended by the officer to elicit self-incriminating admissions from the suspect does not itself establish that interrogation took place; it may, however, strongly tend to show that the officer knew or should have known that the words or conduct were sufficiently likely to elicit the desired response.

The Court has been quite reluctant to characterize situations as involving the functional equivalent of express questioning, as *Innis* itself illustrates. Innis had been apprehended in an area where he was thought to have concealed a firearm used in a murder. Three officers accompanied him in a police vehicle to headquarters. During the trip, one officer said to another that many handicapped children from a local school for the impaired were in the area, and "God forbid one of them might find a weapon * * * and * * * hurt themselves." Innis then interrupted with an offer to show the officers where a weapon (which turned out to be the murder weapon) was located. The Court characterized the officers' actions as "no more

than a few off-hand remarks." No indication was found that the officers intended their remarks to elicit a response from Innis, the Court continued. Further, in the absence of more—such as awareness that Innis was particularly sensitive to appeals concerning handicapped children—the facts did not establish that the officers should have been aware that their comments would move Innis to make a self-incriminating admission as to the location of the gun; therefore, no interrogation occurred.

This tendency to hold *Miranda* inapplicable by finding no interrogation has continued in post-*Innis* Supreme Court decisions, which have somewhat relaxed the *Innis* standard. Permitting a suspect's wife to speak with a suspect arrested for the murder of the couple's young son was held not to constitute interrogation in Arizona v. Mauro.[12] Although there was a possibility that the confrontation would result in the suspect making a self-incriminating admission and the police knew this, the suspect could not have perceived that because of the confrontation he was being coerced into incriminating himself. Otherwise proper law enforcement activity is permissible, even if police know of some chance that it will stimulate a self-incriminatory admission, if the risk of such an admission is low and there is minimal likelihood that the suspect will perceive the situation as coercive.

Even express questions put to a suspect may not constitute interrogation. In South Dakota v. Neville,[13] the Court concluded that police inquiry of a suspect whether he would submit to a blood alcohol test does not constitute "interrogation" under *Miranda.*

Pennsylvania v. Muniz[14] held that no interrogation took place when an officer explained to a suspect how a breathalyzer examination worked, the legal aspects of the applicable Implied Consent Law and then inquired whether he understood and would be willing to submit to the test. Nor was there interro-

---

10. 446 U.S. 291 (1980).
11. Id. at 301.
12. 481 U.S. 520 (1987).

13. 459 U.S. 553 (1983).
14. 496 U.S. 582 (1990).

gation when, during a videotaping, an officer instructed the suspect how he was to perform physical sobriety tests and inquired whether the suspect understood the instructions. In these situations, the procedure is highly regulated and thus quite standardized; it is also normally attendant to proper law enforcement procedures within the meaning of the *Innis* discussion. The instructional part of the procedure is unlikely to be perceived as calling for a verbal response. To the extent that inquiries calling for verbal responses of the suspect are involved, these "limited and focused inquiries" are not likely to be perceived by suspects as calling for *incriminating* responses. Hence even the express posing of questions during routine and otherwise proper procedures does not involve "interrogation," if under the circumstances a reasonable officer would not know that the questions were reasonably likely to elicit an incriminating response from the suspect.

Lower courts have considerable flexibility in characterizing particular situations and generally are quite reluctant to label police action prohibited interrogation. Officers who told a suspect that "this was his last chance to talk with police" and that if he did not "it might be worse" were held to have interrogated him by doing so. But no interrogation was found where officers simply engaged a suspect in "small talk." Similarly, interrogation did not occur when officers, before returning a suspect to his cell, told the suspect they only wanted the truth and to call an officer if he wanted further conversation, or when an officer, while preparing to leave the interrogation room, said to an assault suspect, "You want a lawyer, that's fine with us, but we'll never know [the victim] came at you with a knife."

Exceptions to Miranda Requirements. Miranda does not apply to some situations involving both custody and interrogation as those are defined under the Court's case law.

If the questioning is done by an officer functioning in an undercover capacity, the Court held in Illinois v. Perkins,[15] *Miranda* has no application. Where a suspect is unaware that he is conversing with his captors, the majority reasoned, the situation does not present the interaction between custody and interrogation creating the risk of coercion that justifies the extraordinary *Miranda* protections. *Miranda* also does not apply, the Court held in New York v. Quarles,[16] in certain situations in which police inquiries are motivated by concern for public safety. Where compliance with *Miranda's* mandates would create an immediate and high risk to public safety, the costs are excessive.

A plurality of the Court in Pennsylvania v. Muniz[17] recognized another exception for "routine booking questions" asked during the processing of an arrested suspect. This exception, which is almost certain to be accepted by a majority of the Court, covered questions designed to elicit biographical data necessary to complete the booking process and to provide pretrial services. Thus in *Muniz, Miranda* was regarded by the plurality as inapplicable to questions concerning Muniz's name, address, height, weight, eye color, date of birth, and current age.

§ 150. Self–Incrimination Requirements (c) Prohibition Against Interrogation

It is clear that one undergoing custodial interrogation by law enforcement officers has a right to decline to provide incriminating information and, apparently, the right to remain entirely silent. But does such a person have any right to prevent "interrogation" or efforts to persuade him to submit to interrogation or information?

Under the Fifth Amendment privilege, the *Miranda* opinion itself provided mixed signals. The Court made clear that if the suspect states that he wants an attorney, then "the interrogation must cease until an attor-

15. 496 U.S. 292 (1990).

16. 467 U.S. 649 (1984).

17. 496 U.S. 582 (1990).

ney is present." [1] But other language was broader: "If the individual indicates in any manner, at any time prior to or during questioning, that he wishes to remain silent, the interrogation must cease." [2] This was qualified, however, with the further comment that if an attorney is present and the suspect expresses a desire to remain silent, "there may be some circumstances in which further questioning would be permissible." [3] Self-incriminating responses made in response to interrogation conducted over such objections but in the presence of counsel, the Court indicated, *might* "in the absence of evidence of overbearing" be free of compulsion and thus admissible as having been preceded by a waiver of the right to remain silent.

If an attorney is present, then, *Miranda* itself suggests that the suspect has no absolute right to be free of interrogation. Should interrogation be conducted over objection and prove fruitful, the issue is the effectiveness of the waiver that necessarily preceded or accompanied the self-incriminating admission. The evidence that interrogation continued over objection would tend to show, but would not necessarily establish, that the resulting waiver was involuntary.

The situation presented when a suspect invokes the right to counsel was addressed in Edwards v. Arizona. [4] During interrogation, police and Edwards discussed a possible "deal" and Edwards finally stated, "I want an attorney before making a deal." He was returned to jail but the next morning was interviewed again by two detectives not involved in the earlier discussions. They again warned Edwards and, after waiving his rights, he made an incriminating statement. Holding the statement inadmissible, the Court explained:

> [W]hen an accused has invoked his right to have counsel present during custodial interrogation, * * * [he] is not subject to further interrogation by the authorities until counsel

is made available to him, unless the accused himself initiates further communications, exchanges, or conversation with the police. [5]

Edwards, it is clear, recognizes a *per se* "prophylactic" rule requiring exclusion regardless of the intelligence and voluntariness of a suspect's waiver, if: (a) the suspect invoked his right to counsel; (b) police initiated either further interrogation or discussion as to whether the suspect might submit to interrogation without an attorney present; and (c) the statement at issue resulted from that police-initiated activity.

Edwards was substantially expanded in Arizona v. Roberson, [6] where the suspect was approached by an officer who was unaware that Roberson, during an earlier discussion with another officer, had previously invoked his right to counsel. The second officer successfully questioned Roberson concerning an offense unrelated to the offense with which the first interrogation had been concerned. *Edwards,* the Court explained, is based upon the need to vigorously discourage police activity—reapproaching a suspect who has indicated his belief that he is not capable of undergoing interrogation without a lawyer's help—that creates an especially high risk of involuntary waivers. This rationale applies when the suspect is reapproached concerning a different offense, since there is no basis for concluding that officers investigating such an offense will lack the "eager[ness]" to obtain a confession that in this situation poses the high risk to self-incrimination interests.

The second officer's unawareness that Roberson had invoked his right to counsel was of no significance. *Edwards'* concern is with the state of mind of the suspect rather than that of the officer. *Miranda* creates an obligation to determine whether a suspect has previously requested counsel and a violation of important *Miranda* requirements cannot be excused by an officer's "lack of diligence."

§ 150

1. Miranda v. Arizona, 384 U.S. 436, 474 (1966).
2. Id. at 473–474.
3. Id. at 474 n. 44.

4. 451 U.S. 477 (1981).
5. Id. at 484–485.
6. 486 U.S. 675 (1988).

A suspect's request for counsel, however, may be sufficiently limited that continued questioning or a reapproach of him by officers does not violate *Edwards*. In Connecticut v. Barrett,[7] Barrett made clear to officers that he would not give a written statement until his lawyer was present, but that he had "no problem" in talking orally with the officers about the incident. The state courts, relying upon the proposition that requests for counsel are not to be narrowly construed, held that this was a general invocation of the right to counsel and that the officers' further efforts to elicit an oral confession from Barrett violated *Edwards,* Reversing, the Supreme Court construed Barrett's actions as invoking the right to counsel only with regard to interrogation designed to produce a written statement. Thus *Edwards* did not bar further interrogation to elicit an oral statement. When interpretation of a request for counsel is necessary, the Court agreed, courts should construe such requests broadly. But interpretation is necessary only when the suspect's words are ambiguous. Here, Barrett made clear his meaning, and that meaning was respected by the police.

The *Edwards per se* rule prohibits only further questioning and reapproaches initiated by police officers. In *Edwards* itself, the Court explained that an accused who had invoked his right to counsel would be subject to further interrogation if "the accused himself initiates further communication, exchanges, or conversations with police."[8] This was reaffirmed in Oregon v. Bradshaw,[9] in which the Court considered the more difficult question of the sort of accused-initiated activity that will free law enforcement officers from the *Edwards* ban. In the course of a homicide investigation, an officer offered Bradshaw the officer's theory of the events which assumed that Bradshaw drove the car that caused the fatal accident. Bradshaw responded, "I do want an attorney before it goes

much further." Interrogation ceased. Some time later, Bradshaw was being transferred from the stationhouse to a jail. Before or during the trip, he asked an officer, "Well, what is going to happen to me now?" The officer rewarned Bradshaw, who responded that he understood. A "discussion" followed during which the officer suggested that Bradshaw take a polygraph test and Bradshaw agreed. The test was administered a day later and during post-test discussions Bradshaw admitted guilt.

Eight members of the Court agreed that a suspect's initiative removes the *Edwards* bar only if it demonstrates the suspect's desire for further generalized discussion about the investigation. The plurality acknowledged that some inquiries—such as a request for a drink of water or to use a telephone—would not be sufficient, but found that Bradshaw's question—"[a]lthough ambiguious"—was reasonably interpreted by the officer as intended to open up further discussion concerning the investigation. The three dissenters, in contrast, concluded that under the circumstances Bradshaw's question evidenced no more than a desire to find out where the police were taking him, and thus did not meet the standard.

Edwards is triggered by a suspect's invocation of the *Miranda* right to counsel. It does not affect the holding in Michigan v. Mosely [10] that no absolute bar upon reapproaching a suspect is raised by an accused who invokes his right to remain silent without also invoking his right to counsel. In such a situation, the controlling question is the effectiveness of any ultimate waiver by the suspect considering, among other matters, the showing that he invoked his rights and was nevertheless reapproached by officers.[11]

Edwards applies only if the suspect invokes his right to counsel. A difficult problem is presented when a suspect makes a comment that might possibly be construed as invoking the right to counsel. The Supreme Court has

---

7. 479 U.S. 523 (1987).

8. Edwards v. Arizona, 451 U.S. 477, 484–485 (1981).

9. 462 U.S. 1039 (1983).

10. 423 U.S. 96 (1975).

11. See generally § 151 infra.

noted this problem but not addressed it.[12] Lower courts, however, have generally agreed that in such circumstances officers may make further inquiries of the subject, limited, however, to ascertaining whether the suspect desires the assistance of counsel. If the suspect's action is unambiguous on its face, discussion of the matter must cease. If it does not, the prosecution cannot rely upon the discussion to show that despite his earlier indication, the suspect did not in fact wish the assistance of counsel. A similar approach has been applied where a suspect may have invoked his right to silence.

Edwards itself barred further interrogation until counsel was made available to the suspect. But in Minnick v. Mississippi[13] the Court held that *Edwards* also barred officers from reapproaching a suspect after he had been afforded consultation with counsel. The same considerations that demand a suspect be protected from interrogation before he consults with a lawyer apply when such consultation occurs but ends. "[W]hen counsel is requested," the majority summarized, "interrogation must cease, and officials may not reinitiate interrogation without counsel present, whether or not the accused has consulted with his attorney."[14] Consequently, *Miranda* and *Edwards* were violated when an officer responded to a suspect's desire for an attorney by permitting the suspect to speak to the attorney on a telephone, but then after the conversation inquired of the suspect whether he wanted to tell "his side of what happened."

The *Edwards per se* rule constitutes the major post-*Miranda* development reflecting continuing enthusiasm for both further limitations upon law enforcement practices during custodial interrogation and specific prophylactic rules as a vehicle for imposing such limitations. *Bradshaw's* cavalier willingness to find that an accused's initiative rendered the rule inapplicable cast some doubt upon the Court's continued commitment to the *per se* approach, but *Minnick* makes clear that

the *Edwards* rule continues to have a support of the majority.

§ 151. Self–Incrimination   Requirements (d) Voluntariness of Waivers

Self-incrimination requirements applicable to custodial interrogation demand effective waivers of suspects' right to remain silent and, unless lawyers were present, of the right to counsel. Such waivers must be "voluntary" to be effective. What this requires, however, is somewhat unclear. Most of the case law involves application of *Miranda's* Fifth Amendment version of self-incrimination.

The basic question is whether the standards for determining voluntariness are stricter than those imposed by the due process requirements of voluntariness.[1] The fact of custodial interrogation argues for stricter standards than are embodied in due process voluntariness, since suspects' interests are placed at greater risk by custodial interrogation than they are under in those situations to which only the more general due process standard applies. Correspondingly appropriate protection can perhaps best be afforded by imposing stricter requirements for determining the acceptability of suspects' decisions to provide the prosecution with evidence or with access to them for questioning without the protection of counsel.

On the other hand, suspects protected by the privilege against self-incrimination as construed in *Miranda* will have been provided warnings, and they are protected against "interrogation" until they waive their right to counsel. Perhaps these aspects of self-incrimination law provide adequate protection against the increased threat generated by custodial interrogation. Stricter standards for voluntariness, then, may be unnecessary. Moreover, given the difficulty of articulating useful standards in this area, courts may be

---

12. See Smith v. Illinois, 469 U.S. 91, 99–100 (1984) (per curiam).

13. 111 S.Ct. 486 (1990).

14. 111 S.Ct. at 491.

§ 151

1. See § 147 supra.

unable to distinguish meaningfully between two "levels" of voluntariness.

Under *Miranda* law, the Supreme Court has indicated that no such distinction is to be drawn. In Colorado v. Connelly,[2] the Court commented that "[t]here is obviously no reason to require more in the way of a 'voluntariness' inquiry in the *Miranda* waiver context than in the Fourteenth Amendment confession context." No notice was taken of arguments that such reasons exist, no authority was cited, and no discussion was provided.

Specifically, *Connelly* held that a waiver of *Miranda* rights, like a decision to confess under due process voluntariness, need not constitute an exercise of "free will" or "free choice" by the suspect. "Voluntariness" as is required for a *Miranda* waiver is only put into question if the facts show official coercion or overreaching *and*, as a result, the decision was not voluntary in the more ordinary sense of that term.

A showing that the suspect was psychologically impaired, then, does not raise voluntariness issues under *Miranda* waiver unless there was official overreaching. If such overreaching is shown, however, those conditions of the suspect are relevant to determining whether the overreaching had sufficient impact upon the suspect to render his waiver decision involuntary under the *Miranda* standard. The lower courts have been slow to recognize this and many continue to simply inquire whether on the totality of the circumstances—including any mental impairment—a suspect's *Miranda* waivers or his basic decision to confess are "voluntary."

The same approach seems required with regard to other evidence of impairment, as for example intoxication or even emotional distress caused by the circumstances. *Connelly* makes clear that unless official overreaching is first established, such evidence is irrelevant to voluntariness. Nevertheless, many lower courts continue to simply consider such evidence as among the totality of the circumstances determining voluntariness. Substan-

tial discretion in evaluating the circumstances is given to trial courts, and appellate decisions almost always affirm trial judges' decisions.

The prosecution's burden of showing *Miranda* voluntariness is especially heavy if the suspect was reapproached after earlier invoking his right to remain silent. Under Michigan v. Mosley,[3] officers are not completely barred by a *per se* rule from reapproaching a suspect who has invoked the right to remain silent but not the right to counsel. If such a suspect is reapproached and, in response, waives his *Miranda* rights, the admissibility of any resulting statements depends upon the effectiveness of that waiver, which in turn depends upon "whether [the suspect's] 'right to cut off questioning' was scrupulously honored.' " [4] What constitutes sufficient respect for this right is not entirely clear.

Mosley itself indicates that among the factors tending to show that the standard was met are: (1) a showing that the first session was noncoercive; (2) a significant time interval between the invocation of the right to silence and the reapproach; (3) reapproach by a different officer than the one who first inquired as to the suspect's willingness to make a statement; (4) changes in circumstances between the two inquiries; (5) a significant difference in the matters of interest to the officers in the two situations; and (6) supplementation of the warnings administered during the second approach with clear explanations that the suspect was under no obligation to answer questions (or even submit to questioning) and could avoid further questioning by simply indicating again that he wished to remain silent. The more the reapproach appears to be an effort to persuade the suspect to submit to questioning about matters concerning which he had previously indicated a desire to remain silent, the more difficult the prosecution's burden becomes. Conversely, the more the reapproach appears to concern matters not covered by the suspect's first invocation of his right to re-

---

2. 479 U.S. 157 (1986); see generally § 147 supra.
3. 423 U.S. 96 (1975), discussed in § 150 supra.

4. 423 U.S. at 104.

main silent, the easier is the prosecution's task.

Mosley strongly suggests that the "reapproach" must not simply be a resumption of interrogation but rather an inquiry of the suspect whether, despite his earlier invocation of his right, he is "now" willing to submit to questioning without the presence of an attorney. Curiously, the opinion does not distinguish between a simple resumption of interrogation, on the one hand, and an inquiry concerning the suspect's willingness to submit to interrogation, on the other. This distinction is, however, unquestionably implicit in the analysis.

Generally, the prosecution can meet its burden of proving at least a *prima facie* of voluntariness by eliciting from the interrogating officer that the suspect had not been threatened or promised anything, and appeared to freely decide for himself to forego the assistance of counsel and to provide an incriminating statement. If the defense introduces evidence suggesting official overreaching and a significant impact of that overreaching upon the suspect, of course, the prosecution may well have to respond with more detailed and persuasive evidence in order to meet its burden of persuasion.

§ 152. Self–Incrimination Requirements (e) Intelligence of Waivers

The requirement that waivers of self-incrimination rights during custodial interrogation be "intelligent" is separate and distinct from the demand that such waivers be "voluntary." In the *Miranda* context, the Supreme Court has held that a finding of voluntariness does not satisfy the additional need to find that a suspect understood her right to counsel and intelligently and knowingly relinquished it.[1] As best defined, the demand that the waivers be intelligent addresses the information of which the suspect must have actu-

ally been aware for her decision to be effective.

The difficult task has been that of defining the information a suspect must assimilate to make her waivers effective. In the federal constitutional *Miranda* context, the Supreme Court has required relatively little.

The original *Miranda* opinion could be read as assuming that a waiver would be intelligent and hence effective only if the suspect had considerable and accurate information concerning the facts of her situation and the law applicable to it. Whatever the Court had in mind in 1966, however, its subsequent decisions make clear that the Fifth Amendment requirements can be satisfied much more easily. It has emphasized that suspects need not be aware of the full consequences of their decisions. Apparently the Court has distinguished between the "knowing nature" of decisions, on one hand, and their "wisdom," on the other. The Fifth Amendment, as it applies to custodial interrogation, requires only that the decisions be "knowing."

Consequently, a defendant who has previously made an incriminating statement which is in fact inadmissible against her need not understand the inadmissibility of that statement in order to effectively waive her rights and again admit those same facts.[2] The Court has strongly hinted that a defendant who acknowledges participation in a robbery under circumstances that—unknown to her—create felony murder liability for a killing committed by a companion has made intelligent waivers of her rights despite ignorance as to the legal effect of the admissions.[3] A suspect's waiver of the right to counsel is not rendered ineffective by ignorance concerning the subjects about which the officers intended to question her if she waived counsel's help.[4] In Moran v. Burbine,[5] the Court held that a suspect's waiver of counsel was not rendered unintelligent by his unawareness that there was a specific attorney ready and willing to

---

§ 152

1. Edwards v. Arizona, 451 U.S. 477, 482–483 (1981).

2. Oregon v. Elstad, 470 U.S. 298, 316–318 (1985).

3. California v. Beheler, 463 U.S. 1121 (1983) (per curiam).

4. Colorado v. Spring, 479 U.S. 564 (1987).

5. 475 U.S. 412 (1986).

represent him during questioning if he wished representation.

The Supreme Court's post–1985 cases collectively suggest that "intelligence," as used in *Miranda's* waiver criteria, involves only an understanding of the basic abstract Fifth Amendment rights of which a suspect must be informed: that there is a legal right to remain silent during custodial interrogation; that anything said can be used in evidence to convict her of a crime; that she is entitled to consult with a lawyer and to have a lawyer present during custodial interrogation; and that if she decides to speak to law enforcement officers she is entitled to discontinue such discussion at any time she wishes. It is *not* necessary that she be aware of factual or legal matters bearing upon the wisdom of exercising any of those options. To the contrary, the cases suggest that ignorance of any or all of those matters is totally irrelevant to the effectiveness of the waiver.

Under this approach, one sticky problem remains. *Miranda* requires that the suspect be admonished with regard to one specific evidentiary consequence of her choices—"that anything said" can be used against her in court. In light of this requirement, must a suspect understand that an *oral* admission of incriminating facts is admissible evidence against her? Amazingly, the Court has not clearly answered this question. The analysis suggested by the Court's recent cases indicates that since this is part of the admonishment, the suspect must have at least a basic understanding of the admissibility of oral statements to render her decisions effective. But the result is to place arguably awkward emphasis upon one of the numerous considerations that might affect suspects' decisions.

The Court's position that an intelligent waiver of *Miranda* rights requires at most only an abstract understanding of those legal matters covered in the *Miranda* warnings serves several purposes. First, it avoids the difficult task of determining and articulating what broader information would be required. Second, it eliminates what would sometimes

be an impossible task for the prosecution. Officers in some situations would simply be unable to provide a suspect with sufficient information concerning a crime, their investigation of it, or the suspect's legal position to render any waivers effective. They would, then, be barred from productive interrogation of the suspect. A construction of *Miranda* that so limits officers can reasonably be viewed as excessively solicitous of those interests of suspects that the self-incrimination privilege properly protects.

On the other hand, this position arguably renders *Miranda* ineffective in assuring that suspects' confession decisions reflect what in ordinary terms are "meaningful" decisions. In many situations, awareness of the abstract law would for most persons be only a relatively minor consideration in deciding whether to invoke either or both the rights to representation or counsel. Jerry Beheler,[6] for example, was faced with the choice of invoking these rights when police sought his admission to involvement in a robbery. His awareness of his rights to silence and counsel were of little practical importance to him given his blissful ignorance that admitting the robbery also acknowledged liability for the murder committed by his companion. Most people would likely regard his awareness of abstract interrogation law as insufficient to enable him to make an "intelligent" decision regarding whether to invoke his rights under that law.

Assuring that suspects' choices are "meaningful" in such a broad, tactical sense, however, may be beyond the purposes of the *Miranda* requirements. Custodial interrogation may pose such extreme dangers to suspects' privilege primarily or exclusively because of the danger of unacceptable pressures—such as the fear of prolonged secret detention—influencing their volition. Custodial interrogation may not, in the Court's perception, pose similarly severe risks to suspects' access to factual information or their abilities to intellectually assimilate or use it. Since the *Miranda* requirements are imposed for reasons unrelated to suspects' ability to make

6. See text at note 3 supra.

intellectually informed decisions, waiver crite-ria are perhaps appropriately formulated so as to require relatively minimal intellectual understanding of facts useful in making "wise" decisions.

Once the general standard for intelligence is defined, another problem is presented by Colorado v. Connelly,[7] which held that a *Miranda* waiver can be rendered involuntary only by official coercion.[8] Is official coercion also a prerequisite to consideration of the possibility that a *Miranda* waiver is insufficiently intelligent or knowing? The issue was not addressed in *Connelly* itself.

Connelly's general discussion suggests that official misconduct is necessary. If the "vol-untariness" of a waiver is put into issue only by a preliminary showing of official coercion, a similar showing would seem necessary to challenge the "intelligence" of that waiver. Thus *Connelly* apparently means that a trial court need not consider a defendant's claim that because of mental illness or retardation, intoxication or emotional distress she failed to actually understanding the warnings, unless the court first finds that official coercion oc-curred and played a causal role in this failure to develop the required understanding. Many lower courts, however, have not taken such an approach but rather have continued to characterize such impairments as simply factors to consider in determining whether the suspect had the minimal understanding required for an effective waiver. Appellate analyses, however, generally result in uphold-ing trial court determinations that the requi-site understanding had been developed.

§ 153. General Right to Counsel Requirements

Miranda and analogous state self-incrimi-nation decisions recognize a right to counsel based upon the privilege against self-incrimi-nation as it applies during custodial law en-forcement interrogation. General constitu-tional rights to counsel, such as that in the Sixth Amendment, focus upon representation at trial, but they also apply to certain pretrial situations in which suspects may make self-incriminating admissions. Since an exclu-sionary sanction attaches to violations of these rights to counsel,[1] failures to comply with them permit challenges to the admissi-bility of confessions.

Litigation has emphasized the Sixth Amendment right, which was applied to con-fessions in a line of cases beginning with Massiah v. United States[2] in 1964. Under *Massiah* and its progeny, "once formal crimi-nal proceedings begin, the Sixth Amendment renders inadmissible in the prosecution's case-in-chief statements 'deliberately elicited' from a defendant without an express waiver of the right to counsel."[3] State courts have occa-sionally been willing to construe analogous state constitutional rights as somewhat broad-er in content than the federal right. In ei-ther case, the point at which a suspect be-comes entitled to the protection of this right is obviously critical. After it is triggered, this right overlaps with the self-incrimination right to counsel to some extent, but it also applies to some situations not covered by the self-incrimination rule.

Triggering the Sixth Amendment Right to Counsel. *Miranda* applies if a suspect is in "custody" and police engage in "interroga-tion;"[4] the Sixth Amendment applies if ad-versary judicial proceedings against the sus-pect have begun and police attempt to deliber-ately elicit self-incriminating admissions from the suspect. "Deliberate elicitation" of ad-missions probably differs minimally if at all from "interrogation" in situations where the two might be compared.

The Sixth Amendment requirement that adversary judicial proceedings against the suspect have begun does differ significantly from the *Miranda* requirement of custody.

---

7. 479 U.S. 157 (1986), discussed in §§ 147, 151, supra.

8. See generally § 151 supra.

§ 153

1. See § 166, infra.

2. 377 U.S. 201 (1964).

3. Michigan v. Harvey, 494 U.S. 344, 348 (1990).

4. See generally § 149 supra.

Since custody is not required, the Sixth Amendment applies to some situations not covered by *Miranda*. On the other hand, in those situations in which the suspect is seized by police, the Sixth Amendment is usually not triggered until significantly after *Miranda* has been brought into play.

Precisely when adversary judicial proceedings begin is not entirely clear. Detention by the police or even formal arrest is not sufficient. On the other hand, a formal charge—as by the filing of an indictment—is clearly enough. In Michigan v. Jackson,[5] the Court held that an "arraignment"—by which it meant an arrested person's post-arrest appearance before a judicial officer—does trigger the Sixth Amendment right. In most situations, this post-arrest appearance will be the definitive point.

Application of Sixth Amendment to Overt Police Questioning. Brewer v. Williams,[6] decided in 1977, made clear that the Sixth Amendment applies to overt interrogation of a suspect by law enforcement officers *if* that occurs after adversary judicial proceedings have been commenced. Whatever the uncertainties as to what constitutes deliberate elicitation of self-incriminating admissions, any police conduct constituting "interrogation" is certain to also trigger the Sixth Amendment right. The Sixth Amendment right therefore overlaps *Miranda* to some extent. Since it applies to interrogation of a suspect who is not in custody, however, it also covers some overt interrogation not within *Miranda's* scope.

The critical question is how, if at all, a suspect is more protected during interrogation if that interrogation occurs after the Sixth Amendment right is triggered.

A suspect entitled to Sixth Amendment protection is apparently entitled to at least the same admonishments required by *Miranda*. The Sixth Amendment embodies a version of the *Edwards* rule,[7] so a suspect who invokes

his right to counsel cannot be reapproached by officers. This bar to being approached by law enforcement officers is triggered when during a court appearance a defendant requests generally that counsel be appointed.[8] But the Sixth Amendment right to counsel, unlike *Miranda's* right to representation, is "offense-specific," so a suspect who has by requesting counsel invoked his Sixth Amendment version of the *Edwards* rule may be approached by officers concerning other offenses as to which matters have not progressed sufficiently so as to give him a Sixth Amendment right to counsel as to those other offenses.[9]

The Sixth Amendment right does not, generally speaking, protect a suspect from being approached in the absence of counsel by officers seeking to persuade him to provide a self-incriminating statement. In Patterson v. Illinois,[10] the Court refused to bar police from approaching a suspect who was covered by the Sixth Amendment but had not invoked his right to counsel. Like *Miranda's* Fifth Amendment right to counsel, the Court explained, the Sixth Amendment right to counsel does not generally bar police from inquiring whether a suspect would be willing to undergo questioning without the aid of counsel.

Waiver of Sixth Amendment Right. The Sixth Amendment right to counsel during questioning, like the Fifth Amendment right, can be waived. A waiver of the Sixth Amendment right must, of course, be both voluntary and intelligent or knowing. If suspects' interests protected by both the Fifth and Sixth Amendments are placed at greater risk when an investigation progresses to the point of adversary judicial proceedings, the Sixth Amendment might provide appropriately greater protection if it imposes more stringent waiver requirements than apply under *Miranda*.

In *Patterson*, however, the Court explicitly rejected arguments that the Sixth Amend-

---

5.   475 U.S. 625 (1986).

6.   430 U.S. 387 (1977).

7.   See § 150 supra.

8.   Michigan v. Jackson, 475 U.S. 625 (1986).

9.   McNeil v. Wisconsin, 111 S.Ct. 2204 (1991).

10.   487 U.S. 285 (1988).

ment right is "superior" to the Fifth Amendment right and that consequently waiver standards for the former should be more stringent than for the latter. Its cases provide no support, the majority explained, "for the notion that because a Sixth Amendment right may be involved, it is more difficult to waive than the Fifth Amendment counterpart."[11] At least generally, then, the sort of barebones showing that establishes a prima facie case for an effective waiver of *Miranda* rights will also suffice where the Sixth Amendment right is applicable.

The Court added that it did not mean "that all Sixth Amendment challenges to the conduct of postindictment questioning will fail whenever the challenged practice would pass constitutional muster under *Miranda*." In explanation, it noted that Moran v. Burbine[12] had upheld a *Miranda* waiver although the suspect was not told his lawyer was trying to reach him during the questioning. "[I]n the Sixth Amendment context," the Court commented without elaboration, "this waiver would not be valid."[13] The Court also left open the possibility that the Sixth Amendment right requires that officers warn a suspect, or that a suspect actually be aware, of the prosecution's progression to the point of judicial proceedings. Such a requirement, however, seems inconsistent with the Court's general approach in *Patterson*.

Patterson raises significant doubts as to whether there are any meaningful differences between the Sixth Amendment and self-incrimination rights to counsel, as applied to custodial questioning. In *Patterson,* the Court acknowledged that the content of the right to counsel, and of waiver standards in particular, were appropriately related to the function that the lawyer can serve at the stage of proceeding involved. The transition from earlier interrogation to questioning after formal adversary proceedings begin, it continued, "does not substantially increase the value of counsel to the accused at questioning, or

expand the limited purpose that an attorney serves when the accused is questioned by authorities." As a consequence of these perceptions, the Court is likely to construe the Sixth Amendment as imposing more stringent requirements than the Fifth only if the Court is convinced that this is necessary to protect some legitimate function that counsel might serve during custodial interrogation after adversary judicial proceedings begin but not before. *Patterson* suggests the Court is not likely to find such differences in function.

Sixth Amendment Application to Undercover Elicitation. The Sixth Amendment was first applied to law enforcement questioning conducted surreptitiously in the course of an undercover investigation. Most likely, it is in this context that the Sixth Amendment imposes requirements meaningfully different from those imposed by the Fifth Amendment.

In Massiah v. United States,[14] Massiah and one Colson had been arrested and indicted for drug offenses, but had been released on bail. Colson, cooperating with federal law enforcement officers, permitted installation of a radio transmitter in his car. He then caused Massiah, while in the car, to engage in a conversation during which Massiah made self-incriminating admissions. The Court held that Massiah's Sixth Amendment rights had been violated "when there was used against him at his trial evidence of his own incriminating words, which federal agents had deliberately elicited from him after he had been indicated and in the absence of counsel."[15] The Sixth Amendment, then, bars undercover elicitation from a defendant, after adversary judicial proceedings have begun, of self-incriminating admissions "in the absence of [defense] counsel." Although this bar applies when the suspect is in custody, *Massiah* itself makes clear that it also applies when custody is absent.

Precisely what constitutes deliberate elicitation of self-incriminating statements has proven troublesome. The Court adopted this

---

11. 487 U.S. at 297–298.

12. 475 U.S. 412 (1986); see § 152 supra.

13. Id. at 296 n. 9.

14. 377 U.S. 201 (1964).

15. 377 U.S. at 206.

phraseology rather than *Miranda's* "interrogation" standard, it explained in Kuhlmann v. Wilson,[16] to make clear that the Sixth Amendment covered "indirect and surreptitious interrogations." The Court has characterized deliberate elicitation as the functional equivalent of interrogation, as applied to the situation in which the defendant does not recognize that he is the subject of such efforts.

In United States v. Henry,[17] the informer had not "questioned" Henry while the two were imprisoned together, but had stimulated conversation in an effort to have Henry make incriminating statements. This was held sufficient to constitute the necessary deliberate elicitation. On the other hand, in *Wilson* the undercover officer was instructed only to listen to Wilson in an effort to learn from him the identities of his cofelons. After Wilson had volunteered to the officer the same exculpatory version he had given to the police, the officer commented that this "didn't sound too good." The evidence of this one comment, the Supreme Court held, did not permit the federal courts to override the state court's otherwise supported conclusion that the informant did not take any action, besides listening, to deliberately elicit incriminating remarks.

State Constitutional Rights to Counsel. State courts seeking to impose greater limits upon law enforcement questioning though their state constitutions have tended to rely upon explicit constitutional rights to counsel rather than rights derived from constitutional self-incrimination privileges. This has been the case even if so applying the state rights requires construing them as applicable earlier in the criminal process than the analogous Sixth Amendment right.

State courts' willingness to so apply state constitutional rights has been most common where officers have either or both interfered with counsel's access to a suspect undergoing interrogation or have failed to inform such a suspect of counsel's ready availability. Under Moran v. Burbine, this violates none of *Miranda's* self-incrimination requirements. But

state courts have called state provisions into play to assure such suspects of relief. The Delaware Supreme Court, for example, held that police failure to inform a suspect in custody of counsel's reasonable, diligent and timely efforts to render legal services precluded a knowing waiver of the right to counsel as guaranteed by Article I, section 7 of the Delaware Constitution.

On the other hand, state courts have been less responsive to arguments that they should reject the Sixth Amendment approach taken in *Patterson* and—as a general matter—require more for an effective waiver of this right than is required for a *Miranda* waiver. The Pennsylvania Supreme Court, for example, refused to read the state provision as requiring that officers explain to a suspect the perils of self-representation and perhaps even explain to the suspect the advantages of representation by counsel. The New York court, however, has vigorously developed that state's right to counsel and held—among other things—that under certain circumstances a suspect's right to counsel during questioning is "indelible," meaning that it can only be effectively waived in the presence of counsel.

§ 154. Promises Made to Suspects

From its first articulation by Lord Mansfield, the common law requirement of voluntariness specifically emphasized "promises" as among the influences that might render confessions inadmissible. Modern voluntariness standards, self-incrimination demands, and right to counsel requirements have incorporated at least some of this early "promise law."

During the vigorous application of the voluntariness requirement in the early 1800s, what today would be regarded by most courts as quite innocuous references to possible benefits were regarded as *per se* tainting subsequent confessions. Bram v. United States[1] arguably incorporated such an approach into

---

16. 477 U.S. 436 (1986).
17. 447 U.S. 264 (1980).

1. 168 U.S. 532 (1897).

due process voluntariness. In *Bram,* an officer told the accused, "If you had an accomplice, you should say so, and not have the blame of this horrible crime on your own shoulders." This statement, the Court concluded, might have been understood by Bram as holding out the encouragement that by disclosing his accomplice (and thereby acknowledging his own guilt) he might obtain mitigation of his punishment. Consequently, the promise was among the grounds on which the subsequent confession was found inadmissible.

In Brady v. United States[2] the Court explained and apparently reaffirmed *Bram:*

> [Regarding] a confession given by a defendant in custody, alone and unrepresented by counsel[,] * * * even a mild promise of leniency was deemed sufficient to bar the confession * * * because defendants at such times are too sensitive to inducement and the possible impact on them is too great to ignore and too difficult to assess.[3]

This rationale explains the discrepancy between the rule that promises of leniency render confessions involuntary and the rule that a guilty plea is voluntary despite the inducement of a promise of reduced punishment. Defendants entering guilty pleas are represented by counsel and have adequate opportunity to assess the wisdom of accepting a promise of leniency; such defendants are not so "sensitive to inducement" as to justify the rigorous protection of the confession rule.

But in Arizona v. Fulminante[4] the Court indicated that the *Bram* language suggesting a rigid rule that promises render a confession involuntary does not state the current standard for determining the federal constitutional voluntariness of a confession. Instead, the Court approved the approach previously taken by a number of lower tribunals under which, despite *Bram,* the federal constitution requires no more than that courts consider promises as part of the totality of the circumstances when they determine the voluntariness of defendants' confessions.

Lower courts have taken a variety of positions regarding the effect of promises on the admissibility of confessions, often leaving unclear whether they perceive differences between the requirements imposed by the forum's rules of evidence or its constitution or between self-incrimination standards or general right to counsel demands.

There is general agreement that a promise of complete immunity from prosecution or its equivalent in return for a confession will render a resulting confession involuntary. This may also mean that a promise not to pursue charges for the most serious offenses committed by admitted actions has the same effect. Furthermore, a promise that a confession would be kept confidential has been held to similarly render a confession inadmissible.

Regarding other promises, some courts articulate a rigid criterion similar to the widely applied nineteenth century standard that any promise tending to induce a confession would render a confession involuntary, and a few may actually enforce such a standard. The Arkansas court, in contrast, has indicated that only a "false" promise will render a confession inadmissible. The Texas court—reverting to a functional version of the early English approach—holds that a promise will render a confession involuntary only if the promise was "of such character as would be likely to influence the defendant to speak untruthfully," an approach embodied explicitly in several state statutes.

Representation of "Advantages" and Promises to "Help". Courts have experienced particular difficulty developing a satisfactory approach for the recent cases in which law enforcement officers suggested to suspects the certainty, likelihood, or possibility that cooperation by promptly confessing would be to the suspect's advantage during the later processing of his case. In many cases, the officers express a willingness to communicate the fact of the suspect's cooperation to the prosecutor, judge or both. Sometimes this is supplemented by the officer's offer to endorse the

2. 397 U.S. 742 (1970).
3. 397 U.S. at 754.
4. 111 S.Ct. 1246 (1991).

suspect's plea for leniency or to otherwise, in unspecified ways, "help" the suspect. Generally, however, the officer also formally disclaims any authority to make a binding commitment or to otherwise "promise" or guarantee the advantages under discussion.

Some courts give lip service to the proposition that a "promise" will automatically render a confession inadmissible but hold that officers' formal disclaimers make most such representations only "exhortations to tell the truth" which invoke no exclusionary penalty. Others emphasize the specificity of the advantages which the discussion suggests to the suspect might flow from confessing. A fatal "promise," under this approach, occurs only if the discussion entailed considerable specificity on the part of the officer.

Many courts, however, eschew the task of parsing the precise terminology of officers' representations and simply regard evidence of such representations as invoking a totality of the circumstances analysis, in which the ultimate question is whether the suspect's will was overborne. A trial judge's resolution of this question will be given substantial deference on appeal.

The totality of the circumstances approach, however, provides no assurance of consistency in outcome and permits courts to avoid the real underlying issue: should suspects and law enforcement officers be permitted, at early stages of the processing of a case, to engage in negotiations pursuant to which a defendant agrees not to contest her guilt and to provide incriminating evidence in return for uncertain advantages in the later processing of the case? Traditional promise analysis assumed that suspects at this initial stage were so susceptible to overreaching that such negotiations should be discouraged; the traditional prohibition against almost all promises consequently sought to discourage negotiations of this sort. Most such negotiations now occur in circumstances in which suspects have at least the Fifth Amendment *right* to representation by counsel. Does this theoretical right to counsel, and the realities of plea bargaining, require rejection of the traditional perception that the law should prohibit, or at

least discourage, settlement negotiation at these early stages?

The Second Circuit recently confronted the issue directly. Eschewing any artificial reliance upon the qualifications often attached to officers' representations, the court explicitly affirmed the propriety of such bargaining. The officers had qualified their approach to the defendant by telling him that their offer of leniency would be withdrawn if he consulted a lawyer. This, the court continued, did not render the resulting confession less voluntary, apparently because the officers' legitimate concern regarding the secrecy of their investigation justified conditioning the offer on the noninvolvement of others such as attorneys.

If suspects are troublesomely susceptible to overreaching at the investigatory stages of a criminal case, there is serious question whether the theoretical availability of representation by counsel is as a practical matter sufficient to combat that susceptibility. Any such argument that it is sufficient, however, becomes completely implausible if officers are permitted to burden that right by conditioning their offer upon the suspect's willingness to forego consultation with counsel. The Second Circuit's analysis greatly oversimplifies the problem.

In contrast, the Pennsylvania Supreme Court reacted differently when a suspect, being admonished under *Miranda,* mused that, "Maybe I should talk to a lawyer," and inquired of the officer, "What good would it do me to tell you?" The officer responded that he would tell the prosecutor that the defendant cooperated, but he "had no idea" whether that would help the defendant's case or not. Finding an "impermissible inducement" in this, the court stressed that the *Miranda* warnings must "proceed freely." "Misleading statements and promises by the police," it continued, "choke off the legal process at the very moment which *Miranda* was designed to protect." If offers of assistance or leniency by police are to be countenanced, perhaps it is necessary to insure that suspects retain without penalty the opportunity to consult with counsel during the negotiations.

Requirement of Person in Authority. *Hopt's* statement of the traditional rule required that the inducement or promise be one "held out by one in authority." The Supreme Court has never determined whether this requirement is part of the due process voluntariness standard or other federal constitutional requirements. It is, however, widely accepted, although there are some questions as to what constitutes a person "in authority."

Under this approach, a law enforcement officer is a person in authority, but there is probably no absolute requirement that the promisor be an officer or other public official. It is widely but not universally accepted that the complaining witness or victim of the offense is a person in a position of sufficient authority, apparently on the ground that such persons have practical control, although not formal power, over whether criminal charges are brought and pursued. Several cases have held that defense lawyers are not persons in authority under this rule.

Impact of Promises Upon Suspect. The traditional rule rendered confessions inadmissible *per se* upon proof that certain promises were made, with little inquiry into the effect of those promises upon the specific suspect's decision to confess. As the Supreme Court explained in *Brady,* this was in part because of the difficulty of assessing the impact of such promises. Judicial rejection of *per se* analysis in favor of a totality of the circumstances analysis increases the need to assess the impact, if any, of such promises or representations upon particular decisions by particular defendants during the interrogation process.

Recent cases consequently emphasize the presence or absence of evidence of such an impact. This evidence may consist of the defendant's conduct at the time of her confession or her testimony at the hearing on the motion to suppress the confession. Despite the prosecution's burden of proving the volun-tariness of challenged confession distinction,[5] some cases indicate that a defendant relying upon a promise is required to come forward with evidence that any such promise "caused" his decision to confess.

Promises Solicited by Suspect. A number of discussions of promises have, in the course of upholding the admissibility of confessions challenged on promise grounds, emphasized evidence that the defendant first raised the possibility of the benefit which the authorities later promised. Some decisions even suggest that a showing of this sort totally precludes the defendant from later relying on the solicited promise.

Why the suspect's initial role should have such impact is not clear. *Drew v. State*[6] suggests that such evidence tends to show that the defendant had a propensity and willingness to make an incriminating statement before the promise and thus that the statement was freely made and not induced by the promise. This is difficult to evaluate, given the uncertainty as to the role that a promise must play in the defendant's decisionmaking. But on a general level, it is clear that a showing that the suspect initiated bargaining simply does not exclude the possibility that she was nevertheless overwhelmed during the resulting bargaining. Perhaps such evidence tends to show that at the time she initiated such discussion, the defendant was not overwhelmed which, in turn, suggests that she *may* have retained that autonomy later during the negotiations. Or, perhaps there is an estoppel-like consideration operating here, denying defendants the right to both initiate negotiations and also rely on those negotiations to challenge a confession.

Promises of "Collateral" Benefits. *Hopt's* statement of the traditional promise rule described prohibited promises as those "touching the charge preferred." Promises of benefits not "touching the charge preferred," and thus "collateral," have sometimes been held not to invoke the promise rule at all, or to require suppression of the confession only if

---

5. See § 162 infra.

6. 503 N.E.2d 613 (Ind.1987).

the promise was such as to render the confession untrustworthy.

There is a growing tendency to regard such promises as implicating no *per se* rule—if such a rule is retained for promises touching the charge preferred—and simply as constituting evidence bearing upon whether the defendant's will was overborne. If, as is increasingly the case, most or all promises are given that same effect, "in general such promises [of only "collateral" benefits] are less coercive to the accused than promises directly relating to the criminal proceedings at hand." Some courts, on the other hand, apparently regard the collateral nature of the promised benefit unworthy of consideration or even comment.

Fulminante's reading of the federal due process standard as imposing no special rule regarding the effect of promises will require considerable rethinking of the law in this area. First, consideration must be given to whether the same approach will be taken when the issue is the effectiveness of suspects' waivers of *Miranda* and Sixth Amendment rights. Most likely promises will be held entitled to no more weight on these questions than they are to be given in applying due process voluntariness. Second, *Fulminante* will require that many state courts reconsider their approaches to promise attacks upon the admissibility of confessions. If those tribunals are to continue to somewhat rigidly regard confessions as involuntary because they were made in response to promises, these holdings will have to be based upon state law grounds.

§ 155. Deception of Suspects

Among the most difficult issues raised by confession law is the appropriate effect to be given to evidence that law enforcement officers affirmatively and intentionally deceived the defendant concerning some matter potentially significant to the defendant in making his confession decisions. If such evidence con-

vincingly demonstrates that the defendant lacked some information necessary to make his confession admissible under the applicable legal standard, of course, the evidence necessarily demonstrates that this legal standard was not met. Uncertainty concerning the precise contents of some of the legal standards, however, sometimes creates difficulty applying this principle. Moreover, the legal standards apparently require quite little in terms of a defendant's awareness, and this approach therefore gives little significance to proof of deception.[1] Courts seem open to arguments that deception should have some significance beyond simply "disproving" that the defendant had the awareness required. No consensus has developed, however, on what that significance should be.

The relevance and significance of deception might vary depending upon whether the issue presented is the voluntariness of the confession in the general due process or evidence law sense, the effectiveness of a defendant's waivers of his self-incrimination rights, the effectiveness of a defendant's waiver of his general right to counsel, or whether the deception violated minimal standards of official conduct implicit in the requirement of due process.

Voluntariness. Uncertainty as to whether voluntariness requires awareness of any particular matters at all[2] creates some difficulty in simply regarding evidence of deception as bearing on whether the suspect had the awareness required by the legal standard. Common law voluntariness appears, from the minimal case law available, to have regarded proof of deception as largely if not entirely irrelevant to admissibility.

The Supreme Court addressed the issue under Fourteenth Amendment due process voluntariness in Frazier v. Cupp,[3] decided in 1969. During interrogation concerning a homicide, Frazier informed officers that at the time of the offense he had been with his

---

§ 155

1. See generally § 152 supra, considering the "intelligence" required for *Miranda* waivers.

2. See § 147 supra.

3. 394 U.S. 731 (1969).

cousin Rawls. The officers then falsely told Frazier that Rawls had been taken into custody and had confessed. Frazier subsequently made a confession later used against him in a state criminal prosecution over his claim that the officers' deception rendered it involuntary. Rejecting this argument almost offhandedly, the Supreme Court—offering no authority or discussion of rationale—simply stated, "[T]he fact that the police misrepresented the statements that Rawls had made is, while relevant, insufficient in our view to make this otherwise voluntary confession inadmissible."

Lower courts usually follow this approach, and characterize evidence of deception as relevant to, but not determinative of, the voluntariness of confessions. Some qualify it with caveats that deception may render a confession involuntary if the deception is of a sort likely to stimulate an unreliable confession or extremely offensive to due process or "fairness." Some have heavily emphasized a need for deception to create a risk of inaccuracy, although it is arguable that this emphasis is contrary to the Supreme Court's insistence that voluntariness be determined without regard to the accuracy of particular confessions. Deception is virtually never found to give rise to risks of inaccuracy or to offend notions of "fairness," so as a practical matter evidence of deception is considered—to the extent that it is considered at all—as one of the totality of the circumstances to be considered in determining whether the defendant's will was overborne.

Self-Incrimination (Miranda) Waivers. If a confession is in response to custodial interrogation, and the privilege against self-incrimination therefore applies, the more specific and perhaps more stringent standards may give deception greater significance. Language in Miranda v. Arizona,[4] in fact, suggests that deception is necessarily and automatically controlling on the effectiveness of a suspect's purported waiver of his right to counsel or his right to withhold a self-incrimi-

nating admission. In *Miranda,* the Court—with no substantive discussion or citation of authority—commented, "[A]ny evidence that the accused was * * * tricked * * * into a waiver will, of course, show that the defendant did not voluntarily waive his privilege."[5]

Although *Frazier* was decided after *Miranda,* the Court in *Frazier* amazingly made no mention of the obvious tension between the implications of the *Miranda* dictum and the analysis used in *Frazier.* In several subsequent cases presenting *Miranda* issues, the Court has failed to respond to or reach defendants' claims that their *Miranda* waivers were rendered ineffective by police deception.

If, as seems likely, the requirement that self-incrimination waivers be "intelligent" requires only that defendants understand the abstract propositions of law as to which they must be admonished,[6] deception will almost never tend to show that a waiver was ineffective for being insufficiently intelligent. Deception used during interrogation seldom suggests to suspects that they do not have a formal legal right to withhold self-incriminating admissions or that any self-incriminating admission made will be not be usable against them. Since intelligence does not involve the tactical wisdom of making an incriminating admission, deception about matters bearing upon the wisdom of a waiver is simply irrelevant to the intelligence of the waiver.

On the facts of *Frazier,* for example, the officer's misrepresentation that Frazier's co-felon had confessed bore only on the wisdom of Frazier providing police with a self-incriminating statement nevertheless more favorable to his position than the one he thought his co-felon had provided. While as a result of the police deception Frazier was seriously mistaken as to the strength of the prosecution's evidence implicating him, this would not tend to show that Frazier's decision to forego assistance of counsel and to confess was unintelligent under *Miranda.*

4. 384 U.S. 436 (1966).
5. 384 U.S. at 476.

6. See § 152 supra.

In Colorado v. Spring,[7] however, the Supreme Court recognized and left open the possibility that affirmative misrepresentations by officers might have significance for the effectiveness of a *Miranda* waiver beyond its logical relevance to the intelligence of that waiver.

Despite the tension between the *Miranda* language and the analysis of *Frazier,* lower courts have tended—usually with little concern—to assume that *Frazier* provides the appropriate model for determining the effect of deception on the effectiveness of a self-incrimination waiver. A more critical panel of the Third Circuit, however, noted "a paucity of case law to guide us in the area of deception in the *Miranda* waiver context," and Judge Weinstein of the Eastern District of New York has characterized *Frazier* as of "diminished significance" in light of its failure to consider the effect of *Miranda.* But there seems to be widespread agreement that the *Miranda* suggestion that deception—apparently *any* deception—will render waivers invalid was not carefully considered and thus is not now literally authoritative.

Judicial analyses of deception have failed to identify why deception of suspects might be offensive to interests protected by the various legal rules limiting admissibility of confessions. The limited requirements for knowing and intelligent confession decisions suggest that no interests protected by confession law doctrines are offended by deception which does not deprive a suspect of knowledge necessary to render his decisions intelligent. If confession law is not concerned with suspects' ability to make "wise" or tactically sound decisions, deception affecting only that ability is perhaps properly regarded as irrelevant to the admissibility of confessions.

On the other hand, the limited requirements for intelligent decisions may not rest upon a fundamental determination that suspects' interests in making wise decisions is beyond the legitimate concern of confession law. Rather, these requirements may instead be based upon what courts perceive to be the difficulty or impossibility of assuring wise decisions by developing the legal standards for effective confession decisions. Despite these limited requirements, then, implementing suspects' ability to make wise choices may remain among the general objectives of voluntariness, *Miranda* law, and the general rights to counsel.

Under this approach, some or all official deception affecting suspects' tactical decisions to confess might reasonably be prohibited even if the law does not otherwise seek to protect suspects' ability to make such decisions. Isolating such deception can be justified by the comparative ease with which it can be identified and prohibited combined with the particularly severe threat that it poses to suspects' ability to make meaningful decisions as to whether to invoke their confession rights.

General Constitutional Right to Counsel. If interrogation occurs under circumstances implicating general constitutional rights to counsel, such as that conferred by the Sixth Amendment,[8] do misrepresentations have greater significance than they would if "only" self-incrimination rights applied? Unless—as seems unlikely [9]—these rights to counsel require more for an intelligent waiver than the self-incrimination rights, no greater significance exists if misrepresentations are related to waivers only by virtue of their logical relationship to intelligence.

The Supreme Court's Sixth Amendment case law, however, provides some basis for believing that the Court remains open to the possibility that misrepresentations may have more significance than that and perhaps even more than they are given under federal self-incrimination law. In Patterson v. Illinois,[10] the Court indicated that Sixth Amendment waivers, although not Fifth Amendment ones, would be rendered invalid by officers' failure to inform suspects undergoing interrogation that lawyers already representing them were

---

7. 479 U.S. 564 (1987).

8. See generally § 153 supra.

9. See § 153 supra.

10. 487 U.S. 285 (1988).

trying to reach them. If Sixth Amendment waivers are more susceptible to challenge on such omission grounds than are Fifth Amendment waivers, it seems almost necessarily to follow that they are also more susceptible to challenge on grounds of affirmative misrepresentation.

Patterson, then, suggests at least the possibility of limited *per se* rules, rendering confessions inadmissible where they are given during interrogation which included deception of the suspect of a particularly offensive sort. Such rules are likely to be few in number, however, and limited to deception that endangers values of particular significance to the Sixth Amendment right to counsel, such as represented suspects' interests in having reasonable access to their lawyers.

"Due Process" Violation. Especially if none of the major doctrines generally applicable to law enforcement interrogation practices embodies significant limits upon police deception, the general Fourteenth Amendment due process prohibition against conduct that "shocks the conscience," as developed in Rochin v. California,[11] may render inadmissible confessions obtained by outrageously offensive deception. In Moran v. Burbine,[12] the Court recognized this possibility. But neither *Rochin* nor *Burbine* provides any hint of what sort of deception under what sort of circumstances would present a viable case for a due process violation. Neither decision even suggests the considerations that might render deception so violative of the "traditions and conscience of our people" as to implicate the due process provision.

Application of Totality of the Circumstances Approach. In most situations, regardless of the legal basis for the challenge, courts purport to consider deception as a factor in considering whether, on the totality of the circumstances, a suspect was deprived of an effective choice in deciding whether to forego counsel or to confess. But the reported cases provide no guidance as to what sort of impact upon the suspect must be shown before the suspect's choices are ineffective and little

more guidance as to how deception is to be related to other evidence logically relevant to the voluntariness inquiry. Moreover, despite judicial discussions put in terms of totality of the circumstances, the courts have made little progress in articulating an analysis that meaningfully integrates consideration of deception and other factors universally recognized as relevant to voluntariness. Where the facts suggest that the suspect was impaired or that the officers engaged in aggressive interrogation practices, for example, the courts make little effort to inquire whether these additional considerations combine with evidence of deception to somehow deprive a suspect of the required opportunity for meaningful choice. As a practical matter, this results in deception seldom or never affecting the validity of confession decisions, except perhaps where it convinced the suspect that the conduct he was admitting had not been criminal.

Despite the rhetoric in at least some appellate opinions, most case law leaves the effect to be given evidence of deception entirely within the discretion of trial judges and tacitly approves of trial judges virtually ignoring such evidence in resolving challenges to the admissibility of confessions. This almost certainly reflects the courts' inability to address definitively the nature and seriousness of any offensiveness arising from such deception and consequently the rigor with which the law—either on a constitutional or nonconstitutional level—should seek to discourage it.

§ 156. Delay in Presenting Arrested Person Before Magistrate

Statutes and court rules in virtually every state as well as Rule 5(a) of the Federal Rules of Criminal Procedure require that arrested persons be brought with some dispatch before judicial officers for what, under the Federal Rules, is called the "initial appearance." Controversy continues as to the appropriate effect of violation of the applicable require-

11. 342 U.S. 165 (1952), discussed in § 166 infra.

12. 475 U.S. 412 (1986).

ment on the admissibility of a confession obtained during the delay. The Supreme Court's development of the so-called *McNabb–Mallory* Rule and Congress's modification of it have served as a basis for analysis.

The Supreme Court has never suggested that the *McNabb–Mallory* Rule or any similar prophylactic rule is required by the federal Constitution. Rather, the Court has assumed that delay is merely a factor in constitutional analysis of the voluntariness of a confession and presumably the effectiveness of waivers of Fifth and Sixth Amendment rights.

McNabb–Mallory Rule. In McNabb v. United States,[1] the Supreme Court held that statements elicited from a defendant during a period in which federal officers had failed to comply with the statutory directive for prompt presentation of arrested persons before magistrates were inadmissible at the defendant's subsequent federal criminal trial. This holding, the Court made clear, was not of constitutional dimensions but rather was an exercise of the Court's supervisory power. The substance of the statute enforced in *McNabb* was subsequently incorporated into the Federal Rules of Criminal Procedure and the Court soon applied an identical exclusionary sanction to statements obtained in violation of Rule 5(a)'s requirement of presentation before a magistrate without "unnecessary delay."

The impact of this exclusionary requirement was increased by the Court's construction of the substance of the Rule 5(a) requirement. In Mallory v. United States,[2] the Court held that if officers delayed presenting a defendant before a magistrate in order to interrogate him, the delay was "unnecessary" within the meaning of Rule 5(a). Thus the so-called *McNabb–Mallory* Rule was in part a substantive rule—any delay in presentation for purposes of interrogation was improper under purposes of Rule 5(a)—and in part a remedial rule—a confession obtained during delay that had become unnecessary for Rule 5(a) purposes was for that reason automatical-

ly inadmissible. Whether the Court in fact possessed a supervisory power sufficient to support its development of an exclusionary sanction of this sort has been questioned.

Congressional Rejection of McNabb–Mallory. In 1968, Congress effectively nullified the *McNabb–Mallory* Rule by enacting what was codified as Section 3501 of Title 18 of the United States Code. Section 3501(c) provides that in a federal criminal prosecution, a voluntary confession made by an arrested person within six hours of arrest or detention "shall not be inadmissible solely because of delay in bringing such person before a magistrate * * *." Under Section 3501(a), a confession "shall be admissible [in a federal prosecution] if it is voluntarily given." Section 3501(b) specifies that among the factors to be considered in determining voluntariness is "the time elapsing between arrest and arraignment of the defendant * * *."

Under § 3501, a confession made within six hours of arrest will be excluded in a federal prosecution only upon a determination that it is involuntary. There is less certainty whether a confession given during custody that lasts longer than six hours without presentation before a magistrate can be excluded on the basis of the delay alone. In United States v. Halbert,[3] the Ninth Circuit held that under the statute exclusion is permitted only if the confession is found—on the basis of the delay and all other relevant considerations—to have been involuntarily given. But the more reasonable reading of the statute permits exclusion for delay alone if that delay is longer than six hours. Perhaps a finding of unreasonable delay in this situation merely permits the district court discretion to exclude the confession, although if so neither the statute nor the case law provides criteria for the exercise of that discretion.

State Requirements. There is wide variation among the approaches taken by the states, although the majority regard delay as merely a factor to consider in determining the

1. 318 U.S. 332 (1943).

2. 354 U.S. 449 (1957).

3. 436 F.2d 1226 (9th Cir. 1970).

voluntariness of decisions made during the delay. Some judicial discussions, however, suggest that the delay—and perhaps the intention with which it was caused—are particularly important in making the voluntariness decision.

Some state courts have adopted state versions of *McNabb–Mallory,* requiring suppression of confessions obtained during delay that has become improper because of failure to present the accused before a judicial officer. Others have embraced modified formulations of that rule. Pennsylvania required that the defendant show, in addition to improper delay, prejudice in the sense that the challenged confession must have been reasonably related to the delay. This approach was adopted by the Arkansas court, which expressed concern that the rule, as specifically formulated by the Pennsylvania courts, was little more than a voluntariness test. To remedy this defect, the Arkansas court held that a defendant need only show that "it reasonably appears that the delay contributed to obtaining the confession." This is similar to the approach of the Rhode Island court, which holds that delay will render a confession inadmissible if that delay was operative in inducing the confession.

The Wisconsin court, influenced by what it perceived to be due process considerations, first held that a confession obtained during improper delay must be excluded, but later qualified that by requiring that the officers have used the detention to obtain the challenged statement. Maximum flexibility is provided by the approach of the Kansas court, which has held that trial courts have broad discretion to fashion and apply remedies for violation of the right of prompt presentation, including exclusion.

A number of state legislatures have followed Congress' lead and—often negating case law—have provided by statute that delay in presenting a defendant does not by itself render inadmissible those confessions obtained during improper delay. Furthermore, whatever state judicial enthusiasm for the

McNabb–Mallory approach previously existed may be waning; the Michigan Supreme Court, which adopted an exclusionary requirement in 1960, comprehensively reviewed the issue in 1988 and rejected this approach in favor of the prevailing view under which delay is merely a factor considered in assessing voluntariness of the confession.

Exclusionary Sanction Analysis. As best framed, the basic issue is one of exclusionary sanction analysis:[4] Should an exclusionary sanction be attached to existing legal requirements that arrested suspects be promptly presented before judicial officers? Where legislatures have mandated prompt presentation but not the exclusion of evidence obtained as a result of a violation of this requirement, there is substantial question whether state courts have the legitimate power to develop and apply an exclusionary rule. To the extent that the requirement of prompt presentation is imposed by case law or judicially-promulgated rule rather than legislation, of course, the judicial source of the requirement strengthens the argument that the courts have power to develop an exclusionary remedy.

On the merits, the matter should probably turn upon the importance attributed to the prompt presentation requirement, the extent to which it is likely to be respected in the absence of an exclusionary sanction, and—finally—whether the increased compliance with the requirement likely to be stimulated by an exclusionary rule is worth the loss of reliance evidence that will result.

Prompt presentation requirements, of course, serve some purposes related to the purposes of confession law. Production of an arrested suspect before a magistrate reduces the risks of law enforcement abuse of custodial interrogation and of suspects making unacceptable decisions to incriminate themselves. This can be accomplished in part by implementing pretrial release, which frees suspects from the risks of custodial interrogation. But when the suspect is not released, presentation provides an opportunity for warnings by a

---

4. See generally Chapter 15 infra, and especially §§ 169–172 infra.

presumably impartial person who, unlike law enforcement officers, supposedly has no vested interest in the suspect waiving the rights about which he is informed. Such warnings might be more effective than those administered by police themselves. Moreover, presentation may serve to emphasize to a suspect who remains in custody that his fate depends not simply upon the whim of law enforcement officers but upon the legal process which has now been begun. This may serve to effectively combat the inherent effects of custodial interrogation with which *Miranda* was concerned.

Perhaps prompt presentation so directly serves important confession-law purposes that it, like the *Miranda* requirements, is appropriately enforced by a prophylactic exclusionary rule. Such a remedy requires exclusion of a confession that follows a violation without inquiry into whether, in the case, violation of the requirement affected the suspect's decisions to waive counsel and make a statement. On the other hand, the existence of the *Miranda* rights might weigh against such an approach. The Michigan Supreme Court recently concluded that the development of other rights for suspects undergoing custodial interrogation has greatly reduced the importance of prompt presentation, which suggests that enforcement of prompt presentation by such costly means is inappropriate.

Confession law's difficulty in reaching a satisfactory approach to this issue is closely tied to the law's failure to confront whether, for how long, and under what conditions law enforcement officers should have access to an arrested suspect for purposes of interrogation. Because presentation often involves pretrial release of the suspect, it sometimes constitutes the law's formal denial of law enforcement access to the suspect. Courts, however, quite reasonably recognize that prompt presentation requirements do not reflect a carefully considered decision that law enforcement officers should be permitted to question suspects only insofar as mechanical delays in presenting such suspects incidentally create

opportunities to do so. Unfortunately, neither prompt presentation requirements themselves nor the case law under them adequately address the extent to which presentation may be delayed for purposes of questioning or the circumstances under which such delay is acceptable. Prompt presentation requirements artificially ignore the generally-accepted but largely unarticulated assumption that law enforcement officers should have some opportunity to persuade arrested suspects to cooperate with investigations and provide inculpatory statements. Since the prompt presentation requirements themselves artificially fail to accommodate custodial interrogation, courts are understandably unwilling to exclude reliable confessions simply on the basis that officers violated those requirements.

No fully satisfactory approach to the exclusionary issue can be developed until criminal procedure defines appropriate law enforcement access to suspects for interrogation purposes and then formulates the prompt presentation requirement to permit such access and to bar further access to those suspects unable to secure pretrial release.

§ 157. Confessions as "Fruit" of Improper Arrests or Detentions

If a defendant shows that he was improperly arrested or detained prior to making a confession later offered by the prosecution, the confession may be the excludable "fruit" of that arrest or detention. Such cases, however, often present especially difficult to resolve claims by the prosecution that, under generally-applicable "attenuation of taint" law,[1] the taint flowing from the improper arrest was attenuated and consequently the confession is admissible. Compliance with self-incriminations requirements and the voluntariness of the confession are often relevant to the admissibility of a confession challenged as the fruit of an improper detention, but those considerations are not necessarily controlling.

§ 157

1. See generally § 179 infra.

The leading cases are United States Supreme Court decisions addressing claims that confessions are inadmissible as the "fruit" of an arrest made in violation of the Fourth Amendment to the United States Constitution. Claims that confessions are inadmissible as the tainted results of arrests made in violation of other legal requirements are generally resolved under the analysis developed in this case law, although of course this need not be the case.

In Wong Sun v. United States,[2] the Supreme Court held that oral or written self-incriminating admissions by a suspect could be the tainted "fruit" of a detention in violation of the suspect's Fourth Amendment rights and therefore subject to suppression on that ground. A challenge can also rest upon a claim that a confession is tainted by an improper stationhouse detention for interrogation based on less than probable cause or an unreasonable field detention.

Wong Sun also made clear, however, and numerous subsequent Supreme Court cases have confirmed, that these claims are subject to generally-applicable Fourth Amendment exclusionary rule "fruit of the poisonous tree" analysis, under which evidence which would not have been obtained "but for" the Fourth Amendment violation is nevertheless admissible if the circumstances show that the "taint" of the Fourth Amendment violation was nevertheless attenuated. When the challenged evidence consists of a confession, Fourth Amendment attenuation of taint analysis apparently requires that the prosecution convince the judge that, despite the unlawful arrest and that "but for" the arrest the defendant would not have confessed, the defendant's decision to confess was nevertheless so minimally influenced by that arrest as to make the decision "sufficiently an act of free will to purge the primary taint" of the arrest. As applied to confessions obtained after unlawful arrest, this attenuation analysis has special characteristics worth noting.

In Brown v. Illinois,[3] the Court rejected all proffered *per se* rules. Consequently, although the confession must be voluntary within the meaning of the Due Process requirement and *Miranda's* Fifth Amendment demands must be met, neither showing automatically or necessarily establishes attenuation of taint. Compliance with *Miranda* is no more than "an important factor" suggesting attenuation of taint. Several other factors are also important.

One important factor is the time between the unreasonable arrest and the making of the confession. Generally, the longer that time, the more likely the taint is to have become attenuated. But obviously at some point, prolonged delay during which the defendant is detained becomes a factor tending to overbear the defendant's will and—since it is itself attributable to the unreasonable arrest—suggests that the taint is not attenuated. Several days between the arrest and the confession where the defendant had been released from custody was given substantial weight in *Wong Sun*; differences between two and six hours, on the other hand, have been treated as indistinguishable and as of little value in showing attenuation where the defendant was unrepresented and in police custody during the period between arrest and confessing.

A second consideration is variously called "the presence of intervening circumstances" or "intervening events." In Rawlings v. Kentucky,[4] evidence showed that there had been no questioning of the defendant during most of the detention and that the atmosphere had been "congenial." These were held—apparently as "circumstances"—influential in finding attenuation despite the passage of only 45 minutes. On the other hand, if the intervening events consist of interrogation and other police actions that exploit the custody and are designed to make use of the custody in persuading the defendant to make an incriminating statement, obviously those events or cir-

---

2. 371 U.S. 471 (1963).

3. 422 U.S. 590 (1975).

4. 448 U.S. 98 (1980).

cumstances suggest that attenuation has not occurred.

The Court has suggested that presentation of the suspect before a magistrate and the provision of warnings by that magistrate tends to show attenuation, even if the result of the presentation is a remand to continuing police custody. On the other hand, a showing that an arrest warrant was obtained soon after the improper warrantless arrest was held of minimal significance, at least where that warrant was based in part upon fingerprints taken from the defendant after the arrest and which were thus themselves the tainted fruit of that arrest.

Since the ultimate inquiry seems to be the defendant's motivation in confessing, if the intervening events provide a nontainted motive for making the confession, those events strongly suggest attenuation. During the improper detention in *Rawlings,* for example, the defendant's girlfriend revealed the drugs he had entrusted to her and told him to "take what was his." Attenuation was suggested by this evidence that his decision to confess was motivated by her proposal that he assume responsibility for the situation and thus relieve her of the suspicion he had caused to fall upon her.

A third factor is the extent to which the officers deviated from legal requirements and whether that deviation occurred in a manner causing it to have a particularly severe impact upon the defendant. Thus in *Brown,* attenuation was rendered less likely by a showing that the officers had not simply—and improperly—detained Brown but rather had taken the more intrusive step of arresting him, and that they had accomplished the arrest by a display of firearms that may have been unnecessary. This was a showing of a particularly significant violation of the law's standards and thus weighed heavily against attenuation.

A final concern is the extent to which the officers were motivated by a desire to secure incriminating admissions. Evidence that the officers were so motivated, of course, suggests the absence of attenuation. In *Rawlings,* for example, the officers' purpose in detaining Rawlings was not to interrogate him but rather to "secure" premises while other officers applied for a search warrant; this argued in favor of attenuation. In contrast, evidence that officers made a detention for the specific purpose of interrogation and extraction of the very type of incriminating admission that actually materialized argues strongly against a finding of attenuation.

§ 158. Evidence Obtained as a Result of Inadmissible Confessions

As American confession law developed, courts appeared generally satisfied that the rules demanding suppression of improperly obtained confessions embodied a version of the "fruit of the poisonous tree" doctrine.[1] In the absence of attenuation of taint[2] or some other exception,[3] the prosecution was denied use of the confession and also evidence derived from that confession. Recent developments, however, make clear that, at least on the federal constitutional level, this no longer reflects the law.

At early common law, the involuntariness of a confession did not affect the admissibility of other evidence obtained by use of that statement. If, for example, a suspect was coerced into confessing to a murder and also into revealing the location of the murder weapon, the weapon, if located, could be used in evidence. The rationale for this position was that the confession was excluded because of its untrustworthiness. If the "fruits" of that confession were themselves sufficiently probative of the defendant's guilt, the reason for excluding the confession did not extend to that derivative evidence and hence it was admissible.

American courts applying the voluntariness requirement adopted this position, and some held further that the discovery of corroborat-

---

§ 158

1. See generally § 176 infra.

2. See generally § 179 infra.

3. See §§ 179–182 infra.

ing evidence as a result of the confession rendered part or perhaps even all of the confession admissible.

As criminal evidence became permeated with exclusionary flavor after Mapp v. Ohio [4] and Miranda, American courts quite uncritically adopted for confession cases the "fruit of the poisonous tree" doctrine as developed in Fourth Amendment case law. In a "notable" case addressing the basis for this shift, Justice Schauer of the California Supreme Court explained that the rationale for excluding confessions even under the voluntariness rule had progressed beyond trustworthiness concerns and the expanded rationale for confession rules demanded exclusion of the "fruits" as well as the confessions themselves.[5] He emphasized what the California court regarded as the need to respect the community's sense of fair place and decency, which the court concluded was as offended by use of derivative evidence as by use of the coerced confession itself. His explanation applied equally, however, to the developing perception that confession law doctrines served the important purpose of discouraging improper police practices. Whether it is the need to comply with a sense of fair play or to discourage conduct such as that which led to particular confessions that supports the exclusion of evidence derived from such confessions, the reliability of the derivative evidence does not render the rationale for exclusion inapplicable.

In Oregon v. Elstad,[6] the Supreme Court made clear that not all federal constitutional requirements that mandate exclusion of a confession also embody a fruits doctrine requiring the exclusion of derivative evidence. Elstad's significance differs depending upon the reason why the confession itself must be excluded and—perhaps—upon the nature of the derivative evidence at issue.

Confession Obtained Without Miranda Warnings. Elstad itself held that a violation of Miranda's prophylactic warning requirements did not invoke the "fruit of the poisonous tree" doctrine so as necessarily to demand exclusion of a subsequent confession which was subject to neither Miranda nor voluntariness challenge. The "fruit of the poisonous tree" doctrine, the Court explained, applies where there has been an actual infringement of the suspect's federal constitutional rights. The Fifth Amendment itself prohibits only evidentiary use of compelled confessions. Miranda's prophylactic warning requirements are not actual parts of the Fifth Amendment's mandate but rather are judicially developed standards that sometimes require exclusion of a confession not actually "compelled." In such cases, exclusion of the confession is necessary although there has been no actual underlying violation of the suspect's Fifth Amendment rights.

Freed from the restraints of the fruits doctrine, the Court proceeded to consider whether the nature of the Miranda requirements and other relevant considerations demanded a similar rule. Two considerations, it suggested, might dictate such a rule—a need to deter violations of the sort shown in the case or a need to assure truthworthy evidence. Neither was found controlling. Since Miranda violations are often accidental and do not intrude upon the Fifth Amendment itself, the need for deterrence is somewhat lessened; exclusion of the confession itself meets this reduced need. With regard to trustworthiness, the absence of coercion means that subsequent confessions would not be of questionable accuracy.

On balance, the Court concluded, "If errors are made by law enforcement officers in administering the prophylactic Miranda procedures, they should not breed the same irremediable consequences as police infringement of the Fifth Amendment itself. Consequently, while an unwarned statement must be suppressed, the admissibility of any subsequent statement which was itself preceded by

---

4. 367 U.S. 643 (1961), discussed in § 166 infra.

5. People v. Ditson, 57 Cal.2d 415, 436–440, 20 Cal. Rptr. 165, 176–178, 369 P.2d 714, 725–727 (1962), cert. dismissed 372 U.S. 933.

6. 470 U.S. 298 (1985).

proper warnings "should turn in these circumstances solely on whether it is knowingly and voluntarily made."

Involuntary Confession. If the first of two confessions is inadmissible because it was involuntary within the meaning of the Fourteenth Amendment due process requirement, the extraction of the confession constituted "police infringement of the Fifth Amendment itself" and neither *Elstad* nor its rationale apply. Consequently, the second confession—if it resulted from the first—as well as the first must be suppressed.

This distinction might be explained in terms of either of two considerations found inapplicable in *Elstad.* First, the involuntariness of the first confession may suggest a sufficient risk that subsequent confessions will be unreliable to demand exclusion of at least some of those confessions in order to serve the purpose of assuring accuracy. Second, the need for deterrence might lead to the same conclusion. Violations of *Miranda* prophylactic rules are not so important as to demand maximum preventive efforts; thus exclusion of only the immediately-resulting confessions provides adequate prevention. Official coercion sufficient to render a confession involuntary, on the other hand, is more offensive and therefore demands greater preventive efforts. Exclusion of both the confession and derivative admissions may be necessary to provide discouragement appropriately related to the offensiveness of the official conduct targeted by the preventive efforts.

Elstad, then, leaves no doubt that a defendant may challenge a confession as inadmissible "fruit" or derivative results of a previous involuntary confession. Precisely what standard to apply in determining whether the subsequently-given confession is suppressible derivative evidence, however, is not entirely clear.

In *Elstad,* the Court reaffirmed that a suspect from whom a confession has been coerced is not, as a result, perpetually disabled from thereafter giving an admissible confession. If, however, the subsequent confession was stimulated by the same coercive circumstances that gave rise to the first, it clearly is not admissible. While the Court has not definitively determined whether there is a formal presumption that a confession is involuntary if it was given after an initial involuntary statement, the prosecution's burden of proving voluntariness at least imposes a practical need to overcome an inference of involuntariness. The major question is whether the prosecution establishes admissibility by proving that the second and challenged confession is itself voluntary or whether it must prove more.

Elstad reaffirmed that when the initial illegality consists of a Fourth Amendment violation and the "fruit of the poisonous tree" doctrine therefore applies, a "tainted" confession is not rendered admissible simply by proof that it was voluntary. "Beyond this," the Court emphasized, "the prosecution must show a sufficient break in events to undermine the inference that the confession was caused by the Fourth Amendment violation." Does this same approach apply when the primary illegality is coercion of a confession in direct contravention of the Fifth Amendment instead of an arrest in violation of the Fourth Amendment?

Elstad's reasoning suggests so. Consequently, the prosecution must, under analysis developed primarily in Fourth Amendment cases,[7] show that the taint was "attenuated." Applying this approach, the Ninth Circuit explained:

The following factors have been identified as relevant to the issue of whether a statement made after an involuntary statement is voluntary: (1) a break in the stream of events sufficient to insulate the statement from the effect of all that went on before; (2) "inferences as to the continuing effect of the coercive practices which may fairly be drawn from the surrounding circumstances"; (3) "the time that passes between confessions, the change in the place of interrogations, and the change in the identity of the interrogators"; (4) removal

7. See § 179 infra.

of the conditions which preclude the use of the first statement.[8]

The third consideration identified by the Ninth Circuit—time elapsing between the involuntary statement and the confession at issue—is given particular importance.

Does this analysis require proof that the defendant was aware of the inadmissibility of his earlier and coerced confession?

Harrison v. United States,[9] suggests so. *Harrison* involved a challenge to a defendant's testimony at a prior trial rather than an out-of-court confession. At the first trial, the prosecution had used against Harrison improperly obtained confessions and Harrison testified in his defense. In the second trial, the prosecution made no offer of the confessions but did introduce Harrison's testimony at the first trial over his objection that this testimony was derived from his inadmissible confessions. The Court held that use of Harrison's testimony was error, since the prosecution had failed to show that its illegal action in obtaining and using the confessions did not "induce" the trial testimony.

Harrison's language suggests that the prosecution might well have been unable to carry its burden without showing that Harrison's decision to testify was not influenced by the prosecution's possession and use of his confessions; this in turn would quite likely require proof that he was aware those confessions would ultimately be held inadmissible. *Harrison* strongly suggests that where a reasonable likelihood appears that an involuntary out-of-court confession stimulated a subsequent confession, that later confession is also inadmissible, unless the prosecution shows that the defendant's decision to give the second confession was made for reasons independent of the first confession. Generally, this requires proof that the defendant knew the first confession could not be used or that he was moved to make the second confession by considerations completely independent of the prosecution's ability to use his first confession against him.

Confession Obtained in Violation of Miranda Ban on Interrogation. Does *Elstad* apply if the first confession is itself inadmissible not because of a failure to administer the *Miranda* warnings but because officers failed to comply with their duty to avoid "interrogation" after the suspect invoked his right to counsel or to silence?[10] The Court's language can be read as limiting its holding to nonwarning situations.

Whether *Elstad's* rationale indicates that it be so limited is less certain. This uncertainty arises in part because of uncertainty as to *Elstad's* rationale, generated by ambiguity regarding *Elstad's* basis for distinguishing between *Miranda* warning violations, on the one hand, and official action resulting in an involuntary confession, on the other. If *Elstad* rests upon the relative nonoffensiveness of the illegality involved in failing to admonish a suspect, reasonable persons could differ on whether a failure to respect a suspect's right to avoid interrogation is distinguishably more offensive.

If *Elstad* rests upon the absence of any threat to reliability in a nonwarning situation, perhaps the holding ought to extend to other *Miranda* violations, since improper interrogation or the improper continuation of interrogation does not *necessarily* mean that there was coercion which could cast doubt upon the suspect's later confession as well. On the other hand, improper interrogation may involve a much higher likelihood of coercion than a mere failure to warn. Perhaps this likelihood is sufficiently high that the fruits doctrine should apply, and the prosecution should therefore have the burden of showing either that there was no coerciveness to taint the later confession or that any coercive taint was attenuated before the second confession was given.

On balance, *Elstad* should be read as rendering the fruits doctrine inapplicable when the *Miranda* violation consists of an improper interrogation. Only when the actual involun-

---

8. United States v. Patterson, 812 F.2d 1188, 1192 (9th Cir.1987) (citations omitted).

9. 392 U.S. 219 (1968).

10. See generally § 150 supra.

tariness of a confession is established is there sufficient assurance of highly offensive police conduct or an actual coercive influence that might affect later confessions to justify application of the "fruit of the poisonous tree" doctrine.

"Fruits" Other than Subsequent Confessions. *Elstad* involved challenged evidence consisting of an out-of-court statement of the defendant. Does it apply to other evidence derived from *Miranda* violations? Clearly so in at least one instance. *Elstad* reaffirmed Michigan v. Tucker,[11] holding admissible the testimony of a witness located by means of a statement elicited from the defendant without full compliance with *Miranda's* warning requirements.

Suppose, as a result of a confession obtained in violation of *Miranda,* police obtain an article of evidentiary value.

Elstad emphasized the defendant's voluntary decision in making the confession challenged in that case; *Tucker* similarly stressed the witness's voluntary decision to cooperate. If these voluntary intervening decisions were necessary to "insulate" those confessions from the earlier *Miranda* violations, *Elstad's* rationale does not apply to physical derivative evidence because generally no insulating voluntary decision will have intervened. But most lower courts have reasonably construed *Elstad* as rather resting upon the rationale that the prophylactic nature of the rights violated removed any need to exclude reliable and probative but derivative evidence. This rationale, of course, applies equally if the challenged evidence is physical evidence. *Elstad,* most faithfully construed, means that physical evidence obtained by authorities through exploitation of information obtained in violation of *Miranda* is simply not subject to challenge because it was obtained in this manner.

"Fruits" of Confessions Inadmissible for Other Reasons. *Elstad,* of course, dealt only with the consequences of federal constitutional violations. State courts are free but not required, therefore, to apply its approach to

evidence challenged as the "fruit" of a confession obtained in violation of state law requirements.

Unfortunately, *Elstad* may be uncritically adopted in state law contexts. A Texas court, for example, simply assumed without discussion that *Elstad's* analysis should be applied where a confession was obtained in violation of statutory requirements for eliciting statements from juvenile offenders. A subsequent confession, obtained after those requirements were met, would be admissible if it was voluntary. This approach unfortunately misapplies *Elstad's* analysis.

Properly read, *Elstad* simply suggests that when confessions are obtained in violation of legal requirements that are not core constitutional demands, courts may properly consider more critically and flexibly whether derivative evidence as well as the confessions themselves should be excluded. Attention should focus, first, upon whether the legal requirement is such that its violation creates some risk that derivative evidence—such as a subsequent confession—might be untrustworthy. Second, significance should be given to the importance of the legal requirement and whether, in view of this assessment of its importance, the need for sufficient incentive to comply with it demands exclusion of derivative evidence as well as confessions immediately resulting from violations. *Elstad* provides no basis for quick conclusions that all nonconstitutional legal requirements applicable to confessions are such that their violation should not result in exclusion of derivative evidence.

§ 159. Judicial Confessions, Guilty Pleas, and Admissions Made in Plea Bargaining

Most confession law involves self-incriminating admissions made by suspects to law enforcement officers during the pre-judicial stages of a criminal investigation. But the prosecution sometimes seeks trial use of self-incriminating admissions made by the defen-

11.   417 U.S. 433 (1974).

dant during what is essentially the judicial processing of a case. These efforts can usefully be broken down into three areas: "judicial" confessions, guilty pleas, and admissions made in connection with plea bargaining.

Judicial Confessions. A so-called "judicial confession" may consist of a defendant's testimony in a different (and perhaps civil) proceeding or in a prior hearing during the criminal prosecution then being tried. It may also be a "stipulation" or even the pleadings in this or other litigation. Under the general rules governing admissions,[1] these judicial confessions are admissible, subject of course to compliance with such requirements as any right to counsel the defendant may have had at the time.

If, during pretrial hearings, a defendant testifies in support of a federal constitutional claim, his right to enforce that claim precludes use of the testimony to convict him. This will often also be the case as a matter of state law when such testimony is offered in support of a state law claim. Such testimony is, however, admissible to impeach the defendant if he takes the witness stand at trial and testifies in a manner inconsistent with these earlier admissions.

Guilty Pleas. A defendant's guilty plea and statements made in connection with its offer to and acceptance by the trial court are admissible as admissions. Pleas of guilty to minor offenses may sometimes constitute questionable evidence of actual guilt, but this is best handled by considering on a case-by-case basis the probative value of particular pleas weighed against the risk of undue prejudice likely to arise from their admission into evidence.

If a plea of guilty is withdrawn with permission of the court, perhaps it should be rendered inadmissible only if the reasons for its withdrawal cast doubt upon its reliability. In Kercheval v. United States,[2] however, the Supreme Court held—apparently as a matter of

federal evidence law—that the use of a withdrawn guilty plea in a federal criminal prosecution was impermissible regardless of the reason withdrawal was permitted. Permitting evidentiary use of the plea, the Court reasoned, would frustrate the policy objectives supporting the right to withdraw that plea. This position is now embodied in Federal Rule 410[3] and Rule 9 of the Federal Rules of Criminal Procedure,[4] which also bar the use of statements made in the course of proceedings in which such pleas are submitted to and accepted by the trial court. State statutes or court rules generally are similar. If a plea is withdrawn as a matter of federal constitutional right, the right mandating withdrawal probably also bars use of the plea against the defendant.

Admissions Made in Connection With Plea Bargaining. Self-incriminating admissions made in defendants' efforts to engage in plea bargaining present different and more difficult questions. The extent to which limits on admissibility do or should extend to admissions made to law enforcement officers rather than prosecuting attorneys is a particularly difficult subissue.

There is general agreement that admissions made in connection with plea negotiations that do not result in final pleas of guilty must be excluded in order to encourage the desirable or at least necessary process of plea bargaining. This is provided for by Federal Rule 410[5] and Rule 9 of the Federal Rules of Criminal Procedure;[6] state statutes and court rules often address the matter as well, although there is considerable variation among the provisions.

Courts have encountered considerable difficulty addressing how the prohibition against use of statements made in connection with plea negotiations affects the admissibility of statements made to law enforcement officers. As initially enacted, Federal Rule 410 barred admission of "statements made in connection

§ 159

1. See §§ 257–258 infra.
2. 274 U.S. 220 (1927).
3. Fed.R.Evid. 410(1).

4. Fed.R.Crim.P. 11(e)(6).
5. Fed.R.Evid. 410(4).
6. Fed.R.Crim.P. 11(e)(6)(D).

with any [offer to plead guilty or nolo conten-
dere]." In 1975, this rule and the criminal
rule were amended to require that the statement be "made in connection with, and relevant to" the offer. In 1980, both rules were
further amended to their present form, which
mandates exclusion only of "statements made
in the course of plea discussions with an attorney for the government." The advisory committee's note to the amendment of the criminal rule makes clear that the amendment was
intended to focus—perhaps exclusively—upon
and to encourage negotiations between prosecutors and defense counsel (or unrepresented
defendants). "[C]onfrontations" between law
enforcement officers and suspects, the committee observed, "involve problems of quite
different dimensions" which are best "resolved by that body of law dealing with police
interrogations." Similar state provisions,
perhaps modeled upon the earlier federal
rules, have not always been similarly amended.

It is clear that the 1980 amendments were
designed to reject the position that a defendant's statement is inadmissible, regardless of
to whom it was made, simply because it was
motivated by the defendant's hope of obtaining leniency. But nevertheless the federal
rule may not be limited to statements made
literally to a prosecuting attorney who is
physically present. It is likely, for example,
to also render inadmissible at least some
statements to law enforcement officers who
have been authorized by a prosecuting attorney to negotiate a plea with the defendant
and perhaps some to officers whom the defendant reasonably believes to be so authorized.

State provisions have been varyingly construed. Whether all or most statements
made to law enforcement officers should be
beyond the rule of exclusion simply because
they were made to such officers is doubtful.
Perhaps sound policy suggests that prosecuting attorneys should control negotiations between suspects and criminal justice authorities and that legal rules should encourage
only negotiations between prosecutors and

suspects. On the other hand, many defendants probably believe—with some accuracy—
that "deals can be cut" with law enforcement
officers. A rule that ignores this reality "is
capable of working substantial injustice in
many cases."

A number of state courts have applied a
two part test developed under the pre–1980
federal provisions in United States v. Robertson.[7] Under this analysis, a statement is inadmissible if two matters are established.
First, the defendant must at the time have
had a subjective expectation that he was in
the process of negotiating a plea. Second,
that expectation must have been objectively
reasonable. The fact that discussions were
occurring with a law enforcement officer rather than a prosecuting attorney is a consideration suggesting that the defendant had no
such reasonable expectation, but it is not necessarily conclusive.

A defendant's statement is inadmissible
only if it was part of plea negotiations or
discussions. Some courts have therefore held
admissible statements made to law enforcement officers and even prosecuting attorneys
where the officials have not indicated any
willingness to negotiate pleas and the defendants were only attempting to interest them
in doing so. A few courts have construed plea
discussions literally, and held admissions
made during discussions concerning the drop-
ping of all charges to be unprotected. One
decision quite artificially requires the admissions to be made before an agreement is
reached; thus admissions made after, but pursuant to the terms of, the agreement are not
protected.

The federal provisions permit use in perjury prosecutions of otherwise inadmissible
pleas and statements related to pleas and plea
negotiations. State provisions often but not
always provide similarly. As a result of 1980
amendment, the federal provisions also embody a provision permitting the use of such
statements against a defendant when some
other statement made in the course of the
same plea proceedings or negotiations has

7. 582 F.2d 1356, 1366 (5th Cir.1978).

been introduced and the statement at issue "ought in fairness be considered contemporaneously with it."[8]

Whether an admission otherwise subject to exclusion may be used to impeach a defendant who testifies is not explicitly addressed under the federal provisions. The original version of Federal Rule 410 contained an explicit but limited exception permitting the use of "voluntary and reliable statements" made in court and on the record, even if they were otherwise inadmissible under Rule 410, but only "where offered for impeachment purposes." This language was eliminated in the 1975 amendment of the rule by Congress. The Second Circuit has held that this "unusually clear legislative history" demonstrates a Congressional intention "to preclude use of statements made in plea negotiations for impeachment purposes." State provisions vary.

§ 160. "Tacit" and "Adoptive" Confessions and Admissions

Under the general rules regarding admissions,[1] the prosecution is generally permitted in a criminal case to prove that an accusatory statement was made in the hearing of the defendant and that the defendant's response was such as to justify the inference that he agreed with or "adopted" the statement. The adopting response may, of course, be an express affirmative agreement with the statement. It may also be conduct from which the defendant's belief in the accuracy of the statement can be inferred; where this is the case, the evidence amounts to what in this text is regarded as an adoptive admission.[2] Traditionally, adoption can be also inferred from the defendant's failure to deny the accusation, so a type of adoptive admission can arise from either silence or an "equivocal response" not a clear denial.[3] Where the accusation is so adopted by the defendant's silence, the evi-

dence thereby rendered admissible—the accusation and the defendant's silence—is a "tacit" confession or admission.

The foundation necessary has been articulated in various ways. Best put, admission requires preliminary proof (1) of an accusatory statement that a person who considered himself innocent would, under the circumstances, deny; (2) that the defendant heard and understood the accusatory statement; (3) that the defendant had the opportunity and ability to deny the statement; and (4) that the defendant manifested his adoption of it or—in the case of a tacit admission—adopted it by his silence. Some courts have held that the trial judge's role in passing on admissibility is merely to determine whether a jury could properly find these facts in favor of the prosecution. Under this approach, the jury is to determine whether the defendant in fact heard and adopted the accusatory assertion.

Here, as in civil litigation, admission is based on the assumption that human nature is such that innocent persons will usually deny false accusations. Critical reconsideration of this assumption, especially as it applies in the criminal context, had led to increasing limitations upon adoptive "confessions" in criminal litigation.

Use of this evidence in criminal trials is also constrained by federal and perhaps state constitutional considerations. The Supreme Court's federal constitutional decisions have all involved use of silence to impeach testifying defendants. In this context, the sole established federal constitutional limitation is the due process prohibition against reliance upon silence or action after the suspect has been admonished that he has a right to remain silent.[4] Whether, in the absence of such an admonition, the federal constitution imposes a broader ban upon the prosecution's use of silence to affirmatively prove the guilt of a nontestifying defendant remains uncertain.[5]

---

8. See generally § 56 supra, considering the effect of introducing part of a writing or conversation.

§ 160

1. See § 254 infra as to the nature of admissions.

2. See generally § 261 infra.

3. See generally § 262 infra (admissions by silence).

4. See § 132 supra.

5. See § 132 supra.

Courts have often commented that the evidentiary issues presented by reliance upon silence have constitutional overtones, although the precise relationship between the constitutional and evidentiary issues is not completely clear. This is in large part because of uncertainty as to whether the probative value of silence, clearly critical to the evidentiary issue, is also relevant to the constitutional issues presented by reliance upon silence. In any case, the evidentiary questions do require inquiry into probative value and place less significance upon whether suspects were arrested or warned than is given those considerations in constitutional analysis.

The major evidentiary issue is under what circumstances, if any, the prosecution should be permitted to use a defendant's silence in the face of accusatory circumstances to show his consciousness of guilt and therefore guilt itself. Courts have become more sensitive to the possibility that those accused of crimes may remain silent for a variety of reasons other than their consciousness of guilt, particularly when they are in the custody or even presence of law enforcement officers. A suspect may, for example, be unaware of any obligation to speak or of any value in doing so. Especially if the accusation is hostile, he may perceive that the accusing party will be unresponsive to any claim of innocence and may even be enraged by it. He may be vaguely aware of a legal right to remain silent and believe in some general way that exercising that right may help him avoid unjustified conviction. If law enforcement authorities are present, the suspect may be moved to remain silent by a general sense that anything he says, exculpatory or not, might eventually and in some way he does not precisely understand be to his detriment. Silence may also reflect nothing more than a general hostility towards or distrust of law enforcement representatives.

Judicial acknowledgment of numerous innocent explanations for silence is often accompanied by expressions of doubt as to juries' ability or inclination to consider adequately explanations other than consciousness of guilt and to give evidence of silence only that weight to which it is objectively entitled.

In response to these concerns, some courts have directed trial judges to screen offers of tacit confessions more rigorously. The Connecticut Supreme Court, for example, held that an adoptive admission based on silence is admissible only if no explanation other than assent to the accusatory statement is "equally consistent." Others courts have encouraged trial judges to engage in more critical appraisals of the probative value/risk of undue prejudice balances.

Some courts have more severely curtailed prosecution use of tacit admissions. The Alabama Supreme Court, for example, barred the use of either pre- or post-arrest silence, explaining that "neither logic nor common experience any longer support the tacit admission rule, if indeed, either ever supported it."

On balance, the prosecution should not be permitted to establish a criminal defendant's pretrial "tacit" adoption of an accusatory statement by showing silence if that silence was in the presence of persons whom the defendant knew were law enforcement officers. The variety of possible explanations for such silence creates too great a risk that juries will give such silence unjustified weight.

This position is also supported by two considerations suggested by the constitutional issues.[6] First, barring use of such evidence avoids the unfairness of penalizing a defendant for silence he is likely to believe at the time will be without adverse consequences, a perception for which the government must bear major responsibility. Second, it avoids the risk of placing a burden upon the exercise of a major constitutional right, the right to decline to provide self-incriminating admissions. This might also be accomplished by case-by-case inquiry into whether silence was in fact reliance upon that right, but such inquiries would be time-consuming and suffi-

6. See § 132 supra.

ciently difficult to cast doubt upon the accuracy of their conclusions.

The prosecution should, however, as a general matter be permitted to show either (a) an adoptive confession or admission on the basis of affirmative adoptive conduct even in the presence of law enforcement officers; or (b) an adoptive or tacit confession or admission by either affirmative conduct or silence in situations where the defendant is neither in custody nor in the presence of persons he knew were law enforcement officers. The probative value of proffered admissions of this sort should be carefully evaluated and balanced against the risk that juries will be unable or disinclined to objectively evaluate such evidence. Whether the prosecution has made the necessary preliminary showing should, of course, be informed by the developing recognition that the traditional approach was insufficiently sensitive to the risks posed by adoptive admissions in the criminal litigation context.

§ 161. Use of Otherwise Inadmissible Confessions for Impeachment

The exclusionary sanctions applicable to confessions are subject to the limitations applicable to exclusionary sanctions generally, including the limitation which often permits the prosecution to use inadmissible evidence to impeach a defendant who testifies in his own defense at trial.[1] Confession law's complexity, and especially the distinction between the voluntariness requirement and other exclusionary rules, results in particular difficulties applying the impeachment exception to confession law. The Supreme Court's federal constitutional case law provides the framework most often used for even nonconstitutional analyses.

Harris v. New York [2] made clear that the previously-recognized impeachment exception to federal constitutional exclusionary requirements had survived the Warren Court's "revo-

lution" in criminal constitutional procedure. It also demonstrated that this exception would permit the use of at least some otherwise inadmissible confessions for such impeachment purposes and that impeachment use was permitted despite a showing that a confession was obtained by violations of at least some of Miranda's Fifth Amendment requirements.

Harris rested primarily upon two considerations. First, the violation of Miranda's demands shown there carried no suggestion that the resulting confession was unreliable; therefore, the confession was probative on the particularly important question of whether the defendant was perjuring himself during his in-court testimony. Second, no more than speculation suggested that permitting impeachment use of such confessions would dilute the effectiveness of Miranda's exclusionary sanction in enforcing compliance with Miranda's substantive requirements.

Subsequent cases made clear that a self-incriminating statement may be offered to impeach the defendant regardless of which of Miranda's prophylactic requirements was violated. In Harris, the officer had given the suspect a warning which omitted one of the required elements. In Oregon v. Hass,[3] on the other hand, the suspect had been adequately warned but officers interrogated him after he invoked his right to counsel. Justice Brennan urged in Hass that Miranda's exclusionary sanction would be impaired by permitting impeachment use of confessions obtained in violation of the Miranda requirement that interrogation cease if the suspect invoked his right to counsel. The Hass majority, however, characterized Justice Brennan's concerns as simply "speculative" and rejected them. Apparently, no violation of any of Miranda's per se requirements will require exclusion of a resulting confession offered to impeach a testifying defendant.

A majority of the Court, in Michigan v.

---

§ 161

1. See generally § 182 infra.

2. 401 U.S. 222 (1971).

3. 420 U.S. 714 (1975).

Harvey,[4] adopted the same general impeachment exception to the exclusionary requirement applicable to confessions obtained through violations of defendants' Sixth Amendment right to counsel. But Justice Stevens, writing for four dissenters, characterized *Harris* as resting upon the Court's power to fashion and limit exclusionary remedies where the constitutional provision violated does not itself necessarily demand exclusion. Only then, he reasoned, does the Court have the right to balance the prosecution's need for the evidence against the value of exclusion in preventing future violations of the underlying rule. The Sixth Amendment itself, without any judicially-developed exclusionary requirement, he continued, demands exclusion of confessions obtained in violation of its right to counsel. Consequently, the Court has no legitimate power to hold that exclusion is unnecessary based upon its own perception of the relevant considerations. The majority, however, implicitly rejected the underlying distinction the dissenters drew between the exclusionary sanctions attaching to the Fifth and Sixth Amendments rights to counsel.

This impeachment exception to the federal constitutional exclusionary sanctions attaching to confessions does not extend to certain situations in which voluntariness concerns are implicated. In both *Harris* and *Hass,* the Court carefully noted that no claim had been made and no evidence had been produced that the confessions at issue were coerced or involuntary. In both opinions, the Court carefully commented that its reasoning applied "provided of course that the trustworthiness of the evidence satisfies legal standards." This suggested that a confession inadmissible because it was involuntary would not be admissible even for impeachment. In Mincey v. Arizona[5] the Court confirmed this and found constitutional error in the use of an involuntary confession to impeach a testifying defendant. "*[A]ny* criminal trial use against a defendant of his *involuntary* statement," the

Court announced, "is a denial of due process * * *."[6]

Why this is the case was not made clear. Perhaps the Court viewed the requirement that involuntary confessions be excluded as a part of due process itself and thus the Court has no legitimate authority to develop an exception for impeachment purposes. Or, perhaps the especially important need to prevent those police practices that give rise to involuntary confessions is the controlling consideration. Although the Court has the power to develop an impeachment exception, then, the need to prevent these particularly offensive practices has convinced it that this power should not be exercised.

Trustworthiness considerations suggest another possibility: the trustworthiness of involuntary confessions is, because of their involuntariness, subject to some doubt. Such untrustworthiness makes them less valuable as indicators of defendant perjury at trial. Given this reduced evidentiary value even for impeachment, perhaps considered in light of the increased need to discourage the underlying activity, the balance of the relevant considerations tips back in favor of constitutionally-required exclusion when involuntariness is established.

Does *Mincey* prohibit impeachment use of a confession if the underlying violation consists of eliciting the confession by means of an ineffective waiver of the Fifth or Sixth Amendments right to counsel? In *Harvey,* the Court noted but did not reach Harvey's argument that he had been misled by the officers as to his need for counsel and that his waiver was therefore invalid. Such activity, Harvey argued, violated the "core value" of the Sixth Amendment and demanded the exclusion of the resulting confession for all purposes.

The major problem would be presented by evidence that a waiver of counsel was voluntary but made with sufficient misunderstanding to render it unintelligent. If *Mincey* rests upon an assumption that the inaccuracy of an

---

4. 494 U.S. 344 (1990).

5. 437 U.S. 385 (1978).

6. Id. at 398 (emphasis in original).

involuntary confession renders the rationale for *Harris* inapplicable, a confession resulting from an unintelligent waiver would seem to be admissible for impeachment. Lack of intelligence, unlike coercion, is unlikely to affect trustworthiness. If *Mincey* instead rests upon a need for extraordinarily strong incentives to discourage particularly offensive police behavior, on the other hand, perhaps unintelligence attributable to intentional law enforcement misconduct but not other sources should render a resulting confession inadmissible for impeachment.

As in other exclusionary sanction situations, state courts and legislatures remain free to reject the federal constitutional model and to apply state law exclusionary requirements unqualified by impeachment exceptions. Some have done so. Vigorous disagreement with *Harris,* for example, motivated the Alaska Supreme Court to adopt a broad exclusionary rule that prohibits use of improperly obtained confessions (as well as other illegally obtained evidence) for impeachment.[7]

The rationale for state law limits on the admissibility of confessions may suggest that in construing those limitations state courts eschew adoption of the apparent reasoning of *Harris.* Texas, for example, has long statutorily prohibited evidence that a criminal defendant orally confessed. In Butler v. State,[8] the Texas Court of Criminal Appeals refused to rely on what it perceived as *Harris'* rationale as a basis for construing the statute as having an implied exception which would permit use of oral confessions to impeach a testifying defendant. The Texas court read *Harris* as resting on the premise that *Miranda* violations do not impair the reliability of confessions. The prohibition against evidence of oral confessions, it continued, reflects a legislative judgment that such evidence is unreliable. Consequently, the court was not free to characterize such evidence as reliable enough

for impeachment use, and *Harris* therefore provided no support for the prosecution's argument that an exception could be developed by the court.

§ 162. Determining Admissibility

Considerations bearing upon determining the admissibility of confessions are closely related to those for raising and resolving exclusionary sanction issues generally.[1] Because some factors bearing upon the admissibility of confessions may also affect the credibility of admissible confessions, however, there are some potential differences between the situations.

Roles of Judge and Jury. In Jackson v. Denno,[2] the Supreme Court held that the due process clause of the Fourteenth Amendment required that upon proper demand [3] the trial judge must determine the voluntariness of a challenged confession. *Jackson* held constitutionally impermissible what had previously been known as the "New York procedure," under which the trial judge conducted a preliminary inquiry and excluded a challenged confession only if its involuntariness was so clear as to present no issue. If the evidence presented a fair question as to voluntariness or any factual matters relevant to voluntariness, the confession was submitted to the jury with directions to determine voluntariness and to consider the confession on the issue of guilt or innocence only if it was found to be voluntary.

The New York procedure was found to impermissibly endanger defendants' rights to fair determinations of the voluntariness of challenged confessions and to determinations of guilt or innocence without reference to involuntary confessions. Jurors might, the Court reasoned, first conclude that a defendant committed the crime charged and then turn to the voluntariness of a challenged confession; having concluded that the confession

---

7. Alaska R.Evid. 412.

8. 493 S.W.2d 190 (Tex.Cr.App.1973).

§ 162

1. See § 183 infra.

2. 378 U.S. 368 (1964).

3. See § 183 infra.

was accurate, they might be unable or disinclined to determine voluntariness without regard to that accuracy. This would, of course, violate the right to have voluntariness determined without regard to reliability. Alternatively, the jurors might first address the confession and conclude that it was involuntary but reliable; they might then be unable or disinclined to ignore that confession in assessing the sufficiency of the prosecution's evidence on guilt or innocence. This would endanger the right to have guilt or innocence determined without consideration of an involuntary confession.

Under *Jackson,* of course, it is permissible to give the trial judge sole responsibility for resolving voluntariness issues. Under this "orthodox" approach, then, the trial judge resolves all factual disputes and determines voluntariness. No issues related to voluntariness are submitted to the jury.

Jackson also left states the flexibility to utilize what is known as the Massachusetts or "humane" procedure under which the trial judge makes a full inquiry into and determines voluntariness. If the trial judge finds the challenged confession voluntary, however, the issue is then submitted to the jury for reconsideration of the matter, and the jury is instructed to consider the confession on the defendant's guilt only if it first finds it voluntary. A number of jurisdictions take this approach.

In Lego v. Twomey,[4] the Court held that the Constitution does not require the states to provide for jury consideration of claims of involuntariness rejected by the trial judge. It found no basis for concluding that juries are somehow "better suited" than trial judges to determine voluntariness. Similarly, it discerned no convincing grounds for regarding trial judges' resolutions of voluntariness challenges as sufficiently unreliable to entitle defendants to "a second forum for litigating [their] claim[s]."

The leading recent judicial discussion of the wisdom of the alternative approaches is the

Colorado Supreme Court's 1987 decision in Deeds v. People.[5] Rejecting the Massachusetts approach, the court expressed doubt that juries can isolate and determine voluntariness or disregard confessions they find involuntary. Moreover, permitting a jury to convict a defendant despite having found a confession involuntary "is incompatible with the proscription against a conviction being based upon an involuntary confession." Consequently, under the approach adopted by the Colorado court, the judge makes the only determination of voluntariness. If the judge finds the confession is voluntary, the confession is then submitted to the jury "solely for consideration of the credibility of the testimony relating to the confession and the weight to be given to the testimony and the confession." No instruction on voluntariness is given to the jury. Although special credibility instructions are normally undesirable, the court concluded that the risk of juries giving undue weight to confessions justifies an exception in this situation:

> Accordingly, * * * the trial judge may properly instruct the jury that, although the confession has been admitted into evidence, it is the sole prerogative of the jury to determine what weight, if any, is to be given to the confession and any testimony directly related to the confession.[6]

Deeds' approach seems appropriate. The widely-adopted Massachusetts procedure was developed without careful distinction between credibility considerations and other factors that have become relevant to voluntariness as a criterion for determining admissibility. Accommodating that distinction and a reasonable allocation of responsibility between the trial judge and jury is best achieved by limiting the jury's role to considering the reliability of the specific confession offered in the case. Assessing the credibility of such evidence is a task traditionally entrusted to jurors. The voluntariness requirement serves functions other than assuring the accuracy of specific contested confessions, including the

---

4. 404 U.S. 477 (1972).
5. 747 P.2d 1266 (Colo.1987).

6. Id. at 1272–1273.

discouragement of law enforcement misconduct offensive for reasons completely unrelated to reliability of confessions and discouragement of official misconduct because such conduct in general creates an unacceptable risk that resulting confessions will be inaccurate. Whether a particular confession should be disregarded for these reasons is a matter best left to the trial judge, who is likely to bring to the task broader breadth of experience and perspective.

Hearing on Admissibility. Generally, a trial judge is required to hold a hearing on the admissibility of proffered evidence only if the party against whom it is offered objects and requests such a hearing.[7] This rule is usually applied to confessions as well. A few courts, apparently regarding some confession requirements as too important to fall to defense counsel's default, require that even in the absence of objection and demand for a hearing, trial judges conduct a hearing, entertain evidence, and determine voluntariness of a proffered confession.

Hearings Out of Jury's Presence. Jackson is widely regarded as establishing a right to have the hearing on voluntariness conducted out of the presence of the jury. But apparently no constitutional violation is committed by having the hearing in the presence of the jury if the confession is properly found voluntary by the judge, since the jury hears no evidence it is not otherwise entitled to hear, and the hearing is not somehow deficient because of the jury's presence.[8]

It is likely that if in such a situation the trial judge found the confession involuntary, an instruction to the jury to disregard the evidence produced before it would be inadequate and a mistrial would have to be declared. So proceeding, then, is obviously unwise from an administrative perspective. Moreover, the need to avoid a mistrial may create the appearance and perhaps the reality of unfair pressure to find a contested confession voluntary. This simply reaffirms the

wisdom of holding the proceedings out of the presence of the jury.

Judge's Findings on Admissibility. In Sims v. Georgia,[9] the Court held that a trial judge's conclusion that a challenged confession is voluntary "must appear from the record with unmistakable clarity." It is not constitutionally necessary, however, that the trial judge make formal findings of fact on contested subissues or write a formal opinion. Nevertheless, sound policy and particularly the practicalities of effective appellate review strongly suggest specific findings concerning disputed subquestions of fact as well as a clear ultimate determination of the major issues.

Resolving Confession Issues Other Than Voluntariness. Jackson dealt with the procedure required to resolve a defendant's due process voluntariness challenge to the admissibility of an offered confession. But there has been a general tendency to regard *Jackson's* requirements as also applicable to other federal constitutional challenges to confessions' admissibility. Perhaps voluntariness might be regarded as a uniquely important federal constitutional demand requiring more procedural solicitude than other admissibility demands. Less, then, might be required for resolving *Miranda* challenges. But the Court has developed *Jackson* as imposing such minimal procedural requirements that the tribunal is unlikely to require even less when the challenge raised is based upon a constitutional claim other than that of involuntariness.

Defendants' Right to Contest Credibility. Although under *Lego* a defendant has no federal constitutional right to contest *voluntariness* before the trial jury, in Crane v. Kentucky[10] the Court recognized such a right to contest the *credibility* of a confession. Thus once the prosecution is permitted to introduce evidence that the defendant made incriminating admissions, the defendant is entitled to introduce evidence concerning the circumstances under which he made them if those

7. See § 53 supra.

8. Pinto v. Pierce, 389 U.S. 31 (1967).

9. 385 U.S. 538 (1967).

10. 476 U.S. 683 (1986).

circumstances bear upon the credibility of the admissions.

Burden of Proof. In *Lego,* the Supreme Court held that when a defendant challenges the prosecution's proffer of a confession, the federal constitution requires that the prosecution prove the voluntariness of the confession but that the prosecution need only establish this by a preponderance of the evidence. Voluntariness does not have to be established beyond a reasonable doubt or even by clear and convincing evidence.

Due process requirements, the Court reasoned in *Lego,* are not based upon concern that juries might be unable to recognize the inaccuracy of involuntary confessions. *Jackson* rested instead primarily upon concern that jurors would improperly give weight to involuntary but reliable confessions. Thus the need to safeguard against inaccurate convictions, as might flow from juries' reliance upon inaccurate confessions, does not suggest an extraordinarily high burden for establishing admissibility. Nor do those values in fact served by the voluntariness requirement establish the need for such a burden of proof. Confessions have long been admitted into evidence based upon admissibility established only by a preponderance of the evidence. No basis had been presented for believing that those determinations of admissibility were unreliable or otherwise so "wanting in quality" as to demand a higher standard of proof of admissibility. Whatever might be accomplished by imposing a higher standard, the Court concluded, would be outweighed by the cost of denying juries probative evidence helpful in arriving at truthful decisions regarding defendants' guilt or innocence. Fourteen years later, in Colorado v. Connelly,[11] the Court reaffirmed *Lego* and summarily held that the prosecution's burden of proving compliance with the Fifth Amendment requirements announced in *Miranda* and its progeny is no greater.

Lego and *Connelly,* of course, establish only the minimum demands imposed by the federal constitution. States remain free to impose higher standards, and many do require the prosecution to establish voluntariness and sometimes compliance with other requirements, such as those imposed by self-incrimination demands, beyond a reasonable doubt or at least by clear and convincing evidence.

Appellate Review. Appellate courts differ dramatically regarding the scope of appellate review of confession decisions. Many, of course, apply traditional notions of deference to decisions of trial judges and overturn these decisions only if they are clearly erroneous or an abuse of discretion.

A number of courts take no issue with the proposition that such deference is due trial judges' findings of historical fact, such as those concerning the length of interrogation or whether particular admonitions were given. They do, however, regard certain "ultimate" questions—most often the "voluntariness" of a challenged confession—as different in nature and thus entitled to *de novo* determination by the appellate tribunal.

This position finds support in the Supreme Court's analysis in Miller v. Fenton,[12] holding that a state court's finding of voluntariness challenged in federal habeas litigation is not entitled to the statutory presumption of correctness applicable to findings of fact because "the ultimate issue of 'voluntariness'" is a legal question subject to plenary federal review. Assessments of credibility and demeanor are generally not critical to resolution of the issue of voluntariness, the Court reasoned, which "has always had a uniquely legal dimension." While the matter depends in part "on whether the defendant's will was in fact overborne"—apparently a purely factual matter—it also turns at least as much "on whether the techniques for extracting the statements, as applied to this suspect, are compatible with a system that presumes innocence and assures that a conviction will not be secured by inquisitorial means * * *." Thus the state trial judge who observed the witnesses is not in a uniquely effective position to make the determination.

---

11. 479 U.S. 157 (1986).

12. 474 U.S. 104 (1985).

Miller did not address the standard for review on direct appeal in federal litigation or, of course, any federal constitutional demands that might be imposed upon appellate review in state litigation. Nevertheless, the Court's characterization of the voluntariness question certainly suggests that *de novo* appellate review is appropriate. A number of appellate courts have taken that position, sometimes but not always citing *Miller* in support.

Several courts have limited this approach to the ultimate issue of voluntariness, apparently as required by Fourteenth Amendment due process,[13] and have distinguished *Miranda* self-incrimination waiver issues as subject to the same limited scrutiny on appeal as findings of narrow historical fact. This seems to rest upon the questionable assumption that the general requirement of due process, but not the requirement of a voluntary self-incrimination waiver, involves delicate questions of weighing policy considerations and balancing competing interests.

If a trial court erroneously admitted a confession into evidence, can a conviction nevertheless be affirmed on the ground that the error was harmless? As a matter of federal constitutional law, it has long been clear that improper admission of confessions subject to most challenges—including *Miranda* ones—can constitute harmless error if the appellate court is convinced beyond a reasonable doubt that the improperly admitted confession did not contribute to the jury verdict or conviction. Whether admission of an involuntary confession could constitute harmless error, however, remained open until Arizona v. Fulminante.[14] Four members of the Supreme Court urged that such error should always require reversal of a conviction for several reasons. First, the potential unreliability of an involuntary confession, when combined with the difficulty of accessing the impact of a confession upon a jury, means that use of the harmless error rule in this context creates risks of inaccurate convictions not presented by its application where confessions inadmissible for other reasons were improperly used.

Second and more importantly, use of an involuntary confession—regardless of its accuracy—transforms the criminal justice system into an abhorrent inquisitorial one and thus aborts the basic trial process and renders the trial fundamentally unfair.

The *Fulminante* majority, however, reasoned that appellate courts can reliably determine whether improper uses of an involuntary confession, like other trial errors, affected the outcomes of cases. Thus convictions rendered potentially inaccurate by reliance upon involuntary confessions will be identified and reversed even under the harmless error analysis. The Court also concluded that use of an involuntary confession is not meaningfully different than use of evidence obtained by other reprehensible law enforcement misconduct and therefore has no uniquely fundamental impact upon the fairness of the trial. Consequently, improper admission of an involuntary confession does not require, as a matter of federal constitutional law, reversal of a conviction if the appellate court is convinced beyond a reasonable doubt that the confession did not contribute to the outcome.

States remain free, of course, to apply a different rule as a matter of state procedure. Given the nature and intensity of the disagreement over the propriety of applying harmless error analysis to involuntary confessions, some states are likely to require automatic reversal of convictions if on appeal the trial judge is held to have erroneously admitted an involuntary confession.

§ 163. Future of Confession Law

The last quarter-century of confession law has been dominated, of course, by *Miranda.* The early years saw the Warren Court proceeding with confidence that *Miranda* and its progeny would reform custodial interrogation. This initial enthusiasm has dissipated, and the post-*Warren* Court has clearly failed to develop the *Miranda* requirements as vigor-

---

13. See § 147 supra.

14. 111 S.Ct. 1246 (1991).

ously as the optimism of the later 1960s suggested. Where is confession law likely to go from here?

On the federal constitutional level, there is little likelihood that the Supreme Court will develop prophylactic rules beyond those promulgated in *Miranda* and Edwards v. Arizona.[1] Perhaps the most pressing question is whether the Supreme Court will overrule at least part of *Miranda* itself.

The Court is quite unlikely to abandon *Miranda's* holdings that the Fifth and Fourteenth Amendments require the right to the assistance of counsel, the basic warnings, and effective waivers. But the continued vitality of the prophylactic exclusionary requirement is probably in some jeopardy. A majority might well be persuaded that violations of these requirements no longer require exclusion of resulting confessions, at least where the evidence establishes convincingly that the violations had no effect or only minimal impact upon the defendants' decisions to confess.

Whether or not *Miranda's* prophylactic approach is modified, emphasis will increasingly be placed on a case-by-case consideration of the effectiveness of defendants' confession decisions. At least after judicial procedings have commenced or during custodial interrogation, the Court will continue to insist that those decisions meet minimal requirements of both voluntariness and intelligence. The criteria for applying these requirements, however, are likely to demand relatively little. Voluntariness will be quite generally defined and will leave substantial room for trial court flexibility. Intelligence is unlikely to require more than minimal intellectual understanding of the basic abstract rights to remain silent and to have an attorney and perhaps of the prosecution's ability to use as evidence any self-incriminating admissions made.

The increasingly limited scope of federal constitutional requirements will result in increasing efforts to persuade state courts to develop additional protections for suspects as a matter of state constitutional and nonconstitutional law. State courts will, then, have to confront the difficult questions that have troubled the Supreme Court during the last twenty-five years. What interests of accuseds are protected by state law? More specifically, does state law give suspects a legitimate interest in deciding whether to give the prosecution a usable confession only with a relatively full understanding of the wisdom of doing so? Or are suspects' legitimate interests more limited?

Once they identify the relevant protected interests, state courts will have to address the equally difficult question of how those interests should be protected. Can and should state courts construe state self-incrimination and right to counsel provisions as mandating detailed prophylactic rules of the sort promulgated in *Miranda?* If so, what such rules should be developed? Defendants' decisions will also have to be both voluntary and intelligent as a matter of state law. State tribunals, then, will also have to consider whether to give those state law requirements a more expansive content than the analogous federal constitutional demands.

Increased emphasis upon the effectiveness of suspects' decisions will raise the same difficulty courts experienced administering the pre-*Miranda* voluntariness requirement. Among the most troublesome of these is still the accurate re-creation in court of precisely what occurred during field and stationhouse interrogation sessions.

Hopes that modern technology may reduce these problems has given rise to suggestions that interrogations and confessions be recorded. In 1985, the Alaska Supreme Court held that state due process requires "where feasible" that custodial interrogation sessions be recorded. Other courts, however, have balked at reading so specific a requirement into general state constitutional language.

Whether or not constitutionally required, proof of confessions by means of audio or video recordings might reasonably be encouraged as a matter of prosecution policy or even demanded as a matter of evidence law. Such

§ 163

1. 451 U.S. 477 (1981), discussed in § 150 supra.

recordings are probably quite valuable in presenting juries, trial judges, and appellate courts with as accurate as possible a re-creation of the circumstances of defendants' statements; video recordings are especially valuable in this regard. The advantages are not one-sided; such recordings may be valuable to the prosecution in establishing that defendants did in fact waive their rights and that they did so voluntarily. The major difficulty is assuring that such recordings are "complete," in the sense that they reflect as fully as possible the relevant interaction between law enforcement officers and the defendant. A recording may even misleadingly suggest that the defendant was not influenced by anything not memorialized on the recording. Thus, recording may unfairly increase defendants' already difficult task of establishing—where it occurred—law enforcement misconduct relevant to the admissibility or credibility of a confession.

Overall, confession law is likely to fall significantly short of what some believe is necessary to guard against convictions being influenced by unreliable confessions. Federal constitutional law in particular, given *Connelly,* will place decreased emphasis on accuracy considerations. Perhaps, in light of this, trial courts should more explicitly and vigorously inquire on a case-by-case basis whether there are unacceptable risks that juries will be unable or disinclined to objectively evaluate the credibility of specific confessions offered by the prosecution. This, of course, could be done pursuant to trial judges' general power to exclude logically relevant evidence when its probative value is outweighed by other considerations, including jurors' inability to judge the probative worth of the evidence. Thus a trial judge could properly take into consideration such concerns as jurors' reputed tendency to give great and perhaps excessive weight to evidence that a defendant earlier acknowledged guilt or incriminating facts, as well as defendants' general difficulty in recreating the details of law enforcement interrogation and his own response to that experience. Against such considerations, of course, must be balanced the prosecution's right to have the jury consider all otherwise admissible evidence of the defendant's guilt as well as the traditional assumption that a confession properly elicited is "evidence of the most satisfactory character." If admissibility requirements are relaxed as much as seems likely, then, reliability concerns ought to be addressed directly by giving trial judges greater power and responsibility for assessing the risk that jurors will be improperly influenced by evidence that defendants confessed.

Chapter 15

THE PRIVILEGE CONCERNING IMPROPERLY OBTAINED EVIDENCE

Table of Sections

---

§ 164. Introduction

Traditionally, out-of-court impropriety in the manner by which evidence was obtained did not affect its admissibility. This position rested primarily, of course, upon the need for all probative evidence to assure the most ac-curate resolution of lawsuits. In addition, however, courts' reluctance to inquire into such impropriety was based upon their perception that inquiries would be too costly and time-consuming. Probably the most important recent development in the law of evi-

283

dence as applied in criminal litigation has been the increase in requirements that reject this traditional approach and that mandate exclusion of evidence because of the manner in which it was obtained.

These requirements are appropriately characterized as rules of privilege rather than rules of competency.[1] Generally speaking, their purpose is not to facilitate the accurate ascertainment of facts by safeguarding against unreliable or misleading evidence but rather to further other interests embodied in the requirements violated by the manner in which the evidence was obtained.[2]

Discussions sometimes assume the existence of "the exclusionary rule," suggesting that there is only one remedial requirement involved. This is unfortunate and misleading. Litigation and discussion is often dominated by considerations of the Supreme Court's construction of the Fourth Amendment to the United States Constitution as requiring the exclusion in both state and federal criminal prosecutions of evidence tainted by a violation of that provision.[3] But this ignores that exclusion may be required because evidence was obtained by violating other legal requirements, many of them not embodied in the federal constitution. Moreover, the contents of these exclusionary requirements need not necessarily be the same as that of the Fourth Amendment exclusionary requirement.

Generally, then, discussion best avoids simplistic reference to "the exclusionary rule" as a single rule covering a range of situations. Instead, this area should be conceptualized as containing numerous possible exclusionary rules or sanctions. An exclusionary sanction may attach to any legal requirement that could be violated in the gathering of evidence. There are potentially as many exclusionary sanctions as there are legal requirements of this sort. The Fourth Amendment exclusion-

ary sanction may provide a benchmark for analysis of issues presented by other exclusionary sanctions. But it is important to recognize that other such sanctions may differ in content from the Fourth Amendment's rule. Whether and how they *should* differ are hard issues that tend to be obscured by discussion of "the exclusionary rule."

It is, of course, difficult to separate discussion of exclusionary sanctions from consideration of the underlying rules enforced by these sanctions. On the other hand, the contents of those rules are not matters of evidence law and, in any case, practicality precludes full coverage here of the contents of these rules. Consequently, this chapter focuses upon the exclusionary remedies rather than the rights violated.

Many legal requirements relating to the admissibility of confessions, such as the *Miranda* requirements and directives that an arrested person be promptly presented before a magistrate, are enforced by rules that probably constitute exclusionary sanctions within the meaning of this chapter. For convenience, however, these are treated in Chapter 14, devoted generally to confessions.

§ 165. Policy Bases for Exclusionary Sanctions

The purposes which exclusionary rules might serve have been discussed primarily in the context of the federal constitutional requirements, but this discussion can quite easily be generalized. How the Supreme Court has developed the conceptual bases for these federal constitutional requirements is considered later.[1] While this case law is a model that might be applied in other contexts, the Court's selection of those objectives legitimately served and the comparative significance given them is certainly not beyond reasonable dispute. Some state courts, in devel-

---

§ 164

1. See the discussion in §§ 72 and 72.1 supra concerning the distinction between rules of privilege and those of competency.

2. For a general discussion of the uses of privileges, see Chapter 8, supra.

3. See § 166 infra.

§ 165

1. See § 167 infra.

oping state exclusionary requirements, have rejected at least parts of this model in developing the conceptual bases for these state law rules.[2]

It is clear that exclusionary sanctions result in rejection of what would otherwise be relevant and competent evidence, and therefore they bear a significant burden of justification. Such justification might be provided by several quite different functions which these sanctions might serve.

Promotion of Accurate Results. Can exclusionary rules be defended on the ground that they result in rejection of evidence that might otherwise increase the risk that trials would lead to inaccurate results? Some exclusionary sanctions may be supported, at least to some extent, on this basis. If counsel's presence at lineups reduces the risk of suggestiveness, for example, exclusion of eyewitness testimony tainted by the witness's identification of the defendant at a lineup conducted in violation of this right[3] might to some extent result in rejection of unreliable evidence that might otherwise be credited beyond what can be defended on objective grounds.

Most exclusionary sanctions, however, cannot be supported on these grounds. To the contrary, the fact that the evidence excluded by these requirements is not only relevant and competent but also highly reliable increases the difficulty of justifying the requirements.

Prevention of Future Violations. A major function served by exclusionary sanctions, of course, is the prevention of future violations of the legal requirement enforced by exclusion of evidence. Prevention might be effectuated in at least two quite different ways: deterrence and "education" or "assimilation."

Deterrence consists of motivating persons to consciously choose not to violate legal requirements because of a desire to avoid rendering evidence inadmissible. Usually in exclusionary sanction debates this means encouraging law enforcement officers to comply with legal requirements in a conscious effort to assure

the admissibility of the products of their investigative efforts. But detractors of the exclusionary sanction approach argue that any expectation that deterrence will work effectively is naive, because law enforcement officers will often perceive the threat of exclusion as far less meaningful than other considerations influencing their conduct.

Exclusion will be a possibility only if the case is actively contested. Most criminal cases are not ultimately litigated, so the technical admissibility of evidence will not be a consideration. In the infrequent cases in which exclusion becomes a real possibility, the threat materializes only long after the officers' role in the case is finished. A threat to exclude, made in the context of plea bargaining and protracted processing of criminal cases, may be a threat of such minimal and distant significance that it cannot be expected to overcome, in the officers' minds, other considerations that suggest different courses of action.

In actuality, other considerations may be more immediately pressing and make stronger cases for officers' attention. If an officer believes that compliance with legal requirements endangers his personal safety, he is unlikely to ignore that risk because of the possibility of legal challenges to the admissibility of the products of his actions at some distant time. Similarly, the expectations of the officer's peers and immediate supervisors may well conflict with what the law requires and may compete quite effectively with evidentiary rules for the officer's response.

Moreover, the legal requirements with which the officer is expected to comply may be so unclear as to frustrate efforts to ascertain and follow them. Or they may appear to the officer as unrealistic, meaningless or both, and thus invite circumvention.

There is even a risk that to the extent an exclusionary sanction may convey a meaningful deterrent message to law enforcement officers, the result may be that officers will find it most advantageous to completely forego for-

2. See § 168 *infra.*

3. See § 166 *infra.*

mal prosecution and instead rely upon "street justice" to encourage what they perceive as desirable behavior. If the result of an evidentiary rule is to encourage law enforcement agencies to engage in informal and largely extra-legal activities rather than to encourage them to comply with legal requirements so that prosecution remains possible, the rules have arguably effectuated the worst of all possibilities.

Perhaps the lesson is that generalization about the deterrent effect of exclusionary sanctions is impossible. Some law enforcement activities may be far more subject to being influenced by evidentiary rules than others. Some legal requirements might far more than others lend themselves to effective implementation by means of exclusionary requirements.

Prevention of undesired law enforcement activity, however, may be accomplished in ways other than deterrence. The Supreme Court has noted the possibility that the long-term effect of excluding evidence may be to demonstrate the seriousness with which society regards the underlying legal requirements. This, in turn, may cause law enforcement officers and policymakers to incorporate the requirements into their value system and, presumably, to accept them unconsciously as demanding compliance regardless of the consciously-perceived effect of noncompliance.

How effective exclusionary sanctions are in enforcing various legal requirements in different contexts remains addressed largely on the basis of intuition. Some empirical research has been undertaken, but in part because of severe methodological problems it is inconclusive.

Judicial Integrity Considerations. Proponents of exclusionary sanctions have suggested that exclusion can be justified in whole or in part on the basis of what the Supreme Court in Elkins v. United States[4] called "the imperative of judicial integrity." But two very different approaches are sometimes confused in discussions of judicial integrity.

One argument is that courts' use of improperly obtained evidence is simply and inherently "wrong." Of course, the nature of the argument means that it is incapable of utilitarian analysis or empirical verification. At its base, it rests upon an intuitive notion of "right" or "integrity." Whether any such notion of "right" can provide strong support for an important evidentiary rule, of course, is at best problematic.

But another argument often regarded as a judicial integrity consideration has a clearly utilitarian end and thus is susceptible to efforts to verify it. This approach is attributed to Justice Brandeis' opinion in Olmstead v. United States:

> In a government of laws, existence of the government will be imperiled if it fails to observe the law scrupulously * * *. Crime is contagious. If the Government becomes a lawbreaker, it breeds contempt for law; it invites every man to become a law unto himself; it invites anarchy.[5]

This means, he continued, that the government, like a private litigant, should be denied access to the courts if it comes with unclean hands. If the government bases its request for aid from the courts on illegally obtained evidence, "aid is denied despite the defendant's wrong. It is denied in order to maintain respect for law; in order to promote confidence in the administration of justice; in order to preserve the judicial process from contamination."

Essentially, this argument is that if illegally seized evidence is used by the government acting through its courts, government in general and its courts in particular will lose the respect of the governed and will be rendered less able to perform their governing functions. In the case of courts, this means that they will be rendered unable to resolve disputes among citizens.

Despite the rhetorical flourish with which Justice Brandeis demonstrated this argument can be made, whether it coincides with reality is problematic. Whether the courts' ability to

---

4. 364 U.S. 206 (1960).

5. 277 U.S. 438, 485 (1928) (Brandeis, J., dissenting).

command respect and compliance is affected by evidentiary rules is, of course, open to doubt. But to the extent that it is, this argument may distort the effect of those rules. General respect for the judiciary may well suffer when the courts are perceived as ignoring reliable evidence because of impropriety in the manner it was obtained, particularly if doing so requires the acquittal of persons clearly guilty of serious antisocial acts.

Remedy for Wrongs Done. Superficially, at least, exclusionary sanctions would seem to perform a unique and perhaps appropriate remedial function. The law's objective, the argument might run, should be to place a wronged person as close to his previous condition as is feasible.

In some ways, this is impossible; no legal remedy can erase the experience of having one's privacy invaded or eliminate the present traumatic impact of that memory. In addition, however, before the wrong occurred the person was not facing criminal charges in which the prosecution would have available for evidentiary use against him the results of that wrongful activity. After and because of the wrong, he does face such charges. This is something the law can change, but only by an exclusionary sanction. Only this remedy enables the wronged person to be restored to a condition in which he does not face criminal prosecution on the basis of the results of the wrong done to him.

On the other hand, this effect of exclusion is arguably neither appropriate nor really remedial. Generally, the wrong done to the defendant is regarded as limited to the original action, as for example the search of the defendant's home; the relevant harm for which compensation might be warranted is limited to that occasioned by the wrong itself. Use of the resulting evidence is neither a part of that wrong or its harm nor a new and additional wrong. An evidentiary rule that bars use of the evidence, then, does not serve to make the defendant whole in any relevant sense.

Addressing this problem obviously requires careful consideration of the manner in which the underlying rights are conceptualized. Do the legal requirements violated create a right not simply to be free of the violation but also to be free of the evidentiary consequences of any such violation? If the rights created by the underlying legal requirement include a right not to have resulting evidence used, then an exclusionary sanction is remedial. Alternatively it can be argued that if the original illegality invaded a personal right of the defendant, that right is further or again infringed by the use of the resulting evidence, perhaps because that official use legitimizes the conduct that produced it.

Even if exclusion does tend to respond in a logical manner to the harm done, it may not be "appropriate" because it provides an excessive remedy. This is especially the case if exclusion of evidence frustrates the prosecution. Acquittal of a demonstrably guilty person may simply be too heavy a cost even to make a victimized person whole.

§ 166. Federal Constitutional Exclusionary Sanctions: (a) Development of the Requirements of Exclusion

Federal Constitutional exclusionary sanctions appear to have originated in confusion concerning the substance of Fourth and Fifth Amendment protection. In Boyd v. United States,[1] an unsuccessful claimant in a forfeiture action sought relief from a judgment of forfeiture on the ground that the trial court erred in receiving into evidence an invoice which the claimant had been compelled to produce by order of the trial court. Both the Fourth and Fifth Amendments were invoked. The Supreme Court held that the compulsory production of the document was subject to scrutiny under the Fourth Amendment. To determine whether it was reasonable, the Court turned to the Fifth Amendment's prohibition against compelled self-incrimination. Finding an "intimate relationship" between the two provisions, the Court concluded that compelled production or other seizure of a

§ 166

1. 116 U.S. 616 (1885).

person's private books or papers to be used in evidence against him was violative of the Fifth Amendment. Ultimately, the Court held that the admission into evidence of the invoice, given the manner in which it was obtained, violated both the Fourth Amendment prohibition against unreasonable searches and seizures and the Fifth Amendment prohibition against compelled self-incrimination.

But the Court was unwilling to require exclusion where no Fifth Amendment considerations were present. In Adams v. New York,[2] Adams sought relief from a state conviction on the ground that the state had used in evidence over his objection certain papers obtained from him in an improper search. Finding no Fifth Amendment violation in the seizure of the papers, the Court distinguished Boyd as involving compelled production of items. Apparently then treating the case as one involving a violation of the Fourth but not the Fifth Amendment, the Court applied what it described as "the weight of authority as well as reason," embodied in the rule that courts will not pause to inquire as to the means by which competent evidence is obtained.

Ten years later, however, in Weeks v. United States,[3] the Court held that the Fourth Amendment, as it applied in federal criminal litigation, imposed an exclusionary sanction. Prior to Weeks' trial in federal court for use of the mails for gambling purposes, he moved in the trial court for the return of certain property obtained in what he alleged was an improper search. The trial court denied the motion insofar as it concerned items that were pertinent to Weeks' guilt of the pending charge. When these items were later offered by the Government at trial, Weeks objected and the trial court overruled his objection. Both actions of the trial court were assigned as error on appeal. Addressing only Weeks' complaint concerning the trial court's pretrial refusal to order return of the property, the Court distinguished Adams as involving no

such issue, and found constitutional error. Its explanation, however, was quite broad. "If letters and private documents can thus be [improperly] seized and held and used in evidence against a citizen accused of an offense," the Court reasoned, "the protection of the Fourth Amendment declaring his right to be secure against such searches and seizures is of no value, and, so far as those thus placed are concerned, might as well be stricken from the Constitution."

The manner in which Adams was distinguished in Weeks suggests that the Court's willingness to embrace the exclusionary sanction was in part at least because as presented the issue involved not only the admissibility of evidence but also the right to possession of items improperly taken from the defendant. But any relationship between the right to have evidence excluded and the existence of a right to possession of a tangible item in the possession of the prosecution was rejected by Silverthorne Lumber Co. v. United States,[4] in which the items obtained by the Government pursuant to an unreasonable search were returned to the defendants by order of the court. A subpoena was issued directing the defendants to produce the items; upon their noncompliance the defendants were found in contempt. The Court acknowledged that the Government was seeking to restrict Weeks to situations in which the Government was in wrongful physical possession of items. To accept this view, the Court reasoned, would be to reduce the Fourth Amendment "to a form of words." It concluded that the essence of Weeks "is that not merely [that] evidence [improperly] acquired shall not be used before the Court but that it shall not be used at all."

Weeks, of course, was inapplicable to state litigation, and doubt remained even whether the Fourth Amendment itself was binding on the states. In Wolf v. Colorado,[5] the Court for the first time directly addressed these issues. Concluding that the core of the Fourth Amendment—the security of one's privacy

2.   192 U.S. 585 (1904).

3.   232 U.S. 383 (1914).

4.   251 U.S. 385 (1920).

5.   338 U.S. 25 (1949).

against arbitrary intrusion by the police—was basic to a free society and therefore implicit in the concept of orderly liberty, the Court held that under Palko v. Connecticut [6] the Fourth Amendment prohibition against unreasonable searches and seizures was enforceable against the States through the Due Process clause of the Fourteenth Amendment.

But the Court then distinguished the prohibition against unreasonable searches and seizures from the exclusionary remedy applied in federal criminal litigation and found the latter not binding on the States. A number of American jurisdictions and most of the English–speaking world had rejected the exclusionary sanction. Further, whether to adopt such a remedy raised a number of questions that "are not to be so dogmatically answered as to preclude the varying solutions which spring from an allowable range of judgment on issues not susceptible of quantitative solution." While the states might well be barred from affirmatively sanctioning unreasonable searches and seizures, the Court concluded, the Fourth and Fourteenth Amendments did not require them to exclude evidence obtained by such methods.

In 1952, however, the Court imposed a limited federal constitutional exclusionary requirement on the states, albeit as a matter of general due process law. In Rochin v. California,[7] officers improperly broke into the defendant's bedroom, seized him, and caused him to vomit, thereby obtaining certain capsules of morphine. Without discussing any Fourth Amendment implications of the facts, the Court held that Rochin's conviction in state court of possession of the morphine violated his Fourteenth Amendment right to due process. "It has long since ceased to be true that due process of law is heedless of the means by which otherwise relevant and credible evidence is obtained," the Court commented. Since the law enforcement activity by which the morphine was obtained was conduct that "shocks the conscience," the conviction resting upon that evidence violated due process.

By 1961, the Court was prepared to reconsider *Wolf's* conclusion that the Fourth Amendment exclusionary rule was not binding on the states, and in Mapp v. Ohio,[8] this holding of *Wolf* was reversed. Since *Wolf,* the majority explained, more than half of those states considering whether to adopt an exclusionary sanction as a matter of state law had decided to do so. The weight of the relevant authority, then, could not be said to oppose the *Weeks* rule. More important, however, the Court read experience as contradicting the *Wolf* assumption that remedies other than an exclusionary rule could be relied upon to enforce Fourth Amendment rights. The experience and decisions of the state courts as well as the Supreme Court's own decisions recognized the "obvious futility of relegating the Fourth Amendment to the protection of other remedies * * * " Consequently, the *Weeks* exclusionary rule was held an essential part of both the Fourth and Fourteenth Amendments and therefore binding on the states as well as the federal government.

Having determined that an exclusionary sanction was an essential part of the Fourth Amendment right to be free from unreasonable searches and seizures, the Court proceeded to apply it uncritically to other federal constitutional rights.

The Court did not carefully distinguish when considerations of reliability were relevant to or perhaps even controlled whether a federal constitutional right was construed as imposing an exclusionary sanction. Exclusion of a prior conviction obtained in violation of the defendant's right to counsel at trial, for example, seemed to rest in part at least upon the risk that such convictions will be inaccurate, although the Fourth Amendment cases showed no such concern.

The uncertain role of reliability concerns was most dramatically demonstrated by the trilogy of "lineup" cases decided in 1967. In

6. 302 U.S. 319 (1937).

7. 342 U.S. 165 (1952).

8. 367 U.S. 643 (1961).

Gilbert v. California [9] and *United States v. Wade* [10] the Court held that a criminal suspect against whom judicial proceedings have been begun is entitled by the Sixth Amendment to the presence of counsel when he is viewed by a witness who will later testify at trial. This, the Court reasoned, was necessary to implement the eventual defendant's right at trial effectively to confront and cross-examine such witnesses.

In *Gilbert,* it imposed a *per se* exclusionary sanction, providing that when a witness has identified a defendant at a viewing conducted in violation of this right to counsel the prosecution may not make trial use of evidence that this out-of-court identification occurred. But in *Wade,* the Court held that despite such an identification a witness will nevertheless be permitted to make an in-court identification of the defendant as the perpetrator, if the prosecution establishes that such testimony would have a source independent of the tainted identification procedure. Despite the underlying concern that lineup procedures conducted without counsel might so affect witnesses as to render their later identification testimony unreliable, the Court apparently saw little direct relationship between denial of the right to counsel in a particular case and the reliability of the witness's later testimony. An exclusionary sanction was imposed not to bar the use of unreliable evidence but to encourage police to respect suspects' right to counsel.

In contrast, the third case of the trilogy—as least as later read by the Court—recognized a different right to exclusion closely tied to reliability. In *Stovall v. Denno,* [11] the Court held that a defendant may also attack the admissibility of eyewitness testimony on the ground that the witness was exposed to an identification procedure that was unacceptably suggestive. As later developed, this right rests entirely upon what the Court perceived as the need to guard against unreliability. Consequently, "reliability is the linchpin in determining the admissibility of identification testimony [challenged on this basis]." Only if the procedure creates a very substantial likelihood of "irreparable misidentification" of the defendant by the witness does due process prohibit the use of the testimony.

The Supreme Court has made clear that these various federal constitutional exclusionary sanctions are not identical in content. As a general rule, all evidence obtained by the prosecution as result of a violation of the defendant's Fourth Amendment rights is inadmissible. *Oregon v. Elstad,* [12] however, held that this is not the case where the exclusionary sanction is the result of a violation of the *Miranda* rights. Precisely how the two exclusionary rules differ in this regard is not clear, [13] but there can be no doubt that that they do differ in substance.

Whether *Rochin* has current vitality is somewhat uncertain. Perhaps any impropriety in obtaining evidence that could conceivably meet *Rochin's* "shock the conscience" test would now also clearly violate some other more specific constitutional requirement now enforced by exclusion—usually one imposed by the Fourth Amendment—and therefore be excludable on the basis of that requirement. Thus *Rochin* may reflect only a stage in the Court's transition from *Wolf* to *Mapp* and has perhaps been entirely superceded by *Mapp.* On the other hand, the Supreme Court has never so characterized *Rochin* and continues to consider its applicability on the assumption that it is still a viable alternative to other federal constitutional doctrines. It may remain of some significance in areas simply not addressed by the Fourth Amendment, where it is available upon proof of an extraordinarily offensive intrusion upon interests that, in general, are not within federal constitutional protection.

§ 167. Federal Constitutional Exclusionary Sanctions: (b) The Policy Considerations

In developing the federal constitutional exclusionary requirements, primarily the

9. 388 U.S. 263 (1967).

10. 388 U.S. 218 (1967).

11. 388 U.S. 293 (1967).

12. 470 U.S. 298 (1985).

13. See § 176 infra.

Fourth Amendment sanction, the Supreme Court has narrowed the policy considerations it regards as relevant to those rules. It has also developed a consistently-applied approach to framing the subissues raised in developing the contents of those requirements. In the course of this process, the Court has made three basic choices regarding the potentially-relevant policy considerations.

First, the Court has made clear that the federal rules do not serve a significant legitimate remedial function. This is because as the Court envisions the injury done, exclusion of evidence simply does not tend to make the victim whole. "[T]he ruptured privacy of the victims' homes and effects," it explained, "cannot be restored. Reparation comes too late." [1]

If exclusion of evidence cannot restore the violated privacy, why cannot it at least reduce one effect of the privacy violation by replacing the victim to a position wherein he does not face criminal prosecution based on evidence obtained as a result of the violation of his privacy interests? The Court has not directly addressed this question. But most likely it views the prosecution's possession of and ability to use incriminating evidence as entirely unrelated to the legitimate interests of the defendant. The prosecution has a right to possession of this evidence; the defendant has no ultimate right to withhold it from the prosecution. To the extent that an improper search results in the prosecution being able to implement its interest in obtaining such evidence, the search violates no protected interests, that is, no "rights," of the defendant. The wrong to the defendant consisted entirely of violating his privacy. To the extent that this violation of privacy factually resulted in the prosecution obtaining access to incriminating evidence, this in no way contributes to the offensive aspects of the search, that is, those aspects as to which the defendant has a legitimate claim to remedy.

Consequently, to deprive the prosecution of the ability to use this evidence would in no way restore the defendant in a manner to which he has any legitimate claim. His only legitimate claim is for restoration of his violated privacy, which is in no way accomplished by depriving the prosecution of evidence.

Second, the Court has adopted the view that considerations of judicial integrity have only a "limited role" in Fourth Amendment theory and, consequently, in determining the content of the provision's exclusionary mandate. This is because the "primary meaning" of judicial integrity in this context is such that it is violated when, but only when, courts' use of illegally obtained evidence encourages future violations of the sort that provided the prosecution access to the evidence at issue. [2] Consequently, whether particular use of illegally obtained evidence offends judicial integrity considerations involves essentially the same question as whether it serves a preventive purpose: will the admission of the evidence encourage future illegality of the sort committed to obtain the evidence at issue?

Third, with regard to the preventive function of the exclusionary rule, the Court has suggested that the long-term "educative" effect is "[m]ore important[ ]" than the tendency of the threat of exclusion to consciously deter officers from future violations. [3] Whether it actually follows this approach, however, is doubtful, since its formulations of specific issues tend to frame the questions in terms of deterrence rather than prevention by other mechanisms.

Building on these three basic decisions regarding the relevant considerations, the Court has developed a consistent formula for framing specific subissues regarding the content of the federal constitutional exclusionary rules. First articulated in United States v. Calandra, [4] this approach requires that the issue be put as one of proposed expansion of the exclu-

§ 167
1. Linkletter v. Walker, 381 U.S. 618, 637 (1965).
2. United States v. Janis, 428 U.S. 433, 458 n. 35 (1976).

3. Stone v. Powell, 428 U.S. 465, 492 (1976).
4. 414 U.S. 338 (1974).

sionary requirement beyond the core demand that evidence obtained as a direct result of activity violating the constitutional requirements be excluded when offered by the prosecution to prove the defendant's guilt in the prosecution's case-in-chief at a criminal trial. The analysis requires identification of, first, the increased effectiveness of the exclusionary sanction in accomplishing its purpose that would result from the proposed expansion, and, second, the costs of doing so. The critical question is whether the incremental increase in effectiveness is worth the cost that must be paid.

Generally, in inquiring into the potential for increased effectiveness the Court focuses upon deterrence, and the major question becomes the incremental deterrent effect which would be achieved by the proposed expansion. With regard to the costs, of course, the loss of reliable evidence of offenders' guilt is the major concern. But in addition the Court has taken into account other considerations, such as administrative costs and disruption of the criminal justice system in general and criminal trials in particular. In *Calandra,* for example, the specific issue before the Court was whether the Fourth Amendment exclusionary rule should be applied to grand jury proceedings by permitting witnesses to decline to respond to questions based upon information obtained in violation of the witnesses' Fourth Amendment rights. Permitting this, the majority stressed, would require that grand jury investigations be frequently halted for extended inquiries into the manner in which particular information was acquired. The result would be serious interference with the effective and expeditious discharge by grand juries of their historic role and functions.

This approach is subject to criticism on several grounds. First, it arguably ignores or minimizes the functions of exclusionary sanctions other than conscious deterrence of future violations. But the decision to focus upon deterrence is really a part of the Supreme Court's perception of the rationale for the basic exclusionary requirements rather than a part of its approach to formulating specific exclusionary sanction issues. Second,

and more fundamentally, the *Calandra* approach, even if it is conceptually sound, arguably poses what are essentially unanswerable questions. Given the minimal information available regarding the actual effect of excluding evidence, for example, it is most likely impossible to formulate even a reasonable estimate of the respective deterrent effects of various ways in which exclusionary sanctions might be developed. Similarly, there is little or no useful information on the precise costs that would be incurred by various expansions of the sanctions.

The analysis may also be faulted for providing imprecise criteria for the final balancing decisions. How much in costs should we be willing to pay for how much incremental deterrence or prevention? Or, if these matters are necessarily quite speculative, how certain must we be of how much deterrence before certain costs become excessive? There is, however, no practical way in which to arrive at even a reasonably precise estimate of either the actual costs of various possible expansions of the exclusionary rules or the increased prevention that could be expected from those expansions. Any imprecision in the standard for balancing such estimates, therefore, is probably of little or no significance.

§ 168. State Constitutional Exclusionary Sanctions

Despite the prominence of *Mapp* and Fourth Amendment case law in exclusionary sanction discussion, the exclusionary remedy was first developed in state constitutional litigation. State decisions provide bases of increasing importance for modern exclusionary sanctions, independent of *Mapp* and its progeny.

Several state courts held soon after the turn of the century that evidence obtained in violation of their search and seizure provisions could not be used in criminal trials. Most state courts held to the contrary, however, and the few decisions adopting an exclusionary approach did not effectively advance justifications for doing so. In Wolf v. Colorado [1] the Court relied in part upon "[t]he contrariety of views of the States" in declining to read the Fourth Amendment as imposing an exclusionary requirement on the states. But in *Mapp,* the Court stressed that since *Wolf* more than half of the states addressing the issue had accepted all or part of the *Weeks* rule.

Many observers of the Supreme Court regard the federal tribunal as having recently slowed or reversed the Warren Court's development of the Fourth, Fifth and Sixth Amendments as appropriately vigorous limits on state law enforcement activity. This trend has encouraged litigants to turn to state courts with arguments that state constitutional provisions analagous to the federal provisions be construed "independently" of those federal provisions and more expansively so as to provide greater protections for those being investigated or prosecuted for criminal activity. To the extent that state courts have responded in a sympathetic manner, the resulting "new federalism" has thrust state constitutional provisions into increased prominence. For many litigants, success in persuading state courts to adopt more expansive constructions of state constitutional provisions is meaningful only if those provisions are enforced by exclusionary sanctions.

States' power to accept or reject an exclusionary approach was confirmed by the Supreme Court in California v. Greenwood.[2] Under California law, the warrantless search of Greenwood's trash constituted an unreasonable search under a state constitutional provision similar to the Fourth Amendment, yet this did not require exclusion of the resulting evidence. All agreed that *Mapp* and its rationale did not require, as a matter of Fourth Amendment law, exclusion of evidence obtained in violation of the state constitution but not in violation of any federal provision.

Greenwood argued, however, that the Due Process Clause of the Fourteenth Amendment barred the state from depriving him of a remedy for police conduct violating state but not federal constitutional law. Rejecting this, the Supreme Court reasoned that the state could have defined unreasonable searches as encompassing no more official activity than was covered by the Fourth Amendment. Since the state has the power to permit police activity not barred by the Fourth Amendment, it necessarily has the lesser included power to prohibit such activity but to enforce that prohibition by means other than excluding evidence from criminal trials.

State constitutional provisions, like their federal counterparts, seldom expressly address the admissibility of evidence obtained in violation of them. When a state court is asked to construe such provisions to require the exclusion of evidence, then, it must choose whether or not to interpret its constitution with the same vigor and flexibility exercised by the Supreme Court in *Mapp.* Occasionally the task is made easier by considerations not present in *Mapp.* Especially where a state constitution is of relatively recent origin, reliable evidence of an actual understanding on the part of the framers or adopters may be available. If so, of course, that understanding controls.

As *Mapp* indicated, prior to 1961 a number of state courts had embraced exclusionary sanctions. State courts sometimes read such decisions as committing the state to a reading of the state provision as imposing an exclusionary remedy for violation of its state law requirements. It is not clear, however, that these early decisions carefully distinguished between state remedies for violations of the federal constitution and similar remedies for violations of the state provisions. In fact, the possibility of significant differences in content between the two may simply not have been anticipated or considered. In other jurisdictions, language accepting an exclusionary sanction for violations of state constitutions has simply offhandedly crept into discussion and become accepted law without any focused and careful consideration as to the propriety

1. 338 U.S. 25 (1949).

2. 486 U.S. 35 (1988).

of this position. State constitutional exclusionary rules have sometimes developed with little or no careful scrutiny of their propriety or wisdom.

Several courts have recently addressed in more depth the propriety of construing their state provisions as the Supreme Court construed the Fourth Amendment in *Mapp*. Each has chosen to do so. The most significant consideration in these analyses has been the courts' perceptions that exclusionary sanctions have become generally accepted and thus are appropriately read into a state provision in the absence of a demonstrated reason to read the state provision otherwise. As the intermediate Connecticut appellate court explained in accurately predicting that the state's highest court would recognize a state constitutional exclusionary rule:

> [T]he [exclusionary] rule has gained overwhelming judicial acceptance as the most effective method of guaranteeing the protection against unreasonable invasion of privacy secured by constitutional search and seizure provisions.[3]

Perhaps most amazing is the lack of diversity in the holdings. No highest state court seems recently to have squarely held that a state provision analogous to the Fourth, Fifth or Sixth Amendment does not require exclusion.

It can be argued, of course, that the *Mapp* analysis notwithstanding, neither state constitutional language nor history provides sufficient bases for state courts to develop state constitutional exclusionary sanctions. To the extent that state courts have authority under state provisions to develop exclusionary sanctions, experience under the federal requirements may suggest the wisdom of restraint.

State constitutional—or nonconstitutional—exclusionary sanctions may be particularly inappropriate because they must be superimposed upon the federal constitutional requirements. As a result, law enforcement officers and prosecutors must contend with two or more bodies of law enforced by draconian penalties. "[O]ne of the few things

worse than a single exclusionary rule," the Arizona Supreme Court has complained, "is two different exclusionary rules." This may, however, be a complaint more appropriately directed at a complex governmental and legal system in which legal requirements can and are imposed by numerous bodies of law on both the state and federal level. If state law enforcement agencies are properly subjected to both federal and state constitutional demands, surely they are not entitled to have the latter armed with no effective remedy so that officers can ignore them with impunity.

A state court's adoption of a state constitutional exclusionary rule, and even its explicit approval of *Mapp's* interpretive approach, does not mean that it is technically or logically bound to follow the Supreme Court's lead in developing the state remedy or even in framing the issues. Most importantly, the state court remains free to redefine for state law purposes the considerations bearing upon how the state remedy will be developed and the comparative importance of those considerations.

The Supreme Court has emphasized the federal constitutional exclusionary sanctions' function in deterring future violations of the substantive requirements of the amendments and has framed exclusionary rule issues so as to tailor the remedies to serve that function.[4] A few state courts have rejected this framework in developing their own state constitutional exclusionary sanctions. The Idaho Supreme Court, for example, has indicated that the state exclusionary sanction will give considerable, although secondary, significance to the function of preserving judicial integrity. Both the Washington and Oregon Supreme Courts have, in effect, rejected the Supreme Court's position that exclusionary sanctions have no legitimate or significant remedial function.

State judicial independence in this area has resulted in several modifications of state constitutions. In 1982, the substantive provisions of Florida's search and seizure provision

---

3. State v. Brown, 14 Conn.App. 605, 543 A.2d 750, 763 (1988).

4. See § 167 supra.

were supplemented with a specific directive that it be construed "in conformity with" the Supreme Court's construction of the Fourth Amendment. Previously the provision had expressly provided that evidence obtained in violation of it was inadmissible in evidence. The 1982 amendment limited this directive to those situations in which the evidence "would be inadmissible under decisions of the United States Supreme Court construing the 4th Amendment to the United States Constitution." In the same year, California voters created a state constitutional "Right to Truth-in-Evidence" section providing that except as enacted by a two-thirds vote of both houses of the state legislature, "relevant evidence shall not be excluded in any criminal proceeding." This has effectively deprived the California courts of power to develop state constitutional exclusionary sanctions requiring exclusion of relevant evidence where such exclusion is not mandated by the federal constitution.

§ 169. Exclusion for Nonconstitutional Illegality (a) In General

Both federal and state constitutional requirements apply only where a defendant establishes that challenged evidence was obtained as a result of a violation of his constitutional rights. But with increasing frequency, defendants are seeking exclusion as a remedy for violation of nonconstitutional legal requirements. When, if ever, exclusion is available on such bases presents a more difficult question than is often recognized. Our acceptance of exclusion as a necessary if not appropriate remedy for the violation of constitutional requirements has tended too often to lead to uncritical acceptance of exclusion as similarly available upon a showing of any illegality. This is simply not the case.

Challenges to relevant evidence on grounds that it was obtained in violation of nonconstitutional legal requirements raises several distinguishable concerns addressed in the next three sections. First is whether courts have

legislatively-provided authority to exclude evidence on these bases.[1] Second is whether courts have autonomous authority to exclude evidence on these grounds.[2] Third is the content of any such exclusionary requirements as exist, given that there is widespread agreement that any exclusionary sanctions in this area are properly more limited than those applied to constitutional violations.[3]

§ 170. Exclusion for Nonconstitutional Illegality (b) Legislative Requirements

Legislatures unquestionably have authority to direct that legal requirements be implemented by excluding evidence obtained in violation of those requirements, or to give courts of the jurisdiction discretionary power to develop exclusionary remedies. Exercises of this authority may be explicit or implicit, and the two possibilities are best considered separately. If an exclusionary requirement rests on legislative authorization, this raises some question as to the breadth of judicial authority to construe and develop the requirement.

Explicit Legislative Exclusionary Requirements. A few jurisdictions have relatively broad statutory requirements of exclusion. Since 1925, Texas has statutorily excluded from criminal trials evidence obtained in violation of the laws or constitutions of either the United States or Texas. North Carolina has a somewhat narrower provision, requiring the suppression of certain evidence obtained in violation of its Criminal Procedure Act. These provisions, however, are exceptional. Most states have neither any general explicit legislative directive for exclusion of illegally obtained evidence nor explicit delegation to the courts of authority to develop any such exclusionary requirement.

Somewhat more frequently, legislatures have provided exclusionary remedies for particular statutes. The primary example is the federal electronic surveillance statute, which contains its own statutory exclusionary remedy. Under this statute, states are authorized

§ 169

1. See § 170 infra.

2. See § 171 infra.

3. See § 172 infra.

to provide by state law for state law enforcement officers to engage in certain electronic surveillance, and state statutes enacted pursuant to this contain exclusionary requirements similar or identical to that in the federal statute.

Other statutory provisions also sometimes explicitly require exclusion. Exclusion may be authorized indirectly, as in the Oregon "implied consent" statute which provides that it is not to be construed as limiting the introduction of otherwise competent and relevant evidence in any proceeding other than a criminal prosecution for driving while intoxicated.

Implied Legislative Exclusionary Requirements. Legislative authority to exclude evidence may sometimes be implied from statutory provisions that lack the sort of explicit requirement discussed above, and courts have recognized this. When a statute is appropriately construed as authorizing or requiring exclusion, however, has proved to be a difficult question for many courts.

In several early cases, the Supreme Court uncritically held that evidence obtained in violation of federal statutory requirements must be excluded.[1] It left unclear, however, whether these holdings rested on readings of legislative intent or were rather exercises of the Court's own power to develop exclusionary requirements.

Some lower courts have been willing on quite scant bases to find implied legislative exclusionary requirements. In United States v. Chemaly,[2] for example, the court held that federal legislation limiting currency searches at the border required exclusion of evidence obtained in violation of its terms. Emphasizing the long acceptance among courts of exclusion as a remedy for even nonconstitutional illegality, the court reasoned that Congress assumed that in the absence of an explicit directive to the contrary courts would enforce the statute by excluding evidence obtained in

violation of it; therefore, congressional silence regarding exclusionary sanctions was an implied directive that such a remedy be applied. There is a discernible tendency on the part of some courts to pursue this analysis under statutes imposing requirements similar to, but more stringent than, constitutional mandates. This is apparently on the assumption that when a legislature acts in an area where constitutional exclusionary rules apply, it ordinarily assumes that its statutory directives will also be enforced by such sanctions.

Most courts, however, are more reluctant to find unexpressed legislative directives that exclusionary sanctions be available. Several considerations are emphasized. If other statutes passed by the legislative body have expressly directed exclusion, legislative failure to similarly provide in the statute at issue suggests to many courts a legislative intention that no such remedy be available for statutes silent on the matter. If the overall purpose of legislation is to increase law enforcement power, courts have also reasoned, the legislature is unlikely to have intended to impede this general objective by imposing an exclusionary sanction, and thus courts should be reluctant to read one into such statutes.

On balance, courts should be reluctant to find implied authority in a statute for exclusion of evidence. Exclusion is an exceptionally costly remedy, and its propriety is highly questionable. Legislative silence almost certainly reflects, in most cases, the absence of a consensus that the provisions being enacted are appropriately enforced by such a remedy. Unless there is reasonably clear evidence of such a consensus, generally reflected in the terms of the statute itself, a statute should not be regarded as empowering the courts to exclude evidence obtained in violation of its requirements.

§ 170

1. Grau v. United States, 287 U.S. 124 (1932) (search warrant issued on showing insufficient to support statutorily-required determination that premises were used for storage or manufacture of liquor); Miller v. United States, 357 U.S. 301 (1958) (violation of statutory require-

ment of prior announcement before entering to execute search warrant required exclusion); Sabbath v. United States, 391 U.S. 585 (1968) (same).

2. 741 F.2d 1346 (11th Cir.1984), order granting en banc hearing vacated 764 F.2d 747 (11th Cir.) (en banc).

Construction of Legislative Requirements. When an exclusionary rule based on legislative authority is applicable, the construction of that rule presents particular problems. Perhaps most significant is the extent to which the general requirement of exclusion is subject to exceptions similar to those developed for federal constitutional exclusionary requirements but not specifically provided for in the legislation.[3] Resolving this question is a difficult task of statutory construction. General statutory language might, of course, be construed in some situations at least as a legislative delegation to the courts of authority to develop exceptions modeled upon those recognized as a matter of federal constitutional law.

§ 171. Exclusion for Nonconstitutional Illegality (c) Judicially Developed Requirements

In the absence of legislative or constitutional authorization, courts may nevertheless have independent power to develop and apply exclusionary requirements. This might be based either upon the authority given many courts to promulgate rules relating to procedure and evidence or upon the power claimed by some courts to exercise what is often called "supervisory authority" over litigation and the behavior of some persons whose actions in some way affect that litigation.

Rulemaking Power. Many American courts have power to promulgate rules of evidence and procedure, granted by statute or legislative provision. This power has been implemented through widespread adoption of evidence rules. Might this power permit a court to promulgate an exclusionary rule applicable to violation of nonconstitutional—as well as perhaps constitutional—legal violations?

Such action has been taken by the Alaska Supreme Court, which in 1979 incorporated into its Rule 26 a provision taken from its Criminal Rules. Under Alaska Rule of Evidence 412, evidence "illegally obtained" may not be used over proper objection by the defendant in a criminal prosecution "for any purpose," with limited exceptions applicable to perjury prosecutions.

Whether this is an appropriate exercise of the rulemaking power is at best problematic. Rulemaking authority is given to courts in large part because of their exceptional ability to address such matters as how to most efficiently and effectively arrive at accurate resolutions in litigated cases. The extent to which exclusionary requirements will interfere with these interests is, of course, an important consideration in deciding whether an exclusionary sanction is appropriate.[1] But far more important are such considerations as the extent to which violations occur and whether other measures hold reasonable promise of discouraging them. The final decision must balance the costs of an exclusionary sanction and the potential benefits of it. This decision is no more than peripherally within courts' area of particular expertise and is clearly the sort of judgment that is ordinarily for legislative decision. Given the nature of exclusionary sanctions, despite their "evidentiary" form, they are best regarded as beyond general judicial evidentiary and procedural rulemaking authority.

Federal Courts' "Supervisory" Power. A number of American courts have held, or indicated in dicta, that they have authority to judicially-develop exclusionary requirements invoked by violation of nonconstitutional legal requirements. The contents of these requirements is considered elsewhere.[2] Most troublesome is the power of courts, without statutory or constitutional enabling authority, to develop such requirements. The most available model for such authority is the Supreme Court's development of what it has described as its "supervisory power" authority to develop such a rule for litigation in the lower federal courts. Whether this percep-

---

3. See discussions under those sections infra considering exceptions: § 177 (independent source), § 179 (attenuation of taint), § 180 (inevitable discovery), § 181 ("good faith"), and § 182 (impeachment).

§ 171

1. See § 165, supra.

2. See § 172 infra.

tion of its power is soundly based is, at best, questionable.

The seminal decision is McNabb v. United States,[3] holding that suppression was required of evidence obtained in violation of what was then the statutory requirement that an arrested person be presented before a magistrate without unnecessary delay. In Rea v. United States,[4] the Court held that a federal officer who had obtained evidence in violation of Rule 41 of the Federal Rules of Criminal Procedure should be enjoined from using that evidence in a state prosecution. Implicitly, *Rea* approved the suppression of this evidence in the federal litigation and explicitly held that Rea was entitled to the additional injunctive relief he sought. Both decisions rested upon what the Court described as its "supervisory power." In *McNabb*, the Court equated an exclusionary rule with other rules of evidence, particularly those—apparently rules of privilege—that are based on considerations other than simply "evidentiary relevance." Development of legal requirements of both sorts, the Court concluded, was permissible pursuant to its "duty" to establish and maintain "civilized standards of procedure and evidence" in the federal courts. *Rea's* discussion went further and suggested that the underlying power was not only to provide for the proper processing of litigation but also to "prescribe standards for law enforcement * * * to protect the privacy of the citizen * * *."

Since *Rea*, the Court has continued to insist that it has such power, but it has obviously become more reluctant to exercise it and in fact has not found occasion to do so. In Lopez v. United States,[5] the Court reaffirmed its "inherent power" to exclude "material" evidence because of illegality in the manner it was obtained, but commented that this power should be "sparingly exercised." Since Lopez could show no "manifestly improper" conduct by the law enforcement officers, invoking the power in his case would not be justified. In

United States v. Caceres,[6] the Court suggested that it had the power to exclude evidence on a "limited individualized approach" for the violation of federal administrative regulations. But exclusion under this power would not be appropriate in the case before it, the Court concluded, since the investigators had made a reasonable, good faith attempt to comply with what they understood to be the applicable legal requirements, and the actions they took would clearly have been permitted had they followed the regulations.

Most recently, the Court in United States v. Payner [7] considered an argument that it should exercise its supervisory power to exclude evidence obtained by "gross illegality" from a person other than the defendant who moved to suppress it. Again reaffirming its supervisory exclusionary power, the Court offered that "Federal courts may use their supervisory power in some circumstances to exclude evidence taken from the defendant by 'willful disobedience of law.'" But it then made clear that the exercise of this power is to be informed by the same considerations and conclusions reached in developing the federal constitutional exclusionary requirements. The Fourth Amendment case law made clear that as a general rule, the purposes of exclusion are adequately achieved if the remedy is made available to those whose interests were violated by the underlying illegality.[8] This should also apply where exclusion might be justified under the supervisory power, and thus under that power federal courts should not suppress otherwise admissible evidence on the ground that it was unlawfully obtained from a third party not before the court.

Both the scope and legitimacy of the supervisory power as applied and discussed in this line of cases has been severely criticized. The Supreme Court's refusal, since *McNabb* and *Rea*, actually to exercise what it continues to insist is the federal courts' supervisory power

---

3. 318 U.S. 332 (1943).

4. 350 U.S. 214 (1956).

5. 373 U.S. 427 (1963).

6. 440 U.S. 741 (1979).

7. 447 U.S. 727 (1980).

8. See § 175 infra.

to develop exclusionary rules for nonconstitutional violations suggests that the tribunal is becoming at least ambivalent concerning the legitimacy of this authority.

The lower federal courts continue to assume that some power to develop exclusionary rules exists, perhaps most significantly—implicitly relying on *Rea*—that violations of some of the nonconstitutional requirements for search warrants imposed by Rule 41 of the Federal Rules of Criminal Procedure under some circumstances require or permit exclusion. The courts are, however, increasingly reluctant to exercise this power.

State Court Decisions. State courts may also have supervisory powers similar to that invoked in *McNabb–Rea*, and these might be relied upon as a basis for state court developed exclusionary requirements. Generally, however, state courts have engaged in little discussion of this possibility. When state tribunals mention supervisory power, they tend to avoid explicit comment upon whether they possess such power and whether it would support development of exclusionary sanctions, and simply find that the situation before them is not sufficient to invoke any such sanction as they might have power to develop.

A number of state courts have, without careful consideration of the possible bases for judicially-developed exclusionary requirements, signaled that state law does not require or permit exclusion of evidence for nonconstitutional legal violations. A number of others, however, have without careful explanation developed at least limited exclusionary requirements. Probably the leading recent decision is Commonwealth v. Mason,[9] in which the Pennsylvania Supreme Court held that in selected situations[10] evidence obtained in violation of the Pennsylvania Rules of Criminal Procedure would be suppressed in criminal litigation. The basis for this action was not made clear, although the opinion suggests reliance upon a state law version of supervisory power.

In general, American courts have been insufficiently critical regarding their power, or the lack thereof, to develop exclusionary sanctions for nonconstitutional violations in obtaining evidence. This is no doubt due in large part to the prominence of federal constitutional exclusionary rule case law in any consideration of exclusionary sanction matters. On one hand, this case law encourages an uncritical assumption that courts have power to develop similar exclusionary requirements for nonconstitutional illegality. On the other, resentment at being constitutionally compelled to accept what is regarded by some as an unwise remedy for constitutional violations encourages equally uncritical rejection of exclusion as an authorized remedy where such a remedy is not constitutionally mandated.

Whether the courts of a particular jurisdiction have the power to develop exclusionary sanctions, and whether they should exercise any such power as they may have, must depend in large part upon the nature and breadth of judicial authority in that jurisdiction and the tradition with which it has been applied and developed. Proper resolution of these issues, in any case, can result only after reasonable consideration is given to the argument that the major factors in deciding whether exclusionary sanctions are appropriate are factors that require legislative rather than judicial action.

§ 172. Exclusion for Nonconstitutional Illegality: (d) Substance of Exclusionary Requirements

The exclusionary requirements developed as part of federal constitutional law are, as an initial matter, unqualified. This means that a showing that evidence was obtained as a factual result of a violation of the underlying constitutional requirement demands exclusion of that evidence. Most exclusionary requirements applicable to nonconstitutional violations, on the other hand, are more qualified. A right to exclusion often demands that

9. 507 Pa. 396, 490 A.2d 421 (1985).

10. See discussion in § 172 infra.

a defendant show more than a violation of a nonconstitutional legal requirement and that the challenged evidence was obtained as a factual result of that violation.

The limited nature of these nonconstitutional exclusionary sanctions is developed in this section. Three types of limitations can usefully be distinguished.

First, those nonconstitutional legal requirements whose violation will trigger a possible right to exclusion have been limited. This limitation has been accomplished in several ways. Some courts have indicated that exclusion will be limited to violation of only legal—usually statutory—requirements that resemble constitutional requirements. Presumably this means nonconstitutional requirements that protect the same or similar interests as are protected by constitutional rules, but that are violated by infringements not significant or basic enough to give rise to a constitutional intrusion. A few courts have suggested that the availability of exclusionary sanctions should turn in part at least upon the type of law enforcement activity affected by the legal requirement. If that activity is generally designed to collect evidence for use in prosecution, an exclusionary sanction is more likely to affect the activity and thus is more appropriately imposed.

The exclusionary sanction attached to the federal electronic surveillance regulatory scheme is unqualified. Nevertheless, the Supreme Court has held that it is triggered only by those statutory provisions that "directly and substantially implement" the congressional purpose of reasonably limiting use of electronic surveillance techniques.[1] Consequently, failure to secure approval of an application for a surveillance order from the Attorney General or Assistant Attorney General did require exclusion of the resulting evidence, but a failure simply to specify on the documents the official who had in fact authorized the application did not. State exclusionary requirements embodied in similar state electronic surveillance statutes have been similarly construed.

This approach could be applied in other areas. It would require identification of, first, the basic purposes of the underlying legal requirements and, second, the significance to those purposes of various subrequirements of the legal framework. Violation of only those subrequirements that are in some sense directly or importantly related to achievement of the purposes, then, would trigger a right to have resulting evidence excluded.

A second type of limitation upon nonconstitutional exclusionary sanctions makes exclusion available only to those defendants who show more than simply that the evidence at issue was obtained by means of a violation of a sufficient legal requirement. There are several approaches to defining what more must be shown.

Lower federal courts have often followed the approach of United States v. Burke[2] to arguments that evidence is inadmissible because it was obtained in violation of requirements for issuance and execution of search warrants imposed by Rule 41 of the Federal Rules of Criminal Procedure. Under Burke, exclusion is appropriate if the defendant shows, in addition to a violation of Rule 41, that "(1) there was prejudice in the sense that the search might not have occurred or would not have been so abrasive if the Rule had been followed, or (2) there is evidence of intentional and deliberate disregard of a provision in the Rule."

Some courts have emphasized these same requirements individually. Thus exclusion is required only upon a showing that the underlying violation was in some sense "intentional" or that the defendant was in some often-undefined sense "prejudiced" by the illegality.

A somewhat different approach, urged in the American Law Institute's Model Code of Pre-Arraignment Procedure,[3] is incorporated

§ 172
1. United States v. Chavez, 416 U.S. 562, 578 (1974).
2. 517 F.2d 377 (2d Cir.1975).

3. See Model Code of Pre-Arraignment Procedure § 290.2(2)–(4) (Official Draft 1975).

into the North Carolina statute,[4] which provides for exclusion only upon proof that the violation of the legal requirement was "substantial." Developing what constitutes a "substantial" violation, the North Carolina statute continues:

In determining whether a violation is substantial, the court must consider all the circumstances, including:

a. The importance of the particular interest violated;

b. The extent of the deviation from lawful conduct;

c. The extent to which the violation was willful;

d. The extent to which exclusion will tend to deter future violations of this Chapter.

Results reached under this approach are probably quite similar to those reached by courts which express a willingness to exclude evidence in appropriate situations but decline to do so when violations are only "technical" in nature or if the law enforcement activity failed to violate the "spirit" or "legislative intent" underlying the nonconstitutional legal requirement.

A third type of limitation is imposed by giving defendants no right to exclusion but rather conferring upon trial courts discretion to exclude evidence if a defendant makes the required showing that the evidence was improperly obtained. Sometimes this is simply implicit in the courts' approach. But in Commonwealth v. Mason,[5] the Pennsylvania Supreme Court explicitly announced that a showing that evidence had been obtained in violation of the Pennsylvania Rules of Criminal Procedure established only that "exclusion *may* be an appropriate remedy." Exclusion is to be ordered only if the trial judge, after considering the nature of the case and the particular facts, determines that exclusion and its costs would be proportional to the benefits to be gained, with particular emphasis being given to the likelihood that exclusion would prevent future misconduct similar to that which gave rise to the violation before the court.

§ 173. Use of Illegally Obtained Evidence in Noncriminal Litigation

Most exclusionary sanction issues arise in criminal litigation. Perhaps because of our increasing acceptance of exclusion as a response to illegality in obtaining evidence, however, an increasing number of litigants are attempting to invoke exclusionary remedies in various types of civil litigation. When, if ever, exclusionary sanctions are appropriate outside of criminal litigation presents a number of difficult questions.

Distinctions here as elsewhere must be drawn among the various exclusionary sanctions that do or might exist. The Supreme Court's case law addressing the application of the federal constitutional exclusionary requirements outside of criminal litigation provides an attractive model that has been widely but not universally followed in other contexts.

Soon after *Mapp*, the Supreme Court held the Fourth Amendment exclusionary rule applicable in a state forfeiture proceeding.[1] The action was under a statute that gave the state a right to title of an automobile upon proof that the vehicle had been used in the criminal transportation of illicit liquor. Forefeiture was clearly a penalty for a criminal act, the Court reasoned, and might sometimes constitute a harsher penalty than could be imposed upon criminal conviction. It would therefore be incongruous to exclude the evidence in a criminal prosecution but admit it in a forfeiture proceeding based on the same criminal activity. "[T]he exclusionary rule," the Court announced, "is applicable to forfeiture proceedings such as the one involved here."

The matter was addressed again in United States v. Janis,[2] a civil proceeding for a tax

---

4. N.C.G.S. § 15A–974(2).

5. 507 Pa. 396, 490 A.2d 421 (1985); see § 171 supra.

§ 173

1. One 1958 Plymouth Sedan v. Commonwealth of Pennsylvania, 380 U.S. 693 (1965).

2. 428 U.S. 433 (1976).

refund in which the Government counter-claimed for the unpaid balance of the assessment. The assessment was based upon information concerning Janis' illegal bookmaking activities; that information had been obtained by state law enforcement officers acting pursuant to a defective search warrant but nevertheless in the "good faith" belief that the search was lawful. Use of the evidence was permissible, the Court reasoned, because "exclusion from federal civil proceedings of evidence unlawfully seized by a state criminal law enforcement has not been shown to have a sufficient likelihood of deterring the conduct of the state police so that it outweighs the societal costs imposed by the exclusion."

Janis involved an intersovereign situation, and may have rested in part upon the Court's conclusion that excluding evidence in a *federal* civil proceeding is unlikely to influence *state* officers. In I.N.S. v. Lopez–Mendoza,[3] however, the Court arrived at a similar result in an intrasovereign case. At issue was whether evidence obtained in violation of the Fourth Amendment by federal immigration officers was admissible in a civil deportation proceeding. *Janis,* the Court observed, provided the framework for analysis: the likely social benefits of excluding the evidence must be balanced against the likely costs. The intrasovereign nature of the situation suggested that the deterrent benefits were likely to be greater than in *Janis.* But other considerations suggested they would still be quite small: the Government itself disciplines officers who violate the Fourth Amendment and excludes evidence arising from intentional violations, and INS officers know that there is only a small likelihood that any arrestee will actually challenge the officers' actions in a formal proceeding. On the cost side, application of the rule would impede the busy deportation system. Since immigration enforcement often involves continuing violations of the law, application of an exclusionary rule in this context "would require the courts to close their eyes to ongoing violations of the law," a

cost of a particularly offensive character. The *Janis* balance, the Court concluded, came out against application of the Fourth Amendment exclusionary rule.

Under *Janis* and *Lopez–Mendoza,* whether the federal constitutional exclusionary rules are applicable in civil litigation turns upon whether the increased prevention of unconstitutional conduct accomplished by such application is worth the costs of so expanding those sanctions. The two decisions suggest that the Court is generally satisfied that sufficient prevention is provided by exclusion of unconstitutionally obtained evidence in criminal litigation. A civil litigant seeking to show that exclusion is justified under *Janis–Lopez–Mendoza* has an extremely difficult task. Lower courts are understandably hesitant to exclude evidence in civil contexts but remain reluctant to characterize the sanctions as never applicable to noncriminal litigation.

The *Janis–Lopez–Mendoza* analysis is most likely to lead to exclusion when unconstitutionally obtained evidence is offered in proceedings which, although "civil," are brought by the government for what is essentially a public purpose. Governmental activity may be conducted with the prospect of such litigation in mind, and thus exclusion in such litigation may discourage impropriety in the investigatory activity. The Ninth Circuit, for example, has held that evidence obtained in "bad faith" by state officers would be inadmissible even in a federal civil tax proceeding. Whether evidence must be excluded in administrative proceedings such as those under the Occupational Safety and Health Act of 1970 (OSHA), remains unclear. The Fifth Circuit, relying upon dictum in *Lopez–Mendoza,* has held that the Fourth Amendment exclusionary rule should not be applied to bar the Secretary of Labor from ordering the correction of violations, but is to be applied to those aspects of OSHA procedure that are "for purposes of 'punishing the crime,'" that is, assessing penalties for past violations.[4]

---

3. 468 U.S. 1032 (1984).

4. Smith Steel Casting Co. v. Brock, 800 F.2d 1329, 1334 (5th Cir.1986).

The Second Circuit, in Tirado v. C.I.R.,[5] held that in most situations whether the federal constitutional exclusionary rules apply in civil litigation should be determined by case-by-case consideration of whether application of the rules would have a realistic prospect of achieving marginal deterrence. The "key question" is generally "whether the particular challenged use of the evidence is one that the seizing officials were likely to have had an interest in at the time—whether it was within their predictable contemplation and, if so, whether it was likely to have motivated them." Evidence is more likely to be excluded if it is offered by either the agency that engaged in the wrongful conduct or another having close working connections with that agency.

Under the *Janis–Lopez–Mendoza* approach, it is quite unlikely that the federal constitutional rules will ever be applicable in civil actions between private parties. If the evidence was wrongfully obtained by public officers, exclusion would not penalize them and officers would not likely be influenced in their future conduct by such exclusion. If the evidence was wrongfully obtained by private persons, efforts to exclude it first encounter the difficulty of establishing a violation of the underlying constitutional provision. Private actions generally are not covered by federal constitutional provisions, which protect citizens only against official activity. A private person's wrongful invasion of another's privacy, for example, does not constitute a "search" within the meaning of the Fourth Amendment. If that hurdle is somehow overcome, it is most likely that the Supreme Court would find that the deterrence rationale of the federal sanctions dictates that those sanctions not apply; exclusion would at most deter similar private action in the future, a concern beyond the scope of the underlying federal constitutional rules being enforced.

Particular formulations of exclusionary requirements, especially those in statutes, are sometimes phrased so broadly that they clearly require exclusion in civil as well as criminal cases. This is true, for example, of the exclusionary provision in the federal "wiretap" statutes. Evidence obtained in violation of this statutory scheme is therefore inadmissible in civil litigation.

State courts, of course, are technically free to reject the approach taken in *Janis* and *Lopez–Mendoza* and to construe state constitutional provisions as fully applicable to civil litigation. The Oklahoma Supreme Court took at least a step in that direction in Turner v. City of Lawton.[6] Cocaine found in a firefighter's home was suppressed in a criminal action and then was relied upon in an administrative proceeding to dismiss him. The state's constitutional search and seizure provision, the court held, required exclusion of the cocaine even in a civil personnel proceeding. In support, it stressed the state's commitment to exclusion and the greater substantive protection afforded by the state provision as compared to the Fourth Amendment. To admit the evidence, the court stressed, would be "wholly at odds with our heritage."

At its core, *Turner* rested upon the state court's characterization of the right to exclusion as "a fundamental right under the Oklahoma Constitution," in contrast to a litigant's more limited right under the Fourth Amendment to invoke what is "merely a federal rule of evidence." Implicitly, the court accepted the state provision as creating a right to exclusion as a necessary remedy for the preceding violation of privacy, regardless of the necessity for exclusion to discourage future violations of the underlying legal requirements. In order to achieve the remedial objective of the state exclusionary requirement, then, the Oklahoma court extended its rule to civil litigation in order to replace the wronged person as close as possible to his condition before the wrongful search occurred.

Turner did not make clear whether exclusion would not be required in all civil litigation. Much of the language suggested that the court envisioned its holding as covering all civil litigation. On the other hand, the

---

5. 689 F.2d 307 (2d Cir.1982), cert. denied 460 U.S. 1014.

6. 733 P.2d 375 (Okl.1986), affirming 56 Okl.B.J. 535 (Okl.App.1985), cert. denied 483 U.S. 1007.

Court did stress that the evidence was obtained by a city police officer and then offered by the city in the civil personnel proceeding. Distinguishing *Janis,* it noted that on the facts before it "the deterrent value of applying the exclusionary rule is obvious." Whatever its scope, *Turner* is unlikely to be followed by many state courts.

§ 174. Use of Illegally Obtained Evidence in Criminal Proceedings on Matters Other Than Guilt

Evidence may be offered against a criminal defendant in the course of criminal litigation but other than at the trial on guilt or innocence. It may, for example, be used in an effort to have pretrial release denied or revoked, at a preliminary hearing to determine whether a defendant is to be "bound over" for grand jury consideration or trial, before a grand jury in support of a proposed indictment charging the defendant with an offense, at sentencing in support of a more severe disposition, in support of an effort to revoke probation once granted, or to substantiate a claim that parole after imprisonment should be denied or revoked. A conclusion that illegally obtained evidence must be inadmissible to prove defendants' guilt does not necessarily establish also that such evidence should be unavailable for any or all of these or similar purposes.

There are two distinguishable subissues. One is whether exclusionary rules such as those mandated by the federal constitution are by their own terms applicable in these nontrial contexts. The other is whether, as a matter of the procedural law governing these proceedings, evidence improperly obtained should be excluded from consideration.

The Supreme Court addressed the inherent applicability of the Fourth Amendment exclusionary rule to grand jury situations in United States v. Calandra.[1] Whether that exclusionary requirement should be applied, it

held, turned upon a balance of the "costs" of doing so against the potential benefits of applying the requirement in this context.[2] Any increased preventive effect of doing so, it reasoned, is "uncertain at best." Seldom are officers likely to be motivated to disregard a suspect's rights by a desire to obtain a grand jury indictment by means of evidence which cannot be used at trial. On the other hand, application of the rule here would seriously impede the grand jury. Resolving issues raised by exclusionary rule claims would delay and disrupt the grand jury proceedings. The result, it concluded, would be undue interference with the "effective and expeditious discharge of the grand jury's duties." Consequently, the Court ultimately held, the *Mapp* rule cannot be invoked before a federal grand jury.

The Supreme Court has not addressed the applicability of the federal constitutional exclusionary rules at preliminary hearings. In federal litigation, however, Rule 5.1 of the Federal Rules of Criminal Procedure specifically provides that "[o]bjections to evidence on the ground that it was acquired by unlawful means are not properly made at the preliminary examination."[3] The Advisory Committee that recommended this relied heavily upon dictum in Giordenello v. United States[4] that the judicial officer presiding over a preliminary hearing lacked authority to adjudicate for trial purposes the admissibility of evidence challenged by the defendant. From this the Committee apparently reasoned quite uncritically that the federal constitutional exclusionary rules did not require that evidence obtained in violation of federal constitutional rights be disregarded in making the probable cause determination at the preliminary hearing and that the proper administration of preliminary hearings did not suggest that such evidence be excluded.

Lower courts have generally responded unsympathetically to efforts to invoke both con-

§ 174

1.　414 U.S. 338 (1974).

2.　For a general discussion of this approach, see § 167 supra.

3.　Fed.R.Crim.P. 5.1(a).

4.　357 U.S. 480 (1958).

stitutional and other exclusionary requirements in nontrial contexts. Focusing upon the preventive function of such rules, they have tended to find any incremental deterrence provided by excluding evidence in these situations outweighed by the costs of resulting disruption of the proceedings and the loss of reliable evidence. Most litigation has concerned parole and probation revocation, but similar results have been reached in response to efforts to challenge evidence offered in pretrial release situations and sentencing.

Some judicial discussions have stopped short of embracing a position rendering federal or state constitutional exclusionary requirements totally inapplicable in these situations. Gross or egregious police misconduct, several courts have suggested, might render evidence inadmissible at nontrial stages, perhaps—as the Alaska Supreme Court indicated—because receipt of such evidence would trigger controlling considerations of judicial integrity. Alternatively, or in addition, some courts have indicated that evidence must be excluded if officers who obtained it did so for the specific purpose of using it in the nontrial situation at issue. In these situations, the likelihood that exclusion would provide a significant deterrent motivation is great enough that exclusion may be justified. Even courts generally disinclined to apply exclusionary requirements in nontrial situations may be receptive to evidence that illegally-seized evidence is being so frequently offered in nontrial situations as to suggest that officers are acting illegally in the expectation that such use of the evidence will be permitted. A showing of this sort might persuade these tribunals that a *Calanda*-type balancing analysis must be resolved in favor of applying exclusionary requirements.

Despite the unequivocal position of Rule 5.1, there is significant diversity regarding the applicability of exclusionary requirements at preliminary hearings. The dictum in *Giordenello* found persuasive by the federal Advisory Committee arguably addresses only the preliminary hearing judge's power to make a determination on admissibility that would later be binding upon the trial court. So read,

it does not address a defendant's right to have the preliminary hearing officer exclude—for purposes of the preliminary hearing only—evidence the officer finds to have been obtained illegally. Nor, of course, does it address the wisdom of having the judge do so even if the constitutional exclusionary rule does not mandate this.

A preliminary hearing might be regarded as designed to determine whether the prosecution has sufficient evidence likely to be admissible at trial to justify subjecting the accused to further proceedings. This perception of its role suggests that—as a matter of preliminary hearing law—the decision should be made without reference to evidence clearly inadmissible at trial. On the other hand, perhaps such an important decision on a matter often so critical to the case at trial should not be made by the "lower" preliminary hearing court at this early a stage in the proceedings. In any case, a number of jurisdictions do permit defendants to raise exclusionary rule objections at preliminary hearings, although some have also developed rather elaborate procedures for avoiding a binding determination at this stage and for minimizing the need to litigate these issues several times in the course of one proceeding.

§ 175. "Standing" and Personal Nature of Rights

The Fourth Amendment exclusionary rule and most other exclusionary sanctions permit a criminal defendant to seek suppression of evidence only on the basis of a claim that the evidence was obtained in an improper manner that violated the defendant's own rights. Put negatively, this requirement of "standing" precludes a defendant from objecting to evidence on the basis that it was obtained illegally but in a manner that violated only the rights of another person.

When this requirement is combined with a narrow reading of the underlying rights, the result is that evidence improperly obtained is sometimes admissible even against defendants who were the target of the officers' conduct. This is most effectively illustrated by Rakas v.

Illinois,[1] in which the Supreme Court held that mere legitimate presence in an automobile at the time it was searched was not sufficient to show a privacy interest violated by a search of the car. Consequently, the results of an improper search of an automobile are probably inadmissible against the driver. Mere passengers, however, lack "standing" to object to the evidence because—in the absence of additional facts—they cannot show a Fourth Amendment privacy interest of their own that could have been violated by the search.

The Fourth Amendment standing requirement was first developed under pre–*Mapp* law and was explained in Jones v. United States [2] as based upon language in Rule 41(e) of the Federal Rules of Criminal Procedure authorizing a motion to suppress only by "[a] person aggrieved by an unlawful search and seizure." [3] This was read by the Court as applying the "general principle" that constitutional protections can be claimed only by those parties to litigation that belong to the class of persons for whose sake the constitutional protection is given. The Fourth Amendment exclusionary requirement is not designed to exclude evidence on grounds of unreliability or prejudicial effect. Rather, it is a means of making effective the underlying Fourth Amendment protection against official invasion of privacy and the security of property. "[I]t is," the Court concluded, "entirely proper to require of one who seeks to challenge the legality of a search as the basis for suppressing relevant evidence that he allege, and if the allegation be disputed that he establish, that he himself was the victim of an invasion of privacy." After *Mapp*, this approach was incorporated into the Fourth Amendment exclusionary rule as applied to the states.

As first announced and applied, the standing requirement was sometimes read as invoking a distinct body of law distinguishable from that defining the content of the Fourth Amendment's coverage. In *Rakas*, however,

the Supreme Court rejected such an approach and made clear that the inquiry necessitated by the Fourth Amendment standing requirement involves application of the case law defining the scope of Fourth Amendment coverage and, in particular, the extent of a particular defendant's rights under that provision. When a defendant objects to the admissibility of the results of a search or seizure, the standing question is whether—under substantive Fourth Amendment law—the search or seizure violated the rights of the moving defendant.

Several recent decisions defining the scope of Fourth Amendment protection, when combined with the *Rakas* analysis, have significantly limited many defendants' ability to challenge law enforcement action by which the prosecution obtained evidence implicating the defendants. Prior to *Rakas, Jones* was widely regarded as establishing that anyone legitimately on premises or in an automobile when those premises or that automobile was searched had a sufficient privacy interest in the premises or automobile to give them standing to litigate the propriety of the search. In *Rakas* itself, the Supreme Court held that a mere showing that the defendant was a passenger in a searched automobile did not establish that he had a sufficient privacy interest in that automobile to give him standing to challenge the search. This obviously cast significant doubt upon *Jones* as authority for the proposition that anyone legitimately present in residential premises at the time of a search has, for that reason alone, the ability to challenge the search. Two years later, in Rawlings v. Kentucky,[4] the Court held that a defendant did not have standing to challenge the search of another's property because the defendant had been permitted by that other person to store some of his personal items in that property.

The Fourth Amendment's standing limitation was defended in terms of the underlying

§ 175

1. 439 U.S. 128 (1978).
2. 362 U.S. 257 (1960).
3. Fed.R.Crim.P. 41(e).
4. 448 U.S. 98 (1980).

policy concerns in Alderman v. United States: [5]

> The deterrent values of preventing the incrimination of those whose rights the police have violated have been considered sufficient to justify the suppression of probative evidence even though the case against the defendant is weakened or destroyed. But we are not convinced that the additional benefits of extending the exclusionary rule to other defendants would justify further encroachment upon the public interest in prosecuting those accused of crime and having them acquitted or convicted on the basis of all the evidence which exposes the truth.[6]

The same approach has been vigorously pursued by the Supreme Court in the context of another, nonconstitutional exclusionary requirement. In United States v. Payner,[7] the lower courts had held that evidence had been obtained by a grossly illegal search of a person other than the defendant. Federal courts could properly use their supervisory power, they held, to suppress evidence obtained by gross illegality even if that illegality did not infringe the objecting defendant's rights. Justice Marshall and two other members of the Court agreed, reasoning that the supervisory power was based upon somewhat different considerations than the Fourth Amendment exclusionary requirement. Those considerations include the objective of protecting the integrity of the federal courts, and this integrity is violated by reliance upon illegally obtained evidence regardless of whether the illegality violated the interests of the litigants before the courts. When the supervisory power exclusionary rule is invoked, Justice Marshall concluded, the standing requirement should not apply.

The *Payner* majority rejected this approach, however, and held that the "same social interests" are implicated by both supervisory power exclusionary requirements and the Fourth Amendment exclusionary rule. Moreover, the values assigned to those interests do not change when the basis for the exclusionary sanction is the supervisory power rather than the Fourth Amendment. Consequently, even construction of the supervisory power exclusionary sanction is governed by the Court's conclusion that any increased deterrence that would be provided by abandoning standing is outweighed by the inevitable increased loss of reliable evidence.

In both of these contexts, the standing requirement serves to limit the remedy to those who have been harmed by the underlying illegal activity. To the extent that exclusionary remedies serve a remedial function, standing requirements serve to limit the rule to those situations in which that function is served. Standing requirements deny any possible remedy to those who have suffered no harm and thus cannot be entitled to remedial relief. Since the Fourth Amendment exclusionary rule serves no remedial function,[8] however, this effect of the standing requirement is apparently of no significance in analysis.

Fourth Amendment law had relaxed ordinary standing requirements in limited situations covered by what was characterized as the "automatic" standing rule. Under this rule, a defendant charged with possession of an item at the time of a search or seizure was permitted to challenge that search or seizure regardless of general standing requirements. In part, the automatic standing rule was based on concern that in the cases covered defendants would often have to make an admissible judicial confession of guilt, i.e., possession, to establish standing. Such defendants' testimony establishing standing, given at the hearing on the admissibility of the item, might well be admissible against the defendants at trial. The resulting "dilemma," the Court concluded, was unacceptable. As the Court has recognized in United States v. Salvucci,[9] this part of the rationale was destroyed by Simmons v. United States,[10] holding that testimony given at a motion to

---

5. 394 U.S. 165 (1969).
6. Id. at 174–175.
7. 447 U.S. 727 (1980).
8. See § 167 supra.

9. 448 U.S. 83 (1980).
10. 390 U.S. 377 (1968).

suppress evidence is not admissible against the defendant at a subsequent trial. A defendant who, to establish standing, judicially admits possession need not fear that the prosecution will use that admission at trial to establish his guilt.

But the automatic standing rule was also based in part upon perceived offensiveness of contradictory prosecutorial arguments that defendants had close enough relationships to items to be guilty of possession of them but not sufficient relationships to give them standing to challenge the searches by which the prosecution obtained them. In *Salvucci*, however, the Court considered developments in the Fourth Amendment case law defining privacy rights and concluded that there was no inherent inconsistency between prosecution claims that a defendant was guilty of criminal possession of an item at the time of a search and that he lacks standing to challenge that search. Since the automatic standing rule had "outlived its usefulness in [the] Court's Fourth Amendment jurisprudence," it was overruled.

The standing requirement is firmly entrenched in the Fourth Amendment and probably in those other exclusionary requirements over which the Supreme Court has substantive development power. But in *Alderman* the Court acknowledged that Congress or states could extend the right of exclusion to persons without standing in the Fourth Amendment sense.

The Supreme Court, nevertheless, has been reluctant to construe statutory language as extending exclusionary rights to persons without standing as that has been developed under the Fourth Amendment exclusionary rule. Under the federal electronic surveillance statute, suppression of the results of an improper interception of a covered communication is required upon the motion of any "person against whom the interception was directed." In *Alderman*, however, the Court—without discussing the specific terminology chosen by Congress—offered that the

legislative history of the statute indicated a Congressional purpose to permit objections to evidence only by persons with standing under existent standing rules.[11]

State courts developing state law exclusionary requirements have generally, but not universally, followed the Supreme Court's Fourth Amendment model. The most dramatic deviation was that of the California Supreme Court, which in 1955 announced that all of the reasons persuading it to adopt exclusionary requirements suggested further that defendants should be able to invoke those requirements regardless of whether they had been the victims of the illegality relied upon.[12]

The California court's rejection of standing rested on several bases. First, the California court sought greater assurance of a deterrent effect than satisfied the Supreme Court, and this was provided by requiring exclusion regardless of the challenging defendant's standing. In addition, however, the California tribunal gave greater weight to judicial integrity considerations than has the Supreme Court. It conceptualized judicial integrity as broader than the Supreme Court's later analysis finding judicial integrity implicated only if judicial use of evidence encourages future violations of the underlying legal requirement. Judicial integrity—as broadly conceptualized—was compromised by use of illegally obtained evidence regardless of whether the victims of the illegality were before the court. Whatever the rationale, the California approach was nullified by the 1982 amendment to the state constitution barring judicial development of exclusionary sanctions. The Louisiana Constitution, however, continues to be construed as dispensing with any standing requirement.

Several state courts have retained a standing requirement as a matter of state constitutional law but have held that it is more readily met than the Fourth Amendment requirement as construed by the Supreme Court. Both the New Jersey and Vermont courts have held that a defendant need only assert a

---

11. Alderman v. United States, 394 U.S. 165, 175 n. 9 (1969).

12. People v. Martin, 45 Cal.2d 755, 290 P.2d 855 (1955).

possessory, proprietary or participatory interest in either the area searched or the item seized in order to have standing. Others have retained the automatic standing rule, sometimes expressing broader misgivings as to other aspects of the Fourth Amendment approach.

Exclusionary sanctions attached to nonconstitutional rights may not be qualified by a requirement of standing. Careful consideration of the purpose of the legal requirement enforced by such an exclusionary sanction may indicate that the purposes of that requirement are ill-served by limiting the exclusionary remedy to those defendants with standing in the traditional Fourth Amendment rule sense. The Washington Privacy Act, for example, was construed as intended to protect citizens not only from improper interception of their conversations but also from dissemination of information obtained improperly. The second objective, of course, suggested that the dissemination inherent in evidentiary use of improperly intercepted conversations be avoided regardless of what parties are before the court and without reference to the status of the party raising the objection. Given the legislative objective, the Washington court concluded, the broad language of the statutory exclusionary remedy indicated a legislative intention to allow a defendant to object to the use in his trial of evidence obtained in violation of the act, even if he himself was not a participant in the conversation.

If the Fourth Amendment model is abandoned, what defendants would be entitled to challenge evidence improperly obtained? One possibility, of course, is that no limits whatsoever might apply, and all defendants would be so entitled. Such an approach, however, might reasonably be regarded as unacceptably costly; reliable evidence might well disregarded in numerous situations although doing so served no conceivable preventive purpose. But intermediate positions might be available that more effectively implement the policies involved without abandoning all efforts to limit the loss of reliable evidence. Justice Fortas, concurring and dissenting in *Alderman,* urged a "target" approach under which any person "against whom [a] search was directed" could challenge the admissibility of evidentiary results of that search.[13] Such an approach would provide a disincentive for officers to engage in searches for the specific purpose of seeking evidence against persons they believe might not be able to challenge the search under the traditional approach. Perhaps it is reasonable to expect officers, in deciding how to proceed, to be influenced by the risk of later challenge to evidence by those they recognize as likely to be affected by the search. But they may not be subject to influence by the risk of later challenge by persons whose interests unforeseeably turn out to have been affected by the search. Permitting all "targets" to challenge law enforcement activity, then, might accommodate the primary preventive purpose of exclusionary sanctions by permitting those challenges likely to affect officers' decisions in future cases. It would not, however, permit challenges by those unforeseeably incriminated by a search. Overall, such an approach might best serve to permit challenges to evidence when, but only when, such challenges could reasonably be expected to influence future law enforcement conduct.

In any case, *Rakas* explicitly rejected such a target standard under Fourth Amendment law. Then–Justice Rehnquist explained that such an approach would often involve difficult and time-consuming inquiries into what persons were targets of particular law enforcement behavior. Against this certain administrative cost of such an expansion, the Court weighed the "hypothetical" marginal increase in prevention urged by Rakas and found the balance insufficient to overcome the counsel of the Court's case law against enlarging the class of persons who can invoke the Fourth Amendment exclusionary rule.

---

13. Alderman v. United States, 394 U.S. 165, 208 (1969) (Fortas, J., concurring in part and dissenting in part).

§ 176. Evidence Indirectly Acquired: "Fruit of the Poisonous Tree"

Six years after it imposed the Fourth Amendment exclusionary rule upon federal litigation, the Supreme Court construed that rule to require exclusion of evidence obtained even as an indirect result of violation of defendants' Fourth Amendment rights. In Silverthorne Lumber Company v. United States,[1] certain documents had been obtained in an unconstitutional search of petitioners' office. The trial court had suppressed them and ordered their return to the petitioners. Nevertheless, the government, relying on information obtained from the documents while they were in the government's possession, sought to subpoena the documents from the petitioners.

This, the Court held, was impermissible. Characterizing the government's position as "that the protection of the Constitution covers the physical possession [of the documents] but not any advantages that the government can gain over the object of its pursuit by doing the forbidden act," the Court rejected it: "The essence of a provision forbidding the acquisition of evidence in a certain way is that not merely evidence so acquired shall not be used before the Court but that it shall not be used at all." The resulting rule was given its now widely-used name by Justice Frankfurter in Nardone v. United States,[2] when he referred to a defendant's right to obtain suppression of evidence by establishing that it was "a fruit of the poisonous tree."

During these early discussions, the rule was not carefully discussed or supported by reference to the purposes of the exclusionary requirements being applied. In 1984, however, the Court retrospectively explained:

> The core rationale consistently advanced by this Court for extending the exclusionary rule to evidence that is the fruit of unlawful police conduct has been that this admittedly drastic

and socially costly course is needed to deter police from violations of constitutional and statutory protections.[3]

The Fourth Amendment rule was expanded in Wong Sun v. United States,[4] in which the Court rejected the argument that trial courts need exclude only physical, tangible materials obtained during or as a "direct" result of an unreasonable search. The petitioner successfully urged that his oral admission, made soon after his unreasonable arrest, was the excludable "fruit" of that arrest. Noting with approval that lower courts had excluded testimony as to matters observed during an unlawful search, the Court concluded that the policies underlying the Fourth Amendment exclusionary rule did not invite any logical distinction between physical and verbal evidence. Permitting the government to use verbal evidence resulting from a Fourth Amendment violation, it explained, would endanger the ability of the exclusionary remedy to deter future Fourth Amendment violations and to close the doors of federal courts to use of evidence unconstitutionally obtained. Consequently, verbal evidence obtained as a result of an unreasonable search or seizure "is no less the 'fruit' of official illegality than the more common tangible fruits of the unwarranted intrusion."

To invoke the Fourth Amendment "fruit of the poisonous tree" doctrine, a defendant must show[5] that challenged evidence was obtained by the prosecution as a factual consequence of a violation of his Fourth Amendment rights. The nature of the relationship required was developed in Murray v. United States.[6] Federal officers had made a presumably unreasonable search of a warehouse and in the course of that search had noticed—but not seized—bales of marijuana. They then obtained a search warrant and returned to the warehouse, at which point they executed the warrant and seized the marijuana. At issue was whether that seizure of the marijua-

---

§ 176

1. 251 U.S. 385 (1920).
2. 308 U.S. 338 (1939).
3. Nix v. Williams, 467 U.S. 431, 442–443 (1984).
4. 371 U.S. 471 (1963).

5. Allocation of the burdens of going forward with evidence and of persuasion are considered in § 183 infra.

6. 487 U.S. 533 (1988).

na and thus the marijuana was the "fruit" of the earlier and unreasonable search. The Court acknowledged that this would unquestionably have been the case had the officers in applying for the warrant relied upon their observations during the illegal search and had the magistrate relied upon that in issuing the warrant. But the lower courts had found that the officers had not communicated to the magistrate the results of their earlier search or even the fact that it had been made.

This finding of untainted support for the warrant, however, did not complete the inquiry. The Court then inquired whether the federal officers had been influenced in their decision to seek the warrant by their observations during the illegal search. If this was the case, the Court continued, the warrant and its products would be the fruit of the illegal search. This would be true even if the warrant was obtained entirely on the basis of information which the officers developed prior to the invalid search. The case was consequently remanded for further inquiry into whether the officers would have sought the warrant even if they had not made the illegal search of the warehouse. The necessary consequential relationship is shown, under *Murray*, if a defendant demonstrates that officers were motivated by an unreasonable search or its products to take action for which they already had legally sufficient grounds.

Generally, the taint flows only forward and renders inadmissible only that evidence obtained after, and as a factual consequence of, the unreasonable search. Moreover, part of a search may be reasonable and other parts may be unreasonable. Officers searching pursuant to a valid search warrant, for example, may search within the terms of the warrant and discover and seize some evidence. But at various times, they may exceed the scope of search authorized by the warrant and during some of these transgressions they may find and seize other evidence. Usually, only that evidence located and seized while the officers were engaged in the unreasonable aspects of the search, that is, while they were acting

beyond the authority of the warrant, are tainted by the officers' improper action and thus rendered inadmissible.

New York v. Harris [7] illustrates the effect of this aspect of the requirement. Officers with grounds for arrest improperly entered Harris' residence and there arrested him. Harris was taken to the stationhouse, where he gave a confession. Assuming that the entry into the residence was an unreasonable search, the Court held that the confession could not be regarded as the "product" of that entry. Once Harris was removed from the illegally-entered residence, he was no longer illegally in custody. The situation is no different, Justice White stressed, than it would be if Harris had been arrested on his door step by police who then conducted an unlawful search of his residence and finally interrogated him at the stationhouse, or if they had first unsuccessfully searched his residence for him and then later arrested him when they encountered him on the street. Since Harris' statement was not an exploitation of the illegal entry, it was not subject to suppression because of that entry.

Under some circumstances, the Fourth Amendment exclusionary rule might require suppression of more evidence than that tainted by illegal aspects of a search. This is most likely to be the case where the officers' misconduct poses such an unusually significant threat to the underlying protected interests that a corresponding draconian penalty is justified to discourage such conduct. The Supreme Court has suggested that such an approach might be taken if officers executing a search warrant disregard the limits imposed by the warrant on the places subject to search.[8]

The "fruits" doctrine was developed in Fourth Amendment cases such as *Silverthorne Lumber, Wong Sun*, and *Murray*. In 1985, the Supreme Court indicated that it did not necessarily apply to all other federal constitutional exclusionary sanctions, and suggested that it may have limited applicability

---

7. 495 U.S. 14 (1990).

8. Waller v. Georgia, 467 U.S. 39, 43 n. 3 (1984).

to federal exclusionary sanctions attaching to nonconstitutional legal requirements.

In Oregon v. Elstad,[9] the "poisonous tree" consisted of an interrogation conducted in violation of *Miranda's* requirements, during which Elstad made certain admissions. At issue, however, were not these admissions but a later confession given after *Miranda's* requirements were met. The admissibility of that confession, the Court concluded, was not determined by the "fruits doctrine" as applied in Fourth Amendment cases but rather upon whether it was "knowingly and voluntarily made." This, Justice O'Connor explained, was because the fruits doctrine applies only where the impropriety—the "poisonous tree"—was an actual infringement of the suspect's federal constitutional rights. Violations of *Miranda's* requirements do not in themselves constitute violates of the Fifth Amendment.

Where the illegality is not an actual violation of a constitutional requirement, *Elstad* reasoned, an exclusionary sanction does not *necessarily* extend to "fruits." Whether it *will* extend to such evidence, Justice O'Connor explained, depends upon whether the goals of the underlying constitutional provision invoked suggest a need for such extensive exclusion. In *Elstad* as in Michigan v. Tucker[10], the underlying Fifth Amendment invoked the dual goals of assuring trustworthy evidence and deterring improper police conduct. These goals, she concluded, are adequately served by exclusion of only those later and resulting confessions that are involuntary. This is consistent with *Tucker,* Justice O'Connor added, in which the Court found no need to exclude the testimony of a witness who had been located by use of information obtained from the defendant in violation of *Miranda's* requirements.

What *Elstad* means in the confession context is discussed elsewhere.[11] If it simply holds that the fruits doctrine necessarily applies only where the primary illegality consists of a violation of some federal constitutional right, it may have little consequence in federal constitutional law beyond the *Miranda* context. This is because it would render the fruits doctrine inapplicable only in other situations in which the Court has developed prophylactic requirements based on federal constitutional provisions but whose violation does not constitute violations of the constitutional provisions themselves.

But *Elstad* may have more dramatic implications for nonconstitutional exclusionary requirements. In United States v. Tedford[12] the Fifth Circuit relied upon *Elstad* in holding that the "fruit of the poisonous tree" doctrine is not invoked when the illegality consists of a violation of a nonconstitutional legal requirement. In *Tedford,* Tedford's residence was searched pursuant to a warrant presumably complying with the Fourth Amendment but issued in violation of a requirement in the Federal Rules of Criminal Procedure that a search warrant permit nighttime execution only if the issuing magistrate determines that reasonable cause is shown for such execution.[13] A receipt for storage space was found and seized; when later confronted with that receipt, Tedford consented to a search of the storage unit. A search of that unit resulted in discovery and seizure of certain weapons which Tedford challenged as the inadmissible "fruit" of the improper search of his residence. Rejecting his argument, the court reasoned that Tedford could prevail only if the "derivative evidence" rule applied and that it did not, because he relied upon a violation of a nonconstitutional legal requirement.

Elstad and certainly *Tedford* ignore the complexity of the issue. As *Elstad* recognized, a conclusion that the fruits doctrine does not necessarily apply merely requires consideration of whether it should. This, in turn, requires consideration of, among other matters, the importance of the underlying rule, the need to provide officers with addi-

9. 470 U.S. 298 (1985).
10. 417 U.S. 433 (1974).
11. See § 158 supra.

12. 875 F.2d 446 (5th Cir.1989).
13. Fed.R.Crim.P. 41(c).

tional incentive to comply with that rule, and the loss of reliable evidence that would result if the fruits doctrine were applied to provide this incentive. In *Elstad,* the Court quite cavalierly reached the conclusion that the need to assure compliance with *Miranda* did not suggest the application of the fruits doctrine. In *Tedford,* the Fifth Circuit simply halted analysis once it concluded that the nonconstitutional nature of the illegality shown did not mandate application of the fruits doctrine.

If the fruits doctrine does not apply, of course, some other standard must be used to determine the scope of taint. In *Elstad,* the Court was able to call into play the voluntariness requirement as an alternative standard. That could not be done in *Tedford,* since the evidence at issue did not consist of an out-of-court statement. But the *Tedford* Court made no inquiry whatsoever into what standard might be substituted for the fruits doctrine if that was regarded as inapplicable.

One possibility is the distinction between primary and derivative evidence applied by some courts in limiting the "inevitable discovery" exception.[14] Exclusion might, then, be limited to the "primary" evidence obtained as the result of illegality. Where the illegality consists of an improper search, those items seized during the search would be "primary" evidence and subject to exclusion. But other items found later by using information obtained during the search would be "derivative" evidence beyond challenge as a result of the improper search. Difficulties experienced in applying this distinction in the inevitable discovery context, however, suggest caution in using the concept of "primary" evidence as an alternative to the fruits doctrine.

A major argument for retention of the fruits doctrine, then, may be the difficulty of developing a satisfactory alternative. To the extent that the fruits doctrine provides unsatisfactory results, this might be best accommo-

dated not by abandoning the rule itself but by more rigorously applying the qualification to the fruits rule that permits use of evidence that is the fruit of illegality where the proponent of that evidence establishes that the "taint" is "attenuated."[15]

Perhaps because of these considerations, state law exclusionary sanctions have tended quite uncritically to adopt the Fourth Amendment "fruits" rule. Oregon has embodied it in statutory form. But it is possible that the nature and purposes of at least some state law rights enforced by exclusionary sanctions suggest that the "fruits" doctrine not apply.

§ 177. Admissibility of Evidence With An "Independent Source"

In Silverthorne Lumber Co. v. United States,[1] after articulating what has become the "fruits of the poisonous tree" doctrine,[2] Justice Holmes carefully added that this analysis did not necessarily mean that facts acquired in violation of the Fourth Amendment "become sacred and inaccessible." "If," he explained, "knowledge of them is gained from an independent source they may be proved like any others, but the knowledge gained by the Government's own wrong cannot be used by it [to do so]." This has developed into what is often called the "independent source" rule or "concept." Conceptually, it is simply a label reflecting a conclusion that particular evidence was not obtained in a manner causally related to the Fourth Amendment violation. Thus, it is necessarily included in the "fruits" doctrine. But such situations are so widely discussed under the distinct label of "independent source" that separate consideration of them under this terminology is appropriate.

In Murray v. United States,[3] the Supreme Court emphasized that the independent source "concept" has been used in two distinguishable ways. Justice Holmes' *Silverthorne*

---

14. See § 180 infra.
15. See § 179 infra.

1. 251 U.S. 385 (1920).

2. See § 176 supra.

3. 487 U.S. 533 (1988).

Lumber Co. dictum used it to describe situations in which the prosecution has both tainted and untainted evidence of a particular fact and offers only the untainted evidence to prove that fact. For example, police might improperly arrest X, question him, and obtain from him an admission to being in the vicinity of V's home the night it was burglarized. But an alert citizen might report to police seeing X in V's neighborhood on the night of the break-in. The fact that the prosecution obtained inadmissible evidence indicating X's presence near the scene of the offense would not bar it from proving his presence, because it could do so by evidence with an "independence source," that is, evidence obtained in a manner not factually related to the improper arrest. This, *Murray* indicated, was the more specific and most important use of the term independent source.

The other and more general use of the term describes situations in which all of the prosecution's evidence of a particular fact is untainted by its improper activity. For example, police might improperly arrest X and question him, but X may not reveal anything about the location of his victim's body. A citizen, however, may report to police that she observed X hide a body in a particular location; police following up on this information might then discover the body. The state's evidence regarding the body is admissible despite the improper arrest of X because that evidence has an independent source.

Both senses in which the doctrine is applied have been explained in terms of the preventive purpose of the exclusionary sanctions which the doctrine modifies. Adequate incentive for law enforcement to comply with legal requirements is provided if, after law enforcement impropriety is shown, the police are denied all evidentiary benefits of that activity. To exclude evidence which has an independent source would go further and place police in a worse position than they would have been in had they avoided the impropriety. Any incremental prevention of law enforcement illegality accomplished by excluding evidence with independent sources is outweighed by the consequential loss of reliable evidence.

The independent source rule has been applied with particular frequency in lineup and showup cases in which defendants' right to counsel was violated. In United States v. Wade,[4] the Court held that a witness who identified a defendant at a pretrial lineup at which the defendant was denied his right to counsel may nevertheless make an in-court identification of the defendant as the perpetrator if the prosecution convinces the judge that such testimony has a source "independent" of the tainted lineup. That source, of course, will almost inevitably be the witness's observation of the offense. *Wade* held that in that context the independent source burden—apparently that of persuasion—was on the prosecution and that it was the unusually high one of "clear and convincing evidence."[5]

The primary unresolved issue with regard to independent source doctrine is whether in some specific situations it should not be applied and evidence should sometimes be excluded despite the absence of proof that its acquisition was causally related to official impropriety. Such an approach might be justified in two types of cases.

First, perhaps the rule should not be applied in some situations raising particularly difficult factual issues concerning causal links between impropriety and evidence ultimately offered by the prosecution.

The argument was made by Justice Marshall in *Murray*: To avoid defeating the preventive effect of exclusionary sanctions, those sanctions must reasonably assure that evidence actually obtained as a result of illegality be subject to challenge. In some situations, the prosecution's claim that proffered evidence had an independent source will be particularly difficult to resolve with accuracy. Application of the independent source rule in those situations will lead officers to recognize that if they engage in the illegal activity,

---

4. 388 U.S. 218 (1967).

5. Burden of proof on exclusionary sanction issues in general is discussed in § 183 infra.

later challenges to admissibility of the fruits of that activity will often be rejected because of the courts' uncritical willingness to believe that evidence had an independent source. The officers will, then, have less incentive to avoid the illegal activity.

If there is merit in the argument that some situations present unacceptably difficult questions of "causation in fact," can exclusionary sanction law identify and describe those situations in which this risk is sufficiently high that the independent source rule ought not to be applied? Perhaps among the situations presenting an especially high risk of this sort are those in which the same officers engage first in illegal activity and then later in proper activity offered by the prosecution as an independent source for evidence developed by those officers. Whether the officers were caused by the first and illegal activity to engage in the second action requires often difficult analysis of those officers' mental processes and motivation. The difficulty of ascertaining which activity by these officers was the "source" of the evidence may argue strongly for precluding the entire inquiry. This is particularly the case when officers first engage in an improper search and during that search actually observe certain evidence or contraband. Later, the same officers conduct a proper search during which they seize the previously-observed items.

In *Murray*, for example, the evidence convincingly showed that the officers actually observed—during the improper search—at least some of the marijuana offered at trial as having been obtained by a later and "independent" search conducted by the same officers. In such situations, there may be a sufficiently high likelihood that these observations affected later investigatory activities that the court considering the defendant's exclusionary rule challenge to the evidence should not be permitted to engage in high risk speculation as to whether the discovery and seizure of the marijuana during the valid search was in fact independent of the earlier improper search. Under such an approach, the independent

source rule would not apply in cases like *Murray*. But it would remain available in cases such as Segura v. United States,[6] in which the proof showed a presumably improper search without a warrant and a later search pursuant to a search warrant, but failed to establish that the officers observed during the illegal search the items seized during the later and valid search.

The independent source analysis might also or alternatively be inappropriate in cases in which exclusion of evidence obtained as a result of misconduct is unlikely to sufficiently discourage that misconduct. Only exclusion of all evidence subsequently developed—perhaps by the officers who engaged in the illegality—might be sufficient to discourage future conduct of a similar sort. Again, the major issue is whether it is possible to identify those situations in which application of the independent source rule sufficiently blunts the preventive impact of the exclusionary sanction to justify holding the rule inapplicable. One possibility suggested by several cases consists of situations in which defendants show that other parties to conversations with them improperly recorded the conversations. May the party who wrongfully recorded the conversation but also—and properly—participated in it testify to the conversation from his memory of it? His testimony, based on his memory, is not a factual result of his wrongful act in recording the conversation. But perhaps only by excluding his testimony as well as the recording itself can the law provide sufficient incentive to discourage parties from violating prohibitions against such recording of conversations.

Whatever the merits, the Supreme Court's discussion in *Murray* suggests that the tribunal has little sympathy for arguments that the independent source rule should sometimes be inapplicable. It is a firmly entrenched part of the federal constitutional exclusionary requirements. State courts have, perhaps without full and careful consideration, accepted as part of state exclusionary sanctions the independent source rule as developed in the

---

6. 468 U.S. 796 (1984).

Supreme Court's federal constitutional case law.

§ 178. Effect of Illegality Upon "Jurisdiction" Over Criminal Defendants

Conceptually, the very presence of many criminal defendants before the trial court could be regarded as the "fruit" of earlier official illegality and hence in some way tainted by that activity. This is particularly so when the illegality consists of an improper arrest, in the absence of which the defendant would almost certainly have fled and escaped. Nevertheless, there is agreement that ordinary illegality in an investigation does not deprive the trial court of "jurisdiction" in any sense or otherwise interfere with the court's power to proceed with the trial. Thus it does not provide a basis for a motion to dismiss the charges or other relief which automatically ends the proceedings.

As a matter of federal constitutional law, the Supreme Court has held since Ker v. Illinois,[1] decided in 1886, that there is no federal constitutional bar to a court exercising jurisdiction over the person of a criminal defendant regardless of manner in which the presence of the person was obtained. In United States v. Blue,[2] the Court explained why this was not changed by the Court's commitment in *Mapp* and its progeny to exclusionary sanctions as the primary means of implementing many federal constitutional rights:

> Our numerous precedents ordering the exclusion of * * * illegally obtained evidence assume implicitly that the remedy does not extend to barring the prosecution altogether. So drastic a step might marginally advance some of the ends served by exclusionary rules, but it would also increase to an intolerable degree interference with the public interest in having the guilty brought to book.[3]

That interference, of course, would be caused by depriving the prosecution of all possibility of convicting the defendant. Exclusionary sanctions, where applied, always leave open

at least the theoretical possibility that the defendant can be convicted by evidence with an independent source.

Reluctance to read exclusionary sanctions as depriving courts of the power to proceed against defendants may affect analysis of other exclusionary sanction issues. In United States v. Crews,[4] for example, the victim made an in-court identification of the defendant, who had been illegally arrested. The Court of Appeals held that the defendant's presence at trial had been used by the prosecution in presenting that testimony; the witness testified that she was comparing her memory of the perpetrator with the defendant's appearance, with which she was familiar because she observed him in the courtroom, and on that basis she concluded that he was the perpetrator. This constituted an impermissible evidentiary use of the fruits of the illegal arrest, it concluded. A unanimous Supreme Court reversed but split on the rationale. Justice Brennan, speaking for three members, indicated he would leave open Crews' argument that a defendant's person can be considered evidence and thus a fruit of an illegal arrest. Prior to the arrest, he reasoned, the police had obtained all relevant evidence including what the victim ultimately repeated at trial. Thus the illegal arrest did not taint that previously-obtained information. Five members of the Court, however, rejected this approach and expressed the view that Crews' argument was precluded by *Ker* and its progeny. As Justice White explained, a holding that a defendant's face can be considered suppressible evidence "would be tantamount to holding that an illegal arrest effectively insulates one from conviction for any crime where an in-court identification is essential." This, he concluded, was inconsistent with the rationale of *Ker's* successors.

The unanimity of the result makes clear the strength of the perception that exclusionary sanctions should not be expanded to bar proceedings. But this analysis is unconvinc-

---

§ 178

1. 119 U.S. 436 (1886).
2. 384 U.S. 251 (1966).

3. Id. at 255.
4. 445 U.S. 463 (1980).

ing. It is correct, of course, that acceptance of Crews' argument would preclude conviction in those cases where an in-court identification is essential to proof of guilt. But the same is true of other decisions requiring exclusion of particular kinds of evidence; in some cases such evidence is essential to proof of guilt, and in those cases such decisions insulate the defendants from conviction. Crews had identified an argument that was evidentiary in nature, and there appears to be no principled way to distinguish it from other cases in which exclusion of prosecution evidence has the practical effect of precluding prosecution.

State courts have followed the Supreme Court's federal constitutional approach and repeatedly emphasize that the illegality of an arrest or a detention has no effect upon the jurisdiction of the trial court or the state's power to prosecute and convict the defendant. The Connecticut Supreme Court recently overruled its prior position to the contrary, and specifically rejected the argument that the state constitutional search and seizure provision provided adequate support for its previous position. An isolated defense of the position that an unlawful arrest should fatally taint the jurisdiction of the trial court has been predicated largely upon considerations of judicial integrity:

> By basing the court's jurisdiction on an illegal warrantless arrest of the defendant in his home, the court legitimizes the illegal conduct which produced the arrest. Courts should not be parties to invasions of the constitutional rights of citizens.[5]

§ 179. Exceptions to Exclusion (a) Attenuation of Taint

The widely-accepted position that under exclusionary sanctions all "fruit" of the primary illegality is subject to exclusion[1] is usually qualified by adding that exclusion of such fruit is not necessary if the relationship between the illegality and the actual procurement of the challenged evidence was such that the "taint" of the illegality was "attenuated" by the time the challenged evidence was obtained. This approach is based upon case law developed under the Fourth Amendment model, although it is widely—but often uncritically—accepted under state exclusionary sanctions as well. Despite its widespread acceptance and historical pedigree, both the rationale and the scope of the exception remain somewhat unclear.

Development of Fourth Amendment Rule. The Fourth Amendment rule apparently had its genesis in Justice Frankfurter's 1939 discussion in Nardone v. United States.[2] *Nardone* presented the question of whether the exclusionary sanction of the Communication Act of 1934, applied to a telephone conversation intercepted in violation of the Act, required only the exclusion of evidence of that conversation itself or required exclusion of other evidentiary fruits of it as well. The Court of Appeals had held that only evidence of the conversation itself must be excluded, and the Supreme Court reversed. In the course of his discussion for the Court, Justice Frankfurter commented:

> Sophisticated argument may prove a causal connection between information obtained through illegal wire-tapping and the Government's proof. As a matter of good sense, however, such connection may have become so attenuated as to dissipate the taint.[3]

Nardone's offhand reference to attenuation was made in discussion of a statutory exclusionary requirement. The notion was further discussed and actually applied in the context of Fourth Amendment violations in Wong Sun v. United States.[4] After citing *Nardone* for the proposition that the connection between unlawful conduct of the police and the discovery of challenged evidence can become so attenuated as to dissipate the taint and render the evidence admissible, Justice Brennan continued for the Court:

5. State v. Smith, 131 Wis.2d 220, 244, 388 N.W.2d 601, 612 (1986) (Abrahamson, J., concurring).

§ 179

1. See § 176 supra.

2. 308 U.S. 338 (1939).

3. Id. at 341.

4. 371 U.S. 471 (1963).

We need not hold all evidence is "fruit of the poisonous tree" simply because it would not have come to light but for the illegal actions of the police. Rather, the more apt question in such a case is "whether, granting establishment of the primary illegality, the evidence to which instant objection is made has been come at by exploitation of that illegality or instead by means sufficiently distinguishable to be purged of the primary taint." Maguire, Evidence of Guilt, 221 (1959).[5]

It is not entirely clear that Justice Frankfurter in *Nardone* distinguished his attenuation language from his restatement of the "independent source" doctrine. Professor Maguire's discussion, adopted in *Wong Sun,* seemed clearly to confuse the two. Justice Brennan's *Wong Sun* discussion, however, carefully drew the distinction. Consideration of whether the taint had been attenuated, he made clear, was appropriate only after it was established that the evidence at issue "would not have come to light but for the illegal actions of the police." Thus a court should first consider whether the facts before it demonstrate a causal relationship between official illegality and obtaining the challenged evidence. If, but only if, there is no "independent source"[6] and consequently the challenged evidence is the "fruit" or product of the illegality, should the court then consider whether the taint of that illegality was attenuated.

In *Wong Sun* itself, heroin had been obtained from a witness located by means of information obtained from one petitioner, Toy, after his improper arrest. Holding the heroin inadmissible, the Court rejected the government's argument that the taint of the arrest had become attenuated by the time the heroin was obtained from the witness. The other petitioner, Wong Sun, had also been improperly arrested. He was released on his own recognizance; several days later he voluntarily came to the office of federal agents and gave a voluntary confession. That confession, the Court concluded with citation to

Nardone, was admissible because "the connection between the arrest and the statement had 'become so attenuated as to dissipate the taint.' " Neither application of the rule was explained.

Rationale for Fourth Amendment Rule. These early cases did not develop the rationale for the doctrine. In United States v. Leon,[7] however, the Court explained that the attenuation of taint doctrine is the product of the principles underlying the federal constitutional exclusionary rules. To some extent, it identifies those cases in which the taint upon evidence is so minimal that admitting the evidence does not compromise the integrity of the court. More importantly, however:

[T]he "dissipation of taint" concept * * * "attempts to mark the point at which the detrimental consequences of illegal police action become so attenuated that that the deterrent effect of the exclusionary rule no longer justifies its cost."[8]

Application of Fourth Amendment Rule. Cases following *Wong Sun* have made somewhat clearer the factors to be considered in determining whether the taint of illegality has become attenuated. Most have involved confessions given after unreasonable arrests. Several considerations are of major significance:

(1) Time Sequence. The longer period of time between the primary illegality and obtaining the challenged evidence, the more likely it is that the taint of that illegality has become attenuated. In Rawlings v. Kentucky,[9] for example, the defendant had been improperly detained 45 minutes when he made the later-proffered statement. This "relatively short period of time," the Court commented, might under some circumstances not suffice to purge the taint. But on the facts before it, the Court found that attenuation had occurred.

(2) Intervening Circumstances. The number and nature of circumstances intervening

---

5. Id. at 487–489.

6. See § 177 supra.

7. 468 U.S. 897 (1984).

8. Id. at 911, quoting Brown v. Illinois, 422 U.S. 590, 609 (1975) (Powell, J., concurring in part).

9. 448 U.S. 98 (1980).

between the primary illegality and the obtaining of the evidence are clearly relevant. Precisely how they are to be considered is less certain. Some case law suggests that if one of the intervening circumstances involves judicial action, this is entitled to particular significance in finding attenuation.

(3) Magnitude of Misconduct. The "purpose and flagrancy" of the primary illegality is relevant, although neither the rationale for nor the precise method of applying this rule are clear. Perhaps the more egregious the misconduct, the greater the need to prevent future misconduct of the same sort; therefore, attenuation is to be less readily found to increase the preventive impact of the exclusionary sanction in this sort of situation. Or perhaps the more egregious the misconduct, the longer and stronger its likely actual impact; therefore, the less likely it is, other factors being equal, that this impact has decreased sufficiently to render the taint attenuated.

(4) Voluntary Choice. The major thread running through the Court's attenuation cases is the significance of proof that the chain of events involved a voluntary decision by someone to cooperate with investigating authorities. If the decision was that of the defendant, the factor is entitled to particular weight. In *Wong Sun,* for example, the Court's conclusion that Wong Sun's confession was admissible appeared to turn in large part upon the Court's conclusion that his decision to confess was voluntary. When a confession follows an improper arrest, evidence that officers fully complied with *Miranda* will not automatically attenuate the taint of the arrest. It is, however, a major factor tending to suggest attenuation, apparently because it increases the likelihood that the suspect's decision to confess was voluntary and hence sufficiently independent of the arrest to strongly suggest attenuation of the taint. If, on the other hand, the defendant's decision to cooperate was itself affected by the initial illegality, that decision is quite unlikely to attenuate the taint.

The Court's case law makes reasonably clear the factors to be considered but is less helpful in interrelating them and directing an ultimate conclusion. In United States v. Ceccolini,[10] the Court observed that "[o]bviously no mathematical weight can be assigned to any of the [relevant] factors * * *." This is an understatement.

Testimony of Witness as Excludable "Fruit." The difficulty of applying attenuation analysis is illustrated by the Supreme Court's application of it to the situation in which the challenged evidence consists of the in-court testimony of a witness located by exploitation of information obtained as a result of an improper search or seizure.

In *Ceccolini,* the Court refused to adopt a *per se* rule under which such evidence could never be the excludable fruit of a Fourth Amendment violation. But it did hold that the attenuation analysis should be applied in such cases with a particular flavor. When a criminal defendant seeks suppression of live-witness testimony, "a closer, more direct link between the illegality and that kind of testimony is required," as compared to cases in which exclusion of other kinds of evidence is sought. This apparently means that attenuation is to be more readily found.

Some of the Court's *Ceccolini* discussion suggests that its rationale is that witnesses might come forward spontaneously, and thus such cases are ones in which the prosecution is somewhat less likely to ultimately benefit from its wrong despite a causal link between its illegality and discovery of the witness's identity. But the Court explicitly emphasized instead that exclusion of live-witness testimony involves an extraordinarily high cost and for this reason a closer link to the primary illegality is necessary to offset that cost. In any case, *Ceccolini* made clear that the voluntariness of the witness's decision to cooperate and testify for the prosecution is of particular importance. The less significance the illegality had in motivating the witness to cooperate and testify, the more likely it is that the taint of that illegality was attenuated.

10. 435 U.S. 268 (1978).

Attenuation in Other Contexts. Where a defendant invokes an exclusionary requirement other than those based in federal constitutional law, of course, neither the attenuation of taint doctrine nor the Supreme Court's development of its need necessarily apply. Nevertheless, both have tended to be used in implementing state constitutional and nonconstitutional exclusionary requirements. In Bell v. State [11] for example, the Texas court recognized that Fourth Amendment analysis did not necessary apply when an arrest was subject to attack only because of a state law warrant requirement and exclusion of resulting evidence was required only because of a state statutory exclusionary sanction. The issue, it observed, was whether this approach would most effectively implement legislative objectives as reflected in these nonconstitutional requirements. Legislative intent was to make the statutory warrant requirement "at least equal in magnitude" to federal Fourth Amendment rights, and the Supreme Court's attenuation of taint analysis reflects the Court's means of assuring that law enforcement officers could not violate Fourth Amendment rights with impunity. Consequently, it concluded, the state court would use the Fourth Amendment analysis under the state statutory exclusionary sanction to determine whether an improper warrantless arrest required suppression of a resulting confession.

The *Bell* court's analysis somewhat oversimplifies the issue presented. While it is true that the Supreme Court's attenuation analysis reflects an effort to assure that sufficient evidence is excluded to assure that officers are provided with an incentive to comply with federal constitutional requirements, other considerations were also implicated. *Ceccolini,* of course, reflects the Court's general objective of developing the attenuation analysis so as to minimize the unjustified loss of reliable evidence. Perhaps—although this is not clear—the overall analysis reflects an effort to promulgate a standard that assures insofar as possible that evidence is excluded

where, but only where, that exclusion can be expected to have sufficient incremental preventive impact to justify the cost paid in terms of loss of evidence. A court exercising real independence of analysis would have to address for itself whether the attenuation analysis in the Supreme Court's cases in fact does this, or at least does this as well as the task can be performed. The Texas court did not undertake such an evaluation in *Bell.*

As a practical matter, however, there may be no viable alternative. Few if any courts are likely to accept the fruits doctrine unqualified by some assurance that not all evidence obtained in a manner influenced by illegality must be excluded. What alternatives to the Court's attenuation analysis, or something quite similar, are available?

Justice White has suggested that exclusion ought to be required if, but only if, the challenged evidence was foreseen by the officers at the time of their conduct or, in the exercise of reasonable care, should have been foreseen.[12] If discovery of evidence was or could have been foreseen, the threat of its exclusion can be expected to discourage officers in similar situations from engaging in similar conduct; no attenuation should be found, and such evidence should be excluded. But if discovery of the evidence was not and could not have been anticipated, exclusion cannot be expected to affect law enforcement conduct; attenuation should be found, and the evidence should be admitted.

Justice White's approach is, of course, conceptually true to what the Court has identified as the major principle underlying the federal constitutional exclusionary sanctions and the attenuation doctrine in particular. But accurately determining foreseeability in the varying situations presented by criminal cases may be impossible. Consideration of other factors, such as the type (and value) of the evidence challenged and the intervention of a voluntary decision by the defendant or someone else may be both desirable and inevitable. If so, this may be best accommodated

---

11. 724 S.W.2d 780 (Tex.Cr.App.1986), cert. denied 479 U.S. 1046.

12. Harrison v. United States, 392 U.S. 219, 230–234 (1968) (White, J., dissenting).

by a flexible approach—such as that taken by the Court—that expressly provides for consideration of such factors.

§ 180. Exceptions to Exclusion (b) Inevitable Discovery

Federal Constitutional exclusionary rules are subject to an exception often called the "inevitable discovery" exception. Accuracy suggests it would better be labeled the "inevitable legitimate discovery" rule, because it consists of a showing by the prosecution that had the challenged evidence not been improperly secured as it was, the prosecution would nevertheless "inevitably" have obtained it in a "legitimate" manner.

This exception must be distinguished from others with which it might be confused. Both the independent source rule[1] and the inevitable discovery rule rest on assumptions that if the law enforcement agencies involved had eschewed the illegal activity, they nevertheless would have procured the evidence at issue. But the independent source rule applies only upon proof that *in actual fact* the officers did not obtain the challenged evidence as a result of the primary illegality; the inevitable discovery exception assumes that the evidence was in fact obtained as a consequence of the primary illegality but is invoked by proof that—hypothetically—if the officers had not engaged in the primary illegality, they would nevertheless although in a different manner have obtained the challenged evidence. The attenuation of taint doctrine[2] turns upon the characteristics of the actual causal relationship between the primary illegality and the obtaining of the challenged evidence; the inevitable discovery exception, in contrast, depends upon what would have occurred had the primary illegality not taken place.

Federal Constitutional Exception. The doctrine was incorporated into federal exclusionary analysis in Nix v. Williams,[3] a Sixth Amendment right to counsel case. Williams was interrogated in violation of his Sixth Amendment right to counsel, and in the course of this questioning led police to the body of his young murder victim. At trial, the state successfully offered evidence concerning the condition of the victim's body, articles and photographs of her clothing, and the results of chemical and medical tests conducted on the body. An extensive and intensive search had been underway for the victim, but it was called off before discovery of her body when the officers directing it learned that Williams was cooperating with the investigation. No constitutional error arose from the prosecution's use of the evidence, the Supreme Court held, because the lower courts had properly determined that the challenged evidence would ultimately or inevitably have been discovered even if no violation of Williams' rights had occurred.

The inevitable discovery exception, the Court explained, flows from the rationale for the Court's development of federal constitutional exclusionary law. That development reflects a view that prevention of future violations of constitutional norms ordinarily requires that the prosecution be denied any advantages that might flow from its misconduct. It does not, however, reflect any perception that this preventive purpose requires that the prosecution be put in any worse a position than it would be in had it not committed the primary illegality. In fact, the independent source doctrine indicates that in view of the need for probative evidence, exclusionary sanctions should ordinarily not go beyond putting the prosecution in the same position it would have been in had no misconduct occurred. These considerations make clear that no reason exists to deny the prosecution any advantage it can establish that it would have enjoyed had its officers eschewed improper action. To deprive it of such advantages would unjustifiably place it in a worse position because of its illegality.

All members of the Court agreed that the exception was appropriate. Justice Brennan,

---

§ 180

1. See § 177 supra.

2. See § 179 supra.

3. 467 U.S. 431 (1984).

joined by Justice Marshall, argued, however, that the nature of the exception required that the prosecution have an extraordinarily high burden of proof on it. Unlike the other exceptions, he reasoned, the inevitable discovery rule requires a "hypothetical finding" concerning what would have happened if antecedent events had not occurred. The hypothetical nature of the inquiry means that it poses a greater risk of error than does application of the independent source rule, which involves only inquiry into what in fact occurred. To minimize this risk that factfindings will incorrectly determine the prosecution would have discovered the evidence had the primary illegality not occurred, Justice Brennan urged that clear and convincing evidence be required of the prosecution. The majority, however, reasoned that "inevitable discovery involves no speculative elements but focuses on demonstrated historical facts capable of ready verification or impeachment" and consequently presents no justification for requiring more of the prosecution than proof by a preponderance of the evidence.

"Bad Faith." Both the Iowa Supreme Court and the Ninth Circuit in *Williams* assumed that any inevitable exception to the Sixth Amendment exclusionary sanction required that the officers not have acted in "bad faith." Without defining what that required, the Iowa court held that since reasonable persons well-versed in constitutional law have differed on whether the interrogation violated Sixth Amendment standards, "it cannot be said that the actions of the police were taken in bad faith." The Ninth Circuit apparently defined the requirement as demanding that the prosecution actually prove the officers believed their actions proper under applicable law and held that the state courts had not required a sufficient showing of this sort by the prosecution.

But the Supreme Court held that the exception includes no such requirement. Any demand of this sort, the Court noted, would sometimes place the prosecution in a worse position than it would have been in had its officers complied with the law. This is not justified by any need to discourage officers from taking "shortcuts." An officer who is aware that grounds exist for a later claim of inevitable discovery, it reasoned, will have little to gain from taking "dubious 'shortcuts' " to obtain the evidence and to the contrary will try to avoid any questionable conduct.

Whether the Court's conclusion is justified or not is at best problematic. The Court presented no support for its factual assertions and may well have underestimated police officers' incentive to avoid what are perceived by them as cumbersome legal requirements where they see that the law offers them a way to escape any evidentiary penalty for doing so.

A few lower courts have been obviously troubled by *Williams'* elimination of any "good faith" element to the exception. Moreover, it is quite likely that this has encouraged some courts to limit the rule in other ways to avoid the sorts of abuse of the exception that might more directly be addressed by a requirement that the officers have had a good faith—and perhaps objectively reasonable—belief that the actions actually taken were consistent with legal demands.

Issues Under the Federal Exception. Several major questions have been posed by implementation of the federal constitutional exception. First, must the prosecution show that legitimate discovery of the evidence was absolutely certain or is something less sufficient? Most courts state the rule as requiring absolute certainty, although generally this has not been given consideration. A few courts have stated the exception as requiring less—generally a "reasonable probability" that the evidence would have been obtained in a legitimate fashion.

Second, is the exception limited to "derivative" as contrasted with "direct" evidence? Under this distinction, "direct" evidence is that which is actually discovered and seized during the illegal conduct. "Derivative" evidence, on the other hand, is evidence obtained later by means of information derived from illegal conduct. Some courts have limited the exception to evidence of the latter sort.

As the Second Circuit suggested in rejecting such a limitation, *Williams* itself provides no significant support for such a limitation although the evidence there at issue was clearly "derivative" within the meaning of this distinction. In Murray v. United States,[4] the Supreme Court refused to limit the independent source exception to derivative evidence, reasoning in part that such limitation would produce results "bearing no relation to the policies of the exclusionary rule." Given the close conceptual relationship between the independent source and inevitable discovery exceptions, the Court is likely to take the same approach to the latter exception.

Would limiting the exception to derivative evidence produce results reasonably related to the policies of the exclusionary requirements? It is difficult to see how. Neither the truly independent nature of the legal source nor the true inevitability of the evidence's discovery by such means are less susceptible to accurate determination with regard to primary evidence. Perhaps officers are more likely to actually anticipate the "primary" results of their activities and thus application of the independent source to such results creates an especially significant incentive for officers to "shortcut" required steps in reliance upon their later ability to invoke the exception. But *Williams* indicates that the Court is inclined, at a minimum, to require quite persuasive evidence to support any claim that the exception will in fact be abused. No such evidence appears available to support these concerns.

A third implementation issue is whether the legitimate line of investigation relied upon by the prosecution as the hypothetical source of the evidence must actually have been in progress at the time of the illegal activity. A number of courts have imposed such a requirement, primarily on the ground that only in such situations can courts be

sufficiently convinced that legitimate investigations would in fact have resulted in discovery of the challenged evidence. Other courts, however, have rejected a strict requirement of this sort. Such a requirement, then-judge Kennedy noted in a Ninth Circuit decision, comports with the facts of *Williams,* but *Williams'* "rationale * * * is not so limited."[5]

A fourth issue, less directly acknowledged in the cases, is whether the exception is itself subject to one or several exceptions that render it inapplicable in certain situations. Some courts have so held. The Arizona Supreme Court, for example, found the exception inapplicable to evidence seized during a warrantless search of a residence.[6] "[U]nlawful entry into homes and seizure of evidence," the court explained, "cannot be tolerated." This may reflect a view that with regard to situations in which privacy interests are particularly intense, the need to prevent improper intrusions is so great that courts should tolerate no dilution of exclusionary sanctions' deterrent message.

But some lower court cases alternatively suggest judicial discomfort with application of the exception in situations where its application would so often render evidence admissible that the general requirement of exclusion would be deprived of all meaning. A Florida court has noted, for example, that that application of the inevitable discovery exception to situations in which the illegality consisted of improper "no-knock" entries to execute warrants would emasculate the exclusionary remedy, since almost always proper entries would have resulted in the same searches and discovery of the same evidence. This perhaps explains judicial discomfort with application of the exception to situations where officers eschewed the search warrant process and later sought admission of the fruits of their efforts on the ground that had they not ignored the warrant requirement a valid warrant would in fact have issued and produced a valid search.

---

4. 487 U.S. 533 (1988), discussed in § 177 supra.

5. United States v. Boatwright, 822 F.2d 862, 864 (9th Cir.1987).

6. State v. Ault, 150 Ariz. 459, 724 P.2d 545 (1986).

Some cases demonstrate in other ways a similar inclination to seek objectively-defined limits to the inevitable discovery exception. Lower courts, it seems, are with some frequency distressed by the broad terms of the doctrine as developed in *Williams* and, it is likely, particularly with the Court's insistence that the officers' "bad faith" is irrelevant. Since the doctrine cannot be held inapplicable on the explicit grounds of bad faith, some lower courts see a need to struggle to avoid the exception's application to situations in which bad faith circumvention of important legal requirements seems most likely, most costly, or both.

State Law Developments. In addressing the content of state exclusionary requirements, state courts have been less troubled by the inevitable discovery exception than by its breadth as developed in *Williams.* Several courts have adopted state constitutional limits on the exception that may not apply under the *Williams* rule. State constitutional grounds were explicitly relied upon, at least as alternative grounds should federal law develop otherwise, by the New York court in holding the exception inapplicable to "primary" evidence and the Arizona court in holding it inapplicable to the direct results of a warrantless entry into a private residence. Similarly, the New Jersey court has imposed a requirement that the prosecution show inevitability of discovery by clear and convincing evidence, apparently as a matter of state constitutional law.

The Massachusetts court more explicitly imposed, as a matter of state constitutional law, limitations upon the exception that it recognized may be more stringent than those imposed under *Williams.* Noting uncertainty as to the precise meaning of *Williams'* definition of the prosecution's burden of proof, it held that under state law the state need prove factual matters only by the *Williams'* preponderance of the evidence standard. But from the facts so proved, legitimate discovery of the evidence must have been "certain." It is not sufficient that such discovery was more probable than not.

In addition, the Massachusetts court indicated that the courts have flexibility in applying the exception and that the severity of the underlying violation is "critical" in determining whether the exception will be applied. Evidence that the police acted in "bad faith" is relevant and, of course, suggests that the exception ought not to be available. Further, the court offered, the exception might not be applicable where evidence is found and seized in disregard of the requirement of a search warrant, even if the prosecution establishes the inevitability that a valid warrant would have been issued.

There is, in short, widespread judicial perception that the inevitable discovery exception is, in general, a legitimate and appropriate aid in limiting the cost of adherence to exclusion of evidence as a response to official impropriety. But there is almost equally widespread recognition that the exception presents serious risk of misapplication and requires particular care in its development and application. In the words of one court:

> "The [inevitable discovery] doctrine must be used with restraint and circumspection lest it become a vehicle abrogating the right of all citizens to be free from unreasonable searches and seizures." [7]

§ 181. Exceptions to Exclusion (c) "Good Faith"

Whether illegally obtained evidence should be excluded if the officers who gathered it mistakenly believed that their actions complied with legal requirements is perhaps the most controversial issue posed by existing exclusionary requirements. A limited exception to the federal constitutional exclusionary rules for some situations of this sort has been recognized by the Supreme Court. State courts and legislatures have sometimes, but not always, followed suit.

Federal Constitutional Exception. The exception to the Fourth Amendment exclusionary sanction was recognized in two 1984 com-

---

7. State v. Kennedy, 134 Wis.2d 308, 318, 396 N.W.2d 765, 768 (App.1986).

panion cases, United States v. Leon [1] and Massachusetts v. Sheppard.[2] In both cases, the officers had conducted searches on the basis of search warrants that were later assumed violative of Fourth Amendment standards; in *Leon,* the facts on which the warrant issued were insufficient to demonstrate probable cause, and in *Sheppard* the warrant itself failed to describe adequately the items to be searched for and seized. Where officers relied upon a subsequently invalidated search warrant, the Court held, and their belief that the warrant was valid was objectively reasonable, the "extreme sanction" of exclusion of the evidence obtained was inappropriate.

Three years later, in Illinois v. Krull,[3] the Court similarly held that evidence should not be excluded where officers obtained it in a warrantless search conducted pursuant to an invalid statute authorizing such searches, if the officers acted in objectively reasonable reliance on the statute's validity. The tribunal has not addressed whether the exception will cover other situations.

Reemphasizing the preventive purpose of the Fourth Amendment exclusionary rule, *Leon* reasoned that the rule cannot be expected to deter objectively reasonable law enforcement activity and should not be applied in an effort to do so. This is particularly so, it continued, where officers have obtained a search warrant. The magistrate has the responsibility for determining such matters as whether probable cause exists; officers cannot be expected to question magistrates' resolution of those issues. "Penalizing the officer for the magistrate's error, rather than his own," the Court concluded, "cannot logically contribute to the deterrence of the Fourth Amendment violations." Similarly, officers cannot ordinarily be expected to question the judgment of a legislature that passed a statute, so no contribution to deterrence can logically be expected from penalizing the officer for errors of the legislature. Consequently, any benefits derived from excluding such evi-

dence cannot justify the substantial costs of exclusion.

Exclusion might, of course, be justified as a means of discouraging errors in the *Leon* context on the part of magistrates and in the *Krull* context by legislatures. The Court, however, rejected this. Federal constitutional exclusionary sanctions are not aimed at magistrates or legislatures. Nor should they be, given the absence of evidence that lawlessness by them is of sufficient importance to warrant "the extreme sanction of exclusion." Moreover, exclusionary sanctions might well be ineffective in affecting such conduct. Magistrates, the Court suggested, have no stake in the outcome of litigated cases and thus are unlikely to respond to the threat of exclusion.

The Court did, however, somewhat qualify its holdings in *Leon* and *Krull.* Officers' reliance upon a warrant or legislation must be objectively reasonable; simply a subjective "good faith" state of mind is not sufficient. Exclusion is required despite the officers' good faith belief in the legality of their action, then, if the defect in a warrant or a statute is so clear that a reasonably well trained officer would recognize it. In the case of reliance upon a warrant, exclusion is required if the officer in applying for the warrant misled the magistrate by including information he knew was false or would have known was false except for his reckless disregard for the truth.

The remedy also remains necessary if the responsible entity has abandoned its role in the governmental process, but apparently only if that was or should have been apparent to the officer. If in the case of a warrant, for example, the magistrate so participated in the actual search as to preclude his functioning in the objective detached manner required by the Fourth Amendment, an officer could not reasonably rely on the warrant. Moreover, in *Krull* the Court somewhat more puzzlingly commented, "A statute cannot support objectively reasonable reliance if, in passing the statute, the legislature wholly abandoned its responsibility to enact constitutional laws."

§ 181

1.　468 U.S. 897 (1984).

2.　468 U.S. 981 (1984).

3.　480 U.S. 340 (1987).

The major issue posed by *Leon, Sheppard* and *Krull* is whether the exception recognized in these cases will be extended to other and perhaps all situations where officers acted under a good faith and objectively reasonable belief that their conduct complied with federal constitutional standards. Even before *Leon*, a bare majority of the Fifth Circuit sitting en banc held that it would apply a good faith exception whenever the prosecution could show that the law enforcement officers reasonably and in good faith believed their actions proper.[4] The Bush Administration, in the "Exclusionary Rule Reform Act of 1989," has proposed a federal statutory directive that evidence not be excluded from federal litigation "if the search of seizure [by which it was obtained] was carried out in circumstances justifying an objectively reasonable belief that it was in conformity with the Fourth Amendment." The Court's emphasis in *Leon* and *Sheppard* upon the officers' reliance upon the warrant and in *Krull* upon the statute suggests, however, that *Williams* and the Administration's proposal may have overestimated the breadth of the exception which the Supreme Court is willing to adopt.

The Utah Supreme Court has held that the federal constitutional "good faith" exception applies only if the officers relied upon some "outside authority"—such as an invalid warrant or statute—which expressly authorized their search. Perhaps such a limitation upon the exception is defensible on the rationale that sufficient assurance exists that exclusion will serve no sufficient preventive function where, but only where, the officers can establish reliance upon some objective basis for their belief that they were acting acceptably. Only where the facts show reliance upon a judicially-issued warrant or legislative authorization is there sufficient assurance that the rationale for exclusion is inapplicable. No exception would be applicable, then, where situations leave open the possibility that exclusion would serve some preventive function. Evidence remains inadmissible, for example,

if officers reasonably but mistakenly believed they had grounds for a warrantless investigatory stop. It might also be inadmissible if officers mistakenly believed that a warrant existed or that their actions were within the scope of authority granted by a valid warrant. In these situations, there remains sufficient likelihood that exclusion might encourage greater care in ascertaining the existence or effect of a warrant.

State Constitutional Requirements. More than any other aspect of exclusionary sanction law, the good faith exception issue has stimulated state courts' consideration of whether their state constitutions create exclusionary requirements and, to the extent that they do so, whether those requirements differ in substance from the federal constitutional exclusionary requirements. A significant number of state courts have declined to follow *Leon, Sheppard* and *Krull* in developing their local constitutional exclusionary rules. Others, of course, have followed the Supreme Court's approach and construed their state provisions as subject to a *Leon/Krull*-like exception.

The New Jersey Supreme Court's decision in State v. Novembrino[5] is the leading discussion rejecting *Leon* as a model for construction of a state constitution. To some extent, the New Jersey court's holding rested upon simple disagreement with the Supreme Court as to the impact of the exception upon the deterrent effect of exclusionary sanctions. A good faith exception, the New Jersey court concluded, "will tend to undermine the motivation of law-enforcement officers to comply with the constitutional requirement of probable cause," "will inevitably and inexorably diminish the quality of evidence presented in search-warrant applications," and ultimately "assures us that the constitutional standard [of probable cause] will be diluted."

In addition, however, *Novembrino* rested upon the New Jersey court's position that the state constitutional exclusionary sanction serves purposes broader than those served by

---

4. United States v. Williams, 622 F.2d 830, 846–847 (5th Cir.1980) (en banc), cert. denied 449 U.S. 1127.

5. 105 N.J. 95, 519 A.2d 820 (1987).

its federal counterpart. The state requirement, observed the *Novembrino* court, has
functions other than "merely to deter police
misconduct." It also "serves as the indispen-
sible mechanism for vindicating the constitutional right to be free from unreasonable
searches." Thus the state rule, unlike its
Fourth Amendment analogue, legitimately
serves to remedy underlying violations. Defendants consequently "deserve" a remedy for
wrongs done regardless of whether the officers who wronged them had reasonable and
good faith beliefs at the time that they were
acting within the law. A good faith exception
would mean that some defendants entitled to
a remedy under the rationale of the state rule
would be denied exclusion. This, the Court
suggested, was unacceptable.

The merits of the New Jersey court's first
concern regarding the impact of the *Leon–
Krull* exception depends in large part upon
how that exception is developed. Courts may
construe the requirement of objective reasonableness to require that officers be reasonably
trained and adequately informed and that
they exercise skill and insight when applying
what they regard as the law to the facts
before them; if so, the New Jersey court's
fears may turn out to have little basis. Trial
judges, however, may be hostile to the underlying requirements being enforced, a remedy
that requires them to ignore reliable evidence
of defendants' guilt of serious offenses, or
both. This hostility, combined with the difficulty of effective appellate supervision, may
lead to lax application of the reasonableness
demand. Such implementation of the requirement could, of course, undermine officers' incentive to comply with the underlying
legal requirements.

The Supreme Court's *Leon–Krull* approach
might also be rejected on the basis that it
inappropriately foregoes use of exclusionary
sanctions as a means of encouraging responsible behavior on the part of magistrates and
legislative bodies. Three members of the Mississippi Supreme Court, for example, have
argued that the fundamental error in *Leon's*
analysis was the Court's failure to recognize
that the magistrate's responsibility for the

improper search "suggests a *greater* need for
the exclusionary rule, not a lesser one." No
other recourse exists for those harmed by a
magistrate's error, they explained, since the
issuance of warrants is not appealable and—
unlike the situation where the officer errs—
no civil action for damages lies against the
judicial officer.

*Nonconstitutional Exclusionary Require-
ments.* *Leon* -like good faith exceptions have,
to some extent, been incorporated into state
nonconstitutional exclusionary requirements.
The Texas statutory exclusionary rule, for
example, was amended in 1987 to specifically
permit use of evidence "obtained by a law
enforcement officer acting in objective good
faith reliance upon a warrant issued by a
neutral magistrate based on probable cause."
But other statutory exclusionary requirements containing no such exceptions have
been construed as legislative directives to reject the *Leon* approach. Judicial hostility to
proffered rationales for good faith exceptions
may lead to simple refusal to develop them on
the state level, or in begrudging development
and application of such exceptions when they
are recognized.

The nature of some state law requirements
enforced by exclusionary sanctions may suggest that no "good faith" exceptions to the
exclusionary remedies be recognized. A Maryland court, for example, has suggested that
a state wiretap statute is designed not simply
to "police the police" but also to prevent dissemination of improperly secured information. Consequently, an exception permitting
such dissemination because of the officers'
good faith in intercepting a covered conversation would be inappropriate, since that good
faith in no way indicates that those whose
conversations were overheard have no legitimate interest in minimal dissemination of
the contents of those conversations.

§ 182. Exceptions to Exclusion (d) Use of Illegally Obtained Evidence to Impeach Testifying Defendant

The exceptions discussed in the preceeding
sections, when applicable, permit the prosecu-

tion to use improperly obtained evidence to prove defendants' guilt. Many exclusionary sanctions, however, are subject to a broader exception that permits the use of improperly obtained evidence for the limited purpose of impeaching a defendant who chooses to testify in his own behalf at trial. Again, the Supreme Court's federal constitutional case law provides the point of reference for analysis.

The federal constitutional exception was developed in Walder v. United States,[1] a pre-*Mapp* case. At his trial for sale of narcotics, Walder took the stand and denied the sales. He also denied ever having had any narcotics in his possession, except pursuant to a physician's prescription. The government was then permitted to ask on cross-examination whether a police officer had taken heroin from his home in 1950 and, when he denied that this had occurred, to prove that this had taken place. In earlier litigation, the heroin obtained in the 1950 search had been suppressed as having been obtained in an illegal search.

Nevertheless, the Supreme Court found no impropriety in the use of the heroin in the second trial. A defendant, Justice Frankfurter wrote for the Court, "must be free to deny all the elements of the case against him without thereby giving leave to the Government to introduce by way of rebuttal evidence illegally secured by it * * *." But this, he continued, "is hardly justification for letting the defendant affirmatively resort to perjurious testimony in reliance upon the Government's disability to challenge his credibility." *Walder* was widely read as establishing an exception to the Fourth Amendment exclusionary rule and perhaps also to other federal constitutional exclusionary sanctions, permitting use of otherwise inadmissible evidence to impeach a testifying defendant but only when the defendant's testimony went beyond a simple denial of guilt and addressed "collateral matters."

Walder's continuing vitality was placed in doubt during the 1960s by the Supreme Court's increasing reliance in *Mapp* and its progeny upon exclusion as the primary means of implementing the major constitutional limitations upon law enforcement activity. This was especially so with regard to confessions, given the language of Miranda v. Arizona[2] suggesting that incriminating statements obtained in violation of the requirements established by that case would be inadmissible for all purposes.

In Harris v. New York,[3] however, the Supreme Court reaffirmed *Walder* in the *Miranda* context. Harris's statement had been obtained during custodial interrogation conducted without informing him of his right to appointed counsel under *Miranda*. Nevertheless, the Court held, this was properly used to impeach Harris. Moreover, *Harris* abandoned *Walder's* requirement that the defendant go beyond denial of guilt and testify as to collateral matters. While it is arguable that Harris's trial testimony went into matters that were collateral within the meaning of *Harris,* the Court attributed no significance to this. Rather, noting that *Walder* involved testimony as to "collateral matters," "whereas [Harris] was impeached as to testimony bearing more directly on the crimes charged," it found this distinction insufficient to warrant a result different from that reached in *Walder.*

Subsequent decisions permitted impeachment use of evidence obtained in violation of other federal constitutional exclusionary requirements. In Oregon v. Hass,[4] the Court upheld impeachment of a testifying defendant by a confession obtained after a properly warned suspect requested counsel but was nevertheless interrogated without representation, and in United States v. Havens[5] the Court approved similar use of evidence obtained in violation of the defendant's Fourth Amendment rights. A confession obtained in violation of the Sixth Amendment prophylac-

§ 182

1. 347 U.S. 62 (1954).
2. 384 U.S. 436 (1966); see generally § 148 supra.
3. 401 U.S. 222 (1971).

4. 420 U.S. 714 (1975).
5. 446 U.S. 620 (1980).

tic requirement that officers not reapproach a suspect who has invoked his right to counsel is available for impeachment, the Court held in Michigan v. Harvey.[6]

In James v. Illinois,[7] however, the Supreme Court clarified a major limit upon the exception. At James' trial, the state court had permitted the use of evidence obtained in violation of his Fourth Amendment rights to "impeach" the testimony of a defense witness other than the defendant. This, the Supreme Court held, was impermissible. Thus the *Walder–Harris* exception is limited to situations in which the defendant testifies and the improperly obtained evidence is used to impeach him.

In both *Walder* and *Harris,* the otherwise inadmissible evidence was used to contradict the defendant's testimony on direct examination. Such use of otherwise inadmissible evidence leaves defendants somewhat free, in Justice Frankfurter's *Walder* terminology, to "deny" guilt without enabling the prosecution to use improperly secured evidence. Defense counsel, in conducting the direct examination of a testifying defendant, might be able to avoid reference to matters as to which the prosecution possesses otherwise inadmissible evidence; to the extent that this can be done, the defendant can testify without triggering the prosecution's right to impeach by use of that inadmissible evidence. In *Havens,* however, the Court held that the prosecution can use otherwise inadmissible evidence to contradict a defendant's testimony during cross-examination, as long as that testimony was in response to questions "plainly within the scope of the defendant's direct examination." As a result, a defendant seeking to avoid creation of an opportunity for the prosecution to use excluded evidence must not only consider the questions necessary on direct examination but also the questions that may be asked on cross-examination. If the answers to those likely to be asked on cross-examination are inconsistent with the suppressed evi-

dence, testimony given in his own defense may open the defendant up to impeachment use of that evidence.

The cases are unclear as to the degree of inconsistency required to allow impeachment by otherwise inadmissible evidence,[8] the nature of those assertions by defendants that can be inquired into by cross-examination questions derived from inadmissible evidence, and any "noncollateralness" of the defendant's assertions that will permit the prosecution to go beyond questioning the defendant and permit the prosecution to affirmatively introduce otherwise inadmissible evidence.[9] It is not even clear whether a state court is required by federal constitutional considerations to apply, or apply accurately, the jurisdiction's ordinary rules concerning cross-examination or impeachment in implementing the prosecution's right to use inadmissible evidence for this purpose.

Inadmissible evidence may be used under *Walder–Harris* only to assail the defendant's credibility and not to prove the defendant's guilt. Presumably the defendant is entitled to an instruction to the jury concerning the limited use it is to make of the evidence; the Court has not addressed the constitutional necessity for this. Perhaps the failure of both parties and the Court to address this reflects general recognition that juries are quite unlikely to be able or inclined to follow such instructions, and hence that the giving of the instructions amounts to little more than a ritual.

The federal constitutional exception may be limited to evidence tainted by federal constitutional provisions that do not include exclusion of evidence as a "core" part of the rights afforded defendants. In Michigan v. Harvey,[10] the defendant urged that the Sixth Amendment, unlike the Fourth Amendment and the *Miranda* requirements, is itself violated by trial use of evidence obtained in violation of the right to counsel which it establishes for those formally accused of crime.

---

6.   494 U.S. 344 (1990).
7.   493 U.S. 307 (1990).
8.   See § 34 supra.

9.   See § 45 supra.
10.   494 U.S. 344 (1990).

His statement had been given after his Sixth Amendment right to counsel had attached and—he argued—had been elicited without first securing a voluntary and intelligent waiver of that right; since it was secured in violation of his "core" Sixth Amendment rights, it could not be used even for impeachment. The Court did not reach the issue, as it found that Harvey had not litigated below whether his waiver of counsel was voluntary and intelligent in Sixth Amendment terms and therefore whether the procurement and use of his statement might violate the Sixth Amendment. Thus it remains possible that the impeachment exception is applicable only where the original right to exclusion is a judicially-developed remedy for a right that intrinsically involves no such remedy.

Two major objections to the impeachment use of otherwise inadmissible evidence run throughout *Walder* and its Supreme Court progeny. First, of course, such use of evidence may decrease the effectiveness of exclusionary sanctions in preventing future illegality. Officers faced with a difficult choice as to whether to make a questionable search may be influenced by a perception that if the search is successfully made but ruled improper, the results may nevertheless discourage the defendant from asserting to the jury what officers regard as a fraudulent defense.

Second, impeachment use of improperly obtained evidence may impermissibly burden the exercise of important and constitutionally-protected rights. *Walder* itself reflected the view that a defendant's right to put his personal version of the facts—"to deny all elements of the case against him"—before the trier of fact is so important that it should ordinarily not be discouraged by a threat of impeachment by evidence otherwise unusable by the prosecution. A defendant's interest in similarly testifying as to collateral matters is less important, and perhaps is properly qualified by attaching to his right to do so an obligation to explain to the trier of fact other generally-inadmissible evidence that suggests his testimony is inaccurate.

The Supreme Court's *Walder–Harris* position, as developed in *James,* rests upon several underlying conclusions responding to these objections. First, it reflects the Court's view that any risk that impeachment use of evidence will impede the preventive function of the exclusionary sanctions is at most "speculative" and therefore entitled to little weight. In addition, *Walder* and its progeny reflect the Court's perception that permitting impeachment use of such evidence furthers the truthseeking function of criminal trials by permitting triers of fact to consider quite probative information bearing upon the accuracy of the defendant's version of the events. *Harris* suggests that values of particular importance are served by the tendency of impeachment use of such evidence to discourage perjury by defendants. Perjury, the Court implied, is an offense against the administration of justice and thus, in some senses, is even more serious than the offenses for which defendants are being tried.

Moreover, the Court has concluded that the prosecution's ability to impeach by means of otherwise excludable evidence does not unacceptably discourage defendants from putting their own version of relevant facts before juries. Each defendant controls whether he will testify and what he will say if he chooses to do so; the rule therefore does not deprive defendants of means by which to avoid the prosecution's use of suppressed evidence. Its effect will be less to discourage honest testimony by defendants than to encourage honesty when defendants choose to present their stories to juries. In any case, application of the exception does not make the inadmissible evidence determinative of guilt but simply requires that the defendant address apparent inconsistencies between his trial testimony and other information available regarding the case. He can, of course, undertake to persuade the trier of fact that his trial testimony is accurate and that the impeaching evidence is unreliable or actually consistent with his trial testimony.

James concluded that for several reasons the rationales for permitting impeachment use against testifying defendants did not apply when the defense offered other witnesses. First, the expanded opportunity for trial use of inadmissible evidence provided by such a rule would greatly weaken the deterrent effect of exclusion in general. The costs of admitting the evidence, second, would be different and greater than permitting its use to impeach a testifying defendant. Since defense counsel have less control over nondefendant witnesses than over testifying defendants, defense lawyers would have less opportunity to present legitimate defensive testimony but in a manner avoiding perjury. Consequently, they would often decline to call nondefendant defense witnesses because of the risk that calling those witnesses would permit the prosecution to use inadmissible evidence. The proposed expansion of the impeachment exception would not simply discourage perjury but also dissuade defendants from presenting legitimate defenses through nondefendant witnesses.

Four members of the Court took the position in *James* that the truth-seeking function of the criminal trial justified permitting the prosecution to use inadmissible evidence to impeach nondefendant witnesses for the defense. Testimony by a defendant, Justice Kennedy argued, carries a signal of potential unreliability. But other defense testimony does not, and jurors are likely to assume from the prosecution's failure to produce contradicting evidence that nondefendant witnesses for the defense testify accurately. Recognizing the increased risks of such expanded use of inadmissible evidence, Justice Kennedy suggested that its use be limited in several ways. First, the prosecution should be permitted to use inadmissible evidence only if there is direct conflict between that evidence and the testimony of a defense witness. This would reduce the tendency of an expanded exception to chill defense presentation of defensive cases. Second, *Havens* might be abandoned in this context, and the prosecution might be limited to rebutting testimony elicited from defense witnesses on direct examination by defense counsel. This would reduce defense counsels' concern that presenting defense testimony might unwittingly open the door to otherwise inadmissible evidence.

A major consideration in the Court's recognition and development of the *Walder–Harris* doctrine has been its perception that the evidence admitted under the doctrine is reliable and thus quite highly probative as to the accuracy of the defendant's version. This provides the rationale for the major limit on the rule. In *Harris* itself the Court pointedly observed that Harris made no claim that his statements were coerced or involuntary and suggested that its holding was limited to situations in which the "trustworthiness" of the proffered impeachment evidence "satisfies legal standards." In Mincey v. Arizona,[11] the Court explicitly held that a confession shown by the evidence to be involuntary could not be used under *Harris* to impeach a testifying defendant. This followed from the rationale of *Harris*. Where the inadmissible evidence was rendered inadmissible for a reason that indicates unreliability, the probative value of that evidence on the ultimate question of truth is obviously less, and the balance among the competing considerations tips in favor of exclusion.

It is unclear under *Mincey* how a trial court is to resolve the question of admissibility. Should it merely consider whether the confession is involuntary under traditional standards and then assume that a finding of involuntariness indicates sufficient doubt as to accuracy to preclude use of the confession for impeachment? Or, should it directly address the reliability and hence the accuracy of the statement? Voluntariness could be a relevant and major consideration, and perhaps a prerequisite to a finding of insufficient reliability, but voluntariness would not be the only consideration or the ultimate question. The *Mincey* confession was apparently analyzed under the former approach, but there is no indication that any challenge was raised to that method of analysis.

The Supreme Court's case law leaves unclear what if any substantive violations other than coercion in eliciting a confession may render resulting evidence sufficiently unrelia-

---

11. 437 U.S. 385 (1978).

ble to require that the evidence not be used for impeachment under *Walder–Harris*. Given the rationale for the rule prohibiting exposure of a witness to an extremely suggestive lineup or photo showing,[12] perhaps eyewitness testimony tainted by such a violation must be treated the same as the involuntary confession in *Mincey*. But what of the testimony of a witness who identified the defendant at a lineup conducted in violation of the defendant's Sixth Amendment right to the presence of counsel? Most likely the relationship between this right to counsel and reliability of witnesses' identification testimony is no more direct than that between the Sixth Amendment right to counsel as it applies to custodial interrogation and the reliability of statements obtained in violation of this aspect of the right, but this is not certain.

The *Walder–Harris* approach has been widely, although not universally, followed in other exclusionary sanction contexts. State courts have generally accepted impeachment exceptions to exclusionary requirements found in state constitutions. Oregon's exclusionary rule enforcing its constitutional search provision, however, has been construed as unqualified by an impeachment exception. The state rule has, among other objectives, the remedial function of restoring search victims to the position they would be in had no improper search been conducted; accomplishing those objectives, the Oregon court reasoned, requires that improperly obtained evidence be unavailable to the prosecution for any purpose.

The Massachusetts court has held that impeachment use of evidence obtained in violation of the state constitutional search provision is not permitted, at least where the violation by which it was obtained was of substantial magnitude. An intermediate position was taken by the Vermont Supreme Court, which embraced a more limited exclusionary exception than the *Walder–Harris–Havens* product. Emphasizing what it viewed as the need to preserve a defendant's right to an unfettered opportunity to testify in his own

defense, the court rejected the *Havens* approach and held that evidence obtained in violation of the state provision could only be used to impeach a defendant's testimony on direct examination.

Statutory exclusionary requirements that make no express provision for impeachment use have divided the courts. The federal electronic surveillance statute has been read by lower courts as permitting impeachment use, on the basis that the legislative history makes clear Congressional intent to incorporate the *Walder* doctrine. Exclusionary directives in several state surveillance statutes, however, have been construed as containing no such exception, and thus as barring the use of evidence even for impeachment. Whether other statutory exclusionary requirements permit use of otherwise inadmissible evidence for impeachment presents similar problems of construction.

§ 183. Enforcement of the Right to Exclusion

Because of the special problems raised when criminal defendants invoke exclusionary sanctions, special procedures for raising and resolving exclusionary sanction issues in criminal litigation have evolved. Again, federal constitutional requirements impose minimal demands which state procedure must respect, but substantial flexibility nevertheless exists for states to impose procedural requirements to be followed even when defendants seek to raise federal constitutional objections to the prosecution's use of evidence.

Judge's Determination of Admissibility. There is general agreement that the admissibility of evidence challenged on exclusionary sanction grounds is to be resolved by the trial judge. Hearings on the exclusionary sanction objections are generally held out of the presence of the trial jury. The Supreme Court has indicated, however, that the federal constitution does not always require this even when the objection is on federal constitutional

---

12. See § 166 supra.

grounds.[1] This probably means only that a trial judge who ultimately and properly finds contested evidence admissible has committed no federal constitutional error by conducting the hearing on that matter in the presence of the trial jury, at least as long as the jury has not been exposed to inadmissible and prejudicial evidence as a result.

Pretrial Motions to Suppress. Statutes or court rules in many jurisdictions require that exclusionary sanction issues be raised by pretrial motions, often called motions to suppress evidence. Rule 12 of the Federal Rules of Criminal Procedure, for example, provides that motions to suppress evidence must be "raised" prior to trial and, further, within any shorter period for the making of such motions as is established by the trial court.[2] Failure to raise objections to evidence as Rule 12 demands results in a waiver of the right to exclusion, "but the court for cause shown may grant relief from the waiver." Similar requirements exist in a number of states. The Supreme Court has given no indication that requiring pretrial assertion of the right to exclusion would be an impermissible state procedure requirement for assertion of a federal constitutional right to exclusion.

Some jurisdictions impose additional requirements on the motion to suppress. These are designed to permit trial judges to dispose of as many such motions as possible without the need to hold evidentiary hearings. The motion may have to set out specifically the facts supporting the defendant's claim and be accompanied by an affidavit indicating that, if a hearing is held, the defense has a reasonable chance of proving those facts. The Supreme Court has, in at least a limited context, authorized states to limit factual hearings to those cases in which a specific claim is made and is supported with both reasoning and a preliminary showing by affidavit of the defendant's likelihood of proving the factual basis for his claim. It is likely that similar requirements in other situations will not impermissi-

bly burden defendants' ability to enforce their federal constitutional rights to exclusion.

A pretrial motion, even if required, does not assure that the issue must be resolved before trial. Rule 12, for example, provides that pretrial motions to suppress shall be ruled upon before trial unless the court for "good cause" defers the matter for determination at trial or even after verdict. State provisions vary. Orderly procedure, of course, suggests the wisdom of pretrial resolution unless the evidence bearing on the motion is so intertwined with that on guilt or innocence that full development of the evidence bearing on the motion to suppress would, in effect, require pretrial presentation of the prosecution's entire case on guilt.

Hearing on Admissibility. How formal the hearing on an exclusionary rule issue must be remains somewhat uncertain. It seems obvious that the defendant must have the right to introduce evidence on his objection and to contest the prosecution's evidence, but the extent to which this involves the right of in-court confrontation and cross-examination is unclear. In United States v. Matlock,[3] the Court suggested that such hearings could constitutionally and should as a matter of administrative policy be conducted under the same approach as other preliminary matters concerning admissibility of evidence, pursuant to which evidentiary rules—except perhaps for rules of privilege—are inapplicable. It rejected an "automatic rule against the reception of hearsay evidence in such proceedings," and specifically held that hearsay determined by the trial judge to be credible could be considered in resolving a defendant's challenge to the admissibility of evidence.

A defendant has an important interest in accurate resolution of his Fourth Amendment claims. To avoid discouraging defendants' exercise of their right to raise and pursue such claims, the Supreme Court has held that defendants' personal testimony at hearings on motions to suppress evidence cannot be used by the prosecution at trial to prove the defen-

---

1. Watkins v. Sowders, 449 U.S. 341, 349 (1981).

2. Fed.R.Crim.P. 12(b), (c).

3. 415 U.S. 164 (1974).

dants' guilt.[4] If, however, a defendant who has testified at such a hearing takes the witness stand at trial and testifies inconsistently with his hearing testimony, he may well be subject to impeachment by use of his testimony at that hearing.

Minimal requirements of procedural fairness quite clearly apply at such a hearing. A New York appellate court recently held, for example, that a trial court's restrictions upon defense counsel's questioning of a state police witness would require reversal:

> A fair suppression hearing requires that a defendant be given an adequate opportunity to cross-examine the police officers and fully challenge the constitutionality of their actions.[5]

Of course, the prosecution has a similar right to present its own evidence and to challenge that introduced by the defense.

Burden of Proof. The Supreme Court has not definitively determined what limitations the federal constitution places upon the allocation of the burdens of proceeding and persuasion with regard to criminal defendants' claims of rights to suppression based on the federal constitutional exclusionary requirements. In *Matlock,* however, the Court did comment that "the controlling burden of proof at suppression hearings should impose no greater burden than proof by a preponderance of the evidence."

It seems likely that a defendant raising an exclusionary rule issue is properly required to persuade the court that an illegality sufficient to invoke exclusion occurred, that this illegality infringed the defendant's interests (and therefore he has "standing"), and that the challenged evidence was obtained as a result of that illegality. Lower courts generally hold, however, that if the defense shows that the evidence was obtained by police action without a warrant, the burden of proceeding with the evidence to show the validity of the police action shifts to the prosecution which may also then carry the burden of persuasion.

Once that basic showing has been made, the prosecution most likely has—and perhaps constitutionally must have—the burden of persuading the judge of the applicability of one of the "exceptions" to the general rule requiring exclusion. Thus the prosecution properly bears the burden of proving that despite causation-in-fact between illegality and obtaining evidence, the taint of the illegality was attenuated before the challenged evidence was obtained by the prosecution. If the prosecution relies upon consent as a basis for a search, the prosecution must prove that the consent was voluntary and was given by a person authorized to consent to the search at issue.

The prosecution's burden is generally one of convincing the trial judge by only a preponderance of the evidence, although in at least one situation it is put to a higher standard. In United States v. Wade,[6] the Supreme Court addressed prosecutorial trial use of in-court identification testimony of a witness who identified the defendant at a pretrial lineup conducted in violation of the defendant's Sixth Amendment right to counsel. Such testimony is admissible, the Court indicated, if the prosecution establishes that it would have an "independent source," that is, a source unrelated to the witness's observations at the tainted lineup. The prosecution must establish this "by clear and convincing evidence."

This unusually heavy burden is unlikely to apply in other situations. In Nix v. Williams,[7] the Court refused to apply this high burden of proof when the prosecution invoked the "inevitable discovery" exception to the federal constitutional exclusionary rules. *Wade,* the Court suggested, rested upon the exceptional difficulties of determining the actual "source" of an eyewitness's proffered in-court identification testimony and the resulting need to guard against "speculative" and inaccurate findings that such testimony would not be influenced by identifying a defendant at a tainted lineup.

---

4. Simmons v. United States, 390 U.S. 377 (1968).

5. People v. Cruz, 149 A.D.2d 151, 163, 545 N.Y.S.2d 561, 568 (1989).

6. 388 U.S. 218 (1967).

7. 467 U.S. 431 (1984).

States remain free, of course, to impose a greater burden on the prosecution. Some have done so. Pennsylvania, for example, provides by rule that at a hearing on a motion to suppress evidence the prosecution has both the burden of going forward with the evidence and of establishing that the challenged evidence was not obtained in violation of the defendant's rights.

The complex nature of the issues and the numerous and varying burdens mean that procedure at suppression hearings can be confusing. Special problems are presented when a case involves questions of standing (on which the defense probably has the burdens of production and persuasion) and of the reasonableness of a warrantless police search (on which the prosecution probably has both burdens). In a recent California case of this sort, the parties stipulated that no warrant was involved, but both sides then declined to proceed until the other had met its burden. The appellate court noted the absence of Supreme Court case law on the order of proof and suggested that ordinarily it would not be a matter of constitutional dimensions. In any case, it continued, trial judges would necessarily have substantial discretion in dealing with such questions, and the trial judge here did not abuse that discretion in requiring the prosecution to proceed first.

Appellate Review. A defendant whose exclusionary sanction objection to evidence is overruled and who is subsequently convicted may, of course, assert on appeal error in that ruling. Defendants are, generally, limited to this route in obtaining appellate review; interlocutory appeals by defendants from even pretrial rulings on motions to suppress are unavailable. On the other hand, state law sometimes relieves a defendant of the need to go through a contested trial to secure appellate review. The defendant may, under these provisions, obtain whatever advantage he can from plea bargaining, plead guilty, and nevertheless appeal on the basis of the overruling of his motion to suppress. When appeal is taken from a conviction, the conviction may

be upheld despite error in admitting evidence over an exclusionary sanction objection if the "harmless error" standard is met.

In recognition of the exceptional impact of exclusion upon the prosecution, many jurisdictions have made provision for the prosecution to take interlocutory appeals from trial courts' orders granting pretrial motions to suppress evidence. These often contain requirements to limit prosecution appeals to those cases in which the trial court's ruling constitutes a serious impediment to continuation of the prosecution on the basis of other, unsuppressed, evidence. Under the federal statute, for example, the prosecutor must certify that the appeal is not being taken for purposes of delay and that the suppressed evidence is "a substantial proof of a fact material in the proceeding."

Postconviction Attacks Upon Convictions. Among the potentially most serious costs of exclusionary sanctions is the possibility that they will subject convictions to attack on the basis of theories unavailable or unrecognized by counsel at the time of the original prosecutions. Since some of the most important exclusionary requirements are imposed by federal constitutional law, *Mapp* and its progeny posed the specter of state convictions being perpetually subject to attack in federal postconviction habeas corpus proceedings. Because of the pervasive impact of Fourth Amendment requirements, the Fourth Amendment exclusionary rule posed the most serious concerns of this sort.

The Supreme Court responded in Stone v. Powell,[8] by refining the *Mapp* Fourth Amendment right to challenge the admissibility of evidence as obtained in violation of that provision. Whether the constitutionally mandated remedy requires that state defendants be entitled to raise it in federal habeas corpus, the Court made clear, depends upon whether the incremental preventive effect of so expanding the remedy would outweigh the costs involved. Assuring state defendants of the right to raise claims in federal habeas corpus would contribute little if anything to the pre-

---

8. 428 U.S. 465 (1976).

ventive effect of the federal exclusionary requirement. It would, however, involve a number of costs, including a substantial decrease in the assured finality of state criminal convictions and—when a federal habeas court grants relief denied by an entire state court system—an increase in the friction between federal and state systems of justice.

Consequently, the Court concluded, a defendant convicted in a state criminal trial is not to be granted federal habeas corpus relief simply upon a showing that evidence tainted by an unconstitutional search or seizure was introduced at his trial. The defendant is entitled to relief only if, in addition, he shows that the state failed to afford him an opportunity for full and fair consideration of his search or seizure claim at trial and on direct review of his conviction. If he had such an opportunity but failed to pursue it, he is entitled to no federal relief. Similarly, if he pursued that opportunity but the state courts erroneously resolved his claim against him, he is not to be granted relief.

The Supreme Court has not addressed whether any of the other federal constitutionally-required exclusionary sanctions will be defined so as to be of only limited enforceability in federal habeas corpus litigation.

Whether state exclusionary requirements should be defined as enforceable in state postconviction proceedings is, perhaps, somewhat more problematic. Such enforceability does not endanger the proper relationship among components of our federal system. If the defendant raised the issue in his original prosecution and appeal, postconviction relitigation will ordinarily hold little hope of success; his petition will usually be heard by the same courts that previously rejected his argument. Those defendants who did not raise their claims in the original proceeding can be barred from relief by a requirement that matters be so raised. This would leave state postconviction proceedings available for the exceptional case where excuse exists for not raising the issue in the original proceedings or where there is a basis for believing that it was resolved incorrectly after being so raised.

State courts have tended to make state postconviction proceedings unavailable to defendants seeking to raise exclusionary sanction issues, particularly for the first time. But they have neither carefully engaged in *Powell*-like analyses of state exclusionary requirements nor explored whether the rationales or purposes of those requirements would be sufficiently furthered by defining them as including a right to raise the issues in state postconviction proceedings.

Title 7

RELEVANCY AND ITS COUNTERWEIGHTS

Chapter 16

RELEVANCE

Table of Sections

§ 184. Relevance as the Presupposition of Admissibility

The law of evidence presupposes that in judging the claims of litigants, it is important to discern the true state of affairs underlying the dispute. In pursuing this objective, it proceeds on the premise that the way to find the truth is to permit the parties to present to the court or jury all the evidence that bears on the issue to be decided. Of course, there are many rules that keep probative evidence from the finder of fact. The self-incrimination privilege is one. But unless there is some distinct ground for refusing to hear such evidence, it should be received. Conversely, if the evidence lacks probative value, it should be excluded.

Federal Rule of Evid. 402 and the corresponding Uniform Rule adopt these two "axioms" of the common law. The Federal Rule provides that

All relevant evidence is admissible, except as otherwise provided by the Constitution of the United States, by Act of Congress, by these rules, or by other rules prescribed by the Supreme Court pursuant to statutory authori-

ty. Evidence which is not relevant is not admissible.

§ 185. The Meaning of Relevancy and the Counterweights

To say that relevant evidence is generally admissible, while irrelevant evidence is not would be of little value without a suitable definition of relevance. This section clarifies the meaning of relevance. It then outlines the factors that can make even relevant evidence inadmissible.

There are two components to relevant evidence: materiality and probative value. Materiality looks to the relation between the propositions for which the evidence is offered and the issues in the case. If the evidence is offered to help prove a proposition which is not a matter in issue, the evidence is immaterial. What is "in issue," that is, within the range of the litigated controversy, is determined mainly by the pleadings, read in the light of the rules of pleading and controlled by the substantive law. Thus, in a suit for worker's compensation, evidence of contributory negligence would be immaterial, wheth-

338

er pleaded or not, since a worker's negligence does not affect the right to compensation. But matters in the range of dispute may extend somewhat beyond the issues defined in the pleadings. Under flexible systems of procedure, issues not raised by the pleadings may be tried by express or implied consent of the parties. In addition, the parties may draw in dispute the credibility of the witnesses and, within limits, produce evidence assailing and supporting their credibility. Moreover, considerable leeway is allowed even on direct examination for proof of facts that do not bear directly on the purely legal issues, but merely fill in the background of the narrative and give it interest, color, and lifelikeness. Maps, diagrams and charts, for example, are material as aids to the understanding of other material evidence.

The second aspect of relevance is probative value, the tendency of evidence to establish the proposition that it is offered to prove. Federal Rule and the Revised Uniform Evid. Rule 401, for instance, incorporate these twin concepts of materiality and probative value. They read:

"Relevant evidence" means evidence having any tendency to make the existence of any fact that is of consequence to the determination of the action more probable or less probable than it would be without the evidence.

A fact that is "of consequence" is material, and evidence that affects the probability that a fact is as a party claims it to be has probative force. To have this effect, the evidence must be more (or less) probable when the disputed fact is true rather than false. Such evidence often is said to have "logical relevance," while evidence lacking in probative value may be condemned as "remote" or "speculative."

Under our system, molded by the tradition of jury trial and predominantly oral proof, a party offers his evidence not *en masse,* but item by item. An item of evidence, being but a single link in the chain of proof, need not prove conclusively the proposition for which it is offered. It need not even make that proposition appear more probable than not. Whether the entire body of one party's evi-

dence is sufficient to go to the jury is one question. Whether a particular item of evidence is relevant is quite another. It is enough if the item could reasonably show that a fact is slightly more probable than it would appear without that evidence. Even after the probative force of the evidence is spent, the proposition for which it is offered still can seem quite improbable. Thus, the objection that the inference for which the fact is offered "does not necessarily follow" is untenable. It poses a standard of conclusiveness that very few single items of circumstantial evidence ever could meet. A brick is not a wall.

But if even very weak material items of evidence are relevant, what sort of evidence is irrelevant for want of probative value? The long-standing distinction between "direct" and "circumstantial" evidence helps answer this question. Direct evidence is evidence which, if believed, resolves a matter in issue. Circumstantial evidence may also be testimonial, but even if the circumstances depicted are accepted as true, additional reasoning is required to reach the proposition to which it is directed. For example, a witness' testimony that he saw A stab B with a knife is direct evidence of whether A did indeed stab B. In contrast, testimony that A fled the scene of the stabbing would be circumstantial evidence of the stabbing (but direct evidence of the flight itself). Similarly, testimony of a witness that he saw A at the scene would be direct evidence of the facts asserted, but testimony that he saw someone who was disguised and masked, but had a voice and limp like A's, would be circumstantial evidence that the person seen was A.

In terms of this dichotomy, direct evidence from a qualified witness offered to help establish a provable fact can never be irrelevant. Circumstantial evidence, however, can be offered to help prove a material fact, yet be so unrevealing as to be irrelevant to that fact. For instance, evidence that the government awarded a firm a lucrative contract is irrelevant on the issue of whether the firm damaged property leased to it because there is no reason to suppose that firms that handle large government contracts are more likely to damage such property than other lessees. In short, to say that evidence is irrelevant in the sense that it lacks probative value is to say that knowing the circumstantial evidence does not justify any reasonable inference as to the fact in question. Cases involving such evidence are few and far between.

Yet, how can a judge know whether the evidence could reasonably affect an assessment of the probability of the fact to be inferred? In some instances, scientific research may show that the fact in issue is more likely to be true (or false) when such evidence is present than when it is not. Ordinarily, however, the answer must lie in the judge's own experience, general knowledge, and understanding of human conduct and motivation. If one asks whether an attempted escape by a prisoner charged with two serious but factually unconnected crimes is relevant to show consciousness of guilt of the first crime charged, the answer will not be found in a statistical table of the attempts at escape by those conscious of guilt as opposed to those not conscious of their guilt. The judge can only ask, could a reasonable juror believe that the fact that the accused tried to escape makes it more probable than it would otherwise be that the accused was conscious of guilt of the crime being tried? If the answer is yes, then the evidence is relevant. In other situations, the judge may need to consider explicitly not only whether the evidence reasonably could support the proposition for which it is offered, but also whether its absence might warrant negative inferences.

In sum, relevant evidence is evidence that in some degree advances the inquiry. It is material and probative. As such, it is admissible, at least prima facie. But this relevance does not ensure admissibility. There remains the question of whether its value is worth what it costs. A great deal of evidence is excluded on the ground that the costs outweigh the benefits. Rule 403 of the Federal and Revised Uniform Evidence Rules categorize most of these costs. It codifies the common law power of the judge to exclude relevant evidence "if its probative value is sub-

stantially outweighed by the danger of unfair prejudice, confusion of the issues, or misleading the jury, or by considerations of undue delay, waste of time, or needless presentation of cumulative evidence." Such factors often blend together in practice, but we shall elaborate on them briefly in the rough order of their importance. First, there is the danger of prejudice. In this context, prejudice does not simply mean damage to the opponent's cause. Neither does it necessarily mean an appeal to emotion. Prejudice can arise, however, from facts that arouse the jury's hostility or sympathy for one side without regard to the probative value of the evidence. Thus, evidence of convictions for prior, unrelated crimes may lead a juror to think that since the defendant already has a criminal record, an erroneous conviction would not be quite as serious as would otherwise be the case. A juror influenced in this fashion may be satisfied with a slightly less compelling demonstration of guilt than the law requires. Second, whether or not "emotional" reactions are at work, relevant evidence can confuse, or worse, mislead the trier of fact who is not properly equipped to judge the probative worth of the evidence. Third, certain proof and the answering evidence that it provokes might unduly distract the jury from the main issues. Finally, the evidence offered and the counterproof may consume an inordinate amount of time.

Analyzing and weighing the pertinent costs and benefits is no trivial task. Wise judges may come to differing conclusions in similar situations. Even the same item of evidence may fare differently from one case to the next, depending on its relationship to the other evidence in the cases, the importance of the issues on which it bears, and the likely efficacy of cautionary instructions to the jury. Accordingly, much leeway is given trial judges who must fairly weigh probative value against probable dangers. Nevertheless, discretion can be abused, and some appellate courts have urged trial courts to articulate the reasoning behind their relevance rulings. In certain areas, such as proof of character, comparable situations recur so often that relatively particularized rules channel the exercise of discretion. In others, less structured discretion remains prominent. One way or another, however, admissible evidence must satisfy the cost-benefit calculus we have outlined.

Some courts and textwriters have described this process of weighing marginal costs and benefits as a matter of "legal relevancy," in that "legally relevant" evidence must have a "plus value" beyond a bare minimum of probative value. This notion of "plus value" is at best an imprecise way to say that the probative value and the need for the evidence must outweigh the harm likely to result from admission, and most modern opinions do not rely on such potentially misleading terminology.

Chapter 17

CHARACTER AND HABIT

Table of Sections

§ 186. Character: In General

Evidence of the general character of a party or witness almost always has some probative value, but in many situations, the probative value is slight and the potential for prejudice large. In other circumstances, the balance shifts the other way. Instead of engaging exclusively in the case-by-case balancing outlined in Chapter 16, however, the courts tend to pass on the admissibility of evidence of character and habit according to a number of rules with myriad exceptions that reflect the recurring patterns of such proof and its usefulness.

Before turning to the details of the rules, it may be helpful to sketch two general considerations that are central to shaping and applying these rules. The first factor is the purpose for which the evidence of character is offered. If a person's character is itself an issue in the case, then character evidence is crucial. But if the evidence of character merely is introduced as circumstantial evidence of what a person did or thought, it is less critical. Other, and probably better, evidence of the acts or state of mind usually should be available. Exclusion is therefore much more likely when the character evidence is offered to help prove that a person acted in one way or another. Thus, Federal and Revised Uniform Evidence Rule (1974) 404(a), which basically codify common law doctrine, provide that subject to enumerated exceptions,

Evidence of a person's character or a trait of his character is not admissible for the purpose

342

of proving that he acted in conformity therewith on a particular occasion * * *.

The second consideration is the type of evidence offered to establish the character of an individual. Character is susceptible of proof by evidence of conduct that reflects some character trait, by a witness's testimony as to the witness's opinion based on personal observations, or by testimony as to reputation generally. As one moves from the specific to the general in this fashion, the pungency and persuasiveness of the evidence declines, but so does its tendency to arouse undue prejudice, to confuse and distract, and to raise time-consuming side issues. Traditionally, where character evidence could come in at all, the relatively neutral and unexciting reputation evidence was the preferred type. Thus, prior to the adoption of the Federal Rules, as a general matter, where character was being used as circumstantial evidence of conduct, it could be proved only by reputation evidence. Where character was in issue, it could be proved by specific instances or by reputation.

Federal and Revised Uniform Rule of Evidence (1986) 405(a), however, allows opinion testimony as well as reputation testimony to prove character whenever any form of character evidence is appropriate. And, as at common law, when character is "in issue," as discussed in the next section, it also may be proved by testimony about specific acts.

§ 187. Character in Issue

A person's character may be a material fact that under the substantive law determines rights and liabilities of the parties. For example, in an action of defamation for a publication to the effect that plaintiff's character is bad, the publisher may raise the defense that the statement was true. A complaint for negligence may allege that the defendant allowed an unfit person to use a motor vehicle or other dangerous object, or that an employer was negligent in hiring or failing to supervise an employee with certain dangerous character traits. Likewise, in deciding who should have custody of children, fitness to provide care is of paramount importance.

When character has been put in issue by the pleadings in these and other such cases, evidence of character must be brought forth.

In view of the crucial role of character in these situations, the courts usually hold that it may be proved by evidence of specific acts. The Federal and Revised Uniform Rules follow this approach. The hazards of prejudice, surprise and time-consumption implicit in this manner of proof are more tolerable when character is itself in issue than when this evidence is offered as a mere indication that the defendant committed the acts that are the subject of the suit.

Yet, some courts do not simply permit evidence of specific acts to prove character when it is in issue. They insist on it to the point of excluding opinion and reputation evidence. There seems little point to excluding reputation evidence, which ordinarily is the preferred mode of proof of character. Proof by means of opinion testimony is slightly more debatable, but most of the arguments against opinion evidence do not apply when character is in issue. For example, the possibility that specific acts may be inquired into on cross-examination (which may prompt barring specific act evidence when character is not in issue) is hardly of concern, since the door to such evidence already is open. Because an opinion held by someone familiar with an individual and his conduct may rest on facts too detailed to be worth reciting yet still may be useful in evaluating character, many courts allow such opinion evidence when the character involved is for the so-called nonmoral traits of care, competence, skill or sanity. On the other hand, as to the traits of moral character like peaceableness and honesty, courts that follow the tradition barring opinion evidence of the character of an accused as circumstantial evidence of conduct on a particular occasion presumably would frown on opinion evidence even when character is in issue. In contrast, the Federal and the Uniform Rules, as we have noted, allow opinion evidence as well as reputation and specific act evidence to prove character whenever it is in issue.

§ 188. Character as Circumstantial Evidence: General Rule of Exclusion

Even when a person's character is not itself in issue in the sense we have described, litigants may seek to introduce character-type evidence. In ascertaining whether such evidence is admissible, attention to the purpose for which the evidence is offered remains of the utmost importance. In some cases, even though a person's character is not itself in issue, evidence probative of that character may be relevant to proving a material fact that is distinct from whether the person acted in conformity with her character. Thus, where extortion is charged, the defendant's reputation for violence may be relevant to the victim's state of mind. In these cases the reputation itself, not the character that it tends to prove, is the significant fact; reputation is not used as evidence of how the person with the character traits behaved on a given occasion.

In contrast, evidence that an individual is the kind of person who tends to behave in certain ways almost always has some value as circumstantial evidence as to how the individual acted (and perhaps with what state of mind) in the matter in question. By and large, persons reputed to be violent commit more assaults than persons known to be peaceable. Yet, evidence of character in any form—reputation, opinion from observation, or specific acts—generally will not be received to prove that a person engaged in certain conduct or did so with a particular intent on a specific occasion, so-called circumstantial use of character. The reason is the familiar one of prejudice outweighing probative value. Character evidence used for this purpose, while typically being of relatively slight value, usually is laden with the dangerous baggage of prejudice, distraction, time consumption and surprise.

At the same time, there are important exceptions to this general rule of exclusion. The next six sections consider various applications of the rule and the exceptions.

§ 189. Character for Care in Civil Cases

The rule against using character evidence solely to prove conduct on a particular occasion has long been applied in civil cases. The rule is invoked most uniformly when specific act evidence is proffered. Negligence cases illustrate the point. Evidence of negligent conduct of the defendant or his agent on other occasions may reflect a propensity for negligent acts, thus enhancing the probability of negligence on the occasion in question, but this probative force has been thought too slight to overcome the usual counterweights. The same applies to evidence of other negligent acts of the plaintiff, as well other instances of careful conduct.

Most courts also reject proof of an actor's character for care by means of reputation evidence or opinion testimony. In the past, a minority of courts had admitted these types of evidence, often under the guise of evidence of "habit," when there were no eyewitnesses to the event. A few even did so if there were eyewitnesses with conflicting stories. The Federal and revised Uniform Rules do not make such fine distinctions. The prevailing pattern now is to exclude all forms of character evidence in civil cases when the evidence is employed merely to support an inference that conduct on a particular occasion was consistent with a person's character.

This trend is apparent despite psychological studies of "accident proneness." It has been argued that scientific research establishing that drivers with inadequate training, defective vision, and certain attitudes and emotional traits are at risk for automobile accidents should prompt a relaxation of the rule against evidence of character for negligence. The argument seems to be that because a small number of drivers with identifiable characteristics account for the bulk of the accidents, they must drive improperly as a routine matter, and this provides a better than usual basis for inferring that the accident in issue resulted from such negligent driving. Presumably, the reform would be to admit evidence of previous accidents combined with proof that the particular driver fits the "accident proneness" profile.

A somewhat different proposal that also has yet to be implemented asks that aggregate and individual data concerning the actions of physicians should be admissible in malpractice cases. For example, in deciding whether the removal of a patient's appendix was unnecessary surgery, the jury might be invited to consider whether the defendant physician performs appendectomies far more frequently than other surgeons. Although evidence of previous accidents or similar happenings should not be freely admitted, a suitable expert testifying about a departure from the customary standard of care should be permitted to rely on such information and to explain his analysis to the jury. Moreover, where the statistically measured departure from the customary pattern is itself so great as to make it plain for all to see that the defendant is behaving differently from the norm, this statistic should be provable.

§ 190. Bad Character as Evidence of Criminal Conduct: Other Crimes

If anything, the rule against using character evidence to prove conduct on a particular occasion applies even more strongly in criminal cases. Unless and until the accused gives evidence of his good character, the prosecution may not introduce evidence of (or otherwise seek to establish) his bad character. The evidence of bad character would not be irrelevant, but in the setting of the jury trial particularly the dangers of prejudice, confusion and time-consumption outweigh the probative value.

This broad prohibition includes the specific and frequently invoked rule that the prosecution may not introduce evidence of other criminal acts of the accused unless the evidence is introduced for some purpose other than to suggest that because the defendant is a person of criminal character, it is more probable that he committed the crime for which he is on trial. As Federal and revised Uniform Rule (1986) 404(b) put it:

> Evidence of other crimes, wrongs, or acts is not admissible to prove the character of a person in order to show that he acted in conformity therewith. It may, however, be admissible for other purposes, such as proof of motive, opportunity, intent, preparation, plan, knowledge, identity or absence of mistake or accident.

As the rule indicates, there are numerous other uses to which evidence of criminal acts may be put, and those enumerated are neither mutually exclusive nor collectively exhaustive. Subject to such caveats, examination is in order of the principal purposes for which the prosecution may introduce evidence of a defendant's bad character. Following this listing, some general observations will be offered about the use of other crimes evidence for these purposes. The permissible purposes include:

(1) To complete the story of the crime on trial by placing it in the context of nearby and nearly contemporaneous happenings. In State v. Brown,[1] for instance, evidence that a man accused of robbery lived with and took the earnings of a young prostitute was held admissible where the prostitute confessed that she suggested that the defendant rob her client. The phrases "same transaction" or, less happily, "res gestae" often are used to denote evidence introduced to complete the story. This rationale should be applied only when reference to the other crimes is essential to a coherent and intelligible description of the offense at bar.

(2) To prove the existence of a larger plan, scheme, or conspiracy, of which the crime on trial is a part. Each crime should be an integral part of an over-arching plan explicitly conceived and executed by the defendant or his confederates. This will be relevant as showing motive, and hence the doing of the criminal act, the identity of the actor, or his intention.

(3) To prove other crimes by the accused so nearly identical in method as to earmark

§ 190

1. 199 Conn. 47, 505 A.2d 1225, 1229–1230 (1986).

them as the handiwork of the accused. Much more is demanded than the mere repeated commission of crimes of the same class, such as repeated murders, robberies or rapes. The pattern and characteristics of the crimes must be so unusual and distinctive as to be like a signature.

(4) In some jurisdictions, to show a passion or propensity for unusual and abnormal sexual relations. Initially, proof of other sex crimes always was confined to offenses involving the same parties, but a number of jurisdictions now admit other sex offenses with other persons, at least as to offenses involving sexual aberrations.

(5) To show, by similar acts or incidents, that the act in question was not performed inadvertently, accidentally, involuntarily, or without guilty knowledge. A classic illustration is the "brides of the bath" case, Rex v. Smith.[2] Accused of drowning the woman he had bigamously "married," Smith claimed that she had drowned in the bathtub while he was away. The prosecution was allowed to show that Smith bigamously "married" several wives who also left him their property before he purportedly discovered them drowned in the bath. Under this rationale, the similarities between the act charged and the extrinsic acts need not be as extensive and striking as is required under purpose (3), and the various acts need not be manifestations of a unifying plan, as required for purpose (2).

(6) To establish motive. The evidence of motive may be probative of the identity of the criminal or of malice or specific intent. An application of this principle permits proof of criminal acts of the accused that constitute admissions by conduct designed to obstruct justice or avoid punishment for a crime, or of the crimes that motivated the interference with the enforcement of the law, as when a person is charged with trying to assassinate a witness to a previous crime.

(7) To establish opportunity, in the sense of access to or presence at the scene of the crime or in the sense of possessing distinctive or unusual skills or abilities employed in the commission of the crime charged.

(8) To show, without considering motive, that defendant acted with malice, deliberation, or the requisite specific intent. A typical example is a history of selling narcotics to prove a charge of possession with intent to sell. The use of such "mental propensity" evidence, however, has been questioned.

(9) To prove identity. Although this is indisputably one of the ultimate purposes for which evidence of other criminal conduct will be received, the need to prove identity should not be, in itself, a ticket to admission. Almost always, identity is the inference that flows from one or more of the theories just listed. The second (larger plan), third (distinctive device), and sixth (motive) seem to be most often relied upon to show identity. In addition, the courts tend to apply stricter standards when the desired inference pertains to identity as opposed to state of mind.

(10) To impeach an accused who takes the witness stand by introducing past convictions.

A number of procedural and other substantive considerations also affect the admissibility of other crimes evidence pursuant to these ten exceptions. To begin with, the fact that the defendant is guilty of another relevant crime need not be proved beyond a reasonable doubt. The measure of proof that the defendant is guilty of the other crime has been variously described, ranging from "sufficient * * * to support a finding by the jury," to "a preponderance," to "substantial," to "clear and convincing." If the applicable standard is satisfied, then the other crimes evidence should be potentially admissible even if the defendant was acquitted of the other charge.

Second, the connection between the evidence and the permissible purpose should be clear, and the issue on which the other crimes evidence is said to bear should be the subject of a genuine controversy. For example, if the prosecution maintains that the other crime reveals defendant's guilty state of mind, then his intent must be disputed. Thus, if the

---

2. 11 Cr.App.R. 229, 84 L.J.K.B. 2153 (1915).

defendant does not deny that the acts were deliberate, then the prosecution may not introduce the evidence merely to show that the acts were not accidental. Likewise, if the accused does not deny performing the acts charged, the exceptions pertaining to identification are unavailing.

Finally, even if one or more of the valid purposes for admitting other crimes evidence is appropriately invoked, there is still the need to balance its probative value against the usual counterweights. When the sole purpose of the other crimes evidence is to show some propensity to commit the crime at trial, there is no room for ad hoc balancing. The evidence is then unequivocally inadmissible—this is the meaning of the rule against other crimes evidence. But the fact that there is an accepted logical basis for the evidence other than the forbidden one of showing a proclivity for criminality may not preclude the jury from relying on a defendant's apparent propensity toward criminal behavior. Accordingly, most recent authority recognizes that the problem is not merely one of pigeonholing, but of classifying and then balancing. In deciding whether the danger of unfair prejudice and the like substantially outweighs the incremental probative value, a variety of matters must be considered, including the strength of the evidence as to the commission of the other crime, the similarities between the crimes, the interval of time that has elapsed between the crimes, the need for the evidence, the efficacy of alternative proof, and the degree to which the evidence probably will rouse the jury to overmastering hostility.

§ 191. Good Character as Evidence of Lawful Conduct: Proof by the Accused and Rebuttal by the Government

The prosecution, as we saw in the preceding section, generally is forbidden to initiate evidence of the bad character of the defendant merely to imply that, being a bad person, he is more likely to commit a crime. This rule, in turn, is a corollary of the more general proscription on the use of character as cir-

cumstantial evidence of conduct. Yet, when the table is turned and the defendant in a criminal case seeks to offer evidence of his good character to imply that he is unlikely to have committed a crime, the general rule against propensity evidence is not applied. In both situations, the character evidence is relevant circumstantial evidence, but when the accused chooses to rely on it to exonerate himself, the problem of prejudice is altogether different. Now, knowledge of the accused's character may prejudice the jury in his *favor*, but the magnitude of the prejudice or its social cost is thought to be less. Thus, the common law and the Federal and Revised Uniform Evid.Rules (1974) permit the defendant, but not the government, to open the door to character evidence.

Not all aspects of the accused's character are open to scrutiny under this exception. The prevailing view is that only pertinent traits—those involved in the offense charged—are provable. One charged with theft might offer evidence of honesty, while someone accused of murder might show that he is peaceable, but not vice versa. A few general traits, like being law-abiding, seem sufficiently relevant to almost any accusation.

The common law has vacillated as regards the methods of establishing the good character of the accused. A rule of relatively recent origin limits proof to evidence of reputation for the pertinent traits. This constraint supposedly prevents a witness from giving a personal opinion no matter how well grounded. It also prohibits testimony concerning specific acts or their absence.

The Federal and Revised Uniform Evidence Rules reinstate the earlier common law approach. Rule 405(a) provides, in part, that:

> In all cases in which evidence of character or a trait of character of a person is admissible, proof may be made by testimony as to reputation or by testimony in the form of an opinion.

This liberalization was not achieved without debate. It allows expert opinion testimony about an accused's character traits, subject to the court's residual power to screen for prejudice, distraction, and time-consumption. Like the common law rules, it does not allow evidence of particular incidents.

Where reputation evidence is employed, it may be confined to reputation at approximately the time of the alleged offense. Furthermore, traditionally, only testimony as to the defendant's reputation in the community where the accused resided was allowed, but increasing urbanization has prompted the acceptance of evidence as to reputation within other substantial groups of which the accused is a constantly interacting member, such as the locale where defendant works.

When defendant does produce evidence of his good character as regards traits pertinent to the offense charged, whether by way of reputation or opinion testimony, he frequently is said to have placed his character "in issue." The phrase is misleading. That a defendant relies on character witnesses to indicate that he is not predisposed to commit the type of crime in question does not transform his character into an operative fact upon which guilt or innocence may turn. Defendant simply opens the door to proof of certain character traits as circumstantial evidence of whether he committed the act charged with the requisite state of mind.

Ordinarily, if the defendant chooses to inject his character into the trial in this sense, he does so by producing witnesses who testify to his good character. By relating a personal history supportive of good character, however, the defendant may achieve the same result. Whatever the method, once the defendant gives evidence of pertinent character traits to show that he is not guilty, his claim of possession of these traits—but only these traits—is open to rebuttal by cross-examination or direct testimony of prosecution witnesses. The prosecution may cross-examine a witness who has testified to the accused's reputation in order to probe the witness' knowledge of the community opinion, not only generally, but specifically as to whether the witness "has heard" that the defendant has committed particular prior criminal acts that conflict with the reputation vouched for on direct examination. Likewise, if a witness gives his opinion of defendant's character, then the prosecution

§ 191

can allude to pertinent bad acts by asking whether the witness knew of these matters in forming his opinion. Indeed, eschewing the dubious distinction between questions of the form "Have you heard" as opposed to "Do you know," the remainder of Federal and Revised Uniform Rule 405(a) simply provides that

> On cross-examination, inquiry is allowed into relevant specific instances of conduct.

This power of the cross-examiner to reopen old wounds is replete with possibilities for prejudice. Accordingly, certain limitations should be observed. The general responsibility of trial courts to weigh probative value against prejudice does not vanish because reference to other crimes or wrongs takes the form of insinuation or innuendo rather than concrete evidence. The extent and nature of the cross-examination demands restraint and supervision. As a precondition to cross-examination about other wrongs, the prosecutor should reveal, outside the hearing of the jury, what basis exists for believing in the rumors or incidents. The court should then determine whether there is a substantial basis for the cross-examination.

In this regard, the use of arrest records for cross-examination has troubled many courts. The federal practice, upheld over a vigorous dissent in Michelson v. United States,[1] allows it. Some jurisdictions have declined to follow *Michelson*.

The other prosecutorial counterthrust to the defendant's proof of good character is not so easily abused. The government may produce witnesses to swear to defendant's bad reputation or, currently in most jurisdictions, their unfavorable opinion of defendant's character. As with defense character witnesses, the strictures concerning pertinent traits and remoteness apply. The courts had divided over the admissibility as rebuttal evidence of judgments of convictions for recent crimes displaying the same traits, but with the adoption of the federal rules, few jurisdictions now allow any proof of specific instances of misconduct as rebuttal evidence.

1. 335 U.S. 469 (1948).

§ 192. Character in Civil Cases Where Crime Is in Issue

As explained above in § 191, in criminal cases the law relaxes its ban on evidence of character to show conduct to the extent of permitting a defendant to produce evidence of her good character. It is not unusual in civil litigation, however, for one party to accuse another of conduct that amounts to a criminal offense. For instance, much of the conduct that is the subject of civil antitrust, securities, and civil rights cases as well as a substantial proportion of more traditional civil actions, could also provide grist for the public prosecutor's mill.

Where the homologous crimes are largely regulatory or administrative, it may seem inappropriate to accord the civil party the same dispensation given criminal defendants whose lives or liberties are in jeopardy. But what of the party whose adversary's pleading or proof alleges what would be an offense involving moral turpitude, as in an action for conversion, a complaint arising from an alleged incident of police brutality, or a suit for a breach of a fire insurance policy in which the insurer refuses to pay because it believes that the insured set the fire? Some courts have thought that the damage that may be done to the party's standing, reputation and relationships warrants according the civil defendant the same special dispensation. These courts therefore permitted the party to introduce evidence of her good reputation for the traits involved.

But this never has been the majority view. Since the consequences of civil judgments are less severe than those flowing from a criminal conviction, most courts have declined to pay the price that the concession would demand in terms of possible prejudice, consumption of time, and distraction from the issue. Although the balance may be arguable, the Federal and Revised Uniform Rules of Evidence (1986) adhere to the majority position. Rule 404 bars evidence of character in civil cases to show how a person probably acted on a particular occasion.

§ 193. Character of Victim in Cases of Assault, Murder, and Rape

A well established exception to the rule forbidding character evidence to prove conduct applies to homicide and assault cases in which there is a dispute as to who was the first aggressor. This exception permits the accused in such cases to introduce appropriate evidence of the victim's character for turbulence and violence. In response, the prosecution may adduce evidence that the victim was a characteristically peaceful person.

Federal and Revised Uniform Evidence Rule (1974) 404(a)(2) addresses such situations. It speaks to "pertinent" character traits of the victims of crimes generally and specifically to the trait of nonviolence in homicide cases. It exempts from the usual rule of exclusion

Evidence of a pertinent trait of character of the victim of the crime offered by the accused, or by the prosecution to rebut the same, or evidence of the character trait of peacefulness of the victim offered by the prosecution in a homicide case to rebut evidence that the defendant was the first aggressor.

The fact that the character of the victim is being proved renders inapposite the usual concern over the untoward impact of evidence of the defendant's poor character on the jury's assessment of the case against him. There is, however, a risk of a different form of prejudice. Learning of the victim's bad character could lead the jury to think that the victim merely "got what he deserved" and to acquit for that reason. Nevertheless, at least in murder and perhaps in battery cases as well, when the identity of the first aggressor is really in doubt, the probative value of the evidence ordinarily justifies taking this risk.

In some jurisdictions the fact that the defendant claims that he killed the victim to defend himself from attack may not trigger, in itself, the prosecution's power to introduce rebuttal evidence of the victim's non-violent nature. By one view, such counterproof is allowed only when the accused opens the door specifically by evidence of the victim's bad character for belligerence. The federal rule quoted above clearly follows the contrary view in homicide cases. Since a dead victim cannot attest to his peaceable behavior during the fatal encounter, the last clause of Rule 404(a)(2) provides that whenever the accused claims self-defense and offers *any* type of evidence that the deceased was the first aggressor, the government may reply with evidence of the peaceable character of the deceased.

A similar exception to the general rule against the use of character to prove conduct has pertained to the defense of consent in sexual assault cases. In the past, the courts generally admitted evidence of the victim's character for chastity, although there were diverging lines of authority on whether the proof could be by specific instances and on whether the prosecution could put evidence of chastity in its case in chief.

In the 1970s, however, nearly all jurisdictions enacted "rape shield" laws. The reforms range from barring all evidence of the victim's character for chastity to merely requiring a preliminary hearing to screen out inadmissible evidence on the issue. Federal Rule of Evidence 412 lies between these extremes. Reversing the traditional preference for proof of character by reputation, it bars reputation and opinion evidence of the victim's past sexual conduct, but permits evidence of specific incidents if certain substantive and procedural conditions are met. If the evidence pertains to past sexual behavior of the victim with an accused who claims consent, it may be admitted to prove or disprove consent. If the evidence involves acts of the victim with other individuals, the defendant may be permitted to use it to prove that someone else was the "the source of semen or injury." Finally, in exceptional cases the defendant may have a right under the due process or confrontation clauses, to introduce certain evidence of the victim's prior sexual conduct.

This resort to an undefined, residual provision to avoid an otherwise unconstitutionally

sweeping ban on proof of the victim's character seems inferior to an articulation of the full range of allowable uses of sexual history evidence. It places trial courts in the awkward position of having to make constitutional rulings rather than to apply a self-contained and structured rule of evidence.

Under many state laws, evidence of the victim's sexual experience generally is admissible, upon notice, for specified purposes: to demonstrate that the victim, having had previous voluntary sexual relations with defendant, consented to the alleged attack; that the victim has a motive falsely to accuse defendant; that the witness characteristically fantasizes sexual assaults; that the witness knowingly brings false accusations of sexual misconduct; that a young child who gave a detailed account of a sexual assault already possessed the knowledge to do so; or that someone else may have been the source of semen or trauma to the witness.

These laws have withstood constitutional attacks. They reflect the judgment, evident also in the case law emerging during the period preceding their enactment, that most evidence about chastity has far too little probative value on the issue of consent to justify extensive inquiry into the victim's sexual history.

§ 194. Evidence of Character to Impeach a Witness

The familiar practice of impeaching a witness by producing evidence of her bad character for veracity amounts to using a character trait to prove that a witness is testifying falsely. As such, it constitutes a true exception to the policy against using evidence of character solely to show conduct. The chapter on impeachment discusses the scope of this exception.[1]

§ 195. Habit and Custom as Evidence of Conduct on a Particular Occasion

Although the courts frown on evidence of a person's traits of character when introduced

---

§ 194

1. See supra Ch. 5.

to prove how he acted on a given occasion, they are more receptive to evidence of his habits or of the customary behavior of organizations. To understand this difference, one must appreciate the distinction between habit and character. The two are easily confused. People sometimes speak of a habit for care, a habit for promptness, or a habit of forgetfulness. They may say that an individual has a bad habit of stealing or lying. Evidence of these "habits" would be identical to the kind of evidence that is the target of the general rule against character evidence. Character is a generalized description of a person's disposition, or of the disposition in respect to a general trait, such as honesty, temperance or peacefulness. Habit, in the present context, is more specific. It denotes one's regular response to a repeated situation. If we speak of a character for care, we think of the person's tendency to act prudently in all the varying situations of life—in business, at home, in handling automobiles and in walking across the street. A habit, on the other hand, is the person's regular practice of responding to a particular kind of situation with a specific type of conduct. Thus, a person may be in the habit of bounding down a certain stairway two or three steps at a time, of patronizing a particular pub after each day's work, or of driving his automobile without using a seatbelt. The doing of the habitual act may become semi-automatic, as with a driver who invariably signals before changing lanes.

Evidence of habits that come within this definition has greater probative value than does evidence of general traits of character. Furthermore, the potential for prejudice is substantially less. By and large, the detailed patterns of situation-specific behavior that constitute habits are unlikely to provoke such sympathy or antipathy as would distort the process of evaluating the evidence.

As a result, many jurisdictions accept the proposition that evidence of habit may be admissible to show an act. These courts only reject the evidence if the putative habit is not sufficiently regular or uniform, or the circumstances are not sufficiently similar to outweigh the dangers of prejudice, distraction and time-consumption. The Federal, Revised Uniform, and Model Rules all follow this pattern.

A few state courts, however, exclude evidence of habit altogether. Others admit it only if there are no eyewitnesses to testify about the events that are said to have triggered the habitual behavior.

Even the jurisdictions that are reluctant to accept evidence of personal habits are willing to allow evidence of the "custom" of a business organization, if reasonably regular and uniform. This may be because there is no confusion between character traits and business practices, as there is between character and habit, or it may reflect the belief that the need for regularity in business and the organizational sanctions which may exist when employees deviate from the established procedures give extra guarantees that the questioned activity followed the usual custom. Thus, evidence that a letter was written and signed in the course of business and put in the regular place for mailing usually will be admitted to prove that it was mailed.

The existence of the personal habit or the business custom may be established by a knowledgeable witness's testimony that there was such a habit or practice. Evidence of specific instances may also be used. Naturally, there must be enough instances to permit the finding of a habit, and the circumstances under which the habit or custom is followed must be present.

Chapter 18

SIMILAR HAPPENINGS AND TRANSACTIONS

Table of Sections

§ 196. Other Claims, Suits or Defenses of a Party

To what extent should a party be permitted to demonstrate that an opponent has advanced similar claims or defenses against others in previous litigation? Inescapably, two conflicting goals shape the rules of evidence in this area. Exposing fraudulent claims is important, but so is protecting innocent litigants from unfair prejudice. The easy cases are those in which one of these considerations clearly predominates. If the evidence reveals that a party has made previous, very similar claims and that these claims were fraudulent, then almost universally the evidence will be admissible despite the dangers of distraction and time-consumption with regard to the quality of these other claims, and despite the general prohibition on using evidence of bad character solely to show conduct on a given occasion. At the other pole, if the evidence is merely that the plaintiff is a chronic litigant

with respect to all sorts of claims, the courts consider the slight probative value overborne by the countervailing factors. This evidence they usually exclude.

In between lie the harder cases. Suppose the evidence is that the party suing for an alleged loss, such as fire damage to his property or personal injury in a collision, has made many previous claims of similar losses. The evidence surely is relevant. The probability of so many similar accidents happening to the same person by chance alone can be vanishingly small. Yet, rare events do happen. There will always be some people who suffer the slings and arrows of outrageous fortune. In itself, this fact gives no indication of prejudice. Presumably, a jury can come to a reasonable judgment as to the relative likelihood of the alternatives. Nevertheless, there is a form of prejudice inherent in this situation. The jury may disapprove of a person precisely because that person is litigious. It would seem that the judge, balancing probative value against prejudice, should admit the evidence only if the probability of coincidence seems negligible or if the proponent has distinct evidence of fraud.

So far, we have discussed evidence of a party's other claims introduced to raise a question about the instant claim or suit. Evidence of a witness' past accusations or defenses introduced to attack the veracity of that witness presents comparable problems. In these situations, a litigant might seek to prove that the other accusations have been false as circumstantial evidence that the testimony just delivered is also false. Although this is a species of character evidence to show conduct, it usually will be admissible. More problematically, the very fact that the witness repeatedly accuses many others of the same kind of behavior may seem too extraordinary to be explained as a mere coincidence. The logic and issues here are perfectly analogous to those already addressed with regard to the filing of repeated, similar suits or claims. However, in keeping with the customary relaxation of the standard of admissibility on cross-examination, it is generally easier to elicit admissions about the other claims on cross-examination than it is to introduce the evidence by the testimony of the proponent's witnesses.

§ 197. Other Misrepresentations and Frauds

In cases alleging fraud or misrepresentation, proof that the defendant perpetrated similar deceptions frequently is received in evidence. Such admission is not justified on the theory of "once a cheat, always a cheat." Rather, at least one of three well entrenched alternate theories that do not contravene the ban on using character traits solely as evidence of conduct typically is available. To begin with, evidence of other frauds may help establish the element of knowledge—by suggesting that defendant knew that his alleged misrepresentation was false or by indicating that defendant's participation in an alleged

fraudulent scheme was not innocent or accidental.

Second, the evidence may be admissible with respect to the closely related element of intent to deceive. When other misrepresentations are used to show intent or knowledge, they need not be identical nor made under precisely the same circumstances as the one in issue.

Finally, if the uttering of the misrepresentations or the performance of the fraudulent conduct is contested, then other misrepresentations or fraudulent acts that are evidently part of the same overall plan or scheme may be admissible to prove the conduct of the defendant. For example, in Mudsill Mining Company v. Watrous,[1] evidence that defendants had "salted" ore samples that other prospective buyers took from defendant's mine was admissible "to establish their complicity in the like fraud, now under consideration" since all the fraudulent acts were "in furtherance of the same general design."

The requirement of a common plan or scheme is well recognized, but it appears to be of questionable value in civil cases. When there is conflicting testimony as to the making of the misrepresentation at issue, the value of evidence of other, very similar misrepresentations—whether or not part of the same plan or scheme—in resolving the controversy should be sufficient to outweigh the danger of prejudice. As it is, the courts often manage to discern a larger plan when the various acts could well be described as separate transactions.

§ 198. Other Contracts and Business Transactions

Evidence concerning other contracts or business dealings may be relevant to prove the terms of a contract, the meaning of these terms, a business habit or custom, and occasionally, the authority of an agent. As to many of these uses, there is little controversy. Certainly, evidence of other transactions between the same parties readily is received

§ 197

1. 61 Fed. 163, 179 (6th Cir.1894).

when relevant to show the meaning they probably attached to the terms of a contract. Likewise, when the existence of the terms is in doubt, evidence of similar contracts between the same parties is accepted as a vehicle for showing of a custom or continuing course of dealing between them, and as such, as evidence of the terms of the present bargain. Also, when the authority of an agent is in question, other similar transactions that the agent has carried out on behalf of the principal are freely admitted.

In the past, many courts had balked when contracts *with others* were offered to show the terms or the making of the contract in suit. It is hard to understand why any hard and fast line should be drawn. As an historical matter, these decisions perhaps may be explained as manifestations of the perennial confusion between the concepts of sufficiency and relevancy, or as products of the beguiling power of the mystical phrase *res inter alios acta*. Yet, it seems clear that contracts of a party with third persons may show the party's customary practice and course of dealing and thus supply useful insights into the terms of the present agreement. Indeed, even if there are but one or two such contracts, they may be useful evidence. When, in a certain kind of transaction, a business has adopted a particular mode of handling a bargaining topic or standardized feature, such as warranty, discount or the like, it is often easier for it to cast a new contract in the same mold than it is to work out a new one. Moreover, some practices become so accepted in an industry that they may shape the meaning of most contracts in that field. As to these, evidence in the form of contracts or transactions involving neither of the parties may nevertheless be probative of the commercial relationship that exists between the parties.

Inasmuch as there is no general danger of unfair prejudice inherent in evidence of other business transactions, strict rules or limits on admissibility seem inappropriate. The courts should admit such evidence in all cases where the testimony as to the terms of the present bargain is conflicting and where the judge finds that the risk of wasted time and confusion of issues does not substantially outweigh the probative value of the evidence of the other transactions. Many jurisdictions therefore leave evidence of other contracts or business dealings to the trial judge to evaluate on a case by case basis.

§ 199. Other Sales of Similar Property as Evidence of Value

When the market value of property needs to be determined, the price actually paid in a competitive market for comparable items is an obvious place to look. The testimony of witnesses with first-hand knowledge of other sales, or reliable price lists, market reports, or the like may be received to show the market price.

The less homogeneous the product, the more difficulty there is in measuring market value in this way. Thus, cases involving land valuation, especially condemnation cases, frequently discuss the admissibility of evidence of other sales. A dying rule excludes the evidence entirely save in exceptional circumstances. The dominant view gives the judge discretion to admit evidence of other sales. The inquiry focuses on whether these sales have been sufficiently recent, and whether the other land is sufficiently nearby and alike as to character, situation, usability, and improvements, as to make it clear that the two tracts are comparable in value. A weaker standard for similarity applies when the other sales are used as the basis for an expert judgment as to value instead of being introduced as independent evidence of value.

Since the value sought is what, on average, a willing buyer would have paid a willing seller, prices on other sales of a forced character, such as execution sales or condemnation awards for other tracts, generally are inadmissible. Many courts also exclude the condemnor's evidence of prices it paid to other owners on the theory that sales made in contemplation of condemnation do not approximate the relevant market price. Other courts, following what seems the better reasoned view, allow such evidence in the judge's discretion.

Of course, any other sale must be genuine, and the price must be paid or substantially secured. Likewise, actual sale prices rather than asking prices typically are required.

§ 200. Other Accidents and Injuries

The admissibility of evidence of other accidents and injuries is raised frequently in negligence and product liability cases. In light of the prejudice that such evidence can carry with it, most judges will scrutinize it carefully. The proponent therefore should be prepared to convince the judge of the need for the proof.

The purpose for the evidence is important in determining whether the proof will be admitted and how strictly the requirement of similarity of conditions will be applied. In practice, the various permissible purposes for proof of other accidents tend to blend together in that more than one purpose typically is available, but for clarity of analysis we shall try to isolate each valid purpose.

To begin with, evidence of other accidents sometimes may be admissible to prove the existence of a particular physical condition, situation, or defect. For instance, the fact that several persons slipped and fell in the same location in a supermarket can help show that a slippery substance was on the floor. At the same time, this proof is a bit sensational. Unless the defendant strenuously disputes the presence of the condition, the court may reject the evidence of the similar accidents as unduly prejudicial and cumulative.

Second, the evidence of other accidents or injuries may be admissible to help show that the defect or dangerous situation caused the injury. Thus, instances in which other patients placed on the same drug therapy contracted the same previously rare disease is circumstantial evidence that the drug caused the disease in plaintiff's case. However, since many unsuspected factors could contribute or cause the observed effects, the conditions of the other injuries and the present one must be similar. Although the use of evidence of other accidents to prove the existence of a condition (the first purpose listed above) can overlap the use of the evidence to prove that the condition caused plaintiff's injuries, ordinarily, the need to use the evidence for this second purpose is plainer. Causation is frequently in genuine dispute, and circumstantial evidence may be of great value in pursuing this elusive issue. Thus, receptivity to evidence of similar happenings to show causation is heightened when the defendant contends that the alleged conduct could not possibly have caused the plaintiff's injury.

Third, and perhaps most commonly, evidence of other accidents or injuries may be used to show the risk that defendant's conduct created. If the extent of the danger is material to the case, as it almost always is in personal injury litigation, the fact that the same conditions produced harm on other occasions is a natural and convincing way of showing the hazard. The requirement of substantial similarity is applied strictly here.

Finally, the evidence of other accidents commonly is received to prove that the defendant knew, or should have known, of the danger. Of course, if defendant's duty is absolute, this theory is inapposite. In negligence cases, however, the duty is merely to use reasonable care to maintain safe conditions. Even in many strict product liability cases, demonstrating that the product is defective or unreasonably dangerous for its intended use requires an analysis of foreseeable risks.

When the evidence of other accidents is introduced to show notice of the danger, subsequent accidents are not admissible under this rationale. The proponent probably will want to show directly that the defendant had knowledge of the prior accidents, but the nature, frequency or notoriety of the incidents may well reveal that defendant knew of them or should have discovered the danger by due inspection. Since all that is required is that the previous injury or injuries be such as to call defendant's attention to the dangerous situation that resulted in the litigated accident, the similarity in the circumstances of the accidents can be considerably less than that which is demanded when the same evidence is used for one of the other valid purposes.

Having surveyed the utility of a history of accidents in establishing liability, we now consider the admissibility of a history of no accidents for exculpatory purposes. One might think that if proof of similar accidents is admissible in the judge's discretion to show that a particular condition or defect exists, or that the injury sued for was caused in a certain way, or that a situation is dangerous, or that defendant knew or should have known of the danger, then evidence of the absence of accidents during a period of similar exposure and experience likewise would be receivable to show that these facts do not exist in the case at bar. Indeed, it would seem perverse to tell a jury that one or two persons besides the plaintiff tripped on defendant's stairwell while withholding from them the further information that another thousand persons descended the same stairs without incident.

Yet, many decisions lay down just such a general rule against proof of absence of other accidents. In some cases, excluding such proof of safety may be justified on the ground that the persons passing in safety were not exposed to the same conditions as those that prevailed when the plaintiff's injury occurred. The evidence of a thousand safe descents down the stairs would be far less convincing if it were revealed that all of these were made

in daylight, while the two or three accidents occurred at night in poor lighting. However, the possibility that a very general safety record may obscure the influence of an important factor merely counsels for applying the traditional requirement of substantial similarity to evidence of the absence as well as the presence of other accidents. When the experience sought to be proved is so extensive as to be sure to include an adequate number of similar situations, the similarity requirement should be considered satisfied.

Neither can the broad proscription be justified by the other considerations that affect the admissibility of evidence. The problems of prejudice and distraction over "collateral issues" seem much more acute when it comes to proof of other accidents than when evidence of an accident-free history is proffered. Indeed, the defendant will seldom open this door if there is any practical likelihood that the plaintiff will dispute the safety record.

Consequently, few recent decisions can be found applying a general rule of exclusion. A large number of cases recognize that lack of other accidents may be admissible to show (1) absence of the defect or condition alleged, (2) the lack of a causal relationship between the injury and the defect or condition charged, (3) the nonexistence of an unduly dangerous situation, or (4) want of knowledge (or of grounds to realize) the danger.

Chapter 19

INSURANCE AGAINST LIABILITY

Table of Sections

§ 201. Insurance Against Liability

A formidable body of cases holds that evidence that a party is or is not insured against liability is not admissible on the issue of negligence. This doctrine rests on two premises. The first is the belief that whether one has insurance coverage reveals little about the likelihood that he will act carelessly. Subject to a few pathological exceptions, financial protection will not diminish the normal incentive to be careful, especially where life and limb are at stake. Similarly, the argument that insured individuals or firms are more prudent and careful, as a group, than those who are self-insurers seems tenuous, and also serves to counteract any force that the first argument may have. Thus, the relevance of the evidence of coverage is doubtful. In addition, there is concern that the evidence would be prejudicial—that the mention of insurance invites higher awards than are justified, and conversely, that the sympathy that a jury might feel for a defendant who must pay out of his own pocket could interfere with its evaluation of the evidence under the appropriate standard of proof.

Despite these concerns and the general rule that evidence of the fact of insurance coverage is inadmissible to show negligence or reasonable care, such evidence frequently is received. As with the exclusionary rules discussed in Chapters 17 (Character and Habit) and 18 (Similar Happenings and Transactions), the evidence may be admitted for some other purpose, providing of course that its probative value on this other issue is not substantially outweighed by its prejudicial impact. The purposes for which such evidence may be offered are several. Federal and Revised Uniform Rule (1974) 411 list most of them:

> Evidence that a person was or was not insured against liability is not admissible upon the issue whether the person acted negligently or otherwise wrongfully. This rule does not require the exclusion of evidence of insurance against liability when offered for another purpose, such as proof of agency, ownership or control, or bias or prejudice of a witness.

The hypothesis that persons rarely purchase liability insurance to cover contingencies for which they are not responsible makes the evidence relevant to questions of agency, ownership, and control. The fact of insurance can be relevant to the bias of a witness in a

357

number of ways. For example, the witness may be an investigator or other individual employed by the insurance company. Cross-examination affords the usual means of revealing the relationship between the company and the witness.

Plainly, these purposes do not exhaust the possibilities. Evidence of insurance may be admitted when it is an inseparable part of an admission of a party bearing on negligence or damages. And, there are some less common uses.

Furthermore, there are two other ways in which the fact of insurance can be brought home to the jury. Witnesses have been known to make unexpected and unresponsive references to insurance. In these situations, the judge may declare a mistrial, but it is a rare case in which he will do more than strike the reference and instruct the jury to ignore it. Finally, in the examination of prospective jurors, most jurisdictions allow questions about employment by or interest in insurance companies.

Despite its nearly universal acceptance, the wisdom of the general prohibition on injecting insurance into the trial, as it currently operates, is questionable. When the rule originated, insurance coverage of individuals was exceptional. In the absence of references to insurance at trial, a juror most probably would not have thought that a defendant was insured. Today, compulsory insurance laws for motorists are ubiquitous, and liability insurance for homeowners and businesses has become the norm. Most jurors probably assume that defendants are insured. Yet, few courts will allow a defendant to show that he is uninsured, unless the plaintiff has opened the door to such evidence. At a minimum, such a defendant, and indeed any party, should be entitled to an instruction that there has been no evidence as to whether or not any party is insured because the law is that the presence or absence of insurance should play no part in the case.

More fundamentally, the underlying soundness of the general rule forbidding disclosure of the fact of insurance has been the object of scathing criticism. Stripped to its essentials,

the debate is not really over the application of the doctrines of relevancy and its counterweights. Hardly anyone questions the premise that the evidence is irrelevant to the exercise of reasonable care. Neither does anyone contend that a party has a right to put irrelevant evidence into the record. Rather, the arguments for the abandonment of the policy of secrecy are either pragmatic or idealistic. The pragmatic argument is straightforward. The conspiracy of silence is hard to maintain. Its costs include extensive and unnecessary arguments, reversals, and retrials stemming from elusive questions of prejudice and good faith. This state of affairs might be tolerable if the revelations of insurance were truly fraught with prejudice. But, as we have suggested, most jurors probably presuppose the existence of liability insurance anyway, and the heart of the policy of nondisclosure is surrendered when jurors are examined about their connection with insurance companies. Consequently, the extent to which evidence of coverage or its absence is prejudicial is unclear. Even the direction in which such prejudice might work is obscure. In sum, the rule has become a hollow shell, expensive to maintain and of doubtful utility.

The other principal argument against the rule of secrecy is more difficult to evaluate, but standing alone, it is less persuasive. It arises from a certain conception of fairness—a conception that holds that the jury should know who the "real" parties in interest are. The insurance company, which under its policy has the exclusive right to employ counsel, defend the suit, and control the decision as to settling or contesting the action, is a party in all but name. Unfortunately, this argument begs the question. If the substantive law is that the depth of the defendant's pocket has nothing to do with liability or damages, then why should the jury be apprised of this fact? To be sure, in many cases the relative wealth of the parties is manifest. A multinational corporation cannot disguise itself as a struggling member of the proletariat. But where admittedly irrelevant characteristics can be removed from the courtroom without great strain, it is hard to see why they should be retained. In the end, therefore, it is the more pragmatic analysis that should be decisive. The benefits of a half-hearted policy of secrecy are not worth the costs. If disclosure of the fact of insurance really is prejudicial, the corrective is not a futile effort at concealment, but the usual fulfillment by the court of its function of explaining to the jury its duty to decide according to the facts and the substantive law, rather than upon sympathy, ability to pay, or concern about proliferating litigation and rising insurance premiums.

Chapter 20

EXPERIMENTAL AND SCIENTIFIC EVIDENCE

Table of Sections

§ 202. Pretrial Experiments

The dominant method of factual inquiry in the courts of law is observational. Witnesses relate what they have seen under naturally occurring conditions, and the judge or jury, observing the witnesses, accepts or rejects their stories with some degree of confidence. In many fields of science, naturalistic observations of people or things are also a principal means of gathering information (though the observations are made in a more structured fashion and are presented and analyzed in a different way). In other scientific disciplines, the major method for collecting data involves manipulating the environment. In its simplest and ideal form, a controlled experiment screens out or holds constant all extraneous variables so that the experimenter can measure the impact of the one factor of interest.

The opportunities for applying the experimental method to factual controversies that arise in litigation are immense, but they generally go unrecognized and unused. Some of the more frequently encountered types of experiments are tests of the composition or physical properties of substances or products, tests of the flammability or explosive properties of certain products, tests of the effects of drugs and other products on human beings or other organisms, tests of firearms to show characteristic, identifying features, or capabilities, tests of the visibility of objects or persons under certain conditions, tests of the speed of moving vehicles and of the effectiveness of brakes, headlights or other components. Some of these experiments can be simple affairs, such as driving an automobile along a stretch of road to determine where a particular object on the road first becomes visible. Others are more complicated, requiring sophisticated machinery, statistical analysis of the results, or other specialized knowledge or procedures, and these are taken up in later sections. Testimony describing the experiments may be received as substantive evidence, or it may form the basis for an expert opinion. The simplest experiments are often the most convincing, and expert testimony is not always cost-effective.

Pretrial experiments will be admitted as evidence if their probative value is not substantially outweighed by the usual counterweights of prejudice, confusion of the issues, and time consumption. The only form of prejudice that might operate in this context is that of giving experimental results more weight than they deserve. This should not be a serious barrier to admissibility unless the interpretation of the experiment would require expert testimony and specialized knowledge. The extent to which the presentation will be distracting or time-consuming will vary from case to case. As for probative value, the courts often speak of the need for similarity between the conditions of the experiment and those that pertained to the litigated happening.

In practice, however, this requirement of similarity is not applied to all pretrial experiments, or if it is nominally applied, the notion of "similarity" becomes almost infinitely flexible. The requirement is most meaningful and at its strictest when the experiment expressly seeks to replicate the event in question to show that things could (or could not) have happened as alleged. But even in these case-specific experiments, differences between the experimental and actual conditions that only could make it harder for the experiment to be favorable to the proponent should be no obstacle to admission. Furthermore, an event can never be perfectly reenacted or simulated. There are too many details to keep track of, and some defy precise re-creation. For example, the human agent in the happening to

which the experiment pertains may be deceased, the vehicle may be destroyed, the surrounding circumstances may be known only vaguely, or the process of duplicating what actually happened may be too dangerous. Consequently, although the similarity formula is sometimes overrigidly applied, most courts recognize that the requirement is a relative one. If enough of the obviously important factors are duplicated in the experiment, and if the failure to control other possibly relevant variables is justified, the court may conclude that the experiment is sufficiently enlightening that it should come into evidence. This determination typically is subject to review only for an abuse of discretion.

On the other hand, the similarity requirement either is not applied or is highly diluted when the pretrial experiment does not purport to replicate the essential features of a particular happening. There are many perfectly acceptable experiments of this nature. For example, if one party contends that certain acts or omissions could not produce—under any circumstances—the result in question, then the other party may conduct an experiment to falsify this hypothesis. Of course, the closer the experiment is to the conditions that actually pertained, the more useful the experiment will be, but merely refuting the opposing party's sweeping claim may be sufficiently valuable to make the evidence admissible. Similarly, the proponent may offer to prove that something was not the cause of the actionable result. To do so, he may use an experiment that shows that some other agent can bring about the same result. Finally, the experiment may be introduced solely to illustrate or demonstrate a scientific principle or empirical finding that a jury, perhaps with the aid of an expert witness, can apply to the specifics of the case. Thus, experiments showing general properties of materials are admitted without confining the experiments to the conditions surrounding the litigated situation. Most of these analyses are referred to as tests rather than experiments. When this label is attached, the question becomes one, not of similarity, but of authentication—making sure that the right material was tested and that it underwent no essential alterations before testing. With all these limited purpose experiments, the issue, as always, is whether, on balance, the evidence will assist the jury.

Some courts distinguish between experiments commissioned for a specific lawsuit and those undertaken solely to obtain scientific knowledge of greater generality. Although the latter have the advantage of being untainted by any interest in the litigation, steps can be taken to improve case-specific experimentation as well. Consideration might be given to allowing the judge to exclude experiments unless the adversary has had reasonable notice, an opportunity to make suggestions, and to be present during the experiment. Also worthy of consideration is appointment by the court of an impartial person to conduct or supervise an experiment. Such procedures could lead to findings that would invite much less in the way of time-consuming or distracting attack and defense at trial.

§ 203. Scientific Tests in General: Admissibility and Weight

To deal effectively with scientific evidence, the attorney must know more than the rules of evidence. He must know something of the scientific principles as well. While he can rely on suitably chosen experts for advice about the more arcane points, he must have a sufficient grasp of the field to see what is essential and what is unnecessary detail and verbiage if he is to develop or counteract the evidence most effectively. In this chapter, we cannot explore in any depth the vast body of knowledge that comes into play in the forensic applications of science and medicine. Only a superficial sampling of a few areas will be attempted. We shall focus on some of the problems that can arise in making measurements and in interpreting the data so obtained. Sections 204 through 207 deal with laboratory, clinical, or field tests (organized somewhat arbitrarily by scientific discipline) in which statistical analysis of the data does

not play a major role. Sections 208 through 211 concern studies in which statistical analyses are prominent. In the remainder of this section, we discuss some general points concerning the admissibility of all such evidence and the weight that it should receive.

A. *Admissibility.* Most of the case law centers on the threshold question of admissibility. The principles of relevancy outlined in Chapter 16 are as applicable to scientific evidence as to any other kind, and the doctrines governing all expert testimony discussed in Chapter 3 operate here as well. Federal and Revised Uniform Rule of Evidence (1974) 702 specifically mentions scientific testimony, linking it with expert testimony generally:

> If scientific, technical, or other specialized knowledge will assist the trier of fact to understand the evidence or to determine a fact in issue, a witness qualified as an expert by knowledge, skill, experience, training or education, may testify thereto in the form of an opinion or otherwise.

However, many courts purport to apply special rules of admissibility when expert witnesses are called to testify about scientific tests or findings. The most common special rule is that in addition to satisfying the traditional requirements of relevancy and helpfulness to the trier of fact, the proponent must show general acceptance of the principle or technique in the scientific community.

This notion of a special rule for scientific evidence originated in 1923 in Frye v. United States.[1] *Frye* was a murder prosecution in which the trial court rebuffed defendant's effort to introduce results of a "systolic blood pressure test," a forerunner of the polygraph. On appeal, the defendant relied on the traditional rule governing expert testimony, but the Court of Appeals, without explanation or precedent, superimposed a new standard:

> Just when a scientific principle or discovery crosses the line between the experimental and demonstrable stages is difficult to define. Somewhere in this twilight zone the evidential force of the principle must be recognized, and

§ 203

1. 293 Fed. 1013 (D.C.Cir.1923).

while courts will go a long way in admitting expert testimony deduced from a well-recognized scientific principle or discovery, the thing from which the deduction is made must be sufficiently established to have gained general acceptance in the particular field in which it belongs.[2]

The opinion did not state clearly whether "the thing" that needed "to have gained general acceptance" was the link between conscious insincerity and changes in blood pressure or the ability of an expert to measure and interpret the changes, or both. The court concluded, however, that the deception test lacked the requisite "standing and scientific recognition among physiological and psychological authorities."[3]

The *Frye* standard was adopted by many courts in the ensuing years with scant discussion. Polygraphy, graphology, hypnotic and drug induced testimony, voice stress analysis, voice spectrograms, ion microprobe mass spectroscopy, infrared sensing of aircraft, retesting of breath samples for alcohol content, psychological profiles of battered women, and child abusers, post traumatic stress disorder as indicating rape, astronomical calculations, and blood group typing, all have fallen prey to its influence. In the jurisdictions that follow *Frye,* the proponent of the evidence must prove general acceptance, by surveying scientific publications, judicial decisions, or practical applications, or by presenting testimony from scientists as to the attitudes of their fellow scientists.

Especially in the last two decades, however, the *Frye* standard has been subjected to critical analysis, limitation, modification, and finally, outright rejection. Some courts have found the *Frye* standard satisfied in the teeth of expert testimony that the technique in question was too new and untried and the test results too inconclusive for court use. While asserting the continuing vitality of the *Frye* standard, other courts have held that general acceptance goes to the weight rather than the admissibility of the evidence. Still others have reasoned that the standard applies only

to tests for truthfulness, to relatively esoteric applications of science, or to the underlying principles or methodology rather than the particular studies or results based on those principles or that methodology. Many opinions have simply ignored the standard, and many others have blithely equated it with a requirement of showing the accuracy and reliability of the scientific technique. Finally, several jurisdictions expressly have rejected *Frye,* leaving the task of regulating the admission of scientific evidence to the normal doctrines of relevancy and helpfulness of expert testimony. The adoption of the Federal Rules of Evidence only intensified this process. These rules do not explicitly distinguish between scientific and other forms of expert testimony, and they permit experts to rely on facts or data not otherwise admissible into evidence as long as they are "reasonably relied upon by experts in [the] particular field." Plainly, "reasonable reliance" is not synonymous with general acceptance.

A drumbeat of criticism of the *Fyre* test provides the background music to the movement away from the general acceptance test. Proponents of the test argue that it assures uniformity in evidentiary rulings, that it shields juries from any tendency to treat novel scientific evidence as infallible, that it avoids complex, expensive, and time-consuming courtroom dramas, and that it insulates the adversary system from novel evidence until a pool of experts is available to evaluate it in court. Most commentators agree, however, that these objectives can be attained satisfactorily with less drastic constraints on the admissibility of scientific evidence. In particular, it has been suggested that a substantial acceptance test be substituted for the general acceptance standard, that courts look directly to reliability or validity rather than to the extent of acceptance, that scientific evidence be admitted freely, coupled with testimony of an expert appointed by the court if it finds that the testimony would be subject to "substantial doubt in peer review by the scientific community," that a panel of scientists rather

---

2. Id. at 1014.

3. Id.

than the usual courts screen new developments for acceptance, and that the traditional standards of relevancy and the need for expertise—and nothing more—should govern.

The last mentioned method for evaluating the admissibility of scientific evidence is the most appealing. It avoids the difficult problems of defining when "scientific" evidence is subject to the general acceptance requirement and how general this acceptance must be, of discerning exactly what it is that must be accepted, and of determining the "particular field" to which the scientific evidence belongs and in which it must be accepted. General scientific acceptance is a proper condition for taking judicial notice of scientific facts, but it is not a suitable criterion for the admissibility of scientific evidence. Any relevant conclusions supported by a qualified expert witness should be received unless there are distinct reasons for exclusion. These reasons are the familiar ones of prejudicing or misleading the jury or consuming undue amounts of time.

This traditional approach to the evidence does not make scientific testimony admissible on the say-so of a single expert. Neither does it go to the other extreme and insist on a fully formed scientific concensus. It permits general scientific opinion of both underlying principles and particular applications to be considered in evaluating the worth of the testimony. In so treating the yeas and nays of the members of a scientific discipline as but one indication of the validity, accuracy, and reliability of the technique, the traditional balancing method focuses the court's attention where it belongs—on the actual usefulness of the evidence in light of the full record developed on the power of the scientific test. Furthermore, unlike the general or the substantial acceptance standards, it is sensitive to the perceived degree of prejudice and unnecessary expense associated with the scientific technique in issue. Not every scrap of scientific evidence carries with it an aura of infallibility. Some methods, like bitemark identification and blood spatter analysis, are demonstrable in the courtroom. Where the methods involve principles and procedures that are comprehensible to a jury, the concerns over

the evidence exerting undue influence and inducing a battle of the experts have less force. On the other hand, when the nature of the technique is more esoteric, as with some types of statistical analyses and serologic tests, or when the inferences from the scientific evidence sweep broadly or cut deeply into sensitive areas, a stronger showing of probative value should be required. This could result in the categorical exclusion of certain types of evidence, such as statements made while under the influence of "truth" serum. By attending to such considerations, the rigor of the requisite foundation can be adjusted to suit the nature of the evidence and the context in which it is offered.

B. *Weight.* Whatever the standard for admissibility may be in a particular jurisdiction, arguments as to the weight that the jury should give to the evidence will be important. Indeed, skills in building cases with admissible scientific evidence and demolishing these same structures are becoming increasingly valuable as the forensic applications of science are becoming more commonplace. Attention to possible infirmities in the collection and analysis of data can cut superficially impressive scientific evidence down to its proper size. To begin with, one might consider the process by which the forensic scientist makes his raw measurements. Does subjective judgment play any role? If so, do different experts tend to find very different measured values, so that the measurement process can be described as unreliable? Are the variations randomly distributed about some true mean, or are they biased in one direction or another, so that even if they are reliable, their accuracy is suspect? Then there are problems of interpretation. Is the quantity being measured the real item of interest, or at least a suitable proxy for that variable? In brief, considering the probable errors introduced at each stage of the scientific analysis, is the final result likely to be reliable, accurate, and meaningful? The remainder of this chapter addresses these questions with regard to particular scientific tests and studies.

§ 204. Particular Tests: Physics and Electronics: Speed Detection and Recording

Forensic applications of physics and electronics include motor vehicle accident reconstruction, analysis of tape recordings, and detecting and recording speed and other aspects of the movements of vehicles. This section surveys the evidentiary features of speed detection and recording devices.

The branch of classical mechanics that deals with the motion of objects is called kinematics. The physicist defines average velocity as the distance travelled along a given direction in a specified time period divided by the length of this time period. Speed is the absolute value of velocity. The difference between speed and velocity is that the latter includes information as to the direction of travel, while the former merely states how fast the object moved. Acceleration is the change in velocity for a unit of time divided by the time elapsed. It states how quickly an object is speeding up or slowing down. Measuring such quantities without some mechanical aid is difficult to do accurately, although it can be easy enough to ascertain whether one vehicle is moving faster or slower than another. A more elaborate application of these principles of kinematics to the detection and conviction of traffic offenders is recorded in an English case at the turn of the century in Gorham v. Brice,[1] which a constable took readings from a watch with a second hand. A progression of more sophisticated timing mechanisms followed, culminating in the Visual Average Speed Computer and Record (VASCAR). When a suspected violator's vehicle reaches a clearly marked point, such as an intersection, the operator activates the timer. When the police car reaches the same point, the operator activates a mechanism for recording the distance the police car travels as measured by its odometer. When the target vehicle reaches a second clearly marked point down the road, the police officer shuts off the timer, and when the police car arrives at this second point, he turns off the distance

switch. The computer divides the measured distance by the measured time elapsed and displays this average speed.

Initially, the courts required expert testimony concerning the principles and operation of the VASCAR. However, the kinematic principles, which date back to the time of Galileo and Newton, are so well established that they, like the ability of an electronic computer to divide two numbers, easily can be the subject of judicial notice. The more serious issue, which goes to the weight and (in an extreme case, the admissibility) of the evidence, is the accuracy of the device under operational conditions. Errors can arise from a poorly calibrated odometer, from turning on and off the switches at the wrong times, and so on. A foundation indicating that the device is properly calibrated and the operator well trained in its use is usually required.

A speed detector and recorder not so closely tied to police work is the tachograph. It consists of a tachometer and a recording mechanism that furnishes, over time, the speed and mileage of the vehicle to which it is attached. It is used on trains, trucks and busses. Its readings have been admitted in civil and criminal cases, on a showing the particular device works accurately and an identification of which portion of the record generated pertains to the events in issue.

A more advanced kinematic recording instrument is the aircraft flight recorder. It records time, airspeed, altitude, attitude (orientation of axes relative to some reference line or plane, such as the horizon), magnetic heading, vertical acceleration, and other instrument readings. These records can be extremely valuable in analyzing aircraft crashes. Admissibility turns on evidence of authenticity and expert testimony to explain how the machine operates and to interpret the marks on the chart.

Radar equipment provides another means of measuring velocity. Military or aircraft pulse-type radar involves more or less direct applications of the velocity-distance-time rela-

1. 18 T.L.R. 424 (K.B.Div.1902).

tionships previously discussed, but police radar relies on a different theory. In its simplest form, the radar speedmeter used by police agencies transmits a continuous beam of microwaves of uniform frequency, detects the reflected signals, and measures the difference in frequency between the transmitted and reflected beams. It converts this frequency difference into a number for the speed of the object that has reflected the radiation. This conversion is based on a quantitative description of the phenomenon known as the Doppler effect. On both theoretical and experimental grounds, it is well established that electromagnetic radiation coming from an object moving relative to the observer is shifted to a higher frequency if the object is approaching, and to a lower frequency if the object is receding. For the range of velocities of interest in traffic court, the extent of this Doppler shift is directly proportional to the relative speed. When the radar set is at rest relative to the ground (earth's surface), it therefore gives the speed of the vehicle being tracked.

A more complicated version of the Doppler shift detector processes signals received at two distinct frequencies. This refinement allows the unit to be used conveniently in a moving vehicle. The shift in frequency of the beam as reflected off the road surface gives the speed of the police vehicle. The shift in frequency as reflected off the target vehicle gives its speed relative to the police car. In effect, circuitry in the radar unit adds the relative speed to the police car's speed to yield the ground speed of the target.

Most of the early cases admitting radar evidence of speeding involved testimony showing not only that the target car had been identified and that a qualified operator had obtained the reading from a properly functioning device, but also explaining the Doppler effect, its application in the radar speedmeter, and the scientific acceptance of this method of measuring speed. Within a few years, the courts began to take judicial notice of the underlying scientific principles and the capability (in theory) of the device to measure speed with tolerable accuracy. Ex-

pert testimony on these subjects is no longer essential.

The question of what must be proved to establish that the specific instrument was operating accurately has provoked more controversy. Decisions range from holdings that the evidence is inadmissible without independent verification of the accuracy of the system at the time and place of the measurement to holdings that lack of evidence of testing goes to the weight but not the admissibility of the results. Revelations that police radar units operating under field conditions may not be as reliable as had once been assumed should encourage adherence to the more stringent standards.

Regardless of whether the jurisdiction has a particularized rule for the extent and type of testing needed for admissibility, evidence pertaining to the accuracy of the reading is admissible. There are many ways in which errors can creep into the system. Stationary radar readings will be wrong if the transmission frequency changes, if the receiver misevaluates the frequency difference, if the radar is not held motionless, or if radiation from another source is attributed to the suspect's vehicle. Moving radar, being a more complex device, has more room for error. Acceleration of the patrol car, "cosine error," and "shadowing" can lead the instrument to underestimate the patrol car's speed, and hence to overstate the target vehicle's speed.

Some of these potential sources of error can be minimized or excluded by careful operating procedures and on-site tests. These include the use of tuning forks vibrating at frequencies such that their linear motions will cause the speedmeter to register particular speeds if it is receiving properly, use of an internal, electronically activated tong for the same purpose, and simply checking that, when aimed at another police car, the radar reading corresponds with that car's speedometer reading. Of course, after a few years of use, tongs may not vibrate at the presumed frequency, an internal oscillator may need adjustment, and a car's speedometer may not be accurate. At least on the question of admissibility, however, most courts recognize that independent errors are unlikely to be identical. They tend to hold that some combination of these methods is sufficient to warrant admissibility. Furthermore, a number of decisions, sometimes aided by statute, hold that tested radar readings can amount to proof beyond a reasonable doubt.

§ 205. Particular Tests: Biology and Medicine: Drunkenness, Blood, Tissue and DNA Typing

The forensic applications of the biological sciences and medicine are far too extensive and varied to be discussed fully here, but we shall consider two groups of laboratory tests of biological samples that commonly provide crucial evidence. These are chemical tests for drunkenness and immunogenetic and other tests for blood, tissue and DNA types.

A. *Drunkenness.* Physiologically, the amount of alcohol in the brain determines the degree of intoxication. Except in an autopsy, however, a direct measurement of this quantity is not feasible. Nevertheless, samples of blood, urine, saliva, or breath can be taken, and the alcohol level in these samples can be measured. Using these measurements to determine whether a person is intoxicated raises two technical problems—the accuracy of the measurement itself, and the extent of the correlation between the concentration of alcohol in the sample and the degree of intoxication. There is room for concern on both these points.

Analysis of blood samples gives the most accurate and reliable results. Various chemical techniques are available to measure the concentration of ethyl alcohol in the sample. When proper laboratory procedures are followed and the sample is correctly obtained and preserved, these give reliable estimates. Of course, there is always room for error in these measurements, but the more fundamental problem lies in moving from an estimated value for the blood alcohol concentration (BAC) to a correct statement about the degree of intoxication during the crucial period. Even where the measured values are reliable and accurate, the substantial variability in

tolerances for alcohol, absorption rates, and clearance rates, both among individuals and within the same individual from one situation to another, complicates efforts to deduce the true extent of intoxication at the time of an arrest or accident. For these reasons, extrapolations based on direct measurements of BAC seem more perilous than is generally recognized.

Determinations resting exclusively on concentration of alcohol contained in a sample of a person's breath (BrAC) are even more questionable. Again, the problem is not the accuracy of the instrumentation as maintained and used in laboratory studies. Although errors can arise from field operating conditions, individual variability, and extrapolation to the time in question, there is a further problem. A formula must be used to convert BrAC to BAC. A single number presently is used as a multiplier in making this conversion, but the exact value of this parameter is debatable, and there are strong indications of substantial variability in the figure among individuals and within the same individual over time.

These cautions concerning the scientific proof as applied in particular cases do not necessarily make the blood and breath test evidence inadmissible. On the contrary, when the tests are properly conducted and analyzed, the evidence can be of great value in deciding questions connected with intoxication. Since the links from breath alcohol concentration to blood alcohol level to intoxication, as well as the accuracy of measurements made under ideal conditions is well established, under the usual principles governing scientific evidence, the test results should be admissible if founded on a showing of authenticity and satisfactory care in the collection of the sample and its analysis. Expert testimony ordinarily would be needed to establish that the party with the measured or inferred BAC was intoxicated during the period in question.

In the context of traffic offenses, however, specialized statutes and regulations provide shortcuts to the application of the common law principles and evidence codes in determining the admissibility of blood and breath test evidence. The Uniform Vehicle Code illustrates some common provisions. In proceedings involving driving or control of a vehicle while under the influence of intoxicating liquor, it makes chemical test evidence of BAC admissible as long as it is obtained by certified persons following procedures that the state department of health has prescribed. If the procedures are sufficiently rigorous, then the results of this testing can trigger two rebuttable presumptions: if BAC at the relevant time was .08% or more, that the individual was under the influence; and if BAC was .05% or less, that he was not. An intermediate reading is deemed "competent evidence" for consideration along with the other evidence in the case. In most jurisdictions, a party offering test results pursuant to such a statute must lay a foundation by producing witnesses to explain the way the test is conducted, to identify it as duly approved under the statutory scheme, and to vouch for its correct administration in the particular case. In more recent years, all but six states have placed still more emphasis on chemical testing by enacting "per se" laws that make it a crime to drive while having a BAC or a breath alcohol concentration in excess of a specified amount. The typical result is a set of overlapping offenses with various statutory provisions for admitting evidence of BAC or BrAC in traffic cases superimposed on the more general evidence code or common law rules.

B. *Blood, Tissue, and DNA Types.* Another group of chemical tests—those that identify blood, tissue and DNA types—are often the subject of courtroom testimony. Elucidating the biochemical mechanisms by which a multicellular organism distinguishes between self and non-self—between its own cells and foreign substances—is a major research problem in biology. The topic is fundamental to understanding the way in which the body responds to infections from microorganisms, to grafts of foreign tissues or materials, and to blood transfusions, and it is central to the study of allergies, tumors, and autoimmune diseases. Research in this field reveals that sticking out of the surface of cells are various molecules, called in this context, antigens. For instance, a person with type A blood has the molecule known as an A antigen on his red blood cells. Of course, red blood cells are not the only ones to possess antigens. Human Leucocyte Antigens (HLA) are found on the surface of most human cells, and there is an elaborate nomenclature for these. The full set of antigens that a cell possesses thus distinguishes it from the cells of other organisms. It is conceivable that each person is uniquely identifiable in this way. However, no one really knows exactly how many antigens there are. New ones continue to be discovered. In addition to the immunologically crucial antigens, cells and bodily fluids contain chemicals such as enzymes and other proteins that can differ from one person to another.

Most enzymes and serum proteins are identified by a technique called electrophoresis, in which an electric field is applied to separate the molecules according to their electric charge. Although electrophoresis is a standard technique in biochemistry, its application to aged or dried blood stains has proved intensely controversial. Difficulties arise because thin gel multisystem testing is used only in crime laboratories, because few outside investigations of the effects of aging and environmental contamination have been undertaken, and because crime laboratories do not submit to routine proficiency testing. Nevertheless, almost all appellate courts that have encountered challenges to electrophoretic identifications have concluded that both the multisystem and the more generally used electrophoretic procedures are scientifically accepted and that the findings can be admitted into evidence.

A different type of test is used to detect antigens. The antigens react with other biologically produced molecules, called antibodies. Serologic tests consist of exposing a suspected antigen to its corresponding antibody and observing whether the expected reaction occurs. Errors involving misinterpretation, mislabeling, poor reagents, and the like are always possible, but workers in this field report that with stringent procedures and quality control standards, the risk of error can be made very small.

The forensic use of these tests arises principally in two areas—identifying the perpetrators of violent crimes or sexual offenses from traces of blood or semen and ascertaining parentage in child support cases or other litigation. In general, the courts have moved from an initial position of mistrust of such evidence to the present stage of taking judicial notice of the scientific acceptance or acceptability of serologic and related tests. From the outset, it was recognized that if the suspect's antigens do not match those in the sample found at the scene of a crime, then the incriminating trace does not consist of his blood. For a considerable time, however, there was a difference of judicial opinion concerning evidence of a match. Since some combinations of antigens are relatively common, a few courts dismissed the positive test results for these antigens as irrelevant. The better view—and the overwhelming majority position—is that positive findings are neither irrelevant nor so innately prejudicial as to justify a rule against their admission.

Serologic tests have been used for the last half-century in paternity litigation. The underlying logic is based on a few principles of human genetics. Roughly speaking, portions of the DNA contained in the chromosomes of the nucleus of a cell—the genes—direct the synthesis of proteins. Different versions (or alleles) of these genes oversee the synthesis of the different antigens. Consequently, by ascertaining which antigens are present in an individual (the phenotype), one learns something about that individual's alleles (the genotype). As such, the antigens can be thought of as genetic markers. Knowing the phenotypes of the child, mother, and putative father and applying the laws of inheritance, a geneticist can say whether it would be possible for a child with the observed phenotype to have been born to the mother and the alleged father. That is, the medical expert can state that whoever the biological father was must have had certain genetic characteristics, which can be compared to those that the alleged father has. In this way, a man falsely

accused—one who does not have the necessary characteristics—can be excluded.

With an appropriate foundation, such negative test results are nearly always admissible, although the weight accorded to an exclusion varies. A few cases can be found upholding liability despite serologic proof of nonpaternity. In other states, a properly conducted blood test that excludes the defendant is conclusive.

Positive immunogenetic findings are another matter. Although European countries allow positive test results as tending to prove paternity, the traditional rule in this country was that serologic tests are inadmissible for this purpose. At one time, when only a few, widely shared antigens were known, this approach made some sense. For example, under the early ABO system, a positive test result merely meant that, on average, the accused was one of the 87% of the male population possessing the requisite genotypes. Such evidence is not very probative, and the fear that the jury would give it more weight than it deserved, cloaked as it was in the garb of medical expertise, prompted many courts to exclude it as unduly prejudicial. For decades, however, this situation has been changing steadily. With the plethora of genetic markers now known, it is commonplace to determine that the biological father has genetic traits shared by one in several thousand men of the same race. Many laboratories are equipped to test reliably for enough antigens that such positive test results are simply too probative to be ignored.

As a result, evidence that the accused has immunogenetic traits that are consistent with the claim that he is the biological father is received regularly. In most states, this is a consequence of statutory innovation—sometimes, poorly drafted or conceived. In other instances, it is an example of the common law lugubriously digesting a technological advance. The battle over the admissibility of serologic and related tests to prove paternity is over, but disputes over efforts to give an exact statement of the "probability of paternity" linger.[1]

In contrast to the widespread acceptance of red blood cell grouping, blood serum protein and enzyme analysis, and HLA typing, the evidentiary status of forensic applications of recombinant-DNA technology is in flux. A proper evidentiary analysis must attend to the fact that there is no single method of DNA typing. As with conventional immuno-genetic testing, the probative value of the laboratory findings depends both on the procedure employed and the genetic characteristics that are discerned. We shall describe some of these procedures and the theory that lies behind them, and then consider the developing case law.

DNA is a long molecule with two strands that spiral around one another, forming a double helix. Within the double helix are molecules, called nucleotide bases, that link one strand to the other, like the steps of a spiral staircase. There are four of these bases, which can be referred to by their initials, A, T, G and C. The A on one strand pairs with T on the other, and the G bonds to C. The lengthy sequence of AT and GC "stairs" within the DNA contained in human cells includes all the genes and control sequences (for turning certain genes on and off). The genes are stretches of base pairs whose order determines the composition of proteins and related products synthesized by various cells. Oddly enough, however, much of the DNA has no known function.

Examining cell surface antigens (such as the ABO and HLA systems) or blood serum enzymes or proteins gives some information about the DNA sequences that code for these particular substances; if the markers differ, then the underlying DNA must differ. In contrast, DNA analysis is not limited to identifying variations in these coding sequences. With appropriate "DNA probes," one can detect differences in the base pair sequences anywhere in the DNA. A probe is a short piece of a single strand of DNA with a radio-

active or other readily identifiable component attached, like a sticker or tag on a suitcase. If the bases in the target DNA are in an order matching those in the probe, the probe will bind to the target DNA.

Because 99.9 percent of the DNA sequence in any two people is identical, the technical challenge is to detect the relatively rare stretches of DNA, sometimes called alleles, that vary among individuals. Various procedures to do this are in use. In one, fragments of DNA are "amplified" by heating and cooling with an enzyme called DNA polymerase. Even if the sample contains only one or two copies of the allele, the polymerase induces a chain reaction that increases the number to about 10 million. The amplified DNA is "spotted" onto a membrane, and a probe added. If the sequence complementary to the probe is there, it will be tagged. If a radioactive element is used for the tag, for example, the spot will become radioactive and a dark dot will appear if the membrance is placed on X-ray film. The analyst simply looks to see whether the dot, and hence the allele, is present. This test resembles serologic tests in giving a categorical answer: either the allele is present or it is not.

The great advantage of the polymerase chain reaction over conventional immunogenetic and other DNA typing techniques is that it requires very little biological material. As with serologic tests, however, a single allele may be common in the population, and hence not especially revealing. Of course, a series of probes may narrow the percentage of the population that could have been the source of the sample, but the procedure cannot identify any one individual as the only possible source.

The more frequently used procedure for identifying DNA variations ("polymorphisms") does not rely on the presence or absence of the base pair sequence detected by the probe. Instead, it detects variations in the lengths of DNA fragments produced by "digesting" DNA into fragments with "restriction" enzymes. The lengths are mea-

§ 205

1. See infra § 211.

sured by separating the fragments by gel electrophoresis, blotting them onto a nylon membrane, tagging them with a probe, then placing X-ray film to the membrane to give an image with dark bands at the locations of the tagged fragments. The pattern of bands is the DNA "print" or "profile."

How many people have a given DNA profile (and hence, how valuable that profile is for identification) depends on where the restriction enzyme cuts the DNA (the restriction sites) and on the probe that picks out some of the resulting fragments. Suppose that some people have two restriction sites 32,000 bases apart, while others have an extra site located 12,000 bases inside this 32,000 base region. If the probe recognizes a sequence that occurs only on the shorter side of the extra restriction site, people with the extra site will have a profile consisting of one band for the 12,000 base fragment. People without the extra site also will have one band, but it will correspond to a fragment 32,000 bases long. Because the shorter 12,000 base band will migrate farther down the gel during electrophoresis, by placing DNA from two samples in parallel lanes on the same gel, an observer can tell whether one sample produces the smaller fragment while the other does not. The extra site thus gives rise to a restriction fragment length polymorphism (RFLP) detectable with a particular enzyme-probe combination. However, there may be many people with each of the two possible bands, and this one simple site RFLP may not be very revealing.

Other enzyme-probe combinations generate many more possible length measurements within a population. Suppose that the 32,000 base pair sequence differs among individuals, not by a change in a single base pair at a given locus, creating or deleting an interior restriction site, but instead by the insertion of a short sequence starting at this locus and repeating itself many times. The more tandem repeats there are inside the restriction fragment, the longer it will be. A probe that detects the core repetitive sequence starting at this single site will detect these variable length fragments. A person with a single copy of the core sequence will have a band at the 32,000 point, someone with a hundred

repeats of a core sequence ten base pairs long will have a band at the 33,000 point, and so on. Because the number of repeating units at a "variable number tandem repeat locus" (VNTR locus) can vary greatly within a population, the probes that detect this type of repetitive DNA are generally much more informative than probes for simple site polymorphisms.

In addition to single-locus probes for VNTR loci, multiple-locus probes for VNTR loci have been developed and employed for forensic purposes. Some core sequences have tandem repeats not just at one locus, but in many places. Under proper conditions, a probe based on these core sequences detects length polymorphisms from all these loci scattered amidst many fragments, all at once. The developers of such probes call the set of 10 to 20 bands obtained with them "fingerprints." In effect, the multiple-locus VNTR probes are like a powerful cocktail of single-locus probes.

Initial journalistic and judicial praise for applications of RFLPs in homicide, rape, paternity, and other cases has been effusive. Indeed, one judge proclaimed "DNA fingerprinting" to be "the single greatest advance in the 'search for truth' * * * since the advent of cross-examination."[2] In this first wave of cases, expert testimony for the prosecution rarely was countered, and courts readily admitted RFLP findings.

Yet, the early enthusiasm for these techniques has led to second thoughts. The problems arise at two levels: controlling the experimental conditions of the analysis, and interpreting the results. Declaring matches or non-matches among the RFLPs due to VNTR loci in two samples is not always trivial. Furthermore, many forensic calculations of the probability of a coincidentally matching pattern have been oversimplified.

Despite these concerns, the recent cases continue to find forensic RFLP analyses to be generally accepted, and a number of states have provided for admissibility of DNA tests by legislation. Concerted attacks by defense experts of impeccable credentials, however, have produced a few cases rejecting specific

---

2. People v. Wesley, 140 Misc.2d 306, 533 N.Y.S.2d 643 (Albany County Ct.1988).

proffers on the ground that the testing was not sufficiently rigorous.

In evaluating the general acceptance (as well as the validity and reliability of any DNA analysis), one must recognize that most of the probes used in criminal and paternity cases have no other medical or scientific application. To be sure, the use of suitable restriction enzymes followed by separation by gel electrophoresis and radioactive tagging of the fragments is a well established and fruitful research and diagnostic tool in medical genetics. In most such applications, however, there is no need to measure precisely the position of bands or to estimate the frequency of these bands in the population; moreover, the information available in diagnostic work makes spurious or missing bands a much less serious problem. Consequently, the outcome of an inquiry into general acceptance depends largely on the generality with which the question is posed. If all that need be accepted is the theoretical basis for DNA identification, there is no doubt that the technique is potentially admissible. If proof that molecular biologists and geneticists believe that DNA analysis of possibly contaminated samples with probes of largely forensic interest are as infallible as some forensic analysts have maintained, then general acceptance is far more doubtful. Given the ongoing debate over the standards and controls that should be used, perhaps the findings of laboratories that have yet to establish a track record on independently administered, blind proficiency tests should be inadmissible, while proof that a laboratory has participated successfully in blind proficiency tests and has applied a similar or more rigorous protocol to the samples at bar should satisfy the threshold test for admissibility. In addition, the performance of the laboratory on the proficiency tests should accompany the case-specific findings. In this way, the trier of fact will be in a better position to assess the ability of the laboratory, using whatever type of DNA analysis and quality controls it has adopted, to obtain and interpret test results correctly.

§ 206. Particular Tests: Psychology: Eyewitness Testimony, Lie Detection, Drugs, Hypnosis, and Profiles

The law and its procedures have long attracted the interest of psychologists. Of late, that profession's courtroom-related activities have expanded dramatically. Although the preeminent contributions of psychologists and psychiatrists as expert witnesses have come in presenting clinical diagnoses or evaluations in criminal and mental health cases, at this point, we shall describe less conventional forensic applications. Specifically, this section surveys issues arising from expert testimony about the accuracy of eyewitness identifications, physiological indicators of deception, "truth" drugs and hypnosis, and "profiles" of certain types of offenders or victims.

A. *Eyewitness Testimony.* For many years, expert testimony has been received to show that mental disorders may have affected the testimony of eyewitnesses. More recently, criminal defendants have called on psychologists to offer expert opinions on the factors that ordinarily influence the reliability of eyewitness identifications. Typically, the expert testifies to generalizations from experiments in which students or other subjects have witnessed a film or other enactment or description of the kind of events that are the subjects of courtroom testimony. In such studies, the accuracy of the recall of faces or facts is then tested under a variety of conditions. The overall findings indicate that such witnesses often make mistakes, that they tend to make more mistakes in cross-racial identifications as well as when the events involve violence, that errors are easily introduced by misleading questions asked shortly after the witness has viewed the simulated happening, and that the professed confidence of the subjects in their identifications bears no consistent relation to the accuracy of these recognitions.

Testimony about such research findings has been received in some cases and rejected in others. Given the extreme deference usually accorded trial court decisions on the need for expert testimony, these decisions seem almost invariably to be upheld. Although a handful of courts have held that exclusion of expert testimony on highly pertinent aspects of eyewitness identifications constitutes an abuse of discretion or that this testimony is not categorically excluded, many of the appellate opinions display a distinct distaste for such testimony. These opinions argue that since an appreciation of the limitations on eyewitnesses' perceptions and memory is within the ken of a lay jury, broad brush psychological testimony about these mechanisms would not appreciably assist the jury. They point also to the standard concerns with scientific evidence—that lay jurors will overstate its importance and that its introduction will entail undue expense and confusion. The more poorly reasoned opinions speak of invading the province of the jury.

The matter cannot be disposed of this easily. Concern over the reliability of eyewitness testimony lies at the heart of the Supreme Court's right to counsel and due process decisions in cases involving lineups and other pretrial identification procedures. It may well be that without some counteracting influence, juries give too much weight to the witness's assertions of recognition. To contend that juries know how to evaluate the reliability of the identifications without expert assistance, while simultaneously maintaining that the assistance would have too great an impact on the jury's deliberations, smacks of makeshift reasoning. Admittedly, there are dangers—some obvious and some subtle—in translating laboratory and classroom demonstrations of witness fallibility into conclusions about the accuracy of a particular witness's identification in a real life setting. Nevertheless, it would seem that the researchers have something to offer, and that where a case turns on uncorroborated eyewitness recognition, the courts should be receptive to expert testimony about the knowledge, gleaned from methodologically sound experimentation, concerning the factors that may have produced a faulty identification. Although the researcher must be circumspect in stating inferences about a particular witness's testimony, the pertinent research findings should assist the jury in evaluating a crucial piece of evidence. While expert testimony on the psychology of eyewitness identifications may not be necessary or appropriate in many cases, in those instances where the case turns on the eyewitness testimony and the expert's assistance could make a difference, the scientific knowledge generally should be admitted, either through expert testimony or judicial instructions concerning factors affecting eyewitness accuracy that are important to assessing the identification in question and that are not well understood by most jurors.

B. *Detection of Deception.* Popular belief has it that lying and consciousness of guilt are accompanied by emotion or excitement that expresses itself in bodily changes—the blush, the gasp, the quickened heartbeat, the sweaty palm, the dry mouth. The skilled cross-examiner may face the witness with his lies and involve him in a knot of new ones, so that these characteristic signs of lying become visible to the jury. This is part of the demeanor of the witness that the jury is told it may observe and consider upon credibility.

Internal stress also has been thought to accompany the process of lying. It is said that more than 4,000 years ago the Chinese would try the accused in the presence of a physician who, listening or feeling for a change in the heartbeat, would announce whether the accused was testifying truthfully. The modern "lie detectors" operate on the same general principle. While an interrogator puts questions to the suspect, the polygraph monitors and records several autonomic physiological functions, such as blood pressure, pulse rate, respiration rate and depth, and perspiration (by measuring skin conductance). In the most commonly used procedure, the "diagnosis" is made by comparing the responses to "control" questions with the reactions to "relevant" questions. If the autonomic disturbance associated with the relevant items seems greater or more persistent, then the subject is judged to be dissembling.

The validity and reliability of this procedure are hotly contested. Polygraph examiners claim that, properly administered, it is a highly effective means of detecting deception, and they cite figures such as 92%, 99%, and even 100% for its accuracy. Although some controlled experiments suggest that such accuracy is possible, most psychologists reviewing the literature are not impressed with these bold assertions. They see methodological flaws undermining the conclusions, they suggest figures in a much lower range, and they point out that the percentage figures of "accuracy" are inappropriate measures of validity. Attempts to determine the rate of false positives—of saying that someone is lying when he is actually telling the truth— have also been controversial. Some writers claim that these errors rarely occur but there are also studies and analyses that put the expected rate of false positives in excess of 35%. The skeptics also dispute the underlying theory. At best, the technique described above registers physiological correlates of anxiety, which is not quite the same thing as consciousness of guilt or lying. Questions can provoke inner turmoil even when they are answered truthfully. As one critic has put it, "the polygraph pens do no special dance when we are lying."[1] In addition, there are numerous countermeasures that a suspect can use to mislead the analyst, some of which are said to be effective and difficult to detect. It is feared that if the polygraph came into widespread use in court cases, these could cause the rate of false negatives—saying that the suspect is telling the truth when he is lying— to become intolerably high.

A variation on the polygraph examination procedure outlined above avoids some of these objections. This "conscious concealment" or "guilty knowledge" test does not necessarily attempt to evaluate the truthfulness of any verbal response. It requires that the examiner know facts that a guilty subject, but not an innocent person, would know. The examiner presents multiple choice questions about these facts. Consistently high autonomic responses to the incriminating choices indicates

some involvement in the offense. Experimentation with this technique suggests that it can achieve false positive error rates of ten percent or less.

Another group of devices that measure a physiological response to detect when a person is consciously concealing knowledge are the voice stress analyzers. They analyze the frequency spectrum of a speaker's voice to detect subaudible, involuntary tremors said to result from emotional stress. As of this writing, most of the scientific literature on these lie detection devices concludes that they have no validity.

The courts have not greeted the modern methods of lie detection with enthusiasm. Indeed, the case that announced the general-acceptance standard for the admissibility of scientific evidence involved a primitive version of the polygraph.[2] In the succeeding decades, many courts treated the early decision as if it established that polygraph results were inadmissible regardless of any improvements in the technology. With the erosion of the general-acceptance requirement and the accretion of polygraphy in government and business, however, a substantial number of courts have been willing to take a fresh look at the evidentiary value of the most commonly used polygraph tests. Three principal positions on admissibility can now be seen, with some back and forth movement into and out of each category. First, there is the traditional rule that the test results are inadmissible when offered by either party, either as substantive evidence or as relating to the credibility of a witness. As a corollary, the willingness or unwillingness of a party or witness to submit to examination is also inadmissible. Second, a substantial minority of jurisdictions have carved out an exception to the majority rule of unconditional exclusion. In these jurisdictions the trial court has the discretion to receive polygraph testimony if the parties stipulated to the admission of the results prior to the testing and if certain other condi-

§ 206

1. Lykken, as quoted in Kleinmuntz & Szucko, On the Fallibility of Lie Detection, 17 Law & Soc'y Rev. 85, 88 (1981).

2. See supra § 203.

tions are met. Third, in a handful of jurisdictions, admissibility even in the absence of a stipulation is said to be discretionary with the trial judge.

The widespread and strongly rooted reluctance to permit the introduction of polygraph evidence is grounded in a variety of concerns. The most frequently mentioned is that the technique is "unreliable" due to inherent failings, a shortage of qualified operators, and the prospect that "coaching" and practicing would become commonplace if the evidence were generally admissible. Yet, by themselves, such doubts are not sufficient to warrant a rigid exclusionary rule. A great deal of lay testimony routinely admitted is at least as unreliable and inaccurate, and other forms of scientific evidence involve risks of instrumental or judgmental error.

Rather, the argument against admissibility is, as usual, two-pronged. If the probative value of polygraph readings is slight (or would be if the barriers to admissibility were dropped), then their value easily is outweighed by the countervailing considerations. These counterweights are the danger that jurors would be unduly impressed with the "scientific" testimony on a crucial and typically determinative matter, that judicial and related resources would be squandered in producing and coping with the expert testimony, and that routine admissibility would put undesirable pressure on defendants to forfeit the right against self-incrimination.

Some of these concerns may be overstated, and the miscellaneous other reasons that courts sometimes give for excluding polygraph tests may not withstand analysis. Nonetheless, it would seem that opening up the matter to the discretion of the trial courts—without providing more detailed standards than the usual balancing prescription—could lead to untoward results. Nor is the "stipulation only" approach satisfactory. Whether polygraph testimony should be admitted is doubtful, but if it is to be received, clear standards should be developed as to whether such testimony is admissible solely for impeachment purposes, how important the testimony must be in the context of the

other evidence in the case for admissibility to be warranted, what type of examination should be administered, what level of training and competence examiners should have, what precautions should be taken against deceptive practices on the part of examinees, and what procedures would be best to give an independent or opposing expert a meaningful opportunity to view or review the examination and analysis.

C. *Drugs and Hypnosis.* Psychologists and psychiatrists have used hypnosis and hypnotic drugs for diagnosis and therapy. Resort to these techniques became prevalent in the treatment of traumatic war neuroses during World War II, and the methods have been applied to the treatment of hysterical amnesias, catatonic conditions, and psychosomatic disorders. They have also been employed to test the truthfulness of a witness' testimony as well as to enhance recall.

Although the scientific study of hypnosis began over 200 years ago, a single, satisfactory explanation of the phenomenon has yet to emerge. The scientific studies do make it clear, however, that people who are hypnotized or given so-called "truth serum" do not always tell the truth. On the other hand, the most directly pertinent studies do suggest that in certain circumstances hypnosis can enhance memory. The problem is that it also appears that it can *alter* memory. Hypnotized persons are highly suggestible, and some authorities believe that when a hypnotist encourages a subject to relate everything he can possibly remember, the subject produces fragments and approximations of memory in an effort to be cooperative. In addition, the subject may accept as his own recollections distortions inadvertently suggested by the hypnotist. Finally, the hypnotic session may reinforce the witness' confidence in erroneous memories.

Forensic applications of hypnosis can generate a variety of constitutional and evidentiary issues. A party may seek admission of statements a witness made while under hypnosis or narcoanalysis to show directly the existence of certain facts, to impeach or buttress credibility, or to show the basis for a psychiatric or psychological opinion. Similarly, a party may offer the in-court testimony of a witness even though this testimony may be influenced or "tainted" by this person's prior exposure to such interrogation.

The courts have been most reluctant to admit such statements or testimony. In People v. Ebanks,[3] the first case to raise the issue, a California court stated in 1897 that "the law of the United States does not recognize hypnotism." Since then the courts nearly always have excluded statements made under hypnosis or narcoanalysis, regardless of whether these statements are offered as substantive evidence or as bearing on credibility. Posthypnotic testimony as to recollections enhanced or evoked under hypnosis has produced more divergent holdings. A few courts have said that such testimony is generally admissible, with objections as to its accuracy bearing on the weight that the finder of fact should give it. But even in these jurisdictions there is a trend toward insisting that rigorous safeguards be observed before the hypnotically refreshed memories are admissible. The far more prevalent view is that testimony about the posthypnotic memories is inadmissible, although the once hypnotized witness may be permitted to testify to memories demonstrably held prior to hypnosis, and the Supreme Court held in Rock v. Arkansas[4] that the constitution precludes categorical exclusion of the hypnotically refreshed testimony of a criminal defendant who cannot present a meaningful defense without that testimony.

Typically, the courts adopting a strict exclusionary rule rely on the *Frye* test of general scientific acceptance, although the same result probably could be reached by inquiring directly into the relative costs and benefits of the testimony. Indeed, the more modern cases support their invocation and application of the general acceptance standard by examining scientific testimony or literature on the value of hypnosis for recovering memories and by referring to the usual concerns with scientific evidence—its suspected tendency to over-awe the jury and to consume time and resources—in a matter of particular sensitivity.

When an expert uses narcoanalysis or hypnosis in his or her examination of a person to determine whether the individual is insane, incompetent, or mentally incapacitated, the case for admissibility is much stronger. A few courts have excluded expert opinions based on these techniques, but this position seems difficult to defend even under the restrictive general acceptance standard. Most courts recognize that the opinions of the experts may be admitted and that the revelation of the details of what the subject said while under hypnosis or drugs is within the trial judge's discretion. Thus, the trial court may permit the expert to give his opinion and an explanation of the information on which the expert relied, but curb the introduction of the statements made under hypnosis or narcoanalysis.

D. *Profiles.* Psychological studies sometimes show a correlation between certain traits or characteristics and certain forms of behavior. When this is the case, one can construct a diagnostic or predictive "profile" for such behavior. For instance, retrospective analysis of individuals apprehended while smuggling drugs through airports shows that these persons tend to arrive from major points of distribution, to have little or no luggage with them, to look nervously about, to arrive in the early morning, and to have large amounts of cash in small bills. Studies of "accident prone" persons indicate that such factors as having poor eyesight, being relatively young or old, and acting impulsively, aggressively or rebelliously are prevalent in this group. Physicians regard certain patterns of physical injuries in children, which they designate the "battered child syndrome," as indicating repeated physical abuse. Indeed, we all evaluate information in the light of some such "profiles." Jurors, for example,

---

3. 117 Cal. 652, 665, 49 P. 1049, 1053 (1897), overruled on other grounds People v. Flannelly, 128 Cal. 83, 60 P. 670 (1900).

4. 483 U.S. 44 (1987).

can be said to bring to the courtroom their preconceived "profiles" which they then apply to decide who is lying and who is telling the truth, and who is likely to have committed an offense and who is innocent. Although there is no fundamental difference between the psychological and medical profiles and the more common, impressionistic ones, some of the former may have been derived in a more or less systematic and structured way, and some may have been tested by verifying that they give correct diagnoses or predictions when applied to new cases. The correlations obtained in such prospective studies measure the validity of the profiles.

In a growing number of cases, litigants have sought to introduce expert testimony as to the scientifically constructed or validated profiles. Women accused of murdering their husbands have pointed to the "battered wife syndrome" to support a plea of self-defense. Prosecutors in sexual abuse cases have relied on the "rape trauma syndrome" to negate a claim of consent, to explain conflicting statements or actions of the complainant, to prove criminal sexual penetration, and defendants have introduced evidence that a complainant did not experience the syndrome's symptoms. In sexual abuse cases involving children, prosecutors have relied on a similar "sexual abuse accommodation syndrome" for children to prove the fact of abuse or to explain the child's delay in reporting the abuse his or her retraction of the accusation, or other behavior apparently inconsistent with abuse. They also have relied on expert testimony that children who report sexual abuse generally are truthful. In child abuse and homicide cases, prosecutors have called witnesses to establish that defendants exhibited the "battering parent syndrome." And defendants accused of sexual offenses have offered testimony to the effect that they did not fit the profiles for sexual offenders.

When the plaintiff or the government offers evidence that the defendant fits an incriminating profile, it may be excluded under the rule that prohibits evidence of character to show conduct on a particular occasion.[5] Yet, arguably the rule should not bar admission in all such cases. After all, the rule rests on the premise that the marginal probative value of character evidence generally is low while the potential for distraction, time-consumption and prejudice is high. Where the profile is not itself likely to arouse sympathy or hostility, the argument for applying the rule against character evidence to prove conduct on a particular occasion is weakened. Conversely, if it were shown that the profile was both valid and revealing—that it distinguishes between offenders and non-offenders with great accuracy—then the balance might favor admissibility. It is far from clear, however, that any existing profile is this powerful.

When the profile evidence is used defensively (to show good character, to restore credibility, or to prove apprehension in connection with a claim of self-defense), it falls under an exception to the rule against character evidence.[6] Admissibility then should turn on the extent to which the expert testimony would assist the jury viewed in the light of the usual counterweights. The qualifications of the expert, the reliability and validity of using the profile, and the need for the evidence in light of what most jurors know about the behaviors in question, and whether the expert crosses the line between the general and the specific or tries to evaluate the truthfulness of the witness or a class of witnesses, thus affect the admissibility and of course the weight of the profile evidence.

In some ways, profile evidence resembles expert testimony, considered at the outset of this section, describing the results of psychological research into eyewitness identifications. In both instances, the expert provides background information that may contradict lay impressions and that the jury can apply to the case at hand, if persuaded to do so. Perhaps the greater receptivity of the appellate courts to psychological profile evidence stems from the fact that this type of testimony seems more like the clinical assessments rou-

---

5. See § 190 supra.

6. See supra §§ 191, 194.

tinely received from psychologists and physicians. In addition, considering the subject matter of most of the psychological profiles that have come to the attention of the courts, it is possible that a growing sensitivity to women's and children's issues has played some role.

§ 207. Particular Tests: Criminalistics: Identifying Persons and Things

Many of the techniques of scientific criminal investigation, or criminalistics, are aimed at identifying people or things. Fingerprinting, studying the trajectories and characteristics of bullets and firearms, examining questioned documents, detecting and identifying poisons and other drugs, microscopically comparing hair samples and fibers, and matching blood stains are among the better known examples. In addition, there is a vast array of less familiar techniques for detecting and analyzing what might be called "trace evidence" of criminal or other activity. These include other applications of microanalysis, forensic odontology, anthropology, entomology, and somewhat esoteric chemical and physical tests used in connection with fingerprints, firearms, glass fragments, hair, paints, explosions and fires, and questioned documents.

While these methods are unquestionably of great value in many investigations, their use in the courtroom can pose problems. Perhaps to emphasize the scientific quality of the analysis, or merely in an effort to be as precise as possible, expert witnesses may state the results or implications of their tests in quantitative, probabilistic terms—a practice that causes difficulty for the courts. Furthermore, a few of these analytic procedures or tests are themselves specially adapted or developed for forensic purposes and well known primarily in law enforcement circles. Consequently, the test of general scientific acceptance does not always work well in this context, and this incongruity can result in important opinions on the standards governing the admissibility of scientific evidence.

The spectrographic analysis of human voices illustrates this last point. Complex

sound waves, such as those involved in speech, can be understood mathematically as sums of simple waveforms of various frequencies. The frequency spectrum of such a sound wave is, in effect, a list of each such constituent frequency and its relative importance in describing the composite sound. For at least 40 years, electronic devices that analyze sound waves into these frequency components have been available. A spectrogram is a graphic representation of this information, that is, a picture of the frequency spectrum of a sound wave. In the 1960's, it was proposed that the spectral characteristics of a speaker's voice could serve to identify that speaker. The theory behind this suggestion was that individuals have different but largely stable patterns in the way they manipulate their lips, teeth, and so on in speaking. From the outset, this hypothesis has been controversial. If it is false, then comparisons of spectrograms should not produce consistently correct identifications. Despite a few early (and seemingly extravagant) claims of accurate identifications, subsequent studies providing better approximations of realistic forensic conditions report misidentifications at rates ranging from 18% (12% false negatives and 6% false positives) to 70 and 80% (including 42% false positives). Many scientists continue to express doubts about the reliability and validity of the current technique.

Most courts applying the general scientific acceptance test to voice spectrographic evidence have held the evidence inadmissible. In fact, this evidence has inspired some of the most spirited and thoughtful defenses of the general acceptance standard for scientific evidence. On the other hand, faith in the method and a belief that jurors will not find it overly impressive have prompted some courts to bend the *Frye* test to the breaking point in order to conclude that the evidence should be admissible. Whatever standard may be applied, however, it seems that until further research makes the validity of the technique plainer, the courts will remain divided over the admissibility of voice spectrographic identification.

§ 208. Statistical Studies: Surveys and Opinion Polls

Samuel Johnson once remarked that "You don't have to eat the whole ox to know the hide is tough." In the past, courts required litigants to dismember and devour an ox or two in order to prove a point. However, with the development and implementation of scientific survey methods, the courts are much more receptive to proof based on sample data. The Federal and Uniform Rules sweep aside traditional hearsay objections and allow the evidence to come in, if it is reasonably reliable, as the basis for an expert opinion. Specially commissioned surveys, and especially opinion polls, have been used to support motions for a change of venue in criminal cases, to show consumer perceptions in trademark and misleading advertising cases, to unmask community standards in obscenity prosecutions, and for numerous other purposes. Advocates have also relied on pre-existing research involving sample data in product liability, food and drug, environmental, and other cases. The modern opinions have said that case-specific surveys are generally admissible if they are conducted according to the principles accepted by social scientists and statisticians for gathering and analyzing survey data. This section therefore attempts to give an overview of these principles—adherence to which affects the weight as well as the admissibility of survey evidence. As the material collected in the notes will show, the courts have carefully examined whether the conclusions of the survey researchers rest on sample data collected in such a way as to permit fair inferences about the relevant factual questions.

Although many refinements are possible, the basic ideas behind scientific survey techniques are simple enough. The researcher tries to collect information from a manageable portion (a sample) of a larger group (a population) in order to learn something about the population. Usually some number or numbers are used to characterize the population, and these are called parameters. For example, the proportion of all consumers who

would mistake one product for another because of a similarity in the brand names is a population parameter. Sample data leads to statistics, such as the proportion of the persons in the sample who are confused by the similarity. These sample statistics are then used to estimate the population parameters. If 50% of the sample studied exhibited confusion between the products with the similar brand names, then one might conclude that 50% of the population would be confused. Under some circumstances, statistical methods enable the researcher not only to make an estimate, but to state the probability that such an estimate would differ from the unknown parameter by a given amount—that is, to quantify the error that may be lurking in the estimate.

Sampling underlies almost every pertinent research effort. Descriptive surveys, like those introduced in connection with change of venue motions, are almost always confined to a sample of the entire population. Surveys looking for causal explanations (such as a survey of homicide rates in states that do and states that do not have capital punishment) usually involve samples. Even experiments designed to investigate causation, such as a trial of a new drug, typically produce only sample data. Many such surveys are nonverbal. Since an employer's records can be inspected, no one needs to poll the current employees to obtain data on the distribution of wages paid to men as opposed to women. Other surveys are personal or verbal, using survey interviewers or written questionnaires.

What factors are likely to make such surveys produce accurate as opposed to misleading estimates? We can identify two major categories of errors: random errors and non-random errors. There are many potential sources of non-random, or systematic errors. In personal surveys, these include the specification of the population to be sampled, the technique for eliciting responses, the wording of the questions, the method for choosing and finding respondents, and the failure to pose questions that address the proper issues. Unless those sources of non-random error cancel each other out, any estimates made on the basis of the sample data will be biased. Making the sample size larger offers no protection against bias. It only produces a larger number of biased observations.

Random errors arise at two levels. The first is with respect to the observations on each unit sampled. In a nonverbal study, a measuring instrument (such as an instrument to determine breath alcohol content) might well give slightly different readings even on identical samples. A person seeking to get rid of an interviewer may say whatever pops into mind. The process for making individual measurements or observations is rarely perfectly reliable. The second kind of random error results from variability from one sample to the next. One sample of air expelled from the lungs may be slightly different from the next in its concentration of alcohol. Even though great care may be taken to assure that the people selected for interviews are representative of the population, there can be no guarantee that another sample selected by the same procedure would give identical responses. As such, even if all the answers or measurements are individually free from error, sampling variability remains a source of statistical, or chance error.

If methods known as probability sampling are employed, however, the magnitude of the sampling error (but not of the non-random errors) can be estimated. Probability sampling also has been shown to be very effective in producing representative samples. The reason is that unlike human beings, blind chance is impartial. Probability sampling uses an objective chance process to pick the sample. It leaves no discretion to the interviewers. As a result, the researcher can compute the chance that any particular unit in the population will be selected for the sample. Stated another way, a probability sample is one in which each unit of the sampling frame has a known, non-zero probability of being selected. So-called "convenience" or "quota" samples do not have this property, and they are acceptable only in very special circumstances. A common type of probability sampling is simple random sampling, in which

every unit has the same probability of being sampled. It amounts to drawing names at random without replacement.

The statistics derived from observations or measurements of random samples permit one to estimate the parameters of the population. In a consumer confusion survey for instance, some proportion of the sample of consumers who are interviewed will indicate confusion between the products. If the sample is a simple random sample, and if there are no non-random errors, then this sample proportion is an unbiased estimator of the proportion for all consumers. But it is only an estimate. After all, another random sample probably would not include precisely the same persons, and it probably would produce a slightly different proportion of responses indicating confusion. There is no single figure that expresses the extent of this statistical error. There are only probabilities. If one were to draw a second random sample, find the proportion of confused consumers in this group, then do the same for a third random sample, a fourth, and so on, one would obtain a distribution of sample proportions fluctuating about some central value. Some would be far away from the mean, but most would be closer. Pursuing this logic in a rigorous way, the statistician computes a "confidence interval" and gives an "interval estimate" for the population proportion. He or she may report that at a 90% confidence level, the population proportion is 50% plus or minus 10%. What this means is that if the same method for drawing samples and interviewing the customers were repeated a very large number of times, and if a 90% confidence interval were computed about each sample, 90% of these interval estimates would be correct. This many would include the population proportion, whatever that number happens to be.

Although testimony as to confidence intervals often is received in cases involving survey evidence, its meaning apparently remains obscure in many cases. Note that a confidence of, say 90% does not necessarily mean that the interval estimate has a 90% probability of being correct. Strictly speaking, all that the classical statistical methodology reveals is that the particular interval was obtained by a method that gives intervals that would capture the true proportion in 90% of all possible samples. But each such interval estimate could be different. Thus, the "confidence" pertains to the process rather than to any particular result. Despite this difficulty in interpreting a confidence interval, the technique does give the finder of fact some idea of the risk of error in equating the sample proportion to the population figure. If the interval is small, even for a high level of "confidence," then the sample proportion is reasonably accurate, at least in the sense that taking more, or larger samples probably would give similar results.

The width of the confidence interval depends on three things. For a given sample, there is a trade-off between the level of confidence and the narrowness of the interval. One can be sure that the population proportion lies somewhere between zero and one. The confidence is 100% but the interval is so broad as to be useless. Lowering the confidence level narrows the range of the estimate; but there is more risk in concluding that the population value lies within the narrower interval. Second, for a given confidence and a fixed sample size, the width of the interval depends on how homogeneous the population is. If nearly every consumer would be confused (or nearly no one would be), then there will be minimal sampling variability, since almost all the possible samples can be expected to look alike. Hence, the confidence interval for any sample will be very narrow. On the other hand, if the population is highly variable, then there are more chances to draw aberrant samples, and the computed confidence interval for any sample will be larger. Third, whatever the makeup of the population, larger samples give more reliable results than smaller ones. However, the point of diminishing returns rapidly is reached in that adding the same amount to the sample size does little to narrow the confidence interval. It is wrong to believe that one always needs to sample a substantial proportion of a large population to obtain an accurate estimate of a population parameter.

In assessing the statistical error of a survey, therefore, the courts should look to the interval estimates rather than to untutored intuitions as to how large a sample is needed. Deciding what level of confidence is appropriate in a particular case, however, is a policy question and not a statistical issue. Finally, in making use of surveys, it is important to remember that the statistical analysis does not address the non-random sources of error. A small confidence interval is not worth much if the data collection is badly flawed.

§ 209. Statistical Studies: Correlations and Causes: Statistical Evidence of Discrimination

Survey evidence, as we described it in the previous section, involved sampling from some population, deriving statistics from the sample data, and offering some conclusion about the population in light of these sample statistics. In this section, we describe applications and extensions of this approach used to supply and interpret evidence on the issue of causation. In environmental or drug litigation, for instance, a party may seek to prove that a chemical is toxic or carcinogenic. Laboratory experiments, clinical tests, or epidemiologic studies may be relied on, but the conclusions of the scientific studies will involve statistical assessments. In civil rights cases, a party may seek to prove that a class or an individual has been subjected to unlawful discrimination. Again, statistical evidence may be useful. In antitrust litigation, a party may use statistical analysis to show illegal conduct and its effects. In business litigation generally, a party may apply statistical techniques to estimate lost profits or other damages resulting from illegal conduct. In these and other sorts of cases, the statistics, and inferences drawn from them, usually will be admissible via the testimony of a suitably qualified expert.

The weight that may be given such testimony will depend, of course, on the skill of counsel and the ability and preparation of the witness. In addition, the methods that the expert uses to analyze and interpret that data, so as to assist the court or jury in understanding it, may be of great importance in determining the outcome. This section outlines one of the statistical concepts most frequently encountered in connection with sophisticated statistical proofs. Because most cases addressing the usefulness of this concept currently arise in the context of discrimination issues, we shall draw on a few of the developments in this area to illustrate some general points about the presentation of statistical evidence.

The courts have relied heavily on statistical evidence in cases in which a criminal defendant alleges that he was indicted by an unconstitutionally selected grand jury or an unconstitutionally empaneled petit jury. There is no constitutionally permissible basis for systematically excluding, say, members of defendant's race from the population of citizens who are eligible for jury duty. Where direct evidence of discrimination is unavailable, or where additional proof is desired, statistical methods have been pressed into service. The usual procedure is to compare the proportion of the persons eligible for jury service who are in the class allegedly discriminated against with the corresponding proportion appearing on jury venires or pools over some period of time. Substantial underrepresentation is taken as evidence of discrimination. In early cases, the courts made purely intuitive assessments of the disparity in the proportions.

Many recent cases use formal statistical reasoning to evaluate the quantitative evidence. The logic begins from the assumption that selection of potential jurors is a random process, like blindly drawing differently colored marbles from an urn, in which the chance that a person in the protected class will be selected is the same in each instance. Under the "null" hypothesis, which is consistent with the position that there is no discrimination, the probability of picking a member of the protected class each time is simply the overall proportion of these individuals in the eligible population. The alternative to this hypothesis is not always specified clearly. The statistical analyst calculates the probability that so few members of the protected class

would be chosen for jury service if each selection were made by the random process described above with the parameter stated in the null hypothesis. This probability is called a "P-value." It states the chance that the observed disparity resulted from bad luck, or coincidence. If it is very small, it is taken to indicate that the null hypothesis is implausible. If the P-value, or probability of the data given the assumptions behind the null hypothesis, is large, it is taken to indicate that this hypothesis of no discrimination is consistent with the data. The P-value thus serves as an index of the statistical force of the quantitative evidence. The smaller the P-value, the more unlikely it is that the statistical disparity was the result of the chance process.

But it is not the only such index, and some statisticians do not think that it is the best. One problem with its use in court is the tendency of some expert witnesses or judges to assume that because there is an arbitrary convention of insisting on P-values of .05 or less before labelling scientific findings "statistically significant," this same number should be required before the factfinder may rely on the quantitative results. If the P-value is not to be misleading, its meaning must be clearly understood. The factfinder must realize that the P-value is not itself evidence. It is not the statistic that directly states how large the observed underrepresentation is. It is merely one measure of the probative force of statistical evidence, and an incomplete measure at that. This is not to deny that it is a useful concept. Properly understood, it may assist the court (or, in appropriate cases, the jury) in assessing the statistical evidence.

This approach also is used in employment discrimination cases. There is more difficulty in defining the relevant population from which employees are drawn, there are more variables to consider, the sample sizes tend to be smaller, and the mechanics of computing P-values may differ, but the meaning of the P-value and of "statistical significance" is the same. When complicated statistical models are used to account for the effects of many variables, however, many subtle errors are possible, and an uncritical acceptance of the estimates derived from these models and their calculated P-values can be misleading. In short, for this form of scientific testimony, the battle is not usually over the admissibility of the statistical evidence or the use of concepts like the P-value to assess the evidence. Rather, the battlelines are drawn when it comes to the weight that should be given the evidence and to transforming methods and conventions of statistical inference into rules of law.

§ 210. Probabilities as Evidence: Identification Evidence Generally

The previous two sections discussed the use of probability calculations in connection with statistical studies. When the statistical analyst takes properly collected sample data, computes some statistics such as a proportion, a difference between two means, or a regression coefficient, and calculates a P-value or a confidence interval for each such statistic, the courts are willing to rely on the probabilities in assessing the force of the statistical evidence. Especially in criminal cases, however, the courts are substantially more reluctant to admit probability calculations intended to show the identity of a wrongdoer. This section examines the admissibility of probability calculations relating to the myriad forms of identification evidence—eyewitness testimony, blood tests, fingerprints, bitemarks, questioned document examinations, microanalysis, and so on. The next section focuses on the role of probability calculations in paternity litigation.

In one important sense, all evidence is statistical. Admittedly, courts sometimes suggest that evidence about a class of objects cannot be used to support a conclusion about a particular member of the class. But we rely on such evidence all the time. Law schools admit students with high grades and test scores because they have had favorable experiences with other such students, surgeons perform drastic operations on patients because they have had beneficial effects in some proportion of cases in the past, legislatures enact statutes making it an offense to drive with a blood alcohol concentration exceeding

an amount seen to impair the functioning of a sample of persons, and juries tend to convict or acquit defendants because of hunches or beliefs about how certain classes of people behave, and they award damages in wrongful death cases with the assistance of mortality tables that reflect the experiences of many other men or women.

So, too, any expert giving any opinion on whether the scientific test identifies the defendant as being the person who left the incriminating trace, such as a fingerprint, bullet, or bloodstain, necessarily bases this conclusion on an understanding or impression of how similar the items being compared are and how common it is to find items with these similarities. If these beliefs have any basis in fact, it is to be found in the general experience of the criminalists or more exacting statistical studies of these matters. In brief, the reluctance to allow testimony or argument about probabilities must be justified, if at all, on the basis of something other than an undifferentiated claim about the logical weakness of relying on probabilities derived from statistics about other persons or things. In fact, a variety of more conventional concerns about "probability evidence" surface in the decisions in this area. These relate to the probative value of the explicit quantification and the tendency of the seemingly impressive numbers to mislead or confuse the jury.

To begin with, for more than a hundred years there have been attempts to compute the probability of observing a conjunction of certain incriminating characteristics by assuming that each characteristic is statistically independent and that the probabilities of these presumably independent characteristics could be obtained by introspection. In what may be the most notorious of these cases, police apprehended a man and a woman fitting descriptions supplied by eyewitnesses near the scene of a robbery. The prosecutor proposed figures for the frequencies of such things as an interracial couple in a car, a girl with a pony tail, a partly yellow automobile, a man with a mustache, and so on. A mathematics professor testified to the rule that the joint probability of a series of independent events is the product of the probabilities of each event. Applying this rule to the "conservative estimates" that he had propounded, the prosecutor concluded that there was but one chance in 12 million that any couple possessed the distinctive characteristics of the defendants, and he argued that "the chances of anyone else besides these defendants being there, * * * having every similarity, * * * is something like one in a billion."[1]

In these cases, the appellate courts hold that it is error to admit such testimony on the ground that the hypothesized values used in computing the probability of the joint event are sheer speculation. Because such computations therefore have little basis in fact and are presented in the guise of expert analysis, they are excluded under the principle that their prejudicial impact clearly outweighs their probative value.

In another group of cases, some data can be employed in calculating the joint probability. While many forensic experts are content to describe the points of similarity between the incriminating traces and material taken from the defendant or his belongings and to leave it to the jury to decide how unlikely it would be to find all these similarities by mere coincidence, from time to time, the experts testify to vanishingly small probabilities. The appellate responses to estimates that have some empirical basis are more divided. In the exceptional case that finds error in the admission of computations that the court considers well founded, the rationale seems to be that the jury would misconstrue the meaning of the probability or overemphasize the number, or that it would be too difficult to explain its true meaning.

In evaluating these decisions, it is important to distinguish between explicit calculations of the probability of guilt or coincidence and the presentation of relevant background statistics. If the offender, whoever he or she may have been, left a bloodstain at the scene of the crime that matches the defendant's blood types, the scientific evidence cannot be interpreted intelligently without some knowledge of how frequently these blood types occur in the relevant population. We have already remarked that the expert who offers any conclusion as to whether the defendant left the incriminating trace is relying, either explicitly or *sub rosa*, on estimates of these quantities. Without being informed of such background statistics, the jury is left to its own speculations. Where reasonable estimates of the population frequencies are available, they should not be kept from the jury. Thus, courts routinely admit testimony estimating such frequencies, often without objection. To be sure, there are risks in this policy. A juror who hears that only one out of every five, or for that matter, one out of every 10,000 persons, possesses the traits that characterize the true offender, may be tempted to subtract this statistic from one to arrive at the incorrect conclusion that the remainder is the probability that the defendant is guilty. Nevertheless, it should not be so difficult for defense counsel to correct any such misapprehension by pointing out that the frequency estimate merely establishes that the defendant is one member of a class of persons who have the incriminating characteristics. The distribution of these characteristics in the population at large simply determines whether this class of persons whom the scientific evidence would identify as a possible offender is large or small.

In principle, a statistician could do more than state the frequency at which the scientific tests would implicate persons. First, in those cases in which the identifying characteristics were not the very basis on which the defendant was picked from the general population, the expert could be explicit about the P-value for the findings. Second, valiant efforts have been made to calculate conditional probabilities pertaining to the number of people in some populations who have the incriminating characteristics. One could imagine ad-

§ 210

1. People v. Collins, 68 Cal.2d 319, 66 Cal.Rptr. 497,

438 P.2d 33 (1968).

mitting testimony about these probabilities. Finally, and perhaps most satisfying from the mathematical standpoint, it has been proposed that the expert apply Bayes' rule to show jurors how the frequency data would increase a previously established probability that the person tested is the one who left the incriminating traces. The mechanics of this approach are briefly stated in the next section. The usual suggestion is that the expert present an illustrative chart showing how, in view of the frequency with which the incriminating traits are to be found in the relevant population, the identification evidence would affect a broad spectrum of prior probabilities. The expert need not ask the jurors to choose any particular prior probability to express their estimate of the strength of the non-test evidence. A few writers suggest that statisticians go beyond this, and counsel jurors to form prior and posterior probabilities.

This last proposal has been attacked on both philosophical and practical grounds. It has been said in reply that the pragmatic objections are the more persuasive. Certainly, having an expert testify to the "probability of guilt" given the evidence would be inadvisable. But whether the benefits of using this method of statistical inference solely to educate the jury by displaying the probative force of the evidentiary findings would be worth the costs in terms of time-consumption and possible confusion is a closer question. Outside of the parentage testing area, however, Bayesian calculations rarely are seen in court.

In general, it appears that the explicit use of the theories of probability and statistical inference, either as a basis for the opinions of the experts themselves or as a course of education for jurors in how to think about scientific identification evidence, remains controversial. As long as counsel and the experts do not try to place a scientific seal of approval on results not shown to be scientifically based, however, it would seem that there is room for some judicious use of these theories to put the identification evidence in reasonable perspective.

§ 211. Probabilities as Evidence: Paternity Testing

Problems of questioned or disputed parentage have plagued mankind, perhaps ever since the origin of the species. The Talmud tells of a case in which a widow married her brother-in-law before the required three month waiting period after the death of her husband. She gave birth to a child scarcely six months later. The rabbis reasoned that either the child was a full term baby fathered by the deceased husband or a premature child of the second husband. Since the mother had shown no visible signs of pregnancy three months after her first husband's death, the matter was not easy to settle. As one rabbi said, "it is a doubt."

Many legislators, courts, and commentators now think that newly discovered serologic and statistical methods permit such doubts to be dispelled in the vast majority of cases. In section 205(B) we described the methods of detecting genetic markers and the principles of human genetics that allow this information to be applied to resolve cases of disputed parentage. We saw that a majority of states now admit the results of blood and tissue typing tests not merely to exclude the alleged father as the biological father, but, when he is not excluded, to help prove that he is the biological father. In most, if not all of these jurisdictions, an expert may go beyond reporting the positive test findings. To assist the trier of fact in interpreting these positive results, he or she, under generally applicable evidentiary principles,[1] may give reliable estimates of the frequencies that characterize the distribution of the incriminating genetic markers in the population of males of the pertinent race. That is, if the population data warrant it, the expert may testify to the proportion of the relevant male population that the test would exclude—a parameter that is sometimes converted into the "probability of exclusion." To this extent, the procedures are

1. See supra § 210.

essentially the same as those that apply to scientific identification evidence generally.

Yet, many experts believe that testimony limited to the test results and the probability of exclusion is incomplete and sometimes misleading. They would prefer to testify to "the probability of paternity," and many jurisdictions allow such testimony. Although most states have statutes that permit positive test results to be received into evidence, not all of these statutes say whether the probabilities derived from the test results also are admissible. At the other extreme, a few statutes—of dubious value—not only allow such testimony, but rely on the "probability of paternity" to trigger a presumption of paternity. In the absence of a statute explicitly authorizing the expert to give the "probability of paternity," admissibility should turn on whether probability testimony is sufficiently likely to aid the jury in properly assessing the probative value of the positive findings. To answer this question, one must first understand what the "probability of paternity" is. For this reason, this section indicates how this probability is computed. It then argues that at least one version of this approach is not suited for courtroom use and suggests some alternative methods of assisting the jury or court to weigh the positive test results along with the other evidence in the case to reach a decision as to paternity. Finally, it describes special difficulties in probability computations involving DNA typing.

The probability of paternity, as conventionally computed, is a deceptively simple application of an elementary result in probability theory discovered by the Reverend Thomas Bayes in the nineteenth century. Bayes' formula can be interpreted as showing the effect of a new item of evidence on a previously established probability. Suppose, to save space, we let B stand for the event that the alleged father is the biological father, we let Odds(B) designate the odds in favor of this event (before we learn the outcome of the laboratory tests), and we use the letter T to denote the test evidence (the phenotypes of the mother, child and father). Most testifying experts who realize how the probability of paternity is calculated take the prior odds to be 1 (i.e., 50–50) on the theory that doing so shows that they are neutral as between plaintiff and defendant. Adopting these odds amounts to assuming that the accusation of paternity is as likely to be true as to be false. Bayes' rule tells us how to update these Odds(B) to account for the test results T. In particular, it says to multiply the prior odds by a quantity called the likelihood ratio to produce the new odds that the alleged father is the biological father, which we write as $\text{Odds}(B > T)$, for the odds of B given the test results T. In symbols, $\text{Odds}(B \mid T) = LR \times \text{Odds}(B)$, where LR is an abbreviation for likelihood ratio. For the standard assumption that the prior odds are 1, the posterior odds of paternity are just $\text{Odds}(B \mid T) = LR$.

This likelihood ratio can be computed as the ratio of two probabilities. The numerator is the probability that the phenotypes T would be found if the alleged father really were the biological father. The denominator is the probability that the phenotypes T would be found if the alleged father were not the biological father. In other words, the likelihood ratio states how many times more likely it is that the tests would show the phenotypes T if the alleged father were the biological father than if he were not. It often is referred to as the "paternity index." The computation of the numerator is relatively simple. It is just the probability that a man with the phenotypes of the alleged father and a woman with the mother's phenotypes would produce an offspring with the child's phenotypes. The computation of the denominator is trickier. The denominator is the probability that a man other than the alleged father would produce an offspring with the child's phenotypes. But which man? Some "alternative men" could not produce this type of child. They are the ones whom the tests would exclude. Others would have the same probability of producing this type of child as does the alleged father. These are the ones who have the same phenotypes that he does. Still others would produce this type of child with other probabilities. Their phenotypes differ from the alleged father's but are still consistent with the genotypes of the biological father. The conventional solution is to invent a "random man"—a hypothetical entity whose genotypes (and hence phenotypes) are a kind of average across all these men. Assuming that the estimates of the population gene frequencies are completely free from error, the computation can proceed.

Suppose, for example, that given the estimated gene frequencies, it is 50 times more likely to obtain a child with the observed phenotypes from a man with the alleged father's phenotypes than from the imaginary "random man." Bayes' formula then states that Odds $(B \mid T) = 50 \times$ Odds(B). For prior odds of 1, this means that the odds that the alleged father is the biological father are 50 to 1. The corresponding probability of paternity is $50/51 = .98$, or 98%. These are the kind of numbers of which the experts testifying to the "probability of paternity" speak.

Should the results of these calculations ever be admissible? Resorting to the "random man" to form the likelihood ratio and postulating prior odds of 1 create grave problems for any courtroom presentation. It is tempting to dismiss the choice of the prior odds as contrived, speculative, and lacking any scientific basis. It sounds like some of the classic cases in which an expert multiplied together probabilities that had no basis in fact.[2] Here, however, there are some hard data suggesting that these prior odds understate the incidence of truthful accusations of paternity and therefore favor the alleged father, who would be the objecting party.

Nonetheless, to serve up any single number computed in this fashion as "the" probability of paternity connotes more than the mathematical logic possibly can deliver. Most persons hearing that the probability of paternity is 98% would think that the alleged father's role in the affair is conclusively confirmed. Indeed, the experts have developed standardized phrases, which they call "verbal predicates," to characterize the numbers. Yet, in view of the way in which the "probability of paternity" is calculated, many men—all those

who share the alleged father's phenotypes—would have "probabilities of paternity" of 98%. Some non-excluded men might have even higher "probabilities of paternity." In more than one case, a man later shown to be sterile had a "probability of paternity" of this magnitude as determined from HLA typing. Unless an expert can somehow explain that the calculated "probability of paternity" is not the chance that the alleged father, as distinguished from all other possible fathers, is the biological father, the expert should not be allowed to put this "probability" before the jury. Furthermore, it would appear that any accurate explanation of why the "probability of paternity" does not mean the probability that the alleged father, rather than any other man, is the biological father, and then of what it does mean, would be hopelessly confusing. Consequently, testimony as to the "probability of paternity," computed with a fixed and undisclosed prior probability of one-half, should not be allowed. Such testimony seems unable to fulfill its only legitimate function— assisting the jury in weighing the positive test results along with the other evidence in the case. The same rule of exclusion should apply to the "verbal predicates" that some experts attach to probabilities of paternity computed in this way.

This rule would not prohibit the introduction of the serologic evidence and an explanation of its significance. The fact that competently performed serologic tests prove the alleged father's phenotypes to be consistent with the claim of paternity is always relevant and useful evidence. The strength of this evidence, like other forms of identification evidence, can be shown to some extent by testimony about the probability of exclusion or related concepts.

There is also a strong argument for using a Bayesian approach to help the jury evaluate the evidence. Instead of viewing the evidence from the position of a laboratory, which, having nothing else to go on, is driven to such artifacts as using prior odds of one, one can adjust the focus to the trial, where other

2. See supra § 210.

evidence is available to the decisionmaker. As noted in section 210, the expert could show the jury how the test results would affect not merely a prior probability of one-half, but a whole spectrum of prior probabilities. It could be made clear to the jurors that the purpose of this exposition is not to compel them to assign a prior probability to the other evidence in the case, but to permit them to gauge the strength of the positive test findings and to weigh these findings, along with the other evidence, in the manner that they think best. By using variable instead of fixed prior odds, the expert can display the statistical force of the evidence without attempting to quantify—on the basis of incomplete information—the one thing that the jury must decide with the benefit of all the evidence in the case: the probability of paternity.

Even if an illustrative rather than a fixed prior probability is used to generate the probability of paternity, however, it is important to recognize that the likelihood ratio does not include all the information pertinent to assessing the laboratory findings. As we have described it (and as it typically computed), this ratio assumes that there is no ambiguity or doubt about the determination of phenotypes and the frequencies of the related genotypes in the relevant population.

Although these assumptions are defensible in some cases involving red blood cell, HLA or serum protein tests, they have been forcefully attacked with regard to certain types of DNA tests. The traditional paternity tests, which detect gene products, can be supplemented by tests of the genetic material itself. The overall logic of the probability calculation—multiplying prior odds by a likelihood ratio—is the same, but restriction fragment length polymorphism (RFLP) matching entails measurement error that poses problems in declaring a match and in determining population frequencies for specific bands. In principle, this uncertainty can be incorporated into the likelihood ratio for single-locus VNTR probes, but even with this refinement, the validity of the assumption of statistical independence of bands detected with VNTR probes and the relevant population in which to measure the frequencies of these bands are debatable. Nevertheless, it has been suggested that the exquisite power of some DNA probes to discriminate individual characteristics may yet obviate the need for detailed calculations of the troublesome "probability of paternity."

Title 8

DEMONSTRATIVE EVIDENCE

Chapter 21

DEMONSTRATIVE EVIDENCE

Table of Sections

§ 212. Demonstrative Evidence in General

There is a type of evidence which consists of things, e.g., weapons, whiskey bottles, writings, and wearing apparel, as distinguished from the assertions of witnesses (or hearsay declarants) about things. Most broadly viewed, this type of evidence includes all phenomena which can convey a relevant firsthand sense impression to the trier of fact, as opposed to those which serve merely to report the secondhand sense impressions of others. Thus, for example, demeanor evidence, i.e. the bearing, expression, and manner of a witness while testifying,[1] is an instance of the type of evidence here considered, but the statements which he utters are not.

Evidence from which the trier of fact may derive a relevant firsthand sense impression is almost unlimited in its variety. As a result, the problem of satisfactorily labeling and classifying has proved a difficult one, and it will be seen variously referred to as real, autoptic, demonstrative, tangible, and objective. For present purposes, the term "demonstrative" will be used to refer to the generic class, though it should be noted that some courts employ this term in a more limited sense.[2]

Since "seeing is believing," and demonstrative evidence appeals directly to the senses of the trier of fact, it is today universally felt that this kind of evidence possesses an immediacy and reality which endow it with particularly persuasive effect. Largely as a result of this potential, the use of demonstrative evi-

---

§ 212

1. While demeanor evidence is analytically a type of demonstrative evidence, it is inseparably related to oral testimony and is thus treated elsewhere. See § 245, infra.

2. I.e., as contrasted with "real" evidence. See discussion at p. 392–3 infra.

dence of all types has increased dramatically during recent years, and the trend seems certain to continue in the immediate future. At the same time, demonstrative evidence remains the exception rather than the rule, and its use raises certain problems for a juridical system the mechanics of which are essentially geared to the reception of *viva voce* testimony by witnesses. Some of these problems are so commonly raised by the offer of demonstrative evidence, and are so frequently made the bases of objections to its admission, that they deserve preliminary note.

It has already been noted that evidence from which the trier of fact may derive his own perceptions, rather than evidence consisting of the reported perceptions of others, possesses unusual force. Consequently, demonstrative evidence is frequently objected to as prejudicial, a term which is today generally defined as suggesting "decision on an improper basis, commonly, though not necessarily, an emotional one." A great deal of demonstrative evidence has the capacity to generate emotional responses such as pity, revulsion, or contempt, and where this capacity outweighs the value of the evidence on the issues in litigation, exclusion is appropriate.

Again, even if no essentially emotional response is likely to result, demonstrative evidence may convey an impression of objective reality to the trier. Thus, the courts are frequently sensitive to the objection that the evidence is "misleading," and zealous to insure that there is no misleading differential between objective things offered at trial and the same or different objective things as they existed at the time of the events or occurrences in litigation.

Further, and apart from its bearing on the issues of the case, demonstrative evidence as a class presents certain essentially logistical difficulties for the courts. Since the courts are basically structured, architecturally and otherwise, to receive the testimony of witnesses, the presentation of demonstrative evidence may require that the court physically move to receive it, or that unwieldly objects or para-

phernalia be introduced into the courtroom, actions which may occasion delay and confusion. Finally, while oral testimony is easily incorporated into a paper record for purposes of appellate review, demonstrative evidence will sometimes be insusceptible to similar preservation and transmission.

The cogency and force of the foregoing objections to the introduction of demonstrative evidence will obviously vary greatly with the nature of the particular item offered, and the purpose and need for its introduction in the particular case. Since the types of demonstrative evidence and the purposes for which it is sought to be introduced are extremely varied, it is generally viewed as appropriate to accord the trial judge broad discretion in ruling upon the admissibility of many types of demonstrative evidence.[3]

Despite its great variety, certain classifications of demonstrative evidence appear both valid and useful. First, like other evidence, it may be either direct or circumstantial. If a material issue in the case is whether an object does or does not possess a perceptible feature, characteristic, or quality, the most satisfactory method of demonstrating the truth of the matter will ordinarily be to produce the object so that the trier of fact may perceive the quality, or its absence, for himself. Thus, where a party seeks damages for the loss of a limb or for an injury leaving a disfiguring scar, exhibition of the person will constitute direct evidence of a material fact. Similarly, exhibition of the chattel purchased in an action for breach of warranty will, at least if the quality or characteristic warranted is a perceivable one, constitute direct evidence on the issue of condition. In these cases no process of inference, at least in the ordinary sense, is required. Similarly, exhibition of a person to establish such facts as race and age may perhaps also be considered examples of demonstrative evidence of a direct sort, though the immediate perceptability of these qualities may on occasion be subject to more doubt.

Demonstrative evidence may also be offered for its circumstantial value, i.e., as the basis

---

3. E.g., the types of demonstrative evidence discussed in §§ 213–216 infra.

for an inference beyond those facts which are perceivable. Such is the case when the exhibition of a person is made for the purpose of demonstrating his relationship to another, as in a filiation proceeding. The use of demonstrative evidence is even more clearly circumstantial when articles of clothing worn at the time of his arrest by the defendant in a robbery prosecution are exhibited to the jury to demonstrate their conformity with the descriptions of the robber given by witnesses.

The practical significance of the foregoing distinction lies in the fact that direct evidence, because of its eminently satisfactory character, will generally be admitted even where it is likely to occasion some prejudice or physical difficulty. Thus, gruesome photographs which directly show a material fact have been held properly admitted in innumerable criminal cases, often without regard to their obvious capacity to inflame the jury. The better view, reflected in some recent decisions, is that the admission even of demonstrative evidence which directly portrays material facts calls for the exercise of judicial discretion.

When circumstantial evidence is involved, in the present context as elsewhere, the trial judge will generally be viewed as possessing a broader discretionary power to weigh the probative value of the evidence against whatever prejudice, confusion, surprise and waste of time are entailed, and to determine admissibility accordingly.

As with other circumstantial evidence, of course, demonstrative evidence offered for its circumstantial value may give rise to more than one inference. Thus introduction of a firearm taken from the defendant on his arrest and shown to be similar to that used in the commission of the offense charged may imply both that the defendant was the robber and that the defendant is a dangerous individual given to carrying firearms. If a permissible inference is present, admission will generally be upheld, a limiting instruction being deemed sufficient to prevent any untoward damage.

Again, demonstrative evidence may be classified as to whether the item offered did or did not play an actual and direct part in the incident or transaction giving rise to the trial. Objects offered as having played such a direct role, e.g., the alleged weapon in a murder prosecution, are commonly called "real" or "original" evidence and are to be distinguished from evidence which played no such part but is offered for illustrative or other purposes. It will be readily apparent that when real evidence is offered an adequate foundation for admission will require testimony first that the object offered is *the* object which was involved in the incident, and further that the condition of the object is substantially unchanged. If the offered item possesses characteristics which are fairly unique and readily identifiable, and if the substance of which the item is composed is relatively impervious to change, the trial court is viewed as having broad discretion to admit merely on the basis of testimony that the item is the one in question and is in a substantially unchanged condition. On the other hand, if the offered evidence is of such a nature as not to be readily identifiable, or to be susceptible to alteration by tampering or contamination, sound exercise of the trial court's discretion may require a substantially more elaborate foundation. A foundation of the latter sort will commonly entail testimonially tracing the "chain of custody" of the item with sufficient completeness to render it reasonably probable that the original item has neither been exchanged with another nor been contaminated or tampered with. It should, however, always be borne in mind that foundational requirements are essentially requirements of logic, and not rules of art. Thus, e.g., even a radically altered item of real evidence may be admissible if its pertinent features remain unaltered.

Real evidence consisting of samples drawn from a larger mass are also generally held admissible, subject to the foregoing requirements pertaining to real evidence generally, and subject to the further requirement that the sample be established to be accurately representative of the mass.

Demonstrative evidence, however, is by no means limited to items which may properly be classed as "real" or "original" evidence. It is today increasingly common to encounter the offer of tangible items which are not themselves contended to have played any part in the history of the case, but which are instead tendered for the purpose of rendering other evidence more comprehensible to the trier of fact. Examples of types of items frequently offered for purposes of illustration and clarification include models, maps, photographs, charts, and drawings. If an article is offered for these purposes, rather than as real or original evidence, its specific identity or source is generally of no significance whatever. Instead, the theory justifying admission of these exhibits requires only that the item be sufficiently explanatory or illustrative of relevant testimony in the case to be of potential help to the trier of fact. Whether the admission of a particular exhibit will in fact be helpful, or will instead tend to confuse or mislead the trier, is a matter commonly viewed to be within the sound discretion of the trial court.

§ 213. Maps, Models, and Duplicates

Among the most frequently utilized types of illustrative evidence are maps, sketches, diagrams, models and duplicates. Unlike real evidence, the availability of which will frequently depend upon circumstances beyond counsel's control, opportunities for the use of the types of demonstrative evidence here considered are limited only by counsel's ability to recognize them. The potential of these aids for giving clarity and interest to spoken statements has brought about their widespread use, which will undoubtedly continue in the future.

While all jurisdictions allow the use of demonstrative items to illustrate and explain oral testimony, there is some diversity of judicial opinion concerning the precise evidentiary status of articles used for this purpose. Thus, while most jurisdictions treat items used to illustrate testimony as fully admissible, a few have singled out such items for distinct treatment. Of the various restrictions which have been imposed, the most supportable is that which limits jury access to illustrative items during deliberation. There would appear to be no reason why this policy, even if adopted, necessitates denying "admission" to such items.

Even in the majority of jurisdictions where there is no apparent bar to, or restriction upon, their full admission, it is not uncommon for maps, models, etc., to be displayed and referred to without being formally offered or admitted into evidence. While no absolute prohibition would appear to be justified concerning such informal use of illustrative items, numerous appellate courts have commented upon the difficulties created on appeal when crucial testimony has been given in the form of indecipherable references to an object not available to the reviewing court. By the more common, and clearly preferable practice, illustrative objects will be identified by the witness as substantially correct representations and will be formally introduced as part of the witness' testimony, in which they are incorporated by reference. When the record is not so perfected many courts have presumed that the illustrative items and testimony referring to them support the verdict, making it in the interest of both parties to clarify the record.

Illustrative exhibits may often properly and satisfactorily be used in lieu of real evidence. As previously noted, articles actually involved in a transaction or occurrence may have become lost or be unavailable, or witnesses may be unable to testify that the article present in court is the identical one they have previously observed. Where only the generic characteristics of the item are significant no objection would appear to exist to the introduction of a substantially similar "duplicate." While the matter is generally viewed as within the discretion of the trial court, it has been suggested that it would constitute reversible error to exclude a duplicate testified to be identical to the object involved in the occurrence. On the other hand, if there is an absence of testimony that the object to be illustrated ever existed the introduction of a "duplicate" may foster a mistaken impression of certainty and thus merit exclusion.

Models, maps, sketches, and diagrams (as distinguished from duplicates) are by their nature generally not confusable with real evidence, and are admissible simply on the basis of testimony that they are substantially accurate representations of what the witness is endeavoring to describe. Some discretionary control in the trial court is generally deemed appropriate, however, since exhibits of this kind, due to inaccuracies, variations of scale, etc., may on occasion be more misleading than helpful. Nevertheless, when the trial court has exercised its discretion to admit, it will only rarely be found in error, at least if potentially misleading inaccuracies have been pointed out by witnesses for the proponent, or could have been exposed upon cross-examination.

§ 214. Photographs, Movies, and Sound Recordings

The principle upon which photographs are most commonly admitted into evidence is the same as that underlying the admission of illustrative drawings, maps and diagrams. Under this theory, a photograph is viewed merely as a graphic portrayal of oral testimony, and becomes admissible only when a witness has testified that it is a correct and accurate representation of relevant facts personally observed by the witness. Accordingly, under this theory, the witness who lays the foundation need not be the photographer nor need he know anything of the time, conditions, or mechanisms of the taking. Instead he need only know about the facts represented or the scene or objects photographed, and once this knowledge is shown he can say whether the photograph correctly and accurately portrays these facts. Once the photograph is thus verified it is admissible as a graphic portrayal of the verifying witness' testimony into which it is incorporated by reference. If the photograph fails to portray the relevant facts with complete accuracy, such as where changed conditions have been brought about by lapse of time or other

factors, the photograph may still be admissible in the trial court's discretion if the changes are not so substantial as to be misleading.

The foregoing doctrine concerning the basis on which photographs are admitted is clearly a viable one and has undoubtedly served to facilitate the introduction of the general run of photographs. It is doubtful, however, whether this theory should be pressed to its logical limits, as some few courts have done, by limiting photographs admitted on this basis to "illustrative" status and denying them "substantive" effect. This distinction has been cogently criticized, and in any event does not seem to warrant the procedural consequences seen to flow from it. A majority of jurisdictions have either rejected the distinction explicitly or ignored it altogether.

The products of certain applications of the photographic process do not readily lend themselves to admission in evidence on the foregoing theory. X-ray photographs are a common example, and are of course constantly admitted, despite the fact that no witness has actually viewed the objects portrayed. The foundation typically required for X-rays is calculated to demonstrate that a reliable scientific process was correctly utilized to obtain the product offered in evidence. Earlier recognized only sporadically, this same approach has in recent years found greatly increased acceptance as applied to various products of the photographic process. Under this doctrine, commonly referred to as the "silent witness" theory of admission, photographic evidence may draw its verification, not from any witness who has actually viewed the scene portrayed on film, but from other evidence which supports the reliability of the photographic product. Most commonly, such evidence has been directed at establishing the validity of the photographic process by means of a foundation closely resembling that required for the admission of the products of other scientific processes. However, it has been pointed out that other types of foundation may properly support the admission of "silent witness" evidence. Today the "silent witness" doctrine affords an alternative route to the introduction of photographic evidence in virtually all jurisdictions. However, since the foundation required will generally be more elaborate than the relatively simple one sufficient under the traditional theory, resort to the latter remains preferable where circumstances permit.

The interest and vividness of photographs may be heightened by utilization of various techniques of photography, such as having the photographs taken in color, or having them enlarged so that pertinent facts may be more readily observed. While the use of these techniques clearly increases the number of factors subject to distortion, the basic standard governing admission of photos generally remains applicable. Thus color and enlarged photographs have generally been viewed as admissible provided the photo represents the scene depicted with substantial accuracy.

A somewhat more troublesome problem is presented by posed or artificially reconstructed scenes, in which people, automobiles, and other objects are placed so as to conform to the descriptions of the original crime or collision given by the witnesses. When the posed photographs go no further than to portray the positions of persons and objects as reflected in the undisputed testimony, their admission has long been generally approved. Frequently, however, a posed photograph will portray only the version of the facts supported by the testimony of the proponent's witness. The dangers inherent in this situation, i.e., the tendency of the photographs unduly to emphasize certain testimony and the possibility that the jury may confuse one party's reconstruction with objective fact, have led some courts to exclude photographs of this type. The orthodox theory of photos as merely illustrated testimony, however, can be viewed to support the admission of any photo reflecting a state of facts testified to by a witness and the current trend would appear to be to permit even photos of disputed reconstructions in some instances.

Motion pictures, when they were first sought to be introduced in evidence, were frequently objected to and sometimes excluded on the theory that they afforded manifold

opportunities for fabrication and distortion. Even those older decisions which upheld the admission of motion pictures appear to have done so on the basis of elaborate foundation testimony detailing the methods of taking, processing, and projecting the film. More recently, however, it appears to have become generally recognized that, as with the still photograph, the reliability and accuracy of the motion picture need not necessarily rest upon the validity of the process used in its creation, but rather may be established by testimony that the motion picture accurately reproduces phenomena actually perceived by the witness. Under this theory, though the requisite foundation may, and usually will, be laid by the photographer, it may also be provided by any witness who perceived the events filmed. Of course, if the foundation testimony reveals the film to be distorted in some material particular, exclusion is the proper result.

The "silent witness" theory of admissibility is as fully applicable to the motion picture as to the still photograph, and in fact many of the explicit applications of that theory have been with reference to movies.

Both the "pictorial testimony" and "silent witness" doctrines previously discussed will readily be seen to be equally applicable to the newer technology of the videotape, despite the fact that the latter operates upon quite different principles. The videotape has several practical advantages over the motion picture, and in fact seems largely to have displaced it as the common mechanism for presenting representations of motion to the trier of fact. While the admissibility of videotape evidence has sometimes been specifically provided for by rule or statute, such treatment is not a necessary precondition to reception of this type of evidence.

Judicial discretion in the admission or exclusion of representation of action is constantly emphasized in the decisions, and is perhaps largely attributable to the fact that the presentation of this kind of evidence will involve considerable expenditure of time and inconvenience. At the same time, however, when motion pictures are offered which reproduce the actual facts or original events in controversy, such as films of an allegedly incapacitated plaintiff shoveling snow or playing baseball, or post-arrest films of an allegedly intoxicated driver, the cogency of the evidence is such that the taking of considerable time and trouble to view the evidence would appear amply warranted.

Somewhat more difficult questions are posed by moving pictures taken of an injured party pursuing ordinary day-to-day activities, offered for the purpose of bringing home to the trier of fact the implications and significance of the injury for which damages are sought. With respect both to their relevance and to the possible objections which may legitimately be raised against them, these films are closely akin to bodily demonstrations of injuries in court. Both species of evidence therefore ought to be governed by the same rule, to wit, both should be admissible only in the sound discretion, and under the strict control, of the trial court.

A still different set of problems is presented by photographs or videotapes which do not portray original facts in controversy, but rather represent one party's staged reproduction of those facts. Here the extreme vividness and verisimilitude of pictorial evidence is truly a two-edged sword. For not only is the danger that the jury may confuse art with reality particularly great, but the impressions generated by the evidence may prove particularly difficult to limit or, if the film is subsequently deemed inadmissible, to expunge by judicial instruction. The latter difficulty may be largely eliminated by a preliminary viewing by the court in chambers, and the decided cases suggest that this expedient is widely employed.

Experiments and demonstrations must today be mentioned in the present context because of the frequency with which these are today filmed or taped so that the jury may observe the results rather than merely having them reported. While the fact of filming does not alter the basic principles applicable to

experiments and demonstrations,[1] it does raise the additional problem that the evidence may be presented in such a way as to cause the jury to confuse the filmed event with the actual one in litigation. Thus, where the film or tape appears to present a replication of the original event it will generally be required that the experiment be conducted under substantially similar circumstances. Where the purpose of the evidence is not to present a graphic reproduction of the event and there is little chance of jury confusion this similarity requirement is not imposed. Experiments intended to demonstrate the nature or capacity of physical objects are generally placed in this latter category, and films and tapes of such experiments have frequently been admitted.

Sound recordings will sometimes be offered as an integral part of a motion picture, but a recording alone may of course also be probative of relevant facts. When a sound recording consists of spoken words, questions concerning the "best evidence" rule and the rule of completeness may be raised. Where a sound recording itself does constitute the "best evidence," it is not uncommon to find a transcript of the recorded words offered to assist the jury in following the recording. Clearly such transcripts can serve a beneficial demonstrative function where no question exists as to the accuracy of the transcription, but serious theoretical and practical problems arise when a legitimate question is presented as to what words the recording contains.

Sound recordings may also be offered as reproducing relevant nonverbal sounds, and when this is the purpose the considerations potentially affecting admissibility are substantially similar to those relating to motion pictures. Thus, the recording will generally be admitted if a witness testifies that the recording as played is an accurate reproduction of relevant sounds previously audited by the witness. On occasion, too, sound recordings may be admitted upon a foundation analogous to that sometimes recognized for films taken by surveillance cameras. This will consist of a showing of the accuracy and

§ 214

1. See § 202, supra.

completeness of the recording by scientific and corroborative evidence.

§ 215. Bodily Demonstrations: Experiments in Court

The exhibition of a wound or physical injury, e.g., the injury sustained by a plaintiff in a personal injury action, will frequently be the best and most direct evidence of a material fact. Not surprisingly, therefore, exhibitions of physical injuries to the jury are commonly allowed. In most jurisdictions the matter is viewed as subject to the discretion of the trial court, but has sometimes been said to be a matter of right on the part of the injured party. Further, in those jurisdictions which hold the matter to be discretionary, a trial court is rarely reversed for permitting a bodily exhibition. Thus, when the exhibition is permitted no abuse of discretion is generally found present even though the injury displayed was particularly shocking, or even where the injury's nature or existence need not have been proved because admitted.

The physical characteristics of a person may also constitute relevant evidence in a criminal prosecution. For example, the scars or physical condition of the victim may tend to prove the nature of an assault, or a physical trait of a person may be relevant to prove or disprove the identity of the perpetrator of an offense. Though some awkwardness is encountered in treating persons as exhibits, bodily exhibitions for purposes such as those indicated are viewed as within the trial court's discretion and have frequently been allowed. When the prosecution desires to exhibit traits of the defendant, the question has long been considered under the heading of self-incrimination and the demonstration allowed so long as it may be classed as "non-testimonial." Similarly, it has generally been held that it is open to the defendant to display his physical characteristics to the trier of fact without incurring the necessity of taking the stand.

Judicial opinion has been somewhat more divided concerning the propriety of going be-yond the mere exhibition of an injury or physical condition by having the injured person perform actions or submit to manipulation by a physician. The dangers inherent in demonstrations of this latter type include undue emotional response on the part of the jury and the fact that manifestations of pain and impairment of function are easily feigned and difficult to test by cross-examination. Nevertheless, this matter too is commonly left to the discretion of the trial courts, and that discretion is frequently exercised in favor of permitting the demonstration. Occasional cases have, however, held the allowance of a particular demonstration to be an abuse of trial court discretion, a fact which may suggest that the tactic is a somewhat hazardous one for the party utilizing it.

In addition to active demonstrations of physical injuries, in-court reenactment of material events by witnesses has been held permissible to illustrate testimony.

Whether demonstrations in the form of experiments in court are to be permitted is also largely subject to the discretion of the trial judge. Unlike experiments performed out of court, the results of which are generally communicated testimonially, in-court experimentation may involve considerable confusion and delay, and the trial judge is viewed as in the best position to judge whether the game is worth the candle. Simple demonstrations by a witness are usually permitted, and may be strikingly effective in adding vividness to the spoken word.

In addition to the limitations arising from the desirability of orderly and expeditious proceedings, in-court experiments are held to the same basic requirement of similarity of conditions which is applicable to experimental evidence generally.[1] This requirement may be particularly difficult to meet under courtroom conditions, and many proposed courtroom experiments have been held properly excluded on this ground. Nevertheless, the well-planned courtroom experiment may provide extremely striking and persuasive evi-

§ 215

1. See § 202 supra.

dence, and the opportunities for utilizing such experiments should not be overlooked.

§ 216. Views

The courts, like the prophet, have sensibly recognized that if a thing cannot be brought to the observer, the observer must go to the thing. Venturing forth to observe places or objects which are material to litigation but which cannot feasibly be brought, or satisfactorily reproduced, within the courtroom, is termed a "view." While statutes or court rules concerning views are in effect in nearly all states, it is frequently said that even without express statutory authorization there is an inherent power in the trial judge to order a view by the jury, or, in a judge-tried case, to take a view personally. This power extends to views of personalty, realty, and to criminal as well as civil cases.

Since a view is often time-consuming and disruptive of the ordinary course of a trial, the trial judge is in most instances vested with a wide leeway of discretion to grant or refuse a view. It is to be noted, however, that a number of state statutes provide that in certain types of cases, notably eminent domain, either party is entitled to a view upon request as a matter of right. Where the grant of a view is discretionary with the trial court, as is usually the case, factors which are commonly stated to be appropriate for consideration by the court in determining whether to a grant a view include the importance to the issue of the information to be gained by the view, the extent to which this information has or could have been secured from maps, photographs, or diagrams and the extent to which the place or object to be viewed has changed in appearance since the controversy arose.

The appropriate procedures to be followed in connection with views are widely regulated by statute. At common law, and generally in civil cases today, the presence of the trial judge at a view is not required, the more common practice being for the jury to be conducted to the scene by "showers," expressly commissioned for the purpose. Attendance at the view by the parties and their counsel is generally permitted though subject to the discretion of the trial judge. In criminal cases, the rights of the defendant to have the judge present at the view, and to be present personally, are frequently provided for by statute. Moreover, when testimony is taken at the view, or the view itself is deemed to constitute evidence, the right of the defendant to be present in all probability possesses a constitutional underpinning.

Statutory and constitutional considerations aside, the advisability of trial court attendance at views is strongly suggested by the numerous cases in which unauthorized comments, obviously hearsay, have been made to the jury, or other improper events have occurred during the course of the view. Presence of the trial judge would seem to afford the best guarantee available against the occurrence of events of this nature. On the other hand, where the trial judge is present to rule on admissibility, and provision for preparation of a proper record is made, there would appear no inherent vice in receiving testimony or allowing demonstrations or experiments during a view. These practices, however, have often been looked upon with disfavor by appellate courts, and some jurisdictions appear to hold reception of testimony or experiments during a view improper under any circumstances.

Closely related to the above questions is the troublesome problem of what evidentiary status a view possesses. A large number of jurisdictions, probably a majority, holds that a view is not itself evidence, but is only to assist the trier of fact in understanding and evaluating the evidence. This doctrine undoubtedly rests in large part upon the consideration that facts garnered by the jury from a view are difficult or impossible to embody in the written record, thus rendering review of questions concerning weight or sufficiency of the evidence impracticable. At the same time, however, this doctrine ignores the fact that many other varieties of demonstrative evidence are to some extent subject to the same difficulty, and further that it is unreasonable to assume that jurors, however they may be instructed, will apply the metaphysical distinction suggested and ignore the evidence of their own senses when it conflicts with the testimony of the witnesses. Commentators have uniformly condemned the downgrading of views to non-evidentiary status, and a substantial number of courts holds a view to be evidence like any other. The latter position appears to be the preferable one, at least when modified by the caveat that where the question is one of sufficiency, a view alone cannot logically be considered to constitute sufficient evidence of a fact the establishment of which ordinarily requires the introduction of expert testimony.

§ 217. Exhibits in the Jury Room

Under modern American practice it is common to allow many types of tangible exhibits to be taken by the jury for consideration during the deliberations, provided that the exhibits have been formally admitted into evidence. The question whether a particular exhibit may be taken by the jury is widely viewed as subject to discretionary control by the trial judge, but in some jurisdictions jury access to at least certain types of exhibits is apparently made mandatory either by judicial holding or legislative enactment.

The current practice extends, unlike that at common law, to written exhibits generally except for those which are testimonial in nature, such as depositions, dying declarations in writing, etc. The reason underlying this latter exception is that writings which are merely testimony in a different form should not, by being allowed to the jury, be unduly emphasized over other purely oral testimony in the case. As an exception to the exception, however, written or recorded confessions in criminal cases, despite their obvious testimonial character, are in many jurisdictions allowed to be taken by the jury, apparently on the theory that their centrality in the case warrants whatever emphasis may result.

The practice of allowing nontestimonial written evidence generally to be taken by the

jury would appear to be supported by many of the same considerations which underlie the so-called "Best Evidence Rule."[1] Legal rights and liabilities are frequently a function of particular words and figures, and may be drastically affected by seemingly minor variations in phraseology. Thus crucial documents, such as deeds, contracts, or ledger sheets may frequently be of vital help to the jury. On the other hand, where a writing is of only minor relevance, despatch to the jury may induce an emphasis upon it out of proportion to its intrinsic worth.

The case for allowing the jury to take with it tangibles other than writings is somewhat weaker, at least if in-court examination of the tangible by the jury has been had. As noted in an earlier section, demonstrative evidence has peculiar force which arguably does not stand in need of yet additional augmentation. Further, the relevant characteristics of many tangible exhibits are sufficiently gross as not to require the close perusal appropriate to writings, while at the other end of the spectrum there appears some anomaly in allowing independent jury inspection of tangibles the relevant features of which are so fine as to require expert exposition and interpretation. Nevertheless, the sending of tangible exhibits to the jury room is today probably so well established as to be practically irreversible.

A major problem stemming from relatively free jury access to tangible exhibits other than writings is that of controlling jury use of them for purposes of experimentation. The general limitations upon the introduction of evidence of experiments obviously become largely meaningless if the jury is allowed to conduct experiments of its own devising in the jury room. In attempting to distinguish between proper and improper jury use of tangible exhibits, the most commonly drawn distinction is between experiments which constitute merely a closer scrutiny of the exhibit and experiments which go "beyond the lines of the evidence" introduced in court and thus constitute the introduction of new evidence in the jury room. The decisions reached under

§ 217

1. See generally Chapter 23 infra.

the aegis of this rubric are perhaps not totally reconcilable. Most courts, however, emphasize the immunity of jury-conducted experiments from adversary scrutiny as their pre-eminently objectionable feature. Thus it would seem correct to say that jury experimentation is improper if reasonable grounds existed for an adversary attack on the experiment by the complaining party and, in addition, if nothing transpiring during the in-court proceedings rendered such an attack inappropriate. Specifically, experiments which are merely reruns of in-court experiments, or which use techniques of examination not markedly different from those employed during trial are not generally held to fall within the proscribed class. On the other hand, jury experiments utilizing techniques or equipment substantially different from any employed in court tend to be held error, at least where counsel has not specifically acquiesced in the experiment, such as by arguing that the jury should be allowed certain tools.

Title 9

WRITINGS

Chapter 22

AUTHENTICATION

Table of Sections

§ 218. General Theory: No Assumption of Authenticity

The concept of authentication, although continually used by the courts without apparent difficulty, seems almost to defy precise definition. Some writers have construed the term very broadly, as does Wigmore when he states that "when a claim or offer involves impliedly or expressly any element of *personal connection with a corporeal object,* that connection must be made to appear * * *." [1] So defined, "authentication" is not only a necessary preliminary to the introduction of most writings in evidence, but also to the introduction of various other sorts of tangibles. For example, an article of clothing found at the scene of a crime can hardly constitute relevant evidence against the defendant unless ownership or previous possession of the article is shown. Since authentication of tangibles other than writings, has been treated elsewhere, however, the term authentication will here be used in the limited sense of proof of authorship of, or other connection with, writings.

It is clear that the relevancy of a writing to a particular issue raised in litigation will frequently be logically dependent upon the exist-

§ 218
1. 7 Wigmore, Evidence § 2129 at 564 (Chadbourn rev. 1978).

ence of some connection between that writing and a particular individual. If Y sues X for libel and attempts to introduce into evidence a writing containing libelous statements concerning Y, it will readily appear that the writing is relevant only if some connection between the writing and X exists, as where X authored or published it. The real question, however, is not whether such a connection is logically necessary for relevancy, but rather what standards are to be applied in determining whether the connection has been made to appear. In some instances testimony concerning a writing will be offered rather than the writing itself. Where this is permissible through the operation of the so-called "best evidence" rule or its exceptions, is the requirement of authentication excused? The answer should necessarily be that it is not, for the connection between the writing and the individual is rendered no less logically significant because of the form of evidence concerning the writing.

In the everyday affairs of business and social life, it is the custom to look merely at the writing itself for evidence as to its source. Thus, if the writing bears a signature purporting to be that of X, or recites that it was made by X, we assume, nothing to the contrary appearing, that it is exactly what it purports to be, the work of X. At this point, however, the law of evidence has long differed from the commonsense assumption upon which each of us conducts her own affairs, adopting instead the position that the purported signature or recital of authorship on the face of a writing will *not* be accepted as sufficient preliminary proof of authenticity to secure the admission of the writing in evidence. The same attitude has traditionally extended as well to the authority of agents, with the result that if an instrument recites that it is signed by A as agent for P, not only must additional proof be given that A actually did the signing, but also of the fact that she was P's agent and authorized to sign.

The principal justification urged for this judicial agnosticism toward the authorship of documents is that it constitutes a necessary check on the perpetration of fraud. Thus it is quite conceivable that the libelous writing previously adduced by way of example is not the work of X but of some third person who, for reasons of her own, wishes to embroil X in difficulties, or to libel Y without suffering any adverse consequences. It is also possible that Y has fabricated the writing to provide herself with a cause of action.

Another possibility against which traditional authentication is sometimes suggested to guard is that of mistaken attribution of a writing to one who fortuitously happens to possess the same name, etc., as the author.

On the other side of the coin, requiring proof of what may correctly be assumed true in 99 out of 100 cases is at best time-consuming and expensive. At the worst, the requirement will occasionally be seen to produce results which are virtually indefensible.

Thus, while traditional requirements of authentication admittedly furnish some slight obstacles to the perpetration of fraud or occurrence of mistake in the presentation of writings, it has frequently been questioned whether these benefits are not outweighed by the time, expense, and occasional untoward results entailed by the traditional negative attitude toward authenticity of writings.

§ 219. Authentication by Direct Proof: (a) In General

The simplest form of direct testimony authenticating a writing as that of X, is the production of a witness who swears that he saw X sign the offered writing. Other examples would be the testimony of X, the signer, acknowledging execution, or the admission of authenticity by an adverse party in the present action, either made out of court and reported by another witness or shown by the party's own letter or other writing, or in the form of the party's testimony on the stand.[1] It is generally held that business records may

§ 219

1. See Ch. 23 infra.

be authenticated [2] by the testimony of one familiar with the books of the concern, such as a custodian or supervisor, who has not made the record or seen it made, that the offered writing is actually part of the records of the business.

§ 220. Authentication by Direct Proof: (b) Requirement of Production of Attesting Witnesses

Our rules about the production of subscribing witnesses are survivals of archaic law. They have their origins in Germanic practice earlier than jury trial, when pre-appointed transaction-witnesses were the only kind of witnesses that could be summoned or heard in court. When jury trial came in, the attesting witnesses at first were summoned along with the jurors themselves, and this practice seems to have lingered until the middle fifteen hundreds. The rule in its modern common law form requires, when a document signed by subscribing witnesses is sought to be authenticated by witnesses, that an attesting witness must first be called, or all attesters must be shown to be unavailable, before other witnesses can be called to authenticate it.

The requirement has no application where the foundation for introducing the document is the opponent's judicial admission of its genuineness, either by stipulation of the parties in writing or in open court, or under modern rules and statutes by the opponent's failure to deny the genuineness of the writing. Though it has been suggested that extra-judicial admissions also, if in writing, might properly be held to dispense with the production of attesters, such American authority as exists seems to deny that extra-judicial admissions of any sort have this effect.

The requirement is that the attesting witnesses be called before other authenticating witnesses are heard, but it is not required that the attesters give favorable testimony establishing the writing. So even if they profess want of memory or even deny that they

attested, the writing may be established by other proof, and conversely if they support the writing, other proof may establish that it is not authentic. Moreover, since the party calling the attester is required by law to do so, the prohibition upon impeaching one's own witness is held inapplicable.

This requirement of calling particular persons, or accounting for them, to authenticate the writing is often inconvenient, and of doubtful expediency, and various exceptions have been carved out by the courts, as for ancient documents, writings only "collaterally" involved in the suit, and for certified copies of recorded conveyances, where the original is not required to be produced. A more sweeping reform, generally effected by statute but on occasion by judicial decision, has been to dispense with the requirement of calling attesting witnesses except when the writing to be offered is one required by law to be attested.

§ 221. Authentication by Direct Proof: (c) Proof of Handwriting

A witness is placed on the stand. "Will you state whether you are acquainted with the handwriting of X?" "I am." "Will you look at this letter (or this signature) and tell me whether it is in the handwriting of X?" "It is." These or similar questions and answers are part of the familiar routine of authenticating writings, a routine which might be supposed to possess a rationale until note is taken of the qualifications typically required to be shown as part of his testimony by the witness through whom such a foundation is laid. These qualifications are minimal to say the least. Thus it is generally held that anyone familiar with the handwriting of a given person may supply authenticating testimony in the form of his opinion that a writing or signature is in the handwriting of that person. Adequate familiarity may be present if the witness has seen the person write, or if he has seen writings *purporting* to be those of the

---

2. Merely supplying the requirement that the books be identified as such, though other foundation proof may be required before the records will be accepted as evidence of the facts recorded under the hearsay exception for Business Records. See §§ 284–294 infra.

person in question under circumstances indicating their genuineness. Examples of the latter situation include instances where the witness has had an exchange of correspondence with the person, or has seen writings which the person has asserted are his own, or has been present in an office or other place where genuine writings of a particular person in the ordinary course of business would naturally be seen. Finally, it is not required that the authenticating witness' identification be categorical in nature.

The same assumptions which underlie lay witness authentication based upon familiarity with individual handwriting may be seen to justify another well-established doctrine, that of authentication by handwriting specimens or "exemplars." The common law limited the use of exemplars for comparison purposes to writings otherwise admissible in the case, but this rule has generally been modified by rule or statute to allow handwriting samples to be admitted solely for the purpose of comparison. Some conflict of authority exists concerning the standard by which the authenticity of such specimens is to be determined. Once admitted, however, an apparent majority of jurisdictions hold that the genuineness of other offered writings alleged to be the work of the same author becomes a question for the trier of fact who may, but need not, be assisted in this task by expert comparisons. Analogous holdings may be found in the relatively rarer cases of authentication by typing technique or word usage patterns (psycholinguistics), both of which, like handwriting identification, proceed on the basis of comparisons between the document in question and exemplars of known origin.

Demonstration is available, if demonstration is thought to be needed, that evidence of the foregoing varieties is essentially meaningless in cases where the authenticity is actually disputed. If a writing is in fact questioned no layperson is competent to distinguish a skilled forgery from a genuine writing. Certainly it is incredible that an unskilled layman who saw the person write once a decade before could make such a differentiation. In the event of an actual controversy over genu-

ineness, both logic and good advocacy demand a resort to evidence of greater reliability and persuasiveness, principally, according to the prevalent view, the testimony of bona fide handwriting experts.

The minimal qualifications required of the ordinary witness authenticating a writing by identification of handwriting are defensible only on the basis that no more than one in a hundred writings is questioned. The current permissive standards allow the admission of the general run of authentic documents with a minimum of time, trouble, and expense. The latter argument, however, may prove too much since even greater savings in these commodities might safely be achieved by simply presuming the authenticity of writings for purposes of admissibility in the absence of proof raising a question as to genuineness.

§ 222. Authentication by Circumstantial Evidence: (a) Generally

As has been seen there are various ways in which writings may be authenticated by direct evidence. Nevertheless, it will frequently occur that no direct evidence of authenticity of any type exists or can be found. Resort must then be had to circumstantial proof and it is clear that authentication by circumstantial evidence is uniformly recognized as permissible. Certain configurations of circumstantial evidence have in fact been so frequently held to authenticate particular types of writings that they have come to be recognized as distinct rules, e.g., the ancient documents rule, the reply doctrine, etc. These more or less formalized rules are treated in succeeding sections.

It is important to bear in mind, however, that authentication by circumstantial evidence is not limited to situations which fall within one of these recurrent patterns. Rather, proof of any circumstances which will support a finding that the writing is genuine will suffice to authenticate the writing.

§ 223. Authentication by Circumstantial Evidence: (b) Ancient Documents

A writing which has been in existence for a number of years will frequently be difficult to authenticate by direct evidence. Where the maker of an instrument, those who witnessed the making, and even those familiar with the maker's handwriting have over the course of years died or become unavailable, the need to resort to authentication by circumstantial evidence is apparent. The circumstances which may, in a given case, raise an inference of the genuineness of an aged writing are of course quite varied, and any combination of circumstances sufficient to support a finding of genuineness will be appropriate authentication. Facts which may be suggested as indicative of genuineness include unsuspicious appearance, emergence from natural custody, prompt recording, and, in the case of a deed or will, possession taken under the instrument. Age itself may be viewed as giving rise to some inference of genuineness in that an instrument is unlikely to be forged for fruition at a time in the distant future.

The frequent necessity of authenticating ancient writings by circumstantial evidence plus the consideration that certain of the above facts probative of authenticity are commonly found associated with genuine older writings have led the courts to develop a rule of thumb for dealing with the question. Under the common law form of this rule a writing is sufficiently authenticated as an ancient document if the party who offers it produces sufficient evidence that the writing is thirty years old, that it is unsuspicious in appearance, and further proves that the writing is produced from a place of custody natural for such a document. The Federal Rules of Evidence and most state derivatives continue the rule but reduce the required documentary age to twenty years. In addition to the foregoing requirements, some jurisdictions, if the writing is a dispositive one such as a deed or a will, impose the additional condition that possession must have been taken under the instrument. The documents which may be authenticated under the rule here described, however, are not limited to dispositive instruments, and the rule has been applied to allow authentication of a wide variety of writings.

In the case of a writing which purports to be executed by an agent, executor, or other person acting under power or authority from another, proof of the facts which authenticate the writing as an ancient document gives rise to a presumption that the person signing was duly authorized.

It should be borne in mind that, despite the utility of the rule here discussed, it is merely a rule of authentication, the satisfaction of which does not necessarily guarantee the admission of the writing authenticated. Thus, it is sometimes forgotten that a writing may be proved perfectly genuine and yet remain inadmissible as being, e.g., hearsay or secondary evidence. This source of confusion is compounded by a partial overlap between the requirements of the present rule and those of the distinct doctrine which holds that recitals in certain types of ancient instruments may be received as evidence of the facts recited. The latter doctrine, however, constitutes an exception to the rule against hearsay and is quite distinct from the present rule concerning authentication. It is discussed in another place.[1]

The preferable and majority view is that satisfaction of the ancient document requirements will serve to authenticate an ancient copy of an original writing. And a fresh certified copy of an instrument of record for thirty years will prove the ancient writing, though perhaps with the additional qualification that before the copy can come in, the original documents rule must be satisfied by showing the unavailability of the original. Admission of a writing as an ancient document does, however, dispense with the production of attesting witnesses.[2]

§ 224. Authentication by Circumstantial Evidence: (c) Custody

If a writing purports to be an official report or record and is proved to have come from the proper public office where such official papers

1. See § 323 infra.

2. See § 220 supra.

are kept, it is generally agreed that this authenticates the offered document as genuine. This result is founded on the probability that the officers in custody of such records will carry out their public duty to receive or record only genuine official papers and reports, and thus it is the official duty to record and maintain the document, rather than the duty to prepare it, which constitutes the document a public record. Similarly, where a public office is the depository for private papers, such as wills, conveyances, or income tax returns, the proof that such a purporting deed, bill of sale, tax return or the like has come from the proper custody is usually accepted as sufficient authentication. This again can be sustained on the same principle if it appears that the official custodian had a public duty to verify the genuineness of the papers offered for record or deposit and to accept only the genuine.

As is discussed in a subsequent section, any need for testimonial proof of production from proper official custody is today frequently avoided by resort to certification procedures or "self-authentication." However, it is significant to note that such procedures are not exclusive or mandatory, and that proof of the facts necessary to secure admission of a public record may be made by any witness with competent knowledge.

As is true with ancient documents, the question of the authenticity of official records should not be confused with the ultimate admissibility of such records. It is quite possible for a public record to be perfectly genuine, and yet remain inadmissible for some distinguishable reason, e.g., that it is excludable hearsay.

Some question exists whether the rule which accepts, as prima facie genuine, documents which are shown to emerge from official custody should be extended beyond the field of public duty and recognized as to writings found in private custody. Since the circumstances of private custody are infinitely more varied than those of public custody, a new rule in an already rule-ridden area seems inadvisable. No such rule, in fact, is needed, provided that, in their discretion, courts recognize that proof of private custody, together with other circumstances, is frequently strong circumstantial evidence of authenticity.

§ 225. Authentication by Circumstantial Evidence: (d) Knowledge: Reply Letters and Telegrams

When a letter, signed with the purported signature of X, is received "out of the blue," with no previous correspondence, the traditional "show me" skepticism of the common law trial practice [1] prevails, and the purported signature is not accepted as authentication, unless authenticity is confirmed by additional facts.

One circumstance recognized as sufficient is the fact that the letter discloses knowledge that only the purported signer would be likely to have. Moreover, a convenient practice recognizes that if a letter has been written to X, and the letter now offered in evidence purports to be written by X and purports to be a reply to the first letter (that is either refers to it, or is responsive to its terms) and has been received without unusual delay, these facts authenticate it as a reply letter. This result may be rested upon the knowledge-principle, mentioned above. In view of the regularity of the mails the first letter would almost invariably come exclusively into the hands of X, or those authorized to act for him, who would alone know of the terms of the letter. It is supported also by the fact that in common experience we know that reply letters do come from the person addressed in the first letter.

Considerations concerning reliability of the mails are significant only to demonstrate the likelihood that the purported author of the response did in fact receive the original communication. Thus, where receipt of the communication referred to in the reply can be established by other means, and the reply is timely received, these facts will be sufficient to authenticate.

§ 225

1. See § 218 supra.

These same arguments apply to reply telegrams, but with a reduced degree of certainty. Some of the employees of the telegraph company, as well as the addressee, know the contents of the first telegram. Moreover, the instances of misdelivery of telegrams may be more numerous relatively than misdeliveries of letters. These considerations have led some courts to reject for reply telegrams this theory of authentication. The contrary view, that the inference of authenticity of the reply telegram is substantial and sufficient, seems more reasonable and expedient.

When the reply letter purports to be signed by an agent or other representative of X, the addressee of the first letter, the authority of the signing representative is presumed.

The first step in authentication of the reply letter is to prove that the first letter was dated and was duly mailed at a given time and place addressed to X. Seemingly oral testimony to these facts should suffice as to the first letter if the reply letter refers to it by date.[2] If, however, the reply letter only refers to it by reciting or responding to its terms, then since the terms of the first letter become important,[3] probably it would be necessary to satisfy the Best Evidence Rule. If X, as usually would be the case, is the party-opponent, and has the first letter in his hands, it would be necessary to give him notice to produce it, before a copy could be used to prove its terms.

§ 226. Authentication by Circumstantial Evidence: (e) Telephone Messages and Other Oral Communications

Modern technology makes commonplace the receipt of oral communications from persons who are heard but not seen. The problems of authentication raised by these communications are substantively analogous to the problems of authenticating writings. Thus, if the witness has received, e.g., a telephone call out of the blue from one who identified himself as "X", this is not sufficient authentication of the call as in fact coming from X. The requisite additional proof may take the form of testimony by the witness that he is familiar with X's voice and that the caller was X. Or authentication may be accomplished by circumstantial evidence pointing to X's identity as the caller, such as if the communication received reveals that the speaker had knowledge of facts that only X would be likely to know. These same modes of authentication are also recognized where communications have been received by radio.

Whatever the means of transmission, oral communications today will frequently be perpetuated in some type of recording. Where such is the case the authentication of the communication is likely to be facilitated simply because otherwise unavailable proof of various kinds may be generated by use of the recording. However, it must be constantly born in mind that authentication does not necessarily equate with admissibility, and that recordings will often raise evidentiary problems other than authentication.[1]

A somewhat easier problem is presented when the witness testifies that she placed a telephone call to a number listed to X, and that the person answering identified himself as X. In such a situation the accuracy of the telephone system, the probable absence of motive to falsify and the lack of opportunity for premeditated fraud all tend to support the conclusion that the self-identification of the speaker is reliable. Thus most courts today view proof of proper placing of a call plus self-identification of the speaker as sufficient proof of authenticity to admit the substance of the call. Moreover, it is likewise held that where it is shown that the witness has called the listed number of a business establishment and spoken with someone purporting to speak for the concern, with respect to matters within its ordinary course of business, it is presumed that the speaker was authorized to speak for the employer.

§ 226

2. See § 233 infra.

3. See § 233 infra.

1. See, e.g., § 214 supra; Ch. 23 infra.

§ 227. Functions of Judge and Jury in Authentication

If direct testimony of the authorship of a writing or of an oral statement is given, this is sufficient authentication and the judge has no problem on that score.[1] The writing or statement comes in, if not otherwise objectionable. When the authenticating evidence is circumstantial, however, the question whether reasonable men could find its authorship as claimed by the proponent, may be a delicate and balanced one, as to which the judge must be accorded some latitude of judgment.[2] Accordingly, it is often said to be a matter of discretion. It must be noticed, however, that authenticity is not to be classed as one of those preliminary questions of fact conditioning admissibility under technical evidentiary rules of competency or privilege. As to these latter, the trial judge will permit the adversary to introduce controverting proof on the preliminary issue in support of his objection, and the judge will decide this issue, without submission to the jury, as a basis for his ruling on admissibility.[3] On the other hand, the authenticity of a writing or statement is not a question of the application of a technical rule of evidence. It goes to genuineness and conditional relevance, as the jury can readily understand. Thus, if a prima facie showing is made, the writing or statement comes in, and the ultimate question of authenticity is left to the jury.

§ 228. Escapes From the Requirement of Producing Evidence of Authenticity: Modern Theory and Practice

As the foregoing sections clearly imply, the authentication of writings and other communications by formal proof may prove troublesome, time consuming, and expensive even in cases where no legitimate doubt concerning genuineness would appear to exist. The ultimate explanation for the continuing insistence upon the furnishing of such proof, justi-

fiable only upon assumptions which accord very little with common sense, is of course obscure. It may be speculated, however that in part the explanation is to be found in various procedural devices which afford escape from authentication requirements. Use of these devices will avert some of the impatience which might otherwise be engendered by formal authentication requirements. The legislatures, too, have frequently nibbled at the problem by enacting statutes relieving the rigors of authentication in what would otherwise be particularly troublesome contexts. Among these "escapes from authentication," the following are particularly noteworthy.

Requests for Admission. Under the practice in the Federal courts as provided by Rules 36 and 37(c) of the Federal Rules of Civil Procedure, and under analogous rules or statutes in many states, a party may serve upon an adversary a written request for admission of the genuineness of any relevant document described in the request. If the adversary unreasonably fails within a specified time to serve an answer or objection, genuineness is admitted. If genuineness is denied and the requesting party thereafter proves the genuineness of the document at trial, the latter may apply for an order of court requiring the adversary to pay her the reasonable costs of making the authenticating proof.

Securing Admission at Pretrial Conference. Under Rule 16 in the Federal courts and under analogous rules and statutes in many states, it is provided that a pretrial conference of the attorneys may be called by the court to consider among other things, "the possibility of obtaining admissions of fact and of documents which will avoid unnecessary proof." Of course, similar stipulations often are secured in informal negotiation between counsel, but a skilful judge may create at a pretrial conference an atmosphere of mutual concession unusually favorable for such admissions. This function of the pretrial practice

§ 227

1. See §§ 219–221 supra.

2. See §§ 222–226 supra.

3. See § 53 supra.

has been considered one of its most successful features.

Statutes and Rules Requiring Special or Sworn Denial of Genuineness of Writing. A provision of practice acts and rules of procedure may require that when an action is brought upon a written instrument, such as a note or contract, copied in the complaint, the genuineness of the writing will be deemed admitted unless a sworn denial be included in the answer.

Writings Which "Prove Themselves:" Acknowledged Documents, Certified Copies, and Law Books Which Purport to be Printed by Authority. There are certain kinds of writings which are said to "prove themselves" or to be "self-identifying." In consequence one of these may be tendered to the court and, even without the shepherding angel of an authenticating witness, will be accepted in evidence for what it purports to be. This convenient result is reached in two stages. First, by statutes which often provide that certain classes of writings, usually in some manner purporting to be vouched for by an official, shall be received in evidence "without further proof." This helpful attribute is most commonly given by these statutes to (1) deeds, conveyances or other instruments, which have been acknowledged by the signers before a notary public, (2) certified copies of public records, and (3) books of statutes which purport to be printed by public authority.

But in the first two of these classes of writings, which can qualify only when the acknowledgment is certified by a notary or the copy certified by the official who has custody of the record, how is the court to know without proof that the signature or seal appearing on the writing is actually that of the official whose name and title are recited? This second step is supplied by the traditional doctrines which recognize the seal or signature of certain types of officers, including the keeper of the seal of state, judicial officers, and notaries public, as being of themselves sufficient evidence of the genuineness of the certificate. Moreover in many state codes particular provisions supplement or clarify tradition by specifying that the seals or signatures of certain classes of officialdom shall have this self-authenticating effect.

Federal Rules of Evidence. The concept of self-authentication, previously recognized by statute in the case of the certain relatively limited classes of writings noted above, is given an expanded ambit of operation by the Federal Rules of Evidence. Rule 902 accords prima facie authenticity not only to those types of writings such as acknowledged writings and public records which have commonly enjoyed such treatment by statute but also to various other types of writings not previously so favored. Among these new classes of self-authenticating writings are included books, pamphlets and other publications issued by public authority, newspapers and periodicals, and trade inscriptions and labels indicating ownership, control or origin. Presumptive authenticity, as provided for by the rule, does not preclude evidentiary challenge of the genuineness of the offered writing, but simply serves to obviate the necessity of preliminary authentication by the proponent to secure admission. This commonsense approach was long overdue and might well be extended to apply to all writings purporting to have a connection with the party against whom offered.

The concept of self-authentication was subsequently extended dramatically in federal criminal proceedings by enactment of a statute which confers self-authenticating effect on foreign records of regularly conducted activity which are certified by the custodian in accordance with the statute. This development in turn motivated the Conference of Commissioners on Uniform State Laws to amend Uniform Rule 902 to provide for self-authentication of "certified" business records, domestic as well as foreign.

Chapter 23

THE REQUIREMENT OF THE PRODUCTION OF THE ORIGINAL WRITING AS THE "BEST EVIDENCE"

Table of Sections

§ 229. The "Best Evidence" Rule

Thayer tells us that the first appearance of the "best evidence" phrase, is a statement in 1700 by Holt, C.J. (in a case in which he admitted evidence questioned as secondary) to the effect that "the best proof that the nature of the thing will afford is only required." This statement given as a reason for receiving evidence, that it is the best which can be had—a highly liberalizing principle—not surprisingly gives birth to a converse and narrowing doctrine that a man must produce the best evidence that is available—second-best will not do. And so before 1726 we find Baron Gilbert in one of the earliest treatises on Evidence saying, "the first and most signal rule in relation to evidence is this, that a man must have the utmost evidence the nature of the fact is capable of * * *." [1] Blackstone continues the same broad generalizing and combines both the positive and negative aspects of the "best evidence" idea when he says, " * * * the best evidence the nature of the case will admit of shall always be required, if possible to be had; but if not possible then the best evidence that can be had shall be allowed." [2] Greenleaf in this country in 1842 was still repeating these wide abstractions.[3]

Thayer, however, writing in 1898, points out that these broad principles, though they had some influence in shaping specific evidence rules in the 1700s, were never received as adequate or accurate statements of governing rules, and that actually "the chief illustration of the Best Evidence principle, the doctrine that if you would prove the contents of a writing, you must produce the writing itself" is an ancient rule far older than any notion about the "best" evidence. While some modern opinions still refer to the "best evidence" notion as if it were today a general governing legal principle most would adopt the view of modern textwriters that there is no such general rule. The only actual rule that the "best evidence" phrase denotes today is the rule requiring the production of the original writing.

§ 230. Original Document Rule

The specific context in which it is generally agreed that the best evidence principle is applicable today should be definitely stated and its limits clearly defined. The rule is this: in proving the terms of a writing, where the terms are material, the original writing must be produced unless it is shown to be unavailable for some reason other than the serious fault of the proponent. The discussion in the following sections is directed to adding content to this basic framework.

§ 231. The Reasons for the Rule

Since its inception in the early 18th century, various rationales have been asserted to underlie the "best evidence rule." Many older writers have asserted that the rule is essentially directed to the prevention of fraud. Wigmore, however, vigorously attacked this thesis on the analytical ground that it does not square with certain recognized applications and non-applications of the rule. Most modern commentators follow his lead in asserting that the basic premise justifying the rule is the central position which the written word occupies in the law. Because of this centrality, presenting to a court the exact words of a writing is of more than average importance, particularly in the case of operative or dispositive instruments such as deeds, wills or contracts, where a slight variation of words may mean a great difference in rights. In addition, it is to be considered (1) that there has been substantial hazard of inaccuracy in some of the commonly utilized methods of making copies of writings, and (2) oral testimony purporting to give from memory the terms of a writing is probably subject to a greater risk of error than oral testimony concerning other situations generally. The danger of mistransmitting critical facts which accompanies the use of written copies or recollection, but which is largely avoided when an original writing is presented to prove its terms, justifies preference for original documents.

At the same time, however, it would appear a mistake totally to disregard all other justifications for the rule. It has long been observed that the opportunity to inspect original writings may be of substantial importance in the detection of fraud. At least a few modern courts and commentators appear to regard the prevention of fraud as an ancillary justification of the rule. Unless this view is accepted it is difficult to explain the rule's frequent application to copies produced by modern

---

1. Gilbert, Evidence (2d ed.) 4, 15–17, quoted in Thayer, Preliminary Treatise on Evidence 490 (1898).

2. Blackstone, Commentaries 368, quoted Thayer op. cit. 491.

3. 1 Greenleaf, Evidence Part 2, ch. 4, §§ 82–97 (1842), quoted and analyzed in Thayer, op. cit., 484–487.

techniques which virtually eliminate the possibility of unintentional mistransmission.

Finally, one leading opinion intimates that the rule should be viewed to protect not only against mistaken or fraudulent mistransmissions but also against intentional or unintentional misleading through introduction of selected portions of a comprehensive set of writings to which the opponent has no access. This seems to engraft upon the best evidence rule an aspect of completeness not heretofore observed.

Whatever rationale is viewed to support the rule, it will be observed that the advent of modern discovery and related procedures under which original documents may be examined before trial rather than at it, have substantially reduced the need for the rule. Nevertheless, it has been pointed out that at present limitations on the availability of these alternatives leaves the original documents rule a continuing and important sphere of operations.

§ 232. What Are Writings? Application to Objects Inscribed and Uninscribed

A rule which permitted the judge to insist that all evidence must pass the court's scrutiny as being the "best" or most reliable means of proving the fact would be a sore incumbrance upon the parties, who in our system have the responsibility of proof. In fact, as we have seen, no such general scrutiny is sanctioned, but only as to "writings" is a demand for the "best," the original, made. This limitation on the ambit of the rule rests largely on the practical realization that writings exhibit a fineness of detail, lacking in chattels generally, which will often be of critical importance. Prevention of loss of this fine detail through mistransmission is a basic objective of the rule requiring production of documentary originals.

But while writings may be generally distinguished from other chattels with respect to

the amount and importance of the detail they exhibit, chattels bearing more or less detailed inscriptions are far from uncommon. Thus, when an object such as a policeman's badge, a flag, or a tombstone bears a number or legend the terms of which are relevant the problem is raised as to whether the object shall be treated as a chattel or a writing. It is here clearly unwise to adapt a purely semantic approach and to classify the object according to whether its written component predominates sufficiently to alter the label attached to it in common parlance. At the same time, however, it would seem also unnecessary to classify as writings, as apparently do the Federal and Revised Uniform Rules (1974), any object which carries an inscription of any sort whatsoever. In the final analysis, it is perhaps impossible to improve upon Wigmore's suggestion, followed by a number of courts, that the judge shall have discretion to apply the present rule to inscribed chattels or not in light of such factors as the need for precise information as to the exact inscription, the ease or difficulty of production, and the simplicity or complexity of the inscription.

Within this general framework, certain types of chattels warrant specific mention. Thus, sound recordings, where their content is sought to be proved,[1] so clearly involve the identical considerations applicable to writings as to warrant inclusion within the present rule. Somewhat more questionable are the provisions of the Federal and Revised Uniform Rules of Evidence (1974) which bring photographs within the rule in those relatively rare instances in which their contents are sought to be proved. However, while it is difficult to accept that photographs of objects exhibit more intricacy of detail than do the objects photographed, concentrating attention upon content does provide a rationale for bringing photographs within it where their contents are sought to be proved. Certainly, the original of a photograph may afford indices of chicanery which secondary evidence of its contents would not betray, and this is

§ 232

1. For a discussion of those instances in which content

is sought to be proved, see § 233 infra.

likely to be of unusual importance where photographic products are offered "to speak for themselves." Further, it should be noted that X rays were frequently held to be within the rule even before the advent of the recent codifications.

§ 233. What Constitutes Proving the Terms

It is apparent that this danger of mistransmission of the contents of the writing, which is the principal reason for the rule, is only important when evidence other than the writing itself is offered for the purpose of proving its terms. Consequently, evidence that a certain document is in existence or as to its execution or delivery is not within the rule and may be given without producing the document.

In what instances, then, can it be said that the terms of a writing are sought to be proved, rather than merely its identity, or existence? First, there are certain writings which the substantive law, e.g., the Statute of Frauds, the parol evidence rule, endow with a degree of either indispensability or primacy. Transactions to which substantive rules of this character apply tend naturally to be viewed as written transactions, and writings embodying such transactions, e.g., deeds, contracts, judgments, etc., are universally considered to be within the present rule when actually involved in the litigation. Contrasted with the above described types of writings are those, essentially unlimited in variety, which the substantive law does not regard as essential or primary repositories of the facts recorded. Writings of this latter sort may be said merely to happen to record the facts of essentially nonwritten transactions. Testimony descriptive of nonwritten transactions is not generally considered to be within the scope of the present rule and may be given without producing or explaining the absence of a writing recording the facts. Thus, evidence of a payment may be given without production of the receipt, or evidence of a marriage without production of the marriage certificate.

While, however, many facts may be proved without resort to writings which record them, the party attempting to prove a fact may choose to show the contents of a writing for the purpose. Thus, for example, a writing may contain a recital of fact which is admissible under an exception to the hearsay rule. Here the recited fact might possibly be established without the writing, but if the contents are relied upon for the purpose, the present rule applies and oral testimony as to its contents will be rejected unless the original writing is shown to be unavailable.

Distinguishable from the situation in which the witness undertakes to state the fact based upon what he has seen in a writing, is the situation in which the witness testifies that the fact did not occur because relevant records contain no mention of it. This negative type of testimony is usually held not to constitute proof of contents and thus not to require production of records. But it will be seen that care in the application of this exception is required, since testimony as to what does not appear may easily involve a questionable description by the witness of the details which do appear. Perhaps a better approach would be to treat such "non-entry" testimony as a form of summary, which in fact it is, and to subject it to the safeguards employed in that context.

It has long been held that records too voluminous to be conveniently produced and examined in court may be summarized and their import testified to by a witness, usually an expert, who has reviewed the entirety. The Federal and Revised Uniform Rules of Evidence (1974) recognize and clarify this helpful practice, and also provide appropriate safeguards by requiring that the originals be made available for examination and copying by other parties. These requirements, of course, tacitly assume that reasonable notice be given of the intent to offer summaries. And, since the summaries admitted under this rule are being introduced substantively in place of the matters summarized, it has reasonably been held that a foundation is required for such evidence which establishes both the admissibility of the underlying data and the accuracy of the summary.

Certain criticisms may be leveled at the commonly applied distinction between facts the legal efficacy of which is affected by recordation, and facts which are legally effective whether or not contained in a writing. Thus it has been suggested that in modern law there are few if any instances in which a writing is anything more than a recordation of some nonwritten fact. For example, a written contract, it may be contended, merely records the operative legal fact, which is the agreement of the parties. Moreover, the distinction has proved a difficult one to apply, and does not adequately serve to reconcile various common applications and nonapplications of the rule. Thus it is commonly held that oral evidence of a witness's prior testimony is receivable even though that testimony is embodied in a transcript. But when a confession has been both orally made and reduced to writing, numerous courts require the writing. Dying declarations both spoken and reduced to writing have produced a similar contrariety of opinion.

Perhaps the most satisfactory solution to the problem would be to abandon the distinction between transactions essentially written and nonwritten and allow the application of the rule to turn upon the trial judge's determination of such factors as the centrality of the writing to the litigation, the importance of bringing the precise words of the writing before the trier, and the danger of mistransmission or imposition in the absence of the original. The result would simply be to merge the present confusing and confused doctrine with the collateral documents exception discussed below, or at least to enlarge the scope of the latter.

§ 234. Writings Involved Only Collaterally

At nearly every turn in human affairs some writing—a letter, a bill of sale, a newspaper, a deed—plays a part. Consequently any narration by a witness is likely to include many references to transactions consisting partly of written communications or other writings. A witness to a confession, for example, identifies the date as being the day after the crime because he read of the crime in the newspaper that day, or a witness may state that he was unable to procure a certain article because it was patented. It is apparent that it is impracticable to forbid such references except upon condition that the writings (e.g., the newspaper, and the patent) be produced in court. Recognition of an exception exempting "collateral writings" from the operation of the basic rule has followed as a necessary concession to expedition of trials and clearness of narration, interests which outweigh, in the case of merely incidental references to documents, the need for perfect exactitude in the presentation of these documents' contents.

While writings are frequently held to be collateral within the meaning of the present exception, the purposes for which references to documents may be made by witnesses are so variegated that the concept of collateralness defies precise definition. Three principal factors, however, should, and generally do, play a role in making the determination of collateralness. These are: the centrality of the writing to the principal issues of the litigation; the complexity of the relevant features of the writing; and the existence of genuine dispute as to the contents of the writing. Evaluation and weighting of these factors in the particular instance may perhaps best be left to the discretion of the trial judge, and as elsewhere in the application of this essentially administrative rule, exercise of that discretion should be reviewed only for grave abuse.

§ 235. Which Is the "Writing Itself" That Must Be Produced? Telegrams, Counterparts

What should be the application of the basic rule where two documents, X and Y, exist, X having been created first and Y being some variety of reproduction of X? Copies, of course, are frequent and in most cases the document first prepared will be the one whose initial production is required by the rule.

But the problem is not always so simple. For example, X may be a telegram written by the sender and handed to the company for transmission; or X may be a libelous handwritten letter given to a stenographer for copying and sending, and Y the letter actually received by the addressee; or X may be a ledger sheet in the creditor's books and Y the account rendered made up therefrom and sent to the debtor.

In any of the above cases, if a party in court offers document Y in evidence, what determines whether the document is "the writing itself" offered to prove its own terms, or merely a "copy" offered to establish the terms of X? The answer here clearly does not depend upon the chronology of creation or the ordinary semantic usage which would denominate Y as a "copy." Instead it will depend upon the substantive law of contracts, defamation, property, and the like. The question to be asked, then, is whether, under the substantive law, the creation, publication, or other use of Y may be viewed as affecting the rights of the parties in a way material to the litigation. If the answer to this question is affirmative, the fact that Y happens to be a copy of another writing is completely immaterial. Decisions illustrative of instances in which the terms of "copies" are the facts sought to be proved are cited below.

It will also frequently occur that a written transaction, such as a contract or deed, will be evidenced by several counterparts or identical copies, each of which is signed by the parties or, at any rate, intended to be equally effective as embodying the transaction. Such multiple counterparts are frequently termed "duplicate (or triplicate, etc.) originals". Each of these counterparts is admissible as an "original" without producing or accounting for the others, but before secondary evidence may be resorted to, all of the counterparts must be shown to be unavailable.

§ 236. Reproductions: Carbons: Printed and Multigraph Copies: Photo and Xerographic Copies

The treatment of copies under the rule requiring the production of the original document can only properly be understood when viewed in light of the technological history of copying itself. In its earliest stages, the rule appears to have developed against a background of copying performed by individuals of the Bob Cratchit sort, transcribing manually not always under the best of conditions. Errors under such circumstances were routinely to be expected. Only marginally greater reliability was to be found in the so-called letterpress. Here the original was written or typed in copying ink or with copying pencil. Presumably influenced by the infirmities present in such modes of copying, the courts generally declined to accept subsequently created copies as equivalent to originals.

The advent of carbon paper, however, made possible the creation of copies of substantially greater reliability and legibility. Here, since the copy is made by the same stroke as the original, there was an apparent factual distinction between these copies and copies produced subsequent to the original by the older methods. It moreover became common, as it is today, to create multiple counterparts of a contract or transaction through the use of carbon paper, with each copy duly signed either through the same medium or individually. What makes such writings counterparts, of course, is the signing with intent to render each co-equal with the others, and the doctrine of counterparts can therefore hardly apply to a retained carbon copy which is not intended as a communication at all. However, the fact that many true counterparts are made by the use of carbons coupled with the notion that writings generated simultaneously by the same stroke are in some way superior, has caused a great number of courts to treat all carbons as if they were duplicate originals, i.e., as admissible without accounting for the original.

More comprehensibly, there is warrant for believing that the courts will accept as primary evidence of the contents of a given book or a given issue of a newspaper any other book or newspaper printed from the same sets of fixed type, or the same plates or mats. A like result should be reached as to all copies run off from the same mat by the multigraph, lithoprint or other duplicating process.

In the present day, copying by various photographic and other processes has become commonplace, replacing the carbon for many purposes. Various types of photographic copying, of course, produce facsimiles of an extremely high degree of verisimilitude, and thus might have been expected, as have carbons, to win recognition as duplicate originals. In fact, an early judicial step in this direction was taken in a celebrated federal court of appeals decision which held that "recordak" photographs of checks which had been paid, preserved by a bank as part of its regular records were admissible under the Federal Business Records Act. Subsequently, a uniform act was prepared under which photographic copies, regularly kept, of business and public records are admissible without accounting for the original. This act has been widely adopted. In the cases, however, in which photographs of writings have been offered to show the terms of the original, without the aid of specific statutes, they have been almost uniformly treated as secondary evidence, inadmissible unless the original is accounted for.

The resulting state of authority, favorable to carbons but unfavorable to at least equally reliable photographic and xerographic reproductions, appears inexplicable on any basis other than that the courts, having fixed upon simultaneous creation as the characteristic distinguishing of carbons from copies produced by earlier methods have on the whole been insufficiently flexible to modify that concept in the face of newer technological methods which fortuitously do not exhibit that characteristic. Insofar as the primary purpose of the original documents requirement is directed at securing accurate information from the contents of material writings, free of the infirmities of memory and the mistakes of hand-copying, we may well conclude that each of these forms of mechanical copying is sufficient to fulfill the policy. Insistence upon the original, or accounting for it, places costs, burdens of planning, and hazards of mistake upon the litigants. These may be worth im-

posing where the alternative is accepting memory or hand-copies. They are probably not worth imposing when risks of inaccuracy are reduced to a minimum by the offer of a mechanically produced copy.

At the same time, however, if the original documents requirement is conceded to be supported by the ancillary purpose of fraud prevention, it will be seen that even copies produced by photographic or xerographic processes are not totally as desirable as the original writing. Many indicia of putative fraud such as watermarks, types of paper and inks, etc., will not be discernable on the copy. The most reasonable accommodation of the purposes of the basic rule to modern copying to date would appear to be that of the Federal Rules of Evidence. Under Federal Rule 1001(4) copies produced by photography or chemical reproduction or equivalent techniques are classed as "duplicates," and, under Rule 1003 are declared admissible as originals unless a genuine question is raised as to the authenticity of the original or it appears under the circumstances that it would be unfair to admit the duplicate in lieu of the original.

An even more recent challenge to the flexibility of the rule requiring documentary originals has appeared in the form of machine readable records stored on punch cards or magnetic tape. Obviously, where records are originally deposited in such media nothing akin to a conventional documentary original will be created. To the credit of the courts, records there stored have generally fared well in the face of objection predicated on the original document rule, and machine printouts of such records have been admitted.

§ 237. Excuses for Nonproduction of the Original Writing: (a) Loss or Destruction

The production-of-documents rule is principally aimed, not at securing a writing at all hazards and in every instance, but at securing the best *obtainable* evidence of its contents. Thus, if as a practical matter the document cannot be produced because it has been lost or destroyed, the production of the original is excused and other evidence of its contents becomes admissible. Failure to recognize this qualification of the basic rule would in many instances mean a return to the bygone and unlamented days in which to lose one's paper was to lose one's right. Recognition of the same qualification also squares with the ancillary purpose of the basic rule to protect against the perpetration of fraud, since proof that failure to produce the original is due to inability to do so tends logically to dispel the otherwise possible inference that the failure stems from design.

Loss or destruction may sometimes be provable by direct evidence but more often the only available evidence will be circumstantial, usually taking the form that appropriate search for the document has been made without discovering it. It would appear that where loss or destruction is sought to be proved by circumstantial evidence of unavailing search, the declarations of a former custodian as to loss or destruction may be admitted to show the nature and results of the search, though if offered as direct evidence of loss or destruction itself such declarations would be incompetent as hearsay.

Where loss or destruction is sought to be shown circumstantially by proof of unsuccessful search, it is obvious that the adequacy of the showing will be largely dependent upon the thoroughness and appropriateness of the search. It was laid down in certain early decisions that when the writing is last known to have been in a particular place or in the hands of a particular person, then that place must be searched or the person produced, and statements to the same effect are to be found in modern decisions. It is believed, however, that these statements are best considered as general guides or cautions, rather than strict and unvarying rules. Virtually all jurisdictions view the trial judge as possessing some degree of discretion in determining the preliminary question as to whether it is feasible to produce the original document. Such discretion is particularly appropriate since the character of the search required to show probability of loss or destruction will, as a practical matter, depend on the circumstances of each case. Factors such as the relative importance of the document and the lapse of time since it was last seen have been seen to bear upon the extent of search required before loss or destruction may be inferred. The only general requirement, however, should be that all reasonable avenues of search should be explored to the extent that reasonable diligence under the circumstances would dictate.

If the original document has been destroyed by the person who offers evidence of its contents, the evidence is not admissible unless, by showing that the destruction was accidental or was done in good faith, without intention to prevent its use as evidence, he rebuts to the satisfaction of the trial judge, any inference of fraud.

§ 238. Excuses for Nonproduction of the Original Writing: (b) Possession by a Third Person

When the writing is in the hands of a third person who is within the geographical limits of the trial court's subpoena power, the safest course is to have a writ of subpoena duces tecum served on the possessor summoning him to bring the writing to court at the trial, though some decisions will excuse resort to subpoena if the possessor is privileged not to produce it, and others suggest that proof of a hostile or unwilling attitude on his part will be a sufficient excuse.

If the writing is in the possession of a third person out of the state or out of the reach of the court's process, a showing of this fact alone will suffice, in the view of many courts, to excuse production of the writing. This practice has the merit of being an easy rule of thumb to apply, but the basic policy of the original document requirement would tend to support the view of a substantially equal number of courts that a further showing must be made. These latter courts require that, before secondary evidence is used, the proponent must show either that he has made reasonable but unavailing efforts to secure the original from its possessor, or circumstances which persuade the court that such efforts, had they been made, would have been fruitless.

§ 239. Excuses for Nonproduction of the Original Writing: (c) Failure of Adversary Having Possession to Produce After Notice

A frequently used method of showing that it is impracticable for the proponent to produce the original writing is to prove, first, that the original is in the hands of his adversary or under his control, and second, that the proponent has notified him to produce it at the trial and he has failed to do so. Observe that the notice is without compulsive force, and is designed merely to account for nonproduction of the writing by the proponent, and thus to enable him to use secondary evidence of the writing's terms. If the proponent actually needs the production of the original itself he will resort to subpoena duces tecum or under modern rules the motion for an order to produce. But when the notice is offered as an excuse for resorting to secondary evidence the adversary cannot fairly complain that he was only given opportunity, not compelled, to make the writing available.

An oral notice may be sufficient, but the safest and almost universal practice is to give written notice beforehand to the party or his attorney, describing the particular documents, and then to call upon the adversary orally at the trial for the writings requested. It is held that the nature of the complaint or of the defense may constitute a sufficient implied notice that the pleader is charging the adversary with possession of the original and that he considers its production essential. As to the time of serving notice it is sufficient if it allows the adversary a fair opportunity under the existing circumstances to produce the writing at the trial. Accordingly, if it appears at the trial itself that the adversary has the original paper in the courtroom, an immediate notice then and there is timely.

Some exceptions, under which notice is unnecessary before using secondary evidence of a writing in the adversary's possession, have been recognized. The first is well sustained

in reason. It dispenses with the need for notice when the adversary has wrongfully obtained or fraudulently suppressed the writing. The others seem more questionable. There is a traditional exception that no notice is required to produce a writing which is itself a notice. This is understandable in respect to giving notice to produce a notice to produce, which would lead to an endless succession of notices, but there seems little justification for extending the exception, as the cases do, to notices generally. Finally an exception is made by the majority view for writings in the hands of the accused in a criminal prosecution. Under this view, secondary evidence may be received without notice to the accused to produce. The logic of deriving this position, as seems to have been done, from the privilege against self-incrimination is dubious. For while a demand upon the accused to produce which is delivered before the jury clearly has a tendency to coerce the defendant and thus cheapen the privilege, there is no logical necessity that the demand be so delivered. Since the object of notice is to protect against imposition upon the opponent, and since this object may be achieved in the case of the criminal defendant by notice before trial, the minority view under which the prosecution must give notice as a necessary precondition to the use of secondary evidence seems the fairer and more reasonable stand.

§ 240. Excuses for Nonproduction of the Original Writing: (d) Public Records

If the contents of the judgment of a court or of an executive proclamation are to be proved, shall the proponent be required to produce the original writing? The accepted view is that, in general, public and judicial records and public documents are required by law to be retained by the official custodian in the public office designated for their custody, and courts will not require them to be removed. To require removal would be inconvenient for the public who might desire to consult the records and would entail a risk of loss of or damage to the official documents. Accordingly, statutes and rules have provided for the issuance of certified copies and for their admission in evidence in lieu of the original. In addition, examined copies, authenticated by a witness who has compared it with the original record, are usually receivable.

§ 241. Preferences Among Copies and Between Copies and Oral Testimony

The basic policy of the original document requirement is that of specially safeguarding the accuracy of the presentation in court of the terms of a writing. If the original is unavailable does the same policy require a preference among the secondary methods of proving the terms? Some means of proof are clearly more reliable than others. In order of reliability the list might go something like this: (1) a mechanically produced copy, such as a photograph or xerograph, a carbon, a letter-press copy, etc.,[1] (2) a firsthand copy by one who was looking at the original while he copied (immediate copy, sworn copy), (3) a copy, however made, which has been compared by a witness with the original and found correct (examined copy), (4) a secondhand or mediate copy, i.e., a copy of a firsthand copy, (5) oral testimony as to the terms of the writing, with memory aided by a previously made memorandum, and (6) oral testimony from unaided memory. There are many additional variations.

There is one rule of preference that is reasonable and is generally agreed on by the courts, namely, that for judicial and other public records, a certified, sworn or examined copy is preferred, and other evidence of the terms of the record cannot be resorted to unless the proponent has no such copy available, and the original record has been lost or destroyed so that a copy cannot now be made.

As to writings other than public records, there are two general approaches to the problem. First there is the view, fathered by some of the English decisions and espoused by a minority of the American cases, that "there are no degrees of substantive evidence." This position has the virtues of simplicity and easi-

ness of application. In addition, it may be observed that failure to apply the basic rule as between varieties of secondary evidence leaves unimpaired a substantial practical motivation to produce more satisfactory secondary evidence where it appears to exist. This practical motivation, of course, stems from apprehension of the adverse inference which may be drawn from failure to produce more satisfactory secondary evidence indicated to exist and not shown to be unavailable. These considerations have led the draftsmen of most modern codes of evidence to adopt the so-called "English" view.

The second view is followed by a majority of the courts which have passed on the question. Here a distinction is recognized between types of secondary evidence, with a written copy being preferred to oral testimony, and, under circumstances varying from state to state, and an immediate copy being preferred to a more remote one. This view is justifiable chiefly on the ground that there is some incongruity in pursuing the policy of obtaining the terms of writings with fullest accuracy, by structuring a highly technical rule to that end, only to abandon it upon the unavailability of the original. In formulating this general approach of discrimination among types of secondary evidence, the courts following the American rule have sought to avoid a position which would require the proponent to produce or account for all possible copies that may have existed. A reasonable standard is suggested by an early New York judge, who said:

"I do not mean to contend that there are any arbitrary or inflexible degrees of secondary evidence, rendering it necessary for a party, who is driven to that description of proof, to show affirmatively, in every instance that there is no higher degree within his power, than the one he offers; but I think it may be safely said, that where it appears in the very offer, or from the nature of the case itself, or from the circumstances attending the offer, that the party has better and more reliable evidence at hand, and equally within

1. See § 236 supra.

his power, he shall not be permitted to resort to the inferior degree first".

§ 242. Adversary's Admission as to the Terms of a Writing

Many American courts have followed the lead of Baron Parke's decision in Slatterie v. Pooley and have held admissions by a party opponent admissible to prove the terms of a writing. Upon reflection, however, it will be seen that Baron Parke's decision squares rather poorly with the primary modern day policy in favor of obtaining the contents of writings with accuracy. The evidence determined admissible in Slatterie v. Pooley was actually at two removes from the writing itself, being witness' report of the defendant's comment. Perhaps the policy of holding admissible any admission which a party-opponent chooses to make will suffice to justify the first step, but the second frequently raises the possibility of erroneous transmission without corresponding justification. Accordingly, some American decisions have rejected testimony relating oral admissions concerning contents of writings.

It will be observed, however, that the second possibility of mistransmission noted above is effectively eliminated where no testimonial report of the admission is required. Thus, the desirable solution, towards which it is believed the decisions may be drifting, is to receive admissions to evidence a document's terms (1) when the admission itself is in writing and is produced in evidence, or (2) when the party himself, on the stand in this or some other trial or hearing, makes the admission about the contents of the writing or concedes that he made such an admission on a former occasion. Oral testimony by a witness that he heard the party's admission as to the terms of the writing, despite the authority of Slatterie v. Pooley, should be excluded.

§ 243. Review of Rulings Admitting Secondary Evidence

It will be seen from the earlier sections of this chapter that the requirement of the production of original writings, with the several excuses for nonproduction and the exceptions to the requirement itself, make up a fairly complex set of regulations for administration by the trial judge. Mistakes in the application of these rules are, understandably, not infrequent. The purpose of this system of rules, on the other hand, is simple and practical. That purpose is to secure the most reliable information as to the contents of documents, when those terms are disputed. A mystical ideal of seeking "the best evidence" or the "original document," as an end in itself is no longer the goal. Consequently when an attack is made, on motion for new trial or on appeal, upon the judge's admission of secondary evidence, it seems that the reviewing tribunal, should ordinarily make inquiry of the complaining counsel, "Does the party whom you represent actually dispute the accuracy of the evidence received as to the material terms of the writing?" If the counsel cannot assure the court that such a good faith dispute exists, it seems clear that any departure from the regulations in respect to secondary evidence must be classed as harmless error.

*

Title 10

THE HEARSAY RULE AND ITS EXCEPTIONS

Chapter 24

THE HEARSAY RULE

Table of Sections

§ 244. The History of the Rule Against Hearsay

In an oft-quoted passage, Wigmore calls the rule against hearsay "that most characteristic rule of the Anglo–American Law of Evidence—a rule which may be esteemed, next to jury trial, the greatest contribution of that eminently practical legal system to the world's methods of procedure." [1] How did this rule come about?

The development of the jury was, no doubt, an important factor. It will be remembered that the jury in its earlier forms was in the nature of a committee or special commission of qualified persons in the neighborhood to report on facts or issues in dispute. So far as

necessary its members conducted its investigations informally among those who had special knowledge of the facts. Attesting witnesses to writings were summoned with the jurors and apparently participated in their deliberations, but the practice of calling witnesses to appear in court and testify publicly about the facts to the jury is a late development in jury trial. Though something like the jury existed at least as early as the 1100's, this practice of hearing witnesses in court does not become frequent until the later 1400's. The change-over to the present conception that the normal source of proof is not the private knowledge or investigation of the jurors, but the testimony of witnesses in open court, is a matter of gradual evolution thereafter. Finally, in the 1500's it has become,

§ 244

1. 5 Wigmore, § 1364 at 28 (Chadbourn rev. 1974).

though not yet the exclusive source of proof, the normal and principal one.

It is not until this period of the gradual emergence of the witness testifying publicly in court that the consciousness of need for exclusionary rules of evidence begins to appear. It had indeed been required even of the early witnesses to writings that they could speak only of "what they saw and heard"[2] and this requirement would naturally be applied to the new class of testifying witnesses. But when the witness has heard at firsthand the statement of X out of court that she has seen and heard a blow with a sword, or witnessed a trespass on land, as evidence of the blow or the trespass, a new question is presented. Certainly it would seem that the earlier requirement of knowledge must have predisposed the judges to skepticism about the value of hearsay.

Accordingly, it is the value of hearsay, its sufficiency as proof, that is the subject of discussion in this gestation period. And so through the reigns of the Tudors and the Stuarts there is a gradually increasing drumfire of criticism and objections by parties and counsel against evidence of oral hearsay declarations. While the evidence was constantly admitted, the confidence in its reliability was increasingly undermined. It was derided as "a tale of a tale"[3] or "a story out of another man's mouth."[4] Parallel with this increasingly discredited use of casual oral hearsay was a similar development in respect to transcribed statements made under oath before a judge or judicial officer, not subject to cross-examination by the party against whom it is offered. In criminal cases in the 1500's and down to the middle 1600's the main reliance of the prosecution was the use of such "depositions" to make out its case. As oral hearsay was becoming discredited, uneasiness about

the use of "depositions" began to take shape, first in the form of a limitation that they could only be used when the witness could not be produced at the trial. It will be noted that the want of oath and the unreliability of the report of the oral statement cannot be urged against such evidence but only the want of cross-examination and observation of demeanor.

It was in the first decade after the Restoration that the century or so of criticism of hearsay had its final effect in decisions rejecting its use, first as to oral hearsay and then as to depositions. Wigmore finds that the period between 1675 and 1690 is the time of crystallization of the rule against hearsay. For a time the rule was qualified by the notion that hearsay, while not independently admissible, could come in as confirmatory of other evidence, and this qualification survived down to the end of the 1700's in the limited form of admitting a witness's prior consistent statements out of court to corroborate his testimony.

Whether the rule against hearsay was, with the rest of the English law of evidence, in fact "the child of the jury"[5] or the product of the adversary system may be of no great contemporary significance. The important thing is that the rule against hearsay taking form at the end of the seventeenth century was neither a matter of "immemorial usage" nor an inheritance from Magna Charta but, in the long view of English legal history, was a late development of the common law.

Holdsworth thinks that the immediate influences leading to the crystallization of the rule against hearsay, at the particular time in the late 1600's when this occurred, were first, a strong dictum by Coke in his Third Institute denouncing "the strange conceit that one may be an accuser by hearsay,"[6] and second, the

---

2. Thayer, Preliminary Treatise on Evidence, pp. 101, 519 (1898).

3. Colledge's Trial, 8 How.St.Tr. 549, 663 (1681) (counsel for prosecution warning his own witness), cited in 5 Wigmore, supra note 1, at n. 32.

4. Gascoigne's Trial, 7 How.St.Tr. 959, 1019 (1680) (warning by judge, but evidence finally admitted) cited in 5 Wigmore, supra note 1, at n. 32.

5. Thayer, Preliminary Treatise on Evidence 47, also 2–4, 180 (1898).

6. Coke thus condemned the holding in Thomas's case, Dyer 99b (1553) to the effect that under a statute of Edward VI requiring two witnesses in treason if one accuser speaks from his own knowledge, "and he relate it to another, the other may well be an accuser." Coke Third Inst. 25 (1641).

rejection of the attempt to naturalize in English law the canon and civil law requirement of "two witnesses" and the consequent urge to provide some compensating safeguard.[7] As we have seen, a century of increasing protests against the use of hearsay had preceded the establishment of the rule. However, most of the specific weaknesses of hearsay, which were the underlying reasons for the adoption of the rule, and which have explained its survival, were not clearly pointed out until after the beginning of the 1700's when the newly established rule came to be rationalized by the judges and the text writers.

§ 245. The Reasons for the Rule Against Hearsay: Exceptions to the Rule

The factors upon which the credibility of testimony depends are the perception, memory, and narration of the witness. (1) *Perception.* Did the witness perceive what he describes, and did he perceive it accurately? (2) *Memory.* Has the witness retained an accurate impression of his perception? (3) *Narration.* Does his language convey that impression accurately? Some writers subdivide inaccuracy of narration into ambiguity and insincerity, resulting in four rather than three factors. However, it seems apparent that ambiguity and insincerity, as well as honest mistake, all manifest themselves as inaccuracy of narration.

In order to encourage witnesses to put forth their best efforts and to expose inaccuracies which might be present with respect to any of the foregoing factors, the Anglo–American tradition evolved three conditions under which witnesses ordinarily will be required to testify: oath, personal presence at the trial, and cross-examination. The rule against hearsay is designed to insure compliance with these ideal conditions, and when one of them is absent the hearsay objection becomes pertinent.

In the hearsay situation, two "witnesses" are involved. The first complies with all three of the ideal conditions for the giving of testimony, but his testimony consists of reporting what the second "witness" said. The second "witness" is the out-of-court declarant; his statement was not given in compliance with the ideal conditions, yet it contains the information that is of concern in the case.

Oath. Among the earliest of the criticisms of hearsay, and one often repeated in judicial opinions down to the present, is the objection that the out-of-court declarant who made the hearsay statement commonly speaks or writes without the solemnity of the oath administered to witnesses in a court of law. The oath may be important in two aspects. As a ceremonial and religious symbol it may induce in the witness a feeling of special obligation to speak the truth, and also it may impress upon the witness the danger of criminal punishment for perjury, to which the judicial oath or an equivalent solemn affirmation would be a prerequisite condition. Wigmore considers that the objection for want of an oath is incidental and not essential, and suggests that this is demonstrated by the fact that a hearsay statement, even if under oath, is still rejected.[1] But the fact that the oath is not the only requirement of the rule against hearsay does not prove that it is not an important one. Nor does the fact that the oath may have diminished in significance with the passage of time mean that today it is without significance; no disposition to abolish it (other than to allow affirmation as a substitute) is apparent.

Personal presence at trial. Another objection early asserted and repeated of late is the want of opportunity, in respect to the out-of-court declarant, for observation of his demeanor, with the light that this may shed on his credibility, that would be afforded if he were a witness on the stand.

The solemnity of the occasion and possibility of public disgrace can scarcely fail to impress the witness, and falsehood no doubt becomes more difficult if the person against whom directed is present.

---

7. 9 Holdsworth, History of English Law 217, 218 (3d ed. 1944).

§ 245
1. 5 Wigmore, Evidence, p. 10 (Chadbourn rev. 1974).

Moreover, personal presence eliminates the danger that in the oral reporting of an out-of-court statement the witness reporting the statement may do so inaccurately. It seems probable that the reporting of words spoken is subject to special dangers of inaccuracy beyond the fallibility common to all reproduction from memory of matters of observation, and this seems a substantial danger in the admission of hearsay. It is true as Wigmore points out [2] that not all hearsay is subject to this danger. Written statements can be produced in court and can be tested with reasonable accuracy for genuineness and freedom from alteration. Moreover, as Morgan has suggested, the reporting in court of spoken words for nonhearsay purposes, as in proving the making of an oral contract or the utterance of a slander,[3] is subject to this same risk of misreporting. Neither argument seems conclusive. In any event, no distinction is in general made between written and spoken hearsay.

Cross-examination. It would be generally agreed today that noncompliance with the third condition is the main justification for the exclusion of hearsay. This is the lack of any opportunity for the adversary to cross-examine the absent declarant whose out-of-court statement is reported by the witness. Thus as early as 1668 we find a court rejecting hearsay because "the other party could not cross-examine the party sworn."[4] Judicial expressions stress this as a principal reason for the hearsay rule. Cross-examination, as Bentham pointed out,[5] was a distinctive feature of the English trial system, and the one which most contributed to the prestige of the institution of jury trial. He called it "a security for the correctness and completeness of testimony." The nature of this safeguard which hearsay lacks is indicated by Chancellor Kent: "Hearsay testimony is from the very nature of it attended with * * * doubts and difficulties and it cannot clear them up. 'A person who relates a hearsay is not obliged to enter into any particulars, to answer any questions, to solve any difficulties, to reconcile any contradictions, to explain any obscurities, to remove any ambiguities; he entrenches himself in the simple assertion that he was told so, and leaves the burden entirely on his dead or absent author.' * * * *"[6] In perhaps his most famous remark, Wigmore described cross-examination as "beyond any doubt the greatest legal engine ever invented for the discovery of truth."[7]

Hearsay that is admitted. It is easy, however, to overplay the unreliability of hearsay. Eminent judges have spoken of its "intrinsic weakness."[8] If this were meant to imply that all hearsay of its very nature is unworthy of reliance in a court of law, of course the implication is quite insupportable. The contrary is proved by the fact that courts are constantly receiving, as we shall see, hearsay evidence of various kinds under the numerous exceptions to the hearsay rule, and by the doctrine established in most jurisdictions that when hearsay evidence, which would have been excluded if objected to, is let in without objection, it may be taken into consideration if it appears to be reliable in the particular case, as sufficient to sustain a verdict or finding of the fact thus proved.[9] The truth, of course, is that hearsay evidence, ranging as it does from mere third-hand rumors to sworn affidavits of credible observers, has as wide a scale of reliability, from the highest to the lowest, as we find in testimonial or circumstantial evidence gener-

2. 5 Wigmore, supra note 1, at § 1363(1).

3. Where the utterance of the words is an "operative fact," see Morgan, A Suggested Classification of Utterances Admissible as Res Gestae, 31 Yale L.J. 229 (1922). See § 249, infra.

4. 2 Rolle's Abr. 679, pl. 9 (1668), cited by Morgan, Jury Trials and the Exclusionary Rules of Evidence, 4 U.Chi.L.Rev. 247, 253 (1937).

5. Rationale of Judicial Evidence, b. II, ch. IX, and b. III, ch. XX (1827) quoted 5 Wigmore, supra note 1 at § 1367.

6. Coleman v. Southwick, 9 John. 50 (N.Y.1812), in 5 Wigmore, supra note 1, § 1362 at p. 6.

7. 5 Wigmore, supra note 16, at p. 32.

8. Marshall, C.J. in Mima Queen v. Hepburn, 11 U.S. (7 Cranch) 290 (1813) and Story, J. in Ellicott v. Pearl, 35 U.S. (10 Pet.) 412, 436 (1836), both cited 5 Wigmore, supra note 1, § 1363 at p. 11.

9. See § 54, supra, where the matter is developed.

ally, depending as they all do upon the frailties of perception, memory, narration, and veracity of men and women. Notice may also be taken at this point that hearsay is widely used and usable in our judicial system in proving probable cause. Much of our learning comes in the form of hearsay. Indeed, it is the failure to adjust the rules of admissibility more flexibly and realistically to these variations in the reliability of hearsay that as we shall see has constituted one of the pressing needs for liberalization of evidence law.[10]

Few persons question the desirability of a general policy of requiring that testimony be given by witnesses in open court, under oath, and subject to cross-examination, which is the objective of the rule against hearsay. The problem area is found in the operation of the rule in excluding evidence as a means of effectuating that policy.

§ 246. A Definition of Hearsay

A definition cannot, in a sentence or two, furnish ready answers to all the complex problems of an extensive field, such as hearsay. It can, however, furnish a helpful general focus and point of beginning, as well as a memory aid in arranging some of the solutions.

The following definition is from the Federal Rules of Evidence, in effect in about half the states as well as in the federal courts. It has, in addition, been quoted with approval or adopted outright on a case-by-case basis in states where the Federal Rules have not been adopted in their entirety, and is generally consistent with the views now expressed in common law jurisdictions. Federal Rule of Evidence 801 provides:

    (a) **Statement.** A "statement" is (1) an oral or written assertion or (2) nonverbal conduct of a person, if it is intended by the person as an assertion.

    (b) **Declarant.** A "declarant" is a person who makes a statement.

    (c) **Hearsay.** "Hearsay" is a statement, other than one made by the declarant while testifying at the trial or hearing, offered in evidence to prove the truth of the matter asserted.

Before going into the sections of text that follow, dealing with various aspects of what is and is not hearsay, certain preliminary observations should be made.

The word "assert" appears prominently in the quoted rule but is nowhere defined. What does it mean? The contemporary dictionary meaning is to state positively or strongly, and accordingly a person may be described as being assertive. However, in the world of evidence, the word "assert" carries no connotation of being positive or strong. A favorite of writers in the field for at least a century and a half, the word simply means *to say that something is so,* e.g. that an event happened or that a condition existed.

The definition of hearsay contained in Federal Rule of Evidence 801(a)–(c), quoted above, is affirmative in form; it says that an out-of-court assertion, offered to prove the truth of the matter asserted, is hearsay. For example, witness W reports on the stand that declarant D has stated that X was driving a car at a given time and place. Proponent is trying with this evidence to prove that X did so act. The out-of-court assertion is being offered to prove the truth of the matter asserted, and by definition it is hearsay. Alternatively, if the out-of-court statement is measured against the policy underlying the hearsay rule, its evidentiary value depends upon the credibility of the declarant without the assurances of oath, presence, or cross-examination, and again the result is classification as hearsay.

The definition in the rule does not in terms say that everything not included within the definition is not hearsay. However, exclusion from the definition of everything not included within its terms was the intended effect of the rule, according to the Advisory Committee's Notes which accompanied the rules during their submission to the public, submission to the Supreme Court, transmission to the Congress, consideration by the Congress, and eventual adoption. No challenge to this read-

---

10. See § 325 infra.

ing of the rule was offered. The rule's definition must, therefore, be taken as meaning that out-of-court conduct that is not an assertion, or that, even though assertive, is not offered to prove the truth of the matter asserted, is not hearsay. What is, or is not, an assertion thus becomes an important inquiry in some situations. Moreover, if the policy underlying the hearsay rule is stretched to include all situations where the evidentiary value of a statement depends on the credibility of an out-of-court declarant, in however slight a degree or without regard to offsetting factors, there exists the possibility of conflict between the rule's underlying policy and the definition. These matters will be considered in the sections which follow.

Not in presence of party against whom offered. A remarkably persistent bit of courthouse folklore is the practice of objecting to out-of-court statements because not made in the presence of the party against whom offered. From the foregoing discussion, the lack of relationship between this objection and the concept of hearsay is apparent. The presence or absence of the party against whom an out-of-court statement is offered has significance only in a few particular situations, e.g., when a statement spoken in her presence is relied upon to charge her with notice,[1] or when failure to deny a statement spoken in her presence is the basis for claiming that she acquiesced in or adopted the statement.[2]

§ 247. Distinction Between Hearsay Rule and Rule Requiring Firsthand Knowledge

There is a rule, more ancient than the hearsay rule, and having some kinship in policy, which is to be distinguished from it. This is the rule that a witness is qualified to testify to a fact susceptible of observation, only if it appears that he had a reasonable opportunity to observe the facts.[1] Thus, if a witness testifies that on a certain day flight

450 arrived at the airport at X on time, and from his other evidence it appears that he was not in X at the time in question, and hence could only have spoken from conjecture or report of other persons, the proper objection is not hearsay but want of personal knowledge. Conversely, if the witness testifies that his brother *told* him that he came in on the flight and it arrived on time, the objection for want of knowledge of when the plane arrived is inappropriate, because the witness purports to speak from his own knowledge only of what his brother said, and as to this he presumably had knowledge. If the testimony in this latter case was offered to show the time of the plane's arrival, the appropriate objection is hearsay. The distinction is one of the form of the testimony, whether the witness purports to give the facts directly upon his own credit (though it may appear later that he was speaking only on the faith of reports from others) or whether he purports to give an account of what another has told him and this is offered to evidence the truth of the other's report. However, when it appears, either from the phrasing of his testimony or from other sources, that the witness is testifying on the basis of reports from others, though he does not in terms testify to their statements, the distinction loses much of its significance, and courts may simply apply the label "hearsay."

§ 248. Instances of the Application of the Hearsay Rule

A few examples of the rejection of evidence under the general hearsay rule excluding extra-judicial assertions offered to prove the facts asserted will indicate the scope of its operation. Evidence of the following oral statements has been excluded: on the issue whether deceased had transferred his insurance to his new automobile, testimony that he said he had made the transfer; to prove that veniremen had read newspaper articles, testi-

§ 246

1. See § 249, infra.
2. See § 250, infra.

§ 247

1. See § 10 supra.

mony of deputy sheriff that attorney said that one venireman said that other venireman had read the articles; to prove that driver was driving with consent of insured owner, testimony that owner said after the accident that the driver had his permission; in rebuttal of defense of entrapment, criminal reputation of defendant to show predisposition; to show defendant's control of premises where marijuana was found, testimony of police officer that neighbors said person of same name occupied the premises; statements of child to social workers describing sexual abuse.

Instances of exclusion of written statements as hearsay when offered in court as evidence of their truth are likewise frequent. Thus, the following have been determined to be hearsay: written estimates of damages or cost of repairs, made by an estimator who does not appear as a witness; written appraisal of stolen trailer by appraiser who did not testify; invoices, bills, and receipts as independent evidence of the making of repairs, payment, and reasonableness of charges; the written statement of an absent witness to an accident; newspaper accounts as proof of matters of fact reported therein; statements in will that testator's second wife had agreed to devise property to his children, as proof of that agreement; medical report, by a physician who did not testify, to prove that plaintiff had sustained injuries in a subsequent accident; manufacturer's advertising claims as proof of reliability of "Intoximeter."

§ 249. Some Out-of-Court Utterances Which Are Not Hearsay

The hearsay rule forbids evidence of out-of-court assertions to prove the facts asserted in them. If the statement is not an assertion or is not offered to prove the facts asserted, it is not hearsay. A few of the more common types of nonhearsay utterances are discussed in the present section.

Verbal acts. When a suit is brought for breach of a written contract, it would not occur to anyone, when a writing is offered as evidence of the contract sued on, to suggest that it is hearsay. Similarly proof of oral utterances by the parties in a contract suit constituting the offer and acceptance which brought the contract into being, are not evidence of assertions offered testimonially but rather of utterances—verbal conduct—to which the law attaches duties and liabilities. Other obvious instances are evidence of the utterance by the defendant of words relied on as constituting a slander or deceit for which damages are sought.

Verbal parts of acts. The legal significance of acts taken alone and isolated from surrounding circumstances may be unclear. Thus the bare physical act of handing over money to another person is susceptible of many interpretations. The possibilities include loan, payment of a debt, bribe, bet, gift, and no doubt many other kinds of transactions. Explanatory words which accompany and give character to the transaction are not hearsay when under the substantive law the pertinent inquiry is directed only to objective manifestations rather than to the actual intent or other state of mind of the actor. Similar considerations are commonly said to prevail when the character of an establishment is sought to be proved by evidence of statements made in connection with activities taking place on the premises.

Utterances and writings offered to show effect on hearer or reader. When it is proved that D made a statement to X, with the purpose of showing the probable state of mind thereby induced in X, such as being put on notice or having knowledge, or motive, or to show the information which X had as bearing on the reasonableness or good faith or voluntariness of the subsequent conduct of X, or anxiety, the evidence is not subject to attack as hearsay. The same rationale applies to proof by the defendant, in cases of assault or homicide, of communicated threats made to him by the person whom he is alleged to have killed or assaulted. If offered to show his reasonable apprehension of danger it is not offered for a hearsay purpose;[1] its value for

§ 249

1. See § 275 infra.

this purpose does not depend on the truth of the statement.

In the situations discussed above, the out-of-court statement will frequently have an impermissible hearsay aspect as well as the permissible nonhearsay aspect. For example, the inspector's statement that the tires were defective is susceptible of being used improperly by the trier of fact as proof that the tires were in fact defective, rather than only as notice of defective condition, with other proof being required of the fact of defective condition. Or the evidence that the man who lit the match said he was from the gas company might improperly be taken as proof of agency, rather than as a circumstance bearing on the reasonableness of plaintiff's conduct. Generally the disposition has been to admit the evidence with a limiting instruction, unless the need for the evidence for the proper purpose is substantially outweighed by the danger of improper use.[2] However, one area of apparently widespread abuse should be noted. In criminal cases, an arresting or investigating officer should not be put in the false position of seeming just to have happened upon the scene; he should be allowed some explanation of his presence and conduct. His testimony that he acted "upon information received," or words to that effect, should be sufficient. Nevertheless, cases abound in which the officer is allowed to relate historical aspects of the case, replete with hearsay statements in the form of complaints and reports, on the ground that he was entitled to give the information upon which he acted. The need for the evidence is slight, the likelihood of misuse great.

Indirect versions of hearsay statements; group statements. If the purpose of offered testimony is to use an out-of-court statement to evidence the truth of facts stated therein, the hearsay objection cannot be obviated by eliciting the purport of the statement in indirect form. Thus evidence as to the purport of "information received" by the witness, or testimony of the results of investigations made by other persons, offered as proof of the facts asserted out of court, are properly classed as hearsay.

Whether this approach should be applied to collective or group decisions presented by the testimony of one of the group is a matter of some uncertainty. The situation most likely to arise is probably a decision reached after consultation by a group of doctors. Authority on the hearsay question is scattered. In any event, the problem seems largely academic in view of the liberalization of the expert opinion rule to allow opinions to be based on reports of others[3] and of the regular entry rule to include opinions and diagnoses.[4]

Reputation. In the earlier stages of jury trial, when the jurors were expected to seek out the facts by neighborhood inquiries (instead of having the witnesses bring the facts through their testimony in court) community reputation was a frequent source of information for the jurors. When in the late 1600's the general doctrine excluding hearsay began to take form[5] the use of reputation either directly by the jurors or through the testimony of the witnesses, in certain areas of proof, was so well established that exceptions to the hearsay rule for reputation in these ancient uses soon came to be recognized.

Reputation is a composite description of what the people in a community have said and are saying about a matter. A witness who testifies to reputation testifies to his generalized memory of a series of out-of-court statements. Whether reputation is hearsay depends on the same tests we have applied to evidence of other particular out-of-court statements.[6] Accordingly proof of reputation will often not be hearsay at all. Thus, in an action for defamation, where an element of damages is injury to the plaintiff's reputation, and the defendant offers on the issue of damages, evidence that the plaintiff's reputation was bad before the slander, the evidence is not hearsay. Another example is proof of

---

2. See § 59 supra.
3. See § 15 supra.
4. See § 287 infra.

5. See § 244 supra.
6. See § 246 supra.

reputation in the community offered as evidence that some person in the community had knowledge of the reputed facts.

Applying again the general definition we may conclude that evidence of reputation is hearsay only when offered to prove the truth of the fact reputed and hence depending for its value on the veracity of the collective asserters. There are moreover, exceptions to the rule against hearsay, for reputation of particular facts, often restricted to certain uses and issues.[7]

Evidence of reputation, not falling within the established exceptions, when offered to prove the fact reputed, is constantly being excluded as hearsay, as for example, when reputation is offered to prove ownership, sanity, the existence of a partnership, or a predisposition to commit crime, to rebut a defense of entrapment.

Prior statements of witnesses; admissions of party-opponents. The status of prior statements of witnesses[8] and of admissions by party-opponents[9] as hearsay is discussed in later sections.

§ 250. Conduct as Hearsay: "Implied Assertions"

Nonverbal conduct. Thus far our examination into what is and is not hearsay has been confined to out-of-court words, either spoken or written. Under the definition in § 246, if they constitute an assertion and are offered as proof that the matter asserted happened or existed, they are hearsay.

Additional inquiry readily shows that nonverbal conduct may unmistakably be just as assertive in nature as though expressed in words. No one would contend, if, in response to a question "Who did it?," one of the auditors held up her hand, that this gesture could be treated as different from an oral or written

statement. Other illustrations are the act of pointing to a particular person in a lineup as the equivalent of saying "That's the person," or the sign language used by persons with impaired speech or hearing. These are clear instances of "non-verbal conduct of a person, if it is intended by him as an assertion," which under our hearsay definition receives the same treatment as oral or written assertions. The only difference is that an oral or written assertion is assumed, without further ado, to have been intended as such by virtue of being assertive in form, while in the case of the non-verbal conduct an intent to assert must be found by the judge as a precondition to classification as hearsay.

In contrast to the examples of clearly assertive nonverbal conduct given in the preceding paragraph, other situations may arise in which the conduct is just as clearly nonassertive. Thus an uncontrollable action or reaction by its very nature precludes any intent to make an assertion. Two cases will illustrate the difference. In the first, People v. Clark,[1] a murder suspect was described by witnesses as wearing a jacket with a fur-lined collar. The officer who arrested defendant at his home testified that he asked defendant if he had a jacket with a fur-lined collar, and that defendant turned to his wife and said, "I don't have one like that, do I dear?" The wife fainted. In the second case, Stevenson v. Commonwealth,[2] also a prosecution for murder, an officer testified he went to defendant's home and asked the wife for the shirt defendant was wearing when he arrived home after the time the murder was committed, and that she handed him a shirt. (Blood stains were found on the shirt.) In the first case, the conduct was held to have been nonassertive and hence not subject to the hearsay rule, while in the second it was held that the wife intended to assert that the shirt was the one

7. See § 322 infra.

8. § 251 infra.

9. Chap. 25 infra.

§ 250

1. 6 Cal.App.3d 658, 86 Cal.Rptr. 106 (1970). It is, of course, possible that the wife feigned the fainting, or that

it was genuine but caused by the general stress of the situation rather than by the reference to the jacket. These aspects are discussed at a later point in the text.

2. 218 Va. 462, 237 S.E.2d 779 (1977).

in question, and her conduct was within the hearsay rule.

The disputed area lies between these extremes.

So-called "implied assertions." In the early part of the 19th century, the celebrated case of Wright v. Tatham [3] wound its way through the English courts. John Marsden, a country gentleman, had by will left his estate to one Wright, who had risen from a menial station to the position of steward and general man of business for Marsden. The legal heir, Admiral Tatham, brought proceedings to recover the manors of the estate, alleging that Marsden was not competent to make a will. Defendant Wright, supporting the will, offered in evidence several letters that had been written to the deceased by third persons no longer living. The theory of the offer was that the letters indicated a belief on the part of the writers that Marsden was mentally competent, from which it might be inferred that he was in fact competent. The letters were admitted and the will sustained. However, upon retrial after reversal, the letters were excluded, and the verdict was against the will. The House of Lords ended eight years of litigation by upholding the ruling that the letters were inadmissible as being equivalent to hearsay evidence of the opinions of the writers. The holding was perhaps most pithily put by Baron Parke in these words:

> The conclusion at which I have arrived is, that proof of a particular fact which is not of itself a matter in issue, but which is relevant only as implying a statement or opinion of a third person on the matter in issue, is inadmissible in all cases where such a statement or opinion not on oath would be of itself inadmissible; and, therefore, in this case the letters which are offered only to prove the competence of the testator, that is the truth of the implied statements therein contained, were properly rejected, as the mere statement or opinion of the writer would certainly have been inadmissible.[4]

To describe the evidence in Wright v. Tatham as "implied statements," i.e. implied assertions, as suggested by Baron Parke is, of course, to prejudge the issue, for it is to extrajudicial assertions that the hearsay rule aplies.

During the progress of the case hundreds of pages of opinions were written by the judges and numerous examples posed, including these:

(1) proof that the underwriters have paid the amount of the policy, as evidence of the loss of a ship; (2) proof of payment of a wager, as evidence of the happening of the event which was the subject of the bet; (3) precautions of the family, to show the person involved was a lunatic; (4) as evidence of sanity, the election of the person in question to high office; (5) "the conduct of a physician who permitted a will to be executed by a sick testator;" (6) "the conduct of a deceased captain on a question of seaworthiness, who, after examining every part of the vessel embarked in it with his family."

Taking example (6) as an illustration, the line of reasoning suggested is (a) that the captain's conduct tends to prove that he believed the ship to be seaworthy, and (b) that from this belief the conclusion might be drawn that the ship was in fact seaworthy. This, the judges said, was the equivalent of an out-of-court statement by the captain that the ship was seaworthy and hence inadmissible hearsay. Functional equivalence can, however, be misleading. The vital element of intent to assert is missing from each of the examples.

In many of the cases after Wright v. Tatham the presence of an arguable hearsay issue went unrecognized. The earlier cases tended to favor the objection, but the current trend is much in the opposite direction. The Federal Rule,[5] for example, as well as numerous decisions, requires that nonverbal conduct must be intended to be an assertion if it is to be classed as hearsay.

---

3. 7 Adolph. & E. 313, 112 Eng.Rep. 488 (Exch.Ch. 1837), and 5 Cl. & F. 136 (H.L.1838).

4. 7 Adolph. & E. at 388, 112 Eng.Rep. at 516.

5. See § 246 supra.

Is this trend consistent with the policies that underlie the hearsay rule? A satisfactory resolution can be had only by making an evaluation in terms of the dangers which the hearsay rule is designed to guard against, i.e., imperfections of perception, memory, and narration. It is believed that such an analysis can result only in rejecting the view that evidence of conduct, from which may be inferred a belief, from which in turn may be inferred the happening of the event which produced the belief, is the equivalent of an assertion that the event happened and hence hearsay. People do not, prior to raising their umbrellas, say to themselves in soliloquy form, "It is raining," nor does the motorist go forward on the green light only after making an inward assertion, "The light is green." The conduct offered in the one instance to prove it was raining and in the other that the light was green, involves no intent to communicate the fact sought to be proved, and it was recognized long ago that purposeful deception is less likely in the absence of intent to communicate. True, the threshold question whether communication was in fact intended may on occasion present difficulty, yet the probabilities against intent are so great as to justify imposing the burden of establishing it upon the party urging the hearsay objection.

Even though the risks arising from purposeful deception may be slight or nonexistent in the absence of intent to communicate, the objection remains that the actor's perception and memory are untested by cross-examination for the possibility of honest mistake. However, in contrast to the risks from purposeful deception those arising from the chance of honest mistake seem more sensibly to be factors useful in evaluating weight and credibility rather than grounds for exclusion. Moreover, the kind of situation involved is ordinarily such as either to minimize the likelihood of flaws of perception and memory or to present circumstances lending themselves to their evaluation. While the suggestion has been advanced that conduct evidence ought to be admitted only when the actor's behavior has an element of significant reliance as an assurance of trustworthiness, a sufficient response here too is that the factor is one of evaluation, not a ground for exclusion. Undue complication ought to be avoided in the interest of ease of application. The same can be said with respect to the possibility that the conduct may be ambiguous so that the trier of fact will draw a wrong inference. Finally, a rule attaching the hearsay tag to the kind of conduct under consideration is bound to operate unevenly, since the possibility of a hearsay objection will more often than not simply be overlooked.

Out-of-court assertions not offered to prove the truth of the matter asserted. The preceding discussion relates to hearsay aspects of nonassertive conduct. Wright v. Tatham, on which the discussion is largely based, did not, however, involve nonassertive conduct; it involved conduct that was, in a measure at least, assertive. The hearsay status of assertive conduct must now be considered. If one of the letters had said, "Marsden, you are competent to make a will," it would clearly fall within the definition of hearsay, an out-of-court assertion offered to prove the truth of the matter asserted. But that was not the case: the letters, though assertive in form, were not offered to prove the truth of what was asserted. The letter from the cousin describing conditions found on his voyage to America for example was not offered as evidence of conditions in America but as evidence that the writer believed Marsden to be of reasonable intelligence, from which belief competency might be inferred. Under these conditions, should the evidence be treated as hearsay?

The pattern of the current decisions and the Federal Rules and their counterparts [6] is to answer the question in the negative: the out-of-court assertion is not hearsay if offered as proof of something other than the matter asserted. The supporting arguments, however, are somewhat less compelling than is so with respect to nonassertive conduct, since the presence of an assertion reintroduces intent as an element of risk to be considered.

6. See § 246 supra.

This risk is believed not to be of such dimension as to mandate treatment as hearsay: the intent does not embrace the inference suggested, and the likelihood of purposeful deception is accordingly lessened.

At this point it is apparent from the treatment of what is and what is not hearsay that the definition of hearsay previously advanced is less inclusive than the logical and analytical possibilities would allow. At a fairly early stage of his career, Professor Morgan, whose bright mind contributed much to the law of evidence, suggested:

A comprehensive definition of hearsay * * * would include (1) all conduct of a person, verbal or nonverbal, intended by him to operate as an assertion when offered either to prove the truth of the matter asserted or to prove that the asserter believed the matter asserted to be true, and (2) all conduct of a person, verbal or nonverbal, not intended by him to operate as an assertion, when offered either to prove both his state of mind and the external event or condition which caused him to have that state of mind, or to prove that his state of mind was truly reflected by that conduct.[7]

Further thought and observation, however, apparently convinced him that a definition of hearsay expanded to the outer limits suggested by logic and analysis was undesirable, with needless complication of the hearsay rule that outweighed any supposed advantage. He first advocated removing nonassertive conduct from the hearsay definition.[8] Then he took the final step of removing from the definition assertive conduct not offered to prove the matter asserted.

The adoption of Uniform Rule 62(1) and Rule 63 defining hearsay evidence would be a boon to lawyers and judges. Rule 62(1) reads " 'Statement' means not only an oral or written expression but also non-verbal conduct of a person intended by him as a substitute for words in expressing the matter stated." And Rule 63 states: "Evidence of a statement which is made other than by a witness while testifying at the hearing offered to prove the truth of the matter asserted is hearsay." These provisions would avoid all the conflicts in the decisions where the evidence describes conduct from which a relevant inference may be drawn and where very careful analysis is required to determine whether the process of reasoning requires the trier to treat the party exhibiting the conduct as if he were testifying.[9]

One further word should be added. The decision that a given item of evidence is not hearsay, or that it is hearsay but falls within an exception to the hearsay rule, may not in every case be conclusive when the evidence is attacked as contrary to the values sought to be protected by the hearsay rule. One class of litigants, namely accused persons in criminal cases, are the objects of special solicitude. Among the rights conferred upon them by the Sixth Amendment is the right of confrontation, and though evidence may not be classed as hearsay the possibility that it may violate the right of confrontation may require further examination.[10]

Knowledge. On an issue whether a given person was alive at a particular time, evidence that she said something at the time would be proof that she was alive. Whether she said, "I am alive," or "Hi, Joe," would be immaterial; the inference of life is drawn from the fact that she spoke, not from what was said. No problem of veracity is involved. In terms of the definition of hearsay, the first statement is not offered to prove what is asserted, since that is merely coincidence; the second statement is not even an assertion. Neither is hearsay.

An extension of this analysis is applicable to declarations evincing knowledge, notice, or awareness of some fact. Proof that one talks about a matter demonstrates on its face that she was conscious or aware of it, and veracity does not enter into the situation. Caution is, however, indicated, since the self-proving aspect is limited strictly to what is said. Thus,

7. Morgan, Hearsay and Non–Hearsay, 48 Harv. L.Rev. 1138, 1144 (1935).

8. Morgan, Hearsay, 25 Miss.L.J. 1, 8 (1953).

9. Morgan, Basic Problems of Evidence 253 (1962).

10. See § 252 infra.

the statement, "I know geometry," establishes no more than that the speaker is aware of the term "geometry", not that she has command of that subject. On the other hand, if the statement is itself a proposition of geometry, it is self-evident that the speaker does know geometry pro tanto; whether she prefaces her statement with "I know," is immaterial.

When the existence of knowledge is sought to be used as the basis for a further inference, the possibility of infringing upon the hearsay rule is apparent. That possibility becomes a reality when the purpose of the evidence of knowledge is to prove the existence of the fact known. Statements of memory or belief are not generally allowed as proof of the happening of the event remembered or believed, since allowing the evidence would destroy the hearsay rule.[11] For this purpose, knowledge seems to be indistinguishable from memory and belief. There remains, however, the possibility of drawing from evidence of knowledge an inference other than the existence of the fact known.

Cases of establishing the identity of a person offer the possibility of an inference of this kind. Thus evidence that a person made statements indicating knowledge of matters likely to have been known only to X is receivable as tending to prove that she was in fact X. In somewhat different vein, the often discussed case of Bridges v. State,[12] a prosecution for taking indecent liberties with a female child, involved the admissibility of evidence that the victim, in reporting the incident, gave a description of the house and its surroundings and of the room and its furnishings, where the alleged offense occurred. Other evidence showed that the description fitted the house and room where the defendant lived. While it has been suggested that the evidence depended for its value upon the observation, memory, and veracity of the child, and thus shared the hazards of hearsay, the testimony nevertheless had value independently of these factors. Other witnesses had described the physical characteristics of the locale, and her testimony was not relied

upon for that purpose. Once other possible sources of her knowledge were eliminated, which the court was satisfied was the case, the only remaining inference was that she had acquired that knowledge through a visit to the premises. The evidence was not within the ban of the hearsay rule.

Silence as hearsay. One aspect of the conduct-as-hearsay problem is presented by cases where a failure to speak or act is offered to support an inference that conditions were such as would not evoke speech or action in a reasonable person. The cases are likely to fall into two classes: (1) evidence of absence of complaints from other customers as disproof of claimed defects of goods or food or from other persons who would have been affected as disproof of a claimed injurious event or condition, and (2) evidence from members of a family that a particular member never mentioned an event, or claim to or disposition of property, to prove nonoccurrence or nonexistence. Often the presence of an arguable hearsay question is neither noted nor discussed.

While the cases at common law were divided as to the hearsay status of this kind of evidence, it appears under the definition of hearsay in Section 246 supra that the evidence, not being intended as an assertion, is not hearsay. It should be noted, however, that the support for admissibility, aside from any question of hearsay, may be stronger in the cases of absence of complaints than in other cases of silence. The other cases present a variety of situations which in some instances suggest motivations for silence other than nonoccurrence of the disputed event, calling for evaluation in terms of whether the probative value of the evidence is outweighed by its prejudicial effect.

Negative results of inquiries. Somewhat related questions arise in respect to testimony by a witness that she has made inquiries among the residents of a given place where a certain person is claimed to live, and that she

---

11. See § 276 infra.

12. 247 Wis. 350, 19 N.W.2d 529 (1945), rehearing denied 247 Wis. 350, 19 N.W.2d 862.

has been unable to find anyone who knows her or has any information about her. When offered upon an issue as to whether due diligence has been exercised in attempting to locate a missing witness or other person, it is clear that testimony as to the results of the inquiries is not hearsay but is merely a narration of acts and efforts showing due diligence. However, the evidence of inquiries and inability to secure information may be offered as proof of the nonexistence of the person sought to be located, or of the fact that no such person lives at the place in question. Then it may be argued that this is merely an indirect way of placing in evidence the statements of those of whom inquiry was made for the purpose of proving the truth of what they asserted. It is true that the residents of whom inquiry was made could be brought in to testify as to their want of knowledge but only at the price of substantial inconvenience and loss of time. However, application of the hearsay definition[13] yields a satisfactory avoidance of the hearsay argument. The question asked would in essence have been, "Do you know, or have you ever heard of, a person named Mary Jones in this community?", with the answer, "No." The assertion in the answer is that the declarant has not heard of the person, but the inference suggested from the aggregate of the answers is not that the declarants had not heard of such a person, but rather that such a person does not exist. Almost all the cases have in any event ruled in favor of admitting the evidence, influenced no doubt by considerations of convenience, probable accuracy, and the difficulties that often attend the proving of a negative, often without reference to a possible hearsay problem but classifying as nonhearsay when the question is raised.[14]

Silence as an admission by a party-opponent is treated elsewhere.[15]

13. See § 246 supra.

14. The analogy to public opinion polls and surveys will be apparent. Compare the discussion of reputation in § 249 supra.

15. See the general coverage in § 262 infra, and the discussion of the particular problems of treating the silence of a criminal defendant as an admission or confession in § 161 supra.

§ 251. Prior Statements of Witnesses as Substantive Evidence

As previously observed,[1] the traditional view had been that a prior statement of a witness is hearsay if offered to prove the happening of matters asserted therein. This categorization has not, of course, precluded using the prior statement for other purposes, e.g., to impeach the witness by showing a self-contradiction if the statement is inconsistent with his testimony or to support his credibility under certain circumstances when the statement was consistent with his testimony.[2] But the prior statement has been admissible as proof of matter asserted therein, i.e. as "substantive" evidence, only when falling within one of the exceptions to the hearsay rule. This position has increasingly come under attack in recent years on both logical and practical grounds.

The logic of the orthodox view is that the previous statement of the witness is hearsay since its value rests on the credit of the declarant, who, when the statement was made, was not (1) under oath, (2) in the presence of the trier, or (3) subject to cross-examination.

The counter-argument goes as follows: (1) The oath is no longer a principal safeguard of the trustworthiness of testimony. Affidavits, though under oath, are not exempted from the hearsay rule. Moreover, of the numerous exceptions where evidence is admitted despite its being hearsay, in only one instance is the out-of-court statement required to have been under oath. And that instance, namely prior testimony, may arguably be regarded as a case of nonhearsay rather than as a hearsay exception.[3]

(2) With respect to affording the trier of fact the advantage of observing the demeanor

§ 251

1. See § 34 supra with respect to prior inconsistent statements, and § 47 supra as to prior consistent statements.

2. See § 47 supra.

3. See § 301 infra.

of the witness while making the statement, Judge Learned Hand's classic statement puts it:

> If, from all that the jury see of the witness, they conclude that what he says now is not the truth, but what he said before, they are none the less deciding from what they see and hear of that person and in court.[4]

(3) The principal reliance for achieving credibility is no doubt cross-examination, and this condition is thought to be satisfied. As Wigmore, who originally adhered to the traditional view, expressed it:

> Here, however, by hypothesis the witness is present and subject to cross-examination. There is ample opportunity to test him as to the basis for his former statement. The whole purpose of the hearsay rule has been already satisfied.[5]

The question remains whether cross-examination in order to be effective must take place at the time when the statement is made. The opinion where the orthodox view finds its most vigorous support urges:

> The chief merit of cross-examination is not that at some future time it gives the party opponent the right to dissect adverse testimony. Its principal virtue is the immediate application of the testing process. Its strokes fall while the iron is hot. False testimony is apt to harden and become unyielding to the blows of truth in proportion as the witness has opportunity for reconsideration and influence by the suggestions of others * * *.[6]

Yet the fact in the case was that the witness did change his story very substantially; rather than hardening, his testimony yielded to something between the giving of the statement and the time of testifying. This appears to be so in a very high proportion of the cases, and the circumstances most frequently suggest that the "something" which caused the change was an improper influence.

An additional persuasive factor against the orthodox rule is the superior trustworthiness of earlier statements, on the basis that memory hinges on recency. The prior statement is always nearer and usually very much nearer to the event than is the testimony. The fresher the memory, the fuller and more accurate it is. The requirement of the hearsay exception for memoranda of past recollection, that the matter have been recorded while fresh in memory,[7] is based precisely on this principle.

These various considerations led to a substantial movement to abandon the orthodox view completely. Thus the Model Code of Evidence provided:

> Evidence of a hearsay declaration is admissible if the judge finds that the declarant * * * is present and subject to cross-examination.[8]

Substantial support for this position began to appear in the decisions.

Under the Model Code Wigmore position, all prior statements of witnesses, regardless of their nature, were exempted from the ban of the hearsay rule. This complete rejection of the orthodox rule resulted in uneasiness that a practice might develop among lawyers whereby a carefully prepared statement would be offered in lieu of testimony, merely tendering the witness for cross-examination on the statement. The practice seems not in fact to have materialized in the jurisdictions where the orthodox rule was rejected, but the potential for abuse nevertheless remained. As a consequence, the Advisory Committee on Federal Rules of Evidence adopted an intermediate position, neither admitting nor rejecting prior statements of witnesses *in toto*, but exempting from classification as hearsay certain prior statements thought by circumstances to be free of the danger of abuse. The exempt statements are (A) inconsistent statements, (B) consistent statements when admissible to rebut certain attacks upon the credibility of the witness, and (C) statements of

---

4. Di Carlo v. United States, 6 F.2d 364 (2d Cir.1925).

5. 3A Wigmore, Evidence § 1018, p. 996 (Chadbourn rev. 1970).

6. State v. Saporen, 205 Minn. 358, 362, 285 N.W. 898, 901 (1939).

7. See § 281 infra. Note also that the regularly kept records exception requires that the entry be made at or near the time of the transaction recorded. Infra § 286.

8. Model Code of Evidence Rule 503(b).

identification. Federal Rule of Evidence 801(d)(1) provides:

(d) Statements which are not hearsay.— A statement is not hearsay if—

(1) Prior statement by witness.—The declarant testifies at the trial or hearing and is subject to cross-examination concerning the statement, and the statement is (A) inconsistent with the declarant's testimony, and was given under oath subject to the penalty of perjury at a trial, hearing, or other proceeding, or in a deposition, or (B) consistent with the declarant's testimony and is offered to rebut an express or implied charge against the declarant of recent fabrication or improper influence or motive, or (C) one of identification of a person made after perceiving the person; or

(A) Prior inconsistent statements. The witness who has told one story aforetime and another today has opened the gates to all the vistas of truth which the common law practice of cross-examination and re-examination was invented to explore. The reasons for the change of face, whether forgetfulness, carelessness, pity, terror, or greed, may be explored by the two questioners in the presence of the trier of fact, under oath, casting light on which is the true story and which the false. It is hard to escape the view that evidence of a prior inconsistent statement, when declarant is on the stand to explain it if he can, has in high degree the safeguards of examined testimony. In addition, allowing it as substantive evidence pays a further dividend in avoiding a limiting instruction quite unlikely to be heeded by a jury.

When is a prior statement inconsistent? [9] On the face of it, a prior statement describing an event would not be inconsistent with testimony by the witness that he no longer remembers the event. Yet the tendency of unwilling or untruthful witnesses to seek refuge in forgetfulness is well recognized. Hence the judge may be warranted in concluding under the circumstances the claimed lack of memory of the event is untrue and in effect an implied denial of the prior statement, thus qualifying it as inconsistent and nonhearsay.

In the absence of such a finding, the presence of inconsistency is difficult to maintain.

As originally drafted by the Advisory Committee and transmitted to the Congress by the Supreme Court, the Federal Rule contained no requirement as to the conditions under which the prior inconsistent statement must be made. The Congress, however, imposed strict limitations, adding the language "given under oath subject to the penalty of perjury at a trial, hearing, or other proceeding, or in a deposition * * *." The result of the limitation is to confine substantive use of prior inconsistent statements virtually to those made in the course of judicial proceedings, including grand jury testimony, although allowing use for impeachment without regard to the Congressional limitation. Where both are present in the same case, the likelihood of jury confusion is evident.

(B) Prior consistent statements. While prior consistent statements are hearsay by the traditional view and inadmissible as substantive evidence, they have nevertheless been allowed a limited admissibility for the purpose of supporting the credibility of a witness, particularly to show that a witness whose testimony has allegedly been influenced told the same story before the influence was brought to bear. No sound reason is apparent for denying substantive effect when the statement is otherwise admissible. The witness can be cross-examined fully. No abuse of prepared statements is evident. The attack upon the witness has opened the door. The giving of a limiting instruction is needless and useless.

The Federal Rule's exemption of prior consistent statements from the hearsay rule has given rise to some controversy with regard to the admissibility of statements that do not come within the language of Rule 801(d)(1)(B). The rule exempts consistent statements "offered to rebut an express or implied charge against the declarant of recent fabrication or improper influence or motive" from the hearsay rule. Are other consistent statements admissible based on the traditional view that

---

9. See § 34 supra, as to the requirement of inconsistency in prior statements used for impeachment.

they support the witness's credibility? Some courts have said that consistent statements are either admissible under Rule 801 or inadmissible for any purpose. Others have held that the rule applies only to the substantive use of such statements and that consistent statements not falling within the language may be admissible for purposes of supporting credibility. Under the latter view, statements not within the language of Rule 801(d)(1)(B) would, of course, be subject to a relevancy analysis. Such an analysis would preclude the admission of most such statements.

(C) Statements of identification. When A testifies that on a prior occasion B pointed to the accused and said, "That's the man who robbed me," the testimony is clearly hearsay. If, however, B is present in court, testifies on the subject of identity, and is available for cross-examination, a case within the present section is presented. Similarly if B has himself testified to the prior identification. Admissibility of the prior identification in all these situations has the support of substantial authority in the cases, often without recognition of the presence of a hearsay problem. Justification is found in the unsatisfactory nature of courtroom identification and the safeguards which now surround staged out-of-court identifications.

The requirement of cross-examination. With respect to each of the categories of prior statements discussed above, the Federal Rule requires that declarant testify at the trial or hearing and that he be "subject to cross-examination concerning the statement * * *."[10] The requirement that he testify appears to offer no problem, but the requirement that he be subject to cross-examination concerning the statement calls for exploration. The problem area will usually be prior inconsistent statements. As has been observed, if the witness testifies that he does not remember the event and the judge finds the asserted lack of memory to be genuine, the prior statement is not inconsistent with the testimony and does not fall within the exemption, and

the question of cross-examination upon the statement is not reached. If the asserted lack of memory is found to be false under the circumstances, and the witness does not deny making the statement but offers explanation of his change of position, he may be cross-examined as to the circumstances and as to his explanation, and the cross-examination requirement is satisfied. If he denies making the statement, and also denies the event, it has been held that the result is more favorable to the cross-examiner than could be produced by eliciting an admission that the statement was made and an explanation of change of position, and that cross-examination requirements are satisfied.

Statements of identification, introduced under Rule 801(d)(1)(C), present a somewhat different set of problems where the witness claims lack of memory of either the statement or the underlying events. Because identification statements do not depend upon their inconsistency with prior statements for their admissibility, they come within the meaning of the rule even if the witness genuinely says that he has no memory, provided the witness is considered to be "subject to cross-examination" concerning the statement. Despite a persuasive argument that effective cross-examination is precluded under such circumstances, the United States Supreme Court, in *United States v. Owens,*[11] held that neither Rule 801(d)(1) nor the Confrontation Clause is violated by the introduction of prior statements of identification where the witness claims a lack of memory. The court held that both the constitutional and hearsay exceptions were satisfied by the opportunity to cross-examine the witness about his bad memory.

§ 252. Constitutional Problems of Hearsay: Confrontation and Due Process

A discussion of the constitutional problems of hearsay must focus primarily on the Confrontation Clause of the Sixth Amendment.

---

10. Fed.R.Evid. 801(d)(1). Constitutional aspects of cross-examination generally are discussed in § 252 infra.

11. 484 U.S. 554 (1988).

The clause requires "that in all criminal prosecutions, the accused shall enjoy the right * * * to be confronted with the witnesses against him." Nearly every state constitution has a like provision. In 1965, the Supreme Court ruled that the Fourteenth Amendment made the federal Confrontation Clause obligatory upon the states.[1]

The Confrontation Clause is applicable only to criminal prosecutions and may be invoked only by the accused. Thus it is unavailable to the prosecution in a criminal proceeding or to either party in civil litigation. So basic, however, are the values thought to be served by confrontation that confrontation requirements on occasion are found constitutionally extended to persons other than the accused in a criminal case as an aspect of due process.

Certain facets of the right of confrontation and the right to due process, while relevant to the values sought to be protected by the hearsay rule, do not bear directly upon it. Of these facets, one is the right of an accused to be present at every stage of her trial as an aspect of confrontation. Another is the defense right to disclosure by the prosecution of material exculpatory evidence as an element of due process. In the same vein, though ostensibly not constitutionally based, is the disclosure of prior statements of government witnesses mandated by the *Jencks* decision and the statute that it sired.[2] The right to counsel is a thread running through much of this constitutional fabric.

Turning to examination of the relationship between the hearsay rule and constitutional right of confrontation, the similarity of their underpinnings is evident.[3] The hearsay rule operates to preserve the ability of a party to confront the witnesses against him in open court. The Confrontation Clause does the same for an accused in a criminal case. The hearsay rule has numerous exceptions and so does the Confrontation Clause. To what extent do these exceptions overlap?

In the late 1700's when confrontation provisions were first included in American bills of rights, the general rule against hearsay had been accepted in England for a hundred years,[4] but it was equally well established that hearsay under certain circumstances might be admitted. One could certainly argue that the purpose of the American provision was to guarantee the maintenance in criminal cases of the hard-won principle of the hearsay rule, without abandoning the accepted exceptions which had not been questioned as to fairness, but forbidding especially the practice of using depositions taken in the absence of the accused. This latter practice was later abandoned by the English judges and forbidden by statute.

The debate that has raged in the courts and the law journals has boiled down to whether the Confrontation Clause merely constitutionalizes the hearsay rule for the accused in a criminal case or whether it operates to limit the introduction of evidence admissible under the rule and its exceptions. The more recent decisions of the Supreme Court seem to point strongly in the direction of the former analysis. A secondary question, if the Clause constitutionalizes the hearsay rule, is at what point did it do so? In other words, to what extent may modern expansions of the rule run afoul of the constitutional limitation? Here the issue is still an open one.

The Supreme Court's progression toward its present view of the relationship of the hearsay rule and the Confrontation Clause effectively began with the case of California v. Green.[5] In *Green,* the Court found that the clause did not limit the introduction of prior statements of witnesses actually produced at the trial. Ten years later, in Ohio v. Roberts,[6] the court laid down a two-part test for the application of the Confrontation Clause to hearsay evidence. First, "the prosecutor must either produce, or demonstrate the unavailability of, the declarant whose statements

§ 252

1. Pointer v. Texas, 380 U.S. 400 (1965).
2. See § 97 supra.
3. As to hearsay, see § 245 supra.

4. See § 244, supra.
5. 399 U.S. 149 (1970).
6. 448 U.S. 56 (1980).

it wishes to use against the defendant." [7] Secondly, if the declarant is unavailable, the statement must have been made under circumstances providing sufficient "indicia of reliability." The Court in *Roberts* further noted that sufficient reliability to satisfy the demands of the confrontation clause "can be inferred without more in a case where the evidence falls within a firmly rooted hearsay exception. In other cases, the evidence must be excluded at least absent a showing of particularized guarantees of trustworthiness." [8]

In United States v. Inadi,[9] the Court backed away from the unavailability requirement pronounced in *Roberts*. In *Inadi*, the Court found no need to produce or demonstrate the unavailability of a conspirator whose statement was used against the accused. The statements in *Roberts* were limited to instances involving the introduction of prior testimony, which has always required unavailability under the hearsay rule. In the case of co-conspirator's statements, the Court found that such statements "provide evidence of the conspiracy's context that cannot be replicated, even if the declarant testifies to the same matters in court." [10] The Court also noted that the benefits of an unavailability rule for co-conspirator declarants would be slight and the burdens substantial, and concluded that "the Confrontation Clause does not embody such a rule."[11]

Both *Roberts* and *Inadi* leave open the impact of the Confrontation Clause in cases, such as those involving former testimony, where the hearsay exception itself requires unavailability. Earlier decisions, such as Barber v. Page,[12] seem to dictate a more rigorous test for unavailability for the prosecution in a criminal case than for the defense or for either party in a civil case.

Inadi did not expand on the other prong of the *Roberts* test, i.e., when are sufficient "in-dicia of reliability" present? The issue of whether co-conspirators statements were within a "firmly rooted" exception to hearsay rule was resolved in the affirmative in Bourjaily v. United States.[13] The co-conspirator exception was held to be firmly enough rooted in our jurisprudence that a court need not independently inquire into the reliability of such statements.

In 1990, some constitutional limitations on the creation of nontraditional exceptions to the hearsay rule were imposed. In Idaho v. Wright,[14] the Court dealt with statements of a child to a doctor, admitted pursuant to Idaho's residual hearsay exception. The Court held that the introduction of the statements violated the Confrontation Clause, noting that the residual exception is not a "firmly rooted" exception for Confrontation Clause purposes [15] and that therefore statements admitted under it would be constitutionally admissible based only upon a finding of "particularized guarantees of trustworthiness." [16] The Court directed the search for such guarantees to the totality of circumstances surrounding the making of the statement "that render the declarant particularly worthy of belief." [17] The Court expressly rejected the use of evidence corroborating the truth of a hearsay statement to support the guarantees of trustworthiness.

In summary, hearsay falling within a traditional or "firmly rooted" exception to the rule will be admissible under the Confrontation Clause. Where the exception does not require unavailability, it is unlikely that the Court will hold that the Constitution requires it. The Court confirmed this analysis in 1992, holding that the Constitution does not require a showing of unavailability with regard to statements otherwise admissible under a state's exceptions for spontaneous declarations and statements made in the course of

---

7.   Id. at 65.
8.   Ibid.
9.   475 U.S. 387 (1986).
10. Id. at 395.
11. Id. at 400.
12. 390 U.S. 719 (1968). See discussion § 253, infra.

13. 483 U.S. 171 (1987).
14. 110 S.Ct. 3139 (1990).
15. Id. at 3147.
16. Id. at 3148.
17. Id. at 3149.

procuring medical services.[18] Where the exception requires unavailability, the clause will also require such a finding and will likely require a more rigorous demonstration by the prosecution than by other parties. Where the hearsay is admissible under a residual exception on behalf of the prosecution in a criminal case, the courts will look for "particularized guarantees of trustworthiness," a test apparently more demanding than the "equivalent circumstantial guarantees of trustworthiness" required by the Federal Rules and their state counterparts. In addition, the prosecution will have to rely on the trustworthiness of the statement itself, rather than on its likely truth in light of corroborating circumstances. Newly created statutory hearsay exceptions arguably should be subject to the test set forth in *Wright*.

Some questions still remain for adjudication, probably by the United States Supreme Court. What are the firmly rooted exceptions to the hearsay rule? To what extent will the Confrontation Clause limit the application of traditional hearsay exceptions to nontraditional circumstances. For example, is a state free to apply the traditional exception for public records to permit the introduction of police reports against the accused in a criminal case? How far can a state go in admitting statements against penal interest of nondefendants which implicate the accused?[19] In such instances, will the Court look only to the existence of a traditional hearsay exception as in *Bourjaily,* regardless of how unorthodox the application, or will it require at least a specific finding of particularized guarantees of trustworthiness as in *Wright?* Furthermore, could a state dispense with a traditional requirement of unavailability, for example, for declarations against interest?[20] Logic and policy favor a limit on the state's ability to expand hearsay exceptions to assist the prosecution in instances such as those posed here,

but in this area as in so many, the Court is capable of some surprising decisions.

In contrast to the right of confrontation, which results in exclusion when ruled to be applicable to an item of hearsay, the due process clause may require the admission of hearsay, though inadmissible under applicable hearsay rules, if of sufficient reliability and importance. In Chambers v. Mississippi,[21] the Supreme Court ruled that due process was denied by the exclusion of several confessions exculpating the accused given "under circumstances that provided considerable assurances of their reliability," coupled with the inability of the accused to cross-examine the confessing person, who testified as a witness, because of the local "voucher rule." The decision was carefully limited to the situation presented and is of uncertain constitutional dimension, though suggesting possibilities of further application.

§ 253. The Hearsay Exceptions: Unavailability of the Declarant

In the concluding portion of the earlier section discussing the reasons for the rule against hearsay, the point was made that the difficulty with the rule lies in the procedure of excluding evidence as a means of effectuating the policy of requiring that testimony be given in open court, under oath, and subject to cross-examination. The problem arises from the wide variation in the reliability of evidence which by definition is classed as hearsay. The traditional solution has been found in recognition of numerous exceptions where it has been thought that "circumstantial guarantees of trustworthiness"[1] justified departure from the general rule excluding hearsay. These exceptions are the subjects of several of the chapters which follow.

The pattern of the exceptions as evolved by the decisional process of the common law and

---

18. White v. Illinois, 112 S.Ct. 736 (1992).
19. See §§ 318, 319, infra.
20. See §§ 318–320, infra.
21. See also the discussion of third-party confessions in § 318, infra.

§ 253

1. 5 Wigmore, Evidence § 1422 (Chadbourn rev. 1974).

generally in effect today divides the hearsay exceptions into two groups. In the first, the availability or unavailability of the declarant is not a relevant factor: the exception is applied without regard to it. In the second group, a showing of unavailability is a condition precedent to applying the exception. The theory of the first group is that the out-of-court statement is at least as reliable as would be his testimony in person, so that producing him would involve pointless·delay and inconvenience. The theory of the second group is that, while it would be preferable to have live testimony, if the declarant is unavailable, the out-of-court statement will be accepted.[2] The pattern to a large extent is the product of history and experience, and, as might be expected of a body of law created by deciding cases as they arose in necessarily random fashion, it is not in all respects consistent. Nevertheless, it has stood the test of time and use, and offers a substantial measure of predictability. While the number of the exceptions may at first glance appear extraordinarily complex, many are encountered only rarely; the actual working collection probably numbers no more than 10 or a dozen.

The importance accorded unavailability in the scheme of hearsay exceptions requires that it be considered in some detail.

Preliminarily it may be observed that while the rather general practice is to speak loosely of unavailability of the witness, the critical factor is actually the unavailability of his testimony. As will be seen, the witness may be physically present in court but his testimony nevertheless unavailable. Of course if the unavailability is by procurement of the party offering the hearsay statement, the requirement ought not to be regarded as satisfied.

In principle, probably anything which constitutes unavailability in fact ought to be considered adequate. However, the rules have grown up around certain recurring fact situations, and the problem is therefore approached in that pattern. Depositions receive special treatment at the end of the section.

Federal Rule of Evidence 804(a) provides a convenient list of the generally recognized unavailability situations, as follows:

(a) Definition of Unavailability. "Unavailability as a witness" includes situations in which the declarant—

(1) is exempted by ruling of the court on the ground of privilege from testifying concerning the subject matter of the declarant's statement; or

(2) persists in refusing to testify concerning the subject matter of the declarant's statement despite an order of the court to do so; or

(3) testifies to a lack of memory of the subject matter of the declarant's statement; or

(4) is unable to be present or to testify at the hearing because of death or then existing physical or mental illness or infirmity; or

(5) is absent from the hearing and the proponent of his statement has been unable to procure the declarant's attendance (or in the case of a hearsay exception under subdivision (b)(2), (3), or (4), his attendance or testimony) by process or other reasonable means.

A declarant is not unavailable as a witness if exemption, refusal, claim of lack of memory, inability, or absence is due to the procurement or wrongdoing of the proponent of a statement for the purpose of preventing the witness from attending or testifying.

(1) Exercise of privilege. The exercise of a privilege not to testify renders the witness unavailable to the extent of the scope of the privilege.

(2) Refusal to testify. If a witness simply refuses to testify, despite the bringing to bear upon him of all appropriate judicial pressures, the conclusion that as a practical matter he is unavailable can scarcely be avoided, and that is the holding of the great weight of authority.

---

2. The usual exceptions requiring a showing of unavailability are former testimony, § 302 infra; dying declarations, § 310 infra; declarations against interest,

§ 320 infra; and statements of pedigree and family history, § 322. See Fed.R.Evid. 804.

(3) Claimed lack of memory. A claim of lack of memory made by the witness on the stand should satisfy the requirement of unavailability. If the claim is genuine, the testimony is simply unavailable by any realistic standard. The earlier cases, however, indicated concern that the claimed lack might not be genuine, particularly in former testimony cases, where the witness who learns that the adversary has discovered new fuel for cross-examination or for other reasons seeks refuge in forgetfulness. This concern appears not to be well grounded, especially when the parallel to the witness who simply refuses to testify, discussed above, is noted. The witness who falsely asserts loss of memory is simply refusing to testify in a way that he hopes will avoid a collision with the judge. He is present in court, by definition, and subject to cross-examination. If his claim is false, he is in principle at least liable to contempt proceedings, though perhaps less effectively than in cases of simple refusal. The trend is to recognize asserted loss of memory as sufficient. If the forgetfulness is only partial, the appropriate solution would appear to be resort to present testimony to the extent of recollection, implementing with the hearsay testimony to the extent required.

(4) Death; physical or mental illness. Death was the form which unavailability originally assumed with most of the relevant exceptions. Physical disability to attend the trial or testify is a recognized ground. Mental incapacity, including failure of faculties due to disease, senility, or accident, is also a good ground of unavailability. The relative scarcity of decisions passing upon the required degree of permanency of either physical and mental incapacity supports the conclusion that most of the cases are handled by continuance. Some authority accepts a relatively temporary disability as sufficient. The matter would appear to be appropriate generally for the exercise of discretion by the judge, with due regard for the prospects for recovery, the importance of the testimony and the prompt administration of justice. In criminal cases where absence is relied upon to establish unavailability of a witness against the accused, a higher standard may be required with respect to disability.

(5) Absence. Mere absence of the declarant from the hearing, standing alone, does not establish unavailability. Under the Federal Rule, the proponent of the hearsay statement must in addition show that he is unable to procure declarant's attendance (1) by process or (2) by other reasonable means. State requirements vary, especially with respect to (2). Furthermore, the requirements of the confrontation clause must be observed. (1) The relevant process is subpoena, or, in appropriate situations, writ of habeas corpus ad testificandum. If a witness is beyond the reach of process, obviously process cannot procure his attendance. Substantial differences in the reach of process exist between civil and criminal cases. For example, service of a civil subpoena is relatively limited while a criminal subpoena may be served anywhere in the country and under some circumstances even abroad. And, while in State courts process in civil cases will usually not be effective beyond State boundaries, all States have enacted the Uniform Act To Secure the Attendance of Witnesses from Without a State in Criminal Proceedings,[3] which in effect permits extradition of witnesses from another State in criminal cases. If a witness against the accused in a criminal case is within the reach of process, the prosecution must resort to process in both State and federal cases. If a witness cannot be found, it is evident that resort to process cannot be effective. The proponent of the hearsay statement must, however, show that the witness cannot be found. In criminal cases, the showing required of the prosecution with regard to witnesses against the accused is strict, described as a "good-faith effort," [4] applicable in both State and federal prosecutions. A lesser showing may be adequate as to defense witnesses in criminal cases and witnesses generally in civil cases, where confrontation requirements do not apply. (2) In addition to inability to procure attendance by

---

3. 11 U.L.A. 1.

4. Ohio v. Roberts, 448 U.S. 56, 74 (1980).

process, the confrontation clause requires the prosecution, before introducing a hearsay statement of the type where unavailability is required, also to show that declarant's attendance cannot be procured through good-faith efforts by other means. Here, too, the standard is strict. In Barber v. Page,[5] the confrontation clause was held to require a State prosecutor, before using at trial the preliminary hearing testimony of a witness presently incarcerated in a federal penitentiary in an adjoining State, to take appropriate steps to induce the federal authorities to produce him at the trial. When the witness is beyond the reach of process for reasons other than imprisonment, the least that would seem to satisfy confrontation requirements would be a request to appear, with reimbursement for travel and subsistence expenses. When the confrontation clause does not apply, i.e. civil cases and defense witnesses in criminal cases, the authorities are divided as to whether attempts must be made to induce the witness to attend voluntarily. Some authorities, including the Federal Rule, require an effort through reasonable means. Others require no more than a showing that the witness is beyond the reach of process.

When absence is relied upon as grounds of unavailability, some jurisdictions impose a further requirement that inability to take the deposition of the missing witness also be shown.

Depositions. Unavailability may appear as a requirement at two different stages in connection with depositions: (1) the right to take a deposition at all may be subject to certain conditions, of which the most common is unavailability to testify at the trial, or (2) the right to use a deposition at the trial in place of the personal appearance of the deponent is usually conditioned upon his unavailability. The matter is largely governed by statute or rule, and those in force locally should be consulted.

The use of depositions in criminal cases requires particular consideration in view of the higher standards of confrontation applicable to evidence presented against an accused. Legislation providing for depositions in criminal cases, sometimes by express constitutional sanction, is in effect in a number of jurisdictions. No constitutional problems are apparent when the deposition is to be taken and used by the accused. When, however, the deposition is to be used *against* the accused, it seems evident that the unavailability standards of Barber v. Page, previously discussed in this section, are applicable. If these standards are met, there must, of course, be meaningful opportunity to confront and cross-examine, with its concomitant right to counsel, when the deposition is taken.

Children. Children, particularly in sexual abuse cases, often present difficult questions of unavailability for purposes of the application of both a hearsay exception and the Confrontation Clause. In at least some jurisdictions, a finding of incompetence will make a witness unavailable. Other courts have found unavailability based upon the inability of the child to remember the events. Often, a finding of unavailability is justified based upon a determination that testifying will cause emotional trauma to the child and that therefore the child is unavailable. Courts finding the child unavailable within the meaning of the hearsay rule have usually also found any Confrontation Clause requirement of unavailability also satisfied. Some states have enacted statutes making a child unavailable, and permitting either the introduction of videotaped statements or closed-circuit testimony, based upon a finding that the child would suffer emotional or mental distress if required to testify in open court. In Maryland v. Craig,[6] an individualized finding of potential serious emotional distress was held sufficient to permit a child to give testimony via closed circuit television outside the physical presence of the accused. In White v. Illinois,[7] the Court held statements made by an available child witness could be admitted under firmly rooted exceptions to the hearsay rule, without a finding of the kind required in *Craig.*

5.   390 U.S. 719 (1968).
6.   110 S.Ct. 3157 (1990).

7.   112 S.Ct. 736 (1992).

Chapter 25

ADMISSIONS OF A PARTY–OPPONENT

Table of Sections

§ 254. Nature and Effect

"Anything that you say may be used against you," according to the familiar phrase. It offers a convenient point of beginning for the examination of the use of admissions in evidence.

Admissions are the words or acts of a party-opponent or a representative that are offered as evidence against the party. They may be *express* admissions, which are statements of the opposing party or an agent whose words may fairly be used against the party, or ad-

missions by *conduct.* Among the theories on which the probativity and admissibility of admissions have been explained and supported, the following seem most helpful.

Morgan's view was that admissions came in as an exception to the hearsay rule, assuming hearsay is given the usual definition of declarations made out of court, not subject to cross-examination, and received as evidence of the truth of the matter declared. Exceptions to the hearsay rule usually are justified on the ground that evidence meeting the requirements of the exception possesses special reliability, plus perhaps special need because of the unavailability of the declarant. Yet no objective guaranty of trustworthiness is furnished by the admissions rule. The party is not required to have firsthand knowledge of the matter declared; the declaration may be self-serving when made; and the declarant is probably sitting in the courtroom. As Morgan himself admitted, "The admissibility of an admission made by the party himself rests not upon any notion that the circumstances in which it was made furnish the trier means of evaluating it fairly, but upon the adversary theory of litigation. A party can hardly object that he had no opportunity to cross-examine himself or that he is unworthy of credence save when speaking under sanction of an oath."[1]

Wigmore, after pointing out that the party's declaration has generally the probative value of any other person's assertion, argued that it had a special value when offered *against* the party. In that circumstance, the admission discredits the party's statements inconsistent with the present claim asserted in pleadings and testimony, much like a witness impeached by contradictory statements. Moreover, he continued, admissions pass the gauntlet of the hearsay rule, which requires that extra-judicial assertions be excluded if there was no opportunity for the opponent to cross-examine because it is the opponent's own declaration, and "he does not need to cross-examine himself." Wigmore then added that "the Hearsay Rule is satisfied" since the party "now as opponent has the full opportunity to put himself on the stand and explain his former assertion."[2]

Strahorn suggested a further theory that classified all admissions when offered against a party, whether words or acts, as being *conduct* offered as circumstantial evidence rather than for its assertive, testimonial value. This circumstantial value is, as noted by Wigmore, the quality of inconsistency with the party's present claim:

The hearsay rule applies to those statements for which the only justification is their narrative content. It is inapplicable to those which are conduct, i.e., for which the trustworthiness of the utterance is a matter of indifference. So it is with admissions. The writer feels that inasmuch as all admissions, express and otherwise, can be rationalized as the relevant conduct of the speaker, it is unnecessary to predicate their admissibility on the basis of a possible narrative effect not possessed by all of them.[3]

On balance, the most satisfactory justification of the admissibility of admissions is that they are the product of the adversary system, sharing on a lower level the characteristics of admissions in pleadings or stipulations. Under this view, admissions need not satisfy the traditional requirement for hearsay exceptions that they possess circumstantial guarantees of trustworthiness. Rather admissions are simply classed as nonhearsay and outside the framework of exceptions to the hearsay rule.

Federal Rule 801(d)(2) takes the view that admissions are not hearsay. It provides:

A statement is not hearsay if—* * * The statement is offered against a party and is (A) the party's own statement, in either an individual or a representative capacity, or (B) a statement of which the party has manifested an adoption or belief in its truth, or (C) a statement by a person authorized by the party to make a statement concerning the subject, or (D) a statement by the party's agent or servant concerning a matter within the scope of the agency or employment, made during the existence of the relationship, or (E) a statement by a coconspirator of a party during the course and in furtherance of the conspiracy.

Regardless of the precise theory of admissibility, it is clear that admissions of a party are received as substantive evidence of the facts admitted and not merely to contradict the party. As a result, no foundation by first examining the party, as required for impeach-

§ 254

1. Morgan, Basic Problems of Evidence 265–266 (1963).

2. 4 Wigmore, Evidence § 1048 (Chadbourn rev. 1972).

3. Strahorn, A Reconsideration of the Hearsay Rule and Admissions, 85 U.Pa.L.Rev. 484, 576 (1937).

ing a witness with a prior inconsistent statement,[4] is a prerequisite for proof of admissions.

When the term admission is used without any qualifying adjective, the customary meaning is an evidentiary admission, that is, words in oral or written form or conduct of a party or a representative offered in evidence against the party. *Evidentiary* admissions are to be distinguished from *judicial* admissions. Judicial admissions are not evidence at all. Rather, they are formal concessions in the pleadings in the case or stipulations by a party or its counsel that have the effect of withdrawing a fact from issue and dispensing wholly with the need for proof of the fact.[5] Thus, the judicial admission, unless allowed by the court to be withdrawn, is conclusive in the case, whereas the evidentiary admission is not conclusive but is always subject to contradiction or explanation.[6]

Confessions of crime are a particular kind of admission, governed by special rules discussed in the chapter on Confessions.[7] Admissions do not need to have the dramatic effect or be the all-encompassing acknowledgement of responsibility that the word confession connotes. They are simply words or actions inconsistent with the party's position at trial, relevant to the substantive issues in the case, and offered against the party. Moreover, while generally received in evidence because of their substantial probative value in most situations, admissions may be excluded if their probative value is substantially outweighed by the prejudicial impact.

A type of evidence with which admissions may be confused is evidence of declarations against interest. The latter, treated under a separate exception to the hearsay rule,[8] must have been against the declarant's interest when made. No such requirement applies to admissions. For example, if a person states that a note is forged and then later acquires

the note and sues upon it, the previous statement may be introduced as an admission although the party had no interest when he or she made the statement. Of course, most admissions are actually against interest when made, but there is no such requirement. Hence the common phrase in judicial opinions, "admissions against interest," is an invitation to confuse two separate exceptions to the hearsay rule and erroneously to engraft upon admissions an against-interest requirement.

Other distinctions between admissions and declarations against interest are that admissions must be the statements of a party to the lawsuit. Also, admissions must be offered against the party opponent. By contrast, declarations need not be made by a party but may be, and typically are, made by some third person, and they may be offered by either party.[9] Finally, the declaration against interest exception admits the statement only when the declarant has become unavailable as a witness, while unavailability is not required of admissions of a party.

§ 255. Testimonial   Qualifications: Mental Competency; Personal Knowledge

The nature of admissions as a general proposition denies any significance to the question whether the party making the admission must meet standards of competency established for witnesses.[1] Thus, disqualifications arising from the marital relationship or "dead man's" acts, for example, lack relevancy in the case of admissions. No reason exists to exclude an otherwise receivable admission because the party making it was married or is now dead.

The single exception calling for consideration is lack of mental capacity. Some cases involve statements by badly injured persons, possibly also under sedation. While the older

---

4. See supra § 37.

5. See infra § 257.

6. As to admissions in pleadings other than the effective pleadings in the case, see infra § 257.

7. See supra Ch. 14.

8. See infra § 316.

9. See infra § 316.

§ 255

1. See supra Ch. 7.

decisions tended to examine the capacity of the declarant and to exclude the evidence if capacity was found not to exist, more recent opinions view the question as going to weight rather than admissibility. The latter position represents a preferable allocation of the functions of judge and jury and is consistent with current treatment of mental competency as a qualification of witnesses.[2] The adversary roots of admissions by parties make caution appropriate in applying this reasoning to statements by children. Substantive rules of liability for torts may suggest acceptable standards of responsibility for such admissions. Hearsay exceptions such as that for excited utterances should be explored as possibly offering a more satisfactory avenue to admissibility in evidence in a particular case.[3]

The requirement that a witness speak from firsthand knowledge is applicable to hearsay declarations generally,[4] and it has on some rare occasions been applied to admissions. However, the traditional view espoused by the vast majority of courts and adopted by the Federal Rules[5] is that such firsthand knowledge is not required of admissions.

The general theory supporting the elimination of firsthand knowledge as a requirement is supported by a number of arguments. First, when people speak against their own interest, it is generally to be supposed that they have made an adequate investigation. While this disserving feature might attach to most admissions, we have seen that admissions are competent evidence though not against interest when made, and as to these, the argument does not apply. However, a sufficient basis for generally dispensing with the requirement of firsthand knowledge qualification rests on the argument that admissions that become relevant in litigation usually concern some matter of substantial importance to declarants upon which they would likely have informed themselves. As a result, such admissions possess greater reliability

than the general run of hearsay, even when not based on firsthand observation. Moreover, the possibility is substantial that the declarant may have come into possession of significant information not known to the opponent.

The validity of dispensing with firsthand knowledge in the case of admissions by agents has been questioned vigorously by a leading text on the Federal Rules, advocating the insertion of such a requirement by construction.[6] The proposal has not been accepted by the courts, however.

§ 256. Admissions in Opinion Form; Conclusions of Law

If the lack of firsthand knowledge of the party does not exclude an admission, as indicated in the preceding section, it would seem clear that the opinion rule should not. As we have seen, the purpose of the latter rule is to regulate the in-court interrogation of a witness so as to elicit answers in a more concrete form rather than in terms of inference. In its modern form, it is a rule of preference for the more concrete answers, if the witness can give them, rather than a rule of exclusion.[1]

This rule, which is designed to promote the concreteness of answers on the stand, is grotesquely misapplied to out-of-court statements such as admissions where the declarant's statements are made without thought of the form of courtroom testimony. While counsel may reframe the question in the preferred form if an objection is sustained regarding in-court testimony, the rule can only be applied by excluding an out-of-court statement. Accordingly, the prevailing view is that admissions in the form of opinions are competent.

Most often the question arises in connection with statements of a participant in an accident that the mishap was the speakers fault.

---

2. See supra § 62.

3. See infra § 272.

4. See, e.g., infra §§ 280, 290, 313.

5. Advisory Committee's Note to Federal Rule 801(d)(2).

6. 4 Weinstein & Berger, Weinstein's Evidence ¶ 801(d)(2)(C)[01], at 277–280 (1990).

§ 256

1. See supra § 18.

Additionally, it is often argued that such statements should be excluded because they are conclusions of law. While conceivably a party might give an opinion on an abstract question of law, such are not the typical statements actually offered. These statements normally include an application of a standard to the facts; thus they reveal the facts as the declarant thinks them to be, to which the standard of "fault" or other legal or moral standard involved in the statement was applied. In these circumstances, the factual information conveyed should not be ignored merely because the statement may also indicate the party's assumptions about the law. However, it is conceivable that the legal principle may be so technical as to deprive an admission of significance or the party may indeed give an opinion regarding solely an abstract issue of law. In those cases, exclusion is warranted. In addition, it should be generally remembered that evidentiary admissions are subject to explanation.

§ 257. Admissions in Pleadings; Pleas of Guilty

The final pleadings upon which the case is tried state the contentions of each party as to the facts, and by admitting or denying the opponent's pleading, they define the factual issues that are to be tried by the process of proof. Thus, the court must look to the pleadings as part of the record in passing on the relevancy of evidence and to determine the issues to be submitted to the jury. For these purposes, it is not necessary to offer the pleadings in evidence. They are used as judicial and not as evidentiary admissions, and for these purposes, they are conclusive until withdrawn or amended.

A party may also seek to use an averment or admission in an adversary's final pleading as a basis for arguing the existence of some subordinate fact or as the foundation for an adverse inference. Some courts permit the party to do this by quoting or reading the

pleading as part of the record, while others require that the party, in order to make this use of the final pleading, introduce the relevant passage from the opponent's pleading as part of its own evidence during the course of the trial. Such a requirement allows the pleader to give explanatory evidence, such as that the allegation was made through inadvertence or mistake, and avoids the possibility of a surprise inference from the pleading in closing argument. These considerations may justify the departure from consistency.

Subject to the qualifications developed later in this section, pleadings are generally usable against the pleader. If they are the effective pleadings in the case, they have the standing of judicial admissions. Amended, withdrawn, or superseded pleadings in the case are no longer judicial admissions, but may be used as evidentiary admissions. A party's pleading in one case may generally be used as an evidentiary admission in other litigation. These same principles apply to the use in a subsequent trial of counsel's oral in-court statements representing the factual contentions of the party, even including assertions made during opening statement.[1]

How closely is it necessary to connect the pleading with the party against whom it is to be introduced as an admission? Certainly if it be shown to have been sworn to, or signed by, the party that would be sufficient. More often, however, the pleading is prepared and signed by counsel, and the older view holds that it is not sufficient to show that the pleading was filed or signed by the party's attorney of record, and statements therein will be presumed to be merely "suggestions of counsel" unless other evidence is produced that they were actually sanctioned by the client. The dominant current position, however, is that pleadings shown to have been prepared or filed by counsel employed by the party are prima facie regarded as authorized by the client and are entitled to be received as his admissions. The party opposing admission

§ 257
1. See generally infra § 259 regarding vicarious ad- missions by representatives of the party.

may offer evidence that the pleading was filed upon incorrect information and without his or her actual knowledge, but, except in extraordinary circumstances, such a showing goes only to the weight and not to the admissibility of the pleading.

An important exception to the use of the pleadings as admissions must be noted. A basic problem which attends the use of written pleadings is uncertainty whether the evidence as it actually unfolds at trial will prove the case described in the pleadings. Traditionally a failure in this respect, i.e., a variance between pleading and proof, could bring disaster to the pleader's case. As a safeguard against developments of this kind, the common law permitted the use of counts, each a complete separate statement of a different version of the same basic claim, combined in the same declaration, to take care of variance possibilities. The same was done with defenses. Inconsistency between counts or between defenses was not prohibited; in fact it was essential to the successful use of the system. Also essential to the success of the system was a prohibition against using allegations in one count or defense as admissions to prove or disprove allegations in another.

Under the influence of the Field Code of 1848, the view prevailed for a time that there could exist only one set of facts in a case and that inconsistent statements and defenses were therefore not allowable. Nevertheless, uncertainty as to how a case will in fact develop at trial is now recognized as a reality, with a concomitant need for some procedure for dealing with problems of variance. The modern equivalent of the common law system is the use of alternative and hypothetical forms of statement of claims and defenses, regardless of consistency. It can readily be appreciated that pleadings of this nature are directed primarily to giving notice and lack the essential character of an admission. To allow them to operate as admissions would frustrate their underlying purpose. Hence the decisions with seeming unanimity deny

them status as judicial admissions, and generally disallow them as evidentiary admissions.

Some courts have exhibited sensitivity to the potential unfairness involved in admitting pleadings where a more skillful pleader would have avoided the pitfalls of creating an admission, particularly where the pleading at issue concerned the conduct of third parties. Another approach is to recognize the potential of receiving an inconsistent pleading to unfairly prejudice a party and to be overvalued in relation to its true probative worth, excluding the pleading in appropriate cases after balancing the relevant factors. A final possible exception, not widely recognized, is denial of status as an admission to amended, withdrawn, or superseded pleadings on the theory that to admit them into evidence contravenes the policy of liberality in amendment.

A recurring question is whether a plea of guilty to a criminal charge should be allowed in evidence in a related civil action. Generally the evidence is admitted. While a plea of guilty to a traffic offense is in theory no different from a plea of guilty to other offenses, recognition that people plead guilty to traffic charges for reasons of convenience and with little regard to guilt or collateral consequences has led to some tendency to exclude them from evidence.[2] Pleas of *nolo contendere* or *non vult,* in jurisdictions where allowed, are generally regarded as inadmissible, and in fact that attribute is a principal reason for use of such pleas.

A related question involves whether a plea of guilty can be introduced as an admission in a criminal case where the accused is allowed to withdraw the guilty plea and is subsequently tried on the charge. The result depends on the resolution of competing considerations of policy. On the one hand, a plea of guilty if freely and understandingly made is so likely to be true that to withhold it from the jury seems to ask them to do justice without knowledge a very significant item of evidence. On this basis, some courts have received admissions in civil cases, leaving it to the adversary to rebut or explain. The competing con-

2. See infra § 298.

cern is that if the withdrawn plea is admitted the effectiveness of the withdrawal itself is substantially impaired. In addition, admitting the guilty plea virtually compels the accused to explain why it was initially entered, with resultant encroachment upon the privilege against self-incrimination and intrusion into sensitive areas of the attorney-client relationship. The Federal Rules Advisory Committee accepted the policy arguments against receiving evidence of a withdrawn guilty plea, and Rule 410 excludes such evidence in both civil and criminal cases.[3]

§ 258. Testimony by the Party as an Admission

While testifying on pretrial examination or at trial, a party may admit some fact that is adverse, and sometimes fatal, to a cause of action or defense. If at the end of the trial the party's admission stands unimpeached and uncontradicted, then like unimpeached and uncontradicted testimony generally it is conclusive against the party. Frequently this situation is what the courts are referring to when they say somewhat misleadingly that a party is "bound" by his or her own testimony. The controversial question is whether the party is bound by such testimony in the sense that the party will not be allowed to contradict it with other testimony, or if contradictory testimony has been received, the judge or jury is required to disregard it and to accept as true the party's disserving testimony as a judicial admission.

Three main approaches are reflected in the decisions, which to some extent tend to merge and do not necessarily lead to different results in particular situations. First, some courts take the view that a party's testimony in this respect is like the testimony of any other witness called by the party, that is, the party is free (as far as any rule of law is concerned) to elicit contradictory testimony from the same witness or to call other witnesses to contradict the statement. Obviously, however, the problem of persuasion may be a difficult one when the party seeks to

explain or contradict his or her own words, and equally obviously, the trial judge would often be justified in ruling on motion for directed verdict that reasonable minds could only believe that the party's testimony against interest was true.

Second, others take the view that the party's testimony is not conclusive against contradiction except when testifying unequivocally to matters in his or her "peculiar knowledge." These matters may consist of subjective facts, such as the party's own knowledge or motivation, or they may consist of objective facts observed by the party.

Third, some courts adopt the doctrine that a party's disserving testimony is to be treated as a judicial admission, conclusive on the issue, so that the party may not bring other witnesses to contradict the admission, and if the party or the adversary does elicit such conflicting testimony, it will be disregarded. Obviously, this third rule demands many qualifications and exceptions. Among these are the following: (1) The party is free to contradict, and thus correct, his or her own testimony; only when the party's own testimony taken as a whole unequivocally affirms the statement does the rule of conclusiveness apply. The rule is inapplicable, moreover, when the party's testimony (2) may be attributable to inadvertence or to a foreigner's mistake as to meaning, (3) is merely negative in effect, (4) is explicitly uncertain or is an estimate or opinion rather than an assertion of concrete fact, or (5) relates to a matter as to which the party could easily have been mistaken, such as the swiftly moving events just preceding a collision in which the party was injured.

Of these three approaches the first seems preferable in policy and most in accord with the tradition of jury trial. It rejects any restrictive rule and leaves the evaluation of the party's testimony and the conflicting evidence to the judgment of the jury, the judge, and the appellate court, with only the standard of reason to guide them.

---

3. For full text of Rule 410, see infra § 266.

The second theory, binding as to facts within the party's "peculiar knowledge," is based on the assumption that as to such facts the possibility that the party may be mistaken largely disappears. If the facts are subjective ones (e.g., knowledge, motivation), the likelihood of successful contradiction is slight, but even then the assumption may be questioned. "Knowledge may be 'special' without being correct. Often we little note nor long remember our 'motives, purposes, or knowledge.' There are few if any subjects on which plaintiffs are infallible."[1]

The third theory is also of doubtful validity. In the first place the party's testimony, uttered by a layman in the stress of examination, cannot with justice be given the conclusiveness of the traditional judicial admission in a pleading or stipulation,[2] deliberately drafted by counsel for the express purpose of limiting and defining the facts in issue. Again, a general rule of conclusiveness necessitates an elaboration of qualifications and exceptions, which represents a transfer to the appellate court of some of the traditional control of the jury by the trial judge, or in a nonjury case of the judge's factfinding function. These duties call for an exercise of judgment by the judge who has heard and seen the witnesses. Supervision by appellate judges of this process can best be exercised under a flexible standard, rather than a rule of conclusiveness.

Moreover, the third rule leads to mechanical solutions, unrelated to the needs of justice and calculated to proliferate appeals, in certain special situations. One is the situation where the opponent, by adroit cross-examination, has maneuvered the party into an improvident concession. Another is the case of the defendant who is protected by liability insurance testifying to facts that will help the plaintiff to win. Yet another is the situation where both parties testify against their respective interests. Here the rule of conclusiveness may be thought to decide the issue against the party who has the burden of proof.

Finally, the moral emphasis is wrong. Early cases where the rule of conclusiveness was first used may have been cases where judges were outraged by apparent attempts by parties to play fast and loose with the court. However, examination of numerous decisions demonstrates that this is far from being the typical situation of the party testifying to disserving facts. Instead of the unscrupulous party, it is either the one who can be pushed into an admission by the ingenuity or persistence of adverse counsel or the unusually candid or conscientious party willing to speak the truth regardless of its consequences who is penalized by the rule of conclusiveness. Courts should employ the more flexible practice, which is older and simpler.

§ 259. Representative Admissions; Co-conspirator Statements

When a party to the suit has expressly authorized another person to speak, it is an obvious and accepted extension of the admission rule to admit against the party the statements of such persons. In the absence of express authority, how far will the statements of an agent be received as the principal's admission by virtue of the employment relationship? The early texts and cases used as analogies the doctrine of the master's substantive responsibility for the acts of the agent and the notion then prevalent in evidence law that words accompanying a relevant act were admissible as part of the *res gestae*. Together, these concepts produced the inadequate theory that the agent's statements could be received against the principal only when made at the time of, and in relation to, some act then being performed in the scope of the agent's duty.

A later theory that gained currency in the writings and opinions was that the admissibility of the agent's statements as admissions of the principal was measured by precisely the same tests as the principal's substantive responsibility for the conduct of the agent, that is, the words of the agent would be received as

---

§ 258

1. Alamo v. Del Rosario, 98 F.2d 328, 332 (D.C.Cir. 1938).

2. As to judicial admissions, see supra § 254.

the admissions of the principal if they were spoken within the scope of the authority of the agent to speak for the employer. This formula made plain that the statements of an agent employed to give information (a so-called "speaking agent") could be received as the employer's admissions, regardless of want of authority to act otherwise, and conversely that authority to act, e.g., the authority of a chauffeur to drive a car, would not carry with it automatically the authority to make statements to others describing the duties performed.

Probably the most frequent use of these tests occurred in the exclusion of statements made by employees involved in an accident to someone at the scene regarding the accident, not made in furtherance of the employer's interest, but as a "mere narrative." This result represents the logical application of these tests, but the assumption that the determinant of the master's responsibility for the agent's *acts* should be the test for using the agent's statements as *evidence* against the master is a shaky one.

The rejection of such post-accident statements coupled with the admission of the employee's testimony on the stand resulted in preferring the weaker to the stronger evidence. Typically the agent is well informed about acts in the course of the business, the statements are offered against the employer's interest, and while the employment continues, the employee is not likely to make the statements unless they are true. Moreover, if admissions are viewed as arising from the adversary system, responsibility for statements of one's employee is consistent with that theory. Accordingly, even before adoption of the Federal Rules, the predominant view was to admit a statement by an agent if it concerned a matter within the scope of the declarant's employment and was made before that relationship was terminated. Of course, admissibility of the traditional authorized statement was continued as well.

Federal Rule 801(d)(2)(C) & (D) follow the expansive view described in the preceding paragraph. They provide:

A statement is not hearsay if—

    * * *

The statement is offered against a party and is * * * (C) a statement by a person authorized by the party to make a statement concerning the subject, or (D) a statement by the party's agent or servant concerning a matter within the scope of the agency or employment, made during the existence of the relationship.

The party offering evidence of the alleged agent's admission must first prove the fact and scope of the agency of the declarant for the adverse party. This may, of course, be done directly by the testimony of the asserted agent, or by anyone who knows, or by circumstantial evidence. Traditionally, courts held that evidence of the purported agent's past declarations asserting the agency were inadmissible hearsay when offered to show the relation. This analysis no longer appears correct under the Federal Rules, although it likely remains true that statements of the purported agent alone are not sufficient to establish agency.[1] If the preliminary fact of the declarant's agency is disputed, the question is one to be decided by the court under Rule 104(a).[2]

The question also arises whether a statement by an agent, in order to qualify as an admission, must be made to an outsider rather than to the principal or to another agent. Typical instances are the railway conductor's report of an accident or a letter to the home office from a manager of a branch office of a bank. Historically, though plainly made in the scope of authority, some courts refused to admit such statements unless they were adopted by the principal. Others admitted them in either situation. Those courts which excluded such statements relied chiefly on the fact that the doctrine of *respondeat superior* does not apply to transactions between the

§ 259

1. See Bourjaily v. United States, 483 U.S. 171, 175–181 (1987), analysis by analogy to treatment of coconspirator statements, infra § 259.

2. Id. at 175–178.

agent and the principal, determining the hearsay question by the rules of substantive liability of principals. However, other analogies could just as reasonably control, such as the fact that statements made by a party not intended for the outside world—entries in a secret diary, for example—are receivable as admissions.

Reliability also favors admissibility of such in-house statements. While slightly less reliable as a class than the agent's authorized statements to outsiders, intra-organization reports are generally made as a basis for some action, and when this is so, they share the reliability of business records. They will only be offered against the principal when they admit some fact damaging to the principal, and this kind of statement by an agent is likely to be trustworthy. No special danger of surprise, confusion, or prejudice from the use of the evidence is apparent.

The drafters of the Federal Rule found the arguments in favor of receiving such in-house admissions persuasive. The expansion has been held to apply both to statements by agents authorized to speak and by those without "speaking authority" but only authorized to act for the principal.

While the Federal Rule greatly expands the scope of statements within a corporation that will qualify as admissions, it leaves a number of difficult issues to be resolved by analysis of the individual facts of the situation. For example, even though statements made by corporate officers or employees are found to be admissions of the corporation, further inquiry is required before such statements can be used as vicarious admissions of other corporate employees. Also, while firsthand knowledge is not required for vicarious admissions of corporate employees, uncertainty about the identity of the person who was the source of a statement may result in exclusion because of a failure to establish that the statement concerned a matter within the scope of the declarant's employment as opposed to mere "gossip."

The general principles developed above are applied in the remainder of this section to special categories of agents and to types of vicarious admissions that are frequently encountered:

Attorneys. If an attorney is employed to manage a party's conduct of a lawsuit, the attorney has *prima facie* authority to make relevant judicial admissions by pleadings, by oral or written stipulations, or by formal opening statement, which unless allowed to be withdrawn are conclusive in the case.[3] Such formal and conclusive admissions should be, and are, framed with care and circumspection, and historically these admissions were often contrasted with an attorney's oral out-of-court statement. The latter were characterized as "merely a loose conversation," and it is often said that the client is not "bound" by the "casual" statements of counsel made outside of court. The use of the word "bound" is obviously misleading. The issue is not whether the client is "bound," as he or she is by a judicial admission, but whether the attorney's extrajudicial statement is admissible against the client as a mere evidentiary admission made by an agent.

A natural, if unconscious, tendency to protect the client and, perhaps the attorney, against the hazard of evidence of statements by counsel produced a tendency in the older cases to restrict introduction of such statements more than statements by other types of agents. More recent cases generally measure the authority of the attorney to make out-of-court admissions by the same tests of express or implied authority as would be applied to other agents, and when they meet these tests, admit as evidentiary admissions the statements of attorneys. These admissions occur, for example, in letters or oral conversations made in the course of efforts for the collection or resistance of claims, or settlement negotiations, or the management of any other business in behalf of the client.[4]

Partners. A partner is an agent of the partnership for the conduct of the firm's busi-

---

3. See the discussion of judicial admissions supra § 257.

4. Possible application of the rule excluding offers of compromise should not be overlooked. See infra § 266.

ness. Accordingly, when the existence and scope of the partnership have been proved, the statement of a partner made in the conduct of the business of the firm is receivable as the admission of the partnership. What of statements of a former partner made after dissolution? The cases are divided, but since a continuing power is recognized in each former partner to do such acts as are reasonably necessary to wind up and settle the affairs of the firm, one former partner should be regarded as having authority to speak for the others in making statements of fact as are reasonably incident to collecting the claims and paying the debts of the firm. Beyond this, it seems that one partner's admissions should be competent only against that partner.

Coconspirator. Conspiracies to commit a crime or an unlawful or tortious act are analogous to partnerships. If A and B are engaged in a conspiracy, the acts and declarations of B occurring while the conspiracy is actually in progress and in furtherance of the design are provable against A, because they are acts for which A is criminally or civilly responsible as a matter of substantive law. But B's declarations may also be introduced against A as representative admissions to prove the truth of the matter declared. Only statements of the latter sort are at issue within this section on representative admissions. However, courts have seldom discriminated between declarations offered as conduct constituting part of the conspiracy and declarations offered as vicarious admissions of the facts declared. Instead, even when offered as admissions, courts have generally imposed the same test applicable to statements that form part of the conduct of the crime, namely that the declaration must have been made while the conspiracy was continuing and must have constituted a step in furtherance of the venture.

Federal Rule 801(d)(2)(E) is generally consistent with the foregoing analysis. When offered against a party, it treats as "not hearsay" "a statement by a coconspirator of a party during the course and in furtherance of the conspiracy."

Literally applied, the "in furtherance" requirement calls for exclusion of statements possessing evidentiary value solely as admissions, yet in fact more emphasis seems to be placed upon the "during the course" aspect and any statement so qualifying temporally may be admitted without much regard to whether it in fact furthered the conspiracy. These latter decisions may represent a parallel to the cases allowing in evidence against the principal declarations of an agent which relate to the subject of the agency, even though the agent was not authorized to make a statement.

Both the "in furtherance" and the "during the course" requirement call for exclusion of admissions and confessions made after the termination of the conspiracy. Questions arise, of course, as to when termination occurs. Under some circumstances, extending the duration of the conspiracy beyond the commission of the principal crime to include concomitant and closely connected disposition of its fruits or concealment of its traces appears justifiable, as in the case of police officers engaged in writing up a false report to conceal police participation in a burglary, disposal of the body after a murder, or continuation of a racketeering enterprise that involved on-going concealment to effectuate the scheme. The Supreme Court's conclusion in Krulewitch v. United States [5] that it was error to admit evidence of a coconspirator's statement regarding concealment efforts after arrest of the participants established the position of the federal courts and was cited with approval in the Advisory Committee Note to the Federal Rule. As a result, attempts to expand the so-called "concealment phase" to include all efforts to avoid detection have generally not been accepted by the courts. While statements made after the termination of the conspiracy are inadmissible, subsequent acts which shed light upon the nature of the conspiratorial agreement have been held admissible.

5. 336 U.S. 440 (1949).

Preliminary questions of fact with regard to declarations of coconspirators are governed by Federal Rule 104(a) and must be established by a preponderance of the evidence.[6] Changing longstanding practice in the federal courts, the Supreme Court held in Bourjaily v. United States [7] that the putative coconspirator statement itself can be considered by the trial court in determining whether a conspiracy exists and its scope.[8] However, the Court left undecided whether the trial court could have relied exclusively on the purported conspirator statement to make this determination.[9]

The existence of a conspiracy in fact is sufficient to support admissibility, and a conspiracy count in the indictment is not required and the declarant need not be charged. The evidence is similarly admissible in civil cases, where the conspiracy rule applies to tortfeasors acting in concert.

Statements of government agents in criminal cases. In a criminal prosecution, statements by the agent of an accused may be admitted against the accused, but statements by agents of the government have been held not admissible against the government. "This apparent discrimination is explained by the peculiar posture of the parties in a criminal prosecution—the only party on the government side being the government itself whose many agents and actors are supposedly uninterested personally in the outcome of the trial and are historically unable to bind the sovereign." [10] A more plausible explanation is the desirability of affording the government a measure of protection against errors and indiscretions on the part of at least some of its many agents.

The cases ruling against admissibility involve statements by agents at the investigative level, with statements by government attorneys after the initiation of proceedings having been held admissible. A dividing line in terms of the relative position of the agent in question may well serve to balance the conflicting interests involved. While Federal Rule 801(d)(2) does not specifically address the question, it is very hard to find any support in its language or structure for a blanket exclusion of statements by government agents. However, a balancing approach of the type suggested above appears consistent with its basic approach and the various policy concerns involved.

§ 260. Declarations by "Privies in Estate," Joint Tenants, Predecessors in Interest, Joint Obligors, and Principals Against Surety

Historically, courts generally accepted the notion that "privity," or identity of interest between the declarant and a party justified introduction of the statement of the declarant as an admission of the party. Thus, the declaration of one joint tenant or joint owner against another could be received, but not that of a tenant in common, a co-legatee or co-devisee, or a co-trustee—so strictly is the distinction derived from the law of property applied in this context.

The more frequent and important application of this property analogy was the use of declarations of a predecessor in title to land, personalty, or choses in action against a successor. The successor was viewed as acquiring an interest burdened with the same liability of having declarations used against him or her as could have been used against the predecessor. The declarations had to relate to the declarant's transactions, intent, or interest in the property, and they must have been made while the declarant was the owner of the interest now claimed by the successor. Under this theory, courts have received the declarations of grantors, transferors, donors, and mortgagors of land and personalty against the transferees and mortgagees; of decedents against their representatives, heirs and next of kin; by a prior possessor against one who claims prescriptive title relying on

---

6. See generally supra § 53.

7. 483 U.S. 171 (1987).

8. Id. at 176–179.

9. Id. at 181.

10. United States v. Santos, 372 F.2d 177, 180 (2d Cir.1967).

such prior possession; and of former holders of notes and other choses in action against their assignees. Of course, concepts such as bona fide purchaser and holder in due course may make the evidence irrelevant and therefore inadmissible.

Similarly, it is asserted that when two parties are jointly liable as obligors, the declarations of one are receivable as an admission against the other. However, the element of authorization to speak in furtherance of the common enterprise, as in the case of agency, partnership, or conspiracy can hardly be spelled out from the mere relationship of joint obligors, and admissibility of declarations on this basis has been criticized. In fact, most of the cases found in support are cases involving the special situation of declarations of a principal offered as admissions against a surety, guarantor, indemnitor, or other person secondarily liable. These declarations were usually held admissible.

Morgan criticized importing into the law of evidence the property doctrines of identity of interest and privity of estate:

> The dogma of vicarious admissions, as soon as it passes beyond recognized principles of representation, baffles the understanding. Joint ownership, joint obligation, privity of title, each and all furnish no criterion of credibility, no aid in the evaluation of testimony.[1]

Following Morgan's view, the Model Code omitted any provision for admitting these declarations, and the Federal Rules followed the same pattern. Most meritorious cases will qualify as a declaration against interest, vicarious admissions of agents, or some other hearsay exception more soundly grounded than an admission based on privity.

§ 261. Admissions by Conduct: (a) Adoptive Admissions

One may expressly adopt another's statement. That is an explicit admission like any

other and calls for no further discussion. In this treatise, the term adoptive admission is used somewhat restrictively to apply to evidence of other conduct of a party which manifests circumstantially the party's assent to the truth of a statement made by another.[1]

Adoptive admissions under the Federal Rules are governed by Rule 801(d)(2)(B). In conformity with traditional practice, it provides that a statement is not hearsay if offered against a party and is "a statement of which the party has manifested an adoption or belief in its truth."

The fact that the party declares that he or she has heard that another person has made a given statement is not alone sufficient to justify finding that the party has adopted the third person's statement. The circumstances surrounding the party's declaration must be examined to determine whether they indicated an approval of the statement.

The question of adoption often arises in life and accident insurance cases when the defendant insurance company offers statements which the plaintiff beneficiary attached to the proof of death or disability, such as the certificate of the attending physician or the coroner's report. The fact that the beneficiary has thus tendered it as an exhibit accompanying a formal statement of "proof" presented for the purpose of having the company act upon it by paying the claim would appear to be enough to secure the admission of the accompanying statements. In actuality, however, the surrounding circumstances often show that an inference of adoption would be most unrealistic. This is clear when the beneficiary expressly disavows the accompanying statement,[2] and it seems that exclusion of the attached statement should likewise follow when the statements of the beneficiary in the proofs are clearly contrary to those in the

---

§ 260

1. Morgan, Admissions, 12 Wash.L.Rev. 181, 202 (1937).

§ 261

1. Admissions by silence are treated separately. See infra § 262.

2. In the absence of disavowal, it is arguable that the case is one of admission by failure to deny. See infra § 262.

exhibits. Moreover, when the company's agent prepared the proof for signature and procured the accompanying documents, as is frequently done as a helpful service to the beneficiary, the inference of adoption of statements in the exhibits should not be drawn if the agent has failed to call the beneficiary's attention to inconsistencies between the proof and the exhibits. By similar reasoning, furnishing a copy of an examining physician's report to the opponent under the requirement of a discovery rule should not be considered an adoption. The argument for exclusion is particularly strong if accompanying statements, such as the certificate of the attending physician regarding particular facts, are required under the terms of the policy. In such cases, the statements are not attached at the choice of the beneficiary, and the sponsorship generally to be inferred from a voluntary tendering of another's statement cannot be made.

Does the introduction of evidence by a party constitute an adoption of the statements therein, so that they may be used against the party as an admission in a subsequent lawsuit? The answer ought to depend upon whether the particular circumstances warrant the conclusion that adoption in fact occurred and not upon the discredited notion that a party vouches for its own witnesses. When a party offers in evidence a deposition or an affidavit to prove the matters stated therein, the party knows or should know the contents of the writing so offered and presumably desires that all of the contents be considered on its behalf since only the portion desired could be offered. Accordingly, it is reasonable to conclude that the writing so introduced may be used against the party as an adoptive admission in another suit.

With respect to oral testimony, however, the inference of sponsorship of the statements is not always so clear. However, here too circumstances may justify the conclusion that, when the proponent placed the witness on the stand to prove a particular fact and the witness so testified, the party has created an adoptive admission of the fact that may be admitted in a later suit. But how is the party offering the testimony in the later suit to show that a given statement of the witness at the former trial was intended to be elicited by the party who called the witness or was contrary to or outside that intention? The form and context of the question would usually, but not always, give the clue. In view of the prevailing practice of interviewing one's witnesses before putting them on the stand, it would seem that a practical working rule would admit against the proponent the direct testimony of its own witness as presumptively elicited to prove the facts stated, in the absence of counter proof that the testimony came as a surprise to the interrogator or was repudiated in the course of argument. By contrast, testimony elicited on cross-examination may be drawn out to reveal the witness' errors and dishonesty and should not be assumed to have been relied on by the examiner as evidence of the facts stated. To constitute an adoptive admission, reliance must be affirmatively established.

In the main, preliminary factual issues arising with regard to whether a statement was adopted are to be decided as questions of conditional relevancy under Rule 104(b).[3]

Similar to adoptive admissions are the instances where the party has referred an inquirer to another person whose anticipated statements the party accepts in advance. However, these admissions by reference to a third person are probably more properly classifiable as representative or vicarious admissions, rather than adoptive.[4]

§ 262. Admissions by Conduct: (b) Silence [1]

When a statement is made in the presence of a party containing assertions of facts

§ 262

3. See discussion of related issues regarding adoption by silence in infra § 262.

4. See generally supra § 259.

1. The general question whether silence is hearsay is treated in supra § 250 and particular aspects of silence as

which, if untrue, the party would under all the circumstances naturally be expected to deny, failure to speak has traditionally been received as an admission. Whether the justification for receiving the evidence is the assumption that the party has intended to express its assent and thus has adopted the statement or that the probable state of belief can be inferred from the conduct is probably unimportant. Since it is the failure to deny that is significant, an equivocal or evasive response may similarly be used against the party on either theory, but if the total response adds up to a clear-cut denial, this theory of implied admission is not properly available.

Despite the offhand appeal of this kind of evidence, courts have often suggested that it be received with caution, an admonition that is especially appropriate in criminal cases. Several characteristics of the evidence should be noted. First, its nature and the circumstances under which it arises often amount to an open invitation to manufacture evidence. Second, ambiguity of inference is often present. Silence may be motivated by many factors other than a sense of guilt or lack of an exculpatory story.[2] For example, silence may be valued. As indicated at the beginning of this chapter, everyone knows that anything you say may be used against you. Third, the constitutional limitations of *Miranda* apply to the use of this type of evidence in criminal cases, but only where there is custodial interrogation.[3] Fourth, while in theory the statement is not offered as proof of its contents but rather to show what the party accepted, the distinction is indeed a subtle one; the statement is ordinarily highly damaging and of a nature likely to draw attention away from the basic inquiry whether acquiescence did in fact occur.

Despite the array of circumstances raising doubts regarding the reliability of this kind of evidence, the Supreme Court has not found any absolute federal constitutional barriers

against its use other than those imposed in some circumstances by *Miranda*. Nevertheless, courts have evolved a variety of safeguards against misuse: (1) The statement must have been heard by the party claimed to have acquiesced. (2) It must have been understood by the party. (3) The subject matter must have been within the party's knowledge. At first glance, this requirement may appear inconsistent with the general dispensation with firsthand knowledge with respect to admissions, yet the unreasonableness of expecting a person to deny a matter of which he or she is not aware seems evident.[4] Otherwise the party simply does not have the incentive or the wherewithal to dispute the accusation. (4) Physical or emotional impediments to responding must not be present. (5) The personal makeup of the speaker, e.g., young child, or the person's relationship to the party or the event, e.g., bystander, may be such as to make it unreasonable to expect a denial. (6) Probably most important of all, the statement itself must be such as would, if untrue, call for a denial under the circumstances. Beyond the constitutional issues that can be raised, the fact that the police are present when an accusatory statement is made may constitute a critical circumstance that eliminates the naturalness of a response.

The above list is not an exclusive one, and other factors will suggest themselves. The essential inquiry in each case is whether a reasonable person under the circumstances would have denied the statement, with answers not lending themselves readily to mechanical formulations.

Most preliminary questions of admissibility in connection with admissions by acquiescence fall within the category of conditional relevancy. While some preliminary issues involved with admissions by silence are entrusted to final determination by the court, questions such as whether the statement was made in the person's hearing and whether there was an opportunity to reply should be

---

an admission in criminal cases are discussed in supra § 160.

   2. See supra § 160.

   3. See supra § 132.

   4. The general absence of a firsthand knowledge requirement for admissions is discussed in supra § 255.

submitted for jury determination if the court concludes sufficient evidence has been introduced so that a reasonable jury could find that those facts have been established.[5]

Failure to Reply to Letter or other Written Communication. If a written statement is given to a party and read in the presence of others, the party's failure to deny its assertions may be received as an admission, when under the circumstances it would be natural for the person to deny them if he or she did not acquiesce. The principle in operation here is similar to the failure to deny an oral statement. Moreover, if a party receives a letter containing several statements, which he or she would naturally deny if untrue, and states a position as to some of the statements but fails to comment on the others, this failure will usually be received as evidence of an admission to those omitted.

More debatable is the question whether the failure to reply at all to a letter or other written communication should be received as an admission by silence. Certainly such a failure to reply will often be less convincing than silence in the face of an oral charge. Indeed, it is sometimes announced as a "general rule," subject to exceptions, that failure to answer a letter does not constitute an admission. The negative form of the rule seems undesirable in that it tends toward over-strict rulings excluding evidence of material value. The preferable view is that the failure to reply to a letter containing statements which it would be natural under all the circumstances for the addressee to deny if he or she believed them untrue is receivable as evidence of an admission by silence. Two factors particularly tend to show that a denial would be naturally forthcoming: first, where the letter was written as part of a mutual correspondence between the parties, and second, where the proof shows that the parties were engaged in some business, transaction, or relationship which would make it improbable that an untrue communication about the transaction or relationship would be ignored.

The most common instance of this latter situation is the transmission by one party to a business relationship to the other of a statement of account or a bill. Failure to question such a bill or statement is uniformly received as evidence of an admission of its correctness. On the other hand, if the negotiations have been broken off by one party's taking a final stand, thus indicating a view that further communication would be fruitless or if the letter was written after litigation was instituted, these circumstances tend to show that failure to answer should not be received as an admission.

§ 263. Admissions by Conduct: (c) Flight and Similar Acts

"The wicked flee when no one pursues."[1] Many acts of a defendant after the crime seeking to escape are uncritically received as admissions by conduct, constituting circumstantial evidence of consciousness of guilt and hence of the fact of guilt itself. In this class are flight from the scene, from one's usual haunts, or from the jurisdiction after the crime; assuming a false name; shaving off a beard; resisting arrest; attempting to bribe arresting officers; forfeiture of bond by failure to appear or departure from the trial while it is proceeding; escapes or attempted escapes from confinement; and suicide attempts by the accused.

If the flight is from the scene of the crime, evidence of it seems to be wholly acceptable as a means of locating the accused at the critical time and place. However, in many situations, the inference of consciousness of guilt of the particular crime is so uncertain and ambiguous and the evidence so prejudicial that one is forced to wonder whether the evidence is not directed to punishing the "wicked" generally rather than resolving the issue of guilt of the offense charged. Particularly troublesome are the cases where defendant flees when sought to be arrested for another crime, is wanted for another crime,

---

5. See the general treatment of preliminary questions in supra §§ 53, 58.

§ 263
1. Proverbs 28:1 (New Rev. Standard).

or is not shown to know that he or she is suspected of the particular crime. Some courts appear to accept a general sense of guilt as sufficient. Perhaps the chief offenders are the cases of attempted suicide.

A leading case suggests with respect to evidence of flight:

> Its probative value as circumstantial evidence of guilt depends upon the degree of confidence with which four inferences can be drawn: (1) from the defendant's behavior to flight; (2) from flight to consciousness of guilt; (3) from consciousness of guilt to consciousness of guilt concerning the crime charged; and (4) from consciousness of guilt concerning the crime charged to actual guilt of the crime charged.[2]

In recent years, a number of courts have begun to look with particular care at the timing of the flight relative to the offense and the strength of the inference that in fleeing the defendant was aware of, and motivated by fear of apprehension for, a particular offense. The potential for prejudice of flight evidence should also be weighed against its probative value. Critical scrutiny of the balance between the often weak probative value of this type of evidence and its prejudicial impact is appropriate in each case.

While the great bulk of the decisions involve criminal prosecutions, flight also finds recognition in civil actions.

§ 264. Admissions by Conduct: (d) Failure to Call Witnesses or Produce Evidence; Refusal to Submit to a Physical Examination

When it would be natural under the circumstances for a party to call a particular witness, or to take the stand as a witness in a civil case,[1] or voluntarily to produce documents or other objects in his or her possession as evidence and the party fails to do so, tradition has allowed the adversary to use this failure as the basis for invoking an adverse inference. An analogous inference may be drawn if a party unreasonably declines to submit, upon request, to a physical examination or refuses to furnish handwriting exemplars.

Most of the controversy arises with respect to failure to call a witness. The classic statement is:

> [I]f a party has it peculiarly within his power to produce witnesses whose testimony would elucidate the transaction, the fact that he does not do it creates the presumption that the testimony, if produced, would be unfavorable.[2]

The cases fall into two groups. In the first, an adverse inference may be drawn against a party for failure to produce a witness reasonably assumed to be favorably disposed to the party. In the second, the inference may be drawn against a party who has exclusive control over a material witness but fails to produce him or her, without regard to any possible favorable disposition of the witness toward the party. Cases in the second group are increasingly less frequent due to the growth of discovery and other disclosure requirements. In either group, if the testimony of the witness would be merely cumulative, the inference is unavailable.

Despite an abundance of cases recognizing the inference, refusal to allow comment or to instruct rarely results in a reversal, while erroneously instructing the jury on the inference or even an erroneous argument by counsel much more frequently requires retrial. The appellate courts often counsel caution. A number of factors support a conservative approach. Conjecture or ambiguity of inference is often present. The possibility that the inference may be drawn invites waste of time in calling unnecessary witnesses or in presenting evidence to explain why they were not called. Failure to anticipate that the inference may be invoked entails substantial possi-

---

2. United States v. Myers, 550 F.2d 1036, 1049 (5th Cir.1977).

§ 264

1. See supra § 134 as to extent to which an accused waives the privilege against self-incrimination by testifying.

2. Graves v. United States, 150 U.S. 118, 121 (1893).

bilities of surprise. Finally, the availability of modern discovery and other disclosure procedures serves to diminish both the justification and the need for the inference. In recognition of these factors, courts often require the party expecting to make a missing witness argument or intending to request such an instruction to give notice as early as possible.

It is often said that if a witness is "equally available" to both parties, no inference springs from the failure of either to call the witness. This can hardly be accurate, as the inference may be allowed when the witness could easily be called or subpoenaed by either party. What is in fact meant is that when so far as appears the witness would be as likely to be favorable to one party as the other, there will be no inference. But even here, it seems that equality of favor is nearly always debatable and that although the judge thinks the witness would be as likely to favor one party as the other, either party should be permitted to argue the inference.

A party may be at liberty to call a witness, but may have a privilege against the witness' being called by the adversary, as when in a criminal case the accused may call his or her spouse but the state may not. Similarly, it may be clear that all the information that a witness has is subject to a privilege which the party may exert, such as the doctor-patient privilege. In these situations probably the majority of courts would forbid an adverse inference from a failure to call.[3] Of course, an inference from the failure of the criminal defendant to take the stand is constitutionally forbidden.[4] The policy considerations with respect to comment upon the exercise of evidentiary privileges are discussed elsewhere.[5]

The specific procedural effect of the inference from failure to call a witness is seldom discussed. Some courts have said that the party's failure to call the witness or produce the evidence creates a "presumption" that the testimony would have been unfavorable. It is usually phrased in terms, however, of "may" rather than "must" and seemingly could at

most be only a "permissive," not a mandatory presumption, i.e. an inference described as a presumption in order to avoid local prohibitions against judges commenting on the evidence.[6] Moreover, unlike the usual presumption, it is not directed to any specific presumed fact or facts which are required or permitted to be found. The burden of producing evidence of a fact cannot be met by relying on this "presumption." Rather, its effect is to impair the value of the opponent's evidence and to give greater credence to the positive evidence of the adversary upon any issue upon which it is shown that the missing witness might have knowledge.

Instead, most courts speak of the party's failure to call the witness as creating an "inference." Some of these courts consider that the party has a right to have such inference explained in the instructions on proper request while others consider that the instruction is proper but not required. Still others would condemn an instruction as a comment on the evidence. Of course, all courts permit counsel to argue the inference where the inference is an allowable one.

In jurisdictions where the judge retains the common law power to comment on the evidence, a fair comment on failure to produce witnesses or evidence is traditionally allowable. Furthermore, there is no harm in permitting judicial discretion to instruct on the inference. However, a practice that gives a party a right to such instruction is undesirable. If made a matter of right, it is hard to escape the development of elaborate rules defining the circumstances when the right exists. To make instruction a matter of right has the advantage, it is true, of focusing past experience on the problem presented at the trial, but the cost here of complex rules far outweighs the gain.

A web of rules also can develop by tightly controlling counsel's argument on the inference. It is wiser to hold that if an argument on failure to produce proof is fallacious, the

---

3. See supra § 74.1.

4. See supra § 132.

5. See supra § 74.1.

6. See discussion of these terms in infra Ch. 36.

remedy is the answering argument and the jury's good sense. Thus, the judge should be required to intervene only when the argument, under the general standard, can be said to be not merely weak or unfounded, but unfair and prejudicial.

§ 265. Admissions by Conduct: (e) Misconduct Constituting Obstruction of Justice

We have seen in the preceding section that a party's failure to produce evidence that he or she is free to produce or withhold may be treated as an admission. As might be expected, wrongdoing by the party in connection with its case amounting to an obstruction of justice is also commonly regarded as an admission by conduct. By resorting to wrongful devices, the party is said to provide a basis for believing that he or she thinks the case is weak and not to be won by fair means, or in criminal cases that the accused is conscious of guilt. Accordingly, the following are considered under this general category of admissions by conduct: a party's false statement about the matter in litigation, whether before suit or on the stand; subornation of perjury; fabrication of documents; undue pressure by bribery, intimidation, or other means to influence a witness to testify favorably or to avoid testifying; destruction or concealment of relevant documents or objects; attempt to corrupt the jury; and hiding or transferring property in anticipation of judgment.

Of course, it is not enough to show that a third person did the acts charged as obstructive. They must be connected to the party, or in the case of a corporation to one of its superior officers, by showing that an officer did the act or authorized it by words or other conduct. Moreover, the circumstances of the act must manifest bad faith. Mere negligence is not enough, for it does not sustain the inference of consciousness of a weak cause.

A question may well be raised whether the relatively modest probative value of such evidence is not often outweighed by its prejudicial effect.[1] The litigant who would not like to have a stronger case must indeed be a rarity. It may well be that the real underpinning of the rule of admissibility is a desire to impose swift punishment, with a certain poetic justice, rather than concern over niceties of proof. In any event, the evidence is generally admitted, despite incidental disclosure of another crime.

What is the probative reach of these various kinds of "spoliation" admissions, beyond their great tactical value in darkening the atmosphere of the party's case? They should entitle the proponent at least to an instruction that the adversary's conduct may be considered generally as tending to corroborate the proponent's case and to discredit that of the adversary. This result is worthwhile in itself, and it carries with it the corresponding right of the proponent's counsel to argue these inferences.

However, a crucial and perplexing question remains, namely, does the adverse inference from the party's obstructive conduct substitute for evidence of a fact essential to the adversary's case? Certainly the primitive impulse to answer "yes" is strong, and an analogy has been suggested to the practice under statutes and rules permitting the court to enter a default against a party who refuses to provide discovery. Certainly, when the conduct points toward an inference about a particular specific fact, as in the case of bribing an attesting witness to be absent or destroying a particular document, there is likely to be a greater willingness to allow an inference of that fact although the only available information regarding it is the proponent's claim in the pleadings. Where the conduct is not directed toward suppression of any particular fact, as in attempts to "buy off" the prosecution, to suborn the jury, or to defeat recovery by conveyance of property, an inference as to the existence of a particular fact not proved is more strained. Without adverting to this distinction, many decisions have supported the general doctrine that the inference from obstructive conduct will not satisfy the need for

§ 265
1. See generally supra § 185.

proof of a particular fact essential to the proponent's case.

Some recent cases have indicated a willingness to rethink these traditionally established principles. Several cases have found intentional actions that result in the destruction of evidence either to shift the burden of proof or to provide affirmative evidence on a critical issue. Other cases have begun to develop a separate tort for spoliation of evidence. This area of the law appears to be in the process of rather rapid change, although the patterns of the new order are not yet entirely clear.

§ 266. Admissions by Conduct: (f) Offers to Compromise Disputed Claim in Civil Suits and Plea Negotiations in Criminal Cases

In general. Arguably an offer to accept a sum in compromise of a disputed claim might be used against the party as an admission of the weakness of the claim. Conversely, an offer by the adversary to pay a sum in compromise might be used against that party as an admission of the weakness of his or her position. In either situation, there is general agreement that the offer of compromise is not admissible on the issue of liability, although the reason for exclusion is not always clear.

Two grounds for the rule of inadmissibility are advanced: lack of relevancy and policy considerations. First, the relevancy of the offer will vary according to circumstances, with a very small offer of payment to settle a very large claim being much more readily construed as a desire for peace rather than an admission of weakness of position. Relevancy would increase, however, as the amount of the offer approaches the amount claimed. Second, the policy aspect is to promote the settling of disputes, which would be discouraged if offers of compromise were admitted. Resting the rule on this basis has the advantage of avoiding difficult questions of relevancy. On this ground, the rule is available as an objection to one who made the offer and is a party to the suit in which the evidence is offered.

To invoke the exclusionary rule, there must be an actual dispute, preferably some negotia-

tions, and at least an apparent difference of view between the parties as to the validity or amount of the claim. An offer to pay an admitted claim is not privileged since there is no policy of encouraging compromises of undisputed claims. They should be paid in full. If the validity of the claim and the amount due are undisputed, an offer to pay a lesser sum in settlement or to pay in installments would accordingly be admissible.

What is excluded? The offer is excluded, of course, as well as any suggestions or overtures of settlement. How far do any accompanying statements of fact made by either party during oral negotiations or correspondence looking to settlement share the privilege? The historically accepted doctrine held that an admission of fact in the course. of negotiations was not privileged unless it was stated hypothetically ("we admit for the sake of the discussion only"); expressly made "without prejudice"; or inseparably connected with the offer so that it could not be correctly understood without reading the two together.

This traditional doctrine of denying the protection of the exclusionary rule to statements of fact had serious drawbacks, however. It discouraged freedom of communication in attempting compromise and, taken with its exceptions, involved difficulties of application. As a result, the trend has been to extend the protection to all statements made in compromise negotiations.

Federal Rule 408, set forth below, is consistent with the foregoing observations, including an extension of its protection to all statements made in compromise negotiations.

Evidence of (1) furnishing or offering or promising to furnish, or (2) accepting or offering or promising to accept, a valuable consideration in compromising or attempting to compromise a claim which was disputed as to either validity or amount, is not admissible to prove liability for or invalidity of the claim or its amount. Evidence of conduct or statements made in compromise negotiations is likewise not admissible. This rule does not require the exclusion of any evidence otherwise discoverable merely because it is presented in the course of compromise negotiations. This rule also does not require exclusion when the evidence is offered for another purpose, such as proving bias or prejudice of a witness, negativing a contention of undue delay, or proving an effort to obstruct a criminal investigation or prosecution.

The exclusionary rule is designed to exclude the offer of compromise only when it is tendered as an admission of the weakness of the offering party's claim or defense, not when the purpose is otherwise. Thus, for example, the rule does not call for exclusion when the compromise negotiations are offered to explain delay in taking action, prior statements, or failure to seek employment to mitigate damages or to show the extent of legal services rendered in conducting them. As in other situations where evidence is admissible for one purpose but not for another, an evaluation is required in terms of weighing probative value and need against likelihood of prejudice, with due regard to the probable efficacy of a limiting instruction.[1]

Evidence of present party's compromise with third persons. In an action between plaintiff (P) and defendant (D), a compromise offer or a completed compromise by D with a third person having a claim similar to P's arising from the same transaction may be relevant as showing D's belief in the weakness of the defense in the present action. Nevertheless, the same consideration of policy which prompts exclusion of a compromise offer made by D to P, namely the danger of discouraging such compromises, also applies here. Accordingly, the prevailing view is that the compromise offer or payment made by the present defendant is privileged when offered as an implied admission of liability.

Although inadmissible to show liability, the completed compromise agreement may be admissible for another purpose. A defendant in a personal injury case, for example, may call a witness who was injured in the same collision. If the witness has made a claim account against the defendant, inconsistent with the witness' present favorable testimony, this

may be proved to impeach the witness. Furthermore, if the witness has been paid or promised money in compromise of his or her claim, this may likewise be shown as evidence of bias or used more generally to impeach.[2] The need to evaluate properly the credibility of the witness is, like the policy of encouraging compromise, an important interest. If, however, the witness sought to be impeached by showing the compromise with a third person, is one of the present parties, the question is more debatable. The danger that the evidence will be used substantively as an admission is greater, and, as the party's interest is apparent, the need for additional evidence on credibility is less. This impeachment of party-witnesses, however, has occasionally been sanctioned.

Effect of acceptance of offer of compromise. If an offer of compromise is accepted and a contract is thus created, the party aggrieved may sue on the contract and obviously may prove the offer and acceptance. Moreover, if after such a contract is made and the offering party repudiates it, the other may elect to sue on the original cause of action and here again the repudiating party may not claim privilege against proof of the compromise. The shield of the privilege does not extend to the protection of those who repudiate the agreements, which the privilege is designed to encourage.

Compromise evidence in criminal cases. The policy of protecting offers of compromise in civil cases does not extend to efforts to stifle criminal prosecution by "buying off" the prosecuting witness or victim. Indeed, such efforts are classed as an implied admission and generally admissible. The public policy against compounding crimes is said to prevail. On the other hand, the legitimacy of settling criminal cases by negotiations between prosecuting attorney and accused, whereby the latter pleads guilty in return for some leniency, has been generally recognized. Effective criminal law administration would be difficult if a large proportion of the charges were not disposed of by guilty pleas. Public policy

§ 266

1. See supra § 59.

2. See supra § 39.

accordingly encourages compromise, and as in civil cases, that policy is furthered by protecting from disclosure at trial not only the offer but also statements made during negotiations.

Federal Rule 410 provides:

Except as otherwise provided in this rule, evidence of the following is not, in any civil or criminal proceeding, admissible against the defendant who made the plea or was a participant in the plea discussions:

(1) a plea of guilty which was later withdrawn;

(2) a plea of nolo contendere;

(3) any statement made in the course of any proceedings under Rule 11 of the Federal Rules of Criminal Procedure or comparable state procedure regarding either of the foregoing pleas; or

(4) any statement made in the course of plea discussions with an attorney for the prosecuting authority which do not result in a plea of guilty or which result in a plea of guilty later withdrawn.

However, such a statement is admissible (i) in any proceeding wherein another statement made in the course of the same plea or plea discussions has been introduced and the statement ought in fairness be considered contemporaneously with it, or (ii) in a criminal proceeding for perjury or false statement if the statement was made by the defendant under oath, on the record and in the presence of counsel.

The original version of the rule did not explicitly state that its protection extended only to offers and statements made in the course of negotiations between the accused and the United States Attorney or representative. As a consequence, some decisions held that efforts to make deals with a considerable variety of federal law enforcement officers were within the rule. The rule accordingly was amended as stated above to make clear that only negotiations "with an attorney for the prosecuting authority" fall within its protection.

While the rule permits use of statements made as part of plea negotiations for certain limited purposes, impeachment of the defendant's subsequent testimony is not one of those permissible purposes. If the transaction on which the prosecution is based also gives rise to a civil cause of action, a compromise or offer of compromise of the civil claim should be privileged when offered at the criminal trial, assuming that no agreement to stifle the criminal prosecution is involved.

§ 267. Admissions by Conduct: (g) Safety Measures After an Accident; Payment of Medical Expenses

Remedial Measures. After an accident causing injury, the owner of the premises or the enterprise will often take remedial measures, such as repairing a defect or changing safety rules. Are these new safety measures, which might have prevented the injury, admissible to prove negligence as an implied acknowledgment by conduct that due care required that these measures should have been taken before the injury? Particularly when the remedial measures follow the injury immediately, they may be very persuasive of the owner's belief as to the precautions required by due care before the accident. Nevertheless, courts occasionally broadly assert that the evidence is irrelevant for this purpose. While such remedial changes permit varying explanations, some of which are consistent with due care, the evidence would often meet the usual standards of relevancy if treated only as raising issues of the admissibility of circumstantial evidence and admission by conduct.[1]

The predominant reason for excluding such evidence, however, is not lack of probative significance, but rather a policy against discouraging the taking of safety measures.[2] At all events, courts do exclude evidence of remedial safety measures taken after an injury when offered as admissions of negligence or fault. These include: repairs and alterations in construction; installation of new safety

1. See supra § 185.

2. See supra § 72.1.

devices, such as lights, gates, or guards; changes in rules and regulations or the practice of the business; or the discharge of an employee charged with causing the injury. However, when the remedial measures are taken by a third person, the policy ground for exclusion is no longer present, and the tendency is to admit the evidence.

The ingenuity of counsel in suggesting other purposes has made substantial inroads upon the general rule of exclusion. Thus evidence of subsequent repairs or changes has been admitted as evidence of the defendant's ownership or control of the premises or duty to repair where these are disputed; as evidence of the possibility or feasibility of preventive measures, when properly in issue; as evidence to explain that the situation at the time of accident was different where the jury has taken a view or where the opposing party has introduced a photograph of the scene; as evidence of what was done later to show that the earlier condition as of the time of the accident was as plaintiff claims, if the defendant disputes this; as evidence that the faulty condition later remedied was the cause of the injury by showing that after the change the injurious effect disappeared; and as evidence contradicting facts testified to by the adversary's witness.

Federal Rule 407, which is in conformity with the foregoing discussion, provides as follows:

> When, after an event, measures are taken which, if taken previously, would have made the event less likely to occur, evidence of the subsequent measures is not admissible to prove negligence or culpable conduct in connection with the event. This rule does not require the exclusion of evidence of subsequent measures when offered for another purpose, such as proving ownership, control or feasibility of precautionary measures, if controverted, or impeachment.

The encouragement of remedial measures, as has already been indicated, is the principal reason for the rule excluding evidence that such measures were taken. Liberal admission of remedial measure evidence for purposes other than as an admission of negligence seriously undercuts the basic policy of the rule. Hence Rule 407 specifically requires that, when the evidence is offered for another purpose, that purpose must be controverted. Ownership, control, and feasibility of precautionary measures are mentioned as illustrations of other purposes. If the other purpose is not controverted, the evidence is inadmissible. The fact that the other purpose is controverted should not be taken as a guarantee of admissibility; the possibility of misuse of the evidence as an admission of fault still requires a balancing of probative value and need against potential prejudice under Rule 403. The availability of other means of proof is an important factor in this balancing process.[3]

Of particular concern is the provision of the rule that permits evidence of remedial measures to be admitted for impeachment, an exception which, if applied expansively, could "swallow up" the rule.[4] At the same time, there will be situations where impeachment should be permitted. One example is when the statement of the witness constitutes, not simply a general denial of negligence, but a statement that is directly contradicted by the remedial conduct.

In product liability cases, a trend away from the basic rule of exclusion of evidence of subsequent remedial measures was initiated by Ault v. International Harvester Co.[5] It has been suggested that the difference in result is warranted by the fact that negligence cases focus on the conduct of the defendant, while product liability cases focus on the nature of the product. However, the true bases of the departure are probably a rejection of the assumption that admitting the evidence discourages remedial steps when the enterprise involved is a large manufacturer and a general desire to spread the cost of injuries. A number of courts have followed *Ault,* either

3. See supra § 185.

4. Bickerstaff v. South Cent. Bell Telephone Co., 676 F.2d 163, 168 (5th Cir.1982).

5. 13 Cal.3d 113, 117 Cal.Rptr. 812, 528 P.2d 1148 (1974).

as a matter of construing Rule 407 or as common law, while others have rejected both its reasoning and its results.

The admissibility of recall letters has been approached in somewhat similar vein, as the first step in the taking of remedial steps. The courts have divided on the question, those admitting the letters often taking the view that the action should not be protected since it is not likely to be deterred because undertaken under regulatory command and not voluntarily.

Payment of medical expenses. Similar considerations of doubtful relevancy and of public policy underlie the generally accepted exclusion of evidence of payment or offers to pay medical and like expenses of an injured person. Federal Rule 409 accordingly provides:

> Evidence of furnishing or offering or promising to pay medical, hospital, or similar expenses occasioned by an injury is not admissible to prove liability for the injury.

The rule is in general conformity with the run of common law decisions.

Unlike compromise negotiations covered by Rule 408, where the discussion of issues is an essential part of the process and requires protection against disclosure, communications are unnecessary to the providing of care and hence are unprotected.

Chapter 26

SPONTANEOUS STATEMENTS

Table of Sections

§ 268. Res Gestae and the Hearsay Rule

The term *res gestae* seems to have come into common usage in discussions of admissibility of statements accompanying material acts or situations in the early 1800's. At this time the theory of hearsay was not well developed, and the various exceptions to the hearsay rule were not clearly defined. In this context, the phrase *res gestae* served as a convenient vehicle for escape from the hearsay rule in two primary situations. In the first, it was used to explain the admissibility of statements that were not hearsay at all.[1] In the second, it was used to justify the admissibility of statements which today come within the four exceptions discussed in this chapter: (1) statements of present sense impressions, (2) excited utterances, (3) statements of present bodily condition, and (4) statements of present mental states and emotions. Despite the increased sophistication of the hearsay rule and its exceptions today, however, courts still occasionally speak in terms of *res gestae* rather than a more precise hearsay doctrine.

Initially the term *res gestae* was employed to denote words which accompanied the principal litigated fact, such as the murder, collision, or trespass, which was the subject of the

§ 268

1. See infra § 269.

471

legal action. However, usage developed to the point where the phrase seemed to embody the notion that evidence of any concededly relevant act or condition might also bring in the words which accompanied it. Two main policies or motives are discernible in this recognition of *res gestae* as a password for the admission of otherwise inadmissible evidence. One is a desire to permit each witness to tell his or her story in a natural way by telling all that happened at the time of the narrated incident, including those details that give life and color to the story. Events occur as a seamless web, and the naturalness with which the details fit together gives confirmation to the witness' entire account. The other policy, emphasized by Wigmore and those following his leadership, is the recognition of spontaneity as the source of special trustworthiness. This quality of spontaneity characterizes to some degree nearly all the types of statements which have been labeled *res gestae*.

Commentators and, with ever greater frequency, courts have criticized use of the phrase *res gestae*. Its vagueness and imprecision are, of course, apparent. Moreover, traditional limitations on the doctrine, such as the requirement that it be used only in regard to the principal litigated fact and the frequent insistence of concurrence (or at least a close relationship in time) between the words and the act or situation, have restricted its usefulness as a tool for avoiding unjustified application of the hearsay rule. Historically, however, the phrase served its purpose. Its very vagueness made it easier for courts to broaden its coverage and thus permit the admissibility of certain statements in new situations. However, the law has now reached a stage where expanding admissibility will be best accomplished by other means. The ancient phrase can well be jettisoned, with due acknowledgment that it served its era in the evolution of evidence law.

§ 269. Spontaneous Statements as Nonhearsay: Circumstantial Proof of a Fact in Issue

The types of spontaneous statements discussed in this chapter are often treated by courts as hearsay, and thus to be admissible they must come within an exception to the general rule excluding hearsay. In many cases, however, this maneuver is unnecessary because the statements are not hearsay in the first place. As suggested in an earlier section,[1] hearsay is most appropriately defined as assertive statements or conduct offered to prove what is asserted. But many so-called spontaneous statements are in fact not assertive statements or, if assertive, are not offered to prove the truth of the assertions made. For example, it is clear that the statements, "I plan to spend the rest of my life here in New York" and "I have lost my affection for my husband" are hearsay, when offered to prove the plan to remain in New York or the loss of affection. On the other hand, statements such as "I have been happier in New York than in any other place," when offered to show the speaker's intent to remain in New York, and "My husband is a detestable wretch," offered to show lack of affection for the husband, will or will not be classed as hearsay, depending upon the position taken with respect to the long debated question whether "implied assertions" are to be classed as hearsay. That issue is discussed elsewhere.[2]

If the statement which is offered in evidence is not classed as hearsay, then no further consideration of the matters developed in this chapter is required. If, however, it is classed as hearsay, then these matters may become pertinent to the question of admissibility. Nevertheless, the issue is often almost entirely academic, for statements offered to prove the declarant's state of mind, if relevant, are admissible either as an exception to the hearsay rule[3] or as nonhearsay.

---

§ 269

1. See supra § 246.

2. See supra § 250.

3. See infra § 274.

§ 270. "Self–Serving" Aspects of Spontaneous Statements

The notion that parties' out-of-court statements could not be evidence in their favor because of the "self-serving" nature of the statements seems to have originated with the now universally discarded rule forbidding parties to testify.[1] When this rule of disqualification for interest was abrogated by statute, any sweeping rule of inadmissibility regarding "self-serving" statements should have been regarded as abolished by implication. This, however, was often not the case.

The hearsay rule excludes all hearsay statements unless they fall within some exception to the rule. Thus, no specific rule is necessary to exclude self-serving out-of-court statements if not within a hearsay exception. If a statement with a self-serving aspect falls within an exception to the hearsay rule, the judgment underlying the exception that the assurances of trustworthiness outweigh the dangers inherent in hearsay should be taken as controlling, and the declaration should be admitted despite its self-serving aspects.

Historically, most courts agreed that this was the proper approach when the self-serving statement fell within one of the well-established exceptions, such as the exclusion of business records, excited utterances, and spontaneous statements of present bodily sensations or symptoms. However, with regard to the somewhat more recently developed exceptions, such as statements of present state of mind or emotion, there was less agreement. Some courts applied a purported general rule of exclusion of self-serving statements in this area. Others rejected any blanket rule of exclusion, although the self-serving aspects of the declaration were taken into account in applying a requirement that the statements must have been made under circumstances of apparent sincerity.

The Federal Rules covering hearsay exceptions for spontaneous statements, discussed in the remaining sections of this chapter, make no special provision for self-serving statements. What is clear, however, is that since spontaneity is the principal, and often the only, guarantee of trustworthiness for the exceptions in this chapter, its absence should result in exclusion of the statement. Circumstances indicating a lack of spontaneity, which may be related to the self-serving character of the statement, are accordingly extremely important to the determination of admissibility.

While some issues can be determined by reference to spontaneity, a very difficult issue remains: may courts properly exclude statements because of judicial doubts about the sincerity of the declarant as evidenced by the self-serving nature of the statement? There is no theoretical impediment to judicial consideration of credibility in determining an issue of preliminary-fact-finding of the type involved in admitting or excluding hearsay. The chief problem with this approach under hearsay rules modeled on the Federal Rules is one of legislative intent. The rules give no authorization to such considerations, and indeed the omission of a requirement found in the original Uniform Rule that the statement must not be made in "bad faith" strongly indicates a contrary legislative intent. Moreover, in some other exceptions, the self-serving character of a statement, appearing in the form of motive to falsify, is specified as a ground for exclusion.[2]

A somewhat more comfortable place for the general exercise of such judicial judgment is under the balancing of probativity and prejudice authorized by Rule 403, although this home is hardly secure since neither the rule itself nor its history gives explicit authorization. Nevertheless, in exercising discretion to exclude evidence where the danger of prejudice, confusing the issues, misleading the jury, or wasting time outweighs its probative value, circumstantial or direct evidence revealing a self-serving motive should logically have a

---

§ 270

1. The rule forbidding parties to testify is discussed in supra § 65.

2. E.g., accident reports, infra § 288, and police reports, infra § 296.

place.[3] Rarely, however, should statements of substantial importance to the case be excluded even under this rule based upon judicial doubts about the declarant's motivation. Under the structure of the Federal Rules, judgments about credibility should generally be left to the jury rather than preempted by a judicial determination of inadmissibility. This is particularly true when the credibility issue can be readily appreciated by the jury, as is generally the case when the reason to question credibility rests upon the declarant's self-serving motivation.

§ 271. Unexcited Statements of Present Sense Impressions

Although Wigmore's creative work did much to clarify the murky concept of *res gestae,* his analysis of spontaneous declarations may have led to one unfortunate restricting development of this exception. Professor Thayer, reviewing the *res gestae* cases in 1881, concluded that this was an exception based on the contemporaneousness of statements. He read the law as creating an exception for statements "made by those present when a thing took place, made about it and importing what is present at the very time."[1] Wigmore, however, saw as the basis for the spontaneous exclamation exception, not the contemporaneousness of the exclamation, but rather the nervous excitement produced by the exposure of the declarant to an exciting event. As a result, the American law of spontaneous statements shifted in its emphasis from what Thayer had observed to an exception based on the requirement of an exciting event and the resulting stifling of the declarant's reflective faculties. This, as Professor Morgan noted, was unfortunate. Given the danger of unreliability caused by the very emotional impact required for excited utterances, it makes little sense to admit them while excluding other out-of-court statements that may have equal assurances of reliability and lack the inherent defects of excited utterances.[2]

Under Morgan's leadership, arguments were made for restoring Thayer's view of the law by recognizing another exception to the hearsay rule for statements concerning nonexciting events that the declarant was observing while making the declaration. Although these statements lack whatever assurance of reliability is produced by the effect of an exciting event, other factors offer safeguards. First, since the report concerns observations being made at the time of the statement, it is safe from any error caused by a defect of the declarant's memory. Second, a requirement that the statement be made contemporaneously with the observation means that there will be little or no time for calculated misstatement. Third, the statement will usually have been made to a third person (the witness who subsequently testifies to it), who was also present at the time and scene of the observation. Thus, the witness in most cases will have observed the situation and thus can provide a check on the accuracy of the declarant's statement and furnish corroboration. Moreover, since the declarant will often be available for cross-examination, his or her credibility will be subject to substantial verification before the trier of fact.

The courts generally did not rush to the support of the proposed exception for unexcited statements of present sense impressions. A considerable number continued to admit contemporaneous statements under *res gestae* language without emphasis on the presence or absence of an exciting event. In a large proportion of these decisions, an arguably exciting event was present. However, cases recognizing the exception for unexcited statements of present sense impressions began to emerge. The case most commonly cited to illustrate judicial recognition of the exception is Houston Oxygen Co. v. Davis.[3] Although an apparently exciting event transpired, the opinion disclaimed reliance upon it and instead expressly based its decision upon the exception for unexcited declarations of present sense impressions.

---

3. See generally supra § 185.

§ 271

1. Thayer, Bedingfield's Case—Declarations as a Part of the Res Gesta, 15 Am.L.Rev. 1, 83 (1881).

2. Morgan, A Suggested Classification of Utterances Admissible as Res Gestae, 31 Yale L.J. 229, 236 (1922).

3. 139 Tex. 1, 161 S.W.2d 474 (Com.App.1942).

A more compelling case on its facts, decided in the same year, is Tampa Electric Co. v. Getrost.[4] There a statement by the deceased to a fellow lineman that he had just given the order to deactivate the electric line on which repairs were to be made was admitted in a wrongful death action, the declarant having been electrocuted by his subsequent contact with the still live line.

Judicial acceptance gradually gained momentum. The relative infrequence of such cases results from the fact that unexciting events do not often give rise to statements that later become relevant in litigation.

The principal impetus for recognition of the hearsay exception for unexcited statements of present sense impressions came through the rulemaking process. The Model Code of Evidence and the original Uniform Rules included such an exception. Federal Rule 803(1) provides a hearsay exception, without regard to the availability of the declarant, for "a statement describing or explaining an event or condition made while the declarant was perceiving the event or condition, or immediately thereafter."

In addition to the absence of any requirement of an exciting event, the hearsay exception for statements of present sense impressions differs from the exception for excited utterances in two other significant respects. First, while excited utterances "relating to"[5] the startling event or condition are admissible, present sense impressions are limited to "describing or explaining" the event or condition perceived. This more restrictive limitation is consistent with the theory underlying the present sense impression exception. Although fabrication and forgetfulness are precluded by the absence of time lapse between perception and utterance, the absence of a startling event makes the assumption of spontaneity difficult to maintain unless the statements immediately pertain to that perception. Second, while the time within which an excited utterance may be made is measured by the duration of the stress caused by the exciting event,[6] the present sense impression statement may be made only while the declarant was actually "perceiving" the event or "immediately thereafter." This shortened period is also consistent with the theory of the present sense impression exception. While principle might seem to call for a limitation to exact contemporaneity, some allowance must be made for the time needed for translating observation into speech. Thus, the appropriate inquiry is whether sufficient time elapsed to have permitted reflective thought.

The suggestion has been made that corroboration by an "equally percipient" witness should be a further requirement for admitting statements of present sense impression into evidence. The proposal represents a significant departure from the general pattern of exceptions to the hearsay rule. The only instance in which a requirement of corroboration is found is where a statement against penal interest by a third person—a third-party confession—is offered by way of exculpation of an accused person. There, the common law had a firmly established position against admission. In order to increase the acceptability of a reversal of this position, the Advisory Committee incorporated into Federal Rule 804(b)(3) a requirement that the hearsay statement must be corroborated.[7] The present sense impression exception presents no such need. Its underlying rationale offers sufficient assurances of reliability without the additional requirement of corroboration, and neither the Federal Rule nor the decisions have required it.

It is true that the limitation of the exception in terms of time and subject matter usually insures that the witness who reports the making of the statement will have perceived the event or at least observed circumstances strongly suggesting it. This aspect has been mentioned by the writers as an added assurance of accuracy, but a justification for admission is not the same as a requirement for admission. The matter is bet-

---

4.   151 Fla. 558, 10 So.2d 83 (1942).

5.   See infra § 272.

6.   See infra § 272.

7.   See infra § 318.

ter left for consideration by the judge or jury as an aspect of weight and sufficiency of the evidence, rather than becoming a needlessly complicating requirement for admissibility.

§ 272.   Excited Utterances

While historically often lumped together with the amalgam of concepts under the term *res gestae*,[1] an exception to the hearsay rule for statements made under the influence of a startling event is now universally recognized. Formulations of the exception differ, but all agree on two basic requirements. First, there must be an occurrence or event sufficiently startling to render inoperative the normal reflective thought processes of the observer. Second, the statement of the declarant must have been a spontaneous reaction to the occurrence or event and not the result of reflective thought. Although additional requirements will be discussed subsequently, these two elements constitute the essence of the exception.

Federal Rule 803(2) creates an exception, without regard to the availability of the declarant, for statements "relating to a startling event or condition made while the declarant was under the stress of excitement caused by the event or condition."

The rationale for the exception lies in the special reliability that is furnished when excitement suspends the declarant's powers of reflection and fabrication. This factor also serves to justify dispensing with any requirement that the declarant be unavailable because it suggests that testimony on the stand, given at a time when the powers of reflection and fabrication are operative, is no more (and perhaps less) reliable than the out-of-court statement.

The entire basis for the exception is, of course, subject to question. While psychologists would probably concede that excitement minimizes the possibility of reflective self-interest influencing the declarant's statements, they have questioned whether this might be

outweighed by the distorting effect of shock and excitement upon the declarant's observation and judgement. Despite these questions concerning its justification, however, the exception is well established.

The sufficiency of the event or occurrence itself to qualify under this exception is seldom questioned. Physical violence, though often present, is not required. An automobile accident, pain or an injury, an attack by a dog, a fight, or even seeing a photograph in a newspaper all may qualify. The courts look primarily to the effect upon the declarant, and, if satisfied that the event was such as to cause adequate excitement, the inquiry is ended.

A somewhat more serious issue is raised by the occasional requirement of establishing the exciting event by some proof other than the statement itself. Under generally prevailing practice, the statement itself is taken as sufficient proof of the exciting event, and therefore the statement is admissible despite absence of other proof that an exciting event occurred.[2] Some courts, however, have taken the position that an excited utterance is admissible only if other proof is presented which supports a finding of fact that the exciting event did occur. The issue has not yet been definitively resolved under the Federal Rules. Fortunately, only a very few cases need actually confront this knotty theoretical problem if the courts view the independent evidence concept broadly, as they should where the circumstances and content of the statement indicate trustworthiness.

The question most frequently raised when a purported excited utterance is offered involves the second requirement. In all cases, the ultimate question is whether the statement was the result of reflective thought or whether it was rather a spontaneous reaction to the exciting event. Initially, it is necessary that the declarant be affected by the exciting event. The declarant need not actually be involved in the event; an excited utterance by a bystander is admissible. However, if the identity of the bystander-declarant is undis-

---

§ 272

1. See supra § 268.

2. See also supra § 53.

closed, the courts have been reluctant to admit such statements, principally because of uncertainty that a foundation requirement has been satisfied, such as the impact of the event on the declarant.

Probably the most important of the many factors entering into this determination is the temporal element. If the statement occurs while the exciting event is still in progress, courts have little difficulty finding that the excitement prompted the statement. But as the time between the event and the statement increases, courts become more reluctant to find the statement an excited utterance. However, passage of time viewed in isolation is not an entirely accurate indicator of admissibility. For example, while courts have held statements made twelve or more hours after a physical beating to be the product of the excitement caused by the beating, other courts have held statements made within minutes of the event not admissible.

A useful rule of thumb is that where the time interval between the event and the statement is long enough to permit reflective thought, the statement will be excluded in the absence of some proof that the declarant did not in fact engage in a reflective thought process. Testimony that the declarant still appeared "nervous" or "distraught" and that there was a reasonable basis for continuing emotional upset will often suffice. The nature of the exciting event and the declarant's concern with it are relevant, of course. Thus, a statement made by the victim's wife one hour after a traffic accident was held admissible where the husband was still in the emergency room and the wife was obviously still concerned about his condition.

Other factors may indicate the opposite conclusion. Evidence that the statement was self-serving or made in response to an inquiry, while not justification for automatic exclusion, is an indication that the statement was the result of reflective thought. Where the time interval permitted such thought, those factors might swing the balance in favor of exclusion. Proof that the declarant performed tasks requiring relatively careful thought between the event and the statement provides strong evidence that the effect of the exciting event had subsided. Because of the wide variety of factual situations, appellate courts have recognized substantial discretion in trial courts to determine whether a declarant was still under the influence of an exciting event at the time of an offered statement.

Whether the excited utterance should be required to concern the exciting event and the strictness of the necessary relationship between the exciting event and the content of the statement has been the subject of historical disagreement. One of the major positions in this debate was set out by District of Columbia Circuit in Murphy Auto Parts Co. v. Ball.[3] There the court concluded that a requirement that the statement "explain or illuminate" the event was, if "mechanically and narrowly construed," a "spurious element," but that failure to describe the exciting event was a factor to consider in evaluating the spontaneity of the statement. On the facts of the case, the court sustained admission of a driver's statement following an accident that he had to call on a customer and was in a hurry to get home, which statement helped to established agency.

Federal Rule 803(2) takes a somewhat different position but reaches a similar result to that in *Murphy Auto Parts*. The rule *requires* a connection between the event and the content of the statement, but it defines that connection reasonably broadly as "relating to" the event. This terminology is intended to extend beyond merely a description or an explanation of the event. The courts have been quite liberal in applying this requirement.

The formulation used by Rule 803(2) has the advantage of simplicity while at the same time preserving the trustworthiness gained by requiring a relationship between the exciting event or condition and the resulting statement. It also permits clarification of the difference in theory between excited utterances

---

3. 249 F.2d 508 (D.C.Cir.1957), cert. denied 355 U.S. 932.

and statements of present sense impressions, discussed in the preceding section.

Another major issue frequently encountered with excited utterances is whether the declarant meet the tests of competency for a witness. In a modified manner the requirement that a witness have had an opportunity to observe that to which he or she testifies is applied.[4] Direct proof is not necessary; if the circumstances appear consistent with opportunity by the declarant, the requirement is met. If there is doubt, the question is for the jury.[5] Especially in cases where the declaration is of low probative value, however, the statement is usually held inadmissible if there is no reasonable suggestion that the declarant had an opportunity to observe.

On the theory that there is a countervailing assurance of reliability in the excitement of the event, the other aspects of competency are not applied. Thus, an excited utterance is admissible despite the fact that the declarant was a child and would have been incompetent as a witness for that reason, or the declarant was incompetent by virtue of mental illness, or the declarant was a spouse of the defendant in the criminal case in which the statement was offered.

Some courts have argued that an excited utterance must not be an opinion. Such a blanket limitation is unjustified, in view of the nature and present standing of the opinion rule.[6] Where the declarant is an in-court witness, it is probably appropriate to require testimony in concrete terms rather than conclusory generalizations. But in everyday life, people often talk in conclusory terms, and when these statements are later offered in court, there is no opportunity to require the declarant to testify in more specific language. Here, as elsewhere, the opinion rule should be applied sparingly, if at all, to out-of-court speech. Nevertheless, courts have sometimes excluded excited utterances on the grounds that they violate the opinion rule, especially in situations in which the declarants' statements place blame on themselves or others.

Despite possible danger that these opinions may be given exaggerated weight by a jury, the need for knowledge of the facts usually outweighs this danger, and the better view admits excited statements of opinion.

§ 272.1 Excited Utterances and Other Hearsay Exceptions in Sexual Abuse Cases

Rape cases and other sexual offenses, particularly those involving minors, raise a number of difficult hearsay issues. Several different exceptions may be involved, including statements for the purpose of medical diagnosis and the catchall exception, which are treated elsewhere.[1] The application of the excited utterance exception and several new specific exceptions developed to deal with issues involved with the prosecution of offenses against children are treated below.

Before moving into modern developments, one historical artifact should be noted. In rape cases, out-of-court statements that the victim made a complaint were historically admissible to corroborate the assault. The only time requirement is that the complaint must have been made without a delay that is either unexplained or inconsistent with the occurrence of the offense, which is generally less demanding in terms of the temporal element than would be the case under typical excited utterance analysis. In its origin, the theory of admissibility was to rebut any inference that, because the victim did not immediately complain, no crime had in fact occurred. Accordingly, if the victim did not testify, evidence of the complaint was not admissible, and only the fact that a complaint was made could be admitted.

Moving to modern practice, particularly where children are the victims of sexual offenses, many courts have liberally interpreted the allowable period of time between the exciting event and the child's description of it. The theory of these courts is that the general

---

4. See supra § 10.
5. See supra §§ 53, 58.
6. See supra § 18.

§ 272.1

1. See infra §§ 277–278 & 324.

psychological characteristics of children typically extend the period that is free of the dangers of conscious fabrication. In addition, a growing number of states have enacted specific hearsay exceptions to cover the situations where children are involved as witnesses or victims. One of the advantages of this latter approach is that it reduces the pressure to distort the traditional time limitations of the excited utterance exception to deal with this difficult set of cases.

The new exception is illustrated by the Washington statute, which has become a model for many other states. It admits a child's extrajudicial statement if (1) the court finds after a hearing that the time, content, and circumstances of the statement provide sufficient indicia of reliability, and (2) the child either testifies at the proceeding or is unavailable as a witness and, if unavailable, corroborative evidence is produced to support trustworthiness.

States have also undertaken a major effort to ameliorate the trauma associated with the judicial process by changing the mechanics of the trial in child abuse and related cases. Part of this process has involved the development of new methods of receiving testimony, some of which include the development of new hearsay exceptions. Drawing on a broad base of statutory and other material, the drafters of the Uniform Rules added Rule 807 to help address this set of problems. The rule exempts from the ban of the hearsay rule the audio-visually recorded statement of a child victim or witness describing an act of sexual abuse or physical violence if the court finds that (1) the minor will suffer severe emotional or psychological stress if required to testify in open court; (2) the time, content, and circumstances of the statement provide sufficient circumstantial guarantees of trustworthiness; and (3) other enumerated requirements are followed regarding the conduct of the recording process. Presence of judge, accused, or counsel is not required or apparently contemplated; any person may conduct the interview. However, before the admission of a statement under the rule, the court, on defendant's request, shall provide for further questioning of the minor in a manner as the court may direct. Finally, the rule provides that admission of a statement under these provisions does not preclude the court from permitting any party to call the child as a witness if the interests of justice require it.

Another provision of Uniform Rule 807 permits the taking of testimony by either deposition recorded by audio-visual means or by contemporaneous examination communicated to the courtroom by closed-circuit television if the court concludes the child will suffer severe emotional or psychological harm if required to testify in open court. In this proceeding, the court may order the testimony to be taken outside the presence of any party, including the defendant, if it finds such presence would contribute to the likelihood of harm to the child, and the court shall in that situation place the excluded party so that he or she may see and hear the testimony of the child and may consult with counsel but not be seen by the child.

These provisions, and others like them, raise difficult constitutional issues involving the Confrontation Clause. Two of those issues have been treated extensively by the courts. First, the provisions similar to those of the Uniform Rules that permit the creation and introduction of a recording of the child's statement as part of the state's case, which is made without the opportunity for contemporaneous cross-examination by defense counsel, have been held by several state supreme courts to violate the Confrontation Clause. Second, a procedure which shields the child witness from facing the defendant while testifying is constitutionally valid only if resting upon an individualized finding that the child will suffer trauma otherwise. Clearly, it will take some time for the courts and the legislatures to accommodate the special needs for preservation and presentation of the testimony of child victims or witnesses and the constitutional commands of Due Process and the Confrontation Clause.

§ 273. Statements of Physical or Mental Condition: (a) Statements of Bodily Feelings, Symptoms, and Condition

Statements of the declarant's present bodily condition and symptoms, including pain and other feelings, offered to prove the truth of the statements have been generally recognized as an exception to the hearsay rule. Special reliability is provided by the spontaneous quality of the declarations, assured by the requirement that the declaration purport to describe a condition presently existing at the time of the statement. This assurance of reliability is almost certainly not always effective, however, since some of these statements describing present symptoms are probably not spontaneous but rather calculated misstatements. Nevertheless, a sufficiently large percentage are undoubtedly spontaneous to justify the exception.

Being spontaneous, the hearsay statements are considered of greater probative value than the present testimony of the declarant. Moreover, the alternative of insisting upon the in-court testimony of the declarant, when he or she is available, promises little improvement since cross-examination and other methods of exposing deliberate misrepresentation are relatively ineffective. Together, these factors of trustworthiness and necessity not only provide a basis for admitting statements of this type but also justify dispensing with any requirement of unavailability of the declarant.

Despite occasional indications to the contrary, declarations of present bodily condition generally do not have to be made to a physician in order to qualify for the present exception. Any person hearing the statement may testify to it. The exception is, however, limited to descriptions of present condition and therefore excludes description of past pain or symptoms, as well as accounts of the events furnishing the cause of the condition.

Federal Rule 803(3) defines a hearsay exception, without regard to the unavailability of the declarant, for "a statement of the declarant's then existing * * * physical condition (such as * * * pain and bodily health) * * *." Not only does the rule mandate that the statement must be spontaneous by its requirement that the statement describe a "then existing" physical condition, but also it

is clear from the Advisory Committee's Note to the Federal Rule that the rule is a specialized application of the broader rule recognizing a hearsay exception for statements describing a present sense impression, the cornerstone of which is spontaneity. If circumstances demonstrate a lack of spontaneity, exclusion should follow.

§ 274. Statements of Physical or Mental Condition: (b) Statements of Present Mental or Emotional State to Show a State of Mind or Emotion in Issue

The substantive law often makes legal rights and liabilities hinge upon the existence of a particular state of mind or feeling. Thus, such matters as the intent to steal or kill, or the intent to have a certain paper take effect as a deed or will, or the maintenance or transfer of the affections of a spouse may come into issue in litigation. When this is so, the mental or emotional state of the person becomes an ultimate object of search. It is not introduced as evidence from which the person's earlier or later conduct may be inferred but as an operative fact upon which a cause of action or defense depends. While a state of mind may be proved by the person's actions, the statements of the person are often a primary source of evidence.

In many instances, statements used for this purpose are not assertive of the declarant's present state of mind and are therefore not hearsay.[1] Courts, however, have tended to lump together statements asserting the declarant's state of mind, hence arguably hearsay, with those tending to prove the state of mind circumstantially, arguably nonhearsay, applying a general exception to the hearsay rule and ignoring the possibility that many of these statements could be treated simply as nonhearsay.

The special assurance of reliability for statements of present state of mind rests, as in the case of statements of bodily condition, upon their spontaneity and resulting probable

§ 274

1. See supra § 246.

sincerity.[2] This has been assured principally by the requirement that the statements must relate to a condition of mind or emotion existing at the time of the statement. In addition, some formulations of the exception require that the statement must have been made under circumstances indicating apparent sincerity, although Federal Rule 803(3) imposes no such explicit condition.[3]

Such statements are also admitted because of a form of the same necessity argument that underlies most hearsay exceptions. Often there is no better way to prove a relevant mental or physical condition than through the statements of the individual whose condition is at issue, and the alternative of using the declarant's testimony, even with cross-examination, is likely to be no better, and perhaps an inferior, manner of proof. As was said in a famous case, if the declarant were called to testify, "his own memory of his state of mind at a former time is no more likely to be clear and true than a bystander's recollection of what he then said."[4] As a result, unavailability of declarant is not required.

Common examples of statements used to prove mental state at the time of the statement include: statements of intent to make a certain place the declarant's home offered to establish domicile, statements expressive of mental suffering to prove that element of damages, statements by customers regarding anger to prove loss of good will, statements of patients regarding lack of knowledge of risk of taking medication in malpractice suit, statements of willingness to allow one to use the declarant's automobile offered to prove that the car was used with the owner's consent, statements accompanying a transfer of property showing intent, or lack of intent, to defraud creditors, statements of ill will to show malice or the required state of mind in criminal cases, and statements showing fear.

Although the statement must describe a state of mind or feeling existing at the time of the statement, the evidentiary effect of the statement is broadened by the notion of the continuity in time of states of mind. For example, if a declarant asserts on Tuesday a then-existing intention to go on a business trip the next day, this will be evidence not only of the intention at the time of the statement, but also of the same purpose the next day when the declarant is on the road. Continuity may also look backwards. Thus, when there is evidence that a will has been mutilated by the maker, the declarant's subsequent statements of a purpose inconsistent with the will are received to show his or her intent to revoke it at the time it was mutilated. Similarly, whether payment of money or a conveyance was intended by the donor as a gift may be shown by statements made before, at the time of, or after the act of transfer. Since, however, the duration of states of mind or emotion varies with the particular attitudes or feelings at issue and with the cause, it is reasonable to require that the statement mirror a state of mind, which in light of all the circumstances, including proximity in time, is reasonably likely to have been the same condition existing at the material time. The decision on whether a state of mind continues is a decision left to the determination of the trial judge.[5]

Declarations such as those involved here frequently include assertions other than state of mind. For example, the victim may assert that the defendant's acts caused the state of mind. The truth of those assertions may coincide with other issues in the case, as where the defendant is charged with acts similar to those described. When this is so, the normal practice is to admit the statement and direct the jury to consider it only as proof of the state of mind and to disregard it as evidence of the other issues.[6] Compliance with these instructions is probably beyond the jury's ability and almost certainly beyond their will-

---

2. See supra § 273.

3. See generally supra § 270.

4. Mutual Life Ins. Co. v. Hillmon, 145 U.S. 285, 295 (1892).

5. See generally supra § 53.

6. The legitimacy of inferring from state of mind the happening of the act claimed to have caused the state of mind is discussed in infra § 276.

ingness. Where there is adequate evidence on the other issues, this probably does little harm. But in a case where the mental state is provable by other available evidence and the danger of harm from improper use by the jury of the offered declarations is substantial, the judge's discretion to exclude the statements has been recognized.

Federal Rule 803(3) provides a hearsay exception, without regard to unavailability of declarant, for a "statement of the declarant's then existing state of mind, emotion, sensation * * * (such as intent, plan, motive, design, mental feeling * * *)." The rule is generally consistent with the hearsay exception as developed by the courts at common law.

Insanity. A main source of proof of mental competency or incompetency is the conduct of the person in question, showing normal and abnormal response to the circumstances of his or her environment. By this test, every act of the subject's life, within reasonable limits of time, would be relevant to the inquiry. Whether the conduct is verbal or nonverbal is immaterial, and the same is true as to whether it is assertive or nonassertive in form. It is offered as a response to environment, not to prove anything that may be asserted, and is accordingly not hearsay.[7] Thus it makes no difference whether declarant says "I am King Henry the Eighth" or "I believe that I am King Henry the Eighth." Both are offered as evidence of irrationality, and niceties of form should not determine admissibility. If, nevertheless, it is argued that abnormal conduct can be simulated, thereby becoming assertive and therefore hearsay, a short answer is that in that event the evidence would be admissible under the hearsay exception that is the subject of this section. Such inquiries are largely superfluous, and little effort should be spent by courts determining whether the statement should be treated as nonhearsay or as a hearsay evidence showing an abnormal state of mind.

7. See supra §§ 246, 250.

§ 275. Statements of Physical or Mental Condition: (c) Statements of Intention Offered to Show Subsequent Acts of Declarant

As the previous sections made clear, statements of mental state are generally admissible to prove the declarant's state of mind when that state of mind is at issue. But the probative value of a state of mind obviously may go beyond the state of mind itself. Where a state of mind would tend to prove subsequent conduct, can the two inferential processes be linked together, with the declarations of state of mind being admitted as proof of the conduct? For example, can the declarant's statements indicating an intent to kill another be admitted to prove not only intent but also that the declarant did in fact subsequently commit the murder? The answer involves both concerns of hearsay and relevancy.

These issues are somewhat more difficult than the matter of admissibility of statements to show only the state of mind. The special reliability of the statements is less in the present situation since it is significantly less likely that a declared intention will be carried out than it is that a declared state of mind is actually held. A statement of intention to kill another is much stronger proof of malice toward the victim at the time of the statement (or subsequently) than it is proof that the declarant committed the murder. Nevertheless, a person who expresses an intent to kill is undeniably more likely to have done so than a person not shown to have had that intent. The accepted standard of relevancy, i.e., more probable than without the evidence,[1] is easily met.

Despite the failure until fairly recently to recognize the potential value of statements of state of mind to prove subsequent conduct, it is now clear that out-of-court statements that tend to prove a plan, design, or intention of the declarant are admissible, subject to the usual limitations as to remoteness in time

§ 275

1. See supra § 185.

and perhaps apparent sincerity [2] common to all statements of mental state, to prove that the plan, design, or intention of the declarant was carried out by the declarant.

The leading case is Mutual Life Insurance Co. v. Hillmon,[3] which concerned a suit on life insurance policies by the wife of the insured, Hillmon. The principal issue was whether Hillmon had in fact died; a body had been found at Crooked Creek, Kansas, and the parties disputed whether the body was that of Hillmon. Plaintiff's theory was that Hillmon left Wichita, Kansas, about March 5, 1879, with a man named Brown and that on the night of March 18, 1879, while Hillmon and Brown were camped at Crooked Creek, Hillmon was killed by the accidental discharge of a gun. The defendants, on the other hand, maintained that another individual named Walters had accompanied Hillmon and that the body found at Crooked Creek was Walters'.

Defendants offered testimony that Walters had, on or about March 5, 1879, written to his sister that "I expect to leave Wichita on or about March 5, with a certain Mr. Hillmon." [4] An objection to this and similar evidence was sustained. The United States Supreme Court reversed on the ground that the evidence of the letters should have been admitted:

> The letters * * * were competent not as narratives of facts communicated to the writer by others, nor yet as proof that he actually went away from Wichita, but as evidence that, shortly before the time when other evidence tended to show that he went away, he had the intention of going, and of going with Hillmon, which made it more probable both that he did go and that he went with Hillmon than if there had been no proof of such intention.[5]

While Federal Rule 803(3) does not explicitly address the question of admitting intent for the purpose of proving the doing of the intended act, there can be no doubt that the *Hillmon* rule continues. In fact, the Federal Advisory Committee's Note states, "The rule of Mutual Life Ins. Co. v. Hillmon, 145 U.S.

285 (1892), allowing evidence of intention as tending to prove the doing of the act intended, is, of course, left undisturbed." A number of subsidiary problems remain to be considered, however, under the rule and the common law decisions.

The suggestion has been made that unavailability of the declarant should be a requirement. In fact, in virtually all the cases admitting the statements of intent as proof of the doing of the intended act, the declarant has been unavailable, and it may well be that the resulting need for the evidence influenced the courts in the direction of admissibility. However, neither the decisions nor the Federal Rule require unavailability.

In somewhat similar vein, in virtually all the cases admitting the evidence the intent stated was quite concrete, e.g., to do a specific act at a specific time. Again, this quality of specificity is not generally stated as a requirement, but undeniably probative value is enhanced by its presence. Its absence not only detracts from probative value but, in its vague generality, may tend to stray into areas of character evidence that is inadmissible against a criminal defendant.

The danger of unreliability is greatly increased when the action sought to be proved is not one that the declarant could have performed alone, but rather is one that required the cooperation of another person. If completion of a plan or design requires not only the continued inclination and ability of the declarant to complete it, but also the inclination and ability of someone else, arguably the likelihood that the design or plan was completed is substantially less. In *Hillmon* itself, Walters' successful completion of his plan to leave Wichita depended upon the continued willingness of Hillmon to have Walters as a companion and upon Hillmon's willingness and ability to leave at the time planned. However, it was common ground to all parties that Hillmon did in fact go to Crooked Creek, and the

---

2. See supra § 274.

3. 145 U.S. 285 (1892).

4. Id. at 288.

5. Id. at 295–296.

Supreme Court had no occasion to consider this aspect of the case.

The issue is made more difficult when the cooperative actions between the declarant and another are themselves at issue. For example, in the homicide prosecution of Frank, a witness testifies that on the morning of the killing the victim said, "I am going out with Frank tonight." While this tends to prove the victim's acts, it also tends to prove that the defendant "went out" with the victim, a fact very much in issue. Despite some objection, courts have admitted these statements. The result is that the statement is used as proof of the other person's intent and as proof that this intent was achieved. The additional dangers present here have, however, prompted some courts to impose additional limitations, restrictions, or requirements. These include: instructing the jury to consider the evidence only to prove the conduct of the declarant, requiring independent evidence to establish the defendant's conduct, permitting the declaration to be used only to explain the declarant's intent, and limiting use of such statements only to cases where the declarant is dead or unavailable and to situations where both the statement of intent is shown to be serious and the event realistically likely to be achieved.

Acceptance of the use of statements of state of mind to prove subsequent conduct and recognition of occasions for its application by the courts have differed among types of situations. In will cases, for example, it is now generally established that when the acts of the decedent are at issue, previous declarations of intention are received as evidence of his or her later conduct. Such statements are admissible on issues of forgery, alteration, contents of a will, and whether acts of revocation were done by the testator. Despite early decisions to the contrary, or decisions greatly restricting their use, statements of intent to commit suicide have been admitted when offered by the accused in homicide cases to prove that the victim took his or her own life and similarly in insurance cases to show suicide. Historically, there has been some greater resistance, however, to admitting threats of a third person to commit the act with which the accused is charged as evidence that the act was committed by the third person and therefore not by the accused. Although some opinions suggest an absolute exclusionary rule, others recognize a discretionary power in the trial judge to admit threats upon finding sufficient accompanying evidence of motive, overt acts, opportunity, or other circumstances giving substantial significance to them. Greater liberality should follow under the Federal Rules since Rule 803(3) provides no basis to restrict admission of threats by others, and the Federal Rules' flexible approach to relevancy should provide fewer reasons to treat this as a special class of evidence.

Homicide and assault cases present other special problems. If the accused asserts self-defense and knows of threats of the victim against the accused, these threats are admissible to prove the accused's apprehension of danger and its reasonableness. When used for this purpose, of course, the statements of the victim are not hearsay. But uncommunicated threats pose a more serious problem. They are only admissible to show the victim's intention to attack the accused and further that the victim carried out this intention, thus committing the first act of aggression in the fatal altercation. Fear that juries will abuse the evidence has led some courts to admit proof of uncommunicated threats only under qualification. No qualification appears in the Federal Rule 803(3), and under its influence changes in the qualifications imposed can be anticipated. However, even under the Federal Rule, courts can certainly impose reasonable restrictions on admissibility of such statements to reduce dangers of confusion and misleading under relevancy concerns, which provide the principal focus for determining admissibility of these statements rather than the hearsay doctrine.

The matter of the admissibility of declarations of state of mind to prove subsequent conduct is a far different question from that of the sufficiency of these statements, standing alone, to support a finding that the conduct occurred. In the typical case, it is reasonable to hold that the declarations are themselves insufficient to support the finding and therefore that statements of intention must be admitted in corroboration of other evidence to show the acts.

§ 276. Statements of Physical or Mental Condition: (d) Statements of State of Mind to Show Memory or Belief as Proof of Previous Happenings

As was seen in the preceding section, under the *Hillmon* doctrine, statements of intent to perform an act are admissible as proof that the act was in fact done. By contrast, a statement by the declarant that he or she had in fact done that act would be excluded by the hearsay rule. Thus Walters' statement that he intended to go to Crooked Creek is admissible, but a later statement by him that he had been to Crooked Creek would be excluded. As a matter of common experience, this result seems wrong. It would appear that the first statement, which is admissible, is inferior as evidence to the second, which would be excluded. This is because while both statements involve the truthfulness of the declarant, the second statement involves the further risk that supervening events may prevent the stated intent from being accomplished. Minds are changed, tickets are lost; popular sayings, literature, and experience are filled with plans that went awry. Accordingly, the argument goes, if the inferior evidence of intent is admitted as proof that the act was done, the superior statement that the act was in fact done should certainly be admitted. In other words, hearsay statements of memory or belief should be admitted as proof that the matter remembered or believed did happen.

Forty years after *Hillmon,* in Shepard v. United States,[1] the Supreme Court dealt with an aspect of this argument. In *Shepard,* the trial court had admitted in a murder prosecution testimony that the victim, the wife of the physician-defendant, had stated to a nurse, "Dr. Shepard has poisoned me." Reversing, the Supreme Court rejected the argument

that the statement was admissible as a declaration of state of mind:

> [*Hillmon*] marks the high water line beyond which courts have been unwilling to go. It has developed a substantial body of criticism and commentary. Declarations of intention, casting light upon the future, have been sharply distinguished from declarations of memory, pointing backwards to the past. There would be an end, or nearly that, to the rule against hearsay if the distinction were ignored.
>
> The testimony now questioned faced backward and not forward. This at least it did in its most obvious implications. What is even more important, it spoke to a past act by someone not the speaker.[2]

In more formal hearsay terms, forward-looking statements of intention are admitted while backward-looking statements of memory or belief are excluded because the former do not present the classic hearsay dangers of memory and narration. The weakness inherent in forward-looking statements—the uncertainty that the intention will be carried out—may lead to exclusion, but this is under the relevancy doctrine rather than hearsay analysis.

Nevertheless, after the decision in *Shepard,* the blanket exclusion of statements of memory or belief to prove past events was the subject of substantial re-examination. From the blanket exclusion of statements of memory or belief to prove past events, the courts carved out an area of admissibility for statements by a testator made after the execution of an alleged will. Thus, the testator's statements that he or she has or has not made or revoked a will or made a will of a particular purport were excepted from the ban of the hearsay rule by a preponderance of the decisions. Impetus to recognize such an exception is furnished by the unavailability of the person who best knew the facts and often was the only person with that knowledge, *viz.,* the testator. Special reliability is suggested by the undeniable firsthand knowledge and lack

1. 290 U.S. 96 (1933).

2. Id. at 105–106.

of motive to deceive, though the possibility may exist that the testator wished to deceive his or her relatives. Federal Rule 803(3) admits statement that "relates to the execution, revocation, identification, or terms of declarant's will," exempting such statements from the general prohibition against receiving declarations of state of mind offered to prove the happening of the event causing the state of mind.

More broadly, occasional statutes allowed receipt of statements by deceased persons made in good faith and upon personal knowledge before the commencement of the action. The Model Code of Evidence went much further by allowing any hearsay statement by an unavailable declarant. The original Uniform Rules represented a substantial retreat: they broadly excluded statements of "memory or belief to prove the fact remembered or believed," but opened up a small area by allowing statements by an unavailable declarant describing an event or condition recently perceived while the declarant's recollection was clear and made in good faith prior to the commencement of the action.

The Federal Rules, as presented to and adopted by the Supreme Court, incorporated this base, with the added limitation that the statement must not be in response to the instigation of a person engaged in investigating, litigating, or settling a claim. The Rules as finally enacted prohibit the introduction of statements of memory or belief to prove the fact remembered or believed, except as to wills, omitting the liberalizing provision for statements of unavailable declarants. That latter provision is, however, included for civil cases in the Revised Uniform Rules (1986), although courts generally have shown unwillingness to move to the liberal treatment of the original Uniform Rules in the absence of legislative direction.[3]

A recurring problem arises in connection with the admissibility of accusatory statements made before the act by the victims of homicide. If the statement is merely an expression of fear—i.e., "I am afraid of D"—no hearsay problem is involved, since the statement falls within the hearsay exception for statements of mental or emotional condition. This does not, however, resolve the question of admissibility. The victim's emotional state must relate to some legitimate issue in the case. For example, the victim's emotional state may permit the inference of some fact of consequence, such as lack of consent where the prosecution charges that the killing occurred during the commission of either a kidnapping or rape.

However, the most likely inference that jurors may draw from the existence of fear, and often the only logical inference that could be drawn, is that some conduct of the defendant, probably mistreatment or threats, occurred to cause the fear. The possibility of overpersuasion, the prejudicial character of the evidence, and the relative weakness and speculative nature of the inference, all argue against admissibility as a matter of relevance.[4] Moreover, even if the judgment is made that evidence of fear standing alone should be admitted, statements of fear are rarely stated pristinely. Instead, that state of mind usually assumes the form either of a statement by the victim that the accused has made threats, from which fear may be inferred, or perhaps more likely a statement of fear because of the defendant's threats. Not only does the evidence possess the weaknesses suggested above for expressions of fear standing alone, but in addition it seems unlikely that juries can resist using the evidence for forbidden purposes in the presence of specific disclosure of misconduct of the defendant.

In either event, the cases have generally excluded the evidence. While the same pressing need for the evidence may be present as that which led to the development of the hearsay exception for dying declarations, the case for trustworthiness is much weaker, and need alone has never been thought sufficient to support a hearsay exception. Exclusion is not universal, however, for in some circumstances statements may be admissible under

---

3. See infra § 326.

4. See supra § 185.

other hearsay exceptions, such as that for startled utterances or dying declarations.[5] Moreover, the decedent's fear may be relevant for other legitimate purposes beyond proof of the defendant's act or state of mind. There is broad agreement that such statements are admissible where the defense claims self-defense, suicide, or accidental death, because in each of those situations the decedent's fear helps to rebut aspects of the asserted defense.

5.   See supra § 272 & infra Ch. 32.

Chapter 27

STATEMENTS FOR THE PURPOSE OF MEDICAL DIAGNOSIS OR TREATMENT

Table of Sections

§ 277. Statements of Bodily Feelings, Symptoms, and Condition: (a) Statements Made to Physicians Consulted for Treatment

Statements of a presently existing bodily condition made by a patient to a doctor consulted for treatment [1] have almost universally been admitted as evidence of the facts stated, and even courts that otherwise limited the admissibility of declarations of bodily condition have admitted statements made under these circumstances. Since statements made to physicians are usually made in response to questions, they are not likely to be entirely spontaneous. However, their reliability is assured by the likelihood that the patient believes that the effectiveness of the treatment received will depend upon the accuracy of the information provided to the physician.

As this exception developed, many courts expanded it to include statements made by a patient to a physician concerning *past* symptoms because of the strong assurance of reliability. This is generally sound, as patients are likely to recognize the importance to their treatment of accurate statements as to past, as well as present, symptoms. Some courts continued, however, to admit the testimony only for the limited purpose of "explaining the basis for the physician's conclusion" rather than to prove the fact of the prior symptoms.[2]

A major issue involving the scope of the exception is the treatment of statements made to a physician concerning the cause or the external source of the condition to be treated. In some cases, the special assurance of reliability—the patient's belief that accura-

§ 277

1. Statements made to nontreating physicians are discussed in infra § 278.

2. Bases for expert opinions are discussed in supra § 15.

cy is essential to effective treatment—also applies to statements concerning the cause. Moreover, a physician who views cause as related to diagnosis and treatment might reasonably be expected to communicate this to the patient and perhaps take other steps to assure a reliable response. However, the result is different when statements as to causation enter the realm of establishing fault. It is generally unlikely that the patient or the physician regards them as related to diagnosis or treatment. In such cases, the statements lack any assurance of reliability based on the declarant's interest in proper treatment and should properly be excluded. "Thus a patient's statement that he was struck by an automobile would qualify, but not his statement that the car was driven through a red light." [3]

Federal Rule 803(4) provides a hearsay exception, regardless of availability of declarant for

> [s]tatements made for purpose of medical diagnosis or treatment and describing medical history, or past or present symptoms, pain, or sensation, or the inception or general character of the cause or external source thereof insofar as reasonably pertinent to diagnosis or treatment.

The statement need not have been made to a physician; one made to a hospital attendant, ambulance driver, or member of the family may qualify. Nor does the rule require that the statement be made by the patient. The rule is broadly drawn as to subject matter, including medical history and descriptions of past and present symptoms, pain, and sensations. The test for admissibility is whether the subject matter of the statements is reasonably pertinent to diagnosis or treatment—an apparently objective standard. Descriptions of cause are similarly allowed if they are medically pertinent, but statements of fault are unlikely to qualify.

§ 278. Statements of Bodily Feelings, Symptoms, and Condition: (b) Statements Made to Physicians Consulted Only to Testify

Historically, many courts drew a sharp line between statements made to physicians consulted for purposes of treatment and those made to physicians consulted solely with the anticipation that the physician would testify in court on the declarant's behalf. Courts were hesitant to admit statements made to doctors consulted only for diagnosis under the instant exception. This restriction was based on the conclusion that, where the declarant does not anticipate that the effectiveness of treatment depends upon the accuracy of his or her statement, the underlying rationale for the exception does not exist. Indeed, if the declarant anticipates that enhancement of symptoms will aid in the subsequent litigation, there is an affirmative motive to falsify or at least exaggerate.

The precise nature of the restrictions upon statements made to doctors not consulted for treatment differed among the jurisdictions, although a very common pattern permitted the doctor to recite the statements of the declarant for the limited purpose of providing a basis for the doctor's medical opinion. The dubious propriety of these restrictions was probably at least partially responsible for the restrictive view taken by the courts as to what constituted consultation solely for purposes of obtaining testimony. An inquiry was made to determine whether there was any significant treatment motive; if this existed, an additional motive to obtain testimony was ignored.

These restrictions were abandoned by the drafters of the Federal Rule. The Advisory Committee concluded that permitting statements to be admitted as a basis for a medical expert's opinion but not for their truth was likely to be a distinction lost on juries, and rejected the limitation.[1] The Rule was enact-

---

3. Adv.Comm. Note, Fed.R.Evid. 803(4).

1. The bases of expert opinion are discussed in supra § 15. A quasi-hearsay exception for data relied upon by experts is discussed in infra § 324.3.

ed without congressional modification. The general reliance upon "subjective" facts by the medical profession and the ability of its members to evaluate the accuracy of statements made to them is considered sufficient protection against contrived symptoms. Within the medical profession, the analysis of the rule appears to be that facts reliable enough to be relied on in reaching a diagnosis have sufficient trustworthiness to satisfy hearsay concerns.

The result also has its practical dimension. Under prior practice, contrived evidence was avoided at too great a cost and in substantial departure from the realities of medical practice. Rule 803(4) eliminates any differences in the admissibility of statements made to testifying, as contrasted with treating, physicians. Here, as for statements made to receive treatment, the test for admissibility is whether the statement is medically pertinent to the diagnosis.

The changes in the hearsay exception for statements made for medical diagnosis or treatment have had their biggest impact in cases pertaining to child sexual abuse. In this area, a number of courts have admitted a broad range of statements by children, including statements identifying a particular individual as the perpetrator of the offense. This evidence is admitted under the rationale that such information is pertinent to treatment of the abused child. Statements have been received when made to a rather wide array of professionals and in a number of different situations. These uses of the expanded hearsay exception challenge the wisdom of its extension to cover statements made without any treatment purpose and may raise constitutional problems regarding the right of confrontation in criminal cases.

Chapter 28

RECORDS OF PAST RECOLLECTION

§ 279. History and Theory of the Exception

By the middle 1600's it had become customary to permit a witness to refresh a failed memory by looking at a written memorandum and to testify from a then-revived memory.[1] Frequently, while examination of the writing did not revive memory, the witness recognized the writing as one that he or she had prepared and was willing to testify on the basis of the writing that the facts recited in it were true. By the 1700's this later procedure was also accepted as proper, although the theoretical difficulty of justifying the new practice was often avoided by labeling it with the somewhat ambiguous term of "refreshing recollection," which clearly was not strictly accurate. Beginning in the early 1800's, courts began to distinguish between the two situations and to recognize that the use of past recollection recorded was a far different matter from permitting the witness to testify from a memory refreshed by examining a writing.

As the rule permitting the introduction of past recollection recorded developed, it required that four elements be met: (1) the witness must have had firsthand knowledge of the event, (2) the written statement must be an original memorandum made at or near the time of the event while the witness had a clear and accurate memory of it, (3) the witness must lack a present recollection of the event, and (4) the witness must vouch for the accuracy of the written memorandum.

With the passage of time, these requirements have been the subject of modifications and refinements, discussed in the sections that follow. The exception appears as Rule 803(5) of the Federal Rules of Evidence with no formal unavailability of the declarant specified. It reads as follows:

A memorandum or record concerning a matter about which a witness once had knowl-

§ 279

1. See supra § 9.

edge but now has insufficient recollection to enable the witness to testify fully and accurately, shown to have been made or adopted by the witness when the matter was fresh in the witness' memory and to reflect that knowledge correctly. If admitted, the memorandum or record may be read into evidence but may not itself be received as an exhibit unless offered by an adverse party.

The usefulness of the hearsay exception is apparent from the variety of items the courts have admitted into evidence under its sponsorship: hospital records, reporter's transcripts of testimony, police reports, statements of witnesses, and safe deposit box inventories.

Whether recorded recollection should be classed as a hearsay exception, or as not hearsay at all, is arguable since the reliability of the assertions rests upon the veracity of a witness who is present and testifying.[2] Which way the argument is decided seems not to have affected the requirements for admissibility, however, and it is convenient to treat recorded recollection as a hearsay exception since at least some failure of memory is required.

Should the writing be admitted into evidence and be allowed to be taken to the jury room? Some difference of opinion is apparent. However, the testimonial character of the writing makes a strong argument against the practice, just as depositions are generally not given to the jury.[3] Federal Rule 803(5) solves the problem by resort to the ancient practice of reading the writing into evidence but not admitting it as an exhibit unless offered by the adverse party.

§ 280. Firsthand Knowledge

The usual requirement of firsthand knowledge [1] that applies to witnesses and hearsay declarants, since in reality they are witnesses, is also enforced in regard to past recollection recorded. Thus, where an inventory was offered and the witness produced to lay the

necessary foundation testified that it had been made only partly from his own inspection and partly from information provided by his assistant, the inventory was inadmissible.

§ 281. Written Statement Made While the Witness' Memory Was Clear

Despite some cases suggesting the contrary, the exception as generally stated requires that there be a written formulation of the memory. Federal Rule 803(5) uses the somewhat broader terms "memorandum or record," which a tape recording, for example, should satisfy. Moreover, the original memorandum must be produced or accounted for as is generally required when the contents of documents are sought to be proved.[1]

This writing need not, however, have been prepared by the witness personally if the witness read and adopted it. Multiple-participant situations are considered further in section 283, below.

The writing must have been prepared or recognized as correct at a time close enough to the event to ensure accuracy. Some opinions use the older strict formulation that requires the writing to have been either made or recognized as correct "at or near the time" of the events recorded. This finds some support in psychological research suggesting that a rapid rate of memory loss occurs within the first two or three days following the observation of an event. But the trend is toward accepting the formulation favored by Wigmore, which would require only that the writing be made or recognized at a time when the events were fairly fresh in the mind of the witness. The formula of Federal Rule 803(5) is "when the matter was fresh in the witness' memory." The cases vary as to the length of time lapse allowable, and while the period of time between the event and the making of the memorandum or record is a critically important factor, a mechanical approach that looks only to the length of time that has passed, rather than focusing on indications that the

---

2. Compare the treatment of prior inconsistent statements of a witness in supra § 251. As to possible constitutional problems of confrontation, see supra § 252.

3. See supra § 217.

§ 280

1. See supra § 10.

§ 281

1. See generally supra Ch. 23.

memory remained fresh, should not be employed.

§ 282. Impairment of Recollection

The traditional formulation of the rule requires that, before a past recollection recorded statement can be received in evidence, the witness who made or recognized it as correct must testify that he or she lacks any present memory of the event and therefore is unable to testify concerning it. A few courts have rejected this requirement in circumstances suggesting that, although the witness may have sufficient present recollection to cause the offer not to meet the traditional requirement, the prior recorded statement would appear to be more complete and more reliable than testimony based upon the witness' present memory. An occasional case has supported complete abandonment of the requirement, arguing that failure of memory adds nothing to the credibility of the statement.

It is undoubtedly true that present recollection, clouded by the passage of time, is often less accurate than a statement made at a time when recollection was fresh and clear. However, complete abandonment of the requirement that the witness must have some memory impairment would likely encourage the use of statements prepared for purposes of the litigation under the supervision of claims adjusters or attorneys or under other circumstances casting significant doubt upon the reliability of the statement.

Phrasing the requirement not in absolute terms but as a lack of sufficient present recollection to enable the witness to testify fully and accurately accommodates these competing concerns. This standard, which is used in the Federal Rule, has gained increasing judicial adherents in preference to a total elimination of any requirement of impaired memory.

Is the requirement of "insufficient recollection to enable the witness to testify fully and accurately" satisfied where an apparently reluctant witness seeks to avoid testifying to a particular fact by claiming no memory? Courts have answered this question affirma-

tively. Perhaps that result does no great violence to the underlying hearsay concerns since the witness is still required to establish the accuracy of the statement and since he or she is available for at least some limited cross-examination. However, it is far from clear that this pattern meets the literal requirement of the rule that the witness "has insufficient recollection" as found by the court or that it is consistent with either the historical function of this exception or the legislative intention of its framers.

§ 283. Proving the Accuracy of the Written Statement; Multi–Party Situations

As a final assurance of reliability, it has traditionally been required that either the person who prepared the writing or one who read it at a time close to the event testify to its accuracy. This may be accomplished by a statement that the person presently remembers recording the fact correctly or remembers recognizing the writing as accurate when he or she read it at an earlier time. But if the present memory is less effective, it is sufficient if this person testifies that he or she knows it is correct because of a habit or practice to record such matters accurately or to check them for accuracy. At the extreme, it is even sufficient if the individual testifies to recognizing his or her signature on the statement and believes the statement correct because the witness would not have signed it if he or she had not believed it true at the time.

No particular method of proving the accuracy of the memorandum is prescribed by Federal 803(5), which merely requires that it be "shown * * * to reflect that knowledge correctly." If an adequate foundation has been laid, it is not grounds for exclusion that the witness' testimony as to the accuracy of the statement is contradicted by other testimony. However, the witness must acknowledge at trial the accuracy of the statement. An assertion of its accuracy in the acknowledgment line of a written statement or such an acknowledgment made previously under oath will not be sufficient.

The courts have been relatively liberal in finding that the witness has acknowledged the accuracy of a prior statement, particularly where the witness is apparently hostile or reluctant to testify. A special danger of misuse of the exception occurs when this weak proof of the statement's accuracy operates in combination with the argument, discussed in the preceding section, that a refusal to testify satisfies the exception's requirement that a witness have insufficient memory of the event.

The traditional past recollection recorded was a one-person affair with a single witness making the original observation, recording it, and verifying its accuracy. When the verifying witness did not prepare the report but merely examined it and found it accurate, the matter involved what might be called a coop-erative report. But in this situation, the substantive requirements of the exception could be met by calling only the person who read and verified the report. A somewhat different type of cooperative report exists when a person reports orally facts to another person who writes them down. A store clerk or timekeeper, for example, may report sales or time to a bookkeeper. In this type of situation, courts have held the written statement admissible if the person reporting the facts testifies to the correctness of the oral report (although at the time of this testimony, the detailed facts may not still be remembered) and the recorder of that statement testifies that he or she faithfully transcribed that oral report. While subject to some ambiguity because of inartful drafting by Congress, the Federal Rule continues to permit such multi-party statements to be admitted.

Chapter 29

REGULARLY KEPT RECORDS

§ 284. Admissibility of Regularly Kept Records

Regularly kept records may be offered in evidence in many different situations, although in almost all, the record is offered as evidence of the truth of its terms. In such cases, the evidence is clearly hearsay and some exception to the hearsay rule must be invoked if the record is to be admitted. Often no special exception is needed, however, as the record comes within the terms of another exception. For example, if the record was made by a party to the suit, it is admissible against that party as an admission.[1] If the entrant is produced as a witness, the record may be used to refresh memory,[2] or it may be admissible as a record of past recollection.[3] Sometimes the record may be admissible as a declaration against interest.[4] The present chapter is concerned only with those situations in which none of these alternative theories of admissibility is available or, if available, is not utilized, and a specific exception to the hearsay rule for regularly kept records must be invoked.

§ 285. The Origin of the Regularly Kept Records Exception and the Shopbook Vestige

By the 1600's in England, a custom emerged in the common law courts of receiv-

---

§ 284
1. See generally supra § 254.
2. See generally supra § 9.

3. See generally supra Ch. 28.
4. See generally infra Ch. 33.

ing the "shop books" of tradesmen and crafts-men as evidence of debts for goods sold or services rendered on open accounts. Since most tradesmen were their own bookkeepers, the rule permitted a reasonable means of avoiding the harsh common law rule prevent-ing a party from appearing as its own witness. Nevertheless, theoretical objections to the self-serving nature of this evidence, apparent-ly coupled with abuse of it in practice, led to a statutory curb in 1609 that limited the use of a party's shopbooks to a period of one year after the debt was created unless a bill of debt was given or the transaction was between merchants and tradesmen. The higher courts refused to recognize the books at all after the year had elapsed, although in practice such evidence was received in the lower courts with small claims jurisdiction.

During the 1700's a broader doctrine began to develop in the English common law courts. At first, this doctrine permitted only the use of regular entries in the books of a party by a deceased clerk, but it was expanded to cover books regularly kept by third persons who had since died. By 1832 the doctrine was firmly grounded, and its scope was held to include all entries made by a person, since deceased, in the ordinary course of the mak-er's business.

The development of the doctrine in Amer-ica was less satisfactory, however. In the colonies, limited exceptions for the books of a party based on the English statute of 1609 and Dutch practice were in force. In addition to requiring that the entries be regularly made at or about the time of the transaction and as a part of the routine of the business, other common restrictions were that (1) the party using the book not have had a clerk, (2) the party file a "supplemental oath" to the justness of the account, (3) the books bear an honest appearance, (4) each transaction not exceed a certain limited value, (5) witnesses testify from their experience in dealing with the party that the books are honest, (6) the books be used only to prove open accounts for goods and services furnished the defendant (thus making them unavailable for proof of loans and goods and services furnished under special contract or furnished to third persons on defendant's credit), and (7) other proof be made of the actual delivery of some of the goods.

Not until the early 1800's did the American equivalent of the English general exception for regular business entries by deceased per-sons emerge. As the doctrine gained accept-ance, however, often no provision was made for the "shop books" of a party, whose admis-sibility continued to be controlled by the re-strictive statutes. This made little sense, es-pecially in view of the fact that abolition of the party's disqualification as a witness [1] re-moved the justification for treating the books of a party as a special problem.

Most courts today take the reasonable posi-tion that shop book statutes, where they re-main, are to be regarded as an alternative ground of admissibility. As a result, when a party offers its books in evidence, they may be admissible either if they meet the shop book act requirements or if they meet the tests for regularly kept records generally.

§ 286. The Regularly Kept Records Ex-ception in General

The hearsay exception for regularly kept records is justified on grounds analogous to those underlying other exceptions to the hear-say rule. Unusual reliability is furnished by the fact that regularly kept records typically have a high degree of accuracy. The very regularity and continuity of the records are calculated to train the recordkeeper in habits of precision; if of a financial nature, the records are periodically checked by balance-striking and audits; and in actual experience, the entire business of the nation and many other activities function in reliance upon records of this kind. The impetus for resort to these hearsay statements at common law arose when the person or persons who made the entry, and upon whose knowledge it was based, were unavailable as witnesses because

§ 285

1. See supra § 65.

of death, insanity, disappearance, or other reason.

The common law exception had four elements: (1) the entries must be original entries made in the routine of a business, (2) the entries must have been made upon the personal knowledge of the recorder or of someone reporting the information, (3) the entries must have been made at or near the time of the transaction recorded, and (4) the recorder and the informant must be shown to be unavailable. If these conditions were met, the business entry was admissible to prove the facts recited in it.

The regularly kept records exception had evolved within the context of simple business organizations, with the typical records of a double-entry system of journal and ledger. In this setting, the common law requirements were not unduly burdensome. Control and management of complex organizations require correspondingly complicated records, however, and the organizations of business, government, and institutions in general were becoming increasingly intricate. While the theory of the exception was sound, some of the common law requirements were incompatible with modern conditions. The limitation to records of a business was unduly restrictive. The requirement of an "original" record was inconsistent with modern developments in record keeping. The need to account for nonproduction of all participants in the process of assembling and recording information was a needless and disruptive burden in view of the unlikelihood that any of the persons involved would remember a particular transaction or its details. And there were uncertainties as to what witnesses were required to lay the necessary foundation for the records. Since the courts seemed unable to resolve these difficulties, relief was sought in legislation, and even before the enactment of the Federal Rules, the exception was governed by statute or rule virtually everywhere.

The Commonwealth Fund Act and the Uniform Business Records as Evidence Act provided the principal models for the early legislative reforms. Their essential features are now incorporated in Federal Rule 803(6), which provides a hearsay exception, without regard to unavailability of declarant, as follows:

A memorandum, report, record, or data compilation, in any form, of acts, events, conditions, opinions, or diagnoses, made at or near the time by, or from information transmitted by, a person with knowledge, if kept in the course of a regularly conducted business activity, and if it was the regular practice of that business activity to make the memorandum, report, record, or data compilation, all as shown by the testimony of the custodian or other qualified witness, unless the source of information or the method or circumstances of preparation indicate lack of trustworthiness. The term "business" as used in this paragraph includes business, institution, association, profession, occupation, and calling of every kind, whether or not conducted for profit.

§ 287. Types of Records; Opinions; Absence of Entry

The usual statement of the "business records" exception to the hearsay rule suggests that oral reports are not within it, even if the other requirements for admissibility are met. The common law cases tended to speak in terms of entries in account books, the subject usually under consideration.[1] The Commonwealth Fund Act used the terms "writing or record," the Uniform Act spoke of "record," and the Federal Rule includes a "memorandum, report, record, or data compilation." Of these, only the term "report" in the Federal Rule is arguably broad enough to include an oral report, and there, the provision that the report be "kept" negates the idea that oral reports are within the rule. Nevertheless, the English position is that oral reports may qualify under the exception, and some American courts have admitted oral reports on the basis of a partial analogy to business records.

Under the common law exception, the entries were required to be "original" entries

§ 287

1. See supra § 285.

and not mere transcribed records or copies. This was based on the assumption that the original entries were more likely to be accurate than subsequent copies or transcriptions. In business practice, however, it is customary for daily transactions, such as sales or services rendered, to be noted upon slips, memorandum books, or the like by the person most directly concerned. Then someone else collects these memoranda and from them makes entries in a permanent book, such as a journal or ledger. In these cases, the entries in the permanent record sufficiently comply with the requirement of originality. They would certainly be admissible if the slips or memoranda disappeared and should be admissible as the original permanent entry without proof as to the unavailability of the tentative memoranda. This practice also serves the interest of convenience, since it is much easier to use a ledger or similar source than slips or temporary memoranda when the inquiry is into the whole state of an account. Of course, the slips or memoranda would also be admissible if they should be offered. The Federal Rule does not require that the entry be original, but allows "any form."

With regard to opinions in business records, two types of issues arise. The first concerns lay opinions or conclusions, which are largely conclusory forms of expression. The opinion rule should be restricted to governing the manner of presenting live testimony where a more specific and concrete answer can be secured if desired and should have little application to the admissibility of out-of-court statements, including business records.[2] The second and more difficult issue regards so-called expert opinions within business records. Federal Rule 803(6) specifically provides that an admissible regularly kept record may include opinions. These will ordinarily be expert opinions, and they will be subject to requirements governing proper subjects for expert opinions and qualifications of experts. For further discussion in connection with hospital records, see infra section 293.

Sometimes the absence of an entry relating to a particular transaction is offered as proof that no such transaction took place. For example, a car rental agency's records showing no lease or rental activity for a certain vehicle may be offered to prove that the defendant, found in possession of the car, had stolen it. The majority of courts have admitted the evidence for this purpose, and Federal Rule 803(7) specifically so provides:

> Evidence that a matter is not included in the memoranda reports, records, or data compilations, in any form, kept in accordance with the provisions of paragraph (6), to prove the nonoccurrence or nonexistence of the matter, if the matter was of a kind of which a memorandum, report, record, or data compilation was regularly made and preserved, unless the sources of information or other circumstances indicate lack of trustworthiness.[3]

§ 288. Made in the Routine of a "Business"; Accident Reports

The early cases construed the requirement of a "business" literally and excluded, for example, records kept in connection with loans made by an individual not in the business of loaning money to others on the basis that they were not concerned with "business". The Commonwealth Fund Act defined "business" much more expansively to "include business, profession, occupation and calling of every kind." The Uniform Act added "operation of institutions, whether carried on for profit or not."

In Federal Rule 803(6), the term includes "business, institution, association, profession, occupation, and calling of every kind, whether or not conducted for profit." This rule, applying to a "memorandum, report, record, or data compilation, in any form," of a "business" thus broadly defined, is of great scope. It has been held to encompass such diverse items as a diary of tips kept by a blackjack dealer, notations on calendar of daily illegal drug sales, a catalog, attaching envelopes to bids upon opening, a hospital's scrapbook of

2. See supra § 18.

3. For paragraph (6), see supra § 286.

newspaper articles showing visiting hours, prison counselor's report to staff psychiatrist of incident involving prisoner, invoices from suppliers, a bill of lading, an automobile lease by dealer, a logbook of malfunctions of a machine, and an appraisal of a painting for purposes of insurance. These examples are all in addition, of course, to account books and their counterparts, which might more readily fall within the usual concept of business records. Hospital records are specially treated below in section 293 and computer-stored records are the subject of section 294.

Records, such as diaries, if of a purely personal nature not involved in declarant's business activities, do not fall within the rule, but if kept for business purposes are within the rule. Memoranda of telephone conversations are treated similarly. The breadth of the exception is also demonstrated by cases holding that the activity need not be legal for the record to qualify. Some church records are covered generally by the business records exception while those related to the family history of members are the subject of Federal Rule 803(11).

Under the English rules, both the matter or event recorded and the recording of it must have been performed pursuant to a duty to a third person. This is not the case under the American law.

How far the rule goes in requiring not only that the record must be made in the regular course of a business but that it "be the regular practice of that business to make the memorandum" is disputed. What might be termed nonroutine records, which are nevertheless made in the course of regularly conducted activities, are the focus of concern here. Often such records, because not regularly made, will be outside the expertise of the organization and properly excluded. Other records of this type will be properly excluded because of motivational concerns arising from the fact they were generated for litigation purposes, discussed immediately below. Where these specific threats to trustworthi-

ness are absent but, nevertheless, the record is nonroutine, the authorities reach contrary decisions depending upon whether the focus is on the basic concern of trustworthiness or the apparent intention of Congress as reflected in the literal requirement of the rule.

An important set of concerns revolves around the purpose of the report and the circumstances of its preparation, particularly reports of accidents. The leading case is Palmer v. Hoffman,[1] a suit against railroad trustees arising out of an accident at a railroad crossing. The engineer of the train involved was interviewed two days after the accident by a representative of the railroad and a representative of the state public utilities commission. He signed a statement giving his version of the incident. The engineer died before trial, and the statement was offered by the defendants, who contended that the railroad obtained such statements in the regular course of its business. Affirming the trial court's exclusion of the report, the Supreme Court of the United States stated:

> [The report] is not a record made for the systematic conduct of the business as a business. An accident report may affect that business in the sense that it affords information on which the management may act. It is not, however, typical of entries made systematically or as a matter of routine to record events or occurrences, to reflect transactions with others, or to provide internal controls * * *. Unlike payrolls, accounts receivable, accounts payable, bills of lading and the like, these reports are calculated for use essentially in the court, not in the business. Their primary use is in litigating, not in railroading.[2]

Consequently, the report was held not to have been made "in the regular course" of the business within the meaning of the federal statute then providing for the admissibility of business records.[3]

While *Palmer* has been subject to various interpretations, the most reasonable reading of it is that it did not create a blanket rule of

1. 318 U.S. 109 (1943).

2. Id. at 113–114.

3. Id. at 114–115.

exclusion for accident reports or similar records kept by businesses. Rather, it recognized a discretionary power in the trial court to exclude evidence which meets the letter of the business records exception, but which, under the circumstances, appears to lack the reliability business records are assumed ordinarily to have. The existence of a motive and opportunity to falsify the record, especially in the absence of any countervailing factors, is of principal concern. The Federal Rule incorporates this reading of *Palmer* by permitting admission if the report otherwise complies with the requirements of the rule, "unless the source of information or the method or circumstances of preparation indicate lack of trustworthiness."

Police reports and records can, of course, meet the requirements for the regularly kept records exception to the hearsay rule. They can also qualify under the hearsay exception for public records and reports. Federal Rule 803(8) contains certain restrictions upon the use of police reports in criminal cases, and the question has arisen whether those restrictions can be avoided by offering police reports under the regularly kept records exception, which imposes no such limitations. The answer, while somewhat complicated, has generally been in the negative. This subject is discussed in greater detail in section 296 infra.

§ 289. Made at or Near the Time of the Transaction Recorded

A substantial factor in the reliability of any system of records is the promptness with which transactions are recorded.

The formula of Federal Rule 803(6) is "at or near the time." Whether an entry made subsequent to the transaction has been made within a sufficient time to render it within the exception depends upon whether the time span between the transaction and the entry was so great as to suggest a danger of inaccuracy by lapse of memory. In addition, the failure to make a timely record may suggest nonregularity in the making of the statement and may indicate motivational problems re-

lated to records prepared for litigation purposes.

§ 290. Personal Knowledge; All Participants in Regular Course of Business

The common law exception for regularly kept records required that the entries have been made by one with personal knowledge of the matter entered or upon reports to the maker by one with personal knowledge. The entrant was required to be acting in the regular course of business, and if the information was supplied by another, that person also was required to be acting in the regular course of business. If the information was transmitted through intermediaries, they were subject to the same requirement. The application of the regular course requirement to all participants in the process of acquiring, transmitting, and recording information was consistent with, indeed mandated by, the theory of the hearsay exception.

Reform legislation in general has not dealt clearly with the question whether the information must initially be acquired by a person with firsthand knowledge and whether that person and all others involved in the process must be acting in the regular course of the business. The Commonwealth Fund Act required that the record be "made in the regular course of * * * business" and provided that "other circumstances * * *, including lack of personal knowledge by the entrant or maker, may be shown to affect its weight, but they shall not affect its admissibility." The Uniform Act also required that the record be "made in the regular course of business," and in addition required that "in the opinion of the court, the sources of information, method and time of preparation were such as to justify its admission." Federal Rule 803(6) requires that the record be "made * * * by, or from information transmitted by, a person with knowledge, if kept in the course of a regularly conducted business activity."

Assuming, as is reasonable, that "knowledge" means firsthand knowledge, then Rule 803(6) answers the first part of the above question affirmatively, to the effect that the person who originally feeds the information into the process must have firsthand knowledge. As to whether the person making the record must be in the regular course of business, both the acts and Rule 803(6) answer in the affirmative, the first two using the term "made" and the latter "kept" to describe records produced in the regular course of business. However, stretching "made" and "kept" to include both the original acquisition of the information and its transmission to the recorder is troublesome.

These doubts have largely been resolved by referring to the underlying theory of the exception, namely, a practice and environment encouraging the making of accurate records. If any person in the process is not acting in the regular course of the business, then an essential link in the trustworthiness chain fails, just as it does when the person feeding the information does not have firsthand knowledge. The leading case is Johnson v. Lutz,[1] decided under the New York version of the Commonwealth Fund Act, holding inadmissible a police officer's report insofar as it was not based upon his personal knowledge but on information supplied by a bystander. Wigmore was bitterly critical of the decision,[2] but the courts generally have followed its lead in requiring all parts of the process to be conducted under a business duty. The reasoning of Johnson v. Lutz has been applied to various formulations of the exception.

When the matter recorded itself satisfies the conditions of some other hearsay exception, the requirement that the person initially acquiring the information must be in the regular course of the business is not enforced. For example, a police officer may include in a report of an automobile accident a damaging statement by one of the drivers, who later becomes a party to litigation. The statement qualifies as an admission, and the report may be used to prove it was made. That the officer has no firsthand knowledge of the correctness of the statement is immaterial. This matter is discussed further in connection with multiple hearsay.[3]

Direct proof that the maker of the statement had actual knowledge may be difficult, and it may even be impossible to prove specifically the identity of the informant with actual knowledge. Evidence that it was someone's business duty in the organization's routine to observe the matter will be prima facie sufficient to establish actual knowledge. This does not dispense with the need for personal knowledge, but permits it to be proved by evidence of practice and a reasonable assumption that general practice was followed with regard to a particular matter, or by other appropriate circumstances.

§ 291. Unavailability

Historically, if the person who made a business record was present as a witness, the record could be used to refresh recollection, or if that person could not then recall the facts, his or her testimony might be such as to qualify the record as past recollection recorded. If, however, the witness for some reason could not be produced in court—i.e., was unavailable—then these alternative avenues to admissibility for the business record could not be used. A need for a special hearsay exception for business records in such cases was apparent. Unfortunately, as sometimes happens, the reason why the rule came into existence was incorporated into the rule as a requirement, in this instance a requirement of unavailability.

The process of calling a series of participants, only to have them testify that referring to the business record did not refresh their recollection, or at best to give rote testimony that it was their practice to be accurate, was a manifest waste of the court's time and disruptive to the business involved with no corresponding benefit. Yet no other response could reasonably be expected from participants in the keeping of records under modern conditions. The reliability of the record could

---

§ 290

1. 253 N.Y. 124, 170 N.E. 517 (1930).

2. 5 Wigmore, Evidence § 1561a, at 490, § 1561b, at 507 (Chadbourn rev. 1974).

3. See infra § 324.1.

be shown by evidence other than the testimony of participants, as had been done when a participant was unavailable. Accordingly, unavailability virtually disappeared as a requirement.

The Commonwealth Fund Act and the Uniform Act did not in terms address the unavailability requirement, but their silence was clearly meant to do away with that requirement. Federal Rule 803(6) specifically eliminates the unavailability requirement by including the regularly kept records exception in a rule dealing with a group of exceptions where the hearsay rule does not operate to exclude the evidence "even though the declarant is available as a witness." The unavailability requirement has now almost entirely disappeared from American jurisdictions.

§ 292. Proof; Who Must Be Called to Establish Admissibility

The demise of the requirement of unavailability, discussed in the preceding section, had its impact upon the method of proving business records, as was intended. No longer was it necessary to call each available participant and exhaust the possibility of refreshing memory or establishing the record as past recollection recorded; compliance with the requirements for regularly kept records could be proved by other means. Thus any witness with the necessary knowledge about the particular recordkeeping process could testify that it was the regular practice of the business to make such records, that the record was made in the regular course of business upon the personal knowledge of the recorder or of someone reporting to him or her in the regular course of business, and that the entries were made at or near the time of the transaction. The Commonwealth Fund Act did not deal with the matter of proof expressly, although a principal purpose of the act was to alleviate the burdensome requirements of proof imposed by the common law. The Uniform Act, however, provided that the foundation might be laid by "the custodian or other qualified witness," and this language is incorporated in Federal Rule 803(6).

Perhaps the most commonly used foundation witness is a person in authority in the recordkeeping department of the business. Whether or not such a person falls within the term "custodian" may be questioned, but certainly he or she is "a qualified witness." In fact, anyone with the necessary knowledge is qualified; there is no requirement that this witness must have firsthand knowledge of the matter reported or actually have prepared the report or observed its preparation.

Problems may arise when one business organization seeks to introduce records in its possession but actually prepared by another. It seems evident that mere possession or "custody" of records under these circumstances does not qualify employees of the possessing party to lay the requisite foundation, and that the transmittal of information by the custodian regarding the contents of records in the custodian's possession does not qualify the recipient to lay the foundation. However, when the business offering the records of another has made an independent check of the records, or can establish accuracy by other means, the necessary foundation may be established.

In order to facilitate the introduction of regularly kept records, Congress recently enacted a statute providing a certification procedure for foreign records in criminal cases.

§ 293. Special Situations: (a) Hospital Records

In some jurisdictions, specific statutory authority for the admission of hospital records exists. Although some courts hesitated to expand the business record exception by decision to noncommercial establishments such as hospitals, all would concede today that hospital records are admissible upon the same basis as other regularly kept records. This result is appropriate, for the safeguards of trustworthiness of records of the modern hospital are at least as substantial as the guarantees of reliability of records of business establishments generally. Progress in medical skills has been accompanied by improvements and standardization of the practice of recording facts concerning the patient, and these recorded facts are routinely used to make decisions upon which the health and life of the patient depend.

History. Under standard practice, a trained attendant at hospitals enters upon the record a "personal history," including an identification of the patient, an account of the present injury or illness, and the events and symptoms leading up to it. This information, which may be obtained from the patient directly or from a companion, is elicited to aid in the diagnosis and treatment of the patient's injury or disease. Is this history admissible to prove assertions of facts it may contain? Two layers of hearsay are involved here, with the first being the use of the hospital record to prove that the statement was made. The primary issue is whether the specific entry involved was an entry made in the regular course of the hospital's business. If the subject matter falls within those things which under hospital practice are regarded as relevant to diagnosis or treatment or other hospital business, it is within the regular course of business.[1] If, on the other hand, the subject matter does not relate to those concerns, the making of the entry is not within the regular course of the hospital's business, and thus it is not admissible even for the limited purpose of proving that the statement was made.

Assuming that the hospital record is admissible to prove that the statement contained in the history was made, is this statement admissible to prove the truth of assertions made in it? In accordance with the general rule, the business record exception cannot support admission of the history because the declarant's action in relating the history was not part of a business routine of which he or she was a regular participant. Here as elsewhere, however, if the history comes within one of the other exceptions to the hearsay rule, it is admissible.[2] The statements may,

for example, constitute admissions of a party opponent when the patient is a party, dying declarations,[3] declarations against interest,[4] excited utterances,[5] and most frequently, statements for the purpose of diagnosis or treatment.[6]

Diagnostic statements. Professional standards for hospital records contemplate that entries will be made of diagnostic findings at various stages. These entries are clearly in the regular course of the operations of the hospital. The problem which they pose is one of the admissibility of "opinions."[7] In the hospital records area, the opinion is usually one of an expert who would unquestionably be permitted to give it if personally testifying. While the requirement of qualification does not disappear, if the record is shown to be from a reputable institution, it may be inferred that regular entries were made by qualified personnel in the absence of any indication to the contrary.

When an expert opinion is offered by a witness personally testifying, the expert is available for cross-examination on that opinion. If the opinion is offered by means of a hospital record, no cross-examination is possible. Consequently, the courts have tended to limit the scope of opinions that can be introduced by this method. The admissibility of ordinary diagnostic findings customarily based on objective data and not presenting more than average difficulty of interpretation is usually conceded. By contrast, diagnostic opinions which on their face are conjectural have generally been excluded.

Given that Federal Rule 803(6) specifically includes opinions or diagnoses, this historical distinction based on whether the opinion is objective or conjectural does not appear to survive, at least directly. However, admissibility of all such entries is not assured. First, where there are indications of lack of trustworthiness, which may result from a lack of

§ 293
1. See supra §§ 277–278.
2. See infra § 324.1.
3. See infra Ch. 32.
4. See infra Ch. 33.

5. See supra § 272.
6. See supra Ch. 27.
7. See supra § 287.

expert qualifications or from a lack of factual support, exclusion is warranted under the rule. Moreover, inclusion of opinions or diagnoses within the rule only removes the bar of hearsay. In the absence of the availability of the expert for explanation and cross-examination, the court may conclude that probative value of this evidence is outweighed by the danger that the jury will be misled or confused.[8] This is of particular concern if the opinion involves difficult matters of interpretation and a central dispute in the case, such as causation. Under these circumstances, a court operating under the Federal Rules, like earlier courts, is likely to be reluctant to permit a decision to be made upon the basis of an un-cross-examined opinion and may require that the witness be produced.

Privilege. In most states, patients have been afforded a privilege against disclosure by physicians of information acquired in attending the patient and necessary for diagnosis and treatment.[9] It is possible to interpret the privilege broadly as including any information obtained by hospital personnel related to treatment. While hospital records are generally privileged to the extent that they incorporate statements made by the patient to the physician and the physician's diagnostic findings, application of the privilege to information obtained by nurses or attendants presents a greater problem. On one hand, it is arguable that privilege statutes should be strictly construed, and most do not mention nurses or attendants. On the other hand, information is usually gathered and recorded by them as agents for the physician and for the purpose of aiding the physician in treatment and diagnosis. The problem is one of interpreting the underlying privilege. If it would bar the direct testimony of a nurse or attendant, it should also bar use of their hearsay statement under this exception; if it would not, such statements in hospital records should not be held privileged.

§ 294. Special Situations: (b) Computer Records

Even though the scrivener's quill pens in original entry books have been replaced by computer printouts, magnetic tapes, and microfiche files, the theory behind the reliability of regularly kept business records remains the same. Provided a proper foundation is laid, computer-generated evidence is no less reliable than original entry books and should be admitted under the exception.

With the explosive development of electronic data processing, most business and business-type records are generated by computers. Courts have agreed that their admissibility is governed by the hearsay exception for regularly kept records, whether at common law or in the form of a statute or rule. Federal Rule 803(6) specifically applies to a "data compilation, in any form," terminology intended to include records stored in computers.

The usual conditions for the exception are applicable.[1] The differences between traditional record-keeping methods and sophisticated electronic equipment, however, require some further exploration of foundation requirements. While paper records can be inspected visually and the process of keeping the record can often be tracked in a step-by-step manner, electronically processed data is not a visual counterpart of the machine record and for the most part is not subject to visual inspection until it takes the final form of a printout.

The theory of trustworthiness supporting the regularly kept records exception assumes a reliable method for entering, processing, storing, and retrieving data. Moreover, the rule excludes statements when "the source of information or the method or circumstances of preparation indicate lack of trustworthiness." Issues may arise at any of the stages of the handling of the data regarding (1) computer hardware, (2) software or programming, and (3) accuracy and/or security.

---

8. See generally supra § 185.

9. See supra Ch. 11.

§ 294

1. See supra §§ 286–290.

Serious problems are rarely presented regarding computer hardware because most computer equipment used to produce records otherwise meeting the requirements of the exception is both standard and highly reliable, with few data errors resulting from defects in equipment. Hence testimony describing equipment should ordinarily be limited to the function that each unit performs in the process and that each is adequate for the purpose. Excursions into theory are not required or ordinarily appropriate.

Much more realistic potential for errors is presented by human factors involved in the programming of the computer and the development of software. However, the trend here is not to require the proponent of the statement to call the programmer to lay the foundation for admission.

With regard to questions of inaccuracy and data security, the courts have moved in the direction of not imposing rigid requirements. Thus, in the typical case, the proponent is not required initially to show periodic testing for programming errors or the elimination of all possibilities of data alteration or errors in data entry or programming.

While a well-laid foundation will touch upon each of these three general areas noted above, the trend among courts has been to treat computer records like other business records and not to require the proponent of the evidence initially to show trustworthiness beyond meeting the general requirements of the rule. The fact that the organization relies upon the record in the regular course of its business may itself provide sufficient indication of reliability, absent realistic challenge, to warrant admission.

While it was suggested initially that the Federal Rules should be amended by adding a rule specifically dealing with computer-generated evidence, the courts have generally dealt competently with the admissibility of such evidence by applying Rule 803(6) or its common law or statutory counterparts. Any attempt at more specific treatment ought to be

undertaken only with awareness of unfortunate English experience with efforts to enact specific statutes.

As noted in an earlier section, in order to qualify under the hearsay exception for regularly kept records, a record must have been made in the regular course of business, and documents made for use in litigation do not meet that requirement. Because of the motivation factor, such records often lack the trustworthiness contemplated by the exception.[2] Also, the regularly kept records exception requires that entries must be made at or near the time of the event recorded.[3]

The application of these general principles to the creation of a computer printout raise several specific problems. These issues are presented by a computer printout that is made (1) long after the data were entered into the system and (2) after litigation has commenced.

The question as to the timeliness of the creation of the record is answered by observing that the time requirement refers to when the entry into the data bank was originally made, not the time the printout was produced. With regard to documents prepared for use in litigation, the arrangement of the data in a form designed to aid the litigation should not result in exclusion if the data and the retrieval processes are themselves reliable. For example, when information is recorded in the computer in the sequence in which it was received rather than organized by customers or transactions, reordering the data by computer should not present a barrier to its admission greater than a manual collation of related business records would. The evidence should not be rejected merely because it is not a visual counterpart of the machine record. However, the court must carefully consider whether the process producing the printout is reliable and whether the record may have been compromised in any way by that process.

Another specific issue encountered with regard to computer records is whether such records when self-generated by the computer

2. See supra § 288.

3. See supra § 289.

are hearsay at all. A frequently encountered example of a record of this type is the trace report produced by telephone company computers when tracking a call made to a specific number. Because records of this type are not the counterpart of a statement by a human declarant, which should ideally be tested by cross-examination of that declarant, they should not be treated as hearsay, but rather their admissibility should be determined on the basis of the reliability and accuracy of the process involved.

Chapter 30

PUBLIC RECORDS, REPORTS, AND CERTIFICATES

Table of Sections

§ 295. The Exception for Public Records and Reports: (a) In General

The common law developed an exception to the hearsay rule for written records and reports of public officials under a duty to make them, made upon firsthand knowledge of the facts. These statements are admissible as evidence of the facts recited in them. The common law formulation of this hearsay exception has been relaxed and broadened by decisions, statutes, and rules, discussed in the sections that follow. The most important of these modern formulations of the exception is the Federal Rule.

Federal Rule 803(8) provides, without regard to the unavailability of the declarant, a hearsay exception for the following:

Records, reports, statements, or data compilations, in any form, of public offices or agencies, setting forth (A) the activities of the office or agency, or (B) matters observed pursuant to duty imposed by law as to which matters there was a duty to report, excluding, however, in criminal cases matters observed by police officers and other law enforcement personnel, or (C) in civil actions and proceedings and against the Government in criminal cases, factual findings resulting from an investigation made pursuant to authority granted by law, unless the sources of information or other circumstances indicate lack of trustworthiness.

The special trustworthiness of official written statements is found in the declarant's official duty and the high probability that the duty to make an accurate report has been

507

performed.[1] The possibility that public inspection of some official records will reveal any inaccuracies and cause them to be corrected (or will deter the official from making them in the first place) has been emphasized by the English courts, which have imposed a corresponding requirement that the official statement be one kept for the use and information of the public. This limitation has been criticized, and the American courts reasonably have not adopted it. Although public inspection might provide a modest additional assurance of reliability, strictly limiting admissibility to records that are open to public inspection would be unwise because many documents with sufficiently reliability to justify admission would be excluded.

The impetus for the development of this hearsay exception is found in the inconvenience of requiring public officials to appear in court and testify concerning the subject matter of their records and reports. Not only would this disrupt the administration of public affairs, but it almost certainly would create a class of official witnesses. Moreover, given the volume of business in public offices, the official written statement will usually be more reliable than the official's present memory. For these same reasons, there is no requirement that the declarant be shown to be unavailable.

The convenience of proving by certified copy [2] and the simplicity of foundation requirements in most cases [3] make the official records exception an attractive choice over business records when an option is afforded.

§ 296. The Exception for Public Records and Reports: (b) Activities of the Office; Matters Observed; Investigative Reports; Restrictions on Prosecutorial Use

Under Federal Rule 803(8) matters falling within the hearsay exception for public records and reports are divided into three groups. This grouping offers a convenient approach also to the common law and statutory background.

(A) Activities of the office. The first group includes probably the oldest and most straightforward type of public records, records of the activities of the office itself. An example is the record of receipts and disbursements of the Treasury Department. In addition to the assurances of reliability common to public records and reports generally, this group also has the assurances of accuracy that characterize business records. Accordingly, they are routinely admitted.

(B) Matters observed pursuant to duty. The second group consists of matters observed and reported, both pursuant to duty imposed by law. Rainfall records of the National Weather Service are illustrative. These records are also of a relatively noncontroversial nature, except where the matter is observed by a police officer or other law enforcement personnel. This limitation is discussed in the concluding portion of (C) below.

(C) Investigative reports. Investigative reports have produced the greatest division among the courts due to their considerable range of potential content. In Beech Aircraft Corporation v. Rainey,[1] however, the Supreme Court resolved one of the issues that had previously divided lower federal courts. In that case, the Court rejected the narrow interpretation of "factual findings," holding that "factually based opinions and conclusions" may be included within the exception.[2] The Court noted that the primary protection against admission of unreliable evidence was the rule's escape provision that directs exclusion of all elements of the report—both factual and evaluative—if the court determines that they lack trustworthiness. In making the determination of trustworthiness, the four factors to be examined include: the timeliness of the investigation, the skill or experience of

§ 295

1. See also supra § 286 concerning regular entries.
2. See supra § 240.
3. See supra § 224.

§ 296

1. 488 U.S. 153 (1988).
2. Id. at 163.

the investigator, whether a formal hearing was held, and the bias of the investigator.

As the name indicates, these reports embody the results of investigation and accordingly are often not the product of firsthand knowledge of the declarant, which is required under most hearsay exceptions. Nevertheless, the nature and trustworthiness of the information relied upon, including its hearsay nature, is important in determining the admissibility of the report.

In order to meet the requirements of the exception, the statement must constitute the conclusion of a governmental agency as opposed to mere accumulation of information, and it must not be merely an interim or preliminary document.

Restrictions on use by prosecution in criminal cases. As submitted by the Supreme Court and enacted by the Congress, clause (C) of the Federal Rule prohibits the use of investigative reports as evidence against the accused in a criminal case. The limitation was included because of "the almost certain collision with confrontation rights which would result" from using investigative reports against accused.[3]

As transmitted by the Supreme Court to the Congress, clause (B) simply provided for including in the pubic records and reports exception "matters observed pursuant to duty imposed by law." In the course of debate on the floor of the House, concern was expressed that the provision might allow the introduction against the accused of a police officer's report without producing the officer as a witness subject to cross-examination. Accordingly, the provision was amended by adding the italicized words to read "(B) matters observed pursuant to duty imposed by law *as to which matters there was a duty to report, excluding, however, in criminal cases matters observed by police officers and other law enforcement personnel.*" It was enacted as so amended.

The amendment raises a number of questions of varying importance. (1) Can the accused in a criminal case use a report falling under (B)? Clearly the criminal defendant can use an investigative report which falls under (C). However, the language of (B) appears to prohibit the admission of all records of matters observed in criminal cases, which would exclude use by both prosecution or defense if read literally. This meaning is quite evidently not what the Congress had in mind, and the cases have construed the provision to permit the defendant to introduce police reports under clause (B). (2) Who are "other law enforcement personnel"? In its broadest form, this term has been construed to include "any officer or employee of a governmental agency which has law enforcement responsibilities."[4] In specific, "law enforcement personnel" has been held to include a Customs Service chemist analyzing the seized substance in a narcotics case, border inspectors, and I.R.S. agents, but not a city building inspector or judge. This second inquiry has, however, become somewhat less important as the courts have developed the exceptions examined below for routine or nonadversarial governmental records and for circumstances where the declarant testifies at trial. (3) Does the limitation of clause (B) apply to routine records? The courts have consistently answered that Congress did not intend to exclude observations characterized as "objective" and "nonadversarial" even though these observations are incorporated into law enforcement reports.

(4) Can the limitation of (B) and also that of (C) be avoided by resorting to some other hearsay exception? This question arises when the statement satisfies the requirements of some other hearsay exception that does not prohibit the use of police records and reports or investigative reports against the accused. For example, police reports can often meet the exception for recorded past recollection, and laboratory tests of materials have often been admitted as business records. Neither of these hearsay exceptions contains any limitation like those of Rule 803(8)(B) & (C).

The case first considering this issue answered with an unequivocal and uncompromising

---

3. Adv.Comm. Note, Fed.R.Evid. 803(8)(C).

4. United States v. Oates, 560 F.2d 45, 68 (2d Cir. 1977).

"no." It concluded that Congress meant to exclude law enforcement and investigative reports against defendants in criminal cases whatever route around the hearsay rule was chosen.[5] Further consideration by other courts, however, has led to a most substantial modification: the limitations of (B) and (C) will not be extended to other hearsay exceptions if the maker is produced in court as a witness and subject to cross-examination, since the essential purpose of Congress was to avoid admission of evidence not subject to cross-examination. Similar analysis indicates that this limitation is inapplicable to proof of the absence of an entry in a governmental record.

§ 297. The Exception for Public Records and Reports: (c) Vital Statistics

If the requirement that the out-of-court declarant must have an official duty to make the report were strictly enforced, such matters as a clergyman's return upon a marriage license indicating that the ceremony had been conducted and the report of an attending physician as to the fact and date of birth or death would not be admissible. Consequently this requirement has been relaxed with regard to matters involving various general statistics. Where the report was made to a public agency by one with a professional, although not necessarily an "official," duty to make the report, such as a minister or a physician, the courts have generally admitted the record to prove the truth of the reporter's statement. An alternative approach is to regard the maker of the report as acting as an official for purposes of making the report. However, the mere fact that a report is required by law is not sufficient to convert it into a public report. The person making the report—a motorist, for example, completing a required accident report—can scarcely be regarded as acting in a temporary official capacity or under a professional duty.

The law concerning records of vital statistics is largely statutory, and states generally have legislation on the subject. Federal Rule

803(9) provides a hearsay exception for the following:

> Records or data compilations, in any form, of births, fetal deaths, deaths, or marriages, if the report thereof was made to a public office pursuant to requirements of law.

While the rule looks largely to local law to determine the duty to make the report and for its content, it should not be regarded as borrowing and incorporating the local law as to admissibility. The federal rule governs on that issue.

As to routine matters, such as place and date of birth or death and "immediate" cause of death, such as drowning or gunshot wound, admissibility is seldom questioned. However, entries in death certificates as to the "remote" cause of death, such as suicide, accident, or homicide, usually are made on the basis of information obtained from other persons and predictably involve the questions that have been raised with regard to investigative reports generally, and courts have divided on admissibility. When conclusions of this type are involved, the provisions of Rule 803(8), which is equally applicable and involves a much more careful treatment of the issues, should be applied. Thus, the restrictions on using police and investigative reports against accused persons contained in Federal Rule 803(8)(B) & (C) should be applied to this aspect of records of vital statistics. Similar tests for the admissibility of investigative reports under Federal Rule 803(8)(C), such as the broad scope of investigative reports and analysis of the expertise of the preparer, should prevail.

§ 298. The Exception for Public Records and Reports: (d) Judgments in Previous Cases, Especially Criminal Convictions Offered in Subsequent Civil Cases

Insofar as reports of official investigations are admissible under the official written statement exception, it would seem that the judgment of a court, made after the full investigation of a trial, would also be admissible in subsequent litigation to prove the truth of those things necessarily determined in the

---

5. Id. at 78.

first action. Guilty pleas and statements made in the course of litigation may constitute declarations against interest [1] or admissions of a party-opponent [2] and under those exceptions avoid the bar of the hearsay rule. Where the doctrines of res judicata, collateral estoppel, or claim or issue preclusion make the determinations in the first case binding in the second, not only is the judgment in the first case admissible in the second, but, as a matter of substantive law, it is conclusive against the party. If neither res judicata nor collateral estoppel applies, however, the courts have traditionally been unwilling to admit judgments in previous cases. The judgments have been regarded as hearsay and not within any exception to the hearsay rule.

A variety of reasons have been advanced for this rule. Civil cases often involve numerous issues, and it may be difficult to determine what issues a judgment in fact determined. This, however, argues only for a requirement that one offering a judgment establish as a prerequisite for its admissibility that it did in fact determine an issue relevant to the instant litigation. It is also argued that the party against whom the judgment is offered may not have had an opportunity to be present and to participate in the first action. This misses the point, however, as the appropriate question in deciding whether the hearsay should be admitted in this context is not the party's opportunity to have been present at the official investigation, but rather whether that investigation provided adequate assurance of reliability. In many cases, the party will in fact have been present and have had not only an opportunity but a strong motive to defend.

The argument against admissibility does have merit with regard to judgments offered against a criminal defendant when that judgment was rendered against another. Admitting such judgments violates the defendant's constitutional right of confrontation. Admitting civil judgments rendered against the defendant directly raises constitutional issues as well. Other arguments against admissibility

of prior judgments relate to the danger of undue prejudice and the need for orderly administration of trials. Also juries may have difficulty grasping the distinction between a prior judgment offered as evidence and one that is conclusive, giving the judgment binding effect even if this is contrary to substantive law. Finally, it is argued that, if prior judgments are admissible, parties offering them will tend to rely heavily upon them and not introduce significant amounts of other evidence. The result feared is that the evidence available in the second case will be inadequate for a reliable decision.

These arguments have caused many courts to exclude a prior civil judgment offered in a subsequent civil case. There is, however, a growing tendency to admit a prior conviction for a serious criminal offense in a subsequent civil action. In these situations, the party against whom the judgment is offered was generally the defendant in the criminal case and therefore had not only the opportunity but also the motive to defend fully. In addition, because of the heavy burden of proof in criminal cases, a judgment in such a situation represents significantly more reliable evidence than a judgment in a civil case. The tendency is most noticeable when the judgment is offered in a subsequent civil case in which the convicted defendant seeks affirmatively to benefit from his criminal offense— for example, a convicted arsonist sues to recover upon his fire insurance policy. The strong desire to prevent this result undoubtedly influenced courts to permit the introduction of the judgment of conviction, and some courts also held that the judgment was conclusive proof that the party committed the relevant acts with the state of mind required for criminal liability.

It was but a short step from this position to the general admissibility of a prior criminal conviction in a civil action against the party who was previously the criminal defendant. A number of courts limited this rule to convictions for serious offenses, reasoning that

§ 298

1. See infra Ch. 33.

2. See supra Ch. 25. As to guilty pleas, see especially supra § 257.

convictions for misdemeanors do not represent sufficiently reliable determinations to justify dispensing with the hearsay objections. Judgments of acquittal, however, are still inadmissible in large part because they may not present a determination of innocence, but rather only a decision that the prosecution has not met its burden of proof beyond a reasonable doubt.

Federal Rule 803(22) incorporates these general developments. It provides a hearsay exception for the following:

> Evidence of a final judgment, entered after a trial or upon a plea of guilty (but not upon a plea of nolo contendere), adjudging a person guilty of a crime punishable by death or imprisonment in excess of one year, to prove any fact essential to sustain the judgment, but not including, when offered by the Government in a criminal prosecution for purposes other than impeachment, judgments against persons other than the accused. The pendency of an appeal may be shown but does not affect admissibility.

The following characteristics of the exception should be noted: (1) Only criminal judgments of conviction are included. Judgments in civil cases are not included, their effect being left to the law of res judicata or preclusion. (2) Only crimes of felony grade, i.e., punishable by death or imprisonment for more than one year, are included, thus eliminating problems associated with convictions of lesser crimes. (3) The rule does not apply to judgments of acquittal. (4) When offered by the government in criminal prosecutions, judgments of conviction of persons other than the accused are admissible only for purposes of impeachment. When the judgment of conviction is offered in a civil case, however, it is treated as are investigative reports generally, and there is no restriction as to the parties against whom the evidence is admissible. (5) Judgments entered on pleas of nolo contendere are not included within the exception.[3] (6) The provision merely excludes a qualifying

judgment from the bar of the hearsay rule. It does not purport to dictate the use to be made of the judgment once it is admitted in evidence. Applicable rules of res judicata or preclusion will be given effect. Otherwise the evidence may be used "substantively" or for impeachment, as may be appropriate.

§ 299. The Exception for Official Certificates: (a) In General

For purposes of the law of evidence, a certificate is a written statement issued to an applicant by an official that recites certain matters of fact. It is not a part of the public records of the issuing office, although a common form of certificate is a statement that a document to which it is attached is a correct copy of such a record.[1] The common law was strict about admitting certificates as hearsay exceptions, for the most part requiring statutory authority.

The relation between certification and a public record may be illustrated by proof of marriage. If the celebrant of a marriage issues a certificate that he or she has performed the marriage and gives it to the parties, this document is not a public record, and admission in evidence must be under some other hearsay exception. If, however, the celebrant makes a "return" of the license, i.e., a redelivery to the issuing official with an endorsement of the manner in which the authority was exercised, then the return becomes a part of the public record, admissible under that hearsay exception.

Federal Rule 803(12) provides a certification procedure with respect to marriage and similar ceremonies:

> Statements of fact contained in a certificate that the maker performed a marriage or other ceremony or administered a sacrament, made by a clergyman, public official, or other person authorized by the rules or practices of a religious organization or by law to perform the

---

3. See supra § 257.

§ 299

1. Certification of copies of public records receives further treatment in infra § 300.

act certified, and purporting to have been issued at the time of the act or within a reasonable time thereafter.

Certification is also provided for a large variety of matters by statutes, with corresponding provisions for admissibility in evidence. These statutes are continued in effect under Federal Rule 802.

§ 300. The Exception for Official Certificates: (b) Certified Copies or Summaries of Official Records; Absence of Record

When a purported copy of a public record is presented in court accompanied by a certificate that the purported copy is correct, a two-layered hearsay problem is presented. First, is the public record within the hearsay exception for that kind of record? Second, is the certificate within the hearsay exception for official certificates? The first question has been considered in the earlier sections of this chapter. The second question involves a specialized application of the certification procedure discussed generally in the immediately preceding section.

The early common law generally required a statutory duty to certify. The Supreme Court of the United States, however, long ago rejected this position with respect to certification of copies of public records, and the American common law rule remains that a custodian has, by virtue of the office, the implied duty and authority to certify the accuracy of a copy of a public record in the custodian's official possession. Present-day usual practice is to prove public records by copy certified to be correct by the custodian, and many statutes so provide. Federal Rule 1005 allows proof of public records by copy, without producing or accounting for the original,[1] and Rule 902(4) provides for authentication by certificate as follows:

A copy of an official record or report or entry therein, or of a document authorized by law to be recorded or filed and actually recorded or filed in a public office, including

data compilations in any form, certified as correct by the custodian or other person authorized to make the certification, by certificate complying with paragraph (1), (2), or (3) of this rule or complying with any Act of Congress or rule prescribed by the Supreme Court pursuant to statutory authority.

In the absence of a statute to the contrary, the usual view has been that the authority to certify copies of public records is construed literally as requiring a copy and does not include paraphrases or summaries. Thus a certificate saying "our records show X" is not admissible to prove X.

By analogy to the rule that nonoccurrence of an event may be proved by a business record containing no entry of the event where the practice was to record such events,[2] proof of nonoccurrence may be made by absence of an entry in a public record where such matters are recorded. However, absence of the entry or record could at common law be proved only by testimony of the custodian. This limitation has been modified by many statutes, and Federal Rule 803(10) provides the following:

To prove the absence of a record, report, statement, or data compilation, in any form, or the nonoccurrence or nonexistence of a matter of which a record, report, statement, or data compilation, in any form, was regularly made and preserved by a public office or agency, evidence in the form of a certification in accordance with rule 902, or testimony, that diligent search failed to disclose the record, report, statement, or data compilation, or entry.

The rule is phrased to include not only proving nonoccurrence of an event of which a record would have been made, but also the nonfiling of a document allowed or required by law to be filed. The courts have insisted that the requirement of a "diligent search" must be satisfied but have not required that a specific form of words be used to meet that requirement.

§ 300

1. See supra § 240.

2. See supra § 287.

Chapter 31

TESTIMONY TAKEN AT A FORMER HEARING OR IN ANOTHER ACTION

Table of Sections

§ 301. Introduction; Is It Hearsay? Scope of Statutes and Rules

Upon compliance with requirements designed to guarantee an adequate opportunity for cross-examination and after showing that the witness is unavailable, testimony given previously may be received in the pending case in the form of a written transcript or an oral report of that testimony. This testimony may have been given during a deposition or at a trial. It may have been received in a separate proceeding or in an earlier hearing of the present case.

Depending upon the precise formulation of the rule against hearsay, this evidence, which is usually called "former testimony," may be classified as an exception to the hearsay prohibition, or it may be considered as nonhearsay under the theory that the requirements of the hearsay concept have been met. The former view is accepted generally today; the latter was espoused by Wigmore.[1] In this treatise, former testimony is classified as a hearsay exception under the general definition of hearsay developed earlier which defines hearsay as including all prior testimony that is offered for its truth.[2]

§ 301
1. 5 Wigmore, Evidence § 1370 (Chadbourn rev. 1974).

2. See supra § 246.

Cross-examination, oath, the solemnity of the occasion, and, in the case of transcribed testimony, the accuracy of reproduction of the words spoken all combine to give former testimony a high degree of credibility. Accordingly, to allow its use only upon a showing of unavailability may seem to relegate "former testimony" to an undeserved second-class status. The result is, however, explained by the strong preference to have available witnesses testify in open court.

Many of the exceptions to the hearsay rule have been developed almost solely through the judicial process while others have been widely regulated by statute. The present exception is of the latter class, which had important implications for interpreting the exception prior to the recent trend for most American jurisdictions to adopt general evidence codes.

In many instances the predecessor statutes have been replaced by rules that are identical to, or modeled upon, the Federal Rule 804(b)(1), which provides:

> (b) **Hearsay exceptions.** The following are not excluded by the hearsay rule if the declarant is unavailable as a witness:
>
> > (1) **Former testimony.** Testimony given as a witness at another hearing of the same or a different proceeding, or in a deposition taken in compliance with law in the course of the same or another proceeding, if the party against whom the testimony is now offered, or, in a civil action or proceeding, a predecessor in interest, had an opportunity and similar motive to develop the testimony by direct, cross, or redirect examination.

It is important to notice at the outset that former testimony may often be admitted without meeting the requirements discussed in this chapter, such as opportunity and motive to cross-examine and the unavailability of the witness. These requirements are applicable only when the evidence is offered under this particular exception. When the former testimony is offered for some nonhearsay pur-

pose—to show the commission of the act of perjury, to show that testimony against the accused furnished the motive for the murder of the witness, to refresh recollection, or to impeach a witness at the present trial by proving that earlier testimony was inconsistent—the restrictions of the hearsay exception do not apply. Likewise, if offered for a hearsay purpose but under some other exception, e.g., as the admission of a party-opponent or past recollection recorded, only the requirements of that other exception, and not those of the former testimony exception, must be satisfied.

§ 302. The Requirement of Oath and Opportunity for Cross–Examination; Confrontation and Unavailability

To be admitted under this exception to the hearsay rule, former testimony must have been given under the sanction of an oath or affirmation. More important, and more often drawn into question, is the requirement that the party against whom the former testimony is now offered, or perhaps a party in like interest, must have had a reasonable opportunity to cross-examine.[1]

Actual cross-examination is not required if the opportunity was afforded and waived. Whether cross-examination was conducted or waived, admissibility under this exception is not judged by the use made of the opportunity to cross-examine but rather the availability of the opportunity. This point is amply demonstrated in cases holding that the opportunity to cross-examine at a preliminary hearing in a criminal case provides sufficient opportunity even though few litigants, for a number of reasons, fully exercise that opportunity. However, circumstances may differ sufficiently between the prior hearing and the present trial to bar admission under this requirement, as where questions on a particular subject would have been largely irrelevant at the earlier proceeding. Moreover, as discussed in later sections, the opportunity to cross-exam-

---

§ 302

1. For consideration of when a party is "in like interest," see infra § 303.

ine must have been such as to render the cross-examination actually conducted or the decision not to cross-examine meaningful in the light of the circumstances prevailing when the former testimony was given.[2]

If a right to counsel exists when the former testimony is offered, a denial of counsel when the testimony was taken renders it inadmissible. However, a general finding of ineffective representation at the prior hearing does not automatically require rejection of the testimony; the adequacy of the cross-examination under the facts must be determined. Improper judicial interference may render the opportunity to cross-examine inadequate. However, restrictions upon cross-examination do not have this consequence unless very substantial, some courts holding that they must render the testimony inherently unreliable.

Is the opportunity for direct and redirect examination the equivalent of the opportunity for cross-examination? If a party calls and examines a witness and this testimony is offered against that same party in a subsequent trial, may the direct testimony be admitted over the objection that there was no opportunity to cross-examine? The decisions sensibly hold that it may.

If evidence is offered under the former testimony exception to the hearsay rule, it is offered as a substitute for testimony given in person in open court, and the strong policy favoring personal presence requires that unavailability of the witness be shown before the substitute is acceptable. If the witness is present in court and is available for cross-examination, his or her former testimony may be admitted under some circumstances as a prior statement of a witness.[3] Thus, exclusion of prior testimony for reasons relating to availability will generally occur only when the witness is absent from court but does not meet the unavailability definition used under either the Federal Rules or the

Confrontation Clause. The definition of unavailability under the hearsay rule and problems of confrontation, which are common to a number of hearsay exceptions, are discussed elsewhere.[4] By contrast, if the former testimony is used as a prior inconsistent statement for impeachment or as an admission of a party-opponent, unavailability is not required.[5]

§ 303. Identity of Parties; "Predecessor in Interest"

The haste and pressure of trials cause lawyers and judges to speak in catchwords or shorthand phrases to describe evidence rules. Thus "identity of parties" is often spoken of as a requirement for the admission of former testimony. It is a convenient phrase to indicate a situation where the underlying requirement of adequacy of the present opponent's opportunity for cross-examination would usually be satisfied. But as a *requirement*, identity of parties (or, for that matter, identity of issues [1]) is hardly a useful generalization. It both obscures the true purpose of the requirement and must be hedged with too many qualifications to be helpful.

Historically, courts recognized a number of situations where identity of parties has not been required. It is clear, for example, that if the two present adversary parties, both the proponent and opponent of the evidence, were parties in the former proceedings where the testimony was taken, the presence of additional parties in either or both proceedings is immaterial. A second more important inroad upon strict identity of parties results from the recognition, developed under Wigmore's guidance,[2] that it is only the party *against* whom the former testimony is now offered whose presence as a party in the previous suit is significant. Older decisions that insisted on "reciprocity" or "mutuality," requiring that the party *offering* the former testimony in the

---

2. See infra § 304.

3. See supra § 251.

4. See supra §§ 252, 253.

5. See supra § 37 (prior inconsistent statements) and § 254 (admissions).

§ 303

1. See infra § 304.

2. 5 Wigmore, Evidence § 1388, at 111 (Chadbourn rev. 1974).

present suit must also have been a party in the prior proceeding, are without any supporting basis and are now historical relics.

Furthermore, if the party against whom the former testimony is now offered, though not a party to the former suit, actually cross-examined the witness (personally or by counsel) about the relevant matters or was accorded a fair opportunity for such cross-examination and had a like motive for such examination, then the former testimony may be received. Finally, identity of parties is not required as to a party against whom prior testimony is offered when that party is a successor in interest to the corresponding party in the former suit. This notion, to which the label "privity" is attached, is considered to offer adequate protection to the party-opponent.

The next step in this progression away from the formalistic requirement of identity of parties would be to treat neither identity of parties nor privity as requirements, but merely as means to an end. Under this view, if a party in the former suit who had a motive similar to the present party to cross-examine about the subject of the testimony and was accorded an adequate opportunity for such examination, the testimony could be received against the present party. Identity of interest in the sense of motive, rather than technical identity of cause of action or title, would satisfy the test. Under this perspective, the argument that it is unfair to force upon a party another's cross-examination or decision not to cross-examine loses its validity with the realization that other hearsay exceptions involve no cross-examination whatsoever and that the choice is not between perfect and imperfect conditions for the giving of testimony but between imperfect conditions and no testimony at all.

The impact of the enactment of Federal Rule 804(b)(1) in this area remains uncertain. As sent to Congress by the Supreme Court, the prior testimony exception would clearly have taken that next step described above. It would have admitted prior testimony if the party against whom that testimony is now offered, or a party "with similar motive and interest," had an opportunity to examine the witness. The House Judiciary Committee, however, objected to this formulation on the ground that "it is generally unfair to impose upon the party against whom the hearsay evidence is being offered responsibility for the manner in which the witness was previously handled by another party." [3] Accordingly, it substituted a requirement that "the party against whom the testimony is now offered, or in a civil action or proceeding a *predecessor in interest*, had an opportunity and similar motive" to examine the witness, [4] and this version of the rule was enacted.

While the impact of this congressional modification is cloudy in civil litigation, at least one point is clear when the testimony is offered against a criminal defendant: the defendant must have been a party to the former proceeding. The rule as enacted eliminates doubts under the Confrontation Clause raised by the Court's version, which would have allowed examination by a substitute. However, by its literal terms the rule insists on identity of prosecution also, which would appear to bar a defendant in a federal prosecution from introducing exculpatory testimony from a related state case given by an unavailable witness. Exclusion of such evidence implicates due process considerations, and quite likely was not intended by Congress.

For civil cases this unfortunately oblique legislative history is more troubling, providing no definitive meaning for the term "predecessor in interest." As enacted, the rule requires that there have been opportunity to examine the witness by the party against whom now offered or by a "predecessor in interest" with similar motive. The explanation offered by the report of the House Committee is only modestly helpful. After asserting the general unfairness of requiring a party to accept another's examination of a witness, quoted above, the report

---

3. House Comm. on Judiciary, H.R.Rep. No. 650, 93d Cong., 1st Sess. 15 (1973) reprinted in 1974 U.S.Code Cong. & Admin.News 7075, 7088.

4. Id. (emphasis added).

stated, "The sole exception to this, in the Committee's view, is when a party's predecessor in interest in a civil action or proceeding had an opportunity and similar motive to examine the witness. The committee amended the Rule to reflect these policy determinations." [5] Presumably in adding the language regarding a predecessor in interest, the House Committee meant to make some change. The Senate Committee, however, characterized the difference between the version transmitted by the Supreme Court and that developed by the House Committee as "not great," [6] and the Conference Committee remained silent on this point.

This state of legislative history has left little concrete guidance in determining congressional intent. Having taken the view in the 1978 Pocket Part that privity was required between the parties to satisfy the "predecessor in interest" requirement and the view in the 1984 Third Edition that the intention was to leave the Supreme Court version intact in civil cases, it is perhaps appropriate that this treatise now take an intermediate position. That, indeed, appears to be the proper course of action.

Recent scholarship has shed some new light on this issue, revealing that the House Subcommittee that drafted this modification intended it to require a "formal relationship" between the parties. How much weight to give such obscure indications of legislative intent is itself uncertain, particularly since even the Senate Judiciary Committee did not appear to understand the significance of the modification, which suggests no figurative Congressional meeting of the minds. Nevertheless, it is difficult to ignore entirely the addition of the predecessor in interest language by the House Committee and to construe the provision to mean precisely what it did prior to that change. Thus, those courts that have read the language to mean no more

than the general requirement that the prior party have a similar interest appear to have misconstrued the provision. On the other hand, construing the actions of Congress to require a strict privity approach, while not unreasonable, appears too rigid.

Courts construing the "predecessor in interest" language have taken several discrete approaches, which appear consistent with the murky intent of Congress. One interesting approach is the so-called community of interest analysis. This approach requires some connection—some shared interest, albeit far less than a formal relationship—that helps to insure adequacy of cross-examination. A second approach appears consistent with congressional concerns about fairness and is even more broadly applicable than the community of interest analysis. This approach requires the courts to insure fairness directly by seriously considering whether the prior cross-examination can be fairly held against the later party. The testimony can be excluded if the objecting party shows that the cross-examination was inadequate by, for example, setting out the additional questions or lines of inquiry that he or she would have pursued. The opportunity to challenge the adequacy of the prior cross-examination directly, while ostensibly available in all situations, is not applied with rigor where there is no change in the identity of the party between the different proceedings.[7] The suggested interpretation accomplishes all that we know for certain was intended by the published legislative history—an interpretation of the term predecessor in interest that makes it fair to hold the present party responsible for the actions of another.

§ 304. Identity of Issues; Motive to Cross–Examine

Questions of identity of the issues involved in the former and present proceedings often

5. House Comm. on Judiciary, H.R.Rep. No. 650, 93d Cong., 1st Sess. 15 (1973), reprinted in 1974 U.S.Code Cong. & Admin.News 7075, 7088.

6. Senate Comm. on Judiciary, S.Rep. No. 1277, 93d Cong., 2d Sess. 28 (1974), reprinted in 1974 U.S.Code Cong. & Admin.News 7051, 7074.

7. See infra § 304 regarding, for instance, preliminary hearings.

arise in association with questions about identity of parties. This is to be expected because any supposed requirement of identity of issues is, like the rule about parties,[1] merely a means of fulfilling the policy of securing an adequate opportunity and sufficient motive for cross-examination.

While occasionally stated as a requirement that the issue in the two suits must be the same, the policy underlying this exception does not require that all the issues (any more than all the parties) in the two proceedings must be the same. At most, the issue on which the testimony was offered in the first suit must be the same as the issue upon which it is offered in the second. Additional issues or differences with regard to issues upon which the former testimony is not offered are of no consequence. Moreover, insistence upon precise identity of issues, which might have some appropriateness if the question were one of res judicata or estoppel by judgment, is out of place with respect to former testimony where the question is not of binding anyone, but merely of salvaging, for what it may be worth, the testimony of an unavailable witness. Accordingly, even before the enactment of the Federal Rules, the trend was to demand only "substantial" identity of issues.

It follows that neither the form of the proceeding, the theory of the case, nor the nature of the relief sought needs be the same between the proceedings. Though scattered cases have in the past imposed requirements of this sort, such formalism is not warranted by a policy of insuring adequacy of opportunity and motive for cross-examination, and such a wooden approach has been rejected by the body of caselaw. Thus, in criminal cases where the first indictment charges one offense (robbery), and the second another distinct offense (murder of the person robbed), it is usually considered sufficient that the two indictments arise from the same transaction.

The requirement has become, not a mechanical one of identity or even of substantial identity of issues, but rather that the issues in the first proceeding, and hence the purpose

for which the testimony was offered, must have been such that the present opponent (or some person in like interest) had an adequate motive for testing on cross-examination the credibility of the testimony. How this requirement has been worked out in practice gives definition to the general rule.

One important pattern involves introducing at the trial of a criminal case testimony given at the preliminary hearing, or analogously, in a civil case introducing testimony given at a discovery deposition. In another frequently encountered situation, testimony given against the accused in an earlier criminal trial is offered against the same accused in a civil case to which the criminal defendant is a party. Prior testimony is generally ruled admissible in all of these situations.

Courts do not require that the party at the earlier proceeding actually have conducted a full cross-examination of the witness. The cases emphatically hold that judgments to limit or waive cross-examination at the earlier proceeding based on tactics or strategy, even though these judgments were apparently appropriate when made, do not undermine admissibility. Instead, the courts look to the operative issue in the earlier proceeding, and if basically similar and if the opportunity to cross-examine was available, the prior testimony is admitted. However, at some extreme point, differences in the nature of the proceeding, the stakes involved, and even factual details with regard to the same core issue will result in exclusion of the prior testimony.

§ 305. The Character of the Tribunal and of the Proceedings in Which the Former Testimony Was Taken

If the accepted requirements of the administration of the oath, adequate opportunity to cross-examine on substantially the same issue, and present unavailability of the witness, are satisfied, then character of the tribunal and the form of the proceedings are immaterial, and the former testimony should be received. Accordingly, when these conditions are met, testimony taken before arbitrators, or before a committing magistrate at a pre-

§ 304

1. See supra § 303.

liminary hearing, or in a sworn examination before the comptroller by the corporation counsel of a person asserting a claim against a city, or at a driver's license revocation hearing, or at a broker's license revocation hearing, or at a Coast Guard hearing, or a hearing on motion to suppress, or a bankruptcy proceeding has been held admissible. For lack in the particular proceeding of some of these requisites, testimony given in the course of a coroner's inquest or a legislative committee hearing has been excluded. Also, exclusion in particular situations may be mandated by statute.

Some courts have held that, if the court in the former proceeding lacked jurisdiction of the subject matter, the former testimony is inadmissible, but others have concluded that the fact that it may ultimately be held that the court is without power to grant the relief sought does not deprive the court of power to compel attendance of witnesses and to administer oaths, and accordingly the former testimony was held admissible. The question should not be one of regularity but of reliability. A glaring usurpation of judicial power would call for a different ruling, but where the first court has substantial grounds for believing that it has authority to entertain the proceeding, and the party called upon to cross-examine should consider that the existence of jurisdiction is reasonably arguable, it seems that the guaranties of reliability are present. The question should be viewed, not as one of limits of jurisdiction, but whether the sworn statement of a presently unavailable witness was made under such circumstances of opportunity and motive for cross-examination as to make it sufficiently trustworthy to be received in evidence. In like vein, no significance attaches to the circumstance that the earlier trial resulted in a mistrial or a hung jury.

§ 306. Objections and Their Determination

May objections to the former testimony, or parts thereof, which could have been asserted when it was first given, be made for the first time when offered at the present trial? There are sweeping statements in some opinions that this may always be done and in others that it is never allowable. The more widely approved view, however, is that objections which go merely to the form of the testimony—as on the ground of leading questions, unresponsiveness, or opinion—must be made at the original hearing when they can be corrected. On the other hand, objections that go to the relevancy or the competency of the evidence may be asserted for the first time when the former testimony is offered at the present trial.

Whether the former testimony meets the requirements of the present exception to the hearsay rule may depend on a question of fact. For example, is the witness unavailable? This and other preliminary questions of fact are treated elsewhere.[1] Likewise, impeachment of witnesses whose former testimony is introduced is considered under the topic of impeaching hearsay declarants generally.[2]

§ 307. Methods and Scope of Proof

When only a portion of the former testimony of a witness is introduced by the proponent, the result may be a distorted and inaccurate impression. Hence the adversary is entitled to the introduction of such other parts as fairness requires and to have them introduced at that time rather than waiting until the presentation of his or her own case. The adversary is permitted, however, to choose to wait.

In proving the former testimony at least four theories of admissibility may be employed.

1. Any firsthand observer of the giving of the former testimony may testify to its purport from *unaided memory*. This and the next method were used much more frequently before court stenographers became commonplace. To qualify, the reporting witness need

1. See supra § 53.

2. See supra § 37; infra § 324.2.

not profess to be able to give the exact words of the former witness but must satisfy the court that he or she is able to give the substance of all that the former witness has said, both on direct and cross-examination, about the subject matter relevant to the present suit. By the more convenient practice, the proponent need not prove all of the former testimony relevant to the present case but only such as desired, leaving to the adversary to call for such of the remaining part as desired.

2. A firsthand observer may testify to the purport of the former testimony by using a memorandum, such as the judge's, counsel's, or stenographer's notes, or the stenographer's transcript, to *refresh the present memory* of the witness.[1]

3. In most states the magistrate's report of the testimony at a preliminary criminal hearing and the official stenographer's transcribed notes of the testimony at the trial of a case, civil or criminal, are admitted, when properly authenticated, as evidence of the fact and purport of the former testimony, either by statute or under the hearsay exception for *official written statements.*[2] There is generally no rule of preference for these reports, however, and any observer, including the stenographer, may be called to prove the former testimony without producing the official report or transcript.

4. A witness who has made written notes or memoranda of the testimony at the time of the former trial, or while the facts were fresh in his or her recollection, and who will testify that he or she knows that they are correct, may use the notes as memoranda of *past recollection recorded.*[3]

§ 308. Possibilities of Improving Existing Practice

This treatise has long argued that hearsay admitted under the former testimony excep-

tion should be admitted regardless of the availability or unavailability of the declarant because few exceptions measure up in terms of the reliability of statements under former testimony. However, given the Supreme Court's recent analysis of the Confrontation Clause that treats former testimony as perhaps uniquely inferior hearsay and requires for that reason a showing of unavailability,[1] this proposed change has no real prospects of being accepted when the prior testimony is offered against the criminal defendant.

In spite of the Supreme Court's characterization of prior testimony as weaker form of live testimony, it remains incongruous to accord second-class status to former testimony. The anomaly is apparent when prior testimony is compared to hearsay exceptions that possess generally inferior guarantees of trustworthiness, such as declarations of present bodily or mental state, or excited or spontaneous utterances, where no showing of unavailability is required. The fears that the proponent of prior testimony would routinely resort to the use of such testimony when witnesses are available appears overblown, and when the witness is available, the opponent is able to conduct meaningful cross-examination under Rule 806 even if the declarant is not called on direct examination.[2]

Improvement would be gained from a procedure under which prior testimony is admitted in civil cases after giving the opposing party notice of intent to offer the testimony, thus affording an opportunity to produce the witness in person if desired and if the witness is available. In fact, in civil cases the matter might well be left to the ordinary processes of discovery, with no formal notice procedure at all.

A second area where reform regarding the admissibility of prior testimony should be con-

---

§ 307

1. As to refreshing recollection generally, see supra § 9.

2. For the requirements of this exception, see supra Ch. 30.

3. For the requirements of this theory of admissibility, see supra §§ 279–283.

§ 308

1. United States v. Inadi, 475 U.S. 387, 394 (1986).

2. See infra § 324.2.

sidered concerns the application the predecessor in interest concept. Under Federal Rule 804(b)(1), prior testimony is admissible in civil cases "if the party against whom the testimony is now offered or * * * a predecessor in interest, had an opportunity and similar motive to develop the testimony." A very substantial issue is raised by the meaning of predecessor in interest and in particular whether the concept applies to situations where there is absolutely no economic or legal relationship between the parties.[3]

This problem in defining a predecessor in interest might be avoided if the courts recognized explicitly that the dimensions of the opportunity and motive to cross-examine may differ between the situation where the party itself was involved in the previous litigation and one where an unrelated party conducted

the cross-examination. In the former situation, as exemplified by the use of preliminary hearing testimony against criminal defendants at trial, parties have been, and should be, held responsible for previous strategic or tactical judgments and just plain poor lawyering. By contrast, in the situation where the parties are unconnected, the quality of the cross-examination should be scrutinized much more carefully. Even if opportunity and motive for cross-examination are fully adequate, the costs of poor lawyering should not be imposed on a separate party. Once courts become willing to examine directly and meaningfully the adequacy of the testing of the prior testimony, then issues about what constitutes a predecessor in interest will become much less important.

---

3. See supra § 303.

Chapter 32

DYING DECLARATIONS

Table of Sections

§ 309. Introduction

Of the doctrines that authorize the admission of special classes of out-of-court statements as exceptions to the hearsay rule, the doctrine relating to dying declarations is the most mystical in its theory and traditionally the most arbitrary in its limitations. The notion of the special likelihood of truthfulness of deathbed statements was, of course, widespread long before the recognition of a general rule against hearsay in the early seventeen hundreds. It is natural enough, then, that about as soon as we find a hearsay rule we also find a recognized exception for dying declarations.

§ 310. Requirements That Declarant Must Have Been Conscious of Impending Death and That Declarant Must Be Dead or Otherwise Unavailable

The central notions of the popular reverence for deathbed statements are embodied in two important limitations upon the dying declaration exception as evolved at common law. Unlike several other limitations, which will be discussed in the next section, these two were arguably rational, although they drew the lines of restriction too sharply.

The first of these two limitations was that the declarant must have been conscious that death was near and certain when making the statement. The declarant must have lost all hope of recovery. A belief in the mere probability of impending death would arguably make most people strongly disposed to tell the truth and hence guarantee the needed special reliability. But belief in the certainty of impending death, not its mere likelihood or probability, is the formula that was rigorously required. Perhaps this limitation reflected some lack of confidence in the reliability of "deathbed" statements generally.

The description of the declarant's mental state in the Federal Rules is less emphatic than in the common law cases, merely saying "while believing that declarant's death was imminent." Evidence that would satisfy the common law would clearly satisfy the rule, and a growing number of courts are recognizing that a lesser showing will suffice.

Often this belief in the imminence of death is proved by evidence of the declarant's own statements of belief at the time—an expression of a "settled hopeless expectation." That the deceased should have made such a statement is not required, however. Such belief may be shown circumstantially by the apparent fatal quality of the wound, by the statements made to the declarant by the doctor or by others that his or her condition is hopeless, and by other circumstances. These preliminary questions of fact are to be determined by the court.[1]

The second historical limitation related to the popular reverence for deathbed statements was that the declarant must be dead when the evidence is offered. However, the Federal Rules do not generally contain any requirement that the declarant must be dead. Rather, they require that the declarant must be unavailable, which of course includes death as well as other situations.[2] Since the declarant need not die from his or her wounds or injuries, it is clear that the length of time between a statement and death is not dispositive of the statement's admissibility under the exception, and even under the earlier formulations it was not required that the death must have followed at any very short interval after the declaration. The critical issue throughout is the declarant's belief in the nearness of death at the time the statement is made, not the actual swiftness with which death ensues after the statement or the immediacy of the statement after the injury.

§ 311. Limitation to the Use in Criminal Homicide Cases, and Other Arbitrary Limitations

If the courts in their creation of rules about dying declarations had stopped with the limitations discussed above, the result would have had a narrow, but rational and understandable, exception. The requirement of consciousness of impending death arguably tends to guarantee a sufficient degree of special reliability, and the requirement that the declarant must have died and thus be unavailable as a witness provides an ample showing of the necessity for the use of hearsay. This simple rationale of dying declarations sufficed until the beginning of the 1800's, and these declarations were admitted in civil and criminal cases without distinction and seemingly without untoward results. The subsequent history of the rule is an object lesson in the use of precedents to preserve and fossilize the judicial mistakes of an earlier generation.

The first error occurred in limiting admissibility to homicide prosecutions. Sergeant East, in his widely used treatise of 1803, Pleas of the Crown, wrote:

> Besides the usual evidence of guilt in general cases of felony, there is one kind of evidence more peculiar to the case of homicide, which is the declaration of the deceased, after the mortal blow, as to the fact itself, and the party by whom it is committed. Evidence of this sort is admissible in this case on the fullest necessity; for it often happens that there is no third person present to be an eye-witness to the fact; and the usual witness on occasion of other felonies, namely, the party injured himself, is gotten rid of.[1]

This statement was seized upon for a purpose obviously not intended, namely, an announcement that the sole justification of the

---

§ 310

1. See generally supra § 53.
2. Unavailability is discussed in supra § 253.

§ 311

1. East, 1 Pleas of the Crown 353 (1803).

admission of dying declarations is the necessity of punishing murderers who might otherwise escape for lack of the testimony of the victim. This need may exist, but the proposition that the use of dying declarations should be limited to instances where it exists surely does not follow. Nevertheless, this proposition was further developed into a series of largely arbitrary limiting rules.

The first of these was the rule that the use of dying declarations was limited to cases of criminal homicide. Although the English courts in the 1700's had not done so, nearly all courts, building upon the theory of necessity, refused to admit dying declarations in civil cases, whether death actions or other civil cases, or in criminal cases other than those charging homicide as an essential part of the offense. Thus, in prosecutions for rape, for example, the declarations were held inadmissible even though death of the victim may have ensued. Probably this restriction proceeded from a feeling on the part of judges that dying declarations both rest on a somewhat questionable guarantee of trustworthiness and constitute a dangerous kind of testimony, which a jury is likely to handle too emotionally. However, these dangers are not likely to be less serious in a murder prosecution, where the statements are admitted, than they are in a civil action for wrongful death or in a prosecution for rape, where they are excluded.

As promulgated by the Supreme Court, the Federal Rule contained no limitation as to type of case in which dying declarations were admissible. However, led by the House Judiciary Committee, Congress amended the exception. As enacted, the exception is limited to prosecutions for homicide and civil actions or proceedings. Thus, under the Federal Rule, dying declarations are admissible in all cases except nonhomicide criminal cases.

The concept of necessity, limited to protection of the state against the slayer who might go free because of the death of his victim, produced another consequence. This was the

further limitation that not only must the charge be homicide, but the defendant in the present trial must have been charged with the death of the declarant. In a case in which a marauder shot a man and his wife at the same time and the defendant was put on trial for the murder of the husband only, the dying declaration of the wife identifying the defendant as the assailant was offered by the state. It was excluded under this doctrine. Wigmore's comment is: "Could one's imagination devise a more senseless rule of exclusion, if he had not found it in our law?"[2] No such limitation appears in the Federal Rule.

Less arbitrary, but a source of controversy, is the third of these corollary limitations, i.e., that the declarations are admissible only insofar as they relate to the circumstances of the killing and to the events more or less nearly preceding it in time and leading up to it. Under this version, declarations about previous quarrels between the accused and the victim would be excluded, while transactions between them leading up to and shortly before the present attack would be received. Some limitation as to time and circumstances is appropriate, but proper phrasing of the limitation is difficult. Federal Rule 804(b)(2) requires only that the statement be one "concerning the cause or circumstances of what he believed to be his impending death." Within this more liberal framework, decisions may be made in terms of remoteness and prejudice under Rule 403.[3]

Finally, in some jurisdictions, dying declarations are limited with regard to statements elicited by questions of a leading sort. However, no blanket limitation against statements in response to questions is generally recognized or appropriate.

§ 312. Admissible on Behalf of Accused as Well as for Prosecution

One might have anticipated that the historical limitation on admissibility of dying declarations to homicide cases, based on the ex-

---

2. 5 Wigmore, Evidence § 1433, n. 1 (Chadbourn rev. 1974).

3. See supra § 185.

treme necessity in those cases of admitting the statements of the decedent *and* the sense of rough justice that admitting such statements against the murderer was only fair, might have led the courts to restrict the use of dying declarations to introduction by the prosecution. However, the unfairness of such a result was too apparent, and it has long been established that they will be received on behalf of the defendant as well.

§ 313. Application of Other Evidentiary Rules: Personal Knowledge; Opinion; Rules About Writings

Other principles of evidence law present recurrent problems in their application to dying declarations. If it appears that the declarant did not have adequate opportunity to observe the facts recounted, the declaration will be rejected for lack of firsthand knowledge. This knowledge requirement has sometimes been confused with the opinion rule, and in some instances this confusion may have led courts to make the statement that opinions in dying declarations will be excluded. Of course the traditional opinion rule, designed as a regulation of the manner of questioning of witnesses in court, is entirely inappropriate as a restriction upon out-of-court declarations.[1] Accordingly, most courts, including some that have professed to apply the opinion rule here, have admitted declarations such as: "He shot me down like a dog," [2] "He shot me without cause," [3] "He done it a-purpose," [4] and the like, which at one time would have been excluded as opinions if spoken by a witness on the stand.

Another problem is the application of the so-called best evidence rule.[5] Often the dying victim will make one or more oral statements about the facts of the crime and, in addition, may make a written statement or the person hearing the statement may write it down and

have the declarant sign it. When must the writing be produced or its absence be explained? As to any separate oral statement, it is clear that this is provable without producing a later writing. It is equally clear that the terms of a written dying statement cannot be proved as such without producing or accounting for the writing.[6] What if the witness who heard the oral statement, which was taken down and signed, offers to testify to what he or she heard? Wigmore argued that the execution of the writing does not call into play the parol evidence rule since that rule is limited to contracts and other "legal acts." [7] To a limited extent the courts have held otherwise. They have not excluded evidence of other oral statements made on the same occasion although not embraced in the writing. However, oral declarations embodied in a writing signed or adopted by the deceased have been held not to be provable by one who heard them, but only by producing the written statement itself where available. Even though it represents a departure from the usual practice of freedom in proving oral statements and an extension of the doctrine of integration into a new field, the result may be justified by the need here for accuracy in transmitting to the tribunal the exact terms of the declarant's statement.

§ 314. Instructions Regarding the Weight to Be Given to Dying Declarations

There has been much theorizing in texts and opinions as to the weight to be given to dying declarations, abstractly or in comparison with the testimony of a witness. In consequence, the practice has grown up in some states of requiring or permitting the judge to instruct the jury that these declarations are to be received with caution or that they are not to be regarded as having the same value and weight as sworn testimony. In other

---

§ 313

1. See supra § 18.
2. State v. Saunders, 14 Or. 300, 12 P. 441 (1886).
3. State v. Williams, 168 N.C. 191, 83 S.E. 714 (1914).
4. Pippin v. Commonwealth, 117 Va. 919, 86 S.E. 152 (1915).

5. See supra Ch. 23.
6. See supra § 233.
7. 5 Wigmore, Evidence § 1450(b) (Chadbourn rev. 1974).

jurisdictions, such instructions have been held to be improper. Others have considered it proper to direct the jury that they should give the dying declaration the same weight as the testimony of a witness.

While there may be merit in a standardized practice of giving cautionary instructions, the direction to give the declaration a predetermined fixed weight seems of questionable wisdom. The weight of particular dying declarations depends upon so many factors varying from case to case that no standardized instruction will fit all situations. Certainly in jurisdictions where the judge retains common law power to comment on the weight of the evidence, the dying declaration is an appropriate subject for individualized comment. But where the judge lacks this power, as in most states, it seems wiser to leave the weight of the declaration to the arguments of counsel, the judgment of the jury, and the consideration of the judge on motion for new trial.

§ 315. Decisional and Statutory Extensions of Common Law Admissibility

In a landmark decision,[1] the Kansas court had before it an action by the executor of the seller to recover on a land sale contract. Should the dying statement of the seller of "the truth about the sale" be admitted? An affirmative answer required departure from traditional common law limitations in two respects: (1) the case was civil, not a criminal homicide prosecution, and (2) the statement was unrelated to the cause or circumstances of death. "We are confronted," the court said, "with a restrictive rule of evidence commendable only for its age, its respectability resting solely upon a habit of judicial recogni-

tion, formed without reason, and continued without justification," and ruled in favor of admissibility.

As observed in earlier sections of this chapter, there has been some willingness to expand admissibility with respect to the type of case, as witnessed by the Revised Uniform Rules (1986), which would admit dying declarations in all cases. The exclusion of such hearsay under the Federal Rules from criminal cases other than prosecutions for homicide because of Congressional concern about the reliability of this form of hearsay seems to strike the wrong balance. Only a sense of very rough justice will admit statements in the most serious types of cases because the murder of the witness threatens to rob the court of valuable testimony but exclude them because of questionable trustworthiness in less serious criminal prosecutions. Under the terms of the Federal Rule, the need for the testimony is frequently just as great in nonhomicide cases because the declarant, while not the victim of murder, must be unavailable to testify. As a result, extension of the exception beyond its current limited scope would appear appropriate.

While the limitation on statements admissible under the exception to the circumstances of the declarant's death was not in the original Uniform Rules, it is a requirement of the Federal Rule, and departure from this limitation is found only in occasional rules and statutes. The restriction is generally sound because the connection between these circumstances and the statement helps to enhance its trustworthiness by reducing the dangers of poor memory and insincerity.

---

§ 315

1. Thurston v. Fritz, 91 Kan. 468, 138 P. 625 (1914).

Chapter 33

DECLARATIONS AGAINST INTEREST

Table of Sections

§ 316. General Requirements; Distinction Between Declarations Against Interest and Admissions

To satisfy the instant exception to the hearsay rule in its traditional form, two main requirements have been imposed: first, either the declaration must state facts that are against the pecuniary or proprietary interest of the declarant or the making of the declaration itself must create evidence that would harm such interests;[1] second, the declarant must be unavailable at the time of trial.[2] Under the theory that people generally do not lightly make statements that are damaging to their interests, the first requirement provides the safeguard of special trustworthiness justifying most of the exceptions to the hearsay rule. The second is largely an historical de-

velopment but operates usefully as a limiting factor. Minor qualifications may be added. The interest involved must not be too indirect or remote. The declarant, as in the case of hearsay exceptions generally, must have had the opportunity to observe the facts.

While sometimes erroneously called an admission against interest, the instant exception and the admission exclusion[3] are distinct. The traditional distinctions developed by Wigmore,[4] are generally followed. Thus, the admissions of a party-opponent may be introduced without satisfying any of the requirements for declarations against interest. First, while frequently admissions are against interest when made, they need not be and may, in fact, have been self-serving.[5] Second, the party making the admission need not be,

---

§ 316

1. See infra §§ 317–319.
2. See infra § 320.
3. See supra Ch. 25.

4. 5 Wigmore, Evidence § 1475 (Chadbourn rev. 1974).
5. See supra § 254; infra § 319.

528

and seldom is, unavailable.[6] Third, the party making the admission need not have had personal knowledge of the fact admitted.[7] Accordingly, when the opponent offers a statement of a party, it should be submitted as, and tested by, the requirements for parties' admissions and not those for declarations against interest. On the other hand, statements of nonparties, which may not be introduced as admissions, may be admitted if they are against interest and if the declarant is unavailable. Moreover, since the Federal Rules appear not to recognize admissions by persons in "privity" with parties,[8] the instant exception provides one of the principal alternative methods for introducing damaging statements made by a party's predecessor.

The Federal Rules preserve the hearsay exception as broadly developed at common law with respect to statements against pecuniary or proprietary interest and, in addition, expand the definition to include statements against penal interest. Rule 804(b)(3) admits statements of unavailable declarants as follows:

> A statement which was at the time of its making so far contrary to the declarant's pecuniary or proprietary interest, or so far tended to subject the declarant to civil or criminal liability, or to render invalid a claim by the declarant against another, that a reasonable person in the declarant's position would not have made the statement unless believing it to be true. A statement tending to expose the declarant to criminal liability and offered to exculpate the accused is not admissible unless corroborating circumstances clearly indicate the trustworthiness of the statement.

§ 317. Declarations Against Pecuniary or Proprietary Interest; Declarations Affecting Claim or Liability for Damages

The traditional field for this exception has been that of declarations against proprietary or pecuniary interest. Common instances of the former are acknowledgments that the declarant does not own certain land or personal property, or has conveyed or transferred it. Moreover, a statement by one in possession that he or she holds an interest less than complete ownership has traditionally been regarded as a declaration against interest, though it is obviously ambiguous, and in England has even been received when offered to establish the existence of the interest claimed by the declarant.

The clearest example of a declaration against pecuniary interest is an acknowledgment that the declarant is indebted. Here the declaration, standing alone, is against interest on the theory that to owe a debt is against one's financial interest. This theory is routinely followed even though it may not be applicable in particular circumstances. Less obviously an acknowledgment of receipt of money in payment of a debt owing to the declarant is also traditionally classed as against interest. Here the fact of payment itself is probably advantageous to the receiver, but the acknowledgment of it is regarded as against interest because it is evidence of the reduction or extinguishment of the debt. Of course, a receipt for money which the receiver is to hold for another is an acknowledgment of a debt. Similarly, a statement that one holds money in trust is against interest.

The development of the exception by English courts narrowly focused it in the areas of debt and property, but the American cases extended the field of declarations against interest to include acknowledgment of facts which would give rise to a liability for unliquidated damages for tort or seemingly for breach of contract. A corresponding extension to embrace statements of facts that would constitute a defense to a claim for damages otherwise available to the declarant has been recognized in this country.

Federal Rule 804(b)(3) is broadly drawn to include statements against pecuniary or proprietary interest in general, and more specifically those tending to subject declarant to civil liability, without being limited to tort or

6. See supra § 254.
7. See supra § 255.

8. See supra § 260.

contract, and those tending to invalidate a claim by the declarant against another. This aspect of the rule thus occupies the entire area developed by the common law except for some of the more fanciful English decisions in tenancy cases.

§ 318. Penal Interest; Interest of Prestige or Self–Esteem

In 1844, in the Sussex Peerage Case,[1] the House of Lords, ignoring precedents, determined that a declaration confessing a crime committed by declarant was not receivable as a declaration against interest. This decision was influential in confining the development of this exception to the hearsay rule within narrow materialistic limits. It was generally followed in this country in criminal cases for many years. Courts, while not repudiating the limitation, have sometimes justified admission of a third person's confession of crime in the civil context on the basis that the particular crime was also a tort and thus the statement was against material interest by exposing the declarant to liability for damages.

Was the practice of excluding third-person confessions in criminal cases justified? It certainly could not be justified on the ground that an acknowledgment of facts rendering one liable to criminal punishment is less trustworthy than an acknowledgment of a debt. The motivation for the exclusion was no doubt a different one, namely, the fear of opening the door to a flood of witnesses testifying falsely to confessions that were never made or testifying truthfully to confessions that were false. This fear was based on the likely criminal character of witness and declarant, reinforced by the requirement that declarant must be unavailable, which made perjury easier to accomplish and more difficult to punish.

Wigmore rejected the argument of the danger of perjury, since that danger is one that

attends all human testimony, and concluded that "any rule which hampers an honest man in exonerating himself is a bad rule, even it if also hampers a villain in falsely passing for an innocent."[2] Under this argument, accepted by Justice Holmes in a famous dissent,[3] courts began to relax the rule of exclusion of declarations against penal interest in particular situations or generally. The inclusion of declarations against penal interest in the Federal Rule 804(b)(3) has given great impetus to the use of this exception, and most of the recent case law and literature dealing with declarations against interest has centered on this aspect and its concomitant problems.

During the course of the expansion of the hearsay exception to include declarations against penal interest, the situation principally examined was whether a confession or other statement by a third person offered by the defense to *exculpate* the accused should be admissible. The traditional distrust of declarations against penal interest had evolved in that setting, and, as a result, the Federal Rule included a prohibition against admitting an exculpatory statement in evidence "unless corroborating circumstances clearly indicate the trustworthiness of the statement." While the possibility was recognized that statements against penal interest by third parties inculpating both the declarant and the defendant might also be offered by the prosecution to *inculpate* the accused, prior to the adoption of the Federal Rules the possibility of their admissibility was raised infrequently in cases or the literature. Under Rule 804(b)(3), admission of such statements has been far more common. As will be seen in the section that follows, exculpatory and inculpatory statement raise some different as well as some similar questions.

Whether the hearsay exception for declarations against interest should be enlarged to include declarations against "social" interests has been the occasion of differences of opin-

---

§ 318

1. 11 Cl. & F. 85, 8 Eng.Rep. 1034 (1844).

2. 5 Wigmore, Evidence § 1477, at 359 (Chadbourn rev. 1974).

3. Donnelly v. United States, 228 U.S. 243, 277–278 (1913) (Holmes, J., dissenting).

ion. Traditionally, interests of this nature were not regarded as sufficiently substantial to ensure reliability. Following the pattern of the original Uniform Rule, the Federal Rule, as promulgated by the Supreme Court, included statements tending to make the declarant "an object of hatred, ridicule, or disgrace," but it was deleted from the rule as enacted by Congress. The provision was reinstated in the Revised Uniform Rule (1986) and has been adopted in a handful of states.

§ 319. Determining What Is Against Interest; Confrontation Problems

(a) *The time aspect.* As observed at the beginning of this chapter, the theory underlying the hearsay exception for declarations against interest is that people do not make statements that are harmful to their interests without substantial reason to believe that the statements are true. Reason indicates that the harm must exist at the time the statement is made; otherwise it can exert no influence on declarant to speak accurately and truthfully. That the statement may at another time prove to be damaging—or, for that matter, beneficial—is without significance. This characteristic of contemporaneity is implicit in the cases, although it is only rarely discussed. Occasionally it is suggested that this requirement is ignored to some extent when the admissibility of contextual statements, discussed below, is involved.

(b) *The nature of the statement.* The statement must be such "that a reasonable person in the declarant's position would not have made the statement unless believing it to be true," in view of the statement's adversity to declarant's interest. As indicated earlier, the traditional declaration against interest was a statement that could be used in evidence in a manner adverse to declarant's pecuniary or proprietary interest. A declaration against penal interest is one that would be admissible against declarant in a criminal prosecution; it need not be a confession, but must involve substantial exposure to criminal liability.

A controversial area has been the so-called "contextual" or related statements. In the seminal case of Higham v. Ridgway,[1] in order to prove the date of birth of an individual, an entry in the record book of a midwife was introduced, showing a charge for attendance upon the mother for birth of a child, together with an entry six months later showing payment of the charge. The entry of payment, said the court, "was in prejudice of the party making it." But, though the entry of payment may have been against interest, the issue in the case was not payment, but the birth six months earlier. To this objection, the court replied, "By the reference to the ledger, the entry there [of the birth] is virtually incorporated in the other entry [of payment], of which it is explanatory." In civil cases, as in Higham v. Ridgway, to admit the critical related statement or part of the statement is acceptable, even though not itself against interest, if it is closely enough connected and neutral as to interest.

Judicial scrutiny in criminal cases may be somewhat more exacting. When a statement both incriminates the declarant and exculpates the accused, complete rejection of related or contextual statements is not required, although a rather tight integration between its two aspects is occasionally suggested. When the statement incriminates both the declarant and the accused and is offered by the prosecution against the accused, some commentators and decisions adopt an even stricter approach under the requirements of the confrontation clause, rejecting any part or related statement not in itself against interest. In general, however, the trend in the federal cases is to admit the entire statement if the two parts are reasonably closely connected.

(c) *The factual setting.* Whether a statement was against interest will often require a delicate examination of the circumstances under which it was made. That determination may depend on outside facts that existed at the time the statement was made but were not disclosed in the statement. For example,

§ 319

1. 10 East 109, 103 Eng.Rep. 717 (K.B.1808).

whether a statement that declarant is a member of a certain partnership is against his or her pecuniary interest depends upon whether the firm is clearly solvent or is on an uncertain economic footing. Likewise, a statement that one has a contract to purchase a commodity, such as wheat, at a certain price is against or for interest depending upon the price in the market at the time the statement was made.

If the factual setting suggests that declarant anticipated no damaging disclosure, is the circumstantial guarantee of trustworthiness present? A relation of trust and confidence between speaker and listener arguably militates against awareness that the making of the statement might be against declarant's interest. The question was raised in the *Sussex Peerage* case, where the statement was to declarant's son, and was answered in the negative. The case has not, however, been followed, and the fact that the statement was made to declarant's daughter, or to a friend and cellmate, or "in the course of a conversation with friends over cards," [2] has not ruled out admissibility. The always-existent possibility of disclosure appears to be enough. In fact, the existence of a friendly relationship is on occasion mentioned as a factor supporting admissibility.

The factual setting in which the statement is made is given particular importance in cases of statements against penal interest inculpating the accused, since admissibility must be measured against standards fixed by the Confrontation Clause of the Sixth Amendment, as well as by the rule of evidence. Particular significance is attached to the fact that the declarant was at the time in the custody of law enforcement authorities, if such was the case, since under these circumstances statements that also implicate the accused may be self-serving. While courts generally do not accord conclusive effect to the fact of custody, great weight is attributed to it. Most courts have imposed an additional factual safeguard upon the use of statements inculpating an accused person under the Confrontation Clause by requiring that they be corroborated. The effect is to read into Federal Evidence Rule 804(b)(3) with regard to inculpatory statements a similar requirement of corroboration that is expressly stated with regard to exculpatory statements.

(d) Motive: Actual state of mind of declarant. In strictest logic, attention in cases of declarations against interest, as with other hearsay exceptions, should focus on the actual state of mind produced in the declarant by the supposed truth-inducing circumstances, and a "reasonable-person" standard would be irrelevant. That, of course, is not the case: the usual standard is that found in Federal Evidence Rule 804(b)(3), "that a reasonable person in the declarant's position would not have made the statement unless believing it to be true." Difficulties of proof, probabilities, and the unavailability of the declarant all favor the accepted standard. It can scarcely be doubted, however, that statements of declarant disclosing his or her ostensible actual mental state would be received and would control in an appropriate case.

The exception has often been stated as requiring that there have been no motive to falsify. This is too sweeping, and the limitation can probably best be understood merely as a qualification that even though a statement must be against interest in one respect, if it appears that declarant had some motive, whether of self-interest or otherwise, which was likely to lead to misrepresentation of the facts, the statement should be excluded.

§ 320. Unavailability of the Declarant

The Federal Rule and the vast majority of the states require unavailability. While the requirement of unavailability followed its own course of development at common law with respect to declarations against interest, as was the case with other hearsay exceptions requiring unavailability of the declarant, the pattern is now largely standardized. See supra section 253 for discussion in detail of what satisfies the requirement.

2. United States v. Barrett, 539 F.2d 244 (1st Cir. 1976).

Chapter 34

VARIOUS OTHER EXCEPTIONS AND THE FUTURE OF THE RULES ABOUT HEARSAY

Table of Sections

§ 321 Learned Writings, Industry Standards, and Commercial Publications

When offered to prove the truth of matters asserted in them, learned writings, such as treatises, books, and articles regarding specialized areas of knowledge, are clearly hearsay. Nevertheless, Wigmore argued strongly for an exception for such material.[1] According to his view, permitting such sources to be proved directly would not be as great a change as might at first be supposed because much of the testimony of experts consists of information they have obtained from such sources. Also, admitting the sources would greatly improve the quality of information presented to trial courts in litigated cases. Wigmore concluded that there were sufficient assurances of trustworthiness to justify equating a learned treatise with the live testimony of an expert. First, authors of treatises have no bias in any particular case. Second, they are acutely aware that their material will be read and evaluated by others in their field,

§ 321
1. 6 Wigmore, Evidence §§ 1690–1692 (Chadbourn rev. 1976).

533

and accordingly there is strong pressure to be accurate.

Virtually all courts permit some use of learned materials in the cross-examination of an expert witness. Historically, several patterns developed. Most courts permitted use where the expert relied upon the specific material in forming the opinion to which he or she testified during direct examination. Some of these courts extended the rule to situations in which the witness admitted to having relied upon some general authorities although not the particular impeaching material. Other courts required only that the witness acknowledge that the material offered for impeachment was a recognized authority in the field and, on that basis, permitted use of the material in spite of the fact that the witness may not have personally relied upon it. Finally, some courts permitted use of such material to impeach without regard to whether the witness relied upon or acknowledged the authority of the source if either the cross-examiner established, or the court judicially noticed, the general authority of the material.

Traditionally, the material used to impeach was not admissible as substantive evidence received for its truth. Instead, its only impact was upon the witness' competency or the accuracy of the opinions rendered. Under the common law development of the practice, most courts were unwilling to adopt a broad exception to the hearsay rule for treatises and other professional literature. Wigmore suggested a number of arguments in support of this position, although he concluded that none of them justified the refusal to recognize the exception: (a) professional skill and knowledge shift rapidly, so printed material is likely to be out of date; (b) a trier of fact is likely to be confused by being exposed to material designed for the professionally-trained reader; (c) the opportunity to take sections of material out of context creates a danger of unfair use; (d) most matters of expertise are really matters of skill rather than academic knowledge of the sort put in writing and therefore personally-appearing witnesses are likely to

be better sources of evidence than written material. The only arguably meritorious objection according to Wigmore is the basic hearsay objection that the author is not available for cross-examination, but he concluded that this concern is outweighed by the need for the evidence and the other assurances of its accuracy.[2]

The Federal Rules addressed these various issues by creating a hearsay exception for "learned treatises." Federal Rule 803(18) provides:

> To the extent called to the attention of an expert witness upon cross-examination or relied upon by the expert witness in direct examination, statements contained in published treatises, periodicals, or pamphlets on a subject of history, medicine, or other science or art, established as a reliable authority by the testimony or admission of the witness or by other expert testimony or by judicial notice. If admitted, the statements may be read into evidence but may not be received as exhibits.

The rule is broadly worded as to subjects— "history, medicine, or other science or art"— and is sufficient to include standards and manuals published by government agencies and industry or professional organizations. The reliability of the publication must be established as provided in the rule, which has the purpose of demonstrating that it is viewed as trustworthy by professionals in the field. A significant limitation is that the publication must be called to the attention of an expert on cross-examination or relied upon by the expert in direct examination. This provision is designed to ensure that the materials are used only under the sponsorship of an expert who can assist the fact finder and explain how to apply the materials. This policy is furthered by the prohibition against admission as exhibits, which prevents sending the materials to the jury room.

While Rule 803(18) defines a hearsay exception, its requirements have an impact beyond hearsay concepts, in effect setting the general limits on the use of such documents to impeach. At the same time the rule has this

---

2. 6 Wigmore, Evidence § 1690 (Chadbourn rev. 1976).

impact beyond the hearsay area, satisfying its requirements does not automatically guarantee admissibility. Documents that meet the terms of the rule are still excluded if their probative value is outweighed by their prejudicial impact or potential to confuse or mislead.

Courts have developed a somewhat related hearsay exception that includes publications such as reports of market prices, professional directories, city and telephone directories, and mortality and annuity tables used by life insurance companies. The justification for this exception is that the motivation for accuracy is high, and public acceptance depends upon reliability.

Federal Rule 803(17) defines a hearsay exception for such publications, covering "market quotations, tabulations, lists, directories, or other published compilations, generally used and relied upon by the public or by persons in particular occupations." While the precise definition of this exception is somewhat difficult, other than by example, some of its basic characteristics are clear. The list must be published in written form and circulated for use by others; it must be relied upon by the general public or by persons in a particular occupation; and it must pertain to relatively straightforward objective facts.

§ 322. Statements and Reputation as to Pedigree and Family History, Land Boundaries, and General History

A. Statements and Reputation Concerning Pedigree and Family History

One of the oldest exceptions to the hearsay rule encompasses statements concerning family history, such as the date and place of birth and death of members of the family and facts about marriage, descent, and relationship. Under the traditional rule, declarations of the person whose family situation is at issue are admissible, as are declarations by other members of the family. Under a liberal view adopted by some courts, declarations by non-

family members with a close relationship to the family are also admitted. These statements were admissible, however, only upon a showing that the declarant is unavailable, that the statement was made before the origin of the controversy giving rise to the litigation in which the statement is offered (i.e., *ante litem motam*), and that there was no apparent motive for the declarant to misrepresent the facts.

Under the strict traditional view, the relationship of declarant to the family had to be proved by independent evidence, but this requirement did not apply where declarant's own family relationships were the subject of the hearsay statement. Firsthand knowledge by declarant of the facts of birth, death, kinship, or the like was not required. The general difficulty of obtaining other evidence of family matters, reflected in the unavailability requirement, furnished impetus for the hearsay exception. Reliability was assured by the probability that, in the absence of any motive for lying, discussions with relatives (and others intimately associated) regarding family members would be accurate.

Federal Rule of Evidence 804(b)(4), continuing the requirement of unavailability of the declarant,[1] provides a hearsay exception for statements of personal or family history:

(A) A statement concerning the declarant's own birth, adoption, marriage, divorce, legitimacy, relationship by blood, adoption, or marriage, ancestry, or other similar fact of personal or family history, even though declarant had no means of acquiring personal knowledge of the matter stated; or (B) a statement concerning the foregoing matters, and death also, of another person, if the declarant was related to the other by blood, adoption, or marriage or was so intimately associated with the other's family as to be likely to have accurate information concerning the matter declared.

The rule follows the liberal view in allowing statements by intimate associates of the family. It eliminates the traditional requirements that the statement have been made *ante litem*

1. As to unavailability, see generally supra § 253.

motam and without motive to misrepresent, leaving these aspects to be treated as questions of weight, or possibly excluded under Rule 403 in extreme cases.[2] The narrow view of what is included in family history is continued.

The traditional hearsay exception went beyond the statements described above and allowed the use of contemporary records of family history, such as entries in a family Bible or on a tombstone, even though the author may not be identifiable. Federal Rule 803(13) follows this pattern in providing a hearsay exception, without regard to availability of the declarant, for the following:

> Statements of fact concerning personal or family history contained in family Bibles, genealogies, charts, engravings on rings, inscriptions on family portraits, engravings on urns, crypts, or tombstones, or the like.

Matters of family history traditionally have also been provable by reputation in the family, or, under some decisions, in the community. The tradition is continued in Federal Rule 803(19), by a hearsay exception for the following:

> Reputation among members of a person's family by blood, adoption, or marriage, or among a person's associates, or in the community, concerning a person's birth, adoption, marriage, divorce, death, legitimacy, relationship by blood, adoption, or marriage, ancestry, or other similar fact of his personal or family history.

Also continuing a traditional exception is the admissibility of judgments as proof of family history under Federal Rule 803(23):

> Judgments as proof of matters of personal family or general history, or boundaries, essential to the judgment, if the same would be provable by evidence of reputation.

B. Reputation Regarding Land Boundaries and General History

When the location of boundaries of land is at issue, reputation is admitted to prove that location. Traditionally, the reputation not only had to antedate the beginning of the present controversy, but also it had to be "ancient," i.e., to extend beyond a generation. Some recent cases suggest that the requirement is only that the monuments or markers of the original survey must have disappeared. Federal Rule 803(20), set forth below, dispenses completely with a requirement that the reputation be ancient or that the passage of time have rendered other evidence of the boundaries unavailable.

Reputation is also admissible to prove a variety of facts which can best be described as matters of general history. Wigmore suggested that the matter must be ancient "or one as to which it would be unlikely that living witnesses could be obtained."[3] Federal Rule 803(20) does not impose that requirement, although by use of the term "history" some requirement of substantial age is imposed. In addition, the matter must be one of general interest, so that it can accurately be said that there is a high probability that the matter underwent general scrutiny as the community reputation was formed. Thus when the navigable nature of a certain river was at issue, newspaper accounts and histories describing the use made of it during the nineteenth century were admissible to prove its general reputation for navigability at that time.

Federal Rule 803(20) provides a hearsay exception consistent with the foregoing observations for proof by reputation evidence of boundaries and matters of general history:

> Reputation in a community, arising before the controversy, as to boundaries of or customs affecting lands in the community, and reputation as to events of general history important to the community or State or nation in which located.

In addition to these well-developed exceptions, reputation evidence is sometimes admitted under statute or local law to prove a variety of other miscellaneous matters, such as ownership of property, financial standing, and maintenance of a house as an establishment for liquor-selling or prostitution.

---

2. See supra § 185.

3. 5 Wigmore, Evidence § 1597 (Chadbourn rev. 1974).

§ 323. Recitals in Ancient Writings and Documents Affecting an Interest in Property

As observed in a preceding section,[1] a writing has usually been regarded as sufficiently authenticated if the offering party proves that it is at least thirty years old, the trial judge finds that it is unsuspicious in appearance, and the party proves that it was produced from a place of custody natural for such a writing. This "ancient documents" rule, however, traditionally has related only to authentication. Nevertheless, American courts sometimes recognized a hearsay exception for statements in a writing which met these requirements. Thus, what originated as an aspect of authentication also became, in some jurisdictions, an exception to the hearsay rule.

The primary stimulus for such a hearsay exception is found in the same reasons which gave rise to the special authentication rule: necessity. After passage of a long period of time, witnesses are unlikely to be available or, if available, to recall reliably the events at issue. As to assurances of trustworthiness, the mere age of the writing, it may be contended, offers little assurance of truth; it is unlikely that lying was less common twenty or thirty years ago.

Advocates of the exception argue, however, that sufficient assurances of reliability exist. First, the dangers of mistransmission are minimized since the rule applies only to written statements. Second, the age requirement virtually assures that the assertion will have been made long before the beginning of the present controversy. Consequently, it is unlikely that the declarant had a motive to falsify, and, in any case, the statements are almost certainly uninfluenced by partisanship. Finally, some additional assurance of reliability is provided by insistence, insofar as practicable, that the usual qualifications for witnesses and out-of-court declarants be met. As a result, the writing is inadmissible if the declarant lacked the opportunity for firsthand observation of the facts asserted.[2]

Well before the drafting of the Federal Rules, a number of courts accepted a hearsay exception for recitals in an ancient deed. Thus, recitals of the contents and execution of an earlier instrument, of heirship, and of consideration are nearly everywhere received to prove those facts. Arguably these cases involve unusual assurances of reliability, especially where possession has been taken under the deed, and the rule should be limited to them. However, a number of courts applied the exception to other types of documents.

Federal Rule 803(16) contains a broadly worded hearsay exception for statements in ancient documents: "Statements in a document in existence twenty years or more the authenticity of which is established." While the rule itself contains no limitation as to the kind of document that may qualify, as long as it is at least twenty years old and properly authenticated,[3] several limitations are imposed that provide additional assurance of trustworthiness. The declarant under this rule is subject to the general requirement of firsthand knowledge, and the document must not be suspicious with regard to its genuineness and reliability.

A related hearsay exception is recognized by Federal Rule 803(15):

> A statement contained in a document purporting to establish or affect an interest in property if the matter stated was relevant to the purpose of the document, unless dealings with the property since the document was made have been inconsistent with the truth of the statement or the purport of the document.

This exception has no requirement of age of the document, but it is limited to title documents, such as deeds, and to statements relevant to the purpose of the document. The circumstances under which documents of this nature are executed, the character of the statements that will qualify, and the inapplicability of this exception if subsequent deal-

---

§ 323

1. See supra § 223.

2. See supra §§ 10, 247.

3. See supra § 233.

ings have been inconsistent with the truth of the statement or the purport of the document, are considered sufficient guarantees of trustworthiness. A companion rule deals with the evidentiary status of recording such documents.

§ 324. The Residual Hearsay Exceptions

Despite the extensive array of specific hearsay exceptions in the Federal Rules, the Advisory Committee felt that "[i]t would * * * be presumptuous to assume that all possible desirable exceptions to the hearsay rule have been catalogued and to pass the hearsay rule to oncoming generations as a closed system." Therefore the Committee proposed for both available and unavailable declarants admission of "statement[s] not specifically covered by any of the forgoing exceptions but having comparable circumstantial guarantees of trustworthiness." As a precaution against excessive resort to these provisions as a means of effectively destroying the hearsay rule, the Advisory Committee observed, "They do not contemplate an unfettered exercise of judicial discretion, but they do provide for treating new and presently unanticipated situations which demonstrate a trustworthiness within the spirit of the specifically stated exceptions." [1]

While the rules were under consideration in the Congress, the House Judiciary Committee deleted the provisions in their entirety: too much uncertainty was injected into the law of evidence; any additional hearsay exceptions should be created by amending the rules. The Senate Committee did not agree with this extreme position but suggested further restrictions to be incorporated. The differences were compromised, and, as enacted, Federal Rule 803(24) provides a hearsay exception for the following:

A statement not specifically covered by any of the foregoing exceptions but having equivalent circumstantial guarantees of trustworthiness, if the court determines that (A) the statement is offered as evidence of a material fact; (B) the statement is more probative on the point for which it is offered than any other evidence which the proponent can procure through reasonable efforts; and (C) the general purposes of these rules and the interests of justice will best be served by admission of the statement into evidence. However, a statement may not be admitted under this exception unless the proponent of it makes known to the adverse party sufficiently in advance of the trial or hearing to provide the adverse party with a fair opportunity to prepare to meet it, the proponent's intention to offer the statement and the particulars of it, including the name and address of the declarant.

Rule 804(b)(5) differs only in requiring the unavailability of the declarant.

The rules contain five requirements, three of which impose substantial limitations on the admission of hearsay. They are considered below.

Equivalent circumstantial guarantees of trustworthiness In applying the residual exceptions, the most important issue is whether the statement before the court offers "equivalent circumstantial guarantees of trustworthiness" to those offered by the various other specific hearsay exceptions. In making the admissibility determination, courts frequently employ the technique of comparing the circumstances surrounding the statement at issue to the closest hearsay exception. Courts also focus on particular factors suggesting trustworthiness of those statements. However, since the specific exceptions themselves vary widely in the degree of trustworthiness possessed by each, a rather substantial variation in the types of statements admitted under the residual exceptions could properly be anticipated and has eventuated. Indeed, because the factors supporting and undermining trustworthiness are so varied and can occur in so many combinations, providing useful categorization is difficult. However, as the volume of decided cases increases, certain recurring factors are acquiring recognition as

---

§ 324

1. Adv.Comm.Note, Fed.R.Evid. 803(24).

significant to the determination of admissibility under the residual exception.

Among these factors are: whether the declarant had a motivation to speak truthfully or otherwise, whether the statement was under oath, the duration of the time lapse between event and statement, whether the declarant had firsthand knowledge, and other factors going to the declarant's credibility. These are factors that bear upon the declarant at the time of making the statement, as is characteristic of the specific hearsay exceptions generally, and fairly fall within the description "equivalent circumstantial guarantees of trustworthiness."

In addition, the courts have recognized further facts which did not bear upon declarant at the time he or she was speaking, but which, viewed in retrospect, tend to support the truthfulness of the statement. The most important of these has been corroboration. Courts utilizing this factor have examined whether the other evidence in the case supports the truth of the declaration. The recent opinion of the United States Supreme Court in Idaho v. Wright appears, however, to restrict the analysis of trustworthiness to the circumstances surrounding the making of the statement and to exclude any consideration of corroboration by external facts establishing the accuracy of the statement.[2] Another important factor is whether the declarant is available for cross-examination. A number of courts have used the availability of the declarant as a basis to admit testimony that would not otherwise be admissible. Other courts have ascribed precisely the opposite effect to this factor, ruling that the presence of the declarant renders the hearsay statement inadmissible because superior alternative evidence exists through the live testimony of the declarant.

Other miscellaneous factors have also been employed from time to time by the courts pertaining to both the circumstances of making the statement and to subsequent events. These include whether the statement was spontaneous and/or produced in response to leading questions, whether the declarant was subject to cross-examination at the time the statement was made, and whether the declarant has recanted or reaffirmed the statement.

Relative "Necessity" A second factor given varying significance by the opinions is the requirement that the statement must be "more probative on the point for which it is offered than any other evidence the proponent can procure through reasonable efforts." Many courts interpret this as a general necessity requirement. However, it does not mean that the hearsay evidence must be essential. Indeed, some courts view the requirement as providing a basis for a trial court to evaluate the need for the statement in the case as compared to the costs of obtaining alternative evidence. Others view it as imposing a requirement of diligence.

Notice Another substantial requirement of the rule is that notice be given sufficiently in advance of trial to enable the adverse party to prepare to meet the hearsay evidence. While occasionally strict compliance with this requirement is enforced, courts generally have been willing to dispense with notice if the need for the hearsay arises on the eve of, or during, trial when possible injustice is avoided by the offer of a continuance or other circumstances.

Other requirements The remaining requirements lettered (A) and (C) in the rules, have had no appreciable impact upon the application of the residual exception. Provision (A), requiring that the statement be offered as evidence of a material fact, is a restatement of the general requirement that evidence must be relevant. Requirement (C), that the general purposes of the rules and the interests of justice will be served by admitting the evidence, in effect restates Rule 102.

In restoring the residual exception after the House deleted it, the Senate Judiciary Committee stated that it intended that the residual exceptions should be used "very rarely, and

---

2. 110 S.Ct. 3139, 3149 (1990) (quoting 5 Wigmore, Evidence § 1420, at 251 (Chadbourn rev. 1974)).

only in exceptional circumstances." [3] Nevertheless, use of the exceptions has been substantial. Courts have employed the exceptions most extensively in admitting statements made by child witnesses, particularly in sexual abuse cases. The courts admitting such statements under these exceptions have emphasized factors such as the spontaneity and consistency of the statement, the general proposition that young children do not invent allegations of the type involved, and the unusualness of explicit sexual knowledge by a young child. Statements tend to be excluded in cases where a court finds that they are not spontaneous or that the child has a source for sexual knowledge outside of the offense, or it disagrees with the premise that young children are generally more trustworthy than adult declarants.

§ 324.1 Hearsay Within Hearsay; Multiple Hearsay

"On principle it scarcely seems open to doubt that the hearsay rule should not call for exclusion of a hearsay statement which includes a further hearsay statement when both conform to the requirements of a hearsay exception." The common law followed this reasoning, and it is incorporated into Federal Rule 805:

> Hearsay included within hearsay is not excluded under the hearsay rule if each part of the combined statements confirms with an exception to the hearsay rule provided in these rules.

In the usual situation, two stages of inquiry are involved. First, does the primary statement qualify under a hearsay exception? If so, the hearsay rule allows its use to prove that the included statement was made, which may end the inquiry. Ordinarily, however, the included statement will be offered to prove the truth of the facts that it asserts. In that event, the second stage of inquiry is required: Does the included statement also qualify under a hearsay exception? If the

answer again is in the affirmative, the requirements of Rule 805 are met. However, if the included statement is inadmissible, the rule is not satisfied, and the statements are excluded.

Police reports of accident investigations frequently provide examples of multiple hearsay, with admissibility depending upon the nature of the secondary statement. The primary statement—the written report of the officer—is admissible as a business or public record. Statements of individuals made to the officer either qualify under various exceptions, such as excited utterances or dying declarations, or they fail to meet any additional exception and must be excluded as violating the rule. The rule is not satisfied, for example, when a police officer testifies that A stated that B confessed to the crime. Although B's confession to A—the included statement—is against penal interest, A's statement to the police officer—the primary statement—meets no hearsay exception.

An oft-recurring version of multiple hearsay involves a primary hearsay exception in the form of a regularly kept business record which includes a further hearsay statement. If both the primary and the included statements are by persons acting in the routine of the business, then both are admitted under the regularly kept records exception, and no further exception need be invoked. However, if the person whose statement is included is not acting in the routine of the business, resort must be had to a further exception.

It might be argued that, even if the included statement met some other hearsay exception, the primary statement could not qualify under a hearsay exception because the regularly kept records exception requires that the informant must be produced in the routine of the business. The courts, however, have not so held. They have imposed, however, the requirement that the recorder must have a business duty to record the information provided by the outsider.

---

3. Senate Comm. on Judiciary, S.Rep. No. 1277, 93d Cong., 2d Sess. 18–20 (1974), reprinted in 1974 U.S.Code Cong. & Admin.News 7051, 7065–66.

Such a requirement will lead to a different result depending upon the nature of the business involved. For instance, a hospital intake worker has a business-related interest in a narrower and different type of information when talking to an assault victim about the circumstances surrounding the injury than a police officer. The statement that the victim was shot by a person of a particular race would not be material to treatment and not admissible through the business records exception when made to a hospital employee even if the included statement met another hearsay exception. By contrast, the same statement would be highly relevant to the "business" of the police officer in locating the assailant, and accordingly the primary statement would be admissible as a public or business record.

At common law, one of the hearsay statements might consist of an admission, which was regarded as a hearsay exception. Since admissions are not classed as hearsay under the Federal Rules, the question arises whether an admission may qualify as a hearsay exception for purposes of the multiple hearsay rule. One answer has been that admissions are within the spirit and purpose of the rule. An easier answer may be that only one level of hearsay exists since an admission is not hearsay under the Federal Rules, and if the other statement satisfies an exception, no further hearsay difficulty remains. Similar arguments may be made concerning other out-of-court statements treated as not constituting hearsay by Federal Rule 801(d)(1).

§ 324.2 Impeachment of Hearsay Declarant

When a hearsay statement is introduced, often the declarant does not testify. It is, however, ultimately the declarant's credibility that determines the value that should be accorded to the statement. How should that credibility be attacked or, where appropriate, supported?

Federal Rule 806 provides:

When a hearsay statement, or a statement defined in Rule 801(d)(2), (C), (D), or (E), has been admitted in evidence, the credibility of the declarant may be attacked, and if attacked may be supported, by any evidence which would be admissible for those purposes if declarant had testified as a witness. Evidence of a statement or conduct by the declarant at any time, inconsistent with the declarant's hearsay statement, is not subject to any requirement that the declarant may have been afforded an opportunity to deny or explain. If the party against whom a hearsay statement has been admitted calls the declarant as a witness, the party is entitled to examine the declarant on the statement as if under cross-examination.

The rule treats the hearsay declarant as effectively a witness for impeachment purposes.

The rule covers both statements admitted under hearsay exceptions and admissions, but it does not apply to statements that are non-hearsay and not admitted for their truth.

The declarant may be impeached by any of the standard methods of attacking credibility, including prior convictions, inconsistent statements, bias or interest, and character for untruthfulness. With regard to impeachment by prior inconsistent statements, the rule eliminates the requirement otherwise applicable to statements made by witnesses who testify in person [1] that an opportunity be afforded for them to explain or deny the inconsistency.

The rule also provides that, if the hearsay declarant takes the stand to testify, the party seeking to impeach the declarant is entitled to examine on the statement "as if under cross-examination." This provision clearly permits the use of leading questions. Moreover, when the statement is admitted against a criminal defendant, the accused can invoke the compulsory process clause to require assistance in securing the declarant's presence.

§ 324.3 Basis for Expert Opinion as a Quasi–Hearsay Exception

Under Federal Rule 703, an expert may base an opinion on facts or data that are not

§ 324.2

1. See generally supra § 37.

"admissible in evidence" if of a type reasonably relied upon by experts in the field. The expert should as a general matter be allowed to disclose to the trier of fact the basis for his or her opinion, because otherwise the opinion is left unsupported with little way for the jury to evaluate its correctness. The result is often that the expert may testify to evidence even though it is inadmissible under the hearsay rule. However, this does not mean that the expert becomes the sole judge of the admissibility of the basis facts. The facts must still be of a type reasonably relied upon by experts in the field, and they are subject to such general evidentiary principles as exclusion for prejudice or irrelevancy.[1]

Subject to these restrictions, the expert may testify to the basis of his or her opinion, and accordingly that supporting information is to some degree in evidence. What, however, is the status of the evidence thus admitted? The Third Edition of this treatise took the position that such evidence should be received for its truth because the trustworthiness of the evidence was assured by the requirements of Rule 703 that the evidence must be of a type reasonably relied upon by the expert.

That position is now believed to be in error. Such statements are admissible for the limited purpose of informing the jury of the basis of the expert's opinion. In most situations, the difference between limited admissibility and admission for the truth of the statement will make no difference; indeed, it is probably unrealistic to believe that the jurors will be able or willing to follow limiting instructions. However, limiting instructions are appropriate when requested, and where such evidence is the only substantial evidence on a critical issue—such as the identity of the assailant in a child sexual abuse case—this theoretical distinction will prove decisive.

§ 325. Evaluation of the Present Rules

In his treatise on evidence in 1842, Professor Greenleaf wrote:

The student will not fail to observe the symmetry and beauty of this branch of the law * * * and will rise from the study of its principles convinced, with Lord Erskine, that "they are founded in the charities of religion,—in the philosophy of nature,—in the truths of history,—and in the experience of common life.[1]

Few today would apply this evaluation to the rule against hearsay developed in the common law tradition, and probably more would agree with the description of Professors Morgan and Maguire approximately a century later that the exceptions appear like "an old-fashioned crazy quilt made of patches cut from a group of paintings by cubists, futurists and surrealists."[2]

It is hard to quarrel with the common law's insistence upon a high quality of evidence for judicial fact-finding. However, the hearsay rules appear not to have yielded a quality fully commensurate with the high price they have exacted. As the above quotation by Morgan and Maguire suggests, the chief criticisms are that the rules are too complex and that in reality they fail to achieve their purpose of screening good evidence from bad.

First, with respect to the complexity of the rule against hearsay and its exceptions, the number of exceptions naturally depends upon the minuteness of the classification. The Federal Rules contain thirty-one exceptions and exclusions. Wigmore requires over a thousand pages to cover hearsay, and its treatment occupies one quarter of the original edition of the present work.

Most of the complication, of course, arises in connection with the exceptions, leading readily to the conclusion that a general rule so riddled with exceptions is "farcical." The conclusion may be too facile. Probably less than ten, and possibly no more than a half-dozen, of the exceptions are encountered with any frequency in the trial of cases. To require mastery of these, plus an awareness of the others and a working knowledge of what is and is not hearsay, should not unduly tax

---

§ 324.3

1. See generally supra § 185.

§ 325

1. Greenleaf, Evidence § 584 (1st ed. 1842).

2. Morgan & Maguire, Looking Backward and Forward at Evidence, 50 Harv.L.Rev. 909, 921 (1937).

the intellectual resources of the legal profession.

The second complaint—that the rule against hearsay and its exceptions fail to screen reliable from unreliable hearsay on a realistic basis—is of more serious proportion. The trustworthiness of hearsay statements ranges from the highest reliability to almost utter worthlessness. It includes: history books, newspapers, business records, official records and certificates, affidavits, letters and other written statements, simple oral hearsay, multiple hearsay, reputation, and gossip or rumors.

Whether these almost infinitely varying, plastic situations can ever be completely and satisfactorily treated by a set of rules may well be doubted. Yet similar doubts pervade most other areas of the law and are not generally regarded as cause for despair. If the heart of the problem is that the exceptions are unacceptable in detail, a perusal of the preceding chapters dealing with hearsay indicates that much has been done in recent years to rationalize the rules and to improve their practical workability, albeit more along evolutionary than revolutionary lines. But if the basic difficulty is simply that no hearsay system based on classes of exceptions can truly succeed, a totally different approach would be required.

§ 326. Basic Shifts in the Contemporary Pattern

Wholesale efforts to reformulate the traditional common law hearsay pattern have been for the most part legislative in nature rather than judicial, and some of the more notable legislative efforts are discussed below.

Pursuant to a suggestion from Thayer, the Massachusetts Hearsay Statute of 1898 was enacted as follows: "A declaration of a deceased person shall not be inadmissible in evidence as hearsay if the Court finds that it was made in good faith before the commencement of the action and upon the personal knowledge of the declarant." After a quarter century of experience under the act, a questionnaire was addressed to the lawyers and judges of the state regarding its merits. The vast majority of those responding thought that its effects were positive. The American Bar Association in 1938 recommended a liberalized version of the act for adoption by the states.

The English Evidence Act of 1938 allowed the introduction of written statements, made on the personal knowledge of the maker or in the regular course of business, if the maker was called as a witness or was unavailable. Even though the maker was neither called nor unavailable, the judge might admit the statement if satisfied that undue delay or expense would otherwise be involved. Statements made by interested persons when proceedings were pending or instituted were excluded from the act. It applied only in civil cases.

These limitations were relaxed and new ones added in 1968. Under the act, hearsay statements, whether written or oral, are admissible to the extent that testimony of the declarant would be admissible, regardless of whether he or she is called as a witness, though prior statements are not ordinarily admissible at the request of the proponent if the declarant is called. Notice is required of intent to offer a hearsay statement under the act, and the opposite party has the right to require production of declarant as a witness, if available. The act is far more complex than the foregoing summary would indicate. Like its predecessor of 1938 and the Massachusetts statute, it applies only in civil cases. Efforts to reform in any substantial way the English law of evidence in criminal cases have not succeeded.

The drafters of the Model Code of Evidence of the American Law Institute took a bold course about hearsay. They drafted a sweeping new exception to the hearsay rule as follows:

> Evidence of a hearsay declaration is admissible if the judge finds that the declarant
>
> (a) is unavailable as a witness, or
>
> (b) is present and subject to cross-examination.

This rule, however, was qualified and safeguarded by other rules which (1) limited its application to declarations by persons with personal knowledge and excluded hearsay upon hearsay, and (2) empowered the trial judge to exclude such hearsay whenever its probative value was outweighed by the likelihood of waste of time, prejudice, confusion, or unfair surprise. The traditional exceptions, in addition to the new sweeping one, were generally retained. The liberalizing of the use of hearsay was a chief ground of opposition to the Model Code in professional discussion and no doubt substantially accounted for the failure of the code to be adopted in any jurisdiction.

Nevertheless, the controversy over the Model Code awakened a new interest in the improvement of evidence law. Accordingly, the Commissioners on Uniform State Laws, in cooperation with the American Law Institute and building on the foundation of the Model Code, drafted and adopted a more modestly reformative code, the Uniform Rules of Evidence. The American Bar Association approved this action.

Instead of admitting virtually all firsthand hearsay of an unavailable declarant, the original Uniform Rules, like the Model Code rule quoted above, substituted a hearsay exception for statements by unavailable declarants describing a matter recently perceived and made in good faith prior to the commencement of the action. A similar provision is found in Rule 804(b)(5) of the Revised Uniform Rules, but its counterpart was dropped from the Federal Rules by the Congress. As to prior statements by witnesses present at the hearing, the original Uniform Rules adopted substantially the broad provisions of the Model Code rule quoted above, but the Revised Uniform Rules (1986) follow the much narrower congressional version of the Federal Rule of Evidence 801(d)(1).[1] The original Uniform Rules, like the Model Code, retained and liberalized the other traditional exceptions.

§ 326

1. See supra § 251.

The Advisory Committee on the Federal Rules of Evidence approached its task with awareness of the criticisms that had been leveled against the common law system of class exceptions to the hearsay rule. It also was aware that the Model Code's lack of acceptance was largely the result of having exceeded the profession's willingness to accept a fundamentally altered approach to hearsay that permitted broad admissibility of prior statements of unavailable declarants.

In its first draft circulated for comment, the committee endeavored to rationalize the hearsay exceptions in general terms, while at the same time maintaining continuity with the past. For these ends, two rules were included, one covering situations where it made no difference whether the declarant was available and the other applying only when the declarant was unavailable. The first of these rules opened with the following general provision:

> A statement is not excluded by the hearsay rule if its nature and the special circumstances under which it was made offer assurances of accuracy not likely to be enhanced by calling the declarant as a witness, even though he is available.

This general provision was followed by twenty-three illustrative applications derived from common law exceptions, which were not to be considered an exclusive listing. The second of the rules again opened with a general provision:

> A statement is not excluded by the hearsay rule if its nature and the special circumstances under which it was made offer strong assurances of accuracy and the declarant is unavailable as a witness.

It was also followed by a list, albeit a shorter one, of illustrative applications derived from the common law with again a caution that the enumeration not be considered exclusive.

While the response indicated a willingness to accept a substantial revision in the area of hearsay, the legal community opted for a larger measure of predictability than the proposal was thought to offer. As a result, the two general provisions quoted above were withdrawn, and the two rules were revised by converting the illustrations into exceptions in the common law tradition, with the addition of two residual exceptions to take care of unforeseen situations that might arise. Many of the exceptions were clarified and revised to take advantage of the common law experience and to conform with present-day thinking. In this form, the rules, with some alterations, were enacted into law by the Congress as Rules 803 and 804. In addition, rules modeled on the Federal Rules are now in effect in over thirty states, with local changes of varying significance. The pattern of a general rule excluding hearsay, subject to numerous exceptions, has shown substantial resilience.

§ 327. The Future of Hearsay

This book and scores of others on the law of evidence are testimony that this area of the law of evidence can and does change. For example, in the general field of protecting triers of fact against false testimony, there has been a virtually complete shift from treating interest as a ground for exclusion to regarding it as bearing on weight and credibility.[1] Is a similarly dramatic shift in store for hearsay?

Regardless of whether the hearsay rule was as a matter of history the child of the jury system,[2] clearly the concern for controlling the use of hearsay is more pronounced in jury cases than in nonjury cases. In part, this attitude may be a product of the close association between the right to a jury and the right of confrontation in criminal cases. The English developments in the direction of relaxing limitations on hearsay in civil cases were apparently inspired by the virtual disappearance there of jury trials in such cases. Corresponding changes have not transpired with respect to criminal cases where the jury remains.

In the United States, the constitutional rights of confrontation and jury trial combine to make unlikely any wholesale opening of the gates to hearsay in criminal cases or, for that matter, radical changes in the traditional hearsay exceptions. One may, however, reasonably assume that the civil jury will continue to decline somewhat in importance. As noted in an earlier section,[3] courts exhibit a somewhat more relaxed attitude in administering the exclusionary rules of evidence in nonjury cases, including the rule against hearsay. An even more relaxed attitude prevails in administrative proceedings.[4] Perhaps no more than an acceleration of this process is involved in the vigorous advocacy by some reformers to eliminate the hearsay rule entirely in nonjury civil cases.

In a somewhat different vein is the suggestion that admissibility of hearsay in civil cases, jury or nonjury, be based upon the judge's ad hoc evaluation of its probative force, with certain procedural safeguards. Obviously a substantially greater measure of discretion by the judge is contemplated, with a corresponding decrease in the impact of precedent and predictability. Moreover, the judge is thrust squarely into the area of credibility, which has traditionally been reserved to juries. Suggested procedural safeguards are: notice to the opponent of the intention to use hearsay, expanding the judge's ability to comment on the weight of such evidence, greater control by judges over juries, and greater control by appellate courts over trial courts. However, a notice requirement has the disadvantage of adding a further complication to an already overcrowded array of pretrial procedures and is contrary to modern theories of general pleading implemented by discovery. Also, as with admissibility in the first instance, the controls envisioned find their roots in discretionary judicial evaluation of the evidence. These objections are by no means conclusive and might prove less objectionable than the deficiencies of the existing system.

§ 327

1. See supra § 65.
2. See supra § 244.

3. See supra § 60.
4. See infra §§ 352–353.

More than fifty years ago, Professor McCormick wrote, much in the Benthamic tradition:

Eventually, perhaps, Anglo–American court procedure may find itself gradually but increasingly freed from emphasis on jury trial with its contentious theory of proof. With responsibility for the ascertainment of facts vested in professional judges, the stress will be shifted from the crude technique of admitting or rejecting evidence to the more realistic problem of appraising its credibility. Psychologists meantime will have built upon their knowledge of the statistical reliability of witnesses in groups a technique of testing the veracity of individual witnesses and assessing the reliability of particular items of testimony. Judges and advocates will then become students and practitioners of an applied science of judicial proof.[5]

It becomes increasingly evident that this optimistic statement represents a long-term view indeed.

Some take a completely opposed view, advocating instead a sort of hyperextension of Professor Morgan's finetuned analysis and definition of hearsay, with the result of increasing the complexity of the management of hearsay rather than simplifying it. Somewhere in between are those who, though not maintaining that traditional hearsay principles are carved in granite, point to certain reasons to be cautious about radical change. These reasons include: the likelihood that oral statements may be misreported, the potential effect of relaxing hearsay rules on the advantage that the prosecution and wealthy organizations enjoy in litigation due to superior facilities for generating evidence, a distrust of the ability and impartiality of trial judges, and the fact that the hearsay rules presently are applied more liberally than they are written.

The divergence of these points of view offers assurances that the law of hearsay will in the future be no more static than in the past, that it will continue to challenge its observers, and that proposals for its change will receive the most searching scrutiny. Other than to say that changes will generally move in the direction of liberalizing admission of hearsay, prediction is hazardous.

---

5. McCormick, Evidence, 3 Encyclopedia of the Social Sciences 637, 645 (1931, reissue of 1937).

Title 11

JUDICIAL NOTICE

Chapter 35

JUDICIAL NOTICE

Table of Sections

§ 328. The Need for and the Effect of Judicial Notice

The traditional notion that trials are bifurcated proceedings involving both a judge and a panel of twelve jurors has obviously had a profound impact on the overall development of common law doctrine pertaining to evidence. The very existence of the jury, after all, helped create the demand for the rigorous guarantees of accuracy which typify the law of evidence, witness the insistence upon proof by witnesses having first-hand knowledge, the mistrust of hearsay, and the insistence upon original documents and their authentication by witnesses. Thus it is that the facts in dispute are commonly established by the jury after the carefully controlled introduction of formal evidence, which ordinarily consists of the testimony of witnesses. In light of the role of the jury, therefore, it is easy enough to conclude that, whereas questions concerning the tenor of the law to be applied to a case fall within the province of the judge, the determination of questions pertaining to propositions of fact is uniquely the function of the jury. The life of the law has never been quite so elementary, however, because judges on numerous occasions take charge of questions of fact and excuse the party having the burden of establishing a fact from the necessity of producing formal proof. These hybrid questions of fact, dealt with by judges as if they were questions pertaining to law, are the raw materials out of which the doctrine of judicial notice has been constructed.

A moment's reflection on the law-fact distinction is in order. The statement that it is necessary in a certain jurisdiction to have a testator's subscription attested by three witnesses if the document is going to be admitted to probate is an assertion that a certain state of affairs obtains. A speaker might actually preface the assertion with the words, "As a matter of fact * * *" Whether the statement is true or false presents, in the everyday vernacular, a question of fact. Persons engaged in social conversation might not agree on the accuracy of the statement, but agree to settle their difference by a straw poll of the other persons present. All of which would be of no moment, provided always no one present actually planned his or her estate on the basis of the result of the poll.

If this same conversation took the form of an argument between lawyers in a courtroom during an official proceeding wherein the answer was germane to the disposition of the matter at hand, very different considerations would come into play. The answer could not be seen to vary between cases in the same courtroom and between courtrooms across the jurisdiction. There must exist a standardized answer if the law *qua* system of dispute resolution is to maintain the necessary appearance of fairness and rationality. It is the apparatus of appellate review and one ultimately highest court in the jurisdiction which guarantees uniformity. Thus it is the case that, within the vernacular of the law, a question which can have only one right answer must be answered in a courtroom by a judge and is, therefore, a question of law.

The question who did what to whom when, where and in what state of mind implicates another set of considerations. The concrete human actions or inactions which precipitate lawsuits are water over the dam, history as it were. Reflection may suggest that history is actually a current event, because history is our present best judgment as to what happened in the past. Past events cannot be reconstituted; only a facsimile of them can be constructed in the mind's eye on the basis of the evidence presently available. In a courtroom the evidence available is a factor of the rules of evidence and the cleverness as well as industry of the opposing counsel.

If there is produced at trial enough evidence upon which seriously to deliberate about what actually happened in the past,

and provided that in a civil case the evidence is not so overwhelming as to make deliberation unnecessary, there is no scientific litmus by which to assay the accuracy of the opposing versions of the affair. A verdict either way is possible. In the law's vernacular, we are met with a question of fact, which in Anglo–American tradition is meet for a jury to decide. But this compels the conclusion that a question of fact is one to which there are two right answers.

This model finds its roots in Lord Coke.[1] *Ad questionem facti non respondent judices: ad questionem juris non respondent juratores.* To questions of fact judges do not answer: to questions of law the jury do not answer. Implicit in this model, however, is the notion inherent in the adversarial system that a judge presides over a trial after the fashion of an umpire who governs the play according to known rules but who does not participate in it. Implied, too, are the notions that trials involve straightforward contract or tort disputes, that complaints are abruptly dismissed if they do not state a familiar cause of action and that the concise elements of a well pleaded common law cause of action make the issues of fact at trial, if it comes to that, few and simple. Finally, the model presupposes that the law itself is composed primarily of private law rules which by and large remain immutable over the life of any one generation.

If during a trial a proposition of fact were to be implicated, the truth of which brooked no dispute among reasonable persons, this proposition would not fit comfortably within the principle that either of two answers is appropriate to a question of fact. The application of common sense to the principles thus far rehearsed leads inexorably to the conclusion that the existence of one right answer signals a question of law. Thus, at least if requested to do so, a judge would have to treat this question of fact as one of law and instruct the jury that the proposition could simply be taken as established in its own right.

§ 328

1. I Co.Litt. 155b (1832 ed.).

With what manner of questions pertaining to facts do judges concern themselves? Whether a well known street was in fact within a local business district as alleged by a litigant, in which case a certain speed limit obtained, may be dealt with by the judge during the trial of a negligence case. That is to say, the judge may instruct the jury that the street in question was within a business district, dispensing thereby with the need to introduce evidence to this effect. Then again, questions of fact arise about which reasonably intelligent people might not have in mind the information in question, but where they would agree that the facts are verifiable with certainty by consulting authoritative reference sources. At a time when Sunday contracts were taboo, for example, the question arose during the trial of a warranty action whether the relevant sales instrument, dated June 3, 1906, had been executed on a Sunday. In this instance the trial judge was reversed for leaving the question to the jury to deliberate upon as a question of fact. Experience reveals, therefore, that two categories of facts clearly fall within the perimeters of judicial notice, these being facts generally known with certainty by all the reasonably intelligent people in the community and facts capable of accurate and ready determination by resort to sources of indisputable accuracy.

In both of the examples enumerated thus far it should be carefully noted that the facts of which judicial notice was taken were "adjudicative" facts. They were facts about the particular event which gave rise to the lawsuit and, like all adjudicative facts, they helped explain who did what, when, where, how, and with what motive and intent. Further, either because they were facts so commonly known in the jurisdiction or so manifestly capable of accurate verification, they were facts reasonably informed people in the community would regard as propositions not reasonably subject to dispute.

Another species of facts figures prominently in discussions of judicial notice which, to employ the terminology coined by Professor K.C. Davis, are denominated "legislative" facts. Judicial notice of these facts occurs when a judge is faced with the task of creating law, by deciding upon the constitutional validity of a statute, or the interpretation of a statute, or the extension or restriction of a common law rule, upon grounds of policy, and the policy is thought to hinge upon social, economic, political or scientific facts. Illustrative of this phenomenon was Hawkins v. United States [2] in which the Court refused to discard the common law rule that one spouse could not testify against the other, saying, "Adverse testimony given in criminal proceedings would, we think, be likely to destroy almost any marriage." This conclusion rests upon a certain view of the facts about marriage but, needless to say, the facts taken to be true in this instance were hardly indisputable. Observe, moreover, that these facts were not part and parcel of the disputed event being litigated but bore instead upon the court's own thinking about the tenor of the law to be invoked in deciding that dispute.

The generic caption "legislative facts" fails to highlight any distinction between the use of extra-record data by judges when they craft a rule of law, whether of the constitutional or private law variety, and when they resort to extra-record data to assay whether there exist circumstances which constitutionally either legitimate the exercise of legislative power or substantiate the rationality of the legislative product. Resort to a new subdivision like "law-making facts" might not, in its turn, bring home the reality that judges regularly resort to extra-record data not only when enunciating new substantive doctrine, but employ them in deciding questions which pertain to everything from the alpha of civil jurisdiction to the omega of criminal sentencing.

Concern for legislative facts does signal the recognition both that judges do not "find" the law but rather make it, and that questions of public law have become a staple of the case law menu. A judge may no longer be quite the disinterested umpire in the steady state system suggested by the common law model,

---

2. 358 U.S. 74, 78 (1958).

but more an active participant making work what has come to be seen as process of adapting law to a volatile socio-political environment. In a very real sense it may be that a judge used to a steady diet of private law cases and a judge dealing with disputes arising out of a multiplicity of administrative agency actions may actually live in different worlds. At the same time modern procedure and trial practice have served to create a complexity that would confound the serjeants of yesteryear.

The picture is further complicated by a tendency of any brite-line distinction between adjudicative and legislative facts to dissolve in practice. Posit, for example, a statute making it a crime to possess coca leaves or any salt, compound or derivative thereof. If believed the testimony of witnesses, lay and expert, establishes that defendant possessed a quantity of cocaine hydrochloride and that the item is indeed a salt, compound or derivative of coca leaves. The last proposition is indisputable and subject to judicial notice. If this is an adjudicative fact, a federal judge would not feel free to instruct the jury that, if they were to find the defendant possessed this item, they must find the item was a proscribed one.[3] No such compunction would obtain if it were a legislative fact. Yet one judge might visualize the question in terms of, "What is it that defendant possessed?", which is part of the who, what, when and where litany signalling an adjudicative fact, while another judge might inquire, "What was it that the legislature intended to criminalize?", access door to the realm of legislative facts. All of which may warn the reader that the judicial notice of fact phenomenon has many of the characteristics of an universal solvent: it cannot be totally contained in any known vessel.

It is axiomatic, of course, that the judge decides whether a given set of facts constitutes an actionable wrong or a certain line of

cross-examination is relevant. A judge, unless he is to be reversed on appeal, is bound to know the common and statutory law of his own jurisdiction. Commonly enough even this truism has been incorporated into the law of evidence by saying that judges must judicially notice the law of their own forum. This manner of speaking has served to interpolate into the field of judicial notice the procedural mechanisms by which the applicable law is fed into the judicial process. Foreign law, of course, was once more germane to the topic of judicial notice because that body of law was (for convenience) treated as fact, so much so that the law of a jurisdiction other than the forum had to be pleaded and proved just like any other question of fact, but a peculiar one which only the judge came to decide, and hence its inclusion within the topic of judicial notice. Indeed, lumped along with foreign law as a proper subject for treatment under the caption of judicial notice has been the forum's own administrative law and local municipal ordinances, together with a hotchpot of internal judicial administrative details concerning the courts themselves, such as their own personnel, records, organization and jurisdictional boundaries. The recognition appears to be growing, however, that the manner in which the law is insinuated into the judicial process is not so much a problem of evidence as it is a concern better handled within the context of the rules pertaining to procedure.

§ 329. Matters of Common Knowledge

The oldest and plainest ground for judicial notice is that the fact is so commonly known in the community as to make it unprofitable to require proof, and so certainly known as to make it indisputable among reasonable men. Though this basis for notice is sometimes loosely described as universal knowledge, manifestly this could not be taken literally[1] and the more reflective opinions speak in

---

3. Fed.R.Evid. 201(g).

§ 329

1. The late Dean F. McDermott of Suffolk Law School aptly exposed the absurdity of this approach by succinctly

translating it into the rule that "Judicial notice may only be taken of those facts every damn fool knows."

terms of the knowledge of "most men," or of "what well-informed persons generally know," or "the knowledge that every intelligent person has." Observe that these phrases tend progressively to widen the circle of facts within "common knowledge." Moreover, though usually facts of "common knowledge" will be generally known throughout the country, it is sufficient as a basis for judicial notice that they be known in the local community where the trial court sits.

What a judge knows and what facts a judge may judicially notice are not identical data banks. A famous colloquy in the Year Books shows that a clear difference has long been taken between what judges may notice judicially and the facts that the particular judge happens personally to know.[2] It is not a distinction easy for a judge to follow in application, but the doctrine is accepted that actual private knowledge by the judge is no sufficient ground for taking judicial notice of a fact as a basis for a finding or a final judgment, though it may still be a ground, it is believed, for exercising certain discretionary powers, such as granting a motion for new trial to avoid an injustice, or in sentencing.

Similarly, what a jury member knows in common with every other human being and what facts are appropriately circumscribed by the doctrine of judicial notice are not the same thing. Traditionally those facts so generally known within the community as not to be reasonably subject to dispute have been included within the perimeters of judicial notice under the caption of common knowledge. At the same time, however, it is often loosely said that the jury may consider, as if proven, facts within the common knowledge of the community.

When considering the award to make in a condemnation case, a jury were properly concerned whether the value of the remaining fee was diminished by the installation of a natural gas pipeline in the easement which

was the discrete subject of the taking. The jurors factored in an amount to compensate for the contingency that, the fee being a farm, deep chisel-style plowing might rupture the pipe and cause an explosion, the very notoriety of which would put off future purchasers of the farm. This possibility was taken seriously by the jurors, themselves residents of a farming community and familiar with local practices. Even though there had not been introduced into evidence any matter pertaining to deep chisel plowing, a court was willing to sustain the award precisely because, given the fund of common knowledge shared by this rural jury, there was no need for formal evidence to establish the point.

Had the same case been transferred for trial to an urban venue, deep chisel plowing would not likely have ever been considered by a jury absent the introduction of evidence alerting them to the practice. It would be manifestly improper were a juror to investigate farming practices and to introduce the subject for the first time in the privacy of the jury room. This juror should testify as a witness. This leaves open the possibility that a former rural resident might introduce the subject into an urban jury room, pooling with his compatriots his distinct share of the fund of common knowledge. If the fund the jurors can draw upon is knowledge common to the community as a whole, this datum would appear to be illicit specie in an urban venue.

A similar problem would arise were evidence introduced pro and con the existence of a real threat posed by deep chisel plowing and one or more of the jurors shared their unique experience with the practice with the rest of the panel. Jurors do not think evidence; jurors think about the evidence, and to think at all requires a person to draw upon his or her experience. Still, it has been held improper to invite jurors with personal experience on farms to share it with their fellows in a case

2. Anon., Y.B. 7 Hen. IV, f. 41, pl. 5 (1406), from which the following is an excerpt: "Tirwhit: Sir, let us put the case that a man kills another in your presence and sight, and another who is not guilty is indicted before you and is found guilty of the same death, you ought to respite the judgment against him, for you know the

contrary, and report the matter to the King to pardon him. No more ought you to give judgment in this case * * * Gascoigne, C.J. One time the King himself asked me about this very case which you have put, and asked me what was the law, and I told him just as you say, and he was well pleased that the law was so."

which turned on the question whether an insured horse had indeed been killed by a lightning bolt. It has been held appropriate, however, to invite jurors with personal experience in and about saw mills to share their insights in a personal injury case arising out of an accident at a saw mill.

The parameters of the jury fund of common data may be vague precisely because trial lawyers find themselves embarrassed to insist upon brite-line rules when they themselves regularly employ summations to expose jurors to non-evidenced facts cross-dressed as rhetorical hypotheses. What with voir dire examinations and challenges being available to exclude from juries anyone privy to information in excess of the local common denominator, any eccentric scenarios which do occur may simply be chalked up to self-inflicted hardship upon the part of counsel. Even so, all of this assumes that by and large each venue's jurors share relatively homogenous cultural roots so that, in fact, there does exist a rough hewn common fund of knowledge in which they all share.

In an increasingly multi-racial, multi-lingual, tri-gendered, ethnicity-fixated and highly mobile society, further fractured by class divisions, there may no longer exist a common fund of knowledge shared by the jurors resident in any venue. Out of academe there has come the suggestion that a common fund can be guaranteed by imposing a definition of that fund's parameters community to community. This judge imposed construct would not only be the basis for an instruction confining deliberating jurors to this fund, but would serve as a benchmark during voir dire examinations and in determining relevancy. The efficacy of any instruction purporting to limit the data jurors use in their thinking about the outcome of a case may be questionable at best. Whether the very notion of imposing a chatechistical homogeneity on the ideational materials upon which jurors may draw is compatible with the evolving ethos of a diverse society promises, if it is taken seriously, to catalyze vigorous debate.

Thus it is very easy to confound into one common denominator facts to which the evi-

dentiary discipline of judicial notice applies and the residual data the jury members bring along with them as rational human beings. Whereas in the typical vehicular accident case the well-known character of a street can be dealt with informally as background information which helps everyone visualize the scene, the question becomes a formal one to be dealt with as part of the doctrine of judicial notice if the precise character of the street becomes an adjudicative fact in the case being tried. Again, while the meaning of words is normally left to the informal common sense of the jury, the precise meaning of a word in a contract case which may be outcome determinative should be dealt with formally as a problem of judicial notice.

The cases in which judicial notice is taken of indisputable facts commonly known in the community where the facts noticed are actually adjudicative ones appear to be relatively rare. In most instances, notwithstanding the invocation of the language of judicial notice, the facts either involve background information helpful in assaying the evidence relevant to the adjudicative facts or involve facts relevant to the process of formulating the tenor of the law to be applied to the resolution of the controversy. Indeed, there is a growing recognition that the common knowledge variety of fact plays only a very minor role on the judicial notice scene.

§ 330. Facts Capable of Certain Verification

The earlier and probably still the most familiar basis for judicial notice is "common knowledge," but a second and distinct principle has come to be recognized as an even more significant ground for the invocation of the doctrine. This extension of judicial notice was first disguised by a polite fiction so that when asked to notice a fact not generally known, but which obviously could easily be ascertained by consulting materials in common use, such as the day of the week on which January 1 fell ten years ago, the judges resorted to calendars but purported to be "refreshing memory" as to a matter of common knowledge. Eventually it was recognized that involved here was an important extension of judicial notice to the new field of facts "capable of accurate and ready demonstration," "capable of such instant and unquestionable demonstration, if desired, that no party would think of imposing a falsity on the tribunal in the face of an intelligent adversary," or "capable of immediate and accurate demonstration by resort to easily accessible sources of indisputable accuracy." It is under this caption, for example, that courts have taken judicial notice of the scientific principles which, while verifiable but not likely commonly known, justify the evidentiary use of radar, blood tests for intoxication and nonpaternity, handwriting and typewriter identification, and ballistics. Whether the person employing any of this hardware was qualified to do so, whether the hardware was properly maintained and whether it was used correctly remain questions of fact.

Attempts to formulate inventories of verifiable facts of which courts will take judicial notice have begun to fall into disrepute because the principle involved can better be illustrated by way of example. Thus in State v. Damm [1] defendant was on trial for rape after one of his stepdaughters gave birth to a child. The defense sought a court order authorizing blood tests by which it was hoped to prove his innocence by way of negative results. Even if the tests produced a negative result, however, the testimony recounting the tests would be relevant to the question of guilt or innocence only if it was true that properly administered blood tests evidencing a negative result excluded the possibility of paternity. To leave this preliminary question pertaining to the then present state of scientific knowledge to the jury to decide as best they could on the basis of possibly conflicting testimony would appear absurd. There being only one right answer to the question whether the principle was accepted in the appropriate scientific circles, the question fell within the province of judicial notice. Even so, the trial judge in this particular case was held not to

have erred in refusing the request because, given the time and place, the defense was not able to produce the data necessary to illustrate to him that the principle was an accepted one within the scientific community. Presumably, of course, an opposite result would obtain today.

Thus it is that while the various propositions of science are a suitable topic of judicial notice, the content of what will actually be noticed is subject to change as the tenets of science evolve. It is manifest, moreover, that the principle involved need not be commonly known in order to be judicially noticed; it suffices if the principle is accepted as a valid one in the appropriate scientific community. In determining the intellectual viability of the proposition, of course, the judge is free to consult any sources that he thinks are reliable, but the extent to which judges are willing to take the initiative in looking up the authoritative sources will usually be limited. By and large, therefore, it is the task of counsel to find and to present in argument and briefs such references, excerpts and explanations as will convince the judge that the fact is certain and demonstrable. Puzzling enough in this regard, it has been noted that "nowhere can there be found a definition of what constitutes competent or authoritative sources for purposes of verifying judicially noticed facts." [2] And, it should be noted, after a number of courts take judicial notice of a principle, subsequent courts begin to dispense with the production of these materials and to take judicial notice of the principle as a matter of law established by precedent.

Illustrative as they are, scientific principles hardly exhaust the verifiable facts of which courts take judicial notice. Historical facts fall within the doctrine, such as the dates upon which wars began and terminated. Geographical facts are involved, particularly with reference to the boundaries of the state in which the court is sitting and of the counties, districts and townships thereof, as well as the location of the capital of the state and the

1. 64 S.D. 309, 266 N.W. 667 (1936).

2. Comment, The Presently Expanding Concept of Judicial Notice, 13 Vill.L.Rev. 528, 545 (1968).

location and identity of the county seats. Whether common knowledge or not, courts notice the identity of the principal officers of the national government and the incumbents of principal state offices. Similarly, while obviously not necessarily a matter of common knowledge, judges take notice of the identity of the officers of their courts, such as the other judges, the sheriffs, clerks, and attorneys; of the duration of terms and sessions, and of the rules of court.

It would seem obvious that the judge of a court would take notice of all of the records of the institution over which he presides, but the courts have been slow to give the principle of judicial notice its full reach of logic and expediency. It is settled, of course, that the courts, trial and appellate, take notice of their own respective records in the present litigation, both as to matters occurring in the immediate trial, and in previous trials or hearings. The principle seemingly is equally applicable to matters of record in the proceedings in other cases in the same court, and some decisions have recognized this, but many courts still adhere to the needless requirement of formal proof, rather than informal presentation, of recorded proceedings in other suits in the same court. Matters of record in other courts are usually denied notice even though it would appear manifest that these public documents are logically subject to judicial notice as readily verifiable facts.

In the increasingly important practice of judicial notice of scientific and technological facts, some of the possibilities of error are, first, that the courts may fail to employ the doctrine of judicial notice in this field to the full measure of its usefulness; second, that they may mistakenly accept as authoritative scientific theories that are outmoded or are not yet received by the specialists as completely verified; and third, that in taking judicial notice of accepted scientific facts, the courts, in particular cases may misconceive the conclusions or applications which are supposed to flow from them. Of these, it seems that the first has thus far been the most frequent shortcoming.

In determining relevancy an informal system of judicial notice has always obtained, as for example, when it is decided that burglar tools are admissible evidence on the premise that only burglars likely possess such items. Whether the results of negative blood tests were admissible was again a question of relevancy, but the results were not admitted until it was established as incontrovertible fact that the principle behind the test itself was valid. It seemed at the time quite self evident that juries could not pass upon the validity of the test principle because, a rule of science being implicated, there had to be only one right answer. Concomitantly, there might have been worry that juries might be overawed by scientific evidence and that the risk of prejudice ought not be run unless the principle met the stringent test of absolute truth. Whether the classic model ought still to be followed, however, is a question which has to be faced. In a technological era scientific truths are more readily recognized as theorems themselves subject to modification rather rapidly and juries are likely aware of the frailties inherent in technological equipment and analysis, the meanest juror being owner of electronic gear soon obsolete and always in need of fine tuning during its short life. This suggests that judicial notice, with its premise that facts must be indisputably true, be abandoned as the avenue by which scientific tests be admitted into evidence. Instead, the usual test of relevancy would obtain in which the question would be whether the test was supported by enough expert opinion to suggest that its results ought to be considered by the jury for whatever it was worth. The dogmatic theology of judicial notice would be replaced by pragmatism.

§ 331. Social and Economic Data Used in Judicial Law–Making: "Legislative" Facts

It is conventional wisdom today to observe that judges not only are charged to find what the law is, but must regularly make new law when deciding upon the constitutional validity of a statute, interpreting a statute, or extending or restricting a common law rule.

The very nature of the judicial process necessitates that judges be guided, as legislators are, by considerations of expediency and public policy. They must, in the nature of things, act either upon knowledge already possessed or upon assumptions, or upon investigation of the pertinent general facts, social, economic, political, or scientific. An older tradition once prescribed that judges should rationalize their result solely in terms of analogy to old doctrines leaving the considerations of expediency unstated. Contemporary practice indicates that judges in their opinions should render explicit their policy-judgments and the factual grounds therefor. These latter have been helpfully classed as "legislative facts," as contrasted with the "adjudicative facts" which are historical facts pertaining to the incidents which give rise to lawsuits.

Constitutional cases argued in terms of due process typically involve reliance upon legislative facts for their proper resolution. Whether a statute enacted pursuant to the police power is valid, after all, involves a twofold analysis. First, it must be determined that the enactment is designed to achieve an appropriate objective of the police power; that is, it must be designed to protect the public health, morals, safety, or general welfare. The second question is whether, in light of the data on hand, a legislature still beholden to reason could have adopted the means they did to achieve the aim of their exercise of the police power. In Jay Burns Baking Co. v. Bryan,[1] for example, the question was whether, concerned about consumers being misled by confusing sizes of bread, the Nebraska legislature could decree not only that the bakers bake bread according to distinctively different weights but that they wrap their product in wax paper lest any post-oven expansion of some loaves undo these distinctions. A majority of the court held the enactment unconstitutional because, in their opinion, the wrapping requirement was unreasonable. Mr. Justice Brandeis, correctly anticipating the decline of substantive due process, dissented, pointing out that the only question

was whether the measure was a reasonable legislative response in light of the facts available to the legislators themselves. Then, in a marvelous illustration of the Brandeis-brief technique, he recited page after page of data illustrating how widespread was the problem of shortweight and how, in light of nationwide experience, the statute appeared to be a reasonable response to the environmental situation.

Given the bent to test due process according to the information available to the legislature, the truth-content of these data are not directly relevant. The question is whether sufficient data exist which could influence a reasonable legislature to act, not whether ultimately these data are true. This is not the same case as when a court proceeds to interpret a constitutional norm and, while they still rely upon data, the judges *qua* legislators themselves proceed to act as if the data were true. In Brown v. Board of Education,[2] for example, the Court faced the issue whether segregated schools, equal facility and teacher-wise, could any longer be tolerated under the equal protection clause. The question was not any longer whether a reasonable legislator could believe these schools could never be equal, but whether the *judges* believed that the very act of segregating branded certain children with a feeling of inferiority so deleterious that it would be impossible for them to obtain an equal education no matter how equal the facilities and teachers. Thus the intellectual legitimacy of this kind of decision turns upon the actual truth-content of the legislative facts taken into account by the judges who propound the decision. While not necessarily indisputably true, it would appear that these legislative facts must at least appear to be more likely than not true if the opinion is going to have the requisite intellectual legitimacy upon which the authority of judge-made rules is ultimately founded.

When it comes to the utilization of these law making facts, three problems can beset constitutional law decisions. The first is that

---

§ 331

1. 264 U.S. 504 (1924).

2. 347 U.S. 483 (1954), supplemented 349 U.S. 294.

the forest can sometimes be lost sight of for the trees. That is to say, so much historical and sociological data are rehearsed that an opinion appears to be bottomed upon purely pragmatic considerations and not upon any compelling constitutional norm. The second is that an outpouring of learning appears to be almost an exercise in the narcissus that afflicts academics, the problem at hand not demanding an expenditure of wit and learning on any such scale. The third is that data can appear to be fired off as an exercise in fustian excess, often in a losing cause. The first would appear to be a problem of draftsmanship, hard cases perhaps making bad law, but the latter two tend to give lie to the notion that judges lack for time.

When making new common law, judges must, like legislators, do the best they can assaying the data available to them and make the best decision they can of which course wisdom dictates they follow. Should they, for example, continue to invoke the common law rule of *caveat emptor* in the field of real property, or should they invoke a notion of implied warranty in the instance of the sale of new houses? Should they require landlords of residential units to warrant their habitability and fitness for the use intended? While sociological, economic, political and moral doctrine may abound about questions like this, none of these data are likely indisputable.

Thus it is that, in practice, the legislative facts upon which judges rely when performing their lawmaking function are not indisputable. At the same time, cognizant of the fact that his decision as lawmaker can affect the public at large, in contradistinction to most rulings at trials which affect only the parties themselves, a judge is not likely to rely for his data only upon what opposing counsel tender him. Obviously enough, therefore, legislative facts tend to be the most elusive facts when it comes to propounding a codified system of judicial notice. This seems to be confirmed by the fact that the Federal Rules of Evidence

are a confession of intellectual bankruptcy in this regard.

There are, however, efforts being made to rationalize this subject-matter. If one were to examine social science materials looking for help in enunciating a rule of law, one would be searching for authority much in the same fashion as one would be if one were looking to unearth decisional precedential authority. This has suggested to Professors John Monahan and Laurens Walker that a foray into social science materials is more akin to an effort to answer a question of law than one of fact.[3] Thus judges should not see themselves taking judicial notice of legislative facts but promulgating law. Social science materials would not be introduced into the system by expert testimony but by way of written briefs, and judges would have no hesitation at all carrying on their own independent researches. The very recognition that a question of law was involved would catalyze a more critical attitude toward these materials, because they would carry more *gravitas,* being law, than do the only arguably true episodic facts of the current approach. Soon enough a canon of precedential authority would come into being based upon a calculus of the precise court which relied on particular data and the peer review each decision received in the law reviews and other opinions. Thus these materials could be quickly accessed *in puisne* courts by simple reference and citation.

§ 332. The Uses of Judicial Notice

Judges have been prone to emphasize the need for caution in applying the doctrine of judicial notice. The great writers of evidence, on the other hand, having perhaps a wider view of the needs of judicial administration, advocate a more extensive use of the doctrine. Thus Thayer suggests: "Courts may judicially notice much that they cannot be required to notice. That is well worth emphasizing; for it points to a great possible usefulness in this doctrine, in helping to shorten and simplify

3. Monahan & Walker, Social Authority: Obtaining, Evaluating, and Establishing Social Science in Law, 134   U.Pa.L.Rev. 477 (1986).

trials. * * * The failure to exercise it tends daily to smother trials with technicality and monstrously lengthens them out." [1] And Wigmore says, "The principle is an instrument of usefulness hitherto unimagined by judges." [2]

The simple litany that judicial notice encapsulates facts commonly known and facts readily verifiable is useful as a rule-of-thumb but not as a precise litmus test. The courts' willingness to resort to judicial notice is apparently influenced by a number of less specifically definable circumstances. A court is more willing to notice a general than a specific fact, as for example, the approximate time of the normal period of human gestation, but not the precise maximum and minimum limits. A court may be more willing to notice a fact if it is not an ultimate fact, that is, a fact which would be determinative of a case. Suppose, for example, that a plaintiff in a vehicular negligence action specifically alleged that the defendant was driving too fast in a business district and the testimony, if believed, would indicate that the automobile in question caused a long skid mark on the highway surface. The trial judge might be less willing to notice that the street in question was within the business district than he would to notice that any properly equipped automobile travelling at the maximum speed appropriate in such a district could be stopped within x feet of the braking point. In the first example, the trial judge would appear to be invading the province of the jury to determine the facts pertinent to what had happened, whereas in the second he would be merely establishing rather quickly a piece of data which would aid the jury during their deliberations on the ultimate issue of negligence.

Agreement is not to be had whether the perimeters of the doctrine of judicial notice enclose only facts which are indisputably true or encompass also facts more than likely true. If, on the one hand, the function of the jury is to resolve disputed questions of fact, an argument can be made that judges should not purport to make decisions about facts unless they are indisputable facts. If this argument is accepted, it follows that once a fact has been judicially noticed, evidence contradicting the truth of the fact is inadmissible because by its very nature, a fact capable of being judicially noticed is an indisputable fact which the jury must be instructed to accept as true. If, on the other hand, the function of judicial notice is to expedite the trial of cases, an argument can be made that judges should dispense with the need for time-consuming formal evidence when the fact in question is likely true. If this argument is accepted, it follows that evidence contradicting the judicially noticed fact is admissible and that the jury are ultimately free to accept or reject the truth of the fact posited by judicial notice.

A facile resolution of this conflict suggests itself readily enough. That is, the controversy might be exposed as a misunderstanding caused by a failure to take into account the distinction between "adjudicative" and "legislative" facts. This would be true if the instances where judicial notice was restricted to indisputable facts involved only adjudicative facts whereas potentially disputable facts were only noticed within a legislative context. Whether the decided cases sustain this symmetry is itself a matter of dispute because authority exists which illustrates that some courts are not loathe judicially to notice a potentially disputable fact within what is at least arguably an adjudicative context.

The most recent efforts to deal with judicial notice have exhibited a trend away from extrapolating an all-inclusive definition of a doctrine in favor of promulgating modest guidelines which would regularize what are perceived to be the essential applications of judicial notice. One approach would restrict formalized judicial notice regulation to those situations in which only adjudicative facts are involved. Limiting judicial notice to adjudicative facts and then only to indisputable ones

§ 332

1. Thayer, Preliminary Treatise on Evidence 309 (1898).

2. 9 Wigmore, Evidence § 2583, p. 819 (Chadbourn rev. 1981).

leaves unresolved the question whether a jury in a criminal case should be instructed that they must accept the inexorable truth of the noticed fact. In terms of logic and pure reason it would appear that a jury as a rational deliberative body must accept proper judicially noticed facts. Viewed through the lens of democratic tradition as a protection against an overbearing sovereign, a criminal trial jury may be a body which ought to be free to return a result which as an exercise in logic flies in the face of reason.

Another approach would narrow the range of judicial notice by de-escalating the significance of the conflict between questions peculiarly the province of juries and questions of fact handled by judges. Judges have, for example, always dealt with preliminary questions of fact even in jury trials. Thus, while the admissibility of the results of blood tests raises a question of fact pertaining to the reliability of such tests, the judges deal with this question as a preliminary step in ruling on relevancy, a function that is itself peculiarly a judicial one. Indeed, if trials are examined functionally, it can be demonstrated that judges have always had to decide questions pertaining to facts without any apparent infringement of the jury's domain, whether this be in ruling on demurrers, during pretrial hearings, on motions for nonsuit or to set aside verdicts, or at sentencing. This may indicate, after all, that the scope of judicial notice varies according to the function the judge is performing when judicial notice is taken.

It may be the case that there is no easy rule-of-thumb technique adequate unto the day to serve as an easy capsulation of the judicial notice phenomenon. Protagonists of the indisputable-only definition of judicial notice concede that in criminal cases the jury must be left free in the ultimate analysis to determine the truth or falsity of any adjudicative fact. Protagonists of the disputability thesis might be expected to resolve the controversy by suggesting that, whereas in jury cases there is some merit in the notion that judicial notice should be restricted to indisputable facts in order not to infringe on the role of the jury, the disputable theory works quite efficiently within the context of the jury-waived cases, which probably means that it applies in most cases which come to trial. The fact of the matter is that this solution has not received as much notoriety as might be expected.

The very fact that the trend of these recent investigations has been calculated to resolve the problems associated with judicial notice by narrowing the dimensions of that concept has, however, raised a new problem which must be dealt with in the future. If judicial notice is restricted to instances where judges deal with facts in an adjudicative context, the instances where judges deal with legislative facts is left unregulated insofar as procedural guide-lines are concerned. The significance of this problem can be best illustrated within the context of the next section.

§ 333. Procedural Incidents

An elementary sense of fairness might indicate that a judge before making a final ruling that judicial notice will be taken should notify the parties of his intention to do so and afford them an opportunity to present information which might bear upon the propriety of noticing the fact, or upon the truth of the matter to be noticed. Although the original version of the Uniform Rules of Evidence required it, only a rare case insists that a judge must notify the parties before taking judicial notice of a fact on his own motion, and some authorities suggest that such a requirement is needless. It may very well be the case that a trial judge need only consider notifying the parties if on his own motion he intends to take judicial notice of a less than obviously true fact. In every other instance, after all, the request by one party asking the judge to take judicial notice will serve to apprise the opposing party of the question at hand. While there may, nevertheless, exist in practice a rough consensus with regard to procedural niceties when trial judges take judicial notice of adjudicative facts, this is not the end of the matter. The cases universally assume the nonexistence of any need for a structured adversary-style ancillary hearing with regard to legislative facts. Indeed, even with regard to adjudicative facts, the practices of appellate courts tend to support the argument that there exists no real felt need to formalize the practice of taking judicial notice.

Legislative facts, of course, have not fitted easily into any effort to propound a formalized set of rules applicable to judicial notice. These facts, after all, tend to be less than indisputable ones and hence beyond the pale of judicial notice. What then of the requirement that, before judicial notice is taken, the parties be afforded a reasonable opportunity to present information relative to the propriety of taking judicial notice and the tenor of the matter to be noticed? By and large the parties have this opportunity during arguments over motions as to the appropriate law to be applied to the controversy, by exchanging briefs, and by employing the technique exemplified by the Brandeis brief. It appears, therefore, that there exists no felt need to formalize the procedures pertaining to the opportunity to be heard with reference to legislative facts. Even so, there are cases where the legislative facts which form the basis of an appellate opinion first appear in the decision itself and counsel never have the opportunity to respond to them. Presumably current practice relies upon the sound discretion of judges to maintain discipline in this regard by presupposing a peer-group style general insistence among the judges on a fundamental notion of elementary fairness. However ill-defined because rooted in a sense of due process rather than bottomed on a precise calculus of rules, this notion of fairness may prove to be the common denominator which will continue to link together judicial notice of legislative and adjudicative facts.

With regard to the treatment of adjudicative facts by appellate courts, the common starting point is the axiom that these tribunals can take judicial notice to the same extent as can trial courts. At the very least, this rule suggests the obvious fact that appel-late courts can review the propriety of the judicial notice taken by the court below and can even take judicial notice on their own initiative of facts not noticed below. Nonetheless the recitation of these principles fails to portray the full flavor of the actual practice of appellate courts in taking judicial notice on their own initiative of what would appear to be adjudicative facts.

In this regard the case of Mills v. Denver Tramway Corp.,[1] may be instructive. Plaintiff had alighted from a trolley car, walked behind it and crossed the parallel set of tracks, where he was struck by a car going in the opposite direction. Plaintiff appeared to be manifestly guilty of contributory negligence, a sound enough conclusion plaintiff next attempted to overcome by invoking the doctrine of the last-clear-chance. That is, at the penultimate moment of the trial, plaintiff requested a jury instruction to the effect that, if the motorman had had a chance to sound the trolley bell, the harm might still have been avoided, in which case plaintiff was entitled to prevail. The trial judge refused the instruction because no evidence was ever introduced to indicate that the trolley had a bell. The appellate tribunal reversed, giving plaintiff a new trial, reciting the fact that "streetcars have bells." If all trolley cars had bells, a fact the trial court could have taken judicial notice of had it ever been requested to do so, it would be quite appropriate for the appellate court to take notice of the very same fact. But was it an indisputable fact that *all* streetcars had bells? Arguably most did, in which case the appellate court was taking judicial notice, not of an indisputable fact, but only of a more-than-likely-true fact. More plausibly, the court reasoned that, in all likelihood, the trolley had a bell, in which instance plaintiff should have, as part of his case, proceeded to introduce evidence to substantiate a plausible claim on the last-clear-chance theory. Alternatively, had no bell existed, plaintiff should have made that omission the basis of his claim. In either event, a sense of justice cried out for a trial of the case with all the facts fully developed. If, how-

§ 333

1. 155 F.2d 808 (10th Cir.1946).

ever, this was the sense of justice which moved the appellate tribunal, their invocation of the statement that "all streetcars have bells," a disputable proposition, sheds no real light either on the question whether judicial notice extends to disputable adjudicative facts or whether the parties must be afforded a hearing before judicial notice is taken. Given the need for appellate courts on occasion to reverse results below on a factual basis, judicial notice serves as a convenient device by which to give the practice the appearance of legal propriety. This being true, it would appear that the chances of adequately formalizing judicial notice even of adjudicative facts at the appellate level may be a slim one indeed.

§ 334. Trends in the Development of Judicial Notice of Facts

It appears that, by and large, agreement has been reached on a rough outline of the perimeters of judicial notice as applied to adjudicative facts at the trial level.[1] A workable procedural schemata which would appear to guarantee fairness already exists in the event that judicial notice is restricted to indisputable facts. The only question remaining is whether, in order to expedite the trial of cases, judges should be allowed to excuse the proponent of a fact likely true of the necessity of producing formal evidence thereof, leaving it to the jury to accept or reject the judicially noticed fact, and of course, allowing the opponent to introduce evidence contradicting it. Indeed, the present controversy might be put in a new light by limiting judicial notice to indisputable facts and then raising the question, whether, as part of the law associated with the burden of proof and presumptions, a judge can properly expedite trials by himself ruling that very likely true facts are presumptively true unless the jury care to find otherwise.

Whatever the ultimate doctrinal synthesis of judicial notice of adjudicative facts comes to be, a viable formulation of rules laying down a similarly rigid procedural etiquette

with regard to legislative facts has not proved feasible. Given the current recognition that nonadjudicative facts are inextricably part and parcel of the law formulation process in a policy-oriented jurisprudence, there may be no need to formulate a distinctly judicial notice-captioned procedure with regard to nonadjudicative facts. These data are fed into the judicial process now whenever rules of law are brought to the attention of judges in motions, memoranda and briefs. Thus, whatever rules govern the submission of law in the litigation process have already preempted the nonadjudicative field and made unnecessary separate treatment thereof within the context of judicial notice.

There has been an increasing awareness, moreover, that quite apart from judicial notice, the trial process assumes that the participants therein bring with them a vast amount of everyday knowledge of facts in general. To think, after all, presupposes some data about which to think. In an automobile accident case, for example, both the judge and the jury constantly draw on their own experiences as drivers, as observers of traffic, and as live human beings, and these experiences are reduced in their minds to propositions of fact which, since they have survived themselves, are probably fairly accurate. This substratum of data the participants bring into the courthouse has, however, tended to confuse the judicial notice scene. On the one hand, this subliminal-like data is sometimes confused with the "common knowledge"-style of adjudicative facts with which formal judicial notice is concerned. On the other hand, judges constantly invoke references to these same everyday facts when they write opinions because, when formally articulated, it is impossible "to think" without reference to them. It may very well be the case that judges have tended, when extrapolating the obvious, to invoke the words, "I take judicial notice of" to explain the presence of these facts in their minds, thereby unnecessarily glutting the encyclopedias with trivia which are, when for-

1. See Fed.R.Evid. and Unif.R.Evid. 201.

mally collected, highly misleading indices of the true scope of judicial notice as such.

Federal Rule of Evidence 201 only applies to adjudicative facts, which might suggest that legislative facts simply cannot be fitted into the concept of judicial notice. If they cannot, legislative facts would have to come into the judicial process in the form of "evidence." A problem would then arise if a trial court had to decide the question of law whether it was constitutional totally to exclude from a bifurcated jury in a capital case persons opposed to the death penalty. After hearing testimony and accepting documentary material, the court might conclude on the basis of available social science materials that either death disqualification produced conviction prone juries or it did not. The court might bottom its decision of the constitutional issue on this "finding of fact." If the social science materials were not clearly inclined to sustain only one conclusion, and the ruling were treated as a factual ruling, the ruling whichever way it came out could not be reversed because it would not be clearly erroneous. Law would come to turn on fact and be susceptible to two right answers. This is not going to happen. Legislative facts are not "evidence" in the normal sense of the word, and judicial notice doctrine still obtains as to them. The problem is one of refining that doctrine, and not confusing it with evidentiary proof of adjudicatory facts.

Arguably legislative facts might better be handled by treating them as one would a search for law amidst a canon of conflicting cases, ruling on the tenor of the applicable economic or social rule as if it were a question of law. But as we have seen, judges are constantly asserting facts to be true in many contexts and at many stages of the judicial process, "facts" which while they appeal to common sense and prudence as work-a-day truths, lack the dignity and permanence of something that could be called "law." Law

requires more than cracker-barrel folk wisdom behind it to command respect and obedience. What is needed is a new concept, perhaps oriented around the study of thinking-about-facts techniques involved throughout the judicial process. Judge Robert E. Keeton has spearheaded just such an endeavor in the most appropriate context of a William B. Lockhart Lecture, taking as his cue the notion that facts are the premise of innumerable rulings.[2] Oddly enough, this trend if continued would represent a return to Thayer.[3]

§ 335. The Judge's Task as Law–Finder: Judicial Notice of Law

It would appear to be self-evident that it is peculiarly the function of the judge to find and interpret the law applicable to the issues in a trial, and in a jury case, to announce his findings of law to the jury for their guidance. The heavy-footed common law system of proof by witnesses and authenticated documents is too slow and cumbrous for the judge's task of finding what the applicable law is. Usually this law is familiar lore and if not he relies on the respective counsel to bring before him the statutes, reports, and source books, and these everyday companions of judge and counsel are read from informally in discussion or cited and quoted in trial and appellate briefs. Occasionally the judge will go beyond the cited authorities to make his own investigation. In the ordinary process of finding the applicable law, the normal method then is by informal investigation of any sources satisfactory to the judge. Thus this process has been traditionally described in terms of the judge taking judicial notice of the law applicable to the case at hand. Indeed, when the source-material was not easily accessible to the judge, as in the case of "foreign law" or city ordinances, law has been treated as a peculiar species of fact, requiring formal proof. We shall see, however, that as these materials

---

2. Keeton, Legislative Facts and Similar Things: Deciding Disputed Premise Facts, 73 Minn.L.Rev. 1 (1988).

3. See, Preliminary Treatise on Evidence at the Common Law 278–279 (1898) ("Whereabout in the law does the doctrine of judicial notice belong? Wherever the

process of reasoning has a place, and that is everywhere. Not peculiarly in the law of evidence. * * * The subject of judicial notice, then, belongs to the general topic of legal or judicial reasoning.")

become more accessible, the tendency is toward permitting the judges to do what perhaps they should have done in the beginning, that is, to rely on the diligence of counsel to provide the necessary materials, and accordingly to take judicial notice of *all* law. This seems to be the goal toward which the practice is marching.

Domestic law. As to domestic law generally, the judge is not merely permitted to take judicial notice but required to do so, at least if requested, although in a particular case a party may be precluded on appeal from complaining of the judge's failure to notice a statute where his counsel has failed to call it to the judge's attention. This general rule that judicial notice will be taken of domestic law means that state trial courts will notice Federal law, which is controlling in every state, and has been held to mean that in a Federal trial court the laws of the states, not merely of the state where it is sitting, are domestic and will be noticed. Similarly all statewide or nationwide executive orders and proclamations, which are legally effective, will be noticed. Under this same principle, even the laws of antecedent governments will be noticed.

State and national administrative regulations having the force of law will also be noticed, at least if they are published so as to be readily available. When such documents are published in the Federal Register it is provided that their contents shall be judicially noticed. Private laws and municipal ordinances, however, are not commonly included within the doctrine of judicial notice and these must be pleaded and proved. To the extent that these items become readily available in compilations, it may be expected that they will become subject to judicial notice; whereas, in the meantime, it would appear appropriate for judges to take judicial notice of both private laws and municipal ordinances if counsel furnish a certified copy thereof.

The law of sister states. It is easy to see how the difference of languages and inaccessibility of source books should have led the English courts to develop the common law rule that the laws of foreign nations would not be noticed but must be pleaded and proved as facts. The assumption in the earlier cases in this country that the courts of one state must treat the laws of another state as foreign for this purpose is less understandable and to the afterview seems a deplorable instance of mechanical jurisprudence. Yet it remains today, in nearly every one of the increasingly few states which have not yet adopted a reformatory statute, the common law rule that notice will not be given to the laws of sister states. This is probably the most inconvenient of all the limitations upon the practice of judicial notice. Notice here could certainly be justified on the principle of certainty and verifiability, and the burden on the judge could be minimized by casting the responsibility upon counsel either to agree upon a stipulation as to the law or to produce on each side for the benefit of the court all materials necessary for ascertaining the law in question.

Under this hoary practice when a required pleading and proof of the foreign law has been overlooked, or has been unsuccessfully attempted, the resulting danger of injustice is somewhat mitigated by the presumption that the law of the sister state is the same as that of the forum, or more simply the practice of applying local law if the law of the other state is not invoked and proven. But this presumption-tool is too rough for the job in hand, particularly when the materials for ascertaining the laws of sister states are today almost as readily accessible as those for local law, and in any event counsel as officers of the court are available to find and present those materials to the judge in just the same informal and convenient fashion as if they were arguing a question of local law.

In 1936 the Conference of Commissioners on Uniform Laws drafted the Uniform Judicial Notice of Foreign Law Act which was adopted in substance by more than half the states. This legislation provides that every court within the adopting state shall take judicial notice of the common law and statutes of every other state. While the Act removes the necessity to prove the law of another state, most courts do not feel obliged by it to notice the law of another state on their own initiative. Indeed, in order to invoke the benefits of the Foreign Law Act a litigant must give reasonable notice in the pleadings or otherwise to the adverse party of his intention to do so, failing which the courts are apt to refuse to take judicial notice or admit evidence as to the sister-state law relied on, invoking once again the presumption that it is the same as the law of the forum.

The Uniform Judicial Notice of Foreign Law Act pertained to the law of sister states and did not address the issue of the law of other nations. It was supplanted in 1962 when the National Conference of Commissioners on Uniform Laws approved Article IV of the Uniform Interstate and International Procedure Act. Calculated to address judicial notice of true foreign law, the new Act implicates the law of sister states as well because it imposes the same discipline when the law of *any* extraforum jurisdiction is invoked. Thus a party who intends to raise an issue of the law of a sister state should give notice of an intention to do so, either in the pleadings or by any other reasonable method of written notice. It is the court which determines the tenor of what actually will be noticed about the law of a sister state, and the court may go beyond the materials furnished it by the parties in arriving at its own determination. Article IV, however, has yet to win widespread adoption.

The law of foreign countries. At common law, foreign law was treated as a matter of fact: pleading and proof were required, and the jury decided what the foreign law was. As early as 1936 the Uniform Judicial Notice of Foreign Law Act reflected the idea that the tenor of the law of a foreign country was a question for the court and not for the jury. What is significant is the fact that this selfsame 1936 Act, adverted to in the preceding section, contained no provision for the judicial notice of the law of other nations. The parties were left not only to pleading but proving, albeit to a judge and not a jury, the law of other nations.

The longevity of the ancient notion that a party had "to prove" the law of another na-

tion was likely rooted in the fact that the sources of extranational law were not easily accessible even in urban centers. A healthy pragmatism seems to have ameliorated the harshness of any rule demanding strict proof. Sworn to or certified copies of extranational statutes or decisions gave way to the use of copies thereof in a book printed by the authority of the foreign state or proved to be commonly recognized in its courts.

Even so, the very idea that a party was engaged in "proving" a point of extranational law fairly invited complications. The written text of any law suggests that its "black letter" be interpreted in light of any germane decisions, treatises or commentaries. This under common law proof must be accomplished by taking the testimony in person or by deposition of an expert in the foreign law. The adversary of course is free to take the testimony of other experts if he can find them on his side, and the cross-examination of conflicting experts is likely to accentuate the disagreements. This method of proof seems to maximize expense and delay and hardly seems best calculated to ensure a correct decision by our judges on questions of foreign law. It could be vastly improved by pre-trial conferences in which agreements as to undisputed aspects of the foreign law could be secured, and by the appointment by the court of one or more experts on foreign law as referees or as court-chosen experts to report their findings to the court.

Following the lead of several states which by statute have provided that the court must take judicial notice or permit the court to do so in its discretion, the practice obtaining in the federal courts has been codified to make the tenor of foreign law a question of law for the court. Thus it is that a party who intends to raise an issue of foreign-nation law must give notice of his intention to do so, either in his pleadings or by any other reasonable method of written notice. Once the issue of foreign law is raised, the court need not, in its effort to determine the tenor of that law, rely upon the testimony and other materials proffered by the litigant, but may engage in its own research and consider any relevant material thus found.

In turn the new Uniform Interstate and International Procedure Act's Article IV will, if generally enacted, unify state practice along the lines of the federal model. Thus again the invocation of extranational law would necessitate written notice, by way of the pleadings or any reasonable alternative, and the court, licensed to engage in its own researches, would ultimately fix the actual tenor of whatever was noticed. Concomitantly, recourse to the law of a sister state is included within the same process so that a single procedure will obtain whenever the law of a jurisdiction outside the forum becomes an issue.

The unwillingness of the courts to notice the laws of other countries creates difficulties where the party whose case or defense depends, under conflicts rules, upon foreign law and he fails to prove that law as a fact. There are several solutions. First, the court may decide the issue against him for failure of proof. This is often a harsh and arbitrary result. Second, the court may simply apply the law of the forum on the ground that no other law is before it, especially if the parties have tried the case as if local law were applicable. Third, the court may presume that the law of the other country is the same as that of the forum, thus reaching the same result as under the second theory but raising intellectual difficulties because the presumption is so frequently contrary to fact. When the doctrine involved is one of common law, but the other nation is not a common law country, some courts will decline to apply the presumption. On the other hand, when the common law rule invoked is a part of the common fund of all civilized systems, such as the binding force of ordinary commercial agreements, the presumption is applied though the foreign country is not a common law country. Moreover, by what is probably the prevailing and more convenient view, if the question would be governed locally by a statute, a like statute in the foreign country may be presumed.

International and Maritime Law. The rules, principles and traditions of "international law," or "the law of nations," will be noticed in Federal and state courts. Maritime law is similarly subject to judicial notice but only insofar as these rules have become part of the general maritime law. Less widely recognized maritime rules of foreign countries are treated like foreign law generally and are required to be proved, unless they have been published here by government authority as the authentic foreign law, or they have been embodied in a widely adopted international convention. Peculiarly enough, the presumption of identity of foreign law with the local law, which would seem to be unusually convenient and realistic in the maritime field, has been narrowly restricted.

The future of judicial notice of law. When a judge presiding in the presence of a jury decides a question of fact, a sufficiently unique event occurs to merit special treatment because the jury is thought to perform the factfinding role in common law countries. This appears to explain why judicial notice of facts has been a topic of evidence law ever since Thayer authored his pioneering treatise. There is nothing very remarkable about a judge ruling on the tenor of the law to be applied to the resolution of the controversy, however, because by definition this is the very function judges are supposed to perform. When the sources of law were dubious at best, the job of sorting out the applicable law was shifted to the jury, witness how foreign law and municipal ordinances were treated as questions of fact. When next judges began to rule on the tenor of this law, even though it was still "fact" to be developed by the parties, there may have been some justification for describing this process as judicial notice. As all law has become increasingly accessible and judges have tended to assume the duty to rule on the tenor of all law, the notion that this process is part of judicial notice has become increasingly an anachronism. Evidence, after all, involves the proof of facts. How the law is fed into the judicial machine is more appropriately an aspect of the law pertaining to procedure. Thus it is that the electronic bleeps sounded by today's data processing equipment are actually tolling the intellectual death knell of this discrete subject-matter hitherto dealt with as a subdivision of the law of evidence.

Title 12

BURDENS OF PROOF AND PRESUMPTIONS

Chapter 36

THE BURDENS OF PROOF
AND PRESUMPTIONS

Table of Sections

§ 336. The Burdens of Proof: The Burden of Producing Evidence and the Burden of Persuasion

"Proof" is an ambiguous word. We sometimes use it to mean evidence, such as testimony or documents. Sometimes, when we say a thing is "proved" we mean that we are convinced by the data submitted that the alleged fact is true. Thus, "proof" is the end result of conviction or persuasion produced by the evidence. Naturally, the term "burden of proof" shares this ambivalence. The term encompasses two separate burdens of proof.

One burden is that of producing evidence, satisfactory to the judge, of a particular fact in issue. The second is the burden of persuading the trier of fact that the alleged fact is true.

The burden of producing evidence on an issue means the liability to an adverse ruling (generally a finding or directed verdict) if evidence on the issue has not been produced. It is usually cast first upon the party who has pleaded the existence of the fact, but as we shall see, the burden may shift to the adversary when the pleader has discharged its ini-

568

tial duty.[1] The burden of producing evidence is a critical mechanism in a jury trial, as it empowers the judge to decide the case without jury consideration when a party fails to sustain the burden.

The burden of persuasion becomes a crucial factor only if the parties have sustained their burdens of producing evidence and only when all of the evidence has been introduced. It does not shift from party to party during the course of the trial simply because it need not be allocated until it is time for a decision. When the time for a decision comes, the jury, if there is one, must be instructed how to decide the issue if their minds are left in doubt. The jury must be told that if the party having the burden of persuasion has failed to satisfy that burden, the issue is to be decided against that party. If there is no jury and the judge is in doubt, the issue must be decided against the party having the burden of persuasion.

What is the significance of the burden of persuasion? Clearly, the principal significance of the burden of persuasion is limited to those cases in which the trier of fact is actually in doubt. Possibly, even in those cases, juries disregard their instructions on this question and judges, trying cases without juries, pay only lip service to it, trusting that the appellate courts will not disturb their findings of fact. Yet, even if an empirical study were conclusively to demonstrate both a regular disregard for jury instructions and a propensity on the part of judges to decide issues of fact without regard to their express statements concerning the allocation of the burden of persuasion, rules allocating and describing that burden could not be discarded by a rational legal system. A risk of nonpersuasion naturally exists any time one person attempts to persuade another to act or not to act. If the other does not change her course of action or nonaction, the person desiring change has, of course, failed. If no burden of persuasion were acknowledged by the law, one possible result would be that the trier of

fact would purport to reach no decision at all. The impact of nondecision would then fall by its own weight upon the party, usually the plaintiff, who sought a change in the status quo. Although this is generally where the law would place the burden anyhow, important policy considerations may dictate that the risk should fall on the opposing party.[2]

Another possibility would be that the trier of fact would itself assign a burden of persuasion, describing that burden as it saw fit by substituting its own notions of policy for those now made available to it as a matter of law. Such a result would be most undesirable. Considerations of policy that are sufficient to suggest that in some instances the burden of persuasion be assigned to the party desiring a maintenance of the status quo are strong enough to dictate the need for a consistent rather than a case by case determination of the question. Other policy considerations, such as those that have led the law to require that the prosecution in a criminal case prove the defendant guilty beyond a reasonable doubt,[3] are sufficient to require that the jury be explicitly and clearly instructed as to the measure of the burden as well as its allocation. Although judges and juries may act contrary to the law despite the best attempts to persuade them to do otherwise, we can at least give them the benefit of thoughtful guidance on the questions of who should bear the burden of persuasion and what the nature of that burden should be. In jury trials, perhaps the problem has not been in the concept of a burden of persuasion, but rather in the confusing jury instructions that abound on this point of law. In nonjury trials, if judges are not in fact following rules of law allocating the burden, the fault may lie not in the concept but with thoughtless judicial and legislative allocations and descriptions of the burden.

§ 337. Allocating the Burdens of Proof

In most cases, the party who has the burden of pleading a fact will have the burdens of

1. See § 338 infra.

2. See § 337 infra.

3. See § 341 infra.

producing evidence and of persuading the jury of its existence as well. The pleadings therefore provide the common guide for apportioning the burdens of proof. For example, in a typical negligence case the plaintiff will have the burdens of (1) pleading the defendant's negligence (2) producing evidence of that negligence and (3) persuading the trier of fact of its existence. The defendant will usually have the same three burdens with regard to the contributory negligence of the plaintiff.

However, looking for the burden of pleading is not a foolproof guide to the allocation of the burdens of proof. The latter burdens do not invariably follow the pleadings. In a federal court, for example, a defendant may be required to plead contributory negligence as an affirmative defense and yet, where jurisdiction is based upon diversity of citizenship, the applicable substantive law may place the burdens of producing evidence and persuasion with regard to that issue on the plaintiff. More significantly, reference to which party has pleaded a fact is no help at all when the rationale behind the allocation is questioned or in a case of first impression where there are no established pleading rules.

The burdens of pleading and proof with regard to most facts have been and should be assigned to the plaintiff who generally seeks to change the present state of affairs and who therefore naturally should be expected to bear the risk of failure of proof or persuasion. The rules which assign certain facts material to the enforcibility of a claim to the defendant owe their development partly to traditional happen-so and partly to considerations of policy.

The determination of appropriate guidelines for the allocation of the burdens has been somewhat hindered by the judicial repetition of two doctrines, one erroneous and the other meaningless. Statements are found primarily in older cases to the effect that even though a party is required to plead a fact, it is not required to prove that fact if its averment is negative rather than affirmative in form. Such a rule would place an entirely undue emphasis on what is ordinarily purely a matter of choice of forms. Moreover, these statements were probably to be understood as properly applying only to the denial by a party of an opponent's previous pleading, and now one who has the burden of pleading a negative fact as part of its cause of action generally has the accompanying burdens of producing evidence and persuasion. The second misleading doctrine is that the party to whose case the element is essential has the burdens of proof. Such a rule simply restates the question.

The actual reasons for the allocation of the burdens may be no more complex than the misleading statements just discussed. The policy of handicapping a disfavored contention probably accounts for the requirement that the defendant generally has all three burdens with regard to such matters as contributory negligence, statute of limitations, and truth in defamation. Convenience in following the natural order of storytelling may account for calling on the defendant to plead and prove those matters which arise after a cause of action has matured, such as payment, release, and accord and satisfaction.

A doctrine often repeated by the courts is that where the facts with regard to an issue lie peculiarly in the knowledge of a party, that party has the burden of proving the issue. Examples are the burdens commonly placed upon the defendant to prove payment, discharge in bankruptcy, and license. This consideration should not be overemphasized. Very often one must plead and prove matters as to which his adversary has superior access to the proof. Nearly all required allegations of the plaintiff in actions for tort or breach of contract relating to the defendant's acts or omissions describe matters peculiarly in the defendant's knowledge. Correspondingly, when the defendant is required to plead contributory negligence, it pleads facts specially known to the plaintiff.

Perhaps a more frequently significant consideration in the fixing of the burdens of proof is the judicial estimate of the probabilities of the situation. The risk of failure of proof may be placed upon the party who contends that the more unusual event has occurred. For example, where a business relationship exists, it is unlikely that services will be performed gratuitously. The burden of proving a gift is therefore placed upon the one who claims it. Where services are performed for a member of the family, a gift is much more likely and the burden of proof is placed on the party claiming the right to be paid.

In allocating the burdens, courts consistently attempt to distinguish between the constituent elements of a promise or of a statutory command, which must be proved by the party who relies on the contract or statute, and matters of exception, which must be proved by its adversary. Often the result of this approach is an arbitrary allocation of the burdens, as the statutory language may be due to a mere casual choice of form by the draftsman. However, the distinction may be a valid one in some instances, particularly when the exceptions to a statute or promise are numerous. If that is the case, fairness usually requires that the adversary give notice of the particular exception upon which it relies and therefore that it bear the burden of pleading. The burdens of proof will not always follow the burden of pleading in these cases. However, exceptions generally point to exceptional situations. If proof of the facts is inaccessible or not persuasive, it is usually fairer to act as if the exceptional situation did not exist and therefore to place the burden of proof and persuasion on the party claiming its existence.

As has been stated, the burdens of producing evidence and of persuasion with regard to any given issue are both generally allocated to the same party. Usually each is assigned but once in the course of the litigation and a safe prediction of that assignment can be made at the pleading stage. However, the initial allocation of the burden of producing evidence may not always be final. The shifting nature of that burden may cause both parties to have the burden with regard to the same issue at different points in the trial.[1]

Similarly, although the burden of persuasion is assigned only once—when it is time for a decision—a prediction of the allocation of that burden, based upon the pleadings, may have to be revised when evidence is introduced at trial.[2] Policy considerations similar to those that govern the initial allocation of the burden of producing evidence and tentatively fix the burden of persuasion govern the ultimate assignment of those burdens as well.[3]

In summary, there is no key principle governing the apportionment of the burdens of proof. Their allocation, either initially or ultimately, will depend upon the weight that is given to any one or more of several factors, including: (1) the natural tendency to place the burdens on the party desiring change, (2) special policy considerations such as those disfavoring certain defenses, (3) convenience, (4) fairness, and (5) the judicial estimate of the probabilities.

§ 338. Satisfying the Burden of Producing Evidence

Let us suppose that the plaintiff, claiming an estate in land for John Smith's life, had the burden of pleading, and has pleaded, that John Smith was alive at the time the action was brought. She seeks to fulfill the burden of producing evidence of this fact.

To do this she may offer *direct* evidence, e.g., of witness Jones, who saw Smith alive in the clerk's office when the complaint in the action was filed. From this the inference of the truth of the fact to be proved depends only upon the truthfulness of Jones. Or, she may offer *circumstantial* evidence, which requires a weighing of probabilities as to matters other than merely the truthfulness of the witness. For example, she may secure the testimony of Jones that Jones received a letter in the mail which was signed "John Smith" one month before the action was brought and that she recognized the signature as Smith's. Patently in this latter case, the

§ 337

1. See § 338 infra.

2. See § 344 infra.
3. See § 343 infra.

tribunal may be satisfied that Jones is speaking the truth, and yet the tribunal may decline to infer the fact of Smith's being alive when the action began.

How strongly persuasive must the offered evidence be to satisfy the burden? A "scintilla" of evidence will not suffice. The evidence must be such that a reasonable person could draw from it the inference of the existence of the particular fact to be proved or, as put conversely by one federal court, "if there is substantial evidence opposed to the [motion for directed verdict], that is evidence of such quality and weight that reasonable and fair-minded men in the exercise of impartial judgment might reach different conclusions, the [motion] should be denied." [1]

One problem that has troubled the courts is whether the test for the granting of a directed verdict should vary, depending upon the required measure of persuasion if the case goes to the jury. For example in a criminal case where the prosecution must persuade the jury beyond a reasonable doubt,[2] should the test for a directed verdict be whether the evidence could satisfy reasonable people beyond a reasonable doubt? Some courts have said no, perhaps believing with Judge Learned Hand that, although the gravity of the consequences often makes judges more exacting in criminal cases, the line between proof that should satisfy reasonable men and the evidence that should satisfy reasonable men beyond a reasonable doubt is, in the long run, "too thin for day to day use." [3]

However, most courts applied the stricter test. A clear trend toward universal adoption of the stricter test was effectively solidified into a constitutional dictate in Jackson v. Virginia,[4] where the Court held that a federal court reviewing a state court conviction on a *habeas corpus* petition must determine whether a rational factfinder could have found the petitioners guilty beyond a reasonable doubt.

Arguably no trial judge should apply a lesser standard on a motion for a directed verdict.

Generally no difficulty occurs where the evidence is direct. Except in rare cases, it is sufficient, though given by one witness only, however negligible a human being she may be. But if the evidence is circumstantial, forensic disputes often arise as to its sufficiency to warrant a jury to draw the desired inference. In fact, in few areas of the law have so many words been spoken by the courts with so little conviction. One test frequently expounded in criminal cases is that where the prosecution relies upon circumstantial evidence, the evidence must be so conclusive as to exclude any other reasonable inference inconsistent therewith. The test is accurate enough in criminal cases, but adds little at least to the stricter test for criminal cases discussed above. A similar formula is sometimes expounded in civil cases but seems misplaced in civil litigation. It leaves little for the jury and far exceeds what is needed to prevent verdicts based upon speculation and conjecture. Courts rejecting the formula in civil cases have stated that the burden of producing evidence is satisfied, even by circumstantial evidence, if "there be sufficient facts for the jury to say reasonably that the preponderance favors liability." [5]

Other tests and other phrasings of the tests discussed here are myriad, but irrespective of the test articulated, in the last analysis the judge's ruling must necessarily rest on her individual opinion, formed in the light of her own common sense and experience, as to the limits of reasonable inference from the facts proven. However, certain situations recur and give rise repeatedly to litigation, and a given judge, in a desire for consistency and the consequent saving of time and mental travail, will rule alike whenever the same situation is proved and its sufficiency to warrant a certain inference is questioned. Other judges follow suit and a standardized practice

---

§ 338

1. Boeing Co. v. Shipman, 411 F.2d 365, 374 (5th Cir.1969).

2. See § 341 infra.

3. United States v. Feinberg, 140 F.2d 592, 594 (2d Cir.1944), cert. denied 322 U.S. 726.

4. 443 U.S. 307 (1979), rehearing denied 444 U.S. 890.

5. Smith v. Bell Telephone Co., 397 Pa. 134, 153 A.2d 477 (1959).

ripening into a rule of law results. Most of these rules are positive rather than negative. They announce that certain types of fact-groups are sufficient to enable the person who has the first duty to go forward with evidence to fulfill that burden, i.e., they enable the party to rest after proving them without being subject to the penalty of an adverse ruling.

Suppose the one who had the initial burden of offering evidence in support of the alleged fact, on pain of an adverse ruling, does produce evidence barely sufficient to satisfy that burden, so that the judge can just say, "A reasonable jury *could* infer that the fact is as alleged, from the circumstances proved." If the proponent then rests, what is the situation? Has the duty of going forward shifted to the adversary? Not if we define that duty as the liability to a peremptory adverse ruling on failing to give evidence, for if at this juncture the original proponent rests and the adversary offers no proof, the proponent will not be entitled to the direction of a verdict in her favor on the issue, but rather the court will leave the issue to the decision of the jury. But it is frequently said that in this situation the duty of going forward has shifted to the adversary, and this is unobjectionable if we bear in mind that the penalty for silence is very different here from that which was applied to the original proponent. If she had remained silent at the outset she would irrevocably have lost the case on this issue, but the only penalty now applied to her adversary is the risk, if she remains silent, of the jury's finding against her, though it may find for her. Theoretically she may have this risk still, even after she has offered evidence in rebuttal. It is simpler to limit "duty of going forward" to the liability, on resting, to an adverse ruling, and to regard the stage just discussed (where the situation is that if both parties rest, the issue will be left to the jury) as one in which neither party has any duty of going forward.

In the situation just discussed, the party who first had the duty, i.e., the necessity, of giving proof, has produced evidence which

requires the judge to permit the jury to infer, as it chooses, that the fact alleged is or is not true. It is a permitted, but not a compulsory, inference. Is it possible for the original proponent of evidence to carry her proof to the stage where if she rests, she will be entitled to a directed verdict, or its equivalent, on the issue? Undoubtedly, with a qualification to be noted, this is possible, and when it occurs there is a shifting to the adversary of the duty of going forward with the evidence, in the strictest sense. Such a ruling means that in the judge's view the proponent has not merely offered evidence from which reasonable people could draw the inference of the truth of the fact alleged, but evidence from which (in the absence of evidence from the adversary) reasonable people could not help but draw this inference. Thus, as long ago as 1770, Lord Mansfield told the jury that upon the issue of whether defendant had published a libel, proof of a sale of the book in defendant's shop was, being unrebutted, "conclusive." [6]

In the case first supposed at the beginning of this section, if the plaintiff brought forward the *direct* evidence of Jones that Smith was alive when the complaint was filed, and there is no contrary evidence at all, or if she brings forward circumstantial evidence (that is, evidence that Smith was seen alive in perfect health 10 minutes before the complaint was filed) which is, in the absence of contrary circumstances, irresistibly convincing, the jury should not be left to refuse to draw the only rational inference.

If we do not permit the jury to draw an inference from insufficient data, as where the proponent has failed to sustain her initial duty of producing evidence, we should not permit the jury to act irrationally by rejecting compelling evidence. Here again the ruling, from repeated occurrence of similar facts, may become a standardized one. However, the statement that one who has the duty of going forward can go forward far enough not merely to escape an adverse peremptory ruling herself, but to subject her opponent to one if the latter declines to take up the gage by producing evidence, has the following qualifi-

---

6. Rex v. Almon, 5 Burr. 2686, 98 Eng.Rep. 411 (K.B. 1770).

cation. Obviously if the testimony were conflicting as to the truth of the facts from which the inference of the fact in issue is desired to be drawn, and the judge believes the inference (conceding the truth of the premise) is irresistible to rational minds, he can only make a conditional peremptory ruling. He directs the jury, if you believe the evidence that fact A is so then you must find fact B, the fact in issue. In some jurisdictions, if the party seeking the ruling has the burden of persuasion on the issue, as assigned on the basis of the pleadings, she can only get a conditional ruling, though her witnesses are undisputed and unimpeached. But, in either event, if the inference is overwhelming, the jury is instructed not to cogitate over that, but only over the truthfulness of those who testify to the basic data.

We have seen something of the mechanics of the process of "proceeding" or "going forward" with evidence, viewed from the point of view of the *first* party who is stimulated to produce proof under threat of a ruling foreclosing a finding in her favor. She may in respect to a particular issue pass through three states of judicial hospitality: (a) where if she stops she will be thrown out of court; (b) where if she stops and her adversary does nothing, her reception will be left to the jury; and (c) where if she stops and her adversary does nothing, her victory (so far as it depends on having the inference she desires drawn) is at once proclaimed. Whenever the first producer has presented evidence sufficient to get her to the third stage and the burden of producing evidence can truly be said to have shifted, her adversary may in turn pass through the same three stages. Her evidence again may be (a) insufficient to warrant a finding in her favor, (b) sufficient to warrant a finding, or (c) irresistible, if unrebutted.

§ 339. Satisfying the Burden of Persuasion: (a) The Measure of Persuasion in Civil Cases Generally

According to the customary formulas a party who has the burden of persuasion of a fact must prove it in criminal prosecutions "beyond a reasonable doubt," [1] in certain exceptional controversies in civil cases, "by clear, strong and convincing evidence," [2] but on the general run of issues in civil cases "by a preponderance of evidence." The "reasonable doubt" formula points to what we are really concerned with, the state of the jury's mind, whereas the other two divert attention to the evidence, which is a step removed, being the instrument by which the jury's mind is influenced. These latter phrases, consequently, are awkward vehicles for expressing the degree of the jury's belief.

What is the most acceptable meaning of the phrase, proof by a preponderance, or greater weight, of the evidence? Certainly the phrase does not mean simple volume of evidence or number of witnesses. One definition is that evidence preponderates when it is more convincing to the trier than the opposing evidence. This is a simple commonsense explanation which will be understood by jurors and could hardly be misleading in the ordinary case. It may be objected, however, that it is misleading in a situation where, though one side's evidence is more convincing than the other's, the jury is still left in doubt as to the truth of the matter. Compelling a decision in favor of a party who has introduced evidence that is simply better than that of his adversary would not be objectionable if we hypothesize jurors who bring none of their own experience to the trial and who thus view the evidence in a vacuum. Of course, no such case could exist. We expect and encourage jurors to use their own experience to help them reach a decision, particularly in judging the credibility of witnesses. That experience may tell them, for example, that although the plaintiff has introduced evidence and the defendant has offered nothing in opposition, it is still unlikely that the events occurred as contended by the plaintiff. Thus, it is entirely consistent for a court to hold that a party's evidence is sufficient to withstand a motion

§ 339

1. See § 341 infra.

2. See § 340 infra.

for directed verdict and yet to uphold a verdict for its adversary.

The most acceptable meaning to be given to the expression, proof by a preponderance, seems to be proof which leads the jury to find that the existence of the contested fact is more probable than its nonexistence. Thus the preponderance of evidence becomes the trier's belief in the preponderance of probability. Some courts have boldly accepted this view.

Other courts have been shocked at the suggestion that a verdict, a truth-finding, should be based on nothing stronger than an estimate of probabilities. They require that the trier must have an "actual belief" in, or be "convinced of" the truth of the fact by this "preponderance of evidence." Does this mean that they must believe that it is certainly true? Hardly, since it is apparent that an investigation by fallible people based upon the testimony of other people, with all their defects of veracity, memory, and communication, cannot yield certainty. Does it mean a kind of mystical "hunch" that the fact must be true? This would hardly be a rational requirement. What it would most naturally be understood to mean by the jury (in the unlikely event that it should carry analysis so far) is that it must be persuaded that the truth of the fact is not merely more probable than not, but highly probable. This is more stringent than our tradition or the needs of justice warrant, and seems equivalent to the standard of "clear, strong and convincing proof," hitherto thought to be appropriate only in exceptional cases.[3]

Much of the time spent in the appellate courts over the metaphysics of "preponderance" has been wasted because of the courts' insistence upon the cabalistic word. This bemusement with word-magic is particularly apparent in the decisions dealing with the use of the word "satisfaction" or its derivatives in referring to the effect of the evidence on the jury's mind. Some courts, with more logic than realism, have condemned its use as

equivalent to proof beyond a reasonable doubt unless qualified by the word "reasonable." Other courts have pragmatically, although perhaps reluctantly permitted its use, even without the qualification. Although certainly juries should be clearly and accurately instructed with regard to the question of the measure of persuasion in civil cases, it is hard to believe that variations in language such as those involved in the courts' difficulties with the use of the word "satisfaction" lead to any differences in jurors' attitudes. Thoughtfully drafted pattern jury instructions should prove helpful in reducing unnecessarily spent appellate court time on these questions. Where no pattern instruction is available, however, trial judges would be wise to search for the locally accepted phraseology and to adhere to it religiously.

§ 340. Satisfying the Burden of Persuasion: (b) Requirement of Clear and Convincing Proof

While we have seen that the traditional measure of persuasion in civil cases is by a preponderance of evidence,[1] there is a limited range of claims and contentions which the party is required to establish by a more exacting measure of persuasion. The formula varies from state to state, but among the phrases used are the following: "by clear and convincing evidence," "clear, convincing and satisfactory," "clear, cogent and convincing," and "clear, unequivocal, satisfactory and convincing." Some courts have used all of these phrases and then some to describe the applicable standard. The phrasing within most jurisdictions has not become as standardized as is the "preponderance" formula, but even here the courts sometimes are surprisingly intolerant of slight variations from the approved expression. No high degree of precision can be attained by these groups of adjectives. It has been persuasively suggested that they could be more simply and intelligibly translated to the jury if they were instructed

---

3. See § 340 infra.

§ 340

1. See § 339 supra.

that they must be persuaded that the truth of the contention is "highly probable." But as former Chief Justice Burger stated:

> We probably can assume no more than that the difference between a preponderance of the evidence and proof beyond a reasonable doubt probably is better understood than either of them in relation to the intermediate standard of clear and convincing evidence. Nonetheless, even if the particular standard-of-proof catchwords do not always make a great difference in a particular case, adopting a "standard of proof is more than an empty semantic exercise." * * * In cases involving individual rights, whether criminal or civil, "[t]he standard of proof [at a minimum] reflects the value society places on individual liberty." [2]

To this end, the United States Supreme Court has held that proof by a clear and convincing or similar standard is required, either by the United States Constitution or by the applicable federal statute, in a variety of cases involving deprivations of individual rights not rising to the level of criminal prosecution, including commitment to a mental hospital, termination of parental rights, denaturalization and deportation.

Not all instances of requirements of proof more than usually convincing concern cases involving individual liberty. Indeed, the requirement of proof of this magnitude for certain types of contentions seems to have had its origins in the standards prescribed for themselves by the chancellors in determining questions of fact in equity cases. However, it has now been extended to certain types of actions tried before juries, and the chancellors' cautionary maxims are now conveyed to the jury in the form of instructions on the burden of persuasion.

Among the classes of cases to which this special standard of persuasion commonly has been applied are: (1) charges of fraud and undue influence, (2) suits on oral contracts to make a will, and suits to establish the terms of a lost will, (3) suits for the specific performance of an oral contract, (4) proceedings to set aside, reform or modify written transactions, or official acts on grounds of fraud, mistake or incompleteness, and (5) miscellaneous types of claims and defenses, varying from state to state, where there is thought to be special danger of deception, or where the court considers that the particular type of claim should be disfavored on policy grounds.

The appellate court, under the classical equity practice, tried the facts *de novo*, upon the deposition testimony in the record, and thus it was called on to apply anew the standard of clear and convincing proof in its study of the evidence. But in the modern system there are usually restrictions upon appellate review of a judge's findings of fact, even in equity issues. Thus, in the federal courts under Rule 52(a) the trial court's findings will be reversed only when "clearly erroneous." And in jury-tried cases the verdict will be reviewed only to the extent of determining whether there was evidence from which reasonable people could have found the verdict. Will the appellate court, then, today, if there was substantial evidence from which the judge or jury could have made the findings it did, consider the questions whether the evidence met the "clear and convincing" standard, in a case where it applies? The United States Supreme Court, in reviewing a summary judgment in a libel case where the plaintiff's burden was to prove actual malice by clear and convincing evidence, stated that the test on appeal should be "whether the evidence in the record could support a reasonable jury finding either that the plaintiff has shown actual malice by clear and convincing evidence or that the plaintiff has not." [3] However, in some jurisdictions it is for the trial court, not the appellate court, to draw a distinction between evidence which is clear and convincing and evidence which merely preponderates.

§ 341. Satisfying the Burden of Persuasion: (c) Proof Beyond a Reasonable Doubt

As we have seen with reference to civil cases, a lawsuit is essentially a search for

---

2. Addington v. Texas, 441 U.S. 418, 425 (1979).

3. Anderson v. Liberty Lobby, Inc., 477 U.S. 242, 255–256 (1986).

probabilities. A margin of error must be anticipated in any such search. Mistakes will be made and in a civil case a mistaken judgment for the plaintiff is no worse than a mistaken judgment for the defendant. However, this is not the case in a criminal action. Society has judged that it is significantly worse for an innocent person to be found guilty of a crime than for a guilty person to go free. The consequences to the life, liberty, and good name of the accused from an erroneous conviction of a crime are usually more serious than the effects of an erroneous judgment in a civil case. Therefore, as stated by the Supreme Court in recognizing the inevitability of error even in criminal cases, "[w]here one party has at stake an interest of transcending value—as a criminal defendant his liberty—this margin of error is reduced as to him by the process of placing on the other party the burden * * * of persuading the factfinder at the conclusion of the trial of his guilt beyond a reasonable doubt." [1] In so doing, the courts may have increased the total number of mistaken decisions in criminal cases, but with the worthy goal of decreasing the number of one kind of mistake—conviction of the innocent.

The demand for a higher degree of persuasion in criminal cases was recurrently expressed from ancient times, but its crystallization into the formula "beyond a reasonable doubt" seems to have occurred as late as 1798. It is now accepted in common law jurisdictions as the measure of persuasion by which the prosecution must convince the trier of all the essential elements of guilt. In 1970, the Supreme Court explicitly held that the due process clause "protects the accused against conviction except upon proof beyond a reasonable doubt of every fact necessary to constitute the crime with which he is charged." [2]

A simple instruction that the jury will acquit if they have a reasonable doubt of the defendant's guilt of the crime charged in the indictment is ordinarily sufficient. Courts, however, frequently paint the lily by giving the jury a definition of "reasonable doubt." A famous early instance was the oft-echoed statement of Chief Justice Shaw in the trial of Prof. Webster for the murder of Dr. Parkman: "It is that state of the case, which, after the entire comparison and consideration of all the evidence, leaves the minds of jurors in that condition that they cannot say they feel an abiding conviction, to a moral certainty, of the truth of the charge." [3] It is an ancient maxim that all definitions are dangerous and this one has been caustically criticized as raising more questions than it answers. Other definitions, often more carefully balanced to warn against the overstressing of merely possible or imaginary doubts, have become customary in some jurisdictions. Reasonable doubt is a term in common use almost as familiar to jurors as to lawyers. As one judge has said it needs a skillful definer to make it plainer by multiplication of words, and as another has expressed it, the explanations themselves often need more explanation than the term explained. A definition in terms locally approved is proper, but if not requested by accused is not required. Whether if so requested it is the judge's duty to define the term, is a matter of dispute, but the wiser view seems to be that it lies in the court's discretion, which should ordinarily be exercised by declining to define, unless the jury itself asks for a fuller explanation.

There are certain excuses or justifications allowed to the defendant, which although provable for the most part under the plea of not guilty, are spoken of for some purposes as "affirmative defenses." Among these are self-defense, duress, insanity, intoxication and claims that the accused is within an exception or proviso in the statute defining the crime. Sometimes only the burden of producing evidence will be assigned to the defendant. Under certain circumstances the burden of persuasion with regard to some of these defenses may be allocated to the defendant and correspondingly, the prosecution may be relieved

---

§ 341

1. Speiser v. Randall, 357 U.S. 513, 525–526 (1958).
2. In re Winship, 397 U.S. 358, 364 (1970).

3. Commonwealth v. Webster, 59 Mass. (5 Cush.) 295, 320 (1850).

of proving the absence of the defense. The allocation and operation of the burdens of proof with regard to these defenses present difficult policy, as well as constitutional, problems. These problems will be discussed together with the special problems related to presumptions in criminal cases.[4]

Despite occasional statements to the contrary, the reasonable doubt standard generally has been held inapplicable in civil cases, regardless of the nature of the issue involved. For example, when a charge of crime is at issue in a civil action, the threatened consequences of sustaining the accusation, though often uncommonly harmful to purse or prestige, are not generally as serious as in a prosecution for the crime. Accordingly the modern American cases have come around to the view that in the interest of justice and simplicity a reasonable doubt measure of persuasion will not be imposed. Most courts have said that a preponderance of the evidence is sufficient, although some have increased the standard to "clear and convincing."

§ 342. Presumptions: In General

One ventures the assertion that "presumption" is the slipperiest member of the family of legal terms, except its first cousin, "burden of proof." One author has listed no less than eight senses in which the term has been used by the courts.[1] Agreement can probably be secured to this extent, however: a presumption is a standardized practice, under which certain facts are held to call for uniform treatment with respect to their effect as proof of other facts.

Returning for a moment to the discussion of satisfying the burden of producing evidence,[2] assume that a party having the burden of producing evidence of fact A, introduces proof of fact B. The judge, using ordinary reasoning, may determine that fact A might reasonably be inferred from fact B, and therefore that the party has satisfied its burden, or as sometimes put by the courts, has made out a "prima facie" case. The judge has not used a presumption in the sense of a standardized practice, but rather has simply relied upon a rational inference. However, in ruling on a motion for directed verdict the judge may go beyond her own mental processes and experience and find that prior decisions or existing statutes have established that proof of fact B is sufficient to permit the jury to infer the existence of fact A. The judge has thus used a standardized practice but has the court necessarily used a presumption? Although some courts have described such a standardized inference as a presumption, most legal scholars have disagreed. They have saved the term to describe a significantly different sort of a rule, one that dictates not only that the establishment of fact B is sufficient to satisfy a party's burden of producing evidence with regard to fact A, but also at least compels the shifting of the burden of producing evidence on the question to the party's adversary. Under this view, if proof of fact B is introduced and a presumption exists to the effect that fact A can be inferred from fact B, the party denying the existence of fact A must then introduce proof of its nonexistence or risk having a verdict directed or a finding made against it. Further some authorities state that a true presumption should not only shift the burden of producing evidence, but also require that the party denying the existence of the presumed fact assume the burden of persuasion on the issue as well.[3]

Certainly the description of a presumption as a rule that, at a minimum, shifts the burden of producing evidence is to be preferred, at least in civil cases. Inferences that a trial judge decides may reasonably be drawn from the evidence need no other description, even though the judge relies upon precedent or a statute rather than personal experience in reaching a decision. In most instances, the

---

4. Sections 346–348 infra.

§ 342

1. Laughlin, In Support of the Thayer Theory of Presumptions, 52 Mich.L.Rev. 195, 196–207 (1953).

2. See § 338 supra.

3. See § 344 infra.

application of any other label to an inference will only cause confusion. In criminal cases, however, there are rules that traditionally have been labeled presumptions, even though they do not operate to shift even the burden of producing evidence. The jury is permitted but not required to accept the existence of the presumed fact even in the absence of contrary evidence.[4] Recently, the Supreme Court resurrected the term "permissive presumption" to describe these rules.[5] The term presumption will be used in this text in the preferred sense discussed above in referring to civil cases, but with the qualification suggested in referring to criminal cases.

There are rules of law that are often incorrectly called presumptions that should be specifically distinguished from presumptions at this point:

Conclusive presumptions. The term presumption as used above always denotes a rebuttable presumption, i.e., the party against whom the presumption operates can always introduce proof in contradiction. In the case of what is commonly called a conclusive or irrebuttable presumption, when fact B is proven, fact A must be taken as true, and the adversary is not allowed to dispute this at all. For example, if it is proven that a child is under seven years of age, the courts have stated that it is conclusively presumed that she could not have committed a felony. In so doing, the courts are not stating a presumption at all, but simply expressing the rule of law that someone under seven years old cannot legally be convicted of a felony.

Res ipsa loquitur. Briefly and perhaps oversimply stated, res ipsa loquitur is a rule that provides that a plaintiff may satisfy his burden of producing evidence of a defendant's negligence by proving that the plaintiff has been injured by a casualty of a sort that normally would not have occurred in the absence of the defendant's negligence. Although a few jurisdictions have given the doctrine the effect of a true presumption even

to the extent of using it to assign the burden of persuasion, most courts agree that it simply describes an inference of negligence. Prosser called it a "simple matter of circumstantial evidence."[6] Most frequently, the inference called for by the doctrine is one that a court would properly have held to be reasonable even in the absence of a special rule. Where this is so, res ipsa loquitur certainly need be viewed no differently from any other inference. Moreover, even where the doctrine is artificial—where it is imposed for reasons of policy rather than logic—it nevertheless remains only an inference, permitting but not requiring, the jury to find negligence. The only difference is that where res ipsa loquitur is artificially imposed, there is better reason for informing the jury of the permissibility of the inference than there is in the case where the doctrine simply describes a rational inference. Although theoretically a jury instruction of this kind might be viewed as violating a state rule prohibiting comment on the evidence, the courts have had little difficulty with the problem and have consistently approved and required, where requested, instructions that tell the jury that a finding of negligence is permissible. Obviously these instructions can and should be given without the use of the misnomer "presumption."

The presumption of innocence. Assignments of the burdens of proof prior to trial are not based on presumptions. Before trial no evidence has been introduced from which other facts are to be inferred. The assignment is made on the basis of a rule of substantive law providing that one party or the other ought to have one or both of the burdens with regard to an issue.[7] In some instances, however, these substantive rules are incorrectly referred to as presumptions. The most glaring example of this mislabeling is the "presumption of innocence" as the phrase is used in criminal cases. The phrase is probably better called the "assumption of innocence" in that it describes our assumption

---

4. See § 346 infra.

5. County Court of Ulster County v. Allen, 442 U.S. 140 (1979).

6. Prosser, Torts, § 40 at 231 (4th Ed.1971).

7. See § 337 supra.

that, in the absence of contrary facts, it is to be assumed that any person's conduct upon a given occasion was lawful. In criminal cases, the "presumption of innocence" has been adopted by judges as a convenient introduction to the statement of the burdens upon the prosecution, first of producing evidence of the guilt of the accused and, second, of finally persuading the jury or judge of his guilt beyond a reasonable doubt. Most courts insist on the inclusion of the phrase in the charge to the jury, despite the fact that at that point it consists of nothing more than an amplification of the prosecution's burden of persuasion. Although the phrase is technically inaccurate and perhaps even misleading in the sense that it suggests that there is some inherent probability that the defendant is innocent, it is a basic component of a fair trial. Like the requirement of proof beyond a reasonable doubt, it at least indicates to the jury that if a mistake is to be made it should be made in favor of the accused, or as Wigmore stated, "the term does convey a special and perhaps useful hint * * * in that it cautions the jury to put away from their minds all the suspicion that arises from the arrest, the indictment, and the arraignment, and to reach their conclusion solely from the legal evidence adduced." [8]

§ 343. Reasons for the Creation of Presumptions: Illustrative Presumptions

A presumption shifts the burden of producing evidence, and may assign the burden of persuasion as well. Therefore naturally the reasons for creating particular presumptions are similar to the considerations which have already been discussed,[1] that bear upon the initial or tentative assignment of those burdens. Thus, just as the burdens of proof are sometimes allocated for reasons of fairness, some presumptions are created to correct an imbalance resulting from one party's superior access to the proof. An example of such a

presumption is the rule that as between connecting carriers, the damage occurred on the line of the last carrier. Similarly, notions, usually implicit rather than expressed, of social and economic policy incline the courts to favor one contention by giving it the benefit of a presumption, and correspondingly to handicap the disfavored adversary. A classic instance is the presumption of ownership from possession, which tends to favor the prior possessor and to make for the stability of estates. A presumption may also be created to avoid an impasse, to reach some result, even though it is an arbitrary one. For example, presumptions dealing with the survivorship of persons who died in a common disaster are necessary in order that other rules of law may operate, even though there is actually no factual basis upon which to believe that one party or the other was likely to have died first. Generally, however, the most important consideration in the creation of presumptions is probability. Most presumptions have come into existence primarily because the judges have believed that proof of fact B renders the inference of the existence of fact A so probable that it is sensible and timesaving to assume the truth of fact A until the adversary disproves it.

Obviously, most presumptions are based not on any one of these grounds alone, but have been created for a combination of reasons. Usually, for example, a presumption is based not only upon the judicial estimate of the probabilities but also upon the difficulties inherent in proving that the more probable event in fact occurred.[2] Moreover, as is the case with initial allocations of the burdens, the reasons for creation of presumptions are often tied closely to the pertinent substantive law. This is particularly true with regard to those presumptions which are created, at least in part, to further some social policy.

Although it would be inappropriate to attempt to list the hundreds of recognized pre-

8. 9 Wigmore, Evidence § 2511 at 407 (Chadbourn rev. 1981).

§ 343

1. See § 337 supra.

2. See § 337.

sumptions, following is a brief discussion of a few illustrative presumptions and the reasons for their creation:

Official actions by public officers, including judicial proceedings, are presumed to have been regularly and legally performed. Reason: probability and the difficulty of proving that the officer conducted himself in a manner that was in all ways regular and legal.

A letter properly addressed, stamped and mailed is presumed to have been duly delivered to the addressee. Reason: probability and the difficulty of proving delivery in any other way.

When the plaintiff has been injured by the negligent operation of a vehicle, then upon proof of further facts he may have the benefit of presumptions in moving against the non-driving defendant. The plaintiff seeking to prove agency may secure the advantage of the presumption that the person driving the vehicle was doing so in the scope of his employment and in the course of the business of the defendant, merely by proving that the defendant was the owner. In a number of states the plaintiff must not only prove ownership to gain the benefit of the presumption of agency, but also that the driver is regularly employed by the defendant. If the plaintiff seeks to prove liability in a state having a statute making the owner liable for acts of one driving with the owner's consent, the plaintiff may secure the advantage of the presumption that the person driving was doing so with the owner's consent merely by showing ownership. In some states the plaintiff must not only prove ownership to gain the benefit of the presumption but also that a special relationship existed between the driver and the defendant. Reasons behind these presumptions: probability, fairness in the light of defendant's superior access to the evidence, and the social policy of promoting safety by widening the responsibility in borderline cases of owners for injuries caused by their vehicles.

When a bailor proves delivery of property to a bailee in good condition and return in a damaged state, or a failure to return after due demand, a presumption arises that the damage or loss was due to the negligence or fault of the bailee. Reason: fairness in the light of the superior access of the bailee to the evidence of the facts surrounding the loss; probability.

Proof that a person has disappeared from home and has been absent for at least seven years and that during this time those who would be expected to hear from the person have received no tidings and after diligent inquiry have been unable to find the person's whereabouts, raises a presumption that the person died at some time during the seven year period. The rule, though not very ancient, is already antiquated in that the seven year period is undoubtedly too long considering modern communications and transportation. Reasons: probability and the social policy of enforcing family security provisions such as life insurance, and of settling estates.

In the tracing of titles to land there is a useful presumption of identity of person from identity of name. Thus, when the same name appears in the chain of title first as grantee or heir and then as grantor, it will be presumed that it was the same person in each case. Reasons: the convenience of enabling the court and the parties to rely upon the regularity of the apparent chain of title, until this is challenged by evidence contesting identity; the social policy of quieting claims based on the face of the record; and probability.

Proof that a child was born to a woman during the time when she was married creates the presumption that the offspring is the legitimate child of the husband. Despite the controversy over whether presumptions generally shift the burden of persuasion upon the opponent,[3] it is universally agreed that in the case of this presumption, the adversary contending for illegitimacy does have the burden. This burden, moreover, is usually measured not by the normal standard for civil cases of preponderance of the evidence, but rather by the requirement of clear, convincing, and satisfactory proof, as most courts say, or even by the criminal formula, beyond a reasonable

---

3. See § 344, infra.

doubt. In addition, as pointed out elsewhere in this work, the contender for illegitimacy is further handicapped by a rule rendering incompetent the testimony or declarations of the spouses offered to show nonaccess, when the purpose is to bastardize the child.[4] Reasons: social policy, to avoid the visitation upon the child of the sins of the parents caused by the social stigma of bastardy and the common law rules (now generally alleviated by statutes) as to the incapacities of the *filius nullius*, the child of no one; probability.

When violent death is shown to have occurred and the evidence is not controlling as to whether it was due to suicide or accident, there is a presumption against suicide. Reasons: the general probability in case of a death unexplained, which flows from the human revulsion against suicide, and, probably, a social policy which inclines in case of doubt toward the fruition rather than the frustration of plans for family protection through insurance.

§ 344. The Effect of Presumptions in Civil Cases

The trial judge must consider the effect of a presumption in a civil jury trial at two stages: (1) when one party or the other moves for a directed verdict and (2) when the time comes to instruct the jury.

Sometimes the effect of a presumption, at either stage, is easy to discern; it follows naturally from the definition of the term. Thus, where a party proves the basic facts giving rise to a presumption, it will have satisfied its burden of producing evidence with regard to the presumed fact and therefore its adversary's motion for directed verdict will be denied. If its adversary fails to offer any evidence or offers evidence going only to the existence of the basic facts giving rise to the presumption and not to the presumed fact, the jury will be instructed that if they find the existence of the basic facts, they must

also find the presumed fact. To illustrate, suppose plaintiff proves that a letter was mailed, that it was properly addressed, that it bore a return address, and that it was never returned. Such evidence is generally held to raise a presumption that the addressee received the letter.[1] Defendant's motion for a directed verdict, based upon nonreceipt of the letter, will be denied. Furthermore, if the defendant offers no proof on this question (or if she attempts only to show that the letter was not mailed and offers no proof that the letter was not in fact received) the jury will be instructed that if they find the existence of the facts as contended by plaintiff, they must find that the letter was received.

But the problem is far more difficult where the defendant does not rest and does not confine her proof to contradiction of the basic facts, but instead introduces proof tending to show the nonexistence of the presumed fact itself. For example, what is the effect of the presumption in the illustration given above, if the defendant takes the stand and testifies that she did not in fact receive the letter? If the plaintiff offers no additional proof, is the defendant now entitled to the directed verdict she was denied at the close of the plaintiff's case? If not, what effect, if any should the presumption have upon the judge's charge to the jury? The problem of the effect of a presumption when met by proof rebutting the presumed fact has literally plagued the courts and legal scholars. The balance of this section is devoted to that problem.

(A) The "Bursting Bubble" Theory and Deviations from It

The theory. The most widely followed theory of presumptions in American law has been that they are "like bats of the law flitting in the twilight, but disappearing in the sunshine of actual facts."[2] Put less poetically, under what has become known as the Thayer or "bursting bubble" theory, the only effect of a

---

4. See § 67 supra.

§ 344

1. See § 343 supra.

2. Lamm J. in Mackowik v. Kansas City, St. Josephs & Council Bluffs Railroad Co., 196 Mo. 550, 571, 94 S.W. 256, 262 (1906), quoted in 9 Wigmore, Evidence § 2491 (Chadbourn rev. 1981).

presumption is to shift the burden of producing evidence with regard to the presumed fact. If that evidence is produced by the adversary, the presumption is spent and disappears. In practical terms, the theory means that, although a presumption is available to permit the party relying upon it to survive a motion for directed verdict at the close of its own case, it has no other value in the trial. The view is derived from Thayer,[3] sanctioned by Wigmore,[4] adopted in the Model Code of Evidence,[5] and seemingly been made a part of the Federal Rules of Evidence.[6] It has been adopted, at least verbally, in countless modern decisions.

The theory is simple to state, and if religiously followed, not at all difficult to apply. The trial judge need only determine that the evidence introduced in rebuttal is sufficient to support a finding contrary to the presumed fact. If that determination is made, certainly there is no need to instruct the jury with regard to the presumption. The opponent of the presumption may still not be entitled to a directed verdict, but if its motion is denied, the ruling will have nothing to do with the existence of a presumption. As has been discussed, presumptions are frequently created in instances in which the basic facts raise a natural inference of the presumed fact. This natural inference may be sufficient to take the case to the jury, despite the existence of contrary evidence and despite the resultant destruction of the presumption. For example, in the case of the presumption of receipt of a letter, referred to above, the defendant may destroy the presumption by denying receipt. Nevertheless, a jury question is presented, not because of the presumption, but because of the natural inference flowing from the plaintiff's showing that she had mailed a properly

addressed letter that was not returned. On the other hand, the basic facts may not present a natural inference of sufficient strength or breadth to take the case to the jury. In such an instance, the court may grant a directed verdict against the party who originally had the benefit of the presumption.

Deviations from the theory—in general. The "bursting bubble" theory has been criticized as giving to presumptions an effect that is too "slight and evanescent" when viewed in the light of the reasons for the creation of the rules.[7] Presumptions, as we have seen, have been created for policy reasons that are similar to and may be just as strong as those that govern the allocation of the burdens of proof prior to the introduction of evidence.[8] These policy considerations may persist despite the existence of proof rebutting the presumed fact. They may be completely frustrated by the Thayer rule when the basic facts of the presumption do not give rise to an inference that is naturally sufficient to take the case to the jury. Similarly, even if the natural inference is sufficient to present a jury question, it may be so weak that the jury is unlikely to consider it in its decision unless specifically told to do so. If the policy behind certain presumptions is not to be thwarted, some instruction to the jury may be needed despite any theoretical prohibition against a charge of this kind.

These considerations have not gone unrecognized by the courts. Thus, courts, even though unwilling to reject the dogma entirely, often find ways to deviate from it in their treatment of at least some presumptions, generally those which are based upon particularly strong and visible policies. Perhaps the best example is the presumption of legitimacy arising from proof that a child was born dur-

---

3. Thayer, Preliminary Treatise on Evidence, ch. 8, *passim*, and especially at 314, 336 (1898).

4. 9 Wigmore, Evidence § 2491(2) (Chadbourn rev. 1981).

5. Model Code of Evidence Rule 704(2) (1942): " * * * when the basic fact * * * has been established * * * and evidence has been introduced which would support a finding of the nonexistence of the presumed fact * * * the existence or nonexistence of the presumed fact is to be determined exactly as if no presumption had ever been

applicable * * *.," and Comment, "A presumption, to be an efficient legal tool must * * * (2) be so administered that the jury never hear the word presumption used since it carries unpredictable connotations to different minds * * *."

6. Fed.R.Evid. 301.

7. Morgan & Maguire, Looking Backward and Forward at Evidence, 50 Harv.L.Rev. 909, 913 (1937).

8. See § 343 supra.

ing the course of a marriage. The strong policies behind the presumption are so apparent that the courts have universally agreed that the party contending that the child is illegitimate not only has the burden of producing evidence in support of the contention, but also has a heavy burden of persuasion on the issue as well.[9]

Another example of special treatment for certain presumptions is the effect given by some courts to the presumption of agency or of consent arising from ownership of an automobile.[10] The classic theory would dictate that the presumption is destroyed once the defendant or the driver testifies to facts sufficient to support a finding of nonagency or an absence of consent. Some courts have so held. However, other courts have recognized that the policies behind the presumption, i.e., the defendant's superior access to the evidence and the social policy of widening the responsibility for owners of motor vehicles, may persist despite the introduction of evidence on the question from the defendant, particularly when the evidence comes in the form of the party's own or her servant's testimony. These courts have been unwilling to rely solely upon the natural inferences that might arise from plaintiff's proof, and instead require more from the defendant, such as, that the rebuttal evidence be "uncontradicted, clear, convincing and unimpeached." Moreover, many courts also hold that the special policies behind the presumption require that the jury be informed of its existence.

Deviations from the theory—conflicting presumptions. Frequent deviations from the rigid dictates of the "bursting bubble" theory occur in the treatment of conflicting presumptions. A conflict between presumptions may arise as follows: W, asserting that she is the widow of H, claims her share of his property, and proves that on a certain day she and H were married. The adversary then proves that three or four years before W's marriage to H, W married another man. W's proof gives her the benefit of the presumption of the validity of a marriage. The adversary's

proof gives rise to the general presumption of the continuance of a status or condition once proved to exist, and a specific presumption of the continuance of a marriage relationship. The presumed facts of the claimant's presumption and those of the adversary's are contradictory. How resolve the conflict? Thayer's solution would be to consider that the presumptions in this situation have disappeared and the facts upon which the respective presumptions were based shall simply be weighed as circumstances with all the other facts that may be relevant, giving no effect to the presumptions. Perhaps when the conflicting presumptions involved are based upon probability or upon procedural convenience, the solution is a fairly practical one.

The particular presumptions involved in the case given as an example, however, were not of that description. On the one hand, the presumption of the validity of a marriage is founded not only in probability, but in the strongest social policy favoring legitimacy and the stability of family inheritances and expectations. On the other hand, the presumptions of continuance of lives and marriage relationships are based chiefly on probability and trial convenience, and the probability, of course, varies in accordance with the length of time for which the continuance is to be presumed in the particular case. This special situation of the questioned validity of a second marriage has been the principal area in which the problem of conflicting presumptions has arisen. Here, courts have not been willing to follow Thayer's suggestion of disregarding both rival presumptions and leaving the issue to the indifferent arbitrament of a weighing of circumstantial inferences. They have often preferred to formulate the issue in terms of a conflict of presumptions and to hold that the presumption of the validity of marriage is "stronger" and should prevail. The doctrine that the weightier presumption prevails should probably be available in any situation which involves conflicting presumptions, and where one of the pre-

---

9. See § 343 supra.

10. See § 343 supra.

sumptions is grounded in a predominant social policy.

Another and perhaps even better approach to the problem is to sidestep the conflict entirely and create a new presumption. Such a presumption has evolved in cases involving conflicting marriages. Under this rule, where a person has been shown to have been married successively to different spouses, there is a presumption that the earlier marriage was dissolved by death or divorce before the later one was contracted. While of course the presumption is rebuttable, as in the case of the presumption of legitimacy, many courts place a special burden of persuasion upon the party attacking the validity of the second marriage by declaring that the presumption can only be overcome by clear, cogent, and convincing evidence.

Deviations from the theory—instructions to the jury. Because of the strength of the natural inferences that generally arise from the basic facts of a presumption, judges are seldom faced with the prospect of directing a verdict against the party relying upon a presumption. Similarly, conflicting presumptions are relatively rare. However, far more frequently courts have justifiably held that the policies behind presumptions necessitate an instruction that in some way calls the existence of the rule to the attention of the jury despite the Thayerian proscription against the practice. The digests give abundant evidence of the widespread and unquestioning acceptance of the practice of informing the jury of the rule despite the fact that countervailing evidence has been adduced upon the disputed inference.

Given the frequency of the deviation, however, the manner in which the jury is to be informed has been a matter of considerable dispute and confusion. The baffling nature of the presumption as a tool for the art of thinking bewilders one who searches for a form of phrasing with which to present the notion to a jury. Most of the forms have been predictably bewildering. For example, judges have occasionally contented themselves with a statement in the instructions of the terms of the presumption, without more. This leaves

the jury in the air, or implies too much. The jury, unless a further explanation is made, may suppose that the presumption is a conclusive one, especially if the judge uses the expression, "the law presumes."

Another solution, formerly more popular than now, is to instruct the jury that the presumption is "evidence," to be weighed and considered with the testimony in the case. This avoids the danger that the jury may infer that the presumption is conclusive, but it probably means little to the jury, and certainly runs counter to accepted theories of the nature of evidence.

More attractive theoretically, is the suggestion that the judge instruct the jury that the presumption is to stand accepted, unless they find that the facts upon which the presumed inference rests are met by evidence of equal weight, or in other words, unless the contrary evidence leaves their minds in equipoise, in which event they should decide against the party having the burden of persuasion upon the issue. It is hard to phrase such an instruction without conveying the impression that the presumption itself is "evidence" which must be "met" or "balanced." The overriding objection, however, is the impression of futility that it conveys. It prescribes a difficult metaphysical task for the jury, and, in actual use, may mystify rather than help the average juror.

One possible solution, perhaps better than those already mentioned, would be for the trial judge simply to mention the basic facts of the presumption and to point out the general probability of the circumstantial inference as one of the factors to be considered by the jury. By this technique, however, a true presumption would be converted into nothing more than a permissible inference. Moreover, the solution is simply not a feasible one in many jurisdictions without at least a new interpretation of another aspect of the law. The trial judge in most states must tread warily to avoid an expression of opinion on the facts. Although instructions on certain standardized inferences such as *res ipsa loqui-*

tur are permitted,[11] the practice, wisely or not, may frown on any explanation of the allowable circumstantial inferences from particular facts as "invading the province of the jury."

Where the "bursting bubble" rule is discarded in favor of a rule which operates to fix the burden of persuasion, the problem of alerting the jury to the presumption should not exist. Under this theory, a presumption may ordinarily be given a significant effect without the necessity of mentioning the word "presumption" to the jury at all. There is no more need to tell the jury why one party or the other has the burden of persuasion where that burden is fixed by a presumption than there is where the burden is fixed on the basis of policies apparent from the pleadings. The jury may be told simply that, if it finds the existence of the basic facts, the opponent must prove the non-existence of the presumed fact by a preponderance of evidence, or, in some instances, by a greater standard. Even in those instances in which the presumption places the burden of persuasion on the same party who initially had the burden, there would seem to be no reason to mention the term. If the courts feel that the operation of the presumption warrants a higher standard of proof, the measure of persuasion can be increased as is now done in the case of the presumption of legitimacy. However, unless we are willing to increase the measure of persuasion, nothing can be gained by informing the jury of the coincidence. The word "presumption" would only tend to confuse the issue.

(B) Attempts to Provide a Single Rule Governing the Effect of Presumptions

Perhaps, the greatest difficulty with the "bursting bubble" approach is that, in spite of its apparent simplicity, the conflicting desires of the courts to adopt it in theory and yet to avoid its overly-rigid dictates have turned it

into a judicial nightmare of confusion and inconsistency. This state of affairs has caused legal scholars not only to search for a better rule, but for a single rule that would cover all presumptions.

Many writers came to the view that the better rule for all presumptions would provide that anything worthy of the name "presumption" has the effect of fixing the burden of persuasion on the party contesting the existence of the presumed fact. A principal technical objection to such a rule has been that it requires a "shift" in the burden of persuasion something that is, by definition of the burden, impossible. The argument seems misplaced, in that it assumes that the burden of persuasion is fixed at the commencement of the action. However, as we have seen,[12] the burden of persuasion need not finally be assigned until the case is ready to go to the jury. Thus, using a presumption to fix that burden would not cause it to shift, but merely cause it to be assigned on the basis of policy considerations arising from the evidence introduced at the trial rather than those thought to exist on the basis of the pleadings.[13] Certainly there is no reason why policy factors thought to be controlling at the pleading stage should outweigh factors bearing upon the same policies that arise from the evidence. Just the reverse should be true.

Certainly, some presumptions have been interpreted consistently as affecting the burden of persuasion without a great deal of discussion of a "shifting" burden of proof.[14] The real question is more fundamental: should this rule which is applicable to some presumptions be applicable universally? The answer to that query depends, not on theoretical distinctions between shifting as opposed to reassigning the burden of persuasion, but upon whether the policy behind the creation of all presumptions is always strong enough to affect the allocation of the burden of persuasion as well as the burden of producing evidence.

11. See § 342 supra.

12. See § 336 supra.

13. The policies behind the allocation of the burden of persuasion are discussed generally in § 337 supra. The

policies behind the creation of presumptions are discussed in § 343 supra.

14. See § 343 supra, concerning the presumption of legitimacy.

One of the leading proponents of the rule allocating the burden of persuasion as a universal rule was Professor Morgan. Although Professor Morgan served as a reporter for the Model Code of Evidence, he was unable to persuade the draftsmen of that code to incorporate into it a provision embracing this view of the effect of presumptions. The Model Code instead takes a rigid Thayerian position.[15] However, Morgan also was active in the drafting of the original Uniform Rules of Evidence where he had considerably more success in inducing an adoption of his theory. The original Uniform Rules provided that where the facts upon which the presumption is based have "probative value" the burden of persuasion is assigned to the adversary; where there is no such probative value, the presumption has only a Thayerian effect and dies when met by contrary proof.[16]

The Uniform Rules, although having much to commend them, presented problems. Obviously, they did not provide for a single rule. Different courts could give different answers to the question whether a particular presumption has probative value. The possibilities of inconsistency and confusion, although reduced by the rules, were still present. Further, the distinction made was a thin one that disregarded the existence of strong social policies behind some presumptions that lack probative value. Certainly if a presumption is not based on probability but rather is based solely upon social policy, there may be more, and not less, reason to preserve it in the face of contrary proof. A presumption based on a natural inference can stand on its own weight either when met by a motion for a directed verdict or in the jury's deliberations. A presumption based on social policy may need an extra boost in order to insure that the policy is not overlooked. Morgan apparently recognized the weakness of the distinction made by the rule and seemed to have agreed to it only to allay fears that a provision giving to all presumptions the effect of fixing the burden of persuasion might be unconstitutional.

An approach almost directly opposite to the one taken in the Uniform Rules is taken in California's Code of Evidence, adopted in 1965. Under the California Code, presumptions based upon "public policy" operate to fix the burden of persuasion;[17] presumptions that are established "to implement no public policy other than to facilitate the determination of a particular action" are given a Thayerian effect.[18] The California approach is an improvement over the Uniform Rules but is still not completely satisfactory. The line between presumptions based on public policy and those which are not may not be easy to draw. Furthermore, although the California distinction is sounder than that made in the Uniform Rules, it is not completely convincing. The fact that the policy giving rise to a presumption is one that is concerned with the resolution of a particular dispute rather than the implementation of broader social goals, does not necessarily mean that the policy is satisfied by the shifting of the burden of producing evidence and that it should disappear when contrary proof is introduced. California asks the wrong question about the policies behind presumptions. The inquiry should not be directed to the breadth of the policy but rather to the question whether the policy considerations behind a certain presumption are sufficient to override the policies that tentatively fix the burdens of proof at the pleading stage.

The Federal Rules of Evidence, as adopted by the Supreme Court and submitted to the Congress, took the approach advocated by Morgan. The proposed Rule 301 provided that "a presumption imposes on the party against whom it is directed, the burden of proving that the non-existence of the presumed fact is more probable than its existence." However, the draft did not survive congressional scrutiny and Rule 301, as enacted, has a distinct Thayerian flavor:

In all civil actions and proceedings not otherwise provided for by Act of Congress or by

---

15. Model Code of Evidence Rule 704.

16. Original Unif.R.Evid. 14 (1953).

17. West's Ann.Cal.Evid.Code §§ 605–606.

18. Id. §§ 603–604.

these rules, a presumption imposes on the party against whom it is directed, the burden of going forward with evidence to rebut or meet the presumption but does not shift to such party the burden of proof in the sense of the risk of non-persuasion, which remains throughout the trial upon the party of whom it was originally cast.[19]

Some legal scholars have argued that Federal Rule 301 does not preclude instructions which at least alert the jury to the strength of logic and policy underlying a presumption, even though evidence contrary to the existence of the presumed fact has been introduced. Furthermore, there has been willingness on the part of the federal courts to find that certain acts of Congress create presumptions of greater vitality than that provided by Rule 301 or even that certain presumptions in existence at the time of the adoption of Rule 301 are not subject to the procedure set forth in that rule. On the other hand, the rule has also served as a guideline for courts wishing to give a "bursting bubble" effect to a presumption, even where the court may not necessarily believe itself bound by the dictates of Rule 301.

The matter is further complicated by the fact that many of the states thus far adopting new evidence rules based upon the federal rules, have taken the approach of original Rule 301 and allocate the burden of persuasion based upon the presumption. Likewise, the Revised Uniform Rules of Evidence (1974), reject the "bursting bubble" and contain a Rule 301 almost identical to the rule submitted by the Supreme Court to the Congress.[20]

(C) The Search for the Grail

Despite the best efforts of legal scholars, instead of having one rule to govern all presumptions in all proceedings, we are left in some ways in a more confusing state than that which existed prior to the adoption of the Federal Rules. Neither Morgan's view that all presumptions operate to assign the burden of persuasion nor the Thayerian concept of a disappearing presumption has yet to win the day.

The problem may be inherent in the nature of the concept of a "presumption." At least one author has argued that the concept is an artificial one, an attempt to do through a legal fiction what courts should be doing directly;[21] that the term "presumption" should be eliminated from legal usage and the functions which it serves replaced by direct allocations of the burdens of proof and by judicial comment accurately describing the logical implication of certain facts. In one sense, the suggestion is attractive. The courts should indeed be discussing the propriety of allocating the burdens of proof, rather than the conceptual technical application of a presumption. Yet, both the term and concept of a presumption, however misunderstood, are so engrained in the law that it is difficult to imagine their early demise. Furthermore, as the author recognizes, there are instances in which the evidence introduced at the trial may be such as to give rise to a rule of law which shifts or reassigns the burdens of proof. He calls this a "conditional imperative" and recognizes that in such a case the allocation of the burdens of proof cannot be made prior to trial. While the term "conditional imperative" may be just as good as "presumption," it is no better and the same set of problems which exist with regard to presumptions are just as likely to occur regardless of the label employed.

The answer may be that there is no single solution to the problem. The resistance of the courts and legislatures to a universal rule of presumptions is reflective of the fact that there are policies of varying strength behind

---

19. Fed.R.Evid. 301.

20. Rev. Uniform Rule Evid. (1986) 301(a) provides:
In all actions and proceedings not otherwise provided for by statute or by these rules, a presumption imposes on the party against whom it is directed the burden of proving that the nonexistence of the presumed fact is more probable than its existence.

21. Allen, Presumptions, Inferences and Burden of Proof in Federal Civil Actions—An Anatomy of Unnecessary Ambiguities and a Proposal for Reform, 76 Nw. U.L.Rev. 892 (1982); Allen, Presumptions in Civil Actions Reconsidered, 66 Iowa L.Rev. 843 (1981).

different presumptions and therefore a hierarchy of desired results. In one instance, the policy may be such as only to give rise to a standardized inference, a rule of law which gets the plaintiff to the jury but does not compel a directed verdict in its favor. In another instance, the policy may be strong enough to compel a directed verdict in its favor, thus shifting the burden of producing evidence to the opposing party, but not strong enough to reassign the burden of persuasion. In still another instance, the policy may be strong enough to reassign the burden of persuasion.

Attempts to categorize presumptions according to policy considerations have been thoughtful and well-meaning. Unfortunately, they have fallen short of the mark, largely because of the inherent difficulty of the task. Each presumption is created for its own reasons—reasons which are inextricably intertwined with the pertinent substantive law. These substantive considerations have a considerable impact on the procedural effect desirable for a particular presumption. The diversity of the considerations simply defies usable categorization. The law and lawyers are accustomed to considering the dictates of the substantive law in determining the initial allocation of the burdens of proof. The task should not be thought too onerous in connection with the operation of presumptions which, after all, simply operate to reallocate those burdens during the course of the trial.

Rather than attempting to provide a single rule for all presumptions, a task which has thus far proved futile, the draftsmen of evidence codes might instead provide guidelines for the appropriate but various effects which a presumption may have on the burdens of proof. The courts and legislatures would then have the opportunity to select the appropriate effect to be given to a particular presumption. The term presumption seems likely to be with us forever; it also seems likely that different presumptions will continue to

be viewed as having different procedural effects; we can only hope to insure that the concept which the term "presumption" represents is applied constructively and rationally.

§ 345. Constitutional Questions in Civil Cases

Serious questions under the United States Constitution are raised by the creation and use of presumptions in criminal cases. Those questions are discussed in subsequent sections.[1] Although there are constitutional considerations involved in the use of presumptions in civil cases, the problems are simply not of the same magnitude. In a criminal case, the scales are deliberately overbalanced in favor of the defendant through the requirement that the prosecution prove each element of the offense beyond a reasonable doubt.[2] Any rule that has even the appearance of lightening that burden is viewed with the most extreme caution. However, there is no need for this special protection for any one party to a civil action. The burdens of proof are fixed at the pleading stage, not for constitutional reasons, but for reasons of probability, social policy, and convenience.[3] There is no reason why the same policy considerations, as reflected in the operation of a presumption, should not be permitted further to effect an allocation of the burdens of proof during the course of the trial.

Nevertheless, the courts articulate a "rational connection" test in civil cases, which requires that such a connection exist between the basic facts and the presumed facts in order for the presumption to pass constitutional muster. Recent cases have applied the test, but upheld the presumption. Perhaps under certain circumstances a presumption could operate in such an arbitrary manner as to violate fundamental due process considerations, even in a civil case. But to impose a strictly applied "rational connection" limita-

---

§ 345

1. Sections 347–348 infra.

2. See § 341 supra with regard to the nature of the prosecution's burden; see § 347 infra with regard to the

constitutional limits on the effect that a presumption may have upon that burden.

3. See § 337 supra.

tion upon the creation of presumptions in civil cases would mean that only presumptions based on probability would be permissible. Such a limitation would ignore other, equally valid, reasons for the creation of the rules. Considerations which have been either explicitly rejected or severely limited in criminal cases, such as the comparative knowledge of the parties with regard to the facts and the power of the legislature to do away with a claim or a defense entirely, should remain significant in determining the validity of a civil presumption.

Perhaps the most difficult question with regard to civil presumptions is whether a presumption may operate to assign the burden of persuasion. The question arises from the contrast between two Supreme Court cases considering the validity of presumptions of negligence operating against railroads. In the first, Mobile, J. & K. C. R. Co. v. Turnipseed,[4] decided in 1910, the Court considered a Mississippi statutory presumption of negligence operating against a railroad in an action for death of an employee in a derailment. The statute provided that proof of injury inflicted by the running of railroad cars would be "prima facie evidence of the want of reasonable skill and care" on the part of the railroad. Noting that the only effect of the statute was to impose on the railroad the duty of producing some evidence to the contrary, the court held that the rational connection between the fact proved and the fact presumed was sufficient to sustain the presumption.

However, in 1929, in Western & Atlantic R. R. v. Henderson,[5] the Court struck down a Georgia statute making railroads liable for damage done by trains, unless the railroad made it appear that reasonable care had been used, "the presumption in all cases being against the company." In Henderson the plaintiff alleged that her husband had been killed in a grade crossing collision. The jury was instructed that negligence was presumed from the fact of injury and that the burden

was therefore on the railroad to show that it exercised ordinary care. The Court held that the mere fact of a collision between a train and a vehicle at a crossing furnished no basis for any inference as to negligence and that therefore the presumption was invalid. Turnipseed was distinguished on the ground that the Mississippi presumption raised "merely a temporary inference of fact" while the Georgia statute created "an inference that is given effect of evidence to be weighed against opposing testimony and is to prevail unless such testimony is found by the jury to preponderate."[6]

Although perhaps a grade crossing collision differs from a derailment and therefore Turnipseed and Henderson can be distinguished on their facts, it is nevertheless fair to read Henderson as imposing constitutional limitations on the effect of at least some presumptions. However, Henderson may simply no longer be valid law. The case assumed the necessity of a showing of negligence. But the concept of negligence has lost most of its sanctity since 1929. Although there is considerable doubt as to what the Court would have done in that year, there is little doubt today that a legislature would be permitted at least to relegate lack of negligence to the status of an affirmative defense. If negligence could be so reduced, a presumption which assigned the burden of persuasion could logically be treated no differently.

Since Henderson, the Court has, on at least one occasion, approved a state presumption that operated to fix the burden of persuasion on the party controverting the presumed fact. In that case, Dick v. New York Life Insurance Co.[7] the Court approved a North Dakota common law rule that imposed on the defendant insurance company, defending against the operation of an accidental death clause, the burden of persuading the jury that the death of the insured was due to suicide.

The questionable status of Henderson in light of recent developments in tort law, the

4. 219 U.S. 35 (1910).

5. 279 U.S. 639 (1929).

6. Id. at 643–644.

7. 359 U.S. 437 (1959).

holding of the Court in *Dick,* and the illogic of treating presumptions differently from other rules of law allocating the burden of persuasion, all make it extremely unlikely that there are now serious constitutional limits on the effect that may be given to presumptions in civil cases.

§ 346. Affirmative Defenses and Presumptions in Criminal Cases: (a) Terminology

As has been earlier pointed out, the courts and legislatures do not always use the term presumption in the sense either that the term is used in this text or by the same courts and legislatures on other occasions.[1] The use of loose terminology is perhaps even more prevalent in dealing with presumptions operating in criminal cases than in civil cases. The best example is one that has already been given. The "presumption of innocence" is not a presumption at all, but simply another way of stating the rule that the prosecution has the burden of proving the guilt of the accused beyond a reasonable doubt.[2]

Similarly, the courts and writers have struggled to define and distinguish presumptions and affirmative defenses. Certainly, these procedural devices have factors in common. Yet, as the devices are traditionally defined, there are some significant variations between them that have caused the courts to treat them differently.

1. Affirmative defenses. The term affirmative defense is traditionally used to describe the allocation of a burden, either of production or of persuasion, or both, to the defendant in a criminal case. The burden is fixed by statute or case law at the beginning of the case and does not depend upon the introduction of any evidence by the prosecution. For example, a crime may be statutorily defined as consisting of elements A and B. However, the accused may be exonerated or the offense reduced in degree upon proof of C. C is an affirmative defense. In some instances, the defendant may simply have the burden of production of evidence with regard to C; in the event that burden is satisfied, the prosecution will then have the burden of persuading the jury of elements A, B, *and* C beyond a reasonable doubt. In other instances, the defendant will have both the burden of production and the burden of persuasion. Thus, the prosecution will have no burden with regard to C; the defendant must both introduce proof of C and persuade the jury of its existence. Usually, the measure of persuasion imposed on the defendant with regard to an affirmative defense is a preponderance of the evidence.

2. Presumptions. Presumptions have already been defined as a standardized practice under which certain facts are held to call for uniform treatment with respect to their effect as proof of other facts.[3] In civil cases, the term presumption is properly reserved for a rule that provides that upon proof of certain basic facts, at least the burden of producing evidence with regard to certain presumed facts shifts. As has been discussed, a presumption may in some instances operate to allocate the burden of persuasion as well.[4]

A somewhat different terminology has been used more or less consistently in criminal cases. The tendency in criminal cases has been to describe any standardized rule which permits the inference of one fact from another as a presumption, regardless of whether the rule operates to shift the burden of production. Thus, assume a crime with three elements, A, B and C. A rule of law provides that fact C may be inferred from proof of A and B. Such a rule is usually described as a presumption, whether or not any burden is actually shifted to the defendant. In most instances, no burden shifts; the presumption operates only to permit the prosecution to make out a prima facie case by proof of A and B alone. The jury will be instructed that it

---

§ 346

1. See § 342 supra.
2. See § 342 supra.

3. Section 342 supra.
4. Section 344 supra.

may, but is not required to, infer the existence of fact C from proof of facts A and B.

The United States Supreme Court has resurrected terminology used in the first edition of this text to describe the different effects of presumptions in criminal cases. In County Court of Ulster County v. Allen,[5] the court distinguished between mandatory and permissive presumptions. A mandatory presumption is one which operates to shift at least the burden of production. It tells the trier of fact that it must find the presumed fact upon proof of the basic fact, "at least unless the defendant has come forward with some evidence to rebut the presumed connection between the two facts."[6] The Court further sub-divided mandatory presumptions into two parts: presumptions that merely shift the burden of production to the defendant and presumptions that shift the burden of persuasion. A permissive presumption is one which allows, but does not require, the trier of fact to infer the presumed fact from proof of the basic facts. Under the *Allen* decision, these various kinds of presumptions differ not only procedurally, but also with regard to the tests for their constitutional permissibility as well.

§ 347. Affirmative Defenses and Presumptions in Criminal Cases: (b) Constitutionality

Recent years have brought some noteable developments with regard to the constitutionality of both affirmative defenses and presumptions.

1. Affirmative defenses. Historically, many states placed both the burden of production and the burden of persuasion on the accused with regard to several classical affirmative defenses, including insanity and self-defense. The allocation to the defendant of the burdens of proof with regard to insanity survived constitutional challenge in 1952. In Leland v. Oregon,[1] the Supreme Court held

that the defendant could be required to prove his insanity at the time of the alleged crime beyond a reasonable doubt. On the other hand, some limitations were imposed on the creation or effect of affirmative defenses. For example, one United States Court of Appeals held unconstitutional a state's allocation of the burden of persuasion to the accused with regard to alibi. The court reasoned that an alibi was a mere form of denial of participation in the criminal act, not a true affirmative defense.

Although perhaps foreshadowed by the treatment given the defense of alibi, the real revolution in thought with regard to affirmative defenses occurred in the mid–1970's with two pivotal Supreme Court decisions.

In Mullaney v. Wilbur,[2] the Court reversed a Maine murder conviction where the jury had been instructed, in accordance with longstanding state practice, that if the prosecution proved "that the homicide was both intentional and unlawful, malice aforethought was to be conclusively implied unless the defendant proved by a fair preponderance of the evidence that he acted in the heat of passion on sudden provocation," in which event the defendant would be guilty only of manslaughter. The placing of this burden on the defendant was said to violate the dictates of In re Winship[3] that the due process clause requires the prosecution to prove beyond a reasonable doubt every fact necessary to constitute the crime charged. Although recognizing that under Maine law murder and manslaughter were but degrees of the same crime, the Court noted that *Winship* applied to instances in which the issue is degree of criminal culpability as well as to cases of guilt or innocence.

The *Mullaney* case was surprising in view of the long history in some jurisdictions of placing the burden of reducing the degree of a homicide on the defendant. However, given the holding and rationale of *Winship,* it was not totally unexpected. It was certainly pos-

---

5. 442 U.S. 140 (1979).

6. Id. at 157.

§ 347

1. 343 U.S. 790 (1952) rehearing denied 344 U.S. 848.

2. 421 U.S. 684, 686 (1975).

3. 397 U.S. 358 (1970). See § 341 *supra.*

sible, and perhaps fair, to read the *Mullaney* case broadly so as to require the imposition of the burden of persuasion on the prosecution with regard to many, if not all, of the traditional affirmative defenses. Indeed, the opinion was read by several state courts as constitutionally compelling the prosecution to bear the burden of persuasion with regard to various affirmative defenses. Only the existence of the *Leland* opinion, not expressly overruled in *Mullaney*, prevented one federal court from applying *Mullaney* to impose upon a state the burden of persuasion with regard to an insanity defense.

The first real indication that the holding in *Mullaney* had far more narrow limits came when the Court, in Rivera v. Delaware,[4] dismissed, as not presenting a substantial federal question, an appeal from a conviction in which the defendant had borne the burden of proving his insanity. The indication became a certainty when the Court decided Patterson v. New York.[5] In *Patterson*, the Court upheld a New York procedure under which an accused is guilty of murder in the second degree if he is found, beyond a reasonable doubt, to have intentionally killed another person. The crime may be reduced to manslaughter if the defendant proves by a preponderance of the evidence that he had acted under the influence of "extreme emotional disturbance." The Court held that the New York procedure did not violate due process noting, in the language of *Winship*, " 'every fact necessary to constitute the crime with which [Patterson was] charged had to be proved beyond a reasonable doubt.' "[6] *Mullaney* was distinguished as dealing with a situation in which the defendant was asked to disprove an essential element of the prosecution's case—malice aforethought. New York, unlike Maine, did not include malice aforethought in its definition of murder. By this omission, New York had avoided the defect found fatal in *Mullaney*, even though the defense involved in the *Patterson* case was but an expanded version of the "heat of passion on sudden provocation" involved in *Mullaney*.

The Court in *Patterson* decided the constitutionality of the allocation of the burden of proof by a formalistic analysis of state law: due process was not violated because the defendant did not have the burden of proof on any fact that state law had identified as an element of the offense. Despite significant and persistent criticism, the durability of this approach was confirmed ten years later in Martin v. Ohio[7]. In *Martin*, Ohio had defined the crime of murder as purposely causing the death of another with prior calculation or design and placed the burden of proving self-defense on the defendant. The Court upheld the conviction because the defendant did not have the burden of proving any of the elements included by the state in its definition of the crime. The dictates of *Winship* were not violated so long as the instructions to the jury made it clear that State had the burden of proving all of the elements—including prior calculation and design—beyond a reasonable doubt, and that the self-defense evidence could also be considered in determining whether there was reasonable doubt about any element of the State's case.

The lower courts have, of course, followed the pattern of *Patterson* and *Martin*, holding invalid allocations of the burden of persuasion thought to involve nothing more than the rebuttal of an element of the offense and sanctioning allocations where the jury has been instructed that the affirmative defense is held to come into play only after the state has proven the elements of the crime beyond a reasonable doubt.

The analysis in *Patterson* and *Martin* deals only with the allocation of the burden of persuasion. As suggested by dicta in *Patterson*, the courts have had no trouble with an affirmative defense which simply requires the defendant to bear a burden of production. For example, even though a state includes absence of self-defense as an element of a crime so as to prohibit the allocation of the

---

4. 429 U.S. 877 (1976).

5. 432 U.S. 197 (1977).

6. Id. at 206.

7. 480 U.S. 228 (1987).

burden of persuasion to the accused, the accused may be required to introduce at least some evidence of self-defense in order for the issue to go the jury.

2. *Presumptions.*

Like affirmative defenses, the Supreme Court's analysis of the constitutionality of presumptions has evolved significantly in recent years. The 1979 decisions in County Court of Ulster County v. Allen[8] and Sandstrom v. Montana[9], constitute the watershed in the Court's analysis of the issue.

Prior to *Allen* and *Sandstrom,* the Court had set limitations on the creation and application of presumptions in criminal cases in a series of cases beginning with Tot v. United States.[10] In *Tot,* the Court invalidated a presumption contained in a federal firearms statute stating that possession of a firearm was presumptive evidence that the weapon was received in interstate commerce. The Court stated that "a statutory presumption cannot be sustained if there be no rational connection between the fact proved and the ultimate fact presumed, if the inference of the one from proof of the other is arbitrary because of lack of connection between the two in common experience." [11]

Tot was followed by two 1965 cases dealing with presumptions enacted to aid the government in prosecuting liquor cases. In United States v. Gainey,[12] the Court applied the rational connection test of *Tot* to uphold the validity of a statute which provided that presence at the site is sufficient to convict a defendant of the offense of carrying on the business of distilling without giving bond, "unless the defendant explains such presence to the satisfaction of the jury." However, in United States v. Romano,[13] the Court struck down as violative of *Tot* an identical presumption with regard to the companion offense of possession of an illegal still. The Court distinguished *Gainey,* noting that the crime of

carrying on an illegal distilling business, involved in *Gainey,* was an extremely broad one. A person's unexplained presence at the still made it highly likely that he had something to do with its operation. However, no such natural inference existed with regard to the presumption of *possession* from unexplained presence involved in *Romano.*

Tot, Gainey and *Romano* left several questions unanswered. Most significantly, the "rational connection" test was vague. Was it a test of relevancy or a test of probative sufficiency? If it was a test of sufficiency, the existence of the presumed fact would have to be shown to be more likely than not to exist or perhaps even have to be shown to exist beyond a reasonable doubt.

The question was partially answered in 1969 and 1970 by two cases involving presumptions in narcotics prosecutions. In Leary v. United States,[14] the Court considered a presumption providing that possession of marihuana was sufficient evidence to authorize conviction of transporting and concealing the drug *with knowledge of its illegal importation* unless the defendant explained his possession to the satisfaction of the jury. The Court held that the presumption of knowledge was unconstitutional, stating:

"The upshot of *Tot, Gainey* and *Romano* is, we think, that a criminal statutory presumption must be regarded as 'irrational' or 'arbitrary,' " and hence unconstitutional, unless it can be said with substantial assurance that the presumed fact is more likely than not to flow from the proved fact on which it is made to depend * * *." [15]

In a footnote to this statement, the Court added that because of its finding that the presumption was unconstitutional under this standard, it would not reach the question "whether a criminal presumption which passes muster when so judged must also satisfy the criminal 'reasonable doubt' standard if

---

8. 442 U.S. 140 (1979).

9. 442 U.S. 510 (1979).

10. 319 U.S. 463 (1943).

11. Id. at 467.

12. 380 U.S. 63 (1965).

13. 382 U.S. 136 (1965).

14. 395 U.S. 6 (1969).

15. Id. at 36.

proof of the crime charged or an essential element thereof depends upon its use." [16]

The next year, the Court dealt with two presumptions in Turner v. United States.[17] One was identical with the presumption struck down in *Leary,* except that the drugs involved in *Turner* were heroin and cocaine rather than marihuana. The other provided that the absence of appropriate tax paid stamps from narcotic drugs found in the defendant's possession would be "prima facie evidence" that he purchased or distributed the drugs from other than the original stamped package. The Court extensively reviewed the legislative records with regard to the statutes and surveyed the records of other narcotics cases for evidence to support or rebut the inferences called for by the statutes. It concluded that the "overwhelming evidence" was that the heroin consumed in the United States is illegally imported and that Turner therefore must have known this fact. Based upon this conclusion, the Court upheld the presumptions of illegal importation and "stamped package" as to heroin. In contrast, the Court struck down the same presumptions with regard to cocaine, finding that it could not be "sufficiently sure either that the cocaine that Turner possessed came from abroad or that Turner must have known that it did," and that there was "a reasonable possibility" that Turner had in fact obtained the cocaine from a legally stamped package.

In *Turner,* the Court again found it unnecessary specifically to adopt a test that would require that the presumed fact be shown to exist beyond a reasonable doubt. However, the Court's frequent reference to that standard in *Turner,* coupled with its decision in In re Winship [18] recognizing that such a measure of proof is constitutionally required in criminal cases, seemed to make it likely that the reasonable doubt standard would be applied to test the validity of presumptions.

Not long after *Turner,* the Court applied the rationale of the cases involving statutory presumptions to a common law presumption. In Barnes v. United States,[19] the Court upheld a conviction for possession of stolen treasury checks in which the jury had been instructed in accordance with the traditional common law inference that the knowledge necessary for conviction may be drawn from the unexplained possession of recently stolen goods. The Court still refrained from adopting either a more-likely-than-not or a reasonable doubt standard in its review of the presumption, but held rather that the presumption in question satisfied both. The only question that seem to remain after *Barnes* whether the Court ultimately would require that all presumptions be tested by a reasonable doubt standard. Surprisingly, a whole new set of considerations arrived in 1979.

The New York prosecution in County Court of Ulster County v. Allen [20] was for illegal possession of, inter alia, handguns. Four persons, three adult males and a 16–year–old girl, were tried jointly. The evidence showed that two large-caliber handguns were seen in the front of the car in an open handbag belonging to the 16–year–old. A New York statute provided that, with certain exceptions, the presence of a firearm in an automobile was presumptive evidence of its illegal possession by all persons then occupying the vehicle. The jury was instructed with regard to the presumption but told that the presumption "need not be rebutted by affirmative proof or affirmative evidence but may be rebutted by any evidence or lack of evidence in the case."

The federal Court of Appeals affirmed the District Court's grant of habeas corpus, holding that the New York statute was unconstitutional on its face because it swept within its compass many individuals who would in fact have no connection with a weapon even though they were present in a vehicle in which the weapon was found.

The Supreme Court reversed, stating that the Court of Appeals had improperly viewed

16. Id. at 36 n. 64.

17. 396 U.S. 398 (1970).

18. 397 U.S. 358 (1970). See § 341 supra.

19. 412 U.S. 837 (1973).

20. 442 U.S. 140 (1979).

the statute on its face. The Court stated that the ultimate test of any device's constitutional validity is that it not undermine the factfinder's responsibility at trial, based on evidence adduced by the state, to find the ultimate facts beyond a reasonable doubt. Therefore, mandatory and permissive presumptions must be analyzed differently. It is appropriate to analyze mandatory presumptions on their face. Where a mandatory presumption is used, the defendant may be convicted based upon the presumption alone as the result of the failure of the accused to introduce proof to the contrary. The Court reasoned that in such an instance the presumption would be unconstitutional unless the basic facts, standing alone, are sufficient to support the inference of guilt beyond a reasonable doubt. In the case of a permissive presumption the jury is told only that it may, but need not, find the defendant guilty based upon the basic facts. Thus, the validity of the presumption must be tested, not in the abstract, but rather in connection with all of the evidence in the case. The Court stated:

> "Because this permissive presumption leaves the trier of fact free to credit or reject the inference and does not shift the burden of proof, it affects the application of the 'beyond a reasonable doubt' standard only if, under the facts of the case, there is no rational way the trier could make the connection permitted by the inference. For only in that situation is there any risk that an explanation of the permissible inference to a jury, or its use by a jury, has caused the presumptively rational factfinder to make an erroneous factual determination." [21]

The Court found that the instruction in *Allen* created a permissive, not a mandatory, presumption. The Court considered all of the evidence in the case and found a rational basis for a finding of guilty beyond a reasonable doubt, noting that the jury could have reasonably rejected the suggestion advanced on appeal by the adult defendants that the handguns were solely in the possession of the 16–year–old.

In Sandstrom v. Montana,[22] the defendant was charged with deliberate homicide, which under Montana law would consist of purposely and knowingly causing the death of another. Defendant claimed that the degree of the offense should be reduced in that he suffered from a personality disorder aggravated by alcohol consumption. The jury was instructed in accordance with Montana law that the "law presumes that a person intends the ordinary consequences of his voluntary acts." Defendant was convicted and his conviction was upheld by the Montana Supreme Court. The United States Supreme Court reversed, holding that the jury could have interpreted the instruction with regard to the presumption of intention of the ordinary consequences of voluntary acts as creating either a conclusive presumption or shifting the burden of persuasion with regard to the question of intent to the defendant. Citing *Mullaney* and *Patterson* as well as *Ulster,* the Court found that such a shift of the burden would be constitutionally impermissible. The fact that the jury could have interpreted the instruction either as permissive or as shifting only the burden of production did not matter so long as the instruction could also have been interpreted as imposing heavier burdens on the defendant.

Several years later, in Francis v. Franklin,[23] the Court held that an instruction in a Georgia homicide prosecution, stating that the "acts of a person of sound mind and discretion are presumed to be the product of a person's will, but the presumption may be rebutted," violated *Sandstrom.* The Court held that the instructions had created the kind of mandatory presumption prohibited by *Sandstrom,* even though Georgia had interpreted such language as amounting to no more than a permissive inference. The fact that the presumption was expressly made rebuttable was not controlling so long as the jury could have interpreted the instruction as shifting the burden of persuasion to the accused.

21. Id. at 157.
22. 442 U.S. 510 (1979).

23. 471 U.S. 307 (1985).

The upshot of all of these cases seems to be as follows: Presumptions in criminal cases will be divided into mandatory and permissive presumptions. A permissive presumption is one that will permit the jury to find the presumed facts, but neither compels the acceptance of such facts nor allocates a burden of persuasion to the defendant with regard to those facts. Regardless of how the state characterizes the presumption, the courts will analyze the jury instructions to determine their possible effect on the jury. A permissive presumption will be constitutionally acceptable if, considering all of the evidence in the case, there is a rational connection between the basic facts proved by the prosecution and the ultimate fact presumed, and the latter is more likely than not to flow from the former. A mandatory presumption is one that shifts the burden of production or persuasion to the defendant. Although the Supreme Court has not specifically so held, dictum in *Allen* and the holdings of lower court decisions seem to make it clear that a presumption that clearly shifts nothing other than the burden of production will be scrutinized in the same way as a permissive presumption and pass constitutional muster if it meets a rational connection test. Could a presumption that shifts the burden of persuasion be created? The Court in *Allen* suggests the possibility that such a presumption could be constitutional if a rational juror could find the presumed fact beyond a reasonable doubt from the basic facts. Some authors have suggested that such a presumption may not constitutionally exist after *Allen* and *Sandstrom*. The courts have not had occasion to rule on the question. Certainly, the test suggested in *Allen* is a stiff one.

§ 348. Affirmative Defenses and Presumptions in Criminal Cases: (c) Special Problems

Not surprisingly, several questions remain from the active constitutional development in this area of the law.

1. The creation of affirmative defenses. The *Patterson* case tied the question of the constitutionality of affirmative defenses di-

rectly to the formalistic notion that a true affirmative defense is one that does not simply go to negative an element of the offense. The question remains as to when something is an element of an offense. Many cases have looked only to the language of the statute although some have considered how the statute has been interpreted by the state courts.

Can the state create an affirmative defense simply by carefully excluding it from the elements of the offense? The answer to this question seems to be a qualified yes. In *Patterson,* the Court suggested that there were constitutional limitations on the creation of affirmative defenses. Those limits may depend upon whether the state may, under the U.S. Constitution, punish the activity without reference to the affirmative defense. For example, assume an offense which has consisted of the elements A, B, C, all of which had to be proved by the prosecution beyond a reasonable doubt. The legislature carefully amends the statute covering the offense so as to make the elements of the offense A and B only, but provides that the accused may be exonerated if the defense proves C by a preponderance of the evidence. Such a new statute would be constitutional if the state may, consistent with the Eighth Amendment and substantive due process, punish the individual to the extent provided by the statute based upon proof of A and B only.

Such an analysis has suggested another, less formalistic, approach to the treatment of affirmative defenses to some legal scholars. Under this approach, if the state can constitutionally exclude an element from an offense, it can require the defendant to bear the burden of persuasion with regard to that element. In other words, in the above example, if the state could exclude C from the definition of the crime, it could make the accused prove C, whether or not C is formally removed as an element of the offense. Other scholars have rejected an Eighth Amendment approach entirely and have proposed tests that would more severely limit the state's options in the creation of affirmative defenses.

As yet, no court has struck down an affirmative defense because the Eighth Amendment prohibited punishment based only upon the elements assigned to the definition of the offense. Indeed, the Eighth Amendment and related concepts of substantive due process have not proved to be an effective check on legislative decisions with regard to punishment. Moreover, no court has used an alternative approach suggested in the law journals to limit the creation of affirmative defenses. Instead, the courts have relied upon the safer, formalistic notions of *Patterson*.

One possible approach to assessing the validity of affirmative defenses that is neither inconsistent with case law nor directly tied to the Eighth Amendment was suggested by Justice Powell in his dissent in *Patterson*. Powell suggested that the prosecution be required to prove beyond a reasonable doubt at least those factors which "in the Anglo–American legal tradition" had made a difference in punishment or stigma.[1] Although troublesome if taken to its logical extent, the notion that we should consider historical factors has merit. At the very least, it would be appropriate for a court in assessing the validity of the creation of an affirmative defense to take into account not only the statutory language and judicial statements of the elements of the offense, but also the nature of the burden traditionally borne by the state with regard to the same or analogous factors.

2. Affirmative defenses or presumptions? Despite the differences between affirmative defenses and presumptions as the terms are used by the courts and legal scholars, the impact of these procedural devices on the accused can be identical. Thus, in one state, the accused may have the burden of producing evidence that she acted in self-defense— an affirmative defense. In another jurisdiction, the law may provide that, once the state has proved that the defendant intentionally killed the deceased, there is a presumption of unlawfulness that requires the defendant to introduce evidence with regard to self-defense,

although the ultimate burden of persuasion remains with the state. The defendant must introduce some evidence of self-defense in order for the jury to be instructed on the issue. The effect of this presumption is identical to that of the affirmative defense. Both devices used in this way have been held to be constitutional.

An affirmative defense that places the burden of persuasion on the defendant with regard to a factor that is not an element of the offense may be constitutional. Could the state accomplish the same allocation of the burden of persuasion in the form of a presumption, i.e., a rule that states that once the state has proven the elements of the offense, the defendant is presumed guilty unless he proves some other factor? Such a rule simply delays the allocation of the burden of persuasion until after the state has proved its case. It places no different burden on the accused than would an affirmative defense. However, as framed, the presumption would seem to run directly afoul of *Sandstrom*. The matter may simply be one of legislative drafting. The prudent legislature will choose the affirmative defense route rather than the presumption language. It is yet to be seen whether the courts will look to the designation of a procedural device as a presumption or as an affirmative defense or whether they will more realistically decide the constitutionality of the procedural device based upon its actual effect on the defendant.

3. When is it Proper to Submit an Issue Involving A Presumed Fact to the Jury? In deciding the question whether a case involving a presumed fact should be submitted to the jury, the trial judge must necessarily be guided by the dictates of Jackson v. Virginia:[2] a jury verdict will be upheld, even against collateral attack, only if the evidence was sufficient for a reasonable person to find the defendant guilty beyond a reasonable doubt. In the rare instance in which a mandatory presumption is involved, the problem is not

§ 348

1. Patterson v. New York, 432 U.S. 197, 226–227 (1977).

2. 443 U.S. 307 (1979), rehearing denied 444 U.S. 890; see § 338 supra.

difficult. *Allen* suggests that the presumption will be tested by the constitutional test of whether the presumed fact flows beyond a reasonable doubt from the basic facts. If the presumption meets that test, it is by definition sufficient to get to the jury, provided the other elements of the crime are supported by sufficient evidence. However, because of the rigid requirements for the validity of mandatory presumptions, virtually all presumptions will be permissive. Therefore, under the *Allen* case, the trial judge must look to the rational effect of the presumption in connection with all of the other evidence in the case. Perhaps the best statement of a test for the sufficiency of the evidence under these circumstances is contained in Revised Uniform Rule (1974) 303(b):

> *(b) Submission to the jury.* The court is not authorized to direct the jury to find a presumed fact against the accused. If a presumed fact establishes guilt or is an element of the offense or negatives a defense, the court may submit the question of guilt or of the existence of the presumed fact to the jury, but only if a reasonable juror on the evidence as a whole, including the evidence of the basic facts, could find guilt or the presumed fact beyond a reasonable doubt. If the presumed fact has a lesser effect, the question of its existence may be submitted to the jury provided the basic facts are supported by substantial evidence or are otherwise established, unless the court determines that a reasonable juror on the evidence as a whole could not find the existence of the presumed fact.

Given the dictates of Jackson v. Virginia and County Court of Ulster County v. Allen, no other proposed formulation of the rule seems acceptable.

4. Instructing the Jury on Presumptions. The distinction made in the *Allen* case between permissive and mandatory presumptions, makes the exact language of instructions on presumptions critical. Unless a presumption is strong enough to meet the stringent test for mandatory presumptions, the trial judge must use caution in charging the jury so as to place no burden whatsoever on the defendant.

Again, the Revised Uniform Rules provide a suggested pattern for such an instruction. Uniform Rule 303(c) provides:

> *Instructing the Jury.* Whenever the existence of a presumed fact is submitted to the jury, the court shall instruct the jury that it may regard the basic facts as sufficient evidence of the presumed fact but is not required to do so. In addition, if the presumed fact establishes guilt or is an element of the offense or negatives a defense, the court shall instruct the jury that its existence, on all the evidence, must be proved beyond a reasonable doubt.

This instruction seems to meet most of the problems raised in the *Allen* case, as well as those suggested by Sandstrom v. Montana. One additional problem has been suggested. In *Allen,* the court stated that the prosecution could not rest its case entirely on a presumption unless the facts proved were sufficient to support the inference of guilt beyond a reasonable doubt. Therefore, where the prosecution relies solely upon a presumption and not any other evidence, as in *Allen,* not only must the presumed fact flow beyond a reasonable doubt from the basic facts, but the jury must be able to find the basic facts beyond a reasonable doubt. At least two states have adopted the essence of the Revised Uniform Rule, but, in order to cover this situation, have added language which requires that the basic facts be proved beyond a reasonable doubt.[3]

§ 349. Choice of Law

The significance of the burdens of proof and of the effect of presumptions upon those burdens has already been discussed. Certainly the outcome of litigation may be altered depending upon which party has the burden of persuasion.[1] Where there is little evidence available on an issue, the burden of producing

---

3. Hawaii Evidence Rule 306; Oregon Evidence Rule 309.

1. See § 336 supra.

evidence may also control the outcome.[2] Recognizing the impact of these rules upon outcome, the federal courts, applying the doctrine of Erie Railroad Co. v. Tompkins,[3] have consistently held that where an issue is to be decided under state law, that law controls both the burdens of proof and presumptions with regard to that issue. Federal Rule of Evidence 302 limits the operation of this rule with respect to presumptions to cases in which the presumption operates "respecting a fact which is an element of a claim or defense as to which state law supplies the rule of decision." "Tactical presumptions," those that operate as to a lesser aspect of the case, will be governed by the federal rule. While no court has specifically made the distinction contemplated in the rule, the reasoning is sound. Although tactical presumptions may in some instances influence the outcome of a case, their effect is no greater than that of a rule governing the admission or exclusion of a single item of evidence. As in the case of those rules, the desirability of providing a uniform procedure for federal trials through a fixed rule governing tactical presumptions outweighs any preference for increased certainty of identity of result in state and federal courts.

Of course *Erie* problems are not the only choice of law problems. The question remains, even for federal courts having resolved to apply state rather than federal law: what state's law is applicable? Unlike the federal courts applying the *Erie* rule, the state courts generally have not considered the impact of the burdens of proof and presumptions on the outcome of the lawsuit to be controlling. The general rule expressed is that both the burdens of proof and presumptions are "procedural" in the sense that the law of the forum governs rather than the law of the state whose substantive rules are otherwise applicable. However, as in the case of most general rules with regard to the subject matter of this chapter, instances in which an exception

to this general rule has been held applicable are perhaps as numerous as instances in which the rule has been applied. The principal exception to the basic dogma has been variously phrased but its gist is that the forum will apply the rule of a foreign jurisdiction with respect to the burdens of proof or presumptions where that rule is inseparably connected to the substantive right created by the foreign state.

The general rule and its principal exception have proved difficult to apply. The plethora of conflicting decisions under the test amply illustrates the problems inherent in attempting to distinguish between rules that are inseparably connected with substantive law and those that are not. The distinction is indeed a hollow one. Regardless of the nature of the claim or defense, rules with respect to the burdens of proof always have the same potential effect upon the decision in the case. If insufficient evidence is available, the party having the burden of producing evidence will lose the decision. If the jury is in doubt, the party having the burden of persuasion will lose. As has been observed, cases in which the burden of proof is so closely interwoven with the substantive right as to make a separation of the two impossible constitute either all or none of the litigated cases.

A somewhat better approach to the problem is taken by the Second Restatement of Conflict of Laws which states that the forum will apply its own local law in determining which party has the burdens of proof "unless the primary purpose of the relevant rule of the otherwise applicable law is to affect decision of the issue rather than to regulate the conduct of the trial."[4] The rule sounds very much like the test applied in *Erie* cases. However, the comments and illustrations to the applicable sections of the Restatement indicate that the Restatement is to be interpreted in much the same way as the more

---

2. See § 338 supra. See also §§ 342 and 344 supra as to the operation of presumptions with regard to both the burden of producing evidence and the burden of persuasion.

3. 304 U.S. 64 (1938).

4. §§ 133, 134 (1971).

traditional statements just discussed; the assumption is that the rule is one concerned with "trial administration," not the decision of the issue. The assumption seems wrong. The burdens of proof are almost always allocated for the primary purpose of affecting the decision in the case where there is no evidence or where the jury is in doubt. To say that these rules merely govern the conduct of the trial, as in the case of rules concerning the admission and exclusion of evidence, gives far too much emphasis to form over substance.

A better approach to the choice of law problem would be to adopt the federal rule used in *Erie* cases as a rule of general application. Such a rule would provide that the law of the state or states supplying the substantive rules of law should govern questions concerning the burdens of proof as well as presumptions operating with regard to a fact constituting an element of a claim or defense.

*

Title 13

ADMINISTRATIVE EVIDENCE

Chapter 37

ADMINISTRATIVE EVIDENCE

Table of Sections

§ 350. Introduction to Administrative Adjudication

As the problems facing federal and state governments have multiplied in number and complexity, these governments have created administrative agencies to devise and enforce new policies. This growth has been uneven and with few exceptions relatively slow. Even as late as 1960 the federal government exercised major regulatory responsibility in only five fields: antitrust, communications, financial markets and institutions, food and drugs, and transportation. Beginning in the mid–1960's, however, the number of federal regulatory agencies and the scope of regulatory activity greatly expanded. For example, between 1960 and 1990 the number of federal agencies substantially regulating some aspect of private activity grew from 34 to over 100; whereas in 1930 there were but 18 federal regulatory bodies. This expansion is also reflected in other measures of agency activity. In 1970, federal regulatory agencies spent $800 million and employed 28,000 people. By 1980 these agencies employed 90,000 people and spent $6 billion. During the 1970's the pages of federal regulations in the Federal Register tripled, federal regulatory budgets increased sixfold, agency personnel grew from under 30,000 to over 80,000, and the amount of the gross national product produced by industries regulated by state or federal governments jumped from under 10 to around 25 percent.

Much, perhaps most, of this growth has focused on the use of agency rulemaking to write new regulations. At the same time administrative trials—denominated "adjudications" by the federal Administrative Procedure Act (APA)[1]—have continued to grow and the federal government now employs approximately 1050 administrative law judges. (By contrast, there are approximately 500 federal district judges hearing all federal civil and criminal cases.) The number of administrative trials annually dwarfs the number of cases heard each year in federal court. Yet the range of administrative trials is as great as those heard by federal judges. That is, administrative adjudications extend from relatively insubstantial workers' compensation claims to precedent-setting antitrust merger rulings involving millions of dollars and affecting thousands of employees.

At first glance many, and perhaps most, administrative rulemaking hearings and hearings constituting formal adversarial adjudications appear to be merely carbon copies of judicial trials. Such an administrative hearing is usually public, and in most cases the hearing is conducted in an orderly and dignified manner, although not necessarily with the formality of a judicial trial. Evidence is admissible only if reliable and material; cross-examination is frequently relied upon to challenge witness credibility; and the administrative judge's decision must be supported by substantial evidence.

Closer analysis, however, reveals several differences. Agency hearings, especially those dealing with rulemaking, often tend to produce evidence of general conditions as distinguished from facts relating solely to the respondent. Administrative agencies in rulemaking and occasionally in formal adversarial adjudications more consciously formulate policy than do courts. Consequently, administrative adjudications may require that the administrative law judge consider more consciously the impact of his decision upon the public interest as well as upon the particular respondent. In addition, testimonial evidence and cross-examination often play less important roles in administrative hearings, especially when rulemaking is involved.

An administrative hearing is tried to an *administrative law judge* and never to a *jury*. Since many of the rules governing the admission of proof in judicial trials are designed to protect the jury from unreliable and possibly confusing evidence, it has long been asserted that such rules need not be applied at all or with the same vigor in proceedings solely before an administrative law judge.[2] The administrative judge decides both the facts and the law to be applied. Usually a lawyer, he is generally experienced on the very question he must decide. Consequently, the technical common law rules governing the *admissibility* of evidence have generally been abandoned by administrative agencies.[3]

Courts accept whatever cases the parties present; their familiarity with the subject matter is accidental. Agencies, on the other hand, have only limited jurisdictions and handle selected cases; administrative law judges and agency members who review the adjudicative decisions of administrative law judges are often either experts or have at least a substantial familiarity with the subject matter. The administrative agency may therefore be allowed greater leeway and deference (on appellate review) in deciding questions of fact and law. In addition, an agency usually is staffed by experts whose reports, commonly relating to matters adjudicated before the agency, are made available to administrative judges and commissioners alike.

While this development of agency experience and expertness is commonly offered as a justification for administrative agencies, it also creates a basic conflict between assuring fairness to the private respondent on the one hand and promoting efficient use of reliable information on the other. The respondent, for example, wants an opportunity to rebut or explain all the "evidence" which the administrative judge or agency relies upon in making its decision. Yet the agency, especially in rulemaking, wishes to avoid the burden of having to prove once again previously established "facts." This conflict has led to the

---

§ 350

1. 5 U.S.C.A. §§ 551(7), 554.

2. See § 60 and Ch. 34 supra. Compare § 351 infra.

3. See §§ 352 and 353 infra.

development of the concept of official notice, specifically recognized in the APA (Administrative Procedure Act), which regularizes the procedure for agency reliance on proven facts.[4]

§ 351. Law Governing Administrative Evidence

The legal framework governing the conduct of formal administrative adjudication is not complex and can be best understood by first examining the law which determines the kind of proof an agency can receive into evidence.

(a) *Federal Law.* Until the passage of the Administrative Procedure Act of 1946,[1] the receipt of evidence in federal administrative proceedings was limited only by general constitutional requirements of fairness and privilege together with the vague directions implicit in the standard for judicial review developed by appellate courts or written into agency enabling acts.

The requirement of fairness generally means only that the respondent

shall have an opportunity to be heard and cross-examine the witnesses against him and shall have time and opportunity at a convenient place, after the evidence against him is produced and known to him, to produce evidence and witnesses to refute the charges * * * [2]

The test for judicial review typically provides that "[t]he finding of the Commission as to the facts, if supported by substantial evidence, shall be conclusive." [3]

Either standard could be read as a command that administrative agencies must rely upon common law rules of evidence barring hearsay and other secondary evidence, since the private respondent could neither confront nor cross-examine upon the evidence, or since the evidence was not competent and therefore not substantial. Neither the agencies nor the courts have accepted these contentions. The exclusionary rules of evidence were designed in part to assure that evidence admitted would be relevant and reliable. But the opportunity for confrontation is not the sole measure of reliability.

As early as the turn of this century, the Supreme Court ruled that the Interstate Commerce Commission—the first regulatory agency to conduct formal adjudicatory hearings— was not bound by the exclusionary rules:

The [ICC's] inquiry should not be too narrowly constrained by technical rules as to the admissibility of proof. Its function is largely one of investigation, and it should not be hampered in making inquiry pertaining to interstate commerce by those narrow rules which prevail in trials at common law * * * [4]

Occasionally federal authority has held that the admission of legally incompetent evidence is reversible error. But these decisions are exceptional and erroneous unless other grounds can be established for rejecting the evidence. Indeed, by 1941 the Supreme Court had confidently noted that "it has long been settled that the technical rules for the exclusion of evidence applicable in jury trials do not apply to proceedings before federal administrative agencies in the absence of a statutory requirement that such rules are to be observed." [5]

With the adoption of the federal Administrative Procedure Act in 1946, Congress appeared to be codifying this case law by providing that "[a]ny oral or documentary evidence may be received" in an administrative adjudication.[6] Specific statutes may, however, override the application of the APA to agency hearings. In a few instances over the immediately ensuing years, Congress either exempted an agency's hearings from the APA or specified that the rules of evidence governing

---

4. 5 U.S.C.A. § 556(e). See § 359 infra.

§ 351

1. 5 U.S.C.A. §§ 551–59, 701–06, 3105, 3344, 5362, 7521.

2. N.L.R.B. v. Prettyman, 117 F.2d 786, 790 (6th Cir. 1941).

3. 15 U.S.C.A. § 45(c) (Federal Trade Commission Act).

4. I.C.C. v. Baird, 194 U.S. 25, 44 (1904).

5. Opp Cotton Mills, Inc. v. Administrator, Department of Labor, 312 U.S. 126, 155 (1941).

6. 5 U.S.C.A. § 556(d).

civil nonjury cases should be applied "so far as practicable." Moreover, Congress' adoption of the "substantial evidence" standard for judicial review of formal adjudications [7]—partly in response to a perceived lack of rigor in the proof required in agency trials—fostered the notion that the rule against hearsay or other restrictions might still be mandated in particular circumstances (e.g., where specific facts were in issue and witness credibility was key). This view seemed at least plausible where the congressional objective was not made clear.

In 1971, in Richardson v. Perales,[8] the Supreme Court gave strong evidence that narrow interpretation of agency authority to admit and rely on reliable hearsay and other evidence was not favored. There the Court sustained the Social Security Administration's denial of a claim for disability benefits even though the only testimony presented at the administrative hearing was by Perales, his doctor, and a fellow employee—and all supported Perales' claim. The agency, in denying the claim, relied on hospital records and the written reports of four examining physicians. Its decision had been overturned by the Court of Appeals which had ruled that hearsay uncorroborated by oral testimony could not constitute substantial evidence when the hearsay was directly contradicted by the testimony of live medical witnesses and by the claimant in person. The Supreme Court, however, upheld the Social Security Administration. It emphasized that the reports were impartial, consistent, and based on personal examinations by competent physicians. Moreover, Perales had not exercised his right to subpoena the examining physicians in order to cross-examine them. It argued that the "sheer magnitude" of the administrative burden and desirability of informal procedures supported this approach. In the circumstances, the procedure satisfied both the congressional design as well as requirements of "fundamental fairness."

(b) *State Law.* The constitutional limitations applied to federal agencies also impose restraints upon state hearings. The states in turn have freed their administrative agencies from the "rules of evidence," but not always for the same reasons. Most state agencies were created as political-administrative bodies rather than as quasi-judicial commissions. Thus, writing in 1965, Professor Cooper observed

Fifty years ago, the typical state agencies would include, perhaps, rural township supervisors who as members of local boards of assessors would estimate the value of their neighbors' farms, and statehouse politicians who as a railroad commission would bargain with railroad attorneys concerning the granting of franchises and the fixing of rates, and insurance commissioners who would watch with a wary eye the premiums charged by fire insurance companies * * *, and—in the more progressive states—"committees of arbitration" who would informally arbitrate compensation claims of workers injured in industrial accidents under the newfangled workmen's compensation laws.[9]

Neither these state agencies nor the parties appearing before them could have followed judicial rules of evidence. As the agencies became more sophisticated, and their hearings more formal, the presentation of evidence was formalized. Now, as with federal agencies, their hearings are often indistinguishable from nonjury civil trials. Nevertheless, the original approach that state agencies are not restricted by common law rules in the admission of evidence has continued. Professor Cooper contended that this liberal approach had long ago outrun its reasons. Attributing its continuance to legislative lethargy, to arbitrary agency desire to operate with a free hand, and to the judicial trend toward relaxation of exclusionary rules in court cases, he decried this laxity concerning the application of common law rules and suggested that state agencies be "required to follow the rules of evidence to about the same

---

7. 5 U.S.C.A. § 706(2)(E) (Administrative Procedure Act).

8. 402 U.S. 389 (1971).

9. 1 Cooper, State Administrative Law 379 (1965) (footnotes omitted).

extent and in about the same way as judges do when trying cases without juries." Whatever the then merits of Professor Cooper's position, the 1961 Model State Administrative Procedure Act's provision,[10] that the rules of evidence applicable in nonjury civil cases be followed in state agency adjudications was adopted in only six states. The Model Act was revised once again in 1981, this time adhering more closely to the federal model. Section 4–212 provides that the hearing officer shall exclude evidence on proper objection only if it is "irrelevant, immaterial, unduly repetitious" or because it is privileged.[11] It further specifically provides that "[e]vidence may not be excluded solely because it is hearsay."

Enactment of the Federal Evidence Rules in 1975 brought about a perceptible change in attitude in Congress and in several of the administrative agencies themselves. No longer was it simply assumed that the rules of evidence would not apply in any given administrative agency hearing. As of the mid 1980's, either through congressional action or voluntarily by the federal administrative agencies themselves, of the 280 evidentiary regulations 37 made reference to the Federal Rules of Evidence, most requiring their use "as far as practical." Alarmed by this trend the Administrative Conference of the United States on June 20, 1986 adopted Resolution 86–2(1) which states as follows:

> Congress should not require agencies to apply the FRE, with or without the qualification, "so far as practicable," to limit the discretion of presiding officers to admit evidence in formal adjudications.[12]

For years Professor Davis has opposed the introduction of formal rules of evidence in administrative agency hearings.[13] His opposition forcefully expressed to the Administrative Conference was undoubtedly influential.

Not everyone agrees. In 1987, the United States Department of Labor undertook examination of the Federal Rules Evidence with a view towards adopting a modified version for application solely in formal adversarial adjudications, not rulemaking. Modifications were drafted in recognition of the civil nonjury nature of such hearings and in appreciation of the broad underlying values and goals of the administrative process. The United States Department of Labor Rules of Evidence, 29 C.F.R. §§ 18.101–18.1104, were promulgated on April 9, 1990. Additional hearsay exceptions and self-authentication provisions were added to the Federal Rules of Evidence to reflect the practical realities of formal adversarial administrative adjudication while maintaining the overall integrity of the rule against hearsay. Whether the approach of the Department of Labor will have broad implications remains to be seen.

§ 352. Admissibility of Evidence

Administrative agencies generally are not restricted in the kind of evidence they can admit. The mere admission of proof that would be excluded as irrelevant, immaterial, incompetent, or redundant under the rules of evidence adopted in a jury trial will not restrict enforcement of an agency's decision. The APA confirms this practice in section 556(d) by providing that "[a]ny oral documentary evidence may be received, but the agency as a matter of policy shall provide for the exclusion of irrelevant, immaterial, or unduly repetitious evidence."[1]

Note that the APA opens the door to *any* evidence which the administrative law judge admits and only *suggests* that insignificant and redundant evidence should be rejected, giving the agencies broad discretion. Moreover, the APA pointedly omits hearsay or other "incompetent" evidence from the list of

---

10. Revised Model State Administrative Procedure Act § 10(1) (1961).

11. Revised Model State Administrative Procedure Act § 4–212 (1981).

12. Pierce, Use of the Federal Rules of Evidence in Federal Agency Adjudications, 39 Ad.L.Rev. 1, 2 (1987).

13. See, e.g., Davis, Hearsay in Administrative Hearings, 32 Geo.Wash.L.Rev. 689 (1964); Davis, The Residuum Rule in Administrative Law, 28 Rocky Mtn.L.Rev. 1 (1955); Davis, Evidence Reform: The Administrative

Process Leads the Way, 31 Minn.L.Rev. 584 (1950); Davis, An Approach to Problems of Evidence in the Administrative Process, 55 Harv.L.Rev. 364 (1942); Gellhorn, Rules of Evidence and Official Notice in Formal Administrative Hearings, 1971 Duke L.J. 1.

References to the dominance of the position asserted by Professor Davis on the admissibility of hearsay can be found throughout §§ 352 and 353 infra.

§ 352

1. 5 U.S.C.A. § 556(d).

evidence which should not be received. Thus, the exclusion of otherwise legally inadmissible evidence from an administrative hearing may be error. Furthermore, it is clear that the exclusion of relevant, material, and competent evidence by the administrative law judge will be grounds for reversal if that refusal is prejudicial.

The courts have pressed the agencies to abide by the spirit of these rules. The leading example of such pressure—which in fact antedates the APA—is found in Samuel H. Moss, Inc. v. FTC,[2] where a distinguished panel of the Second Circuit admonished a hearing examiner for rigidly following the rules of evidence:

> [I]f the case was to be tried with strictness, the examiner was right * * *. Why either he or the [Federal Trade] Commission's attorney should have thought it desirable to be so formal about the admission of evidence, we cannot understand. Even in criminal trials to a jury it is better, nine times out of ten, to admit, than to exclude, evidence and in such proceedings as these the only conceivable interest that can suffer by admitting any evidence is the time lost, which is seldom as much as that inevitably lost by idle bickering about irrelevancy or incompetence. In the case at bar it chances that no injustice was done, but we take this occasion to point out the danger always involved in conducting such a proceeding in such a spirit, and the absence of any advantage in depriving either the Commission or ourselves of *all evidence which can conceivably throw any light upon the controversy*.[3]

More recent cases have repeated their admonition.

Many reasons support the open admission of hearsay and other legally incompetent evidence in administrative hearings. Foremost among them is the fact that the exclusionary rules do not determine the probative value of the proffered evidence. Professor Davis, the leading proponent that hearing officers should make no distinction between hearsay and nonhearsay evidence, makes the point this way:

> [T]he reliability of hearsay ranges from the least to the most reliable. The reliability of non-hearsay also ranges from the least to the most reliable. Therefore the guide should be a judgment about the reliability of particular evidence in a particular record in particular circumstances, not the technical hearsay rule with all its complex exceptions.[4]

Most hearsay in administrative hearings is documentary. The standard of admissibility thus applied by both reviewing courts and administrative law judges is that "an administrative tribunal is not required to exclude hearsay evidence in the form of a document if its authenticity is sufficiently convincing to a reasonable mind and if it carries sufficient assurance as to its truthfulness."[5]

To require that an administrative law judge refuse to admit hearsay makes no sense where there is no jury to protect and the trier of fact is equally exposed to the evidence whether he admits or excludes it. Admission without a ruling—as long as the evidence has some element of reliability—does no harm and can prove more efficient than requiring a ruling which may later be held erroneous. Discarding the exclusionary rules of admission eliminates the need for the parties to interpose protective objections—the objections being preserved by their briefs to the law judge or agency—and relieves the law judge of making difficult rulings before all the evidence is available. It assures a complete, yet not necessarily unduly long, record and might well avoid the need to reopen the record. Hearsay, of course, is not subject to current, in-court cross-examination, but that limitation affects the weight the evidence carries, not its admissibility.

---

2. 148 F.2d 378 (2d Cir.1945), cert. denied 326 U.S. 734, rehearing denied 326 U.S. 809, motion denied 155 F.2d 1016 (2d Cir.) (per curiam, decision by Clark, A. Hand and L. Hand, JJ.).

3. Id. at 380 (emphasis added).

4. Davis, Hearsay in Administrative Hearings, 2 Geo. Wash.L.Rev. 689 (1964).

5. Fairfield Scientific Corp. v. United States, 222 Ct. Cl. 167, 611 F.2d 854, 859 (1979), appeal after remand 655 F.2d 1062.

The fact that administrative hearings need not follow the exclusionary rules and the fact that the admission of remote or repetitious evidence is not reversible error does not suggest that "anything goes" or that all proffered evidence, whatever is relevance or trustworthiness, should be admitted. Wholesale admission would only add to delay and further expand records which are already often very long. Nor can an efficient adjudicatory system decide anew each time the question is presented whether some particular evidence should be admitted. However, most agencies have not fully developed regulations governing the extent to which the exclusionary rules should not be applied. Nonetheless, the admissibility of evidence in administrative hearings depends more upon the *importance* of the evidence in relation to the ultimate issues rather than upon the legal standards of relevance and materiality.

Several significant and useful deviations from the judicial pattern appear in administrative hearings. The first, already noted, involves the relatively free receipt of hearsay evidence. Equally important is the manner in which oral testimony is received. Witnesses in agency hearings are frequently permitted freedom to testify in a simple, natural and direct fashion, without unnecessary interruptions from either the attorney who is directing the questioning or his adversary. Only when the witness strays far afield, or the question is remote will an objection be sustained. A third departure permitted from judicial practice occurs when the administrative law judge is uncertain whether to exclude the evidence on the grounds of incompetency, irrelevancy, or immateriality. In administrative hearings the tendency is to admit the evidence. Other techniques, principally the use of written presentations and shortened hearings, are discussed below.[6]

Since the administrative hearings differ so widely in scope and significance, it is impossible to suggest a single standard to govern the admission of all evidence. It is probably still true, however, as one keen observer noted over 40 years ago, that the more closely administrative proceedings approach judicial proceedings in formality and in the nature of the issues to be tried, the greater the degree to which the exclusionary rules will be applied. Nor has improvement been made to the standard suggested by the Attorney General's Committee on Administrative Procedure in 1941: "The ultimate test of admissibility must be whether the proffered evidence is reliable, probative and relevant. The question in each case must be whether the probability of error justifies the burden of stricter methods of proof."[7]

§ 353. Evaluation of Evidence

In contrast to the effect of a trial court's decision to receive hearsay evidence in a jury trial, an administrative law judge's decision to receive hearsay in an administrative adjudication is only the first step in determining its impact upon the tribunal's decision. The admission of evidence in a jury trial is often considered the last effective legal control over the use (or abuse) of such evidence because of the assumption that the jury will rely upon or be swayed by it regardless of whether its reliability has been established. In an administrative hearing, on the other hand, as in the case of nonjury trials, it is generally assumed that the law judge will not rely upon untrustworthy evidence in reaching his decision. Thus if there is "competent" or trustworthy evidence to support the decision, the reviewing court usually presumes that the administrative law or trial judge relied on that evidence in reaching his decision.

Nevertheless, the more difficult—and often crucial—question for the hearing officer is the determination of whether he should rely upon hearsay evidence in reaching his decision. The administrative law judge's concern is with the reliability or probative worth of the evidence. Jury trial rules of evidence exclude hearsay on the theory that it is untrust-

---

6. See § 358 infra.

7. Final Report of Attorney General's Committee on Administrative Procedure, S.Doc. No. 8, 77th Cong., 1st Sess. 71 (1941).

worthy unless within an exception.[1] More specifically, the risk that hearsay evidence is untrustworthy and that it might be relied upon by the decision maker is, in general, so great that it must be excluded unless some other reason justifies its admission. The party against whom the evidence is admitted can neither confront nor cross-examine the out-of-court declarant to test its probative worth.

But on the other side of the ledger is the fact that each of us constantly relies upon hearsay evidence in making important decisions. Without hearsay, commerce would stop, government would cease to function, and education would be reduced to each teacher's personal experience (and even the latter would often be based upon hearsay). It is not surprising, then, that no legal system outside the Anglo–American realm has adopted so restrictive a rule of evidence. Scholars have argued against its across-the-board application and the courts and Legislatures are increasingly liberalizing its application, even in jury cases.

Nonetheless, the fact that some hearsay may prove reliable is no guarantee that all hearsay is reliable. Nor is it responsive to observe that the rules of evidence already admit much that is worthless. Why, it could be asked, should more that is worthless be admitted in order to find some that is trustworthy, particularly when there is no assurance that the factfinder will rely on the latter and disregard the former? It could also be contended that unless probative evidence could be distilled or some alternative protection devised, the admission of hearsay would not promote justice. The administrative regulations governing the receipt and evaluation of evidence indicate that the agencies themselves have not adequately wrestled with this issue.

The courts have provided only scant guidance in upholding administrative reliance on some hearsay evidence. Judge Learned Hand has offered the classic formulation:

> [The examiner] did indeed admit much that would have been excluded at common law, but the act specifically so provides * * * [N]o doubt, that does not mean mere rumor will serve to "support" a finding, but hearsay may do so, at least if more is not conveniently available, and if in the end the finding is supported by *the kind of evidence on which responsible persons are accustomed to rely in serious affairs.*[2]

Administrative law judges and agencies have adhered to this commonsense standard instinctively. At the same time, several criteria applied in evaluating the reliability of hearsay can be discerned.

The following are the most significant:

(a) What is the "nature" of the hearsay evidence? If the hearsay is likely to be reliable, it usually becomes an exception to the hearsay rule. Moreover, if the evidence is intrinsically trustworthy, agencies have taken the next logical step and relied, if necessary, upon this evidence in deciding cases, even though it technically constitutes hearsay and does not fall within any of the recognized exceptions. One example of intrinsically reliable hearsay, intra- and inter-corporate documents not shown to be within the business records exception, was the subject of a celebrated opinion by Judge Wyzanski in a nonjury trial not dissimilar from an administrative hearing.[3] An even clearer example of the reliability criteria is newspaper reports. Stories of significant news events are likely to be reliable. Newspapers normally do not report accidents which did not occur. On the other hand, newspaper summaries of public comments are commonly inaccurate—at least if one may believe those who claim to be misquoted—because of the difficulty of hearing and then summarizing another's views. Even so-called verbatim transcripts commonly suffer from significant errors as a result of the

§ 353

1. See § 245 supra.
2. N.L.R.B. v. Remington Rand, 94 F.2d 862, 873 (2d Cir.1938), cert. denied 304 U.S. 576 (emphasis added), reversed on other grounds 110 F.2d 148 (2d Cir.).

3. United States v. United Shoe Machinery Corp., 89 F.Supp. 349, 355, 356 (D.Mass.1950), 60 Yale L.J. 363 (1951).

pressure of time deadlines. Note that the hearsay quality of each report is identical. Yet the accident report will be treated as solid support for an administrative decision and the speech summary, unless corroborated, will not.

(b) Is better evidence available? The necessary substantiation for the reliability of hearsay evidence may arise from the failure of respondent to controvert the hearsay when the necessary proof is readily available to him, even though there is no testimonial or documentary exhibit of such available "support." A leading example of this position is United States ex rel. Vajtauer v. Commissioner,[4] where the Supreme Court upheld a deportation order based on a finding that the alien had advocated the overthrow of the government by force. The alien gave his name as Emanuel Vajtauer, a "Doctor of Psychology" and editor of the "Spravedlvost." In making his finding the director relied upon two items of hearsay: a pamphlet bearing the name of Dr. E.M. Vajtauer as author; and a newspaper report of a speech by a Dr. Vajtauer, editor of the "Spravedlvost," supporting revolution. Both items became convincing evidence when "the appellant, confronted by this record, stood mute. * * * His silence without explanation other than that he would not testify until the entire evidence was presented, was in itself evidence that he was the author."[5]

(c) How important or unimportant is the subject matter in relation to the cost of acquiring "better" evidence? Many examples are available. If the out-of-hearing declarant is readily available and the question involves the respondent's livelihood or security—as is often the case in security and deportation matters—hearsay by itself carries little weight. If, however, the matter is but one of thousands of compensation claims—as in social security and workers' compensation cases—and the declarant's appearance would be relatively costly or time-consuming, hearsay alternatives such as letters or other written evidence might prove decisive. It has

likewise been held that in the granting of a license an agency may rely upon evidence which would not be adequate in revoking the same license.

(d) How precise does the agency's factfinding need to be? The Interstate Commerce Commission's reliance on "typical evidence" and the Federal Trade Commission's use of survey evidence are examples of agency dependence on statistical averages to determine facts in particular cases where legal or policy decisions are not dependent upon exact determinations. For instance, survey evidence of consumer understanding indicating that a substantial proportion of the public were misled by respondent's advertising will support a finding that it constitutes an unfair or deceptive act. Still another example is the fixing of a rate for commodities transported by one carrier on the basis of costs incurred by similarly situated carriers.

(e) What is the administrative policy behind the statute being enforced? The range of necessary reliability is affected by the type of policy which the administrative hearing is designed to promote. For example, the social security and workers' compensation programs are intended to provide benefits quickly at low cost. The refusal to rely upon reports in such hearings would run counter to the purposes for which the statutes are designed.

When focusing on these criteria, it is essential to consider the central point that evaluation of hearsay and other technically incompetent evidence cannot be accomplished in the abstract; the evidence must be examined in the light of the particular record. This includes, at a minimum, an examination of the quality and quantity of the evidence on each side, as well as the circumstantial setting of the case.

§ 354. The Substantial Evidence Rule

Once the agency has determined that legally incompetent evidence can be admitted and relied upon in making an administrative deci-

---

4. 273 U.S. 103 (1927).

5. Id. at 111.

sion, it might appear that the subject of hearsay evidence in administrative hearings has been exhausted. While the agency's admission and use of legally incompetent evidence is subject to judicial review, this review of administrative determinations of fact should be confined to determining whether the decision is supported by the evidence in the record. Judicial review of administrative evidence has not been so limited, however. As a substitute for rules of admissibility, courts apply the so-called "substantial evidence" rule to judicial review of agency action in seeking to assure fairness to the parties.

As applied to administrative findings, the substantial evidence rule possesses two branches, one of which is sound, and the other unsound. The first consists of an overall standard of review of the findings of fact. Except for the distinctive features of judicial review of administrative action, it does not differ conceptually from the "sufficiency" standard applied in judicial review of jury verdicts.[1] In this sense, substantial evidence is evidence

> affording a substantial basis of fact from which the fact in issue can be reasonably inferred. * * * [I]t must be enough to justify, if the trial were to a jury, a refusal to direct a verdict when the conclusion sought to be drawn from it is one of fact for the jury.[2]

This standard measures both the quantitative and qualitative sufficiency of the evidence. Its proper application takes into account the rationale of the exclusionary rules of evidence, the reliability of the hearsay evidence—including the opportunity for cross-examination, the availability of better evidence, and the appearance of corroborating evidence—and the needs of administrative economy. According to the still leading opinion of Universal Camera Corp. v. NLRB,[3] this judicially evolved standard of review of administrative factfinding is incorporated into the Administrative Procedure Act, except that the Act broadens judicial review to as-

sure that the reviewing court takes "into account whatever in the record fairly detracts from its weight."[4] In other words, the reviewing court should review the whole record to determine whether there is a rational basis in it for the findings of fact supporting the agency's decision.

In reviewing administrative decisions, some appellate courts—primarily state—added a second branch to the substantial evidence test, warping the test into a rigid rule for denying credibility to uncorroborated hearsay evidence. Known as the "legal residuum rule" because it required that an administrative finding be supported by some evidence admissible in a jury trial—that is, by a residuum of "legal" evidence—it has been severely criticized by scholars, and its application has strained judicial reasoning.

The residuum rule is both logically unsound and administratively impractical. In a trial before a lay jury hearsay evidence admitted without objection is given its natural, probative effect and may be the sole support for a verdict. But under the residuum rule hearsay cannot support a decision by an experienced or expert administrator. The rule ignores the reliability of technically incompetent evidence, rendering all such evidence ineffective unless corroborated. However, if corroborated, regardless of how slight the legal evidence, the same hearsay evidence will provide the substantial evidence needed to support the administrative finding.

This rule may also become a trap for the unwary, particularly where the administrative law judge is not expert in the rules of evidence or where the parties are not represented by counsel. In fact it encourages administrative law judges to apply the hearsay rule and exclude probative evidence in order to avoid possible error. In its instinctive protection of fairness in administrative hearings, through assuring that the decision is supported by evidence subject to confrontation

---

§ 354

1. See § 339 supra.
2. N.L.R.B. v. Columbian Enameling & Stamping Co., 306 U.S. 292, 299–300 (1939).

3. 340 U.S. 474 (1951).
4. Id. at 488.

and cross-examination, the residuum rule seems unassailable. What it fails to consider, however, is that much "legal" evidence within the hearsay exceptions is equally untested. Yet the latter is accepted even in jury trials because of its probable reliability. Consequently the residuum rule's mechanical prohibition against uncorroborated hearsay is unsound. Its sound objectives can be secured through the sensitivity of the hearing officers and the wise application of the substantial evidence test which measures the quantity and quality of the supporting evidence regardless of its category or label.

As others have recounted at substantial length, the residuum rule generally lacks acceptance in federal courts. Increasingly the states refuse to apply it.

§ 355. Opinion Evidence and Expert Testimony

The presentation of expert and nonexpert opinions is increasingly common in administrative hearings. Medical issues arising in workers' compensation claims are often complex, technical and beyond the knowledge of either the hearing officer or the agency. An administrative decision to license a hydroelectric plant, to locate a public housing project, to discontinue a bus line, or to grant a liquor license invariably evokes strong community concern. The public views advanced are likely to be expressed in terms of opinions and to include reference to the views of others. To deny the public an opportunity to testify is to invite public rejection of the agency decision or judicial reversal because public participation is required under the agency's enabling legislation.

The general admissibility of expert and nonexpert testimony in administrative hearings is no longer open to question, but doubt still exists regarding the weight an expert's views should be given. For a time agencies and reviewing courts followed early judicial

reasoning and refused to hear expert testimony on the very question that the agency was created to decide. Other courts took the position that it would be unfair for an agency to rely on its own expertness or the expert testimony of its staff when their opinions were contradicted by outside experts. In rejecting these contradictory appeals to ignorance, courts now recognize legislative intention to establish expert agencies. Therefore, agency decisions which rely on the agency's own expertness are upheld when the respondent offers no contrary expert testimony or when expert testimony offered by staff members and outside experts conflicts. Some courts have gone even further and given excessive deference to the knowledge of the administrative agency by upholding its decision in the face of uncontradicted expert testimony to the contrary. However, the demands of fairness are now generally accepted, and an agency seeking to rely on its expertise must present expert testimony subject to cross-examination on the record or give the respondent fair notification that official notice will be taken of such "facts."

§ 356. Privilege in Administrative Proceedings

Witnesses in administrative hearings have the same general duty incumbent on all citizens in judicial trials to give testimony; "the public has a right to every man's testimony."[1] Because the demand comes from the community as a whole, rather than from the parties, and because the obligation is essential to any search for justice, "all privileges of exemption from this duty are exceptional."[2] Read literally, the APA's provision in section 556(d) that "[a]ny oral or documentary evidence may be received,"[3] authorizes the receipt of privileged evidence in administrative hearings.

Nevertheless, administrative hearings have generally followed the judicial lead in recognizing numerous exceptions to the obligation

---

§ 356

1. 12 Cobbett's Parliamentary History 675, 693 (1812), quoted in 4 Wigmore, Evidence 2965–66 (1st ed. 1905).

2. 8 Wigmore, Evidence § 2192, p. 73 (McNaughton rev. 1961).

3. 5 U.S.C.A. § 556(d).

to testify. The exceptions are of two kinds. A few, such as the exclusion of illegally obtained evidence and the assertion of the right against self-incrimination, are constitutional commands. Others, such as the privileges protecting attorney-client and the attorney's work product, are founded upon the need to protect interests without constitutional dimension yet having sufficient social importance to warrant the sacrifice of full factual disclosure.[4]

Even though administrative agencies do not as a rule impose criminal penalties, their adjudicative procedures are not exempt from constitutional limitations, and the chapters of this text which deal with the various constitutional privileges should be consulted. In Camara v. Municipal Court,[5] and See v. Seattle,[6] the Supreme Court applied the Fourth Amendment's strictures against unreasonable searches and seizure of property to administrative health and fire inspections, albeit in somewhat qualified form. These decisions left open the possibility that warrants would not be required for administrative searches where a license was required to conduct the business in question and the grant of a license was effectively conditioned on the applicant's consent to warrantless searches. Later cases confirmed that warrantless searches were permissible in industries subject to a licensing system which involved intensive regulation, i.e., "closely regulated."[7] Compare Marshall v. Barlow's, Inc.,[8] where the Supreme Court ruled that businesses subject to oversight by the Occupational Safety and Health Administration were not "pervasively regulated" and thus could assert the Fourth Amendment privilege against surprise inspections of the workplace. The privilege against unreasonable search is also limited to that which is truly private. Thus a warrant is not necessary if the evidence gathered by the inspector is in "plain view."

While these cases involved direct challenges to administrative inspections, it is also clear that the constitutional objection is available at the hearing even though no objection is asserted at the time the inspection is made. And, in Knoll Associates, Inc. v. FTC,[9] the Court of Appeals of the Seventh Circuit set aside an FTC order on the ground that the Commission's acceptance and use of corporate documents, known to be stolen on behalf of the government, violated the Fourth Amendment.

Many cases uphold the Fifth Amendment privilege against self-incrimination in administrative proceedings. For the Fifth Amendment privilege to apply certain conditions must be met. First, the threatened penalty must be criminal rather than civil in nature.[10] In many regulatory areas, the sanction which the witness fears may be labeled a "civil penalty," a "forfeiture" or a similar term rather than a crime. When this occurs, the court must determine whether the statutory penalty is sufficiently punitive in purpose or effect to be considered criminal. Second, the privilege is available only to natural persons and therefore does not protect corporations and other legal entities.[11] The purpose of the self-incrimination provision is to protect individuals from the government's use of the "third degree" and similar coercive tactics to extract confessions of personal wrong-doing. Thus it does not exempt the officers of corporations and other business associations from testifying about the records of their organizations. Because the privilege is personal to the witness, an individual cannot refuse to testify on the ground that his testimony might incriminate some other person. Third, the privilege attaches only to compelled testimonial utterances and not to other communications. Numerous cases have dealt with the question of whether a particular statement has been coerced or whether it is testimonial in nature. Recent cases have, in general, taken a restric-

---

4. See Chapter 8 supra.

5. 387 U.S. 523 (1967).

6. 387 U.S. 541 (1967).

7. See, e.g., New York v. Burger, 482 U.S. 691 (1987).

8. 436 U.S. 307 (1978).

9. 397 F.2d 530 (7th Cir.1968).

10. See § 121 supra.

11. See § 129 supra.

tive view of the privilege. Thus, even if the documents being sought are personal records, are in his possession, and contain handwritten notations, the agency may still be able to obtain them through use of a search warrant.[12] On the other hand, the Fifth Amendment analysis may be different if the agency seeks to compel an individual to report information rather than trying to get access to existing documents. That is, where the government requires an individual or business to keep business records and make them available to government on demand, such "required records" are not immune from disclosure so long as the underlying regulatory program was a proper exercise of governmental power and the recordkeeping requirement was not designed to make otherwise lawful conduct illegal.[13] Finally, the privilege can be defeated by the grant of immunity from criminal prosecution.[14] Federal agencies commonly have been authorized to grant immunity and compel a witness to testify even if the evidence implicates him.[15] The agency must find that the testimony is "necessary to the public interest," and it must obtain the approval of the Attorney General before immunizing the witness.[16]

On the federal level, neither the Congress nor the agencies have focused on whether administrative agencies must recognize testimonial privileges not constitutionally required. In a leading case concerning the enforcement of an SEC subpoena, Judge Learned Hand expressly assumed that agency proceedings are "subject to the same testimonial privileges as judicial proceedings."[17] Other federal courts have either made the same assumption or considered the matter a question of federal law. Applying the law of privilege applicable in judicial proceedings has considerable merit. Accordingly federal agencies have accorded privileged treatment to communications between attorney and client and husband and wife. But they have

not been anxious to extend such privileges. For example, the accountant-client privileges recognized by a few states has not been accepted by federal agencies. Business secrets have been protected grudgingly, although agencies have become more sophisticated in recent years in protecting both the witness and the adjudicative process by *in camera* receipt of sensitive data.

Claims of privilege for government secrets are particularly important in administrative hearings. Any attempt to probe the government's case by discovery, subpoena of agency witnesses, or cross-examination is quickly met by claims that the information sought is privileged. Actually, government secrets privilege is asserted as an umbrella for three types of information: state secrets involving military or diplomatic information; requests that executive officers testify; and official government information which may range from the identity of informers and internal management materials to staff studies unrelated to any litigation.[18] Only the third, omnibus exception has special significance for administrative adjudications; the judicial rules applicable to state secrets and executive officer testimony are followed in agency hearings. An exploration of all the twists and turns given agency applications of the omnibus exception is beyond the scope of this chapter. In any event, exculpatory information in an agency's possession or file data which may aid respondent's preparation or presentation of his case must be disclosed by the agency. The alternative is to drop the prosecution against the respondent. Anything less would violate the commands of procedural due process which every adjudication must observe.

Almost half the states provide that rules of privilege applicable in court proceedings must apply in administrative hearings. Courts and agencies in other states have reached the same position as a matter of policy. The scope of the statutory recognition of privi-

---

12. See § 127 supra.

13. See discussion of required reports in § 142 supra.

14. See § 143 supra.

15. 18 U.S.C.A. §§ 6001–6005.

16. 18 U.S.C.A. § 6004.

17. McMann v. Securities & Exchange Commission, 87 F.2d 377, 378 (2d Cir.1937), cert. denied 301 U.S. 684.

18. See Ch. 12 supra.

leged communications in the states tends to exceed the testimonial exception recognized by federal courts. On the other hand, where agency proceedings are excepted or where no statutory mandate exists, state agencies have on occasion relaxed or avoided testimonial privileges where the rationale for the privilege is weak or not particularly appropriate. For example, several states have held that the physician-patient privilege cannot bar a worker's compensation commission's search for the truth.

§ 357. Presentation of Case: Burden of Proof and Presumptions

The customary common law rule that the moving party has the burden of proof—including not only the burden of going forward but also the burden of persuasion—is generally observed in administrative hearings. Section 556(d) of the APA, for example, provides: "Except as otherwise provided by statute, the proponent of a rule or order has the burden of proof." [1] State courts have reached the same result in connection with state administrative proceedings.

In most hearings the burden of persuasion is met by the usual civil case standard of "a preponderance of evidence." The rule applicable to federal administrative adjudications was not settled, however, until 1981. In Steadman v. SEC,[2] a broker-dealer being prosecuted by the commission for fraudulent activities had challenged the proceeding, arguing that violation of the antifraud provisions of the securities laws must be proved by the equity standard of clear and convincing evidence. He contended that the potentially severe sanctions (revocation of his license) as well as the circumstantial and inferential nature of the evidence used to prove intent to defraud, required the higher standard of proof. A divided Court rejected his argument. The Court held that the language of Section 556(d) of the APA and the legislative history both show Congress intended that administra-

tive adjudications be measured by the usual standard.

On the other hand, where Congress has not spoken and grave issues of personal security are at stake in an administrative hearing, as in a deportation proceeding, the courts are free to exercise their traditional oversight powers and fashion appropriate standards. Thus in Woodby v. INS,[3] the Supreme Court ruled that in deportation proceedings where liberty is at stake, the government must establish its allegations by "clear, unequivocal, and convincing evidence."

It is also not uncommon for courts to employ the substantial evidence standard to impose a special burden of proof on administrative agencies. This is particularly true in compensation benefits cases where the legislative design is read as favoring awards despite inadequate evidentiary support. A series of cases involving social security and other compensation proceedings has required that the agency accept the claimant's uncontroverted evidence even though the claimant has the burden of proof. Nor can these cases be explained away on the grounds of judicial acceptance of uncontradicted medical testimony in support of the claim, since the agencies are also dealing with malingering and false claims. On the other hand, reviewing courts are more concerned with the remedial, risk-spreading purposes of the statutes and the comparative inability of the claimant to present additional proof. Similar tendencies occasionally appear in such diverse areas as police suspension matters and draft exemption cases where the courts have given increasing scrutiny to the overall fairness of administrative adjudications.

These cases can also be viewed as establishing a presumption in certain administrative adjudications since they affect the burden of proof. The history of workers' compensation illustrates this alternative analysis. Although many state acts have created a presumption in favor of the claimant, several

---

1. 5 U.S.C.A. § 556(d).

2. 450 U.S. 91 (1981).

3. 385 U.S. 276 (1966).

state courts formerly gave these provisions no effect. In interpreting a federal compensation act in Del Vecchio v. Bowers,[4] the Supreme Court held that this "benefit" presumption was sufficient to carry claimant's burden of persuasion in the absence of opposing evidence. However, once rebuttal evidence is introduced, the statutory presumption is overcome and the agency must decide the case solely on the evidence in the record. Similar analysis supports the presumption of the correctness of official administrative action.

On the other hand, the opposite approach is often taken in administrative adjudications where the activities of business respondents are tested. For example, an advertiser may have the burden of establishing any advertising claim, and if it is the type of claim whose truth can be determined only by scientific tests—for example, a claim that respondent's tires will stop a car 25 percent more quickly than other tires—the advertiser's fully-documented proof must *antedate* the representation; the prosecuting agency need only show that the claim was made. That is to say, substantive law interpretations can affect the burden of proof as much as procedural requirements.

§ 358. Presentation of Case: Written Evidence and Cross–Examination

Perhaps the most distinctive feature of many administrative hearings, particularly in contrast to nonjury trials, is the substitution of written evidence for oral testimony. This written evidence takes several forms. In its simplest and least productive aspect, some witnesses appear, if at all, simply for cross-examination, with the written questions and answers read into the record in lieu of the usual oral question-answer format. This "canned dialogue" has been criticized as leading to the withholding of the true facts from the administrative law judge and assuring

that the case will be decided on grounds other than the evidence in the record. But if applied more sensitively, written evidence can expedite and simplify formal administrative proceedings through reducing the controversy to verified written statements which are then exchanged by the parties for the purpose of rebuttal. Federal administrative agencies have frequently relied upon this technique, the Interstate Commerce Commission for almost half a century. With the cooperation of the parties, this procedure can result in greater precision than where the facts are presented orally.

The ICC's written procedures are probably the most sophisticated of all agencies. In time, the Commission's "modified" procedure has been streamlined into an administrative version of summary judgment. Under the ICC's rules of procedure, any party may request use of the modified procedure by filing a verified statement setting forth the facts, argument, and exhibits on which he relies.[1] The opposing party must either admit or deny each material allegation, explaining each exception he takes to the facts and argument of his adversary. Unless there are material facts in dispute or the objecting party explains why he cannot properly present his case by affidavits, a decision will then be rendered on the written case. This rule exceeds the concept of summary judgment currently applied under the Federal Rules of Civil Procedure by placing the burden on the parties to prove that an oral hearing is necessary. An oral hearing is not presumed to be the proper method for hearing a case.

Written evidence has been relied upon most successfully in rate or price control proceedings, where economic and expert analysis rather than sensorily-perceived phenomena provide the bulk of the evidence. Credibility based upon conflicting stories relating what each witness observed is seldom involved. Often the advance preparation of written evi-

---

4. 296 U.S. 280 (1935).

1. 49 C.F.R. § 1100.45; see id. §§ 1100.49, 1100.50, 1100.53.

dence is limited to the contentions of the party having the burden of proof; in others the opposing party's evidence is included. The elimination of surprise cannot be objected to since surprise has no proper place in the hearing when credibility is not in issue. Cross-examination is not used to establish a party's case. Its major purpose here is "not to reduce * * * [the expert] witness to a shattered hulk by the admission of error, but to explore all of the considerations entering into what must remain a matter of judgment."[2]

As explained by the Second Interim Administrative Conference, the benefits of written evidence are manifold:

(1) [The] exchange of written evidence facilitates settlement techniques in situations in which there is staff participation; (2) the hearing examiner, after studying the direct evidence of the parties prior to hearing, can participate in the case in an intelligent fashion, leading to more effective use of conference techniques and more informed rulings at the hearing; (3) in a substantial number of cases, particularly those of less moment, the parties may be satisfied with their written presentations, and an oral hearing becomes unnecessary; and (4) the efforts of the parties at the oral hearing, if one is necessary, are confined to clarifying the major issues through informed cross-examination. Properly handled, written procedures should result in a more adequate record being produced in a shorter space of time.[3]

Section 556(d) of the APA recognizes the propriety of written presentations with only limited cross-examination: "In rule making or determining claims for money or benefits or applications for initial licenses any agency may, when a party will not be prejudiced thereby, adopt procedures for the submission of all or part of the evidence in written form."[4] Existing case law supports the use of written presentations by any agency in a type

of proceeding where the interest of any party is not prejudiced.

Where cross-examination is necessary for protection against untrustworthy evidence, it cannot be avoided. Section 556(d) of the APA specifically preserves the right of cross-examination in agency adjudications: "A party is entitled * * * to conduct such cross-examination as may be required for a full and true disclosure of the facts."[5] State law is identical. Through this provision the APA recognizes one of the fundamentals of a fair hearing—namely a reasonable opportunity to test and controvert adverse evidence whether or not such evidence is a statement of opinion, observation, or consideration of the witness. Cross-examination has several potential uses: to bring out matters left untouched by direct examination; to test the accuracy of a witness' perception as well as his ability to observe; to probe his truthfulness; to question his memory and narration; and to expose the basis of any opinions he has expressed. In other words, "cross-examination is a means of getting at the truth; it is not truth itself."[6] Yet unless credibility is directly in issue—and then only on occasion—cross-examination usually does no more than demonstrate forensic talent or score trial points irrelevant to the final decision.[7] As an experienced agency practitioner, who later became an eminent federal judge, observed: "Only rarely * * * can you accomplish something devastating on cross-examining an expert * * *. [M]ore often it is love's labor lost."[8]

Perception of this point is the key to a reconciliation of the right of cross-examination with the seemingly inconsistent administrative practice of relying on hearsay testimony and written evidence whether or not the declarant is unavailable. The legislative history of the APA makes clear that Congress was seeking to draw a line between an unlimited right of unnecessary cross-examination and a reasonable opportunity to test opposing

2. Selected Reports of the Administrative Conference of the United States 1961–1962, S.Doc. No. 24, 88th Cong., 1st Sess. 92 (1963).

3. Id. at 93.

4. 5 U.S.C.A. § 556(d).

5. Id.

6. W. Gellhorn & Byse, Administrative Law 713 (5th ed. 1970).

7. See § 30 supra.

8. Leventhal, Cues and Compasses for Administrative Lawyers, 20 Ad.L.Rev. 237, 246 (1968).

evidence. The test, stated abstractly, is that cross-examination must be allowed when it is required for determining the truth. If witness veracity and demeanor are not critical, there is no requirement for cross-examination so long as sufficient opportunity for rebuttal exists; if credibility is a key factor, and the objecting party can show that the absence of cross-examination of the witness may have prejudiced his case, the denial of cross-examination could be fatal to an agency decision. Statistical compilations and surveys are admissible only if the person responsible for—and having full knowledge of the preparation of—the exhibit is available. In addition, the raw data upon which the exhibit is based should be available to the opposing party.[9] It has been proposed that the right to cross-examine in at least some administrative proceedings be reduced to a privilege "to be granted only in the virtually unlimited discretion of the hearing officer." This proposal is only part of a recommended restructuring of the administrative hearing into a conference proceeding where almost all the evidence would be submitted in written form.[10]

Finally, administrative agencies are required to apply the "*Jencks* rule"—namely, that after a government witness has testified, the prosecution must disclose prior statements by the witness relating to his testimony.[11] Application of this rule in agency hearings has been the subject of controversy. The Administrative Conference has suggested that prior statements be made available to the respondent at the prehearing conference.[12] If this view were adopted the question would no longer be one of evidence but rather one of discovery.

§ 359. Official Notice [1]

Official notice, like its judicial notice counterpart, involves reliance by the presiding officer—in this case the administrative law judge—on extra-record information. That is, the law judge in making a decision bypasses the normal process of proof and relies upon facts and opinions not supported by evidence "on the record." Several characteristics of official notice should be observed. First, a specific procedure similar to that for judicial notice has been established to receive extra-record facts, with the parties receiving notice and an opportunity to rebut the "noticed" facts.[2] Second, extra-record facts usually have first been developed by the agency's expert staff or accumulated from previous agency decisions. But official notice is not limited to information in agency files. In fact, it may be taken at the initiation of one of the parties. Third, agency recognition of extra-record facts is clearly not limited to "indisputable" facts. Rather, official notice may extend to almost any information useful in deciding the adjudication as long as elemental fairness is observed.[3]

On the other hand, in administrative adjudication, official notice is frequently confused with the process of decisionmaking. In reaching a conclusion, the administrative law judge or agency may rely on its special skills, whether they include particular expertness in engineering, economics, medicine, or electricity, just as a federal or state judge may freely use his legal skills in reading statutes and applying decided cases in the preparation of his opinion. But such evaluations are not within the concept of official notice. Official notice is concerned with the *process of proof,* not with the *evaluation of evidence.* The difference between an administrative tribunal's use of non-record information included in its expert knowledge, as a substitute for evidence or notice, and its application of its back-

---

9. See generally § 208 supra.

10. Westwood, Administrative Proceedings; Techniques of Presiding, 50 A.B.A.J. 659, 660 (1964).

11. Jencks v. United States, 353 U.S. 657 (1957). See generally § 97 supra for discussion of the rule in its present form.

12. ACUS Recommendation No. 70–4, 1 C.F.R. § 305.-70–4.

§ 359

1. See § 333 supra.

2. 5 U.S.C.A. § 556(d). See Fed.R.Evid. 201(e) and § 333 supra.

3. The kinds of facts noticeable in judicial proceedings are discussed in Chapter 35 supra.

ground in evaluating and drawing conclusions from the evidence that is in the record, is, however, primarily a difference of degree rather than of kind. In principle, reliance upon the administrative law judge's knowledge in the process of proof is permissible only within the confines of official notice, whereas the administrative judge's use of his experience in the evaluating "*proof* is not only unavoidable but, indeed, desirable."[4]

The troublesome problem, as with most questions of law, is that a fine line cannot be drawn with precision. Benjamin illustrates the point:

> When the State Liquor Authority concludes, from evidence in the record as to the size of food bills and gas bills paid (in relation to the volume of liquor business), that the holder of a restaurant liquor license is not conducting a *bona fide* restaurant, is the Authority using its experience and knowledge to evaluate and draw conclusions from the evidence, or is it using its experience and knowledge as a substitute for further evidence as to the normal relation of the size of food and gas bills to the volume of food business? * * * My own view is that * * * the procedure described is permissible [evaluation]; but until the courts have decided specific questions of this character, it is impossible to anticipate with any certainty what their decision would be.[5]

Beyond this or other examples, little guidance can be offered.

The primary thrust behind official notice is to simplify or ease the process of proof. Where facts are known or can be safely assumed, the process of proving what is already known is both time-consuming and unduly formal. When facts have been proven before, further proof becomes tiresome, redundant, and lacking in common sense. At times even the obvious could be difficult or time-consuming to prove, without affecting the final result, which was never in doubt. Moreover, administrative agencies were often created to become repositories of knowledge and experience. It would defeat their existence to require adherence to traditional methods of proof when alternative and equally fair methods are readily available. On the other hand, in developing an alternative method, it is necessary to safeguard the elements of a fair trial preserved by the traditional forms of proof. The 1941 Attorney General's Committee accurately summarized the need:

> The parties, then, are entitled to be apprised of the data upon which the agency is acting. They are entitled not only to refute but, what in this situation is usually more important, to supplement, explain, and give different perspective to the facts upon which the agency relies. In addition, upon judicial review, the court must be informed of what facts the agency has utilized in order that the existence of supporting evidence may be ascertained.[6]

The Congress sought to recognize and reconcile these concerns by a single sentence in section 556(e) of the APA: "When an agency decision rests on official notice of a material fact not appearing in the evidence in the record, a party is entitled, on timely request, to an opportunity to show the contrary."[7] The procedure is simple. Official notice is a means by which an agency can avoid hearing further evidence on a material fact in the case if it notifies the parties that unless they prove to the contrary the agency's findings will include that particular fact and allows the parties an opportunity to present contrary evidence.

Federal Trade Commission cases illustrate the practice. After hearing dozens of cases indicating that consumers preferred American to foreign-made goods—and holding, therefore, that a failure to disclose the foreign origin of these goods was a false and deceptive act—the commission advised respondents in Manco Watch Strap Co.[8] that it would not hear evidence on this issue in the future.

---

4. Interstate Commerce Commission v. Louisville & Nashville Railroad Co., 227 U.S. 88, 98 (1913). See the discussion of "legislative" facts in § 331 supra.

5. Benjamin, Administrative Adjudication in the State of New York 212 (1942).

6. Final Report of the Attorney General's Committee on Administrative Procedure, S.Doc. No. 8, 77th Cong. 1st Sess. 72 (1941).

7. 5 U.S.C.A. § 556(e).

8. 60 F.T.C. 495 (1962).

Then, in subsequent cases where the FTC took official notice and the respondents could not prove that American consumers preferred their foreign goods or that the consumers had no particular preference, the Commission upheld orders barring sales of goods not bearing the requisite disclosures. On the other hand, if respondents could show that consumers preferred French over American perfumes, for example, the "noticed finding" would not apply.

Practically, then, the primary effect of taking official notice is to transfer the burden of proof on that material fact—usually from the agency to the respondent. The significance of this tactic varies in proportion to the difficulty of the proponent in establishing that fact originally, and of the cost and effort of the opponent in disproving it. In most instances where agencies have taken official notice, the costs have been slight since the result has seemed obvious. Where the fact is less obvious, however, that cost could prove substantial.[9]

The academic controversy over official notice has centered upon the limitation of judicial notice to undisputed facts and attempts to categorize the types of facts which can be officially noticed. The former is examined elsewhere in this text.[10] On the other hand, the APA's guidance of what facts can be noticed is essentially nonexistent; it merely sets forth the procedure which must be followed for taking notice of "material facts." By omission it appears to suggest that facts which are not material can be noticed in the manner of a judge at a judicial trial, but it does not tell how to determine which facts are material and can therefore be noticed. In any event, the term "material" seems not to be used in its classic sense.

The Attorney General's Committee on Administrative Procedure suggested a distinction between "litigation" and "non-litigation" facts:

If information has come to an agency's attention in the course of investigation of the pending case, it should be adduced only by the ordinary process. * * * But if the information has been developed in the usual course of business of the agency, if it has emerged from numerous cases, if it has become part of the factual equipment of the administrators, it seems undesirable for the agencies to remain oblivious of their own experience [and, they should take notice of such facts].[11]

Professor Davis, on the other hand, rejects the notion that significance could be attached to the time when the factual data was collected. His criticism of the Committee's distinction stems from his conclusion that it would "encourage guesswork" and "discourage extra-record research of the kind that is especially needed for creation of law or policy. It would mean [for example, that] an agency could notice only those statutes that it has previously encountered!" This criticism seems somewhat unfair since the Committee's basic point defining reliable facts—those previously established by the agency—is sound. Davis is right, however, when he points out that the Committee rule is too narrow. As an alternative, he offers a different standard for deciding whether an administrator may use extra-record facts:

When a court or an agency finds facts concerning the immediate parties—who did what, where, when, how, and with what motive or intent—[it] is performing an adjudicative function, and the facts are conveniently called adjudicative facts. When a court or an agency develops law or policy, it is acting legislatively; the courts have created the common law through judicial legislation, and the facts which inform the tribunal's legislative judgment are called legislative facts. * * * Legislative facts are ordinarily general and do not concern the immediate parties.[12]

On this basis, Davis asserts that legislative facts usually need not be brought into the record by official notice; where critical, a

9. See §§ 342, 343, supra.

10. Ch. 35 supra.

11. Final Report of the Attorney General's Committee on Administrative Procedure, supra note 6 at 72.

12. 2 Davis, Administrative Law Treatise § 15.03, at 353 (1958).

party should be able to challenge them by brief and argument. He contends that adjudicative facts, on the other hand, must be brought into the record—unless they are indisputable—either through direct proof or by official notice. Nothing less will meet the cardinal principles of a fair hearing—notice and an opportunity to test and rebut opposing evidence. Whether adjudicative facts can be officially noticed or must be established by direct proof depends, he says, on three variables: how close the facts are to the center of the controversy; the extent to which the facts are adjudicative or legislative; and the degree to which the facts are certain. As the adjudicative facts move closer to the basic issues of the hearing, relate to the parties, and are disputed, the usual methods of proof must be observed; as they move in the opposite direction, official notice is permissible.[13]

Professor Jaffe has suggested an attractive alternative approach:

> [W]here the facts bear closely and crucially on the issue, and are prima facie debatable, they should be developed in evidentiary fashion— by which is meant simply that they should be referred to in such a manner as to enable the opponent to offer rebuttal. Such facts will not necessarily be "adjudicative" * * *.[14]

Thus, as Davis himself concedes, the categories he defines do not in themselves resolve which facts can be noticed in particular cases. He is certainly correct when he points out that the central problem is to reconcile procedural fairness with convenience and the use of agency knowledge. The difficulty with his analysis lies not in his categories which are original and helpful, but rather that many cases fall outside his definitions. A sampling of cases illustrates this point. The existence of the Great Depression is a "legislative" fact which an agency can include in its findings without notice to the parties, but a specific price trend, also a general legislative fact,

cannot be used to update the figures in the record without notice to the parties.[15] Since a specific price trend can be readily verified, taking notice is appropriate; the burden of proving any substantial error is not likely to be significant. Similarly, the courts have upheld agencies' official notice of scientific data, technical facts, and articles in academic journals, although many courts contend that this places too great a burden on the opponent to refute the "noticed evidence."

Of greater consequence is the fact that reliance upon Davis' categories distracts from the central question of fairness—that is, is it fair in the particular hearing to take official notice and *transfer the burden of proof* to the opposing party? Two cases involving the use of the record of a related hearing, each of which reaches an opposite result, are perhaps the clearest examples of this suggested "fairness of the transfer of the burden of proof" analysis. In United States v. Pierce Auto Freight Lines, Inc.,[16] the ICC held two separate hearings on competing applications for truck service between San Francisco and Portland. Each applicant intervened in the other hearing, but the cases were not consolidated. In reaching its decision, the Commission relied on evidence appearing in only one record. The procedure was upheld because both applicants were parties to both proceedings and both had ample opportunity to present evidence, to cross-examine witnesses, and otherwise to protect their interests.

In the second case, Dayco Corp. v. FTC,[17] the FTC sought to take official notice of the distribution system and practices used by the respondent, a manufacturer of auto replacement parts, since the system had been the subject of a prior proceeding. That prior proceeding, in which respondent was only a witness, was brought against his customers. The court ruled that the FTC's attempt to take official notice of these "adjudicative facts"

---

13. Id. § 15.10.

14. Jaffe, Administrative Procedure Re–Examined: The Benjamin Report, 56 Harv.L.Rev. 704, 719 (1943).

15. Ohio Bell Telephone Co. v. Public Utilities Commission, 301 U.S. 292 (1937); West Ohio Gas Co. v. Public Utilities Commission, 294 U.S. 63 (1935).

16. 327 U.S. 515 (1946).

17. 362 F.2d 180 (6th Cir.1966).

from the first proceeding was improper because the manufacturer was not a party, but only a witness to the prior proceeding. To allow official notice in this circumstance, the court reasoned, would have eliminated the commission's entire burden of proof. The agency had asserted that its reliance on prior knowledge merely shifted the burden of going forward to respondent and this burden (of correcting any FTC errors in describing respondent's distribution system) was minimal when compared with the cost of proving these same facts again. The FTC's argument is not persuasive. If the agency merely sought to shift the burden of going forward, it could have introduced the prior record as reliable hearsay evidence subject to rebuttal or as written evidence with an offer to make the witnesses available for cross-examination. If handled in this manner—rather than under the official notice rubric—the fact-trier would still have to determine whether the prior record accurately portrayed respondent's distribution system. The court may also have perceived that there was no compelling need to approve the commission's proposal since the FTC could (and should) have avoided the

burden of re-proof by joining the respondent as a party in the first proceeding. Official notice, in other words, is not properly a procedural device to avoid the requirement of section 556(e) of the APA that the moving party has the burden of proof. If that burden is to be placed on respondent as a condition of doing business, it should be accomplished openly through a shift in substantive policy rather than covertly by manipulation of procedural devices.

When the issue of official notice is viewed in this manner, the Davis criteria and the Attorney General's Committee's distinctions are helpful, but not dispositive. On the other hand, judging from the small number of reported cases, the doctrine of official notice has apparently not been used extensively or creatively by many agencies. This reluctance may be partly the result of uncertainties in the applicable legal standards. Without clear tests indicating when official notice is proper, agencies may be unwilling to risk reversal by taking notice of nonrecord facts. Nonetheless, it remains a potentially useful device for simplifying and expediting hearings.

Appendix

EVIDENCE LAW
RESEARCH ON WESTLAW

Analysis

Section 1. Introduction

The discussion of the law of evidence in this text provides a strong base for analyzing evidence problems. Analyzing an evidence problem can be a complex task, requiring the examination of case law, statutes, court rules and orders, administrative materials and commentary. Along with West books, WESTLAW is an excellent source of research materials.

WESTLAW evidence databases contain rules, commentaries, statutes, cases and administrative materials. Each database is assigned an identifier, which you use to access the database. You can find identifiers for all WESTLAW databases in the WESTLAW Directory and in the *WESTLAW Database List*. When you need to know more detailed information about a database, use the SCOPE command. SCOPE displays unique commands and related databases for each WESTLAW database and service.

You can retrieve documents on WESTLAW by accessing a database and entering a query; by using FIND, a one-step document retrieval service; or by using such services as Insta–Cite®, Shepard's®, Shepard's PreView™ and Quick*Cite*™. You can also use West's menu-driven research system, EZ ACCESS™, for additional help.

Additional Resources

If you have not used WESTLAW or have questions not addressed in this appendix, see the *WESTLAW Reference Manual* or contact the West Reference Attorneys at 1–800–688–6363.

Section 2. Evidence Law Databases

Because new information is continually being added to WESTLAW, you should check the WESTLAW Directory for any new database information.

Database Description	Database Identifier	Coverage
Federal Databases		
U.S. Supreme Court Cases	SCT	From 1945 [1]
U.S. Courts of Appeals Cases	CTA	From 1945 [1]
Individual Courts of Appeals	CTA1–CTA11 CTADC CTAF	See SCOPE for the specific court.
U.S. District Courts Cases [2]	DCT	See SCOPE for the specific court.
U.S. Code Annotated	USCA	Current
U.S. Public Laws	US–PL	Current [3]
Federal Rules	US–RULES	Current
Federal Orders	US–ORDERS	Current
Federal Register	FR	From July 1980
Code of Federal Regulations	CFR	Current [3]
State Databases		
Case Law from all 50 states and the District of Columbia	ALLSTATES	From 1945 [1]
Individual State Cases [3]	XX–CS	See SCOPE for the specific state.
State Statutes—Annotated Statutes and annotations from all available states, the District of Columbia, Puerto Rico and the Virgin Islands	ST–ANN–ALL	See SCOPE for the specific state.
State Statutes—Unannotated Unannotated statutes from all available states, the District of Columbia, Puerto Rico and the Virgin Islands	STAT–ALL	See SCOPE for the specific state.
Individual State Statutes—Annotated [4]	XX–ST–ANN	See SCOPE for the specific state.
Individual State Statutes—Unannotated [4]	XX–ST	See SCOPE for the specific state.
Multistate Legislative Service Documents passed by the legislative bodies from all available states, the District of Columbia, Puerto Rico and the Virgin Islands	LEGIS–ALL	See SCOPE for the specific state.
Individual State Legislative Service [3] Documents passed by the legislative bodies of each state, district or territory	XX–LEGIS	See SCOPE for the specific state.
Individual State Statutes [3] General index references for the statutes and constitutions of all available states and the District of Columbia	XX–ST–IDX	See SCOPE for the specific state.

Database Description	Database Identifier	Coverage
Individual State Attorney General Opinions [3] Attorney general opinions from 49 states	XX–AG	See SCOPE for the specific state.
Individual State Court Rules [4] State court rules from all available states, Puerto Rico and the Virgin Islands	XX–RULES	See SCOPE for the specific state.
Individual State Court Orders [4] State court orders from all available states	XX–ORDERS	See SCOPE for the specific state.

SPECIALIZED MATERIALS

Database Description	Database Identifier	Coverage
Federal Military Law—Manual for Courts–Martial	FMIL–MCM	From 1941
Military Criminal Law Evidence	MCLE	From July 1987
WESTLAW Topical Highlights—Federal Practice and Procedure	WTH–FPP	Current

Texts & Treatises

Database Description	Database Identifier	Coverage
Federal Rules Decisions [5] (articles)	FEDRDTP	From 1986

(1) Cases dated before 1945 are contained in databases whose identifiers end with the suffix—OLD. For example, the identifier for the U.S. Supreme Court Cases—Before 1945 database is SCT–OLD. Coverage for federal databases whose identifiers end with the suffix—OLD is 1789–1944. Coverage for the ALLSTATES–OLD database varies by state.

(2) Case law from the *Federal Rules Decisions*® reporter can be found in the U.S. District Courts Cases database (DCT).

(3) To search for historical versions of the C.F.R. or U.S. Public Laws, access the appropriate database by typing **db cfrxx** or **db us-plxx**, where xx is the last two digits of a year. For example, to access the C.F.R. as it existed in 1986, type **db cfr86**. To access U.S. Public Laws for 1990, type **db us-pl90**.

(4) XX is a state's two-letter postal abbreviation.

(5) Case law from the *Federal Rules Decisions* reporter can be found in the U.S. District Courts Cases database (DCT), articles from the *Federal Rules Decisions* reporter can be found in the Federal Rules Decisions database (FEDRDTP).

Section 3. EZ ACCESS™

EZ ACCESS is West Publishing company's menu-driven research system. It is ideal for new or infrequent WESTLAW users because it requires no experience or training on WESTLAW.

EZ ACCESS assists you in performing the following research tasks on WESTLAW:

1. Retrieving a document using its citation or title

2. Retrieving cases using a West topic or key number

3. Retrieving documents using significant words

4. Retrieving references to a document using Insta–Cite®, Shepard's® Citations, Shepard's PreView™ and WESTLAW as a citator.

To access EZ ACCESS, type **ez.** Whenever you are unsure of the next step, or if the choice you want is not listed, simply type **ez**; additional choices will be displayed. Once you retrieve documents with EZ ACCESS, use standard WESTLAW commands to browse your documents. For more information on EZ ACCESS, see the *Guide to EZ ACCESS*. For more information on browsing documents, see the browsing commands listed later in this appendix or Section 9 of the *WESTLAW Reference Manual.*

Section 4. FIND

Overview: FIND is a WESTLAW service that allows you to retrieve a document by entering its citation. FIND allows you to retrieve documents from anywhere in WESTLAW without accessing or changing databases or losing your search result. FIND is available for many documents including federal court rules, case law (federal and state), state statutes, *United States Code Annotated*®, *Code of Federal Regulations* and *Federal Register* materials, and state and federal public laws.

☐ To use FIND, type **fi** followed by the document citation.

☐ When you are finished using FIND, you have several options. You can access other services, such as Insta–Cite, Shepard's Citations, Shepard's PreView or Quick*Cite*™. You can also return to the last database or service accessed before using FIND by typing **gb** or **map**.

To FIND This Document	**Type**
Jones v. Goodyear Tire & Rubber Co., 1991 WL 128474	**fi 1991 wl 128474**
Wardwell v. United States, 758 F.Supp. 769	**fi 758 fsupp 769**
United States Public Law ** 102–40	**fi us pl 102–40**
Federal Rules of Evidence Rule 803	**fi fre rule 803**
137 Cong.Rec. S8486 (daily ed. June 24, 1991) (statement of Sen. Grassley)	**fi 137 cr s8486**

Section 5. Query Formulation

Overview: A query is a request you make to WESTLAW specifying the information you wish to retrieve. The terms in a query are words or numbers that you include in your request so that WESTLAW will retrieve documents containing those words or numbers. These terms are linked together by connectors, which specify the relationship in which the terms must appear.

5.1 Terms

Plurals and Possessives: Plurals are automatically retrieved when you enter the singular form of a term. This is true for both regular and irregular plurals (e.g., **child** retrieves *children*). If you do not want to retrieve the plural form, you can turn off the automatic pluralizer by typing the # symbol in front of the singular form. If you enter the plural form of a term, you will not retrieve the signular form.

If you enter the non-possessive form of a term, WESTLAW automatically retrieves the possessive form as well. However, if you enter the possessive form, only the possessive form is retrieved.

Automatic Equivalencies: Some terms have alternative forms or equivalencies; for example, *5* and *five* are equivalent terms. WESTLAW automatically retrieves equivalent terms.

Compound Words and Acronyms: When a compound word is one of your search terms, use a hyphen to retrieve all forms of the word. For example, the term **cross-examination** retrieves *cross-examination, cross examination* and *crossexamination.*

** FIND retrieves public laws from the current congressional session. To search for historical versions of U.S. public laws, access the appropriate database by typing **db us-plxx**, where xx is the last two digits of a year. For example, to access the United States Public Laws—1990 database (US–PL90), type **db us-pl90.**

When using an acronym as a search term, place a period after each of the letters in the acronym to retrieve any of its forms. For example, the term **a.p.a.** retrieves *apa, a.p.a., a p a* and *a. p. a.*

Root Expander and Universal Character: Placing a root expander (!) at the end of a root term generates ALL other terms with that root. For example, adding the ! symbol to the root *confess* in the query

confess! /s miranda

instructs WESTLAW to retrieve such words as *confess, confesses, confessed, confessing, confession,* and *confessions.*

The universal character (*) stands for one character and can be inserted in the middle or at the end of a term. For example, the term

withdr*w

will retrieve *withdraw* and *withdrew.* More than one universal character can be used in a term. But adding only two asterisks to the root *jur* in the query

jur**

instructs WESTLAW to retrieve all forms of the root with up to two additional characters. Terms like *jury* or *juror* are retrieved by this query. However, terms with more than two letters following the root, such as *jurisdiction,* are not retrieved. Plurals are always retrieved, even if more than two letters follow the root.

Phrase Searching: To search for a phrase on WESTLAW, place it within quotation marks. For example, to search for references to the doctrine of *res gestae,* type **"res gestae".** You should use phrase searching only when you are certain that the phrase will not appear in any other form.

5.2 Alternative Terms

After selecting the terms for your query, consider which alternative terms are necessary. For example, if you are searching for the term *custody,* you might also want to search for the terms *detain!* and *detention.* You should consider both synonyms and antonyms as alternative terms.

5.3 Connectors

After selecting terms and alternative terms for your query, use connectors to specify the relationship that should exist between search terms in your retrieved documents. The connectors you can use are described below:

Connector	Meaning	Example
or (space)	Retrieves documents containing either term or both terms.	**coerc! force***
& (and)	Retrieves documents containing both terms.	**waiver & privilege**
/p	Retrieves documents containing both terms in the same paragraph.	**withdr*w /p plea**
/s	Retrieves documents containing both terms in the same sentence.	**refresh! /s recollection**
+s	Retrieves documents in which the first term precedes the second within the same sentence.	**marital +s privilege**
/n	Retrieves documents in which terms are within a specified number of terms of each other.	**business /3 record**

Connector	Meaning	Example
+n	Retrieves documents in which the first term precedes the second by no more than the specified number of terms.	**parol +2 evidence**
% (but not)	Excludes all documents containing the term(s) following the % symbol.	**los* /3 evidence** **% to (110)**

5.4 Restricting Your Search by Field

Documents in each WESTLAW database consist of several segments, or fields. One field may contain the citation, another the title, another the synopsis, and so forth. A query can be formulated to retrieve only those documents that contain search terms in a specified field. Not all databases contain the same fields. Also, depending on the database, fields of the same name may contain different types of information.

To view the fields and field content for a specific database, type **f** while in the database. Note that in some databases, not every field is available for every document. To restrict your search to a specific field, type the field name or its two-letter abbreviation followed by search terms enclosed in parentheses.

The following fields are available in some WESTLAW databases you might use for evidence law research:

Digest and Synopsis Fields: The digest and synopsis fields, available in cases published by West Publishing Company, summarize the main points of a case. A search in these fields is useful because it retrieves only cases in which a search term was significant enough to be included in a summary.

Consider restricting your search to one or both of these fields if

☐ you are searching for common terms or terms with more than one meaning, and you need to narrow your search; or

☐ you cannot narrow your search by moving to a smaller database.

For example, suppose you want to retrieve cases that discuss whether parol evidence is admissible in a contract dispute to explain ambiguity in the contract. Access an appropriate database, such as the Connecticut Cases database (CT–CS) and type a query like the following:

sy,di(parol extrinsic /p ambigui! /s contract agreement)

Headnote Field: You can also restrict your search to the headnote field. The headnote field, which is part of the digest field, does not include the topic number, the key number, the citation or the title. A headnote field search is useful when you are searching for references to specific code sections or rule numbers.

For example, to retrieve cases that discuss rule 803(24) of the Federal Rules of Evidence, access a database such as the U.S. Court of Appeals for the Fifth Circuit Cases database (CTA5), and type a query like the following:

he(803(24))

Topic Field: The topic field includes the West digest topic number, topic name, key number and text of the key line for each key number. You should restrict your search to the topic field in a case law database if

☐ a digest field search retrieves too many documents; or

☐ you want to retrieve cases with digest paragraphs classified under more than one topic.

For example, the topic *Evidence* has the topic number 157. To retrieve Illinois cases that discuss the work product doctrine, access the Illinois Cases database (IL–CS) and type a query like the following:

to(157) /p work-product

To retrieve West headnotes classified under more than one topic, search for the topic name in the topic field.

For example, to search for Illinois cases that discuss privilege and the work product doctrine, access the Illinois Cases database (IL–CS) and type a query like the following:

to(privilege!) /p work-product

Be aware that cases from slip opinions and looseleaf services do not contain the digest, synopsis, headnote or topic fields.

Prelim and Caption Fields: Restrict your search to the prelim and caption fields in a database containing statutes, rules or regulations to retrieve documents where your terms are important enough to appear in the heading or name of a statute or rule.

For example, to retrieve the federal rules of evidence discussing character evidence, access the Federal Rules database (US–RULES) and type

pr,ca(character & evidence)

☐ To look at sections surrounding those your query retrieved, use the DOCUMENTS IN SEQUENCE command. When you are viewing rule 404 you can retrieve the section preceding it by typing **d-**. To retrieve the section immediately following a retrieved document, type **d.** To cancel this command and return to your original search result, type **xd.**

☐ To see if a rule has been amended or repealed, use the UPDATE service. Simply type **update** while viewing the rule to display any court order that amends or repeals the rule.

5.5 Restricting Your Search by Date

You can instruct WESTLAW to retrieve documents decided or issued before, after, or on a specified date, as well as within a range of dates. The following are examples of queries that contain date restrictions:

da(bef 1991 & aft 1986) & los* /3 evidence

da(1990) & los* /3 evidence

da(1988 1989) & los* /3 evidence

da(4/26/90) & los* /3 evidence

da(april 26, 1990) & los* /3 evidence

da(aft 1-1-89) & los* /3 evidence

You can also instruct WESTLAW to retrieve documents added to a database on or after a specified date, as well as within a range of dates. The following are examples of queries that contain added date restrictions:

ad(5-10-91) & los* /3 evidence

ad(aft 1-1-89) & los* /3 evidence

ad(aft 2-1-91 & bef 3-1-91) & los* /3 evidence

Section 6. Insta–Cite®

Overview: Insta–Cite is West Publishing Company's case history and citation verification service. It is the most current case history service available. Insta–Cite provides the following types of information about a citation:

Direct History: In addition to reversals and affirmances, Insta–Cite gives you the complete reported history of a litigated matter including any related cases. Insta–Cite provides direct history for federal cases from 1754 and for state cases from 1879.

Related References: Related references are cases that involve the same parties and facts as your case, but deal with different legal issues. Insta–Cite provides related references from 1983 to date.

Negative Indirect History: Insta–Cite lists subsequent cases that have a substantial negative impact on your case, including cases overruling your case or calling it into question. Cases affected by decisions from 1972 to date will be displayed on Insta–Cite. To retrieve negative indirect history prior to 1972, use Shepard's Citations (discussed in Section 7).

Secondary Source References: Insta–Cite also provides references to secondary sources that cite your case. These secondary sources presently include legal encyclopedias such as *Corpus Juris Secundum*®.

Parallel Citations: Insta–Cite provides parallel citations for cases including citations to *Callaghan's Federal Rules Service, Federal Rules Decisions* (cases only), and many other looseleaf reporters.

Citation Verification: Insta–Cite confirms that you have the correct volume and page number for a case. Citation verification information is available from 1754 for federal cases and from 1920 for state cases.

Commands

The following commands can be used in Insta–Cite:

ic xxx or **ic**	Retrieves an Insta–Cite result when followed by a case citation (where xxx is the citation), or when entered from a displayed case, Shepard's result or Shepard's PreView result.
pubs	Displays a list of publications and publication abbreviations available in Insta–Cite.
sc	Displays the scope of Insta–Cite coverage.
expand	Displays the Insta–Cite result with chronological case history. (LOCATE is not available in an expanded Insta–Cite result.)
Loc xxx	Restricts an Insta–Cite result to direct or indirect history or to secondary source references when followed by the appropriate code. For example, **Loc dir** restricts the Insta–Cite result to direct history, including related references.
xLoc	Cancels your LOCATE request.
Loc auto xxx	Automatically restricts subsequent Insta–Cite results according to your LOCATE request (where **XXX** is a LOCATE request).
xLoc auto	Cancels your LOCATE AUTO request.
gb or **map2**	Returns you to your previous service or search result, if one exists.

Section 7. Shepard's Citations®

Overview: Shepard's provides a comprehensive list of cases and publications that have cited a particular case. Shepard's also includes explanatory analysis to indicate how the citing cases have treated the case, e.g., "followed," "explained."

In addition to citations from federal, state, and regional citators, Shepard's on WESTLAW includes citations from specialized citators, such as *Civil Procedure Reports, Federal Rules Decisions* (cases only), and many other looseleaf reporters.

Commands

The following commands can be used in Shepard's:

sh xxx or **sh**	Retrieves a Shepard's result when followed by a case citation (where xxx is the citation), or when entered from a displayed case, Insta–Cite result or Shepard's PreView result.
pubs	Displays a list of publications that can be Shepardized® and their publication abbreviations.
sc xxx	Displays the scope of coverage for a specific publication in Shepard's, where xxx is the publication abbreviation (e.g., **sc civ. proc. n.s.**).
cmds	Displays a list of Shepard's commands.
Loc	Restricts a Shepard's result to a specific category when followed by the analysis code, headnote number, or state/circuit or publication abbreviation to which you want the display restricted. For example, **Loc 5** restricts the Shepard's result to cases discussing the point of law contained in headnote number five of the cited case. Type **xLoc** to cancel LOCATE.
gb or **map2**	Leaves Shepard's and returns you to your previous service or search result, if one exists.

Section 8. Shepard's PreView™

Overview: Shepard's PreView gives you a preview of citing references from West's® National Reporter System® that will appear in Shepard's Citations. Depending on the citation, Shepard's PreView provides citing information days, weeks or even months before the same information appears in Shepard's online. Use Shepard's PreView to update your Shepard's results.

Commands

The following commands can be used in Shepard's PreView:

sp xxx or **sp**	Retrieves a Shepard's PreView result when followed by a case citation (where xxx is the citation), or when entered from a displayed case, Insta–Cite result or Shepard's result.
pubs	Displays a list of publications and publication abbreviations that are available in Shepard's PreView.
sc xxx	Displays the scope of citing references.
cmds	Displays a list of Shepard's PreView commands.
Loc xxx	Restricts a Shepard's PreView result by date, publication or jurisdiction, where xxx is the abbreviation.
gb or **map2**	Leaves Shepard's PreView and returns you to your previous service or search result, if one exists.

Section 9. Quick*Cite*™

Overview: Quick*Cite* is a citator service on WESTLAW that enables you to retrieve the most recent citing cases, including slip opinions, automatically.

There is a four- to six-week gap between citing cases listed in Shepard's PreView and the most recent citing cases available on WESTLAW. This gap occurs because cases go through an editorial process at West before they are added to Shepard's PreView. To retrieve the most recent citing cases, therefore, you need to search case law databases on WESTLAW for references to your case; this search technique is known as using WESTLAW as a citator. Quick*Cite* makes using WESTLAW as a citator automatic.

After you've checked your case in the other citator services on WESTLAW, type **qc** to display the Quick*Cite* screen. From this screen, you can press **ENTER** to retrieve the most recent citing cases on WESTLAW, including slip opinions. You can also type **qc** and the citation to display the Quick*Cite* screen, e.g., **qc 96 sct 1569.**

Quick*Cite* formulates a query using the title, the case citation(s), and an added date restriction to retrieve cases more recent than those listed in Shepard's PreView. Quick*Cite* then accesses the appropriate database, either ALLSTATES or ALLFEDS, and runs the query for you.

Quick*Cite* also allows you to choose a different date range and database for your query so you can tailor it to your specific research needs.

Commands

The following commands can be used in Quick *Cite:*

qc xxx or qc   Retrieves a Quick*Cite* result when followed by a case citation (where xxx is the citation), or when entered from a displayed case, Insta–Cite result, Shepard's result or Shepard's PreView result.

scope   Displays the scope of Quick*Cite* coverage.

Press ENTER   Updates Shepard's and Shepard's PreView by retrieving documents added to ALLFEDS within the last three months that cite this decision.

all   Retrieves all ALLFEDS documents that cite this decision.

Database
  Identifier   Retrieves documents added to WESTLAW within the last three months that cite this decision in the selected database.

q   Displays the Quick*Cite* query for editing in ALLFEDS.

map1   Leaves your Quick*Cite* result and returns you to the WESTLAW Directory.

Quick*Cite* is designed to retrieve documents that cite cases. To retrieve citing references to other documents, such as statutes and law review articles, use WESTLAW as a citator.

Section 10.   WESTLAW as a Citator

Using WESTLAW as a citator, you can search for documents citing a specific statute, regulation, rule or agency decision. To retrieve documents citing Miss.R.Evid. 804(b), *Hearsay exceptions,* access the Mississippi Cases database (MS–CS) and search for the citation alone:

804(b)

If the citation is not a unique term, add descriptive terms. For example, to retrieve documents citing Miss.R.Evid. 404, discussing character evidence, type a query like the following:

404   /p   character   /3   evidence

Section 11.   Research Examples

1.   A colleague refers you to a periodical article surveying the federal law of privileges. How can you retrieve the article on WESTLAW?

Solutions

☐ If you know the publication in which the article appeared, in this case, *Litigation,* check the WESTLAW Directory to see if the publication is online and find the database identifier. Access the database by typing **db litig.** At the Enter Query screen, type a query like the following:

evidence /p privilege

☐ If you know that the title of the article is *The Federal Law of Privileges,* but you don't know the journal in which it appears, access the Journals & Law Reviews database (JLR). Search for key terms in the title field:

ti(federal /s law /s privilege)

☐ If you know that the article citation is 16 Litigation 32 (1989), access the Litigation database (LITIG). Search for terms from the citation in the citation field:

ci(16 +5 32)

2. Your client, who lives in Oregon, is charged with a sex crime against a child. You need to retrieve court rules governing the competency of children as witnesses.

Solution

☐ Access the Oregon Rules database (OR–RULES) and type a query like the following:

child /p witness /p competen!

☐ To see if a rule has been amended or repealed, use the UPDATE service. Simply type **update** while viewing the rule to display any court orders that amend or repeal the rule.

To run your original query in the Oregon Criminal Justice Cases database (ORCJ–CS), type **sdb orcj-cs.**

3. Your client is injured in an automobile accident with an out of state driver. You have brought the action in federal court because of diversity of parties. The defendant has indicated that pursuant to Fed.R.Evid. 609, he intends to impeach the plaintiff by introducing evidence of the plaintiff's past conviction for issuing a bad check with the intent to defraud.

☐ When you know the citation for a specific rule, use FIND to retrieve it. For example, to retrieve Fed.R.Evid. 609, *Impeachment by Evidence of Conviction of Crime,* type the following:

fi fre 609

☐ To view preceding and subsequent rules, use the DOCUMENTS IN SEQUENCE command. To view Fed.R.Evid. 608, type **d-.** To view Rule 610, type **d.**

☐ To see if a rule has been amended or repealed, use the UPDATE service. Simply type **update** while viewing the rule to display any court orders that amend or repeal the rule.

When you retrieve Fre.R.Evid. 609, you also retrieve historical and statutory notes, advisory committee notes, cross references, references to law review commentaries and notes of decisions. Use the LOCATE command to quickly zero in on any annotations in Fed.R.Evid. 609 that discuss bad checks. Type Loc and your query, e.g., **Loc check.**

One of the cases noted is *Petty v. Ideco, Div. of Dresser Industries, Inc.,* 761 F.2d 1146 (5th Cir.1985). Use FIND to retrieve this case by typing **fi 761 f2d 1146.**

You wish to see if this case is still good law and if other cases have cited this case.

Solution

☐ Use Insta–Cite to retrieve the direct and negative indirect history of *Petty*. While viewing the case, type **ic.**

☐ You want to Shepardize® *Petty*. Type **sh.**

Limit your Shepard's result to decisions containing a reference to a specific headnote, such as headnote 12. Type **Loc 12.**

☐ Check Shepard's PreView for more current cases citing *Petty*. Type **sp.**

☐ Check QuickCite for the most current cases citing *Petty*. Type **qc** and follow the online instructions.

4. In a personal injury action, you want to introduce thermographic evidence to substantiate your client's chiropractor's diagnosis and treatment. You have not found any cases on this subject. How can you retrieve cases discussing the admissibility of thermographic evidence?

Solution

☐ Access the ALLSTATES database and type a query like the following:

thermogra! /p admiss! admit! inadmissib!

5. Your client is chemically dependent and at times forgets to feed her children and clean the house. She went to a social worker for family therapy. Her ex-spouse has commenced an action for change in custody and intends to call the social worker to testify about your client's problems. There are physician-patient and psychotherapist privileges in New York, but you are unsure if these privileges cover social workers or other mental health therapists and counselors engaged in marriage and family therapy.

Solution

☐ Access the New York Cases database (NY–CS), and type a query like the following:

sy,di(privilege* /p social mental family /3 worker counselor therapist)

6. With the advent of computer simulations, it is now possible to display the movement of a car under specified conditions and in compliance with the laws of physics based on mathematical calculations.

While driving in her car, your client's spouse was hit and run over by a semi-truck, killing her instantly. The truck apparently was forced into the spouse's lane when the road narrowed and a red Corvette passed the truck on the right.

Your accident reconstruction expert has a computer-generated simulation that graphically demonstrates, based on the skid marks and the speed of the vehicles, that the truck driver lost control of his vehicle and literally ran over your client's car. How can you get this simulation admitted into evidence?

Solution

☐ Access the Pennsylvania Cases database (PA–CS), and type a query like the following:

computer! /s animat! simulat! /p evidence admiss! admit! inadmissib!

☐ If you don't retrieve any cases in your jurisdiction, you will want to run the same query in the ALLSTATES database by typing **sdb allstates.**

☐ Run the same query in the Journals & Law Reviews database (JLR) by typing **sdb jlr.** The JLR database contains articles from law reviews, Continuing Legal Education course handbooks and bar journals.

7. As a new associate in the firm, you are expected to keep up with and summarize recent legal developments in the area of evidence. How can you monitor developments in evidence efficiently?

Solution

☐ One of the easiest ways to stay abreast of recent developments in evidence is by regularly accessing the WESTLAW Topical Highlights—Federal Practice and Procedure database (WTH–FPP). The WTH–FPP database summarizes recent legal developments, including court decisions, legislation and materials released by administrative agencies that pertain to the issues of jurisdiction, evidence, the rules of civil and appellate procedure, limitations and the mechanics of practicing law in the federal courts.

☐ To access the database, type **db wth-fpp**. You automatically retrieve a list of documents added to the database in the last two weeks. To read a summary of a document listed, type its corresponding number.

☐ You can also search this database. To display the Enter Query screen, type **s** from anywhere in the database. At the Enter Query screen, type your query. For example, to retrieve references discussing evidence and discovery of business records, type a query like the following:

business /3 record file

Section 12. WESTLAW Commands

General Commands

ez	Accesses the EZ ACCESS system; when entered from EZ ACCESS, displays additional choices.
help	Displays explanatory messages.
scope	Displays a database description when followed by a database identifier or when entered from a database; displays the scope of coverage when entered from a service, such as Insta–Cite.
time	Displays the amount of chargeable time used in your research session.
off	Signs off WESTLAW.
pr	Displays the Offline Printing and Downloading Menu.
opd	Displays the Offline Print Directory.
client	Allows you to change your client identifier.
options	Displays the WESTLAW Options Directory.

Search Commands

s	New search—displays the Enter Query screen.
q	Edit query—displays the last query for editing.
x	Cancels a search in progress.
db	Returns to the WESTLAW Directory from a database; accesses a database when followed by a database identifier: **db sct**.
sdb xxx	Runs the same query in a different database, where **xxx** is the database identifier: **sdb allfeds**.
qdb xxx	Displays the query for editing in a different database, where **xxx** is the database identifier: **qdb allstates**.
read	In selected databases, retrieves the most recent documents when entered at the Enter Query screen.

List   In selected databases, retrieves a list of the most recent documents when entered at the Enter Query screen.

Browsing Commands

t   Term mode—displays the next page containing the terms in the requested relationship; **t-** displays the previous page containing the terms in the requested relationship.

p   Page mode—displays the next page of a document; **p-** displays the previous page of a document. To display a specific page, type **p** followed by the page number: **p5**.

Loc   LOCATE—locates selected terms in retrieved documents; also restricts a Shepard's display to selected categories, such as history and treatment codes, headnote numbers and citing publications.

LLoc   Retrieves a citations list of LOCATE documents.

xLoc   Cancels a LOCATE command.

r   Displays the next ranked document; displays a specific document when followed by the document's rank number: **r3**.

L   Displays a citations list.

Lr#   Displays a citations list beginning with a specific rank number: **Lr8**.

g   Search summary—displays the query and the number of documents retrieved by it.

h+   Advances one half page in a document.

h−   Moves back one half page in a document.

d   DOCUMENTS IN SEQUENCE—displays sections preceding or following the retrieved document: **d+#, d−#**.

xd   Cancels DOCUMENTS IN SEQUENCE and displays the document you were viewing when you entered the DOCUMENTS IN SEQUENCE command.

f   Displays a list of fields in a database; restricts your display to a selected field or fields when followed by the field name: **f opinion**.

xf   Cancels your command to restrict your display by field.

Service Commands

fi   FIND—retrieves a document when followed by its citation: **fi 93 sct 2357**.

ic   Retrieves an Insta–Cite result when followed by the case citation, **ic 93 sct 2357**, or when entered from a displayed case, Shepard's result or Shepard's PreView result.

sh   Retrieves a Shepard's result when followed by the case citation, **sh 93 sct 2357**, or when entered from a displayed case, Insta–Cite result or Shepard's PreView result.

sp   Retrieves a Shepard's PreView result when followed by the case citation, **sp 93 sct 2357**, or when entered from a displayed case, Insta–Cite result or Shepard's result.

qc   Retrieves a QuickCite result when followed by the case citation, **qc 93 sct 2357**, or when entered from a displayed case, Insta–Cite result, Shepard's result or Shepard's PreView result.

pdq   Personal Directory of Queries—displays a list of saved queries for selection and update.

di   Enters the Black's Law Dictionary® service or displays a definition when followed by the word or phrase: **di presumption**.

update	Displays any document amending or repealing the statute, rule or regulation you are viewing.
rm	Displays the Related Materials Directory for a statute, legislative service document, rule or order.
gm	Displays General Materials, which are references and tables applicable to the entire title, chapter and subchapter containing the displayed statute.
annos	Displays annotations (Notes of Decisions) for the displayed statute.
refs	Displays references to the unannotated statutory document you are viewing.
st-ann	Displays the annotated statute(s) amended or repealed by the displayed document.
stat	Displays the unannotated statute(s) amended or repealed by the displayed document.
rules	Displays the court rule(s) affected by the displayed court order.
gb	GO BACK—returns to a previous location in WESTLAW from a service, e.g., Insta–Cite, Shepard's, FIND.
map	Displays a list containing the most recent database and services accessed and allows you to return to them.
map1	Returns to the WESTLAW Directory.
map2	Returns to your search result, if one exists.

*

Table of Cases

L

M

N

O

P

Palko v. Connecticut—§ 166; § 166, n. 6.
Palmer v. Hoffman—§ 288; § 288, n. 1.
Patterson v. Illinois—§ 153; § 153, n. 10; § 155; § 155, n. 10.
Patterson v. New York—§ 347; § 347, n. 5; § 348, n. 1.
Patterson, United States v.—§ 158, n. 8.
Payner, United States v.—§ 171; § 171, n. 7; § 175; § 175, n. 7.
Pennsylvania v. Muniz—§ 124; § 124, n. 2; § 149; § 149, n. 14, 17.
Pennsylvania v. Ritchie—§ 74.2; § 74.2, n. 8.
People v. ____(see opposing party)
Philadelphia, City of v. Westinghouse Elec. Corp.—§ 87.1; § 87.1, n. 3.
Philadelphia & Trenton R. Co. v. Stimpson—§ 24, n. 2.
Phillips v. Chase—§ 74.1; § 74.1, n. 3.
Pierce Auto Freight Lines, United States v.—§ 359; § 359, n. 16.
Pinto v. Pierce—§ 162, n. 8.
Pippin v. Commonwealth—§ 313, n. 4.
Plimpton v. Spiller—§ 17, n. 1.
Pointer v. Texas—§ 252, n. 1.
Procter & Gamble Company, United States v.—§ 113; § 113, n. 3.

Q

Queen v. ____ (see opposing party)
Queen Caroline's Case—§ 28; § 28, n. 2; § 37; § 37, n. 1.

R

Radiant Burners, Inc. v. American Gas Ass'n, 320 F.2d 314—§ 87.1, n. 2.
Radiant Burners, Inc. v. American Gas Ass'n, 207 F.Supp. 771—§ 87.1, n. 1.
Raffel v. United States—§ 132; § 132, n. 5.
Rakas v. Illinois—§ 175; § 175, n. 1.
Rawlings v. Kentucky—§ 157; § 157, n. 4; § 175; § 175, n. 4; § 179; § 179, n. 9.
Rea v. United States—§ 171; § 171, n. 4.
Rex v. ____ (see opposing party)
Reynolds v. United States—§ 110.
Rhode Island v. Innis—§ 149; § 149, n. 10.
Richardson v. Perales—§ 351; § 351, n. 8.
Rivera v. Delaware—§ 347; § 347, n. 4.
Robertson, United States v.—§ 159; § 159, n. 7.
Rochin v. California—§ 155; § 155, n. 11; § 166; § 166, n. 7.
Rogers v. Richmond—§ 147; § 147, n. 12.
Rogers v. United States—§ 122, n. 4; § 140; § 140, n. 1.
Romano, United States v.—§ 347; § 347, n. 13.
Roviaro v. United States—§ 74.2, n. 6.
Rudd's Case—§ 146, n. 1.

S

Sabbath v. United States—§ 170, n. 1.
Salvucci, United States v.—§ 175; § 175, n. 9.
Samuel H. Moss, Inc. v. F T C—§ 352; § 352, n. 2.
Sandstrom v. Montana—§ 347; § 347, n. 9, 22.
Santos, United States v.—§ 259, n. 10.
Saporen, State v.—§ 251, n. 6.

Saunders, State v.—§ 313, n. 2.
Schmerber v. California—§ 118, n. 1; § 124; § 124, n. 5.
Schneckloth v. Bustamonte—§ 147, n. 16.
See v. Seattle—§ 356; § 356, n. 6.
Segura v. United States—§ 177; § 177, n. 6.
Sells Engineering, Inc., United States v.—§ 113; § 113, n. 1.
Seper, Matter of—§ 140, n. 4.
Shapiro v. United States—§ 142; § 142, n. 1.
Shenton v. Tyler—§ 85.
Shepard v. United States—§ 276; § 276, n. 1.
Silverthorne Lumber Co. v. United States—§ 166; § 166, n. 4; § 176; § 176, n. 1; § 177; § 177, n. 1.
Simmons v. United States—§ 175; § 175, n. 10; § 183, n. 4.
Sims v. Georgia—§ 162; § 162, n. 9.
Slochower v. Board of Higher Ed. of City of N.Y.—§ 126, n. 2.
Smith v. Bell Tel. Co. of Pa.—§ 338, n. 5.
Smith v. Illinois—§ 150, n. 12.
Smith, Rex v.—§ 190; § 190, n. 2.
Smith, State v.—§ 178, n. 5.
Smith v. United States—§ 145; § 145, n. 5.
Smith Steel Casting Co. v. Brock—§ 173, n. 4.
South Dakota v. Neville—§ 124; § 124, n. 10; § 125; § 125, n. 4; § 149; § 149, n. 13.
Speiser v. Randall—§ 341, n. 1.
Spevack v. Klein—§ 126, n. 3.
State v. ____ (see opposing party)
Steadman v. S. E. C.—§ 357; § 357, n. 2.
Stevens v. Marks—§ 141; § 141, n. 3.
Stevenson v. Commonwealth—§ 250; § 250, n. 2.
Stewart v. United States—§ 132, n. 11.
Stone v. Powell—§ 167, n. 3; § 183; § 183, n. 8.
Stovall v. Denno—§ 166; § 166, n. 11.
Sussex Peerage Case—§ 318; § 318, n. 1.

T

Tampa Electric Co. v. Getrost—§ 271; § 271, n. 4.
Tedford, United States v.—§ 176; § 176, n. 12.
Terry v. Ohio—§ 149; § 149, n. 8.
Thomas's Case—§ 244, n. 6.
Thorn v. Worthington Skating Rink Co.—§ 17, n. 1.
Thurston v. Fritz—§ 315, n. 1.
Tirado v. C.I.R.—§ 173; § 173, n. 5.
Tooley v. Bacon—§ 52, n. 3.
Tot v. United States—§ 347; § 347, n. 10.
Turner v. City of Lawton—§ 173; § 173, n. 6.
Turner v. United States—§ 347; § 347, n. 17.

U

(Under Seal), United States v., 794 F.2d 920—§ 123; § 123, n. 4.
(Under Seal), United States v., 745 F.2d 834—§ 127, n. 7.
United Shoe Machinery Corp, United States v.—§ 353, n. 3.
United States v. ____(see opposing party)
United States ex rel. v. ____(see opposing party and relator)
Universal Camera Corp. v. National Labor Rel. Bd.—§ 354; § 354, n. 3.
University of Pennsylvania v. E.E.O.C.—§ 76.2; § 76.2, n. 5.
Upjohn Co. v. United States—§ 87.1; § 87.1, n. 4; § 96; § 96, n. 2, 6.

*

Table of Statutes and Rules

Index

References are to Sections

†